THE

BIRTH, MARRIAGE AND DEATH

REGISTER,

CHURCH RECORDS AND EPITAPHS

OF

LANCASTER, MASSACHUSETTS.

1643-1850

EDITED BY

HENRY S. NOURSE, A. M.

LANCASTER:

1890

Notice

In many older books, foxing (or discoloration) occurs and, in some instances, print lightens with wear and age. Reprinted books, such as this, often duplicate these flaws, notwithstanding efforts to reduce or eliminate them. The pages of this reprint have been digitally enhanced and, where possible, the flaws eliminated in order to provide clarity of content and a pleasant reading experience.

Originally published
Lancaster, Mass.
1890

Reprinted by:
Janaway Publishing, Inc.
2013

Janaway Publishing
732 Kelsey Ct.
Santa Maria, California 93454
(805) 925-1038
www.janawaygenealogy.com

ISBN 978-1-59641-297-2

Made in the United States of America

INTRODUCTION.

AT its annual meeting in March, 1889, the town of Lancaster made appropriation for the preservation in print of its older records of births, marriages and deaths. The publication was by vote entrusted to Doctor Horace M. Nash, town-clerk, and Henry S. Nourse. The latter was designated as editor of the work, and is solely responsible for the manner of its execution.

The returns of the town's first Clerk of the Writs, Ralph Houghton, until October, 1674, were made to the recorder of the Middlesex County Court as required by a law enacted June 14, 1642. A single ragged and discolored leaf of his original manuscript, containing the record of fifty births before 1666, is preserved in the town's archives, having been fortuitously discovered, in 1826, among family papers. More than ten years had elapsed after the setting up in the Nashua valley of the first roof-tree by white men, before Ralph Houghton entered upon his duties as clerk of the writs, and his records are chargeable with some omissions.

The returns of the second clerk, Cyprian Stevens, are found in the Middlesex Registry duly copied from 1680 to 1687. During the interval of six years in which no reports were made to the recorder, there occurred two bloody raids by Indians upon Lancaster, and a temporary abandonment of the settlement. The lists of the numerous victims in the massacres by savages have been compiled from various authorities.

Records of marriages in Lancaster, in obedience to a law dated December 1, 1716, began to be annually given in to the Clerk of the Sessions of the Peace for Middlesex in 1718, and are found registered until 1730. Between 1686 and 1726 all regular town records are wanting, a volume having, it is conjectured, been destroyed by fire. During the whole of this period John Houghton was probably the town-clerk. The church records extant open with the settlement of Reverend John Prentice in 1708.

A volume of the ancient records of the town, printed by the editor of the present compilation in 1884, contains in its appendix memoranda of such births, marriages and deaths in Lancaster families, previous to 1700, as could be anywhere found duly attested. To make the present register complete in itself, these memoranda are now reprinted with suitable re-arrangement.

The oldest book containing continuous registry of "Marriages, Deaths, Births and Publishments in Lancaster," was opened by Jonathan Houghton, fourth town-clerk, upon his election to office in 1726. Many earlier dates have been inserted by him and other clerks, probably derived from family memorials. He began his chronicles upon the tenth page, as though reserving room for those of previous years, if by chance any should be recovered; but his successors used the sheets he left blank for miscellaneous items. This book sufficed for the town's use during about ninety years, and contains three hundred and sixty pages, crowded with a disorderly mass of material, which is here copied without impertinence of alteration in order, orthography or even punctuation.

Until the statute of 1844 enforced a special form of registry, the town-clerks continued the records in two volumes — one devoted to births and deaths, the other to publishments and marriages. With these two books the plan of the present work might appropriately end — thus covering two hundred years from the building of the first house by Englishmen upon Lancaster soil. As, however, numerous items of dates earlier than 1844 are found in a fourth book, and for the convenience of a more definite period, the lists of births, deaths and marriages have been brought down to January 1, A. D. 1850. To perfect this printed register so far as is practicable, not only county, town and church records have been transcribed, when not duplicate, but numerous names and dates have been added from the inscriptions in burial grounds, the bible records of old families, and other sources duly specified.

By comparing the town records with those of the church, or epitaphs, numerous discrepancies in dates will be noticed. The frequent omission of middle names by the recorders, and peculiarities in orthography, cause some confusion of persons; this has been remedied, so far as possible, in the index which has been studiously revised.

The first birth certified to by Ralph Houghton was that of Joseph, son of Lawrence Waters, April 29, 1647. As both the Prescott and Waters families were resident on the Nashua two years before, and the births of Adam Waters and Jonathan Prescott were not recorded at Watertown, there is good reason for supposing that they were born in Lancaster during 1645 or 1646. Houghton also omits the birth of Jonas Prescott in 1648.

The first attested death in the town was that of Rachel, infant daughter of Lawrence Waters, in March, 1649.

The first marriage consummated in Lancaster was doubtless that of Jonas Fairbank and Lydia Prescott, in May, 1658; for solemnizing which Mr. John Tinker received special license from the court. Before that year the several couples joined in wedlock — after their intention had been three times published

INTRODUCTION. 5

in open meeting, or advertised for fourteen days by a notice affixed to the meeting-house doors—were forced to journey, on horseback, to Sudbury, Concord, or even Boston, to obtain some magistrate's seal to the civil contract.

<small>All Marriages in New England were formerly performed by the Civil Magistrate, but of late [1720] they are more frequently solemnized by the Clergy, who imitate the Method prescribed by the Church of England except the Collects and the Ceremony of the Ring.—*Daniel Neal's History of New England*</small>

For the aid of those who may be unfamiliar with the "old-style" method of reckoning time, it is deemed expedient here to state that, during the lives of the first clerks of Lancaster, the heathen names of months and days were seldom used, the ordinal numbers being substituted therefor. In English Church and Court the year began with Lady Day; March being therefore the first month, and January the eleventh. The present mode of computing time from January 1 as New Year's Day was already in use in Scotland and other states of Europe, and signs of the growing change in custom are visible in our early records. In all dates between January 1 and March 25, it became the fashion to indicate not only the year according to English reckoning, but that recognized in Scotland. The change from the Julian to the Gregorian calendar was, by act of parliament, adopted September 2, 1752, when eleven days were dropped, the next day becoming the fourteenth. For all dates previous to that, therefore, in order to bring them into accord with the present calendar, it is necessary to add twelve days to the date, if before March, 1700; or eleven days, if subsequent to that day. Thus the destruction of Lancaster would be recorded as 10, 12mo., 1675; or February 10, 1675-6; or $\frac{2.10}{1675}$; being according to the modern calendar, February 22, 1676.

Words or syllables enclosed in brackets are interpolations by the editor, usually to supply omissions, or to suggest explanation or correction of the record. The numerals at the left margin indicate the paging of the original books.

THE CLERKS OF LANCASTER.

1643-1850.

The first pages of Lancaster's oldest records are by the hand of Master John Tinker, who, as scribe for the first prudential managers, copied some earlier records from "the old book"; but by whom that lost volume was kept is unknown.

RALPH HOUGHTON, clerk of the writs 1656 to 1682.
CYPRIAN STEEVENS, clerk of the writs 1682 to 1686.
JOHN HOUGHTON (son of first John), 1686 (?) to 1725,—40 years.
JONATHAN HOUGHTON, 1726 to 1728, and 1730 to 1736.—Died in office.
JOSEPH OSGOOD, 1729.
JUDGE JOSEPH WILDER, SR., 1737 to 1743.
JOSEPH WILDER, JR., 1744 to 1752.
ABIJAH WILLARD, 1753 and 1754.
COLONEL SAMUEL WILLARD, 1755.
WILLIAM RICHARDSON, October 8, 1755, "in room of Samuel Willard, absent on his majesties service."
LEVI WILLARD, 1756 to 1760, and 1761 to 1769.
ABEL WILLARD, 1760, "in place of Levi Willard going out of town."
DANIEL ROBBINS, 1770, 1772, 1773, 1775 and 1776.
CAPTAIN SAMUEL WARD, 1771, 1774, and 1782 to 1787.
COLONEL WILLIAM GREENLEAF, 1777, 1779, 1781.
NATHANIEL BEAMAN, September, 1777, to May, 1778.
CYRUS FAIRBANK, May, 1778.
DOCTOR JOSIAH LEAVITT, 1780, to May, 1781.
COLONEL EDMUND HEARD, 1788 to 1790.
JOSEPH WALES, 1791 to 1794.
WILLIAM STEDMAN, 1795 to 1800.
JOSIAH FLAGG, 1801 to 1835, except 1828,—34 years.
MAJOR JACOB FISHER, 1828.
JOSEPH W. HUNTINGTON, 1836 and 1837.
JOHN G. THURSTON, 1838 to 1853.

CONTENTS.

		Page.
I.	A Leaf from the first Town Clerk's Register of Births.	9
II.	The Middlesex County Court's Register of Lancaster Births, Marriages and Deaths to 1687.	11
III.	The Victims in the Indian Raids.	15
IV.	The Middlesex Court's Register of Lancaster Marriages, 1718-1726.	17
V.	Marriages and Deaths of some Early Residents not found in the Town's Records.	19
VI.	Book I. Town Records of Births, Publishments, Marriages and Deaths, begun 1726.	21
VII.	Book II. Town Records of Births and Deaths, 1796-1843.	174
VIII.	Book III. Town Records of Publishments and Marriages, begun 1815.	228
IX.	Births, Marriages and Deaths of dates previous to 1850, found in Book IV. of Town Records.	253
X.	Records of First Church. Book I, 1708-1793; including the Pastorates of Reverends John Prentice and Timothy Harrington: Admissions to Membership, Baptisms, Dismissions, and a Register of Deaths, 1747-1793.	270
XI.	Records of First Church. Book II, 1794-1847; including the Pastorates of Nathaniel Thayer, S.T.D., and Reverend Edmund Hamilton Sears: Membership, Baptisms, Deaths, sundry Marriages not recorded in Town Books, and a List of Deacons.	333
XII.	Records of the Second or Chocksett Church, 1744-1781.	374
XIII.	Records of the Hillside Church, 1830-1843.	392
XIV.	Records of the Evangelical Congregational Church.	393
XV.	Records of the Universalist Church.	395

CONTENTS.

		Page.
XVI.	Death Register kept by Rev. George M. Bartol, 1847-1849.	396
XVII.	Judge Joseph Wilder's Memoranda of Births and Marriages.	397
XVIII.	Epitaphs in the Old Burial Field.	398
XIX.	Epitaphs of the Old Common Burial Ground to 1850.	408
XX.	Epitaphs of the Chocksett Burial Ground, 1736-1781.	416
XXI.	Epitaphs of the Middle Cemetery to 1850.	420
XXII.	Epitaphs in the Burial Place of the Shakers to 1850.	445
XXIII.	Epitaphs of the North Burial Field to 1850.	446
XXIV.	Epitaphs of the North Village Cemetery to 1850.	449
XXV.	Appendix.	451
XXVI.	Index of Places.	455
XXVII.	Index of Persons.	457

his wife was borne the
mary daughter of master Joseph Row[...]
mary his wife was borne the
mary the daughter of Ralph Houghton and
his wife was borne the
John the son of Ralph Houghton and [...]
wife was borne the
Joseph the son of Ralph Houghton and [...]
wife was borne the
Experience [...] of Ralph [Houghton] and [...]
his wife [was borne] the
[...] Atherton [...]
wife was borne the
[...] Atherton [...]
wife was borne the
[...]
his wife [...]
[...]
[...]
[...] daughter [...]
wife was borne the
mary and [...] daughters of Edm[und]
Elizabeth his wife were borne the
Debora the daughter of Edmund Parker and
his wife was borne the
two children of John [...] and martha [...]
were borne the
Joseph the son of Lawrence waters and Ann [his]
wife was borne the
Jacob and Rachell son and daughter of Lawr[ence]
waters and Ann his wife was borne the
Samuell the son of Lawrence waters and Ann
wife was borne the
Johana the daughter of Lawrence waters and
his wife was borne the
Ephra[im] the son of Lawrence waters and Ann

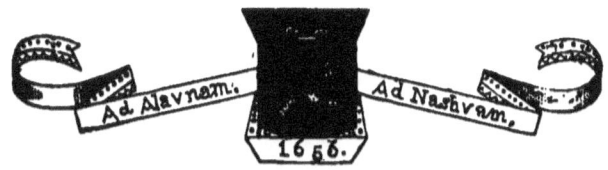

TOWN RECORDS.

The veteran town-clerk, Josiah Flagg, in transcribing the subjoined list of births upon pages 198, 199 and 200 of Book 1, prefaced it with this statement:

The following is a true copy of a record taken from a leaf of an ancient Record Book which I found among the papers of the late Capt. Hezekiah Gates, who died about fifty years ago.
LANCASTER, March 28th, 1826.

The aged manuscript is in the neat handwriting of Ralph Houghton, the first clerk of Lancaster. A photographic reproduction of the first page, in lineal dimensions two-thirds the size of the original, is herewith presented.

A RECORD OF BIRTHES AND DEATHS

LANCASTER
20 : 12 : mon
1660

I'mis   Henry the sonn of Henrie Kerley and Elizabeth his wife : was borne the   11=11 mon 1657

Marie daughter of Master Joseph Rowlandson and Marie his wife : was borne the   15=11 mon 1657

Marie the daughter of Ralph Houghton and Jane his wife : was borne the   4=11 mon 1653

John the sonn of Ralph Houghton and Jane his wife : was borne the   28=2ᵈ mon 1655

Joseph the sonn of Ralph Houghton and Jane his wife : was borne the   1=5 mon 1657

Experience daughter of Ralph Houghton and Jane his wife : was borne the   1=8 mon 1659

James sonn of James Atherton and Hanna his wife : was borne the   13=3 mon 1654

Joshua son of James Atherton and Hanna his wife : was borne the   13=3 mon 1656

Hanna daughter of James Atherton and Hanna his wife : was borne   10=11 mon 1657

Marie the daughter of John More and Ann his wife : was borne the   4=9 mon 1655

Elizabeth the daughter of John More and Ann his wife : was borne the   27=9 mon 1657

Marsa [Mercy] and Ester daughters of Edmund Parker and Elizabeth his wife : were borne the   28=8 mon 1654

Debora the daughter of Edmund Parker and Elizabeth his wife : was borne the   6=11 mon 1655

Two Children of John Rugg and Martha his wife : were borne the   17=11 mon 1655

Joseph the sonn of Lawrence Waters and Ann his wife ; was borne the — 29=2 mon 1647

Jacob and Rachell sonn and daughter of Lawrence Waters and Ann his wife ; was borne the — 1=1 mon 1649

Samuell the sonn of Lawrence Waters and Ann his wife ; was borne the — 14=11 mon 1651

Johanna the daughter of Lawrence Waters and Ann his wife ; was borne the — 26=1 mon 1653

Ephraim the sonn of Lawrence Waters and Ann his wife ; was borne the — 27=11 mon 1655

A child of Nathaniell Josllin and Sara his wife : was borne the — 15=5 mon 1657

Grace daughter of Jonas Fairbank and Lidia his wife was borne the — 15 : 9ᵐ: 1663

Elizabeth daughter of Thomas Sawyer and Marie his wife was borne the — 5 : 11ᵐ: 1663

Samuell sonn of Daniell Allin and Marie his wife was borne the — 17 : 2 : 1664

Joseph sonn of Abram and Beatrix Josllin was borne yᵉ — 26 ; 5ᵐ: 1663

Marie daughter of Abram and Beatrix Josllin was borne — 14 : 10ᵐ: 1666

Sara daughter of Nathaniell Josllin & Sara his wife ; was borne the — 15 : 5 mon 1660

Marie the daughter of Samuell Davis and Marie his wife : was borne the — 26=11 mon 1657

A Child of Richard Smith & Marie his wife : was borne the — 23=3 mon 1654

John the sonn of Richard Smith and Johanna his wife : was borne the — 20=11 mon 1655

ffrances sonn of Richard Smith and Johanna his wife ; was borne the — 26=6 mon 1657

William the sonn of Henrie Kerley and Elizabeth his wife : was borne the — 22=11 mon 1658

Thomas the sonn of Thomas Sawyer and Marie his wife ; was borne the — 2=5 mon 1649

Ephraim the sonn of Thomas Sawyer and Marie his wife : was borne the — 16=11 mon 1650

Marie the daughter of Thomas Sawyer and Marie his wife : was borne the — 4=11 mon 1652

Joshua the sonn of Thomas Sawyer and Marie his wife ; was borne the — 13=1 mon 1655

James the sonn of Thomas Sawyer and Marie his wife : was borne the — 22=1 mon 1657

Caleb the sonn or Thomas Sawyer and Marie his wife : was borne the — 20=2 mon 1659

Marie daughter of Jonas ffairbanke and Lidia his wife : was borne the — 20=4 mon 1659

Ichabod sonn of Jeremiah Rogers and Bia his wife : was borne the — 9=11 mon 1659

Nathaniell the sonn of Nathaniell Josllin and Sara his wife ; was borne the — 21 of June 1658

Joseph the sonn of Simon Willard and Marie his wife : was borne the — 4 : 11. mon 1660

Samuell sonn of George Benit and Lidia his wife : was borne ; — 22 July 1665

Josua sonn of Jonas ffairbanke and Lidia his wife : was borne the : — 6 : 2 : mon: 1661

Abigaill daughter of Ralph Houghton & Jane his wife was borne the — 15 : 5ᵐ 1664

Noah sonn of Gamaliel Beman and Sara his wife : was borne the — 3 : 2 mon 1661

MIDDLESEX REGISTER. 11

John sonn of Thomas Sawyer and Marie his wife: was borne the — 6 : 2 mon 1661
Lidia daughter of John More and Ann his wife: was borne the — 6 : 2 mon 1660
John sonn of John More and Ann his wife; was borne the — 7 : 2 mon 1662
Rachell daughter to Arklous Courser & Rachell his wife was borne the — 8 ; 10 mon 1662

MIDDLESEX COUNTY RECORDS.

The lost leaves of Ralph Houghton's manuscript, and subsequent records for many years, must be supplied from the copies of returns made to the Middlesex County court by him and his successors. These are found in the Records of Births, Deaths and Marriages, Liber III, pages 115 and 196; and Liber IV, pages 39 to 40, 121, 195, 206, 212 to 214. The recorder, it is evident, did not always copy the orthography of Lancaster's scribe :

John sonne of George Bennitt & Lidea his wife was borne 31 . 5 . 1659.
Mary daughter of George Bennitt & Lidea his wife was borne 19 . 6 . 1661.
Steeven sonne of Steeven Gates, & Sarah was borne 17 . 5 . 1665.
Joseph sonne of Mr Joseph Rowlason, & Mary his wife was borne 7 . 1 . 1661.
Mary daughter of Mr Joseph Rowlason, & Mary his wife was borne 12 . 6 . 1665.
Waytestill daughter of Roger Sumner, & Mary his wife was borne 20 . 10 . 1661.
Mary daughter of Roger Sumner, & Mary his wife was borne 5 . 6 . 1665.
Sarah daughter of Ralph Houghton, & Jane his wife was borne 17 . 12 . 1661.
Joseph sonne of Jno. Moore, & Ann his wife was borne 20 . 8, mo. 1664.
Beatrix daughter of Jno. Houghton, & Beatrix his wife was borne 3 . 10.mo. 1665.
Josiah sonne of Josiah Whetcombe, & Rebeccah his wife was borne 12 . 9.mo. 1665.
Jacob sonne of Richard Wheeler, & Sarah his was borne 25 . 9.mo. 1663.
Zebediah sonne of Richard Wheeler, & Sarah his wife was borne 2 . 11 . 1664.
Hannah daughter of Simon Willard, & Mary his wife was borne 6 . 8.mo. 1666.
Rebeccah daughter of Jno. Lewis, & Hannah his wife borne 8 . 6,mo. 1665.
Bethia daughter of Jno. Lewis, & Hannah his wife borne 13 . 5 . 1666.
Josiah sonne of Josiah Whetcombe, & Rebeccah his wife was borne 7 . 11 . 1666.
Jonathan sonne of Jonas ffairbanke, & Lidea his wife was borne 7 . 8 . 1666.
Elnathan sonne of Daniel Allen, & Mary his wife was borne 7 . 11 . 1666.
Dorothy daughter of Nathaniel Joslin, & Mary his wife was borne 4 . 1 . 62.
Peter sonne of Nathaniel Joslin, & Mary his wife was borne 22 . 12 . 1665.
Hannah daughter of Henry Kerly, & Elizabeth his wife was borne 8 . 5.mo. 1663.
Mary daughter of Henry Kerly, & Elizabeth his wife was borne 14 . 8 . 1666.
Sarah daughter of Richard Wheeler & Sarah his wife was borne 1 . 12 . 1666.
Ann daughter of Jno. Moore, & Ann his wife was borne 17 . 5.mo. 1666.
Mary daughter of James Atherton, & Hannah his wife was borne 17 . 11.mo. 1660.
Elizabeth daughter of James Atherton, & Hannah his wife was borne 6 . 8.mo.1666.

MARIAGES.

Jonas ffairebanke & Lidea Prescott were maryed 28 . 3.mo. 1658.
George Bennitt & Lidea Kibby were maried the 13 . 4,mo. 1658.
Richard Wheeler & Sarah Prescott were maryed 2 . 6.mo. 1658.
Willm. Kerly & Brichett Rowlandson were maryed ye 31 . 3,mo. 1659.
William Kerly & Rebeccah Joselin were maryed 16 . 3 . 1664.
John Deuall & Hannah White were maryed the 23 , 10,mo. 1663.
Josiah Whetcombe & Rebeccah Waters were maryed ye 4th. 11mo. 1664.

DEATHS.

A Child of Jno Rug & Martha his wife died. 18 . 11mo. 1655.
A Child of Jno Rug & Martha his wife died. 24 . 11 . 1655.
Martha wife of Jno Rug died. 24 . 11 . 1655.

LANCASTER RECORDS.

Joane the wife of Jno. White died— 18.3.1654.
Mary the wife of Richard Smith died— 27.3.1654.
Elizab. the wife of Edmund Parker died— 6.9.1657.
Thomas Rowlandson died— 17.9.1657.
A Child of Nathaniel Joslin & Sarah his wife died. 16.5.1657.
Rachel daughter of Laurance Waters, and Ann his wife, died. 31.1.49.
Joanna daughter of Laurance Waters, and Ann his wife, died. 21.2.54.
Mary wife of Jno. Smith died— 27.10.59
Ann wife of William Kerly Senr. died— 12.1.1658.
Ephraim sonne of Laurance Waters, and Ann his wife died. 17.4.59.
Josiah sonne of Josiah Whetcombe, & Rebeccah his wife, died. 12.9.65.
Thomas James died ye 13.1.1660.
Mary daughter of Mr Joseph Rowlandson, & Mary his wife died. 20.11.1660.
Hittabel daughter of Jeremiah Rogers, & Biah his wife died. 20.11.60.
Rebeccah daughter of Jno. Lewis, & Hannah his wife died. 20.7.1665.
Jno. Whetcombe, Senr. died. 24.7.1662.
Elizabeth daughter of James Atherton, and Hannah his wife died. 10.6.1665.
Richard Linton died 30.1^{mo}. 1665.
Henry Renie Servant to Roger Sumner died, 15.4^{mo}. 1662.
Brichett wife of William Kerly Senr. died. 14.4^{mo}. 1662.
Jacob sonne of Richard Wheeler, & Sarah his wife died. 21.12.1663.
Deborah daughter of Thomas Sawjer, & Mary his wife died. 17.5thm. 1666.

BIRTHS.

Ann daughter of Daniel Hudsun, & Joanna his wife borne. January 1st. 1668 [1648?]
Daniel sonne of Daniel Hudsun, & Joanna his wife borne, May, 26, 1651.
Mary daughter of Daniel Hudsun, & Joanna his wife borne. Sept. 7, 1653.
Sarah daughter of Daniel Hudsun, & Joanna his wife borne. Jan. 1 1656.
Elizabeth daughter of Daniel Hudsun, & Joanna his wife borne. Janu. 11. 1658.
Johanna daughter of Daniel Hudsun, & Joanna his wife borne. Jan. 6. 1660.
John sonne of Daniel Hudsun, & Johannah his wife borne. March, 10. 1662.
William sonne of Daniel Hudsun, & Johannah his wife borne. June, 12. 1664.
Abigail daughter of Daniel Hudsun, & Joanna his wife borne. Septem. 7 : 1667.
Simon sonne of Arculas & Rachel Courser, borne. August, 3. 1667.
Hittabel daughter of Jeremiah, and Abiah Rogers, borne. Octob. 1. 1667.
Jehosophat sonne of Jeremiah, and Abiah Rogers, borne. Octob. 4. 1663.
Abyah daughter of Jeremiah & of Abyah Rogers, borne. July, 6. 1666.
Hannah, daughter of Ralph & Jane Houghton. borne. Octob. 16. 1667.
John sonne of John & Hannah Divell borne. Sept. 28. 1664
Hannah daughter of Jno. & Hannah Divell borne. June, 12. 1667
John sonne of Jno Ruge & Hannah his wife borne, June, 4, 1662.
Marra daughter of Jno & Hannah Ruge borne, July, 11. 1664.
Thomas sonne of John & Hannah Ruge borne, Sept. 15, 1666.
Bathsheba daughter of Jeremiah & Abyah Rogers borne, Jan. 6, 1667.
Benjamin sonne of John & Beatrix Houghton borne, May, 25, 1668.
Mary daughter of John & Mary farrer borne, June, 18, 1668.
Jaahzoniah sonne of Roger and Mary Sumner borne, Aprill, 11, 1668.
Hannah daughter of Jonathan, & Hannah Whetcombe borne, Sept, 17. 1668.
George sonne of George & Lidea Bennitt borne, March, 26, 1668.
David sonne of Josiah & Rebeccah Whetcombe borne, febr. 20, 1668.
Joseph sonne of John & Hannah Ruge borne, Decem^r. 15, 1668.
John sonne of Thomas & Deborah Wedge borne, April, 28, 1667.
Mary daughter of Thomas & Deborah Wedge borne, May, 12, 1668
Elizabeth daughter of Nathaniel & Sarah Joselin borne, June, 7, 1657 [67?]
John sonne of John and Elizabeth Rigby, borne, July, 2, 1663.
Thankefull daughter of Gamaliel and Sarah Beeman borne. Aprill, 18, 1663
Mehettabell daughter of Gamaliel and Sarah Beman borne, May, 26, 1667
Hazadiah daughter of Jonas & Lidea fairebanks borne Febr. 28, 1668.
Jonathan sonne of John and Ann Moore borne, May 19, 1669
Josiah sonne of John and Hannah Divell borne, Sept. 27, 1669.
Sarah daughter of Joseph & Mary Rowlandson borne, Sept, 15, 1669.

Barachia sonne of John & Hannah Lewis borne, July 31, 1663.
Patience daughter of John & Hannah Lewis borne, Jan. 2, 1668.
Mary daughter of John & Sarah Prescott borne, febr. 2, 1669.
Elizabeth daughter of Richard & Sarah Wheeler borne, May, 24, 1669.
Jonathan sonne of Jonathan & Hannah Whetcombe borne, febr. 26, 1669.
Jonathan sonne of Simon & Mary Willard, borne, Decem. 14, 1669.
Thomas sonne of Daniel & Mary Allin borne, febr. 20, 1669.
Joseph sonne of Henry & Elizabeth Kerly borne, March 28, 1669
John sonne of John & Mary ffarrer borne, Nov. 28, 1669
Mary daughter of Arculeas & Rachell Courser borne, May, 11, 1670
A Child of W^m. & Elizab[eth] Lincorne borne, July, 17, 1670
Deborah daughter of James & Hannah Atherton borne, June, 1, 1669
Joshua sonne of Thomas & Deborah Wedge borne, March, 30, 1670.

Deaths

Thomas Wilder died. Octob. 23. 1667
Hittabell daughter of Jeremiah Rogers died. Novem. 7. 1662
Hannah daughter of Jonath. Whetcomb died. Decem. 9. 1668
Nathaniel sonne of Nath. Josline died. June, 8, 1667
John Smith died July 16, July, 16, 1669
Isabell Walker died Aprill, Aprill, 3, 1669
Hope daughter of Major Simon Willard died. Decem. 23, 1663
Simon sonne of Arculeas Courser died. June 15, 1669
John farrer died Novemb. Novem. 3. 1669
A Child of W^m. Lincorne died. July, 17, 1670
Willm. Kerly Senr. died. July, 14, 1670.

Mariages

Jonathan & Hannah Whitcombe were maryed, Novem' 25, 1667
John & Mary farrer were maryed June, 30. 1667
John Rug and Hannah [Prescott] his wife maryed May, 4, 1660.
John Prescott & Sarah [Hayward] his wife were maryed Novem. 11, 1668.
Thomas Wilder & Mary [Houghton] his wife were maryed June 25, 1668.
Jacob farrer & Hannah [Hayward] his wife were maryed Novem. 11, 1668
John Rigby & Elizabeth his wife were maryed Aug. 30, 1662
Reuben Luxford & Margarett his wife were marryed June. 22, 1669.
Henry Maze and Ales his wife were maryed Sept. 14, 1669.
John Whetcombe and Mary his wife were maryed May, 19, 1669.

9, 7, 1670, per RALPH HOUGHTON *Clark of ye writts for Lanchaster.* Entered by THOMAS DANFORTH *Recorder.*

1670.   LANCHASTER

Jacob of Jacob and Hannah ffarer born, 29 . 1 . 69
Jonath. of Jno. & Elizab. Kettle born, 24 . 9 . 70
Nath^{ll}. of Tho. & Mary Sawjer born. 24 . 9 . 70
Hannah of John & Hannah Rug, born, 2 , 11 . 70
Maria of Jno. & Ann Moore born, 10 , 1 . 70–1
Child of Jonath. & Dorathy Prescott born, 2 , 3 . 71
Samuel of Rich. & Sarah Wheeler. 29 . 2 . 71
Jabez of Jonas & Lidea ffairbanks, 8 . 11 . 70
Joseph of Jacob & Ann ffarer 6 . 6 . 60
George of Jacob & Ann ffarrer 16 . 6 . 70.
Rebecca of Josiah & Rebecca Whetcomb, 12 . 9 . 71
Rebecca of Roger & Mary Sumner, 9 . 8 . 71
Benjamin, Hannah, of Benj. & Hannah Allin, 10 . 7 . 71
Mary of Job & Mary Whetcomb, 27 . 10 . 71
Hannah of Mordecay & Lidea Mackload 16 . 9 . 71
Mary of Tho. & Sarah Sawyer 30 . 11 . 71
Israel of Jereh. & Abigail Rogers, 26 . 9 . 71
Jno. of Jno. & Hannah Lewis, 20 . 4 . 71

Hannah of Jonath. & Han. Whetcomb. 29.6.71
Nathll. of Danl. & Johannah Hudsun, 15.3.71
Jonath. of Jonath. & Dorathy Prescott, 10.2.72
Rebeccah of Nath. & Sarah Joselin, 14.3.72.
W^m. of Jno. & Hannah Divell, 8.2.72
Ruth of Jno. & Mary Whetcomb, 27.4.72
Sarah of Jno. & Beatris Houghton, 30.5.72
Mary of Ciprian & Mary Steevens, 22.9.72
Joseph of James & Hannah Atherton, 28.2.72
W^m. of Georg & Lidea Bennett, 5.1.71-2
Jno. of Jno. & Sarah Prescott, 24.9.72
Priscilla of Ephr. & Priscilla Roper, 26.11.72
Jno. of Jno. & Mary Houghton, 13.12.72
Jonas of Jonas & Lidea ffairbank, 6.3.73
Jno. of Jno. & Hannah Wilder, 11.5.73
Martha of Hen. & Elizab. Kerly, 10.4.72
W^m. of John & Hannah Lewis, 2.11.73
Abigail of Benj. & Mary Allin, 12.1.72-3
Rebeccah of Jno. & Hannah Rug, 16.3.73
Martha of Tho. & Mary Sawyer, 10.6.73
W^m. of Roger & Mary Sumner, 26.11.73
W^m. of W^m. & Elizab. Lincorne, 26.6.72
Elizab. of W^m. & Elizab. Lincorne, 26.12.73
Saml. of Saml. & Mary Waters, 23.1.73
Johannah of Josiah & Rebecca Whetcomb, 8.1.73-4
Jacob of Jno. & Mary Houghton 17.2.74
Beatris of Abram & Ann Joslyn, 9.3.74
Abigal of Jonath. & Hannah Whetcomb, 5.3.74
Susannah of Jer. & Abiah Rogers, 2.11.73
Lidea of Georg & Lidea Bent, [Bennett] 7.6.74

Deaths

Ann wife of Jno. Moore dyed, 10.1,70-71
Child of Jonath & Dorathy Prescott, 2.3.71
W^m. Lewis 3.10.71
ffr[ances] Whetcomb 17.3.71
Jonath. of Jonath. Prescott, 4.3.72
Mary daughter of James Atherton, 4.9.70
Benj. son of Georg Adams, 26.8.72
Isaac Wright, 20.10.63
Tho. Joslin, 3.11.60
Sarah wife of Tho. Sawyer, 2.1.71-2
W^m. son of Georg Bennett, 14.1.71
Jno. son of Jno ffarer, 2.8.73

Mariages

Jonath. Prescott & Dorathy his wife, 4.6.70
Thomas Sawyer & Sarah his wife, 11.8.70
Jno. Whetcomb & Mary his wife. 16.1.70-1
Benj. Bosworth & Beatris his wife, 16.9.71
Mordecay Mackload & Lidea his wife, 31.11.70
Cipryan Steevens & Sarah [Mary Willard] his wife: 22.11.71
John Wilder & Hannah his wife, 17.5.72
John Houghton & Mary his wife, 22.11.71
Tho: Sawyer & Hannah his wife, 21.9.72
Jeremiah Rogers & Dorcas his wife, 11,10.72
Abram Jocelyn & Ann his wife, 29.9.72
Samuel & Mary Waters, 21.1.72
Nathaniel Wilder & Mary his wife, 24.11.73
Jonas Prescott & Mary his wife, 14.9.72

Received from Ralph Houghton, 6.8.74, and ent^d. by Tho: Danforth, R

MIDDLESEX REGISTER.

MARRIAGES

John Sawyer marryed to Mary Bull of Worcester by Mr W^m. Brimsmead Minister   June 16. 1686
Recorded Decemb. 15th. 1686 By L. HAMMOND, Record^r

John Moor & Mary Whitcomb, both of Lancaster were Married, August 23. 1683.
John Pope & Beatrix Haughton, both of Lancaster were Married, Sept. 20, 1683.
*Jonah [Jonas] Haughton of Lancaster & Mary Berbeane of Wooburn were Marryed, February 15, 1681.
James Atherton & Abigail Hudson, both of Lancaster, were Marryed, June 6, 1684.

BIRTHS

Ebenezer, Sonne of Jno & Sarah Prescott, borne, July 6th, 1682
Elizabeth, Daughter of Joseph & Elizabeth Waters, borne. Augst. 11, 1679.
Joseph, Sonne of Joseph, & Elizabeth Waters, borne, April, 2. 1682
Hezekiah, Sonne of *Joseph [Josiah] & Rebecca Whitcomb, borne, Sept. 14, 1681.
Joseph. Sonne of Thomas & Mary Wilder, borne, July, 5, 1683
Ebenezer, Sonne of John & Hannah Wilder, borne, June. 23, 83
Josiah, Sonne of Josiah [Jonas] & Mary Haughton borne, July 2, 82
John, Sonne of Josiah [Jonas] & Mary Haughton borne, January, 24, 83
Hannah, Daughter [of] Robert & Esther Houghton borne, Novemb. 2. 83
John, Sonne of John & Mary Hines borne, January 19, 83
Deborah, Daughter of Josiah & Rebeccah Whitcomb, borne, Decemb: 26, 83
Abigail, Daughter of Abraham & Tabitha Wheeler borne, March 2, 83
John, Sonne of Jonathan & Hannah Whitcomb borne, May, 12, 84
Susanna, Daughter of John & Beatrix Pope borne, Octob. 7, 84
Isaac, Sonne } of Isaac & Experience Wheeler borne, Novemb. 22, 84
Experience, Daughter }
Anna, Daughter of John and Mary Haughton borne, May 8, 84
Sarah, Daughter of John & Priscilla Bemon borne. January. 25, 81
Gamaliel, Daughter [son] of John & Priscilla Bemon borne Febry. 29, 84.
Martha, Daughter of Joseph & Elizabeth Waters borne January 17, 83.
Sarah, Daughter of Josiah & Mary White borne Octobr: 21, 80.
Joseph, Sonne of Josiah & Mary White borne Sept. 15, 82
John, Sonne of Josiah & Mary White borne Sept. 29, 84
James, Sonne of James & Abigail Atherton borne Febry. 27, 84
Jonathan, Sonne of Nathaniel & Mary Wilder borne April 20, 82
Beatrix, Daughter of Robert & Esther Haughton borne Sept. 3, 85.
Sarah, Daughter of Thomas & Mary Wilder borne January 22, 85
Jonathan, Sonne of John & Mary Haughton borne Febry. 20, 85
John, Sonne of Isaac & Experience Wheeler borne July 24, 86
Peter, Sonne of Peter & Sarah Gosling [Joslin] borne Decemr. 8, 86
Edward, Sonne of John & Mary Sawyer borne March 30, 87

DEATHS

John Whitcomb dyed, April 6, 1683
Experience, Daughter of Isaac & Experience Wheeler Novemb. 22, 84
Isaac, Sonne of Isaac & Experience Wheeler Novemb. 26, 84

As Attests   CYPRIAN STEVENS Cler.
Recorded January 25th, 1687 By L. HAMMOND Cler.

VICTIMS OF INDIAN RAIDS.

The following lists have been compiled from numerous authorities, chiefly contemporary with the massacre :

KILLED IN MONOCO'S RAID, SUNDAY P. M., AUGUST 22, 1675, O. S.

Mordecai McLeod—"MacLoad a Scotsman."
Lydia, [Lewis], wife of Mordecai McLeod.
Hannah, daughter of Mordecai McLeod, aged three years.

---
* Accurately copied, but the Recorder must have erred in these two names.

An infant child of Mordecai and Lydia McLeod.
George Bennett.
Jacob Farrar, Junior.
William Flagg, a soldier from Watertown.
Joseph Wheeler, probably a non-resident soldier.

VICTIMS OF THE MASSACRE OF FEBRUARY 10, 1676.

Jonas Fairbank.
Joshua Fairbank, son of Jonas, aged fifteen years.
Richard Wheeler.
Ephraim Sawyer, son of Thomas, aged twenty-five years.
Henry Farrar, son of Jacob, Senior.
John Ball.
Elizabeth Ball, wife of John.
An infant child of John and Elizabeth Ball.
Ensign John Divoll.
John Divoll, Jr., aged twelve years, died in captivity.
Josiah Divoll, son of John, aged seven years.
Hannah Divoll, daughter of John, aged nine years, died captive.
Abraham Joslin, Jr., aged twenty-six years.
Ann Joslin, wife of Abraham, killed in captivity.
Beatrice, daughter of Abraham and Ann Joslin, aged two years, killed in captivity.
Daniel Gains.
Thomas Rowlandson, aged nineteen years, nephew of Reverend Joseph.
John Kettle, aged about thirty-seven years.
Joseph Kettle, son of John, aged about ten years.
John Kettle, son of John, aged about sixteen years.
Elizabeth [White], wife of Captain Henry Kerley.
Henry Kerley, son of Captain Henry, aged eighteen years.
William Kerley, son of Captain Henry, aged seventeen years.
Joseph Kerley, son of Captain Henry, aged seven years.
Priscilla Roper, wife of Ephraim.
Priscilla Roper, daughter of Ephraim, aged about three years.
Sarah Rowlandson, daughter of Reverend Joseph, died of wound, February 18.
John McLeod, brother of Mordecai.
George Harrington, a soldier of Watertown, killed February —.
John Roper, killed March 26,

NOTE.—A few others, probably six or seven, were slain at this time, the names of whom have not been found.

THE MASSACRE OF JULY 18, 1692.

Sarah [Howe] Joslin, wife of Peter.
Peter Joslin, Jr., aged six years, killed in captivity.
Three young children of Peter Joslin.
Hannah Whitcomb, widow of Jonathan.

Abraham Wheeler, son of Richard, aged thirty-six years, killed by Indians November ?, 1695. Inventory dated November 6.

THE MASSACRE OF SEPTEMBER 11, 1697.

Reverend John Whiting, aged thirty-three years.
Daniel Hudson.
Joanna Hudson, wife of Daniel.
Joanna Hudson, daughter of Daniel, aged thirty-seven years, killed captive.
Elizabeth Hudson, daughter of Daniel, aged forty years, killed captive.
Two children of Nathaniel and Rebecca Hudson.
Ephraim Roper.
Hannah [Goble] Roper, wife of Ephraim.
Elizabeth Roper, daughter of Ephraim, aged fourteen years.
John Scate.
The wife of John Scate.

MIDDLESEX REGISTER.   17

Joseph Rugg, aged about twenty-nine years, son of John.
The wife of Joseph Rugg.
Three young children of Joseph Rugg.
Hannah [Prescott] Rugg, widow of John.
Jonathan Fairbank, aged thirty-one years.
Grace Fairbank, daughter of Jonathan.
Jonas Fairbank, son of Jonathan.

KILLED IN ASSAULT BY FRENCH AND INDIANS, JULY 31, 1704.

Lieutenant Nathaniel Wilder, aged fifty-four years.
Abraham How, a soldier of Marlborough.
Benjamin Hutchins, a soldier of Marlborough.
John Spalding, a soldier.

Jonathan White, son of Josiah, aged fifteen years, killed by Indians July 16, 1707.

KILLED IN INDIAN FIGHT, AUGUST 17, 1707.

Jonathan Wilder, son of Nathaniel and Mary, aged twenty-two years.
Richard Singleterry, of Marlborough.
Ensign John Farrar, son of Jacob, Jr., & Hannah, aged thirty-five years.

An Indian Servant of Nathaniel Wilder, killed by Indians Aug. 5, 1710.

MIDDLESEX REGISTRY OF LANCASTER MARRIAGES.

By a province law, passed December 1, 1716, every town-clerk was enjoined to give in a list of marriages, annually, for record, to the Clerk of the Sessions of the Peace. The Middlesex Registry contains such returns of marriages in Lancaster from April, 1718, to the year 1730, after which the town returns were made to the Worcester Court. Only the lists previous to March, 1726, are here copied, as marriages of later date are found duly recorded in the town book.

AN ACCOUNT OF THE MARRIAGES CONSUM'ATED BY REV^d. MR. JNO. PRENTICE.

Joseph Fairbank and Mary Brown were married 21st, April, 1718.
John Bennett & Bathsheba Phelps were married July 23^d, 1718.
Jethro Eams & Abigail Wheelock were married Septemb: ye 10th, 1718.
Joseph Sawyer & Abigail Wilder were married Novembr. ye 10th, 1718.
Edward Phelps & Mary Bennett were married Novembr. ye 24th, 1718.
Deliverance Brown & Elisabeth Fairbank were married Decembr. 24th, 1718
Jabez Fairbank Junr. & Hepsibah Sawyer were married Janur. 28th, 1818-9
Ephraim Brown & Mary ffairbank were married ffebruary ye 9, 1718-9
Jabez ffairbank Sr; & Elisabeth Whetcomb were married March ye 25th, 1719

MARRIAGES CONSUM'ATED PER JNO. HOUGHTON ESQ. JUST. PEACE.

Thomas Sawyer & Mary White were married July 15th, 1718.
John Houghton & Mehetabel Wilson were marryed Novembr. 18th, 1718.
John Goodman & Mary Atherton were married January ye 20th, 1718-9.
Jonathan Whitney & Alice Willard were married February ye 25th, 1718-9.
Eliezer Houghton & Elisabeth Divoll were married March ye 11th, 1718-9.
Joshua Houghton & Elisabeth Bennit were married April ye 8th, 1719.
Amos Sawyer & Abigail Houghton were married May ye 14th, 1719.

All entered in ye Register at Lancaster pr. John Houghton *Town Clerk*
Recd. July 1719 of Jno. Houghton, Clerk of Lancaster and Entered
By SAM^{ll}. PHIPPS *Cler. pacs.*

AN ACCO^t. OF MARRIAGES CONSUM'ATED AT LANCASTER. 1719, 1719-20.

Imps. Nathan^{ll}. Whitney & Mary Holeman were married By ye Reverend Mr John Prentice Minister. Novemb. ye 18th- 1719.

It: Jonathan Willard & Keziah White were married by John Houghton Esqr: Augst. ye 17, 1719

Jno Smith & Martha Butler were married by Justice Houghton Decem^r. 14, 1719

Jno. Houghton & Sarah Gulliver were married by Mr Justice Houghton January ye 7th, 1719-20

Joseph Atherton & Hannah Rogers were Married by Justice Houghton Janu, ye 9th, 1720.

Benjamin Houghton Junr. & Ruth Wheelock were married by Justice Houghton July: 20, 1720.

Benjamin Houghton Senr. & Zerviah Moore were married by Justice Houghton July 28, 1720.

Sd marriages entered at Lancaster & ye list brought & exhibited for Registering Augst. 30th, 1720 By JNO. HOUGHTON *Town Clerk*.

Recd & accordingly entered   By SAM^{ll}. PHIPPS *Cler pacs*

AN ACCOT. OF MARRIAGES CONSUM'ATED BY JOHN HOUGHTON, JUSTICE OF YE PEACE.

Ephraim Wheeler & Meriah Glazier married Novembr: ye first *an: dom*: 1720.

John Longley & Deborah Houghton were married Novembr. 30th. *an: dom*: 1720

John Nicholls & Mary Priest Sr. were married ye 20th Day of March *an: dom*: 1720-1

Jeremiah Holeman & Anna Priest were married ye 23^d. day of March *an: dom*: 1720-1

Ebenezer Houghton & Mary Priest were married 23^d, day March *an: dom*: 1720-1

Thomas Tucker & Mary Divell were married May ye 25th. *an: dom*: 1720-1

All ye sd marriages accordingly entered at Lancaster

pr JOHN HOUGHTON, *Town Clerk*

Recd. June 20th. 1721, and Entered pr.   SAM^{ll}. PHIPPS. *Cler pac*'s

AN ACCOUNT OF LANCASTER MARRIAGES: FROM 1721-2: &c.

Marriages consum'ated pr. me John Houghton, Justice of ye Peace &c.

Richard Wilds & Ruth Houghton were married March 2^d: 1721-2.

Jonathan Whetcomb & Rachel Woods were married Decembr. 12th, 1722.

Joshua Osgood & Ruth Divell were married Decembr. 20th: 1722.

—— Fairbank [Fairbank Moore] & Judith Bellows were married April. 30th, 1723.

Israel Houghton & Martha Wheelock were married July 31st: 1723.

Jonathan Rand of Stow & Abigail Whitney of Lancaster were married Febry. 27th, 1723-4.

Abraham Willard & Mary Sawyer both of Lancaster were married Febry. 27th, 1723-4.

James Butler & Hannah Wilson both of Lancaster were married March 19th, 1723-4.

John Moore & Susannah Willard both of Lancaster were married March 19th, 1723-4:

Peter Joslin & Alice Woods of sd Lancaster were married April 30th. 1724.

John Whitney of Lancaster & Beckah Whitney of Stow were married May ye 20th, 1724.

A true Coppy of the marriages above mentioned & are accordingly entered

pr me JOHN HOUGHTON *Town Clerk for Lancaster*.

Recd June ye 9th, 1724: and accordingly entered per

SAM^{ll}: PHIPPS *Cler pac*^{s}.

Lancaster marriages consum'ated by ye Rev^d. Mr John Prentice.

William Richardson of Woburn and Mary Wilder of Lancaster were married Dec. 27. 1721

Tilley Merick of Brookfield & Elizabeth Wilder of Lancaster were married Nov. 28, 1722

Samuel Chamberlin of Chelmsford & Rebeccah Whetcomb of Lancaster were married Jany. 2: 1722-3

UNREGISTERED.

Jonas Wilder & Eunice Beaman both of Lancaster were married May: 29: 1724
John Houghton Senr. & Hannah Wilder both of Lancaster were married Jany, 27, 1724-5
William Houghton & Experience Houghton both of Lancaster were married June: 4: 1724
David Osgood & Eunice Carter both of said Lancaster were married Nov. 3, 1724
Aaron Willard of Lancaster & Mary Wright of Rutland were married Dec. 16: 1724
Ezra Sawyer & Rebecca Whetcomb both of Lancaster were married Jany: 16: 1725-6

Marriages consum'ated by John Houghton Esqr.

Jonathan Smith of Marlborough and Sarah Jewel of Stow were married Jany, 18. 1724-5
Samuel Parker ot Groton & Sarah Houghton of Lancaster were married Jany. 18. 1724-5
Jacob Houghton & Mary Willard both of Lancaster were married Febry 3: 1724-5
William Johnson & Ruth Rugg both of ye Town of Lexington were married Febry. 11. 1724-5
Gershom Houghton & Elizabeth Rugg both of Lancaster were married Febry. 23. 1724-5
Josiah Willard & Prudence Keyes both of Lancaster were married July, 7, 1725
Henry Houghton of Lancaster & Elizth. Rand of Stow were married Novemb. 24: 1725.
Thomas Houghton & Meriah Moore both of Lancaster were married Dec: 2: 1725
Joseph Joseline & Katharine Reed both of Marlborough were married Decr. 6. 1725
Daniel Albert & Mary Houghton both of Lancaster were married Decr. 9. 1725
Ebenezer Polley & Dorcas Houghton both of Lancaster were married Jany. 11: 1725
Jonathan Houghton & Mary Houghton both of Lancaster were married Jany. 20, 1725
Joseph Whetcomb & Damaris Priest both of Lancaster were married Jany. 20, 1725
Saml. Carter & Jemimah Houghton both of Lancaster were married Febry. 14, 1724-5

An acct. of sd Marriages taken and Entered by JOHN HOUGHTON SEN^r. *Town Clerk for Lancaster.*

   1726, April 20th Rec^d and Entered By SAM^{ll}. PHIPPS *Cler Pacs.*

DEATHS OF SUNDRY EARLY PROPRIETORS AND RESIDENTS OF LANCASTER AS ATTESTED BY WILLS, INVENTORIES, DIARIES, RECORDS OF OTHER TOWNS, ET CETERA.

Sholan alias Showanon, Sachem of the Nashaways, October —, 1654.
Shoshanim alias Sam, Sachem of the Nashaways, hanged at Boston, Sept. 26, 1676.
Monoco alias One-eyed John, Sachem of the Nashaways, hanged at Boston, Sept. 26, 1676.
Thomas King, purchaser of Nashaway from Sholan; at Watertown, December 3, 1644.
Henry Symonds, partner of King; at Boston, September —, 1643.
Stephen Gates, at Cambridge; inventory dated 29. 7 mo. 1622.
John Tinker, in Connecticut, October —, 1662.
Stephen Day, at Cambridge, December 22, 1668.
Abraham Joslin, at sea; will proved April 17, 1670.
John White, at Lancaster; will proved May 28th, 1673.
Dorothy Prescott, wife of Jonathan, at Lancaster, ——— 1674.
Major Simon Willard, at Charlestown; Sewall's Diary; April 24, 1676.
Jeremiah Rogers, at Dorchester, September 26, 1676.
Jacob Farrar, Sen., at Woburn, August 14, 1677.
Mary Hudson, wife of Daniel, at Concord, November 4, 1677.

Abigail Rogers, daughter of Jeremiah, at Dorchester, 6 . 1 mo. 1678.
Bathsheba Rogers, daughter of Jeremiah, at Dorchester, 10 . 1 mo. 1678.
Abiah Rogers, widow of Jeremiah, at Dorchester, 10 . 1 mo. 1678.
Gamaliel Beaman, Sen., at Dorchester, 23 . 1 mo. 1678.
Samuel Rugg, son of John and Hannah, at Concord, 20 . 4 mo. 1678.
Benjamin Allen, at Charlestown, 20 . 7 mo. 1678.
Rev. Joseph Rowlandson, at Wethersfield, Ct., aged forty-seven years — Bradstreet's Journal — November 23, 1678.
Nathaniel Wilder, infant son of Nathaniel and Mary, in Sudbury, May 19, 1679.
Archelaus Courser, in Boston, —— 1679.
Hannah Houghton, daughter of Ralph, aged twelve years, at Charlestown, October 8, 1679.
John Houghton, son of Ralph, aged twenty years, at Charlestown, Oct. 10, 1679.
Ann Waters, wife of Lawrence, at Charlestown, February 6, 1680.
James Butler, Senr. "Irishman," at Billerica, 20 day, 1 mo. 1681.
John Prescott, founder of Lancaster, aged about seventy-seven years; nuncupative will proved December 20, 1681.
William Whittborn; inventory dates February 23, 1682.
John Whitcomb, drowned in Nashua River; inquest April 7, 1683.
William Kerley, Jun., at Marlborough, January 11, 1684.
Lawrence Waters, at Charlestown, December 9, 1687.
John Bush, September 1, 1688.
John Glazier, Sen., inventory dated October 29, 1688.
Jonathan Whitcomb; inventory dated February 25, 1691.
Samuel Wheeler, son of Richard; inventory dated April 7, 1691.
Rev. Samuel Carter, in Groton; administration granted October 30, 1693.
Nathaniel Joslin, at Marlborough, April 8, 1694.
Daniel Allen, at Watertown, March 7, 1694.
George Adams, at Cambridge, October 10, 1696.
John Rugg; inventory dated January 19, 1797.
Alice and Fannie, twin daughters of Rev. John Whiting, aged two years ten months, May 19, 1697.
Eunice, daughter of Rev. John Whiting, November 4, 1697.
Deacon Roger Sumner, aged sixty-six years, at Milton, May 26, 1698.
Philip Goss, at Lancaster; administration granted May 26, 1698.
James Smith, at Lancaster; inventory dated December 23, 1700.
Ensign John Moore, at Lancaster; inventory dated September 23, 1702.
John Moore, Sen., at Lancaster; nuncupative will proved November 26, 1703.
Rev. Andrew Gardner, killed at Lancaster, aged twenty-nine years, Oct. 25, 1704.
John Priest, at Lancaster; inventory dated December 21, 1704.
John Carter, a soldier; by funeral account, March 26, 1704-5.
John Brabrook, a soldier; by funeral account, March 31, 1704-5.
Ralph Houghton, at Milton, April 15, 1705.
James Atherton, aged eighty-four years, at Sherborn; will dated Jany. 3, 1708.
Capt. Henry Kerley, at Marlborough; will proved January 7, 1714.
Thomas Ross; administration granted June 10, 1718.
John Hinds, March —, 1720.

MARRIAGES OF SUNDRY EARLY PROPRIETORS AND RESIDENTS OF LANCASTER NOT FOUND IN THE PRECEDING LISTS.

1648. Thomas Sawyer and Mary Prescott.
1654. John Rugg and Martha Prescott.
1654. 6 mo. 2 day, Richard Smith and widow Joanna Quarlls, in Boston.
1654. November 2, Henry Kerley and Elizabeth White, in Sudbury.
1654. November 16, John Moore and Ann Smith, in Sudbury.
1656. Joseph Rowlandson and Mary White.
1656. Nathaniel Joslin and Sarah King of Marlborough.
1656. Roger Sumner and Mary Joslin.
1656. Samuel Davis and Mary Waters.
1658. April 5, John Maynard and Mary Gates, in Sudbury.
1661. Archelaus Courser and Rachel Roper.

BOOK I.

1 Dinah servant of the Rev.d Mr. Harrington Departed this life in full & certain hopes of a better, June 14, 1783 at 3 OClock P. M.
Phinehas Sawyer son to Phinehas & Mary Sawyer Born April y⁰ 15——

2   *Marriages Consumated by y⁰ Rev.d John Mellen.*

Asa Whitcomb with Eunice Sawyer Decem.r y⁰ 26 1744
Jacob Smith with Esther Burpee August 27 1745
Gideon Brockway with Lois Beman October 10 1745
Joshua House with Prudance Sawyer Novem. 6 1745
Zacheus Boynton with Hanah Pebody Dec.m 9 1746
Jonathan Bayley with Abigail Whitney March 26. 1747
Abiathar Houghton of Leominster & Mileasant Carter of Lancaster was married by Josiah Converse Esq July y⁰ 3. 1750

Marriages consumated by Revd. Mr Timothy Harrington.

Ebenezer Taylor & Mary Houghton March y⁰ 9.th 1748–9
Nathaniel White & Lydia Phelps Novemb.r y⁰ 29.th 1749
Ye Rev.d John Mellen & M.rs. Rebekah Prentice Novem.r 30, 1749
the Rev.d John Rogers of Leominster & M.rs. Releaf Prentice of Lancaster March y⁰ 27 1750

Marriages consumated by Joseph Wilder Jun.

George McFarling of Lunenburg & Margret Torrance of Lancaster April y⁰ 16, 1752
John Phelps & Zipporah Wilder February y⁰ 3, 1747–8
Sherebiah Ballard & Keziah Osgood March 17 1747–8
Robert Fletcher & Elizabeth Houghton May y⁰ 25 1748
Joshua Fletcher & Mary Allen May y⁰ 25 1748
Ebenezer Bigelow & Hephzibah Dufore Decem.r 1748
Jonathan Harris & Annis Houghton May y⁰ 26 1749
Daniel Johnson & Lidia Willard November y⁰ 8 1749
Gershom Flagg & Mary Willard·December y⁰ 6.th 1750 both of Lancaster

Marriages consumated by y⁰ Rev.d Timothy Harrington.

Mathias Larkin and Demaras Sawyer both of Lancaster May y⁰ 8 1751
April [17] 1751 Wm Phelps & Mary Nichols Both of Lancaster
May y⁰ 22, Mr John Beaman & the Widow Sarah Page both of Lancaster
May y⁰ 28.th Jonas Fletcher of Groton & Ruth Fletcher of Lancaster
December y⁰ 4.th Mr David Wilder & Mrs Martha White both of Lancaster
January y⁰ Second [1752] Josiah Cutting of Shrewsbury & Orph[a] Houghton of Lancaster
Jan y⁰ 22 Joseph Kilburn & Mary Sawyer both of Lancaster these according to y⁰ Dates were married by me T. Harrington.

3   *Ye births & Deaths of ye Children of Oliver & Abigail Moor.*

Abijah Moor born September ye 14 1730 & Deceased July 28 : 1740
Levi Moor born May ye 23 1732
Israel Moor Born April ye 12 1744
Uriah Moor born January ye 9 1735 & Deceased September ye 17 1736
Abigail Moor born January ye 27 1737-8
Prudance Moor born August 25 1740
Jonathan Moor born Iuly 26 1742
Hannah Moor born April ye 6th 1746 & Deceased September ye 1st 1749

Ye births of ye Children of Revd Timothy Harrington & Mrs Anna Harrington.

Henrietta Born at Lexington August 8 1744
Arethusa Born at Lexington Octobr 4th [16] 1747 [Died Nov. 17, 1844.]
Timothy at Lancaster October 22d 1749

Pamela Mellen Daughter of ye Revd John Mellen & Rebecca Mellen was Born Sept 5. 1750
John Mellen son of John & Rebecca Mellen was born June ye 27 1752
John Manning & Prudance Houghton was married by Oliver [Wilder] Esq. April ye 28 1753
Rebecka Mellen Daughter to ye Revd John Mellen & Rebecka Born April ye 16 : 1754

Marriages Consumated by ye Revd John Mellen

Ephraim Roper [&] Michal Houghton April ye 8 1748
Ebenezer Buss & Keziah Houghton April ye 8 1748
John Brooks & Parnie Houghton October 20 1748
Ezekiel Newton & Dorathy Osgood June 21 1749
David Willard & Sarah May June 23 1749
Abner Wilder & Eunice Osgood June 27 1750
John Whetcomb & Susanah Gary September 5. 1750
Tilley Richardson & Elisabeth Sawyer July 10th 1751
Jonas Kendal & Elisabeth Bennitt August 8 1751
Solomon Houghton & Deliverance Ross Novemr 7 1751
Samll Newton & Sarah Douglas Decemr 19th 1751
4 Jesse Ross & Ruth Rugg was married by Colo. Oliver Wilder Nov. 1. 1759
Rachel Daught. to Lin & Hanah Jock born June 25th: 1766.

6   *The Births of the Children of Jonas & Thankfull Fairbank*

Martha Fairbank Born January 13 : 1731-2
Josiah Fairbank Born May 22 : 1734
Elijah Fairbank Born December 21 : 1734? [1735]
Cyrus Fairbank Born May 2. 1737   Sarah Fairbank Born October 22 . 1745
Mary Fairbank Born October 15. 1741 Abijah Fairbank Born April 29, 1748
Jonas Fairbank Born November 2, 1743 Elezabeth Fairbank Born April 18, 1750

Elezabeth Wilder Daughter of Ephraim and Anna Wilder Born May 16 1748

8   *Marriages Consumated.*

James Cleland of Lime in ye Coloni of Coneticut with Thankfull Wilder of Bolton

Ye Births of ye Children of James Clealand & Thankfull Clealand of Lyme in Connecticook. I bleve there is two of these Children in another plaee.

Hannah Cleland born Feb 17th 1742-3   Jonas born August 1st 1748
Samuel Born May ye 27th 1744   John was born —— 1st 1749-50
James born October ye 12 1745   Mary September ye 7 1751

Thomas Lagget Son of Thomas & Magdelen Lagget born October ye 7 1734
Mary Lagget Daughter of Thomas & Magdelen Lagget born July 23 1737
Robert Lagget Son of Thomas & Magdelen Lagget born July 26 1742

BOOK FIRST.

Elisabeth Lagget Daughter of Thomas & Magdelen Lagget born October y⁰ 4 1743
Samuel son of Samuel & Hannah Churchel born Oct y⁰ 20ᵗʰ 1749
Luce Wallingsford Daughter of Ezekiel & Lidia Wallingsford born August the 1 1741
Mary Wallingsford Daughter of Ezekiel & Lidia Wallingsford Born June y⁰ 26ᵗʰ 1743

The Children of Roger and Lucy Robins

Silis born Novemʳ y⁰ 24 1749. [46].   Luke was born April y⁰ 25 1749 [48]
Jacob December yᵉ 16 1750.   [See p. 147]

9   *Intentions of Marriage*

Aaron Sawyer Entered his Intentions of marriage with Abigail Moor. Both of Lancaster : March y⁰ 30ᵗʰ 1754.
Joseph Wilder Ter. of Lancaster Entered his Intentions of mariage with Elisabeth Hawyard of Lunenburge May y⁰ 15 : 1754.
Moses Wilder of Lancaster Entered his Intentions of mariage with Submit Ross of Sudbury June y⁰ 7 : 1754.
Ephraim Goss of Bolton Entered his Intentions of mariage with Kezia Gary of Lancaster June 22 : 1754.
Nathaniel Seaver of Naregansett No 2 Entered his Intentions of mariage with Judith Treadaway of Framingham. Lancaster June y⁰ 26 : 1754.
Amasa Turner of Lancaster and Margrett Gross of Hingham Entered their Intentions of mariage. Lancaster September y⁰ 14. 1754
William Richardson y⁰ third Entered his Intentions of mariage with Easter Jipe September y⁰ 14 : 1754
Joseph Whetcomb Jur of Lancaster Entered his 'Entions of mariage with Elesibeth Wheelock of Leominster. Lancaster Sept y⁰ 28 : 1754
Asaph Wilder Entered his 'Entions of mariage with Lidea Rugg Both of Lancaster October y⁰ 23 : 1754
Aamos Sawyer Jur Entered his 'Entions of mariage with Mary Rugg Both of Lancaster Novembʳ 23 : 1754.
Samˡˡ. Prentice Entered his 'Entions of mariage with Prudence Osgood Both of Lancaster Decmʳ y⁰ 30 : 1754.
Tirus Houghton Entered his 'Entions of mariage with Rachel House Both of Lancaster Decmʳ y⁰ 30 : 1754.
Willᵐ Dunsmore of Lancaster Entered his 'Entions of mariage with Hannah Sumner of Kilnerley [Killingly, Ct.] January y⁰ 2ᵈ : 1754 [55].
Nathᵃ: Wilder Jur. Entered his 'Entions of mariage with Lidia Kendall of Lancaster Jan : y⁰ 2 : 1754.-[55.]
Nathan Meriam of Narigansett No. 2 Entered his In'tions of mariage with Mary Hosmore of Concord Jan y⁰ 11 : 1755
Jonathan Fairbank Juʳ. Entred his 'Entions of mariage with Ruth Houghton Both of Lancaster Jan y⁰ 11. 1755
Thomas May Entered his 'Entions of mariage with Thankfull Whetcomb Both of Lancaster January y⁰ 18. 1755
10 Jonathan Houghton & Thankfull White both of Lancaster were married by yᵉ Revᵈ. Mr John Prentice y⁰ : 6. day of November : 1712
Amos Sawyer & Abigail Houghton Both of Lancaster were married the : 14 : day of May, 1719.
Hooker Osgood & Mary Whellock Both of Lancaster were married By the Reverand Mr John Prentice, January y⁰ 23 : 1716-7
John Bennitt & Bathshebah Phelps both of Lancaster were married By yᵉ Reverand Mr John Prentice July yʳ 23, 1718.
Joseph Abbott Son of Joseph & Hannah Abbot born 29 Day of March 1742
Hannah Daughter of Joseph Abbott born September y⁰ 23, 1743
Elizebeth Daughter of Joseph & Hannah Abbott was born July 6ᵗʰ 1746
11 Abraham Beaman & Mary Rice Both of Marlborough were married by John Houghton Esqʳ. the 16 day of March, 1725-6.
Joseph Osgood of Lancaster & Catharine Witherbey of Stow were married by John Houghton Esqʳ. the 12 day of May, 1726.

Samuel Rogers & Isabella Houghton Both of Lancaster were married by John Houghton Esq'. the 4 day of August, 1726.
Phinehas Pratt & Martha Puffer Both of Sudbery were married by John Houghton Esq'. the 4 day of August. 1726.
John Divol & Sarah Osgood both of Lancaster were married by John Houghton Esqr. the 16 day of November, 1726.
Joseph Moore & Rebekah Houghton both of Lancaster were married by John Houghton Esq'. the 17 day of November, 1726.
John Snow & Hannah Sawyer both of Lancaster were married by John Houghton Esq'. the 19 day of January, 1726-7.
Daniel Albertt & Abigail Houghton Both of Lancaster were married by John Houghton Esq'. the 25 day of January, 1726-7.
Thomas Littlejohns & Mary Butler Both of Lancaster were married By John Houghton Esqr. the 26 day of January 1726-7.
Benjamin Atherton & Eunice Preist Both of Lancaster were married by John Houghton Esq'. the 23 day of March, 1726-7.
Jonathan Moor & Mary Wheller Both of Lancaster were married by John Houghton Esq'. the 19 day of April 1727.
Edward Houghton of Lancaster & Abigail Coy of Pomphritt were married by Joseph Levins Esqr. the 16 day of November, 1727.
Henry Willard & Abigail fairbank both of Lancaster was married by y'e Rever'd. Mr John Prentice y'e 24 day of May. 1726.
Joseph Wilson & Rebecca Phelps both of Lancaster was married by y'e Rever'd. Mr John Prentice y'e 21 day of September, 1726.
William Pollard & Experience Wheller both of Lancaster was married by the Rever'd. Mr John Prentice y'e 23 day of november. 1726.
Ephraim Houghton & Sarah Sawyer both of Lancaster was married by y'e Reverand Mr John Prentice y'e 15 day of December, 1726.
Seth Sawyer & Dinah farrar both of Lancaster was married by the Reverand Mr Johh Prentice y'e 11 of January, 1726-7.
The Reverand Mr Job Cushing & Mrs Mary Prentice was married by the Reverand Mr John Prentice y'e 16 of March, 1726-7.
Jeremiah Belknap of Framingham & Martha Rugg of Lancaster was married by y'e Rev'd. Mr John Prentice y'e 23 day of March, 1726-7.
Eleazar Ball & Abigail Rogers was married by y'e Reven'd. Mr John Prentice y'e 23 day of March 1726-7
Eleazar Haywood & Azubah Stevens was married by y'e Reven'd. Mr John Prentice y'e 23 of October, 1727
Phillip Brookins & Sarah Keyes was married by y'e Reven'd. Mr John Prentice the 7 day of november, 1727.
12 John Haywood & Ruth Carter were married by y'e Rever'd Mr John Prentice April 30th : 1728.
Peter Atherton & Experience Wright was married by y'e Rever'd. Mr John Prentice June y'e 13th; 1728.
Joshua Church and Annis Johnson was married by y'e Rever'd Mr John Prentice november y'e 19th. 1728.
Shubael Bayley and Anna Houghton was married by y'e Rever'd. Mr John Prentice november y'e 21st, 1728.
Josiah Bennett of Shrewsbury and Hannah Ross of Lancaster was married by y'e Rever'd Mr John Prentice november y'e 27th, 1728.
Sam'll. Sawyer and Deborah Rugg was married by y'e Rever'd. Mr John Prentice february y'e 20th: 1728-9.
Robert Barnard of Marlborough, and Elizabeth Bayley of Lancaster was married by y'e Rever'd Mr John Prentice, May y'e 28th. 1729.
Benjamin Harris and Deborah Temple was married by y'e Reverend Mr John Prentice november y'e 18th. 1729.
Thomas Wright & Abigail Sawyer, was married by y'e Reverend Mr John Prentice, november y'e 18th 1729.
Hezekiah Whitcomb and Rachel Preist was married by Joseph Wilder Esq'. April y'e 3d. 1729.
Tho. fairbancks and Dorothy Carter was married by Joseph Wilder Esq'. April y'e 24th. 1729.

BOOK FIRST.

Aaron Osgood and Eunis White was married by Joseph Wilder Esqr. May ye 15th. 1729.
Joseph Wood and Hannah White was married by Joseph Wilder Esqr. May ye 15th. 1729
Nathaniel Nueton and Mary Temple was married by Joseph Wilder Esqr. October ye 21st. 1729.
Nathaniel Wilder and Mary Beman was married by Joseph Wilder Esqr. December ye 11. 1729.
Oliver Moor and Abigail Houghton was married by Joseph Wilder Esqr. December ye 18th. 1729.
Hezakiah Gates and Mary Sawyer was married by Joseph Wilder Esqr. february ye 17th: 1729-30
William Whitcomb and Hepthzaba Sawyer was married by Joseph Wilder Esqr. february ye 25th 1729-30.
Benjamin Goodridge & Sarah Phelps was married by ye Rev^d Mr John Prentice April ye 8th. 1730.
Amos Atherton & Elizabeth Harries was married by Joseph Wilder Esqr. Novem^b ye 18, 1730.
John Atherton & Phebey Wright was married by the Rev^d Mr John Prentice July 1, 1730.
Josiah Richardson & Dorothy Wilder was married by ye Rev^d Mr John Prentice Dec^m. ye 3, 1730.
Jonathan Powers & Hannah More was married by ye Rev^d Mr John Prentice Dec^m. ye 17 : 1730.
Zadok Sanborn & Sarah Knight was married by ye Rev^d Mr John Prentice feb^r. 22 : 1730-1.
Samuel Sterns & Keziah Robins of Littleton was married by Joseph Wilder Esqr. Jan^u. 1 : 1730-1
David Whetcomb & Bettey White of Lancaster was married by Joseph Wilder Esqr. Jan^u. 13 : 1730-1
Reubin Rugg & Lydiah Ross of Lancaster was married by Joseph Wilder Esqr. March 10, 1730-1
Elijah Whitney & Mercy Heald of Lancaster was married by Joseph Wilder Esqr. March 11: 1730-1
Jonas Fairbank & Thankful Wheler both of Lancaster was married by ye Reverand Mr John Prentice April ye 8. 1731.
Joseph Sawyer & Tabathy Prescott of Lancaster was married by ye Revn^d Mr John Prentice May ye 19. 1731.
Ephraim Wilder & Anna Wilder of Lancaster was married by ye Rev^d Mr John Prentice June 17: 1731.
Nathaniel Carter & Thankfull Sawyer of Lancaster was married by ye Rev^d Mr John Prentice feb. 9, 1731-2.
James White & Margret M'Colister of Lancaster was marryed by ye Rev^d Mr John Prentice March 1: 1731-2.
Jabez Beaman & Dinah Moore of Lancaster was married by ye Revn^d Mr John Prentice October 4: 1732.
Seth Sawyer & Hephzibah Whetney of Harvard was married by ye Rev^d Mr John Prentice October 12 : 1732
Joseph Sawyer & Abigail foskett of Harvard were married by Joseph Wilder Esqr. March 9: 1732-3.
Josiah Whetney & Elisabeth Whetney was married by Joseph Wilder Esqr. April 24: 1733.
William Butrick & Elisabeth Whetcomb was married by the Rev^d Mr John Prentice January ye 17: 1732-3
Joseph Brown & Grace fairbank was married March ye 27: 1733: by the Rever^d Mr John Prentice
13 James Smith & Sarah Atherton was married by Joseph Wilder Esqr May 29. 1733.
Joseph Wilder & Deborah Joslin was married by Joseph Wilder Esqr July ye 4 : 1733
John Joslin & Luce Wilder was married by Joseph Wilder Esqr. July 4: 1733.

Simon Whetcomb & Thankful Houghton was married by Joseph Wilder Esqr July ye 12 : 1733.
Jonathan Wilson & Hephzibah Wilder was married by Joseph Wilder Esqr August ye 2. 1733.
Robert Powers & Mary Glazier was married by Joseph Wilder Esqr August ye 2. 1733
Jonathan White & Easter Wilder was married by Joseph Wilder Esqr June ye 22: 1732.
Nathaniel Butler & Experience Glazier was married Novem. 22 : 1733 by Joseph Wilder Esqr.
Benjamin Corey of Lunenburgh & Judeth Beaman of Lancaster was married May ye 23 ; 1733, by Mr Prentice.
Daniel Knight & Anna Carter both of Lancaster was married July ye 3^d: 1733: by ye Rev^d Mr Prentice.
Thomas Sawyer & Anna Ross both of Lancaster was married Decemb. 31: 1733, by ye Rev^d. Mr Jno. Prentice.
Peter Kendal & Hephzibah Ruck was married february 14: 1733-4, pr Joseph Wilder Justice of peace
Daniel Powers & Mary Wilder both of Lancaster was married March the 6; 1733-4 pr Joseph Wilder Justice of ye peace.
William Willard & Sarah Gates were married October the 7th: 1734, by Samuel Willard Esqr.
Amos Knight & Hannah Beaman was married November ye 28th: [27th in Joseph Wilder's Memoranda] 1734: by Joseph Wilder Esqr.
James Wilder & Martha Broughton was married December ye 24 : 1734 : by Joseph Wilder Esqr.
Nathaniel Wilson & Eunice Davenport was married ye 20 day of february : 1734-5 ; by Sam^{ll}. Willard Esqr.
Hezekiah Snow & Martha Carly was married — 1734-5. by Sam^{ll}. Willard Esqr.
John Whetcomb & Mary Carter were married by ye Rev^d Mr John Prentice June the 12: 1735.
Jonathan Osgood & Aseneth Sawyer were married by ye Rev^d Mr John Prentice June ye 18: 1735.
Jonathan Wheelock & Elisabeth Russel was married ye 11: day of September: 1735: by Sam^{ll}: Willard Esqr.
Benjn. Ballard & Ruth Wilder was married Janu'ry ye 17: 1734-5: by Joseph Wilder Esqr.
Nathaniel Sawyer & Mary Houghton was married by Joseph Wilder Esqr. ye 19: of March: 1734-5.
John White & Lois Wilder was married by Joseph Wilder Esqr. the 19 of March: 1734-5
John Houghton & Hephzibah Preist was married by Joseph Wilder Esqr. ye 13 of Novemb^r. 1735
James Willard & Rebeckah Gates was married by Sam^{ll}. Willard Esqr. ye 12 of Novembr. 1735
The Revnd. Mr David Sterns & Ruth Hubart of Lunenburgh was married by Revnd. Mr John Prentice of Lancaster, the seventh day of April, 1736.
Abner Sawyer & Mary Wilder of Lancaster was married by Mr Prentice, April ye 8, 1736
William Goss & Lucy Heald of Stow was married by ye Rev^d Mr John Prentice June the 16: 1736.
Gardner Wilder & Mary Phelps both of Lancaster, was married June ye 30: 1736: by ye Rev^d Mr John Prentice.
Thomas Sawyer & Elisabeth Osgood were married October ye 21: 1736. by the Rev^d Mr John Prentice.
John Chamberlin with Sarah Snow June ye 4th 1741.
Jonathan Knight with Mary Johnson Sept. ye 4th 1741.
Amos Rugg with Mary Burpee December ye 29th. 1741.
Daniel Rugg with Sarah Wilder January ye 7th 1741.
Ezekel Kendal with Hanna Perpoint March ye 3^d 1742.
Ebenezer Snow & Elisebeth Carley was married by Oliver Wilder Esqr. Octr. ye 10 1745.

BOOK FIRST. 27

William Richards Junr. —— was married by Oliver Wilder Esqr. June 18, 1749
Benj^a Glaizer and Lidia Daken was married July ye 5 1749 by Oliver Wilder Esqr.
Abiathar Houghton of Leominster &, Melisant Carter of Lancaster was Joyned in marriage July the 3^d, 1750 by Josiah Converse Justice of ye Peace.
14   Caleb Wilder and Abigil Carter February ye 23^d 1736 pr Jos. Wilder Esq.
Thomas Wetherby and Elisabeth Heald March ye 23^d 1736,   "
John Carter and Abigail Joslin March ye 10th 1736-7, pr Rev^d Mr John Prentice
Ephraim Carter and Mary Osgood March 24. 1736-7   "   "
Thomas Sawyer and Abigail White April ye 27. 1737   "   "
Simon Butler and Annah Fairbank April ye 5th 1738 pr Joseph Wilder
Phinehas and Mary Sawyer June ye 1, 1737.   "   "
Joshua Fairbank and Eunice Wilder 1737. December ye 7th.
Edward Robins and Bathsheba Bennet 22 of April 1737.
James Butler and Deborah Harris April 22^d, 1737.
James Ross and Abigail Buss 1737-8 March 2^d.
Charls Wilder, Martha Sawyer May 13 1738, Rev^d Mr Prentice
John Hinds and Alis Smith May ye 25 1738 — Sent to Record.
Benjamin Sterns and Dina Wheeler September ye 11th 1738
David Johnson and Mary Warner February ye 22 1738-9
Mr James Cleland and Thankfull Wilder February ye 22^d 1738
Jonathan Wilder and Zirviah Houghton was married Feb. 23^d 1738-9
Barzillai Holt and Elisabeth Goss was married August ye 27th 1738 by Collonal Willard
Marthew Wiman and Abigail Willard March ye 8 1738-9 by Collonal Willard
Josiah White and Deborah Hous March ye 14th 1738-9 Joseph Wilder
Zechariah Glazier and Thankfull Butler March ye 16th 1738-9   "   "
Israel Whetcomb and Azubah Houghton was maried May ye 8 1738 pr Col Willard.
Thomas White and Sarah Broughton was married October ye 31st 1739.
Oliver Ston of Harvard & Mariah Priest of Bolton November ye 29th 1739
Andrew Wilder and Elisabeth Carter February ye 20th 1739
Isaac Butler and Sarah Harris October ye 22^d 1740.
Phinihas Beman and Joannah White October ye 23^d 1740.
Manassa Divol and Susannah Sollindine June ye 19th. 1740
Daniel Priest and Elisabeth Kilborn June ye forth 1741
David Wilder and [Mrs.] Anna [Willard] Prentice June ye 10th 1739
David Juet and Elisabeth Beman June ye 21st 1739
Jacob Fowl and Phebe Osgood June ye 28 1739
Zacheus Boyinton and Anna Ross July ye 12 1739
Oliver Wilder and Sarah Townsend January ye 16th 1739.
Daniel Robbins and Elisabeth Prentice May ye 27th 1740
Mr Josiah Brown and Mrs Preudence Prentice November the 19th 1740.
Josiah and Abigail Sawyer December ye 11th 1740.
Elisha Sawyer of Bolton and Ruth White January ye 7th 1740
Jeremiah Haskil and Thankfull Beman May ye 14th 1741
Joseph Rugg of Worcester and Ruth Glazier June 15th 1738
Moses Osgood and Martha Powers April ye 19th 1739
    These last twelve by ye Rev^d Mr John Prentice. turn back.
15   William Divol of Lancaster and Sarah Davenport Entered their Intentions of marriage May ye 21 . 1739 and had their intentions then posted.
Mr Thomas Prentice of Lancaster and Mrs Abigail Willard of Lunenburg entered their intentions of marriage June the 15th 1737 and had the same then made Publick at Lancaster as the Law directs.
Joshua Fairbank and Eunice Wilder entered their Intentions of marriage ye 15th of June 1737 and had their Intentions then made Publick as the Law directs at Lancaster.
Edward Robbins and Bathsheba Bennet entered their Intentions of marriage October ye 8th 1737 and were then made Publick
Benj Townsend and Sarah Wheeler at ye same time above said
James Butler and Deborah Harris entered their Intentions of marriage October 27th 1737 and their Intentions were made Publick at ye same time as the Law Directs.

November y⁰ 12 John Buss and Mary Wood James Ross and Abigail Buss Entered their Intentions of marriage y⁰ Date above

Ezekiel Wallinsford Entered their Intention of marriage with Lediah Brown of Concord January y⁰ 18 1737 and Abraham Whetney of Harvard with Sarah Whetney y⁰ same time.

Simeon Houghton of Lancaster and Jerushah Taylor of Stow entered their Intentions of marriage Febr. y⁰ 4th 1737-8.

Joseph Ston and Elisabeth Taylor on the 8 of said month afore said.

Simon Butler entered his Intention of marriage with Annah Fairbank March y⁰ 14th 1737-8

Benjamin Baly entered his Intention of marriage with Sebillah How April y⁰ 4th 1738

John Hinds entered his Intention of marriage with Allis Smith April y⁰ 8th 1738

Joseph Rugg his Intentions of marriage with Ruth Glazier April 14th 1738

Benjamin Sterns entered his Intentions of marriage with Dinah Wheeler July y⁰ 8. 1738

Barzillai Holt entered his Intention of marriage with Elisabeth Goss July y⁰ 16 1738

Josiah Sawyer entered his Intention of marriage with Sarah Fairbank July 28. 1738.

John Dakin entered his Intention of marriage with Abigail Willard August y⁰ 5th 1738

Oliver Carter entered his Intention of marriage with Bulah Wilder Sept y⁰ 2 1738

November y⁰ 25th 1738 Then Jonathan Wilder of Lancaster Entered his Entention of mariage with Zeruiah Houghton of said Town.

December y⁰ 1st 1738 David Farrar of Lancaster appeared and forbid ye banes of mariage being out asked betwix y⁰ above Said Jonath. Wilder and Zeruiah Houghton, and aledged this Reson that shee had Promised him y⁰ said farrar marriage from which shee cannot Losly depart

Jacob Fowle entered his Entention of marriage with Phebe Osgood Feb 4 1738-9

Josiah White entered his Intention of marriage with Debrah Hous Feby 4th 1738-9

David Jewett entered his Intention of marriage with Elisabeth Beman Feb. 4th 1738-9

James Cleland of Lime entered his Entention of marriage with Thankfull Wilder of Bol— February y⁰ 4 1738-9

Marthew Wymand of Woborn Entered his Entention of marriage with Abigail Willard of Lancaster February y⁰ 4th 1738-9.

Moses Osgood of Lancaster entered his Intention of marriage with Martha Powers of sd Town Feb 17th 1738-9

Elexander Scott of Lancaster Entered his Intention of marriage with Margaret Robb of Lunenburg February y⁰ 24th 1738-9

Aholiab Wilder entered his Intention of marriage with Catherine Wetherbee March y⁰ first 1738-9

16 Ephraim Carter of Lancaster entered his Intention of marriage with Abigail Wilder March y⁰ seventeenth 1738-9

David Wilder entered his Intention of marriage with Annah Prentice May y⁰ 23d 1739.

Zaccheus Boyenton entered his Intention of marriage with Annah Ross May y⁰ 26th 1739

Thomas White entered his Intention of marriage with Sarah Broughton May y⁰ 28th. 1739.

Andrew Wilder entered his Intention of marriage with Elisabeth Carter Sept. y⁰ 14th. 1739.

Oliver Wilder entered his Intention of marriage with Sarah Townsend Octo. y⁰ 19th 1739

Shubal Bailey entered his Intention of marriage with Mehetabel Hough [Howe] Nov. y⁰ 10th 1739.

Manasa Divol Entered his Intention of marriage with Susanah Sollind[ine] Jan. y⁰ 19th 1739

Thomas Carter of Lancaster with Bety Sawyer of Bolton January y⁰ 19th 1739.

David Nelson entered his Intention of marriage with Margarrit Rugg Feb. 13th 1739.
John Houghton of Bolton with Susanah Sollindine of Lancaster F. yᵉ 19th. 1739.
March yᵉ 3ᵈ 1739. Then William Cerly of Lancaster entered his purpos of marriage with Abigail Venham of Mendon.
Mr Daniel Robbins Entered his Intention of Marriage with Mrs Elisabeth Prentice April yᵉ 17th. 1740.
Daniel Knights entered his Intention of marriage with Sarah Kindal July yᵉ 14th 1740.
Phinehas Beman with Joannah White July yᵉ 16th 1740
Elijah Sawyer with Ruth White July yᵉ 18th 1740
Isaac Butler with Sarah Harris September yᵉ 26th 1740
Daniel Priest with Elisabeth Kilborn October yᵉ 18th 1740
Mr Josiah Brown entered his Intention of mariag with Mrs Prudence Prentice Nov. 6, 1740.
Josiah Sawyer entered his Intention of marriage with Abigail Sawyer Novemᵇʳ. yᵉ 15th. 1740.
Joseph Osgood Entered his Intention of Marriage with Elisabeth Carter Febru 1740 and Jonath Nelson with Hannah Buss Febru 1740
William Scot Entered his Intention of marriage with Margaret Gregg of Lundon Dery March yᵉ 13th 1740
Moses Bailey of Lancaster Entered his Intention of marriage with Mary Houghton April yᵉ 19th 1741
Nathan Rugg Entered his Intention of marriage with Zerviah Frost of Groaton April yᵉ 21ˢᵗ 1740
Jeremiah Haskil entered his Intention of mariag with Thankfull Beman March yᵉ 19th 1740
Joshua Smith Entered his Intention of marriage with Mrs Sarah Prentice May yᵉ 17. 1741
Phinihas Ball entered his intention of marriage with Martha Bigsbe May 27 1741
Henry Willard Entered his Intention of marriage Sarah Proctor June yᵉ 14 1741
John Rugg Entered his Intention of marriage with Lidiah Phelps [Fletcher added by another hand] September yᵉ 5th 1741
Daniel Rugg entered his Intention of marriage with Sarah Wilder September yᵉ 5 1741
Amos Rugg entered his Intention of marriage with Mary Burpie September 1741.
Jonathan Knight entered his Intention of marriage with Mary Johnson October 1741.
Ephraim Divol entered his intention of marriage with Elisabeth Woods of Groton De 12th 1741
David Jewet enterd his intention of marriage with Easter Hought[on] Decem 6 1741
Nathaniel Bigsbee of Shrewsbury entered his intention of marriage with Jerusha Houghton of Lancaster August yᵉ 27th 1742.
17 John Harbart Entered his Intention of mariag with Mary Beman December yᵉ 28 1742
Ezekiel Kendal entered his Intention of Marriage with Hanna Perpoint January yᵉ 27th 1742

Silas Houghton yᵉ son of Benj and Zeruiah Houghton was born October yᵉ 7 1742

John Prescot ju entered his Intention of marriage with Mary White March yᵉ 5 1742
John Creford entered his intention of marriage with Margaret Anderson March yᵉ 22 1742
Samuel Willard entered his intentiⁿ of marriage with Susannah Wilder April 12 — 1743
Thomas Burpe ju entered his Intention of marᵉ with Ann Chaplin April yᵉ 23ᵈ 1743
Isaac Rugg of Lancaster entered his intention of marriage with Jane Wright of Woborn March 1743
Nathaniel Wiman entered his Intention of Marriag with Mary Sawyer April yᵉ 28th 1743 [Married June 29.]

Dinah y⁰ Daughter of William and Luce Goss was Born July y⁰ 18th 1737
Lucy y⁰ Daughter of William and Luce Goss was Born March y⁰ 15 1739
Daniel Goss y⁰ Son of William and Lucy Goss was Born Sept. y⁰ 14th 1741
Oliver Goss y⁰ Son of William and Lucy Goss was Born November y⁰ 18th 1742
Batrix y⁰ Daughter of John and Sarah Wilder was Born October y⁰ 2d 1742
Elisabeth Jewet y⁰ Daughter of David and Elisabeth Jewet was born in May 1740
Persillah y⁰ Daughter of David and Easter Jewet was Born November y⁰ 20 1742

Steven Buss of Leominster entered his intention of marriage with Prudance Carter of Lancaster October y⁰ 29 1743.
Assa Phelps with Elisabeth Wilder October y⁰ 29 1743 ⎫ Entered their intention of marriage
Darius Sawyer with Deborah Sawyer October y⁰ 29 1743 ⎭
Jonathan Kindal with Admonition Tooker December 1743.
Silas Bridgham of —— with Tabitha Sawyer of Lancaster January y⁰ 13th 1743 Entered his Intention of marriage.
Robert Mitchell Luningburg with Alles Harris of Lancaster Entered [his intention] of marriage March 10 : 1744, and accordingly was posted as the Law Direts.
Josiah Ballard with Sarah Carter Entred there intention of marrige March the 23 : 1744.
Josiah Wilder of Lancaster Entered His Intentions of marrige with Miriam Gates of Stow March the 30 : 1744
Isaac Kilburn Entered His Intentions of Marriage with Joanah Clerk of Rowley April y⁰ 4 1744
Thomas Dole Entered His Intentions of Marriage with Hannah Plumer of Newbury April y⁰ 7 : 1744.
Thomas Holte Entered His intentions of marriage with Susanah Parker April y⁰ 21. 1744
John Goss Entered his intentions of marriage with Abigail Ball of Bolton May y⁰ 5. 1744.
David Wilder Entered his intentions of marriage with Eunice Jenison June the 16 : 1744
John Fletcher Junr. Entered his Ententions of marriage with Joanna Farrer of Wilmington June the 23 : 1744
Asa Harris Entered His Intentions of marriage with Eunice Kent of Harvard June the 25th. 1744
Phillep Goss of Brookfield Entered his intentions of marriage with Mary Kendal of Lancaster June 7th: 1744.
Abijah Wyman Entered His intentions of marriage with Abigail Smith of Newbury July the 14th 1744.
Asa Whitcomb entered his intentions of marriage with Eunice Sawyer August the 2d 1744.
Tilley Wilder Entered His Intentions of marriage with Percis House August 4th: 1744:
Joshua Phelps Entered his Intention of marriage with Rebekah Beman August 18th. 1744.
Oliver Wilder Junr. Entered his intention of marriage with Ruth Russel of Bolton August 25. 1744.
18 Jacob Smith Entered His Intentions of marriage with Hester Burpee Septemr 15th: 1744.
the Revd Mr Elisha Marsh of a new town Called Narraganset No 2 Entered his Intentions of marriage with Mrs Deborah Lothrop of Hingham Octr 6th: 1744
Timothy Knight of Worcester, Entered His Intentions of marriage with Rebekah Kendal of Lancaster Octr. y⁰ 9th. 1744
Mr Roger Robins Entered His Intentions of marriage with Mrs Lucy Smith of Lexinton Octr 17th. 1744.
Frances Butterick Entered His intentions of marriage with Hannah Gilson of Luningburg November the 9th: 1744
Danael Whitney of Stow Entered His Intentions of marriage with Dorothy Goss of Lancaster Novemr 9th. 1744.
Thomas Kendal Entered His Intentions of marriage with Abigail Ames Novemr the 16th, 1744.

BOOK FIRST. 31

Asaph Wilder Entered His intentions of marriage with Zipporah Whealer of Westborough January ye 16th. 1744.
John Russel of Luningburg Entered His intentions of marriage with Thanckfull Harris of Lancaster March ye 8, 1744-5
Silas Rice of Westborough Entered His Intentions of marriage with Copia Broton of Lancaster March ye 10. 1744-5.
Joshua House Entered his intentions of marriage with Prudence Sawyer May ye 13th. 1745.
Gideon Brockway of Lyme Entered His Intentions of marriage with Loes Beman of Lancaster May ye 18th. 1745.
Josiah Carter Entered His Intentions of marriage with Tabitha Hough [Howe] May ye 24th. 1745
Benjamin Willard Entered His Intentions of marrage with Hannah Goodfry of Harvard ——
Joseph Gibbs of a new township Called Narriganset No 2 Entered His Intentions of marriage with Abigail Woodbury of Lancaster May ye 6th. 1745.
John Cheney of Sudbury Entered his Intentions of marriage with Keziah Kendal of Lancaster June 12th. 1745.
Daniel Willard Entered his Intentions of marriage with Luce Butler of Luningburg Septem^r ye 14th, 1745
Joseph White of Lancaster Entered his Intentions of marriage with Patitiance Ball of Westborough Sept ye 27th. 1745
Jerahmeel Bowers of Lancaster Entered his Intentions of marrage with Meriam Houghton of Luningburg Sept 27 : 1745.
David Robins of Lancaster Entered his Intentions of marriage with Persillah Beman of sd town Octo^r 4 1745
John Crosbe Entered his intentions of mariage with Mindwell Houghton of Bolton Novem^r 15 1745.
19 Abraham Willard Entered His Intentions of marriage with Mary Haskel of Harvard February the 18th 1745-6.
William Fife Entered His Intentions of marriage with Deliverance Wilder March ye 3 : 1745-6

Hannah Daughter of John & Hannah Snow was born Feb ye 7th 1746

the births of ye Children of Joshua & Alles Church

Joseph Church July 22. 1729
Alles July 7 — 1731.
Mary January 1st 1734.
Vashty October 3 — 1736

Prudance April 5 — 1739
Caleb June 3 — 1741
Joshua Church August 6 — 1743
Silas Church June 18 — 1745

20 Daniel Halburt of Lancaster Entered his Intentions of marrag with Sarah Perce of Harvard March the 28. 1746.
Arter Gram [Arthur Graham] of Londondery Entered his Intentions of marriage with Ellenor Scott of Lancaster March ye 28th 1746.
Jonathan Prescott Entered His Intentions of marriage with Vashty Houghton of Lancaster April ye 11th. 1746.
Saul Houghton of Lancaster Entered His Intentions of marriage with Mary Marthews of Framingham April ye 11th 1746.
Mr Timothy Sabin of Pomphret Entered His Intentions of marriage with ye Widdow Experience Houghton of Lancaster Septem^r the 8th 1746.
Ebenezer Prescott Jun. of Lancaster & Jerusha Mathews of Southborough Entered their intentions of marriage Septem^r ye 28 : 1746.
Zackeus Boyington Entred his intentions of marriage with Hannah Pebody, they being both of Lancaster October y^e — 1746
Joshua Houghton of Lancaster Entered his intentions of marriage with Elisibeth Gaffel of Shrewsborough October : 1746.
Ebenezer Begilow of Lancaster Entered his intentions of marriage with Anna Harris October ye 3^d 1746.
Jotham Wilder of Lancaster Entered his intentions of marriage with Phebe Wheeler of Leominster October ye 3 1746.
Jonathan Houghton of Leominster Entered his Intentions of marriage with Sarah Houghton of Lancaster October ye 22, 1746.

Lucy Daughter of John & Lidia Rugg was born y⁰ 17 Day of August 1746.

Josiah Houghton of Lancaster Entered his Intentions of marriage with Bethesda Brabrook of Bolton February the 2. 1746-7

John Samson Entered his intentions of marriage with Prudance Ames February y⁰ 2ᵈ, 1746-7

Mr Jonathan Bayley Entered his intentions of marriage with Abigail Whitney of Lancaster February y⁰ 25ᵗʰ 1746-7.

William Richardson Junʳ Entered His Intentions of marriage with Patiance Broughton March — 1746

Abijah Houghton Entered his intentions of marriage with Alles Joslin March — 1746

Hezekiah Walker of Shrewsbury Entered His Intentions of marriage with Sarah Prescott 6f Lancaster Septemʳ y⁰ 4 1747

Capt Abijah Willard of Lancaster Entered his Intentions of marriage with Mrs Elizabeth Prescott of Groton Septʳ y⁰ 19ʳʰ 1746.

John Phelps Entered his intentions of marriage with y⁰ Widdow Zipporah Wilder of sd town Decemʳ y⁰ 10ᵗʰ 1747.

Obediah Townsend Entered his Intentions of marriage with Hannah Trask of sd Town Decemʳ y⁰ 10ᵗʰ 1747

Joshua Osgood Juʳ. Entred his Intentions of marriage with Luce Carter January y⁰ 2ᵈ 1747.

Robert Fletcher of Lancaster Entered his intentions of marriage with Elisibeth Houghton of Lunenburg January y⁰ 2 1747

21 Sherebiah Ballard Entered his Intentions of Marrïage with Keziah Osgood January y⁰ 16, 1747 [-8]

Ebenezer Buss Entered his Intentions of marriage with Keziah Houghton January y⁰ 21ˢᵗ 1747. [-8]

Ephraim Roper Entered His Intentions of marriage with Michal Houghton March y⁰ 6 1747-8.

Ezra Houghton Entered his Intentions of marriage with Dinah Houghton March y⁰ 6 1747-8.

Joshua Fletcher Entered His Intentions of marriage with Mary Allen March y⁰ 12ᵗʰ 1747-8.

Phillep Goss Entered his Intentions of marriage with Hannah Ball of Bolton, April y⁰ 16 1748.

Mr Josiah Converse of Brookfield & Mrs Doratha Carter of Lancaster Entered their Intentions of marriage May y⁰ 15ᵗʰ 1748.

David Robins of Leominster Entered his intentions of marriage with Mrs Elizabeth Knight of Lancaster June y⁰ 10 1748.

Jotham White of Leominster Entered his Intentions of marriage with Mrs. Sarah House of Lancaster June y⁰ 10ᵗʰ 1748

Mr John Brooks Entered His Intentions of marriage with Parmer Houghton September the 9 1748

Ebenezer Begelow Entered His Intentions of marriage with y⁰ widdow Hephzibah Dufore November y⁰ 26, 1748.

Peter Joslin Jun of Lancaster Entered His Intentions of marriage with Elisabeth Greenleaf of Bolton Decemʳ y⁰ 10ᵗʰ. 1748.

Jonathan Harris of Lancaster Entered His Intentions of Marriage with Annis Houghton of Bolton January the 28. 1748 [-9]

Ebenezer Harris Entered His Intentions of marriage with the widdow Lidia Warrensford Feb y⁰ 11 1748-9.

Ezekiel Newton of Shrewsbury Entered His Intentions of marriage with Dorotha Osgood Jur of Lancaster February y⁰ 10ᵗʰ 1748-9.

Ebenezer Talor Entered His Intentions of marriage with Mary Houghton Feb. y⁰ 17ᵗʰ 1748-9.

David Willard Entered His Intentions of marriage with Sarah May April the 30ᵗʰ 1749.

John Henderson of Lancaster Entered His Intentions of marriage with Jane Turner of Lunenburg May y⁰ 6ᵗʰ 1749.

Benjᵃ. Glazier Entered His Intentions of marriage with Lidia Dakin May y⁰ 17ᵗʰ 1749

Daniel Johnson Entered his Intentions of marriage with Lidia Willard July the 11th 1749.
22 Colonal Oliver Wilder Entered His Intentions of marriage with Mrs Rebekah Barns of Chelmsford July the 1st 1749
Nathaniel White Entered His intentions of marriage with Lidia Phelps October the 18th 1749
Alexander Kid of Grafton Entered His Intentions of marriage with Martha Dunsmoor of Lancaster October ye 18th 1749
The Revd Mr John Mellen Entered His Intentions of marriage with Mrs Rebekah Prentice October ye 28th 1749
Abner Wilder Entered His Intentions of marriage with Eunice Osgood Feb ye 1 1749 [- 50]
The Revd Mr John Rogers of Leominster Entered His Intentions of marriage with Mrs Releaf Prentice of Lancaster February ye 27th 1749 [- 50]
Abiathar Houghton of Leominster Entered His Intentions of marriage with Mileasant Carter of Lancaster March ye 17th 1749 [- 50]
Jonathan Begelow of Holden Entered His Intentions of marriage with Mary Richardson March ye 24 1750
Robert Fletcher Entered His Intentions of marriage with Rebecca Edmuns June ye 16th 1750
John Whitcomb Entered His Intentions of marriage with Susanah Garey August ye 10th 1750
John Nichols Junr of Lancaster Entered His Intentions of marriage with Marcey Warner of Harvard October — 1750
David Tailler Entered His intentions of marriage with Betty Houghton of Lancaster October — 1750
Gershum Flagg Entered his Intentions of marriage with Mary Willard November ye 14th 1750
Mr Ephraim Sawyer of Lancaster Entered His Intentions of marriage with Mrs Sarah Richardson of Woburn November ye 20th 1750
Tilley Richardson Entered His Intentions of marriage with Elsabeth Sawyer Both of Lancaster Decem ye 29 1750
Mr Ammasa Turner of Lancaster Entred his Intentions of marriage with Mrs Eunice Sanderson of Groton January the 23d 1750. [- 51]
Tilley Richardson Entered his Intentions of marriage with Mrs Elsabeth Sawyer January ye 24 1750. [- 51]
February ye 28 1750 [- 51] then Peter Larkin Entered His Intentions of marriage with Azubah Wheeler of Shrewsbury.
Samuel Thirston of Lancaster Entered His intentions of marriage with Prisilla Burpee of Rowley March ye 7th 1750 [-51]
Matthias Larkin Entered His intentions of marriage with Demaras Sawyer March ye 21st 1750 [- 51]
Benjamin Rogers of Boxford and Loes Rice of Lancaster Entered their Intentions of marriage March 14th 1750 [- 51]
23 Mr John Beaman Entered His Intentions of marriage with ye widdow Sarah Page April the 19 1751
Jonas Fletcher of Groton Entered his Intentions of marriage with Ruth Fletcher of Lancaster May ye 3d 1751
Elisha Bennitt Entered his Intentions of marriage with Loes Wilder May the 18 1751
John Fairbank Entered His intentions of marriage with Releaf Houghton May the 8th 1751.
Jonas Kendal Entered His intentions of marriage with Elisabeth Bennitt May the 22d 1751
Joseph James of Lancaster Entered His Intentions of marriage [with] Lidia Parker of Andivour May the 30th 1751
Solomon Houghton Entered His intentions of marriage with Deliverance Ross July ye 11th 1751
Mr David Wilder Entered His Intentions of marraige with Mrs Martha White Second —— 1751
Joseph Wheelock of Lancaster Entered his Intentions of marriage with Alles Page of Lunenburg September the ye 11 1751

Josiah Cutting of Shrewsbury Entered his Intentions of marraige with Orpha Houghton of Lancaster October y⁰ 1 1751
Samuel Newton of Shrewsbury Entered His Intentions of marrage with Sarah Douglas of Lancaster November y⁰ 31 1751
Joseph Kilburn Entered his Intentions of marriage with Mary Sawyer Decem^r y⁰ 19th 1751
Thomas Conant of Narragansett No 2: Entered his Intentions of marriage with Hannah Rolph of Lancaster February y⁰ 1th 1752
Ephraim Sawyer Entered his Intentions of marriage with Susannah Richardson January y⁰ 31 1752.
William Fife of Bolton Entered His Intentions of marriage with the widow Abigail Gorss of Lancaster February — 1752
George McFarling [McFarland] of Lunenburg Entered his Intentions of marriage with Margaret Torrance of Lancaster March y⁰ 20th 1752.
Timothy Whitney Entered His Intentions of marriage with Alles Whitney of Harvard March y⁰ 20th 1752
Reuben Lipingwell Entered His intentions of marriage with Anna Wyman March y⁰ 20th 1752

John Abbott son of Joseph & Hannah Abbott was born October y⁰ 8th 1751.

Andrew Grims of Lancaster Entered His Intentions of marrage with Submitt Davenport of Leominster June y⁰ 27 1752.
Ephraim Goss of Bolton Entred his Intentions of marriage with Zilpha Turner of Lancaster July y⁰ 29 1752 and on y⁰ 3 Day of August said Zilpha Turner appeared & forbid the Banns being Published aney further.
Primus Luce of Groton Entered his Intention of marrage with Roes Cantebury of Lancaster September y⁰ 27th 1752
Russel Knight of Lancaster Entered his Intention of marriage with Mary Bruce of Marlborough September y⁰ 30th 1752
Capt. Abijah Willard Entered His Intentions of marriage with Anna Prentice October y⁰ 4th 1752.
Nathanael Joslin Entered his Intentions of marriage with Martha Fairbank October y⁰ 22 1752,
Ezekiel Kendal Entered his Intentions of marriage with Mary May —— the 18th 1752
James Richardson of Leominster and Hannah House of Lancaster Entered their Intentions of marriage November y⁰ 28th 1752.
Asa Harris Entered his Intentions of marriage with Abigail Bennitt Decem^r y⁰ 9 1752
Joseph Bayley & Lidia Parker's Intentions of marriage was entered the 26 Day of January 1753.
Jeramell Bowers Entered his Intentions of marriage with Mary Houghton March y⁰ 10th 1753
John Maning Entered his Intentions of marriage with Prudance Houghton both of Lancaster April the 16th 1753
Benj^a. Osgood Ju^r Entered his Intention of marriage with Mary Carter Both of Lancaster May 20th. 1753.
John Divoll Enterd his Intention of Marriage with Elesabeth Beaman Both of Lancaster July y⁰ 12 1753.
Joshua Read Enterd his Intention of mariage with Susanna Houghton November y⁰ 2^d 1753
William Smith of Townshend Entered his Intentions of mariage with Martha Dunsmore November y⁰ 2^d 1753
Thomas Beaman of Lancaster Entred his Intentions of mariage with Elsabeth White of Shirley November y⁰ 10th. 1753
Nathan Burpey Jun En^d his Intentions of mariage with Azubah Osgood Both of Lancaster Decem^r y⁰ 15th: 1753
Oliver Howe of Leominster and Silance Houghton of Lancaster Entred his intentions of mariage Decem^r y⁰ 22' 1753
Levi Moors Entred his Intentions of mariage with Rebecka Sawyer Both of Lancaster Decem^r y⁰ 28 : 1753.

Reuben Miles of Narigansett No 2 Entered his Intention of mariage with Ann Rice of Concord January y⁰ 4 : 1754
Sam¹¹. Rice of Shrousborough Entered his Ententions of mariage with Mary Bennitt of Lancaster Febury y⁰ 12 : 1754.
Aaron Osgood Jun Entered his Ententions of mariage with Hannah Warner Both of Lancaster Febuary y⁰ 12 : 1754
25 Amos Powers of Lancaster Entered his Intentions of mariage with Zerbille Gibb [Sibyl Gibbs] of Sudbury Febuary y⁰ 11 1755
George Parkes of Lancaster entered his 'Entions of mariage with Keziah Whitcomb of Bolton March y⁰ 3ᵈ 1755
Capt⁰ John Curtis of Worster Entered his Intentions of marige with Mrs Elisebeth Robins of Lancaster October y⁰ 17ᵗʰ 1755
David Whitne of Harvard Entered his Intentions of marige with Sarah Hill of Lancaster October y⁰ 25ᵗʰ 1755
Josiah Houghton of Lancaster Entered his Intentions of marige with Grace Whitne of Harvard November y⁰ 15ᵗʰ 1755
Laiᵗᵉ Jabez Fairbank of Lancaster Entered his Intentions of marige with Mrs Neomi Dupe of Leominster December y⁰ 13ᵗʰ 1755
Israel Moor of Lancaster Entered his Intentions of marige with Abigel How of said Lancaster December y⁰ 13ᵗʰ 1755
Joseph Osgood Juner Entered his Ententions of marige with Catharine Sawyer both of Lancaster January y⁰ 7ᵗʰ 1756
Elisha Sawyer of Lancaster enter'd his Intentions of Marriage with Susanah Huck of Bolton March 3, 1756
Elijah Houghton of Lancaster entered his Intention of marriage with Katharine Sparhawk of Cambridge May 31 1760
Joshua Johnson junʳ of Lancaster entered his Intentions of marriage with Hannah Avery of Groton June 27. 1760
Edward Houghton entered his Intentions of Marriage with Lucretia Richardson both of Lancaster July 19 A D 1760
Bezaleel How of Lancaster entered his Intentions of Marriage with Sarah Biglow of Marlborough July 25 1760
John Gibbs entered his Intentions of marriage with the Widʷ Elisabeth Kendall both of Lancaster July 25 1760
26 Ezra Sawyer jun. of Lancaster entered his Intentions of Marriage with Kezia Sawyer of Lancaster August 14 1760
Gardner Wilder of Lancaster entered his Intentions of Marriage with Martha Wilder of Lancaster August y⁰ 23 1760
Seth Harrington of Westminster entered his Intentions of Marriage with Widʷ. Priscilla Houghton of Lancaster, August y⁰ 28 1760
Israel Moor of Lancaster entered his Intentions of Marriage with Katharine Sawyer of Lancaster, September 6 1760
Elijah Osgood of Lancaster entered his Intentions of Marriage with Mary Wallingsford of Lancaster September 12 1760
John Glazier of Lancaster entered his Intentions of Marriage with Widʷ. Mary Brooks of Bolton - Septʳ. 20 1760
John Ball of Westborough entered his Intentions of Marriage with Abigail Wilder of Lancaster - October 3ᵈ. 1760
Joseph Wilson juʳ. of Petersham entered his intentions of Marriage with Hannah Osgood of Lancaster October y⁰ 21 1760
Samuel Ross of Lancaster entered his Intentions of Marriage with Katharine Gary of Lancaster, November 8 1760
Josiah Osgood of Lancaster entered his Intentions of Marriage with Jane Boynton of Lancaster, November 21 1760
Josiah Fairbank of Lancaster entered his Intentions of Marriage with Abigail Carter of Lancaster, December y⁰ 4 1760
Josiah Divoll of Lancaster entered his Intentions of Marriage with Jenny Mucklewaine of Bolton December y⁰ 6 1760
Deaⁿ. John Heywood of Lunenburgh entered his Intentions of Marriage with Silence White of Lancaster, December 9 1760
Benjamin Priest of Lancaster entered his Intentions of Marriage with Hannah Johnson of Lancaster December 20 1760

George Peterson a Negro man of Shrewsbury entered his Intentions of [marriage with] Margarett Dorchester of Lancaster mollatto woman January 24 1761

Joel Houghton of Lancaster entered his Intentions of Marriage with Sarah Pearson of Shrewsbury, January 28 1761

James Willard of Lancaster entered his Intentions of Marriage with Sarah Longley of Shirley Destrict January 30 1761

27 Jonathan Kendall ye 3^d of Lancaster entered his Intentions of Marriage with Patience Frost of Groton January 31. 1761.

William Shattuck of Hollis entered his Intentions of Marriage with Zilpah Turner of Lancaster February 7, 1761.

John McCarty of Lancaster entered his Intentions of Marriage with Wid^w Margaret Mcfarland of said Lancaster February 21 1761

Nath^{ll}. Wyman of Lancaster & Submit Brooks of Woborn enter'd their Intentions of Marriage March 13 1761. [Married May 14, 1761.]

Thos. Gates & Abigail Wilder Both of Lancaster entered their Intentions of Marriage March 14 1761

James Goss of Lancaster & Mary Stickney of Billerica enter'd their Intentions of Marriage March 14 1761

John Beman Ju^r. of Lancaster & Prudence Bullard of Petersham enter'd their Intentions of Marriage April 19, 1761.

Jonas Goodenough of Shrewsbury & Eunice Hastings of Lancaster enter'd their Intentions of Marriage April 19. 1761.

John Boyinton of Shrewsbury & Elisabeth Jewet of Lancaster Declar'd the Intentions of Marriage July 1 1761

Roger Ross & Molly Rugg Both of Lancaster Declar'd their Intentions of Marriage Augt. 1. 1761

Jon^a Whetcomb & Tamer Ross Both of Lancaster Declar'd their Intentions of Marriage Augt. 1 1761

Aaron Willard Ju^r. of Lancaster & Elis^a. Brewer of Sherburne Declar'd ther Intentions of Marriage Augt: 15. 1761

Joseph Sawyer & Agnus Dunsmoor Both of Lancaster Declared their Intentions of Marriage July 1 1761

Willm. Phelps & Mary Flagg Both of Lancaster Declar'd their Intentions of Marriage Augt. 20th. 1761

28 Tilly White of Lancaster & Katurah Soames of Harvard Declar'd their Intentions of Marriage Octr. 1, 1761.

Peter Thurston & Dorrethy Gates Both of Lancaster Declar'd their Intentions of Marriage Novr. 5, 1761

Jeremiah Stewart of Leominster & Hanah Stewart of Lancaster Declar'd their Intentions of Marr^e. Decr. 4, 1761

Capt. Asa Whetcomb & Betty Sawyer Declar'd their Intentions of Marriage Dec^r, 21, 1761

Nath^{ll} Willard of Lancaster & Elis^a Haskell of Harvard Declar'd their Intentions of Marriage Decr 21, 1761

James Lock & Rebeckah Wilder Both of Lancaster Declar'd their Intentions of Marriage Jany. 3 1762

Joseph Houghton of Bolton & Martha Snow of Lancaster Declar'd their Intentions of Marriage Jany. 21 1762

Stanton Carter & Peninnah Albert Both of Lancaster Declar'd their Intentions of Marriage Feby. 5 1762

Mathew Knight of Leominster Enter'd his Intentions of Mar^e. with Dinah Carter of Lancaster Jany. 15 1762

Sam^{ll}: Bixpy Ju^r. of Prince Town Enter^d his Intentions of Marriage w^h. Hanah Powers of Lancaster January 22^d. 1762.

Nath^{ll}. Wilder of Lancaster Declar'd his Intentions of Marriage w^h. Lucy Knight of Do. March 4th. 1762

Richard Proutee of Lancaster Declar'd his Intentions of Marriage with Esther Smith of Do. March 6. 1762

Elisha Bennit & Mary Larkin Both of Lancaster Declar'd their Intentions of Marriage March 20th. 1762

BOOK FIRST.

John Phelps & Elis⁸. Walker both of Lancaster Declar'd their Intentions of Marriage April 11, 1762
John Hastings of Shrewsbury & Betty How of Lancaster Declar'd their Intentions of Marriage April 16. 1762
29 Nath¹¹. Jones & Phebe Burpe Both of Lancaster Declar'd their Intentions of Marriage April 16 1762
Joel Phelps & Prudence Brown Both of Lancaster Declar'd their Intentions of Marriage April 17. 1762
Josiah Wilder Ju'. & Abigail Osgood both of Lancaster Declar'd their Intentions of Marriage April 24 1762
Tilly Moors & Zilpah Whiting both of Lancaster enter'd their Intentions of Marriage May 15. 1762
Stephen Smith of Shrewsbury & Lucy Kendall of Lan. Declar'd their Intentions of Marriage June 15 1762
Ebenezer Hills of Swanzey & Abibail Nicholls of Lancaster Declar'd their Intentions of Marriage July 11, 1762
Oliver Dresser & Olive Osgood Both of Lancaster Declar'd their Intentions of Marriage July 11, 1762
James Houghton Ju'. of Lancaster & Anna Eveleth of Rutland Declar'd their Intentions of Marriage Augt. 13th, 1762
Enoch Dole & Eunice Richardson Both of Lancaster Declar'd their Intentions of Marriage October 15, 1762
Doct. Daniel Greenleaf of Bolton & Mrs Dorathy Richardson of Lancaster Declar'd their Intentions of Marriage Octo^r. 22^d, 1762
Cyrus Fairbank & Lucy Wilder Both of Lancaster Declar'd their Intentions of Marriage November 6th. 1762
Doc^r. Nathan Raymond of Littleton & Rebeckah Richardson of Lancaster Declar'd their Intentions of Marriage Novr 6 1762
Moses Sawyer Ju^r. & Mary Sawyer Both of Lancaster Declar'd their Intentions of Marriage Decr. 3. 1762
John Boynton of Shrewsbury & Elis⁸. Beman of Lancaster Declar'd their Intentions of Marriage December 16 1762
Peter Hilt of Worcester & Margret Zweier of Lancaster Declar'd their Intentions of Marriage Decem^r. 28, 1762
30 Nath¹¹. Willard Ju^r of Lancaster & Eunice Farwell of Stow Enter'd their Intentions of Marriage May 6, 1763
David Moors of Bolton & Betty Whetcomb of Lancaster Enter'd their Intentions of Marriage May 7. 1763
Sam¹¹. Hancock of Harvard Inter'd His Intentions of Marriage with Abigail Snow of Lancaster June 18, 1763
Willm. Longley of Shirley & Lydia Wallinsford of Lancaster Declar'd their Intentions of Marriage July 20th, 1763
Willm Brown & Elis⁸. Houghton Both of Lancaster Declar'd their Intentions of Marriage August 14th, 1763
Benj⁸. Houghton Tert. & Axey [Achsa] Whetcomb both of Lancaster Declar'd their Intentions of Marriage Sept. 21, 1763
Tho⁸. Brooks of Lancaster & Hanah Cutter of Charlestown Declar'd their Intentions of Marriage October 1st. 1763
Levi Houghton & Anna Richardson both of Lancaster Declar'd their Intentions of Marriage October 7, 1763
Silas How of Lancaster & Abigail Moor of Bolton Declar'd their Intentions of Marriage October 16 1763
Nath¹¹. Hastings Junr & Elis⁸. Goodenow both of Lancaster Declar'd their Intentions of Marriage October 16 1763
William Willard of Petersham & Kath^{ne}. Wilder of Lancaster Declar'd their Intentions of Marriage Octr. 22^d 1763
Jacob Bennit & Anna Boynton Both of Lancaster Declar'd their Intention of Marriage Nov. 10 1763.
Josiah Sawyer of Bolton & Mary Tucker of Lancaster Declar'd their Intentions of Marriage Nov. 12, 1763.
Josiah Houghton & Abigail Goodfree Both of Lancaster Declar'd their Intentions of Marriage Decem^r. 1, 1763

31 Benj^a. Wilder of Lancaster & Patience Newton of Marlbro' Declar'd their Intentions of Marriage Dece^r. 2. 1763.
Andrew McClwin [McElwain] of Bolton & Rebeckah Seever of Lancaster Declar'd their Intentions of Marriage Jany. 10 1764.
Josiah Lock of Lancaster & Esther Kitteridge of Teukesbury Declar'd their Intentions of Marriage Jany 24 1764.
Nathan Gary & Hepzebeth Wilder Both of Lancaster Declar'd their Intentions of Marriage March 10 1764
Joseph Fairbank of Lancaster & Anna Dole of Littleton Declar'd their Intentions of Marriage April 20 1764
John Nicholls of Lancaster & Silence Stow of Townsend Declar'd their Intentions of Marriage April 25th 1764.
Eph^m Beman of Shrewsbury & Thamer How of Lancaster Declar'd their Intentions of Marriage April 29, 1764.
Joseph Russ of Lunenburg & Susanah Priest of Lancaster Declar'd their Intentions of Marriage May 26 1764
Benj^a. Warrin of Littleton & Mrs Elis^a. Haywood of Lancaster Declar'd their Intentions of Marriage August 7, 1764
Thos. Mears of Lancaster & Mary Stewart of Leominster Declar'd their Intentions of Marriage Augt. 26, 1764.
Elijah Houghton & Mary Allen Both of Lancaster have Declar'd their Intention of Marriage Sept. 14, 1764.
Phinehas Wilder & Bridget Baily Declar'd their Intentions of Marriage Sept, 21, 1764.
Jon^a. Wilder Ju^r. & Deborah Sawyer both of Lancaster Declar'd their Intentions of Marriage Sept, 21, 1764.
Robert Procter & Ruth Fowle Both of Lancaster Declar'd their Intentions of Marriage Sept 30, 1764
Heman Kendall & Mary Fairbank both of Lancaster Declar'd their Intentions of Marriage Novr. 3, 1764.
Sam^{ll} Peirce of Groton & Lucy Wallinsford of Lancaster Declar'd their Intentions of Marriage Novr. 10, 1764.
32 Hananiah Rand of Westminster & Martha Osgood of Lancaster Declar'd their Intentions of Marriage Nov. 17, 1764
Robert Phelps of Lancaster & Rachel Richardson of Billerica Declared their Intentions of Marriage Nov. 25, 1764.
Joshua Church & Keziah Goss both of Lancaster Declar'd their Intentions of Marriage Decem: 1, 1764.
John Hadley Ju^r. of Lancaster & Eunice Maynard of Sudbury Declared their Intentions of Marriage Decr. 1, 1764
Jedediah Wood of Warwick & Mary Bixby of Lancaster Declar'd their Intentions of Marriage Decr. 1, 1764
Doc^r. Stephen Ball of Westbro' & Mary Fairbank of Lancaster Declar'd their Intentions of Marriage Decr. 21, 1764
Thos. Cleveland of Bolton & Hanah Rugg of Lancaster Declar'd their Intentions of Marriage Jany. 26 1765
John Stearnes & Anna Joyner both of Lancaster Declar'd their Intentions of Marriage January 26, 1765
Gardnier Wilder & Dorothy Richardson both of Lancaster Declar'd their Intentions of Marriage Feb^{ry}. 18 1765
John Lock & Lucy Wilder Both of Lancaster Declar'd their Intentions of Marriage Feb^{ry}. 18 1765
Isaac Stone of Lancaster & Rachel Fisk of Shrewsbury Declar'd their Intentions of Marriag Feb^{ry}. 28 1765
Daniel Perry & Mary Newton both of Lancaster Declar'd their Intentions of Marriage March 1, 1765
Daniel Cook of Lancaster & Sarah Morse of Southbro' Declar'd their Intentions of Marriage March 1st, 1765
James Goodwin & Barsheba Robbins both of Lancaster Declar'd their Intentions of Marriage March 11th, 1765.
Daniel Warner & Susanah Rugg both of Lancaster Declar'd their Intentions of Marriage March 20 1765.

BOOK FIRST. 39

Jon⁸. Carter Ju^r. of Leominster & Damaras Whitcomb of Lan^r. Declar'd their Intentions of Marriage April 2. 1765.
Thos. Rugg of Lancaster & Eunice Stickney of Leominster Declar'd their Intentions of Marriage April 2 1765
33 Benj^a. Thompson & Susanah Tilly both of Lancaster Declar'd their Intentions of Marriage April 5 1765.

Zeruah Daughter to Benj^a. & Mehetibal Keech born May 25, 1764
Isaac Son to Asa & Lydia Wilder born April 19. 1765

Elkanah Woodcock of Swanzy & Susanah Nicholls of Lancaster Declar'd their Intentions of Marriage June 14, 1765
Jon^a: Whitney & Mary Wyman both of Lancaster Declar'd their Intentions of Marriage Augt. 20, 1765.
Thos. Gary Ju^r, & Priscillia Jewet both of Lancaster Declar'd their Intentions of Marriage August 25 1765
Daniel Rugg Ju^r. & Elis^a. Divoll both of Lancaster Declar'd their Intentions of Marriage Sept. 1. 1765
Joseph Bennit of Lancaster & Sarah Dole of Littleton declar'd their Intentions of Marriage Septem^r. 11 1765
Joseph Boynton of Winchendon & Zerviah Wilder of Lancaster declar'd their Intentions of Marriage Sept. 12, 1765.
James Kendall Junr & Elisebeth Mason declar'd their Intentions of Marriage October the 5th. 1765.
Elisha Sawyer Jur. & Patience Bennit both of Lancaster declar'd their Intentions of Marriag October 11, 1765.
Bartholemew Pearson & Elis^a. Powers both of Lancaster Declared their Intentions of Marriag Octo^r. 21, 1765.
Manasseh Bixby of Shrewsbury & Betty Dunsmoor of Lancaster declar'd their Intentions of Marri'ge Octr. 25 1765
John Richardson of Petersham & Eunice Green of Lancaster Declar'd their Intentions of Marriage Octr 25 1765
Timothy Fullum & Elis^a. Thompson both of Lancaster Declared their Intentions of Marriage Nov. 26 1765
Wyatt Gunn of Swanzey & Martha Houghton of Lancaster Declared their Intentions of Marriage Decem^r. 9th 1765
34 Thos. Bennit & Lydia Longley both of Lancaster declar'd their Intentions of Marrige Decem^r. 13, 1765.
Jothem Sawyer & Dinah Goodale both of Lancaster declared their Intentions of Marriage Decem^r, 13, 1765.
James Ross Ju^r. & Phebe Gary both of Lancaster declared their Intentions of Marriage Feb'y 22, 1766
John Daby of Westminster & Hanah Gary of Lancaster declared their Intentions of Marriage Feb'y 22 ; 1766
Jacob Emerson of Westminster & Sarah Dole of Lancaster declared their Intentions of Mariage Feb'y 22 : 1766
Joseph Horsley Ju^r. of Westminster & Abigail Kendall of Lancaster declared their Intentions of Mariage Feb'y 22 : 1766
Josiah Hosmer & Eunice Whetcomb Both of Lancaster declared their Intention of Marrige March 9, 1766
Paul Dickinson of Groton & Demaris Knight of Lancaster declared their Intention of Marrige Jany 1766
Ephraim Richardson of Lancaster & Sarah Mellen of Hopkinton declared their Intentions of Marr'g April 27, 1766
Abel Willard of Lancaster & Elesebeth Rogers of Littleton Declar'd their Intentions of Marriage April 27, 1766
John White Junr. of Lancaster & Lydia Jeffes of Harvard Declared their Intentions of Marriage May 21, 1766. [Married Jan. 29, 1767.[
John Phelps of Lancaster & Achsah Whiting of Bilrica Declared their Intention of Marriage May 31 : 1766
Joseph Wheelor & Sarah Allen both of Lancaster declared their Intentions of Marriage July 31, 1766

Paul Kendall of Templetown & Mary Baily of Lancaster declared their Intentions of Marriage July 31. 1766.
35 Henry Wyman of Lancaster & Lydia Bruce of Framingham declared their Intention of Marriage Augt. 14th 1766
Ichabod Gary & Sarah Rugg Both of Lancaster declar'd their Intention of Marriage Augt. 16th, 1766
Willm. Kendall & Mary Knight, Both of Lancaster, declard their Intention of Marriage Aug^t- 22 : 1766
Benj^a. Dole & Releaf Thompson Both of Lancaster declar'd their Intention of Marriage Augt. 23 1766
John Leitch of Lunenburg & Abigail Phillips of Lancaster Declar'd their Intentions of Marriage Augt. 29, 1766.
Shubal Baily of Lancaster & Hanah Whittemore of Leominster declared their Intentions of Marriage Septem^r. 1, 1766.
John Dunsmoor & Sarah Winn both of Lancaster declared their Intentions of Marriage September 13, 1766.
George Hall & Elis^a. Richardson both of Lancaster declared their Intention of Marriage Octr. 10: 1766
Solomon Jewet & Elis^a. Osgood both of Lancaster declared their Intentions of Marriage October 18, 1766
Moses Russel of Littleton & Sarah Phelps of Lancaster declared their Intentions of Marriage October 24 1766
Gardnier Maynard & Anna Ross both of Lancaster declared their Intentions of Marriage Novem^r, 1, 1766.
William Dunsmoor of Lancaster & Ruth Moors of Shirley declared their Intention of Marriage Novem^r. 22, 1766.
Capt. Aaron Willard of Lancaster & Miss Mary Bracket of Boston declared their Intention of Marriage Decem^r. 22^d, 1766
Jothem Rice of Rutland Destrict & Hanah Snow of Lancaster declared their Intention of Marriag Dec. 26; 1766
Capt. Willm. Williams of Marlborough & Zilpah Wilder of Lancaster declar'd their Intention of Marriage Jany, 17 : 1767
36 Jona. Powers & Love Pearson Both of Lancaster declar'd their Intention of Marriage Jany. 23 : 1767
Joshua Moseman & Anne Joyner both of Lancaster Declar'd their Intention of Marriage Feby. 19 1767
James Goodfree of Lancaster & Mary Prat of Harvard declared their Intentions of Marriag March 19, 1767
Dec^n. Daniel Spooner of Petersham & Wid^w. Bethiah Nicholls of Lancaster declared their Intentions of Marriage July 30 1767
Francis Prouty & Mary Kendall both of Lancaster declared their Intentions of Marriage August 29. 1767.
John Brooks 3^d of Lancaster & Mary Brown of Cambridge declared their Intentions of Marriage Septr. 5, 1767
David Nims Jur of Keene & Jemima Carter Junr. of Lancaster Declar'd their Intentions of Marriage October 6th. 1767.
Andrew Poor & Esther Snow both of Lancaster declared their Intentions of Marriage October 17, 1767
Silas Fairbank & Lydia Proutee both of Lancaster Declared their Intention of Marriage October 19 1767.
Daniel Nicholls of Leominster & Mary Jewet of Lancaster Declared their Intention of Marriage Octr. 24, 1767.
Samuel Wilder of Ashburnham & Dorrethy Carter of Lancaster Declared their Intentions of Marriag Novr. 4, 1767
James Parker of Shirley & Sarah Dickerson of Lancaster declared their Intentions of Marriage Novr. 6, 1767
Ephraim Carter Jun. & Abigail Carter both of Lancaster declared their Intentions of Marriage Novem^r. 6, 1767
Jacob Maynard of Sudbury & Hanah May of Lancaster Declared their Intentions of Marriage November 18, 1767
Henry Wyman of Lancaster & Sarah Mason of Lexington Declared their Intentions of Marriage Novem^r. 18, 1767.

BOOK FIRST. 41

37 Samuel Ward of Lancaster & Dolly Chandler of Worcester Declared their Intentions of Marriage Novem^r. 21, 1767.
Joseph Page & Eunice White both of Lancaster Declared their Intention of Marriage December the 5, 1767.
Silas Carter & Lucy Sawyer both of Lancaster Declared their Intentions of Marriage December 12, 1767.
Manasseh Sawyer & Lucy Richardson Declared their Intentions of Marriage December 16, 1767.
Amos Jewet Jun. of Lancaster & Priscillar Jones of Concord Declared their Intentions of Marriage Decem^r. 18 1767.
Sam^{ll} Sawyer of Templeton & Phebe Cooper of Lancaster Declared their Intentions of Marriage Jany. 2^d 1768
Jona Kendall 4th & Hanah Johnson both of Lancaster Declared their Intentions of Marriage Jany. 14 1768
Richard Rand & Relief Sawyer both of Lancaster declared their Intention of Marriage February 8 1768
Daniel Goodfree & Sarah Wyman both of Lancaster Declared their Intentions of Marriage February 17 1768
John Barnerd of Bolton & Elisabeth Fairbank of Lancaster Declar'd their Intentions of Marriage March 2^d, 1768.
Jacob Bennit of Leominster & Elisabeth Wilder of Lancaster declared their Intentions of Marriage March 12. 1768.
Ephraim Hale of Leominster & Hanah Spofford of Lancaster declared their Intentions of Marriage March 12, 1768.
Oliver Powers & Lydia Winn both of Lancaster Declared their Intentions of Marriage March 26. 1768
Timothy Temple & Deborah Ball both of Lancaster declared their Intentions of Marriage July 9th. 1768
Francis Moors of Cambridge & Susanah Richardson of Lancaster declared their Intentions of Marriage July 16, 1768
John Wilder of Lancaster & Katharine Sawyer of Bolton Declared their Intentions of Marriage April 29. 1769.
38 Samuel Wilder & Sarah Ballard both of Lancaster Declared their Intentions of Marriage Feby — 1768
James Crosman Jun. of New Marlbro' & Mary Priest of Lancaster Declared their Intentions of Marriage August 10, 1768   August 20 1768 the abovesaid Mary Priest this day forbid the bands of Matrimony with James Crosman. Sept. 1 1768, the above James Crosman & Mary Priest declared their Intentions of Marriage.
Silas Houghton & Eunice Sawyer both of Lancaster declared their Intentions of Marriage August 27th: 1768
John Hammon & Lucy Powers Both of Lancaster Declared their Intentions of Marriage Septr. 15. 1768
Francis Eager of Paxton & Sarah Fairbank of Lancaster declared their Intentions of Marriage Septr. 27, 1768
Paul Richardson of Winchester & Eucebia Harrington of Lancaster declared their Intentions of Marriage Octr. 20 1768.
Francis Davies & Peggy Lahee both of Lancaster declared their Intentions of Marriage Nov. 14, 1768
David Dufar of Lancaster & Vashty Walker of Marlbro' declared their Intention of Marrig Novr. 27 1768
Joshua Sawyer & Esther Jewet Jun. both of Lancaster declared their Intention of Marriage Decem^r. 17, 1768
Aaron Dresser & Wid^w. Margrett Stratton both of Lancaster declared their Intentions of Marr^s. Decem^r. 30, 1768
Joseph Goss & Sarah Wilder both of Lancaster declared their Intentions of Marriage December 31 1768
Ebenezer Ross of Templeton & Achsah Wilder of Lancaster Declared their Intentions of Marriage Decem^r. 31 1768
Joseph House & Allice Houghton both of Lancaster Declared their Intentions of Marriage Januy. 11, 1769

39 Joseph Carter & Beulah Carter both of Lancaster Declared their Intentions of Marriage January 21 1769

Desire French & Abigail Whitcomb both of Lancaster Declared their Intentions of Marriage Febry. 2, 1769

Amos Rugg Ju^r. & Sarah Willard both of Lancaster declared their Intentions of Marriage Feby. 8, 1769

Jesse Byam of Templeton & Lydia Walker of Lancaster Declared their Intentions of Marriage Febry. 11, 1769

Samuel Blodget of Lancaster & Lydia Bennit of Lancaster Declared their Intentions of Marriage February 11, 1769

De^n Israel Houghton & Wid^w. Elisabeth Wilder both of Lancaster Declared their Intentions of Marriage February 18, 1766

Solomon Steuart & Elisabeth Moors both of Lancaster Declared their Intentions of Marriage February 24 1769

Benjamin Son to Benj^a. & Susanah Thompson born Augt. 27, 1766
Susanah Daug^r to Benj^a & Susanah Thompson born Decem^r. 3, 1768

Joseph Johnson & Hanah Wilder both of Lancaster declared their Intentions of Marriage March 25 1769

James Diggins of Lancaster & Lydia Hale of Leominster Declared their Intentions of Marriage April the 6th. 1769

Jacob Winn Ju^r. & Phebe Grout both of Loncaster declared their Intentions of Marriage April ye 6 1769

Israel Houghton & Allice Campbell both of Lancaster declared their Intentions of Marriage April 8, 1769

John Jones of Colerain & Abigail Atherton of Lancaster declared their Intentions of Marriage April 15, 1769

Ebenezer Brooks & Releif Moors both of Lancaster Declared their Intentions of Marriage April 22^d 1769

William Shaw of Peterborough & Barbera Zwaer of Lancaster Intend marriage April 22^d, 1769

40 Simon Ross & Abigail Ross both of Lancaster declared their Intentions of Marriage June 9, 1769

Joseph Bixpy of Shrewsbury & Meriam Bryant of Lancaster declared their Intentions of Marriage June 24, 1769

Joseph Moors of Lancaster & Hepzebeth Bush of Shrewsbury Declared their Intentions of Marriage July 8, 1769

Timothy Haywood of Lancaster & Patience Stebbins of Leominster Declared their Intentions of Marriage July 19 1769

Andrew Haskell & Lois Bullen both of Lancaster Declared their Intentions of Marriage July 22^d. 1769

William Haywood of Lunenburg & Rebecca Kendal of Lancaster Declared their Intentions of Marriage July 30th, 1769

Abijah Houghton Jun. & Mary Sawyer Ju^r. both of Lancaster Declared their Intentions of Marriage August 2, 1769

James Carruth of Templeton & Lucy Gary of Lancaster Declared their Intentions of Marriage August 29, 1769

John Huit of Ashby & Sarah Priest of Lancaster Declared their Intentions of Marriage September 2^d, 1769

Joseph Dunsmoor & Ruth Newton both of Lancaster Declared their Intentions of Marriage September 9, 1769

David Dufar of Lancaster & Ruth Gregory of Marlbro' Declar'd their Intentions of Marr'g Sept. 26 1769

Joshua Goodridge Ju^r. of Lunenburg & Elis^a. Phelps of Lancaster Declar'd their Intentions of Marriage Sep. 30 1769

Silas Wilder & Elisabeth Sawyer both of Lancaster Declared their Intentions of Marriage Octo^r. 18, 1769

James Pratt & Zerviah Rugg both of Lancaster Declared their Intentions of Marriag Octo^r. 21, 1769

Edward Poor of Worcester & Eunice Goodridge of Lancaster Declar'd their Intentions of Marriage October 28 1769

BOOK FIRST. 43

41 Sampson Ayner of Lancaster & Lucy Lue of Littleton Declared their Intentions of Marriage Novr. 9 1769
Silas Smith of Hatfield & Lavina Houghton of Lancaster Declared their Intentions of Marriage November 11, 1769
James Richardson & Wid^w. Mary Spafford both of Lancaster Declar'd their Intentions of Marriage Novr. 15, 1769
James Elder of Worcester & Sarah Gates of Lancaster Declared their Intentions of Marriage November 17. 1769
William Grimes Junr. of Swanzey & Mary Willard of Lancaster Declared their Intentions of Marriage Novem^r. 20 1769
Frederick Albert of Lancaster & Mary Blood of Bolton Declared their Intentions of marriage December 16th, 1769.
Joshua Fairbanks and Rebekkah Richardson Both of Lancaster Declared their Intentions of Marriage December 16th. 1769
Nathaniel Beman of Lancaster & Thankful Farnsworth of Leominster Declared their Intentions of Marriage Jany. 13, 1770
Thomas Holt of Lancaster & Dinah Corah of Harvard Declar'd their Intentions of Marriage Febru'y 17, 1770.
Abishal Phelps & Katharine Richardson Both of Lancaster Declared their Intentions of Marriage March 9th. 1770
James Lock and Martha Wright Both of Lancaster Declared their Intention of marriage March ye 10th 1776
Ephraim Forster of New Ipswich and Hannah Priest of Lancaster Declared their Intention of marage march ye 12th, 1770
John Priest and Mary Longly Both of Lancaster Declaired their Intention of marage march ye 12, 1770
Philemon Whetcomb of Lancaster and Martha Sawyer of Luninburg Declared their Intention of marage march ye 23^d, 1770
Salmon Goodfre and Rebeckah Phelps Both of Lancaster Decl'red their Intention of marage march ye 28th. 1770
42 Nathanel Wright Ju^r. and Ruth Richardson Both of Lancaster Declared their Intention of mariage march the 29th. 1770
Daniel Norcross and Thankfull Sawyer Both of Lancaster Declared their Intentions of marriage march ye 29th, 1770
William Tompson and Elisabeth Jewet Both of Lancaster Declared their Intentions of marrage march ye 31th, 1770
Joseph Brown of Lemenster and Anis Knight of Lancaster Declaired their Intention of marraige may ye 1th, 1770
Jonathan Hastings of Lancaster and Mary Fay of Northbury Declaired their Intentions of marrage may ye 10th, 1770
Samuel Brooks & Ruth Sawyer Both of Lancaster, Declared their Intention of marrage may ye 12th 1770.
Joshua Piper & Bette Proctor Both of Lancaster Declar'd their Intention of Marrage may ye 12th, 1770
Nathaniel Weight of Broockfield and Sarah Holdman of Lancaster Delivered their Intention of marrage may ye 19th, 1770
Elisha Sawyer Ju^r. of Lancaster and Mary Belknap of Woburn Declaired their Intentions of marrage may ye 19th. 1770
Thomas Rugg and Mahetabel Houghton Both of Lancaster Declaired their Intention of marrage may ye 31th, 1770
Josiah Hedley and Martha Bixby Both of Lancaster Declaired their Intention of marrage June ye 1th, 1770
Stephen Wilder of Lancaster and Betty Sawyer of Harvard Declaired their Intention of marrage June ye 9th, 1770
Josiah White and Parne Brooks both of Lancaster Declaired their Intention of marrage June ye 9th, 1770
43 Daniel Zwear of Lancaster and Abigail Willard of Harvard Declaired their Intentions of marrage June ye 19th, 1770
John Townsend of Bolton and Eunice Fairbank Ju^r. of Lancaster Declaired their Intentions of marrage June ye 20th, 1770.
William Brook and Thankfull Fairbank both of Lancaster Declaired their Intentions of marrage June ye 29th 1770.

Henry Prentice and Sarah Blocket both of Lancaster Declaired their Intentions of marrage June ye 21th, 1770.

Nathaniel Josling and Sarah Bennett Both of Lancaster Declaired their Intentions of marrage August ye 16th 1770

Derias Sawyer of Westminster and Sarah Gary of Lancaster Declaired their Intention of marrage August ye 30th, 1770

Ephraim Willard Jur, and Lois Gary Both of Lancaster Declaired their Intention of marrage August ye 30th 1770

John Brown of Chairlemount and Lucy Rugg of Lancaster Declaired their Intention of marrage Sep. ye 3th. 1770

Elijah Ball and Rebecca Moor both of Lancaster Declaired their Intentions of marrage Sept. 21th 1770.

Solomon Goodale of New Brantery and Parces Bayley of Lancaster Declaired their Intentions of marrage Sept. ye 21th 1770

David Wilson of Leominster and Dorcas Osgood of Lancaster Declaired their Intentions of marrage Sepr: ye 29th 1770

Jonathan Carter of Sudbury and Debroh Hunt of Lancaster Declaired their Intentions of marrage Octobr. ye 1th 1770

Jonas Fairbank Junr. and Elisabeth Wilder Both of Lancaster Declaired their Intentions of marrage Octobr ye 26th 1770.

Hiram Prescott and Phebe Boughcor [Bowker] both of Lancaster Declaired their Intentions of marrage October ye 27th 1770.

Micah Briand and Rebeckah Ball both of Lancaster Declaired their Intentions of marrage October ye 27th 1770

Thomas Holt Junr. and Moley Corey both of Lancaster Declaired their Intentions of marrage October ye 27th 1770

Nathaniel Whetney of New Molbury and Moley Houghton of Lancaster Declaired their Intentions of marrage Octobr ye 30th 1770

Moses Smith and Abigail Green both of Lancaster Declaired their Intentions of marrage October ye 30th 1770

David Holt of Luningburge and Hannah Kendall of Lancaster Declaired their Intentions of marrage October ye 30th 1770.

Revd Mr Caleb Prentice of Reading and Mrs Parmelea Mellen of Lancaster Declaired their Intentions of marrage November ye 22d, 1770.

James White of Chairlemount and Ruth Ballard of Lancaster Declaired their Intentions of marrage November ye 22d 1770.

John Bennett and Lucy Phelps both of Lancaster Declaired their Intentions of marrage Novm. ye 22d 1770

Thomas Stearns Junr of Leominster and Molley White of Lancaster Declaired their Intentions of marrage November ye 22d 1770.

Thomas Gary and Rebecca How Both of Lancaster Entred their Intentions of marraige December ye 5th 1770

John Fillips of Lancaster and Anna Parker of Worcester Declaired their Intentions of marrage Decm, ye 14th 1770.

Joshua Smith – Southbury and Abigaiel Wilder of Lancaster Entred their Intentions of marrage January ye 3th 1771

Joshua Kendall of Lancaster and Dorothy Warner of Harvard Declaired their Intentions of marrage Jany. ye 16th 1771

Joseph Whettecor and Mary Whitney Both of Lancaster Declaired their Intentions of marrage January ye 17th 1771

Jacob Zwear and Abigaiel Priest Both of Lancaster Declaired their Intentions of marrage Jany. ye 26th 1771

Stephen Haywood of Templeton and Ruth Dunsmoor of Lancaster Declaired their Intentions of marrage Feby: the 12th 1771.

James Houghton of Lancaster & Margret Ball of Paxton Declaired their Intentions of marrage Feby: ye 12th 1771

Jacob Fowle of Lancaster & Prisila Abbut of Andover Declaired their Intentions of marrage Feby. ye 18th 1770

Amos Knight Junr. of Lancaster & Susannah Maynerd of Framingham Entred their Intentions of marriage march 26th 1771

Antepas Bartlet of Northborough & Lois White Junr. of Lancaster Declared their Intentions of Marriag April 12 1771

BOOK FIRST. 45

Eathan Kendall & Thankfull Moors both of Lancaster Declared their Intentions of marriage May 1st, 1771.
Thomas Blodgett of Lancaster & Lydia Walker of Lancaster Declared their Intentions of marriage May 3d, 1771.
Eliphalet Rogers of Prince Town & Eunice Bennett of Lancaster Declared their Intentions of marriage May 3d, 1771.
Daniel Bigelow of Worcester & Mary Ballard of Lancaster Declared their Intentions of marriage May 3d, 1771.
Jonathan Buss of Leominster & Mary Steward of Lancaster Declared their Intentions of marriage May 22d, 1771.
46 Aaron Kendall & Katherine Wyman both of Lancaster Declared their Intentions of marriage June 1st, 1771.
Jonas Johnson & Damarus Rugg both of Lancaster Declared their Intentions of marriage June 1st, 1771.
Paul Gibbs of Westminster Entered his Intentions of marriage with Eunice Brucklebank of Lancaster June 21st, 1771.
Jedediah Boynton & Elizabeth Holt both of Lancaster Declared their Intentions of marriage September 23d, 1771.
Benjamin Houghton & the Widw. Margaret Houghton both of Lancaster Declared their Intentions of marriage September 26th, 1771.
John Robins & Lydia Haskell both of Lancaster Declared their Intentions of marriage October 10th, 1771.
Lemuel Haskell of Harvard & Lucy Green of Lancaster Declared their Intentions of marriage October 10th, 1771.
Jonas Wyman & Hannah Smith of Shrewsbury Declared their Intentions of marriage October 20th, 1771.
Nathaniel Sawyer of Lancaster & Katherine Ellis of Medway Declared their Intentions of marriage October 20th, 1771.
John Wilder & Abigail Kendall both [of] Lancaster Declared their Intentions of marriage November 9th, 1771.
William Win of Shrewsbury & Anna Bryant of Lancaster Declared their Intentions of Marriage Novr. 14th, 1771
Samuel Wilder & Martha Rugg both of Lancaster declared their Intentions of Marriage November 16th 1771.
Daniel Goss & Eunice Wilder both of Lancaster declared their Intentions of Marriage Nov. 16; 1771.
47 Samuel Gerish & Abigail Moor both of Lancaster Declared their Intentions of marriage Novem'r 19th. 1771.
Samuel Crosby of Billerica & Abigal Bailey of Lancaster Declared their Intentions of marriage December 8th, 1771.
Joshua Whitcomb of Templeton & Eunice Prescott of Lancaster Declared there Intention of marrige December 27th, 1771
James Wilder Junr. of Lancaster & Jemima Johnson of Bolton Declared their Intentions of marriage January 10th: 1772
Elisha Allen of Lancaster & Meriam Goodale of Marlboro' declared their Intentions of Marriage Febry, 1st: 1772.
Abraham Stone of Westminster & Mary Osgood of Lancaster Declared their Intentions of marriage February 4th, 1772.
John Kindrick & Keziah Baldwin both of Lancaster Declared their Intentions of marriage February 6th: 1772
William Locke declared his Intentions of marriage with Mary Fowle, both of Lancaster, February 15th, 1772
Oliver Fairbank of Lancaster declared his Intentions of marriage with Susanna Gates of Littleton, February 15th. 1772
Asa Smith & Sarah Steward Junr. both of Lancaster declared their Intentions of marriage February 28th: 1772
Jonathan Moor & Elizabeth Richardson both of Lancaster declared their Intentions of marriage March 2d 1772
David Goodale and Dorothy Newton both of Lancaster Declaird their Intentions of marriage March ye 2d. 1772
Samuel Holman of Lancaster & Lyda Brunson of Princton Declaired their Intentions of marrage April ye 4th, 1772

48 Joseph Sever & Abigail Sawyer Both of Lancaster Declaired their Intentions of marrage April ye 12th 1772
Jiles Wills & Relief Wilder Both of Lancaster Declaired their Intentions of marrage April 18th 1772.
Nathan Eager of Lancaster and Dinah Sawyer of Harvard Entred their Intentions April 23 1772
Daniel Allen and Rebeccah Houghton both of Lancaster Declaired their Intentions of marrage April ye 20th 1772.
Samuel Mason of Winchendon and Sarah Whetney of Lancaster Declaired their Intentions of marrage may ye 20th 1772.
Ezra Hall of Leominster and Thankfull Brabrook of Lancaster Declaired their Intentions of marrage may ye 20th 1772.
Jonathan Bozworth and Mary Holt both of Lancaster Declard their Intentions of marrage may ye 26th 1772.
Jonathan Butterick of Dunsterabell [Dunstable] and Hannah Wilder Sawyer of Lancaster Declaired their Intentions of marrage may ye 30th 1772
David Jewett and Ruth Sawyer both of Lancaster Declaired their Intentions of marrage July ye 10th. 1772
Luther Graves and Phebe Jewett both of Lancaster Declaired their Intentions of marrage July ye 17th 1772
Moses Wilder and Eunice Furbush Both of Lancaster Declaired their Intentions of marrage July ye 25th 1772
Ebenezer Allen Ju^r. of Lancaster and Mary Henry of Luningburg Declaired their Intentions of marrage July ye 30th 1772
Do^e Israel Araton [Atherton] & Rebecca Prentice both of Lancaster Declared their Intentions of marrage August ye 22^d. 1772
Fransces Cory and Elizabeth Kendall Both of Lancaster Declared their Intentions of marrage August ye 22^d, 1772
49 David Bennett of Shrewsbury and Parses Cutting of Lancaster Entred their Intentions of marrage August ye 29th 1772
Jones Whitney of Shrewsbury and Tamer Houghton of Lancaster Entred their Intentions of marrage August ye 29th 1772
Asa Rugg and Betty Piper Both of Lancaster Entred their [intentions] of marrage Sept. ye 21th, 1772
Dudley Bayley of Lancaster and Reuame [Ruhamah] Durster of Westminster Declaired their Intentions of marrage Sept. ye 21 1772
Timothy Mosman of Lancaster and Lucy Bond of Weston Entred their Intentions of marrage October ye 10th 1772
Colo Abijah Willard of Lancaster Entred his Intention of marrage with Mrs Mary McKown of Boston october the 24th 1772.
Obediah Groce and Lucy Houghton both of Lancaster Enterd their Intentions of marrage Octo^r ye 24th 1772.
Samuel Kilburn of Luningburge and Sarah Cook of Lancaster Entred their Intentions of marrage Octr. ye 29th 1772
John Lock of Templeton and Henreta Herington of Lancaster Entred their Intentions of marrage oct^r. ye 29th 1772.
Aaron Gary and Lucy Beard both of Lancaster Entred their Intentions of marrage oct^r. ye 29th 1772
John Sprague of Lancaster and Katharine Foster of Charlestown Entred their Intentions of marrage Novr. ye 18th 1772
John Dresor and Elisabeth Nelson both of Lancaster Entred their Intentions of marrage Dec^r.- ye 5th 1772
50 Josiah Sawyer ye Son of William and Mary Sawyer was born ye 13 day of august 1714

the births of the Children of Peter and Alles Joslin

Peter Was born the 7th of December 1724
Alles Was born the 25th. of September 1726
Nathanael Was born 11 of November 1729
Hester was born 11 of September 1731
Joseph was born the 19 of May 1733
Sam^ll the 19th. of May 1738

Yͤ births of the Children of Joshua & Hannah Johnson with some of their Deaths

Joshua Johnson was born July the first 1739
Abigail Johnson was born September 24 1743
Hannah Johnson was born April yͤ 15 1749
Samᵘˡˡ Johnson was born August yͤ 4ᵗʰ 1741 & Deceased Decemʳ. 1745
Elisabeth Johnson [was] born August 24 1745 & Deceased 1746
Elisabeth born September 22 1747 Deceased July 6ᵗʰ 1749

The Births of the Children of Mr Josiah & Prudance Brown

William Born July yͤ 6 1741.   Joseph July yͤ 5, 1746.
Prudance Born October 20 1746   Elisabeth May yͤ 25, 1749.
John August yͤ 25 1744

The Births of the Childern of Thomas & Susanah Holt.

Thomas Holt Jun. Born March 1. 1749.   Susanah Holt Born August 8, 1755.
David Holt Born February 22, 1752.   Jabez Holt born January 10. 1758.
Mary Holt Born February 17, 1753.

51   Ezra Houghton yͤ son of Benjamin & Ruth Houghton was born July 2 : 1722
Abijah Houghton yͤ son of Benjamin & Ruth Houghton was born Septem. 23 : 1723
Releef yͤ daughter of Benjamin & Ruth Houghton was born October yͤ 23 : 1726
Elijah Houghton yͤ son of Benjamin & Ruth Houghton was born June yͤ 16: 1728.
Parnee Houghton yͤ daughter of Benjamin & Ruth Houghton was born April yͤ 14: 1730
Philemon Houghton yͤ son of Benjamin & Ruth Houghton was born June yͤ 3: 1731
Naham Houghton yͤ son of Benjamin Houghton & Ruth Houghton was born October 1: 1732
Ruth Houghton yͤ Daughter of Benjamin & Ruth Houghton was born April 3: 1734
Lemuel Houghton yͤ son of Benjamin & Ruth Houghton was born Septemʳ. 25: 1735
Benjamin Houghton yͤ son of Benjamin & Ruth Houghton was born May yͤ 10 1740
Ephraim ——
Amos son of Amos & Elisebeth Atherton was born October 5ᵗʰ: 1731
David Son of Amos & Elisebeth Atherton was born February 10ᵗʰ: 1732-3
Luce Daughter of Amos & Elisebeth Atherton was born September 14: 1735
Sary Daughter of Amos & Elisebeth Atherton was born March the 9ᵗʰ 1738-9
Phinehas Son of Amos & Elisebeth Atherton was born February 17ᵗʰ 1742-3
Abigail Atherton Daughter of Amos & Elisebeth Atherton [was] born May yͤ 27 1746
Peter Son of Amos & Elsabeth Atherton was born yͤ 11ᵗʰ of October 1750
Annah Daughter of Amos & Elsabeth Atherton was born April yͤ 22ᵈ 1753.
Tamar yͤ Daughter of Nathaniel & Jane Hutson was born October 5ᵗʰ 1727
Beriah yͤ Son of Nathaniel & Jane Hutson was Born Sept yͤ 29ᵗʰ 1729
William Hutson yͤ Son of Nathaniel & Jane Hutson was Born August yͤ 18ᵗʰ 1731
Elisabeth yͤ Daughter of Nathaniel & Jane Hutson was born Sept 30 1732
Nathaniel yͤ Son of Nathaniel & Jane Hutson was Born Janu 27 1733-4
Sollomon yͤ Son of Nathaniel & Jane Hutson was born Janu 17 1735-6
Martha yͤ Daughter of Nathaniel & Jane Hutson was born Febry yͤ 13 1736-7 and Deceased april yͤ 8ᵗʰ 1737
Darious yͤ Son of Nathaniel & Jane Hutson was Born Feb yͤ 3ᵈ 1738-9
Ezekiel yͤ Son of Nathaniel & Jane Hutson was Born August yͤ 1ˢᵗ 1740
Martha yͤ Daughter of Nathaniel & Jane Hutson was Born octo 22 1741
Mary yͤ Daughter of Nathaniel & Jane Hutson was Born april 22 1743

The births of the of Childeren of Mr Jacob & Rebekah Barret

Jacob August first: 1741
John May the 17ᵗʰ: 1743
Jonathan June the 11 : 1744.

Keziah Daug^r. to John & Keziah May Born June 20, 1761
Nath^{ll}. Son to Thos. & Abigail Kendall Born Sept. 21, 1759
John son to John & Prudence Warner Born June 16, 1758
Prudence Daug^r. to John & Prudence Warner born Sept. 4, 1759
Levi Son to John & Prudence Warner born May 22, 1761
52 Nathaniel & Jonathan Wilder ye sons of Nathaniel & Damaris Wilder was born Novem^h: 26: 1708: & sd Jonathan Deceased the same day
Charls Wilder ye son of Nathaniel & Damaris Wilder was born Sept^m. 15: 1710
Joshua Wilder ye son of Nathaniel & Damaris Wilder was born Sept^m. 20: 1712
Bezaleel Wilder ye son of Nathaniel & Damaris Wilder was born Nov^m. 24: 1714
Aholiab Wilder ye son of Nathaniel & Damaris Wilder was born febry y^e: 5: 1716-17
Damaris the daughter of Nathaniel & Damaris Wilder was born January y^e: 1: 1719-20
Jaramahell Wilder ye son of Nathaniel & Damaris Wilder was born May y^e: 8: 1721
Prudence the Daughter of Nathaniel & Damaris Wilder was born June y^e: 24: 1723 [2]
Aaron Wilder ye son of Nathaniel & Damaris Wilder was born August y^e: 21: 1723
Sam^{ll} Wilder ye son of Nathaniel & Damaris Wilder was born January: 19: 1724-5
Elias Wilder ye son of Nathaniel & Damaris Wilder was born January: 17: 1726-7
Eunice Sawyer ye Daughter of Bezaleel & Judith Sawyer was born November y^e: 27: 1716.
Josiah Sawyer ye Son of Bezaleel & Judith Sawyer was born November y^e: 7: 1718.
Derias Sawyer ye Son of Bezaleel & Judith Sawyer was Born November y^e: 4, 1720.
Bezaleel Sawyer ye Son of Bezaleel & Judith Sawyer was born March ye 25, 1723.
Hannah Sawyer ye Daughter of Bezaleel & Judith Sawyer was born September y^e: 13, 1725.
And said Hannah Sawyer Daughter of said Bezaeel & Judith Sawyer, Deceased January y^e: 30: 1726-7.
Hannah ye Daughter of Bezaleel & Judeth Sawyer was born January y^e: 4: 1727-8.
Moses Sawyer ye Son of Bezaleel & Judeth Sawyer was born August the 20. 1730.
Paul Sawyer ye Son of Bezaleel & Judeth Sawyer was born May y^e: 19, 1733.
John Buss the Son of John & Hannah Buss was born April y^e: 2^d: 1712.
Abigail Buss ye Daughter of John & Hannah Buss was born January y^e: 4: 1713-14.
Hannah Buss ye Daughter of John & Hannah Buss was born June y^e: 7: 1716.
Stephen Buss ye Son of John & Hannah Buss was born August y^e: 8: 1718.
Jonathan Buss ye Son of John & Hannah Buss was born June y^e: 19: 1721.
Ebenezer Buss ye Son of John & Hannah Buss was born January y^e: 27': 1723-4.
Uzziah Kendal ye Son of Ralph & Abigail Kendal was born April y^e: 11: 1721.
Abiather Kendal ye Son of Ralph & Abigail Kendal was born february y^e:22:1723
Ruth Kendal ye Daughter of Ralph & Abigail Kendal was born february y^e: 9: 1725
Abigail Kendal ye Daughter of Ralph & Abigail Kendal was born July y^e: 20: 1728
Benjamin Kendal ye Son of Ralph & Abigail Kendal was born September y^e: 12: 1731
Eunice Kendal ye Daughter of Ralph & Abigail Kendal was born May y^e: 14: 1732.
Joseph Bealey the Son of Shubael & Anna Bealey was born May y^e: 11: 1730
Hannah Bealey the Daughter of Shubael & Anna Bealey was born April y^e: 2: 1732
Jonathan Bealey ye Son of Shubael & Anna Bealey was born November ye 24: 1733
53 Josiah Wilder ye Son of John & Sarah [Sawyer] Wilder was born June ye 6th: 1700.

Jonas Wilder y⁰ Son of John & Sarah Wilder was born November 16th, 1701
Mary Wilder y⁰ Daughter of John & Sarah Wilder was born July y⁰ 9th, 1705
Hannah Wilder y⁰ Daughter of John & Sarah Wilder was born March 4th: 1707-8
Jonathan Wilder y⁰ Son of John & Sarah Wilder was born October 5th, 1710
John Wilder y⁰ Son of John & Sarah Wilder was born April 3d, 1713
Thankfull Wilder y⁰ Daughter of John & Sarah Wilder was born April 15: 1715
William Wilder the Son of John & Sarah Wilder was born September 4th: 1717

NOTE.—In the Book of the Wilders, Jonas is recorded as born in 1699, and Josiah in 1701.

Jonas More y⁰ Son of Fairbank & Judith More was born October y⁰ 6, 1725
Fairbank More y⁰ Son of Fairbank & Judith More was born July y⁰: 25: 1728
William More y⁰ Son of Fairbank & Judith More was born January y⁰: 17: 1730-31
Samuel Willard y⁰ Son of Henry & Dorcas Willard was born May the 31: 1690.
Elisabeth Phelps y⁰ Daughter of Edward & Ruth Phelps was born January y⁰: 27: 1689-90
Samuel Willard & Elisabeth Phelps was married August y⁰: 19: 1717.
Samuel Willard the Son of Sam¹¹. & Elisabeth Willard was born November y⁰: 12; 1718.
Abijah Willard y⁰ Son of Sam¹¹. & Elisabeth Willard was born July y⁰. 8: 1720.
Naham Willard y⁰ Son of Sam¹¹. & Elisabeth Willard was born May y⁰: 28: 1722.
Abijah Willard y⁰ Son of Sam¹¹. & Elisabeth Willard was born July y⁰: 27: 1724.
Levi Willard y⁰ Son of Sam¹¹. & Elisabeth Willard was born April y⁰: 19: 1727
Joshua Willard y⁰ Son of Sam¹¹. & Elisabeth Willard was born January y⁰: 24: 1729
Abel Willard y⁰ Son of Sam¹¹. & Elisabeth Willard was born January y⁰: 12; 1731-2.
Olive Whelock y⁰ Daughter of Joseph & Abigail Whelock was born January y⁰. 10; 1725-6.
Olive[r?] Whelock y⁰ Son of Joseph & Abigail Whelock was born December y⁰: 7: 1727.
Joseph Whelock y⁰ Son of Joseph & Abigail Wheelock was born february y⁰: 14: 1729-30
Phenihas Whelock y⁰ Son of Joseph & Abigail Whelock was born November y⁰: 9: 1731.
John Whelock y⁰ Son of Joseph & Abigail Whelock was born September y⁰: 9: 1733.
Jonathan Atherton y⁰ Son of Benjamin & Eunice Atherton was born June y⁰: 14; 1729.
Bettey Atherton y⁰ Daughter of Benjamin & Eunice Atherton was born October y⁰: 8: 1731.
Eunice Atherton y⁰ Daughter of Benjamin & Eunice Atherton was born November y⁰: 28: 1733.
54 Hannah Whetcomb y⁰ Daughter of Josiah Whetcomb Ju. and Mary Whetcomb was born March y⁰ 28: 1694
Josiah Whetcomb y⁰ Son of Josiah Whetcomb Ju. and Mary Whetcomb was born y⁰ 10 day of November, anno domini 1701
James Whetcomb y⁰ Son of Josiah Whetcomb Ju. and Mary Whetcomb was born y⁰ first of November 1704
Elisabeth Whetcomb y⁰ Daughter of Josiah Whetcomb Ju. and Elisabeth Whetcomb was born y⁰ 24 of September 1713
Josiah White the son of Josiah & Mary White was born September y⁰: 16. 1682.
Abigail Whetcomb y⁰ daughter of Josiah & Rebekkah Whetcomb was born March y⁰. 13: 1687-8.

Josiah White & Abigail Whetcomb were married June the 26, 1706.

Mary White the daughter of Josiah & Abigail White was born March y⁰, 31, 1707.
Jonathan White y⁰ Son of Josiah & Abigail White was born October y⁰: 4: 1709. [8?]
Hannah White y⁰ daughter of Josiah & Abigail White was born March y: 14: 1709-10
Abigail White y⁰ Daughter of Josiah & Abigail White was born January y⁰: 26: 1711-12.

Josiah White y*e* Son of Josiah & Abigail White was born January y*e*: 3: 1713–14.
Ruth White y*e* Daughter of Josiah & Abigail White was born February y*e*: 9: 1715-16
Martha White y*e* Daughter of Josiah & Abigail White was born November y*e*: 24: 1717.
Joseph White y*e* Son of Josiah & Abigail White was born November y*e*: 1: 1719.
Joanna White the Daughter of Josiah & Abigail White was born September y*e*: 20: 1721.
Jotham White the Son of Josiah & Abigail White was born April y*e*: 20: 1723.
Silence White the daughter of Josiah & Abigail White was born June y*e*: 26: 1725.
John & James White y*e* Sons of Josiah & Abigail White was born January y*e*: 24: 1727-8.
John White the Son of Josiah & Abigail White was born Aprill y*e*: 10: 1729.
Elisha White the Son of Josiah & Abigail White was born March y*e*: 8: 1730-31.
Mary Phelps y*e* Daughter of Edward & Mary Phelps was born August: 13: 1719.
Asahel Phelps y*e* son of Edward & Mary Phelps was born July: 18: 1721
John Phelps y*e* Son of Edward & Mary Phelps was born february: 18: 1723-4
Lydiah Phelps y*e* Daughter of Edward & Mary Phelps was born february: 18: 1726-7
Edward Phelps y*e* Son of Edward & Mary Phelps was born february: 13: 1729-30
Phinehas Phelps y*e* Son of Edward & Mary Phelps was born January: 16: 1732-3
John Priest the Son of Gabriel & Abigail Priest was born November, 21*st*. 1717
Gabriel Priest the Son of Gabriel & Abigail Priest was born June y*e*. 17. 1720
Jeremiah Priest the Son of Gabriel & Abigail Priest was born April y*e*. 30, 1722
55 Sarah Houghton y*e* Daughter of James & Sarah Houghton was born May y*e*. 24: 1723
Bettey Houghton y*e* Daughter of James & Sarah Houghton was born December y*e*. 4: 1725
James Houghton y*e* Son of James & Sarah Houghton was born March y*e*: 31: 1728
Edward Houghton y*e* Son of James & Sarah Houghton was born December, 25, 1730.
Susanna Houghton y*e* Daughter of James & Sarah Houghton was born October y*e*: 1: 1733.
Levi Houghton Son of James & Sarah Houghton [was] born March y*e* 1 1736
Hannah Beaman y*e* Daughter of Ebenezer & Rebekkah Beaman was born May y*e*. 8. 1714
Thankfull Beaman y*e* Daughter of Ebenezer & Rebekkah Beaman was born Janua*r*. 1, 1715-16
Joseph Beaman y*e* Son of Ebenezer & Rebekkah Beaman was born July, 29, 1718.
Rebeckah Beaman y*e* Daughter of Ebenezer & Rebekkah Beaman was born Septem: 11: 1726
Sarah Beaman y*e* Daughter of Ebenezer & Rebeckah Beaman was born Septem: 27, 1723
Pricilla Beaman y*e* Daughter of Ebenezer & Rebeckah Beaman was born June: 22: 1726.
Ebenezer & Patience Beaman y*e* Son & Daughter of Ebenezer & Rebeckah Beaman was born Aug*t*. 1: 1728
Thomas Beaman y*e* Son of Ebenezer & Rebeckah Beaman was born Septem*b*. 16, 1729
Sarah Sawyer y*e* daughter of John & Sarah Sawyer was born April y*e*: 14: 1723.
Sarah Sawyer y*e* daughter of John & Sarah Sawyer was born August y*e*: 20: 1724
Dorothy Sawyer y*e* daughter of John & Sarah Sawyer was born March y*e*: 3: 1725-6.
John Sawyer y*e* Son of John & Sarah Sawyer was born August y*e*. 7. 1728.
Moses Sawyer y*e* Son of John & Sarah Sawyer was born November the, 3: 1730.
Miriam Sawyer the daughter of John & Sarah Sawyer was born August y*e*: 29. 1731.
Aaron Sawyer y*e* Son of John & Sarah Sawyer was born y*e* above said 29 of August, 1731
Deliverance Sawyer Son of John & Sarah Sawyer was born y*e* 11 Day of Decem 1746.

John flecher y° Son of John & Hannah flecher was born March y°: 3: 1713
Timothy flecher y° Son of John & Hannah flecher was born December y°. 19: 1714
Lydiah flecher y° Daughter of John & Hannah flecher was born Novem^b. 26: 1716
Robert flecher y° Son of John & Hannah flecher was born May, y°. 19. 1719.
Hannah flecher y° Daughter of John & Hannah flecher was born August y°: 10: 1721
Joshua flecher y° Son of John & Hannah flecher was born December y°. 26. 1725
Ruth flecher y° Daughter of John & Hannah flecher was born March y°: 16: 1727-8
Samuel fairbank y° son of Thomas & Dorithy fairbank was born April; 8: 1730.
John fairbank y° son of Thomas & Dorithy fairbank was born May y°: 4: 1731
Jonathan fairbank y° son of Thomas & Dorithy fairbank was born November: 12: 1732
56 Hooker Osgood Son of Hooker and Dorothy Osgood was born y°. 26th. of March, 1693;
Mary Whelock Daughter of Joseph and Elezabeth Whelock was born y°: 11: of May; 1695.
Mary Osgood Daughter of Hooker and Mary Osgood was born y°: 7th of April: 1718.
Joseph Osgood Son of Hooker and Mary Osgood was born y°: 25th: of Jenuary: 1720-21.
John Osgood Son of Hooker and Mary Osgood was born y°: 12th: of Jenuary: 1723-4
John Osgood Son of Hooker and Mary Osgood was born y°: 5th: of June: 1725.
Kezia Osgood Daughter of Hooker and Mary Osgood was born y°: 7th of March. 1727-8
Hannah Wilder the daughter of Oliver & Mary [Fairbank] Wilder was born y° 15 of January, 1715-16
Mary Wilder the daughter of Oliver & Mary Wilder was born y° 24 of December, 1717
Oliver Wilder the son of Oliver & Mary Wilder was born the 7 of March, 1719-20
Tilly Wilder the son of Oliver & Mary Wilder was born the 23 of June, 1722
Keziah Wilder the Daughter of Oliver & Mary Wilder was born y° 27 of february, 1724-5
Tamar Wilder the daughter of Oliver & Mary Wilder was born y° 23 of May, 1727.
Phinehas Wilder the son of Oliver & Mary Wilder was born y° 14: of April, 1730
Abigail Wilder the Daughter of Oliver & Mary Wilder was Born December y° 16th 1740
Benjamin Bellows y° Son of Benjamin & Dorcas Bellows was born May y° 26, 1712
Admonition Tooker y° Daughter of Thomas & Mary Tooker was born february y°: 20: 1721-2

Y° births of the Children of John & Mary Johnson

Nathanael born August y° 20th 1730
John was born August y° 12 1733
Doratha born March 22 1736

John Johnson Junr Deceased April y° 22 1737.

Sasanah Wood Daughter of Nehemiah & Mary Wood born May y° 9 1743
Hannah Wood Daughter of Nehemiah & Mary Wood born Novem^r y° 2^d 1745
Mary Wood Daughter of Nehemiah & Mary Wood born November y° 13 1748.
Silas Houghton the Son of Jonas & Mary Houghton was born October y° 26: 1713
Bettey Houghton y° daughter of Jonas & Mary Houghton was born March y° 20: 1715-16
Mary Houghton y° daughter of Jonas & Mary Houghton was born March y° 8: 1720-21

Prudence Houghton y⁶ daughter of Jonas & Mary Houghton was born October, 21, 1723.
Persis Houghton y⁶ daughter of Jonas & Mary Houghton was born July, 31, 1726.
Jonas Houghton y⁶ son of Jonas & Mary Houghton was born April the 21. 1728
Phinehas Willard y⁶ son of Hezekiah & Anna Willard was born October. 22: 1714
Benjamin Townsend the Son of Hezekiah & Sarah Townsend was born februar. 24: 1714-5.
Sarah Townsend the Daughter of Hezekiah & Sarah Townsend was born Octob. y⁶. 18. 1717.
Mary Townsend y⁶ Daughter of Hezekiah & Sarah Townsend was born March y⁶. 10. 1719-20.
Obadiah Townsend y⁶ Son of Hezekiah & Sarah Townsend was born februar. y⁶. 7. 1724-5
John Larkin y⁶ Son of Phillip & Mary Larkin was born May y⁶. 7. 1722
Mattathias Larkin y⁶ Son of Phillip & Mary Larkin was born January y⁶: 5, 1724-5
Peter Larkin y⁶ Son of Phillip & Mary Larkin was born July y⁶. 29. 1727
William Larkin y⁶ Son of Phillip & Mary Larkin was born March y⁶: 13: 1730-1
Edmon Larkin y⁶ Son of Phillip & Mary Larkin was born March y⁶: 11 : 1733-4
57 Jonathan Houghton the Son of John & Mary Houghton was born y⁶ 20 of february 1685-6
Thankfull White y⁶ Daughter of Josiah & Mary White was born y⁶ 27 of March, 1689
Thankfull Houghton y⁶ Daughter of Jonathan & Thankfull Houghton was born y⁶ 3 day of March, 1713-14
Mary Houghton y⁶ Daughter of Jonathan & Thankfull Houghton was born y⁶ 19 of September, 1715
Keziah Houghton y⁶ Daughter of Jonathan & Thankfull Houghton was born y⁶ 31 of May, 1717
Jonathan Houghton y⁶ Son of Jonathan & Thankfull Houghton was born y⁶ 28 of March, 1719
Azubah Houghton y⁶ Daughter of Jonathan & Thankfull Houghton was born y⁶ 20 of November, 1720
Rufus Houghton y⁶ Son of Jonathan & Thankfull Houghtou was born y⁶ 9 of November, 1722
Achsa Houghton y⁶ Daughter of Jonathan & Thankfull Houghton was born y⁶ 16 of January, 1724-5
Ephah Houghton y⁶ Daughter of Jonathan & Thankfull Houghton was born y⁶ 26 of June, 1727.
Zerish Houghton y⁶ Daughter of Jonathan & Thankfull Houghton was born y⁶ 18 day of february. 1728-9
Ephah Houghton y⁶ Daughter of Jonathan & Thankfull Houghton was born August y⁶ 19, 1731.
Abiather Houghton y⁶ Son of Gershom & Elizabeth Houghton was born y⁶ 21 of January, 1725-6
William Tooker y⁶ Son of Thomas & Mary Tooker was born y⁶ 15 of January, 1725-6
Abigail Willard y⁶ daughter of James & Hannah Willard was born y⁶ 17 of April, 1726.
Abner Wilder y⁶ son of Josiah & Prudence Wilder was born y⁶. 4. of November, 1725.
Jonathan Witherby y⁶ son of John & Elisabeth Witherby was born y⁶ 17 of August, 1725.
Josiah Johnson y⁶ son of Josiah & Anness Johnson was born y⁶ 5 day of June, 1726.
Patience Butler y⁶ Daughter of James & Hannah Butler was born y⁶ 1 day of May. 1726.
Joseph Preist y⁶ Son of Joseph & Mary Preist was born y⁶ 28 day of November, 1717.

Benjamin Preist yᵉ Son of Joseph & Mary Preist was born yᵉ 29 day of february, 1719-20
Mary Preist yᵉ daughter of Joseph & Mary Preist was born yᵉ 23 of March, 1721-22
Susanah Preist yᵉ daughter of Joseph & Mary Preist was born yᵉ 22 day of March, 1723-24
Ruth Willard yᵉ Daughter of Henry & Sarah Willard was born yᵉ 22 day of May, 1726.
Olive Whelock yᵉ Daughter of Joseph & Abigail Whelock was born yᵉ 7 day of January, 1725-6
Peter Houghton yᵉ Son of Thomˢ. & Joannah Houghton was born yᵉ 11 day of January: 1723-4
Joannah Houghton yᵉ Daughter of Thomas & Joannah Houghton was born yᵉ 6 day of April, 1726
Israel Houghton yᵉ Son of Israel & Martha Houghton was born yᵉ 13 day of December, 1723
Joseph & Benjamin Houghton yᵉ Sons of Israel & Martha Houghton was born yᵉ 3 of Deceᵐ. 1724
Uriah Holt yᵉ Son of Uriah & Sarah Holt was born yᵉ. 10. day of May, 1726
John Benitt yᵉ Son of John & Bathsheba Benitt was born January yᵉ 23 day, 1718-9
Bathsheba Benitt yᵉ Daughter of John & Bathsheba Benitt was born yᵉ 18 day of December, 1720
Nathan Benitt yᵉ Son of John & Bathsheba Benitt was born yᵉ 28 day of October, 1722.
Jotham Benitt yᵉ Son of John & Bathsheba Benitt was born yᵉ 8 day of May, 1726
Elisha Benitt yᵉ Son of John & Bathsheba Benitt was born yᵉ. 7. day of July. 1728.
Jacob Benitt yᵉ Son of John & Bathsheba Benitt was born September yᵉ: 16: 1734.
Thomas Benitt yᵉ Son of John & Bathsheba Benitt was born August yᵉ 3ᵈ 1736
Mary Houghton yᵉ daughter of James & Mary Houghton was born yᵉ 2 day of August, 1726.
Eleazer Preist yᵉ Son of Joseph & Mary Preist was born yᵉ 23 day of August, 1726.
Phinehas Houghton yᵉ Son of Israel & Martha Houghton was born yᵉ 22 day of September, 1726
Robert Houghton yᵉ Son of Eleazer & Elisabeth Houghton was born yᵉ 12 day of April, 1720
Lois Houghton yᵉ Daughter of Eleazer & Elisabeth Houghton was born yᵉ 22 day of July, 1722
Derias Houghton yᵉ Son of Eleazer & Elisabeth Houghton was born yᵉ 20 day of January, 1723-4
Miriam Houghton yᵉ Daughter of Eleazer & Elisabeth Houghton was born yᵉ 22 day of february, 1725-6
Dorothy Whetcomb yᵉ Daughter of Jonathan & Rachel Whetcomb was born yᵉ 2 day of June, 1726
Oliver Atherton yᵉ Son of Joseph & Hannah Atherton was born yᵉ 1 day of August, 1721
Mary Atherton yᵉ Daughter of Joseph & Hannah Atherton was born yᵉ 8 day of March, 1722-3
Moses Warner yᵉ Son of John & Rebekah Warner was born yᵉ 10 day of August, 1726
Phinehas Houghton yᵉ Son of John & Mehitable Houghton was born yᵉ 10 of April, 1725
Mary Houghton yᵉ daughter of John & Mehitabel Houghton was born yᵉ 2 day of January, 1718-19
Ralph Houghton yᵉ son of John & Mehitabel Houghton was born yᵉ 19 day of May, 1722.
Abia Houghton yᵉ daughter of Henry & Anna Houghton was born yᵉ 21 day of March, 1725-6.
Phinihas ffairbank yᵉ son of Joseph & Mary ffairbank was born yᵉ 8 of April, 1719.
Mary ffairbank yᵉ daughter of Joseph & Mary ffairbank was born yᵉ 17: of October, 1721

Joseph ffairbank y" son of Joseph & Mary ffairbank was born y" 4 of november, 1722
Mercy ffairbank y" daughter of Joseph & Mary ffairbank was born y" 6. day of february, 1724-5.
Cyrus ffairbank y" son of Joseph & Mary ffairbank was born y" 23 day of may, 1726.
Millisant Carter y" daughter of Samuel & Jemimah Carter was born y" 29 of August: 1726.
Releef Houghton y" daughter of Benja^m. & Ruth Houghton was born y" 23 of October, 1726.
Ephraim Willard y" son of Hezekiah & Anna Willard was born y^e: 13 day of October: 1726.
Jerusha y" daughter of Joshua & Elisabeth Houghton was born y" 6 day of January: 1719-20
Saul Houghton y" son of Joshua & Elisabeth Houghton was born y" 6. day of may, 1722.
Orpah Houghton y" daughter of Joshua & Elisabeth Houghton was born y" 6 day of november: 1724
Joshua Houghton y" son of Joshua & Elisabeth Houghton was born y" 6 day of may: 1721: & he deceased y" same day
Abigail Houghton y" daughter of Jonathan & Mary Houghton was born y" 7 day of September, 1726.
Josiah Carter y" son of Samuel & Dorithy Carter was born y" 26 day of January, 1726-7.
Abigail Houghton y" daughter of Stephen & Abigail Houghton was born y" 14 of January, 1726-7.
Ebenezer Polly y" son of Ebenezer & Dorcas Polly was born y" 24 day of October, 1726.
Asa Houghton y" son of Henry & Elisabeth Houghton was born y" 28. of January, 1726-7
Elisabeth Wilder y" Daughter of James & Abigail [Gardner] Wilder was born y" 18. day of September, 1726
Prudence Sawyer y" Daughter of Elias & Beatrix Sawyer was born y" 24 day of September. 1726
Samuel Benit y" son of Samuel & Tabatha Benit was born y^e. 13. day of January, 1715-6
Ephriam Benit y" son of Samuel & Tabatha Benit was born y^e. 14. day of October, 1717
Phenihas Benit y" son of Samuel & Tabatha Benit was born y^e. 12. day of november, 1719
Silas Bennit y" son of Samuel & Tabatha Bennit was born y^e. 12. day of April, 1721.
Tabatha Bennit y" daughter of Samuel & Tabatha Bennit was born y^e. 27. day of October, 1724.
Azubah Bennit y" daughter of Samuel & Tabatha Bennit was born y^e. 5. day of may. 1727.
Joseph Wilder y" son of Jonas & Eunice [Beaman] Wilder was born y" 14. day of January, 1724-5
Hannah Wilder y" daughter of Jonas & Eunice Wilder was born y" 25. day of february, 1726-7
Olliver Pollard y" son of William & Experience Pollard was born y^e. 8 day of September: 1727
Sarah Broughton y" daughter of Edward & Martha Broughton was born y^e. 13 of January, 1722-3
Copiah Broughton y" daughter of Edward & Martha Broughton was born y" 28 of October, 1724
Patience Broughton y" daughter of Edward & Martha Broughton was born y" 27 of January, 1726-7
Aaron Willard y" son of Aaron & Mary Willard was born y^e. 10 of September, 1725.
Simon Willard y" son of Aaron & Mary Willard was born y" 29 of September,: 1727

Cylence Houghton yᵉ daughter of James & Mary Houghton was born yᵉ. 2. of December, 1727.
Thomas Townsend yᵉ son of Hezekiah & Sarah Townsend was born yᵉ 26 of October, 1727
Elisabeth Atherton yᵉ daughter of Joseph & Hannah Atherton was born yᵉ. 5. of may, 1727.
Ruth Carter yᵉ Daughter of Thomas & Ruth Carter was born yᵉ. 26. day of April, 1708.
Abigail Carter yᵉ Daughter of Thomas & Ruth Carter was born yᵉ. 29. day of December, 1711.
John Carter yᵉ Son of Thomas & Ruth Carter was born yᵉ. 23. day of April, 1713.
Thomas Carter yᵉ Son of Thomas & Ruth Carter was born yᵉ. 12. day of february, 1714-15.
Thomas Carter yᵉ Son of Thomas & Ruth Carter was born yᵉ. 30. day of April, 1716.
Elisabeth Carter yᵉ daughter of Thomas & Ruth Carter was born yᵉ. 17. day of January, 1718-19.
James Carter yᵉ Son of Thomas & Ruth Carter was born yᵉ. 8. day of february, 1720-21.
Sarah Carter yᵉ daughter of Thomas & Ruth Carter was born yᵉ. 6. of november, 1722.
Sarah Carter yᵉ daughter of Thomas & Ruth Carter was born yᵉ. 10. day of november, 1725.
Phenihas Carter yᵉ Son of Thomas & Ruth Carter was born yᵉ. 5. day of Deber, 1727.
59 Amos Sawyer yᵉ son of Nathaniel & Mary Sawyer was born yᵉ 20 day of June, 1693.
Abigail Houghton yᵉ daughter of Robert & Esther Houghton was born yᵉ. 18 day of April, 1689.
Esther Sawyer yᵉ daughter of Amos & Abigail Sawyer was born yᵉ 20 day of April, 1720.
Abigail Sawyer yᵉ daughter of Amos & Abigail Sawyer was born yᵉ. 24 day of April, 1721.
Amos Sawyer yᵉ Son of Amos & Abigail Sawyer was born yᵉ: 1: day of December, 1724.
Deborah Sawyer yᵉ daughter of Amos & Abigail Sawyer was born yᵉ 25: day of April, 1727.
David Sawyer the Son of Amos & Abigail Sawyer was born yᵉ 29 day of march, 1729
Amos Sawyer the Son of Amos & Abigail Sawyer was born September yᵉ: 30ᵗʰ. 1733.
Lucy Carter yᵉ daughter of Samuel & Jemima Carter was born yᵉ. 18. day of August, 1727.
Henry Willard yᵉ son of Henry & Abigail Willard was born yᵉ. 11. day of May, 1727.
Abraham Houghton yᵉ son of Jacob & Mary Houghton was born yᵉ. 27 day of november, 1725.
Timothy Houghton yᵉ son of Jacob & Mary Houghton was born yᵉ. 21. day of August, 1727.
Daniel Whetcomb yᵉ son of Josiah & Ruhamah Whetcomb was born yᵉ. 28. of July, 1727.
John Butler yᵉ son of James & Hannah Butler was born yᵉ. 24 of January, 1727-8.
Experience Willard yᵉ daughter of James & Hannah Willard was born yᵉ. 2. of february, 1727-8.
Dinah Whetcomb yᵉ daughter of Hezekiah & Hannah Whetcomb was born yᵉ. 9 of January, 1727-8
Hannah Wright yᵉ daughter of John & Hannah Wright was born yᵉ. 8 of March, 1727-8
Damaris Sawyer yᵉ daughter of John & Ruth Sawyer was born yᵉ. 1. of April, 1725
Dinah Sawyer yᵉ daughter of John & Ruth Sawyer was born yᵉ. 16. of february, 1727-8

Aaron Witherbey yᵉ son of John & Elisabeth Witherbey was born yᵉ. 17. of february, 1727-8
Damaris Knight yᵉ daughter of Amos & Elisabeth Knight was born yᵉ. 2. day of April, 1728
Tabbitha Houghton yᵉ daughter of Thomas & Joannah Houghton was born yᵉ. 14 of march, 1727-8
Ephraim Houghton yᵉ son of Ephraim & Sarah Houghton was born yᵉ 1 day of november, 1727.
Tamer Huston yᵉ daughter of Nathaniel & Jane Huston was born yᵉ. 5. day of october, 1727.
Rufus Wilder yᵉ son of Josiah & Prudence Wilder was born yᵉ. 7. day of January, 1727-8
Mary Litlejohns yᵉ daughter of Thomas & Mary Litlejohns was born yᵉ 10 day of may, 1728
Elijah Houghton yᵉ son of Benjamin & Ruth Houghton was born yᵉ. 18 day of June, 1728
Keziah Willard yᵉ daughter of Jonathan & Keziah Willard was born yᵉ 15 of october, 1719.
Jonathan Willard yᵉ Son of Jonathan & Keziah Willard was born yᵉ. 26 day of february, 1720-21
Adonijah Willard yᵉ Son of Jonathan & Keziah Willard was born yᵉ. 1. day of June, 1724.
Pethula Willard yᵉ Daughter of Jonathan & Keziah Willard was born yᵉ. 18. day of June, 1726.
Barzilai Willard yᵉ son of Jonathan & Keziah Willard was born yᵉ. 5: day of June, 1728.
Rebekah Prentice yᵉ Daughter of John & Prudence Prentice was born yᵉ. 22 day of September, 1727
Joseph Houghton yᵉ son of Henry & Elisabeth Houghton was born yᵉ. 22. of April. 1728
Bekke Whetcomb yᵉ Daughter of Jonathan & Rachel Whetcomb was born yᵉ. 16. day of January, 1727-8
John Divol yᵉ son of John & Sarah Divol was Born yᵉ. 9. day of August, 1728.
Amos Rugg yᵉ son of Daniel & Elisabeth Rugg was born yᵉ. 13 day of December, 1716
Lemuel Willard yᵉ son of Joseph & Elisabeth Willard was born yᵉ 28 of July, 1725
Joseph Willard yᵉ son of Joseph & Elisabeth Willard was born yᵉ. 17 of May, 1728
Sarah Rugg yᵉ Daughter of Daniel & Elisabeth Rugg was born yᵉ. 9. of September, 1728.
Abigail Whetcomb yᵉ Daughter of Joseph & Damaris Whetcomb was born yᵉ 13 of April, 1728.
Tabitha Priest yᵘ daughter of Joseph & Mary Priest was born yᵉ. 5 of november 1728
Lucy More yᵘ daughter of Joseph & Rebekkah More was born yᵉ. 26 of march, 1727.
Jacob More yᵉ son of Joseph & Rebekah More was born yᵉ 12 of October, 1728.
Elisabeth Whetcomb yᵘ daughter of Josiah & Ruhamah Whetcomb was born yᵘ. 3 of December, 1728
60 Sarah Hapgood yᵉ daughter of Nathaniel & Mercy Hapgood was born yᵉ 21 of December, 1728
Silence yᵉ daughter of Jonathan & Mary Houghton was born yᵉ 4 of September, 1728
Sarah Whetney yᵉ daughter of John & Rebekah Whetney was born yᵉ. 5 of february. 1726-7
Dinah Beman yᵉ daughter of Gamaliel & Mary Beaman was born yᵉ. 20. of September, 1728
John Houghton yᵉ son of John & Mehitebel Houghton was born yᵉ. 7. of June, 1727
Dorithy Osgood yᵉ daughter of David & Eunice Osgood was born yᵉ. 2 day of June, 1728.

Ebenezer Houghton y⁰ son of Stephen & Abigail Houghton was born y⁰. 4. day of July, 1728.
Timothy Whetcomb y⁰ son of Joseph & Elisabeth Whetcomb was born y⁰. 1 day of July, 1724
Sarah & Hannah Whetcomb y⁰ daughters of Joseph & Elisabeth Whetcomb was born y⁰. 6 of march 1725-6.
Cyras Whetcomb y⁰ son of Joseph & Elisabeth Whetcomb was born y⁰. 21 of march, 1727-8
Sarah Holt y⁰ Daughter of Uriah & Sarah Holt born y⁰: 18: of March, 1727-8
Experience Atherton y⁰ Daughter of Peter and Experience Atherton: was born y⁰: 13 of february, 1728-9
Timothy Knocks y⁰ son of Timothy and Jane Knocks was born y⁰: 30th: of December: 1727.
Joseph Willson son of Joseph and Rebeckah Willson was born y⁰: 2d: of Jenuary: 1727.
Solomon Willson son of Joseph and Rebecka Willson was born: y⁰ first of november: 1728.
David Willard son of Abraham and Mary Willard born December y⁰: 20th: 1727.
Mary Fairbancks Daughter of Joseph and Mary Fairbancks born Jenuary: y⁰: 10th: 1729:
Pricila Wilder Daughter of Jonas and Eunis Wilder born: y⁰: 11th: of April: 1729:
John Pollard Son of William and Experience Pollard: born April: y⁰: 20th: 1729.
Mary Whitcomb Daughter of James & Hannah Whitcomb born: March y⁰: 4th: 1729:
Hannah Houghton Daughter of Thomas & Moriah Houghton born: y⁰: 16 of december: 1728-9
Dorothy Carter Daughter of Samll & Jemima Carter was born: y⁰: 21 of June: 1729
Ebenezer Houghton Son of Jonathan & Mary Houghton: was born August; y⁰: 1st. 1729
Joseph Church Son of Joshua & Annis Church: was born: July: y⁰: 22d: 1729.
Ruth Wright Daughter of Samll. & Ruth Wright was born y⁰: 5th of August: 1729:
Nathaniel Houghton son of James & Mary Houghton was born: y⁰: 5 of September: 1729.
Abijah Pratt Son of Josiah and Sarah Pratt was born: february y⁰: 28th: 1726-7.
William Pratt son of Josiah and Sarah Pratt was born July: y⁰: 31st, 1729.
William Glazier son of William and Martha Glazier was born november: y⁰: 7th: 1729.
John Prentice son of John and Anna Prentice was born September: y⁰: 23d: 1729.
Mary Albert Daughter of Daniel and Abigail Albert was born october y⁰: 7th: 1728.
Vastie Houghton Daughter of Joshua and Elezabeth Houghton was born: y⁰ 7 of may: 1727:
Solomon Houghton Son of Joshua and Elezabeth Houghton was born y⁰: fifth of June: 1729
Prudenc Wilder Daughter of Thomas and Susana [Hunt] Wilder was born Jenuary y⁰: 2d: 1729-30:
Elezabeth Atherton Daughter of Joseph and Hannah Atherton was born: y⁰: 7th of September: 1729.
Mary Willard Daughter of Aaron and Mary Willard was born: y⁰: 21st: of Jenuary: 1729-30.
Martha Houghton Daughter of Israel and Martha Houghton was born y⁰: 24th: of April: 1728.
Mary Houghton Daughter of Israel and Martha Houghton was born: y⁰: 8th of Jenuary: 1729-30:
Hannah Wheler Daughter of Benjamin and Hannah Wheler was born y⁰ 22d: of December: 1717.
Jesse Wheler Son of Benjamin and Hannah Wheler was born y⁰ 15th of may: 1720.
Bulah Wheler Daughter of Benjamin and Hannah Wheler was born: y⁰: 1t of march 1724.

Zenas Wheler Son of Benjamin and Hannah Wheler was born y⁶: 29ᵗʰ: of December: 1725;
Abigail Willard Daughter of Henry [and] Abigail Willard was born yᵉ: 6ᵗʰ of September: 1728.
Uriah Holt Son of Uriah and Sarah Holt was born: yᵉ: 7ᵗʰ: of february: 1729-30.
Joshua Osgood Son of Joshua and Ruth Osgood: was born: yᵉ: 13ᵗʰ: day of April, 1724-5.
Ephriam Osgood Son of Joshua and Ruth Osgood was born: yᵉ: 22ᵈ: day of Jenuary: 1726-7.
Ruth Osgood Daughter of Joshua and Ruth Osgood was born: yᵉ: 22ᵈ day of november: 1727.
Sarah Osgood Daughter of Joshua and Ruth Osgood was born: yᵉ: 7ᵗʰ: day of December: 1729.
Phinehas Whitney the Son of Jonathan & Alliss Whitney was born the 5 of Septemᵇ, 1727
Caleb Whitney yᵉ Son of Jonathan & Alliss Whitney was born yᵉ 4 of October, 1729.
Easter Houghton yᵉ Daughter of Thomas & Joanna Houghton was born yᵉ 26 of march, 1729
Mary Sawyer yᵉ Daughter of Samuel & Deborah Sawyer was born february yᵉ: 11, 1729-30.
Asaph Butler yᵉ son of James & Hannah Butler was born march yᵉ. 17ᵗʰ. 1729-30
James Richardson yᵉ Son of William & Mary Richardson was born may yᵉ. 5. 1730.
David Whetcomb the Son of Jonaᵗ. & Rachel Whetcomb was born march yᵉ 6. 1729-30
Aretas Houghton yᵉ Son of Henry & Elisabeth Houghton was born July yᵉ. 17. 1729

61 Thomas Littlejohns yᵉ Son of Thomas & Mary Littlejohns was born July yᵉ. 27. 1730
Susanna Wilds yᵉ Daughter of Richard & Ruth Wilds was born July yᵉ. 27. 1730
Nathaniel Wilder yᵉ Son of Nathaniel & Mary [Beaman] Wilder was born may yᵉ. 23. 1730
Elisabeth fairbank yᵉ daughter of Jabez & Hephzibah fairbank was born July yᵉ. 25. 1727.
Dinah fairbank yᵉ daughter of Jabez & Hephzibah fairbank was born July yᵉ. 29. 1730.
David Houghton yᵉ Son of John & Mehetibel Houghton was born march yᵉ. 14. 1729-30
Zeruiah Houghton yᵉ daughter of Benjamin & Zeruiah Houghton was born may yᵉ. 26. 1721
Mindwel Houghton yᵉ daughter of Benjamin & Zeruiah Houghton was born march yᵉ. 7. 1722-3
Mical Houghton yᵉ daughter of Benjamin & Zeruiah Houghton was born June yᵉ. 22. 1725
Dinah Houghton yᵉ daughter of Benjamin & Zeruiah Houghton was born April yᵉ 8. 1727.
Keziah Houghton yᵉ daughter of Benjamin & Zeruiah Houghton was born May yᵉ. 29. 1729
Mary Tooker yᵉ daughter of Thomas & Mary Tooker was born September yᵉ. 14. 1728
Mary Whetcomb the daughter of William & Hepzibah Whetcomb was born June the. 19. 1730
Joseph Polley yᵉ son of Ebenezer & Darcos Polley was born September. 3. 1728
Thomas Wright the son of Thomas & Abigail Wright was born may yᵉ. 18. 1730.
Susanna Willard the Daughter of James & Hannah Willard was Born July yᵉ. 13. 1730.
Catharine Witherbey the Daughter of John & Elisabeth Witherbey was born november yᵉ. 1. 1730
Abijah Moore the Son of Oliver & Abigail Moore was born September 14: 1730
Azubah Osgood the Daughter of David & Eunice Osgood was born October yᵉ. 19. 1730

Asa Wilder y⁰ son of Josiah & Prudence Wilder was born October y⁰ 16. 1730
Absalom Cutting y⁰ son of Jonas & Dinah Cutting was born December y⁰ 5. 1730.
William Wilson the son of Joseph & Rebecah Wilson was born y⁰. 29 day of Septem^b. 1730
Tilley Moore the son of Joseph & Rebeckah More was born y⁰. 29 day of Novem^b. 1730
Azubah Atherton the Daughter of Peter & Experience Atherton was born Decem^b. 23. 1730
Elizabeth Willard the Daughter of Hezikiah & Anna Willard was born Janu^a. 28: 1730-31
Prudence Sawyer the daughter of Ezra & Rebekah Sawyer was born Sept^m. 29: 1726
Elisabeth Sawyer y⁰ Daughter of Ezra & Rebekah Sawyer was born July. 2^d. 1728
Ezra Sawyer y⁰ Son of Ezra & Rebecah Sawyer was born August, 18: 1730
Mary Gates the Daughter of Hezekiah & Mary Gates was born January y⁰. 15. 1730-31
Ebenezer Knight y⁰ Son of Amos & Elisabeth Knight was born January 12, 1730-31
Lucy Walker y⁰ Daughter of Seth & Eliner Walker was born february y⁰. 7th, 1729-30
Phebey Atherton y⁰ Daughter of John & Phebey Atherton was born februr. 7: 1730-31
Parne Houghton y⁰ Daughter of Benjamin & Ruth Houghton was born April: 14: 1730
Daniel Albertt y⁰ Son of Daniel & Abigail Albert was born february y⁰. 10: 1730-1
Amee Willard y⁰ Daughter of Joseph & Elisabeth Willard was born Decem^b. y⁰. 25, 1730.
Phinehas Divol the Son of John & Sarah Divol was born february y⁰ 6. 1730-1.
Mary Carter y⁰ daughter of Samuel & Jemimah Carter was born february: 17, 1730-1
William Phelps y⁰ son of Robert & Dorithy Phelps was born July y⁰. 24: 1730
Mercy Wright y⁰ daughter of Samuel & Ruth Wright was born march y⁰: 17. 1730-1
Jonas Wilder y⁰ son of Jonas & Eunice Wilder was born may y⁰. 9. 1731.
Sarah Whetcomb y⁰ daughter of Josiah & Ruhamah Whetcomb was oorn march y⁰ 3^d, 1730-1
Elisabeth Houghton the daughter of Henry & Elisabeth Houghton was born April y⁰. 21. 1731
Caleb Willard y⁰ son of Jonathan & Kezeiah Willard was born february y⁰: 2. 1730-1
William Pollard y⁰ son of William & Experience Pollard was born June y⁰ 19, 1731
Annes Church y⁰ Daughter of Joshua & Annes Church was born July y⁰: 6. 1731.
John Harries y⁰ Son of Benjamin & Deborough Harries was born July y⁰: 25: 1731
John Whetcomb y⁰ Son of David & Bettey Whetcomb was born november y⁰: 13: 1731
Mary Bigelow y⁰ Daughter of Jonathan & Mary Bigelow was born July y⁰: 16. 1731.
Lois Whetcomb the Daughter of James & Hannah Whetcomb was born may the 13. 1731
Hannah Atherton y⁰ Daughter of Joseph & Hannah Atherton was born may y⁰. 16. 1731
Abigail Snow y⁰ Daughter of John & Hannah Snow was born October y⁰. 21. 1727.
Moses Snow the Son of John & Hannah Snow was born August y⁰ 26. 1729.
Mary Snow y⁰ Daughter of John & Hannah Snow was born August y⁰. 6. 1730.
Lydiah fairbank y⁰ Daughter of Joseph & Mary fairbank was born August y⁰: 16: 1731
Mary Houghton y⁰ Daughter of Jon^{at}. & Mary Houghton was born September. 5. 1731

John Houghton y⁰ Son of Jonas & Mary Houghton was born february y⁰. 13. 1731-2.
Ammite the Daughter of James & Mary Houghton was born november y⁰. 14. 1731
Abigail y⁰ Daughter of William & Hephzibah Whetcomb was born february, 12: 1731-2.
Tiras Houghton y⁰ Son of Joshua & Elisabeth Houghton was born April y⁰. 16: 1732
Dorithy the Daughter of Thomas & Joanna Houghton was born november. 9: 1732
Moses Wilder y⁰ Son of John & Abigail Wilder was born April y⁰. 29. 1732.
Martha Rugg y⁰ Daughter of Ruben & Lydiah Rugg was born february 26, 1731-2
Azubah Sawyer y⁰ Daughter of Samuel & Deborah Sawyer was born August: 28: 1732
Elijah Gibs y⁰ Son of Samuel Gibs & Lydiah his Wife was born April: 18: 1732.
Bulah fairbank y⁰ Daughter of Jabez & Hephzibah fairbank was born June. 11: 1732.
Sarah Littlejohns y⁰ Daughter of Thomas & Mary Littlejohns was born —:25—
Joseph Woods y⁰ Son of Joseph & Hannah Woods was born April y⁰: 1: 1731.
Joseph Houghton y⁰ Son of Ephriam & Sarah Houghton was born October y⁰: 12; 1731.
Tilley Richardson y⁰ Son of Josiah & Dorithy Richardson was born June the. 26. 1732
Oliver Whetcomb y⁰ Son of Jonathan & Rachel Whetcomb was born October y⁰. 3ᵈ, 1732.
Abisha Phelps y⁰ Son of Robert & Dorithy Phelps was born november: 27: 1731
Mary Knights y⁰ Daughter of Amos & Elisabeth Knights was born Decemᵇ: 31: 1732
Ephraim Moore y⁰ Son of Joseph & Rebecah Moor was born December y⁰: 24: 1732
Benjamin Houghton y⁰ Son of Benjamin & Zeruiah Houghton was born November y⁰. 17: 1732
Levi More y⁰ Son of Oliver & Abigail More was born May y⁰. 23. 1732.
Eunice Carter y⁰ daughter of Samuel & Jemimah Carter was born february: 6, 1732-3
Jacob Powers y⁰ son of Jonathan & Hannah Powers was born December, 8: 1731.
Lydiah Rugg y⁰ daughter of Ruben & Lydiah Rugg was born March y⁰. 22, 1732-3
Bathsheba Priest y⁰ Daughter of Joseph & Mary Priest was born may y⁰: 1: 1731.
Martha Wilder y⁰ Daughter of Josiah & Prudence Wilder was born february y⁰: —: 1732-3
Zadok Sanburn y⁰ Son of Zadok & Sarah Sanburn was born April y⁰: 30, 1733.
Elisabeth the Daughter of William & Mary Richardson was born April: 25: 1733.
Henry Albertt y⁰ Son of Daniel & Abigail Albertt was born may 1. 1733.
Simeon Littlejohns y⁰ Son of Thomas & Mary Littlejohns was born April y⁰: 15: 1733.
Joshua Sawyer y⁰ Son of Aholiab & Bettey Sawyer was born September y⁰: 9: 1732.
Elisabeth Gates y⁰ Daughter of Hezekiah & Mary Gates was born february y⁰. 21, 1732-3.
Nathaniel Willard y⁰ Son of Aaron & Mary Willard was born february; 28: 1731-2.
Russel Knight the Son of Daniel & Sarah Knight was born January: 24: 1731-2.
Paul & Silas Whetcomb y⁰ Sons of Josiah & Ruhamah Whetcomb was born December the. 20, 1732.
John Whetcomb y⁰ Son of Hezekiah & Rachel Whetcomb was born march 27, 1731.
Mary Polley y⁰ Daughter of Ebenezer & Darcos Polley was born november y⁰: 27: 1731.
Elijah Woods y⁰ Son of Joseph & Hannah Woods was born July y⁰: 16ᵗʰ: 1733.

BOOK FIRST. 61

Benjamin Harries y⁰ Son of Benjamin & Deborah Harries was born August y⁰; 14: 1733.
Benjamin More y⁰ Son of ffairbank & Judeth More was born July the; 30: 1733.
Levinah Houghton y⁰ Daughter of Jonathan & Mary Houghton was born August y⁰. 13: 1733
William Osgood y⁰ Son of Joshua & Ruth Osgood was born August y⁰. 20, 1732
63 Samuel More y⁰ Son of John & Susanna More was born March y⁰. 29, 1726.
Abigail More y⁰ Daughter of John & Susanna More was born August y⁰; 12. 1728.
John More y⁰ Son of John & Susanna More was born January y⁰; 3, 1730-31.
Susanna More y⁰ Daughter of John & Susanna More was born May y⁰; 28: 1733.
Dinah Cutting y⁰ daughter of Jonas & Dinah Cutting was born June y⁰; 7: 1733
Tamar Houghton y⁰ daughter of Gershom & Elisabeth Houghton was born December y⁰; 5: 1733
Eunice the daughter of David & Bettey Whetcomb was born December y⁰. 10ᵗʰ. 1733.
Olive Beaman y⁰ Daughter of Jabez & Dinah Beaman was born October; 19: 1733.
Elisabeth Bennitt y⁰ Daughter of Joseph & Elisabeth Bennitt was born May y⁰; 12; 1732.
Phenihas How y⁰ son of Phenihas & Abigail How was born March the; 7ᵗʰ; 1732-33.
Oliver Whitney the son of Jonathan & Aliess Whitney was born July the; 22ᵈ; 1731.
James Houghton y⁰ son of James & Mary Houghton was born December y⁰; 3ᵈ: 1733.
Jonas Pollard y⁰ son of William & Experience Pollard was born December: 3: 1733
Mary Bennitt y⁰ daughter of Joseph & Elisabeth Bennitt was born march y⁰: 13: 1733-4
Ephraim Wilder the son of Ephraim & Anna Wilder was born July y⁰: 8ᵗʰ. 1733.
Mary Ross y⁰ Daughter of Thomas & Mary Ross was born September 28: 1733
David Osgood y⁰ Son of David & Eunice Osgood was born Aprill y⁰: 21, 1734.
Israel More y⁰ Son of Oliver & Abigail More was born April y⁰; 12: 1734.
Amos Powers y⁰ Son of Jonathan & Hannah Powers was born february y⁰; 25: 1733-4
Oliver Houghton y⁰ Son of Thomas & Joanna Houghton was born March y⁰; 17: 1733-4.
Prudence Wilder y⁰ Daughter of John & Abigail Wilder was born January: 12: 1733-4
Joseph Whetcom y⁰ Son of Joseph & Damaris Whetcomb was born March y⁰; 15: 1731-2.
Artimus How y⁰ Son of David & Mary How was born March y⁰; 24: 1733-4.
Sarah Dakin daughter of Ebenezer & Abigail Dakin was born April y⁰; 7ᵗʰ: 1733.
Israel Greenleaf the Son of Daniel & Silence Greenleaf was Born March y⁰; 29: 1734
Thankful Whetcomb y⁰ daughter of William & Hephzibah Whetcomb was born April y⁰; 19. 1734.
Joseph Houghton y⁰ Son of Israel & Martha Houghton was born May y⁰: 21: 1733.
Joshua Holt y⁰ Son of Uriah & Sarah Holt was born May the 18. 1733.
Silvanas Sawyer y⁰ Son of Aholiab & Bettey Sawyer was born the 8ᵗʰ; of June; 1734.
Ephraim Butler y⁰ Son of Nathaniel & Experience Butler was born September the; 3: 1734.
Joshua Wilder the Son of Joshua & Sarah [Keyes] Wilder was born August the; 19; 1734.
Lucy Joslin the Daughter of John & Lucy Joslin was born may the; 6: 1734.
Joanna & Damaris Sawyer the Daughters of John & Sarah Sawyer was born September y⁰; 20ᵗʰ; 1734.
Luke Richardson y⁰ Son of James & Sarah Richardson was born August the; 15ᵗʰ; 1734.

Elisabeth Richardson ye daughter of Josiah & Dorithy Richardson was born April; 24; 1734.
Lois Wilder the Daughter of Oliver & Mary Wilder was born Aprill the; 26; 1733.
Mary Whetcomb ye daughter of Simon & Thankfull Whetcomb was born September y^e; 29; 1734.
Mary Rugg ye daughter of Ruben & Lydiah Rugg was born October y^e: 10; 1734.
William Dunsmore ye Son of John & Eunice Dunsmore was born february y^e: 8; 1733-4.
Joshua Phelps ye Son of Joshua & Rebeckah Phelps was born March y^e: 23; 1732-3.
Rebeckah Phelps ye Daughter of Joshua & Rebeckah Phelps was born May y^e: 12; 1734
William M^c. bride ye Son of Alexander & Mary M^cbride was born June the: 6: 1734
Sarah M^cfaddan ye Daughter of Frances & Margret M^cfaddan was born January: 13; 1734-5
Prudence Houghton ye Daughter of Israel & Martha Houghton was born february y^e; 7th: 1734-5.
Dinah Carter ye Daughter of Samuel & Jemimah Carter was born february y^e: 1; 1734-5.
Nathaniel Rugg the Son of Jonatⁿ. & Dorithy Rugg was born february y^e: 13; 1734-5
64 Martha fairbank ye daughter of Jonas & Thankful fairbank was born January: 13th; 1731-2
Josiah fairbank ye son of Jonas and Thankful fairbank was born may y^e; 22: 1734
Amasa Gibs ye son of Samuel & Lydiah Gibs was born march ye 18: 1734-5
Rebeckah More the daughter of Josep & Rebeckah More was born febru^r: 16: 1734-5
Anna Prentice ye daughter of John & Anna Prentice was born June y^e: 17: 1734.
Ruth Sawyer ye Daughter of Sam^{ll}. & Debrough Sawyer was born march y^e; 10: 1734-5
Lois Osgood the Daughter of Aaron & Eunice Osgood was born may the: 3^d: 1730.
Aaron Osgood ye Son of Aaron & Eunice Osgood was born march y^e. 31; 1732.
Thomas Osgood ye Son of Aaron & Eunice Osgood was born April y^e; 3: 1734
Amos Atherton the Son of Amos & Elisabeth Atherton was born Octob^r. y^e: 5: 1731
David Atherton the Son of Amos & Elisabeth Atherton was born february y^e: 10th: 1732-3
Josiah Tooker ye Son of Thomas & Mary Tooker was born february y^e: 2: 1734-5
Elisabeth Dakin ye daughter of Ebenezer & Abigail Dakin was born June y^e; 18: 1734.
Mindwell Bigelow ye daughter of Jonathan & Mary Bigelow was born April y^e: 30; 1735.
Hiram Houghton ye Son of Joshua & Elisabeth Houghton was born June y^e: 6: 1735.
Tilley Littlejohns ye Son of Thomas & Mary Littlejohns was born May y^e: 26: 1735.
Hephzibah fairbank ye Daughter of Jabez & Hephzibah fairbank was born June y^e: 13: 1735
Pearcis Harries the daughter of Benjamin & Deborah Harries was born August y^e: 3: 1735
Hannah Holt ye Daughter of Uriah & Sarah Holt was born October y^e: 6: 1735
Mary Ballard ye Daughter of Benjamin & Ruth Ballard was born July y^e: 8: 1735
Benjamin Whetcomb ye Son of Joseph & Damaris Whetcomb was born September y^e: 1: 1735
Stephen Greenleaf ye Son of Daniel & Silence Greenleaf was born October y^e: 15: 1735
Ruhamah ye Daughter of Josiah & Ruhamah Whetcomb was born may the 4: 1735.
Levi Woods ye Son of Joseph & Hannah Woods was born march y^e: 31, 1735.

Lucresea y⁰ daughter of William & Mary Richardson was born October: 28: 1735.
Josiah Wilder y⁰ Son of Josiah & Prudence Wilder was born y⁰: 17: —— 1735.
Oliver Sawyer y⁰ Son of Nathaniel & Mary Sawyer was born July y⁰: 24: 1735.
Tamar Whetcomb y⁰ Daughter of Benjamin & Dorithy Whetcomb was born March y⁰: 28: 1735
Prudence Whetcomb y⁰ Daughter of David & Betey Whetcomb was born October y⁰: 29: 1735
Hannah Knight the Daughter of Amos & Hannah Knight was born October y⁰. 6: 1735
Thomas Houghton y⁰ Son of Thomas & Moriah Houghton was born October the: 9th: 1731.
Bezaleel How the son of Phinehas & Abigail How was born february y⁰: 14: 1734-5
Cate Houghton the Daughter of James & Mary Houghton was born november y⁰: 29: 1735
Catharine y⁰ Daughter of Ephraim & Anna Wilder was born October y⁰: 18: 1735.
Joel Phelps y⁰ Son of Robert & Dorithy Phelps was born march y⁰: 5: 1733-4
Mary Heald y⁰ Daughter of Israel & Abigail Heald was born January y⁰: 11: 1735-6
Lydiah Glazier y⁰ Daughter of John & Easter Glazier was born Sept. y⁰ Second: 1735.
Uriah Moor y⁰ Son of Oliver & Abigail Moor was born January y⁰: 9: 1735-6:
Josiah Wilder y⁰ Son of James & Martha Wilder was born October y⁰: 19: 1735.
John Joslin the Son of John & Lucey Joslin was born Sepᵗᵐ. 17, 1735.
Abigail Houghton the daughter of Benjⁿ. & Zerviah Houghton was born July y⁰: 27: 1735.
Abigail Albertt y⁰ daughter of Daniel & Abigail Albertt was born february y⁰: 21: 1735.
Martha Snow the Daughter of John & Hannah Snow was born february y⁰: 9: 1731-2
Keziah Snow y⁰ Daughter of John & Hannah Snow was born September y⁰: 7: 1733.
John Snow y⁰ Son of John & Hannah Snow was born June the, 29: 1735.
Elisabeth Powers the daughter of Jonathan & Hannah Powers was born April y⁰: 23: 1736
Assael Osgood y⁰ Son of Joshua & Ruth Osgood was born March y⁰ 23: 1735-6
William fairbank y⁰ Son of Jonathan & Thankfull fairbank was born March: 2: 1735-6
Releife y⁰ Daughter of William & Hephzibah Whetcomb was born february 29: 1735-6
Mary Osgood y⁰ Daughter of David & Eunice Osgood was born may y⁰: 16: 1736
Jonathan Osgood y⁰ Son of Jonathan & Asseneth Osgood was born may y⁰: 18: 1736
Deliverence Ross y⁰ Son [daughter] of Thomas & Mary Ross was born June: 13: 1735.
John Richardson y⁰ Son of James & Sarah Richardson was born June y⁰: 1: 1736.
Prudence Butler y⁰ daughter of Nathˡˡ. & Experience Butler was born July y⁰: 30: 1736.
Sarah Bennitt y⁰ Daughter of Joseph & Elisabeth Bennitt was born May y⁰ 24: 1736.
Aaron Sawyer y⁰ Son of Joseph & Tabathy Sawyer was born May y⁰: 13: 1732
Moses Sawyer y⁰ Son of Joseph & Tabathy Sawyer was born January: 13: 1733-4
Sarah Sawyer the Daughter of Joseph & Tabatha Sawyer was born March y⁰: 4: 1735-6.
Lois Pollard y⁰ Daughter of William & Experience Pollard was born April y⁰: 4: 1736.
Moses Wilder y⁰ Son of Oliver & Mary Wilder was born May y⁰: 4: 1736.
Sarah Divol y⁰ Daughter of John & Sarah Divol was born March the: 22: 1733-4:
Benjamin Sawyer y⁰ Son of John & Sarah, was born August the: 21: 1736
Elisabeth Carter the daughter of Nathaniel & Thankfull Carter was born february y⁰: 9; 1733-4

Nathaniel Carter y° Son of Nathaniel & Thankfull Carter was born: Decem^br y°: 17: 1735
Rhoda Wilson Daughter of Nathaniel & Eunice Wilson was born Decem^b. 28: 1735.
Ezra Beaman y° Son of Jabez & Dinah Beaman was born October: 4: 1736.
Josiah Pratt y° Son of Josiah & Sarah Pratt was born Decem^b. 31: 1735.
Eunice Osgood Daughter of Aaron & Eunice Osgood was born June: 5: 1736.
Abner Moore y° Son of John & Susannah Moore was [born] September; 28: 1736.
Keziah Whetcomb daughter of Simon & Thankfull Whetcomb was born Septem^b. 12: 1736.
Paul Moore the Son of fairbank & Judeth Moore was born Novem^b. 4: 1736.
Eunice Snow the daughter of Hezekiah & Martha Snow was born Sept^m. 12: 1736.
James Kendal Son of James & Sarah Kendal was born Septem^b. 13: 1736.
Rebeckah Houghton the daughter of John & Hephzibah Houghton was born Janu^ry 25: 1736-7
Hezekiah Whetcomb Son of Hezekiah & Rachill Whetcomb was born May y° 31: 1735
Samuel Carter y° Son of Samuel & Jemimah Carter was born January: 7: 1736-7.
John Wilder the Son of Thomas & Susanna [Hunt] Wilder was born Sept^m. 12. 1705
Dinah Wilder Daughter of John & Abigail Wilder was born Novem^b. 15, 1735
Vashti y° daughter of Joshua & Anes Church was born October; 2: 1736.
Thomas Gates y° son of Hezekiah & Anna Gates was born April y°: 29: 1736.
Silas How y° Sone of Phinehas & Abigail How was born January 26th: 1736-7
Tilly White y° Son of John & Lois White was born September y°: 3^d: 1736.
Agnus y° daughter of Alexander & Mary Macbride was born Novem^b: 1: 1736
Eunice y° Daughter of Israel and Martha Houghton was born Janu^ry: 31: 1736-7
David the Son of Jonathan and Mary Crouch was Born 11 of march 1724
John the Son of Jonathan and Mary Crouch was born in May 1728
Abigil Munroe y° Daughter of Thomas and Elisabeth Munroe was born y° 9th day of april 1737
Sarah y° Daughter of John and Mary Farrar was born Januery y° 9, 1736-7
Paul Gibes the Son of Samuel and Lidiah Gibes was born y° 19 of Januery 1736-7
Nathaniel Johnson Son of John and Mary Johnson was born August y° 20th 1730
John Johnson the Son of John and Mary Johnson was born August y° 12th 1733.
Dorathy y° Daughter of John and Mary Johnson was Born March 22^d, 1735-6
66 Elisabeth the Daughter of Joshua and Rebeckah Phelps was Born april 11th 1736
Abel Wilder y° Son of Joshua and Sarah [Keyes] Wilder was born august y° 31st 1736
Hannah y° Daughter of Joseph and Rebeckah Moors was Born may y° 10th 1737
Eunice y° Daughter of Nathaniel and Eunice Wilson was Born June 23^d 1737
David Greenleaf y° Son of Daniel & Elisabeth Greenleaf was Born July y° 13th 1737
Samuel Snow y° Son of John & Hannah Snow was Born February 11. 1736-7
Thomas Ross the Son of Thomas & Mary Ross was born Dec^b. y° 9th 1736
James Ballard y° Son of Benjamin and Ruth Ballard was born may y° 5th 1737
Abigil the Daughter of Ebenezer and Abigil Dakin was Born July y° 21st 1736
Ruth y° Daughter of Rubin and Lidiah Rugg was born July y° 5th 1737.
Oliver the Son of Edward and Mary Phelps was born Sept y° 7th 1737
Meriam the Daughter of Jonathan & Mary Biggalo was Born octo y° 10th 1737
Mary y° Daughter of Gardner & Mary [Phelps] Wilder was Born Sept 10th 1737
Tamer y° Daughter of James & Mary Houghton was Born Septemb 27th, 1737
Lucy the Daughter of Samuel and Deborah Sawyer was born July y° 8 1737
Elishua the Son of Joseph and Hannah Woods was born August y° 18 1737
Abigail the Daughter of fraindces and Abigail Parker was born december 23 1737
Jacob y° Son of John and Easter Glazier was born October y° 17th 1737.
Joel y° Son of Benjamin and Zuruiah Houghton was born September y° 27th 1737
Elias y° Son of Nathaniel and Thankfull Carter was born november 24th 1737
Damaris y° Daughter of Thomas and Joanna Houghton was born may 28th 1737
Mary y° Daughter of Thomas and Mary [Wheeler] Wilder was Born September y° 2^d 1733

Sarah y⁰ Daughter of Thomas and Mary Wilder was Born March y⁰ 10th 1735
Thomas the Son of Thomas and Mary Wilder was Born September y⁰ 15th 1737
Damaris y⁰ Daughter of Jonathan and Damaris Carter was Born January y⁰ 7th 1737-8
Mary y⁰ Daughter of Nathanil and Mary Sawyer was Born January y⁰ 24th 1737-8
Anna the Daughter of Jonathan and Rachel Whetcomb was born october y⁰ 30th 1737
Tilley the Son of David and Betty Whetcomb was Born november y⁰ 22d 1737
Jonathan y⁰ Son of Jonathan and Mary Houghton was Born november y⁰ 7th 1737
Caleb Wilder the Son of Caleb and Abigail [Carter] Wilder was born march y⁰ 2 1737-8
Abigail Moor y⁰ Daughter of Oliver and Abigail Moor was born January 27th 1737-8
Mary y⁰ Daughter of Ephraim and Mary Carter was Born y⁰ 4th. [January] 1737-8.
Isaah Butler was Born y⁰ 25 of January to Nathaniel & Experience Butler — 1737-8
Sarah y⁰ Daughʳ. of Josiah and Prudence Wilder was Born January 2d 1737-8
Samuel Osgood y⁰ Son of Jonathan Osgood and Asenath Osgood was born y⁰ 1ˢᵗ of december 1737
Elisabeth the Daughter of David and Eunice Osgood was Born January y⁰ 28th 1737-8
Abigail y⁰ Daughter of John and Mary Whetcomb was born y⁰ the 13 of February 1737-8
Abil Osgood y⁰ Son of Joshua & Ruth Osgood was born 25 day of april 1738
Jabez Fairbank y⁰ Son of Jonathan & Thankfull Fairbank was Born march 2d 1738
Joseph Sawyer y⁰ Son of Joseph and Tabitha Sawyer was born april y⁰ 23d 1738
Mary y⁰ Daughter of Samuel and Mary Wilson was born march y⁰ 12th 1736-7
Ezra Hald [Heald] y⁰ Son of Israel Hald was Born august y⁰ 30 1737
Joseph Wilder y⁰ Son of Joseph and Deborah Wilder was born april y⁰ 15th 1734
Deborah Wilder y⁰ Daughter of Joseph and Deborah Wilder was Born 17th november 1736
Sarah Wilder y⁰ Daughter of John and Abigail Wilder was Born march y⁰ 2d 1737-8
67 Ephraim the Son of Peter and Hephzibah Kindel was born June y⁰ 20 1734
Peter the Son of Peter and Hephzibah Kindel was born April y⁰ 20 1735
Levi the Son of Peter and Hephzibah Kindel was born January y⁰ 6 1736-7
Annah Wheeler y⁰ Daughter of Joshua and Annah Wheeler was Born June 27th 1721
Joshua Wheeler y⁰ Son of Joshua and Annah Wheeler was Born December y⁰ 13th. 1723
Elisabeth Wheeler y⁰ Daughter of Joshua and Annah Wheeler was Born november 1ˢᵗ, 1725
Thankfull Wheeler y⁰ Daughter of Joshua and Annah Wheeler was Born July y⁰ 16, 1728
Hannah Whetcomb y⁰ Daughter of William and Hephzibah Whetcomb was Born July y⁰ 19th 1738
Benjamin Whetcomb y⁰ Son of Benjᵐ. and Dorathe Whetcomb was born y⁰ 2d day of July 1737
Annah y⁰ Daughter of Simon and Annah Butler was born September y⁰ 3d 1738
Josiah y⁰ Son of Josiah and Tabithy Kindel was born may y⁰ 23 1738
Joshua y⁰ Son of Joshua and Rebecah Phelps was born y⁰ 14 of June 1738.
John y⁰ Son of John and Lois White was born november y⁰ 30th 1738
Lidiah y⁰ Daughter of Ezekiel and Lidiah Wollinsford was born January y⁰ 15th 1738-9
Nathaniel y⁰ Son of Aaron and Eunice Osgood was Born June y⁰ 19th 1738
Easter y⁰ Daughter of James and Sarah Richardson was Born January 22d 1738
Manasah Wilder y⁰ Son of Ephraim and Anna Wilder was Born march y⁰ 5 1737-8

Lidiah Butler yᵉ Daughter of James and Deborah Butler was born January yᵉ 15 1738

Phradrick [Frederick] Albert yᵉ Son of Daniel and Abigail Albert was born February yᵉ 7ᵗʰ, 1738-9

Bridget yᵉ Daughter of Jonathan and Bridget Baley was born 29 day of January 1736-7

Jonathan Baley yᵉ Son of Jonathan and Bridget Baley was born yᵉ 21 of march 1737-8

Samuel Ross yᵉ Son of Thomas and Mary Ross was born January yᵉ 16ᵗʰ 1738

James Ross yᵉ Son of James and Abigail Ross was Born march yᵉ 12ᵗʰ 1738-9

Samuel Ballard yᵉ Son of Benjamin and Ruth Ballard was Born april yᵉ 7ᵗʰ 1739

Jonathan Biggalow yᵉ Son of Jonathan and Mary Begelow was born may yᵉ 3ᵈ 1739

Ruth yᵉ Daughter of Robert and Dorothy Phelps was born January yᵉ 26ᵗʰ 1738-9

Samuel yᵉ the Son of Joseph and Hannah Woods was born May yᵉ 20 1739

Dorathy yᵉ Daughter of Hezakiah and Anna Gates was born Septemb. yᵉ 6: 1738

Prudence Rugg yᵉ Daughter of Rubin and Lidiah Rugg was born april yᵉ 29ᵗʰ 1739.

Releaf Atherton yᵉ Daughter of Benjamin & Eunice Ather[ton] was Born may yᵉ 29. 1736.

Dorathy yᵉ Daughter of Benjamin and Dorothy Whetcomb was born may yᵉ 13ᵗʰ 1739.

Bulah and Abigail Carter yᵉ Daughters of Oliver and Bula Carter was born Sept yᵉ 18ᵗʰ 1739

Ame yᵉ Daughter of William and Mary Richardson was born June yᵉ 13 1738.

Silvanas Harris yᵉ Son of Benjamin & Deborah Harris was born June yᵉ 4ᵗʰ 1739

John Willard yᵉ Son of Aaron and Mary Willard was Born Sept yᵉ 22ᵈ 1729

Peter Willard yᵉ Son of Aaron and Mary Willard was Born February yᵉ 26, 1736

Mary yᵉ Daughter of Samuel and Lideah Gibbs was born yᵉ 8ᵗʰ of october 1739

Anna yᵉ Daughter of Thomas and Mary Wilder was born June yᵉ 10ᵗʰ 1739

Abigail yᵉ Daughter of Jonathan & Assena Osgood was Born Sept.ᵇʳ. yᵉ 6ᵗʰ 1739

Benjamin. Whetcomb yᵉ Son of Joseph and Damaris Whetcomb was born Sept yᵉ 29 1737

Simon Ross yᵉ Son of Timothy & Elisabeth Ross was born yᵉ 7 day of Sept 1739

Lemuel Holt yᵉ Son of Uriah and Sary Holt was born Febrʸ yᵉ 10ᵗʰ 1737-8

Susannah Carter yᵉ Daughter of Nathaniel & Thankfull Carter was born yᵉ 20ᵗʰ Day of april 1739

Catherine yᵉ Daughter of Joseph & Rebeckah Moor was born June yᵉ 4ᶦᵈ 1739

68 Samuel yᵉ Son of Caleb and Abigail Wilder was born May yᵉ 7 1739

John Buss yᵉ Son of John and Eunice Buss was born January yᵉ 3ᵈ 1739

Eunice Buss yᵉ Daughter of John and Eunice Buss was born January yᵉ 19ᵗʰ 1738

John Carter yᵉ Son of John and Abigail Carter was born January yᵉ 9ᵗʰ 1737

Elisabeth yᵉ Daughter of Gardner and Mary Wilder was born yᵉ 30 day of november 1739

Samuel Sawyer yᵉ Son of Samuel and Debrah Sawyer was born January yᵉ 2ᵈ 1739

David yᵉ Son of John & Elisabeth Farrar was born January yᵉ 10ᵗʰ 1739

Benjamin yᵉ Son of Israel and Martha Houghton was born Sept yᵉ 5ᵗʰ 1739

Eunice yᵉ Daughter of Israel and Martha Houghton was born yᵉ 31 day of Janu 1736-7

Tabitha yᵉ Daughter of John and Mary Farrar was born november yᵉ 6ᵗʰ 1739

Eunice Houghton yᵉ Daughter of Benjamin & Zerviah Houghton was born October yᵉ 15ᵗʰ 1739.

Thomas Fairbank the Son of Thomas and Dorothy Fairbank was born the 29ᵗʰ of august 1736.

Dorathy yᵉ Daughter of Thomas and Dorothy Fairbank was born October 17ᵗʰ 1738

John Glazier yᵉ Son of John and Easter Glazier was born march yᵉ 8ᵗʰ 1739

Abigail yᵉ Daughter of John and Abigail Carter was born Febr yᵉ 14ᵗʰ 1739

Jonathan White yᵉ Son of Jonathan and Easter White was born 26 day of april 1734.

BOOK FIRST.

Easter y* Daughter of Jonathan and Easter White was born y* 11 of June 1736
Easter y* Daughter of Jonathan and Easter White was born 15 of october 1738
Jonathan y* Son of Jonathan and Easter White was born y* 14 of march 1739
Elisabeth Burpe y* Daughter of Samuel and Elisabeth Burpe was born Feb y* 20th 1736-7
Stephen Burpe y* Son of Samuel and Elisabeth Burpe was born December y* 1st. 1739.
Jonathan y* Son of Jonathan and Thankfull Sawyer was born January 25th 1739.
Abigail y* Daughter of Phinihas and Abigail How was born Feb y* 12th 1738
Bety the Daughter of Phinihas and Abigail How was born March y* 26th 1740
Rebeckah Houghton y* Daughter of Thomas and Joanah Houghton was born September y* 18th 1739
Levinah y* Daughter of James and Mary Houghton was born Janu^y y* 2d 1739
James y* Son of James and Rebeckah Willard was born november y* 28th 1736
Rebeckah Willard y* Daughter of James and Rebeckah Willard was born 25 of may 1739
Mary y* Daughter of Marthew and Elisabeth Clerk was born June y* 29th 1740.
Mary Holt y* Daughter of Uriah and Sarah Holt was born april y* 5 1740
Luce the Daughter of Amos & Hanna Knight was born June 3d 1740.
Sary y* Daughter of Joshua and Ruth Osgood was born y* 7 day of december 1740
Roger Son of Thomas and Mary Ross was born y* September y* 20 1740
Keziah Daughter of Abner and Mary Sawyer was born December y* 2 1739
Heman Son of Josiah and tabatha Kendall was born May y* 20: 1740
David Son of David and Anna Wilder was born March y* 13 about Sunrise 1740
Rebeckah Richardson y* Daughter of William & Mary Richardson was born october y* 12 1741
Silas y* Son of Aaron and Eunice Osgood was born December y* 4th 1740
Joseph Fairbank y* Son of Thomas & Dorathie Fairbank was born oct, 27, 1741
Ebenezer Woodbery y* Son of Daniel and Abigail Woodbery was born Feb 13th 1740
Thomas y* Son of Thomas and Sarah White was born September y* 4th 1740
69 Cornellies Son of John & Sarah Sawyer was Born December y* 8: 1739 & Died the: 6: of April folloing Mary & Martha was Born March y* 8th: 1739-40
Stanton y* Son of Samuel and Jamimah Carter was born Febuar y* 15, 1738
Silas y* Son of Samuel and Jamimah Carter was born January y* 16, 1740.
Matha y* Daughter of Zechariah and Martha Glazier was born January y* 31st 1740
Jese Dakin y* Son of Ebenezer and Abigail Dakin was Born second Day of november 1739
Ephraim Carter y* Son of Ephraim and Abigail Carter was born march y* 27 1740.
Abigail y* Daughter of Ephraim and Abigail Carter was Born april y* 9th 1741
Jonathan Priest Whetcomb y* Son of Joseph and Damaras Priest was born Janu y* 14 1740
Samuel Wilder y* Son of John and Prudance Wilder was born august y* 17th 1740 at Nechawogg
Bety Nelson y* Daughter of David and Margeret Nelson was born January y* 9th 1740.
Luce y* Daughter of Joseph and Rebekah Moor was Born March y* 23d. 1740
Aaron Bigelow y* Son of Jonathan and Mary Bigelow was born 29 day of april 1741
Rufus Powers the Son of Daniel and Mary Powers was born august y* 9 1740.
Jonathan Priest y* Son of Hezakiah and Rachel Whetcomb was born y* 12th day of may 1741.
Ezra Wilder y* Son of Oliver and Sarah Wilder was born May y* 27th 1741.
Jerusha the Daughter of Simon and Martha Tomson was Born may y* 4th 1741
Joseph Ballard Son of Benjamin & Ruth Ballard was Born July y* 25th 1741.
Hephziba y* Daughter of William and Hephziba Whetcomb was born Febr 14th 1740.
Peninah y* Daughter of Daniel & Abigail Albert was born may y* 8th 1741.

Thankfull the Daughter of Jeremiah and Thankfull Haskell was born Sept 2ᵈ 1741.
Andrew yᵉ Son of Andrew and Elisabeth Wilder was born Sept yᵉ 21ˢᵗ 1741.
Jotham yᵉ Son of Joseph and Hannah Woods was born March yᵉ 18 1740
Elisabeth the Daughter of Ruben and Lediah Rugg was born novemb yᵉ 4ᵗʰ 1741
Thomas the Son of Stanton & Mercy Prentice was born ——
Abigail yᵉ Daughter of John and Hannah Snow [was born] august yᵉ 5ᵗʰ 1741.
Sarah the Daughter [of] Samuel and Hannah Baley was born november yᵉ 30 1738
Susannah yᵉ Daughter of Samuel and Hannah Baley was born 2ᵈ Febu 1740
Caleb Wilder yᵉ Son of Caleb and Abigail Wilder was Born July 31ˢᵗ 1741
Zephaniah Buss yᵉ Son of John and Unis Buss was born December yᵉ 14ᵗʰ 1741.
Rebeckah Gates yᵉ Daughter of Hezakiah and Anna Gates was born July yᵉ 31ˢᵗ 1740
Abijah White yᵉ Son of John and Lois White was born Febr 27ᵗʰ 1740
Sarah Bennet yᵉ Daughter of Joseph and Elisabeth Bennet was born may yᵉ 23ᵈ 1736
Prudance yᵉ Dauter of Joseph and Elisabeth Bennet was born January yᵉ 17ᵗʰ 1739
Eunice Bennet yᵉ Daughter of Joseph and Elisabeth Bennet was born august yᵉ 6ᵗʰ 1741
Nathan Farrow Son of John and Mary Farrow was born January yᵉ 24 1741
David Butler yᵉ Son of James and Deborah Butler was Born march yᵉ 18ᵗʰ 1741-2.
William yᵉ Son of Charles and Martha [Sawyer] Wilder was born may yᵉ 22ᵗʰ 1739.
John yᵉ Son of James and Sarah Richardson was born yᵉ 18 day of July 1741
Hannah yᵉ Daughter of John and Hannah Snow was born yᵉ 11 day of april 1742
Helen yᵉ Daughter of James and Thankful Cleland was born December yᵉ 25ᵗʰ 1739
Thomas Cleland yᵉ Son of James and Thankfull Cleland was born november 11ᵗʰ 1741
Israel Houghton yᵉ Son of Israel & Martha Houghton was Born February 26ᵗʰ 1741-2
Elijah Whetcomb yᵉ Son of Joseph & Damaris Whetcomb was born October yᵉ 18ᵗʰ 1742.
David Nelson yᵉ Son of David and Rachil Nelson was born may yᵉ 18ᵗʰ 1742
Daniel Son of John & Hanah Warner born April 2ᵈ, 1742
70 Sarah yᵉ Daughter of Thomas and Sarah White was born June yᵉ 3ᵈ 1742
Elijah yᵉ Son of Phinihas and Mary Willard was born august yᵉ 19 1740
Martha Dafter of John and Prudence Wilder was born June yᵉ 26ᵗʰ, 1742
Robert Phelps yᵉ Son of Robert and Dorathy Phelps was Born may yᵉ 24 1741
Ephraim Nelson yᵉ Son of Jonathan and Hanna Nelson was born april 22ᵈ 1742
Joannah the Daughter of Phinihas and Joanna Beman was born 4ᵗʰ april 1741
Phinihas Beman yᵉ Son of Phinihas and Joannah Beman was born 20 of april 1742
Eunice the Daughter of Aaron and Eunice Osgood was born 21 of november 1742.
Dorathy the Daughter of Aaron and Mary Willard was born march yᵉ 1ᵗʰ, 1742
Susannah the Daughter of John and Lidia Rugg was born September yᵉ 21, 1742
John Bowers yᵉ Son of John and Margerit Bowers was born Sepᵗ yᵉ 27ᵗʰ 1742
John Carter yᵉ Son of John and Abigail Carter was born July yᵉ 19ᵗʰ 1742.
John yᵉ Son of Henry and Huldah Haskel was born yᵉ 6 day of January 1740
Ruth yᵉ Daughter of Henry and Huldah Haskel was born march yᵉ 18ᵗʰ 1742.
Annah Daughter of Zacheus Boynton and Anna his Wife was born April yᵉ 18ᵗʰ 1740
Jane the Daughter of Zacheus and Anna Boynton was born march yᵉ 22 1742
Ester yᵉ Daughter of John and Easter Glazier was Born april yᵉ 24 1743
Joseph yᵉ Son of Amos and Hannah Knight was born november yᵉ 8 1742
Catherine yᵉ Daughter of Ephraim and Annah Wilder was born Feb yᵉ 18 1742
Ephraim Carter yᵉ Son of Ephraim and Abigail Carter was born June yᵉ 5 1743

BOOK FIRST. 69

Elisabeth ye Daughter of Joseph and Elisabeth Osgood was born may ye 19th 1742
Lois the Daughter of John and Lois White was Born February ye 28 1742 [Canceled.]
Susannah Richadson ye Daughter of William and Mary Richardson born ye 21 day of may 1743
Joseph Moor Son of Joseph and Rebeckah Moor was Born march ye 28 1743
Nahum Wilder ye Son of Caleb and Abigail Wilder was Born August ye 18, 1743
Timothy Ross ye Son of Timothy and Elisabeth Ross was born december ye 24 1741
Hannah Abbott Daughter of Joseph and Hannah Abbot was born September ye 23^d 1743
Prudance ye Daughter of Samuel and Jemimah Carter was born april ye 15 1743
Ebenezer Tomson ye Son of Simon and Martha Tomson was born march ye 15 1743
Charls Wilder ye Son of Charls & Martha Wilder was born august ye 1st 1742
Oliver Wilder ye Son of Oliver and Sarah Wilder was born ye 17 day of november 1743
Sarah ye Daughter of Oliver and Sarah Wilder was born ye 17 day of november 1743
Loes Daughter of John & Loes White was born the 19th of march 1743.
Elizebeth Daughter of Nathanael and Mary Sawyer was born the 5th Day of July 1741
Elizebeth the Daughter of Nathanael & Mary Sawyer was born 24 of July 1742.
John Son of Joseph and Hannah Woods was born march 14 1744.
Elisabeth Daugh^r: to Benj^e: & Ralph Houghton born Octr. 24. 1743
71 Dina Goss ye Daughter of William and —— Goss was born July ye 18 1737
Lucy Goss ye Daughter of William and —— Goss was born ye 15 march 1739
Daniel Goss ye Son of William and —— Goss was born September 14 1741
Oliver Goss ye Son of William and —— Goss was born november ye 18, 1742
Joshua ye Son of Joshua and Lois Pearce was Born may ye 7th 1741.
Mary the Daughter of Edward and Bathsheba Robins was born Sept 10 1738
Edward Robins ye Son of Edward & Bathsheba Robbins was Born may ye 4th 1741
Bathsheba ye Daughter of Edward & Bathsheba Robins was born Decem 22 1743
Tamer the Daughter of Thomas & Mary Ross was born august ye 9th 1743.
Jonathan the Son of Benjamin and Sarah Townsend was born February y^u 8th 1738
Benjamin the Son of Benjamin and Sarah Townsend was born ——
Nathan ye Son of Benjamin and Sarah Townsend was born ye 9 day of Febr^y 1742-3
Joseph ye Son of John and Susanna Beman was born november ye 29th 1733
Elisabeth ye Daughter of John and Susannah Beman was born February ye 1st 1734
Elijah ye Son of John and Susannah Beman was born october 10th 1736
John ye Son of John and Susannah Beman was born october ye 31st 1738
John Beman ye Son of John and Susannah Beman Deceased december ye 5th 1740.
Oliver ye Son of John and Susannah Beman was born may ye 19th 1741.
Cornelias ye Son of Phinihas and Mary Willard was born august ye 23^d 1743.
Doritha Phelps the Daughter of Robert and Doritha Phelps was Born tne first of Octobber 1743.
Elijah Son to Sam^{ll} & Elisebeth Burpee Botn 28 of February: 1744.
Meriam Daughter [of] Jonathan & Mary Bigelow was born the 3 Day of July 1743.
Nathan Son of Nathan & Zerviah Rugg was born 21 Day of april 1743.
Shuble the Son of Jonathan and Bridget Bailey was born June the 6th 1740: & Elisebeth their Daughter February the 28, 1742-3
Sarah the Daughter of Moses & Mary Bailey was Born the 4th of april 1742:
Anna the Daughter of Reuben and Lidea Rugg was born the 18th day of may 1744

Elesebeth Daughter to Andrew & Elesebeth [Carter] Wilder was born april the 4: 1743
Jonathan the Son of Israel and Martha Houghton was born December 24, 1743
John Beman Son of John and Susanah Beman was born march 29th: 1744
Jonathan Goss Son of John & Mary Goss was Born May the 18th: 1725.
Jeremiah Son of Jeremiah & thankfull Haskel was born the 20: Day of July 1744
Elesebeth Daughter of Ephraim & Elisebeth Divoul was born Decem 12: 1742
Ephraim Son of Ephraim & Elizebeth Divoul was born may 24: 1744
Martha Daughter [of] Isaac & Jane Rugg was Born July the 3: 1744
72 Rezineah the Daughter of John and Abigail Wilder was born November —
Nathan Son of David & Hannah Nelson was born november ye 15th: 1742
Deborah Sawyer the Daughter of Samll & Deborah Sawyer was born October 11th: 1744
Mary the Daughter of David & Eunice Osgood was born July 14: 1744
Jonathan Glazier Son of Zackriah and Thanckfull Glazier [was born] the 5th of June: 1744:
Addam hollerway Son of John and Mary farrer was born Novemr the 14th: 1744:
James Son of James and Abigail Ross was born Novemr the 11th: 1744:
Levi Houghton Son of James & Sarah Houghton born March 8: 1736:
Nathanael Sawyer Son of Thomas & Abigail Sawyer was Born Novemr ye 20: 1737; and Decd. the 22 of the same Instant.
Betty Sawyer Daughter of Thomas & Abigail Sawyer was born Decemr: the 29: 1738
Thomas Sawyer Son of Thomas & Abigail Sawyer was Born April the 29: 1744: [1740?]
Catrine Sawyer Daughter of Thomas & Abigail Sawyer Born Jannuary the 27: 1741
Eunis Daughter of Thomas & Abigail Sawyer born march the 27: 1744
Rebekah Daughter of John & Liddia Rugg Born Septembr the 9th: 1744
James Son of James & Lydea Kendal was Born March the 18: 1742
Pall Son of James & Lydea Kendal was Born April the 30th: 1744
Damaris Knight Daughter of Jonathan and Mary Knight was Born October the 10: 1742.
Jonathan Perce Son of Joshua & Loes Perce was born Jannuary the 20th: 1744-5
Mary Prescott Daughter of John Prescott Junr and Mary Prescott was born December the 24th: 1743
Asseneth Osgood Daughter of Jonathan and Asseneth Osgood was Born Decemr 24th 1744
Bette Daughter of Hezekiah and Rachel Whitcomb was born Septemr the 20th 1744
Sarey Kendal Daughter of Jonathan and Admonition Kendal was Born January 16, 1744-5
73 Thomas Rugg Son of Amos and Mary Rugg was born 27 of Jany. 1742-3.
Amos Rugg Son of Amos and Mary Rugg was born Jannuary ye 6, 1744-5
Prudance Sawyer Daughter of Elisha & Ruth Sawyer was born october the 2nd: 1741:
Elisha Sawyer Son of Elisha & Ruth Sawyer was born February the 9th 1743-4
Samll Bayley Son of Samll & annah Bayley was born Jan 25 1743
Sarey Daughter of Hezekiah & Annah Gates born July the first 1744
Nathaniel Sawyer Son of Nathanael & Mary Sawyer was born February ye: 21: 1744-5.
Thomas Son of Andrew Wilder & Elisebeth was born Febr: 24, 1744-5
Mary Daughter of Nathanael & Mary Wyman was born ye: 16 of may 1744
Benjamin Son of Benjamin & Jain [Robbins] Wilder was born march ye 13 1736:
Jain Daughter of Benjamin & Jain Wilder was Born march ye 28: 1738.
Marcy Daughter of Benjamin & Jain Wilder was Born July ye 2 1739
Hephzibah Daughter of Benjamin & Jain Wilder was Born ye 2d of Septemr 1742
Axey Daughter of Benjamin & Jain Wilder was born February ye 15th: 1744-5
Hanna Powers Daughter of Jonathan & Hanna Powers born January 10: 1739.
Oliver Son of Jonathan & Hanna Powers was Born Septem ye 6: 1741

BOOK FIRST. 71

Jonathan Powers Son of Jonathan & Hanna Powers born July 22: 1744.
Loes Holte Daughter of Thomas & Susanah Holte was born Sept: y° 12: 1744
Luie Daughter of Josiah & Tabitha Kendal was born Nov^m 3: 1743
Joseph Son of Joseph & Elisebeth Osgood Born Novem^r ye 7th: 1744.
David Knight Son of Amos [and] Hannah Knight was Born y° 27 Day of February 1744-5
Sarah Daughter of Daniel & Sarah Rugg was Born Sept y° 18: 1744
Prudence Daughter of Ezra & Rebekah Sawyer born Septr y° 29: 1726 [1722?]
Elisebeth Daughter of Ezra & Rebekah Sawyer born July: 2^d: 1724:
Rebekah Daughter of Ezra & Rebekah Sawyer born Feb: 24: 1736-7 [1727?]
Ezra Son of Ezra & Rebekah Sawyer born August 18th: 1730:
Cornelius Son of Ezra & Rebekah Sawyer born May 9: 1737, & Dec^d. the 23 of the same Instant May.
Keziah Daughter of Ezra & Rebekah Sawyer born Feb 27. 1734-5
Esther Daughter of Ezra Sawyer born the 6 of may 1739.
Nathanael Son of Ezra & Rebekah Sawyer born march 15: 1741
Joseph Moor Son of Joseph & Rebekah Moor Born March y° 28: 1743
Rebekah Moor Daughter of Joseph & Rebekah Moor Born Feb: 12: 1744-5
Maththew Wyman Son of Maththew & Rebekah Wyman was born No^m: 26: 1739
Henry Son of Maththew & Abgail Wyman was born March y° y° 16th 1742.
Benj^a Son of Thomas & Hannah Dole Born May 3^d 1745
Manasseh Osgood Son of Joshua & Ruth Osgood Born april y° 30: 1745
Prudence Daughter of Josiah & Meriam Wilder born March 12 1744
Jonas Son of Sam^ll & Jemimah Carter Born July 4th, 1745.
Rebekah Daughter of John & Sarah Sawyer Born April y° 22: 1744.
David Son of Silas & Tabitha Brigham born april 4: 1745
Abijah Son of Abijah & Abigail Wyman born august 9th 1745.
Susanah Bayley Daughter of Sam^ll & Annah Bayley was Born may y° 6: 1745
74 Samuel Son of David & Eunice Wilder was born June 13th 1745
John Son of John & Prudance Wilder was born July y° 12th. 1744
Prudance Daughter of John & Prudance Wilder was born Septem^r y° 12th 1745
Eunice Daughter of Ephraim & Annah Wilder was Born the 5 Day of September, 1745
Eunice Daughter of John & Loes White was born March 22, 1745
John Houghton Son of Israel & Martha Houghton was born Octo^r y° 14, 1745
Zilpah Daughter of Asaph & Zipporah [Wheeler] Wilder was born Novem^r 14 1745
Elisebeth Daughter of Joshua & Rebekah Phelps was born July y° 13th 1745.
Aaron Son of Isaac & Joanah Kilburn was born February y° 17. 1744-5
Doritha Daughter [of] Josiah & Doritha Richardson Born Novem^r. 27, 1743
Ennice Daughter of Josiah & Doritha Richardson was born January y° 30, 1745-6
Stephen Son of Thomas Burpee Jun born Feb 24: 1745
Joshua Fairbank Son of Jonathan & Thankfull Fairbank was Born Feb. y° 23 1745-6
Elisebeth Daughter of Timothy Ross & Elsebeth Born Febru^y y° 10, 1744-5
Wright Son of Aaron & Mary Willard was Born 20 Feb: 1745-6
Sam^ll. Son of Timothy & Dinah Sterns was born June y° 4: 1745
Asenath Daughter of Jonathan & Aseneth Osgood born may 3^d. 1746.
Joshua Barret Son to Jacob & Rebekah Barret born Decr 18. 1745
Abraham Son of Henry & Huldy Haskel Born Novem y° 18th, 1745
Mary Knight Daughter of Jonathan & Mary Knight was born April 20th 1745
Releaf Tomson Daughter of Simon & Martha Tomson born Jan 6 1745-6
Hannah Daughter of Francis & Hanna Buttrick Born Jany. 14, 1745-6
Joseph Son of John & Abigail Carter was born the 17th of Novem^r 1745
Rebkah Kendal Daughter of Thomas & Abigail Kendal was born y° 28 of Janu 1745-6
Sarah Boyington Daughter of Zaceus & Hanah Boyington born February y° 19, 1745
Dina Daughter of Moses & Martha Osgood was born march y° 10th, 1738-9
Martha Daughter of Moses & Martha Osgood was born June y° 23, 1740
Olive Daughter of Moses & Martha Osgood was born march y° 23, 1742
Moses Osgood Son of Moses & Martha Osgood was born October y° 7 1744

Joel Osgood Son of Moses & Martha Osgood was born march 21, 1746
Ephraim Son of Thomas & Doratha Fairbank born July y® 26. 1742
Mary Daughter of Thomas & Dorathy Fairbank born Feb 22ᵈ, 1744
Sarah Bigelow Daughter of Jonathan & Mary Bigelow was born august 6ᵗʰ, 1746
Abisha Son of Robert & Dorath[y] Phelps was born August 13ᵗʰ, 1746
Reuben Son of Daniel & Sarah Rugg born October 19ᵗʰ. 1746
Elisebeth Daughter of David & Eunice Osgood was born Decᵐ yᵉ 17ᵗʰ. 1746
Abigail Daughter of Caleb & Abigail Wilder was born April yᵉ 21. 1746
Susanah Daughter of John & Liddia Rugg born Sept. 21 1742
Rebeckah Daughter of John & Liddia Rugg born Sepᵐ 9, 1744
Luce Daughter of John & Liddia Rugg born August 17, 1746
Joannah Daughter of John & Joanah Fletcher born May 12, 1746
Doratha Daughter of John & Mary Prescott was Born Novemʳ. yᵉ 6, 1745.
Zerviah Daughter [of] Nathan & Zerviah Rugg born August yᵉ 10: 1745

75 Joseph Wilder Junʳ & Deborah [Joslin] was marred July the 4ᵗʰ. 1733

the Birth of their Children

the Birth of Joseph was on april the 15ᵗʰ: 1734
the Birth of Deborah was on november the 17ᵗʰ: 1736:
the Birth of Gardner was on march the 22ⁿᵈ. 1739.
the Birth of Rebeckah was on may the 18ᵗʰ: 1741
the Birth of Peter & John was on november the 10ᵗʰ 1743.
John Dec'd the Evening after Birth
Luce Wilder Daughter of Joseph & Deborah Wilder born yᵉ 24 Day of april 1747-8
John Wilder Son of Joseph & Deborah Wilder Born august yᵉ 5ᵗʰ. 1750
  NOTE.—The Book of the Wilders adds Sarah, born March 2, 1738.

Hannah Bayley Daughter of John & hannah Snow was born Feb 7 1745
Silas Son of Ebenezer & Hannah Kendal was Born the forth Day of February 1744-5.
Hannah Bayley Daughter [of] Jonathan & Bridget Bayley was Born 26 of march 1746.
Luce Daughter of thomas [and] Susanah Holte born August yᵉ 2ᵈ. 1746
Abiel Son of Berzilla & Elisebeth Holte born June 14 1740
Berzilla Son of Berzilla & Elisebeth Holte was born may yᵉ 12. 1745
James Son of Berzilla Holte & Elisebeth born June yᵉ 6 1746
Mindwell Daughter of Silas & tabatha Brigham born Feb 7. 1746-7
Elisebeth Daughter of Asahel & Elisebeth Phelps Born Decemʳ 6ᵗʰ 1744
Mary Daughter of Asahel & Elisebeth Phelps born June yᵉ 9ᵗʰ 1746

Eunice Daughter of John & Ioes White Dec'd October 2ᵈ 1746
Loes Daughter of John & Ioes White Dec'd October 8ᵗʰ 1746
Abijah Son of John & Ioes White Dec'd October yᵉ 9 1746

Samuel Son of Oliver & Ruth Wilder was Born June yᵉ 30. 1746
Mercy Daughter of David and Margret Nelson was born June 26. 1746
Solomon Son of David & Margret Nelson was born April 30 1747
Nathan Son of David & Margret Nelson was born November yᵉ 15 1743
Joseph Son of Joseph & Elisebeth Osgood was born September yᵉ 18, 1746
Elizebeth Daughter of John & Mary farrer was born Novem yᵉ 7ᵗʰ, 1745
Abigail Atherton Daughter of Amos & Elisebeth Atherton born May 27 1746
Relief Moor Daughter of Joseph & Rebekah Moor born August yᵉ 3, 1747
Luce Daughter of John & Lidia Rugg born August 17ᵗʰ: 1746. *before entered*
Jemima Daughter of Samˡˡ & Jemima Carter Born September yᵉ 15 1747
Sarah Daughter of Matthew & Abigail Wyman born Sep yᵉ 20 1745
Elias Son of Elisha & Ruth Sawyer born August 1ˢᵗ 1747
Thanckful Daughter of Elisha & Ruth Sawyer born August 1, 1747
Elisabeth Daughter of Phinehas & Joanna Beman born July 1ˢᵗ, 1745
Elemuel Son of Phinehas & Joanna Beman born October 2, 1746
Silence Daughter of Phinehas & Joanna Beman born August 31. 1747
Jotham Son of Elisha & Ruth Sawyer born April yᵉ 27 1745
76 Deliverance Sawyer Son of John & Sarah Sawyer ——

BOOK FIRST.

Oliver Son of W^m & Jane Dunsmoor born January ye 23 1739
John Son of W^m & Jane Dunsmoor born September 17 1742
Elisabeth Daughter of W^m & Jane Dunsmoor born ye 7 —— 1744
Joseph Son of W^m & Jane Dunsmoor born July 5 1747
Loes White Daughter of John & Loes White was born April 18 1747
Bulah Daughter of Eaphram & Abigail Carter born October ye 14 1747
Jonas Wyman Son of Abijah & Abigail Wyman was born Novem^r 30 1746
Mary Fowle Daughter of Jacob & Phebe Fowle was born March ye 26, 1747
Amos Knight Son of Amos & Hannah Knight was born March 6 1747-8.
Stephen Wilder Son of Jotham & Febe [Wheeler] Wilder was born Feb 26 1747
Rebekah Wilder Daughter of Benj^a & Jane Wilder born April 18 1747.
Abigail Daughter of James & Abigail Ross Born October 11 1745.
Ebenezer Ross Son of Thomas & Mary Ross born June ye 7 1747
Silas Son of Jonathan & Zerviah [Houghton] Wilder was Born Feb 27, 1747
Abigail Green Daughter of Peter & Abigail Green born Octr 23^d 1741
Eunice Green Daughter of Peter & Abigail Green Born Novem^r 3^d 1743
Peter Green Son of Peter & Abigail Green Born October ye 1st, 1745
Eunice Prescott Daughter of John & Mary Prescott was born Novem^r 12 1747
Ruth Wilder Daughter of Andrew & Elizabeth Wilder was born Decem^r 15th 1746
Amos Rugg Son of Amos & Mary Rugg born March y^e — 1747
Sarah Daughter of Thomas & Hannah Dole borne June ye 3^d 1747.
Elizabeth Daughter of Isaac & Jain Rugg born August ye 1. 1747.
Nathanael Beaman Son of John & Susanah Beaman born October 5 1747.
Phinehas Bayley Son of John & —— [Mary?] Bayley born August 1 1740
Ruth Bayley Daughter of John & —— Bayley born October ye 15 1743
Dudley Bayley Son of John & —— Bayley born December 16, 1744
Mary Bayley Daughter of John & —— Bayley born November 11, 1747
Isaac Rugg Son of Isaac & Jane Rugg born Decem^r ye 2 Day 1745.
Sarah Daughter of William & Sarah Willard born Sept ye 2^d 1735
William Willard Son of William & Sarah Willard born Novem 31 1737
Mary Willard Daughter of William & Sarah Willard born March ye 9 1739 and Deceased ye 28 of September following.
Nathanael Willard Son of William & Sarah Willard born April 3^d 1742
Pall Son of William & Sarah Willard born June 22^d 1743.
Daniel Willard Son of Daniel & Lucy Willard born Sept ye 2. 1747.
Luke Osgood Son of Aaron & Eunice Osgood Born June 8th 1747.
John Wilder Son of David & Eunice Wilder born March ye 20th 1746-7.
Lemuel Osgood Son of Joshua & Ruth Osgood born Novem^r 6, 1747
Releef Rugg Daughter of Nathan & Zerviah Rugg born 29 Day of May 1748
Nathanael Wyman Son of Nathanael & Mary Wyman born 2^d Day of Decem^r 1746
Eunice Daughter of Nathanael & Mary Wyman was born ye 4 of August 1748
Andrew Haskel Son of Jeremiah & Thanckfull Haskel was born ye 25 of July 1748
Mehittabel Daughter of Josiah & Bethesdah Houghton was born February 12 1747-8
Demaras Daughter of Joseph & Demaras Whitcomb born May 21st 1746
Rufus Wilder Son of Josiah & Meriam Wilder born May ye 28th, 1748
Jonathan Son of Jonathan & Mindwell Crosbee Born Decem 26, 1746
John Dresser Son of Aaron & Ahetebal Dresser born May 10th 1748.
Lucy Powers Daughter of Jonathan & Hannah Powers born March 19 1748
Ebenezer Son of Ebenezer & Jerusha Prescott was born February 10th. 1747-8
Hyram Prescott Son of Jonathan & Vashty Prescott was born 16 April 1748
Abigail Carter Daughter of John & Abigail Carter born September ye 4th 1748
Joshua Barritt Son of Jacob & Rebekah Barritt [born] October 26 1746.
Rebekah Barritt Daughter of Jacob & Rebekah Barritt born May ye 22^d 1747
Sarah Osgood Daughter of Jonathan & Aseneth Osgood born October 22 1748
Jonathan Kendal Son of Jonathan & Admonition Kendal born January 8th. 1746
Sarah Daughter of Joshua & Rebekah Phelps born August 22^d, 1748
Easter Jewet Daughter of David Jewet & Ester Jewet born June 9, 1745

Hannah Jewet Daughter of David & Ester Jewet born April 26. 1747
Mary Nelson Daughter of David & Margret Nelson born October 15th 1745
Enock Son of Amos & Mary Jewet was born August ye 13th 1739
Amos Son of Amos & Mary Jewet was born July ye 10 1741
Elisabeth Daughter of Amos & Mary Jewet was born June 10, 1744
Ann Jewet Daughter of Amos & Mary Jewet was born June ye 4th 1747
John Boyenton Son of Zacheus & Hannah Boyenton Born June 30, 1745
Philimon Whitcomb Son of Joseph & Demaras Whitcomb was born October 29th: 1748
Joseph Harpard Son of John & Mary Harpard born October 174[8?]
Hanah Daughter of Thomas & Abigail Kendal Born July 3^d 1748
Joshua Fairbank Son of Joshua & Eunice Fairbank Born Sept 28 1746
Eunice Daughter of Joshua & Eunice Fairbank Born October 9th 1747
Ebenezer Begelow born ye forth Day of October Son of Ebenezer & Anah Begelow was born 1747 and Died the 13 of — in the year 1748
Annah Begelow wife to Ebenezer Begelow Departed this life august ye 25 1748 being 29 year two months & 27 Days old.
William Lock son of Sam^{ll} & Rebeckah Lock born August 28 1748
Tamer Daughter [of] Oliver & Ruth Wilder born May ye 27 1748
James Sawyer Son of Thomas & Abigail Sawyer born Novem^r 20; 1745
Josiah Sawyer Son of Thomas & Abigail Sawyer born Novem^r 21 1748 and Deceased soon after
Abigail Daughter of Thomas & Abigail Sawyer born Novem^r 21 1748
Febe Burpee Daughter of Sam^{ll} & Elisabeth Burpee born May 28 1745
Rebeckah Wilder Daughter of Benj^a & Jane Wilder born April 18 1747
Abigail Daughter of James & Abigail Ross born october 11. 1745
Ebenezer Ross Son of Thomas & Magry Ross born June 7 1747
Silas Son of Jonathan & Zerviah Wilder born febry 17 1747
78 Luce Daughter of Daniel and Sarah Rugg born march 9th 1748-9
Joshua Fletcher Son of Joshua and Mary fletcher born Feb ye 25 1748
Hannah Daughter of Ebenezer & Keziah Buss born 24 of feb 1748
Gamaliel Beman Son of Phenihas & Joannah Beman born Decr 4th: 1748
Mary Daughter of Moses & Mary Bayley Born June 24. 1745
Perses Daughter of Moses & Mary Bayley born April ye 2^d 1747
Hannah Buss daughter of Ebenezer & Keziah Buss born February ye 24. 1748
Gamaliel Beman Son of Phinehas & Joanah Beman born Decem^r ye 4, 1748
Silas Son of Thomas & Doratha Fairbank born April ye 27 1747
Mary Daughter of Jonathan & Mary Knight Born April 31: 1748
Hannah Fletcher Daughter of Robert & Elizabeth Fletcher born June ye 19th 1749
Dinah Houghton Daughter of Ezra & Dinah Houghton born July 2^d 1749.
John Rugg Son of John & Lydia Rugg was born 10th of July 1749.
Eisabeth Wilder Daughter of Ephraim & Anna Wilder born May 16. 1748
Damaras Rugg Daughter [of] Reuben & Annah Rugg Born May ye 15 1749
Dorathy Daughter of Aaron & Eunice Osgood Born Septem^r 10th 1749
Abiel Abbott Son of Joseph & Hannah Abbott Born August ye 23^d 1749
Sarah Daughter of Josiah and Sarah Ballard born January 13th 1744 and Deceased ye 5th of February 1744
Sarah Ballard ye 2^d Daughter of Josiah & Sarah Ballard Born ye 31st of January 1745 & Deceased the first of February following
Sarah Ballard ye 3^d Daughter of Josiah & Sarah Ballard born November the last Day 1747
Ebenezer Wilder Son of Benj^a: & Jain Wilder Born August 30, 1749
Isaac Sterns Son of Timothy & Dinah Sterns born July 1st 1749
Josiah Wood Son of Nehemiah & Mary Wood born Decem^r 20th 1740
Joseph Moor Son of Joseph & Rebekah Moor born June ye 6 1749
Nathanael Son of John & Mary Farrer born March ye 25 1749
Elisabeth Divoul Daughter of Ephraim & Elizabeth Divoul born March ye 4th: 1746
Abigail Daughter of Ephraim & Elizabeth Divoul born December ye 18th 1747
Peninah Halbert Daughter of Daniel & Abigail Halbert born May 18th 1741
Titus Wilder Son of Jotham & Phebe Wilder born Decem^r ye 4 1749

BOOK FIRST.

John Prescott Son of John & Mary Prescott Born December y° 6th 1749
Mary Brigham Daughter of Silas & Tabitha Brigham born March y° 1st 1748-9
Elisabeth Daughter of John & Ester Glaizer was born November y° 20th 1749
Mary Osgood Daughter of John & Sarah Osgood Born Decem y° 22 1747
Susanah Daughter of John & Sarah Osgood Born August y° 17th 1749
William Kendal Son of Jonathan & Admonition Kendal born Septem' y° 14th 1749.
Jacob Son of Isaac & Jane Rugg born 7 of November 1749.
Josiah Ballard Son of Josiah & Sarah Ballard born Jan' y° 4 1749
John Ballard Son of Benj° & Ruth Ballard born April y° 17th 1749
Jacob Fowle Son of Jacob & Phebe Fowle born Septem' 14 1749
Benj°. Glaizer Son of Benj° Glaizier born March y° 30th 1750
79   Joseph Nelson Son of Jonathan & Doratha Nelson born Dec^m 30th 1749
Dorathy Nelson Daughter of Jonathan & Dorathy Nelson born June 27 1747
Joseph Barritt Son of Jacob & Rebecca Barritt Born May y° 11 1750
Abner Moor Son of Sam^ll & Zerish Moor born May y° 7th 1750
Mary Rugg Daughter of Amos & Mary Rugg was born Septem' 8 1749
Paciance Daughter [of] Mathew & Abigail Wyman Born June 3 1748
Danael Son of Mathew & Abigail Wyman born June the — 1744 and Died the 24 Day of October following.
Luce Begilow Daughter of Ebenezer & Hephzabah Begilow born Septem' the 18 1749 and Died the Next Day.
Jonas Knight Son of Amos and Hannah Knight Born July y° 3^d 1750
Abijah Son of Nathan & Zerviah Rugg Born July y° 30th 1750
Eunice White Daughter of John & Loes White Born Feb y° 26 1748-9
Thankfull Moor Daughter of Oliver & Abigail Moor Born June y° 13th 1750
Ledia Johnson Daughter of Daniel & Ledia Johnson Born October y° 3^d 1750
Levi Wilder Son of Caleb & Abigail Wilder Born April y° 2 1750
Mary Ballard Daughter of Sherebiah & Keziah Ballard was Born October y° 11 1750
Ephraim Willard Son of Ephraim & Azubah Willard was Born March y° 2^d 1748
Luce Wallonsford Daughter of Ezekiel & Lidia Wallonsford was Born August y° 1st 1741
Mary Wallonsford Daughter of Ezekiel & Lidia Wallonsford was Born June y° 26 1743
Levi Houghton Son of James & Sarah Houghton was born March y° 1 1737-8
Jonas Baley Son of Moses & Mary Bayley was Born August y° 30th 1750
Jonathan Osgood Son of Joseph & Elisabeth Osgood was Born April the first Day 1749
Hannah Kendal Daughter of Ebenezer Kendal & Hannah Kendal was Born December y° 10 1747
Martha Wright Daughter of Nathanael and Martha Wright was born March y° 25 1748
James Wright Son of Nathanael & Martha Wright was born March y° 22^d 1749-50
Luce Willard Daughter of Daniel & Luce Willard was born Feb y° 3. 1750
Rachel Walker Daughter of Hezekiah & Sarah Walker was born July y° 8. 1748
Hezekiah Walker Son of Hezekiah & Sarah Walker was born Feb y° 14th 1750.
Abigail Daughter of Asa & Eunice Whitcomb was born June y° 19th, 1749
Rebecca Daughter of Asa & Eunice Whitcomb was born January y° 17 1750
Sarah Nelson Daughter of David & Margreet Nelson was born March y° 9 1750
John Phelps Son of John & Zipporah Phelps was born December y° 13th 1748
Joseph Phelps Son of John & Zipporah Phelps was born February y° 28 1750
Anna Gates Daughter of Hezekiah & Anna Gates was born August y° 27 1748
Timothy Fletcher Son of Joshua & Mary Fletcher was born September y° 20: 1750
Martha Daughter of Jonathan Wilder & Zerviah Wilder was born February y° 16th 1750
Moses Son of Jeremiah & Elizabeth Burpee was born August y° 11th 1750
Parnee Brooks Daughter of John & Parnee Brooks was born February the 18th 1751

80 *Births of ye Children of Joseph & Elisabeth Bennitt.*

Elisabeth was born May ye 12 1732
Mary was born March 13 1733
Sary was born May 23 1736
Prudance was born January ye 17 1738
Eunice was born August ye 6 1741
Joseph was born April ye 11 1744.

Jonathan Prescott Son of Jonathan & Vasty Prescott was Born June 8th 1750
William Son of Thomas & Mary Ross was Born Sept ye 17th 1749
Abijah Son of Andrew & Elsabeth Wilder was born Novem^r ye 28th 1750
Ephraim Rugg Son of Danael & Sarah Rugg was born February y^e — 1750
Annis Daughter of Jonathan & Mary Knight was born March ye 22^d 1750-1
Jonathan Ross Son of Timothy & Elsabeth Ross born March ye 2 1750-1
Lucy White Daughter of John & Loes White was born May the 21 1751
Ephraim Son of Zaccheus Bointon & Hannah bointon was born July ye 24th 1751
Abel Son of John & Lidia Rugg was born June ye 23^d 1751
John Serjant Son of John & Hannah Serjant was Born Sepr 13th 1749
Ruth Daughter of Elisha & Ruth Sawyer was born March ye 15th 1750
Sarah Daughter of Thomas & Abigail Sawyer was born August ye 6 1751
Samuel Son of Amos & Mary Jewet was born July ye 25th 1751.
Rebecca Divoul Daughter of Ephraim & Elizabeth Divoul was born Jany. ye 31 1749
Stephen Rugg Son of Amos & —— Rugg was Born October ye 30th 1751
Abijah Whitcomb Son of Joseph & Damaris Whitcomb was born June ye 25th 1751
David Jewet Son of David and Estter Jewet was born July ye Eleventh 1749
Phebe Daughter of David & Estter Juet was born February ye last 1750
Elisabeth Sawyer Daughter of Sam^{ll} & Deborah Sawyer was born Sept. 1750
Estter Osgood Daughter of Aaron & Eunice Osgood was born August ye 13th. 1751
Ruth Daughter of Oliver and Ruth Wilder was born March ye 29 1751
Sarah Daughter of James & Mary Carter was born Septem^r ye 28 1751
Ezra Houghton Son of Ezra & Dinah Houghton was born May ye 23^d 1751
Mary Daughter of Moses & Martha Osgood was Born Septem^r 24 1750
Elisabeth Daughter of Timothy & Dinah Sterns was born Novem^r ye 7 1751.
Mary Osgood Daughter of Jonathan & Asenath Osgood was Born April ye 23^d 1751.
Nathan Barritt Son of Jacob & Rebecca Barritt was born February ye 18th 1752
Abijah Willard Son of Abijah & Elisabeth Willard was Born Novem^r 4th: 1750
Abijah Harris Son of Asa & Eunice Harris was born Decem^r ye 3 1752
Benj^a Ballard Son of Benj^a & Ruth Ballard was born February ye 16th 1752

the berths of the Children of Tilley & Persis Wilder.

Persis Wilder was born Octo^r ye 12: 1745
Elisabeth Wilder was born April ye 11 1747
Tilley Wilder was born May v^e 6, 1749
Mary Wilder was born March ye 14th, 1751
Joseph Henderson Son of John & Jane Henderson was born October ye 25th 1751.
Prudance Daughter of Abner & Prudance Wilder was born July ye 24 1751
Levi Son of John & Mindwell Crosbee was born Feby ye 17 1751
Asa Rugg Son of Reuben & Lidia Rugg was born March ye 23, 1752
Buier Daugnter of Benj^a & Jane Wilder was born Feby ye 14 1751
Hephzabah Houghton Daughter of Josiah & bethesda Houghton was born Decem^r 25: 1751
81 Seth Sarjant Son of John & Hannah Serjant was born Feb^{ry} 1752
Sarah Osgood Daughter of John & Sarah Osgood was born April ye 3 1751
John Abbott Son of Joseph & hannah Abbott was born October ye 8th 1751
Jeremiah Son of Josiah & Sarah Ballard was Born March ye 9th. 1752
E[be]nezer Taler Son of Ebenezer & Mary Taler was born July ye 5th 1749
James & Jonathan Taler Sons of Ebenezer & Mary Taler was born Septem^r ye 20th: 1751
Menasseh Wilder Son of Ephraim & Anna Wilder was born May ye 4 1752
Releaf Daughter of Ephraim & Abigail Carter was born August 10th. 1752

BOOK FIRST.

Doratha Carter Daughter of Ephraim & Abigail Carter was Born May y⁰ 21ˢᵗ 1750
Ephraim Ross Son of James & Abigail Ross was born May y⁰ 11. 1750
Jonathan Glaizer Son of Benjᵃ & Lidia Glaizer was born June — 1752
Elisabeth Daughter of John & hannah Snow was born April y⁰ 28 1750
Rebecca the Daughter of John & Mary Prescott was born March y⁰ 7ᵗʰ 1752
Thanckfull Sawyer Daughter of Nathanael & Mary Sawyer was born October y⁰ 8: 1752.
Ephraim Wyman Son of Nathanael Wyman & Mary Wyman was Born February y⁰ 2 Day 1751.
Sherebiah Ballard Son of Sherebiah & Keziah Ballard was born December y⁰ 26ᵗʰ 1752.
Winslow Phelps Son of William and Mary Phelps was born December y⁰ 28 1752.
Ebenezer Burpee Son of Jeremiah & Elisabeth Burpee was born Sepᵗ 9, 1753
Elizabeth Daughter of Joseph & Rebecca Moor was born February y⁰ 15 1753.
John Goss Son of Phillep Goss & hannah Goss was born Feb y⁰ 5 1748–9
Jonathan Ball Son of Jonathan and Martha Ball was born Sept 16 1751
Martha Sawyer Daughter of Elisha and Ruth Sawyer was born November y⁰ 2ᵈ 1753.
Loes Rugg Daughter of Daniel & Sarah Rugg was born January y⁰ 31 1753.
Timothy Kendal Son of Jonathan & Admonition Kendal was born July 31 1753
Annah Atherton Daughter of Amos and Elisabeth Atherton was born April 2 1753
Abijah Haskel Son of Jeremiah & thanckfull Haskell was born August y⁰ 18 1753
Hannah Ross Daughter of Thomas & Mary Ross was Born March y⁰ 30ᵗʰ 1752
Derias Farrer Son of John & Mary Farrer was Born July 16 1751
Silas Willard Son of William and Sarah Willard was born April y⁰ 16, 1748 Deceased the 16ᵗʰ of December 1750
Mary Willard Daughter of William Willard was born July y⁰ 22ᵈ, 1750.
Mary Daughter of John & Marcy Nicholls was born the 28 of October 1753
Levi Rugg Son of John & Lidia Rugg was born December y⁰ 3 1752.
Patiance Daughter of Ephraim and Elizabeth Divoul was born May 30 1752
Rebecca Divoul Daughter of Ephraim & Elizabeth Divoul was born Jany y⁰ 31 1750
Luce Daughter of Josiah & Tabitha Kendal was born November y⁰ 3 1743
Ethan Son of Josiah & Tabitha Kendal was born Sept y⁰ 25 1748
Esther Daughter of Josiah & Tabitha Kendal was born June y⁰ 23 1750
Eunice Daughter of Ebenezer & Keziah Buss was born Decᵐ 1ˢᵗ 1753
Benjᵃ Son of Ephraim and Mikel Roper was born Jany y⁰ 7 1750
Menasseh Son of Ephraim & Mikel Roper was Born May 26ᵗʰ 1752
Joshua Houghton Son of Saul & Mary Houghton was born Feb y⁰ 25 1753
Thomas Carter Son of John & Abigail Carter was born March y⁰ 8ᵗʰ 1753
Martha Daughter of Joseph and Alles Wheelock was born July 11ᵗʰ 1752
Rebecca Daughter of Matthew and Abigail Wyman was born May 6ᵗʰ 1751
William Son of Eunice Carter was born yᵉ 4ᵗʰ Day of April 1752.
Ephraim & Menasseh Knight Sons of Amos & Hannah Knight was born y⁰ 13 of March 1753
Martha Daughter of Elisha & Ruth Sawyer was born Decemᵣ 3ᵈ 1753
Joel Son of Isaac & Jane Rugg was born October y⁰ 20 1752.
Elijah Rugg Son of Nathan & Zerviah Rugg was born April 4ᵗʰ 1753
Jotham Robens Son of Edward & Barsheba Robins was born April 1. 1746
John Son of Edward & Barsheba Robins was born August 20 1751

Children of James & Martha [Broughton] Wilder, their berths.

Josiah Born October 19 1735
Martha was born Feb 23 1737
Abigail Do Do June 22 1739
James Do Do June 22 1741
Josiah was born May 27 1744
Aseph Do Do July 20 1749
Susanah Do Do April 23 1751

Prudence Samson Daughter to John & Prudence Samson Born June y⁰ 17. 1747
John Samson Born april y⁰ 3ᵗʰ: 1750

Thomas Do. Born april y* 23th: 1752
Mary Daughter to Andrew Grime and Submitt Grime Born May y* 19th: 1753.
Jonas Glazer Son to John Glazer and Easter Glazer Born 19 June 1753
Nathan Willard Son to Daniel & Lucy Willard Born y* 12 of December 1751
Abel Wilder Son to David Wilder & Martha Wilder Born November y* 30 1752
Joseph Wilder Son to Andrew and Elisabeth Wilder Born May 20: 1753

To Joseph White and Paciance White: Childrens Births.

Abigail White Born may 13: 1747.   Joseph White Born august y* 25 1751
Josiah White Born march y* 13 1749   Pacience White Born sept. y* 24; 1753

Ebenezer Son to Joseph Abbott & Annah Abbott Born y* 14 of Octo^r: 1753
Eunice Daughter to Asa & Abigal Haris Born Novem^r y* 3: 1753
Relive [Relief] Daughter [of] John and Sarah Osgood march y* 9: 1753
Stephen & Abigal Son and Daughter to Abijah and Abigal Wyman Born march y* 29: 1752.
83   Elesabeth Daughter to Abijah & Anna Willard Born Janu: y* 15: 1754
Pheneas Son to Joshua and Mary Fletcher Born 29th may 1753
Azubah Daughter to Eph^a; and Azubah Willard Born August y* 15th 1753.
Anna Daughter to Enock and Sarah Hill Born the 25 may 1753
John Ballard Son to Benj^a & Ruth Ballard born may y* 8th, 1753
James Son to James and Mary Carter Born Novem^r y* 9 1753.
Hannah Daughter to Jon^a and Zerfiah Wilder Born y* 22: march 1753.
Luke Son to David & Martha Wilder born y* 20 of Fubuary 1754
Elisha Son to Ebenezer Allen Jr. and Tabitha Allen Born in Weston y* 11 of December 1745
Tabitha Born y* 27: of January 1747
Mary Born in Lancaster 14: of January, 1749
Ebenezer Born 12 of April 1751
Amos Born 1 of August 1753
Abijah Kendal Son of Ezekeal & Hannah Kendal Born July y* 12th. 1743
Aaron Kendal Born May y* 29th: 1746
Joseph Born y* 9th. of June 1749.
Noah Kendal Son to Ezekeal & Mary Kendal Born April y* 30: 1753.
Easter Glazer the wife of John Glazer Deceast July 9; 1753 and Jonas Glazer Son to John & Easter Glazer October y* 15: 1753
Katherine Whitcomb Daughter to Asa Whitcomb and Eunice Born June y* 12 1754
Sam^{ll}. Bowers Son to Jarathmeal & Mary Bowers Born april y* 17: 1754
Ruth Houghton Daughter to Phineas Houghton & Ruth Houghton Born December 5; 1754
Susanna Glazer Daughter of Benj^a: & Lidia Glazer Born June y* 8: 1754
John Wheelock Son to Joseph & Alles Born Sept 22; 1754
Jacob Wilder Son to Benj^a: Wilder and Jane Wilder Born y* 25: May 1754
84   Elesabeth Daughter to Abijah & Abigail Wyman Born Sept. y* 24: 1754
Aaron Son to John & Zipporah Phelps Born November 9: 1754

Children to Ephraim and Mikeal Roper

Benj^a. Roper Born January y* 7: 1751   Silas Roper Born January y* 20 1754
Manasseh Born May y* 26 1752

Solomon Son to Charles & Sarah Stuart Born febury y* 9: 1748
Sarah Stuart Born april y* 8: 1750
Releif Daughter to Thomas & Abigail Kendal Born Fuburary y* 22^d: 1754
Abigail Born august y* 11 1752
Lucresha Daug^h; to Daniel and Sarah Rugg born January y* 5 1755
Luce Daughter to John and Lois White Born March y* 30: 1753
Prudence Daughter to Phineas & Ruth Houghton born Febr. y* 10: 1755
Thankfull Daught to Jon^a. & Doretha Nelson Born Sept^m: y* 5: 1754
Hannah Farrah daughter of John and Mary Farrah Born Sept: the Eighth 1753
Eunice Dafter of William & Mary Richardson Born Jenuery y* 12th 1746-7
Calven Son to Jon^a; & Zerviah Wilder born June 12th, 1755

Rebeckah Daughter to James & Mary Carter born Dec^r: 25, 1755
Reuben Son to Asa & Lydia [Rugg] Wilder born Novr. 13. 1755
Prudence Daugh^r. to Ephraim & Elizabeth Divoll born Janu^r: ye 24th, 1756
Elisabeth Daughter to John & Parnee Brooks born March 12 1756
Jeremiah Son to Jeremiah & Elis^a: Burpee born Octr. 11. 1755
William Son to John & Prudence Sampson born May 16, 1754
Levi Son to John & Prudence Sampson born May 7: 1756
Benj^a: Son to Benj^a: & Mary Osgood Ju^r; Born Decem^r: 17, 1754
Oliver Son to Ditto.   Do.   Ditto. March 30. 1756.

85   BIRTHS OF CHILDREN

Ruth Daugh^r. to Joseph & Ruth Gary Born January 14, 1752
Lois Daug^r. to Joseph & Ditto   Do. June 11, 1754.
Samuel Son to John & Hanah Sergants Born May 3. 1756
Rebeckah Daug^r: to W^m: & Mary Tucker Born March 12. 1756
Asa Son to Eph^m: & Michail Roper born Augt. 16, 1756
Elisha Son of Nathan [&] Zerviah Rugg born April 30. 1755
Lucy Daug: to Ezra & Dinah Houghton born Octo^r: 12. 1754.
Ephraim Son to Jon^r: [&] Admonition Ju^a: Kendall born Feb. 16. 1756
Levi Son to Levi & Katharine Willard born Augt. 13th: 1756
Lydia Daughter to Sherebiah & Keziah Ballard, born November 18th, 1756.
Ruth the Daughter to Jona: & Mary Knight, born Jany. 18th. 1753.
Elisabeth Daughter to Jona; & Mary Knight, born April 10th, 1756.
William Son to George & Keziah Parkhurst born Dec^r; 17. 1755.
Phebe Daug^r. to Amos & Mary Rugg born. June 5. 1756.
Jon^a & Martha Son & Daugh^r. to David & Martha Wilder born April 21st: 1755.
Ebeneazer Son to Benj^a: & Lydia Glaizer born September ye 8th, 1756.
Esther Daugh^r; to William & Esther Richardson 3^d, born March 12 1755.
William Son to Willm: & Esther Richardson 3^d, born Janu^y: 28, 1757.
David Son to Robert & Rebecca Fletcher born, April ye 18th, 1755
Oliver Son to Robert & Rebecca Fletcher born, Febrary ye 4th, 1756
Elijah Son to Asa & Lydia Wilder born, March 22, 1757
Sarah & Deborah Daugh^{rs}: to Timo: & Sarah Whiteing born Jan^u: 17, 1757.
Ebenezer Son to Ebenezer & Keziah Buss born November ye 9th, 1756
Subbiear Daugh^r: to Daniel & Lydia Johnson born March 14th: 1755
John ye 3^d son to John & Mercy Nichols Ju^r. born May 19, 1756
David son to Saul & Mary Houghton born April y^e: 9th. Day, 1757
Martha Daugh^r. to John & Lois White born May, 30th. day, 1757
Phinehas Sawyer Son to Phinehas & Mary Sawyer born April 28, 1742.
John Son to Sam^{ll}. & Rebecah Locke born April y^e: 19th 1742
Oliver Moor Son to Isarel & Abigal Moor born July y^e: 9th, 1757.
Jacob Son to Francis & Susanah Fullum born Sept. 13, 1757.
Relief Whetcomb Daughter to Joseph & Elisabeth Whetcomb borne October y^e: 1st, 1757.

86   *Childerin of Abijah & Abigail Wyman.*

Abijah borne August 9th 1745   Stephin & Abigal borne March 29, 1752
Jonas borne November 30th 1746   Elisabeth borne September 24th 1754
Abel borne June ye 27 1749   Sarah borne December 22^d 1756

Ephraim Osgood Son to Joseph & Katherine Osgood born December ye 4th 1757
David Son to Adam & Margret Fleeman born April 7, 1756
Hephzubeth Crosfield born Aug^t: 3. 1752 } Children of James Crosfield & Elis^a.
Adam Crosfield born Augt. 5. 1755
Thomas Son to Thos: & Abigail Kendall born Sept. 30, 1757
Joseph Son to Joseph & Mary Kilborne born Nov^r: 3. 1755
Timothy Son to Joseph & Mary Kilborne born May 26, 1757.
Samuel Son to Eph^m. & Elis^a; Divoll born Sept. 22, 1758
Phinehas Son to Phinehas & Lois [Brown] Wilder Born Jan^y: 24, 1757
Adam Son to   Ditto   & Do.   Jany. 28 1759
Jothem Son to Jothem & Phebe Wilder born Feby. 19. 1759

The Children of Caleb & Abigail Wilder Born

Sam[ll]: Wilder Born May 7th, 1739
Caleb Wilder Born July 1st, 1741
Nahum Wilder Born Aug[t]. 18: 1743
Anna Wilder born July 10: 1755

Abigail Wilder Born April 21. 1746
Levi Wilder Born April 23, 1750
Sarah Wilder born Aug[t]: 6, 1752

Priscillia Daugh. to Benj[a]: & Priscillia Houghton 3[d]: Born May 25: 1759

Children of James & Sarah May

James May Jr Born June 5, 1757   David May Born Dec[r]. 22, 1758

87   AN ACCOMPT OF THE BIRTHS OF CHILDREN.

Hannah Farrah Daughter of John and Mary Farrah Born Sept: y[e] 8th. 1753
W[m]: Phelps Son of W[m]. and Mary Phelps Born Feb[ry]. y[e] 15: 1755
Mary Williams Daughter of Zepheniah & Damaris Williams Born Apr[ll]. y[e] 24, 1755
Ezra Osgood son of Joseph and Elizabeth Osgood Born May the 23[d]: 1752
Dorothy Osgood daughter of Joseph and Elisabeth Osgood Born Sept[br]: y[e] 22[d]: 1754
Bethesda Houghton daughter of Josiah and Bethesda Houghton Born Aprill y[e] 10th. 1755.
Percis Larking daughter of Peter and Azuba Larking Born Feb[ry]: y[e] 18th: 1753
Hezediah Larking daughter of   Ditto,   Born December y[e] 24th. 1754
Phebe Cooper daughter ef Moses & Ruth Cooper Born January y[e] 12th, 1748
Abigail Buss daughter of Ebenezer & Keziah Buss Born Feb[ry]: y[e] 22[d], 1754.
Solomon Rugg Son of Amos & Mary Rugg Born March y[e] 17th. 1754
Calvin More Son of Joseph & Rebecka More Born ——— 1755
Jonathan White Son of John and Lois White Born May y[e] 15 1755
Sarah White Daughter of Joseph & Patience White Born August y[e] 10th, 1755

Children of Israel & Luce Nicholds

Jane Born Febuary y[e] 24th. 1747
Roger Born July y[e] 13th, 1748
William Born June y[r] 28th 1750

Lidia Born July y[e] 23[d]: 1752
Desire Born Feb[ry]: 14th, 1755
Roger Died Sep[br]: 10th, 1754

——— of Joseph & ——— Baley Born October y[e] 10th 1755

Children of James & Ruth Richardson 3[d].

Ruth Born Sept: 13, 1749   James Born June 4, 1753
Susanah Do: July 10, 1751

Children of Solomon & Diliverance Houghton

Molley Born June 18. 1752   Thamer Born June 3, 1754

88 Deborah Daugh[r]: to John & Abigail Carter Born April 26, 1756
Prudence Daugh[r]. to John & Sarah Osgood Ditto April 2, 1755
Martha Daug[r]. to Josiah [&] Meriam Wilder born April 21, 1756
Ephraim Son to John & Mary Bayley born March 4, 1755
Elijah Son to Nathan & Azubah Burpee Jun born June y[e] 10th, 1756
Joseph Son to Joseph & Ruth Gary Born August 19th. 1756
Sarah Daughter to Phinehas & Ruth Houghton born Novem[r]. 9th, 1756.
Jephthah Son to Converse & Mercey Richardson born December y[e] 28th, 1755.
Susannah Wilder Daughter to Jothem & Phebe Wilder born December y[e] 3[d] 1756
Thankfull Cleland Daugh[r]: to James & Thankfull Cleland born Dec[r]: 5th, 1754.
Abel Son to Ebenezer & Tabetha Allen Jur: born April 26: 1756
John Son to Joseph & Ales Wheelock born Jan[y] y[e]: 28th, 1757
Simon Butler y[e] Son [of] James & Deborah Butler Born Febuary y[e]: 2[d], 1756.
Stephen Son to Daniel & Sarah Rugg born Feb[ry]: 12. 1757
Samuel Phelps Son [of] Will[m]. & Mary Phelps born Jan[y]. y[e] 22[d], 1757

BOOK FIRST.

The Children of Darius & Deborah Sawyer.

Deborah Born Febuary y⁰ 20th, 1744
Darius born July y⁰ 18th, 1746
Olive born May y⁰: 8th, 1749
Jude born May y⁰: 8th, 1751
Jacob born June y⁰ 22d, 1756

Benjᵃ; Prescott Son to Ebenezer & Jerusha Prescott born Octr: 3, 1755
Prudence Daughʳ to James & Abigail Ross born May 17, 1754
Lucy Cutter Daughʳ to Jabez & Lucy Brooks born May 26, 1757
David Son to Zepheniah & Damoras Williams born July 11, 1757
John Son to Joshua & Mary Fletcher born October y⁰: 1ˢᵗ. 1757
Keziah Daughter to Nathan & Zerviah Rugg born May y⁰: 11th, 1757
William Son to Samll. & Rebeckah Lock born August 23d: 1748

The Children of Revd. John Mellen & his Wife Rebeckah.

Parmela Mellen Born Sept: 5: 1750
John   Ditto   " June 27: 1752
Rebeckah Do.   " April 16, 1754
Sophia Mellen Born Janu: 22, 1756
Henry Do.   " Octoʳ: 24. 1757

John Son to Levi & Kathⁿᵉ: Willard Born Febrʸ. 22d: 1758.
Aaron Son to Aaron & Abigail Sawyer Born Augt: 24, 1756

The Children of John & Ziporah Phelps.

John Born December y⁰ 13th, 1748
Joseph Born Feby. 28. 1751
Aaron Born Novemʳ, 9, 1753
Josiah Born March 16, 1756

Habijah Son to Abijah & Anne Willard Born Octoʳ: 31, 1757.

The Childerin of John & Prudence Manning.

John Manning borne July y⁰: 5th, 1753
Elijah Son to Thomas & Hannah Dole born March y⁰ 17th day, 1755
Elijah Son to John & Mary Baily Born August 9. 1757
Rebeckah Daughʳ. to Benjᵃ. & Ruth Ballard Born April 7. 1758
Amos Son to Aseph & Jane Butler, Born Augt. 6: 1755
Annis Daughʳ. to Aseph & Jane Butler, Born Augt. 16, 1757
Abel Son to Ebenʳ: & Hepzʰ: Biglo, Born Decemʳ: 7. 1754

The Children of Gershom & Mary Flagg

Mary Flagg Born April 27, 1753
Ebenezer Flagg Born April 7, 1756
Gershom Flagg Born April 11, 1758

Olive Daughʳ: to Wᵐ, & Jane Dunsmoor Born May 15, 1757
Elijah Son to John & Prudence Samson Born April 26. 1758
Joseph Son to Andrew & Elisabeth Wilder Born Febrʸ: 18, 1757
Vashti Son [daughter] to Jonᵃ. & Vashti Prescott Born May 24, 1753
Johanah Daugʳ to Jonᵃ, & Vashti Prescott Born April 12, 1756
Peter Son to Jonᵃ, & Vashti Prescott Born April 3, 1758
Jacob Son to John & Ziporah Phelps Born June 13, 1758
Keziah Daugʳ: to George & Keziah Parkhurst born March 10. 1758
Molly Daugʳ; to Peter & Zubee [Azuba] Larken Born September 25, 1756
Thomas Son to Willᵐ. & Mary Tucker born July 25, 1758
Deborah Dafter to Andrew & Eliezebeth Wilder Born y⁰ 10th. Day of august 1755
John Son to John & Annah Stewart Born 26th of June 1747
Jane yᵉ Dafter of John and Annah Stewart Born Feberuary y⁰ 6th 1740
Rebackah Dafter of William Richardson Juner and Patienc his wife Born Feberuary y⁰ 18th: 1748
Patince yᵉ Dafter of said William & Patince Richardson Born September y⁰ 7th 1751:
Mary yᵉ Dafter of said William & Patience Richardson Born May y⁰ 6th New Stile 1754.
John Son to John [&] Keziah May Juʳ: Born March 31ˢᵗ, 1758
Hanah Daughʳ to Phillip & Hanah Goss Born Nov. 20, 1755
Phillip Son to Ditto & Do. born Octoʳ. 17, 1757
John Son to Zephb. & Damaris Williams born Novʳ: 7, 1758

The Childer of Nathan & Zube Burpee.

Zube Born Decem^r: 25, 1753 Mary Born Novr. 23, 1758
Marther Born Decem^r. 26, 1755

Oliver Son to Eph^m: & Abigail Carter born Sept: 12, 1757
Lois Daugh^r. to Solomon & Deliverrence Houghton born Oct^r, 18, 1758
Solomon Son to Ditto Do. born Dece^r. 18, 1758

The Children of Phinehas & Ruth Houghton.

Phinehas & Luke born Dece^r: 30. 1758
    Died Jany 6. 1759. Luke died Jany. 22 1759.
Lydya Daugh^r: to Nath^ll: & Lydia [Kendall] Wilder Born Novr. 16, 1757
Bethesda Daug^r. to Josiah & Grace Houghton Born Dece^r. 21, 1756
John Son to John & Sarah Osgood Born Oct^r: 10, 1757

The Children of Reuben & Anna Lipinwill

Elisabeth Born Sept. 19, 1753 Anna Born Janu^y: 2, 1757
Sarah Born Febru^y: 12, 1755 Reuben Born Decem^r. 23, 1758

Anna Daugh^r. to Willm. & Mary Phelps Born Febry: 28, 1759

DEATHS RECORDED

Bethesda wife of Josiah Houghton deces^d: Aprill ye 9th: 1755. O: S:
Sarah the wife of Ebenezer Allen Decesed June ye 15th 1755.

Amos Son to Darius & Deborah Sawyer Born Augu^t. 13 1758
Jacob Son to Eben Allen Jur & Tebatha Allen Born Feb: 13. 1758
Nathan Son to David & Hanah Nellson Born Nov^r: 17. 1758
Prudence Daug^r: to Ebenezer & Prudence Knight born May 3. 1759
Joseph Son to Joseph & Alles Wheelock Born March 23. 1759
Cibbell Daugh^r: to Jon^a: & Mary Knight born Augt. 27, 1758
Katharine Daug^r: to Levi & Katharine Willard born June 15, 1759
Elisha Son to Elijah & Mary Wood Born Jany: 11, 1759
Abijah Son to John & Lois White Born June, 14, 1759

The Children of Elisha & Lois Bennet

Elisha Born July 12. 1754 John Born May 14, 1759
Lois Born Septem^r: 2. 1757

Jonathan Son [of] Jon^a: & Abigail Osgood Ju^r. Born May 10. 1759
Joshua Son to John & Lydia Rugg Born March 31. 1759
John Son to John & Kath^ue. Brooks Ju^r. Born Dece^r. 31, 1758
Lucy Daug^r. to Eben^r: & Keziah Buss Born April 30: 1759
Mary Daug^r. to Oliver & Ruth Wilder Ju^r. Born Dece^r. 8, 1753
Relief Daug^r: to Eph^m: & Abigail Carter born Sept: 13th: 1759
Prudence Daug^t to Asa & Ladia Wilder Born July 17: 1759
Rebeckah Daft. to Israel & Abigal Moors Born Nov. 15, 1758
Zube Daug to Peter & Zube Larkin Born May 22^d. 1759

The Children of Abner & Mary Sawyer.

Keziah Sawyer Born Decem^r: 22^d. 1739
Hanah Wilder Sawyer Do. Febru^y: 11. 1744
Relief Sawyer Do. Dece^r. 29, 1749
Mary Sawyer Do. Dece^r 13, 1751
Prudence Sawyer Do. March 26, 1757

John Son to James & Thankfull Clealeand born Jan^y: 22, 1758
Aaron Son of Daniel & Sarah Rugg Born Augt. 6. 1759
Thomas Son to Thos. & Elis^a: Beman Born Augt. 25, 1759
Nath^a. Son to Nath^a. & Mary Houghton Born July 16. 1759
Sam^ll: Son to Benj^a: & Mary Osgood Ju^r. Born Aug^t: 19 1757
Mary Daug^r: to Benj^a. & Mary Osgood Born Novr. 18, 1759.
Mary Daug^r. to Louis & Mary Conqueret Born April 19, 1759

The Children of Nath^ll: & Martha Wright
Thomas & Eph^m: Born May 20, 1756
The Children of Mark & Mary Lincoln
Mary Lincoln Born Augt. 28, 1758   Oatis Lincoln Born Dece^r. 17, 1758
Marcy Daugh^r: to John & Marcy Nicholls Ju^r. Born October 6, 1758
The Children of Jashar and Dolley Wyman
Mary and Dolley Born January 16: 1760.
Abigail Daug^r. to W^m: & Esther Richardson born Dece^r: 28, 1758
Rebeckah Daug^r. to James & Mary Carter Born Dece^r. 25. 1755
Luke Son to James & Mary Carter Born Dece^r. 12, 1757
Abigail Daug^t to Jabez & Meriam Fairbank born Dece^r. 31, 1739
Thankfull Daug^r to Amos & Cybell Powers Born Nov^r, 10: 1758
Elihue Son to Jon^a. & Zerviah Wilder Born Feb^r. 11, 1760

93   INTENTIONS OF MARRIAGES ENTRED

Ephraim Wilder and Lucretia Lock's Intentions of marriage Entred March the 2^d: 1755.
Converse Richardson and Marcey Nickolds' Intentions of marriage Entred March the 2^d. 1755.
Josiah Cutting of Narragansett No: 2 and Lidia Meriam of Lexinton, their Intentions of marriage Entred March ye 2^d. 1755
Daniel Robbins & Mary Norcross Intentions of marriage Entred May ye 10th, 1755.
Joseph Beaman & Hannah Knight's Intentions of marriage Entred May ye 31st: 1755
Joseph Steuart & Mary Snow's Intentions of marriage Entred June ye 14th: 1755
Phenehas Wilder and Lois Brown's Intentions of marriage Entred Augt ye 25 1755
Thos: Gary Ju^r: & Jane Wilder Both of Lancaster Intentions of Marriage Enter'd March 20. 1756
Daniel Rugg of Lancaster & Sarah Hastings of Leominster. Intentions of Marriage March 27. 1756
James May of Lancaster & Sarah Cobourn of Leominster Declare Intentions of Marriage March 27, 1756
Eben^r: Beman of Lancaster & Sarah Lilly of Woborne Declar'd the Intentions of Marriage April 11. 1756
James Ballard & Mary Robbins Both of Lancaster Declar'd their Intentions of Marriage April 22. 1856
Sam^ll. Burpee Ju^r. & Martha Brocklebank Both of Lancaster Declar'd their Intentions of Marriage May 20, 1756
Ebenezer Maynard of Westborough & Sarah Knight of Lancaster Declar'd their Intentions of Marriage June 13, 1756
Benj^a. Shead of Lunenburge & Elisabeth Bloors of Lancaster Declar'd their Intentions of Marriage June 21 1756
Isaac Eveleth of Brookfield & Eunice Hutson of Lancaster Declar'd their Intentions of marrige July 20 1756
94 Charles Morris of Lancaster & Elis^a. Lagget of Leominster Declar'd their Intentions of Marriage August 8th. 1756.
Willm Deputron of Lancaster & Sarah Rice of Shirley Declar'd ther Intentions of Marriage Aug^t: 22, 1756
Joseph Temple of Lancaster & Mary Whitmore of Grafton Declar'd their Intentions of Marriage Sept. 4th: 1756.
Henry Haskel Ju^r. Rebeckah Willard both of Lancaster Declar'd ther Intentions of Marriage Nov^r: 9th, 1756.
James Cowey of No. 2 & Mary Pearson of Shrewsbury Leg Declar'd their Intention of Marriage November ye 25th, 1756.
Jonas Brooks & Lucy Sawyer Both of Lancaster Declar'd their Intentions of Marriage Jany: 14, 1757

William Kendall & Mary Lipinwill both of Lancaster Declar'd their Intentions [of] Marriage Jany: 14. 1757
Jabez Brooks & Lucy Sawyer Both of Lancaster Declar'd their Intentions of Marriage January 14. 1757
Joseph Woods & Lucy Butler Both of Lancaster Declar'd their Intentions of marriage February 1. 1757
W^m: Brabrook of Lancaster & Thankfull Dutton of Lunenburg Declar'd their Intentions of Marriage Feby. 25, 1757
Josiah Bennit & Mary Ross Both of Lancaster Declar'd ther Intentions of marriage February 25. 1757
Christian Angel & Hannah Bennett Both of Lancaster Declar'd their Intentions of Marriage, March 25, 1757
John May & Kezeiah Sawyer Both of Lancaster Declar'd their Intentions of Marriage April 1, 1757
Daniel Albart Jr. of Lancaster & Rachall Warner of Harvard Declar'd their Intentions of Marriage April 10th, 1757
Benj^a. Houghton 3^d. of L & Prescillia Wilder Declar'd their Intentions of Marriage, June 12, 1757
Rev^d. Elisha Marsh of Narragansett No. 2 and Susanah Willard of Lancaster Declar'd their Intentions of Marriage June 10, 1757
Silvanus Sawyer of Bolton & Susanah Whetcomb of Lancaster Declar'd their Intentions of Marriage June 1st. 1757
Mark Lincoln & Mary Carter Declar'd y^r: Intentions of marriage Sept. 1, 1757
Dea^n. Josiah Whetcomb & Miss Dorrethy Osgood Declared their Intentions of Marriage, Septem^r: 2. 1757
Mr Sam^ll; Gemwell of Westborough & Mrs Eunice Dunsmoor of Lancaster Declared their Intentions of Marriage Sept. 2. 1757
John Farrah & Anna Chandler Both of Lancaster Declar'd their Intentions of Marriage Octo^r: 20, 1757
Tilly Littlejohn & Hanah Brooks both of Lancaster Declar'd their Intentions of Marriage, Octo^r: 20. 1757
Moses Wilder of Lancaster & Submit Frost of Groton Declar'd their Intentions of Marriage, Sept. 2^d. 1757
Edward Hazen of Stow & Sarah Willard of Lancaster Declar'd their Intentions of Marriage, Octr. 1. 1757
John Warner of Lancaster & Prudence Wheelock of Leominster Declar'd their Intentions of Marr^g: Octo^r: 10, 1757
Phinehas Carter & Mary Sawyer Both Lancaster Declar'd their Intentions of Marriage, October 24, 1757
John Bewny of Lancaster & Dinah Beman of Lancaster Declar'd their Intent^n. of Marriage Octo^r. 24, 1757
James Clerk & Ann Freeman both of Lancaster Declar'd their Intentions of Marriage Novr. 26, 1757
David Nellson & Hanah Baily both of Lancaster Declar'd their Intentions of Marriage December 4. 1757
Philimon Houghton & Rebeckah Gates both of Lancaster Declar'd their Intentions of Marriage December ye 4 1757
Jon^a: Wheelock of Leominster & Thankfull Haskell of Lancaster Declar'd their Intentions of Marriage December 4. 1757
Doc^r. Stanton Prentice of Lancaster & Rebeckah Stevens of Groton Declar'd their Inten^n. of marr^g. Dec^r: 9. 1757
Amos Atherton Jur. & Lydia Gould of Shirly Decl^d. their Intentions of Marriage Decem^r. 9, 1757
Paul Sawyer & Lois Houghton both of Lancaster Declar'd their Intentions of Marriage Decem^r. 16th. 1757
John Brooks Ju^r: & Kath^ne. Dunsmoor Both of Lancaster Declar'd their Intentions of Marriage Feby: 1. 1758
William Crofford of Shrewsbury & Mary Dunsmoor of Lancaster Declar'd their Intentions of Marriage Feb^y: 20, 1758
Ebenezer Pike of Shrewsbury & Lydia Glazier of Lancaster Declar'd their Intentions of Marriage Feb^y: 20. 1758

BOOK FIRST. 85

Daniel Rice of Rutland & Keziah Snow of Lancaster Declar'd their Intentions of Marriage March 6. 1758
Sherebiah Hunt & Deborah Wilder Both of Lancaster Declar'd their Intentions of Marriage March 10. 1758
Lemuel Houghton & Dinah Osgood Both of Lancaster Declar'd their Intentions of Marriage April 20, 1758
Elisha White of Lancaster & Alles Sternes of Bilrica Declar'd their Intentions of marriage May 12. 1758
Thomas Ross Ju^r: & Priscilla Cooper Both of Lancaster Declar'd their Intentions of Marriage May 21, 1758
Jon^a: Osgood Ju^r: & Abigail Whetcomb Both of Lancaster Declar'd their Intentions of Marriage June 21. 1758
Jabez Fairbank Ju^r: of Lancaster & Meriam Davis of Rutland Declar'd their Intentions of Marriage July 5. 1758
Louis Conqueret & Abigail Wheeler Both of Lancaster Declar'd their Intentions of Marriage July 5. 1758.
Hezekiah Whetcomb of Lancaster & Submit Ross of Sudbury Declar'd their Intentions of marrige July 30, 1758
Ebenezer Knight of Lancaster & Prudence Church of Harvard Declar'd their Intentions of Marrige Octo^r: 10 1758
Thos. Willard of Lancaster & Elis^a. Devenport of Shrewsbury Declar'd their Intentions of Marrige Octo^r: 15. 1758
Jasher Wyman Lancaster & Dolly Moffett of Stow Declar'd their Intentions of Marriage Novr. 15, 1758

97   MARRIAGES RECORDED.

June the 11th 1752, Married Ephraim Sawyer and Susannah Richardson pr John Millen
Ezekiel Kindall and Mary May married December ye 25 1752 pr John Millen
Joseph Baley and Lidia Parker married Feb^{ry}. ye 13th 1753 pr John Millen
Nathan Burpee and Azubah Sawyer married March ye 14th 1753 pr John Millen
Nathan Burpee and Azubah Osgood married Jan^{ry}. ye 24th 1754 pr John Millen
Oliver Hoar and Silence Houghton married Febry ye 28th 1754 pr John Millen
Levi Moore and Rebeckah Sawyer married March ye 7th 1754 pr John Millen.
Samuel Rice and Mary Bennit married Aprill ye 10th 1754 pr John Millen.
Aaron Sawyer and Abigail Moore married Aprill ye 25th: 1754 pr John Millen
Dorchester and Peggy Negroes married in Hay time 1754 pr John Millen.
Asa Wilder and Lydia Rugg married December ye 12th 1754 pr John Millen
Jonathan Farebanks and Ruth Houghton married Feb^{ry}. ye 3^d: 1755 pr John Millen
Phinehas Wilder & Lois Brown married Sept: 8, 1756 pr Oliver Wilder Just. Peace.
      the above sent to the County Register

98   *Marriages Consumated by the Rev^d. John Mellen vizt.*

Joseph Stewart & Mary Snow August 28. 1755 pr John Mellen
John Curtis & Elis^a: Robbins November 13, 1755.
Josiah Houghton & Grace Whitney Januy. 6, 1756.
Israel Moore & Abigail How Jany. 15, 1756
Joseph Osgood & Catharine Sawyer — 29, 1756
Elisha Sawyer & Susanah Huck March 8, 1756
Thomas Gary Jur. & Jane Wilder April 22, 1756
Samuel Burpee Ju^r & Martha Brocklebank June 10. 1756
Charles Morris & Elis^a. Laggett, Sept. 5, 1756
Jabez Brooks & Lucy Sawyer, Januy. 27, 1757
James Cowey & Mary Pearson, March 3, 1757
Josiah Bennitt & Mary Ross, March 10 1757
Christian Angell & Hanah Bennitt April 14, 1757
John May & Keziah Sawyer June 1, 1757
Benj^a Houghton 3^d. Priscellia Wilder Augt 11, 1757
Ephraim Osgood & Abigail Houghton Novr. 17, 1757
Tilly Littlejohns & Hannah Brooks, Dece^r. 1. 1757

John Bewney & Dinah Beman Dece^r. 26, 1757
David Nillson & Hanah Baily Decr. 29, 1757.
Jona. Osgood Ju^r: & Abig^l: Whetcomb of Lancaster was married by Col^o Wilder June 20, 1758
Jon^a: Coborn & Sarah Harvey was Maried by Ditto April 1759

Marriages Consumated by Peter Atherton Esqr.

Peter Snow of Havarell & Eunice Goodfree of Lancaster Decr. 19. 1754
Henry Haskel Ju^r. & Rebeckah Willard, Jany. 6 1757
Jacob Williams & Abigail Wyman, Novr. 29 1759
James Willard & Sarah Longley, March 31, 1761

99   MARIGES CONSUMATED

Lancaster Jenuary ye 30th 1755 Josiah Jackson & Mary Darbey of Narraganset No: 2: ware marid pr William Richardson
Moses Wilder & Submit Frost of Groton was married Novr 17 1757, by Col^o Oliver Wilder Esqr:

Marriages Consumated By the Rev^d: Timothy Harrington of Lancaster, Vizt:

Ebenezer Taylor and Mrs. Mary Houghton both of Lanc'ter March y^e. 9th 1749.
Mr: Nathaniel White and Mrs: Lydia Phelps both of Lancaster November ye 9th [29] 1749
Rev^d: John Mellen and Mrs: Rebeca Prentice both of Lancaster November 30th. 1749
Rev^d: John Rogers of Leominster & Mrs: Relief Prentice of Lancaster March ye 27 1750
Mr: Jonathan [Jotham] Biglo of Holden & Mrs: Mary Richardson of Lancaster May y^e: 23^d 1750
Mr: David Taylor of Luningburge & Mrs: Bettey Houghton of Lancaster November 29, 1750
Mr: Willm: Phelps & Mrs: Mary Nicholls both of Lancaster April 25th 1751
Mr: John Beaman & the Widow Sarah Page both of Lancaster May 22^d 1751
Mr: Jonas Fletcher of Groton & Mrs: Ruth Fletcher of Lancaster May 23^d 1751
Mr: David Wilder & Mrs: Martha White both of Lancaster, December ye 4th 1751
Mr: Josiah Cutting of Shrewsbury & Mrs: Orpha Houghton of Lancaster January 2^d 1752
Mr: Joseph Kilborn & Mrs. Mary Sawyer both of Lancaster, Jan^y: 22 1732
Mr: David Baldwin of Billerica & ye Widow Kezia Bennitt of Lancaster June 18th 1752
Mr: Rebuen Lippenwell & Mrs: Anna Wyman of Lancaster June 18th 1752
Primas Lew of Groton & Rose Canterbury of Lancaster [free] Negroes October y^e: 18th 1752
Mr: Enock Hill and Mrs: Sarah Rugg of Lancaster, October y^e: 24th 1752
Capt: Abijah Willard & Mrs: Anna Prentice of Lancaster November y^e: 15th 1752
Mr: Nath^{ll}. Joslyn & Mrs: Martha Fairbank of Lancaster November y^e: 30 1752
Mr: James Richardson jur. of Leominster & Mrs: Hannah House of Lancaster, January 10 1753
Mr: Asa Harris & Mrs: Abigal Bennitt of Lancaster January 10 1753
Mr: Phinehas Houghton and Mrs: Ruth Osgood of Lancaster, June ye 6th 1753
Mr: Thomas Haywood of Luningburge & Mrs: Elisabeth Richardson of Lancaster July 11th 1753
Mr: William Smith of Townsend & Mrs: Martha Dunsmoor of Lancaster November ye 6 1753
Mr: Joshua Reed of Lexingtown & Mrs: Susannah Houghton of Lancaster. Novembr. 27 1753
Mr: Benj^a: Osgood jun^r. & Mrs: Mary Carter of Lancaster, December ye 5th 1753
Mr: John Divoll and Mrs: Elisabeth Beaman of Lancaster, December ye 26 1753
Mr: Aaron Osgood jun^r: and Mrs Hannah Warner of Lancaster, March ye 6th 1754

BOOK FIRST.

Docter Willm: Dunsmoor of Lancaster & Mrs: Hannah Sumner of Kellingly Jany: 7th 1755
Mr: Amos Sawyer junr. and Mrs: Mary Rugg of Lancaster, Jany: 9 1755
Mr: Tiras Houghton and Mrs: Rachell House of Lancaster Jany: — 1755
Mr: Samuel Prentice and Mrs: Prudence Osgood of Lancaster, Febuy, 13, 1755
Mr: William Tucker and Mrs: Mary Kendall of Lancaster, Febuay. 20. 1755
Mr: Nathl: Wilder jur. & Mrs: Lydia Kendall of Lancaster, Febuay. 27 1755
100 Mr: George Parkhurst of Lancaster & Mrs: Keziah Whetcomb of Bolton March y^e: 13th 1755
Mr: Converse Richardson and Mercey Nicholls of Lancaster March 27. 1755
Mr: Ephraim Wilder ye 3^d & Mrs: Lucretia Lock of Lancaster, April y^e: 3^d 1755
Mr: David Thomas of Pelham and Mrs: Elisabeth Harper of Lancaster November 18 1755
Mr: Jabez Fairbank of Lancaster & the Widow Naomi Dupee Leominster Jany: 22^d 1756
Mr: Benj^a: Shedd of Luningburge and Mrs: Elisabeth Blowers of Lancaster, July 19 1756
Mr: Isaac Eveleth of Brookfield and ye Widow Eunice Hudson of Lancaster, September 2^h, 1756
William De Pution of Lancaster & Mrs: Sarah Rice of Shirley District, October ye 12th 1756
The Rev^d: Elisha Marsh of Narragansett No 2 & Mrs: Susanna Willard of Lancaster July 25, 1757
Mr: William Kendall and Mrs: Mary Lyppenwill of Lancaster August 15 1757
Mr: Samuel Gemwell of Westbro' and ye Widow Eunice Dunsmoor of Lancaster October 11th 1757
Mr: Mark Lincoln & Mrs: Mary Carter of Lancaster, October y^e: 20, 1757
Dea^n: Josiah Whitcomb of Bolton & Mrs: Dorratha Osgood of Lancaster October ye 24 1757
Mr: Joseph Woods and Mrs: Lucy Butler of Lancaster, November 30 1757
Mr: Jonathan Wheelock of Leominster, and Mrs: Thankfull Haskell Lancaster Dec^r: 27 1757
Mr. Elijah Woods of Lancaster, and Mrs: Mary Goodfree of Harvard February 2^h 1758
Ens: Phinehas Carter & Mrs: Mary Sawyer of Lancaster, Febuary 22^d 1758
Mr: Phillemon Houghton & Mrs: Rebecca Gates of Lancaster, Febuary 23^d 1758
Mr: Paul Sawyer and Mrs: Lois Houghton of Lancaster, March 7 1758
Mr: John Brooks and Mrs: Katherine Dunsmoor of Lancaster, March 8 1758

By Col^o. Jos: Wilder

James Ballard & Mary Robbins Both of Lancaster May 11, 1756.
Ebenezer Maynard of Westborough & Sarah Knight of Lancast^r: July 16, 1756
Phinehas Willard & Rebeckah Willard Both of Harvard Jany. 5, 1758
Sherebiah Hunt & Debora Wilder Both of Lancaster April 2, 1755
Luke Richardson & Damarius Carter Both Leom^r: Sept: 7, 1758
Daniel Knight Lancaster & Elis^a. Houghton Leom^r: May 12. 1758
Levi Nicholls & Elis^a, Sawyer Both Lancaster, Nov. 29, 1759

Marriages Consummated by David Osgood Esqr:

John Gibbs & Elisabeth Kendall both of Lancaster, Septr. 3 1760
Samuel Titus of Ipswich Canada & Ann Bigelow of Westminster Destrict. Septr. 11 1760
Samuel Osgood of Narragansett No: 6 & Thankfull Matthews of Lancaster, Septr. 18 1760
Seth Harrington of Westminster Destrict and Priscilla Houghton of Lancaster, Novr. 13 1760
Josiah Osgood & Jane Boynton both of Lancaster Decr. 9. 1760
101 James Dudley & Mehetable Woodbary both of Concord December ye 25th 1755 pr Joseph Wilder.

Marriages Consumated by the Rev^d. John Mellen

John Farrar and Anna Chandler, January 11. 1758

Lemuel Houghton and Dinah Osgood, May 1 1758
Thomas Ross jun'. and Priscilla Cooper, June 8 1758
Nathaniel Houghton and Mary Richardson, June 29 1758
Lewis Conqueret and Abigail Wheeler, July 23 1758
Daniel Rice and Keziah Snow, Novem'. 2 1758
Barzillai Holt and Lois Allard, February 22 1759
David Osgood jun'. and Sarah Bayley, April 12 1759
Samuel Snow and Sarah Bennitt, July 19 1759
Jonathan Bayley and Eunice Houghton, January 16 1760
Elisha Wilder and Mehitabel Dresser, January 17 1760
Jonathan Osgood and Joanna Beaman, January 17 1760
Josiah Kendall jun'. and Esther Sawyer, March 26 1760
Israel Moor and Katharine Sawyer, October 9 1760
Samuel Ross and Katharine Gary, November 27 1760
Ezra Sawyer jun'. and Kezia Sawyer, December 11 1760
Thos. Gates & Abigail Wilder was Married by Col^o. Oliver Wilder Esqr. April 23^d. 1761

By W^m. Richardson Esqr.

Josiah Jackson & Mary Darby Both of Nar[aganset] No. 2 Jany. 30 1755
Warrin Snow of Leicester & Anna Harvey Octo^r 25 1759
Edward Houghton & Lucretia Richardson, Oct^r: 16 1760
W^m. Phelps & Mary Flagg. Sep^t. 17, 1760
    all the Foregoing Marriages Deliv'd to the County Register

102   INTENTIONS OF MARRIAGE ENTER'D—

David Osgood Ju^r. & Sarah Bailey Both of Lancaster Declar'd their Intentions of Marriage April 10, 1759
Sam^{ll} Snow & Sarah Bennit Both of Lancaster Declar'd their Intentions of Marriage April 10 1759
Hooker Osgood Ju^r: & Susanah Sawyer Both of Lancaster Declar'd their Intentions of Marriage April 15 1759
Joseph Cobley of No. 6 & Mary Wilder of Lancaster Declar'd their Intentions of Marriage May 10, 1759
Thos Page of Leominster & Mary Knight of Lancaster Declar'd their Intentions of Marriage July 15, 1759
Ezekiel Haskell of Lancaster & Rebeckah Howard of Chelmsford Declar'd their Intentions of marriage, Sept, 1, 1759
Levi Nicholls & Elis^a: Sawyer Both of Lancaster Declar'd their Intentions of marriage Sept: 15, 1759
Jesse Ross & Ruth Rugg Both of Lancaster Declar'd ther Intentions of mariage October the 20th, 1759.
Elisha Wilder & Mehetebal Dresser Both of Lancaster Declar'd their Intentions of marriage Novr. 1, 1759
Jon^a. Bailey Ju^r. & Eunice Houghton Both of Lancaster Declar'd their Intentions of mariage Nov. 1. 1759
Jacob Williams of Shirley & Wid^w. Abigail Wyman of Lancaster Declar'd their Intentions of mariage Nov^r: 11. 1759
Jona. Osgood & Joanna Beman Both of Lancaster enter'd their Intentions of marriage Dece^r ye 10 1759
Daniel Willard of Lancaster & Sarah Dickerson of Groton Declar'd their Intentions of marriage Decr 20 1759
Josiah Kendall Ju^r. & Esther Sawyer Both of Lancaster Declar'd their Intentions January 5, 1760
Thos. Grant & the Wid^w: Hanah Churchill Both of Lancaster Declar'd their Intentions of marriage Jany. 15, 1760.
Levi Kendall & Elis^a Dorrety Both of Lancaster & Brookfield Declar'd their Intentions of Marriage May 10 1760
Sam^{ll}. Osgood & Thankfull Matthews Declar'd their Intentions of Marriage May 10 1760

103   Mary ye Dafter of Thomas & Mary Ross Born September ye 28th, 1733
Deliverance ye Dafter of Thomas & Mary Ross Born June ye 13th 1735

Mehetibel Eager wife to fortunatus Died March 29 1759

The Births of the Children of Thomas and Mary Ross

Thomas Born Decr ye 9th 1736
Samuel Born Jany. ye 16th 1738
Roger Born Sept ye 10th 1740
Tamer Born august ye 9th 1743
Ebenezer Born June ye 7th, 1747
William Born Sept ye 17th 1749
Hannah Born march 30th 1752

Mary Ross wife to Thomas Ross Died November ye 29 1765
Jonathan Son of Thomas & Mary Ross Born ye 3^d Day of agust 1754 and Decesed October ye 21st 1755.

Daniel Fleman Son to Adam and Margrett Born March 20: 1760
Achsah Daug^r to Aseph & Jennet Butler Born Feby. 21, 1760
Joshua Son to Eph^m. & Zube Willard Born April 15, 1759
Jonas Son to John & Mary Prescott Born Augt 5, 1754.
Ruth Daugh^r to John & Mary Prescott Born Augt. 16. 1757.
Relief Daug^r. to Joseph & Hauah Abbot Born May 11, 1759.

104   *The Children of Ephr^m. & Mikiel Reper.*

Nath^{ll} Roper Borne ye 23 of Febuary 1757
Enock Roper Borne y^e. 7 of Dece^r. 1758

The Chrildrin of Isaac & Eunice Eveleth

W^m. Borne July 3^d 1757.
Eunice Borne Novb. 28. 1758.
John born December 14 1760

The Children of Jacob & Esther Smith

Mary Smith Born Feby. 11, 1752
Benj^a. Smith born April 6, 1754.
Esther Smith born June 13, 1757.

John Winn Son to Jacob & Sarah Winn was born April 17 1760
Ruth Daughter to Joseph & Ruth Gary was born Sepr 16. 1747
Joseph Son to Joseph & Ruth Gary was born July 19. 1760
Katharine Daughter of Nathan & Ziriviah Rugg was born Nov^r, 29 1759
Dinah ye Daughter of Ezra & Dinah Houghton was born March 20 1760
Molley Daughter of Abner & Martha Haskell born May 20 1760
James Son of Eph^m. & Elis^t. Divoll, born Oct^r: 8 1760
Zerubbabel Son to Nathan & Sarah Eager born August 17 1757
Zilpah Daughter to Nathan & Sarah Eager born Novr. 24 1759
Stephen Son of Amos & Mary Rugg born August 28 1758
Olive Daughter of Amos & Mary Rugg born April 6 1760
Mary the Daughter of Joshua & Mary Fletcher was born June 23 1760
Katharine Daug^r. to Joseph & Catherine Osgood born Octob^r: 18, 1760.
John Son to Peter & Zube Larkin born Jany. 27, 1761.
Zube Daug^r. to David & Sarah Osgood Born April 6, 1760

The Children of Benj^a. Willard

Abigail Born April 12, 1750
Benj^a Born Septr. 18, 1753
Daniel Born Octo^r. 16, 1755
Lois Born Octo^r. 16, 1755
Judah Born Octo^r 18, 1757.

105 Nath^{ll}: Wyman of Lancaster & Submit Brooks of Woburn Declar'd their Intentions of marg. March 13. 1761
Thos Gates & Abigail Wilder Declar'd ther Intention of marriage March 13 1761

Phinias, Son to Phinias & Ruth Houghton Born aprel 9: 1761
Katharine Daug^r: to John & Prudence Samson Born April 9, 1761
Thankfull Daug^r: to Eben^r: & Tabitha Allen Ju^r. Born March 31. 1760
Joseph Son to Nath^{ll}: & Martha Wright Born May 29, 1760
Asa Son to James & Mary Carter Born April 27, 1760
Hanah Daug^r: to Jabez & Meriam Fairbank born March 8, 1761
Sarah Daug^r: to W^m. & Mary Tucker Born april 22, 1761
Peter Son to Andrew & Elisabeth Wilder Born April 10, 1761

7

Oliver Son [to] Jos. & Allis Whelock Born May 6, 1761
Johanah Dafter to Jon^a. & Varshter Prescott Born August 13. 1760
William Son to John & Katharine Brook Jur. born March 10: 1761
Nathaniel Son to Ebenezer & Mary Taylor born Octo^r. 15, 1756
Josiah Son to John & Deborah Hadley Born March 7, 1747
Mary Daug^r. to John & Ditto.   Born Octr. 18, 1749
Elis^a. Daug^r. to John & Do.   Born Novr. 6 1752
Charles Son to John & Do.   born June 22, 1756
Abraham Son to Do.   born Sept. 26, 1759
Roger Son to Willm. & Mary Phelps Born March 1, 1761
Abel Son to Darius & Deborah Sawyer born Novr. 1, 1760
Jacob Son to John & Mary Glazier born Augt. 3, 1761
Eph^m. Son to George & Keziah Parkhurst Born Febuary 28: 1759
106 Mary Dafter to Elijah & Mary Woods borne May 31: 1761
Jonas Son to Josiah & Grace Houghton born Augt. 5, 1760
Elis^a. Daft. to Nathan & Azuba Burpee born febuary 12, 1761
John Son to Elijah & Thankfull Beman born Dece^r. 6, 1760
Peirses Daug^r: to Saul & Mary Houghton born Sept: 12, 1759
Betty Daug^r: to Thos. & Elisabeth Willard born Jany. 12, 1759
John Son to Thos. & Elis^a. Willard born July 6, 1761
Reuben Wheeler Son to Jotham & Phebe Wilder born July 6. 1761.
Philemon Son to Solomon & Deliverance Houghton born march 19 1761
Moses Son to Ezekiel & Rebeckah Haskell born May 25, 1760
Vashti Daug^r: to Ebene^r: & Prudence Knight born Dece^r: 23^d. 1760
Sam^{ll}. Son to W^m. & anna Jewett born Oct^r: 21, 1759
Jon^a. Son to W^m. & anna Jewett born August 17, 1761
Oliver Son to Aaron & Abigail Sawyer Born Feb^r: 2, 1759
Parna Daug^r. to Aaron & Abigail Sawyer Born Sept: 16 1761
Prudence Daug^r. to Sam^{ll}. & Prudence Prentice Born Feb^r. 6: 1756
Anna Daug^r. to Sam^{ll}. & Prudence Prentice Born June 23, 1758
John Son to Sam^{ll}. & Prudence Prentice Born Decem^r. 17. 1760
Nathan Son to Nathan & Sarah Eager Born June 21 1761
Lemuel Son to Jesse & Ruth Ross Born Jany. 5, 1760
Reuben Son to Jesse & Ruth Ross born Dece^r. 26, 1761
Prudence Daugh^r. to Daniel & Sarah Rugg born Dece^r: 17, 1761
Eunice Daug^r. to Jon^a. & Eunice Baily Ju^r born Jany. 19, 1761
Sam^{ll}. Son to W^m: & Esther Richardson ye third born June 27, 1760
Nathan Son to David & Sarah Osgood Ju^r. born July 16, 1761
Luke Son to Robert & Rebeckah Fletcher born Octo. 25 1759
107 Martha Daugh^r. to Jon^a. & Zerviah Wilder Born Novr. 3^d. 1761
David Son to Eben^r. & Lydia Pike Born Dece^r: 29 1758
Eph^m: Son to Eben^r & Lydia Pike Born Feby. 1 1761

Children of Abner & Eunice [Osgood] Wilder.

David Born Nov^r: 21, 1756   Nathan born March 3, 1760
Levi Born Augt. 10, 1758

Thos. Son to Israel & Katharine Moor Born Sept: 3^d. 1761.
Reuben Son to Asa & Lydia Wilder Born Jany. 19 1762

The Children of Levi & Rebeckah Moor &c

Rebeckah Moor Born Nov^r: 26. 1754   Levi Moor born Nov^r: 5. 1759
Prudence Moor born April 28, 1756   Molly Moor born Jany. 28, 1762
Hanah Moor born December 23, 1757
Timothy Son to Jon^a: & Admonition Kendall Ju^r. born July 6th: 1761

The Children of Joseph & Patience White.

Sarah White born July 10th; 1757   Martha White born Jany. 7, 1761
Ruth White born April 17, 1759

Ebenezer Son of Jerem^h: & Elis^a: Burpee born Jany. 9, 1758
Jeremiah Son to Jerem^h. & Elis^a. Barpee born Novr. 15, 1770

BOOK FIRST. 91

Solomon Son to Adam & Margret Fleeman born April 10, 1762
Daniel Son ———
Gardnier Son to Gardnier & Martha Wilder born Sept. 17: 1761 & Deceased Sept. 17, 1761.

the Children of Dorchester & Margret Negro

Margret Born May 7, 1756 Daniel Born April 5 1758
Ishmail Born July 1 1757

108 *The Children of Eph^m. & Lucretia [Locke] Wilder 3^d*

Ephraim Wilder born April 29, 1756 Lucretia Wilder born June 17, 1761
Tim^o. Wilder born Decr. 2. 1757

Jon^a. Son to Jon^a. & Mary Knight Born Jany. 21 1761
Pamela Daugh^r. to Amos & Mary Rugg April 12. 1762
Katharine Daugh^r to Elijah & Katharine Houghton borne June 25, 1762
Benj^a. Son to John & Parna Brooks born June 1, 1762
Eunice Daug^r, to Joseph & Katharine Osgood born Aug^t: 4, 1762
Benj^a. Son to Ebenezer & Keziah Buss born Decem^r. 27, 1761.
Samuel Son to Abner & Eunice Wilder born Aug^t; 21. 1762
Hitte Daught. to Moses & Margrett Burpee Born March 21 1759
Eben^r. Son to Moses & Margrett Burpee Born Jany. 30 1761
Timothy Son to Tim^o. & Sarah Whiting Born June 17, 1758
John Son to Tim^o. & Sarah Whiting Born Feby. 24, 1760
Christopher Son to Tim^o. & Sarah Whiting Born Novr. 27, 1761
Salmon Son to Ezra & Dinah Houghton born Sept 24 1762
John Son to Robert & Rebeckah Fletcher born May 12, 1762
Jon^a. Son to Roger & Mary Ross born april 20. 1762,
Hanah Daug^r. to Reuben & Anna Lipinwill born Sept: 5, 1762
Betty Daug^r. to Thos. & Prissilla Ross Ju^r born April 28, 1762
Martha Daug^r. to Gardnier & Martha Wilder Born Jany. 14th. 1763
Lucy Daug^r. to Nath^ll: & Martha Wright Born August 26, 1762
Zerviah Daug^t. to Jon^a. Ju^r. & Eunice Bayley born Sept. 3 1762

109 *The age of the Children of Iasaac Kilborne*

Hanah borne Augt. 15th. 1750 Calvin Born Novr. 1st. 1757
John born April — 1753 Sarah Born July 15, 1759
Isaac born December 1st. 1754 Mary Born April 1st. 1761
Elisabeth Born March — 1756 William Born Sept. 7 . 1762

Oliver Son to Francis & Susanah Fullum born Novr. 29, 1761
Elihu Son to Jon^a. Ju^r. & Joanna Osgood born Sept. 21 1762
David Son to Amos & Elis^a: Atherton born July 27. 1755
Samuel Son to Ebenez^r: & Tabitha Allen Ju^r. Born June 28, 1762
Phebe Daug^r. to John & Keziah May Ju^r. Born Augt. 16. 1762
Eph^m. Son to Fortunatus & Thamer Eager born May 3, 1762
Eunice Daug^r. to Josiah & Jane Osgood born March 3, 1761
Mary Daug^r. to Josiah & Jane Osgood born May 28 1762
Naomi Daugh^t. to John & Elis^a. Gibb born Novr. 4 1761
Nath^ll. Son to Thos. & Abigail Kendall born March 28. 1763
James Son to James & Mary Ballard born Novr. 1, 1758
Abigal Daugh^t. to Israel & Catharine Moors born Decr. 23 1762
Esther Daugh^t. to Darius [&] Deborah Sawyer born April 4 1763
Ruth & Keziah Daught^s. to Phinehas & Ruth Houghton born May 8 1763
Anna Daugh^r. to David & Hanah Nellson born Dece^r. 20 1760
Marcy Daugh^r: to David & Hanah Nellson born May 2, 1763
Abel Son to Eph^m. & Abigal Carter born Decr. 22 1761
Submit Daug^r to Elijah & Mary Osgood born April 14. 1763
110 Joseph Son to Joseph & Agnus Sawyer born June 6th: 1762
Peter Son to Joshua & Mary Fletcher born Sept. 5 1762
Ephraim Son to Peter & Zuba Larkin born March 28, 1763
Oliver Son to John & Mary Gleizier born May 23 1763
Levi Son to Barz^ll. & Lois Holt born May 6 1760

Abial Son to Barz. & Lois Holt born May 11 1763
Dorrethy Daugh^r. to Nath^{ll}. & Elisabeth Willard born March 8 1763
Martha Daugh^r. to Joseph & Allis Wheelock born Sept: 7: 1763
Jesse Son to Jesse & Ruth Ross born Sept. 29 1763
Sarah Daug^t. to John & Deborah Hadley born march 1 1762
Peter Son to Nath^{ll}. & Lucy [Knight] Wilder born May 25 1763
Anna Daug^r. to John & Prudence Warner born Feby. 17. 1763
James Son to James & Sarah Willard born March 1, 1761
Prudence Daug^t. to Jacob & Sarah Wing born Octr. 29 1763
Manassah Son to Eph^m: & Elisabeth Divoll born Dece^r. 14 1763

The Children of John & Mary Prescott

Jonas was Born augt. 6 1754
Ruth was Born augt. 16 1757
Jon^a. was Born July 4 1761
Joseph was Born augt. 5, 1763

Abner Son to Ezra & Kezia Sawyer Jur. born Novr. 8 1761
Dorrethy Daug^t. to Nath^{ll}. & Elis^a: Willard born March 8 1763
Peter Son to Willm. & Esther Richardson 3^d, born July 2^d, 1762
Elisabeth Daug^r. to John & Elis^a: Phelps born May 6th, 1763
W^m. Son to W^m [&] Anna Jewit Born March 1st. 1763

111   The Children of Sam^{ll}. & Prissilla Thurston

Prissilla was born March 24 1752
John was born Novr. 15 1754
Judith was born Jany. 9 1757
Silas was born Decr. 12 1758
Mary was born Octr. 17 1761
Pearson was born Decr. 9 1763

Lucy Daugh^r. to Tilly & Zilpah Moors born June 18, 1763
Zimri Son to Isaac & Eunice Eveleth born Aug^t, 31. 1763
Abigal Daug^t. to Roger & Mary Ross born Jany. 29 1764
Abel Son to James 3^d. & Anna Houghton born aug^t. 16, 1763
Saml. Johnson Son to Daniel & Lydia Johnson born March 8th. 1758
Frances Daug^r. [of] Aaron & Elisabeth Willard born Sept. 9th. 1762
Jabez Son to Joseph & Hanah Beman born March 20, 1762
Lucy Daug^r. to Joseph & Hanah Beman born Jany. 20th. 1764
Hepsibah Daugh^t. to Moses & Margret Burpee born Sept. 9 1763
Thomas Son to Nathan & Zube Burpee Born July 10th: 1763
Rebeckah Daug^r. to Thos. & Abigail Gates Born June 25. 1762
Benj^a. Son to Benj^a. Ju^r. & Axey Houghton born March 30th 1764

the Children of Amos & Mary Sawyer

Lydea born Decem^r. 19 1755
Relief born Decr. 1 1758
Calvin born Octr. 29 1760
Luther born Augt. 21 1762
Releaf born May 24 1756 [66?]

John Son to Willm: & Esther Richardson 3^d. born April 14th: 1764
Hiram Son to Solomon & Diliverance Houghton born June 25, 1763
Anna Daug^t. to David Ju^r. & Sarah Osgood born May 1 1764
112   Benj^a. Whitemore Son to W^m: & Mary Willard Ju^r. born June 26, 1762
Elisabeth Daug^r. to Adam & Margret Fleeman born April 13. 1764.
Frances Daug^r: to Aaron & Elisabeth Willard Jr. born Sep^t: 9th. 1762
Eben Son to Aaron & Elis^a: Willard Ju^r. born May 19th. 1764
Sarah Daug^t. to Amos & Mary Sawyer born June 7 1764
Silence Daug^r. to Jon^a: & Joana Osgood born March 14 1764
Jothem Son to Elijah & Mary Woods born Jany. 1, 1764
Dorrethy Daug^r: to Joseph & Hanah Abbott born Dece^r: 12, 1762
Elis^a. Daug^r. to Jeremiah & Elis^a. Burpee born oct^r. 19: 1763
Abigail Daug^r. to Reuben & anna Lipinwill born Sept: 6. 1764
Phinehas Son to Phi^s. & Lois Wilder born Feby. 28, 1761.
Abijah Son to Tilly & Katurah White born Sept: 31. 1762
Eunice Daugh^r. to Tilly & Katurah White born October 8th. 1764
Mehetibel Daug^r. to Fortunatus & Thamer Eager born Aug^t: 21. 1764
Levi Son to Silas & Abigail How born October 20 1764
Elisabeth Daug^t. to Jon^a. & Vashti Prescott born Novr. 15 1762

BOOK FIRST.

Birth of the Children of the Rev⁴ John & Rebeckah Mellen

Pamelia born Sept'. 5, 1750
John Ditto. June 27, 1752
Rebeckah Do. April 16, 1754.
Sophia Do. Janu'. 22, 1756
Henry Do. October 24. 1757
Mary born October 16. 1760
Thomas Do. Septem'. 16. 1762
Prentice Do. October 11, 1764.
Charlotte Do. February 23. 1768

Abigail Daug': to Ephraim & Elisabeth Reed born May 8, 1762
Molly Daug'. to David & Keziah Baldwin born Nov'. 25 1764
Elijah Son to Eph^m. & Abigail Carter born Feb'. 21 1754
Abigail Daugt. to Aaron & Abigail Sawyer born July 2ᵈ. 1764
Ruth Daug': to Joseph & Mary Kilborne born Augt. 15 1759
Sam^ll. Son to Jos: & Mary Kilborne born May 23, 1762
113 Abel Son to Josiah & Esther Locke born January 16, 1765
Sam^ll. Son to Josiah & Jane Osgood borne April 29 1764
Jon^a. Son to W^m. & Anna Jewett Died Sept. 7. 1764
Jon^a. 2ᵈ Son to W^m. & Anna Jewett Born Jan'. 12. 1765
Moses Son to Moses & Mary Sawyer Born May 29th, 1764.
Benj^a. Son to Jon^a. Ju'. & Eunis Baley Born May 12 1764

the Names of the Childeren of Isaac & Mary Brooks.

Isaac Brooks born June 3ᵈ, 1748 at Concord
Jacob Brooks Ditto. July 2. 1749 at Lexington
Jonathan Brooks Do. Febry. 24, 1751 Ditto
Seth Brooks Do. Septem'. 10 1752 Harvard.
Mary Brooks Do. Sept'. 15: 1754 at Bolton.
Sarah Brooks Do. June 30 1756, at Ditto.

Lucy Daugh^t. to Nath^ll. & Lucy Wilder born Jany 29: 1765
Silas Son to Ebenez: & Keziah Buss born August 28, 1764.
Rufus Son to Joshua & Mary Fletcher born Oct'. 14 1764
Keziah Daug': to John & Keziah May Ju'. born October 8, 1764

The Children of Josiah & Mary Bennit

Asa Bennitt born October 7, 1757
Ephraim Bennit born Nove'. 4. 1760
Molly Bennit born April 2, 1753

The Children of Thoˢ. & Thankfull May

Benj^a. May born Oct'. 23 1755
Thomas May born July 26, 1757
Levi May born July 25, 1759
Prude May born Dec'. 30, 1762

Ephraim Son to Tilly & Zilpah Moors born March 1ˢᵗ, 1765
Calvin Son to Stephen & Elisᵃ. Keyes born March 17th. 1765
Catharine Daugᵗ. to Israel & Catharine Moors born Feby. 12, 1765
Susanna Daug' to John & Prudence Warner born Decem'. 31, 1764
114 Calvin Son to Andrew & Elisabeth Wilder born October 19th: 1764.

Births of the Children of Phinehas Phelps

Phinehas born Feby. 3 1761
Sarah born Decemb'. 16 1762
Olive born June 3 1764

Ruth Daughter to Ezra & Dinah Houghton May 30 1765
John Son to John & Deborah Headley born January 6. 1765
Rosanah Daug'. to Thos. & Barsheba Hendeson born Sept. 25, 1763
Lucy Daugh': to Peter & Zube Larkin born May 21, 1765
Aaron Son to John Sergeant & Han^h. Sergeant born Octob'. 14 1764
Mary Daugh'. to Josiah & Jane Divoll born August 19th: 1761
Josiah Son to Josiah & Jane Divoll born July 24th. 1763
Levi Son to Josiah & Jane Divoll born October 10, 1765
Ephraim Son to Nath^ll. & Mary Houghton born March 28, 1761
Stephen Son to Nath^ll. & Mary Houghton born May 8, 1765
Samuel Son to Sam^ll. & Prudence Prentice born July 11, 1763
David Kendall Son to Ezekiel & Mary Kendall born Feby. 24, 1757

Sarah Kendall Daug^r. to Ezekiel & Mary Kendall born June 18 1759
Ezekiel & Elisabeth Kendall Son & Daughter to Ezekiel & Mary Kendall born March 9. 1763

Children of Daniel & Mary Robbins.

Hanah Robbins born July 8, 1756
Mary Robbins born Janu^y. 27, 1758
Susan^h. Robbins born April 17 1760
Jemima Robbins born July 17, 1762
Elisabeth Robbins born April 2, 1764

Children of Ephr^m: Sawyer of Lancaster

Ephraim Sawyer Ju^r. Born May 27. 1753
Dorrethy Sawyer Ditto June 6, 1755
Josiah Sawyer Ditto January 27, 1757
John Sawyer Do. September 12. 1759
James Sawyer Born December 10 1761
Peter Sawyer Do. August 10th. 1763
Susanah Sawyer Do. May 2, 1765

115   Children of Peter & Dorethy Thurston
Rebeckah born June 30 1762   Gates born Novr. 6 1764

Ameriah Son to Joseph & Agnus Sawyer born Octob^r. 14, 1765
Ama Daugh^r. to Levi & Ama Houghton born Nov^r: 30, 1764
Deborah Daugh to Jon^s. & Deborah Wilder Ju^r. born Octr. 20: 1765
Thos. Son to Darius & Deborah Sawyer born aug^t. 21: 1765

The Children of Levi & Rebeckah Moor

Ezra born Decr. 23: 1763   Patience born Novr. 20: 1765
Joseph Son to Abner & Martha Haskell born oct^r. 27: 1765
Suse Daugh^t. to David Ju^r. & Sarah Osgood born Jany. 16: 1766
Rachel Daugh^t. to Robert & Rachel Phelps born Decr. 18. 1765
Archeppus Son to Joseph & Allis Wheelock born Jany. 22 1766
Jonas Son to John & Mary Glaizer born Jany. 13, 1766
Mary Daug^t. to David & Hanah Nellson born Feby. 26, 1766
Jothem Son to Jon^a. & Lois Prescott born Jany. 10: 1765
Joseph Son to Manassah & Elisabeth Bixby born Jany. 4: 1766
Jothem Son to Barz^{ll}. & Lois Holt born Jany. 10 1765
Eph^m. & Martha Son & Daug^t. to Sam^{ll}. & Mary Bixby Born April 11 1754.
Mary Son to James 3. & Anna Houghton born March 30: 1765

Children of Nath^{ll}. & Mary Wyman.

Katharine born Septem^r. 17, 1753   Martha born May 13. 1756

Benj^a. Son [to] Nath^{ll}. & Submit Wyman born Septem^r. 21, 1765
Nathan Son to Nathan & Zube Burpee born April 27. 1766.
Zenobia Daugh^t. to Jothem & Rebeckah Flagg born octr. 5, 1765
Longley Son to James & Sarah Willard born March 22, 1764
Susanah Daugh^r. to John & Prudence Warner born August 7th; 1766
Molly Daug^r. to John & Keziah May born Septe^r. 10: 1766
116   Abel Son to Josiah & Esther Locke born August 12th. 1766
Asa Son to Timo. & Sarah Goodenow born Feby: 14: 1766
Daniel Son to Daniel Ju^r. & Elis^a. Rugg born Sept. 13, 1766
Mary Daugh^t. to Amos & Mary Sawyer born Decr 3: 1766
John Son to John & Lucy Locke born Sept. 28: 1766
Thos. Son to Sam^{ll}. & Prudence Prentice born Feby: 11; 1766
Barsheba Daug^t. to Thos & Lydea Bennitt born Jany 2: 1767
Mary Daug^t. to Elisha & Mary Bennitt born march: 22, 1765
Sam^{ll}. Son to Nath^{ll}. & Elis^a. Willard, born June 25: 1765
Joseph Son to Nath^{ll}. & Elis^a. Willard born Sept. 17: 1766
Eunice Daug^t. to Francis & Susanah Fullom born aug^t. 25: 1764

The Children of Joshua & Rebeckah Phelps.

Elisabeth Phelps born July 13, 1745
Rebeckah Phelps Ditto Octob^r. 24 1746
Sarah Phelps   Do. August 22^d. 1748
Abel Phelps   Do: August 7 1750
Lydia Phelps   Do: August 14 1753
Peter Phelps born August 3 1755 & Decas'd April 15. 1757.
Relief Phelps born October 23 1757
Joshua Phelps Ditto Septem^r. 22 1766
Deborah Phelps Do. October 31 1764

Hanah Daug^t. to Christopher & Hanah Osgood Born Decr. 11: 1766
Abigail Daug^t. to Silas & Abigail How born march 10 1766
Mary Daug^t to Roger & Mary Ross born Octr. 28 1766
Sam^{ll}. Son to Jon^a. & Joanna Osgood born March 21 1766
Winslow Son to Fortenatus & Tamer Eager born Feby. 14 1767
Nath^{ll}. Son to Moses & Margret Burpee born Jany. 1 1766
Nahum Son to Sol^o & Deliverance Houghton Born Feby 25 1766

117 *The Children of Stanton & Marcy Prentice.*

Stephen Prentice born February 3^d: 1746
Stanton Prentice born November, 17: 1750
William Prentice Ditto October, 9: 1753

Children of Stanton & Rebecca Prentice.

John Prentice born July, 31, 1761   Peter Prentice born Septemb^r. 10: 1766
Samuel Prentice Do. June, 1, 1763   James Otis Prentice Do.———
Cephas Prentice Do. January 2, 1765

The Children of Levi & Katharine Willard.

Levi Willard born August 13th, 1756
John Willard Ditto February 22^d: 1758
Katharine Willard Do: June, 15, 1759 & Deced December 3. 1759.
Katharine Willard 2^d. born Septem^r: 20, 1761
Hanah Willard born January 1. 1764

The Children of Philemon & Rebeckah Houghton

Dolley Houghton born april 12: 1759
Sophia Houghton born Sept. 5; 1761
Rebeckah Houghton born Feby. 1: 1764 & Died July 5: 1765
Rebeckah Houghton Do. Feby. 15: 1766
Elis^a. Daug^t. to Willm. & Esther Richardson 3 born aug^t. 31: 1766

The Children of Christian Angell & Hanah Angel his Wife.

Henry Angel born March 17, 1759   Stephen Angel born Octob^r. 9. 1764
Hanah Angel born Novem^r 5. 1760   Diadame Angel born March 6, 1767
Augustus Angel born Octob^r. 11, 1762   Patience Angel born April 15 1769

118 Israel Son to Joshua & Esther Green born October 27. 1766.
Hannah Daug^r. to Joseph & Hanah Beman born Januy. 27, 1766
Stephen Son to Isaac & Eunice Eveleth born Septr. 3. 1766

The Children of Moses & Submitt [Frost] Wilder.

Luther Wilder born June 20, 1762   Rebeckah Wilder born April 9 1767
John Wilder born Jany 6. 1765

Mary Daug^r. to William & Mary Kendall born Januy: 3, 1767
Lucy Daug^r. to Thos. & Abigail Gates born April 6. 1765
Wilder Gates Son to Thos. & Abigail Gates born June 18, 1766
Elisha Son to Gardnier & Anna Maynard born April 13, 1767
Hanah Daug^r. to Elijah & Mary Woods born August 11, 1766.
Lucretia Daug^r. to Peter & Zuba Larkin born April 14, 1767.
Betsey Daug^r. to John & Lydia White Ju^r. Jany 26 1767.
Molley Daug^r. to Jonathan & Eunice Bailey born May 6, 1767.
Prudence Daugh^r to Jon^a. & Eunice Bailey born May 6, 1767.
Silas Son to James & Anna Houghton born May 19, 1767
Aaron Son to Nath^{ll}: & Martha Wright born December 9, 1766.
Moses Son to Thos. & Priscillia Ross born April 4, 1765
Phebe Daug^r. to Thos. & Priscillia Ross born Novem^r: 12, 1766
Hanah Daug^r. to Amos & Mary Rugg born June 22. 1764
Solomon Son to Amos & Mary Rugg born July 3. 1766
Silvester Son to Ephraim & Michal Roper born July 29, 1762
Joseph Son to Eph^m. & Michal Roper born Decem^r; 29, 1763
Lucy Daugh^r. to Eph^m. & Michal Roper born Febru^y. 10, 1767

Susanah Daug^r. to Ephraim & Elisabeth Divoll born July 19. 1767
Lydia Daug^r to Ruben & Anna Lipinwill born Dece^r. 29. 1766.
Silvia Daug^r. to John & Parna Brook born Septem^r. 12, 1766.

119 *Births of the Children of Josiah & Sarah Ballard.*

Sarah was born Novem^r. 30, 1747
Josiah Ballard born January 4th. 1750
Jeremiah Ballard Ditto: March 9, 1752
John Ballard   Do. January 19. 1755 Deces^d. Feby. 17, 1755
Mary Ballard   Do. January 28, 1756
James Ballard   Do. July 9. 1757
John Ballard   Do. November 13. 1759
Thomas Ballard   Do. March 28. 1762
William Ballard   Do. March 23. 1764
Dolly Ballard   Do. Septem^r. — 1767

Samuel Son to Job & Mary Spafford born Jany. 5, 1763
Oliver Son to David & Keziah Wilder born Septem^r. 22^d. 1767
Samuel Rugg Son of Daniel & Elis^a. Rugg Ju^r: born Septr. 8. 1767
Anna Daug^r. to William & Anna Jewet born April 29. 1767
Jason Son to John & Mary Glazier born July, 14, 1767
Lois Wilder Daug^r. to Phinihas & Bridget Wilder born June 28 1767
Sarah Daug^r. to Nath^ll. & Lucy Wilder born Decem^r. 25, 1766
Peirson Son to James & Elis^a. Kendall Ju^r. born Januy. 4 1767
Thomas Son to Ephraim & Sarah Richardson born May 21. 1767
Asa Son to Asa & Lydia Wilder born Novemb^r. 17, 1767
Relief Daug^r. to Daniel & Lydia Johnson born Aug^t: 30 1757
Daniel Son to Daniel & Lydia Johnson born Decem^r. 28, 1762
John Son to Ebenezer & Keziah Buss born August 6. 1767
Anna Daugh^r. to Joshua & Mary Fletcher born Septem^r. 29. 1767
Ruth Daug^r. to James & Mary Carter born May 7, 1762
Sally Daug^r. to Tilly & Zilpah Moor born Januy. 17. 1767
Augustus Son to James & Elisabeth Kendall born Febry. 24 1768
Andrew Son to Benj^a. & Hanah Willard born June 15, 1762
Henry Son to Benj^a & Hanah Willard born May 13th. 1766
William Son to Joseph & Agnus Sawyer born Febry. 4th. 1768
Jonas Son to Joseph & Hepzebeth Tower born March 8th: 1768
Eph[ra]im Son to Silas & Abigal How Born November 21 1767

120 *The Children of Simon & Martha Thompson*

Samuel Thompson born May 7, 1747   Asa Thompson born June 21, 1752
Jonathan Thompson born March 3, 1750   Sarah Thompson born June 18, 1754

Elijah Son to James & Mary Crossman June ye 10th 1769
Robert Phelps ye Son of Robert & Rachel Phelps born February 27th: 1768
Dolly Daughter to Aaron & Abigail Sawyer born Nov^r: 12. 1767
Sarah Daug^r. to John & Sarah Dunsmoor born Septem^r. 19. 1767
Levi Son to Samuel & Prudence Prentice born April 19. 1768
Dorcas Daug^r. to Joseph & Mary Kilborne born May 17, 1768
Nahum Son to Ezra & Dinah Houghton born Octob^r. 28, 1767

The Children of Josiah & Jane Osgood.

Samuel Osgood born April 29 1764   Joseph Osgood born April 6, 1768
Josiah Osgood born February 14, 1766

Bezeleel Son [of] Darius & Deborah Sawyer born Febuary 11 1768
Abel Son to Joseph & Allis Wheelock born April 14. 1768

The Births of the Childred of Joseph & Lucy Woods

Samuel Woods born January 2^d: 1759   Ursula Woods born February 24, 1763
Rachel Woods born January 28, 1761

Abner Son to Josiah & Mary Bennit born August 30. 1765
Thomas Son to Josiah & Mary Bennit born July 21 1767

BOOK FIRST. 97

Nabby Daugh'. to Thomas & Nabby Gates born Nov'. 3ᵈ 1768
Rebeckah Daug'. to David & Sarah Osgood born June 15, 1768
Christopher Son to Christopher & Hanah Osgood borne June 12, 1768
James Son to Josiah & Abigail Houghton born Nove'. 18. 1764
Jonathan Son to Josʰ. & Abigail Houghton born August 14, 1766
121 Abigail Smith Daug'. to Timothy and Sarah Goodenow, born May 16, 1768
Sarah Daug'. to Lyn Jock & Hanah Jock born October 22, 1768
Daniel Son to Abiel & Marcy Stone born December 22, 1767
Elisabeth Daug'ʳ: to Isaac & Eunice Eveleth born July 3ᵈ. 1768
Thomas Bennitt Son to Thomas & Lydia Bennit born Januy. 31. 1769
Oliver Son to Nathaⁿˡ, & Elisabeth Willard born Novem'. 4, 1768
James Son to James & Barsheba Goodwin born May 9. 1768
Daniel Brown Son to John & Mary Brooks 3ᵈ born Novem. 27, 1768
Enos Son to Bartholmew & Elisᵃ: Pearson horn July 17: 1767
Hepsibeth Daughter to Moses Burpee born July 10ᵗʰ, 1768.
Burpee Son to Richard & Esther Proutee born March 6: 1763
Dolly Daugh'. to Jona. & Deborah Wilder Ju'. born Nove'. 17 1768
Jacob Son to Oliver & Lydia Powers born Decem'. 21. 1768
Jonathan Son to Phinehas & Bridget Wilder born May 19, 1769
Lucy Daugh'. to John & Elisabeth Loring born Nove'. 14, 1765
Joseph Son to John & Elisabeth Loring born July 19, 1768
Silas Son to Israel & Katharine Moors born Novem'. 17, 1768
William Son to John & Mary Baily born March 6. 1762
Jonathan Son to James & Mary Crossman born June 10 1769 [Crossed out.]
Phinehas Son to Bazeliel & Sarah How born Decem'. 1. 1765
Thomas Son to Bazeliel & Sarah How born March 13, 1768
Cooper Son to Samuel & Phebe Sawyer Jun'. born Novem'. 14ᵗʰ: 1768
Zebina Son to Nathaniel & Lucy Wilder born April 8: 1769

The Children of Thoʳ: & Hannah Brooks

Thomas Brooks born March 17, 1765   Alpheus Brooks born June 4, 1768
Helon Brooks born Septem'. 12, 1767

Daniel Son to Daniel & Mary Robbins born February 1ˢᵗ; 1769
122 Joseph Son to Daniel & Elisabeth Rugg Ju: born June 25, 1769
Benjamin Son to Solomon & Deliverance Houghton born Febry. 3, 1768
Rebekkah Lippinwell Daughter to Reuben & Anna Lippinwell born July 24ᵗʰ. 1769

The births of the Children of Micah & Sarah Harthan

Sarah born January yᵉ 19ᵗʰ. 1763   Samuel born February 18, 1768
David born January 15, 1764   Lois born Dec'. 27 1769
Lydia born February 18, 1765   Eunice born March 22 1772
Lucy born June 10, 1766   Olive born Oct'ʳ: 21ˢᵗ 1774

Betty Daughter to John Jur. & Keziah May Sept'ʳ 2 1769
Jabez Son to George & Dury Hibress born Novem'. 14, 1768
Rebecka Daug'. to Tilly & Zilpah Moor born July 14, 1769
Achsah Daug'. to John & Achsah Phelps born July 15, 1767
Martha Daug'. to John & Achsah Phelps born July 17. 1769
William Son to William & Ruth Dunsmoor born March 11, 1769
Samuel Ward Son of Samuel & Dolley Ward born November 16ᵗʰ: 1769
Rachel Daug'. to Joseph & Meriam Bixpy born Octo'ʳ. 25, 1769
Solomon Son to David & Hanah Nelson born February the 6ᵗʰ, 1769
James Son to James & Elisabeth Kendall Ju'. born Nove'. 3, 1769

The births of the Children of Ezra & Keziah Sawyer of Lancaster.

Abner Sawyer born Nov'. 8, 1762   Thomas Sawyer born April 15, 1766
Ezra Sawyer born March 20, 1764   Nathaⁿˡ: Sawyer Do. Septem'ʳ. 10. 1769

Lydia Kendall Daughter of Jona. the 4ᵗʰ. & Hannah Kendall born March 16ᵗʰ: 1769
John Willard Son to John & Lucy Willard born December 17ᵗʰ: 1768
John White Son of John & Lydia White Jun'. born January 10ᵗʰ. 1769

John, Son of Ephraim & Abigail Carter Junr: born December 9th. 1768
Abigail, Daughter of Ephraim & Abigail Carter Ju^r: born February 13th: 1770

123   *An Acco^t: of Marriages Consumated by Joseph Wilder Esqr:*

Gardner Wilder & Martha Wilder Both of Lancaster Nov^r: 13. 1760
De^n John Haywood & Silence White, Decr. 31. 1760
Benj^a Priest & Hanah Johnson both of Lancaster Jany. 20 1761
Joshua Johnson Jr. of Lancaster Hanah Avery of Groton Jany 20 1761
Mitchel Richards of Shirley & Ester Mitchel of Lunenburg July 2^d, 1761.
Timothy Kendel & Anna Houghton Both of Leom^r. Jany. 20 1762
James Locke & Rebeckah Wilder Both of Lancaster Feby. 2 1762

An Acco^t: of Marriages Consumated by David Osgood Esqr.

Vizt: Zacheus Bemis & Elis^a Lyon Both of Westminster Feby, 10, 1761
Joel Houghton of Lan. & Sarah Pearson of Shrewsbury Feby. 25 1761
Gideon Smith & Mary Biglow Both of Westminster April 16 1761
Jeremiah Steuart of Leom^r. & Hanah Steuart of Lanc^r. Feby. 4, 1762
Sam^ll. Bixpy of Prince Town & Hanah Bowers of Lanc^r: March 4th, 1762
George Peterson & Margret Dorchester — Feby. 26 1761

Eunice Daught. to Jabez & Lucy Brooks born April 13 1759
Deborah Daught. to Jabez & Lucy Brooks Born Feb. 15 1762

Marriages Consumated by David Osgood Esqr.

Willm; Gibbs to Joanna Gleason Both of Prince Town April 14 1762
James Houghton Tert. of Lancaster to Anna Eveleth of Prince Town Sept: 10. 1762
John Boyinton of Shrewsbury to Elis^a. Beman of Lancaster Janu^y. 13. 1763.
Doc. Nathan Raymond of Littletown to Rebeckah Richardson of Lancaster by W^m. Richardson Esqr. December 1, 1762.
The above sent to the County Register

124   *Marriages Consumated by the Rev^d. John Mellen Vizt:*

August 20 1761 Joseph Sawyer to Agnus Dunsmoor
Septem^r. 3   Roger Ross to Molly Rugg
  Ditto.   Jonathan Whetcomb to Tamer Ross
Novem. 26   John Boynton to Elisebeth Jewet
Decem^r. 17   Peter Goodenow to Ann Moseman
Jany. 26 1762 Assa Whetcomb to Betty Sawyer
March 11   Joseph Houghton to Martha Snow
May 6   Richard Proutee to Ephee Smith
May 11   Natha^ll. Jones to Phebe Burpee
June 3.   Josiah Wilder to Abigail Osgood
July 8   Stephen Smith to Lucy Kendall
October 26   Enoch Dole to Eunice Richardson
Novr. 4.   Oliver Dresser to Olive Osgood
"   18   Doc Daniel Greenleaf to Dorrethy Richardson
April 27. 1763 Moses Sawyer to Mary Sawyer
Augt. 11   David Moors to Elisebeth Whetcomb
October 20   William Brown to Elisabeth Houghton
March 8, 1764 Nath^ll. Hastings to Elisabeth Goodenow
April 11.   Nathan Gary to Hepsebeth Wilder
October 3   Elijah Houghton to Mary Allen
  all the Foregoing sent to the County Register

Benj^a. Warrin of Littleton marr^d. to Elis^a. Haywood of Lancaster Sept. 19th. 1764, by W^m: Richardson Esqr:
Zach^h. Harvey Ju^r. Married to Mary Norcross both of Prince Town November 15th. 1764 by W^m: Richardson Esqr:

125   *The Following Marriages Consumated by Joseph Wilder Esqr.*

Kendall Boutel of Lunenburg to Mary Wilder of Leominster April 1, 1762
Solomon Shead to Elis^a. Bointon both of Lunenburg May 24, 1763

BOOK FIRST.

Benj^a. Houghton to Axe Whitcomb both of Lancaster Octob^r. 14, 1763
Josiah Sawyer of Bolton to Mary Tooker of Lancaster January 14, 1764
Joseph Russ to Susanah Priest both of Lancaster July 1. 1764
Gardner Wilder with Dorrethy Richardson } March 8, 1765
John Lock with Lucy Wilder all of Lancaster }
JOSEPH WILDER.

The Following Marriages Consumated by David Osgood Esqr.

Jacob Bennit & Anna Boynton both of Lancaster Decr. 11. 1763
Enoch Jewet of Templetown & Mary Moor of Shrewsbury March 8th, 1764
Jedediah Woods of Warwick & Mary Bixby of Lancaster Janu^y. 21, 1765
Hananiah Rand of Westminster & Martha Osgood of Lancaster Decem^r. 20 1765
Joshua Church & Keziah Goss both of Lancaster Feb^{ry}. 21, 1765
Manasseh Bixby of Shrewsb^y. & Elis^a: Dunsmoor of Lancaster Novr. 12 1765
Amos Powers & Molly Parmiter both of Prince Town Jany. 21 1766
Aaron Stearnes of Prince Town & Esther Glazier of Westminster Feb^{ry}. 6, 1766

Marriages Consumated by Willm. Richardson.

Sam^{ll}. Handcock of Harvard to Abigail Snow of Lancaster July 21, 1763
Levi Houghton & Ama Ricnardson both of Lancaster Novr. 2 1763
Jon^a. Townsend & Hulda Newton both of Westminster March 24, 1765
Jothem Rice Ju^r. of Rutland Destrict & Hanah Snow of Lancaster Feby. 11, 1767
Willm: Williams of Marlbro' & Zilpah Wilder of Lancaster Febr^y. 12, 1767

Sarah Daug^r. to Joel & Sarah Houghton born Septr. 29, 1766
Paul Son to William & Mary Willard born Decem^r. 29. 1764
William Son to William & Mary Willard born June 9, 1767

_{all the Foregoing sent to the Register March 17 1768}

126 *Marriages Consumated by the Rev. Timo: Harrington*

Sept^r: 12 1758: Nath^{ll}. Turner and Anna Gross both of Lancaster
Octob^r. 5 1758 Simon Willard of Lancaster & Elisabeth Willard of Harvard
Nov^r: 16 1758 Richard Baker of Narraganset No. 2 & Mary Sawyer of Lancaster
April 16, 1759 Elijah Beman & Thankfull Nicholls of Lancaster
June 5: 1759 Edmund Parmiter of Sudbury & Sarah Beman of Lancaster
" 29, 1759 Hooker Osgood Jun. & Susanah Sawyer both of Lancaster
August 16 1759 Thos. Page of Leominster & Mary Knight of Lancaster
Novem^r. 13. 1759 John Cobley of Narraganset No. 6 & Mary Wilder of Lancaster
Feby. 7. 1760 Thomas Grant & Hannah Churchill both of Lancaster
May 21, 1760 Edmond Larkin & Abigail Albert both of Lancaster
Nove^r. 19 1760 Elijah Osgood & Mary Wallingford both of Lancaster
Janu^y. 1 1761 Joseph Willson of Petersham & Hanah Osgood of Lancaster
Janu^y: 22. 1761 Josiah Fairbank & Abigail Carter both of Lancaster
Jan^y: 22, 1761 John Ball of Westbro' & Abigail Wilder of Lancaster
March 16 1761 John McCarty & Margret McFarling both of Lancaster
Decem^r. 3 1761 Peter Thurston & Dorrethy Gates both of Lancaster
June 18. 1761 Fortunatus Eager & Thamer Houghton both of Lancaster
March 18 1762 Matthew Knight of Leominster & Dinah Carter of Lancaster
April 17 1762 Nath^{ll}. Wilder & Lucy Knight both of Lancaster
May 12 1762 John Phelps & Elisabeth Walker both of Lancaster
May 26 1762 Joel Phelps & Prudence Brown both of Lancaster
May 27, 1762 Stanton Carter & Peninnah Albert both of Lancaster
August 26 1762 Tilly Moor & Zilpah Whiting both of Lancaster
Octob^r. 19, 1762 Ebenez^r. Hill of Swanzy New Hampshir & Abigail Nicholls of Lancaster
Decem^r. 9, 1762 Cyrus Fairbank & Lucy Wilder both of Lancaster
Febr^y 7, 1763 Peter Hilt of Worcester & Margret Zweir of Lancaster
Novr. 22, 1763 William Willard of Petersham & Katharine Wilder of Lancaster
Febr^y 29 1764 Josiah Lock of Lancaster & Esther Kitteridge of Tewksbury

LANCASTER RECORDS.

Jan.ʸ 24, 1765 Robert Phelps of Lancaster & Rachel Richardson of Bilerica
May 23, 1765 Dr. Stephen Ball of Westbro' & Mary Fairbank of Lancaster
May 28, 1765 James Goodwin & Bathsheba Robbins both of Lancaster
Octobʳ. 30, 1765 Daniel Warner & Susanna Rugg both of Lancaster
October 3, 1765 { Jonathan Whitney & Mary Wyman both of Lancaster
{ Daniel Rugg Junʳ. & Elisabeth Divoll both of Lancaster
127 March 10 1766. Paul Dickerson of Groton & Damaris Knight of Lancaster
Augᵗ. 14 1766. Mr Joseph Wheelor & Sarah Allen both of Lancaster
Septʳ. 18, 1766 William Kendall & Mary Knight both of Lancaster
May 19 1767 Mr James Goodfry of Lancaster & Mrs Mary Pratt of Harvard
Decʳ: 3. 1767 Ephrᵐ. Carter Junʳ. & Abigail Carter Junʳ. both of Lancaster
Jan.ʸ, 12, 1768 } David Nims Juʳ. of Keene & Jemima Carter Ju. of Lancaster
{ Silas Carter & Lucy Sawyer both of Lancaster
Feb.ʸ 9. 1768 Jonathan Kendall 4ᵗʰ: & Hannah Johnson both of Lancaster
Feb.ʸ 18, 1768 Cap. Samˡˡ. Wilder of Ashburnham & Dorethy Carter of Lancaster.

entered March 15 1768 *pr* LEVI WILLARD, *Town Clerk*
March 15. Sent to the Register all the foregoing marriages

Marrages consumated by Abel Willard Esq

Sept 20, 1769 John Huet of Ashby and Sarah Priest of Lancaster
Sent to the Register March ye 2d

128 BIRTHS

Dorrethy Daugʳ. to Nathˡˡ. & Elisabeth Willard born Feb.ʸ 5ᵗʰ: 1770
Moses Son to William & Anne Jewet born April 13ᵗʰ, 1769
Phenehas Son to Jonthan and Joana Osgood born Novembr: 7ᵗʰ 1767
Fortunatus Son to Fortunatus & Tamer Eager Born June yᵉ 7ᵗʰ, 1769
Luke Sawyer Son to Richard and Relief Rand Born March yᵉ 31ᵗʰ, 1769
Charlotte Daughter of John and Anna Person was Born Decembʳ. yᵉ 22ᵗʰ, 1769

The Children of Enoch & Eunice Dole.

Dolly Richardson born December 14: 1763   Iseley [Elsie?] Born Sept. 2 1768
Dunsmore Born May 29: 1766   Polley Born August 2, 1771.

Lucy Daughter of Menasah & Lucy Sawyer was Born March yᵉ 8ᵗʰ 1769.
Mical Daughter to Jonathan and Eunice Bayley Born october 24ᵗʰ 1769

The Beths of the Children of Thomas and Elisa'th Willard

Mary Born May yᵉ 30ᵗʰ 1763 and Died Feb: 29ᵗʰ. 1768
Joseph Born June yᵉ 30ᵗʰ 1765
Dolley Born May yᵉ 30ᵗʰ 1767
Moley Born October yᵉ 5ᵗʰ 1768

The Beths of the Children of Thomas and Mary Mears

Judeth Born Janauary yᵉ 7ᵗʰ 1765   Hannah Born Nov 21, 1772
Moley Born May yᵉ 4ᵗʰ, 1767   Thomas Born May 5, 1775
John Born Feb: yᵉ 11ᵗʰ 1769   Dolly Born Feb.ʸ. 14, 1777
Richard Born Jan.ʸ 9, 1771   Nabby Born July 19, 1779

129 The Beths of the Children of Phineas and Joanna Beman

Jonas Born July yᵉ 12ᵗʰ 1750   Benimin Born April yᵉ 10 1754
Gedion Born July yᵉ 12ᵗʰ 1763   Elisha Born June yᵉ 7ᵗʰ 1757
Josiah Born Octobʳ. 2ᵈ. 1752   Abigail Born July yᵉ 14ᵗʰ 1760

Samuel Son to Samuel & Mary Rice Born July yᵉ 10ᵗʰ 1769
Levi Son to Abner & Martha Haskell Born July yᵉ 20ᵗʰ 1769.
Sofia Daughter of Joshua and Mary Fletcher Born Novembʳ 22ᵈ 1769

The Beths of the Children of Thomas and Eunice Rugg.

Thomas Born May 28ᵗʰ 1765   William Stikney born June 10ᵗʰ 1769
Eunice Born october 22ᵈ 1767

BOOK FIRST.

The Beths of the Children of Jabez and Lucy Brooks

Deborah Born Feb 4th 1762
Mary Born March 3th 1764
Hannah Born March 6th 1766
Rhoda Born Feb: 26th 1768
Ester Born Decemr 15 1774
Betsy Washington Born Novemr 29 1776

The Births of the Children of Josiah and Abigail Fairbanks

Josiah Born Novembr 5th 1761
Abigail Born august 27th 1763
Manassah Born august 20th 1765
Martha Born March ye 1st 1768
Ephraim Born March 16th 1770
James Fairbank Born aprill 19 1772
Buler Fairbank Born July 16 1774
Levi Fairbank Born February 12th 1777

130 The Births of the Children of Joseph and Ann Fairbank

Joseph born ye 19th, of July 1765
Molley born ye 11th, of January 1767
Thomas born ye 20, December 1768
Ephraim born ye 7th, March 1771

Fanny Daughter of Tilly & Zilpah Moor born April 12th 1771

The births of the Children of Levi & Rebeccah Moor

Abijah born ye 7th, November 1767
Uriah born 29th, December 1769

The births of the Children of Joseph & Mary Kilborne.

Dorcas born June 17, 1768
Levi born June 19, 1770

James Son to Willm. & Mary Willard Jur. born Januy. 18, 1770
Jonathan Son of Jone. & Hanah Kendall 4th: born April 27, 1771
Lydia Daughter to Thomas & Lydia Bennett born June 1st, 1771
Nathe, Son to Ruben & Anna Lipinwill born June 21, 1771 & Died July 4, 1771
Sewel Son of Robert & Rachel Phelps born July 28, 1771
Benjamin, Son of Ezra & Dinah Houghton born August 23d: 1771
Anna Daughter of Thomas & Abigail Gates born November 12th: 1770
Annice Daugr: to William & Mary Kendall born December 4th 1769
Hannah Daughter of Phinehas & Bridget Wilder born September 8th 1771
Arethusa Daughter to Joseph & Annes Brown born ye 22d, December 1770
Reuben Son of John Dunsmore & Sarah Dunsmore born March 9th 1771
Joseph Son of Daniel Rugg Junr. & Elizabeth born October 7th. 1771
John Son of John & Anna Phillips born December 3d: 1771
Joshua Fairbank Son of Joshua & Rebecca Fairbank born July 13th: 1770

131 Marriages Consumated by Revd: John Mellen

Novr: 29, 1764,	Jonathan Wilder Junr: & Deborah Sawyer.
Feb: 28, 1765	Thomas Cleland & Anna Rugg.
May 17	"	Daniel Perry & Mary Newton.
June 20	"	Heman Kendall & Mary Fairbanks.
July 4th:	"	Benjamin Tompson & Susanna Tilly.
Octobr: 24th	"	Thomas Geary Junr: & Priscilla Jewet
31st.	"	Elisha Sawyer Junr: Patience Bennet.
Novr: 21st.	"	Bartholomew Peirson & Elisabeth Powers
Jany: 9, 1766,	Jotham Sawyer & Dinah Goodell.
Febr: 13	"	Joseph Boynton & Zurvia Wilder.
April 28	"	Josiah Hosmer & Eunice Whitcomb
May 7th,	"	James Ross Junr & Phoebe Geary
Sepr: 11th:	"	Ichabod Geary & Sarah Rugg.
Octobr: 26.	"	Paul Kendal & Mary Bayly
29th:	"	Timothy Fullam & Elisabeth Tompson
Novr: 16.	"	Gardner Maynard & Anna Ross.
Decr: 25th.	"	Shubael Bayly & Hannah Whitmore
Decr: 9th, 1767	Daniel Nichols & Mary Jewet
Jany: 10, 1768	Manassah Sawyer & Lucy Richardson
April 20	"	Richard Rand & Relief Sawyer
June 21,	"	Oliver Powers & Lydia Winn
Octobr. 26	"	Silas Houghton & Eunice Sawyer
Jan. 19, 1769	Joshua Sawyer & Esther Jewet

March 2d: 1769 Samuel Blodget & Lydia Bennet
March 2d: " Ebenezer Ross & Achsah Wilder
April 10th. " Solomon Stewart & Elisabeth Moores
  30th: " Jacob Winn & Phoebe Grout

132   *Marriages consummated by Revd: Jno: Mellen.*

June 29. 1769 Ebenr: Brooks & Relief Moores
Octobr: 5th: " Abijah Houghton Junr; & Mary Sawyer
Novr: 16th: " Joseph Dunsmore & Ruth Newton
Decr. 28 " Silas Smith & Levina Houghton
Decr. 28, " Silas Wilder & Elisabeth Sawyer.
         Entred by DANIEL ROBBINS *Town Clerk*

The Foregoing marrages sent to the Regesters March ye 2d 1771.

Joseph Houghton Junr. & Lois Ross both of Bolton were Joined in marriage November 29th. 1770. by Abel Willard Esqr.
         Entred pr SAM WARD *Town Clerk*

Ethan Kendall & Thankfull Moor both of Lancaster were Joyned in Marriage July ye 4th. 1771 by Abel Willard Esqr.
    a Coppy   Entered pr SAM WARD *Town Clerk*

Marriages Consumated by Joseph Wilder Esqr.

Jonathan Carter of Leominster & Damarus Whitcomb of Lancaster April 3d: 1765.
Ephraim Robins of Petersham & Joana Holden of Harvard July 25th, 1765.
Elkanah Woodcock of Swansey & Suzanna Nickols of Lancaster September 24th, 1765.
Wyat Gun of Swansey & Martha Houghton of Lancaster February 25th. 1766.
Daniel Spooner of Petersham & Bethia Nickols of Lancaster September 3d, 1767
Samuel Joslin of Lancaster & Abigail Wilder October 1. 1767
William Alexander Jur. of Lunenburge & Ruth Putnam of Harvard May 31, 1769
James Digens & Lydia Hale both of Leominster June 1st, 1769
Abisha Phelps & Katherine Richardson both of Lancaster April 22d. 1770
         Entered January 28th. 1772, by SAM WARD *Town Clerk*

133 *Marriages Consumated by Joseph Wilder Esqr. Viz:*

Jonathan Carter of Sudbury & Deborah Hunt of Lancaster October 25th: 1770.
Silas Church & Mary Osgood of Templeton Novr. 25th. 1771.
John Wilder & Abigail Kendall both of Lancaster December 1st, 1771.
         Entered January 28th. 1772 pr SAM WARD *T. Clerk*

Marriages Consumated by Abijah Willard Esqr. viz:

Thomas Meriam & Sarah Wilder both of Westminster Novemr. 24, 1762
Robert Crawford of Worcester & Elizabeth Leitch of Lunenburge Januy: 13th, 1763
Levi Woods of Petersham & Tamar Houghton of Leominster April 20th: 1763
Nathaniel Willard of Lancaster & Eunice Farwell of Stow May 25th, 1763
William Longley of Shirley & Lydia Wallingsford of Lancaster Augt. 8. 1763
Robert Proctor & Ruth Fowle of Lancaster October 7th, 1764
David Hastings & Dinah Williams both of Shrewsbury May 25th. 1765
John Richardson of Petersham & Eunice Green of Lancaster December 18th 1765
Thomas Bennett & Lydia Longley both of Lancaster December 29th. 1765
Samuel Norcross & Rachel Hervey both of Princetown May'2d. 1766
Moses Russell of Littleton & Sarah Phelps of Lancaster November 27th, 1767
Andrew Poor & Esther Snow both of Lancaster November 1, 1767
John Hammond & Lucy Powers both of Lancaster November 3d, 1768
Andrew Haskell & Lois Bullin both of Lancaster August 10th, 1769
Joseph Moor Junr. of Lancaster & Hepsibeth Bush of Shrewsbury October 26th, 1769

Moses Smith & Abigail Green both of Lancaster, January 24th. 1771
Timothy Blodgett & Lydia Walker both of Lancaster June 3d, 1771
Eliphalet Rogers of Princetown & Eunice Bennett of Lancaster August 14th, 1771
William Tinney & Mehitable Jones both of Bolton October 15th, 1771
Jedediah Boynton & Elizabeth How both of Lancaster February 10th, 1772
   Entered February ye 29th, 1772 pr SAM WARD *Town Clerk*

134 *Marriages Consumated by the Revd. John Mellen*
Viz-1770 May 22d, Nathaniel Wright Junr. & Ruth Richardson.
   30, William Thompson & Elizabeth Jewitt
   June 11, Joshua Piper & Betty Procter
   July 26, Thos. Rugg & Mehitabel Houghton
   Octor. 9th, Daniel Norcross & Thankfull Sawyer
     18, Elijah Ball & Rebecca Moor
     30. Solomon Goodale & Persis Bailey
   Novr. 29th, Ephraim Willard Jur. & Lois Geary
1771 Jany. 1, Revd. Caleb Prentice & Pamela Mellen
  March 6th. Stephen Heywood & Ruth Dunsmoor
  April 25th, Joseph Whitaker & Mary Whitney
  July 4th. Jonathan Buss & Widw. Mary Steward
  Sepr. 25th, David Holt & Hannah Kendall
  Octor. 17th, Jonas Johnson & Damarus Rugg
  Decr. 26th Samuel Gerrish & Abigail Moor
1772 March 29th, Asa Smith & Sarah Stewart
  April 8th, David Goodale & Dorothy Newton
  May 5th, Giles Wills & Relief Wilder
  June 23d, Ezra Hale & Widw. Thankfull Brabrook
  July 2d, Jona. Butterick & Hannah Wilder Sawyer
    7th. Joseph Sever & Abigail Sawyer
    8th, Jonathan Moor & Elisabeth Richardson
  Augt. 13th, Luther Graves & Phebe Jewett
  Octor. 8th, Samuel Mason & Sarah Whitney
1773 April 1st, Obadiah Gross & Lucy Houghton
  May 19th, Lemuel Beman & Prudence Rowe
  Novr. 25th, Elias Farnsworth & Lois Willard
  Decr 7th, Abner Farrington & Joanna Kilborne
    14th, Joseph Lewis & Martha Locke
    16th, Moses Newall & Hannah Robbins
1774 Jany. 20th, Levi Carter & Silence Beman
135 Februy. 1st. Nathaniel Brown & Esther Smith
    10th, John Phelps & Lois Davis.

The above & aforegoing marriages Recvd. March 15th. 1774 & Enterd
          pr SAM WARD *Town Clerk*

The above List is deliver'd to the Register.

Marriages Consumated by the Revd Timothy Harrington Viz.

dates
1768 March 17th. Silas Fairbank & Lydia Prouty both of Lancaster
   April 7th. Jacob Bennett of Leominster & Elizabeth Wilder of Lancaster
     27th. Joseph Page & Eunice White both of Lancaster
   July 21. John Barnard of Bolton & Elizabeth Fairbank of Lancaster
   August 1. Samuel Wilder & Sarah Ballard both of Lancaster
   Augt. 31. Timothy Temple & Deborah Ball both of Lancaster
   Octbr. 17 James Crossman of Monadnuck & Mary Priest of Lancaster
   Novr. 29 { Abel Shead of Groton, & Ruth Haskell of Lancaster
       { Francis Davies free Negro, & Peggy Lahey (molatto free born) both of Lancaster
   Decr. 1. Francis Eager of Paxton & Sarah Fairbanks of Lancaster
1769 Jany. 5th. Paul Richardson of Winchester New Hampshire & Eusebia Harrington of Lancaster
   Jany. 31. Joseph House & Alice Houghton both of Lancaster
   Feby. 22, Joseph Carter & Beulah Carter both of Lancaster

March 14th, Israel Houghton & Elizabeth Wilder both of Lancaster
June 1st, John Wilder of Lancaster & Katharine Sawyer of Bolton
July 12th, John Jones of Colrain, & Abigail Atherton of Lancaster
July 20th, Wm. Shaw of Peterborough, & Barbuza Zweir of Lancaster
Octr. 12th, Wm. Heywood of Lunenburgh & Rebekkah Kendall of Lancaster
Novr. 11th: Edward Poor of Worcester & Eunice Goodrige of Lancaster
Novr. 16, James Pratt & Zerviah Rugg of Lancaster
Decr. 14th. Sampson Ayner of Lancaster & Lucy Lew of Littleton, free Negroes
Decr. 28th. Joshua Goodrige of Lunenburgh & Elizabeth Phelps of Lancaster

1770 Jany 16 James Elder of Worcester & Sarah Gates of Lancaster
April 10th, James Foster of New Ipswich & Hannah Priest of Lancaster
136 May 5th, John Priest Junr. & Mary Longley both of Lancaster
May 29 Joseph Brown & Annice Knight both of Lancaster
May 31 Wm. Grimes Junr. of Swansey (New Hampshire) & Mary Willard of Lancaster
July 25, John Townsend of Bolton, & Eunice Fairbank of Lancaster
Augt. 21st, Salmon Goodfrey & Rebekkah Phelps both of Lancaster
Septr 5th. Nathaniel Joslin & Mary Bennett both of Lancaster
Octr. 1st, John Brown of Chearlimont & Lucy Rugg of Lancaster
Novr. 27, Micah Brian[t] & Rebecca Ball both of Lancaster
Decr. 6th, Jonas Fairbank & Elizabeth Wilder both of Lancaster

1771 Jany. 9th, Thomas Stearns of Fitchburgh & Molley White of Lancaster
Jany 31st, Joshua Smith of Southborough & Abigail Wilder of Lancaster
Feby. 7th. John Bennett & Lucy Phelps both of Lancaster
March 21st. Jacob Zweier & Abigail Priest both of Lancaster
May 22d, Daniel Bigelow of Worcester & Mary Ballard of Lancaster
June 13th. Antipas Bartlett of Northborough & Lois White of Lancaster
Novr. 21st. Aaron Kendall of Leominster & Katharine Wyman of Lancaster
Novr. 27th. John Robbins & Lydia Haskell both of Lancaster
Novr. 28th. Lemuel Haskell of Harvard & Lucy Green of Lancaster
Decr. 20th Daniel Goss & Eunice Wilder both of Lancaster

1772 Jany 15th, Samuel Wilder & Martha Rugg both of Lancaster
Feby. 6th, Samuel Crosby of Billerica & Abigail Bayley of Lancaster
Feby. 26 Joshua Whitcomb of Templeton & Eunice Prescott of Lancaster
June 18th. Wm. Lock & Mary Fowle both of Lancaster
Augt. 6th, Jonathan Butsworth & Mary Holt both of Lancaster
Augst. 26th, Moses Wilder & Eunice Furbush both of Lancaster
Sepr. 6th Dr. Israel Atherton & Rebekkah Prentice both of Lancaster
Novr. 10th, Elijah Rice of Holden & Lenfy Williams of Princeton
Decr. 7th, Samuel Kilburn of Lunenburgh & Sarah Cooke of Lancaster
137 Decr. 23d, John Locke of Templeton & Heneretta Harrington of Lancaster

1773 April 21st. Titus Wilder & Mary Allen both of Lancaster
Augst. 19th, Jotham Woods & Mehetibel Aldis both of Lancaster
Octr. 21st, Moses Russell & Hannah Kendall both of Lancaster
Novr. 10th, William Brooks & Beulah Wilder both of Lancaster
Novr. 17th, Reuben Geary & Lucy Cutter Brooks both of Lancaster
Novr. 18th, Timothy Knight Junr. & Lydiah Wilder both of Lancaster
Novr. 25 { Dr Abraham Haskell of Lunenburgh & Sarah Green of Lancaster
{ Joseph Whitcomb of Leominster & Ruth Knight of Lancaster
Decr.- 9th, Lemuel Fairbank & Phoebe Wyman both of Lancaster
Decr. 16th. Joseph Wilder Junr. of Leominster & Susanna Phelps of Lancaster
Decr. 22d. Benjamin Farmer & Sarah Lippenwell both of Lancaster

1774 Jany. 4th, Phineas Sawyer Junr. of Fitchburgh & Mary Prescott of Lancaster
Jany. 6th, Joel Osgood & Lois Rugg both of Lancaster
March 2d. Jeremiah Sachwell & Hannah Ross both of Lancaster

BOOK FIRST.

The above & foregoing list of marriages consumated by the Rev^d. Mr. Harrington Rec'v'd March 22^d, 1774 and Entred & Exam^d.
pr SAM WARD *Town Clerk.*
The above & foregoing List of marriages is delivered to the Register.

Joseph Nichols & Anna Phillips were joined together in holy matrimony by the Rev^d. Daniel Emerson of Hollis March 24th. 1774. Pr his certif^{te}.
Enter'd pr SAM WARD *Town Clerk*

Marriages Consumated By Ezra Houghton Esqr.

1774 Aug 25 Benj^a: Roper & Azubah Willard both of Lancaster
1775 March 6 Ephraim Sawyer Ju^r. & Mary Allen both of Lancaster
1780 April 4, Examined & Entered By JOSIAH LEAVITT *Town Clerk*

138 *Marriages Consumated by the Rev^d. Tim^o Harrington*

1774 March 24. James Wright of Keene & Elizabeth Rugg of Lancaster
June 1. Benjamin Whitmore & Sarah Thompson both of Lancaster
June 2^d. Henry Powers of Bolton & Hannah Moors of Lancaster
14, David Brooks & Patience White both of Lancaster
Augt. 28. Doc^r. Josiah Wilder & Polley Flagg both of Lancaster
Sep^t. 27th. John Newton Parmentor of Winchendon & Hannott Abbott of Lancaster
October 13th, Asa Thompson & Sarah Osgood both of Lancaster
1775. Jany. 4th. Manasseh Wilder & Sarah White both of Lancaster
Febr^y. 6th. Samuel Johnson & Lydia Phelps both of Lancaster
16th, John Carter & Martha Wilder both of Lancaster
pr TIMOTHY HARRINGTON

A True Copy   Attest SAMUEL WARD *Town Clerk.*

Marriages Consumated by the Rev^d. John Mellen

May 25th, 1775, Peter Green Esqr. & Rebecca Mellen
Novr. 4, 1776, Elijah Bailey & Mary Thompson
pr JOHN MELLEN
Copy   Attest, SAM^L. WARD *Town Clerk.* rec^d & Enter'd March 25th, 1782.

140   *The Children of Josiah & Prudence Brown.*

William Brown born June 6, 1741   Timothy Brown born May, 22^d, 1753
Prudence Brown born Oct^{br} 20th, 1742   Stanton Brown born March 12th, 1755
John Brown born Augst, 25th, 1744   Rebeccah Brown born Decem^{br} 16th, 1757
Joseph Brown born July, 5th, 1746   and Died August 11th 1759
Elisabeth Brown born May, 25th, 1748 Samuel Brown born Decem^{br} 27th 1759
Ruhamah Brown born March, 12th,1750 Rebeccah Brown born Jany. 17th 1761

Parsis Daughter to Joseph & Agness Sawyer Born May the 1 1773
Aaron Born October the 6 1775.

The births of the Children of Nathl. & Mary Houghton

Nath^{ll}. Houghton Ju^r. born July 16th, 1759. Menassah born April 18th, 1771
Ephraim born March 28th, 1761,   Mary   do. Novr. 30th, 1773
Stephen born May 8th. 1765   Tilly   do. March 20th, 1776
Josiah   do. November 20th 1768 Jonas   do. July 25th, 1778

The births of the Children of Nathaniel Willard and Eunice his Wife.

Nathaniel born July 4th, 1765   Silas born August 29th, 1771
Jonathan born Febr^y. 22^d, 1767   Joel born February 22^d, 1774
Eunice born Novr. 4th, 1769

141   *Births of the Children of Moses & Submit [Frost] Wilder*

Tryphena born October 14th. 1759   Aaron born Septr. 19th. 1776
Luther born July 24th. 1762   Abel born October 28th: 1778
John born Jany. 10th. 1765   Polly born April 20th. 1780

8

Rebecca born April 10. 1767
Sarah born May 3ᵈ. 1770
Moses born October 28ᵗʰ: 1773
Submit born February 23ᵈ. 1775

Luke born July 19. 1781
Elias born Deceʳ. 19ᵗʰ. 1782
Betsy born Janʸ. 1ˢᵗ. 1785
Jonas born Novʳ. 9ᵗʰ. 1786

Lucy Daughter of John & Rachel Fletcher born Sepʳ. 24ᵗʰ: 1786

The following record is made at the request of Peter Thacher Vose Esq.

Peter Thacher Vose was born at Milton Massᵗᵗˢ. Sept. 4 1769, Married Ann Austin Sprague by Revᵈ Dr Thayer Octo. 10, 1802.
Their first Child Ann Foster Vose, born at Augusta Maine, August 24, 1803.
Samˡ. John Sprague Vose, Born at Augusta Maine Febʸ. 16. 1805.
Edward Henry " " " " Janʸ. 10, 1807, and died June 23, 1810.
Mary Tucker Vose born at Augusta Maine Octo. 15, 1808.
Walter Spooner, " " " " July 23, 1810.
Catharine Sarah, " " " " Janʸ. 31, 1813
Martha Eliza " " Lancaster ⎫ Twins—Augᵗ. 25, 1816.
Francis Henry " " "   ⎭

Attest JOSIAH FLAGG *town clerk.*
Entered from a Manuscript Feb. 9. 1828.

142 Sparhawk Houghton Son of Elijah Houghton and Mary Houghton was born May 23 1773.
Sophia Houghton daughter of Elijah & Mary Houghton was born June 15. 1775.
143 Silas Son to Silas and Abigail How born Janʸ. yᵉ 19ᵗʰ: 1770
Rebeca Daughter to Ebenezer and Keziah Buss born September yᵉ 11ᵗʰ, 1769
Salvenes [Silvanus?] Son to John and Sarah Dunsmoor born July yᵉ 5ᵗʰ 1769
Phebe Dunsmoor Born March the 9 1773
William, Son to John and Mary Bixby born Feb: yᵉ 5ᵗʰ 1770.
Doley Daughter to Roger and Mary Ross Born July yᵉ 19ᵗʰ 1769.
John Goss Son to Joseph and Sarah Goss Born July yᵉ 15ᵗʰ 1770.
James Son to Marcy Wilder Born May yᵉ 5ᵗʰ 1763
Hovey Son to Bartholomew and Elisabeth Parson born July yᵉ 28ᵗʰ 1770.
Calvin Son to William and Patience Judevine born May yᵉ 28ᵗʰ 1760.
William Son to William and Patience Judevine born January yᵉ 17ᵗʰ· 1765.
John Son to John and Mary Brooks born Octoʳ yᵉ 8 - 1770
Betty Daughter to Jonathan and Joana Osgood born Novembʳ yᵉ 11ᵗʰ 1770
Anne Daughter to Zeph and Damaros Williams Born October yᵉ 28ᵗʰ 1770.
Silas Son to Silas & Elisabeth [Sawyer] Wilder Born November yᵉ 12ᵗʰ 1770.
Solomon Son to Joshua & Esther Sawyer Born august yᵉ 15ᵗʰ 1770
Annas Daughter to Joseph and Ruth Dunsmoor Born November yᵉ 3ᵗʰ 1770
Samuel Son to Samuel and Phebe Sawyer Born October yᵉ 11ᵗʰ 1770.
James, Son to James and Zerviah Pratt Born December yᵉ 8ᵗʰ 1770
Epheraim Son to Edward and Sarah Nuton Born Sept yᵉ 17ᵗʰ 1768.
Annace Daughter to Edward and Sarah Nuton Born March yᵉ 21ᵗʰ 1770

144 *The Beths of the Children of Mr Jonathan and Thankfull Fairbank*

William Born March yᵉ 2ᵗʰ, 1736
Jabez Born March yᵉ 22ᵈ, 1738
Jonathan Born January yᵉ 25ᵗʰ, 1740
Jonathan Born January yᵉ 29ᵗʰ, 1743
Joshua Born February yᵉ 23ᵗʰ, 1746
Jonathan Born May yᵉ 18ᵗʰ, 1748

Lemuel Born May yᵉ 8ᵗʰ, 1751
Thankfull Born July yᵉ 12ᵗʰ, 1753
Seth Born December yᵉ 17ᵗʰ 1755
William Born March yᵉ 7ᵗʰ 1759
Rebeckah Born June yᵉ 20ᵗʰ 1761

Ephraim Son to Ezekiel and Mary Kendall Born December yᵉ 23ᵗʰ 1768.

The Children of Roger and Tamazen Bartlet.

John Born March yᵉ 13ᵗʰ 1766
Moses Born April yᵉ 13ᵗʰ 1768

Hannah Born March yᵉ 13ᵗʰ 1770

Elnathan Son to Ebenezer and Mary Talor Born October yᵉ 7ᵗʰ 1769.

BOOK FIRST.

The Beths of the Children of Ebenezer and Prudance Knight

Abel Brown at Harvard December y⁰ 16ᵗʰ 1763
Salmon Born March yᵉ 29ᵗʰ 1766   Ruth Born March yᵉ 26 1770
Pheabe Born March yᵉ 2ᵈ 1768

145 *The Children of Elijah Houghton and Mary his wife.*

Oliver Houghton Born January yᵉ 19ᵗʰ 1765   Maverick Born Sep: 22ᵈ 1768
Elijah Born Jan: yᵉ 11ᵗʰ 1767   Lockheart Born Janʸ: yᵉ 7ᵗʰ 1771
Polley Daughter to Epraim and Sarah Richardson Born December yᵉ 21ᵗʰ 1769
Nathan Son to Nathan and Dinah Goodell Born Sept. the 11ᵗʰ: 1762.
John Son to Jotham & Dinah Sawyer Born Febʸ. 21ˢᵗ 1767
Dinah Dauʳ. to Jotham & Dinah Sawyer Born July 11ᵗʰ. 1768

The Beths of yᵉ Children of Jabez & Meriam Fairbank.

Abigail Fairbank Born Decʳ. the 31ˢᵗ. 1759   Alpheus Born July yᵉ. 24ᵗʰ 1766
Hannah Born March 8 1761   Salle Born Novʳ. yᵉ 29ᵗʰ 1767
Meriam Born Auᵗ. yᵉ. 31ˢᵗ. 1762   Lieza[Eliza?] Born Decʳ. yᵉ. 11ᵗʰ 1770
Jonathan Born March 13ᵗʰ 1765   Jabez Born May yᵉ 28ᵗʰ, 1772

The Beths of yᵉ Children of Jeams & Ruth Richardson

Releaf Born Augᵗ. yᵉ. 20ᵗʰ, 1758   Lucy Born Augᵗ. yᵉ. 22ⁿᵈ, 1764
Abel Born April yᵉ. 13ᵗʰ 1761   Menassah Born Septʳ. 15ᵗʰ 1766

Solomon Son to Samˡˡ. & Lucy Herring Born Octʳ. yᵉ 13ᵗʰ 1770
Samuel Son of Samuel Hawkins & Patience Wyman born December 2ᵈ, 1779.

146 *The Beths of the Children of Jonathan & Tamar Whitcomb*

Jonathan Born Octʳ yᵉ. 23ʳᵈ. 1762   Betty Born April yᵉ. 30ᵗʰ. 1767
Thoˢ. Born April yᵉ. 20ᵗʰ. 1764   Annis Born April yᵉ. 11ᵗʰ. 1769
John Born Sepʳ. yᵉ. 15ᵗʰ. 1765   Nathan Born Decʳ. yᵉ. 9ᵗʰ. 1770

The Beths of the Children of Zebulon & Susannah Rice

Josiah Born august yᵉ 30ᵗʰ. 1750   John Born Janʸ: yᵉ 2ᵗʰ 1764
Zebulon Born Sepʳ: yᵉ 4ᵗʰ 1752   Luke Born march yᵉ 1ˢᵗ 1765
Simeon Born April yᵉ 10ᵗʰ 1768   Stephen Born Decʳ: yᵉ 31ˢᵗ 1766
Jonas Born Feb: yᵉ 16ᵗʰ 1754   Joseph Born august yᵉ 6ᵗʰ 1769
Eliakim Born april yᵉ 1ᵗʰ 1756   Benimin Born Janʸ; yᵉ 29ᵗʰ 1761
Reubin Born august yᵉ 10ᵗʰ 1757   David Born ——
Susanna Born march yᵉ 22ᵗʰ: 1759   Elizabeth ——
Elisha Born July yᵉ 27ᵗʰ 1760   Dolly ——
Molley Born Janʸ: yᵉ 16ᵗʰ 1762

The Births of the Children of Seth and Martha Haywood

Sarah Born March yᵉ 24ᵗʰ 1766   Mary Born Octoʳ. 24ᵗʰ, 1771
Seth Born Jany. 16ᵗʰ, 1768   Benjamin Born July 10ᵗʰ, 1773-
Anna Born January yᵉ 28ᵗʰ 1770

147 Adam Son to Adam & Margret Freman [Fleeman] Born Febuary yᵉ 25ᵗʰ 1767.
Hannah Daughter to Joseph & Eunice Weson Born Febʸ: yᵉ 23ᵗʰ 1768.
Stephen Son to Joseph and Eunice Weson Born Sepʳ: yᵉ 15ᵗʰ 1770.

The Children of Nathaniel and Phebe Jones.

Nathaniel Born August yᵉ 21ᵗʰ 1763   Salley Born Feb: yᵉ 5ᵗʰ 1769
Phebe Parson Born Feb: yᵉ 15ᵗʰ 1764   Eunice Born Novembʳ yᵉ 18ᵗʰ 1770
Betty Born Novemʳ: yᵉ 13ᵗʰ 1765   Samuel Born May yᵉ 14 1772
Phebe Born April yᵉ 16ᵗʰ 1767

Phebea Daughter to Samuel & Elisabeth Burpee Born May yᵉ 11ᵗʰ 1745.

The Children of Roger and Lucy Robbins

Silas Born Novemb^r: ye 24th 1746
Luke Born April ye 25th 1748
Jacob Born Dec^r: ye 16th 1750
John Born Jan^y: ye 12th 1756

Lucy Born Sept, ye 8th 1758
Levi Born May ye 5th 1761
Jude Born April ye 17th 1765.

Abigael Daughter to Josiah & Abigael Houghton Born august the 8th 1769
Daniel Son to Thomas May and Thankfull his wife Born Sept. ye 16th 1766.
Jonathan Son to Roger & Mary Ross born Feb: ye 14th 1771
John, Son of Christopher & Hannah Osgood born Novem^r. 5th. 1770
Josiah, Son of William Richardson ye 3^d, & Esther, born April 23^d. 1770
Allice Daughter of Joseph & Allice Whelock born May 1st. 1770

The Children of Joseph & Allice Wheelock

Martha Born July 11th 1752
John Do. Septr 22^d 1754
John Ju^r. Do. Jany 28th 1757
Joseph Born March 2^d 1759
Oliver Born May 6th 1761

Martha Born Sept 7th 1763
Archenus Jany 22^d 1766
Abel Born April 14th. 1768
Elijah Born April 13th. 1773

148 The births of ye Children of William & Mary Phelps.

Elisha Phelps Born August 31st. 1762
Elizabeth Do. born Septem^r. 21st. 1765

Dolley Phelps Born May 20th. 1768
Calvin Do. Do. May 10th. 1770

Elce Daughter of Edward & Eunice Poor, born April 23^d, 1770

The births of the Children of Jonathan & Mary Whitney

Mary Whitney born January 14 1767
Elisabeth Do. Do. February 14, 1766
Jonathan Do. Do. March 27, 1771

Jonas Whitney born August 27, 1772
Zaccheus do. do. March 11, 1774

The births of the Children of Jona. & Lucy Whitney

Ephraim born March 28th, 1780.
Nancy, born November 13th, 1784

Sally, born Octr. 19th, 1786

John Son of Lyn & Hannah Jock born 24th, of April 1771
Eunice Daughter of Israel & Katherine Moors born 24th, March 1771
Hannah Daughter to William & Anna Jewett Born may 23^d 1771
Sally Daughter of John White Jur. & Lydia White, born Novem^r: 24th, 1770
Dolly Daughter of Peter Thurston & Dolly Thurston born Novr 6. 1766
Peter Son of Peter Thurston and Dolly Thurston born Septr 23 1768
Anna Daughter to Eph^m Jur & Abigel Carter Dec 3^d 1771
Elisabeth Daughter to Zachariah and Abigail Eager Born Jany. ye 16th 1771.
Mary Daughter [to] Jon^a Ju^r & Debrah Wilder born Feb. ye 5th 1772
Anna Daughter to Phineas and Ruth Houghton born March ye 1th 1772.
Patience Daughter to William and Patience Judevine Born July ye 1th 1771
149 Betty ye Daughter of Ebenezer & Prudance Knight Born April ye 7th 1772.
Patience Daughter to Josiah and Mary Benett Born November ye 16, 1769
Elias Son to Josiah and Mary Bennett Born Jany ye 18th 1772
Ruth Daughter to Thomas Ross Jur and Prisila his wife born March ye 4th 1769
Leynard Son to Thomas Ross Jur and Prissila his wife Born Octo^r ye 18th 1771
Phinas Son to Timothy and Patience Haywood born March ye 12th 1770.
James Son to Timothy and Patience Haywood born July ye 1th 1771.
William Son to William and Thankfull Brook born July ye 28th 1771

The Children of Franses and Mary Prouty

Abel Born Decr ye 23^d 1767
Tirzah Born Feb: ye 15th 1769

Isac Born May ye 23^d 1771

Gardner Son to Eph^m. and Sarah Richardson born March ye 9th 1772
Henry Son to Fradrack Abart and Mary his wife born March ye 25th 1772.
Prisila Daughter to Joseph and Miriam Bixby born april ye 9th 1772
John Son to John and Marcy Manning Juner born may 1st 1771

The Children of John and Prudance Manning

Israel Born Jany. ye 29th 1756.
Peter Born November ye 25th 1757
Prudance Born April ye 6th, 1761
Unity Born october 14th, 1763
Artimus Born august ye 13th, 1766
Joseph Born June ye 24th 1768

Eph^m. Son to Isac & Eunice Evlet Born May ye 11th 1770

150   *The Children of Ebenezer and Lydia Pike Jur.*

William Born august ye 1th 1763
Susanna Born June ye 21th 1765
Elijah Born May ye 17th 1768
Annas Born Jany. ye 20th 1772

Ethan Kendall Son to Ethan and Thankfull Kendall Born May ye 7th 1772.
Tamer Daughter [to] Silas and Abigail How Born Sep^r: ye 1th 1772
Sophe Daughter to Jonathan Osgood and Joann his wife Born Novr. ye 23^d. 1772
Samuel Son to James and Zeviah Prat Born October ye 15th 1772
Betty Daughter to Joshua and Esther Sawyer born Sep ye 17th. 1772
Sophia Daughter to James and Sarah Curtis born august ye 26 1772
Lucy Daughter of Caleb and Anes Whetney born Sepr. 25 1770 and Dyd Feb ye 7th 1771
Eunice Daughter of Levi & Rebeckah Moor born Decr. ye 1 1771
Elijah Ball Son to Elijah and Rebekah Ball born august the 29 1771.
Lucy Daughter to Joseph & Sarah Goss born June 8th 1772
Martha Daughter to Samuel and Phebea Sawyer Jur Born october ye 30th 1772.
Jabez Son to Joseph & Agnes Sawyer born octob^r ye 13th 1770
Dolley Daughter to David and Hannah Nelson born Decr. 20th 1772
Luke Son to Samuel & Prudance Prentice born July ye 17th 1770
John Tower Son to Joseph and Hepsabeth Tower born may ye 14th 1771
Ebenezer Son to Amos & Prisila Jewett Jur born may 13th 1769
Samuel Son to Amos and Priscilla Jewett Jur born Feb^r. 25th 1772
Sarah Daughter to Moses & Margret Burpe Born June 9th 1760
Elisabeth Daughter to Moses & Margret Burpe Born Jany. 29 1773
Mary Daughter to James & Elisabeth Kendall Jur Born December the 3^d 1771

151   *The Beths of the Children of John and Anna Moor*

John Born Decembr 26th 1767
Samuel Born July ye 5th 1769
James Born Sept. 18th. 1771
Thomas Born July 18 1774

Submit Daughter to Aaron & Abigail Sawyer born August ye 5th 1770.

The Berths of the Children of Samuel and Martha Burpe Jur

Hannah born No^r. 25th, 1757
Nathan born Decr. 12th 1758
Elijah born March 1th 1761
Marah born Jany. 29th 1763
Stephen born Oc^r: 16th 1766
Azuba born Jany. 15th 1769
Elisabeth born April 16: 1771

Samuel Son to Edward & Sarah Newton born Feb: 28th 1773.
Ezra Son to John & Kezia May Jur born Jany. ye 7th. 1772

The beths of the Children of Eph^m. and Lucretia Wilder

Elisabeth born July ye 22^d 1763
Rebecah born Sept. ye 7th, 1765 and Dyed May ye 14th, 1766
Joel born July ye 7th, 1767
Josiah born July ye 16th, 1770
Harrison born February 11th, 1774
[Samuel Locke, born May —, 1776. Book of the Wilders.]

The Beths of the Children of Levi & Elizabeth Nicols

Mary born May ye 4th, 1761
Elisabeth born May ye 29th, 1763
Eunice born Novr. ye 25th, 1765
Levi born Oct: ye 30th 1767
Luke born Oct: ye 31th 1769
Sarah born July ye 17th 1771

152   Anna Daughter to Thos & Abigail Gates born Oct: 12th 1770
John Son to Thos & Abigail Gates born Feb^r. ye 1th 1773
Edward Son to James & Bathsheba Goodwin born Oct ye 26, 1770
Charles Son to Samuel & Dolly Ward born April ye 16th 1773

Molley Daughter to Samuel & Abigail Garrish Born April y⁰ 24th, 1772
Sparhuark Houghton Son to Elijah & Mary Houghton Born May 23d 1773.
Reubin Son to Stephen and Martha Holman Born Febr y⁰ 4th 1773.
Dolley Daughter to Joshua & Dorothy Kendall Born May y⁰ 18th 1772.
John Aldis Son to Asa Haven & Eunice his wife Born April y⁰ 25 1771.
Ezekiel Son to Roger & Tamezin Bartlit born June y⁰ 30th 1773.
John Son to John & Keziah Keindrick born July y⁰ 10th 1773.
Anna Daughter to Elisha & Meriam Allen Born March y⁰ 16 1773
William Son to Joshua & Mary Fletcher Born august y⁰ 9th 1772
Jonathan Son to John & Elisabeth Lowring born January y⁰ 20th 1773
Polley Daughter to John & Marcy Maning born Sept y⁰ 15th 1773.
Cornelious Son to Israel & Caterine Moor born April y⁰ 6th 1773
John Son to Brthw. & Elisabeth Person born Sepr: y⁰ 4th 1773.
153 Reubin Son to Timothy & Patience Haywood born Novr: y⁰ 11th 1773.
Enos Son to Shubael & Hannah Bayley born Novr: y⁰ 20th 1771
Tamer Daughter to Fortunatus & Tamer Eager born July y⁰ 9th 1773.
Lucy Daughter to Aaron & Lucy Gary born May y⁰ 13th 1773.
Sarah Sprague Daughter to John & Katharine Sprague born November y⁰ 13th 1773.
Damaras Daughter to Joseph and Anes Brown born Dec: 16th 1772

The Children of Henry and Sarah Wyman

Sarah born Febr, 25th 1768   Rebeccah born Jany: 26th 1772
Mary born Octr 18th 1769

Paul Son to Elisha & Patience Sawyer Jur born October y⁰ 20th 1767
William Son to Elisha & Mary Sawyer Jur born April 13th 1771
Samuel Flagg Son to Elisha & Mary Sawyer Jur born Feby: 20th 1774
Sarah Daughter to Moses and Submit Wilder born May y⁰ 1th 1770.
Moses Son to Moses & Eunice Wilder born Oct 28th 1773.
Anna Daughter to Wm. & Elisabeth Tompson born Feb: 27th 1772
Abel Sone to Mosies and Eunice Wilder Born october 21 1778

154 *The Beths of the Children of Elisha & Susanna Sawyer.*

Thomas Born Sept y⁰ 7th 1757   Hannah Born June 9th 1765
Batrix born Octr 27th 1758   Elisabeth Born Nov. 20th 1767
Susanna Born June 22d 1760

Martha Daughter to Samuel & Martha Burpe Jur born December 26th 1773
Dolley Daughter of Edward & Eunice Poor born April 27th, 1772
Eleazar Son to Edward & Eunice Poor born Monday June 6th, 1774
Samuel Son of John & Anna Phillips born November 18th, 1773
Lucy Daughter of Phineas & Bridgett Wilder born January 29th, 1774
Calvin Son of Samuel Wilder Junr. & Martha his wife born October 30th, 1772.
Allice Daughter to Samuel Wilder Jur. & Martha his wife born April 8th, 1774.
Wyman Son to Ethan & Thankfull Kendall Born April 9th. 1774
David Son to David & Annas Margaret Russell Born Novr 18th, 1773
Artamus Son to Jonath. y⁰ 4th. & Hannah Kendall Born Augt. 31st 1773
Oliver Son to Nathaniel & Elizabeth Willard Born Novr. 4th. 1768
Dorethy Daughter to Nathaniel & Eliza. Willard do Feby 5th. 1770
Elizabeth daughter to Nathaniel & Eliza do. do August 19 1772
Samuel Son of Isaac & Eunice Eveleth born December 12th, 1773.
Abigail Daughter of Moses & Abigail Smith born 29th. July 1774
Ebenezer Allen Son of Ebenezer Allen Junr. & Mary, born October 30th: 1773
Thomas Son of Titus & Mary Wilder born January 21st: 1774
Nabby Daughter of Samuel & Abigail Joslin born Novemr. 24th, 1774
Moses Son of Moses & Abigal Smith born May 15th: 1777.
155 William Son of William & Sarah Deputerene born June 27th. 1758
Sarah Daughter of William & Sarah Deputerene born June 27th. 1760
Elisha Son of Elisha & Meriam Allen born July 24th. 1774 and Decest on October 2 1777 aged 3 yer and 2 months
Betsy Allin Born March 12 1778

The Children of Simon & Elizabeth Willard their berths

Ezra Willard born March 19th. 1761 Amasa Willard born March 1st. 1772
Mary Willard born Decemr 4th. 1762 Sarah Willard born January 27th: 1775
Ama Willard born June 11th. 1765

Sarah Daughter of Levi & Rebecca Moor born March 15th: 1774
Silence Daughter of Aaron & Abigail Sawyer Born December 23d. 1774.
Nathaniel Son of William & Anna Jewitt born 27th. august 1774
Lucy Daughter of John & Lucy Bennett born January 5th. 1774
Mary Daughter of William & Mary Locke born May 11th: 1773

The births of the Children of Thomas & Ruth Burditt.

Joshua born June 3d, 1768 Abel born June 18th, 1774
Polley born July 29, 1771

The beths of the Children of Silas & Lydia Fairbanks

Doley born Feb: 3d 1769 Cate bourn Febr 9th 1773
Lydia born March 3d 1770 Elisher Fairbank Born Apriel 7: 1775
Silas born August 14th 1772 Samuel Fairbank Born Januay 28: 1777

156 Sara Daughter of Benjamin & Sara Whitmore Born Octor 6th 1774
John Son to Solomon & Sarah Holman Born Sept 2d 1766
David Son to Solomon & Sarah Holman Born Jaune 12th. 1770
Dolley Daughter of Joshua & Esther Sawyer Born August 6th 1774
Betty Daughter to Samuel & Abigail Garrish born Novr 10th 1774
Anes Daughter to Ebenezer and Prudence Knight born April 25th. 1775
John Son to James & Bethsheba Goodwin born Sept 13th 1773
Daniel Whiten Son to Obediah & Lucy Grose Born March 30th 1774.
Hannah Daughter to Nathll & Phebea Jones Born December 29th 1774

The Beths of the Children of Nathan & Sarah Eager

Haran Born May ye 17th 1763 Fortunatus Born March 27th. 1767
Ephron Son to Nathan and Dinah Eager Born July 7th 1774
Esther Daughter to John & Keziah May Born March 8 1775.
Jonas Son to John & Elisabeth Lowring born March 13 1775

The Beths of the Children of William & Mary Kendall

Luther Born Febr: ye 7th 1775 Rufus Born Novr: ye 20th 1772
Lydia Daughter to Timothy & Lydia Knight Jur Born august the 13th. 1774.

157 ### The Beths of the Children of Wm. & Tamer Ross

Silas Born Sepr: 6th 1774 Seth Born Sept 6, 1777
Tamer Born Octr: 28th 1775 Simeon Born Sept 17 1779

Ruth Daughter to David & Ruth Jewett Born January 16th 1775
Amos Son to Amos & Mary Sawyer Born august 26th. 1768
Ephm: Son to Simon & Abigail Ross Born Octr: 1st. 1774
Eunice Daughter to Jonathan Wilder Jun & Deborah his wife Born September ye 4th 1775
Sarah Daughter to Daniel & Mary Robbins Born June ye 5th. 1774
David Nelson Son to John & Elisabeth Dresor born January 23d 1774
Hytty Daughter to John and Elisabeth Dresor Born June 21th 7751
Aaron Son to Israel & Katharine Moor Born May 17th 1775

The Beths of the Children of Ebenezer & Achsah Ross.

Ebenezer Son to Ebenezer & Achsah Ross born June 29th 1773
Presila Graves Ross Born Sepr: 29 1775.

Mary Daughter to James & Jemima Wilder Jur Born May 19th 1775.
Ebenezer Son to Ebenezer & Achsah Ross Born March 27: 1777
Ebenezer Son to William & Buler Brooks Born January 2: 1777

158   *The Beths of the Children of Samuel & Priscila Thurstin.*

Sally Born June 14th 1767
Susanah Born April 7th 1769
Hepsabeth Born August 1st 1771
Lydia Born January 24th 1774

Eunice Daughter to David & Dorothy Goodale Born February 26 1774.
Mary Daughter to Wm. & Elisabeth Tompson Born August 31th 1774
Noah Son to Thomas & Thankfull May Born December ye 4th 1775
Prudance Daughter to Jonathan & Elisabeth Moor Born Novr: 13th 1774
Abigaiel Daughter to Samuel & Anna Bayley Born June 29th 1750
Isaac Son to Samuel & Anna Bayley born Febr. 7th 1753
David Commoings Son to Jonas & Joanna Brooks Born Oct 22d 1775
Esther Daughter to Jabez and Lucy Brook[s] born Decr. 15th 1775
Thomas Son to Thomas & Presila Ross born Novr. 12th 1773
Lydia Daughter to Oliver & Lydia Powars born Novr: 12th 1774

The Beths of Thomas & Hannah Brooks' [Children]

159   Phebea Born March 6th 1770
Hannah Cutler Born August 26th 1771
Jabez Born June 1th 1773
Polley Born April 19th 1775

Benjamin Son to Reubin & Lucy Cutter Gary born June 23d 1774
Phebea Daughter to Samuel Sawyer Jur & Phebea his wife born Sept. 1th 1774
Charls Son to Manassah & Hannah Knight born Novr: 2d 1775
Peter Son to Samuel & Lydia Johnson born August 9th 1775
Peter Son to Ephm. & Reelief Divil Born July 8th 1776
Moses Sone to Moses & Hannah Newhall Born Sept 23 1764 & Died Septr 23 1775.
Moses Sone to Moses & Hannah Newhall Born Sept 8 1776
Oliver Sune to Ethan & Thankfull Kendall Born febuy. 17: 1776
Dinah Daughter to Jonathan & Eunice Bayley born Sepr 24th 1775
Betty Daughter to John & Sarah Dunsmoor Born Decr. 20th 1776
Sarah Daughter to Edward & Sarah Newton Born march 12th 1775
James Son to Edward & Sarah Newton Born Decr: 18th 1776
David Son to David & Sarah Osgood Born Decr: 31th 1774
Hannah Daughter [of] For[tunat]us & Tamer Eager born July ye 13th 1776

160   *The beths of the Children of Solomon and Elisebeth Stuart*

Catharine Born Novr. 12th 1769
Sarah Born Decr 10th 1771
Polley Born January 13th 1774
Samuel Born May 12th 1776

Roger Son to Roger and Tamazin [Bartlitt] born July ye 4th 1775
Rufus Son to Stephen & Martha Holman Born august 14th 1776
Cornelas Son to William and Patience Judevine born Novr. 2d 1776
Olive Dafter to Jabez & Meriam fairbank born June ye 9th 1775
Abner Son to Ezra & Keziah Sawyer born Novr. 8th 1762
Katharine Daughter to Edmund [Edward] & Eunice Poor, born the Eleventh day of Nov. 1776
Luke Son to Ephraim & Elizabeth Kendall born March 16th. 1776
Samuel Son to John & Keziah Kendrak born Janavary 3th: 1777.
Elisha Son to Elisha & Mary Bennett born Octr. 3th: 1775.

The births of the Children of Russell and Mary Knights

Daniel born April 14th. 1752
Carter born January 4th. 1756
Sarah born Febuary 14th. 1758
Mary born January 2: 1754

The births of the Children of Ebenezer & [Mary] Allen.

Thankfull. born July 30th. 1775.   Molly, born May 2th; 1777.

Betty, Daughter to Phinehas & Bridget Wilder born Feby. 23th: 1777.
Jonathan; Son born May 30th. 1776. to Jonathan & Rebaca Osgood.
Sarrah, Daughter to Jonathan & Hannah Kendall born July 2th: 1776.

161   *The beirths of the Children of John & Prudance Warrner.*

John, born June 16th, 1758, Elizabeth, born May 28th, 1770,
Prudence, born Sept: 4th, 1759. Frances, Do. Jany. 31th. 1772.
Levi,   Do. May 22th, 1761. Olive. Do. March 28th. 1774.
Anna, Do. Feby: 17th, 1763. Lucy, Do. Dec: 20th, 1776.
Abigail, Do. March 15th, 1768.

Abel, born the 4: April 1775, Son of John & Lydia White Junr.

The births of the Children of Margaret Fleeman.

Mary Magdalene, born 26th: March 1771.   Eunis, born 7th: June 1776.

Putnam born the 23: Augt: 1776: Son of Samuel & Pheby Sawyer Junr:

The births of the Children of Moses and Eunis Wilder.

Submit, born 26th. Feby. 1775.   Aaron, born 16th. Sept: 1776.

The Births of the Children of Nathll & Thankfull Beaman.

Sophia Born Febry. 11, 1771 Betsey Born April 27. 1775
Deborah Born March 1, 1773 Abigail born Feby. 12, 1778

Abraham Son of Asa and Lydia Wilder Born Decr. 20. 1776
Bathsheba Daugt. of James and Bathsheba Goodwin Born Octr. 2, 1777
Edward Son to John and Lidya Robbins born Sept. 17th, 1777

The Births of the Children of Joel and Prudence Phelps

Sylvester Born March ye. 7. 1763 & Died April 7. 1765
Prudance Born January 25, 1765 Isabel Born March ye 1, 1772
Lucretia Born June ye. 13, 1768 Jesse Born January ye 18, 1774
Sylvester Born April 10. 1770 Ruth Born January ye 29, 1776

162   Joel Son of Joel and Louis Osgood Born April 13. 1775.
Sally Down, Daughter of Joseph Abbott Junr. & Hannah his wife Born July 22, 1777

The Births of the Children of Andrew & Louis Haskell

Prudence born Novr. ye 18. 1769 Sarah born Sept. 14. 1775
John Born January ye. 16. 1772

Israel Moor Son of Israel & Katharine Moor Born Novr. 11. 1777
Henry Son of Josiah and Polly Wilder Born March 27. 1777
John Sawyer Son to Elisha and Mary Sawyer Born august 11. 1776.
Fairbank Son to Elisha & Mary Sawyer born January 15. 1778.
David Jewett Son to David & Ruth Jewett Born May 26. 1777.
Rhoda Daughter of Joseph & Hannah Beaman born Sep. 19. 1760
Ephraim Son of Joseph & Hannah Beaman born Novr. 17. 1770
Rebeca Daughter of Joseph & Hannah Beaman born March 19. 1774
Nancy Dr. of Joseph & Hannah Beaman born Octr. 3. 1777

The births of the Children of Jonas and Lydia Powars

Peter Powars Born Sept. 28. 1771   Tryphene Powars Born March 8. 1776
Jesse Powars Born Sept. 28, 1773

James Wilder Son of Marcy Wilder Born May 5 1763

163   *A Record of the Births and Deaths of the Children of Cyrus & Lucy Fairbank.*

Lucy Born December 21 1763 Desest March 1, 1763
Lucy the Second Born February 21; 1765
Cyrus Born March 7: 1767
Anna Born Apriel 9: 1769 Decest on July 16: 1769
Anna the Second Born august 10: 1770 Decest on march 31 1773
Sarah Born Desember 29: 1772
Jonas Born October 7 1774

LANCASTER RECORDS.

Ephraim who was Still Born September 1 day 1776
Lucy Fairbank wife of Cyrus Fairbank Departed this Life September 16 1776 aged 36 yer and 8 Days.
Elesebeth Fairbank wife of Cyrus Fairbank Departed this Life in the 39 yer of her age October 1 1778.

Joshua Houghton Sone to Joseph and Rachill Baley Born November 25. 1776
Saley Daughter to Joseph and Rachill Bayley Born June 16 1778
David Son to Joshua & Esther Sawyer Born November 20: 1776
Polly Daughter of Joseph & Rachel Bailey born July 9th 1780.
Levie Prescott was Born Aprill 15: 1777 Sone to Jonathan and Azube Prescott
William Pitt, Son to Josiah & Polly Wilder born June 11, 1775

164 *The Burths of the Childrin of James & Elizabeth Kindal Junr.*

Person Kindal Born January the 4; 1767
Augustus Kindal Born February the 24; 1768
James Kindal the 3 Born November the 3: 1769
Mary Kendal Born Decr 4: 1771
Lidia Kindal Born February the 22: 1777

Abel Son of Capt. John White born Novr. 24th. 1779
Hanah Daughter of Jonathan and Eunes Bayley Born August 21 1777

The Burths of the Children of Mosies and Mary Sawyer

Mosies Sawyer Born May 29 1764	John Sawyer Born March 16; 1770
Molley Sawyer Born January 18 1766	Sarah Sawyer Born May 10 1772
Bettey Sawyer Born Apriel 18 1768	

the Children the sd Mosies hath had by Bettey Sawyer

Artimas Sawyer Born November 2 1777	Ezra Sawyer born Decr. 6, 1785
Joseph Sawyer born Jany. 21. 1780	Lusena Sawyer born Feby 14, 1788
Nathaniel Sawyer born Apr. 26, 1782	Katy Sawyer born Aug: 13, 1790
Peter Sawyer born Jany 25, 1784	Achsa Sawyer born Decr 25, 1794

Mary Sawyer wife of Mosies Sawyer Departed this Life Apriel 12 1774 in the 33 yer of her age.
165 Calvin Wilder Sone of Jonathan Wilder Jur and Debra Wilder Born May 4 1778.
Katey Moor Daughfter of Anna Margit Russil Born March 7 1776.
Jacob Son of William and Mary Willard Born Desember 14: 1778.
Molley Daughfter of Fortinatus and Tamor Eager Born September 15 1778,
Abraham Rice Son to Samuel & Mary Rice Born May 19 1777.
Sally Horsley Daughfter of David and Lucebe Horsley Born November 6: 1778.
Thankfull Fairbank Daughfter of Lemul and Febe Fairbank Born January 17: 1775.
Barakbokworh Fairbank Son to Lemul [&] Febe Fairbank Born august 16: 1778.
Josiah Bower[s] Son of John and Margret Bower[s] Born July 20 1752.
William Wilder Son to William and Relief [Carter] Wilder Born october 18 1778.
Patty daughter of William Wilder & Relief his wife born october 30, 1788.

166 *The Births of the Children of Manassah & Sarah Wilder.*

Sally Born September 22; 1775	Anna Born November 9 1778
Lucy Born January 9: 1777	

Allice, Daughter of Ephraim Divol Jur. & Releaf his wife born Novr. 3^d. 1785
Keziah Daughter of Eph^m. Divol Jur. & Relief his Wife born 22^d. July 1789
Esther Daughter of Ephraim Divol Junr. & Relief his wife born April 5th. 1783.
Betse Willard Daughter of Simon & Elizabeth Willard born March 28th. 1784.
Darby Son of Simon & Elizabeth Willard born November 16th. 1786.

The Births of the Children of Ephraim Carter Junr and Abigail his wife.

John Born Decem ye 9th 1768	Henry Born Jany 22 1780
Abigail Born Feby 13 1770	Sarah Born Feby. 22 1781

Anna Born Decem. 3ᵈ 1771
Epᵐ. Born Oct. 28 1773
Solomon Born Feby 19 1776
Polly Born March 17 1778

John Born April 27 1782
Susanna Born April 2ᵈ 1784 dec'd
Susanna Born July 20ᵗʰ 1785.

167 *The births of the Children of Frederick & Mary Albert*

Molley born June 18ᵗʰ. 1777   Joseph born Febry. 23ᵈ. 1780

The births of the Children of Frederick & Abigail Albert

Abigail born Febry. 23ᵈ. 1782   Daniel born April 7ᵗʰ. 1784

Patty Daughter of Benjamin & Martha Wyman born July 12ᵗʰ. 1787.

The births of the Children of Abel & Lois Phelps.

Lucy born Febry. 22ᵈ, 1779   Peter born April 17ᵗʰ, 1783
Sally born Octoʳ. 28ᵗʰ. 1780   Abel born Decʳ. 31ˢᵗ 1785

Jonas Morse Son of Sam & Lavina Phelps born Augᵗ. 21ˢᵗ 1788

The Births of the Children of Wᵐ. & Sarah Phelps.

Jonas Phelps, born Decʳ. 20ᵗʰ. 1779   Lucy Phelps born May 6ᵗʰ, 1783.

Births of the Children of Ezra & Mary Willard

Jonathan Wright born Sept 9ᵗʰ 1785   Mary born Octʳ. 12. 1789.
Amasa born Decʳ 12, 1787

168 *Births of the Children of Jonathan and Ruth [Prescott] Wilder*

Jonathan	Born Septʳ, 3ᵈ, 1780.		Luke	Born Septʳ. 9. 1791
David	" Feby. 15. 1781		Cephas	" May 23, 1793
John	" Novʳ. 2ᵈ, 1782		Prescott	" May 8 1795
Patty	" June 22, 1784		Louis	" July 23 1797
Nancy	" Decʳ. 30, 1785		Henry	" Feb. 4ᵗʰ. 1800.
David	" June 4, 1787		Frederick	" Jany 27 1804
John	" April 1. 1789			

Children of Aaron & Sally Phelps their births

Nancy born ——   John born August 4ᵗʰ 1785.   Rebecca born ——
Joseph born ——   Sally " ——   Lucinda " ——

169 *Births of the Children of John Sullivan Vincent a Negro and Lydia Savory a white Woman.*

Lovina born at Warwick Jany 1. 1805 as Lydia Savory saith.
Apica born in Lancaster May 27. 1807.
John,   do.   21ˢᵗ Octo. 1808
Sylvia   do.   15 Octo 1810,
Levi Newell born do.   June 8, 1813,

170 *The Burths of the Children of Samuel and Hannah Chirchil Born*

Samuel Chirchil Born october 31 1749   Abiah Churchil Born August 31 1759

The Burths of the Childrin of Thomas and Hannah Grant

Thomas Born July 26 1763   George Born apriel 27 1770
Katharin Born June 16 1766   Melzer Born Fubuary 6 1772
Hannah Born may 10 1768   William Born august 27 1774

Samuel Churchil Departed this life September 28 in the year 1759 in the 35 year of his age.

The births of the Children of Joseph & Anna Carter

Joel born Decᵗ. 19ᵗʰ. 1775   Anna born Augᵗ. 1, 1782
Joseph born April 19ᵗʰ. 1777   Lucy born June 11ᵗʰ, 1784
William May 11ᵗʰ. 1779   Sophia born Novʳ. 19. 1785
Elizabeth born Octoʳ. 8ᵗʰ, 1780

The births of the Children of Samuel & Martha Wilder

Joel born March 27th: 1777.   Daniel born March 15, 1779
Martha Daughter to Simon & Elizabeth Willard born Feby. 20th. 1779

The births of the Children of John & Lucy Willard

Lucy born May 22th: 1770   John born April 12th. 1774
Mary born June 13th; 1772   Cyrus born Feby. 22. 1778:

Seth, son to Elijah & Mary Woods born April 13th: 1777.
Charlotte daughter to Samuel Moor & Submit Taylor born May 9: 1775
Josiah Prentice Brown, son to Timothy & Eunice Brown born Octr 10. 1778
Jonathan, son to Jonathan & Mary Prescott born March 6th, 1779.
Tamer daughter to Silas & Abigail How born April 3: 1779.
Asa son to Joseph & Sarah Goss born June 14th, 1776.
Becky Daughter to William & Sarah Putrin [Deputrin] born Sept. 26: 1777
Eunice daughter to Jonathan & Deborah Wilder born Sept: 25; 1779
John Son to Joseph & Agnis Sawyer born March 15th, 1779
Nathaniel Son to Nathaniel & Mindwell Sampson born May 12: 1777.
Silas Son to Nathaniel & Mindwell Sampson born Decr 6. 1778.

The births of the Children of Fridrich & Mary Albert

Friderick born June the 18: 1774.   Joseph born Feby. the 21. 1780.
Molly Born June the 18 1777.

Rhoda daughter to Anna Powers born Decr: 17: 1774.
Hannah Daughter to Ephraim May born Novr. 8; 1779.

The birth of the Children of Samuel & Thankfull Bailey.

Dolly born Feby. 1st 1778.   James born March 4th 1780.

Lucy Daughter of Jonas & Damaris Johnson Born March 23 1779
Josiah Thompson Son of Samll. Thompson & Eunice his Wife Born March 2 1779.
Ebenezer Son of Ebenezer & Achsah Ross Born March 27 1777.
Benjamin Wilder Ross Son of Ebenezer & Achsah Ross Born Sept. 20 1778.

Children of John and Elisabeth Loring.

Daniel Born Novemb 27 1777   Betsy Born March 13 1780

The Birth of the Children of Joshua & Dorothy Kendal

Ephraim Born May 21. 1774   Joanna Born Jany ye 5th 1780.
Stephen Born November 13th. 1776

Betsy Daughter of David & Ruth Jewett Born Apr 28 1780.
Hannah Daughter of Edward Waldron Jr. & Hannah his Wife born Apr 29 1779.
Samuel John Sprague, Son of John & Katherine Sprague born June 26 1780
Ann Austin Sprague Daughter of John & Katherine Sprague born Febr 25 1776

Birth of the Children of John and Sarah Weeler.

Sarah Born April 10, 1770   John Born July 1, 1774   Ruth Born Jany 27, 1772
Tamazin Daughter of Roger & Tamazin Bartlet Born novembr 12 1777
Salme Son of Nathan & Sarah Farrow Born Apr 15 1779
Sam Dawkins Son of Patience Wyman Born Decr. 2d. 1779

Birth of the Children of Samuel & Elisabeth Jewet

Elisabeth Born Decemh 2 1774   Samuel Born Jany 14 1777
Betty Daughter of John & Elisabeth Dresser Born Oct 21 1777

Births of the Children of Benja. & Sarah Smith

Ester Born Decr 27 1776   Hannah Sheppard Born Jany 31 1779

BOOK FIRST.

Births of the Children of Edward & Sarah Newton
David Born Dec 21 1778   Ezekiel born Oct 13 1780

Births of the Children of Nathanel & Naomi Roper
Ephraim born Feb 6 1779   Michael born Dec 26 1780

Births of the Children of Elias & Louis Farnsworth
Elias Born Sep^t 9 1776   Ephraim Born Dec^b 8 1780   Asa Born Augt 27 1778
Ruth Daughter to Samuel Sawyer Ju^r & Phebe his Wife born Nov 11 1778
David Son to Jonathan Prescot Jun & Mary his Wife born Feb^r 7 1781

Births & Deaths of the Children of Levi & Rebecca Moor
Sarah Moor born March 15th, 1774   Prudence born Decem^r. 27, 1778
Prudence   Do. Deceased Octo^r. 6th. 1775
Luther Son of Micah & Molly Ross born June 25th. 1780

Births of the Children of Samuel & Lydia Johnson
Abel Born October 12th. 1778 at Ashburnham   Deborah born March 23^d, 1782
Betsey born February 12, 1780
Jonathan White, Son of Jonathan White & Rebecca White Born June 26th. 1781.

Births of the Children of Nath$_{ll}$. & Thankfull Beman
Nathaniel born April 17th, 1780   Jonas Farnsworth Born Feb^r. 14. 1784.
John born March 25th, 1782
Mary Daughter of Joshua & Mary Thomas was Born Novr. 25th, 1778.

173 *The births of the Children of Benjamin & Grizzell Apthorp Gould.*
John born June 26th. 1782   Esther born Octob^r. 31. 1785
Grizzell born Febry. 3^d. 1784   Benjamin born June 15th. 1787

The births of the Children of Timothy Whiting Junr, & Abigail his wife
John born October the 10th, 1782.   Sally Upton born Febry. 2^d. 1786.
Polly Born March the 17th, 1784.   Samuel Kidder born December 18th, 1787

Henry Son of Winslow Phelps & Rebecca his wife born December 27th, 1782
Anna Daughter of Winslow & Rebecca Phelps born November 7th. 1785.
John, Son of Joshua Fairbank & Rebecca his wife born Apr. 13th: 1779
Augustus Abel, Son of Joshua Fairbank & Rebecca born August 2^d, 1781.
Sarah, Daughter of Jotham & Mehitabel Woods born September 24th. 1774.
Betsey Daughter of James Pratt & Zerviah his wife born Decem^r. 31. 1780
Justin Elliott Frink Son of William Frink & Sarah his wife, born May 30th, 1783.

The births of the Children of Abijah & Susannah Rugg.
Nahum born Jany. 13, 1781   Ame born May 5th. 1782

Births of the Children of Jeremiah & Rebecca Ballard.
Josiah born Augt. 8, 1779.   James born Decr. 4th: 1788.
Salley born Augt. 21st, 1781.   Dolly born March 9th, 1794
Liphas born Febry. 1, 1784.

John, Son of Edward & Eunice Poor born April 7th, 1781.
John Son of Thomas & Abigail Gates born Novr. 27th. 1778
174 Levi Son of Levi & Martha Page born April 11th. 1785

The births of the Children of John & Anna Ballard
John born April 13th. 1784.   Henry born Feb 14th. 1794.
Charles born Feb. 27th. 1786   Augustus born Augt. 1. 1795
James born May 18 1788   Mary Nichols born Dec 1. 1798
Nancy born Sept. 11th 1792.

Peter Son of Fredᵏ and Abigail Albert born Decemʳ: 21ˢᵗ, 1785

The births of the Children of Benjamin Whittemore Willard and Annis his wife Viz.

Benjamin born November 12ᵗʰ: 1783　　Annis born Decʳ. 22ᵈ, 1788.
Jacob born June 11ᵗʰ, 1786

Asahel, Son of Asahel & Millicent Tower born August 11ᵗʰ, 1787
Millicent Daughter of Do.　　　　born July 7ᵗʰ. 1790.
William Son of　　Do.　　　　 " Aug: 24, 1792
James　Do.　　　Do.　　　　 " May 16. 1796.

Births of the Children of Jonathan & Rebecca Osgood.

Nahum born July 10ᵗʰ. 1778　　Rebecca Do. Do. May 12ᵗʰ. 1785
Samˡ. Willard Do. October 27ᵗʰ, 1783

175　*The Births of the Children of John & Orpah Whiting.*

Timothy Danforth born Decʳ. 8ᵗʰ. 1785　　Sophia born Apr. 26: 1790.
Julia born May 9ᵗʰ. 1787　　　　　　　Fabius born May 10. 1792
Henry born Novʳ. 28: 1788.　　　　　Maria born March 29. 1794.

The Births of the Children of James & Bathsheba Goodwin Enter'd March 1788, by Edm Heard Town Clerk

James born May 9ᵗʰ, 1768.　　　Bathsheba, Octoʳ. 2ᵈ, 1777.
Edward do. Octoʳ. 26ᵗʰ. 1770,　Polley, Augᵗ. 19ᵗʰ. 1779.
John,　" Sept: 13ᵗʰ; 1773.　　Sarah, April 4ᵗʰ. 1782.

The births of Children of Levi Wilder & Sally his Wife, enter'd April 1788

Sampson Vryling Stoddard born May 20ᵗʰ, 1780 [Died 1864.]
Sally, born Decemʳ. 9ᵗʰ, 1781　　Betsy born Octoʳ. 22ᵈ, 1786
Peggy, born Sept. 7ᵗʰ, 1783　　Nancy " Feby 3ᵈ, 1789
Levi, born　do.　2ᵈ 1785.　　Nabby " July 17. 1791.

The Births of the Children [of] Benjᵃ. Houghton & Hannah his Wife.

Benjᵃ. born April 18ᵗʰ, 1788.　Betsy — Octʳ. 1ˢᵗ, 1792
Polly　—　June 14, 1789　　Cephas — July 7, 1794.
John　—　April 19, 1791

176　*The Children of Josiah & Polly Wilder enter'd April 18th, 1788 pr Edm Heard Town Cler.*

William Pitt, June 11ᵗʰ: 1775　　Augustus, Novʳ: 4ᵗʰ: 1779
Henry, March 27ᵗʰ: 1777　　　Polly, Octoʳ. 8ᵗʰ: 1780
Polly, Augᵗ. 22ᵈ. 1778　　　　Henry, April 27ᵗʰ: 1782

The Births of the Children of William & Mary Locke. Enter'd May 5th: 1788
　　　　　　　　　　　　　　　　　　EDM HEARD

Mary, Born May 11ᵗʰ: 1773　　Josiah, Octoʳ: 1ˢᵗ: 1780
William, April 2ᵈ. 1775　　　James, Augᵗ. 28: 1782
Anna, March 6ᵗʰ: 1777　　　Nancy, do. 26: 1784
Polly, Octoʳ: 29ᵗʰ: 1778　　Lucretia, June 5ᵗʰ: 1787

The Births of the Children of Jonas Wyman and Hannah his wife Enter'd April 1789　Edm Heard Town Cler.

Polly, born 28ᵗʰ, July, 1773.　　Sally, born 23, June, 1782.
Betsy, born 25ᵗʰ, July, 1775.　　Jonas, born 9, Sept. 1784
John, born 1, Nov. 1777.　　　a birth stillborn May 19, 1786
Samˡ. born 12, Mar. 1780.　　Stephen born 3ᵈ June, 1788.

177　Elisha Fletcher son of Rufus & Polly Fletcher born Sept. 5ᵗʰ. 1786.
Sophia Daughter of the above born Octoʳ. 18ᵗʰ. 1788,
Artimas Son born Octʳ. 10ᵗʰ. 1790.
Cynthy, Daughter born Janʳ. 31. 1792.

Births of the Children of Timothy Whiting Jur. & Abigal his Wife

Levi born Jany. 27: 1790.   Nancy, March 8, 1793.

Samuel Johnson Wyman Son of Mathew & Abigal Wyman Born March 8th: 1758: Enter'd Sept. 21st. 1790. EDM HEARD.

Dolly Wyman, Daughter of Saml. Johnson Wyman & Dolly his Wife, Born April 15th. 1787.

Samuel Wyman, Son of Samuel Johnson Wyman & Dolly his Wife, Born May 30th. 1789.   Entered Sept. 21st. 1790. EDM HEARD

The Births of the Children of Jonathan & Betsy Tinney

Jonathan born Dec^r: 12th: 1784.

Births of the Children of Menasseh & Hannah Knights.

Patience born July 17th: 1777   Mary, born June 5th; 1781.
Patty,   "   May 8th: 1779

178   *Births of the Children of Willm. Junr. & Sally Willard*

Polly born March 29th; 1789   Luke, born May 22^d. 1793.
Sally,   "   May 20th: 1791   William, "   Septr. 22^d. 1795.

Births of the Children of Jonas & Dolly Lane.

Jonas, born Decr. 22^d: 1789.

Births of the Children of Salmon & Rebecca Godfrey

Eunice	born June 3^d. 1771.	James	born May 5th: 1780
Sarah	" Feby. 15, 1773	Salmon	" July 18th. 1782
Solomon	" Augt. 20th. 1775.	Debenah	" Novr. 21st. 1785
Rebecca	" Septr. 15th; 1777		

Births of the Children [of] Eben^r. & Ruth Haven

Kesey [Keziah] born Nov. 8th: 1788.

Births of the Children of Nathl. & Nancy Miller

Nathan born Jany. 30th. 1792.

179   *Births of the Children of John and Marcy Manning:*

Peter	born June 5th, 1775	Israel	born Octr. 1^t. 1786
Ephraim	" March 25. 1778	Susannah	" June 20th: 1789
Paty	" April 21st. 1780	Sally	" Feby. 22^d. 1792.
Silvester	" May 12th. 1782.	Sally	" Jany. 16. 1794.
Phyneas	" May 17th. 1784		

Births of the Children of William & Lucy Hudson.

William born April 19. 1787.

Births of the Children of Thos. & Abigail Ballard.

Polly born May 9. 1788.   John born Jany. 1, 1793.
William born Jany. 17. 1790.   Sophia, born December 27. 1794.
John born Octr. 22. 1791.

Births of the Children of Moses & Rebecca Dickerson.

Paul	born May 25. 1774	Saml	born May 18. 1782
Moses	" March 26. 1776	Stephen	" Jany. 19. 1785
James	" Decr. 1. 1777	Lemuel	" Augt. 18. 1789.
Rebecca	" March 14. 1780	Lucy	" June 29. 1793.

180   *Births of the Children of Prudence & Jacob Phelps.*

Oliver,	born April 9. 1781.	Betsey	born Septr. 18. 1789
Jacob	" July 18, 1782	Lucretia	" Octr. 9. 1791
Ephraim	" June 25, 1784	William	" July 12. 1793.

Phineas born Dec.r 12, 1785
Edward   "   Nov.r 9, 1787
Roxana born Jany. 18. 1795
Lidia Phelps born June 26 1791 [7]
William died March 10. 1794

Births of the Children of Benj.a & Martha Wyman.

Patty born July 12. 1787
Polly " Oct.r 28: 1788
Betsey " May 15. 1791
Submit born Dec.r 3, 1792.
Emily   " July 27th. 1794

Births of the Children of Eli & Sarah Haynes

Eli, born June 9. 1793

Births of the Children of Jon.a & Rebecca White.

Jacob born Sept. 26. 1785
Sophia " Nov.r 4. 1789
David born July 12. 1794.

181   Births of the Children of William and Almy Stedman

Christopher Ellery, born May 15. 1792.   Mary Ann, born Oct.r 24th. 1794
 Christopher Ellery was lost at sea, on his voyage to Calcutta East Indies, 9th of August 1809.
 Mary Ann died July 31st, 1807.

Births of the Children of Daniel Jun. & Lucy Willard.

Sally born April 16. 1790.   Lovey born Jany. 27, 1792.

Births of the Children of Phinehas & Mary Fletcher.

Phinehas born May 15. 1791
Polly   "   Oct.r 5. 1792.
Betsy born Sept 25, 1794

Births of the Children of Gardner & Cate Wilder.

Lucy born Feby. 6. 1793.

182   Births of the Children of Leonard & Sarah Farwell.

Sally   born Feby. 6. 1787.
Joseph   "   July 6, 1789.
Benjamin "   Jany. 13, 1792.
Levi born May 22. 1794.
Betsy " July 23, 1799.

Births of the Children of Abner & Axer Pollard.

Abner born Feby. 21. 1790
Polly   " Feby. 26. 1791.
Emily born Nov.r 7. 1793.
Achsah " Nov.r 30. 1795.

Births of the Children of David & Sarah Peirce

Betsy born 13th. July 1793   Dana born 7th. Sept.r 1795.

Births of Children of John White 3d & Sophia his wife

Jonas Beaman, born 23d Apr: 1795

183   Births of the Children of Thomas & Betsy Tooker.

William born Aug: 1, 1784.
Thomas   " Feby. 17, 1786.
Betsy   " July 2d, 1788.
Polly born Jany: 27, 1792.
Nancy " July 2. 1794.

Births of the Children of Elisha & Anna Rugg.

Lucy, born Feby. 17. 1783
Elisha, " Oct.r 22. 1784
Nathan, " Oct.r 22. 1786
Artemas, born Apr: 18, 1793
Anthony, " Jany. 29. 1796.

Births of the Children of James & Sophia Campbell.

Sophia born Dec.r 9. 1795.

David Son of Thomas Holt & Dinah his wife born July 22d, 1772.

Births of the Children of Paul & Martha Willard

Dexter born Apr: 28 1793   Paul born Aug: 4, 1795

Births of the Children of John Maynard & Martha his wife

Dolly   born Septr 15th, 1786   Anna, born Feb 1. 1793 & dec^d. ye 19th
Patty,   "   Decr 16th. 1787   of same month
Gardner,   "   Novr 29. 1789   John born Feby 25, 1794.
Polly,   "   Mar: 14. 1791   Anna, "   Feby 26, 1796.

184 Sarah daughter of Daniel Kies & Jededah his wife born July 17th. 1795.

Births of the Children of Thomas Carter & Sally his wife

Thomas, born Feby. 1. 1787   Abel, born Apr: 3. 1792
Alpheus,   "   Apr. 30 1789   James, "   Feby 6. 1794
Cephas,   "   Nov, 1st. 1790   Eli,   "   Novr 30. 1795.

Births of the Children of James Capen & Elizabeth his wife

James born May 5. 1786   Henry born March 20. 1793
Betsy   "   April 28. 1788   Sally   "   Apr: 29. 1796.
John   "   May 16. 1790

Births of the Children of Eli Stearns & Mary his wife, & deaths of two of them.

A Son born Sept 30th 1786, & dec^d Octr. 18, same year.
Charles, born Novr 15, 1788   Mary, born Jany 25. 1792
Henry,   "   Decr 12. 1790 & dec^d Elizabeth born Nov 18. 1793
    Jany 7. 1791.   Sophia born Sept 26. 1795

Births of the Children of Samuel Allen & Lucy his wife.

Susey born Octr 14, 1788   Cynthia born Octr 29. 1794
Abraham " July 6. 1792

185 *Births of the Children of Moses Sawyer Junr. & Elizabeth his wife*

Sally, born May 7th. 1793.   Charles, born Novr. 2^d. 1795.

Birth of the Children of John Carter & Martha his wife

Abigail, born Aug: 16th. 1796.

Sarah Toppan, daughter of the Revd Nathaniel Thayer & Sarah his wife was born August 21st. 1796.

Births of the Children of Aaron Johnson & Elizabeth his wife.

Jonas   born December 13th. 1772   Sarah born September 7th, 1781
Elizabeth "   January 8th. 1774   Anna   "   June 17th. 1784
Deborah "   June 1st, 1777   Calvin   "   June 12th. 1786
Aaron   "   October 13th. 1779   Luther   "   September 6th. 1788.

Births of the Children of Nathaniel Kendall & Rebecca his wife

Nathaniel born March 2^d, 1783   Samuel born Decr 17, 1788
John   "   Decr 11, 1784   Thomas "   Decr 28. 1789
Rebecca "   Feby 15, 1786   Henry   "   April 2, 1794
Nabby } Twins born Sept 6, 1787   Hannah "   March 18, 1796.
Relief }

186 *Births of the Children of Josiah Flagg & Dolly his wife.*

Samuel Ward born April 22^d 1803.   Dolly   born July 25, 1793
William born July 29, 1790   Rebecca "   May 8th, 1795
Sally   "   Nov. 19, 1791   George Washington born Jany 31, 1797.
    "   "   Obiit Octo. 17, 1819.

William Flagg died Feby. 7th 1806, on his passage from Batavia E. Indies.
Nabby daughter of Robert Phelps & Mary his wife born March 16th 1795.

LANCASTER RECORDS.

Births of the Children of Jonathan Barret & Ruth his wife.

Jonathan born Feby. 5, 1790

Joseph }
Polly } Twins born July 19, 1796.

Births of the Children of John Thurston & Rebecca [Gates] his Wife.

Thomas born July 6, 1783 & dec'd Decr 14 1785.
Betsey   "   March 14 1785   Thomas born Feby. 22, 1794.
Anna   "   Jany. 15, 1788   [Charles ———]
John   "   April 16, 1790   [Lucy ———]
Sophia   "   May 21, 1792

Births of the Children of Silas Thurston & Sarah [Kendall] his wife

Samuel   born August 27, 1787   Harriot born July 24 1797
Cynthia   "   June 4, 1789   David Kendall born July 25 1799
Sally   "   April 5, 1791   Mary   "   June 19 1801
Silas   "   June 10th, 1793   John   "   March 20 1808.
Hannah   "   June 16, 1795.

187   *Births of the Children of Jacob Fisher & Nancy his wife*

[Nancy, born February 13, 1793: family records.]
Jacob born Novr. 5, 1794.
Somes White, son of Abijah White & Bathsheba his wife born March 1, 1795.
Julia Goodwin daughter of Edward Goodwin & Sally his wife born Jany. 18, 1796.

Births of two of the Children of Joseph Rugg & Mary his wife

Mary born June 9, 1793   Joseph born Nov. 21, 1794.

Births of the Children of Abijah Rugg & Susanna his wife

Betsy,   born July 26, 1786   Luke born May 9. 1793.
Susanna   "   Sept. 8. 1789

Births of the Children of Thomas Bennett jun & Isabell his wife, & their deaths.

Dorothy, born Feby 27. 1793 died June 9, 1796.
John, born March 29, 1795 died June 11, 1796.

Births of the Children of Joseph Leach & Susannah his wife.

Henry born Aug: 19, 1793   Sally, born May 1. 1795.

Births of the Children of Timothy Fletcher & Hannah his wife & death of one of them.

Charles, born Jany 14, 1794   George born June 1st. 1796.
Martha deceased July 22^d, 1794 aged 2 years 10 months & 3 days.

188   *Births of the Children of Benj^a Wheelock & Prudence his wife.*

Nancy, born Apr: 16, 1784   Cephas, born Aug 22, 1790
Betsy,   "   Novr 14, 1785   Arathusa, "   Jany 12, 1793
Sophia daughter of Sparhawk & Nancy Houghton born Septr. 8th, 1794.

Births of the Children of James Pratt & Lydia his wife

Sally born Dec 24th, 1794   Hariot born June 7, 1796

Fidelia, daughter to Samuel Rugg & Sarah his wife, born Aug: 29, 1794.

Births of the Children of Samuel Wilder 2d & Elizabeth [Joslyn] his wife

Nathaniel born June 30, 1794   Cynthia born Jany. 14, 1796.

Births of the Children of Samuel Sargeant & Mary his Wife

Hannah born April 3^d. 1781   John born Sept. 18, 1785
Samuel   "   July 13th. 1782   Seth   "   Feby. 21, 1787.
William "   Feby 18th. 1784

189 *Births of the Children of Gates Thurston & Betsey his wife.*
James, Born Novr. 9th 1790.   John, Born March 18 1794.
Henry, Born Augt. 19 1792.

Births of the Children of Salmon Willard and Rachel his wife
Benjamin born Sep^t. 9th 1794   Abraham Carleton born Mar 7th 1796

Births of the Children of Daniel Stearns and Deborah his wife.
Deborah and Martha Stearns born June 1st, 1792.— Twins!

Births of the Children of Elijah Houghton Jr. and Ruthy his Wife
Samuel Fisk born Augt 13th 1793   Harriot born Sept 11 1797.
Elijah born May 28, 1795.   Maria born Mar. 15 1801

Births of the Children of Israel Butler and Anna his Wife.
Benjamin born Feb. 7th 1778   Samuel born January 23 1784
Abel   "   April 19th 1779   Abijah   "   Jany. 18 1786.
John   "   April 10th 1781.

190 *Births of the Children of Joel Osgood and Lois his wife*
Joel Osgood born April 13th 1775.   Aaron Osgood born July 7 1786
Lois Osgood " May 25 1778   Dolly   "   " Jany. 13 1789.
Moses "   " March 31 1781   Daniel Powers Osgood born Octo 26 1790.
Sophia "   " April 18 1783   Appollos   "   "   Sep 31 1792.
Lois Osgood wife of the sd Joel, deceased Nov. 15th 1792

Births of the Children of Joel Osgood above named and Lucretia his Wife.
Lucy born June 8th 1794   David born March 24 1798
Peter " Feb 16 1796
Joel Osgood died Nov. 8, 1821, aged seventy-five years.

Births of the Children of Dr James Carter and Susanna his Wife.
James born Dec. 14 1780.   Susanna born July 8 1793 and deceased
Calvin born Dec 4 1783.   July 25th 1795.
   Sewal born Sept 9, 1796.

191   *Births of the Children of Philemon Allen*
Sophia born May 12th 1782   John born April 9th 1789
Betsy born May 2 1786   Sparhawk born Nov 22^d. 1790

Births of the Children of Joseph White and Rebecca White
Rebecca   born April 10th 1785.   Sally Abbot born Augt. 5th 1795
Elizabeth   "   May 9th 1789   William Hunt " Feb. 4th 1798
Joseph White   "   Nov. 26th 1790   Mary Chase   " May 27 1805
Samuel Farrar "   Nov. 6 1792   James White " Octo 12 1806

Children of Samuel Adams & Elizabeth Adams
Samuel Adams Jun born July 10th 1781.

Births of the Children of David & Luceby Hosley.
Sally born Nov. 6th. 1778.   John born April 21. 1781.

192   *Births of the Children of Nathan & Nabby Puffer.*
Lucy Cotting Puffer born Feb. 15th 1796   Harriot Puffer born March 16th. 1799.
Loring Puffer born July 4th 1797   William born Jany. 17th 1801.
Nabby Puffer, wife of Nathan Puffer died Novr. 23 1802, aged 28 years.
Joseph Osgood Son of Jonathan & Rebecca Osgood was born Augt. 3^d, 1790.
   Attest JOSIAH FLAGG *town Cler.*

John 2 Willard was married to Lucebe Avery in May 1767.
Aaron Willard father of John died May 27th 1784 aged 83 yrs. 4 M. and 3 days.
Sylvia Willard daughter of John Willard died Aug. 29th 1777
Cyrus Willard died April 10th 1780

193 *Births of the Children of John Willard and Lucebe Willard*

John	born	Dec 17th 1768		Abigail	born	June 7th 1780
Lucy	"	May 22d 1770		Josiah	"	April 16 1782
Mary	"	June 13th, 1772		Levi	"	Nov. 22d 1784
Jesse	"	April 12 1774		Lucebe	"	April 2d 1786
Sylvia	"	April 24 1776		Rachel	"	July 2d 1794
Cyrus	"	Feb 22d, 1778		Abel	"	Octo 9th. 1796.

Births of the Children of Joshua & Mary Fletcher.

Joshua	was born	Feb 25 1749		Peter	was born	Sep 5 1762
Timothy	"	Sept 20 1750		Rufus	"	Octo 14 1764
Phinehas	"	May 29 1753		Anne	"	Sep 29 1767
Elisha	"	June 18 1755		Sophia	"	Nov 22 1769
John	"	Octo 1. 1757		William	"	Aug 9th 1772.
Mary	"	June 23 1760				

194 *Births of the Children of Gardner Phelps and Mary his Wife*
Mary born June 19th 1788

Rugg James Son of Daniel and Elizabeth Rugg born February 5th. 1788.
Anna Gates, born Sept 10th 1748, and was married to John Moor March 4th. 1767.

Their Children are as follows viz:

John Moor Jr, born Dec. 26th 1767.
Samuel   "   "   July 5th 1769
James Moore   "   Sep 18th. 1771 Sterling
Thomas   "   July 15 1774 Sterling
William   "   born Augt. 17th. 1778 died Feb 26th. 1808
Nancy   "   "   Augt. 26th, 1782. Sterling
Achibald & Artemas Twins born April 31, 1786 at Worcester
Henry born Nov. 11th. 1790. Sudbury.

Entered by desire of Mrs. Moore.

Henry Moore was killed in a Battle with the British Troops and Indians at Brownstown Aug 3. 1812.

195 Abel Wilder Son of Stephen Wilder & Betty his Wife born June 22, 1780.
George Phelps son of Joel & Prudence Phelps born June 6th. 1778.

The births of the Children of William Greenleaf Jun and Maria his Wife viz:
Edmund Q. Greenleaf was born Octo 30th. 1789.
William Josephus Greenleaf was born July 8th. 1791.

Births of the Children of Nathaniel Eaton and Lucy his Wife viz.
Henry was born Dec 23d 1779.

Births of the Children of Eliakim & Hanah Sawyer.
Lucy Ann born in Boston May 22. 1811   Eliakim, born Lancaster Dec 7, 1812
Helen Ann Byron born in Boston May 15th 1807, and brought to Lancaster by
    Mrs Atherton the wife of Dr Atherton who adopted her into her family.

196 *The births of the Children of James Newhall and Mary his wife*
James Born at Sterling Nov. 12. 1800.
Albert   "   at Leominster April 10, 1802.
Mary Louisa Born at Bernardston August the 5, 1804.
Moreton Born at Bolton Feby 3, 1805.
Jerome   "   at Lancaster June 5, 1806 and died March 6, 1808.
Dalmer Born at Do. Jany. 4, 1809.
Martha Anne Born at Do. March 20, 1811.
Susan   "   "   Sep. 5, 1813.

Jacob son of John Houghton and Anna Houghton his wife was born July 24 1680
Jacob Houghton & Rebecca Whitcomb were Married Dec 16 1704.
Jacob Houghton Son of Jacob Houghton & Rebecka his wife was born January 2, 1708
Jacob Houghton and Mary Willard were Married April 6. 1730.
Abraham Son of Jacob Houghton & Mary his wife was born March 13, 1735.
197 Abraham Houghton & Sarah Divoll was married August 11th. 1750.
Jacob Son of Abraham Houghton and Sarah his wife was born November 26, 1760.

The foregoing are the Descendants of John Houghton from Lancashire England and his wife Anna. Entered by Request of Henry Houghton, of Putney Vermont as his certificate on file will show.
May 16 1825. Attest JOSIAH FLAGG *town Clerk of Lancaster.*

The following entry is made at the request of Henry Houghton one of the posterity of John Houghton Esqr. who died in Lancaster February 3. 1736-7.

Is by tradition from his ancestors, that John Houghton with his wife fled from England to America, to enjoy their Religion: They being the parents of the said John Houghton Esquire, who came with them in his infancy.
Entered by me, JOSIAH FLAGG *town Clerk*

NOTE.—For the records upon pages 198, 199, 200 of Book I, see Ralph Houghton's Register, pages 9 to 11 of this volume.

201 MARRIAGES
Consumated by the Revd. Timothy Harrington.
1775
March 22. John Abbott, and Lois Bennett both of Lancaster.
April 2. Moses Mosman of Sudbury, & Mary Willard of Lancaster.
May 30. Ephraim Kendall, & Elizabeth Knights both of Lancaster
July 20. Joseph Joslyn, & Dorothy Osgood, both of Lancaster —
Sept. 10. Lemuel Sawyer, & Anna Pratt, both of Lancaster
Octr. 5. Eleazer Brown of Swansey, New Hampshire, & Susanna Rugg of Lancaster
Octr. 25. John Prescott Junr. & Mary Ballard, both of Lancaster
Octr. 31. Nathaniel Haskell, & Abigall Sawyer both of Lancaster
Novr. 23. Revd. Jacob Biglow of Sudbury, & Elizabeth Wells of Lancaster.
Decr. 26. Capt. Israel Jennison of Worcester, & Margaret Coolidge of Boston Resident in Lancaster
Decr. 27. Col: Joseph Wilder, & Rebecca Locke, both of Lancaster
1776
Janv. 6, Samuel Moor, & Abigal Hastings, both of Lancaster
Jany. 11, Jonathan Osgood, & Rebekkah Divoll both of Lancaster
Jany. 18, Capt. Samuel Mower, of Worcester. & Esther Locke of Lancaster
Feby. 21, John Hoar of Westminster, & Abigal White, of Lancaster
Feby. 29, John Chandler, & Katy Holman both of Lancaster
July 16, Henry Willard Farmer, & Sybil Knights, both of Lancaster
1777
Feby. 27, Daniel Knights, & Mary Woods both of Lancaster
March 5, Luther Fairbank, & Thankfull Wheelock both of Lancaster
April 23, Moses Sawyer, & Betty Larkin, both of Lancaster
pr me TIMOTHY HARRINGTON.

The above List of Marriages Consumated, I received April 24th, 1777 and Examined and Entered: WILLm. GREENLEAF, *Town Clerk.*

The above List of Marriages, I have deliv'd to the County Register.
April 26th. 1777. pr WM. GREENLEAF *Town Clerk*

202 *Marriages Consumated by the Revd. Timothy Harrington*
1777.
May 1. Mr. Samuel Adams, & Mrs. Elizabeth Nowell both of Lancaster
May 8: Mr. Josiah Sawyer, & Mrs. Susanna Green both of Lancaster

June 2: Mr. Joseph Willson of Keene, & Mrs. Sarah Wilder of Lancaster
June 19. Mr. Samuel Dickerson, & Mrs. Lois Willard both of Lancaster
June 26. Mr. Israel Butler, & Mrs. Anna Phillips both of Lancaster
July 2. Cyrus Fairbank Deacon, & Mrs. Elizabeth Wynne both of Lancaster
Augt 6: Mr. Zebediah Wyman, of Woburn & Mrs. Eunice Wyman of Lancaster
Decr 18: Mr. William Wilder, & Mrs. Relief Carter both of Lancaster

1778

Jany. 12: Mr. Ephraim Munrow, & Mrs. Mary Atherton both of Harvard
April 1. Mr. Samuel Thompson, & Mrs. Eunice Dole both of Lancaster
April 8. Mr. Joseph Farnsworth, & Mrs. Mary Hersey both of Harvard
May 7: Mr. Abel Phelps, & Mrs. Lois Willard both of Lancaster
May 28: Mr. Jonathan White, & Mrs. Rebekkah Haskell both of Lancaster
Sept. 7: Mr. Thomas Cnmming, & Mrs. Dolly Chace both of Lancaster
Dec. 30. Mr. Nathaniel Eaton, & Mrs. Lucy Bennet both of Lancaster

1779

Jany 24. Doctr. R. Perkins Bridge, & Mrs. Anna Harrington both of Lancaster
Jany 31. Mr. Jacob Fowle, & Mrs. Elizabeth Abbot, both of Lancaster
March 2. Mr. Jonathan Wallas of South Brimfield, & Mrs. Elizabeth Osgood, of Lancaster
March 4. Mr. Jeremiah Ballard, & Mrs. Rebecca Joslyn both of Lancaster
March 31. Doctr. Jonas Prescott of Rindge, & Mrs. Susanna Wilder of Lancaster

             pr me TIMOTHY HARRINGTON
The above List examined & Entered.
LANCASTER April 30th, 1779.   pr Wm. GREENLEAF T. Cler.
The above List is sent to the Register; pr Wm. GREENLEAF T. Cler.

203 *Marriages Consumated by Josiah Wilder Esqr.*

1776, May 2 Abijah Warner of Harvard & Elsea Fuller of Lancaster
  Sept 29 Daniel Clarke and Lydia Harris Both of Lancaster
  Octr. 1 Person Richardson and Hannah Jewett both of Lancaster
Feb 13: 1777 Jacob Wilder to Lydia Sawyer both of Lancaster
Decr 4 Benjamin Richardson and Abigail French both of Lancaster,
Decr 8 Jude Piper and Deborah Brooks both of Lancaster
1778 January 1 Joshua Houghton Jur to Ruth Kilburn both of Lancaster
     Entered Feby. 28 1778 pr NATH. BEAMAN T. Clerk

  Marriages Consumated by Joseph Wheeler Esqr.
Jany. 12: 1779. Thomas Sawyer, & Susanna Wilder, both of Lancaster.

204 *Marrages Consumated By the Revd. Reuben Holcomb*

1779 Dec{br}. 9th Wm Goss, & Mary Moor both of Lancaster
 Dec{b}. 9 John Seavery, & Phebe Kendal both of Lancaster
 Dec{h}. 9 Wm. Fairbank, & Kezia Houghton both of Lancaster
 Dec{b}. 12 Oliver Bowker, & Anna Pearson both of Lancaster
1780. March 2 Samuel Wait of Malden & Rebecca Harris of Lancaster
 May 18 Isaac Buck, & Patty Phillips both of Lancaster
 June 8 Solomon Jewett, & Martha Burpee both of Lancaster
 Novr. 29 Peter Smith of Sudbury & Lucy Willard of Lancaster
 Dec{b}. 7. Ebenz. Pope, & Lucrecia Wilder both of Lancaster
1781. Jany 1st. Israel Manning, & Lidia Wright both of Lancaster

here follows an Account of the marriages consumated by the Revd. Timothy Harrington viz:
       in 1779.

June 1st. Benjamin Houghton of Bolton & Rebecca Tucker of Lancaster.
Augt. 17th. Joseph Farwell & Mary Haskell both of Lancaster.
Sepr. 8, John Coolidge of Lancaster & Hannah Preist of Marlboro'.
Sepr. 12, William Phelps Junr. & Sarah Beaman both of Lancaster
Octor. 14, John Wheelock Junr. & Dolly Wilder both of Lancaster.
 Do. 28, Timothy Kendall & Eunice Houghton both of Lancaster

BOOK FIRST. 127

1780
Jany. 26. Jacob Phelps & Prudence White both of Lancaster
Feby. 23^d, Thomas Harrington & Rebecca Ballard both of Lancaster
Do. 24, Jonathan Wilder & Ruth Prescott both of Lancaster.
March 5th, Deacon Cyrus Fairbank & Abigail Wyman both of Lancaster
April 5th. Worcester Winslow of Worcester & Phillis Parkis of Lancaster
Do. 23^d, Henry Winchester of Ashburnham & Lois Phelps of Lancaster.
Do. 23^d. ⎫ Dr. Tim^o. Harrington of Pembrook N. H. & Sarah Wilder of Lan-
[May 8.] ⎬ caster
⎭ Benjamin Kimball of Harvard & Anna Wilder of Lancaster
June 28. Nathl. Tayler & Sarah Fuller both of Lancaster.
Sepr. 19. Samuel Serjant & Mary Darling both of Lancaster.
Octo^r. 10. Elisha White Junr. & Deborah Hunt both of Lancaster
Novr. 21, David Robbins of Ringe & Mary Ballard of Lancaster
Decr. 7th, Benjamin Bennett of Fitz William N. H. & Elizabeth Knight of Lancaster

205 in 1781
July 12th, Amos Allen & Rebecca Thurston both of Lancaster
Do. 19th, Benjamin Gould of Topsfield & Grizzell Apthorp Flagg of Lancaster
Octo^r. 21st. John Ballard & Anna Phelps both of Lancaster
Novr. 10, John Winter of Ashburnham & Phebe Wright of Lancaster
Do. 13th, Enoch Whitcomb of Bolton & Sarah Tucker of Lancaster
Do. 25th, Hon. Levi Lincoln of Worcester & Miss Martha Waldo of Lancaster

1782.
Febry. 5th John Bennett of Weathersfield in Vermont & Sarah Joslin of Lancaster
April 4th. Simon Butler & Elizabeth Butler both of Lancaster.
Do. 18th. Amos Knight & Lydia Johnson both of Lancaster.
June 18th. Jonathan Wheelock Junr. & Lucy Beaman both of Lancaster.
Octo^r. 24th. Oliver Wheelock & Lucretia Smith both of Lancaster
Decr. 11. Asa Carter & Mary Joslin both of Lancaster

1783
Jany. 1. John Thurston & Rebecca Gates both of Lancaster
May 13th. John Munroe, of Harvard & Lucy White of Lancaster
June 22^d. Amos Sawyer of Lancaster & Prudence Geary of Sterling
Sepr. 18. Eliphalet Hills of Newbury & Sarah Wyman of Lancaster
Octo^r. 21st. Benjamin Bancroft of Rindge & Deborah Whiting of Lancaster
Novr. 4. Jonathan Thayer of Charlemont & Lucretia Rugg of Lancaster
Decr. 4. David Bennett & Abigail Chase both of Lancaster.

1784
Febry. 5th. William Deputron & Mary Wyman both of Lancaster
March 11. Thomas Wright of Sterling & Eunice Osgood of Lancaster
April 22^d. Gardner Phelps & Molley Baldwin both of Lancaster
June 20th. Peter Manning & Rebecca Carter both of Lancaster
Aug^t: 29. Samuel Johnson Junr. & Dolly Dole both of Lancaster
Sept. 1. Lemuel Barrett & Rebecca Knowlton both of Lancaster
Novr 25th Oliver Tenny & Deborah Phelps both of Lancaster
" " Ezra Willard & Mary Kendall both of Lancaster
Decr. 27 [23]. Ephraim White & Elizabeth Phelps both of Lancaster

206 in 1785.
Jany. 17. Levi Page of Harvard & Martha White of Lancaster
Feby. 10. Mathias Felton of Fitz William & Releaf Kendall of Lancaster
March 2^d. Ezra Osgood & Suzzanna White both of Lancaster
August 11. Abel Allen & Mary Symmons both of Lancaster
Do. 21. John Wyman & Abigail Lippenwell of Lancaster
Do. 31. Isaac Temple of Shrewsbury & Elizabeth Houghton of Lancaster
October 25th. Capt. John Maynard of Framingham & Martha Wilder of Lancaster
" " Capt. Abijah Wyman of Ashby & Martha Stevens of Lancaster

Novr. 9. Reuben Lippenwell Junr. & Dolly Wyman both of Lancaster
Do. 21. Abner Mitchell; molatto, of Lunenburg & Jenny Blackendon of Lancaster, negro.
Decr. 5. Elijah Carter & Sarah Bridge both of Lancaster
Do. 15. James Divol & Sarah Powers both of Lancaster
Do. 21. Thomas Houghton Junr, of Harvard & Betsy White of Lancaster

A. D. 1786.

Jany. 24th. Simeon Perry & Hannah Newton both of Lancaster
March 9th. Eli Stearns & Mary Whitney both of Lancaster.
June 8th. Oliver Chase & Releaf Beaman both of Do.
July 4th. John Dollison of Sterling & Esther Sawyer of Lancaster
Do. 20th. Thomas Carter & Sally Clarke both of Lancaster
Augt. 23. [30, in family records.] Benjamin Wyman & Martha Joslyn both of Lancaster
Novr. 16. Josiah Houghton of Wendall & Mary Nichols of Lancaster.
Do. 30th. Isaac Rugg & Rebecca Wilder both of Lancaster
Decr. 14th. John Locke & Esther Phelps both of Lancaster.

A. D. 1787.

Jany. 28th. Peter Fletcher of Alstead State of N. H. & Sally Piper of Lancaster
Febry. 28. Ephraim Whitney of Guilford State of Verm^t. & Eliz^a. Clarke of Lancaster
March 19. William Ballard & Elizabeth Whitney both of Lancaster
April 1st, Levi Greenleaf of Bolton & Mary Willard of Lancaster.
May 29, William Bridge & Abigail Carter both of Lancaster
Do. 30th Ebenezer Haven & Ruth Houghton both of Lancaster
June 5th. William Hobart of Townshend & Dolley Smith of Lancaster
Do. 27th. Samuel Allen & Lucy Smith both of Lancaster
July 31. George Wilker of Ashburnham & Martha White of Lancaster
Augt. 2^d Benjamin Houghton the 3^d, & Hannah Newhall both of Lancaster
Do. 8. Joseph Wyman & Lydia Lippenwell both of Lancaster
Novr 12th, Stephen Thurston of Fitchburg & Mary Osgood of Lancaster

Recv^d. the aforegoing return of the Rev^d. Mr. Harrington March 3^d, A. D. 1788, and recorded the same.   pr SAM^L WARD *Town Clerk.*

207   MARRIAGES CONSUMATED,

Decem^r. 23 : 1787. By John Sprague of Lancaster Esqr.

Oliver Brewster of Boston & Anne Ivers Resident in Lancaster were married by John Sprague Esqr.
April 18th: 1788.   Enter'd pr EDM HEARD *Town Cler.*

208   *Marriages Consummated by Josiah Wilder Esqr.*

1776.

May 2^d. Abijah Warner of Harvard & Elsea Fuller of Lancaster [See p. 203.]
Sep^t. 29. Daniel Clerk, & Lydia Harris both of Lancaster   "
Oct^o. 1st. Person Richardson, & Hannah Jewett both of do.   "
Decr. 4th. Benj^a. Richardson, & Abigal French both of do.   "

1777.

Feb 13 Jacob Wilder, & Lydia Sawyer both of Lancaster   "
Dec 18 Jude Piper, & Deborah Brook both of   do.   "

1778.

Jan 1st. Joshua Houghton, & Ruth Kilbourn both of Do.   "
Mar. 5 Seth Fairbank, & Relief Sawyer both of   Do.   "
Apr .. 21. Calvin Moore of Lancaster, & Susanna Cumming of Wobourn
May 19th. Paul Wilson, & Ruth Burnam both of Bolton
June 22^d. Silas Houghton. & Mary Knight both of do.
Do. 29th. Josiah Leavet. & Azubah Osgood both of Lancaster
Oct. 8th. James Townshend of Bolton, & Olive Sawyer of Lancaster.
Do, 15th. Joshua Brook, & Lucretia Wait both of   do.
Do. 28. Elijah Wilder, & Azubah Larkin both of Lancaster.

Nov. 5   Eliakim Rice, & Hannah Kindal both of Winchendon
Do. 30.   Sam¹. Page Capt. of Danvers, & Rebecca Putnam of Lancaster.
Decʳ: 20ᵗʰ.   Timo. Kilbourn, & Relief Richardson both of   do.
   do.   Willis Wilder, & Relief Wheelock both of   do.

1779

Feb. 11ᵗʰ.   Elijah Dressor, & Sarah Houghton both of do.
Lar. 25ᵗʰ.   Aaron Sawyer, & Kezia Sawyer both of do.
Apr: 7ᵗʰ.   Stephen Goss, & Hannah Burpee both of do.
do. 8ᵗʰ.   Richard Leese of Shrewsbury, & Patience Richardson of Lancaster
May 13ᵗʰ.   Abraham How of   do   & Parney Sawyer of Lancaster
do. 23ᵈ.   Ephraim Powers, & Keziah Sawyer both of   do.
do. 30ᵗʰ.   Ephraim Wilder, & Hannah Reed both of   do.
June 30.   Jonathan Whitney, & Lucy Smith both of   do.
Augᵗ. 26.   Jonathan Willard, & Anne Goodenough both of   do.
Octoʳ: 12ᵗʰ.   John Spofford, & Lucy Robbins both of   do.
       27.   Joseph Cutting of New Marlboro' State of New Hampshire, and Dorathy Whitcomb of Lancaster
Novʳ. 17.   John Eaton of Winchendon & Molley Larkin of Lancaster

209

1780

Apr. 7ᵗʰ.   Thomas Burdit, & Lois Sawyer both of Lancaster.
   12ᵗʰ.   Ebenezer Harwood of Sutton, & Elizebeth Lippenwell of Lancaster
May 4ᵗʰ.   John Snow Jur., & Hannah Parker both of   do.
do. 16ᵗʰ.   Sherebiah Hunt, & Ruth White both of   do.
July 12ᵗʰ.   Robert Hudson of Shrewsbury a Briton, & Dinah Butler of Lancaster
Augᵗ. 20ᵗʰ.   Ebenezer Fitch of Rindge State of N. Hampshire, & Persis Bush of Shrewsbury, State of Massachusetts.
Dec. 12ᵗʰ.   John Canouse a German Soldier, & Phebe Butler of Bolton.

1781.

Janʸ. 1ˢᵗ.   Abraham Headly, & Eunice Evelith both of Lancaster
Feb. 14ᵗʰ.   Stephen Fuller of Fitchburg & Anne Lippenwell of Lancaster.
Mar. 13ᵗʰ.   Phillip Corey, & Patience Lees both of   do.
Apr. 19ᵗʰ.   Stephen Corey, & Triphene Wilder both of   do.
June 1ˢᵗ.   Thomas Kyes, & Ruth Davis both of Bolton.
   do.   Moses Fisk, & Lucy Bush both of Shrewsbury
Sept. 19ᵗʰ.   Silas Houghton, & Judah Houghton both of Bolton
Dec 2ᵈ.   Aron Phelps, & Sally Capon both of Lancaster
   13ᵗʰ,   Ruben Moore, & Esther Russel both of Bolton

1782.

Janʸ. 6ᵗʰ.   Philemon Allen, & Allice House both of Lancaster
Apr. 18ᵗʰ.   Benjᵃ. Stow of Harvard, & Abigal Atherton of Bolton
May 19ᵗʰ.   Tilley Richardson of Sterling, & Mary Thurston of Lancaster
do. 23ᵈ.   Paul Sawyer, & Martha Wheelock both of Lancaster
July 4ᵗʰ,   Jacob Sawyer of Sterling, & Esther Coolidge of Shrewsbury
do. 30ᵗʰ   Benjᵃ. Hastings, & Experience Ball both of Bolton
Octʳ. 31ˢᵗ,   Luke Wilder of Leominster, & Anne Wilder of Sterling.
Novʳ. 13ᵗʰ.   Elisha Rugg, & Anne Clerk both of Lancaster
   28ᵗʰ.   Thoˢ. Divol Leominster, & Polley Smith of Lancaster
Dec 9ᵗʰ,   Thomas Kindall, & Lucy Baldwin both of Lancaster

1783.

Feby. 13ᵗʰ.   James Osbourn, & Rebecca Whitney both of Bolton
March 13.   Benjᵃ. May, & Lucy Richardson both of Sterling
210   April 13ᵗʰ.   Ezekiel Russel, & Ruth Hastings both of Bolton
May 5ᵗʰ.   David Baldwin, & Olive Phelps both of Lancaster
July 24ᵗʰ.   Calvin Sawyer, & Relief Houghton both of do.

1784.

Feby. 16ᵗʰ.   Ruben Wilder Sterling, & Mary Peirce of Shrewsbury
Mar. 18ᵗʰ.   Josiah Randal Stow, & Prudence Sawyer of Sterling
April 1ˢᵗ.   Samˡ Snow Juʳ., & Dorothy Richardson both of Sterling
June 23ᵈ.   Danˡ. Willard Fitchburg, & Relief Phelps Lancaster

July 17th. Jonathan Tinney, & Betty Willard both of Lancaster
Octo. 14th. Sam¹. French Fitchburg, & Eunice White of Lancaster.

1785.

Jany. 5th. Sam¹. Woods, & Betty Woods both of Leominster
Mar. 24th. Rufus Moore, & Rachel Moore, both of Bolton
April 25th, Jonas Cutting, & Sally Baker both of Northboro'
June 1st. John Fletcher, & Rachel Woods both of Lancaster
do. 2d. Moses Chase of Lancaster, & Parna Hastings of Berling.
do. 16th. Luther Sawyer, & Zilpha Houghton both of Lancaster
Novr. 16th. Abial Holt, & Dolly Fairbank both of Sterling
Decr. 1st. Solomon Pratt, & Rebecca Richardson both of Sterling

1786.

June 29th. Rufus Fletcher, & Polly Sawyer both of Lancaster
Augt. 18th. Ceasar Corbet, & Caty Hastings both of Sterling

1787.

Febr. 1st. Alexander Patterson of Henaker State of N. Hampshire, & Polly Nelson of Sterling
Augt. 10th. Doct. John Dunsmore Lunenburg & Hannah Dunsmore of Lancaster

1788.

Jany. 13th. Luther Harris of Worcester & Grace Briant of Berling

The foregoing list of marriages I received of Josiah Wilder Esqr. April 18th, 1788 the same Entered & Examied pr me   EDM HEARD *Town Cler.*

July 27th 1788, Jno Hooley & Mittee Belknap both of Sterling

211 April 30th: 1789.
A return of Marriages Consummated by the Revd. Timo. Harrington Viz.
                 Dated 30th. of April, 1788.
April 15th. Caleb Kendal of Ashburnham & Lucey Kendal of Lancaster.
Sept. 24 Abijh. Moore Boylston & Mary Sawyer of Lancaster.
Octor. 5th. 1788, Mr Jonas Lane & Mrs. Dolly Ballard both of Lancaster
  do. 14th " Onissmus Newel of New Ipswich, & Lidia Mead of Harvard.
  Nov.. 20th " Abijh. Wheelock, & Bathsheba Bennet both of Lancaster
  do. 27th " Daniel Sterns, & Deborah Carter both of Lancaster
              Sent to the County Clerk pr. E. HEARD *T. Cler*

Marriages Consumated by the Revd. Timothy Harrington 1789.
May 19th; Mr Abner Pollard to Miss Rachel Phelps both of Lancaster
June 7th: Josiah Flagg to Dolly Thurston both of   do.
Sept. 30. Josiah Bowers to Rebecca Prescott both of   do.
Novr. 26. Jabez Prescott to Naby Gates both of   do.
Decr. 3d. Samuel Stephens to Amy Willard both of   do.
Novr. 30th. Abijah Wilder Keene N. H. to Tamer Wilder Lancaster.

1790.

Jany. 12th. Gates Thurston to Betsy Pollard both of   do
Returned to the Clerk of Sessions for the County of Worcester
                                    EDM HEARD *Town Cler*

Aprl. 4th, 1791. This may certify that I William Stedman a Justice of the Peace for the County of Worcester, have never married any one, for which I desire to be thankful.   WM.. STEDMAN.
    Return'd to the Clerk of the Sessions for sd. County.
                        JOSEPH WALES, *Town Clerk.*

212 *Returns of Marriages Solemnized before Timy. Whiting Jun. Esquire between Aprl. 1790, & Apl. 4th. 1791.*

1790, May 30. Amos Pollard and Martha Phelps both of Lancaster.
    Augt. 16. Fredrick Albert of Boilston and Mary Shaw of Lancaster.
         31. Kendal Boutwel Jur. & Betsey White both of Fitchburg.

Septr. 26. Jona: Johnson and Eunice Willard both of Lancaster
1791. Feby. 14. Uri Sawyer & Lydia Pollard both of Bolton.
Apr^l. 3. Levi White & Polly Dole both of Lancaster.
Returned to the Clerk of the Sessions of the County of Worcester by
JOSEPH WALES *Town Clerk*.

Return of Marriages Solemnized before the Rev^d. Tim^y. Harrington between Ap^l. 1790, & Ap^l. 17, 1791.

1790. Novr. 21. Doct^r. Isaac Hurd of Concord, to M^{rs}. Polly Wilder of Lancaster.
1791. Feby. 15. M^r. Cyrus Fairbanks J^r. to Miss Mary Benit both of Lancaster.
March 13. M^r. Jon^a. Kendall to Miss Polly Clerk both of Do.
Apr. 17. M^r. Moses Jones to Miss Mittee Brooks both of Do.
Returned to the Clerk of the Sessions of the County of Worcester by
J. WALES *T. Clerk*.

Apr^l 10th. 1791. Israel Atherton Esqr. filed a Certificate certifying that he had never Married any one. Returned to the Clerk of the Sessions
J. WALES *T. Clerk*.

A Return of Marriages Solemnized by Tim^oy. Whiting Jur. Esqr. since the Month of April A. D. 1791.

Stephen Baker of Marlborough and Prudence Phelps of Lancaster, were Married November 17th. 1791.
Daniel Tucker Jun. & Sally Hannahs both of Shrewsbury, were Married January 30th. 1792.
Eber Godard & Lucy Johnson both of Lancaster, were Married April 11th. 1792.
Certifyed by TIMO^Y. WHITING JUN. *Just. Pacis*.

LANCASTER April 12th. 1792.
Returned to the Clerk of the Sessions by
JOSEPH WALES *Town Clerk*.

213 *A Return of Marriages Solemnized by Timothy Harrington. Pastor of the Church in Lancaster, since April 1791.*

Simon Butler & Eunice Butler both of Lancaster were married May 18th, 1791.
John Amory Jun. of Boston & Catharine Willard of Lancaster were married Jany. 15. 1792.
Willm: Hunt of Heath & Hannah White of Lancaster were married Jany. 26th, 1792.
Saml. Rugg & Sally Wilder both of Lancaster were married Feby. 21st, 1792.
Josiah Cutting of Southboro, & Merviah Houghton of Lancaster were married Feby. 23. 92.
Certified by TIMOTHY HARRINGTON.

April 23^d. 1792. Returned to the Clerk of the Sessions by
J. WALES *T. Clerk*.

Israel Atherton & Willm. Stedman Esq^{rs}: filed Certificates in the Town Clerk's Office, certifying they have not joined any Persons in Marriage since April 1791.
Ap^l. 23^d, 1792. Returned to the Clerk of the Sessions
J. WALES *T. Clerk*.

WORCESTER SS. I certify that Solomon Nelson of Chitendon in the State of Vermont and Dolly Phelps of Lancaster in the County of Worcester, Common Wealth of Massachusetts, were joined in Marriage on the 27. of January A. D. 1793. And on the 11 of March 1793 Noel Littaye and Sarah Knowlton both of Sterling in the County of Worcester were Joined in Marriage by me
LANCASTER Ap^l. 22^d, 1793. WILLIAM STEDMAN *Justice of Peace*.

A Return of Marriages Solemnized by the Rev⁴. Timothy Harrington of Lancaster between April 1792 & April 1793. viz:

May 28, 1792. Jacob Fisher of Princeton to Nancy Carter of Lancaster.
July 18, 1792. Moses Sawyer Jr to Elizab^h. Divol both of Lancaster
by me TIMOTHY HARRINGTON.

Israel Atherton Esqr. filed a Certificate, certifying he had married no one the preceding year.
April 22^d. 1793.

214 WORCESTER ss. April 20. 1793. I certify that Richard Sawtell of Grauton and Mary Carter of Lancaster were married on the 1st of January 1793. by me JOHN SPRAGUE *Jus Pac₅*.

A Return of Marriages Solemnized before Timothy Whiting Jr. Esqr. from April 12. 1792, to April 22, 1793.

Nathl. Eaton Jur. of Springfield to Eunice Wilder of Lancaster Augt. 16, 1792.
Thos. Bennit Jur. to Isabel Phelps both of Lancaster, " 19, "
Peter White of Sutton to Sally Moore of Lancaster, Sept. 3. "
Daniel Keyes to Jedidah Sawyer both of Boylston, Novr. 8. "
Edm^d. Heard Jun. to Lucy.Bennit both of Lancaster, " 25. "
Joseph Rugg to Mary Hazen both of Do. " 29 "
Seth Sergeant to Elizab^h. Phelps both of Do. Decr. 27 "
Coffin Chapen to Hannah Stiles both of Worcester, April 4, 1793.

True Copy. Returned to the Clerk of the Court of General Sessions at Worcester April 22, 1793. J. WALES *T. Clerk*

Copy   MARRIED.

1793 Octr. 22 Willm. McClallan of Petersham to Lucretia Phelps of Lancaster
Decr. 12 John Campbell, to Nancy Rugg both of Lancaster
" 18. James Godfrey of Westborough to [Mrs.] Lucy Munroe of Lancaster.
1794 Jany. 12. Jacob Kilborne to Polly Fletcher both of Lancaster.
16. Joseph Wales to Eliza Willard both of Lancaster.
30. Peter Hunt of Heath to Kezia Osgood of Lancaster.
April 13. James Pratt to Lydia Goold both of Lancaster.

This certifies, that the above Marriages have been consumated before me, at the Periods respectively mentioned. NATH^L. THAYER.

Copy.   MARRIAGES.

1793. Sept. 8. Joel Osgood to Lucretia Thayer both of Lancaster.
Oct. 8. Abijah White to Barthsheba Robbins both of Lancaster.
" " Jacob Rugg to Polly Ramer both of Leominster.
" 15. Gowen B. Newman of Lancaster to Lucy Smith of Lunenburg.
pr. me W^m. Stedman Justice of the peace for the County of Worcester.

WORCESTER SS. April 8, 1794 The above is a true extract from the Records of each Marriage. Attest W^M. STEDMAN *Just. Pac.*

215

Copy.   MARRIED

1793 July 11. James Campbell Jun. of Shirley to Sophia Fletcher of Lancaster
17. Samuel Wilder 3^d, to Betsy Joslyn both of Lancaster.
Augt. 22. Timo^y. F. Hastings to Persis How both of Boylstone.
Oct. 1. Willm. Wright of Peckerfield to Sally Willard of Lancaster.
" 8. John White 3^d. to Sophia Beaman both of Lancaster.

WORCESTER SS. April 16, 1794. The foregoing is a true Statement of the Marriages which have been solemnized before me since the 22^d. day of April, 1793. TIMO^Y WHITING JUN. *Jus^t; Pacis.*

True Copies   Attest   J. WALES *Town Clk.*

BOOK FIRST.   133

Copy   *Married before John Sprague Esqr.*
1793, Oct. 6. Joshua Burditt to Charlotte Houghton both of Lancaster.
                                    Certifyed by J^{no}. SPRAGUE *Just. Peace*

April 29, 1794. I do hereby certify that I have not joined any persons in Marriage for 12 months last passed.   ISRAEL ATHERTON *Just. P.*

April 29, 1794. I hereby certify that I have not joined any persons in Marriage for twelve months last passed.   TIMOTHY HARRINGTON.
    Attest   J. WALES *T. Clerk.*

216   *To William Stedman Esqr. Town Clerk.*
1794. Novr. 24. Mr Robert Phelps to Miss Polly Todd, both of Lancaster.
    Decr. 11. Mr Paul Faulkner of Lancaster to Miss Nabby Stratton of Concord.
    14. Mr Francis Blake of Rutland to Miss Eliza [Augusta] Chandler of Lancaster.
1795 Jany. 15. Mr Oliver Carter to Miss Emily Harrington; both of Lancaster.
    Feby. 12. Mr Joseph Ellis of Sullivan N. H. to Miss Abigail Divol of Lancaster.
    17. Mr Aaron Sergeant to Miss Polly Goddard: both of Lancaster.
    19. Mr Ralph Coffin of Fort Ann, (S. N. York) to Miss Abigail Chase of Lancaster.
    Mar: 29. Mr Benjamin Whitwell to Miss Sally Sprague; both of Lancaster.
    Apr: 8. Mr Amos Sawyer jun to Miss Polly Allen; both of Lancaster.
    12. Mr Edward Goodwin to Miss Sally Pratt both of Lancaster.

This certifies that the above persons were married since the last return was made, at the times respectively named.
    April 15, 1795.   NATHANIEL THAYER
        Att^r.   W^M STEDMAN *Town Cler.*

217   WORCESTER SS. April 23. 1795
        This certifies that Sparhawk Houghton of Lancaster and Nancy Bagnall of Bolton were joined in Marriage June 1, A. D. 1794. by me
                            TIMOTHY WHITING JUN *Just: pacis*
        Att^r.   W^M STEDMAN *Town Cler.*

WORCESTER SS. April 23. 1795. This certifies that Mr William Homes & Miss Rachael Tyler both of Sterling in said County were married on the ninth day of September A. D. 1794 by me   W^M. STEDMAN *Just: pacis.*
        Att^r.   W^M STEDMAN *Town Cler.*

WORCESTER SS. Be it remembered that Mr John Hawks jun & Miss Alice Allen both of Lancaster in said County on this twenty-sixth day of October in the year of our Lord one thousand seven hundred and ninety-five are married by me   W^M STEDMAN *Just: pacis.*
    LANCASTER April 1. 1796.   Att^r.   W^M STEDMAN *Town Cler.*

218   INTENTIONS OF MARRIAGE.

Josiah Whetemore and Lucy Snow both of Lancaster Entred their Intentions of marrage Decr. ye 18th 1772
Gershom Flagg of Lancaster and Sally Pond of Dedham Entred their Intentions of marrage January ye 9th 1772
Phineas Beman of Princeton & Hannah Buss of Lancaster Entred their Intentions of marrage Feb ye 5th. 1773
Titus Wilder & Mary Allen both of Lancaster Entred their Intentions of marrage Feb ye 5th 1773.
Lemuel Beman and Prudance Row both of Lancaster Entred their Intentions of marrage Feb: ye 15th 1773
John Sollindine and Susannah Farwel both of Lancaster Entred their Intentions of marrage may ye 8th 1773

Nathaniel Brown & Esther Smith both of Lancaster Entred their Intentions of marrage may ye 18th 1773

Jotham Woods and Mehetible Aldes both of Lancaster Entred their Intentions of marriage July ye 3^d. 1773.

Abner Ferrington and Joanna Kilburn both of Lancaster Entred their Intentions of marrage August ye 13th 1773

Joseph Wilder Jur of Leominster and Susanna Phelps of Lancaster Entred his Intentions of marriage Augt. 14th. 1773

William Brooks & Buler Wilder both of Lancaster Entred their Intentions of marrage Sept ye 1th 1773

Reubin Gary & Lucy Cutter Brooks both of Lancaster Entred their Intentions of marrage Sept. ye 1th 1773

Moses Russel & Hannah Kendall both of Lancaster Entred their Intentions of marrage Augt. ye 30th 1773

Joseph Whetmore of Leominster and Ruth Knight of Lancaster Entred their Intentions of marrage Sept. ye 6th 1773

219 Jonathan Ball of Lancaster & Mary Prat of Bolton Entred their Intentions of marrage Sepr. ye 14th 1773.

Abel Right & Lydia Richardson both of Lancaster Entred their Intentions of marrage Sepr. ye 17th 1773.

Elias Farnsworth of Westminster & Lois Willard of Lancaster Entred their Intentions of marrage Sept 20th 1773

Timothy Knight Jur & Lydia Wilder both of Lancaster Entred their Intentions of marrage Sepr 28 1773

Daniel Goodfree of Lancaster & Ruth Belloss of Westbury Entred their Intentions of marrage Oct^r: 8th 1773

Samuel Bixby of Lancaster & Sarah Beman of Shrewsbury Entred their Intentions of marrage Octb^r. ye 8th 1773

Nathl. Farrow of Lancaster & Rachel Fletcher of Chelmsford Entred their Intentions of marrage Octob^r 12th 1773

Levi Carter and Silance Beman both of Lancaster Entred their In'tions of marriage Octob^r: 25th 1773

Doct. Abraham Haskell of Lunenburge & Sarah Green of Lancaster Entred their In'tions of marrage Nov^r: 2^d 1773.

Phineas Sawyer Jur: of Fitchburge and Mary Prescott of Lancaster Entred their In'tions of marrage Nov: 6th 1773

Joseph Lewis & Martha Lock both of Lancaster Entred their In'tions of marrage Novr ye 18th 1773.

Moses Newall & Hannah Robbins both of Lancaster Entred their In'tions of marrage Nov^r: 18th 1773

Benjamin Farmer & Sarah Lipinwell both of Lancaster Entred their Intentions of marrage Nov: 26th, 1773

220 Joel Osgood & Lois Rugg both of Lancaster, Entred their Intentions of marrage Dec^r: ye 15th. 1773

John Phelps of Lancaster & Louis Davis of Littleton Entred their Intentions of marrage Decr. 27th 1773.

James Wright of Keen & Elisabeth Rugg of Lancaster Entred their Intentions of marrage Jany. 3^d 1774

Jeremiah Sachwell & Joanna Ross of Lancaster Entred their Intentions of marrage Feby: 8th 1774

William Ross of Lancaster & Tamer Johnson of Leominster Entred their intentions of marrage Feb: 8th 1774

Elias Sawyer & Hannah Farrow both of Lancaster Entred their In'tions of marrage Febr: 24th 1774

Joseph Wilder Esqr of Lancaster & Mrs Hannah Brigham of Marlboro' declared their Intentions of Marriage March 7th. 1774.

Ephraim Divol Junr. & Leaf Rugg both of Lancaster Enter'd their Intentions of marriage April 2^d. 1774.

John Phillips of Lancaster & Mary Richards of Southboro, Enter'd their Intentions of marriage April 13th. 1774.

Benjamin Whitmore & Sarah Thompson both of Lancaster Enter'd their Intentions of marriage April 23^d. 1774.

Samuel Jewitt & Elizabeth Preist both of Lancaster Declared their Intentions of marriage April 30th. 1774.
Henry Powers of Bolton & Hannah Moors of Lancaster Enter'd their Intentions of marriage May 14th. 1774
David Brooks & Patience White both of Lancaster Entred their Intentions of marriage May 28th. 1774
221 John Baker & Polley Flagg Junr. both of Lancaster Entred their Intentions of marriage June 11th. 1774
Manasseh Knight of Lancaster & Hannah Ames of Leominster Enter'd their Intentions of marriage June 17th: 1774
Josiah Wilder & Polly Flagg both of Lancaster Entered their Intentions of marriage June 26th. 1774.
Elijah Whelocke of Lancaster & Anna Wilds of Shirley Enter'd their Intentions of marriage July 16th. 1775.
Benjamin Roper & Azuba Willard both of Lancaster Enter'd their Intentions of Marriage July 16th. 1774
John Newton Parmenter of Winchendon & Hannah Abbott of Lancaster Enter'd their Intentions of marriage August 22d. 1774.
Joseph Abbott Junr. & Hannah Pitson both of Lancaster Enter'd their Intentions of marriage August 22d. 1774.
Asa Thompson & Sarah Osgood both of Lancaster Enter'd their Intentions of marriage September 17th. 1774
Joseph Carter of Lancaster & Anna Smith of Westown Enter'd their Intentions of marriage October 1st: 1774. [Married Nov. 22, 1774.]
William Deputerene of Lancaster & Sarah Kenney of Nottingham Enter'd their Intentions of marriage Octor: 27th: 1774.
John Powers of Lancaster & Anna Stacy of Shrewsbury Enter'd their Intentions of marriage November 21st. 1774
Manasseth Wilder & Sarah White both of Lancaster Enter'd their Intentions of marriage December 1st. 1774.
222 John Carter & Martha Wilder both of Lancaster Enter'd their Intentions of marriage December 31th. 1774
Moses Burpee Junr. of Lancaster & Elizabeth Kendall of Leominster Enter'd their Intentions of marriage Jany. 2d. 1775
Stephen Wyman of Lancaster & Margery Green of Mendon Enter'd their Intentions of Marriage January 14th. 1775
George Henry of Lancaster & Releaf Bradstreet of Lunenburge Entre'd their Intentions of Marriage Jany. 15th. 1775
Ephraim Kendall & Elizabeth Knight both of Lancaster Enter'd their Intentions of Marriage January 17th. 1775
Joseph Houghton Junr. of Templeton & Hannah Ross of Lancaster Enter'd their Intentions of Marriage January 17th. 1775
Samuel Johnson & Lydia Phelps both of Lancaster Enter'd their Intentions of Marriage January 21th. 1775.
Isaac Clark of Keene & Thankfull Sawyer of Lancaster Enter'd their Intentions of Marriage February 2d, 1775
John Abbott & Lois Bennett both of Lancaster Enter'd their Intentions of Marriage February 4th. 1775.
Moses Moseman of Sudbury & Mary Willard of Lancaster Enter'd their Intentions of Marriage February 9th. 1775
Hugh Moors of Lancaster & Sarah Holland of Shrewsbury Enter'd their Intentions of Marriage February 18th. 1775.
Elisha Bennitt & Mary Goodridge both of Lancaster Enter'd their Intentions of marriage Feby 18th, 1775
223 Ephm. Sawyer Junr. & Mary Allen both of Lancaster Enter'd their Intentions of Marriage Feby. 18th. 1775
Timothy Brown & Eunice Priest both of Lancaster Entred their Intentions of marrage March 17th 1775
John Todd & Sarah Fairwell both of Lancaster Entred their Intentions of marrage March ye 30th 1775
Elmer Brown of Swansey and Lucy Rugg of Lancaster Entred their Intentions of marrage April ye 13th 1775

Peter Green Esqr. of Concord in New Hampshire and Rebeca Mellen of Lancaster Entred their Intentions of marrage May 2ᵈ 1775.
Josiah Wilder & Hezediah Larkin both of Lancaster Entred their Intentions of marrage May 2ᵈ 1775
Rufus Wilder of Ashby & Vashty Prescott of Lancaster Entred their Intentions of marrage June 1ᵗʰ, 1775
Joseph Josling & Dorothy Osgood both of Lancaster Entred their Intentions of marrage June 6ᵗʰ 1775
Nathaniel Haskell & Abigaiel Sawyer both of Lancaster Entred their Intentions of marrage July 22ᵈ. 1775
Lemuel Sawyer & Anna Pratt both of Lancaster Entred their Intentions of marrage August 2ᵈ, 1775
John Prescott Juʳ: & Mary Ballard both of Lancaster Entred their Intentions of marrage August 18ᵗʰ 1775
Andrew Grimes of Lancaster and Elisabeth Hager of Shrewsbury Entred their Intentions of marrage Sept 5ᵗʰ 1775
Ebenezer Johnson of Arvinshire & Prudance Kendall of Lancaster Entred their In'tions of marrage Sept 7ᵗʰ 1775
Joseph Bayley & Rachel Houghton both of Lancaster Entred their Intentions of marrage Sept; 7ᵗʰ. 1775.
224 Cornelus Sawyer & Eunice Buss both of Lancaster Entred their Intentions of marrage Sepʳ: 12ᵗʰ. 1775
Joseph Belknap & Olive Glazer both of Lancaster Entred their Intentions of marrage Sept 12ᵗʰ. 1775
Gamaliel Beman & Prudance Wilder both of Lancaster Entred their Intentions [of marriage] October 10ᵗʰ, 1775
Revᵈ Jacob Biglow of Sudbury & Elisabeth Wells of Lancaster Entred their Intentions of marrage Octʳ: 20ᵗʰ 1775
The Honorable Joseph Wilder Esqʳ & Mʳˢ Rebecca Lock Entred their Intentions of marrage Decʳ: 6ᵗʰ 1775
Silas Rice of Lancaster & Elisabeth Taft of Uxbridge Entred their Intentions of marrage Decʳ: 1ᵗʰ. 1775
Samuel Mower of Worcester & Esther Lock of Lancaster Entred their Intentions of marrage Decʳ: 18ᵗʰ 1775.
Samuel Moors & Abigaiel Hastings both of Lancaster Entred their Intentions of marrage Decʳ: 12ᵗʰ 1775
Jonathan Osgood & Rebecca Divel both of Lancaster Entred their Intentions of marrage Decʳ: 16ᵗʰ 1775.
Paul Boyinton & Anna Man both of Lancaster Entred their Intentions of marrage Decʳ: 22ᵈ 1775
Ebenezer Wilder of Lancaster & Elisabeth Wilson of Leominster Entred their Intentions of marrage Decʳ: 25ᵗʰ 1775
Joseph Kendall & Prisilla Thustin both of Lancaster Entred their Intentions of marrage January yᵉ 5ᵗʰ 1776
John Hoar of Westminister & Abigaiel White of Lancaster Entred their In'tions of marrage January 18ᵗʰ, 1776.
John Chandler and Catey Holman both of Lancaster Entred their Intentions of marrage Febʳ 3ᵈ 1776
225 Eliphelet Whetney of Shrewsbury & Lois Houghton of Lancaster Entred their Intentions of marrage June 16ᵗʰ 1776
Henry Willard Farmer & Sibel Knight of Lancaster Entred their Intentions of marrage June 24ᵗʰ 1776
Samuel Barratt Juʳ: of Lancaster & Abigaiel Houghton of Harvard Entred their Intentions of marrage July 27ᵗʰ 1776
Jonathan Prescott Jur of Lancaster & Mary Brigham of Shrewsbury Entred their Intentions of marage Sepʳ: 10ᵗʰ 1776
Elijah Bayley & Mary Thompson both of Lancaster Entred their In'tions of marrage Sepʳ. 27ᵗʰ 1776
Jeremiah Haskell Jur of Lancaster & Letes Corthall of Sittuate Entred their Intentions of marrage Decʳ: 5ᵗʰ 1776
Aaron Glazer & Orpha Cooting both of Lancaster Entred their Intentions of marrage Decʳ: 11ᵗʰ 1776.

Jacob Kilburn of Lancaster and Hannah Farmer of Lexinton Entred their Intentions of marriage Jany. 18th. 1777

Jacob Wilder & Lydia Sawyer both of Lancaster Entred their Intentions of marrage January ye 20th 1777

Daniel Knight & Mary Wood both of Lancaster Entred their Intentions of marrage Jany. 28th. 1777.

226 Joseph Wilson of Keen and Sarah Wilder of Lancaster Entred their In'tions of marrag Feb^r. ye 20th 1777

Isaac Tompson of Jefre and Relief Osgood of Lancaster Entred their Intentions of marrage Feb^r. 12th 1777

Luther Fairbank & Thankfull Whelock both of Lancaster Entred their Intentions of marrag Feb^r: 18th 1777.

Benjamin Haskell of Lancaster, & Susannah Stone of Groton Entr'd their Intentions of marriage March 12th: 1777.

Samuel Bayley Junr. & Thankfull Nelson both of Lancaster, Enter'd their Intentions of marriage March the 21: 1777.

Moses Sawyer, & Betty Larkin, both of Lancaster Enter'd their Intentions of marriage March 29th. 1777.

Samuel Adams, & Elizabeth Nowell, both of Lancaster, Enter'd their Intentions of marriage April 5th, 1777,

Josiah Sawyer, & Susannah Green both of Lancaster Enter'd their Intention of marriage April 26, 1777

Palatial Morse of Natick & Lidia Glaizer, of Lancaster Enter'd their Intention of marriage April 14th. 1777.

Ivory Wildes of Shirley, & Hannah Esterbrooks of Lancaster Enter'd their Intention of marriage, April 28th, 1777.

Israel Butler, & Anna Phillips both of Lancaster Enter'd their Intentions of marriage May 15th. 1777.

Samuel Stone of Winchendon & Martha Wilder of Lancaster, Jur. Entered their Intentions of marriage May 29th, 1777.

227 Samuel Dickerson & Louis Willard, both of Lancaster, Entered their Intentions of marriage May 30th: 1777.

Dec: Cyrus Fairbanks & Elizabeth Winn both of Lancaster, Entered their Intentions of marriage June 3^d: 1777.

Abel Bigelow of Lancaster, & Sarah Brown of Stow Entered their Intentions of marriage June 15th. 1777.

David Willard, Junr: and Roda Bunson, both of Lancaster Entered their Intentions of marriage June 28th: 1777.

William Kendall & Mary Brooks, both of Lancaster Entered their Intentions of marriage June the 30: 1777.

Zebadiah Wyman of Woburn & Eunice Wyman of Lancaster Enter'd their Intentions of marriage July the 1st, 1777,

Thomas Hubbart of Groton, & Louis White of Lancaster Enter'd their Intentions of marriage July 5th: 1777.

Elisha Prouty, and Prudance Wilder, both of Lancaster Enter'd their Intentions of marriage July 8th: 1777.

Amasa Turner, and Lucy Smith both of Lancaster Entered their Intentions of marriage July 26th: 1777.

Ephraim Boyenton & Mary Burpee both of Lancaster Entefed their Intentions of marriage Augt. 1st. 1777.

Paul Boyenton of Winchendon and Abigail Fairbank of Lancaster Entered their Intentions of marriage Sept. 10. 1777

David Hosley of Lancaster and Lucy Smith of Shrewsbury Entered their Intentions of marriage Sept. 16. 1777.

David Whittecur and Martha Wilder both of Lancaster Entered their Intentions of marriage Octr. 26, 1777.

228 Joseph Maynard of Lancaster & Levinah Barns of Marlbrough Entered their Intentions of Marriage Novemb^r. 12. 1777.

Benjamin Richardson & Abigail French both of Lancaster Entered their Intentions of Marriage Novr. 15, 1777

Willm. Wilder and Relief Carter both of Lancaster Entered their Intentions of Marriage Novr. 27. 1777

10

Jude Piper and Deborah Brooks both of Lancaster Entered their Intentions of Marriage Decr. 1. 1777
David Jones of Dracut and Mary Goodfrey of Lancaster Entered their Intentions of Marriage Decr. 25, 1777.
Samuel Thompson and Eunice Dole Both of Lancaster Entered their intentions of Marriage Decr. 28. 1777.
Jacob Robbins and Sophia Houghton both of Lancaster Entered their Intentions of Marriage Feby. 14, 1778
Abel Phelps and Louis Willard both of Lancaster Entered their Intention of Marriage March 6. 1778
Jonathan White & Rebecca Haskell Both of Lancaster Entered their Intentions of Marriage March 6, 1778
Samuel Peirce of Jeffery & Elisabeth Whitney of Lancaster Entered their Intentions of Marriage March 13. 1778
Abel Houghton & Rebecca Willard both of Lancaster Entered their Intentions of Marriage March 19, 1778
Thos. Cummins and Dolly Chase both of Lancaster Entered their Intentions of Marriage March 21. 1778

229   Nathaniel Roper & Naoma Gibbs both of Lancaster Entered their Intencion of marriag may 27: 1778
Nathan Farrar [&] Sarah Brook both of Lancaster Enterd their Intentcion of marrage June 1: 1778
Doc{r}. Josiah Levett and Azubah Osgood Both of Lancaster Entered their intencion of marig June 28 1778
Peter Manning and Mary Bayley both of Lancaster Entered their intencion of marig July 13 1778
Joshua Brooks Lucretia White both of Lancaster Enterd their intencion of maridg August 17 1778
James Townsend of Bolton Olliv Sawyer of Lancaster Entered their intencion of Maridg September 16 1778
Timothy Kilborn Relief Richardson both of Lancaster Enterd their intencion of Mariag September 16 1778
Samuel Holt of Windham and Mary Abbott of Lancaster Enterd their intencion of marig November 9 1778
Henery Rice of Shusbuery Loas Holt of Lancaster Enterd their intencion of marig November 25 1778
Samuel Page of Danvor Rebecka Putnom of Lancaster Enterd their intencion of maridg Nov'ber 26 1778
Nathanil Eaton Lucy Bennett both of Lancaster Enterd their intencion of marieg November 26 1778

230   Willis Wilder Relef Wheelock Both of Lancaster Enterd their intencion of marig Desember 4 1778.
Stephen Goss and Hanah Burpey both of Lancaster Enterd their intencion of marieg Desember 5: 1778.
Elijah Dresor Sarah Houghton both of Lancaster Enterd their intencion of marieg Desember 8 1778
Thomas Sawyer and Susanah Wilder Both of Lancaster Enterd ther intencion of marieg Desember 29 1778.
Aaron Sawyer Keziah Richardson both of Lancaster Entered their intencion of Marieg January the 4: 1779.
Jacob Fowl & Elezebeth Abbott both of Lancaster Enterd their intencion of Marieg Januy' 6 1779
Richd. Perkins Bridge and Anny Harrington Both of Lancaster Enter'd there intention of Marage January ye 10th 1779
Jeremiah Ballard & Rebeckah Joslyn Both of Lancaster Enterd their intencion of Marieg January 28: 1779
Jonathan Wallis of South Brimfield and Elezibeth Osgood of Lancaster Enterd their intencion of Marieg February 4 1779

231   Doc{t} Jonas Prescott of Rindge & Susanah Wilder of Lancaster Enterd ther intencion of Marieg February 9: 1779.
Beniaman Houghton of Bolton Rebeckah Tucker of Lancaster Enterd their intencion of Mariage February 27 1779.

Richard Lees of Shrewsbury Paciants Richardson of Lancaster Enterd their intencion of mariag February 27: 1779
Abijah Rugg of Lancaster, and Susannah Divoll of Leominster, Enter there Intention of marriage March 20th, 1779.
Ephraim Wilder & Hannah Reed, both of Lancaster, Enter there Intentions of marriage April 5th. 1779.
Abraham How & Parny Sawyer, both of Lancaster Enter there Intentions of marriage April 8th, 1779.
Ebenezer Smith of Ashby, & Abigial Conquorett of Lancaster, Enter there Intentions of marriage April 8th: 1779.
Peter Aires, of Lancaster & Esther Sumner, of Pomfret, Enter there Intentions of marriage April 10th: 1779.
Ephraim Powers & Keziah Sawyer, both of Lancaster Enterd there Intentions of marriage May 16th: 1779.
Joseph Cuttin of New Marlboro', in the State of N: Hampshire & Dolly Whitcomb of Lancaster, Entered there Intentions of marriage June 1st: 1779.
John Eaton, of Winchendon & Molly Larkin of Lancaster Enterd there Intentions of marriage June 1st: 1779.
Joseph Farwell, & Molly Haskell both of Lancaster Enterd there Intentions of marriage June 2d: 1779.
Jonathan Whitney, & Lucy Smith both of Lancaster, Enterd there Intentions of marriage June 19th: 1779.
William Flood, & Mary Wyman both of Lancaster Enterd there Intentions of marriage June 19th: 1779.
232 Levi Wilder, of Lancaster, & Sally Stodard of Chelmsford Enterd their Intentions of marriage June 26th: 1779.
John Savory, & Phebe Kendall, both of Lancaster, Enterd their Intentions of marriage July 27th: 1779.
Jonathan Willard of Lancaster, and Anna Goodnough of Princeton Enterd their Intention of marriage Augt. 2d. 1779
John Spafford, & Lucy Robbins both of Lancaster Enterd their Intentions of marriage Augt. 10, 1779.
John Wheelock the 3: of Lancaster & Sally Willis of Sudbury Enterd their Intentions of marriage Augt. 14th. 1779.
John Coolidge of Lancaster & Hannah Priest of Marlboro', Enterd their Intentions of marriage Augt. 14th: 1779.
Solomon Houghton of Lancaster & Martha White of Hopkinton Enterd their Intentions of marriage Augt. 22d. 1779.
William Phelps Junr. & Sarah Beaman both of Lancaster Enterd their Intentions of marriage Augt 26th 1779.
John Wheelock Junr: and Dolly Wilder both of Lancaster Enterd their Intentions of marriage Sept. 12: 1779.
Timothy Kendall, & Eunis Houghton both of Lancaster Enterd there Intentions of marriage Sep 16th: 1779.
Samuel Bennett of Lancaster & Polly Baldwin of New Milford in the State of Connecticut Enterd there Intentions of marriage Octr. 2: 1779.
Israel Willard of Lancaster and Susannah Longly of Shirly Enterd there Intentions of marriage Octr. 2d: 1779.
William Fairbanks & Kezia Houghton both of Lancaster Enterd there Intentions of marriage Octr. 10th: 1779.
Gershom Flagg of Lancaster & Abigial Biglow of Waltham Enterd there Intentions of marriage Octr 12th: 1779
William Goss & Mary Moor both of Lancaster Enterd there Intentions of marriage Octr 15th: 1779.
233 James Carter Junr: of Lancaster & Susannah Kendall of Leominster Enterd there Intentions of marriage Novr: 1: 1779.
Ebenezer Harwood of Sutton & Elizabeth Lippingwell of Lancaster Enterd their Intentions of marriage November, 4th: 1779.
Oliver Bowker & Anna Persons both of Lancaster, Enterd there Intentions of marriage Decr. 2: 1779.
Joseph Taft, of Worcester & Mary Sawyer of Lancaster Enterd there Intentions of marriage Decr. 4: 1779.

Charles Henry of Lancaster & Happy Smith of Shrewsbury Enterd there Intentions of marriage Dec^r: 12: 1779.

Jonathan Wilder & Ruthe Prescott both of Lancaster Enterd there Intentions of marriage Dec^r: 20th: 1779.

Rev^d. Timothy Harrington of Lancaster & M^m: Anna Bridge of Framingham Enterd their Intentions of marriage Decr. 20th: 1779.

Worcester Winslow of Worcester & Phillis Parker of Lancaster Enterd there Intentions of marriage Dec^r: 26th: 1779.

Levi Moor Junr. & Parny Parker both of Lancaster Enterd there Intentions of marriage Jany. 2; 1780.

Jacob Phelps & Prudance White both [of] Lancaster Enterd there Intentions of marriage Jany: 2: 1780.

Jesse Willis of Sudbury, & Allis Wheelock of Lancaster Enterd there Intentions of marriage Jany: 16: 1780.

Henry Winchester of Ashburnham & Lois Phelps of Lancaster Enterd there Intentions of marriage Jany 30; 1780.

Sherebiah Hunt, & Ruthe White both of Lancaster Enterd there Intentions of marriage Jany 30. 1780.

234 Thomas Harrington & Rebecka Ballard, both of Lancaster Enterd there Intentions of marriage Feby. 5th: 1780.

Samuel Wait Junr. of Molden, & Rebeckah Harris of Lancaster, Enterd there Intentions of marriage Feby, 6: 1780.

Cyrus Fairbank & Abigial Wyman both of Lancaster Enterd there Intentions of marriage Feby 14th: 1780.

Thomas Burditt & Lois Sawyer, both of Lancaster Enterd there Intentions of marriage Feby, 14: 1780

Timothy Harrington of Pembrook in the State of New Hampshire and Sarah Wilder of Lancaster Enterd there Intentions of marriage March 3^d. 1780.

Benjamin Kimbal of Harvard & Anna Wilder of Lancaster Enterd there Intentions of marriage March 3^d. 1780.

Peter Atherton, of Lancaster & Pheba Daby of Harvard Enterd there Intentions of marriage March 4th: 1780

Micah Ross & Molly Moor both of Lancaster, Enter'd their Intentions of Marrage March 15 1780.

Isaac Buck & Patty Phillips both of Lancaster, Enter'd their Intentions of Marrage April 20 1780.

John Snow Junr: & Hannah Parker both of Lancaster, Enter'd their Intentions of Marrage April 25 1780.

The Revd Reuben Holcomb of Lancaster, & Miss Jane Strong of Symsbury in ye State of Connecticut Enter'd their Intentions of Marrage May 13th 1780.

Capt Solomon Jewett, & Martha Burpee both of Lancaster Enter'd their Intentions of Marrage May 11 1780.

Jonathan Thompson, & Prudence Osgood both of Lancaster Enter'd their Intentions of Marrage May 12 1780.

Samuel Seargeant, & Mary Darling, both of Lancaster Enter'd their Intentions of Marrage May 14 1780.

Nathaniel Taylor & Sarah Fuller both of Lancaster, Enter'd their Intentions of Marrage June 1 1780.

235 John Mellen & Lucy Kendal both of Lancaster, Enter'd their Intentions of Marrage June 6 1780.

Robert Hudson of Shrewsbury, & Dinah Butler of Lancaster, Enter'd their Intentions of Marrage June 11 1780.

Ebenezer Fitch of Ringe, in ye State of New Hampshire & Percis Bush of Lancaster, Enter'd their Intention of Marrage July 27 1780

David Woods of New-Brantry & Ruth Holman of Lancaster, Enter'd their Intention of Marrage Augt 30 1780.

Jotham Wilder Junr. and Lucy Moor both of Lancaster, Enter'd their Intention of Marrage Sep^t 14 1780.

Joseph Rogers & Abigal Conqueret both of Lancaster, Enter'd their Intention of Marrage Sep^t 18 1780.

David Robbins of Ringe in the State of New Hampshire and Mary Ballard of Lancaster, Enter'd their Intention of Marrage Septem^b 22^d 1780.

BOOK FIRST. 141

Elisha White Jun[r] and Deborah Hunt both of Lancaster, Enter'd their Intention of Marrage Septem[b] 23[d] 1780.
Ebenezer Pope, and Lucretia Wilder both of Lancaster Enter'd their Intention of Marrage Oct 21 1780.
Luther Rice of Lancaster and Elizabeth Bennet of Shrewsbury Enter'd their Intention of Marrage Oct 24th 1780.
David McClallen Jur of Petersham and Hannah Sawyer of Lancaster Enter'd their Intention of Marrage Oct 30 1780.
Peter Smith of Sudbury, and Lucy Willard of Lancaster, Enter'd their Intention of Marrage Nov[b] 4th 1780.
Israel Manning and Lidia Wright both of Lancaster, Enter'd their Intention of Marrage Nov[b] 9th 1780.
Benj[a] Bennet of Fitz William in the State of New-Hampshire, and Elizabeth Knight Enter'd their Intention of Marrage Nov[b] 10 1780.
Peter Stickney of Shirley, & Eunice Carlton of Lancaster, Enter'd their Intention of Marrage Nov 14 1780.
Leonard Farwell & Sarah Meriam both of Lancaster, Enter'd their Intention of Marrage Nov 17 1780.
Abraham Headley, & Eunice Eveleth, both of Lancaster, Enter'd their Intention of Marrage Nov 29 1780.

236 David Nichols of Holden, & Naomi Newton of Lancaster Enter'd their Intention of Marrage Jany 17 1781.
Stephen Fuller of Fitchburge & Anna Lippingwell of Lancaster Enter'd their Intention of Marrage Jany 18. 1781.
Moses Osgood of Lancaster, & Mary Wilder of Lancaster in the State of New-hampshire, Enter'd their Intentions of Marrage Jan[y] 20 1781.
William Ball, and Thankfull Ball both of Lancaster, Enter'd their Intention of Marrage Jan[y] 29 1781.
Nathan Ball, and Betty Ball both of Lancaster, Enter'd their Intention of Marrage Jan[y] 29 1781.
Joshua Willard and Savia Bailey both of Lancaster, Enter'd their Intention of Marrage Jan[y] 30, 1781
Col Henry Haskell of Shirley & Charity Pratt of Lancaster Enter'd their Intention of Marrage Feb[y] 10 1781.
Philip Corey, and Patience Lees both of Lancaster, Enter'd their Intention of Marrage Feb[y] 24 1781.
Stephen Corey, and Triphena Wilder both of Lancaster Enter'd their Intention of Marrage Feb[y] 24 1781
Nathan Wilder, and Susanna Sawyer both of Lancaster Enter'd their Intention of Marrage March 10 1781.
Timothy Whiting Jr of Lancaster, & Abigal Kidder of Bellerica, Enter'd their Intention of Marrage Ap[r] 12 1781
Amos Allen & Rebeckah Thurston both of Lancaster, Enter'd their Intention of Marrage Ap[r] 13 1781.
Aaron Phelps, & Sally Capon both of Lancaster, Enter'd their Intention of Marrage Ap[r] 21 1781.
Mathias Higgins of Charlestown, & Julian Pansey of Lancaster Enter'd their Intentions of Marrage Ap[r] 22, 1781
Benjamin Gould of Topsfield and Grizzal Apthorp Flagg of Lancaster Enter there Intentions of marrage May 27: 1781.
John Winter of Ashburnham & Phebe Wright of Lancaster Enter there Intentions of marrage June 24th, 1781.
Winslow Phelps of Lancaster and Rebeca Kidder of Billrica Enter there Intention of marrage July 1. 1781.

237 John Ballard, and Anna Phelps both of Lancaster Enter there Intention of Marrage: Oct[r]. 5, 1781.
Enoch Whitcomb, of Bolton & Sarah Tooker of Lancaster Enter there Intentions of marrage Oct[r]. 14, 1781.
Levi Lincoln of Worcester and Martha Waldo of Lancaster Enter there Intintions of marrage Oct[r] 28, 1781.
Philemon Allen and Alies House both of Lancaster Enter there Intentions of marrage Oct 28: 1781.

LANCASTER RECORDS.

Jonathan Wheelock Jun. and Lucy Beaman both of Lancaster Enter there Intentions of marrage Nov. 4, 1781

John Bennett of Wethersfield, and Sarah Joslyn of Lancaster Enter there Intentions of marrage Jany. 6. 1782.

Samuel Smith and Sally Pratt both of Lancaster Enter there Intentions of marrage Jany 6. 1782.

Simon Butler & Elizabeth Butler both of Lancaster Enter'd their Intentions of Marriage March 23^d. 1782

Amos Knight & Lydia Johnson both of Lancaster declar'd their Intentions of Marriage March 26th. 1782.

Paul Sawyer Junr. & Martha Wheelock both of Lancaster declared their Intentions of Marriage May 3^d. 1782.

Tilley Richardson of Sterling & Polly Thurston of Lancaster Enter'd their Intentions of Marriage May 4. 1782.

Samuel Corey of Lancaster Enter'd his Intentions of Marriage with Sabre Sawyer of s^d. Town July 17th. 1782

Oliver Wheelock & Lucretia Smith both of Lancaster Enter'd their intentions of Marriage Augt. 31st. 1782.

238 Thomas Divol of Leominster entered his Intentions of Marriage with Polly Smith of Lancaster September 27th. 1782.

Joseph Wilder of Lancaster enter'd his Intentions of marriage with the wid^w. Hepsibeth Norton, of Royalston October 22^d. 1782.

Benjamin Whittemore Willard, entered his intention of marriage with Annis Willard, both of Lancaster, Octr. 21st. 1782

Elisha Rugg enter'd his intentions of Marriage with Anna Clark both of Lancaster Octr. 21. 1782.

Thomas Kendall entered [his intention] of Marriage with Lucy Baldwin both of Lancaster Novem^r. 22^d. 1782

Asa Carter enter'd his intentions of Marriage with Polley Joslin both of Lancaster, Novem^r. 22^d. 1782.

Nathaniel Kendall enter'd his intentions of Marriage with Rebecca Bodge both of Lancaster Novem^r. 27. 1782

John Thurston & Rebecca Gates both of Lancaster declared their Intentions of Marriage Decem^r. 22^d. 1782

Reuben Wheelor Wilder of Lancaster enter'd his intentions of Marriage with Eunice Bailey of Sterling December 28th. 1782.

John Munroe of Harvard, enter'd his intentions of Marriage with Lucy White of Lancaster January 3^d. 1783.

Aaron Rugg of Lancaster enter'd his intentions of Marriage with Releaf Divol of Leominster January 24th. 1783.

Thomas Wright of Sterling enter'd his intentions of Marriage with Eunice Osgood of Lancaster, Febry. 25. 1783

239 Amos Sawyer of Lancaster entered his intentions of marriage with Prudence Garey of Sterling March 14th. 1783.

Benjamin Wheelock of Lancaster enter'd his intentions of marriage with Prudence Divol of Leominster April 8th. 1783

David Baldwin Junr. & Olive Phelps both of Lancaster enter'd their intentions of marriage April 22^d. 1783

Eliphalet Hill of Newbury entered his intentions of marriage with Sarah Wyman of Lancaster May 30th. 1783.

Elijah Rugg & Eunice Manning both of Lancaster enter'd their intentions of marriage June 14th. 1783. *he forbid it*

Calvin Sawyer & Releaf Houghton both of Lancaster Declared their Intentions of marriage June 28: 1783.

Jonathan Thayer of Charlemont enter'd his intentions of marriage with Lucretia Rugg of Lancaster, Sept^r: 4th. 1783.

Benjamin Bancroft of Ringe enter'd his intentions of marriage with Deborah Whiting of Lancaster Septem^r. 17th. 1783.

William Deputereene Junr. & Mary Wyman both of Lancaster entered their intentions of Marriage Septem^r. 27th. 1783

David Bennett entered his intentions of Marriage with Abigail Chase both of Lancaster November 12th. 1783.

BOOK FIRST.

Daniel Willard of Fitchburge enter'd his intentions of marriage with Releaf Phelps of Lancaster Dece^r. 23^d. 1783.
Ephraim Larkin of Lancaster enter'd his Intentions of Marriage with Dinah Baker of Bolton January 13th. 1784
Gardiner Phelps & Molly Baldwin both of Lancaster declared their Intentions of marriage Jany. 17th. 1784
239 *bis*. Thomas Tooker of Lancaster entered his Intentions of marriage with Betty Houghton of Bolton Jany. 17th. 1784
Daniel Adams of Townsend declared his intentions of marriage with Sarah Phelps of Lancaster April 22^d. 1784.
Joseph White of Lancaster entered his intentions of marriage with Rebecca Hoar of Lincoln May 1st. 1784.
Samuel Johnson Jur. of Lancaster enter'd his intentions of marriage with Dolly Richardson Dole of Lancaster May 8th. 1784.
Zimrie Eveleth of Lancaster enter'd his intentions of marriage with Sally Babbet of Keene May 8th. 1784.
Peter Manning & Rebecca Carter both of Lancaster enter'd their Intentions of marriage May 21st. 1784.
Jonathan Tenny & Betty Willard both of Lancaster Enter'd their intentions of marriage June 5th. 1784.
Lemuel Barrett & Rebecca Knowlton both of Lancaster entered their intentions of marriage August 5th. 1785.
Samuel French of Fitchburge entered his intentions of marriage with Eunice White of Lancaster, Septr. 15th. 1784
Oliver Tenney declared his Intentions of marriage with Deborah Phelps both of Lancaster, this 16th. day of October 1784
Ephraim White and Betsy Phelps both of Lancaster declared their Intentions of marriage Novr. 20th. 1784.
Ezra Willard & Mary Kendall both of Lancaster declared their Intentions of marriage Novr. 3^d. 1784
240 Ebenezer Butler of Lancaster & Polley Bernard of Shrewsbury entered their Intentions of Marriage December 11th. 1784.
Peter Zweir & Suzanna Smith both of Lancaster Entered their Intentions of Marriage December 30th. 1784.
Levi Page of Harvard & Martha White of Lancaster Entered their Intentions of Marriage December 24th. 1784
Matthias Felton of Fitzwilliam & Releaf Kendall of Lancaster Entered their Intentions of Marriage January 4th. 1785
Moses Chase of Lancaster entered his Intentions of Marriage with Parna Hastings of Berlin Jan^y: 8th. 1785.
Ezra Osgood Entered his Intentions of Marriage with Suzannah White both of Lancaster, January 27th. 1785.
Fortune Little of Lunenburge entered his intentions of marriage with Lorana Tanner of Lancaster March 9th. 1785.
Abner Mitchel of Lunenburge entered his Intentions of marriage with Jenny Blaikendon of Lancaster March 9th. 1785
Luther Sawyer & Zilpah Houghton both of Lancaster Entered their Intentions of Marriage April 8th. 1785.
Abel Allen & Mary Simmons both of Lancaster declared their Intentions of Marriage April 16th: 1785.
John Fletcher & Rachel Woods both of Lancaster entered their Intentions of Marriage May 7th. 1785.
John Whiting of Lancaster Entered his intentions of Marriage with Orpah Danforth of Billerica May 7th. 1785.
Elisha Phelps & Sally Burditt both of Lancaster Entered their Intentions of Marriage May 21st. 1775. *the banns forbid by her*
241 Isaac Temple of Shrewsbury entered his Intentions of Marriage with Elizabeth Houghton of Lancaster July 8th. 1785
John Wyman & Abigail Lippenwell both of Lancaster entered their Intentions of Marriage July 21st. 1785.
Abijah Wyman of Ashby entered his intentions of Marriage with Martha Stevens of Lancaster, July 20th. 1785.

Samuel Stevens of Lancaster entered his intentions of marriage with Mary Wallace of Townsend Augt. 6th. 1785
John Maynard of Framingham entered his Intentions of marriage with Patty Wilder of Lancaster Augt. 20th. 1785.
Reuben Lippinwell Junr. and Dolly Wyman both of Lancaster entered their Intentions of marriage Septr. 24th: 1785.
Asa Millar Wyman of Lancaster entered his Intentions of marriage with Jane Richards of Shirley September 30th, 1785.
Elijah Carter & Sarah Bridge both of Lancaster entered their Intentions of marriage November 18th. 1785.
Thomas Houghton of Harvard & Betsey White of Lancaster, entered their intentions of marrige Decr 1 1785
James Divol & Moley Power Both of Lancaster entered their intentions of Marrige Decr. 1 1785
Simeon Perry & Hannah Newton both of Lancaster entered there intentions of marrige Decr. 14, 1785.
Ephraim Osgood of Lancaster Entered his Intentions of marriage with Lucy Richardson of Sterling January 12th. 1786.
Thomas Carter entered his Intentions of marriage with Sally Clarke both of Lancaster, January 12th. 1786.
242 Eli Stearns and Polly Whitney both of Lancaster entered their intentions of Marriage February 9th. 1786.
Oliver Chase and Releaf Beaman both of Lancaster entered their Intentions of marriage, March 11th. 1786.
John Butler of East Sudbury & Lucretia Phelps of Lancaster Entered their Intentions of marriage March 21st. 1786
Benjamin Wyman & Patty Joslin both of Lancaster entered their Intentions of marriage April 8th. 1786.
John Larkin of Lancaster declared his Intentions of marriage with Sarah Robertson of Holden Apr^l. 20th, 1786.
John Dollison of Sterling & Esther Sawyer of Lancaster enter'd their Intentions of marriage May 27th. 1786
Rufus Fletcher & Polley Sawyer both of Lancaster Entered their Intentions of mariage June 17th. 1786
Peter Fletcher of Alstead in N. Hampshire and Sally Piper of Lancaster entered their intentions of marriage July 13th. 1786
Joseph Wyman & Sarah Preist both of Lancaster enter'd their intentions of marriage July 14th. 1786.
Isaac Fisher of Lancaster entered his intentions of marriage with Betsy Glover of Framingham Augt. 12th: 1786
Silas Thurston of Lancaster enter'd his intentions of marriage with Sarah Kendall of Sterling Augt. 12th. 1786
Josiah Houghton of Wendall enter'd his intentions of marriage with Mary Nickols of Lancaster August 25th. 1786.
Jabez Beaman & Prudence Haskell both of Lancaster enter'd their intentions of marriage August 26th. 1786.
243 Ebenezer Haven & Ruth Houghton both of Lancaster entered their intentions of marriage Septr. 30. 1786
Jonathan Willard of Lancaster & Lydia Munroe of Harvard declared their Intentions of marriage Octob^r. 6th: 1786
Isaac Rugg and Rebecca Wilder both of Lancaster entered their Intentions of marriage Octo^r. 21st. 1786.
John Locke & Esther Phelps both of Lancaster enter'd their Intentions of marriage December 2^d. 1786.
Aaron Woods of Shirley Entered his intentions of marriage with the wid^w. Elizabeth Gates of Lancaster Decr. 2^d. 1786
William Ballard & Betsy Whitney both of Lancaster enter'd their intentions of marriage January 4th. 1787.
Joshua Phelps of Lancaster & Elizabeth Whitmore of Harvard enter'd their intentions of marriage Febr^y. 5th. 1787
Ephraim Whitney of Guilford enter'd his intentions of marriage with Elizabeth Clark of Lancaster, Februrry 5th. 1787.

Thomas Ballard of Lancaster declared his intentions of Marriage with Abigail Richardson of Leominster February 9th: 1787
Levi Greenleaf of Bolton and Molley Willard of Lancaster Enter'd their Intentions of marriage Febry. 10th. 1787.
Ignatius Fuller of Lancaster enter'd his intentions of marriage with Anna Reed of Sterling March 3^{d}. 1787.
Samuel Allen and Lucy Smith both of Lancaster Entered their Intentions of Marriage, March 21st. 1787.
George Wilker of Ashburnham & Patty White of Lancaster enter'd their intentions of Marriage March 27th. 1787.
William Hobart of Townsend and Dolly Smith of Lancaster Enter'd their intentions of marriage April 17th. 1787.
William Willard Junr. of Lancaster & Sarah Haskell of Harvard Enter'd their intentions of marriage April 24th. 1787

244 W^m. Bridge & Nabby Carter both of Lancaster entered their intentions of marriage May 11th, 1787.
Benjamin Houghton Junr. & Miss Hannah Newhall both of Lancaster entered their intentions of marriage July 7th. 1787.
Joseph Wyman of New Marlboro' & Lydia Lippenwell of Lancaster enter'd their intentions of marriage July 17th: 1787
Dr John Dunsmore of Lunenburge & M^{rs}. Hannah Dunsmore of Lancaster entered their intentions of marriage July 28th: 1787
Stephen Thurston of Fitchburg entered his intentions of marriage with Polly Osgood of Lancaster Augt. 4. 1787
Elijah Rugg of Lancaster Entered his Intentions of marriage with Lois Wilder of Sterling October 10th, 1787.
John Sprague Esqr. of Lancaster Enter'd his Intentions of marriage with M^{rs}. Mary Ivers of Boston, Novr. 14th. 1787.
William Flood & Sybil Clarke both of Lancaster enter'd their intentions of marriage January 22^d, 1788
Caleb Kendall of Ashburnham & Lucy Kendall of Lancaster Enter'd their intentions of marriage Feby. 20th. 1788.
Jonas Lane & Dolley Ballard both of Lancaster enter'd their intentions of Marriage March 8th: 1788.
Abijah Moore of Boylstone & Molly Sawyer of Lancaster enter'd their Intentions of Marriage April 17th: 1788.
Abijah Wheelock & Bathsheba Bennet both of Lancaster enter'd their intentions of marriage June 5th: 1788.

245 Daniel Stearns & Deborah Carter both of Lancaster Enter'd there intentions of Marriage July 6th: 1788
William Greenleaf Ju^r. of Lancaster & Maria Ayres of Boston enter^d. their intentions of Marriage Novr. 23^d. 1788
Daniel Willard Ju^r. of Lancaster & Lucy Bachelor of Boxborough Intend Marriage enterd Feby. 5th: 1789
Caleb Huston of Rindge & Prudence Haskell of Lancaster enter'd their intentions of Marriage Feby. 8th: 1789.
Abner Pollard & Axah Phelps both of Lancaster enter'd their Intentions of Marriage April 18: 1789.
Josiah Wood of Littleton & Rachel Brown of Lancaster enter'd their intentions of Marriage April 18. 1789.
Josiah Flagg and Dolly Thurston both of Lancaster enter'd their intentions of Marriage May 9th. 1789
Josiah Bowers & Rebecca Prescott both of Lancaster enter'd their Intentions of Marriage June 14th: 1789
Jabez Prescott & Nabby Gates both of Lancaster enter'd their Intentions of Marriage Augt. 4th. 1789
Timo. Barrett Dublin & Betsey Clark of Lancaster entered their Intentions of Marriage Sep^t. 10th. 1789
Gates Thurston & Betsy Pollard both of Lancaster enter'd their Intentions of Marriage Octo^r. 10th, 1789

246 Abijah Wilder of Keen entered his intentions of Marriage with Tamar Wilder of Lancaster November 14th, 1789.

Saml. Stephens & Ame Willard enter'd their intentions of marriage November 16th, 1789, both of Lancaster.

Silas Allen of Leominster & Susannah Thurston of Lancaster entered their Intentions of Marriage Jany. 2^d. 1790

Phinehas Fletcher of Lancaster, & Polly Campell of Shirley enter'd their intentions of Marriage Feby. 10th. 1790

Amos Pollard & Martha Phelps both of Lancaster enter'd their intentions of Marriage March 20th, 1790

Nathaniel Miller of Lancaster enter'd his intentions of Marriage with Nancy Taylor of Shirley, April 3^d, 1790.

Fredrick Albert of Boylstone & Mary Shaw of Lancaster entered their Intentions of Marriage July 31st: 1790.

Jonathan Johnson & Eunice Willard both of Lancaster enter'd their Intentions of Marriage Sep^t. 4th. 1790.

William Stedman Esqr. of Lancaster entered his intentions of Marriage with Miss Almy Ellery of Rhodeisland Sep^t. 29. 1790

Doct. Isaac Hurd of Concord enter'd his intentions of Marriage with [Mrs.] Polly Wilder of Lancaster Oct^o. 22^d. 1790

Cyrus Fairbank enter'd his intentions of Marriage with Mary Bennet, (both of Lancaster) Octo^r. 23^d. 1790

Saml. Worcester Harvard & Relief Johnson Lancaster enter'd their Intentions of Marriage Decr. 10th: 1790

247 Jonathan Kendall enter'd his intentions of Marriage with Polly Clark both of Lancaster Feby. 20th. 1791

Moses Jones enter'd his intentions of Marriage with Mittee Brooks both of Lancaster Feby. 26. 1791

Maj^r. Gardner Wilder of Lancaster enter'd his Intention of Marriage with M^m. Caty Cotting of Sudbury March 14th, 1791.

Intention of Marriage enter'd by M^r. Levi White & Miss Polly Dole both of Lancaster March 15th. 1791.

M^r. Simon Butler & Miss Eunice Butler both of Lancaster enter'd their Intention of Marriage Apr^l. 30th. 1791.

M^r. Thomas Chase of Putney, State of Vermont & Miss Sally Greenlief of Lancaster enter'd their intention of Marriage Augt. 12th: 1791.

Mr Stephen Baker of Marlborough & Miss Prudence Phelps of Lancaster enter'd their intention of Marriage Augt. 27th. 1791.

Doct^r. Josiah Cutting of Southborough & Miss Maverick Houghton of Lancaster enter'd their intention of Marriage Augt. 27th. 1791.

Mr William Hunt of Heath, and Miss Hannah White of Lancaster enter'd their intention of Marriage November 5th, 1791.

M^r. John Amory Jun. of Boston Merch^t: and the *truly amiable & agreeable*, Miss Catharine Willard of Lancaster, enter'd their intention of Marriage November 25th: 1791.   Enter'd by JOSEPH WALES T. C.

Mr Samuel Rugg & Miss Sally Wilder both of Lancaster, enter'd their intended Marriage November 26th 1791.   J. W. T. C.

248 Mr Vashni Hemenway of Shrewsbury and Miss Sarah Heard of Lancaster, enter'd their intention of Marriage Decr. 24th: 1792.

Mr Jacob Fisher of Princton & Miss Nancy Carter of Lancaster, enter'd their intention of Marriage Feby. 22^d. 1792.

M^r. Eber Godard & Miss Lucy Johnson both of Lancaster, enter'd their Intention of Marriage March 28th, 1792.   J. W. TC

M^r. Peter White of Sutton and Miss Sally Moore of Lancaster, enter'd their intention of Marriage, April 21st, 1792.   JW T. C.

Joseph Leach & Susannah Newhall both of Lancaster enter'd their Intention of Marriage May 5th. 1792.

M^r. Moses Sawyer Jun. & Miss Elizabeth Divol both of Lancaster, enter'd their intention of Marriage June 9th, 1792.

M^r. Nathaniel Eaton Jun. of Springfield and Miss Eunice Wilder of Lancaster enter'd their Intention of Marriage July 14th: 1792.

M^r. Thomas Bennit Jun. & Miss Isabel Phelps both of Lancaster, enter'd their Intentions of Marriage Augt. 4, 1792.

BOOK FIRST. 147

Richard Haven of Lancaster & Sally Bemis of Framingham, enter'd their Intention of Marriage Augt. 16, 1792.
Oct 13, 1792, M^r. Solomon Nelson of Chitendon in the State of Vermont & Miss Dolly Phelps of Lancaster, entered their Intention of Marriage. J.W. T.C.
October 13, 1792, M^r. Seth Sargent & Miss Eliza^h. Phelps both of Lancaster, entered their Intention of Marriage. J. W. T. C.
November 3^d, 1792, M^r. Edmund Heard Jun. & Miss Lucy Bennit both of Lancaster, enter'd their Intention of Marriage. J. W. T. C.
Novr. 3^d, 1792. M^r. Richard Sawtell of Grauton & Miss Mary Carter of Lancaster, entered their Intention of Marriage. J. W. T. C.
Novr. 17, 1792. M^r. Joseph Rugg & Miss Mary Hazen both of Lancaster, entered their Intention of Marriage. J. W. T. C.
249 Novr. 24, 1792 Paul Willard and Martha Haskell both of Lancaster, entered their Intention of Marriage. J. W. T C
Decem^r, 8. 1792. David Joy of Ashby, & Eunice Godfrey of Lancaster, entered their Intention of Marriage. J. W. T. C.
Decr. 16 1792 Silas Willard and Hannah Hawks both of Lancaster entered their Intention of Marrage
Jany. 27, 1793 Willm. Wright of Peckerfield N. Hampshire and Sarah Willard of Lancaster entered their Intention of Marrag J. W. T. C.
Jany. 31. 1793, M^r. Elijah Buterfield of Kingsbury N York and Miss Hannah Campbell of Lancaster entered their intention of Marriage J. W.
Feby. 9, 1793, Joshua Johnson Jun. of Worcester, and Sally Wilder of Lancaster, enter'd their Intention of Marriage.
March 30, 1793. M^r. Saml Wilder 3^d. and Miss Betsey Joslyne both of Lancaster entered their Intention of Marriage J. W. T. C.
March 30, 1793 Mr John White 3^d. & Miss Sophia Beaman both of Lancaster entered their intention of Marriage.
John Scarlet of Boston & Rebecca Calahan of Lancaster, entered their intention of Marriage April 9. 1793. J W T. C.
James Campbell of Shirley & Sophia Fletcher of Lancaster, entered their Intention of Marriage June 15. 1793. J W. T. C
Mr Abijah White & Miss Bathsheba Robbins both of Lancaster, entered their Intention of Marriage June 24, 1793. J. W.
Mr Salmon Willard & Rachel Whitney both of Lancaster, enter'd their Intention of Marriage June 24, '93.
250 Joel Osgood & Lucretia Thayer, both of Lancaster, entered their Intention of Marriage July 6th. 1793. J. W. T. C.
William McClallan of Petersham & Lucretia Phelps of Lancaster, entered their intention of Marriage, Augt. 24. 1793. J. W. T C
Gowen Brown Newman of Lancaster & Lucy Smith of Lunenburg :
Calvin Sawyer of Lancaster & Polly Brittian of Shrewsbury :
Joshua Burditt & Charlotte Houghton both of Lancaster, respectively entered their intentions of Marriage, August 24, 1793. J W. T C
Jonathan Barret of Lancaster & Ruth Houghton of Leominster, entered their intention of Marriage Septr. 21, 1793. J. W. T C
Jacob Kilborne & Mary Fletcher both of Lancaster, ent^d. their Intention of Marriage Sept. 21, '93 J. W. T. C.
James Godfrey of Westburry & Lucy Morrison of Lancaster, entered their Intention of Marriage Octr. 12. 1793. J. W. T. C.
Peter Hunt of Heath & Kezia Osgood of Lancaster, entered their intention of Marriage Oct. 19. 1793.
James Pratt & Lydia Goold both of Lancaster entered their intention of Marriage. Novr. 6, 1793.
John Campbell & Nancy Rugg both of Lancaster entered their Intention of Marriage Novr. 23. 1793.
Joseph Wales & Eliza Willard both of Lancaster, entered their intention of Marriage December 15, 1793. J. W. T. C.
251 March 29, 1794. Luke Divoll of Leominster and Sally Low of Lancaster enter'd Inten^t. of Marriage.
May 3, 1794, Abel Rugg & Catharine Rugg both of Lancaster entered their Intentions of Marriage.

May 9, 1794, Spahawk Houghton of Lancaster & Nancy Bagnall of Bolton, enter'd their intention of Marriage.
June 24, 1794, Joseph Ellis of Sullivan, N. H. & Abigail Divol of Lancaster, Enter'd their Intention of Marriage. J WALES, *T Clerk*.
John Wilder 2ᵈ. of Lancaster & Sarah Moore of Boylstone, enter'd their intention of Marriage August 22, 1794.   J. W. T. C.
Robert Phelps and Polly Todd both of Lancaster entered their intention of Mariage Noveʳ. 8ᵗʰ. 1794.   J. W. T. C.
Paul Faulkner of Lancaster and Nabby Straton of Concord entered their intention of Mariage Noveʳ. 8ᵗʰ, 1794.   J W T. C.
Francis Blake of Rutland & Eliza A. Chandler of Lancaster, entered their intention of Marriage Novʳ. 23, 1794.
Oliver Carter & Emily Harrington both of Lancaster, entered their Intention of Marriage December 6. 1794.
Aaron Seargeants and Miss Polly Godard both of Lancaster entered their Intentions of Marriage Janʸ. 10ᵗʰ. 1795.   J. W. T. C.
252 Benjⁿ. Farnsworth & Sarah Haskell both of Lancaster, entered their intention of Marriage Janʸ. 26, 1795.   J. W. T. C.
Aaron Cook & Elizabeth Johnson both of Lancaster, entered their intention of Marriage Febʸ. 7, 1795.   J. W. T. C.
Ralph Coffin of Fourt Ann, N. York & Abby Chase of Lancaster, entered their intention of Marriage Febʸ. 7. 1795.   J. W. T. C.
Amos Sawyer Jun. & Polly Allen both of Lancaster, enter'd their intention of Marriage Febʸ. 21, 1795.   J. W. T. C.
Benjamin Whitwell & Sally Sprague both of Lancaster entered their intention of Marriage March 14, 1795.   Wᴹ. STEDMAN *Town Cler*.

NOTE. William Stedman, clerk of Lancaster 1795-1800, adopted the custom of attesting each entry of "intentions." As the official signatures add nothing to the record, they will be henceforward represented by asterisks.

William Carlton & Hepsey Geary both of Lancaster entered their intention of Marriage March 21, 1795. *
Edward Goodwin & Sally Pratt both of Lancaster entered their intentions of Marriage March 23, 1795. *
Nathan Puffer & Nabby Joslyn both of Lancaster enter their intentions of marriage, Apr: 4, 1795. *
William Sherin of Leominster & Patience Wyman of Lancaster enter their intentions of Marriage, April 4, 1795. *
Levi Davis & Deborah Stone both of Lancaster enter their intentions of Marriage, June 21, 1795. *
253 Sylvester Phelps of Lancaster & Ester Patterson of Shirley enter their intentions of marriage September 6, 1795. *
Calvin Wilder & Sukey Solindine both of Lancaster enter their intentions of marriage September 12, 1795. *
Revᵈ. Nathaniel Thayer of Lancaster & Sarah Toppan of Hampton, State of Newhampshire enter their intentions of marriage, September 26, 1795. *
Daniel Goss jun & Polly Gates both of Lancaster enter their intentions of marriage the same date last above mentioned. *
John Hawks jun & Alice Allen both of Lancaster enter their intentions of marriage Oct. 11ᵗʰ. 1795. *
Perley Whittemore of Thompson, State of Connecticut & Sally Elder of Lancaster enter their intentions of marriage, Novʳ 20. 1795. *
Israel Sawyer of Lancaster & Mary Hicks of Newton enter their intentions of marriage Novʳ. 22. 1795. *
Jonas Joslyn & Betsy Beaman both of Lancaster enter their intentions of marriage Decʳ. 31, 1795. *
William Locke jun & Eleanor Haynes both of Lancaster enter their intentions of marriage Febʸ. 6, 1796. *
John Wilder & Sally Whipple both of Lancaster enter their intentions of marriage March 8, 1796. *
254 Jonas Lane of Lancaster & Eunice Kendall of Leominster enter their intentions of marriage Apr: 4 1796. *

Oliver Sawyer & Polly Burt both of Lancaster enter their intentions of marriage Apr: 4, 1796. *
Thomas McLeod & Alice Wilder both of Lancaster enter their intentions of marriage April 17, 1796. *
Joseph Abbot & Prudence Phillips both of Lancaster enter their intentions of marriage May 3ᵈ. 1796. *
Otis Parker of Lancaster & Mary Nurse of Westborough enter their intentions of marriage May 4, 1796. *
Joel Osgood jun & Becca Beaman both of Lancaster enter their intentions of marriage May 4, 1796. *
Oliver Maynard of Lancaster & Anna Allen of Princeton enter their intentions of marriage May 26, 1796 *
Nathaniel Sawyer of Lancaster & Mʳˢ Lucy Whitcomb of Boxborough enter their intentions of marriage June 3. 1796. *
Elijah Colburn & Sally Hosley both of Lancaster enter their intentions of marriage June 4, 1796. *
Nathaniel Flint Farnsworth of Shirley & Abigail Zwiers of Lancaster Enter their intentions of marriage July 2. 1796. *
William Craig of Fitchburg & Jemima Stone of Lancaster Enter their intentions of marriage June 7. 1796. *
Benjamin Houghton junʳ. & Lydia Bennett both of Lancaster Enter their intentions of marriage July 9. 1796. *
255 Josiah Phelps of Boston & Catherine Clark of Lancaster enter their intentions of marriage July 25, 1796, *
Joseph Rice of Boylston & Betsy Sawyer of Lancaster enter their intentions of marriage Aug: 27, 1796. *
Nathan Bennett & Eunice Clark both of Lancaster enter their intentions of marriage, Sepᵗ 3ᵈ, 1796.
Peter Thurston jun & Miss Sally Sweetser both of Lancaster enter their intentions of marriage Octʳ. 2, 1796
Jotham Snow & Sally Eaton both of Lancaster intend marriage. Oct 14, 1796.
Heywood Kidder of Winchendon & Zilpah Phelps of Lancaster enter their intentions of marriage, Oct 14, 1796 *
Joseph Newman and Elizabeth Stone both of Lancaster entered their intention of Marriage Oct. 29, 1796.
Thomas Sawyer of Bolton & Elizabeth White of Lancaster entered their intention of Marriage Novʳ. 11, 1796.
Jotham Robins & Sarah Godfrey both of Lancaster enter their intentions of marriage Novʳ 17, 1796.
Nahum Ball & Mary Thomas both of Lancaster enter their intentions of marriage Novʳ 17, 1796.
Aaron Jones & Sally Wilder both of Lancaster enter their intentions of marriage Novʳ 19, 1796.
Henry Farwell of Shirley & Damson Phillips of Lancaster enter their intentions of marriage Decʳ 12, 1796.
Ephraim Carter jun. & Mary Maynard both of Lancaster enter their intentions of marriage Jany. 17. 1797. *
256 Elisha Phelps & Polly Parker both of Lancaster enter their intentions of marriage, Jany 20, 1797. *
Nathaniel Hazen of Cherry Valley in the State of New York & Rebecca Haskel of Lancaster enter their intentions of marriage, March 8, 1797. *
Haran Eager & Betsy Dunlap both of Lancaster intend marriage. March 25, 1797. *
Hooker Osgood of Marblehead & Nancy Whetcomb of Lancaster enter their intentions of marriage April 7. 1797. *
Eleazar Robbins of Lancaster & Polly Warren of Shirley enter their intentions of marriage July 7ᵗʰ. 1797. *
Charles Lewis of Lancaster & Hannah Damon of Reading enter their intentions of marriage Sept. 2ᵈ. 1797. *
James Willard of Lancaster & Ame Atherton of Harvard enter their intentions of marriage Sept. 2ᵈ, 1797. *

Moses Thomas of Sterling & Rebecca Whiting of Lancaster enter their intentions of marriage Novr. 6th: 1797. *

Samuel S. Parker of Harvard & Rebeccah Thomas of Lancaster enter their intentions of marriage, Novr. 15, 1797. *

Ezekiel Smith of Heneker State of Newhampshire & Nabby Whipple of Lancaster intend marriage. Novr. 20th. 1797. *

Josiah White of Lancaster & Sarah Kilburne of Sterling intend marriage. Novr. 21st, 1797. *

257 John Goodwin & Rebeccah Godfrey both of Lancaster enter their intentions of marriage, Jany 12th 1798. *

Gilman Thurston of Westminster & Azubah Gillet of Lancaster enter their intentions of marriage, Jany. 12th, 1798.

Nathaniel Butler of Boston & Lydia Mason of Lancaster enter their intentions of marriage Feby. 7, 1798. *

Hon Barzillai Homes of Boston & Sally Flagg of Lancaster enter their intentions of marriage Feby. 24th. 1798. *

Benjamin Geary of Leominster & Lois Osgood of Lancaster enter their intentions of marriage April 11, 1798. *

Reuben Witherbee of Boxboro' & Sukey Zwier of Lancaster enter their intentions of marriage Apr: 15, 1798. *

Jonathan Winch of Barre and Deborah Belknap of Lancaster enter their intentions of marriage, May 31, 1798. *

Reuben Zwier & Levisa Phillips both of Lancaster enter their intentions of marriage, June 9, 1798. *

Thomas Lewis of Lancaster & Jenny Armond of Worcester enter their intentions of marriage June 18, 1798. *

Jonathan Phillips & Rebecca Brown both of Lancaster enter their intentions of marriage June 18, 1798.

Aaron Phelps & Relief Chace both of Lancaster enter their intentions of marriage, Septr. 23^d. 1798. *

258 Nathaniel Whittemore of Lancaster & Sarah Stone of Groton Enter their intentions of marriage, Septr. 30th. 1798. *

Thomas Brooks of Sterling & Eunice Eveleth of Lancaster enter their intentions of marriage, Octr 9. 1798.

Timothy Lewis jun^r. & Nabby Foster both of Lancaster enter their intentions of marriage, Oct. 18, 1798.

Aaron Pollard of Lancaster & Anna Taylor of Harvard enter their intentions of marriage, Octr. 31, 1798.

Ezra Willard & Susannah Tenny both of Lancaster intend marriage. Nov. 14, 1798.

Jesse Willard of Lancaster & Abigail Farnsworth of Harvard enter their intentions of marriage Novr. 30, 1798

Ephraim Sawyer of Templeton & Sarah Houghton of Lancaster enter their intentions of marriage Decr. 1. 1798.

Abijah Rogers of Sterling & Lucy Wilder of Lancaster enter their intentions of marriage Decr. 14, 1798.

Caleb Lincoln & Patty Carter both of Lancaster enter their intentions of marriage, Decr. 26th, 1798.

Ebenezer Sargeant of Lancaster & Mary Ball of Bolton enter their intentions of marriage Decr. 22^d. 1798.

John Watkins of Newton & Sarah Brewer of Lancaster intend marriage. Jany. 11, 1799. Jany. 16, 1799, Sarah Brewer appears in person and disavows her intentions of marriage with the said Jno. Watkins. *

Elisha Bennet jun. & Nancy Wilder both of Lancaster enter their intentions of marriage, Feby. 7, 1799.

Otis Hunt & Arathusa Divoll both of Lancaster enter their intentions of marriage, Feby. 7th, 1799. *

259 Feby. 7th Luther Washburn of Hardwick & Caty Cotting of Lancaster enter their intentions of marriage. also:

Rufus Washburn of Hardwick & Thankful Cotting of Lancaster enter their intentions of marriage. *

16th. Willard Hills of St Armand in the Province of Canada & Susannah Divoll of Lancaster enter their intentions of marriage. *
April 1st. Nathaniel Whittemore junr. of Lancaster, & Polly Stone of Groton enter their intentions of Marriage. *
" 21st. Samuel Pratt & Mary Henry both of Lancaster enter their intentions of marriage. *
May 23d. James Robins & Nancy Houghton both of Lancaster, enter their intentions of marriage. *
July 25th. Daniel G. Wheeler of Worcester & Elizabeth D. Sweetser of Lancaster enter their intentions of marriage. *
Aug: 16. Ephraim Geary of Lancaster & Dolly Moore of Boylston enter their intentions of marriage. *
Septr. 28. Timothy Whiting & Lydia Phelps both of Lancaster enter their intentions of marriage. *
Same day. Asa Warner of Lancaster & Jane Peacock of Cambridge enter their intentions of marriage. *
Octr. 10. Joshua Turner & Lucy Blood both of Lancaster enter their intentions of marriage. *
Decr. 8th. Timothy H Curtis & Subbiear Johnson both of Lancaster enter their intentions of marriage. *
260 1800 Jany 4. Mulford Phillips & Betsy Zwear both of Lancaster enter their intentions of marriage. *
" 6. David Wilder 2d. of Leominster & Lucy Rugg of Lancaster enter their intentions of marriage. *
" 17 Jonadab Moore of Bolton & Thankful Sargeant of Lancaster enter their intentions of marriage. *
" 25 Jabez Brigham & Sophia Hunt both of Lancaster enter their intentions of marriage. *
Feby. 18. Joseph Wilder of Lancaster & Sally Tucker of Leicester enter their intentions of marriage.
April 7. Benjamin Larkin of Boylston and Polly Fuller of Lancaster enter their intentions of marriage- *
26. Oliver Baldwin of Lancaster & Lucy Hosley of Billerica enter their intentions of marriage. *
June 6th. Josiah Barnard of Berlin & Catherine Wilder of Lancaster enter their intentions of marriage. *
18. George Phelps & Sally Jones both of Lancaster enter their intentions of marriage. *
22d. Samuel Atherton of Lancaster & Betsy Henry of Chesterfield Newhampshire enter their intentions of marriage. *
October 5. Eben Preble of Boston and Abigail Torrey of Lancaster enter their intentions of marriage.
Novr. 2d. Daniel Harris of Lunenburg & Nancy Elder of Lancaster enter their intentions of marriage.
22d. Amos Rogers of Harvard & Polly Phillips of Lancaster enter their intentions of marriage. *
261 1801, Jany 17. David Macgregore of Lancaster & Mary Butterfield of Groton enter their intentions of marriage. *
" Joseph Fairbank of Harvard & Mary Willard of Lancaster Enter their intentions of marriage.
24. Jonathan Fiske of Wendell & Prudence Houghton of Lancaster enter their intentions of marriage.
" William Barnard & Bathsheba Goodwin both of Lancaster enter their intentions of marriage.
" Oliver Sawyer & Polly Wilder both of Lancaster enter their intentions of marriage. *
Mar: 1st. Phillip Freeman & Patty Hammond both of Lancaster Enter their intentions of marriage. *
June 13. John Whiting 2nd. and Nancy Carter both of Lancaster enter their intentions of marriage. JOSIAH FLAGG, *Town Clerk.*

NOTE. Josiah Flagg, clerk of the town 1801-1835, never failed to attach his full official signature to each "publishment." As in the case of his predecessor, these attestations will be omitted.

June 13. Moses Wares of Harvard and Rebecca Allen of Lancaster enter their intentions of marriage. *

July 11. Stephen Sargent of Lancaster and Mary Temple of Boylstone enter their intentions of marriage. *

Aug. 13 Thomas Durant and Sophia Osgood both of Lancaster enter their intentions of Marriage. *

262 Augt. 14th Gardner Pollard of Lancaster, and Lucy Heywood of Gardner enter their intentions of Marriage. *

Aug. 14th, John Hunt Jr. and Polly Wilder both. of Lancaster, enter their intentions of marriage.

15 William Wilder Jun. of Portland and Nancy Beaman of Lancaster enter their intentions of marriage. *

Sept. 9th. William Carter of Sullivan in the State of New Hampshire and Sarah Goodwin of Lancaster enter their intentions of marriage. *

" John Martin of Lancaster and Polly Lowe of Leominster, enter their intentions of Marriage. *

Octo. 24. Moses Osgood, and Hannah Sargant both of Lancaster, enter their intentions of Marriage. *

Nov. 28. Joseph Leach of Lancaster and Rebecca Flagg of Boston enter their intentions of Marriage. *

263 Dec. 1. Jesse Smith of Hollis, New Hampshire and Hannah Farnsworth of Lancaster Enter their intentions of Marriage. *

" 19. Jonas Osteinbrooks of Stilwater, State of New York, now resident in Lancaster, and Phebe Woods of Lunenburge persons of Colour enter their intentions of Marriage. N. B. The said Osteinbrooks, is an indented Servant to Major Merrick Rice. *

Jany 8th 1802. Abraham Wheeler Jr. of Bolton and Izze Warner of Lancaster enter their intentions of Marriage. *

.16 Abel Willard and Rebecca Elder both of Lancaster enter their intentions of Marriage. *

Feb. 6. John Sargent and Anne Miller both of Lancaster enter their intentions of Marriage. *

264 Mar 1. 1802. Jonas Johnson, and Mary Lyon both of Lancaster enter their intention of Marriage. *

6th. Edward Holmes and Huldah Robbins both of Lancaster enter their intention of Marriage.

13. John Townshend and Ruth Phelps, both of Lancaster enter their intentions of Marriage. *

20. Daniel Wilder and Lydia Kelsey, both of Lancaster enter their intentions of Marriage. *

23^d. James Godfrey and Polly Goodwin both of Lancaster enter their intentention of Marriage. *

May 8th. William Abbot of Castine and Becca Atherton of Lancaster, enter their intention of Marriage. *

" 11 Joel Wilder and Sophia Prescott both of Lancaster enter their intentions of Marriage. *

10. Nathaniel Chandler of Petersham and Dolly Green of Lancaster enter their intentions of marriage. *

265 June 19, 1802. John Thurston and Polly Sargant both of Lancaster enter their intentions of marriage. *

July 10. John Parker of Lancaster and Lydia Barnard of Harvard enter their intentions of Marriage. *

Augt. 3. James Carter Jun. of Lancaster, and Sally Hall of New Braintree, enter their Intentions of Marriage. *

7. John Ivory Jr. and Betsy Page of Shirley enter their intentions of Marriage. *

Sep. 7. Charles Emes Knight of Lancaster, and Sally Knight of Fitzwilliam, enter their intention of Marriage. *

18. William C. Reed of Charlestown and Susanna Pollard of Lancaster enter their intentions of Marriage. *

266 Sep. 20. Peter T. Vose of Augusta district of Maine and Ann A. Sprague of Lancaster enter their intentions of Marriage. *

BOOK FIRST. 153

Octo. 25. Benjamin Chandler and Elizabeth Pratt both of Lancaster enter their intentions of marriage. *
28. Joseph Carter Jun. and Elizabeth Goss both of Lancaster enter their intentions of marriage. *
Nov. 27. Solomon Carter, and Lucy Joslyn both of Lancaster enter their intentions of marriage. *
Dec. 10. Amasa Willard, and Fanny Willard both of Lancaster enter their intentions of Marriage. *
Jany. 13, 1803. John Wilder 4th and Mary Knight both of Lancaster enter their intentions of Marriage. *
30th. Salmon Godfrey jun. and Lucy Clarke both of Lancaster enter their intention of marriage. *
267 Feb. 10. John Robbins and Prudence Johnson both of Lancaster enter their intentions of marriage. *
April 8. Jonas Whitney and Mary Hawkes both of Lancaster enter their intentions of marriage. *
April 23. Aaron Wilder and Hannah Bemis both of Lancaster enter their intention of Marriage. *
May 20. Wiiliam Damon and Abigail Willard both of Lancaster enter their intentions of Marriage. *
Augt. 6th. Luke Wilder of Lancaster and Mary Rand of Stow enter their intentions of Marriage. *
20. Edward Fuller of Lancaster and Susanna Maynard of Berlin enter their intentions of Marriage. *
268 Sept. 8th. Horatio G. Buttrick, and Nancy Whitney, both of Lancaster enter their intentions of Marriage. *
17. John Carter 3^d. and Betsy Thurston both of Lancaster enter their intentions of Marriage. *
Octo. 15. Mannasah Solindine of Lancaster and Deborah Fairbank of Bolton, enter their intentions of Marriage. *
29th. William Willard and Lucy Haskell both of Lancaster enter their intentions of Marriage. *
Nov. 11th. James Richardson and Lois Bennett both of Lancaster enter their intentions of marriage *
Feb. 11, 1804. Calvin Peabody and Nabby Fairbank both of Lancaster enter their intention of Marriage. *
Mar. 16, 1804. Nathaniel Jones and Susanna Meriam both of Lancaster enter their intentions of Marriage. *
269 April 28. Abel White of Lancaster and Betsy Carter of Lancaster aforesaid enter their intentions of Marriage. *
Aug. 6. Samuel Barrett and Eleanor Arnold both of Lancaster enter their intentions of Marriage. *
Sep^t. 1. Jonathan Hildreth of Lancaster and Elizabeth Wimble Ansart of Dracut, enter their intentions of Marriage. *
Sep^t. 1. Jacob Zwiers jun. of Lancaster and Fanny Adams of Groton enter their intentions of Marriage. *
Octo. 13. William Fletcher and Dorcas Whipple both of Lancaster enter their intentions of Marriage. *
270 Octo. 29th. Calvin Foster of Worcester and Lucy Dickinson of Lancaster enter their intentions of Marriage. *
" 30. Benjamin Goodhue Esq of Salem and Anna Willard, of Lancaster, enter their intentions of Marriage. *
Nov. 6. Ephraim Rugg and Betsy Warner both of Lancaster enter their intentions of Marriage. *
Nov. 10. Abijah Phelps and Mary Phelps 2^d. enter their intentions of Marriage. *
Nov. 28. Samuel Sherman of Leominster and Phebe Atherton of Lancaster enter their intentions of Marriage, *
Nov. 30. Reuben Barrett and Rebecca Haskell both of Lancaster enter their intentions of Marriage. *
271 Dec. 8th. Jonathan Osgood jun. and Ami Fales both of Lancaster enter their intentions of Marriage. *

1805. Jany. 25. Joel Oliver and Esther Divol both of Lancaster enter their intentions of marriage. *
Feb. 16. Samuel Euers and Dolly Wilder both of Lancaster enter their intentions of marriage. *
28. Asa Knowlton, and Alice Divol both of Lancaster enter their intentions of marriage. *
March 29. Samuel Sawyer of Sterling and Hepshibah Thurston of Lancaster enter their intentions of marriage. *
June 29. David Hildreth of Lancaster, and Sarah Bradley of Dracut enter their intentions of Marriage. *
Sep. 8. Benjamin Farnsworth of Groton, and Dorcas Whittemore of Lancaster enter their intentions of Marriage. *

272 Sep. 27th. Charles Barker of Lancaster and Lucy Willard of Lancaster enter their intentions of Marriage. *
Octo. 5. Thomas Burpee of Belfast in the District of Maine and Polly Haskell of Lancaster enter their intentions of Marriage. *
Octo. 5. Ebenezer Taylor of Sterling and Abigail Webb of Lancaster enter their intentions of marriage. *
Octo. 12. Ephraim Phelps and Dolly Divol both of Lancaster enter their intentions of marriage. *
Nov. 18. Moses Smith Jun. of Lancaster and Sally Sawyer of Lunenburge enter their intentions of Marriage. *
Dec. 7, 1805. Benjamin Willard of Lancaster, and Sally Conant of Sterling enter their intentions of Marriage. *

273 1805. Dec. 7th. Jonas Goss of Lancaster, and Judith Andrews of Boylstone enter their intentions of Marriage. *
Dec, 13th. John Lyon and Sally Crooker both of Lancaster enter their intentions of Marriage. *
1806. Jany. 4th. Flavel Coolidge of Cambridge, and Nancy Wilds of Lancaster, enter their intentions of Marriage. *
Feb. 14th. John Adams of Lancaster and Dolly Stuart of Leominster enter their intentions of marriage. *
Feb, 19. Thomas Darby of Leominster and Mary Stone of Lancaster enter their intentions of Marriage. *

274 1806. Feb. 28. James Mallard of Lancaster, and Betsy Brigham of Marlboro' enter their intentions of Marriage. *
Mar. 8th. Jonas Phelps of Amherst New Hampshire and Nancy Phelps of Lancaster enter their intentions of Marriage. *
Mar. 15. Pliny Newhall and Patty Wyman of Lancaster enter their intentions of Marriage. *
Mar. 22d. Jonathan Farwell, and Lois Pond both of Lancaster enter their intentions of Marriage. *
March 29th. Joseph Fletcher of Bolton, and Mercy Warner of Lancaster, enter their intentions of Marriage. *
April 2d. John Haskell, and Tamsin Hayden both of Lancaster enter their intentions of Marriage. *

275 May 8th. Samuel Damon Jr. and Polly Hart both of Lancaster, enter their intentions of Marriage. *
May 31. John Carter 2d and Tempe Fales both of Lancaster enter their intentions of Marriage. *
June 5th. William Lambert of Roxbury, and Lucy Hiller of Lancaster, enter their intentions of Marriage. *
June 11th. Joseph Emerson jun. of Royalston and Lydia Whittemore of Lancaster enter their intentions of marriage. *
June 21. Peter Divol and Susanna Peirce both of Lancaster enter their intentions of Marriage. *

276 1806. June 28. Calvin Carter of Lancaster and Sally Perry of Fitchburge enter their intentions of Marriage. *
Aug. 18. Silas Thurston of Lancaster and Michal Nelson of Sterling enter their intentions of Marriage. *
Lep. 5. Abel Wilder of Lancaster and Hannah Merritt of Templeton enter intentions of Marriage. *

Sept. 20. Artemas Brigham of Concord and Eliza Wilder of Lancaster enter their intentions of Marriage. *
Sept. 24. Stephen Cleverly and Sarah Dixon both of Lancaster enter their intentions of Marriage. *

277 1806 Octo. 9th. Simon Derby of Leominster and Lydia Johnson of Lancaster enter their intention of marriage. *
Nov. 3. Lewis Parker of Lancaster and Elizabeth Seaver of Sterling enter their intentions of Marriage. *
Nov. 26. Benjamin Wyman and Lucretia Thayer of Lancaster enter their intentions of Marriage. *
Dec. 8. Elias Wilder of Lancaster and Rebecca Coudry of Carlisle enter their intentions of Marriage. *

278 1807. Jany. 31. Aaron Cooley of Boston, and Harriet Pownal of Lancaster enter their intentions of Marriage, *
Feb. 23. Elisha Townshend of Bolton and Lucy Rand of Lancaster enter their intentions of Marriage. *
March 2d. Robert Hudson of Lancaster and Polly Fife of Berlin enter their intentions of Marriage. *
Mar. 18. Stephen Wilder jun. and Katy Sawyer both of Lancaster enter their intentions of Marriage.
April 17, Titus Wilder jun. and Eunice Butler both of Lancaster enter their intentions of Marriage. *

279 1807. April 27. Jedediah Buffum and Nancy Wilder both of Lancaster enter their intentions of Marriage. *
May 1. Peter Sawyer and Mary Heywood Sawyer both of Lancaster enter their intentions of Marriage. *
Sept. 1. Daniel Frothingham of Charlestown and Rebecca Barrett of Lancaster enter their intentions of Marriage. *
Octo. 8. Ebenezer Wilder and Lusena Sawyer both of Lancaster enter their intentions of Marriage. *
Octo 17th. Nathaniel Kidder of Prospect in the District of Maine, and Sally Atherton of Lancaster enter their intentions of marriage. *

280 1807 Octo. 20th. Levi Blood and Olive Laughton both of Lancaster enter their intentions of Marriage. *
Octo. 24, 1807. Josiah Rugg and Polly Wyman both of Lancaster enter their intentions of Marriage. *
Nov. 10. Thomas Howe of Lancaster and Sally Miles of Rutland, enter their intentions of Marriage. *
Nov. 16. Reuben Wheeler and Sally Whitney both of Lancaster enter their intentions of Marriage. *
Dec. 11. Stephen Bates of West Cambridge and Nancy Thurston of Lancaster enter their intentions of Marriage. *

281 1807 Dec. 27th. George Robinson jun. of Harvard and Annis Willard of Lancaster enter their intentions of Marriage.
1808, Mar. 12. Thomas Phelps of Lancaster and Betsy Norcross of Princeton enter their intentions of Marriage.
April 9th. Samuel Jones jun. and Nancy Fales both of Lancaster enter their intentions of Marriage. *
May 2, Oliver Brown and Keziah Haven both of Lancaster enter their intentions of Marriage. *
Augt. 1. Joshua Kenney of Orrington and Hannah Stearns of Lancaster enter their intentions of Marriage, *

282 1808. Augt. 13. Jacob Thayer of Boston and Deborah Knowlton of Lancaster enter their intentions of Marriage. *
Sept. 24. John Ballard of Lancaster and Molly Moore of Boylstone enter their intentions of Marriage. *
Sept. 24. Elijah Rugg and Lucy Fairbank both of Lancaster enter their intentions of Marriage. *
Sept. 29. Freeborn Stearns of Lancaster and Clarissa Demery of Dublin N. H. enter their intentions of Marriage. *

283   DEATHS

Mr Josiah Whetcomb j^r Deceased March y^e. 21, 1718-9.
Mr Josiah Whetcomb Deceased April y^e. 12, 1718.
Jonas Houghton j^r Deceased September y^e. 20, 1723.
Josiah Houghton Deceased September y^e. 29: 1723.
Ebenezer Warner Deceased October y^e. 3, 1723.
Edmund Harries Deceased December y^e. 10. 1723.
Dinah the Daughter of Jonas & Mary Houghton Deceased y^e. 23. September 1723.
Daniel Priest Deceased October y^e. 9, 1723.
Lydiah Butler ye wife of James Butler Deceased October y^e. 11, 1723.
Mrs Mary Houghton ye wife of John Houghton Esqr. Deceased April ye 9. 1724.
Leiu^t. John Houghton Deceased April v^e. 5. 1724.
Sarah Beaman the Daughter of John & Abigal Beaman Deceased September y^e: 22, 1723.
Hannah Wilder ye Daughter of John & Sarah Wilder Deceased September y^e: 30. 1723.
Dorithy Joslin ye Daughter of Capt. Peter Joslin Deceased April y^e: 22: 1732.
Lucy Joslin ye Daughter of John & Lucy Joslin December y^e: 1: 1736.
Mr Edward Phelps Departed this life November ye 30th. 1747.
John Beaman Son of John & Susanah Beman Deceased ye 28 of September 1746
Oliver Son of John & Susanah Beaman Deceased September ye 30th 1746.
Sarah Beaman Daughter of John & Susanah Beaman Decea^d October ye 1th 1746.
Rebekah Rugg Daughter of John & Lidia Rugg Deceased July 6th. 1747
Bettey Nelson Daughter of David & Margret Nelson Deceased August 14th 1750
Nathan Nelson Son of David & Margret Nelson Deceased August ye 20 1750
Marcey Nelson Daughter of David & Margret Nelson Deceased August ye 22, 1750
Marey Nelson Daughter of David & Margret Nelson Deceased August ye 23, 1750
Mrs Eunice Osgood Wife of Mr Aaron Osgood Dec'd August 21 1751
Eunice Daughter of Aaron Osgood & Eunice Osgood Deased Jany ye 3^d 1739
Thankfull Daug^r. to Eben^r. & Tabatha Allen Ju^r Decas'd May 9. 1761
Abigail Osgood Daft Jon^a. Osgood Junr. —— May 11: 1761
Daniel Son to Daniel Ju^r & Elis^a. Rugg Deceas^d. Octr. 14: 1766
Josiah Son to Zebulon & Susanah Rice Dec'd September 1756
Zebulon Son to Zebulon & Susannah Rice Dec^d. September 1756
Prudance Daughter of Joseph & Elisabeth Bennett Departed this Life october ye 2^d 1756.
Ephm. Wilder Dyed march ye 7th. 1770
Joshua Fletcher Son to Joshua & Mary Fletcher Departed this Life october ye 13th 1772.
Elisha Fletcher Son to Joshua & Mary Fletcher Departed this Life December 25th 1772

284
Jonathan White ye Son of Josiah & Mary White Deceased ye 16. of July. 1707.
Mr Josiah White Deceased y^e. 11 day of November, 1714.
Capt John White Deceased y^e. 12 day of September, 1725.
Thomas Carter ye Son of Thomas & Ruth Carter Deceased y^e. 3. day of April, 1715
Sarah Carter ye Daughter of Thomas & Ruth Carter Deceased ye 10 day of August: 1723
Hannah Wilder ye Daughter of Oliver & Mary Wilder Deceased ye 22 day of November, 1723
Sarah Sawyer ye Daughter of John & Sarah Sawyer Deceased December, 17: 1723
Mrs Mary Sawyer ye Wife of Mr Thomas Sawyer Deceased August ye 22^d: 1733.
John Houghton Esqr. Deceased february the third: 1736-7

285
Mary ffairbank ye daughter of Joseph & Mary ffairbank Deceased ye 22 of October, 1721.
Mercy ffairbank ye daughter of Joseph & Mary ffairbank Deceased y^e. 17: of february 1724-5
Mary Albert ye wife of Daniel Albertt Deceased ye 23 day of October: 1726.

Esther Sawyer y'' daughter of Amos & Abigail Sawyer, Deceased y''. 6. day of September, 1720.
Amos Sawyer y'' son of Amos & Abigail Sawyer, Deceased y''. 26; day of December, 1726.
Uriah Holt y'' son of Uriah & Sarah Holt Deceased y'' 23 day of December, 1727.
Daniel Whetcomb y'' son of Josiah & Ruhamah Whetcomb Deceased y'' 14 day of —— 1727.
Josiah Johnson Decesed y'' 15 day of October, 1727.
Tabatha Houghton y'' daughter of Thomas & Joannah Houghton Deceased y'' 14 of march, 1725-8
Pethula Willard y'' daughter of Jonathan & Keziah Willard Deceas^d y''. 30. day of October 1727.
Silence Houghton y'' daughter of Jonathan & Mary Houghton Deceased y'' 4 day of Septem^b. 1728
Hezakiah Townsend Deceased: y'': 19th of April· 1729:
Prescila Beman y'' wife of John Beman Sn^r. Deceased: y'': 6th: of August: 1729.
Joseph Houghton y'' Son of Israel and Martha Houghton Deceased: y'': 17th: of november 1726.
Mary Warner Daughter of John and Rebecka Warner: Deceased: y'': 9th: of febrarey: 1729-30.
John Osgood Son of Hooker and Mary Osgood, Deceased: y'': 26th: of August: 1724.
David Sawyer y'' Son of Amos & Abigail Sawyer Deceased y'' 3 day of June, 1729
Ephah Houghton y'' daughter of Jonathan & Thankfull Houghton Deceased September y''. 27, 1729
Patience Beaman y'' Daughter of Ebenezer & Rebeckah Beaman Deceased October 10, 1728
Ebenezer Beaman y'' Son of Ebenezer & Rebeckah Beaman Deceased October, 17. 1728
Moses Sawyer y'' Son of John & Sarah Sawyer Deceased December y''. 4: 1730.
Adonijah Willard y'' Son of Jonathan & Keziah Willard Deceased October y''. 22. 1729.
Moses Snow y'' Son of John & Hannah Snow deceased: October y''. 11. 1729.
M^n Eunice Wilder y'' Wife of Mr Jonas Wilder Deceased: June y''. 15: 1731.
Miriam Sawyer y'' daughter of John & Sarah Sawyer Deceased, September y''; 1, 1731
Aaron Sawyer y'' Son of John & Sarah Sawyer Deceased September y''. 16, 1731
Mr Caleb Townsend Deceased the first day of April, 1732
Mr John Sawyer of Lancaster Deceased October the. 2^d, 1731
Jonathan & Aaron Witherbey Sons of John & Elizabeth Witherbey Deceased April y''. 26: 1731
John & James White the Sons of Josiah & Abigail White Deceased January y'': 24: 1727-8
Abijah Willard y'' Son of Samuel & Elisabeth Willard Deceased October y'': 3. 1722.
M^n. Mary Gates the Wife of Mr Hezekiah Gates Deceased April y'': 3^d. 1733.
M^n. Sarah Knight y'' wife of Mr Daniel Knight Deceased April y''. 29. 1732
Rhoda Wilson y'' Daughter of Benjamin & Rebekah Wilson Deceased August y'' first, 1733
M^n. Mercy Wilder the wife of Mr Ebenezer Wilder Deceased January y'': 7th: 1733-4.
M^n. Mary Whetcomb (y'' widow of Mr David Whetcomb;) Deceased January y'': 15th: 1733-4.
David Sawyer the Son of Amos & Abigail Sawyer Deceased: June y''; 3: 1729.
Oliver Witherbey y'' Son of Jon^a. & Aliess Witherbey: Deceased August y'': 30th, 1731.
Mr John Buss Deceased the thirtieth day of April, 1734.
Joshua Phelps y'' Son of Joshua & Rebeckah Phelps Deceased April y''; 13: 1733
Sam^{ll}. Wilder y'' Son of Nathaniel & Damaris Wilder Deceased May y''; 9: 1725.
Joanna Sawyer y'' daughter of John & Sarah Sawyer Deceased May y'' 30; 1735.
Sarah Kendal y'' wife of James Kendal Deceased September 20; 1736
James Kendal the Son of James & Sarah Kendal Deceased November 20: 1736

Mary Ballard Daughter of Benjamin & Ruth Ballard Deceased October 20: 1736
Benjn. Houghton ye Son of Israel & Martha Houghton Deceased October: 27: 1737
286   Capt Thomas Carter Deceased March ye 31st 1737.
Lev^t Jonathan Houghton Deceased april ye 8th 1737
———— ye Child of Nathaniel Hutson deceased april ye 8th 1737
Hannah ye Wife of John Fletcher Deceased april ye 10 1737
John Johnson Juner Deceased ye 21 of april 1737·
John Wilds ye Son of Richard and Ruth Wilds deceased april ye 24th 1737.
Joseph Sawyer Deceased July ye 10 1737.
Hannah Houghton Deceased January ye 8th 1737-8
Caleb ye Son of Caleb and Abigail Wilder Deceased March ye 5th 1737-8
John Prentice Deceased March ye 12th 1737-8
Jonathan Priest Deceased april ye 23^d 1738.
Mary Houghton Deceased may ye 13th 1738
Mary Carter ye wife of Ephraim Carter Deceased ye 30 of may 1738
Rebeckah Phelps ye Wife of Joshua Phelps Deceased June ye Later end 1738
Samuel Carter Deceased ye 22 day of august 1738.
Rebeckah ye Wife of Joshua Phelps deceased June ye 28th 1738. [See above.]
Mary Osgood ye Daughter of David [&] Eunice Osgood Deceased may ye 17th 1739
James Wilder Esqr Deceased May ye 13th 1739
John Harris Deceased May ye 16th 1739.
Caleb ye Son of Caleb and Abigail Wilder Deceased March ye 5 1738
Eunice Buss ye Daughter of John and Eunice Buss deceased february ye 13th 1738
John Carter ye Son of John & Abigail Carter Deceased October ye 18th. 1739
Joseph Osgood ye Son of Joseph and Mary Osgood Deceased December ye 30th 1738
John Richardson ye Son of James and Sarah Richardson Deceased December ye 6th 1739
Elisabeth Osgood ye Daughter of David and Eunice Osgood Deceased January ye 10 1739
Jonathan ye Son of Jonathan and Easter White Deceased 2 day of December 1736
Easter ye Daughter of Jonathan and Easter White Deceased December 7 1738
Easter ye Daughter of Jonathan and Easter White Deceased January ye 5 1739
Ephraim Moor ye Son of Joseph and Rebeckah Moor Decased June ye 15th 1740.
Hannah the Daughter of Joseph and Rebeckah Moor Deceased June ye 17th 1740
Jacob Moor ye Son of Joseph and Rebeckah Moor Deceased June ye 18th 1740
Catherign ye Daughter of Joseph and Rebeckah Moor Deceased June ye 23^d 1740
Rebeckah the Daughter of Joseph and Rebeckah Moor Deceased June ye 26 1740
Luce Moor ye Daughter of Joseph and Rebeckah Moor Deceased August ye 22^d 1740
Ephraim Carter ye Son of Ephraim and Abigail Carter Deceased April ye 16th 1740.
Samuel Wilder ye Son of John and Prudence Wilder Deceased September ye 12 1740 at Necthiwage.
Martha and Mary Sawyer Daughters of John & Sarah Sawyer Deceased about March Mary ye 13 & Martha ye 27, 1740-1
Abigail Snow the Daughter of John and Hannah Snow Deceased february ye 5 1740
Martha Snow February ye 14
John Snow the Son of John and Hannah Snow February ye 28 1740
Jonathan ye Son of Jonathan and Thankfull Fairbanks Deceased Sept ye 14th 1741
Eunice ye Daughter of Aaron and Eunice Osgood Deceased January ye 4th 1739
Sarah Wilder ye Wife of Oliver Wilder Deceased y^r 9 day of Decemb 1743
287   Elisebeth the Daughter of Nathanael and Mary Sawyer Deceased October the 3 Day 1742.
Joseph Joslin the Son of Peter and Alles Joslin Deseased December the 2nd: 1735
Reziner the Daughter of John & Abigail Wilder Dec^d August, 6: 1744
Joseph Son of Joseph & Elisebeth Osgood: Dec^d. February 27th: 1744

Luce Moor Daughter of Joseph & Rebekah Moor Deca^d: Octo^r. ye 1: 1744
M^n Ruth Phelps Wife of Mr Edward Phelps Deca^d. Feb^r: 1st: 1744-5
Rebekah Sawyer Daughter of John & Sarah Sawyer Dec^d. May ye 6: 1745
Amos Rugg Son of Amos & [Mary] Rugg Deceased September ye 11, 1746
Abisha Son of Robart & Doratha Phelps Deceased ye 22^d of Novem^r. 1739
Doratha Daughter of Robert Phelps & Doratha Phelps Dece'd Novem^r 27, 174-
Doratha Daughter of John Prescott Junr & Mary Prescott Deceased Decem^r 28, 1746.
M^n Bridget Bayley Wife of Mr Jonathan Bayley of Lancaster Departed this life April ye 15. 1746.
Joseph Moor Son of Joseph & Rebekah Moor Deceased October ye 25, 1746
Rebekah Daughter of Joseph & Rebekah Moor Dece^{sd}. Septem^r 22, 1746
Oliver Carter Son of Ephraim & Abigail Carter Dece^d. July ye 30 1747.
Abigail Green Daughter of Peter Green & Abigail Green was born 14 of March 1737 and Deceased ye 26 of ye same month.
Peter Green Son of Peter & Abigail Green was born Apriel 1740 and Deceased ye third Day of Novem^r following.
Elizabeth Fletcher wife of Robert Fletcher Deceased July ye 24 1749
Mr Hooker Osgood Departed this life June the 29th 1748
Benjamin Ballard Son of Benjamin & Ruth Ballard Departed this life Octo ye 27. 1749
Ebenezer Kendal Departed this life May ye 27 1749
Ebenezer Kendal Junr. Departed this life May ye 16 1749
Ruth Sawyer Daughter of Sam^{ll} & Deborah Sawyer Dec^d August 1751
Mrs Eunice Harris Wife of Asa Harris Deceased Decem^r ye 16th 1752
Abijah Harris Son of Asa & Eunice Harris Deceased March ye 3^d. 1752.
Luce White Daughter of John & Loes White Departed this life February 26, 1753
Josiah Wilder Son of James & Martha Wilder Dec^d April ye 4, 1736
Coll^o. Sam^{ll}. Willard Departed this Life Novr. ye 20th. 1752
Mary Knight Daughter to Jon^a. & Mary Knight Dece^d. Febuary ye 5th. 1747
Saray the Wife of John Beman, Decas^d. Decr. 17. 1756
Stephen Son to Amos & Mary Rugs Dece^d. Octr. 19, 1756
Solomon Son to Amos & Do. Do. Dece^d. Novr. 5, 1756
Benj^a. Son to Joseph & Sarah Glaizer Dece^d: May 20. 1756
Susannah Daughter to Benj^a. & Lydia Glaizer Dec^d. October ye 4th 1756
Jane Wilder Wife of Benj^a. Wilder Dec^d. March 26, 1759
Lois Bennit Wife of Elisha Bennit Decas^d; May 28, 1759
288 Abigail Moor Wife of Israel Moor Died Decem^r: 20 1759
Mary Phelps Wife of Wm Phelps Deceased March 17, 1761
Ebenezer Son to Jeremiah & Elis^a. Burpee Deceased Augt. 31, 1756
Jeremiah Son to Jerem^h. & Ditto. Do. Sep^t: 2, 1756
Molly Daug^r. to Jer^h. & Elis^a. Burpee Do. Sep^t. 6, 1756
Katharine Houghton Wife to Elijah Houghton Deceas'd July 4th. 1762
Ruth Daug^r. to Phinehas & Ruth Houghton Deceas'd July 4th. 1762
Eunice Daug^t to Josiah & Jane Osgood Deceas'd Novr. 8 1762
Grace Houghton Wife of Josiah Houghton Deceas'd June 6th. 1763
John Prescott Deceas'd Octr. 7 1749
Dorathy Prescott Wife to John Prescott Deceas'd Sep^t. 25. 1749
Relief Daug^t. to Amos & Mary Sawyer Deceas'd Jany 12 1757
Elisabeth Wife to Aaron Willard Ju^r. Died June 3^d. 1764
Phinehas Houghton Son to Phin^s. & Ruth Houghton Died March 22 1765
Susanah Warner Daug^r. to John & Prudence Warner Died Octo^r: 13. 1765
Martha Houghton Wife to Israel Houghton Died Jany. 1 1768
Capt. John Bennitt Died June ye 5th, 1761
Barsheba Wife to John Bennitt Died February 7. 1762
Elisha Bennitt Died March ye 5th. 1769.
Ebenezer Allen Deseased July the 9: 1770 in ye 94 year of his age.
Sarah Allen Wife of Ebenezer Allen Deseased June the 15: 1755 in the 71 year of her age.
Decon Jonathan Osgood Died Feb: ye 10th 1766 in the 70th year of his age.

Abigail Osgood wife of Jonathan Osgood Died June ye 12th, 1759 in the 27 year of her age.
Daniel Robbins Died march ye 31th 1755 in the 48 year of his age
Elijah Beaman Died august 12, 1771.
289 Jonathan Fairbank son to Jonathan and Thankfull Fairbank Departed this Life Sep^r: the 14th, 1741.
Jonathan Fairbank Son to Jonathan and Thankfull Fairbank Departed this Life october ye 19th 1747
Joshua Fairbank son to Jonathan & Thankfull Fairbank Departed this Life october ye 21st. 1747.
William Fairbank son to Jonathan & Thankfull Fairbank was killed by the French and Indians at an Ingagement with them at Lake George September the Eighth, 1755
Jonathan Fairbank son to Jonathan & Thankfull Fairbank Departed this Life December the 14th, 1750
Abigail White wife to Dec Josiah White Depated this Life Sepr. ye 24th 1771 and was Buried ye 25th 1771
Decon Josiah White Departed this Life may ye 6th 1772 and Buried ye 7th 1772.
Ruth Houghton wife to Benjamin Houghton Departed this Life March ye 2^d 1762, in the 61 year of her age.
Jonathan Bayley Departed this Life Jan^y: 15th 1770 in his 75th year of his age.
Bridget wife to Jonathan Bayley Departed this Life April 1746
Abigaiel wife to Jonathan Bayley Departed this Life Feb 2nd 1771.
Michael Trollet Esqr. Native of Geneva of French Extract deceas'd Sunday Morning July 17th. 1774.
Aaron Sawyer departed this Life December 15th, 1774 aged 42 years 6 months & 23 days
Amos Sawyer departed this Life January 25th 1768
290 Dec Oliver Moor Departed this Life December ye 23^d 1774.
Martha Wilder wife to Majour James Wilder Departed this Life march ye 19th 1774.
John son to Roger and Tamezin Bartlett Departed this Life Sepr. ye 13th 1775
Moses & Ezekiel sons of Roger and Tamezin Bartlett Departed this Life August 31th 1775
Rebeckah Phillips, Daughter to John & Anna Phillips, Departed this life Octr. 26th, 1776.
John Phillips Junr. Son to John & Anna Phillips, Departed this life Octr. 29: 1776
Samuel Phillips, Son to John & Anna Phillips Departed this life November the 2th: 1776.
John Phillips, husband to Anna Phillips, Departed this life Novr. 24th: 1776, in his 56 year of his age
Sylvester Son of Joel and Prudence Phelps Departed this Life April 7, 1765.
Luke Carter Son to James Carter and Mary Carter Departed this Life May 22 1778 aged twenty yers five months and ten Day
Daniel Albert, departed this Life Jany 28: 1769: Aged sixty eight years.
Benj^a: Wilder Ross Son of Ebenezer & Achsah Ross Died Feb^r 20 1780.
Tamazin, Wife to Roger Bartlet Died Feb^r. 24, 1780.
William Dunsmore Esqr. died May 20th. 1784
Mary Albert the wife of Fred^k. Albert deceased May 3^d. 1781 aged 41 years.
Daniel, Son of Fred^k. & Abigail Albert deceased Feby. 1st. 1786, aged 21 months and 21 days.
Wid^w. Hannah Woods deceas'd June 24th. 1786.
291 M^{rs}. Eliz^h. Greenough died March 13th. 1788.

Deaths of the Children of Josiah Wilder Esqr & Polley his Wife.

William Pitt died Sep^t. 1st: 1778   Polly died Sep^t. 17th: 1778
Henry died Sep^t. 19th: 1778   Augustus died Nov^r: 16th: 1779
Henry, the youngest Child of sd Wilder died at Guadaloupe W. Indies in the year 1802.

NOTE. In 1778, Mrs. Wilder, prostrated by the fever that proved fatal to her children, apparently died. The undertaker, when about to place the body in the coffin, noticing some sign of life, summoned her husband, and she was resuscitated. Surviving Doctor Wilder, she married Doctor Isaac Hurd and lived to a ripe old age.

BOOK FIRST.

The Deaths of the Children of W^m. & Mary Locke.
Anna died Augt. 23^d: 1778   Mary died do. 26: 1778
Samuel, Son of Ephraim & Elizabeth Divol died the 18th: of Jany. 1784 A. E. 30 years.
M^rs. Catharine, Widow of Levi Willard Esqr. deceased Jany. 10th. 1791.
Miss Kesey Houghton, Daug^r. of Phyneas Houghton Died March 26. 1787.
Nancy Hawl, Woman of Colour—Transient Person died in Lancaster Novr. 2^d. 1791.
292 John, Child of Thos. & Abigail Ballard, died March 3^d. 1792.
Mary Carter wife of Capt. James Carter deceased April 18, 1795, aged 66 years 13 days,
The Revd Timothy Harrington our Senior Pastor deceased on Fryday even^g. Decr. 18th. 1795. aged 80 years.
  " His flight *Timotheus* took, his upward flight,
  " If ever Soul ascended."
Hannah the wife of Benjamin Houghton jun deceased July 12th, 1794.
Sarah the daughter of Moses Sawyer & Mary his wife deceased, Sept. 3^d 1788
Nathaniel the son of Moses Sawyer & Betty his wife deceased, Feby 13, 1788.

294   MARRIAGES

This certifies that the following persons have been legally married, at the periods respectively mentioned by me.   NATHANIEL THAYER
April 30, 1796.

1795. April 16th. Mr William Carlton to Miss Hepsey Geary both of Lancaster.
May 7. Mr Abel Rugg to Miss Catherine Rugg both of Lancaster.
Aug: 23. Mr Nathan Puffer to Miss Nabby Joslyn both of Lancaster.
Octr 12th. Mr William Sherin of Leominster to Miss Patience Wyman of Lancaster.
Novr 8th. Mr Benjamin Farnsworth to Miss Sarah Haskell both of Lancaster.
" 19. Mr Daniel Goss jun to Miss Polly Gates both of Lancaster
Decr. 13. Mr Perley Whittemore of Thompson (State of Connecticut) to Miss Sally Elder of Lancaster.
" 17. Mr Calvin Wilder to Miss Sukey Solendine both of Lancaster.
1796 Jany 27. Mr Jonas Joslyn to Miss Betsy Beaman both of Lancaster.
Feby 25. Mr William Locke jun. to Miss Eleanor Haynes both of Lancaster.
Apr. 10. Mr John Wilder to Miss Sally Whipple both of Lancaster.
                                Att^r W^m. STEDMAN *Town Clerk.*

COMMONWEALTH OF MASSACHUSETTS.
December 1st. 1796. Nahum Ball of Lancaster and Mary Thomas late of said Lancaster now resident of Boston were legally married by me.
                                JAS. SULLIVAN one of the Justices of the Peace throughout the Commonwealth aforesaid.
                                Att^r. W . STEDMAN *Town Clerk.*

295 Heywood Kidder of Winchendon and Zilpah Phelps of Lancaster, were joined in marriage December 15. A. D. 1796.
Sampson Worcester of Harvard and Phebe Wilder of Sterling were joined in Marriage January 2^d. A. D. 1797.
John Varnum Stevens of Roxbury and Betsy Knight of Bolton were joined in Marriage January 31. A. D. 1797.
Tristam Sanborn and Abigail Knight both of Harvard were joined in marriage March 17. A. D. 1797.

WORCESTER SS. April 8. 1797. The foregoing is a true return of all the names of the persons who have been joined together in marriage within the year last past, by me.   TIMOTHY WHITING JUN. *Just. Pacis.*
Entered, April 24, 1797.   Att^r. W^m. STEDMAN *Town Clerk.*

To William Stedman Esqr. Clerk of the Town of Lancaster:
   The following is a list of persons, whom I have joined together in Marriage the year past, viz :

May 11, 1797.   Jacob Stone with Anna Barns, both of Boylstone.
Aug: 8, 1797.   Jonas Coolidge with Lucy Temple, both of Bolton.
Novr. 28, 1797.   Paul Faulkner of Berlin with Sarah Smith of Boylston.
Novr. 30, 1797.   David Wood with Nancy Eaton both of Leominster.
March 15, 1798.   Samuel Dunlap with Elizabeth Temple both of Boylstone.
   WORCESTER SS.   April 18, 1798.
                    Attest TIMOTHY WHITING JUN : *Just. pacis.*
   Entered April 24th 1798.   Att^r. W^M. STEDMAN *Town Clerk*

296

1796.
May 29.   Mr Thomas Mc:Leod to Miss Alice Wilder, both of Lancaster.
June 7.   Mr Joseph Abbot to Miss Prudence Phillips, both of Lancaster.
    19.   Mr Elijah Colburn to Miss Sally Hosley; both of Lancaster.
Aug: 2.   Mr Nathaniel Flint Farnsworth of Shirley to Miss Abigail Zwiers of Lancaster.
    14.   Mr Josiah Phelps of Boston to Miss Catharine Clark of Lancaster.
    21   Mr William Craig of Fitchburg to Miss Jemima Stone of Lancaster.
Septr. 18.   Mr Joel Osgood junr. to Miss Becca Beaman; both of Lancaster.
    19.   Mr Nathan Bennett to Miss Eunice Clark; both of Lancaster.
    27.   Mr Benjamin Houghton junr. to Miss Lydia Bennett; both of Lancaster.
    29.   Mr Joseph Rice of Boylston to Miss Betsy Sawyer of Lancaster.
Octr. 30.   Mr Jotham Snow to Miss Sally Eaton; both of Lancaster.
Novr. 29.   Mr Joseph Newman to Miss Betsy Stone; both of Lancaster.
Decr. 1.   Mr Thomas Sawyer of Stow to M^m Elizabeth White of Lancaster.
    8.   Mr Peter Thurston Junr. to Miss Sally Sweetser; both of Lancaster.
    11.   Mr Jotham Robbins to Miss Sarah Godfrey both of Lancaster.
    15.   Mr Aaron Jones to Miss Sally Wilder both of Lancaster.
1797. Feby. 2^d.   Mr Ephraim Carter junr. to Miss Mary Maynard both of Lancaster.

297

1797. Feby. 14.   Mr Henry Farwell of Shirley to Miss Damson Phillips of Lancaster
Mar: 29.   Mr Elisha Phelps to Miss Polly Parker; both of Lancaster.

   This certifies that the above marriages were solemnized at the periods respectively named.   Attest NATHANIEL THAYER
   LANCASTER April 30, 1797.   Entered pr W^M. STEDMAN *Town Clerk.*

1797. May 11.   Mr Haran Eager to Miss Betsy Dunlap; both of Lancaster.
    31   Mr Hooker Osgood Jun. of Marblehead to Miss Nancy Whitcomb of Lancaster.
1798. Jany. 4.   Mr Moses Thomas of Sterling to Miss Rebecca Whiting of Lancaster.
    28.   Mr John Goodwin to Miss Rebecca Godfrey; both of Lancaster.
Feby 4.   Mr Ezekiel Smith of Hennaker State of N. Hampshire to Miss Nabby Whipple of Lancaster.
    6.   Mr Gilman Thurston of Westminster to Miss Azubah Gillet of Lancaster.
Apr: 3.   Mr Barzillai Homes of Boston to Miss Sally Flagg of Lancaster.

   This certifies that the above marriages were solemnized, at the periods respectively named.   Attest NATHANIEL THAYER
   LANCASTER April 29 1798.   Entered Pr W^M. STEDMAN *Town Clerk*

298

1798   Aug: 20.   Mr Reuben Zweirs to Miss Levina Phillips; both of Lancaster.

Octr. 29. Mr Thomas Brooks of Sterling to Mrs Eunice Eveleth of Lancaster.
Novr 29. Mr Ezra Willard to Miss Susannah Tenny; both of Lancaster.
Mr Timothy Lewis junr, to Miss Nabby Foster; both of Lancaster.
1799. Jany. 16. Mr Ephraim Sawyer of Templeton, to Miss Sarah Houghton of Lancaster.
Feby 7. Mr Caleb Lincoln to Miss Patty Carter; both of Lancaster.
25. Mr Abijah Rogers of Sterling to Miss Lucy Wilder of Lancaster.
Mr Elisha Bennett junr. to Miss Nancy Wilder both of Lancaster.
Mar: 10. Mr Willard Hills of St Armand in the Province of Canada, to Miss Susannah Divoll of Lancaster.
25. Mr Luther Washburn of Hardwick to Miss Caty Cotting of Lancaster.
Mr Rufus Washburn of Hardwick to Miss Thankfull Cotting of Lancaster.
Apr: 4. Mr Otis Hunt to Miss Arathusa Divoll; both of Lancaster.

This certifies that the above marriages were solemnized at the periods, respectively named.   Attest NATHANIEL THAYER

LANCASTER April 30. 1799.   Entered pr W^M. STEDMAN *Town Clk.*

299

To William Stedman Esqr Clerk of the Town of Lancaster
The following is a list of persons whom I have joined together in marriage the year passed viz :
May 6, 1798. Reuben Wetherbe of Boxborough with Sukey Zwear of Lancaster.
Octr. 25. 1798. Caleb Willard with Rachael Perry both of Harvard.
Jany 10. 1799. Ebenezer Sargeant of Lancaster with Mary Ball of Bolton.
Jany 28. 1799. Jonathan Phillips with Becca Brown both of Lancaster.
Given under my hand this ninth day of April A. D. 1799.
*   TIMOTHY WHITING JUN^R. *Just. pacis.*

WORCESTER ss. This certifies that William Rice of Worcester and Patty Goulding of Shrewsbury were married, September 22^d A D 1799 by me
Apr: 5. 1800. *   TIMOTHY WHITING *Just. pacis.*

WORCESTER ss. Jany 30. 1800 Be it remembered that William Sawyer & Nancy Carter both of Sterling in said county, on this day, are joined in marriage by me.   W^M. STEDMAN *Just: pacis.*
April 30, 1800. *

300

1799. May 5. Mr Samuel Pratt to Miss Mary Henry; both of Lancaster.
26. Mr Aaron Phelps to Mrs Relief Chace, both of Lancaster
June 13. Mr James Robbins to Miss Nancy Houghton both of Lancaster
Septr. 23. Mr Daniel G. Wheeler of Worcester to Miss Elizabeth D. Sweetser of Lancaster.
Octr. 14. Timothy Whiting Esquire to Miss Lydia Phelps, both of Lancaster.
1800. Jany. 29. Mr Daniel Wilder 2^d of Leominster to Miss Lucy Rugg of Lancaster.
Feby. 9. Mr Jabez Brigham to Miss Sophia Hunt, both of Lancaster.
10. Mr Joshua Turner to Miss Lucy Blood; both of Lancaster.
Mar: 6. Mr Timothy H. Curtis to Miss Subbiear Johnson, both of Lancaster.

LANCASTER April 30. 1800.
This certifies, that the marriage of the above named persons was consummated at the periods which are mentioned.
*   Attest NATHL. THAYER

301

To Mr Josiah Flagg Clerk of the town of Lancaster.
The following is a list of persons whom I have Joined in Marriage the year past, viz :

Benjamin Larkin of Boylstone & Polly Fuller of Lancaster, were married June 5th 1800,
Levi Whitney & Rebecca Fasset, both of Boylston were married July 3d, 1800.
Josiah Barnard of Berlin and Caty Wilder of Lancaster were married July 20th 1800,
Jonadab Moore of Bolton & Thankful Sargeant of Lancaster were married Sept. 25th, 1800.

 Given under my hand this twenty-eighth day of April A. D. 1801.
           TIMOTHY WHITING *Jus. Pacis.*

302

Mr Josiah Flagg Town Clerk of Lancaster.

 SIR. This may certify that I have not joined any persons in marriage during the last year.
 April 29th 1801.   SAMUEL WARD *Just pacis*

1800. July 6th. Mr George Phelps was married to Miss Sally Jones; both of Lancaster.
  Nov. 2. Mr Ebenezer Preble of Boston to Miss Abigail Torrey of Lancaster.
1801 Jany. 1. Mr Daniel Harris of Lunenburge to Miss Nancy Elder of Lancaster.
  Feb. 15. Mr Oliver Sawyer to Miss Polly Wilder both of Lancaster.
   19. Mr William Barnard to Miss Bathsheba Goodwin both of Lancaster.
   22. Dr. Jonathan Fiske of Wendall to Miss Prudence Houghton of Lancaster.
  Mar. 23 Phillip Freeman to Patty Hammond both of Lancaster.

 This certifies that the marriages above mentioned were consummated at the periods respectively named before me.   NATHANIEL THAYER.

303 John Whiting 2nd, and Nancy Carter, both of Lancaster, June 28th. 1801.
Thomas Durant and Sophia Osgood, both of Lancaster. were married Sep. 20th A D 1801.
Abel Willard and Rebecca Elder, both of Lancaster were married February 3d A. D. 1801.
Abraham Wheeler Jun. of Bolton, and Izze Warner of Lancaster were married Feb. 21. A. D. 1802.

 WORCESTER SS April 14th 1802. This certifies that the foregoing is a true return of the persons who have been joined in marriage by me the year past.
           TIMOTHY WHITING *Just pacis*

1801 July 20. Moses Wares of Harvard to Rebecca Allen of Lancaster
  Sep 6th. John Hunt Jun to Polly Wilder both of Lancaster.
   8. William Wilder Jun of Portland, to Nancy Beaman of Lancaster.
  Nov. 15. Moses Osgood to Hannah Sargent, both of Lancaster.
1802 Jany. 2. Jonas Ostenbrooks of Lancaster, to Phebe Woods of Lunenburge.
   31. William Carter of Sullivan to Sarah Goodwin of Lancaster.
  Feb. 9. Jesse Smith of Hollis in New Hampshire to Hannah Farnsworth of Lancaster.
  March 10. John Sargent to [Mrs.] Anna Miller both of Lancaster.
  April 6. Edward Holmes to Huldah Robbins both of Lancaster
   22. John Townshend to Ruth Phelps both of Lancaster.
   28. Daniel Wilder to Lydia Kelsey both of Lancaster.

 LANCASTER April 28th 1802. This certifies that the persons above named were married at the time which is mentioned before me
           NATHANIEL THAYER

304

 This certifies that the marriages which follow, were consummated at the times prefixed to their respective names.

1802 May 9. James Godfrey to Polly Goodwin both of Lancaster.
     24. William Abbott of Castine to Rebecca Atherton of Lancaster.
June 13. Joel Wilder to Sophia Prescott both of Lancaster.
July 7. John Thurston to [Mrs.] Polly Sargeant both of Lancaster.
Aug. 17. Nathaniel Chandler of Petersham to Dolly Greene of Lancaster.
Octo. 10. Peter Thacher Vose of Augusta (Maine) to Ann Austin Sprague of Lancaster.
Nov. 9. William Crosby Reed of Charlestown to Susanna Pollard of Lancaster.
     14. Benjamin Chandler to Elizabeth Pratt both of Lancaster.
     28. Joseph Carter jun to Elizabeth Goss both of Lancaster.
Dec. 5. James Carter jun of Lancaster to Sally Hall of New braintree.
305   27. Solomon Carter to Lucy Joslyn both of Lancaster.
1803 Jany. 9. Amasa Willard to Fanny Willard both of Lancaster.
Mar. 2 Salmon Godfrey jun. to Lucy Clarke both of Lancaster,
     18 John Robbins to Prudence Johnson, both of Lancaster.

*   Attest NATH^L. THAYER.

A return of the persons who have been joined in marriage by Timothy Whiting Esq. the year last past, viz:

Joseph Perry and Sally Sawyer, both of Boylstone were married Novem. 2nd. A D. 1803.

*   Attest TIMOTHY WHITING

306 This certifies that the persons herein named were married at the time prefixed to their respective names.

1803. May 8. Aaron Wilder to Hannah Bemis both of Lancaster.
     30. John Wilder 4th. to Mary Knight both of Lancaster.
June 2. Jonas Whitney to Mary Hawkes; both of Lancaster.
     22. William Damon to Abigail Willard both of Lancaster.
Octo. 6. Horatio G. Buttrick to Nancy Whitney both of Lancaster.
     19. John Carter 3^d to Betsy Thurston both of Lancaster.
Dec. 1. James Richardson to Lois Bennett both of Lancaster.
     22 William Willard to Lucy Haskell both of Lancaster.
     26 John Wyman of Ashby to Betsy Osborn of Bolton.
1804 Jany. 1. Manasah Solindene of Lancaster to Deborah Fairbank of Bolton.
Mar. 22. Calvin Peabody to Nabby Fairbank both of Lancaster.

*   Attest NATH^L THAYER.

307 This certifies that the persons herein named were married on the days prefixed to their names.   Attest NATH^L THAYER.

1804. Sep. 15. Samuel Barrett to Eleanor Arnold, both of Lancaster.
Sep. 20 Abel White to Betsy Carter; both of Lancaster.
Nov. 25 Hon. Benjamin Goodhue of Salem; to Anna Willard of Lancaster.
Nov. 29. William Fletcher to Dorcas Whipple both of Lancaster.
Dec. 26. Ephraim Rugg to Betsy Warner both of Lancaster.
1805. Jany. 2. Samuel Sherman of Leominster to Phebe Atherton of Lancaster.
Jany. 24. Abijah Phelps to [Mrs.] Mary Phelps both of Lancaster.
Jany. 28. Jonathan Osgood jun. to Ami Fales both of Lancaster.
Feb. 27. Joel Oliver to Esther Divoll both of Lancaster.
April 2. Asa Knowlton to Alice Divoll both of Lancaster
308   *
1805 Octo. 2. Benjamin Farnsworth of Groton to Dorcas Whittemore of Lancaster.
     13. Charles Barker to Lucy Willard; both of Lancaster.
Nov. 5. Ephraim Phelps to Dolly Divoll; both of Lancaster.
     19. Ebenezer Taylor of Sterling, to Abigail Webb of Lancaster.
1806 Jany. 19. John Lyon to Sally Crooker; both of Lancaster.
April 13, Pliny Newhall to Patty Wyman; both of Lancaster.
     16. John Haskell to Tamsin Hayden; both of Lancaster.

LANCASTER April 17th, 1806.
This certifys that marriage was consummated between the persons above mentioned on the day prefixed to their respective names.
Attest NATHANIEL THAYER.

309 This certifies that the persons herein named were married on the days prefixed to their names, by me   Attest JOSIAH FLAGG *Jus. Pacis.*
1805 Octo. 20th. John Davenport, and Mary M. Beaman both of Boylstone.
Nov 2. Ephraim Boynton jun. and Betsy Smith both of Sterling.

1806. April 8. A return of the persons who have been joined together in Marriage the year past, by Timothy Whiting Esq. viz: Samuel Ewers, and Doris Wilder, both of Lancaster were married May 30th. 1805.

310 A return of marriages solemnized before Timothy Whiting Esq. the past Year, viz:
Joseph Fletcher of Bolton, and Mary Warner of Lancaster, were married April 15 A. D. 1806
John Tenney, and Nancy Thompson both of Leominster were married Augt. 4th. Anno Domini 1806.

This certifies that Salmon Hougnton and Lucy May both of Sterling were married March 5th 1807 by me   JOSIAH FLAGG *Justice of the peace.*

311 LANCASTER May 1, 1807. This certifies that the marriages herein named were solemnized before me   NATHL. THAYER.

1806. May 25. Thomas Darby of Leominster to Mary Stone of Lancaster.
" Jonas Phelps of Amherst N. H. to Nancy Phelps of Lancaster.
June 1. Jonathan Farwell to Lois Pond, both of Lancaster.
Samuel Damon Jr. to Polly Hart both of Lancaster.
July 4. William Lambert Jr. of Roxbury to Lucy Hiller of Lancaster.
6. John Carter Jr. to Tempe Fales, both of Lancaster.
Aug. 31. Peter Divol to Susanna Peirce both of Lancaster.
Octo. 20. Artemas Brigham of Concord to Betsy Wilder of Lancaster.
30 Silas Thurston of Lancaster to [Mrs.] Michal Nelson of Sterling.
Nov 4. Joseph Emerson Jr. of Royalstone to Lydia Whittemore of Lancaster.
27 Simon Darby Jr. of Leominster to Lydia Johnson of Lancaster.
1807. Jany. 4. Benjamin Wyman to Lucretia Thayer both of Lancaster.
April 8. Elisha Townshend of Bolton to Lucy Rand of Lancaster.

312
PUBLISHMENT.

1807 Luke Bennett of Lancaster and Katharine Hadley of Sterling enter their intentions of Marriage May 19, 1807.

MARRIAGES

1807 May 3. Stephen Wilder Jun to Caty Sawyer both of Lancaster.
12th. Jedediah Buffum to Nancy Wilder both of Lancaster.
21. Titus Wilder jun. to Eunice Butler both of Lancaster.
Peter Sawyer to Mary Hayward Sawyer both of Lancaster.
June 16. Aaron Cooley of Boston to Harriet Pownal of Lancaster.
Nov. 3. Ebenezer Wilder to Lucena Sawyer both of Lancaster.
10. Josiah Rugg to Polly Wyman both of Lancaster.
29. Levi Blood to Olive Laughton both of Lancaster.
Dec. 17. Reuben Wheeler to Sally Whitney both of Lancaster.

313 1808 April 20 Stephen Bates of West Cambridge to Nancy Thurston of Lancaster.

LANCASTER April 21 1808. This certifies that the marriage of the persons above named was solemnized at the time prefixed to their respective names before me.   NATHL THAYER.

WORCESTER SS Feby 8th 1809. This may certify that the Marriage was solemnized between David Baldwin jun. of Heath and Susanna Carter of Lancaster by JOSIAH FLAGG *Just. Pacis*

314 *
1808. May 15. Samuel Jones Jun. to Nancy Fales both of Lancaster
June 23. Oliver Brown to Keziah Haven both of Lancaster
July 10. Nathaniel Kidder of Prospect (District of Maine) to Sally Atherton of Lancaster.
Aug. 31. Jacob Thayer of Boston to Deborah Knowlton of Lancaster.
Octo. 23. Elijah Rugg to Lucy Fairbank, both of Lancaster.
Nov. 24. John Goss 2nd. to Rebecca White both of Lancaster.
Dec. 22. John Ballard of Lancaster to [Mrs.] Molly Moore of Boylstone.
1809. Jany. 22. Luther Townshend of Warren (District of Maine) to Dolly Osgood of Lancaster.
Feb. 1. Eliphaz Ballard to Anna Goss both of Lancaster.
315 Mar. 21. Silas Thurston to [Mrs.] Amy Rugg, both of Lancaster.
23. Thomas Hastings to Susanna Allen both of Lancaster.

LANCASTER April 29th, 1809. This certifies, that the marriage of the persons above named was solemnized on the day which is prefixed.
* Attest NATHL THAYER.

316 1809.
A Return of Marriages solemnized by Timothy Whiting Esq. one of the Justices assigned to keep the peace within and for the County of Worcester the past year.
Isaac Stone and Sarah Moore both of Boylstone were married May 1st. A. D. 1808.
Joshua Kenny of Orrington and Hannah Stearns of Lancaster, were married September 5th. 1808. *

317
1809. June 1st. This may certify, that the Marriage of John Allen, and Polly Jones was this first day of June A. D. 1809, solemnized by me.
* JOSIAH FLAGG *Just Pacis.*

1810. Feb. 27. This may certify that Amos Freeman of Brookline, and Mercy Hammond of Lancaster were married this twenty-seventh day of February A. D. 1810, by me   JOSIAH FLAGG *Just pacis.*
*

WORCESTER SS. April 20th 1810 This certifies, that Nathan Burditt and Margaret Darling both of Lancaster, were joined in marriage Sept. 20th, 1809.
318 * By me TIMOTHY WHITING *Jus. Pacis.*

1811 Feb. 21. This may certify that Pliny. Higley of Marlboro' State of Vermont, and Mary Willard of Lancaster were married this twenty-first day of February A. D. 1811, by me   JOSIAH FLAGG *Just Pacis.*
319 *
LANCASTER, April 1st. 1810. This certifies, that the Marriages herein named, were consummated before me on the day which is prefixed to each of them.
Attest NATHL. THAYER, *Minister of Lancaster.*

1809. May 14. Joseph Webb to Lucy Osgood; both of Lancaster.
May 27. Richardson Bigelow of Brattleboro' (Ver.) to [Mrs.] Sarah Hall of Lancaster.
June 11. Benjamin Hawks to Polly Ballard; both of Lancaster.
July 30. Jonas Lane to Sally Hawks both of Lancaster.
Nov. 1. Nathaniel Warner to Polly Rugg, both of Lancaster.
Nov. 29. Charles Bridge to Susanna Rugg both of Lancaster.
320 Dec. 3. Eber Brigham of Sudbury, to Lucy Arnold of Lancaster.
Dec. 26. Calvin Briggs of Marblehead to Rebecca Munroe of Lancaster.
*

Josiah Flagg Esquire Lancaster.
June 10. Nathaniel Alexander of Burlington to Rebecca Nichols of Lancaster.

17. Elijah Wilder to Sophia Thurston both of Lancaster.
24. Israel Woodbury of Boston to Tabitha Wilder of Lancaster.
321 July 3. David Howe to Susan Carter both of Lancaster.
Octo. 7. Josiah Fay to Nancy Fisher both of Lancaster.
Nov. 8. Ebenezer Bragg of Shrewsbury to Martha Wilder of Lancaster.
Dec. 11. Samuel Wilder 2^d. to Mary Carter both of Lancaster.
1811. Jan. 15. Samuel Barrett to Mehitable Burbank, both of Lancaster.
Feb. 12. David Low of Fitchburg to Betsy Damon of Lancaster.
Feb. 17. Darby Willard to Anna Johnson both of Lancaster.
Mar. 24 Jeffery Otis Prentiss to Sarah Harriet Reynolds now both of Lancaster.
Apr. 7. Anthony Phelps to Catharine Hawks both of Lancaster.

322 LANCASTER April 8, 1811. This certifies that the Marriage of the persons above named was consummated on the day which is prefixed, before me
*   NATH_L. THAYER, *Minister of the Church in Lancaster.*

LANCASTER Nov. 3^d. 1811. This certifies that Mr Nahum Rugg, and Miss Betsy Fairbank were married by me.   JOSIAH FLAGG *Just Pacis*.
323   *

LANCASTER April 10. 1812. I hereby certify that on the day which is prefixed, the marriage of the persons herein named was consummated before me.
                                            Attest   NATH_L. THAYER.

1811. June 2. Samuel Winchester of Marlborough to Sarah Farwell of Lancaster.
June 9. Abidan Knight of Harvard to Sally Johnson of Lancaster.
Aug. 18. Moses Haynes of Watertown N. York to Cynthia Thurston of Lancaster.
Sept. 15. Oliver Studley to Elisabeth Gould, both of Lancaster.
Octo. 22. Reuel Roby of Concord to Eliza Safford of Lancaster.
Dec. 26. Horatio G. Buttrick to Mary Barnard both of Lancaster.
Feb. 6. 1812. Jeremiah Fales jun. to Ami Rugg both of Lancaster.
Feby. 19. Asa Willard of Sterling to Lucy Whiting, of Lancaster.
March 25. Samuel Whitney of Bolton to Fanny Hudson of Lancaster.
April 9. Michael B. Green of Newton to Lucebe Willard of Lancaster.
324   *

I hereby certify that I married according to the Laws of this Commonwealth, the following persons viz :
Aug. 11. 1812. Mr Benjamin Houghton jun. of Lancaster to Miss Susan Buttrick of Concord.
Sep. 17, 1712. Mr Oliver Derby with Miss Elizabeth Hadley both of Lancaster.
                    JOSIAH FLAGG *Justice of the Peace.*

LANCASTER April 12 1813. I hereby Certify that the marriages herein named were consummated before me on the day prefixed to the names respectively.
                            Attest   NATHANIEL THAYER.

1812. April 19. James Moor of Concord to Dorinda Haskell of Lancaster.
May 7. Daniel [R.] Newhall to Betsy Wyman both of Lancaster.
10. Joel Rugg to Bathsheba Brown, both of Lancaster.
Octo. 11. Paul Faulkner to Hannah Stratton both of Lancaster.
15. Phinehas Nutting of Groton to [Mrs.] Sophia Durant of Lancaster.
325 Dec. 23. Moses Dickinson jun of Lancaster to Nancy Houghton of Bolton.
27. Calvin Johnson to Nabby Studley, both of Lancaster.
29. Calvin Joslyn to Hannah Robbins both of Lancaster.
31. Nathan Stuart of Leominster to Roxana Phelps of Lancaster.
1813. April 12. Abel Houghton Jr. of Princeton to Lucretia Phelps of Lancaster.   *

326 *To the town Clerk of Lancaster,* Sir.
Calvin Willard Esqr. of Petersham and Mary Thomas Ball of Shirley were joined in marriage June 17th. A. D. 1812.
* By me TIMOTHY WHITING *Jus. pacis*

This certifies that I the subscriber have married Mr Levi Ball of Townshend to Miss Lucy Burbank of Lancaster June 10, 1813.
LANCASTER April 8, 1814. PAUL WILLARD *Justice Peace*
*

This certifies that I the subscriber have married Mr Joseph Upton of Lancaster to Miss Hannah Weatherbee of Shirley.
July 15 1813 PAUL WILLARD *Justice Peace*
327 *

1814. Jany 25 Mr Samuel L Morse of Sodus State of New York and Miss Fanny Whiting of Lancaster were this 25th. day of January A. D. 1814, married by me JOSIAH FLAGG *Just Pacis.*
*

William Ball and Elizabeth Rice both of Lancaster were married Dec. 21, Anno Domini 1813. By me TIMOTHY WHITING *Jus. pacis.*
328 *

1814 April 17 Mr Nathan Peirce and Miss Eliza Mott both of Sterling were this 17th day of April A. D. 1814, married by me
* JOSIAH FLAGG *Just. pacis*

LANCASTER April 27. 1814. This certifies, that the Marriage of the persons herein named was consummated before me on the day which is prefixed.
Attest NATH^L. THAYER.

1813 June 1. Mr Lincoln Morris of Boston to Miss Eliza W. Dollison of Lancaster.
    Sep. 20. Mr Ephraim Hastings of Boylstone to Miss Achsah Sawyer of Lancaster.
    Octo. 24. Mr John Taylor to Mrs Nancy Wilder, both of Lancaster
329 Nov. 25. Mr James Rugg to Miss Submit Wyman both of Lancaster.
  "   "   Mr Charles E. Knight to Miss Catharine A. Lakin both of Lancaster.
  " 28. Mr Windsor Barnard to Miss Phebe Savory both of Lancaster.
    Dec. 12, Mr Prentiss Pond to Miss Lucy Haskell both of Lancaster.
1814 Feb. 13. Thomas Aspinwall Esq. of Boston to Miss Louisa Elizabeth Poignand of Lancaster.
    April 11. Mr William Townshend of Bolton to Miss Martha Wilder of Lancaster.
  " 19. Major Solomon Carter to Miss Elizabeth White both of Lancaster.
  " 24. Mr John Thurston jun. to Miss Lucy Moore both of Lancaster.
*

330   PUBLISHMENTS

1814 Octo. 29. Mr Samuel Dollison of Lancaster and Miss Nancy Peirce of West Boylstone enter their Intentions of Marriage this 29. Octo. 1814 *
1814, Dec. 3. Mr Moses Barrett of Lancaster and Miss Sarah Hill of Mason N Hampshire enter their Intentions of Marriage this third day of December 1814. *
331 1814. Sep. 21. Dr Emory Willard of Marblehead, and Miss Sally Farwell of Lancaster enter their intentions of Marriage this 21. Sep. 1814 *
1814, Octo. 8. Mr Jonas Wilder of Sterling and Miss Sally Fairbank of Lancaster enter their Intentions of Marriage this 8th of Octo. A D 1814. *
1814. Octo. 24. Mr Samuel Richardson of Lancaster, and Miss Susanna Nurse of Bolton enter their Intentions of Marriage this 24th day of October A. D. 1814. *
332 1814, July 30. Mr Samuel Wood Jr. of Keene New Hampshire, and Miss Emily Wyman of Lancaster Enter their intentions of Marriage this thirtieth day of July 1814 *

1814, Sept. 9. Levi McIntire of Lancaster and Miss Rebecca Knight of Reading enter their Intentions of Marriage this ninth day of Sept. A. D. 1814. *

1814, Sept. 18th. Mr Stephen Wilder and Miss Patience Sargent both of Lancaster enter their intentions of Marriage this Eighteenth day of Sept. 1814.

333 1814, April 9. Mr John Thurston 2d and Miss Lucy Moore both of Lancaster enter their intentions of Marriage this ninth day of April A. D. 1814.

1814. April 18. Mr Amzi Langdon of Rowe and Miss Levina Thayer of Lancaster enter their intentions of Marriage this Eighteenth day of April A. D. 1814. *

1814, June 18. Mr William Bridge of Lancaster and Mrs Sally Winchester of Surry N. Hampshire enter their Intentions of Marriage this 18th. June 1814.

334 1814, Mar 12. Major Solomon Carter and Miss Elizabeth White both of Lancaster enter their Intentions of Marriage March 12, 1814. *

1814, April 3. Mr Asa Barrett and Miss Sally Bennett both of Lancaster enter their Intentions of Marriage this 3d of April A. D. 1814. *

1814, April 9. Mr Ephraim Robbins and Miss Polly Gleason both of Lancaster enter their intentions of Marriage. *

335 1814, Feb. 26. Robert Hudson jur. of Lancaster, and Miss Betsy Whitney of Bolton enter their intentions of Marriage this 26 day of Feby. 1814.

1814, Mar. 5, Mr Joseph May of Leominster & Miss Cynthia Thompson of Lancaster enter their Intentions of Marriage this fifth day of March A. D. 1814.

1814, Mar. 9. Mr Charles Cogswell of Marlboro' and Miss Lucy Wilder of Lancaster enter their Intentions of Marriage this ninth day of March A. D. 1814. *

336 1813. Dec. 25. Mr Luther Johnson of Lancaster and Miss Graty Tyler of Leominster enter their Intentions of Marriage this twenty-fifth day of Dec 1813. *

1814 Jany. 14. Mr Asa Wood Jur. of Leominster and Miss Susan Stone of Lancaster enter their intentions of Marriage this 14th. January 1814. *

1814 Feby. 5. Mr William Townshend of Bolton & Miss Martha Wilder of Lancaster enter their Intentions of Marriage, this 5th of Feby. A. D. 1814.

337 1813 Nov. 6. Mr Prentiss Pond and Miss Lucy Haskell both of Lancaster enter their Intentions of Marriage this sixth day of November *Anno Domini* 1813. * .

1813 Dec. 4. Mr Samuel L. Morse of Sodus State of New York, and Miss Fanny Whiting of Lancaster enter their Intentions of Marriage this fourth day of December *Anno Domini* 1813. *

1813 Dec. 4. Mr William Ball. and Miss Elizabeth Rice both of Lancaster enter their intentions of Marriage Dec 4. 1813. *

338 1813, Octo: 12. Mr Emery Harris of Lancaster, and Miss Hezediah Larkin of Berlin enter their intentions of Marriage this twelfth day of Octo. A. D. 1813. *

1813, Octo. 24. Mr Winsor Barnard and Miss Phœbe Severy both of Lancaster enter their Intentions of Marriage this 24th day of October *Anno Domini* 1813. *

Octo. 30. Mr James Rugg and Miss Submit Wyman both of Lancaster enter their Intentions of Marriage this 30th day of October A. D. 1813. *

339 1813, Sep. 4. Mr Ephraim Hastings of Boylston and Miss Achsah Sawyer of Lancaster enter their intentions of Marriage this fourth day of September 1813 *

1813. Octo. 2. Mr John Taylor, and Mrs Nancy Wilder both of Lancaster enter their intentions of Marriage Octo. 2. 1813. *

1813. Octo. 9. Mr Charles E. Knight and Miss Katharine A. Lakin both of Lancaster, enter their intentions of Marriage, this ninth day of October *Anno Domini* 1813. *

340 1813, May 29. Mr Joseph Upton of Lancaster and Miss Hannah Weatherbee of Shirley enter their Intentions of Marriage, this twenty-ninth day of May A. D, 1813. *

1813, June 26. Mr David Richardson of Lancaster, and Miss Patty Joslyn of Leominster, enter their intentions of Marriage this 26th day of June 1813. *

BOOK FIRST. 171

Aug⁺. 25. Capt Moses Emerson of Lancaster and Miss Eunice Wright of Sterling enter their Intentions of Marriage, this 25ᵗʰ. August 1813. *
341 1812, Dec. 12. Mʳ Calvin Johnson, and Miss Nabby Studley, both of Lancaster enter their intentions of Marriage this 12. day of Dec. 1812. *
1813, Mar. 20. Mʳ Abel Houghton jur. of Princeton and Miss Lucretia Phelps of Lancaster, enter their intentions of Marriage this twentieth day of March A. D. 1813. *
1813, April 18. Mʳ Lincoln Morris of Boston and Miss Eliza Whetcomb Dollison of Lancaster enter their intentions of Marriage this eighteenth day of April A. D. 1813. *
May 11. Mʳ Levi Ball of Townshend and Miss Lucy Burbank of Lancester enter their intentions of Marriage this eleventh day of May *Anno Domini* 1813. *
342 1812, Sep. 19. Mʳ Paul Faulkner and Miss Hannah Stratton both of Lancaster enter their Intentions of Marriage this 19 Sep. 1812. *
1812, Nov. 7 Mʳ Calvin Joslyn and Miss Hannah Robbins, both of Lancaster enter their intentions of Marriage this seventh day of November 1812. *
1812, Nov. 19. Mʳ. Moses Dickinson jur. of Lancaster and Miss Nancy Houghton of Bolton enter their intentions of Marriage this 19ᵗʰ day of Nov. 1812. *
1812, Nov. 30. Mʳ Nathan Stuart. of Leominster and Miss Roxana Phelps of Lancaster enter their intentions of Marriage this 30ᵗʰ day of Nov 1812. *
343 1812, June 23. Mʳ Benjamin Houghton Jun 3ᵈ of Lancaster and Miss Susan Buttrick of Concord enter their intentions of Marriage. *
1812, July 3. Mʳ Pliny Newhall of Lancaster, and Miss Katharine White of Lincoln, enter their intentions of Marriage. *
Aug. 22ᵈ. Mʳ Oliver Derby and Miss Elizabeth Hadley both of Lancaster enter their intentions of Marriage. *
Sep. 19. Mʳ Phinehas Nutting of Groton, and Mʳˢ Sophia Durant of Lancaster enter their intentions of Marriage this nineteenth day of September A. D. 1812. *
344 1842, Mar. 4. Mʳ Samuel Whitney of Bolton and Miss Fanny Hudson of Lancaster enter their intentions of Marriage, this fourth of March 1812.
1812 Mar. 13. Mʳ Michael Bird Green of Newton and Miss Lusebe Willard of Lancaster enter their intentions of marriage. *
1812, Mar. 21. Mʳ Moses Jones of Lancaster and Mʳˢ. Sarah Egerton of Shirley enter their intentions of Marriage this twenty-first day of March A. D. 1812. *
1812, April 18. Mʳ Daniel Newhall, and Miss Betsy Wyman, both of Lancaster, enter their intentions of Marriage this eighteenth day of April, A. D. 1812. *
345 1812, Jan. 4. Mʳ Jeremiah Fales Jur. and Miss Ama Rugg both of Lancaster enter their intentions of Marriage. *
1812, Jany. 25. Mʳ Asa Willard of Sterling and Miss Lucy Whiting of Lancaster enter their intentions of Marriage. *
1812 Feb. 3. Mʳ James Moor of Concord and Miss Dorinda Haskell of Lancaster, enter their intentions of Marriage. *
1812, Feb. 16. Mʳ John Sargent 2ᵈ of Lancaster and Miss Nancy Knight of Fitz William enter their intentions of Marriage. *
1812, Feb. 16. Mʳ Joel Rugg and Miss Bathsheba Brown both of Lancaster enter their intentions of Marriage. *
346 1811, Sept. 7. Capt Horatio Gates Buttrick and Miss Mary Barnard both of Lancaster enter their intentions of Marriage. *
1811, Sep. 8. Mʳ Reuel Roby of Concord and Miss Eliza Safford of Lancaster enter their intentions of Marriage. *
1811, Octo. 5. Mʳ Nahum Rugg and Betsy Fairbank both of Lancaster enter their intentions of Marriage. *
1811, Nov. 16. Mʳ Prescott Whittemore of Lancaster, and Miss Lucy Rebecca Geer of Worcester enter their intentions of Marriage. *
347 1811, June 16. Thomas Aspinwall of Boston and Louisa Elizabeth Poignand, of Lancaster enter their intentions of Marriage. *
July 26. Moses Haynes of Watertown State of New York, and Cynthia Thurston of Lancaster enter their intentions of Marriage. *

Aug. 10. Oliver Studly, and Elizabeth Gould, both of Lancaster enter their intentions of Marriage. *

Aug. 22 Mr Oliver Derby and Miss Elizabeth Hadley both of Lancaster enter their intentions of Marriage. * *Duplicate*

348 1811, April 20. Abidan Knight of Harvard and Sally Johnson of Lancaster enter their intentions of Marriage this twentieth day of April A. D. 1811. *

1811 Apr. 29. Samuel Winchester of Marlboro' and Sarah Farwell of Lancaster enter their intentions of Marriage, this twenty-ninth day of April A. D. 1811. *

1811. May 18. Joseph Leach of Lancaster, and Tabitha Dana of Natick enter their intentions of Marriage this eighteenth day of May *Anno Domini* 1811. *

349 1811, Mar. 23^d. Rufus Fletcher of Lancaster, and Faithful Aldrich of Upton, enter their intentions of Marriage, this twenty-third day of March A. D. 1811. *

1811, Apr. 4. Luke Wilder of Leominster, and Mary Harvey of Lancaster enter their intentions of Marriage this fourth day of April A. D. 1811 *

1811, April 5. Benjamin H. Foster of Lancaster and Martha Shed of Billerica enter their intentions of Marriage this fifth day of April A. D. 1811. *

1811. Apr. 8th. Jesse Constandine of Lancaster, and Susan Sawtell of Groton, enter their Intentions of Marriage this eighth day of April A D. 1811. *

350 1810, Dec. 20 Samuel Barrett, and Mehitable Burbank both of Lancaster, enter their Intentions of Marriage. In Meeting house published. *

1811, Jany. 21. Pliny Higley of Marlborough State of Vermont, and Mary Wilder of Lancaster enter their intentions of Marriage. *

1811, Mar. 1. Anthony Phelps and Katharine Hawks both of Lancaster, enter their intentions of Marriage. Published in Meeting house. *

1811, Mar. 2^d. Jeffrey Otis Prentiss, and Sarah Harriet Reynolds, both of Lancaster, enter their intentions of Marriage. Published in the Meeting house.

351 1810, Dec. 1. David Low of Fitchburge and Betsy Damon of Lancaster enter their intentions of Marriage; application made by Saml. Damon Jr. *

1810, Dec. 8th. Jeremiah Ballard of Lancaster and Elizabeth Barnard of Westminster enter their intentions of Marriage. in meeting house. *

1810, Dec. 8. Zedediah Tyler of Lunenburge and Nancy Lawson of Lancaster enter their intentions of Marriage. *

352 Octo. 13. Ebenezer Bragg of Shrewsbury and Martha Wilder of Lancaster enter their intentions of Marriage. *

1810, Nov. 17. Darby Willard and Anna Johnson both of Lancaster enter their intentions of Marriage. *

1810, Nov. 17. John McGaw of Lancaster and Hannah Adams of Londonderry New Hampshire enter their intentions of Marriage. Published in Meeting house by desire. *

1810, Nov. 23. Samuel Wilder 2^d and Mary Carter both of Lancaster enter their intentions of Marriage. Published by desire in Meeting house. *

353 1810, May 26. David Howe and Susan Carter both of Lancaster enter their intentions of Marriage *

June 9th, 1810. Israel Woodbury jun. of Boston and Tabitha Wilder of Lancaster enter their intentions of Marriage. *

July 27th. 1810. Josiah Fay and Nancy Fisher both of Lancaster enter their intentions of Marriage. *

Sep 29th, 1810. Ancill Tyler of Lunenburge and Mary Lawson of Lancaster enter their intentions of Marriage. *

354 1809, May 27th. Benjamin Hawks and Polly Ballard both of Lancaster enter their intentions of Marriage. *

July 15. Jonas Lane and Sally Hawks both of Lancaster enter their intentions of Marriage. *

Augt. 10. Nathan Burditt, and Margaret Darling both of Lancaster enter their intentions of Marriage. *

Sep. 8th. Nathaniel Warner and Polly Rugg both of Lancaster enter their intentions of Marriage. *

355 1809, Apr. 23. Moses Emerson of Lancaster, and Lydia Carleton of Methuen, enter their intentions of Marriage. *

April 29. John Allen and Polly Jones both of Lancaster enter their intentions of Marriage. *
May 1. Maurice Kelly of Harvard and Lucy Peirce of Lancaster enter their intentions of Marriage. *
May 7. Richardson Bigelow of Brattleboro' Vermont and Sarah Hall of Lancaster enter their intentions of Marriage. *
356 1809, Jany. 7. Luther Townshend of Warren District of Maine, and Dolly Osgood of Lancaster enter their intentions of Marriage. *
Feb. 22. Silas Thurston and Amy Rugg both of Lancaster enter their intentions of Marriage. *
Mar. 18. Joshua Thomas of Lancaster and Mary Armstrong of Boston enter their intentions of Marriage *
April 22. Joseph Webb and Lucy Osgood both of Lancaster enter their intentions of Marriage. *
357 1808, Sep. 30. Asa Arnold of Lancaster, and Mary Moore of Sudbury enter their intentions of Marriage. *
Octo. 23. John Goss 2nd. and Rebecca White of Lancaster enter their intentions of Marriage. *
Dec. 2nd. Thomas Hastings and Susanna Allen both of Lancaster enter their intentions of Marriage. *
Eliphas Ballard, and Anna Goss, of Lancaster, enter their intentions of Marriage Jany 1st. 1809. *
David Baldwin Jr. of Heath and Susanna Carter of Lancaster enter their intentions of Marriage Jany 1st. 1809. *
358 1809, Nov. 13. Amos Freeman of Brookline and Mercy Hammond of Lancaster enter their intentions of Marriage. persons of color. *
1800. April 13th. Paul Willard and Polly Damon both of Lancaster enter their intentions of Marriage. *
April 20. Nathaniel Alexander of Burlington and Rebecca Nichols of Lancaster enter their intentions of Marriage. *
May 26. Elijah Wilder and Sophia Thurston both of Lancaster enter their intentions of Marriage. *
359 1809, Sept. 9 John Peterson Dalton of Lancaster and Mary Willard of Lunenburge enter their intentions of Marriage. *
Sep. 23. Eber Brigham of Sudbury and Lucy Arnold of Lancaster enter their intentions of Marriage. *
Octo. 14. Charles Bridge and Susanna Rugg of Lancaster enter their intentions of Marriage. *
Nov. 11. Calvin Briggs of Marblehead and Rebecca Munroe of Lancaster enter their intentions of Marriage. *

BOOK II.

1796—1843.

In this volume, begun September 1, 1796, only births and deaths were registered. The print rigidly conforms to the manuscript, save that sundry duplicate entries are omitted.

1　　　　LANCASTER RECORDS OF DEATHS

Allen, —— daughter of Daniel Allen died June 29, 1798, aged 7 weeks.
Allen, Abel, son of Samuel Allen and Lucy his wife died April 4th 1800.
Allen Rebecca wife of Daniel Allen deceased Dec 31, 1801.
Allen Delilah daughter of Daniel Allen and Rebecca his wife died January 10th, 1802.
Adams, Sarah Widow died at Willm Studley's the 12th. of Octo. 1802 Æ 81.
Allen Sparhawk died October 24th. 1803 aged 13 years.
Arnold William died Novr. 11th 1805.
Allen Samuel son of Samuel and Lucy Allen died the 21st day of January 1807.
Allen Samuel 2nd son of Samuel & Lucy Allen died July 23 1809.
Allen Betsey daughter of Philemon Allen died March 18th. 1810.
Allen Ebenezer died Jany. 26th. 1812. aged 88 yrs.
Allen Polly wife of John Allen died 25, Feb. 1812 at Mr Moses Jones's
Andrews Samuel died April the 15th 1814. *A good Man!*
Allen Mrs. wife of Mr Philemon Allen died Feb 18th. 1817.
2　Allen Philemon died March 4, 1817.
Atherton Peter died April 14, 1819.
Atherton Israel Esqr. an eminent Physician, a good Neighbour & an honest man, died July 20th 1822. aged, 82 years.
Atherton Rebecca relict of the late Doctor Israel Atherton, and former wife of Doctor Staunton Prentiss died Thursday May 15. 1823, 1 ºClock A. M. aged 86.
Atherton Caroline Weeks daughter of the late Abel Atherton and Margarett his wife & widow died Feb 16, 1824.
Allen Sophia, daughter of the late Philemon Allen died at the house of Mr Robert Phelps, February 2. 1826.
Sophia the daughter of Sophia Allen died at the house of Saml. Dollison May 1826.
Adams Amos Gilman son of Amos Adams died Sept 1. 1822.
William B. Andrews died March 31 1833 at the house of Deacon Joel Wilder.
Mrs —· Adams, wife of Samuel Adams died Nov. 27, 1833.
Allen Tabitha daughter of the late Mr Ebenezer Allen died December 17. 1833, aged 87.
3　1838　A son of James Arnold died August 9th Aged 4 months
1839　Mrs Phebe Atherton died October 14 1839 aged 82 years
1841.　Mr Samuel Adams Died Sept. 5 1841, aged 62 yrs.
7　Mr Thomas P. Buttrick Aged 21, was Drowned at Lincoln July 30 1842
1843　Miss Cynthia Bigelow Daughter of Luke Bigelow Died March 3, 1843 Aged 9, yrs Consumption

1844 Bridge, Franklin Thayer, son of Charles and Sophia W. Bridge Died at Lowell May 6, 1844 aged 17 mo 24 days
Bridge George Whitney Son of Charles & Sophia W. Bridge was drowned at Lowell Dec^r: 25th 1844
8 Butler Dinah ———
Bennett Elisha died March 17th 1807.
Ballard Charles, son of John and Anna Ballard, died in Sterling at the house of Capt Thomas Blood April 1st. 1807, Aged 21 years.
Ballard James, Son of Jeremiah Ballard & Rebecca Ballard, killed instantly by falling from a chimney in Leominster, the 7th day of Sept. 1807, aged 18 years.
Ballard Anne wife of John Ballard died March 1st. 1808, aged 49 years.
Brown Mary, daughter of Capt John Brown and Polly Brown died Jany. 7th 1809. aged 21 mo.
Blanchard Eliza daughter of William & Elizabeth Blanchard died Dec 11th. 1807.
Buttrick Nancy Whitney daughter of Horatio G. Buttrick and Nancy his wife, died March 19th, 1810.
Bennett Dolly daughter of Thomas Bennett Jr. & Isabella died June 9th 1796.
Bennett John Son of Thomas Bennett Jr. & Isabella died June 11th 1796.
Barrett Eleanor, wife of Samuel Barrett died May 14th 1810 in a fit of Insanity.
9 Mrs Anna Brewster wife of Oliver Brewster of Boston Merchant deceased at the house of Jno Sprague esqr October 5, 1796.
Brittain, [Polly] wife of John Brittain, died October 28th, 1797- aged 63 years
Brittain John, died March 1st 1798, aged 80 years.
Barnard Jonathan son of Jonathan Barnard & his wife, died Feby 13- 1799, ab^t 3 years old.
Ballard, Sarah, wife of Deac: Josiah Ballard deceased March 31, 1799.
Ballard, Deacon Josiah. deceased August 6th, 1799.
Ballard, Lucy, Daughter of Thomas & Abigail Ballard died August 19, 1799.
Ballard Abigail, Daughter of Thomas & Abigail Ballard died August 25, 1799.
Ballard, Sophia, Daughter of Thomas & Abigail Ballard died Septr. 1, 1799.
Bennett Nancy, daughter of Nathan Bennett died Jan. 21st 1802.
Barker Robert deceased the 30th July 1802.
Butler Simon dec^d. Nov. 4th 1802.
Burbank (Widow) dec^d. Decr. 18, 1802.
Ballard Thomas son of Thomas Ballard and Abigail his wife deceased Nov 26, 1803.
Butler Mary wife of Ebenezer Butler died Sept. 12th 1805.
Barnard Julia daughter of Jonathan and Annis Barnard died ———
Barnard Benajah son of Jonathan and Annis Barnard died Octo 4th 1805.
10 Ballard Rebecca wife of Jeremiah Ballard died June 2nd. 1810.
Bridge Abigail wife of William Bridge died August 13th 1810.
Barrett Samuel Arnold son of Samuel and Eleanor Barrett died May 16, 1806.
Buttrick Nancy wife of Horatio G Buttrick died January 27th 1811.
Bennett Nancy the widow of Elisha Bennett Jur. died May 29th, 1811.
Ballard Josiah Richardson son of Thomas and Abigail Ballard died November 29, 1812.
Bennett James Dexter son of Elias Bennett died January 6, 1813.
Butler Eunice widow of the late Simon Butler died April 17, 1813.
Beaman Joseph died April 24. 1813.
Butler Israel died Feby. 3 1814.
Bennett Caroline daughter of Luke Bennett died Feb. 1, 1814
Bridge Twins of Josiah & Irene Bridge, first died 30th Jany 1815 second died Feb. 1. 1815.
Burpee Polly wife of Thomas Burpee, died April 6. 1816.
11 Reuben Barrett Jun died at the house of his fathers July 26, 1816.
Burpee Lydia wife of Martin Burpee died the 24th March 1817.
Bradish Ebenezer Esq. died at the house of Mr John Ballard April 29. 1818.
Ballard Nancy wife of Eliphaz Ballard died June 22 1818.
Blanchard William died Nov. 13, 1818.
Ballard Molly, the second wife of Mr John Ballard died July 8th 1819, aged 53
Burbank Nathaniel died July 21 1819.

Baldwin Lucy wife of Oliver Baldwin died July 30 1820.
Bridge Abigail died Octo. 10, 1820.
Bennett Charles drowned Dec. 29 1820.
Butler Widow died in Dec. 1820
1821. Butler Lydia daughter of Benj. Butler died Feby. 13 1821.
1822. Bruce Rufus died Jany. 11, 1822.
Billings Mrs. wife of Mr Josiah Billings died August 6. 1822.
Burditt Christopher Columbus died Feb. 28 1817.
12 Bruce Mrs. wife of Jonathan Bruce, died Feb. 19 1824.
Bridge Susan wife of Charles Bridge died Feby 19 1825.
Widow [Mary] Joslin relict of the late Mr. Nathl. Joslyn died Feb 1825.
Baker Elizabeth Dana wife of Dr. George Baker died March 4. 1825.

* * * * *

[Buttrick, Jonathan Sen., died April 15, 1825. *Family records*.]
Ballard John died Sept: 9, 1826, aged 66.
Bragg Horatio Carter son of Eben Bragg died 7th Dec. 1826.
Burditt Sarah Margarett, daughter of Nathan & Margarett Burditt died March 19, 1825.
Butler Nancy daughter of Samuel Butler died July 11, 1827.
Bennett Levi son of Elisha Bennett died May 21, 1828

* * * * *

Bridge Solomon, son of the late William Bridge died at the house of Mr Stedman Nurse, September 24, 1829 aged 27.
Ballard Henry son of the late John Ballard, was killed by a tree which fell on him Jany. 12, 1830.
Barrett Ruth died April 1829 aged 73.
Ballard John Augustus son of the late Henry Ballard, died May 31, 1830.
13 Bowman Henry son of Simeon & Hannah Bowman died Feby 20. 1831.
Bigelow Solon Francis died March 17, 1831; } Children of Capt Luke & Eliza
Bigelow Jane Eliza, " April 5. 1831 } Bigelow.
Barnes Mrs. [Abby E.] Wife of Mr Ira Barnes, died December 16, 1831.
Brigham Widow died at the house of Mr James Mallard Dec 20 1831, aged 71.
Bruce Jonathan died Jany 21, 1832.
Butler David died at the Pauper Establishment January 11th, 1832, aged 90 ^{yrs} 10 ^{mo}
Brown Sarah died at the Pauper Establishment Sept 22 1830.
Burditt Sarah wife of John Burditt, died March 17, 1832.
Burbank Susan Eliza daughter of Saml W Burbank and Hannah his wife died July 22 1825.
Barnes Mrs Nancy, wife of Mr Artemas Barnes, died July 16 1832, aged 30 yrs. 4 mo. 11 days.
Barnard Caleb son of Winsor & Phebe Barnard died Nov. 17, 1810.
1833. Butler Mary died Sep. 29, 1826 } Children of Joseph & Mary Butler
Butler Stephen died Jan 20 1823 }
Barrett Lydia B. daughter of Joseph & Lucy Barrett died Sept 14 1831.
Bethell Thomas J. died at the house of Joseph W. Wilder June 9. 1834. aged 26 years.
Bridgman Mrs Betsey wife of Horatio N Bridgman died June 11th. 1834.
14 Barnard William son of Winsor Barnard died at the house of Emory Harris, October 6. 1834.
1835 Burbank Mrs. widow of the late Nathaniel Burbank died June 5, 1835, aged 82
Barnard Winsor, son of Winsor and Phebe Barnard died Apr: 9, 1835.
1836 Josiah Bowers a Revolutionary Pensioner died August 1836 aged 84 years
1838 Robert Franklin Bradley son of Col. R. M. Bradley died May 9, 1838 aged 5 years and eight months.
1836 Rebecca Bowers, Widow of Josiah Bowers, died Nov. 30 1836
1838 Ballard, Thomas, died June 1, 1838 Aged 76 yrs
Ballard, Jeremiah, died Oct. 2 1838 Aged 86 yrs
1839 Bray William aged 14 yrs Killed by the accidental discharge of a gun February 25 1839
A Daughter of Cyrus Bliss Died July 11 1839 aged 9 months

Charles S. Brown Died August 18 1839 aged 16 years
A Daughter of Reuben Barrett Died September 2 1839 aged 2 years
1842 Robert M. Bradley Died Nov. 15 '42 aged [48] Dropsy
15 1840 Mrs [Hannah] Burbank wife of Saml W. Burbank Died February 17 1840 aged [39] years
*841 Miss Sally Ballard, daughter of the late Jeremiah Ballard, died March 25, 1841 aged 61 years.
1841 Caroline Thayer daughter of Charles and Sophia Bridge, Died Aug. 31, 1841.
1841 Charles A. son of Thomas & Sarah E. Burditt died February 21, 1842 aged 6 months
1842 Thomas Porter Butterick Died at Lincoln (drowned) July 30 1842
Cornelia Asenath Bigelow, Daughter of Luke & Eliza Bigelow Died July 1, 1837
1843 Cynthia Wilder Bigelow, daughter of Capt Luke Bigelow Died February 24. 1843, aged 12½ years
1843 Abigail Ballard widow of Thomas Ballard died August 20th 1843 aged 75 years 3 months & 18 days [Mortification.]
1843 Mr Josiah Billings Died May 23 aged [58] years [Paralysis.]
1843 John A. Bigelow Infant son of Luke Bigelow aged 4 months Died July 12 1843

*   *   *   *   *

1843 Warren, son of Jeremiah Barnard aged 1 yr 8 mo^s. Dysentery Died 18 September 1843
16 Carter Mrs Lucy, wife of Major Solomon Carter died April 5, 1813.
Cleveland Mrs. Mary the wife of Capt William Cleveland died May 7th, 1815.
Childs M^{rs}. Sarah wife of Isaac Childs died October 17, 1815.
Carter John died Nov. 19, 1815.
Carter Betsy wife of John Carter 2^d, died Dec. 28, 1815.
Carleton Mary wife of Mr Moses Carleton died February 7, 1816. aged 23.
Carter Dr. James, died January the 17th, 1817, Aged sixty three !
Cleveland Hiller son of William Cleveland died June 28. 1817.
Carlton James, son of Jonathan Carlton of Boston, a member of the Private School in this town, drowned while bathing in the River Tuesday the 29th. of June 1819, aged [11]
Miss [Eloise R.] Paine at Widow Channing's died July 3^d 1819.
Clark James died July 6, 1819. Æ. 36.
1820 Carter William Henry son of Solomon Carter and Elizabeth Carter died March 9th 1820.
Childs James son of Isaac Childs died Feb 22^d. 1822.

*   *   *   *   *

17 Chapin, the Widow Mary, deceased at her Son Coffin Chapin's house Octr. 13, 1796.
Campbell daughter of Jno Campbell deceased Novr. 29th, 1796.
Champney, Joseph, died July 27, 1797, at the house of Jonas Lane, aged 22 years.
Carter, Ephraim deceas'd May 19, 1798 Æ 55, and was the first person buried in the Center field.
Carter Eli, son of Thomas Carter died Aug: 24 1798. aged 2 years & 9 mo.
Carter, James, deceased July 18th 1800.
Cotting Nancy deceased April 24th 1801.
Chapin Leonard deceased June 18th, 1801.
Chapin Orcily deceased June 17th 1801.
Carter Lucy died September 26th 1803. Æ 19.
Carter Sally wife of William Carter died October 2nd. 1804.
Carter Susanna daughter of James Carter Jun. & Sally his wife died March 29th 1805.
Carter Abigail relict of the late Ephraim Carter Sen died Augt. 20th, 1805, Æ 84.
Cleverly Sarah Widow died Augt. 10th. 1807.
Cook Harriot daughter of Aaron Cook died Octo. 12th. 1807.
Caldwell Lydia daughter of John Caldwell Apr 5, 1808.
Corey Rebecca daughter of the late Stephen Corey died April 19th 1810.
18 Carter Thomas died Feb. 1, 1823, aged 69.

Carlton Theodore son of Moses Carlton and Mary Carlton died at the house of the Widow Sweetser Octo 23, 1823.
Silence Carter Widow of Levi Carter died at the house of Mr John Carter Nov. 23, 1823, aged 76.
Chambers David died Dec. 10 1824.
Carter Polly wife of Capt Ephraim Carter, died June 22nd 1826.
Carter Tempe wife of John Carter died August 31, 1826.
Carter Capt. Ephraim died 31, August 1827. Æ 54
Chambers Hannah widow of the late David Chambers died at the Poor house Dec 1, 1827.
Carlton George [H.] son of Moses & Mary Carleton died Sept. 8th 1829.
Clark Mrs. widow of the late James Clark, died at the house of Mr. Alpheus Carter, Octor. 3, 1829, aged 93.
Carter Major Solomon died November 8, 1829 aged 53.
Carter James, son of Dr Calvin Carter, a student at the University in Cambridge, died there March 19, 1830.
Carter John 2nd died July 3, 1830 aged 48.
Chase Ami Ann daughter of Mr Charles Chase died Feby 4, 1831.
Colburn Sally wife of Elijah Colburn, died February 9th 1831.
19 Carlton Mary wife of Mr Moses Carlton, died May 8th 1832.
Carter Nancy, daughter of John Carter 3d and Betsey Carter, both deceased, died Nov. 22d. 1832 aged 21yrs 7mo
Cleverly Stephen died at the pauper establishment Dec — 1832.
Carter Horatio died Sept. 7th. 1832.
Cutting Stephen son of Stephen Cutting died July 8. [1833]
Chamberlain Mr, died at the house of Nathl Alexander March 22, 1834
Carter Mary Ann Augusta daughter of Doctor Calvin Carter died Jany 17, 1835.
Carter Martha Lincoln daughter of Doctor Calvin Carter & Sally Carter died Mar 20, 1822.
An infant of same parents died Feby 20, 1822.
Chase Albert R. son of Alanson Chase and Maria Chase died April 4, 1825.
Carter Mrs Emily wife of Mr Oliver Carter died March 17, 1835.
Carter William died at the Alms House, Dec. 11, 1835.
Carlton Miss Mary died January 22d 1837.
Carter Martha, widow of the late John Carter Junior, died July 30, 1838 aged 83 years
Carter Sewall, Son of the late Doct James Carter, Died at Boston September 7th, 1838.
20 1838 Mrs Chase, wife of George Chase of Leominster died December 27th suddenly, at the house of Thomas Houghton, 1838.
1840 Miss Mary Conquerette Died February 7 1840 aged 81 years
Mr Isaac Childs died February 23 1840 aged 65 years
1841 Mr John Carter Died August 6, 1841 Aged 63 yrs
1842 Mrs Polly Carter, wife of Mr Oliver Carter died February 28, 1842 aged 27 years.
1843 Mrs Susanna Carleton, wife of Mr Albert Carleton, died June 26, '43 aged 26 years. Consumption.
1843 Mrs Elizabeth Carter, Widow of the late Maj Solomon Carter Died July 26, 1843 aged [54] yrs Consumption
1842 Mr Cephas Carter Died at Boston Died 29 Sep. 1842 aged 52. Consumption

* * * * *

1842 Mr Oliver Carter Died May 19 1842 aged 84 old age
Miss Julia Chandler Died May 8, 1842 aged 20. Consumption
25 Divol, Manassah, deceased Sepr 11, 1797, Æ. 82.
Divol Ephraim, deceased April 7th, 1798. Æ 84.
Dunlap Tyler, deceased July 28 1802, 6 Mo
Dollison Lucy daughter of John Dollison Nov. 3d 1802.
Dunlap Paulina, daughter of Saml Dunlap deceasd April 1st 1803.
Divol, Susanna, relict of Manassah Divol died April 17th, 1806. Ætatis Suae 89!
Deputron William died November 23d 1806.
Divol Ephraim died August 17th 1810.

Divol Peter died January 2, 1812, on his return from Boston at the house of Mr Warner in Weston.
Davis Francis a man of colour died April 23 1812.
Divol, Mrs, relict of the late Ephraim Divol died June 16, 1813.
Danforth Mrs Sarah relict of the late Dr. Danforth of Billerica, died the 22nd April 1814 at the house of the Widow Orpah Whiting, aged 79
Dollison Daniel son of John Dollison & Esther his wife died August 16, 1801.
Dollison Lucy daughter of Jno and Esther Dollison died Nov. 6, 1802.
Dickinson Moses died at Dr James Carter's March 25 1816.
Dickinson Rebecca Widow of Moses Dickinson died January 19 1821.
Deputron Widow [Sarah,] died in Novr. 1820. [December 3]
1823 Damon Hariet Hart daughter of Saml Damon Jr died Octo 9, 1822.
Damon Aaron Alonzo son of Saml Damon Jun died June 6, 1820.
Dyer Mrs. [Susan] wife of Mr Jedediah Dyer died Feb. 16, 1824.
Damon Joseph Willard died at Springfield Sept. 13, 1825.
Damon Abraham Prescott died Sept 29, 1825. Sons of William Damon.
Damon Mrs. [Polly] wife of Samuel Damon died Sept. 9th, 1826.
Dickinson Lemuel son of the late Moses Dickinson died July 1826.
Divol Susan, daughter of Ester Divol deceased, at the house of Mr Henry Ballard Augt 30 1829.
Divol Rebecca wife of Thomas Divol died Dec 12, 1829.
Divol Miss Patience died at the house of her brother Manaseh March 13, 1830. Aged [77]
Dexter Roxanna died at the house of Mr Henry Goss Nov. 12 1830.
Dudley Andrew Jackson, son of John and Esther Eliza Dudley died July 30, 1831.
Dean Charles son of John & Emily Dean died Sep. 18. 1832.
27 Divol Manassah died Novr. 7th 1833.—70 yrs old.
Dean Mrs Emily, wife of Mr John Dean died June 29, 1834.
Dean Sarah Bridges, daughter of John Dean and Emily Dean died June 2, 1834.
Dickinson Stephen, son of the late Moses Dickinson, died at the Pauper Establishment Feb. 16, 1835.
Danforth Sarah, a daughter of the late Doctor Danforth of Billerica died at the house of her Sister Orpah Whiting Sep. 9, 1832.
Mrs Peggy Davis Died at the poor house March 5 1839 aged about 100 years
1839 Mrs Prudence Dinsmoor Died September 6 1839 aged 87 years
" Mr Jonathan Davis died September 25 1839 aged 36 years
1840 Mr Thomas Davis—formerly of Holden, Died May 14 aged 87 years.
1843 Mrs Nancy M. Damon wife of Mr Jno Warren Damon Died Feby 1 1843.
1843 Mrs Lucy Danforth, wife of Mr Elias Danforth, Died Decr 25, 1843, aged 50. Dropsy of the heart.
29 Eveleth —— child of Ephraim Eveleth died Novr 6, 1797, aged 6 months.
Emmerson Lydia, wife of Moses Emmerson died January 13, 1813.
31 Egerton Benjamin died April 2nd 1806, aged 45.
Egerton [Muriel?] daughter of the late Benjamin Egerton deceased, and Sarah Egerton, was drowned May 1st. 1807. aged [3] years.
Emmerson Sally wife of Moses Emmerson died October 16th 1808.
Emmerson Lydia, wife of Moses Emmerson died January 13, 1813.
Emerson Sally Carleton daughter of Moses Emerson and Eunice his wife died Nov. 27 1817.
1822 Emerson Capt Moses died Octo. 20 1722 aged 48 years.
Eaton Nathaniel died Feby 24, 1826, aged 82.
Eager Haran died October 10th 1829, aged 66 A Revolutionary Pensioner.
1835 Emmerson Elias, a Revolutionary Pensioner died June 16, 1835 aged 76.
1839 Eager Farwell died February 1, 1859 Aged 49 yrs.
Everett, Miss Louisa Died Feby 3, 1839 aged 26 yrs.
A child of Felicia Ann Eastman died Feby 8, 1839 aged 5 months
Mrs Betsey Eager wife of Haran Eager Died October 26 1839 aged 72 years
A son of Farwell Eager Died November 21 1839 aged 2 years
32 Fletcher Mary wife of Joshua Fletcher died July 25, 1813 aged 86.
Fletcher Joshua died Nov. 14, 1814.
Fletcher Joseph Warren son of Joshua Fletcher and Nabby Fletcher died May 10, 1816.

Freeman Mercy, wife of Amos Freeman, died at the widow Hammond's May 27, 1816.
Faulkner Mrs. Hannah wife of Mr. Paul Faulkner died October 24, 1817.
Fairbank Elizabeth, wife of Mr. Jonas Fairbank, died April 9 1818
Fletcher Julia Maria daughter of Joshua Fletcher & Nabby his wife died May 2, 1819.
1820. Fletcher Rebecca Widow died at the house of Capt Ephraim Carter, March 6th, 1820.
Flood William died Sept. 14, 1820.
Farmer Sally died in Sept. 1820.
Fales Jeremiah died June 25, 1821.
1822 Fisher Nancy wife of Jacob Fisher Esq, died April 15, 1822.
Farnsworth James, son of Benjamin Farnsworth died June 14, 1822.
33 Fletcher, Hannah, Sister of Joshua Fletcher died at his house, April 17th, 1797, Ætat: 76.
Faulkner, a daughter of Paul Faulkner & his wife deceased Decr, 3d. 1796.
Fisher, son of Isaac Fisher died July 12, 1799 an infant
Fairbank Deac. Cyrus deceased Feby. 28th. 1801 Æ tat. 63.
Fletcher Elijah son of Rufus and Mary Fletcher decd. Sep 4th 1802
Fuller Edward died Dec. 12th, 1802, Ætatis Suae 85.
Faulkner Hariot a daughter of Paul Faulkner and Abigail his wife deceased Sept. 28th. 1803.
Fletcher Roxa daughter of Willm. and Dorcas Fletcher died Octo 23d 1805.
Flagg William, son of Josiah Flagg, and Dolly Flagg, died on his passage from Batavia in the East Indies, the 7th of February A. D. 1806, in the 16th year of his age.
Farnsworth Charles son of Benjamin Farnsworth & Sally his wife died May 23d 1807.
Fletcher Polly wife of Rufus Fletcher died Augt. 29th 1808.
Farwell Sarah, wife of Leonard Farwell died May 31st. 1809, 61 years.
Faulkner Abigail wife of Paul Faulkner died Sept. 23d 1810.
Fisher Joshua died at the house of Mr Thomas W. Lyon January 3. 1813.
34 Major Timothy Fletcher died March 17, 1823.
Farwell Leonard died at Milton County of Saratoga N. York, Octo. 19, 1822 aged 62.
Fletcher Widow Ruth died at the house of Mr Abel Rugg's Feb. 20. 1824.
Fuller Mrs wife of Mr James Fuller died Nov. 21, 1824.
Fairbank Jonas Capt: son of the late Deacon Cyrus Fairbank, died April, 6, 1826, aged 51.
Foster Benjamin H. died May 10, 1826.
Fairbank Mary wife of Mr Cyrus Fairbank died Dec: 13, 1827. aged 53.
Fletcher Martha daughter of the late Major Timothy Fletcher died May 29th. 1829, aged 26.
Fairbank Jonas, died July 17, 1829, aged 86.
Fuller Francis F. drowned July 20, 1829. Son of Ephraim & Susan Fuller.
Farwell Frances Maria, daughter of Levi & Lucy B. Farwell, died Aug. 30 1830
James Fuller died July 23, 1831, aged 81.
Fuller Francis Faulkner son of Ephraim & Susan Fuller, died May 24th, 1832.
35 Fletcher Mrs Hannah relict of the late Major Timothy Fletcher died at Philadelphia of the Cholera. August 4, 1832 aged 75.
1833. Fuller Mrs. Susan wife of Mr. Ephraim Fuller died May 1, 1833.
Fuller Ephraim Heywood, son of Ephraim & Susan Fuller died Sept. 16, 1833.
Fisher an infant of E Carter Fisher died April 13. 1834.
Farwell Joseph, many years a Constable and Collector of this town, and a Revolutionary Soldier, died Sept 16, 1834, aged 75.
Fletcher Rebekah died at the Pauper establishment Feb. 19, 1835
1835. Fairbank Cyrus died May 1, 1835, aged 68 years.
Flagg Dolly, wife of Josiah Flagg Esqr. died June 1, 1835, aged 68 years.
George W Fletcher son of Lewis & Sally P. Fletcher died October 24 1835.
36 Edward Everett Farnsworth, son of Asa D & Betsy Farnsworth Died Oct 22d 1837, aged 10. weeks.

Abigail Farnsworth died March 14, 1838 at Capt Orice King's caused by her Clothes taking fire accidentally

1840 Abigail Fairbank, Widow of the late Deacon Cyrus Fairbank aged 88 years, Died January 14th.

1840. Josiah Flagg Esq formerly clerk of the Town of Lancaster during the long period of 33 years, a man of much mental ability and great industry, Died February 11. 1840 aged 79 Years

Mr Paul Faulkner Died February 7 1840 Aged 73 Years.

Mrs Polly Farnsworth Died February 23 aged 53 years

1841 Mr Ebenezer W. Fuller Died Oct. 11, 1841 aged 72 yrs.

1842. Daniel Willard Farwell Died April 5th 1842 [Child of Levi and Lucy B.]

Ann E. Farwell, daughter of Capt Joseph Farwell died August 31, 1842 aged 17 years & 2 mos

1843 Mrs Fidelia French wife of Mr Seth French Died May 14th. 1843.

1843 Mrs Faithful Fletcher, wife of Mr Rufus Fletcher, died 14th May Aged 74 yrs [Fever.]

37 Jacob Fisher, Esq. Died June 2, 1843. Aged 75 years. with very small advantages of schooling in early life, Major Fisher acquired, by habits of great and untiring industry, a good business education. He represented the Town many years in the Legislature of this Commonwealth, and served his fellow citizens long and usefully in various responsible offices. He was an honest man, a useful citizen, and a kind neighbor.

1843. Mr Torry Fitch Died September 4, 1843. Paralysis. Aged 48.

1843. John William son of George Fitch Died 17 Oct. 1843 Aged 3½ yrs. Canker

*   *   *   *   *   *

1844. Mrs Sarah Farnsworth Died Feb'y 1. 1844 aged 69. Influenza [Widow of Benjamin.]

1844. Mrs Dorcas Fletcher, wife of Mr William Fletcher died May 24, 1844 aged 74 years [Typhus fever.]

39 Gould, Polly, deceased Decr. 28th, 1796, at the house of James Pratt.

Gates, Lucy, daughter of Capt. Thomas Gates decd. July 19th 1797, aged 32 years.

Goss, James, son of John Goss and Mary his wife decd. Decr. 30, 1800.

Goss John son of John & Mary Goss died Octo. 1st 1803.

Goss Joseph son of John & Mary Goss died Aug 16. 1801.

Goss Daniel died Decem. 10th 1809 Aged 69.

Goss Judith daughter of Jonas & Judith Goss died August 21st 1807.

Gates Abigail wife of Thomas Gates died August 5th. 1810. Æ 69.

Goss Eunice relict of the late Capt. Daniel Goss, died January 7, 1813.

Goodwin Bathsheba wife of James Goodwin died Jany. 7, 1814.

Gates Capt Thomas died Dec. 27, 1814, aged 79.

Mr Daniel Godfrey died at the house of Dr James Carter July 9, 1816.

Goodwin Loring, son of the late Mr James Goodwin Junr. died at the house of his grandfather James Goodwin on Tuesday the 22nd. day of April 1817, aged 18yrs, 7mo, 10days.

Goss Ebenezer son of Jonas Goss died Dec 15. 1817.

Geary Mr [Rufus] Died at the house of Mr Aaron Jones August 13th 1818.

40 Guild Mrs. died at the house of Capt Richard Cleavland August 27, 1825.

Goodwin Edward Esq. died January 10th 1828, at Pauper establishment.

Goss John son of John Goss & Mary Goss died Sunday the 13. Jan'y 1828 aged 23.

Gates Mrs Lucy died June 1829.

Goss Henry Laughton son of Henry Goss & Sally his Wife died Sep 2 1830.

Goodspeed Mrs [Elizabeth] died Dec. 28th. 1830. by drowning.

Godard Miss Nabby died Jany 7, 1831, at the house of Capt John Thurston

Goss Nancy, daughter of Jonas Goss and Judith died Jany 25 1831.

Goodwin James died Sept 8th 1831 aged 90 years, a Soldier of the Revolution.

Goldthwait John died at the Pauper establishment January 15 1832, aged 66 years.

Goodwin Susan Emeline daughter of John Goodwin Jun & Susan died Octo 20, 1824

Goodwin Susan wife of Mr John Goodwin Jr. Died March 18, 1825.

Gould William died October 7, 1834 aged 80 years

Godard Eber died May 26, 1835, a Revolutionary Pensioner.

Goodwin Miss Bathsheba daughter of Mr John Goodwin Senior died June 11th, 1835.
41 Goodrich Bulah widow, and Mother of Doctor Goodrich died Dec. 4, 1835 aged 81.
Goodwin Cynthia Jane, daughter of John Goodwin Jr died 19th October 1835.
Goodwin Mrs Rebecca Died Feby 7th 1839 aged 61 yrs.
Edward son of James E. Gould died February 5, 1839 aged 11 months

* * * *

Mrs Elizabeth Gould wife of Nathl Gould Died March 3 1839 aged 84 years
Mr William Gould son of Nathl Gould, Died February 22 1840, aged 56 years
Miss Gould Died 1839
Goss Jonas, Died October 18th 1840 Aged 60 years.
Capt Daniel Goss Died May 11, 1841. Aged 69 years.
A child of Oliver E. Greene Died May 16, 1841, aged 3 years
1843 Charles William, son of Mr H. Gibbs died Oct. 1, 1843 aged 3 months Canker
Mr John Goss, Died March 24 1843, aged 73. Dropsy in the chest
42 Hatch Turner of Scituate died at Dr James Carter's the first day of March 1810.
Hawks Sewall son of John Hawks Jr and Alice his wife died March 22d 1809.
Houghton Capt. Elijah, died July 7th 1810, aged eighty-two years!
Haven Richard jun. son of Richard and Sally Haven died May 2nd 1811.
Haskell Elias died July 1st. 1811.
Hawks Cynthia daughter of John & Alice Hawks died Sep. 6. 1811.
Hastings Thomas, and Benjamin, Sons of Benjamin Hastings of Sullivan New Hampshire, were drowned in Still River, Sabbath Morning, July 4. 1813.
Haskell Charity relict of the late Col. Henry Haskell died Dec. 1813.
Houghton Lockheart, died at the house of his Brother Oliver Houghton Feb. 2, 1814. Aged 43.
Hiller Joseph Esquire, died Feby. 9th. 1814. "When such friends part, 'tis the Survivor dies."
Houghton Achsah relict of the late Deacon Benjamin Houghton died July 5, 1815 aged 72.
43 Houghton, Phinehas, decd. Novr. 10, 1797, aged 71 years.
Houghton Abijah, decd. Jany. 23d. 1802, aged 78 yn.
Houghton Emeline decd. Dec. 18, 1792 aged 4 mo. 25 Day
Hosley David killed at the raising of a building, July 4th. 1802.
Houghton Deacon Benjamin deceased the 31st of July 1802, Ætat. 63.
Houghton John son of Benjamin Houghton deceased the 11th of Octo 1802 Ætat 12.
Houghton Elijah, son of Elijah and [Ruth?] deceased June 12 1803.
Hammond Ceazar a Negro died June 24th 1803.
Holt Dinah Widow of Thomas Holt died Nov 9th. 1803.
Hunt Otis jun son of Otis Hunt died 3d of July 1804.
Houghton Ruth relict of the late Phinehas Houghton died Jany 10th 1805.
Hudson Dinah wife of Robert Hudson died 7th Feb. 1806.

* * * *

Houghton Sparhawk died May 23d 1806. Aged 33.
Hunt Dandridge died April 14th 1807.
Haskell Henry Col. died June 10th 1807.
Houghton Alice widow of the late Abijah Houghton died Feb 5th, 1808 aged 83 years.
Hunt Maria daughter of Otis Hunt died Feb 27, 1809.
Houghton Oliver son of Oliver Houghton died Octo 3d 1809.
Houghton Mary daughter of Oliver Houghton died Aug. 1808.
44 Hammond Levi died Feby 19 1817.
Hawks Anstiss, daughter of John Hawks and Alice died April 1, 1817.
Haven Mrs. Wife of Mr Ebenezer Haven died Feb. 13 1819.
Hildreth Mrs Nancy wife of Mr Richard Hildreth died Nov. 20, 1819.
Harris Hezediah wife of Mr Emery Harris died January 11, 1820.
Hildreth Ezekiel son of Richard and Nancy Hildreth died Jany 25, 1820.
Hyde Solon Whiting son of John Hyde jun. and Julia Hyde died August 1, 1820.

1821. Hyde John died Nov. 17, 1821.
1822. Howe Susan daughter of David & Susan Howe died April 27, 1817.
Howe William son of David & Susan Howe died August 20, 1821.
Hayward, Lois wife of Moses Hayward died 4th March 1822, aged 75.
Harris Sam, an Indian, an aboriginal, one of the Six Nations, an itinerant traveller, died at the house of Capt Joseph Wilder, July 20, 1822, aged as he said 31.
Houghton Mrs. Lydia wife of Capt Benj^a. Houghton died Aug. 8, 1825
45 Hammond Widow Mercy died 5 Feby 1826.
Houghton Lydia daughter of Capt Benj^a. Houghton, died Sept. 14, 1826.
Hammond Pearly died 28th Dec: 1826.
Hawkes Dr John died Jany. 26 1827.
Houghton Mary widow of Capt Elijah Houghton died at her son Elijah Houghton's, May 22^d 1818 Aged 82 years.
Holman John died Dec. 1827, at the house of Capt. Henry Townsend Aged 32.
Howard Mrs. [Sarah M.] wife of Mr. George Howard died Sept. 7, 1830.
Howard Amasa, son of Levi & Mary Howard died July 9. 1830.
Houghton Frederic son of Cyrus Houghton died Feb. 18. 1834.
Houghton Mrs. Martha, wife of Rufus Houghton died Decr. 16, 1834.
Horsely Widow [Luceba] died January 14, 1835. [1834, on grave stone.]
Houghton Benjamin, son of the late Trumpeter Abijah Houghton died at the Poor House Jany 15, 1835.
Haskell John Edward son of John A. Haskell & Sarah, died February 3, 1835.
46 Houghton Oliver, died Sept 20th. 1836. Aed, 71.
Houghton Nabby died Feb 4th 1837 Agd 66 years
Huntington Julia M. Died Sept. 20th: [23] 1833
Huntington Horatio [M.] Died [Sept 17,] 1836
1837 Howard Elizabeth wife of George W Howard died. June 2^d 1837, aged 27. years
1838 Daniel Harris died Oct 22, 1838 aged 80 yrs A Revolutionary Pensioner
" George Harris, born in Lancaster, Son to Emory Harris, died in Wrentham Oct [12] 1838 Aged [23.]
" Emory Harris, died December 31 Aged 50 years
1839 Rebecca Houghton Wife of Stephen Houghton died Jany 20, 1839 Aged 70 yrs
" A Son of Phineas B. Howe Died February 25 1839 Aged 12 yrs
   * * * * *
" A son of Solomon Houghton Died August 26 Aged 1 Year
" Mrs Frances Houghton Wife of Solomon H. Died September 11 1839 Aged 32 Years
Mrs Sarah P. Hodgman Wife of Mr Artemas H. Died February 7 1840 aged — years
1841 Sarah Abigail Hastings daughter of Saml A. Hastings died March 13, 1841 aged 7 yrs 10 months.
47 " Mr Stephen Houghton Died April 17 1841 aged 76 years
" [Joseph] Miller Son of J. W. Huntington Died July 2, 1841 Aged 3 years.
" Horatio [Harrison] Son of J. W. Huntington Died July 8, 1841, Aged 1 year.
1842 Mr Jonathan Holman Died January 5. 1842 Aged 78 yrs
John A. Harriman Son of John and Julia A. Harriman died July 26, 1841 Aged 1 year & 9 mo^s.
1843 Relief Houghton, Widow of Mr A—. Aged 81 years Died June 3, 1843.
1842 Mrs Abigail Harris Widow of the late Mr Daniel Harris Died March 26 1842 aged 78, yrs
1844 Capt Asahel Harris Died Jany 14. 1844 Aged 50 yrs Consumption
1843 Miss Eliza [H.] Harris Died March 28, 1843, aged 22 yrs.
50 Jones Charles son of Moses Jones died in the U. S. Hospital at Avon State of N York, in the U. S. Service April 18, 1815.
Jones Mary Ann, daughter of Aaron Jones and Sally Jones died Aug. 1. 1815.
Jenks Molly, died at the house of Mr Charles Chase May 17. 1817.
Jones Edwin Son of Aaron Jones and Sally Jones died Octo 12, 1816.
Jones Mrs. [Sarah] Wife of Samuel Jones died September 7, 1818.

Jones Mrs Nancy wife of Sam¹ Jones Jun died November 10. 1818.
Johnson Daniel died March 24, 1819
1822. Johnson Luther died, April 24, 1822.
Joslyn Mary relict of Nath¹ Joslyn died at the house of Mr Cyrus Fairbank Feby 18, 1825 aged 88.
Joslyn Samuel died the 15th, Feby. 1826 aged 88
Johnson Aaron died Feby 6. 1826 Æ 78.
Jones Moses died Decr. 5. 1829, Aged 60.
William Hubbard Smith Jewett son of Samuel Jewett died March 14 1832, aged 5 years.
Jones Sullivan son of the late Moses Jones, died July the [18th] 1832.
51 Jones — daughter of Samuel & —— Jones deceased Decr. 25th. 1796.
Johnson — son of Daniel Johnson died July 23, 1797 aged 9 years.
Johnson — daughter of Dan¹ Johnson died July 25, 1797 aged 3 years.
Johnson — daughter of Dan¹ Johnson died July 27, 1797
Johnson — son of Dan¹ Johnson died Aug: 8th, 1797, aged 6 years.
Joslyn Peter son of Nathaniel Joslyn died June 20th 1802.
Joslyn Jonas Jun Son of Jonas and Betsy Joslyn deceased Sunday the 15th of August 1802
Joslyn James son of Jonas Joslyn deceased June 3^d 1804.
Jones Mary relict of the late David Jones died the 29th Sept. 1805 Ætat. 85.
Nathaniel Joslyn died May 27th 1806.
Jones Betsy daughter of Moses Jones died June 22nd 1810 aged 16 years.
Submit Jones Wife of Moses Jones died Dec 18th 1810.
Jones Polly died ——
Joslyn Jonas son of Jonas & Betsy Joslyn died Aug. 15, 1802.
Joslyn James same Parents " June 3, 1804.
Joslyn Abigail, wife of Capt Samuel Joslyn died August 8, 1814.
Jones Solon son of Moses Jones died the 12 August 1814.
52 Jones Sarah J. daughter of Luther & Charlotte Jones, died Octo. 23, 1826
1838 Jonas Joslyn, died August 5th 1838, Aged 64 yrs
1839 Mr Aaron Jones Died September 23 1839 aged 72 years
1842 Marcus L Jones — Son of Mr Luther Jones, died Oct. 17, 1842.
55 Knight, Patience. daughter of Manassah Knight died April 1st. 1797, aged 20 years.
Keyes Dorcas daughter of Simon Keyes died Sep. 4. 1802.
Knight Patty, daughter of Manassah Knight died January 29th 1802, aged 23 years.
Knight Mrs [Lydia] relict of the late Mr Amos Knight died May 1. 1812.
Knight Sally wife of Charles E. Knight died June, 1 1813.
Knight Manasah died 28. Sep 1814.
Keyes Sarah Lane daughter of Amasa Keyes & Sally Keyes, died Sep 12, 1817, Aged 5^{yrs}. 2mo. 22^{days}.
Knight James, son of Charles E Knight and Catharine his wife was drowned Sep 26 1823.
Keyes Amasa died Octo: 11 1826.
Kingsbury Catharine wife of Nath¹. Kingsbury died June 19, 1827.
Kimball Mrs. Polly, wife of Aaron Kimball Esq. formerly of Sterling, July 27. 1832. died, aged 64.
Knight Nathaniel Lakin son of Charles E Knight & Catharine Knight died March 7, 1828.
Knight Sophia Maynard, Same Parents died Dec. 26 1828.
Kilburn Lydia died March 24, 1835, at the House of the South family of Shakers aged 88.
56 Kendal Jane died at the Pauper establishment Dec 22, 1835.
1839 Mr Eben^r Knowlton Died October 6 1839 aged 61 years
1841 A Child of Mr Alfred Knight Died February 1841 aged 2 years
1843 George Gerry, Son of Alfred Knight Died Augt 31, one & a half yrs
60 Leach Rebecca wife of Joseph Leach deceased April 28th. 1810 aged 39 years.
Laughton Capt. Daniel died Aug. 28, 1812
Larkin Polly wife of Benjamin Larkin died 1812.

Lane Sally wife of Col. Lane died March 12, 1813.
Low Abigail daughter of John & Mary Low died Sept. 15. 1813.
Larkin William died Jany. 25, 1814.
Locke Jonathan died Aug. 13. 1814, 66
Laughton Ephraim died March 19 1817.
Lewis Timothy died in June 1816.
Leach Elizabeth, daughter of the late Capt. Kezekiah Gates, died April 18, 1818 aged 86 yrs.
Littaye Noel D^r. died September the 16th *Anno Domini*, 1818.
1821. Mrs [Annis] Lowe, wife of Nathl Lowe died March 11 1821.
" Lincoln Cummings Son of Jacob Lincoln died Jany. 4 1822.
1823. Lyon Willard Son of Thomas W Lyon died Aug. 1812
    Lyon Maria same Parents   died   "   1812
    Lyon Nancy same Parents   died   "   31 1812
1824. Mrs Mehitable Larkin wife of Mr W^m. Larkin died Sep. 22, 1824.
Lincoln Capt Caleb died Octo: 20 1825.
61 Locke, Mrs Mary, wife of Wm Locke, deceased Novr 15, 1796
Longley a child of Ezekiel Longley dec^d. Sepr. 29. 1796.
Lane Dolly Ballard daughter of Jonas Lane & Eunice his wife dec^d March 8th, 1798 — aged 14 months.
Lane Jonas son of Jonas Lane, by Dolly his former wife deceased August 28, 1797, aged 6 years.
Litch, Washington, of the family of John Maynard, drowned, August 11, 1798, aged 22 years.
Leach, Collins a son of Joseph & Susannah Leach: deceas'd Sept. 29th. 1798, aged 19 months.
Leach, Mrs Susannah, wife of Joseph Leach deceased December 31. 1800.
Lyon Aaron died the 24th Nov. 1801.
Leach Mary, daughter of Joseph Leach dec^d. Feb 20th 1802.
Laughton Thomas died March 11th 1805.
Low Saxton Son of Nathl Low Jr. Sept. 15th 1805.
Low Polly, daughter of Nathl Low Jr. Sept. 16 1805.
Lane Elizabeth daughter of Jonas Lane died Septem. 6th 1805 aged 3 Mo^s.
Lane Maryann daughter of Jonas Lane died Sept. 23^d 1805 aged 3 yrs.
Low Mary daughter of John Low died Octo the 15th 1805, aged three years.
Lane Mrs. Eunice wife of Col. Jonas Lane died August 2nd 1807.
Littaye Katharine daughter of Noel Littaye & Sally his wife dec^d Ap 4th 1801.
Low Comfort died at the house of Dr James Carter April 4, 1809.
62 Low Rufus son of Nathl Low died Octo. 14, 1826.
Low Nathaniel died April 29, 1827.
Laughton Marshal, son of Hannibal Laughton, and Dolly his wife, died July 13, 1827.
Lincoln Chloe wife of Jacob Lincoln, died July 10. 1829.
Lowe Almira daughter of the late Nathaniel Lowe died at the house of Dr Carter April 17, 1830.
Lawrence Edmund died June 15, 1830. Verdict of Jury Self Murder
Lane Clarissa daughter of Alvinzey Lane and Lucy his wife died March 20 1830.
Laughton Emily daughter of the late Capt Daniel Laughton died Jany 9 1832, aged 38.
Lewis Martha daughter of Levi Lewis Esq and Abigail his wife died Jany 15 1825.
Lewis Augustus Son of the said Levi & Abigail died November 24, 1831.
Lyon Matilda died in the family of Shakers Jany. 9 1834, aged 73.
Lee Mrs. Ann of Boston, died at the House of Mrs. Southwick, Sept. 11, 1834, Aged 60.
63 Lyon Capt. John died Jany. 9, 1836.
Ladd George Vivian Son of Rufus King Ladd and Emily P. Ladd died March 11th 1838
1839 Major Jonathan Locke died January 26, 1839 Aged 60 yrs
    Levi Lewis Esq Died July 2 1839 Aged 51 Years
1841 A Child of Charles A. Lyman Died April 16, 1841, Aged 18 months
13

1841 Mr Daniel Lawrence Died June 5th 1841 Aged 52 yrs
" Mr John Laughton Died Sept. 18, 1841. Aged 21 yrs.
1843 Miss Hannah Larkin Died 10th Sept 1843 Aged 79, Dysentery.
1842 Miss Mary Ann Laughton Died Aug. 9, 1842. Aged 21. Consumption.
67 Millar, Nathaniel, died Novr 25, 1798, aged 31 years.
Millar Samuel son of Anna Millar died March 3d, 1799.
Mareschallee Pierre a french stranger died May 25th 1804, at the House of Capt Thomas Bennett.
Mallard James Jr. Son of James & Betsy Mallard died Jany 11 1810.
Mallard Maryann daughter of Abraham and Sally Mallard died April 17, 1808.
Mallard James 2d. Son of James Mallard died August 10, 1813.
Miller Nancy died Nov 1814
Manning Rebecca P. daughter of Dr Samuel Manning died Octo. 4 1817.
Mansfield Lydia died at the house of Capt Ephraim Carter January 7. 1820.
McLellan William died Octo 19, 1822.
Maynard Capt John died Jany. 21, 1823 a Hero of the Revolution.
Munroe Aaron died Jany 19 1825
Miller Joseph died February 16, 1827.
Manning Mercy, Widow of the late John Manning, died Nov. 7. 1827, at the Pauper establishment
68 Moore Hariet a daughter of Mr Henry Moore and Achsah his Wife died April 8th 1827.
Maynard Ann daughter of Joseph Maynard and Anna died Dec. 28th 1829.
Maynard Mrs Martha relict of the late Capt John Maynard, died February 19. 1831.
Maynard Esther daughter of Joseph & Betsy Maynard died March 1. 1813.
Miles Miss Catharine daughter of Capt Thomas Miles died Jany. 24 1832.
Maynard Caroline daughter of Joseph Maynard and Anna died Mar. 30 1831.
Manly, Widow [Sarah] died at the house of Mr George Howard Sept 11, 1833.
Morse Joseph died July 29, 1834
1836. Miss Lucretia Murry died August 30th 1836 aged 75 years.
1837. Mrs Susan Morse wife of Joseph Morse died May 20th 1837, aged 52 years & 2 mo
1839 A Daughter of Joseph Maynard Jr Died July 27 1839 aged 2 Years
" William A. Marston at the house of Rev Dr Thayer Died August 4 1839 aged 16 Years
1840 Mrs Ann Matthews Died Novr 3 1840 Aged 25 yrs
1841 Mrs Ruth Miles, Died Oct. 11, 1841 Aged 65 Years
69 1843 Mrs Dinah Merriam of Fitchburg Died Novr 5, 1843, Aged 77.
1843 Miss Ann Mitchell Died 31 Jan. 1843, aged 15 Bowel complaint.
71 Nichols, widow Silence, died at the house of Aaron Johnson, Novr. 7, 1797, aged 72 years.
Newman Edward Selfridge son of Gowen B. Newman, and Lucy his Wife died Octo 24th. 1803.
Newman Daniel son of Gowen B. Newman and Lucy Newman died Dec 20th 1807, aged 3 years.
Nelson George, son of Paul & Rhoda Nelson, died May 8, 1811.
Newman Samuel, son of Gowen B. Newman and Lucy his wife, died March 17. 1813.
Newton Samuel, and a young Mr Felton of Marlboro' were on the evening of the 18th of April 1815, both drowned in Sandy Pond by the upsetting of a Canoe.
Newhall James, died Sept. 6, 1820 Æ 43, an Eminent Teacher of Church Music.
Nichols Joseph died March 8th 1826 aged 82.
Nowell Elizabeth Arnold daughter of Wm. & Elizabeth Nowell died April 8, 1826.
Nowell John William Son of William and Elizabeth Nowell died Feby. 9, 1832.
72 Newman Gowen B. died Decemr. 9th 1833, aged 65.
1843 Newman William, Son of Wm Newman Died June 2 1843. Killed by a limb from a tree. Aged [5] years
1842 Newman, Mrs Lucy, Widow of the late Mr G. B. Newman Died June 2, 1842 Aged 71 Dropsy

77 Osgood, Joseph, deceased Septr. 24, 1797, aged 77 years
Osgood Jonathan deceased July 14th 1808, at the house of Haran Eager.
Osgood Martha relict of the late Moses Osgood died March 17th. 1810 aged 92 years.
Osgood Joseph Son of Ephraim Osgood & Lucy Osgood died Octo 31. 1804
Osgood Jerusha died at the house of M^r. Calvin Peabody, Dec. 12, 1813 aged 96.
Osgood Nahum died at the house of Mr Fales Feb 18, 1815.
Osgood Mrs [Catharine] Relict of the late Mr Joseph Osgood died at the house of Mr Ephraim Osgood, Feby 17th. 1819 aged 92.
Osgood Daniel Powers son of Moses Osgood and Hannah his wife. died Nov. 12, 1818.
Osgood Katherine daughter of the late Mr Joseph Osgood died May 30 1821.
Osgood Joel died Nov. 8, 1821, Æ 75.
Osgood Martha Wyman daughter of Peter Osgood & Mary his Wife died August 31, 1832.
1834 Osgood Ephraim died March 15 1834
  Osgood Mary died at the Shakers, Dec. 3. 1834, aged 87
78 Miss Abigail E. Osgood Died 17th Oct. 1843. Aged 17. Consumption.
82 Phelps Oliver, Son of Jacob & Prudence Phelps lost at Sea the 20th January 1805.
Phelps Anna daughter of Calvin & Asenath Phelps died Sep 7th 1799.
Pratt Zeruiah died May 22nd 1806.
Phelps Mary died Sept 21 1807 aged 78.
Phelps Mary Peirce daughter of Sylvester & Esther Phelps died May 24 1808.
Phelps Lucy 2nd daughter of Gardner & Lucy Phelps died Octo 12th, 1803.
Phelps Louisa daughter of George & Sally Phelps died March 26, 1809.
Phelps Aaron, died December 21st. 1810.
Prescott John Capt. died Aug 18th. 1811.
Phelps Mrs. Elizabeth Widow of Mr. Asahel Phelps died Mar 5, 1812 aged 86.
Pollard Clarissa daughter of Abner and Achsah Pollard died 5th of April 1812.
Peirce Clarissa daughter of Joel Peirce died Dec. 18, 1812.
Phelps David died April 30, 1813.
Phelps Joel died May 27, 1813, 79 yrs
Phelps Dolly died Nov, 18. 1813,—aged 70
Phelps Prudence widow of Joel Phelps died June 3 1813, aged 71.
83 Patten, Richard, one of the Commonwealth's Poor, died April 8th. 1797, at the house of Edwd Goodwin aged 65. years.
Priest, John, died Sept 9, 1797, at the house of Abij: Phelps, aged 88 years.
Priest, Elizabeth, wife of Joseph Priest died March 25th. 1798, at a house of Aaron Johnson, aged 84 yrs.
Priest, Joseph, died May 17, 1798 at Barrett's house aged 83 years.
Phelps Son of Robert Phelps died Aug: 31. 1798 aged 3 weeks.
Phelps Son of Calvin Phelps died Septr. 7, 1798 aged 1 year & 6 months.
Phelps Dolly Lovering, daughter of Luke Phelps died Aug: 31, 1799.
Phelps Lucy, daughter of Gardner Phelps died Dec. 27, 1801, aged 7 years & 10 Mos.
Phelps Elisha died Jany 21st 1802.
Phelps William deceased Feb. 22nd 1802.
Phelps Jacob Jr died at Sea on board the Constitution Frigate April 6, 1799.
Phelps Achsah, relict of John Phelps, died Octo^r. 15th 1802. Ætat 61.
Puffer Abigail wife of Nathan Puffer died Nov. 23^d 1802.
Phelps Ruth died Feb. 6th 1803.
Pollard Polly daughter of Abner Pollard & Achsah his wife died July 15th. 1803 aged 12 Years & 5 Mos.
Pollard Sally daughter of Abner Pollard & Achsah his wife died Augt. 4th 1803, aged 1 yr. & 4 Mos.
84 Pollard John died May 10, 1814. aged 85.
Poor Alice, died at the house of Doctor Israel Atherton August 2, 1814.
Plummer Thomas Son of Farnham Plummer & Nancy his wife died Octo. 2, 1814.
Pollard Achsah wife of Abner Pollard died January 29, 1816.
Pollard Edward Walker son of Abner and Achsah Pollard died Dec. 7, 1815

Pollard Elizabeth relict of the late John Pollard died March 4, 1816, Æ 78.
Plummer Charles son of Farnham Plummer & Nancy Plummer died May 25th, 1818.
Putnam Mrs. Elizabeth, widow of the late Eben[r]. Putnam Esq., died at the House of Major Solomon Carter January 18th, 1820, Aged 50 years.
Phelps Asahel son of Gardner Phelps died January 18th 1820.
Phelps George died August 22, 1821.
1822 Phelps Levinia daughter of George Phelps died at Waltham Nov 15, 1822.
Peaslee Moses died May 18th, 1823.
Phelps Mrs [Asenath] Wife of Calvin Phelps died May [2] 1824

85 Phelps Abiel son of Peter Phelps died 1825
Phelps Meriel died August 15 1819 daughter of Ephraim and Dolly Phelps.
Phelps Samuel same Parents died July 13 1821.
Phelps Jacob died at Leominster August 22 1824.
Phelps Henry son of Sylvester Phelps died August 8, 1826.
Prescott widow Abigail died at the house of Capt Daniel Goss Octo. 3, 1827. aged 59.
Phelps Sewall son of Robert Phelps and Mary his wife died Aug[t]. 31, 1798.
Phelps Clarissa, daughter of Thomas Phelps died Dec. 1, 1827.
Phelps Abijah died June 1829
Pollard Lucy wife of Gardner Pollard died October 17, 1829. Aged 50.
Pollard William died June 16th, 1830
Poignand David died August 28 1830, aged 72.
Peirce Charles Henry son of Harvey & Cynthia Peirce, died Feb 15 1831.
Phelps Mary widow of Abijah Phelps died March 26, 1831.
Plummer Mrs. Nancy, wife of Mr. Farnham Plummer died Dec. 27, 1831.
1833 Poignand Mrs Delicia A. Relict of the late David Poignand died Sep 30th, 1833.
Prouty Martha of the family of Shakers, Died March 16, 1833 aged 31[y]. 7[mo]. 20[days].

86 Phelps Patterson Hezekiah, son of Sylvester Phelps died Dec. 18, 1833.
Parker Edward Samuel, Son of Capt Joel & Czarina Parker, died at the house of Mr Amos Wheeler. Dec. 30 1833. aged 10 years.
Phelps Mary Ann, daughter of Sylvester Phelps, died May 11th, 1833.
Plant Delicia Amiraux daughter of Samuel & Delicia Mary Plant. died January 29. 1834.
1834 Phelps Robert, died June 9. 1834 aged —
Pollard Leonard was killed by Lightning July 17, 1834.
Pitts James died January 13, 1835.
Pollard John W[m]. Gamble son of Leonard and Annis Pollard died April 3, 1834.
1836 Palmer Mr. died 5–6, January 1836
1836 John Chandler Son of Farnham and Abigail Plummer died Nov. 13, 1836.
1839 Joseph Phelps, Son of Sylvester Phelps, Died May 8th. aged 33 years
" Mrs Laura Phelps Died March 6 1839 aged 35 years
" Mrs Emily Pratt Wife of Eben Pratt Died July 10 1839 Aged 42 years
" A Son of Levi Pierce Died October 2 aged 7 Years
1840 Infant of Mr Levi Peirce died May 3rd aged one year
87 Miss Beulah Phelps Died November 8 1739 Aged 86 Years
1842 Mrs Abigail, wife of Farnham Plummer Died February 5th 1842 Aged 42 yrs
1842 Mrs Sarah Phelps died January 25, 1842, Aged 61 years
1841 George J. Persons. Died Sept. 11, 1841 [aged 17 years.]
1842 Miss Dolly Persons, died July 14th Aged 21 years
1843 Mrs Betsey S. Pitts, Wife of Mr [Hiram W.] Pitts died May 12, 1843 aged 29 years
1843 Lewis Hiram, Child of Mr Hiram [W.] Pitts aged 5 months Died Sept. 7 1843. Dysentary
1842 Mr Henry Parker aged about 50 Suicide July 13, 1842
1843 Mrs Relief Phelps aged 83, died Jan 6. 1843 Consumption
90 Rugg Isaac died April 1, 1813. Aged 66.
Rugg Sophia daughter of Samuel & Sarah Rugg died Octo. 5. 1810.

Ross Josiah died Octo. 22, 1814 at the house of Mr Jonas Fairbank, whose death was occasioned by a fall from a Tree.
Rugg Martha wife, ——
Rugg Abijah died Feb 2, 1816.
Rand Harry Son of Nathaniel Rand died March 11, 1816
Rogers Mrs. Abigail wife of Mr Joseph Rogers died Octo. 23 1817 aged --
Robbins John died December 17th, 1820.
Rugg Edward Son of Joseph Rugg, died Octo. 13, 1822.
Rugg Susan Whiting daughter of Luke Rugg & Silome died June 5 1825.
Rice Mary Ann died May 13, 1825
Robbins Mrs. [Lydia] Widow of the late Mr John Robbins died Sep 2nd 1826, aged 78.
Rand Mrs, [Lucy] wife of Nathaniel Rand died Novr. 3d, 1826.

91 Rider, Mr Eleazar. deceased at his house in Lancaster Septr 17, 1796.
Rider Mrs Anna widow of Eleazar Rider, died March 20th, 1797. aged 70 years.
Rugg, John, died Jany 11. 1799, aged 85 years.
Russell Lucretia daughter of Caleb Russell died Aug. 18th 1803.
Rugg Capt. Elisha died January 7th. 1805.
Rugg Lucy daughter of the late Capt Elisha Rugg. died Augt. 10th. 1805.
Rugg Jane died, Sept. 11th 1805, Ætat 93.
Robbins Bathsheba relict of the late Edward Robbins died Octo. 16th, 1805. Ætat 85.
Rugg Zerviah relict of the late Nathan Rugg died April 8th 1807, Aged 86 years.
Rugg Lydia Widow of the late John Rugg, died Novr, 11th 1807, aged 91 years.
Robbins John died March 2nd 1810.
Rugg Elijah died May 1st. 1810, in a fit of insanity
Rugg Aaron died July 6th 1810.
Rugg Augustus, Son of Joseph and Mary Rugg died January 3d, 1812.
Rugg Alpheus Son of Abijah & Susanna Rugg died at Leominster April 21, 1812.
Richardson Widow died at the house of Thomas Ballard Augt. 1812.

92 Richardson Miss [Charlotte] daughter of the 2nd Wife of Mr Paul Faulkner, died Novr: 13, 1827.
Rugg Submit daughter of James & Submit Rugg died March 4 1826.
Rugg Daniel Son of James & Submit Rugg died March 16, 1828.
Rugg Elizabeth daughter of James & Submit Rugg died October 27, 1828.
Rugg Capt Daniel died April 10 1830, aged 87.
Rice Harriet Maria daughter of Josiah Rice died July 21, 1830.
Rice Mary Ann a daughter of Nathl. Rice died Feby. 16th 1831.
Rugg Submit, wife of James Rugg died Sept 1, 1830.
Richardson Susan Nurse daughter of Saml. Richardson died Dec. 9, 1831.
Rugg Susanna relict of the late Abijah Rugg died Jany 11 1832.
Rugg Bathsheba Wife of Joel Rugg died Nov. 13, 1832
1834 Rugg Elizabeth relict of the late Capt Daniel Rugg died April 8, 1834 aged 88.
Richardson Abel a Revolutionary Pensioner died July 17 1834.
Rugg Stephen, Son of the late Daniel Rugg senior died Dec. 23, 1834, Aged 77 yrs. 10 mo. 11 days.

93 Rugg Martin Son of Abel W. and Hannah Rugg died Sep. 4 1819
Rugg Susan W. daughter of Luke Rugg & Silome his wife died June 5, 1825
1835 Rugg John Son of John & Eliza Rugg died July 28, 1832
1838. Rugg Prudence, died March 15, 1838, at Peter Osgoods.
1838. Rand Mrs Nancy — wife of Nathaniel Rand, Esquire, died March 29th
Rugg Miss Mary, Daughter of Joel and Bathsheba Rugg, died August 2nd 1838, aged 24 yrs
1839 Abel Richardson Died August 25 1839 Aged 56 Years
1842 Mrs Anna Rice, wife of Mr Nathaniel Rice, died Sept. 30, 1842 Aged 37 yrs Debility
1843 Mrs Katharine Rugg Widow of Mr Abel Rugg Died Novr 2 1843 Aged 84. Old age
1842 Mr Abel Rugg Died Feby 14, 1842 Aged 92. Old age

97	A child of America Sawyer Died Oct. 18. 1840
1840	Mrs Nancy Sawyer, Wife of Mr Amos Sawyer, Died Decr 29 Aged 63.
1841	An Infant Child of Mr James Stone Died Feby 17. 1841.
1843	Mr Amos Sawyer Died Augt 23, 1843 Aged 85 yrs Dysentery
1844	Miss Louisa Sawyer, Daughter of Mr Elias Sawyer Died Jany 14, [8] 1844 Aged 16. Consumption
1842	Miss Abby Sawyer, daughter of Mr Elias Sawyer, died Oct. 3, 1842. Consumption
1842	An Infant Daughter of Mr James Stone, Died Oct. 11 1842
1843	Mr Elisha Sanderson Died March 14, 1843 aged 81 yrs Old age

98 Solindine Isaac died Sept. 16th 1806.
Solindine John died February 25th 1807.
Stedman Mary ann died July 31st, 1807 aged 12 yrs. 9 Mo.
Sargant Richard died October 14th, 1807.
Solindine Susanna, relict of John Solindine, died at the house of her son-in-law, Calvin Wilder, March 4th 1808. Insanity.
Stephenson Thomas Son of Martin Stephenson died Sept. 1808.
Stedman Christopher Ellery, son of William Stedman and Almy Stedman, was lost at Sea the 9th. of August 1809, on a voyage to Calcutta in the East Indies, in the 18th year of his age.
Stedman William Son of William Stedman and Almy his wife, died April 16th 1810.
Sawyer Charlotte a daughter of Paul Sawyer deceased died Nov. 6th, 1810.
Stearns Timothy died March 22^d 1811.
Stearns Augustus son of Eli and Mary Stearns died Sept 27th, 1811.
Smith Abigail wife of Moses Smith, died January 26. 1812, aged 70 y. 3 Mo. 3 d.
Smith Moses, died Feb. 3, 1812, aged 72.
Smith Charles Henry, son of Moses Smith and Salla Smith died April 3, 1812.
Sawyer Abigail relict of Josiah Sawyer died Nov. 13, 1812. aged abt ninety one.
99 Safford [Catharine] daughter of Thomas Safford died July 4th 1798, aged 15 months.
Sawyer, Son of Amos Sawyer jun, died October 29, 1798.
Sawyer, Elizabeth wife of Thomas Sawyer deceased Feby. 14, 1799.
Sargeant, Hannah wife of John Sargeant died Aug: 26, 1799.
Sprague Hon: John, deceased Septr 28th 1800, Ætat. 61.
Sargeant, Aaron deceased Feby. 5th, 1801.
Sawyer Josiah deceased Mar: 19th, 1801 Ætat. 81
Sawyer Deborah deceased Mar. 2 1802.
Sargent John deceased Dec. 21 1802.
Sawyer Lois Widow deceased June 8 1803.
Sanderson Samuel deceased July 24 1803.
Sprague Mary relict of Hon: John Sprague dec'd Sept. 22^d 1803.
Sargent Stephen Son of Stephen Sargent died Octo 29th 1804
Sprague Samuel John deceased Sept. 10th 1805 Ætat 25.
Sawyer Joseph Son of Moses Sawyer Senior died Octo. 2nd 1805 Ætat 25.
Sawyer Moses died the 3^d of October 1805, Ætat 72.
Sweetser William died at Sea Octo 4th 1805 Aged 21 years
100 Shearer Patience died at the house of Dr James Carter Sunday May 22, 1814.
Sawyer Cynthia daughter of Luther Sawyer and Zilpah his wife, died the first day of April A. D. 1815 aged 15 years.
Stevens Pardon died at the house of Dr. James Carter July 1, 1816.
Simmons Micah died Jany 30th. 1817, aged 83 years.
Simmons Mrs. [Nabby] relict of the late Mr Micah Simmons died June 23, 1817.
Safford Mrs Elizabeth wife of Mr Thomas Safford died March 11, 1818.
Stone Mrs. Anna wife of Jacob Stone died April 12, 1818.
Stearns Daniel, died June 30 1818.
Stone Betsy daughter of Jacob Stone & Anna his wife died Sept 30 1813.

1821	Sawyer Amos Senior died June 13, 1821, Æ 68.
1822	Sargent John died April 1822.
	Sawyer Mrs. [Prudence] wife of Amos Sawyer, 2nd, died Octo. 11, 1822.
	Sawyer Major Eben died Octo. 23 1822, aged 25.

101 Sweetser Jacob died Jan. 23 1823, Æ. 77.
Sawyer Luther died Sep 2 1824. Juror's verdict Insanity!
Sargent Miss [Susan] died at the house of Mr Jonathan Buttrick Sept. 4 1824.
Sawyer Capt Ezra son of Moses. & Betty Sawyer died Jany 18, 1825, aged 40.
Stearns Eli died March 7th 1825 aged 67.
Safford Thomas, died June 20 1825. Insanity!
Solindine John Junr. died Nov 4 1825 at the Pauper Establishment.
Solindine Julia Ann daughter of Manasah & Deborah Solindine died Sep 1825
Sawyer James son of Thomas Sawyer died at the house of his Uncle Amos Sawyer, January 8th. 1827.
Sawyer Sarah Elizabeth, daughter of Charles Sawyer, died April 22nd, 1827, aged 3 yrs, 7 mo. 29 d.
Stevenson Lydia daughter of Martin Stevenson died August 5th. 1827.
Solindine Deborah wife of Manassah Solindine died Novr. 8th, 1827.
Mary Stearns widow of the late Eli Stearns died May 24, 1828
Sawyer Thomas died at the pauper house March 18 1829 aged sixty four.
Sawyer Franklin, Son of Henry Sawyer died July 2, 1829.
102 Sawyer Lucy Ann daughter of Silas & Sarah Sawyer died October 28, 1829.
Stone Jacob Jr Son of Jacob Stone died Octo 9, 1830 aged 27 years.
Seaver Cyrus Son of Joseph Seaver died Octo. 9 1830
Sargeant Seth died Novr 28, 1830, aged 78.
Safford Polly wife of George Safford died Feby. 19, 1831.
Sawyer Moses died March 12, in the 67th year of his age. 1831
Sawyer Charles Francis Son of Charles & Eliza Sawyer died May 12th 1831.
Sawyer Peter died June 2 1831.
Sawyer Martha daughter of Charles & Eliza Sawyer died November 28th 1831.
Sawyer Elmirick Son of the late Peter Sawyer died January 16, 1832.
Studley Consider a revolutionary pensioner died Dec 28, 1832.
Sawyer Sarah Elizabeth daughter of Charles & Eliza Sawyer died Sep 16 1832.
Sawyer Ezra son of the late Peter Sawyer died August 27, 1833, aged 19 years
1834 Shepard Thomas W. Son of Thomas W. Shepard Æ 26. mo. died Feb. 26, 1834
    Stearns Deborah Relict of the late Mr Daniel Stearns died October [10] 1834
    Severy John a Revolutionary pensioner died at the house of Winsor Barnard Sep. 10, 1834 aged 82. years.
103 Smith Widow died Nov. 26, 1834, at the house of Samuel Jewett.
Sawyer Evelina daughter of the late Peter Sawyer died at the house of Capt Asahel Harris, June 23, 1835, aged 26 years.
Smith Moses Esquire, died June 26, 1835, aged 58 yrs.
1836 Tamher Stone daughter of Jacob & Anne Stone died May 19th 1836, aged 20 yrs 4 mo 18 days
    Abel Stone son of Jacob & Anne Stone died at Woonsocket Falls R I aged 30 years [June 11, 1836.]
1838 Mrs Margaret Sweetser, Widow of the late Mr Jacob Sweetser died July 9th 1838 aged 85 years
"   Ruth Sawyer died at the poor house August 16, 1838 Aged 93 yrs
"   Sarah Louisa Stone Died March 6 1838 Daughter of James & Eliza Stone Aged two days
"   Henry Oliver Sawyer Son of America & Lucy H. Sawyer died March 24, 1835.
"   Nelson Spaulding died Oct. 16, 1838 Aged 14 yrs
1840 A Son of Emeline Sawyer Died March 10th aged 7 months.
1839 Mr Martin Stephenson Died
"   Mr Sampson Died
1840 Miss Margaret Sweetser died March 6 Aged 53 years.
104 Thompson William Graves Son of Mr Benjamin Thompson & his wife died 26. Sep 1805
Thompson Caroline daughter of Benjamin Thompson and [Elizabeth] his wife died Dec 13, 1811.
Thurston Sally daughter of Silas Thurston, deceased Sep. 21, 1812.

Thurston Peter, died Dec. 22, 1812 aged 73.
Townshend Richard died at the house of his son Robert Townshend Nov. 28th 1814.
Townshend John died Sunday morning July 2, 1815   Jury's Verdict, Insanity.
Thurston Gates died Feby. 12, 1816 aged 51.
Thompson Benjamin died October 19th 1817.
Thompson Abigail daughter of the late Mr Benjamin Thompson died at the house of David Poignand April 18 1820.
Tower Milecent wife of Capt Asahel Tower died Sept. 20, 1820, Æ 60.
1821   Thurston Polly wife of Capt John Thurston died Sept. 6, 1821.
Townshend Betsy died Dec. 23, 1821.
1822.   Townshend Henry son of Robt Townshend died in Boston Nov. 21, 1822.
105   Thomas, Mrs Nancy, died June 19, 1799 at the house of Henry Haskell.
Tenny, daughter of Jon^a Tenny dec^d Sept. 15, 1800.
Thurston Rebecca wife of John Thurston: deceased May 9th, 1801.
Tenny Rebecca died August, 16, 1802, aged 81.
Tooker William died Nov. 17. 1802
Thurston Abel [Atherton] Son of Gates & Betsy Thurston died April 17th 1803.
Tyler William of Boston died at the house of Mr Jeremiah Ballard's Saturday night the 9th March 1805.
Thurston Sally wife of Silas Thurston died Mar. 12th 1805
Thompson William Graves, Son of Benjamin and Elizabeth Thompson died Sept. 25th 1805.
Thurston Samuel died March 26th. 1806.
Taft Mary died Feby. 10th 1808 aged 73 years.
Thurston Michel wife of Silas Thurston died April 24th 1808.
Thomas Mary wife of Joshua Thomas died May 27th 1808, aged 68 years.
Thurston Priscilla relict of the late Mr Samuel Thurston died Nov. the 8th 1811 aged 83.
106   Thurston an infant of Silas Thurston jun died Mar 21, 1823.
Thomas Mrs. Wife of Joshua Thomas died Nov 22nd 1823, 2nd wife aged 72.
Thurston Peter died Dec 9th 1824 Æ 56.
Tidd Joel, died at the house of his brother July 20, 1825, aged 40.
Townshend Widow of John Townshend died December 14, 1825.
Townshend Elvira daughter of the late John Townshend and Ruth Townshend deceased, died January 7, 1826.
Tindy Cuff a blackman a Revolutionary Pensioner, died January 7, 1826.
Townshend Elizabeth wife of Robert Townshend died July 11 1826.
Townshend Robert died Sept. 2, 1826.
Thurston Lucy, wife of John Thurston Jun. died July 2nd. 1827.
Mrs [Sarah] Todd. Widow of the late Mr John Todd died at the house of Mr Robert Phelps, July 4, 1829.
Thurston Thomas son of Capt John Thurston, died Dec. 14 1830.
Thurston Miss Lucy, daughter of Capt John Thurston died Jany 17th 1831.
107   Thomas Joshua died February 4, 1831, aged 86.
Thurston Dorothy, relict of the late Peter Thurston Senior, died at the house of Saml W. Flagg. February 16, 1831 Aged 92 years 5 mo. 10 days.
Thayer Miss Sally Toppan daughter of the Rev^d Dr Nathl Thayer died Dec. 20, 1831.
Thurston Sally relict of the late Peter Thurston Junior died January 20 1832 aged 55.
Thomas Rebecca, relict of the late Mr Joshua Thomas died Feby 1832
Thurston Charles, son of Capt John Thurston, died November 4, 1832.
Thurston Josephine daughter of John G Thurston and Harriet Thurston died October 15 1832
1833   Tower Capt. Asahel died Aug. 3. 1833 aged 73.
Thayer Miss Abigail daughter of Revd Doctor Thayer died Dec. 11, 1834 aged 22 years.

*   *   *   *   *

Townshend Mrs Almira Wife of Warren Townshend died Feby. 12, 1835.
Toppan Miss [Elizabeth G.] died at the house of Rev^d. Dr Thayer March 17, 1835.

BOOK SECOND.

Tyler Mrs [Eliza H.] Wife of Benjamin Tyler, died May 15. 1835.
108 Thurston Mary Ann daughter of John Thurston Jr. died Nov. 27, 1835, aged 18.
1838 Thurston, Capt John, a Revolutionary Pensioner, died November 9th Aged 84 yrs
1839 Mrs Mary Tyler Wife of Benj Tyler Died March 19 1839 Aged 36 Years
1840 Thayer, Rev^d. Nathaniel D. D., minister of the Church and Society in this Town for more than forty seven years; died after a sudden illness of three hours, at Rochester in the State of New York, while journeying for pleasure and improvement of his health to the falls of Niagara. His labors during the long period of his ministry in this place were devoted to the good of the people of his charge; and his death was sensibly felt and deeply lamented. Aged 71 years. June 23.
1840 Mr Silas Thurston, died March 23^d Aged 81 years.
1841 Russell Gates, Son of Wilder S. and Ann M. Thurston, Died April 17. 1841 aged one year
1842 Miss Martha Townshend Daughter of Mr William Townshend Died December 14, 1842, Aged 21. Consumption
1844 Mrs Elizabeth Tidd Died January 14, 1844 aged 88 yrs Influenza
1842 Mr Henry Thurston Died 30th Sept 1842, aged 50 Paralysis
" Lauriana S. Daughter of S. H. Turner June 19 1842 aged 3 yrs
109 Upton Phebe wife of Joseph Upton died June 11. 1812.
Vincent John Sullivan, a Negro, died the 23^d, March 1813, Servant of Capt B Lee.
Vose Mrs Ann A. wife of Peter T. Vose, and daughter of the late Hon. John Sprague died Sept. 10, 1834, age 58
1840 Vose Francis Henry, Son of Peter T. Vose.
1843 Mrs Hannah W. Upton aged 80. Palsy Died Jany 30, 1843.
110 Willard Stedman Son of William Willard died Aug. 27th 1803.
Wilder Mary Joslyn daughter of Saml Wilder 2^d died July 25 1804
Whetcomb Maria daughter of Josiah & Dolly Whetcomb Octo^r. 10th 1804.
Wyman Submit died Nov. 25th 1804 aged 73.
White Patience relict of the late Deacon Joseph White died Dec. 30th, 1804 Aged 80 years.
Willson Roxa died at the house of Dr James Carter, January the 15th 1805.
Whiting Sarah relict of the late Timothy Whiting, died May 24th, 1805, aged 67 Years.
White Levi Son of Ephraim & Betsy died at Sea in the Mediterranean Service.
Wyman Patty [Martha Joslyn] wife of Capt. Benjamin Wyman died May 4th 1806 Age 40
White Deacon Joseph, died June 30th A. D. 1806 aged 56
Warner Samuel died at the house of Ebenezer Warner Sept. 6th 1807.
Willard Mary relict of the late Col. Abijah Willard died Dec 15th 1807, aged 79 years.
Wilder Frederick Son of Aaron Wilder and Hannah his wife died May 12th, 1806.
Whittemore [Asa] Dunbar Son of Nathaniel Whittemore died Feb. 22^d, 1808, aged 19 years. [Feb. 21, Æ. 23 yrs. 6 m. *See epitaph.*]
Willard Martha wife of Paul Willard died May 22nd, 1808.
Whittemore [Sarah] wife of Nathaniel Whittemore, deceased March 17th 1809.
Wilder Gardner deceased Nov. 25th 1809.
111 White, Capt. John, died Feby. 21, 1797, aged 83 years.
Whittemore [Lydia], wife of Natha^l Whittemore died June 2^d. 1797.
Whiting, Abigail wife of Timothy Whiting Jun deceased Octr. 1. 1798.
Whiting, Joseph, son of Timothy Whiting jun & Abigail his late wife, deceased March 19. 1799.
Whiting Polly, daughter of Timothy Whiting jun & Abigail his late wife, deceased April 7th, 1799.
Whiting, Timothy, died July 12th, 1799.
Willard, Betsy daughter of Simon Willard died Apr: 19 1799.
Woods, Jotham, died Decr 9, 1799.
Wilder, Eunice, wife of Moses Wilder died July 31st, 1800

Ward Samuel Jr. son of Samuel & Dolly Ward died Novr. 29, 1800, Æ 31.
White Prudence wife of Capt Nath White died Feb. 2nd 1802.
Wheelock Martha died May 12th, 1802, Ætatis 94.
Whitney Jonathan died Nov 20th 1802, 66
White Sophia wife of Jno White jun died Æ 32 Apr. 12th 1803.
Peter Willard Son of Amasa & Fanny Willard died August 20
Wilder John died Octo. 4th 1803, son of the late Dea. D. Wilder
Willard Mary died Octo. 4 1803.
Willard Sarah wife of Willm. Willard died June 2^d, 1803.
112 Wilder Betsy wife of Samuel Wilder 2^d. died May 22nd 1810. Æ 38 y. 1 mo, 18 d.
Wilder Malinda daughter of Samuel Wilder 2^d and Betsy Wilder died Augt. 13 1810.
Whiting John, Col. of the 5th Regiment of U. S. Infantry, died at the City of Washington, the 4th, Sept. 1810, Æ 50.
Wilder Anthony Son of Samuel Wilder 2^d died Nov. 20 1810.
Wilder Holman son of Luke Wilder and Mary his wife died January 20th 1807.
Willard Sarah daughter of Salmon and Rachel Willard died Octo 26th 1810.
Wilder Martha relict of the late Deacon David Wilder died November the 6th, 1811, aged 94.
Willard Dexter Son of Paul Willard and Martha his wife, 6th July 1810, died.
Worcester Samuel died Apr. 16 1812
White John died June 8 1812.
Wright Sarah, died at the house of Doctor James Carter Jany. 21. 1813, A Town pauper.
Wilder Moses died March 30. 1814.
Wilder Aaron died April 11, 1814.
Wilder Betty wife of Stephen Wilder died July 14, 1814, aged 74.
113 Wilder Polly died at the house of Mr Luke Wilder the 18th day of August A. D. 1814.
Wilder Martha wife of Samuel Wilder died Nov. 3, 1814 aged 70 years.
Whipple Nathan died at the house of Mr John Wilder the 21st. December 1814
Whipple Abigail relict of the late Nathan Whipple, died at the house of Mr John Wilder March 12th. 1815.

* * * *

Wilder Sally wife of John Wilder died November 28th 1815.
Willard Fanny wife of Amasa Willard died July 8, 1812.
Wilder William died the 20. day of March Anno Domini 1816, Æ 62.
Willard Merrick died at the house of Mr John Goodwin April 2, 1816.
Warner Asa died Dec 30 1816.
Whiting Julia daughter of the late John Whiting Esq. died July 3. 1817.
Whitney Lucy relict of the late Jonathan Whitney died October 11 1817.
114 Willard Charles, son of Benja & Sally Willard died Sep. 19, 1812.
Willard Paul, Esqr. died August 2^d 1817.
Whiting Mary Phelps, daughter of Timothy and Lydia Whiting died March 11 1818.
Warner Sally, daughter of Nathaniel and Polly Warner died March 24, 1818.
Wilder Prescott, son of Mr Jonathan Wilder died July 3. 1818.
Wilder Ephraim Rand, son of Luke Wilder died Sep. 12, 1818.
Wheeler Amos Augustus, son of Amos Wheeler and Prudence his wife, died May 16, 1818.
Willard Miss Lucia, daughter of the late Paul Willard Esq died Nov. 14, 1818.
Ward Mrs Dolly, wife of Saml. Ward Esq. died Dec 31, 1818, aged 73.
Wilder Oliver, Son of Titus Wilder Jun. & Eunice his Wife, died Feby. 11. 1819.

* * * * *

Willard Mary Conant daughter of Benjamin and Sally Willard died March 16 1818.
Willard Lucy, wife of Mr William Willard died June 27th, 1819.
Whittemore Mary Moors daughter of Nathl. Whittemore Jun & Polly his wife died June 16 1819.
115 Wilder Mrs. Sarah relict of the late Mr Levi Wilder, died August 31, 1819 Æ. 66.

Wilder Otis, Son of the late James Wilder died the house of Major Locke Jany 23. 1820.
Worster Mary died Octo 14, 1815 } Children of Sam¹ Worster.
Worster Eliza died June 20, 1818 }
Wilder Stephen died Octo 9ᵗʰ 1820.
Wares Polly died Nov. 28. 1820.
1821 Willard John died May 24 1821.
1822 Whittemore Nathaniel died Jany 3 1822.
     Wilder Sophia wife of Mr Elijah Wilder died June 15. 1822.
     Wales Elizabeth wife of Deacon Joseph Wales, died August 19, 1822.
     Wilder Manassah died Novʳ. 4, 1822.
1823 Whitney Reuben, of Harvard, a Deputy Sheriff, died suddenly at the house of the Widow of Geo Phelps, the 14ᵗʰ Feb. 1823, aged 64.
Wheeler Roxanna daughter of Amos & Prudence Wheeler, died April 30, 1822.
Wetherbee Roxanna Wife of Salathiel Wetherbee, died March 10 1823.
Whitney Mrs. Abigail H. wife of Mr Abel Whitney of Boston died at the house of her Father Robert Townshend Sep 24, 1823.
White Mrs [Lydia] relict of Capt John White died Sep. 26 1823.
116 Wilder Almira wife of Elijah Wilder died Feb. 6, 1824.
Whiting Newell Son of Paul Whiting died Octo 16, 1824.
Wilder Samuel died Octo. 22ⁿᵈ 1824 Aged 81.
Willard Simon died January 9 1825 Aged 97 y. 3 mo. 11 D.
White Joseph C. Son of Abel White was Killed by a Tree which fell on him,— Aged 15.
   *   *   *   *   *

Willard Sarah daughter of Benja. Willard & Sally his wife died Aug 15 1821.
Wilder Lucene wife of Ebenʳ. Wilder died June 25, 1825.
Wilder Lydia wife of Daniel Wilder died July 17. 1825.
Weld William G. Capt. departed this life this 14ᵗʰ day of September 1825 aged –
Whiting Timothy Esqʳ. a Revolutionary Officer, died January 13, 1826 aged 67.
Wilder Horace Son of Jacob Wilder died Jany 31 1826.
Wilder Fredrick Son of Jonathan Wilder, died at Northampton Feb. 5, 1826, Aged 22,—a bright Schollar a graduate of Harvard College.
117 Whitwell Samuel died at the house of Major Jonathan Locke, March 12ᵗʰ 1826 Æ. 27.
Wilder Emily daughter of Elisha & Emily Wilder died 2ⁿᵈ June 1825.
Ward Samuel Esquire, died August 14ᵗʰ, 1826. Aged 87.
Wilder Elijah died Nov. 9, 1826, Aged 42.
Wilder Ruth wife of Jonathan Wilder, died Novʳ: 19, 1826, aged 69.
Whitney son of Shadrach Whitney died Nov: 21, 1826.
Wyman Benjamin Esquire, died Dec: 30 1826.
Wilder Samuel 2 died Nov: 13, 1827, aged 81.
   *   *   *   *   *

White Lucy daughter of Abel White died June 1829.
Wilder Mrs Emily wife of Elisha Wilder died Novʳ. 5ᵗʰ 1830.
Wilson Miss Hannah died at the house of Dr Goodrich June 2, 1831.
Whittemore Nathaniel son of Nathaniel Whittemore, died Dec. 14ᵗʰ, 1831 aged 14.
118 Wilder Mr. Calvin died April 5ᵗʰ 1832 aged 60 years.
Wilder Rebecca, daughter of Mr John Wilder, died April 25, 1832 aged 16 years.
Warner Mrs. [Jane] widow of the late Mr. Asa Warner, died Sept. 2 1832.
   *   *   *

1833. Wilder Titus Jun. Died Dec. 13 1833, aged 55
1834 Whitney Elijah died at the house of the Widow Stearns, January 5, 1834.
     Warner Nathan died March 25, 1834
     Whittemore Amelia, wife of Mr Nath¹. Whittemore died April 18, 1834.
     Walton George, died July 7. 1834 at the house of Mr Davis Whitman's.
     Wyman Martha Thayer daughter of the late Benjamin Wyman Esq. died Sept. 12, [13th, family record] 1834, aged 23, yrs
     Wilder James Jun. died Dec. 22ⁿᵈ 1834 aged 40
Wilder Lydia wife of Josephus Wilder died at the house of her father Joseph Maynard January 23, 1835.

Worcester Molly died May 5, 1835 aged 88, of the South family of Shakers.
119 Wilder Mr Jonathan died Jany. 13th, 1835, aged 80 years 8 months & 23 days, a Revolutionary Pensioner.
1837 White, Francis Jones, died August 18th 1836
White Miss Sally, died January 28th 1837 aged 66 years, 2 mo & 4 days.
Wilder, Dea Joel died May 2d. 1837, aged 70 years
1838 Charlotte Otis, daughter of Snell, and Deborah R. Wade died April 8, 1838 aged 3½ years
1837 Wilder, Titus, a Revolutionary pensioner died at the poor house April 10th 1837
1838 Tryphena Wilder Died March 3d Aged 79 years
Miss Prudence Rugg Died March 16th Aged 77
1839 Wilder, Mrs Maria S. died February 9 1839 Aged 26 yrs
" A Daughter of Thomas Wellington Died June 1 1839 aged 5 years
" Amos White Died August 14 1839 aged 43 years
" A Son of Amos Wyman Died October 1 1839 aged 1 year
" Mr John Willard Died at the Alms House November 22 1839 Aged — years.
120 " Mr Baxter Wood Died December 25 1839 Aged 48 Years
" A Daughter of Capt Salmon Willard Died —
1840 Mr Daniel Wilder, Died May 28th Aged 60 years
1841 A Child of Mrs Williams (Irish) Died February 18, 1841, Aged 1 year.
" An Infant Child [Harriet E.] of Charles L. Wilder Died July 31 1841 Aged one month.
" Samuel B. Wilder Son of the late Samuel Wilder of Sterling Aged 15 yrs Died August 13, 1841.
" Capt Joseph Wilder Died August 23, 1841 Aged 55 years
1842 Mr Ephraim Whitney Died Sept 6th 1842 Aged 62 yrs
1842 Mr Samuel Whitney Died April 12 1842 Aged 95 yrs
" George Wait, Son of Joel Wilder 2d died Novr 8. 1842 Aged 13 years
1843 Mrs Mary Wilder, [widow of Titus,] Died July 12, 1843 Aged 95 yrs Old age
1843 Edward, Son of Mr Volney Wilder of Boston, Aged 11 months died Aug 25 1843, Dysentary
1843 Francis, Son of Mr Volney Wilder of Boston, Died 20 Augt, Aged 11 months Dysentary
121 1842 Mrs Mary M. Wilder Wife of Mr Danl K. Wilder died Nov 24, 1842 aged 39. Consumption
1842 Mr Amasa Willard Died 10 Nov. Aged 70. Cancer
1842 Mrs Eliza Ann Wilson, wife of Col. John Wilson, died 14 July 1842, Consumption
1832 Maj Fabius Whiting. U. S. Army Died May 18, 1842 Aged 50.
1843 Deacon Saml F. White Died March 16, 1843 aged 50. Consumption
1843 Mrs Sarah Wilder Died 28 Jan. 1843 aged 86. Old age
1843 George W. Infant son of Charles J. Wilder Died 10 March 1843 aged 10 weeks Smothered
1844 Mrs Sophia P. Wilder Wife of Mr Joel Wilder died Feby 27. 1844 aged 64.
Wilder Harriet Ellen, Daughter of Charles L. Wilder died July 30, 1841
123 Mrs. [Abigail,] Zwier wife of Jacob Zwier died in December 1820.
Zwier Reuben Jun. died July 1822.
Zwier Ruben died Octo. 1822.

124 The following is a Record of the deaths which have happened among the People called Shakers, in their Village in Lancaster, handed in to the Town Clerks' office Feby 21, 1820, by their Elder Mr Brocklebank. Viz:

The Widow Prudence Warner,	Nov. 13 - 1792.
Ethan Phillips,	Nov. 19. 1792.
Widow Sarah Dodge -	Dec. 23. 1792.
Widow Lydia Kenney -	Feby. 29, 1794.
Deborah Lyon -	Sept. 30. 1794.
Joseph Marble -	Octo. 26, 1797.
Lucy Beckwith.	Dec, 29, 1797.

Anna Procter -	Sep. 30. 1798.
Widow Hannah Woodward -	Octo. 1. 1798.
Ebenezer Pratt -	July 1, 1798.
Sarah Larrabee -	Sep. 14, 1803.
Widow Sarah Wood -	March 15, 1806.
Anna Turner -	Sep. 7 1806.
Hannah Woodward Jun.	March 11, 1809.
Jonathan Cook.	March 11, 1809.
Betty Druse -	March 22, 1809.
Mary Monroe -	Dec 7, 1812.
Louis Hayward -	March 4, 1822.
Peletiah McIntire -	May 16. 1827
Phineas Pratt -	July 18, 1828 age 73.
Eleanor Peirce -	Nov. 17, 1828, 88
Moses Howard [or Hayward]	March 26, 1829, 85
Betty Priest -	August 16, 1830.
Ebenezer Osgood -	May 19, 1831.

1   LANCASTER RECORD OF BIRTHS, 1796-1843

Children's Names.	Parents.	When born.
Allen, Abel, son of	Samuel & Lucy Allen	Novr. 8th. 1796.
Samuel Allen son of	Same	Aug: 22, 1799.
Allen Delilah	Danl. and Rebecca Allen	May 23 1801
Allen Abel	Samuel & Lucy Allen	May 10th 1802.
Allen Lucy Kendall	Samuel & Lucy Allen	May 9th, 1805.
Allen Samuel	Saml & Lucy Allen	July 16, 1808.
Arnold Rebecca	Asa & Mary Arnold	Augt 25 1809.
Allen Sally	Samuel & Lucy Allen	March 2, 1812.
Alexander Rebecca	Nat. Alexander and Rebecca	July 25, 1811
Aspinwall Louisa Elizabeth,	Col. Thomas Aspinwall and Louisa Elizabeth his wife.	Feb. 1 1815.
Alexander Jonas	Nathl Alexander & Rebecca his wife	Apr. 9 1815.
Arnold James A.	Asa & Mary Arnold	Nov. 17, 1810
Arnold William	Same Parents	Octo 20 1812
Arnold Susan	Same Parents	Jany 22 1816
Allen James	John & Polly Allen	Nov 16, 1809.
Allen Mary	Cheney & Lois Allen	Jany — 1817.
Akeley Lucinda Elizabeth	Almus & Harriet Akeley	Feb. 20. 1822.
Arnold Charles	Asa & Mary Arnold	Nov. 30, 1819.
Arnold Mary Ann	Same Parents	Nov. 3. 1821.
Sophia an illegitimate of	Sophia Allen	Nov. 25, 1825
Arnold Caroline Marie	Asa & Mary Arnold	Mar 27 1825
Alexander Nathl.	Nathl & Rebecca Alexander	August 5 1821
Alexander Joseph N.	Same Parents	July 7th 1817
Adams Benj Wyman	Amos & Polly Adams	October 11, 1816.
Adams Amos Gilman	Same Parents	October 3 1820.
Adams Saml Gilman	Ditto.	Decem^r 21, 1822.
Adams Nathaniel	Ditto.	Augt 2 1825.
2 Arnold Daniel Woodward	Asa & Mary Arnold	Octob^r 1828.
Atherton Mary Dyer,	Charles Atherton & Annis,	May 12, 1834.
6 Sarah Adaline Barnes	John W. & Adaline Barnes	Aug. 22, 1836
George Abram	Same Parents	July 26, 1841
Ellen S. Brown	Thomas & Ann S. Brown	June 12, 1841
George Thomas Buttrick	Jonathan & Charlotte Buttrick	April 4 [3] 1842
Solon Francis Bigelow	Luke & Eliza Bigelow	Aug. 19, 1828
Cynthia Wilder Bigelow	Same Parents	Sept. 7, 1830
Eliza Jane Bigelow	Same Parents	Aug. 17, 1832
Theodore Francis Bigelow,	Same Parents. Born in Charlestown	July 12, 1834
Cornelia Asenath Bigelow	Same Parents	May 13, 1836
Mary Elizabeth Tyler Bigelow	Same Parents	Aug. 6, 1838

John Alanson Bigelow	Same Parents	Feby. 18, 1843
Warren Barnard	Jeremiah & Bilhah Barnard	Jany. 1, 1842
Sarah E. W. Burditt	Thomas. and Sarah E Burditt	Dec. 6. 1842
Burditt, Jerome Wayland	William & Sally Burditt	Oct. 10, 1843
Bennett Walter Franklin	Laban & Roxsey Bennett	Apl 30, 1843
Bridge Franklin Thayer	Charles & Sophia Bridge Born at Lowell Nov[r] 12, 1842
7 William Roswell	Roswell and Mary S. Bourne his wife born Octo. 14 1832.
Henry Willard	" " " " "	" Sept. 7, 1834.
Bowman Henry	Simeon & Hannah Bowman	Sept. 9, 1834
1835 Butler Frederick Austin	Abel & Sally Butler.	March 11, 1834
Bridge George Whiting.	Charles & Sophia Bridge	Feby 3. 1834
Balcom Rebecca Jane	Thadeus & Rebecca Balcom.	Mar. 21, 1835.
Burbank Hosea Hurlburt,	Sam[l]. W. & Hannah Burbank	Octo 13 1833.
Bancroft Mary Elizabeth	Tarbel & Lucinda	Octo. 13, 1835
1826 Bancroft Charles Lowell	Tarbel & Lucinda Bancroft	Nov. 13, 1826.
Brigham Harriet Augusta	Franklin Brigham & Ann	Sept. 2 1835.
Burditt John Maffit	John Burditt Jr & Persis	Sept. 5, 1835.
Burditt Franklin Carpenter	John Burditt & Sally	Octo 8, 1835.
Burditt William Draper	William & Sally Burditt	Feb 26, 1835.
Barrett Elisha	Elias & Sarah Barrett	June 2, 1825
Barrett Nathan E.	Same Same	Jany. 7, 1828
Bride James Henry	Wilson & Betsey Bride	Dec 24, 1832
Butler Sidney Smith	Benj[a] & Martha P. Butler	Aug. 9, 1835
Billings Joseph Fife	Josiah Billings	March 31, 1826.
Barnard Lucy	Winsor & Phebee Barnard	Octo. 11, 1835.
Bourne Mary Ann	Roswell & Mary S. Bourne	Sept 21. 1835
1837 Burditt Henry Hiland	William & Sally Burditt	Aug 2[d], 1836
Burbank Eliza Jane	Samuel W & Hannah Burbank	April 17, 1836
Bowman Samuel M.	Simeon & Hannah Bowman	Nov. 9, 1836
Bridge Ellen Augusta	Charles & Sophia W Bridge	May 18, 1836
Bridge William Augustus	John & Catharine M Bridge	Aug 6, 1835
Bridge John Henry	Same parents	May 7, 1837
Bridge Mary Jane	Charles & Sophia W. Bridge	Apl 16, 1838
Burditt Thomas E.	Thomas & Sarah E Burditt	June 8. 1839
Bridge Caroline Thayer	Charles & Sophia Bridge Born at Lowell Feby 26, 1840
Burditt Charles A.	Thomas & Sarah E Burditt	Aug. 1, 1841
8 Bennett Dolly	Thomas Jur & Isabella Bennett	Feb. 27 1793.
Bennett John	Same Parents	Mar 29 1795
Bennett Dolly	Same Parents	Mar 8th 1797,
Bennett Sarah	Same Parents	Sep 15 1799
Bennett John 2	Same Parents	Aug 26 1802
Bennett Lucinda	Same Parents	July 25 1805
Bennett Henry	Same Parents	July 11 1807
Bennett Mary B.	Same Parents	Octo 28 1809
Ballard Elizabeth Ann,	Eliphaz & Nancy Ballard	Feb 5th 1810
Bridge Charles Henry	Charles & Susannah Bridge	April 6 1810.
Barrett Samuel Arnold	Sam[l] & Eleanor Barrett	Aug. 6 1805
Barrett Reuben	Same Parents	April 10 1807
Barrett George Campbell	Same	May 28 1809.
Brown Ruth	John & Polly Brown,	July 26th, 1810.
Baldwin Lucy Hosley	Oliver & Lucy Baldwin	July 13 1811.
Bennett Nancy	Thomas Jr & Isabella Bennett	Aug 18 1811
Barrett Daniel Burbank	Sam[l] & Mehit[ble] Burbank	Aug. 24, 1811
Bennett Lucy Ann	Elias & Sarah Bennett	Dec. 13 1809
Bennett James Dexter	Same Parents	Nov. 1 1811
Buttrick Jane	Jonathan & Jane Buttrick	Nov 5, 1811
Ballard James	Eliphaz & Anna Ballard	Dec 21 1811
Burditt William	Nathan & Margarett Burditt,	Feb. 3 1811
Bridge Nancy	Josiah & Eirene Bridge	April 20 1812
Bennett Lydia	Tho[s] Bennett Jr & Elizabeth	Octo. — 1813
Buttrick Charles	Asa & Hannah Buttrick	June 12 1813
Bridge Sarah	Josiah & Eirene Bridge	Jany. 22 1814

Name	Parents	Date
Ballard Josiah	Eliphaz & Anna Ballard	Apr. 2 1814
9 Ballard, Lucy	Thomas & Abigail Ballard	Octr. 27. 1796.
Bennett, Nancy	Nathan & Eunice Bennett	Decr. 9th, 1796.
Bridge, Mary Nowell	William & Abigail Bridge	Octr 12, 1796
*	*	*
Bridge, Abigail	W^m & Abigail Bridge	June 19 1798
Ballard, Abigail	Thomas & Abigail Ballard	Octr 12th. 1798
Ballard, Abigail	Thomas & Abigail Ballard	Aug: 15th 1800
Brigham Mary-ann	Jabez & Sophia Brigham	Dec 29 1801
Bennett Harriot	Nathan Bennett & Eunice his wife	July 25 1801
Baldwin Sarah	Oliver & Lucy Baldwin	Aug 15 1801
Brigham Francis	Jabez & Sophia Brigham	Feb 21 1800
Ballard Thomas	Thomas & Abigail Ballard	Feb. 12th, 1803.
Butler Benjamin	Benjamin & Polly Butler	Mar. 29 1804
Ballard Thomas	Thomas & Abigail Ballard	Nov 17 1804
Blanchard William	William & Eliza^h Blanchard	Sep. 2 1805.
Buttrick Caroline	Horatio G. Buttrick & Nancy	Dec 4 1805
Ballard Martha	Thomas & Abigail Ballard	Feb. 28 1807.
Buffum Sampson Wilder	Son of Jedediah & Nancy Buffum	Aug 16 1807
Blanchard Elizabeth	Willm. & Elizabeth Blanchard	Feby 7th 1807
Bridge Martha Irene	Josiah & Irene Bridge	July 11 1808.
Bennett Charles	Elisha & Nancy Bennett	July 15 1802
Baldwin Henry	Oliver & Lucy Baldwin	Nov 9 1806
Bridge Eliza	William & Abigail Bridge	June 30 1800
Bridge Solomon	Same Parents	June 5. 1802.
Bridge Joseph	Same Parents	Augt. 1 1804
Bridge John	Same Parents	Jany 14 1806
Ballard Josiah Richardson	Thos. & Abigail Ballard.	Novr 10th 1809
Bridge Asarelah Morse	Josiah & Eirene Bridge	Jany 21 1810.
Buttrick Nancy Whitney	Horatio G Buttrick	Feby — 1810
10 Buttrick Jonathan,	Jon^a. & Jane Buttrick	Aug. 7. 1813.
Brown Julia	Oliver & Kezia Brown	Octo 26 1808
Brown Susan	Same Parents	Octo 21 1810
Brown Silas Law	Same Parents	Dec. 30 1812.
Brown Asaph	Same Parents	Dec. 15, 1814
Twins *died*		Jany 29 1815.
Burditt Eliza	Bridge Josiah & Irene	Dec. 18. 1808
Burditt Nathan	Nathan & Margaret Burditt	May 16, 1813
Burditt Thomas	Same Parents	May 4 1815
Bragg Ebenezer Gott	Ebenezer & Martha Bragg	April 4. 1815.
Bridge Mary Elizabeth	Charles Bridge 2 & Susan	Mar 5, 1815
Bigelow Haskell Derby Pickman	Charles & Sarah Bigelow	Jany. 15, 1816.
Butler David	Benj^a. & Polly Butler	Sep. 4, 1805
Butler Mary	Same Parents	Mar 4 1808
Butler Rachel	Same Parents	July 8 1810
Butler Anne	Same Parents	May 12, 1812
Bridge Josiah	Josiah & Eirene Bridge	May 4, 1816
Ballard Eliphaz	Eliphaz & Nancy Ballard,	April 13, 1816
Burpee Martin Jun	Martin & Lydia Burpee,	Dec. 31 1815
Buttrick Hariot Parker	Asa Buttrick & Hannah,	Aug 7 1815.
Buttrick John Whitman	Jonathan & Jane Buttrick	Dec 10, 1815.
Brown Mary Blood	Oliver & Kezia Brown	Feby 27 1817.
Bennett Elias Dexter	Elias & Sally Bennett	April 6 1814
Bennett Charles	Same Parents	July 5, 1816
Barrett Mary	Moses & Sarah Barrett	Nov 23 1815
11		
Buttrick Hannah Elizabeth	Jonathan Buttrick & Jane his wife	Jany. 23, 1818.
[Buttrick, Thomas Porter.	" " " "	Jany. 10, 1822.]
Bragg Charles Carter	Eben^r. & Martha Bragg	Jany 12, 1818.
Bridge Sarah	Josiah Bridge & Eirene his wife	July 19, 1818.
Ballard Rebecca	Eliphaz and Anna Ballard	May 28 1818
Barrett Sarah	Asa Barrett & Sally	Sep. 20, 1818

Bennett Aaron Sawyer	Elias and Sally Bennett,	Jany 25 1820
1820. Burditt Julia Ann	John Burditt & Sarah	Aug 18, 1814
Burditt Adeline	Same Parents	Jany. 23, 1816
Burdit James	Same Parents	July 5, 1818
1821. Bridge W^m. Frederic	Josiah & Eirene Bridge	Feb. 15 1821.
Burpee John	Martin & Betsy Burpee	Jany 1, 1821.
Bancroft Andrew	Tarbel Bancroft	Aug. 2. 1821.
1822. Burditt Martha Ann	John Burditt & Sarah	Mar 19, 1820
Burditt Thos. Marshall	Same Parents	Nov 30 1821.
1823. Ballard Asa Whetcomb	Luther Ballard & Rebecca	Dec 15, 1822
Burditt Christopher Columbus	Nathan & Margaret Burditt	Feb 28, 1817
Burditt George Washington	Same Parents	Feb 17, 1819
Burditt Mary Ann	Same Parents	Mar 31. 1821
Bartlett Emory Adam	John Bartlett & Mary,	Apr 17, 1822.
Burbank Susan Eliza	Saml. W. Burbank & Hannah	Sep. 2, 1822.
Billings Lydia Whitney	Josiah & Hannah Billings	Sep 1. 1816
Billings Martha Fessenden	Same Parents	July 16, 1818
Billings Josiah	Same Parents	Aug. 14. 1820
Bragg Martha Ann Relief	Eben^r & Martha Bragg	July 10, 1820
Billings Luther	Josiah & Hannah Billings, born in Groton Octo. 18, 1812.	
Billings Horace	Same Parents born in Groton May 27, 1814.	
Bridge Abigail Allen	Josiah & Eirene Bridge	June 30, 1823.
Burditt Fredric William	John & Sarah Burditt	Sep 29 1823.
12 Bowman Henry	Simeon Bowman & Hannah	April 26, 1830.
Brigham Sarah Ann	Franklin & Ann Brigham	Jenuary 7 1831.
Brigham Franklin	Jabez Brigham & Dandridge Hunt	July 19, 1805.
Barnes Sabra	Ira & Abby Barnes	April 8, 1831.
Ballard Louisa Christmas	Henry & Abigail Ballard	June 12 1830
Bennett Clorinda	Otis & Clorinda Bennett	Sep. 11. 1831.
Barnes Betsey Maria	Artemas & Nancy Barnes	Augt 21, 1826
Barnes Nancy Jane	Same Parents	Feby 14 1828
Burbank Sarah Maria	Saml W Burbank & Hannah	Feb 21, 1826
" Hannah Elizabeth	Same Parents	April 5. 1828.
" George Walton	Same "	Nov. 17 1829.
" Lucy Ann	Same "	April 4 1831.
Barnard William	Winsor & Phebe Barnard	March 17, 1814.
" Caleb	Same Parents	July 29, 1816.
" Benajah	Same "	Nov. 15, 1817.
Bridge Sophia	Charles & Sophia Bridge	April 13, 1830
Bridge James William	Same Parents	Feb. 20 1832.
Barnes Sarah Ellen	Artemas & Nancy Barnes	April 15 1832
Brigham Almira Low	Franklin & Ann Brigham	April 27 1832.
1833. Brigham Francis Low	Same Parents	July 22 1833.
Butler Martha	Joseph & Mary Butler	April 19, 1821
Butler Stephen	Same Parents	Jany 4, 1823
Butler Almira	Same Do,	Sept 9 1824
Butler Granville	Same Do,	March 19 1820.
Butler Margarett	Same Do,	July 8, 1827.
Butler Amos Joseph	Same Do,	April 1 1829
Butler May	Same Do,	May 7 1825
Ball Ephraim Edward	Nathan & Abigail Ball	March 31, 1833.
Burditt Sarah Augusta	William Burditt & Sally	Sep 20 1832.
Burditt Louisa Jane	John Burditt Jr & Persis	Aug. 14 1833.
Butler Hamilton Erving	Amos & Mary Butler	May 9. 1817
Barrett Lucy	Joseph & Lucy Barrett	Nov 26. 1820
13 Bigelow Lucius Aurelius	Luke Bigelow & Eliza	Dec 7. 1823.
Brown Moses, an illegitimate Child of Betty Brown		Nov. 9. 1824
1825. Bigelow Jane Eliza	Luke Bigelow & Eliza	Sept. 4 1825.
Bruce Christopher	Hollis & Jerusha Bruce	Aug. 10 1815
Bruce Sarah	Same Parents	Nov. 11 1817
Bruce Hollis	Ditto do.	May 7 1823
Bruce Abigail	Ditto do	June 29, 1825

Barrett Sam¹ Prescott	Moses and Sarah	April 6, 1818
Barrett Moses	Same Parents	Feb. 26 1820
Bowman George	Simeon & Hannah Bowman	May 27 1825
Barnes Wᵐ. Meriam	Artemas & Nancy Barnes	Jany. 3 1825.
Butler George Washington	Abel & Sally Butler	Apr. 10, 1826.
Bragg Horatio Carter	Ebenʳ & Martha Bragg	Aug 9. 1825
Ballard Sarah Elizabeth	Henry & Abigail Ballard	July 17 1826.
Butler Wᵐ. Bartlett	Abel & Sally Butler	June 22. 1827.
Burditt Alfred Augustus	Nathan & Margarett Burditt	June 20 1827
Bragg Abigail Ann	Joseph Maynard	Feb 25, 1814
Bragg George Franklin	Same Parents	Dec 28, 1825
*	* *	*
Butler Nancy	Sam¹ Butler	March 4 1807.
Butler Charles	Same Parents	March 2 1810
Butler Sally	Ditto.	Jany 27 1813
Butler Miranda	Ditto.	May 15 1814
Butler Rufus	Ditto.	Dec. 9 1817.
Butler Merrick	Ditto.	Apr 9ᵗʰ 1820
Butler Sherman	Ditto.	Mar. 19 1822
Butler Albert	Ditto.	Apr 1824
Butler Harriet	Ditto.	Feb 15 1827.
Burditt Francis Wentworth	Jnº & Sara Burditt	April 15, 1828.
Bowman Charles	Simeon & Hannah Bowman	Octo 23. 1828
Ballard Thirza	Henry & Abigail Ballard	May 13 1828
14		
Chandler Wᵐ. Dexter	Benjᵃ Chandler & Elizabeth Chandler	June 17 1805.
Chandler Eliza Ansart	Same Parents	April — 1808.
Chandler Mary Augusta	Same Parents	Mar 1. 1810
Chandler Sarah Ann Goodwin	Same Parents	—— 1812
Chandler James	Same Parents	Octo 8 1815.
Carter Solomon	Solomon and Elizabeth Carter	Jany. 19, 1816.
Cook Geo. Washington,	Aaron & Elizabeth Cook.	Nov. 15, 1798.
Elizabeth Cook	Same Parents	Dec. 15, 1796.
Cook Caroline	Same Parents	Jany 3 1804
Cook Aaron Jun	Same Parents	May 1 1806
Cook James [Madison]	Same Parents	March 13 1809
Cook Horatio Nelson	Same Parents	March 9 1811
Cook Lucia	Same Parents	March 18 1813.
Carter Martha	Solomon & Elizʰ Carter	Octo 22 1817.
Carter Betsy Thurston	Jno. Carter 2ᵈ & Elizabeth	Octo 2 1817.
Chandler Benjamin	Benjᵃ. Chandler & Elizabeth	Dec — 1816.
Childs James	Isaac Childs & Polly	Sep 9, 1818.
Carter William Henry	Solomon and Elizabeth Carter	Aug. 7, 1819.
Chase Moses	Moses Chace & Ruth	Dec. 2. 1817.
Chase Ruth	Same Parents	Nov. 17, 1819.
Childs Mary	Isaac & Polly Childs	Nov 11 1820.
1821. Carter Sarah Carter	Calvin & Sally Carter	Sep 11 1808
Carter Caroline	Same Parents	Feb 24 1812
Carter James	Same Parents	Mar. 24 1813
Carter Mary Ann Augusta	Same Parents	Octo 9 1816
Carter Martha Lincoln	Same Parents	Mar 3 1821.
15 Carter, George,	Oliver & Emily [Harrington] Carter	Apr; 13, 1797.
Carter, Patty Maynard	Ephraim Carter jun & Polly his wife	July 11, 1797.
Carter, Lucinda	Thomas & Sarah Carter,	Apr: 14, 1798.
Carter Susanna	Ephraim & Polly his wife	Nov 2, 1800
Carter Sewal	Dr James & Susanna Carter	Sep 9 1796
Chandler Henry Dana	Benjᵃ & Betsy Chandler	Sep 17 1803.
Carter Eli	Thomas & Sarah Carter	April 27 1800
Carter Susanna	James Carter jun & Wife	Aug 3 1804
Carter Timº Harrington	Oliver & Emily [Harrington] Carter	Dec 23, 1798.
Carter Charles	Same Parents	Aug 21. 1800.
Carter Emily	Same Parents	Mar 21, 1802

14

Name	Parents	Date
Carter Nancy Bridge	Same Parents	Feb 23 1804
Carter Catharine Prescott	Same Parents	Feb 14 1806.
Carter Henry	John Carter 3d & Betsy Carter	Mar 22 1804
Carter Rebecca	Same Parents	June 11 1805
Carter Mary	Same Parents	Feb 8th 1807.
Carter Abigail	Ephraim & Polly Carter	April 24 1805
Caldwell Lydia	John Caldwell & ——	Ap — 1808.
Carter Ephraim	John 3d & Betsy Carter	Dec 2 1808.
Colburn Charles	Elijah & Sally Colburn	Dec 13 1796
Colburn Jonas	Same Parents	June 21 1798
Colburn Lucy Hosley	Same Parents	Mar 27 1800.
Colburn David Hosley	Same Parents	Feb 28 1802.
Colburn Nancy Wilder	Same Parents	May 3 1804.
Chenery Nancy Jackson	Thaddeus Chenery	Feby 10 1807.
Carter Lucy	John Carter Jun & Tempe Carter	Mar 7th 1807.
Chenery Lucy Ann	Thaddeus & Polly Chenery	Jany. 13 1809.
Carter Richard [Bridge]	Oliver & Emily Carter	Aug. 30 1808
Carter Nancy	John Carter 3d and Betsy	April 17. 1811
Carter Lucy Elizabeth	Solomon & Elizabeth Carter	Jany 21, 1815.
16		
1821. Carter William Henry	Solomon & Elizabeth Carter	April 14 1821.
1822. Carter an infant	Dr Calvin Carter	Feb. 12 1822
Carter Charles Myrick	Saml. Carter & Delia	May 3, 1822
Carter Horatio	Oliver & Emily Carter	Feb. 17, 1796
1823. Carter George Putnam	Solomon & Elizabeth Carter	Apr. 13, 1823
Chambers Hiram	Aaron & Catharine Chambers	Octo 19 1821.
Carter Abigail Rebecca	Solomon & Elizabeth Carter	Jan; 6 1825
Carter John	Son of Jno Carter & Tempe	March 24 1816.
Carter Charles	Same Parents	May 25, 1818.
Carter Martha Lincoln	Calvin & Sally Carter	Augt 22 1823.
Chase Mary	Moses & Ruth Chase	Jany 11 1822.
Carter James Coolidge	Solomon & Elizabeth Carter	Octo 14 1827
Carter Daniel Andrew	Saml Carter & Delia	August 30 1824
Cummings Ann Maria	Right Cummings & Mary Cums.	Mar. 6 1828
Carter George Augustus	Saml & Delia Carter.	Dec 17 1827.
Copeland Almira	Charles & Mary Copeland	June 27 1829.
*	*	*
Carter Julia Ann	John Carter 2d & Elizabeth	March 8 1820
Carter Adelia Meriam	Saml & Delia Carter	July 13 1830.
Copeland Charles Henry	Charles & Mary Copeland	Mar; 11 1832
1833. Carter Solon Francis	Samuel & Delia Carter	March 7, 1833
Carter Sarah Catherine	George & Nancy Carter	July 8, 1833.
Cutting Stephen	Stephen Cutting	June 30 —
1834. Carter Ann M.	James G. Carter & Ann M	Aug. 10, 1833
Chase Albert R.	Alanson & Maria Chase	July 16 1824
Chase Charles H.	Same Parents	Feb 19, 1826
Chase Emery	Same Parents	Sep. 12 1829.
Chase Maria Ann	Same Parents	Feb. 1. 1833.
1835. Copeland Delia	Charles & Mary Copeland	April 14, 1834.
Carter Horatio	George & Nancy Carter	March 15 1835
1836. Carter Oliver Warner	Oliver & Polly Carter	April 10 1836
Carter Emily B	George & Nancy	July 16, 1836
Carter Sarah Frances	Oliver & Polly Carter	Decr. 6, 1838
Chandler Mary Elizabeth	Saml W. & Elizabeth F. Chandler	May 16, 1842
Christiana Cunningham	John & Louisa Cunningham	Aug. 8. 1842
25 Dunlap Tyler	Elizabeth and Samuel Dunlap	Jany 28 1802
Dunlap Saml.	Samuel and Elizah Dunlap	Jany. 20 1800.
Damon Jonas Marshall	Samuel Damon Jr. & Polly	April 13, 1807.
Divol Susanna	Peter & Susanna Divol	May 20, 1807.
Damon Jno Warren	Samuel Jr & Polly	Nov. 7 1809.
Divol Peter	Peter Divol & Susanna	Dec 22 1808
Damon Darius	Samuel & Polly Damon	June 16 1811.

Damon Mary Lewis	Same Parents	Nov 15 1813
Dollison Samuel	John & Esther Dollison	Aug. 26. 1786
Dollison John	Same Parents	March 3 1788
Dollison Elizabeth W.	Same Parents	Nov. 29 1789.
Dollison Nancy T.	Same Parents	May 4 1792.
Dollison Esther	Same Parents	April 5 1794.
Dollison Daniel	Same Parents	April 20 1796.
Dollison Lucy	Same Parents	April 23 1798.
Dollison Barzillai	Same Parents	Feby. 21 1800.
Dollison Daniel	Same Parents	April 2 1802.
Dollison Mary Ann	Same Parents	Aug. 6 1804.
Dollison Margaret B.	Same Parents	June 12 1806.
Damon Aaron Alonzo	Sam¹. & Polly Damon	Nov. 23 1815.
Dollison Levi Peirce	Sam¹. Dollison and Nancy his wife	Dec. 31 1815
Dollison Sam¹. Augustus	" " "	Nov 21 1817
Danforth Eliza L.	Elias Danforth & Lucy	March 26 1818
Davis John Buxton	Elisha Davis & Betsy	Octo 1 1818
1820. Dollison Nancy Peirce	Sam¹ Dollison & Nancy	Dec 4 1819.
1821. Davis Catharine	John Davis Jr & Sylvia	Aug. 14th. 1821.
Danforth Sarah Ann	Elias Danforth & Lucy	Dec 16. 1821.
Dean George Bennett	George C Dean & Dolly	Apr. 22 1820.
Dean Francis Porter	Same Parents	Feb. 5. 1822.
26 * *	*	*
Damon Martha Willard	Sam¹ & Polly Damon	Jan 27 1818.
Damon Hariet Hart	Same Parents	June 6. 1820.
1823. Damon Abraham P	Wm Damon & Abigail his Wife	Jany. 10. 1804.
Damon Joseph W.	Same Parents.	Jany 5 1806.
Damon Caroline L.	Same Parents.	April 5, 1808.
Damon Levi W.	Same Parents.	June 25, 1810.
Damon Michael S	Same Parents.	June 26, 1812.
Damon Jerophas E.	Same Parents.	May 26. 1815.
Damon Rachel R.	Same Parents.	March 5, 1821.
Davis Franklin	Elisha Davis & Betsy	Jany. 21, 1822
Dollison Eliza Ann	Sam¹: & Nancy Dollison	May 17. 1823.
Dollison Almira Jane	Same Parents.	Aug: 30. 1825.
Dean John Prentiss	John & Emily Dean	June 4 1827.
Dickinson Eliza	Moses & Nancy Dickinson	April 13. 1815.
Dickinson Alfred	Same Parents.	June — 1816.
Dickinson Lois	Same Parents.	April — 1819.
Divoll Edward	Thos. & Rebecca Divoll	April 11. 1817.
Divoll George	Same Parents.	Octo 31, 1826.
Dudley Andrew Jackson	John & Esther Eliza Dudley	March 4 1829.
Dollison George Alber	Sam¹ & Nancy Dollison	Dec. 6 1831
Dean Charles	John & Emily Dean	June 19 1832
1833. Dean Sarah Bridges	John & Emily Dean	Aug. 10 1833.
1835. Dudley Charles Henry	John & Esther Eliza Dudley	July 15, 1831
Dudley John Edwin	Same Parents.	April 28, 1834
Divol Sarah	Willm. & Dolly Divol	Dec. 29, 1826
Divol Caroline Carter	Same Parents	May 18 1831.
Divol Emily O	Same Parents	March 23. 1833
Divol Julia Ann	Same Parents	May 20. 1835.
27 Danforth Roxana:	Octa Danforth & Nancy	March 25 1835.
1837. William Carlton Divol	William & Dolly Divol	Feb 15, 1837.
Tryphosa Davis	Sumner & Susan Davis	Jany 17, 1837
Harriet Augusta D.	Same Parents	Aug. 18, 1838
Frances Ann Divoll	William & Dolly Divoll	Decr. 9, 1838
Ellen Maria Divoll	Same Parents	June 22 1842
Oscar Augustus Dorrison	Samuel A. & Elizabeth F Dorrison	Oct. 29, 1842
Edwin Heywood Damon	John W. & Nancy M. Damon	Jany. 18, 1843
Dorrison Ellen Elizabeth	Samuel & Nancy Dorrison	Novr. 3, 1837
Dorrison Chas. M.	Same Parents	Oct 31, 1827.
31 Nancy Emerson	Elias Emerson & Phebe his wife	May 29 1801.

Oliver Emerson	Same Parents	May 29 1801.
Charles Emerson	Same Parents	Dec 21 1803.
Sophia Emerson	Same Parents	Feby 15 1806.
Eager Samuel	Haran & Betsy Eager	Aug 29 1803.
Eager Mercy	Same Parents	Aug 25 1805.
Emerson Francis Bradley	Moses & Lydia Emerson	June 27 1810.
Emmerson Hiram	Moses & Lydia Emerson	Aug. 8 1812.
Emerson Sally Carleton	Moses & Lydia Emerson	Octo 30, 1814.
Evans George Washington	Jeremiah & Sarah Evans	April 1st, 1812.
Evans Sarah Osgood	Same Parents	Aug. 5, 1814.
Eager Lewis	Benj^a. Eager & Sally	Dec 8 1815.
Emmerson Charles	Moses Emmerson and Eunice his Wife	July 28, 1816.
1822. Eaton Joseph	Nathl. & Lucy Eaton	May 2 1790.
Emerson Clarissa	Elias Emerson & Phebe	July 31 1808.
Eaton Sally	Nathl & Lucy Eaton	Sep 18 1776.
Eaton Nancy	Same Parents.	Nov. 28 1777.
Eaton Henry	Same Parents.	Dec. 23. 1779.
" Betsy	Ditto.	June 28 1781.
" Mary	Ditto.	Mar: 10 1783.
" John	Ditto.	Octo 21 1784.
" Theophilus	Ditto.	July 16 1786.
" Charles	Ditto.	May 6 1788.
" Catharine Maria	Ditto.	Nov 9 1792.
" Esther	Ditto.	Mar. 24. 1800.
32 Eager John Bigelow	Farwell Eager & Althina	May 6. 1826.
Eager Eliza	Same Parents.	Dec. 8, 1829.
Ellenwood Eliza Ann	Arah & Eliza^h Ellenwood	Sept 17, 1835.

34 Fisher David, Son of Jacob Fisher and Nancy Fisher, Born Sept. 5th 1808.
Fletcher Otis, son of William Fletcher and Dorcas Fletcher born Jany. 24th 1809.
Fuller Alcy daughter of Edward Fuller and Susanna his wife born May 24 1809.
Farnsworth Abigail Meriam   Benj^a & Sally Farnsworth   Dec 17 1808

Fisher Susanna	Jacob Fisher & Nancy Fisher	born Jany. 19th, 1811.
Fuller James	Edward and Susanna Fuller	May 28 1811.
Farnsworth Augustus	Benj^a & Sally Farnsworth	Aug 10. 1811.[1810?]
Fales Susanna	Jeremiah & Ami Fales	July 4 1812.
Fletcher Joseph Warren	Joshua Fletcher 2^d & Nabby	Nov 15 1813.
Fuller Abner	Edward & Susanna Fuller	Sep 19, 1813.
Farnsworth Nancy	Benj^a 2^d & Dorcas Farnsworth	June 25 1810.
Farnsworth Dorcas	Same Parents	July 30 1812.
Fuller Joseph	Sally Fuller	July 5 1809.
Fisher George	Jacob & Nancy Fisher	Dec 1. 1814.
Fletcher Dorcas Warren	Willm & Dorcas Fletcher	Mar 28. 1815.
Farnsworth Andrew Jackson	Benj^a Farnsworth 2^d & Dorcas	Mar 23. 1815.
Farnsworth James	Benj^a & Sally Farnsworth	May 29 [28] 1815.
Fletcher Martha	Timo. & Hannah Fletcher	May 1 1803.
Fletcher Elenor Louisa	Joshua & Nabby Fletcher	March 15, 1815.
Fletcher Julia Maria	Same Parents	March 21 1817
35 Flagg, George Washington	Josiah & Dolly Flagg	Jany 31. 1797.
Fisher, Mary	Jacob & Nancy Fisher	Octr 2^d 1796.
Fletcher, Rufus	Rufus & Polly Fletcher	Mar: 30 1797.
Fletcher, Leonard	Phinehas & Mary Fletcher	Octr 23 1796
Fisher, Ephraim Carter	Jacob & Nancy Fisher	June 25, 1798
Fletcher, Mary Ann	Timothy & Hannah Fletcher	Octr 29, 1798.
Faulkner, Horace	Paul & Abigail Faulkner	Novr 24 1799
Fletcher, Levi	Timothy & Hannah Fletcher	Aug: 21, 1800
Fisher, Sally	Jacob & Nancy Fisher	July 16, 1800
Fletcher Mary	Rufus & Mary Fletcher	Dec. 25 1799
Fletcher Elijah	Rufus & Mary Fletcher	Aug 22 1802
Farnsworth Sally	Benjamin & Sally Farnsworth	July 2 1796
Farnsworth Benjamin	Benjamin & Sally Farnsworth	June 20 1799

Farnsworth Abijah Haskell	Benjamin & Sally Farnsworth	Octo 6 1801.
Flagg Samuel Ward,	Josiah & Dolly Flagg.	April 22d 1803.
Farwell Jonathan	Joseph & Molly Farwell	June 30 1780
Farwell Sarah	Ditto	July 28 1786
Farwell Mary	Ditto.	Dec. 10 1790
Farwell James	Ditto.	Sep. 5 1794
Farwell Martha H.	Ditto.	April 10 1803.
Faulkner Hariot	Paul and Abigail Faulkner	July 13, 1801.
Faulkner Louisa	Same	Nov. 21 1803.
Fuller Caroline	Edward Fuller & Susanna his wife	Aug. 1 1804
Farnsworth Mary	Benjamin & Sally Farnsworth	Feb. 27. 1804
Fisher Alexander	Jacob and Nancy Fisher	Aug. 12 1804
" [James	" " "	Aug 12 1806]
Fuller Joseph Shephard	Edward Fuller & Susanna his wife	Octo 4 1805.
Fletcher Roxa	William & Dorcas Fletcher	Octo 2 1805.
Fletcher Lewis	Rufus Fletcher & Mary Fletcher	Dec 19 1805.
Faulkner Augustus	Paul and Abigail Faulkner	Feb 27 1806.
Fletcher William	William & Dorcas Fletcher	May 19 1807.
Farnsworth Charles	Benja Farnsworth & Sally his wife	Mar 31 1807.
Fuller Mary ann	Edward & Susanna Fuller	July 2 1807.
36 Farnsworth Benjamin Franklin.	Benja Farnsworth 2d and Dorcas his wife.	May 22, 1817.
Fales Warren	Ami & Jereh. Fales Jr.	Nov. 9. 1813.
Fales Martha	Ephm Fales & Olive	July 18 1814
Fales Daniel	Same Parents	Aug. 13 1816
Farwell Elbridge	James Farwell & Mary	June 17 1818.
Fletcher George Henry	Joshua Fletcher & Nabby	Dec 18, 1818.
Faulkner, Mary Daniels	Paul Faulkner & Eunice	May 21, 1819.
Farnsworth Jonas	Benja. Farnsworth 2d and Dorcas his wife	July 10, 1819
Fairbank Sarah	Silas Farbank.	Nov 18 1819
Fales Loisa	Jeremiah & Ami Fales	Aug. 23, 1818
Fales Mary Ann	Same Parents.	May 8, 1820.
1821. Fletcher James Fosdick	Joshua Fletcher & Nabby	Sep. 22, 1820.
Foster Caroline	Benja H. Foster & Martha	Feb. 23. 1812
Foster Martha	Same Same	Mar. 2, 1814
Foster Lavina	Same Same	Dec. 31. 1818
Farnsworth James	Benja Farnsworth & Dorcas	Aug. 19 1821.
1822. Fisher Martha	Jacob Fisher Jr & his wife Orricy	Aug 20, 1819
Fisher Sarah	Same Parents	Jan. 30. 1822.
Fuller Susan Heywood	Ephraim Fuller & Susan	Sep 7. 1819
Fuller Francis Faulkner	Same Parents	Jan. 8. 1822
1823. Farwell Lucius Leonard	Joseph Farwell 2d & Sarah	Octo 31, 1816.
Farwell Sarah Meriam	Same Parents	Aug. 12, 1819
Farwell Lucy Barnard	Same Parents	July 8, 1822.
Farnsworth Lydia	Benja. Farnsworth 2d & Dorcas	June 17. 1823.
Foster Charles Baldwin	Benja. H Foster & Martha	Nov 26 1822
37 Farwell Mary Emerson,	James & Mary Farwell Born	Feb 15, 1824
Fitch Charles Torry.	Torry Fitch & Harriet Fitch Born	July 20 1823.
Fuller Andrew Lowell	Ephraim & Susan Fuller	June 6 1824.
Fisher Charlotte	Jacob Fisher Jr & Orricy	Jan. 25 1824
Fisher Caroline	Same Parents	Sept: 9 1826.
Farwell Ann Elizabeth	Joseph Farwell 2 & Sarah his wife	July 1. 1825.
Farnsworth Angelina	Benja Farnsworth 2d & Dorcas	June 12 1827.
Foster Eliza	Benja. H Foster & Martha	Feb 2 1826.
Fletcher Julia Abigail	Joshua & Nabby Fletcher	April 6. 1823.
Fletcher Charles Thornton	Same Parents.	March 23 1826.
Fisher Eliza	Jacob & Betsy	Augt 1. 1828
Farwell Frederic Holden,	Abel & Mary Farwell	Octo. 29 1828
Faulkner Emily Holman	Horace and Eliza Faulkner	Apr 1 1827
Fitch Francis George	George & Sophronia Fitch	Jany 13, 1829
Fisher Andrew	Jacob Fisher Jr. & Orricy	Feby 24 1829.

Farwell Frances Maria	Levi & Lucy B Farwell	Dec. 30. 1827
Farwell Eliza Willard	Same Parents	Sep. 21, 1829
Fuller Francis Faulkner	Ephraim & Susan Fuller	Feby. 5, 1830.
Fitch Helen Sophronia	George & Sophronia Fitch.	Sep 25, 1830.
Flagg Sarah Elizabeth	Otis Flagg & Theresa	Jany 29, 1831.
Fairbank Elizabeth	Silas & Martha Fairbank,	Octo 9. 1817
Fairbank Martha T.	Same Parents	Jany 27 1816
Fairbank Sarah	Same Parents	Nov. 18. 1819
Fletcher Martha Celestine	Joshua & Nabby Fletcher	Aug. 8. 1830.
Fairbank Martha Ann	Timothy [J.] & Lucy Fairbank	June 25. 1832
1833. Farwell Augusta Maria	Levi & Lucy B. Farwell	July 1. 1831
Fitch Edwin Raymond	Torrey Fitch & Hariet	Octo. 16, 1832.
Fuller Ephraim Heywood	Ephraim & Susan Fuller	April 25. 1833
Fuller Sophronia Mehitable	John & Sophronia Fuller	Jany 18, 1829
Fuller John Thurston	Same Parents	Dec. 28, 1830.
Fuller Samuel Ebenezer	Same Parents	March 31, 1833
Foster Alvan Carpenter	Jeremiah & Sarah Foster	Nov. 2 1832
38. Farwell Daniel Willard	Levi & Lucy B Farwell	Augt. 16, 1833
Farwell Francis Marion	Same Parents	Sep. 4. 1834.
Faulkner George Amasa	Amory & Bathsheba Faulkner	Sep. 11. 1834
Fitch Louisa Maria Tidd	George & Sophronia Fitch	Dec 5. 1832
Fitch Hariet Lane	Same Parents	Dec. 11. 1834.
Fuller George Walton	Ephraim & Judith Fuller	Dec 4, 1834.
1834. Fletcher Sarah P.	Lewis & Sally Fletcher	May 13, 1834.
Fletcher George W.	Same Parents	Octo. 23, 1835.
Fairbank Francis Lyman	Timothy [J.] & Lucy Fairbank	Feb. 18, 1835.
Fales Sophia	Jeremiah & Ami Fales	July 27, 1823.
Fales Martha	Same Parents	June 22. 1826.
Fisher [Emily]	Jacob Jun. & Orricy Fisher	[Feb. 19, 1831.]
1836. Charles T. Fairbanks	Timothy J & Lucy Ann Fairbanks	Sept. 18. 1836
1837. Farwell Abigail J	Geo P & Ruth Farwell	Ap 14. 1836
Farnsworth Benj Sawtell	Asa D. Farnsworth & Betsey	July 15, 1836
Fisher Elizabeth [Hills]	Jacob Jun. & Orricy Fisher	[Aug. 28, 1833.]
Farnsworth Edward Everett.	Asa D. Farnsworth & Betsey.	Aug. 13th, 1837
Fletcher Edward Lewis	Lewis & Sally P Fletcher	July 2^d, 1837.
Fitch Andrew Lucien Houghton	George & Sophronia W. Fitch	Jany 28. 1837
Fitch John William Homer	Same Parents	March 21, 1839
Fairbank Laura Paulina	Timothy [J.] & Lucy Ann Fairbank	Aug. 21. 1840
Farnsworth James Delap	Asa D. & Betsey Farnsworth	June 3. 1839
Farnsworth William Harrison	Same parents	July 3. 1840
Farwell, Mary Ann Russell	Levi & Lucy B. Farwell	Jany 10. 1838
Lucius Andrew Farwell	Lucius L & Mary Farwell	March 31, 1842
David Boynton Fletcher	David B. Sarah A. Fletcher	Novr 21, 1840
Mark Anthony Farnsworth	Andrew J & Catharine M Farnsworth	Sept. 7. 1843
John Edward Farnsworth	Benj F. & Cynthia A. Farnsworth	Sept. 6. 1843
[Fletcher, Jane Augusta.	Otis and Joanna B. Fletcher.	Feb. 1, 1841.]
44 Goodwin Sarah	John Goodwin & Rebecca his Wife	April 12 1809.
Goodwin Mary Ann	Same Parents	July 7. 1811.
Goss Levi.	John Goss & Mary	Nov 1 1813.
Goss Judith 2^d	Jonas & Judith Goss	March 13, 1811
Goss Ebenezer	Same Parents	May 9 1813.
Goss Joseph White	John 2^d & Rebecca Goss	June 2 1812
Goss Samuel	Same Parents	Feb. 4 1813
Goss^s Charles	Same Parents	July 28 1814
Goddard Eber	Eber & Lucy Goddard	July 8 1813.
Goss Lucy Gates	John & Mary Goss	Sep 28 1816
Goodwin Hariot Maria	Jno. Goodwin & Rebecca	June 13, 1815
1822. Goodwin Wm Smith	Jno. Goodwin Jr. & Susan	June 1. 1821.
Goodwin Susan Emeline,	Same Parents	Mar. 10 1823.
Goldthwait Hannah	John & Mehitable	Octo — 1806.
Goldthwait Eunice	Same Parents	Sep — 1808
Goldthwait John	Same Parents	April 2 1810

Goodale Martha Farwell	Obediah Goodale	Jan 22ᵈ 1828
Goss Henry Laughton	Henry & Sally Goss	April 15 1829
Green Charles Frederic	Levi & Achsah Green	Aug 21 1830.
Goss William Dexter	Henry & Sally Goss	Feby 27 1831.
Goss Susan Polly	Henry & Sally Goss	July 29 1832.
Green Ellen Maria	Levi & Achsah	May 7 1832.
*	*	*
Greene Elsy Ann	Levi & Achsah Greene	July 30 1833.
Goodwin George Gibson	John Goodwin Jr. & Katharine	Sep 19 1828
" Susan Emeline	Same Parents	Aug 1 1831
" James Solomon	Same Parents	Jany. 22 1833
45 Goss, William	Daniel Goss junr & Polly his wife	Septr. 27, 1796.
Goss Abigail	Same	May 13, 1799
Goss James	John Goss & Mary his wife	Apr: 28, 1797.
Goss, Joseph	Same.	Octr 14, 1799
Goodwin Loring,	James Goodwin junr. & Abigail,	Sept. 12, 1798.
Goodwin John Adams	Edward Goodwin & Sally his wife	March 22 1800.
Goodwin James Goulding	James Goodwin jur. & Abigail	April 9, 1801.
Goss James	Daniel Goss jun & Polly his Wife	Octo 26 1801.
Goodwin John Jr.	John Goodwin & Rebecca his wife	May 21 1798.
Goss John	John Goss & Mary Goss	Feb. 9 1802
Goodwin Leander	James Goodwin jun & Abigail	Augt. 17 1803
Goodwin Rebecca	John Goodwin & Rebecca his wife	Aug 6 1803.
Goss Henry	Daniel Goss jun & Polly his wife	Sep 10 1803.
Goodwin Edward	Edward Goodwin & Sally his wife	May 1 1804.
Goss John	John Goss & Mary his wife	Octo 13 1804
Goss Elizabeth	Daniel and Polly Goss	May 18 1805.
Goodwin Palmer	James Jr. & Abigail Goodwin	Feb, 9th 1806.
Goodwin Alfred	John Goodwin & Rebecca his Wife	April 15 1806.
Goss Mary Whetcomb	John Goss & Mary Goss	June 4th 1807
Goodwin Caleb Strong	Edward Goodwin & Sally his wife	May 26 1807
Goss Maryann Stedman.	Daniel & Polly Goss	Feb 25 1808
Goss Jonas	Jonas & Judith Goss	Aug 9 1808
Goss Daniel	Same Parents	Jany 4: 1810
Goss Judith	Same Parents	Apr. 4 1807.
Goss Rebecca White	John & Rebecca Goss	Feby 7 1809.
Goss, Martha Ellery	Daniel & Polly Goss	Mar. 7 1810.
Goodwin Samuel	Edward & Sally Goodwin	Sep. 27 1809.
Goddard Mary Carter	Eber & Lucy Goddard	Feb. 21 1810
Goss Sara Edmunds	John & Mary Goss	June 19 1810
Goss Elizabeth Ann		
Goss John	John & Rebecca Goss	May 27 1810.
46 1834. Goss Eunice Wilder	John & Rebecca Goss	Feb 25, 1817.
Goss Sarah White	Same Parents	July 4 1818
Goss Mary Wheeler	Same Parents	July 8. 1822
Goodwin Cynthia Jane	John Goodwin Jun & Catherine	Sep 26 1834
Greene George Manly	Williams Green & Sarah	July 25. 1834
1836. Greenleaf Sarah Eliza.	Edmund Q & Elizabeth W. Greenleaf	May 13, 1835
Greene Daniel Webster	Williams & Sarah M. Greene	April 30, 1836
1838. Greene Eliza Ann H.	Same Parents	Nov 25, 1837
1842. Goddard Artemas Walker	Eber & Mary L Goddard	March 30, 1842
Green, Asa Whitman	Williams & Sarah Green	Novr 2. 1839
Green John Davis	Same Parents	Oct. 23, 1841
Golden James B.	Patrick & Mary Golden	Aug. 8, 1842
Lucy Maria Goddard	Eber & Mary L. Goddard	July 26, 1843
Greenleaf George Ruggles	Edmund Q & Eliz^h W.	Sept. 3 1832

50 Haskell Mary daughter of William & Mercy Haskell born the 7th May 1800.
Houghton Lydia daughter of Benjamin & Lydia Houghton born September 6th 1805.
Holmes Edward Warren son of Edward Holmes & Huldah his wife born September 26th, 1802.

Holmes Miranda daughter of Edward Holmes & Huldah born Feb. 11th 1804.
Haven Caroline daughter of Richard Haven & Sally Haven born the 19th January 1806.
Haven John Son of Eben^r. and Ruth Haven born August 6th 1805.
Hunt Titus Son of John Hunt and Polly Hunt born May 2^d 1805.
Houghton Sophronia Willard daughter of Elijah and Ruth Houghton born Octo 25th 1806.
Houghton Oliver Son of Oliver & Nabby Houghton born Nov. 26 1806.
Haven William Ingraham Son of Richard Haven and Sally his wife born May 1 1808.
Houghton Mary, Elijah & Ruth Houghton's daughter born Dec 21 1808.
Howe Thomas, Son of Thomas Howe & Sally his wife born Dec. 2, 1808.
Hastings Amory Son of Thomas & Susanna Hastings born Sept. 30th 1809.
Hawks Thomas Ballard Son of Benjamin & Polly Hawks born July 20th 1809.
51 Houghton Meriel, daughter of Sparhawk & Nancy Houghton born March 3^d, 1797.
Houghton, Charles, Son of Benjamin Houghton jun & Lydia his wife born Jany 11 1798.
Haven, Richard, Son of Richard Haven & Sally his wife, born March 6th, 1799
Houghton Maria, daughter of Elijah & Betty Houghton his wife, born March 15, 1801.
Haven Sally daughter of Richard Haven and Sally his Wife, born Sep. 22nd. 1801.
Houghton Emeline daughter of Oliver Houghton and Nabby his wife born July 23, 1792.
Houghton Eliza daughter of Oliver Houghton and Nabby his wife born May 22 1794.
Houghton Jeffery Atherton, Son of Oliver Houghton and Nabby his wife born April 27. 1796.
Houghton Edmund Winchester Son of Oliver Houghton and Nabby his wife born May 10, 1798.
Houghton George Washington, Son of Benjamin Houghton & Lydia his wife born Dec 14 1800.
Hunt Sarah Taft daughter of Otis and Arethusa Hunt. born Jany. 27th 1800.
Hunt Otis jun son of Otis and Arethusa Hunt born Nov 16th 1802.
Haven Jonas Son of Eben^r. & Ruth Haven born January 28th 1802.
Hunt John 3^d Son of John Hunt 2^d, born Jany. 29th 1802.
Hunt Jeremiah Son of John Hunt 2^d. born Augt. 26th 1803.
Haven Jubal Harrington Son of Richard Haven and Sally Haven born Sep. 23^d 1803.
53 Hunt Elizabeth Beaman, daughter of Otis and Arethusa Hunt born January 2nd 1810.
Hawks Alice daughter of John Hawks Jun and Alice his wife was born March 10th 1796

Hawks John	the same Parents	born May 7th 1797.
Hawks Sally	Same Parents	" Octo 10 1798.
Hawks Daniel	Same	" April 20th 1800.
Hawks James	Same	" March 19, 1802.
Hawks Hariot	Same	" Nov. 18th. 1803.
Hawks Benjamin	Same	" May 15 1805.
Hawks Sewall	Same	" Jany. 22 1807.
Hawks Cynthia	Same	" June 10th 1809.
William Howe	Thomas & Sally Howe	Aug 11. 1810.
Haven Harriot	Richard & Sally Haven	July 4 1810.
Hawks Rebecca	John & Alice Hawks	Apr. 29 1811.
Howe Fredrick	David & Susan Howe	Aug. 3 1811.
Hunt Martha Ann	Otis Hunt & Arethusa	April 18, 1812.
Howe Francis	Thomas & Sally Howe	Mar 3. 1814.
Houghton Abigail	Oliver & Ruth Houghton	Feb 10 1815.
*	*	*
Hawks Mary Plimpton	Jno & Alice Hawks	Jany 20 1817.
Harris George	Emery & Hezediah Harris	May 20 1815
Harris Hariot	Same Parents	Apr 5 1817

Howe Andrew	Thomas & Sally Howe	Nov. 27 1816
Howard Caleb Alden	Sydney & Sally Howard	Dec 26 1817.
54 Hawks Cynthia Anstiss	Jno Hawks Jr. and Alice	Jany 25 1818.
Hildreth Martha	Richard Hildreth & Nancy	Dec 16 1817.
Hildreth Ezekiel	Same Parents	July 10 1819.
Howard Parney	Sydney & Sally Howard	Nov, 8 1819,
1821. Howe Barzillai Miles	Thomas & Sally Howe	June 21 1819.
Haven Sarah Whetcomb.	Eben^r & Prissa Haven	June 21 1821.
Harris Eliza	Asahel Harris & Abigail	Aug 10. 1820
*	*	*
Howe Henry Peabody	David Howe & Susan	Apr. 4 1813.
Howe David	Same Parents	Mar. 10 1815.
Howe Susan	Same Parents	Feb. 6, 1817
Howe William	Same Parents	July 24 1821.
Howard Sarah Ann	Sydney & Sally Howard	Jany 3 1824.
Howard Geo Fredric	Same Parents	Octo 9 1821.
Houghton Hariet Williams	Rufus & Martha Houghton	Feb 28 1824.
Haven Nancy	Eben^r & Prissa Haven	May 26 1825
Harris Frederic Alonzo	Asahel & Abigail Harris	Feb 7. 1822
Harris Sidney Algernon	Same Parents	Mar. 29 1824
Harris Francis Alonzo	Same Parents	Aug. 6 1825
Harris Bradford,	Polly Deputron	Mar. 21 1825.
Howe Dolly Stratton	Levi & Susan Howe	Augt 7 1821.
Sidney Thomas Howard	Sidney & Sally Howard	April 22 1827
Houghton Josiah	George and Miranda Houghton	Feby 24 1828
Howard Amasa	Levi Howard & Mary	Sept. 28 1828.
Harris Julia Maria	Asahel & Abigail Harris	Sept 1 1828.
Hartwell Abigail Louisa	Leonard Hartwell	July 3 1827
Hartwell Emily Pollard	Same Parents	June 27 1829
Howard Susan Sawyer	Sidney & Sally Howard	Feb 9. 1830.
Harris Alfred P.	Asahel & Abigail Harris	Augt 18, 1830.
Hudson Sarah	Robert Hudson	Dec 26 1794.
55 Houghton Lucy Jane,	Geo W. Houghton & Miranda	Dec 10 1831.
1833. Howland Harriet Louisa	Henry J Howland & Ellen M.	Novr. 6. 1833.
Haven Waldo	William & Harriet Haven	Nov 9 1833.
Hastings Sarah Abigail	Saml. A Hastings.	May 15 1833.
Huntington George Miller	Joseph W. Huntington & Julia M.	Aug 25, 1833.
Howard Sarah Elizabeth	Levi & Mary Howard	March 24, 1831
Houghton Gardner Pollard.	Rufus & Martha Houghton	Dec 8 1825
Houghton Andrew Rufus	Same Parents	June 19, 1827.
Houghton Lucy Heywood	Same Do	Jan. 7. 1830.
Houghton Solon Bridgman	Same Do	Jany. 9, 1832.
1834. Houghton Martha Elizabeth	Geo. W. Houghton & Miranda	Nov 19 1833
Houghton Edward	Cyrus & Eliza Houghton	Nov 15. 1829
Houghton Eliza	Same Parents	Sep 14 1831
Houghton Frederick	Same Parents	June 28, 1833
Harris Jane A.	Sidney & Sally Harris.	June 6, 1831
Harris Christopher C.	Same Parents	March 22, 1832
Haskell John Edward	John A, Haskell & Sarah	May 1. 1834
[Howard, Daniel Manley.	George and Sarah (Manley).	March 25, 1829.]
Howard Louisa [M.]	George & Elizabeth Howard	Aug. 7, 1834
1835. Hildreth Ann V.	Thomas & Mary Hildreth	Feb. 28. 1832
1836. Huntington Horatio M.	Joseph W & Julia M.	June — 1836.
1837. Howard Mary Francis	George W. & Elizabeth Howard	April 1, 1837
Howe Hannah	Phineas B & Nancy Howe	June 22^d 1837
Hastings Laura Lincoln	Samuel A & Olive W.	Oct. 14, 1838
Holman James Henry	Orion and —— Holman	April 20. 1825
Holman Elizabeth Jane	do. do.	Oct. 23. 1829
Holman Amanda Melvina	do. do.	Dec 10. 1833
Holman Helen Maria	do. do.	Oct 9. 1836
Holman Charles Augustus	do. do.	May 26. 1839
Harriman Edwin	John & Julia A. Harriman	Jany. 27. 1842

56 Harris Frederick	Emery Harris & Sally	May 6, 1823.
Harris Emery Jun.	Same Parents	June 11 1830
Hunt Emeline	Thomas T Hunt & Nancy	Nov 29 1831.
Howard Francina	Sidney Howard	May 19, 1832.
Harriet Maria Haynes	John A & Mary Haynes	July 16 1838
Charles Bond Harris	Edmund & Hannah P. Harris	Sep. 10, 1843
Hodgman Oren	Artemas & Louisa	Sept. 9, 1843
Havrety Emma Louisa	Daniel & —— Havrety	April 27, 1841
Havrety Robert Emmett,	Daniel & —— Havrety	July 21, 1843
59 Joslyn Catharine Eliza	Peter and Almira (Carter) Joslyn	March 20, 1828
Johnson Charles Francis	Francis & Sarah Johnson	July 22d 1830.
Jacobs Ira Gardner	Gardner & Emeline Jacobs	April 17 1829.
Jacobs Sullivan	Same Parents	Octo 1, 1830
Jacobs George Sumner	Same Parents	Dec 18 1831.
Joslyn Mary Ann	Peter & Almira Joslyn	October 2 1832.
1833. Johnson Mary Stone	Johnson Nathl & Almira P.	Augt. 13. 1832.
Johnson Orson.	Luther & Sophia Johnson	Jany. 6 1815
Johnson Julia Ann	Same Parents	Aug. 5 1817.
1835. Joslyn William Carter	Peter & Almira Joslyn	Feby 9. 1835.
Jones Sarah J.	Luther & Charlotte.	Sept. 9 1835.
Jones M. Luther	Same Parents	July 9. 1828.
Jones Sarah J. 2d	Same Parents	June 22, 1831.
Jones Lavinia Jane	Same Parents	Octo 20, 1833.
60 Joslin, James	Jonas & Betsy Joslyn	Decr 14 1797
Joslyn Eliza	Same	July 5, 1799
Jones Polly	Moses Jones	May 28 1792
Betsy Jones	ditto.	April 24 1794
Jones Charles	ditto.	Mar 29 1796
Jones Amos Brooks	ditto.	April 27 1798
Jones Cynthia	ditto.	June 25 1800
Jones Almira	Aaron Jones	Feby. 3 1799
Jones Eliza	ditto	Sep 20 1802
Jones Sarah Parker	Moses Jones & Submit	Aug 8 1803
Johnson Rollin	Jonas & Mary Johnson	Sept 26th 1809
Jones Sullivan	Moses & Submit Jones	June 28 1807
Joslyn Peter	Jonas & Betsy Joslin	Octo 21, 1803
Joslyn Nathl.	Same Parents	Octo 11 1810
Joslyn William	Same Parents	Aug. 23 1811.
Johnson Mary	Jonas & Mary Johnson	Nov. 22, 1812.
Johnson Harrison	Calvin & Nabby Johnson	April 6 1814.
Jones Benja. Franklin.	Aaron Jones	Dec 6 1808
Jones Solon	Same	May 12 1812.
Jones Edwin	Same	June 11 1814
Jones David Wilder	Same	Sep 11 1816
Johnson Elizabeth Rider	Jonas & Mary Johnson	Aug. 26 1817.
Johnson Sewall	Calvin & Nabby Johnson	Dec 28 1817
Jones Nancy	Saml Jones Jun & Nancy	March 29 1812.
Jones Christopher	Same Parents	May 29 1814
Jones Samuel 3	Same Parents	April 19 1816.
Jones Edward	Same Parents	July 4 1818
Jones Charlotte Ann	Luther & Charlotte Jones	May 30. 1823.
Johnson Luther Solon	Calvin & Nabby Johnson	Dec 2 1823.
61 Jewett John Stewart	Horace & Jane Stewart	Sept 12, 1839
Jewett Sarah Churchill	Same Parents	Sept. 25, 1842
68 Kies, John	Daniel & Jedidah Kies	Decr 4. 1797.
Kies Mary	Daniel & Jedidah Kies	July 8 1801
Knight Charles	Charles E Knight & Sally	Dec. 27th 1803.
Keyes Lucinda	Daniel Keyes & Jedidah	June 16 1804
Knight Patty	Charles E Knight & Sally	April 9th 1805
Knowlton Charles	Seth & Relief Knowlton	Nov 4th 1803
Knight Sally	Charles E. Knight & Sally	March 24 1807
Keyes Martha	Daniel Keyes and Jedidah his Wife born July 13, 1808	

Knight Mary Wilder	Charles E. Knight and Sally his wife	Dec. 13. 1811.
Knight James Manasseh	Charles E. Knight and Katharine his wife	May 2 1817.
Knight Elizabeth	Same Parents	Nov. 29, 1820.
Knight Nath¹ Lakin	Same	Jan. 17. 1822.
Knight Wᵐ Jackson	Charles E Knight	August 19 1825.
Kilburn Mary Jane	Isaac Kilburn & Nancy	August 13 1818,
Kilburn Calvin	Same Parents	Feby 8. 1827.
1833. Knight Sophia Catherine	Charles E. & Catherine	April 20 1830
Knight Abigail Jane	Same Parents	Sep. 5, 1832.
Knap Charles M	Horace & Martha T	July 18 1834
1835. King Charles E.	Capt Orrice & Mary Ann King	March 18 1834
71 Lincoln Betsy	Jacob Lincoln & Chloe	Dec 1 1801
Lincoln Maria	Same Parents	July 15 1804
Lincoln Jacob	Same Parents	May 14 1809
Lowe Jonathan Porter	Jonᵃ Lowe jun & Susan Lowe	Apr 20 1817.
Leach Luther Dana	Joseph Leach & Tabitha Leach	Octo 31, 1817.
Low Matilda	John Low & Polly Low	Dec 21 1818.
Lewis Levi Jun.	Levi Lewis & Abigail	Dec 21. 1818.
Locke Edward Cutter	Jonᵃ & Mary Locke	Feb 25 1818.
Lyon Martha Ann	John Lyon & Sally	April 6 1817
Lewis Abigail	Levi Lewis & Abigail	June 13 1820.
1820. Locke Sarah Shattuck	Jonᵃ. & Mary Locke	July 29 1820.
1822. Lewis Jackson	Levi Lewis & Abigail	Feb. 1 1822.
1833. Lowe Almira	Nath¹ & Annis Lowe	Jany 19 1806.
Lowe Rufus	Same Parents	Dec 14 1807.
Lowe Eliphaz	Same Parents	Octo 9, 1811.
Lowe William	Ditto.	Dec 14 1815.
Lowe Saxon	Ditto.	Feb 17 1804
Lyon Maria	Thos W Lyon & Nancy	August 1804
Lyon Nancy	Same Parents	—— 1805
Lyon Charles	Ditto.	Sep. 18. 1810
Lyon Thomas	Ditto.	June 15 1813
Lyon Augustus	Ditto.	Octo 9 1816
Lyon Mary	Ditto.	Octo 3 1817
Lyon William	Ditto.	Mar 21 1820.
Lyon Lawson	Ditto.	Octo 13 1822.
Locke Eliza Ann	Jonᵃ Locke & Mary	June 16 1823.
Locke Frances Augusta	Same Parents	June 16 1823.
72 Leach, Collins.	Joseph & Susannah Leach	March 12ᵗʰ. 1797.
Leach, Mary	Same	Octʳ 7ᵗʰ 1799
Lee Elizabeth	Benja: & Elizaʰ. Lee	Aug. 16 1801.
Low Thomas	Nath¹. & Anis Low.	May 31 1801.
Low Polly	Nath¹. & Anis Low.	June 29 1798
Lowe Mary	John Lowe.	Nov 2, 1802
Lowe Sylvia	John Lowe.	Nov 2, 1804
Lyon Sophia	Luther & Mary Lyon	Nov. 28 1804.
Lyon Luther	Luther & Mary Lyon	Sept 11 1806
Low Anson	John & Polly Low	Dec 8ᵗʰ 1806
Lyon Mary Ann	'Luther & Mary Lyon	Feby 2 1808.
Leach Joseph	Joseph & Rebecca Leach	June 1 1804
Leach Lucretia Murray	" "	Jany. 3 1806
Leach Rebecca Luscomb	" "	Feb. 24 1807
Leach Mary Howe	" "	May 5 1808.
Littaye Noel	Noel Littaye & Sally	May 18 1797
Littaye Katy	Same Parents	June 4 1802
Littaye Dolly	Same Parents	May 16 1804
Littaye Katharine	Same Parents	April 4 1795
Leach Josiah	Joseph & Rebecca Leach	May 14 1809.
Low Abigail	John & Mary Low	Sept. 5 1809.
Lyon Willard	Thoˢ. W. & Nancy Lyon	May — 1808.
Lyon Amory Ward,	Jno & Sally Lyon	March 1, 1809
Low Martha	Jno Low & Polly Low.	Aug 30 1811.

Laughton Emily	Daniel & Lucy Laughton	July 4 1798.
Low Caroline	John Low & Polly Low	Nov. 19 1813.
[Low, John W.	" " "	Sept. 16, 1816.]
Low Francis	Nath¹ & Annis Low	Sep 28 1813.
Locke William Stearns	Jonª Locke Jr. & Mary Locke	Nov. 21, 1813.
Locke Phebe Rebecca	Same Parents	Dec. 23 1815.
73 Lewis Martha	Levi Lewis & Abigail Lewis	February 9 1824.
Lewis Crosby	Same Parents	April 24 1825.
Lane Annis Knights	Alvinzey Lane & Lucy	May 2, 1827.
Laughton Caroline Matilda	Stephen & Clarissa Laughton	March 31 1824.
Laughton Mary Waters	Same Parents	May 28 1826.
Laughton Thomas	Hannibal & Dolly Laughton	June 2, 1816.
Laughton Rebecca	Same Parents.	June 7, 1819.
Laughton James	Ditto.	Jany 10 1825
Laughton Marshal	Ditto.	April 20 1826
Lane Diancy Thayer	Alvinzey Lane & Lucy	June 21 1826
Lane Alvinzey Whitcomb	Same Parents	Feb 5, 1830.
Lane George Henry	Same Parents	April 12 1832
Lewis Augustus	Levi & Abigail Lewis	Jany 12 1827
Lewis Martha Jane	Same Parents	Octo 15, 1830
Lewis Francis	Same Parents	Sept 15, 1828
Lewis Susan Augusta	Same Parents	June 28, 1832.
1833. Lewis, George Henry	Henry & Sally B. Lewis	Aug. 15 1830.
Lewis Charles Alfred	Same Parents	May 18, 1833.
Low Albert [Alfred?] William	Henry & Mary Low	Feb. 12 1832.
Low Charles [Francis]	Same Parents	Dec. 4 1833. [34?]
1834. Lawrence George	Sally & Edmund Lawrence	Nov. 16, 1827.
1835. Lewis Sarah Jane	Henry Lewis & Sally B.	April 22 1835.
Laughton Andrew	Hanibal & Dolly Laughton	Sep. 4, 1828.
Laughton Hanibal D.	Same Parents	May 19, 1830.
Laughton Caroline	Same Parents	April 29, 1833.
Lane Alfred Loring	Alvinzy Lane & Lucy	April 7, 1835.
1836. Lyman Alfred Augustine	Charles A & —— Lyman	Feb 10 1834
Lyman Maria Louisa	Charles A. & —— Lyman	July 30, 1836
Lewis Lucy Elizabeth	Levi & Abigail Lewis	Feb 1ˢᵗ 1834
Lewis William Augustus	Same Parents	Feb 1ˢᵗ 1834
Lewis James Ballard	Same Parents	August 21, 1836
1838. Lewis Delia Ann	Henry & Sarah B Lewis	July 4ᵗʰ 1837.
Ladd George Vivian	Rufus K & Emely P. Ladd	Jan 21. 1838
74 Lee, Harriet Thurston	George W. & Laura S. Lee	Novʳ 8ᵗʰ 1837
Lane Helen Mariah	Alvinzey & Lucy Lane	April 3ʳᵈ 1837
Lincoln, Mary Catharine	Henry & Martha B. Lincoln	Jany. 31ˢᵗ 1840
Lincoln Ellen Sears	Same Parents	Septʳ 27ᵗʰ 1841
Lewis Francis Elizabeth	Henry & Sarah B. Lewis	May 17ᵗʰ. 1842
Laughton Austin A.	Thos & Nancy P. Laughton	March 6 1843
Lincoln, William Henry	Henry & Martha B. Lincoln	July 6, 1843
76 McLeod, David.	Thomas & Alice McLeod	Septʳ 21, 1796.
Maynard, Nabby	John & Martha Maynard	Feby. 16, 1798.
Maynard Joseph Warren	John & Martha Maynard	July 11ᵗʰ, 1801.
Maynard Sophia	John & Martha Maynard	April 3ᵈ, 1803.
Maynard Sally Felton	John & Martha Maynard	Octobʳ. 7ᵗʰ, 1805.
Mallard Maryann	Abraham & Sally Mallard	Octo 7ᵗʰ 1805.
McLellan Charles	William & Lucretia McLellan	Aug 11ᵗʰ 1803.
McLellan Susan	Same Parents	Octo 23 1805.
Mallard Eliza B.	James & Betsy Mallard	Feb 2 1807.
Mallard James Jr.	Same Parents	Jany. 19 1809.
Mallard James	Same Parents	Feb. 15 1811.
McGaw Arabell	John McGaw & Hannah	Nov. 15 1811.
Maynard Charles Angier	Joseph & Anna Maynard	July 31 1808.
Maynard Joseph	Same Parents	Apr 25 1810.
Maynard Elizabeth	Same Parents	Mar. 5 1812.
Mallard Albert	Abraham & Sally Mallard	May 4 1807.

Mallard Hariot		Same Parents	Dec 21, 1809.
Manning Joseph Cogswell		Samuel Manning & Lucy Manning	Sep. 13 1812.
Morgan Louis, altered to Otis Norcross,		Morgan Morgan & Caroline Morgan	July 14 1823.
Mallard Adeline		Abra^m. & Sally Mallard	Mar 19 1814.
Manning Rebecca Pratt.		Saml. & Lucy Manning	Ap 14 1814.
Mallard Hannah Dana		Abraham & Sally Mallard	Mar. 10, 1817.
Meed Sarah		Emily Willard	July 22 1817.
Manning Charles Pratt		Samuel & Lucy Manning	Feb. 13, 1817.
Moore Achsah Ann		Henry & Achsah Moore	Nov. 19 1827.
77 Maynard Elvira		Joseph & Betsy Maynard	Octr 4 1807.
"	Mary Esther	Same Parents	Jany 7 1810.
"	John Hapgood	Same Parents	March 1, 1812.
"	Joseph	Same "	Novr 1 1814.
"	Mary Esther	Same "	August 14 1816.
"	Abigail	Same "	Dec. 2, 1819.
"	Rufus	Same "	March 20 1822.
"	Susan	Same "	June 8, 1824.
"	Martha	Same "	Feby 12 1826.
"	Elizabeth	Same "	March 8, 1829.
"	Catharine E	Same "	August 9 1830.
1835. McCollum Mary Francis		Haskell McCollum & Silvia	Dec. 2, 1835.
Morse Susan M		William & Mary Ann Morse,	" 23, 1835.
1838. Morse Curtis Goodwin		William & Mary Ann Morse.	Aug. 8th 1837.
1842. Maynard David Hollon		Camdan & Julia Ann Maynard	Feby 12, 1842
Maynard Julia Ann		Same Parents	July 19, 1843
Maynard John Harrison		John H. & Mary Maynard	15 Nov^r: 1843
82 Newman Lucy Channing		Gowen B. Newman & Lucy his wife	Decr. 7, 1796.
Newman James Homer		Gowen B. Newman & Lucy his wife	Octr 21. 1798.
Newman Sally		Joseph & Betsy Newman	Dec 17 1799
Newman Polly		Joseph Newman & Betsy his wife	Jan. 14 1801.
Newman Edward Selfridge		Gowen B. Newman & Lucy his wife	Aug. 30 1802.
Newman Betsy Stone		Joseph & Betsy Newman	Jany. 17 1803.
Newman Samuel Chittenden		Gowen B Newman & Lucy his wife	June 18 1807.
Nelson George		Paul & Rhodia Nelson	Apr. 17 1809.
Nelson Maryann		Same Parents	Apr. 15 1811.
Nelson Louisa		Same Parents	Mar 27, 1813.
Newhall Jerome		James & Mary Newhall	June 5 1806.
Dalmer Newhall		Same Parents	June 4 1809.
Newhall Martha Anne		Same Do	Mar 20 1811.
Newhal Susan		Same Parents	Sep. 5 1813.
Newhal Henry Abbot		Pliny & Catharine Newhal	May 3 1814
Nelson Horatio		Paul & Rhoda Nelson	Mar. 4, 1815.
Maria Newman		Newman Lucy Channing	Dec 5 1815.
Newhall Daniel Burt		Daniel & Betsy Newhall	July 20 1813.
Norcross Lucy Maria		Henry & Polly Norcross	June 27 1824.
Norcross Sarah Ann		Same Parents	Sep. 12 1826
Nowell Elizabeth Arnold		W^m. & Elizabeth Nowell	Jan. 17 1824
Nowell John William		Same.	Jany 25 1829
Nowell Elizabeth		Same.	July 18 1826
Nowell Lucy Brigham		Same.	Jany 26 1832
Nourse Henry Stedman		Stedman & Patty Nourse	April 9 1831
1833. Nurse Mary P.		Jon^a. P. Nurse & Mary his wife	Sep: 6 1832.
83 Newman Maria Blain		W^m. H Newman & Mary.	Bor Octo 21 1825
Newman Mary Ann		Same Parents	Bor Dec 16. 1826.
Newman Lucy Adeline		Same Parents	Aug. 26 1829.
Newman James Homer		Same Parents	Aug. 19 1833.
Norcross George Henry		Henry & Polly Norcross	Octo. 10 1828.
1835. Norcross Nathl. Francis		Same Parents	Octo. 16, 1835
1836. Nowell, Catharine Ann		William & Elizabeth Nowell	June 5, 1836
Newman William Nichols		William & Mary Newman	July 17, 1838
Nurse Byron Heywood		Jonathan P. & Mary P. Nurse	Sept. 5th. 1838

LANCASTER RECORDS.

1839. Nourse Ann Elizabeth   Stedman & Patty Nourse   Sept. 4, 1839
1840. Nourse Roscoe Henry   Jonathan P. & Mary P. Nourse   Sept. 6, 1840
1841. Nourse Francis Edward   Fordyce & Laura   April 6, 1841.
88 Abigail Oliver daughter of Joel Oliver and Esther Oliver
                                                  born 15th of November 1805.
Osgood Nancy daughter of Ephraim and Lucy Osgood born May 7, 1787
Lucy Osgood   Parents Same   born May 7, 1791
Betsy Osgood   Do.   born Aug 14, 1797
Ruth Osgood   Do.   born Aug 9, 1801
Joseph Osgood   Do.   born Sep 29 1804
               the above are children of said Ephraim.
Osgood Almira   born Novr. 24, 1805.⎫ Children of
Osgood Emily   " Octor. 3, 1808.   Jonathan Osgood
Osgood Samuel W. " March 9, 1811.   ⎬   &
Osgood Ezra   " April 29, 1814.   Ami his
Osgood James   " Jany. 27 1817.⎭   Wife.
Osgood William   born March 30, 1802.⎫
Osgood Dolly   " July 25, 1803.
Osgood Moses   " Dec. 17, 1805.   Births of the
Osgood Roland   " July 15, 1806.   Children
Osgood Vryling   " Jany. 27, 1808.   of
Osgood Hannah   " March 17, 1810. ⎬ Moses Osgood
Osgood Gilson   " Feb. 22, 1812.   &
Osgood Thomas   " Dec. 7, 1813.   Hannah
Osgood Lucy   " June 25, 1815.   his wife.
Osgood Maryann " April 25, 1817.
Osgood Daniel Powers " Octo. 11, 1818.⎭
89 Otis Mary Elizabeth Benja B. Otis & Mary his wife Apr. 23, 1823.
Osgood Abigail Carter Peter & Mary Nowell Osgood Octo 1, 1826.
Osgood Mary Eliza   Same Parents   April 20, 1828.
Osgood Martha Wyman   Same Parents   August 30 1832.
95 Prentiss Martha Bridge John Prentiss & Martha June 8 1807.
Phelps William   Abijah & Mary Phelps   Nov. 8 1805.
Phelps Sally Parker   Same Parents
Phelps John   Same
Phelps Edward   Same   July 23. 1812
Phelps Elizabeth Wilder, Thomas & Betsy Phelps Sep 28 1812.
Plant George Poignand Samuel Plant & Delicia Mary his wife, Mar. 23, 1814
Plant Sarah Ann   Same Parents   Octo. 21, 1815.
Pollard Emily   Gardner Pollard and Lucy his wife Nov. 11, 1815
Plummer Elizabeth Chandler Farnham & Nancy Plummer Aug. 17. 1815.
Pollard Edward Walker   Abner & Achsah Pollard
Prescott Levi Townshend Levi & Mary Prescott Sep 2, 1798 born in Boylston.
Prescott Otis Brigham   Same Parents   Aug. 22, 1800 " Bolton.
Prescott Nancy   Same Parents   April 30 1807
Prescott Mary Brigham   Same Parents   May 31, 1809
Prescott Hannah Merriam Same Parents   Octo 22, 1811
Prescott Alexander   Same Parents   July 6, 1813.
Phelps Lucretia   George & Sally Phelps   Mar. 31, 1815.
Prescott Harrison   Levi & Mary Prescott   June 23 1816
Pollard Emily   Gardner & Lucy Pollard   Novr. 11, 1816.
Peabody Eliphalet Hill   Calvin & Nabby Peabody   Sep 4, 1816
Pollard Susan Augusta   Abner Pollard & Susanna   Sep 7 1817
Phelps Charles   Thomas & Betsey Phelps   Octo 13 1815.
Plant Frederick William Samuel Plant and Delicia Mary his wife. Octo 3 1817.
96
Prentiss, Anna Rebecca James Otis Prentiss & Anna his wife. Octr. 24th, 1796.
Parker Anna.   Joel & Hannah Parker.   Jany 1st. 1797.
Pratt, Nabby   James & Lydia Pratt.   Novr. 23d, 1797.
Pollard Lydia,   Abner & Achsah Pollard   Apr: 6th, 1798
Prentiss, John Adams   John & Martha Prentiss   May 7th, 1798.
Phelps, Parker   Elisha & Mary Phelps.   Feby. 5, 1798.

Phelps, Mary.	Elisha & Mary Phelps	Apr: 25, 1799.
Phelps, Lydia	Jacob & Prudence Phelps	June 26, 1797.
Pollard, Leonard	Abner & Achsah Pollard	March 11, 1800.
Phelps James Baxter	Elisha & Polly Phelps	Decr. 8, 1800.
Phelps Jesse	George & Sally Phelps	Dec 21 1800
Prentiss William	John & Martha Prentiss	May 10th, 1801.
Pollard Lucy	Gardner & Lucy Pollard	Dec 10 1801
Pollard Sally	Abner & Achsah Pollard	March 27 1802.
Potter Harvey	Jacob & Lucy Potter.	May 11 1799.
Prescott James Sullivan	Levi & Mary Prescott	Jany. 26 1803.
Pollard Patty	Gardner & Lucy Pollard	June 19, 1813.
Phelps Lavina	George & Sally Phelps	Sep. 29 1813.
Pollard Amery	Abner and Achsah Pollard	Mar. 19 1804.
Prentiss Josiah	John & Martha Prentiss	Dec 10 1804.
Prescott Amory	Levi & Mary Prescott	Octo 14, 1804
Pollard Levi	Gardner & Lucy Pollard	May 3 1805
Phelps Sarah	George & Sally Phelps	Augt. 2 1805.
Phelps Martha	Calvin & Asenath Phelps	Augt. 12th 1796
Phelps Anna	Same Parents	April 19 1798
Phelps Calvin	Same Parents	Mar. 30 1800.
Phelps Joseph & Mary Twins	Same Parents	Sep 17 1804
Parker Edmond	John & Lydia Parker	Dec 1 1806
Pollard Mary Ann	Abner & Achsah Pollard	May 26 1806
97 Peabody James Longley	Twins of Calvin Peabody &	Octo 25th 1804
Peabody James Amory	Nabby Peabody	
Phelps Meriel	Ephraim & Dolly Phelps	Dec 30 1806.
Phelps Louisa	George & Sally Phelps	Octo 13 1807
Prescott Nancy	Levi & Mary Prescott	April 30 1808.
Pollard Abner Williams,	Abner & Achsah Pollard	Dec 5 1808.
Phelps Henry	Sylvester & Esther Phelps	Jany 13 1796
Phelps Hezekiah Patterson	Same Parents	Sep 19 1797
Phelps Eliza	Same Parents	April 6 1799
Phelps Samuel	Same Parents	Sep 1 1801
Katharine and Caroline Twins	Same Parents	Sep 30 1803
Phelps Joseph	Same Parents	Jany 26 1806
Phelps Mary Peirce	Same Parents	May 6 1808
Pollard Almira	Gardner & Lucy Pollard	Dec 25 1808
Phelps Gardner	Gardner Phelps & Lucy	Nov 8 1784
Phelps Thomas	Same Parents	April 26 1786
Phelps Polly	Same Parents	June 28 1788
Phelps Asahel	Same Parents	March 8 1790
Phelps Lucy	Same Parents	Feb 28 1794
Phelps Abigail	Same Parents	Sep. 29 1796
Phelps David	Same Parents	June 21 1799
Phelps Lucy 2^d	Same Parents	Aug 3 1802
Phelps Darwin	Same Parents	July 19 1804
Phelps Evelina	Same Parents	Nov. 14 1806
98 Phelps Clarissa	Thomas Phelps & Betsy	May 8th 1809.
Phelps Olive	George & Sally Phelps	July 25 1809
Phelps Nancy	Aaron Phelps	Sept 29 1782
Phelps Joseph	Same Parent	Nov 5th, 1783
Phelps John	Same Parent	Augt. 4 1785
Phelps Sally	Same Parent	Sept. 3 1787
Phelps Rebecca	Same Parent	June 29 1789
Phelps Lucinda	Same Parent	Octo. 14 1791.
Peabody Mary	Calvin & Nabby Peabody	Jany 22 1807
Peabody Hannah Willard	Same	June 8 1808
Peabody Clifford Callahan	Same	Sep 8 1810.
Prentiss Mary Ann Wright.	John & Martha Prentiss.	May 25 1810.
Phelps Joel Wright	Sylvester & Esther Phelps	Mar. 28 1810.
Pollard Mary	Gardner & Lucy Pollard	Jany. 30, 1811

Pollard Seth Heywood	Same Parents	March 21st. 1807.
Pollard Clarissa	Abner & Achsah Pollard	June 17 1811.
Plant Ann Hague	Samuel & Delicia Mary Plant	May 20 1810
Plant Louisa Elizabeth	Same Parents	April 3 1812.
Phelps Luther Jones	George & Sally Phelps	Nov. 30 1812.
Phelps Mary Ann	Sylvester & Esther Phelps	Mar. 26 1813.
Follard Betsy	Gardner & Lucy Pollard	May 11 1813.
Pollard Edward Walker	Abner & Achsah Pollard	Octo 10 1814.
Plummer Thomas	Farnham & Nancy Plummer	May 19 1814
*	*	*
99 Phelps Mary Baldwin	Thos. & Betsy Phelps.	Feby 22 1818.
Prescott Willm. Augustus	Levi & Mary Prescott	Octo 17 1818
Peirce Sally Ann	Charles Peirce & Sally	Aug. 9 1818.
Plummer Charles	Farnham Plummer & Nancy Plummer	Jany. 6, 1818
Plummer Charles	Same Parents	July 12, 1819
Pratt Siloma	Ebenr. Pratt & Emily	Octo 20 1818
Phelps Julia Ann	George Phelps & Sally	Octo 3, 1819.
Pollard Clarissa Elizabeth	Abner Pollard & Susanna	Nov. 12, 1819.
Peirce Samuel Harvy	Harvy Peirce & Cynthia	Jany. 31. 1820.
Pollard Nancy	Gardner & Lucy Pollard	Dec 30 1817
Pollard Henry Gardner	Same Parents	Sep. 9 1820.
1821. Plant Samuel	Saml. & Delicia Mary Plant	June 18, 1819.
Plant Alfred	Same Parents	Mar. 2, 1821.
Pitts Seth Grout	James Pitts & Prudence	May 26 1817.
Phelps Levi Whiting	Peter Phelps	April 29, 1821
Pollard Christopher Augustine	Abner & Susanna Pollard	Octo 14, 1821
Peasely Martha Ann	Moses & Sarah Peasely	Jany 4, 1822.
1823. Pratt Betsy	Ebenr. & Emily Pratt	May 23, 1822
Peirce Charles Henry	Henry & Cynthia Peirce	Feb. 27, 1825.
Phelps Maria	Thos. & Betsy Phelps	June 15, 1820
Plant William Marshall	Saml. & Delicia Plant	March 16, 1823.
Plant Henry	Same Parents	July 22 1825.
Phelps Elizabeth	Ephraim & Dolly Phelps	Jan. 8 1814
Phelps Dolly	Same Parents	Nov 2 1815
Phelps Mary Ann	Same Parents	May 10 1818
Phelps Samuel	Same Parents	July 12 1821
Phelps James	Same Parents	Aug 1 1825
Pratt Curtiss	Jesse Pratt & Polly	Aug. 10 1827.
Pratt Joseph Warren	Ebenr. Pratt & Emily	Feby. 11, 1826.
100 Plant Elizabeth Derby Pickman	Samuel & Delicia Plant	July 10, 1827.
Prentiss John	Rhoda Johnson	April 21, 1824.
Phelps Abigail.	Robert & Mary Phelps	March 16 1795.
Phelps Sewall.	Same Parents.	Augt. 11, 1798.
Phelps Sewall 2d.	Same Parents.	May 13, 1809.
Phelps Mary	Same Parents.	Sept 14, 1813.
Phelps Cornelia	Same Parents.	Feby. 11, 1816.
Pratt Abel Solon	Ebenr. & Emily Pratt	March 9, 1829.
Phelps Mary Elizabeth	Henry & Mary Phelps	Jany 18, 1826.
Pollard Charles F.	Leonard Pollard & Annis	March 27 1822.
Pollard Leonard L.	Same Parents.	Nov. 9, 1823.
Pollard Nancy W.	Same Parents.	April 28 1827.
Pollard Alvah H.	Same.	Octo. 9 1829.
Priest Sylvanus C.	Charles & Nancy Priest	Octo 12 1830
Ellen Augusta Pollard	Amory & Persis Pollard	March 27, 1831.
Pollard George Amory	Same Parents	August 15 1832.
Pollard Sylvia Ann	Leonard & Annis Pold	Aug. 26, 1831.
Parker Gilman Cornelius	Gilman B & Sarah F. Parker	June 28 1832
Plant Mary Delicia	Saml & Delicia Plant	Novr 28 1829
Plant Delicia Amiraux	Same Parents	Jany 6, 1832.
1833. Prouty Mary E. Glazier	Jason Prouty & Elizh,	Sep. 20 1828.
Pollard Adelaide Elizabeth	Levi & Lydia Pollard	April 24 1833.
Putney Mariett	Putney Manasah & Mary	Feb 2, 1834.

BOOK SECOND. 217

Phelps Martha Stearns	Thomas & Betsy Phelps	Jany. 30 1832
Pratt Mary Louisa	Eben' & Emily Pratt	Jany. 7, 1832.
Parker Sam¹. Abbot.	Gilman B. & Sarah F. Parker	May 21, 1834.
Pease Abba Elizabeth	Lory Pease & Cathª. W.	May 19, 1834
Priest Adolphus M.	Charles & Nancy Priest born at Cambridge	Sep. 25 1827
Priest Electa	Same Parents	July 4, 1833.
1835. Pollard John Gardner	Levi & Lydia Pollard	Octo. 10, 1834.
Pratt Elsey Frances	Eben & Emily Pratt	Octo 29, 1835.
101 1836. Mary Jane Parker	Gilman B. & Sarah F. Parker	Dec 31, 1835
John Chandler } Twins	Farnham & Abigail Plummer	Apl. 18, 1836
Mary Marsh }		
Parker Sarah Isabella	Gilman B. & Sarah F. Parker	Feby 21, 1838
Henrietta Eliza Phelps	Joel W. Phelps & Lorinda Phelps	July 9, 1837
Mary Ann Phelps	" " "	Sept 5, 1839
Ellen Elizabeth Pitts	William & Dolly T. Pitts	Oct. 8, 1840
Anna Louisa Pitts	Same Parents	Dec. 28, 1842
Francis Mary Pierce	Gilbert & Rhoda Pierce	May 6, 1838
Plummer, Francis John	Farnham & Abigail Plummer	Feby 29, 1840
Phelps Elizabeth	William & Olive Phelps	April 12, 1833
105 Rugg Eliza Ann	Ephraim & Betsy Rugg	June 28 1812
Rugg Julia	Joseph & Mary Rugg	Jan 11 1813
Rugg Sophia	Samuel & Sarah Rugg	July 17 1809
Rugg Warren	Same Parents	July 11 1812.
Rugg Emily Wyman	James Rugg & Submit	May 22 1814
Rugg Harriet	Joseph & Mary Rugg	Jany. 11ᵗʰ 1815.
Rugg Submit Brooks	James Rugg & Submit	Feb. 12 1816
Rugg Ephraim	Ephraim Rugg & Betsy	Dec — 1816
Rugg Benjª. Hazen	Joseph Rugg & Mary Rugg	Dec 29 1816
Rugg Sophia	James Rugg & Submit Rugg his wife	Aug. 11 1817.
Rugg Lewis Patch	Luke Rugg & Salome	Mar. 25 1819
Rugg Elizabeth	James Rugg & Submit	Nov 12 1818
Rugg Asa W.	Ephraim Rugg & Betsy	July 27 1819.
1821. Rugg James	James Rugg & Submit	May 14 1820.
Rugg Susan Whitney	Luke Rugg & Salome	Apr. 19 1821.
1822. Rugg Josiah Newhall	James Rugg & Submit	Feb 17 1822.
1823. Rugg Hannah Martin	Abel Rugg Jr & Hannah	Mar 26 1820
Rugg Martha Fay	Same Parents	July 17 1822.
Rugg Mary	Joel Rugg & Bathsheba	Mar. 14 1814
Rugg Elizabeth	Same Parents	Sep 26 1816.
Rugg Joel Isaac	Same Parents	Feb 13 1819
Rugg Willᵐ Brown	Same Parents	May 1 1822.
Rugg George Henry	Luke Rugg & Salome	Aug 27 1823.
Rugg Hariet Stearns	James & Submit Rugg	Nov 2 1823.
106 Rugg, Sarah Harriman	Joseph & Mary Rugg	Octʳ. 28, 1796.
Rugg, Alpheus.	Abijah & Susanna Rugg	Sept. 26, 1796.
Rugg, Emily,	Samˡ. & Sarah Rugg	May 30 1798.
Robins, Hannah	Eleazer & Mary Robins	May 27, 1798.
Rugg, Edward	Joseph & Mary Rugg	May 27, 1798.
Robbins Robba	Eleazer & Mary Robbins	Nov. 16, 1799.
Rice, Nathaniel	Joseph & Betsy Rice	May 2ᵈ 1800.
Rugg Joseph Arnold	Elisha & Ami Rugg	Feb 26 1801.
Robbins Sarah Manning	Eleazar & Mary Robbins	Sep. 25 1801
Rugg Granville	Joseph & Mary Rugg	May 24 1802.
Rice Joseph	Joseph & Betsy Rice	Nov. 26 1802
Rugg Elijah	Joseph & Mary Rugg	Mar. 10 1804
Rice Sally	Ezekiel & Eliza Rice	Feb. 19 1804.
Rugg Abel Warner	Abel & Katharine Rugg	March 17 1797
Rugg Katharine	Abel & Katharine Rugg	Mar 18 1799
Rugg, Sarah Wilder	Samuel & Sarah Rugg	May 11 1801
Rugg Maryann	Samuel & Sarah Rugg	Sep 15 1803.
Rice Maryann	Joseph & Betsy Rice	July 1 1805.
Rugg Lucy	Joseph & Mary Rugg	Feb. 4 1806.

15

Name	Parents	Date
Rugg Samuel Stillman	Samuel Rugg & ——	July 6th 1807.
Rugg William	Joseph & Mary Rugg	May 24 1808.
Rice Abel	Joseph & Betsy Rice	May 2d 1808.
Rugg Martha Wyman	Josiah & Polly Rugg	Aug 10 1808.
Rugg Sally Warner	Ephraim & Betsy Rugg	Octo 4 1809.
Rugg Christopher } Twins	Joseph & Mary Rugg	April 25 1810.
Rugg Augustus } Twins	Same Parents	April 25 1810.
Ross John	Simeon & Polly Ross	July 5, 1811.
Rice Louisa	Joseph & Betsy Rice	Sep. 14 1811.
Rugg Sewall	Josiah & Polly Rugg	Feb. 22, 1812.
Rugg ——	Nahum & Betsy Rugg	May 18 1812.
107 Rugg Martha [K.]	James Rugg & Submit	March 2 1825
Rugg Harriet Pratt	Abel W. Rugg Jr & Hannah	Sept 21 1824
Rugg Mary Elizabeth	Same Parents	Augt 11, 1826
Rice Mary Eliza	Josiah Rice & Mary	May 2, 1825
Rugg Emeline Elizabeth	Luke Rugg & Siloma.	May 10 1826.
Rand Charles Henry	son of Nath¹ & Nancy E. Rand	Oct' 9 1828
Rice Harriet Maria	Josiah & Mary Rice	Sept 29th 1828
Rugg Lucretia	James Rugg & Submit	Aug 12 1826
Rugg Daniel	Same Parents	Feby 22, 1828
Rugg Daniel [W.]	Same Parents	Mar. 2 1829
Rice Benjⁿ. Franklin	Nath¹ Rice & Anna	Sep 21 1828
Rice Mary Ann	Same	May 16 1830
1833. Rugg Charles Franklin	Luke Rugg & Siloma	Feby. 9, 1831
Rugg Francis	Joel & Bathsheba Rugg	August 26 1832
Rice Sarah Jane	Nath¹ Rice & Anna his Wife	Octo. 7, 1831.
Rice Anna Maria	Same	Feb 24 1833.
1834. Rugg Susan Whitney	Luke Rugg & Silome	Nov. 28, 1834
Richardson Joseph Osgood.	Abel & Elizabeth Richardson	Sept 25 1831
Rugg Lucinda Maria	Abel W. Rugg & Hannah	Octo. 31, 1828
1835. Rugg Sewall T.	John Rugg & Eliza his wife	June 24 1821
Rugg Mary T.	Same Parents	Octo 25 1823
Rugg William	Same Parents	Nov 8, 1825
Rugg John Junʳ.	Same Parents	March 8, 1828
Rugg Lucy H.	Same Parents	May 21, 1832
*	*	*
Richardson Clorinda	Samuel & Betsy Richardson	July 14 1819
Richardson Martha W.	Same Parents	Octo 11 1826
Richardson Harriet Miranda	Same Parents	April 8, 1830
Rice Louisa Elizabeth	Nath¹. & Ann Rice	Nov. 16, 1834
108 Rugg, Henry Howard	John & Eliza Rugg	August 31 1839
Rice Jacob Eynand	Nath¹ & Anna Rice	Oct. 1, 1839
Rice Harriet Augusta	Same Parents	April 2, 1841
William D. Rand	Nathaniel & Ruth Rand	Oct. 5th 1839
Rand Josephine A.	Same Parents	Dec. 22 1841
113 Sawyer John	Moses Sawyer & Elizabeth	Dec 24 1810.
Smith Charles Henry	Moses Smith & Salla	May 25 1811
Studly Frederick Gould	Oliver Studly & Elizabeth	Jany 14 1812.
Sawyer Eliakim	Eliakim & Hannah Sawyer	Dec 7, 1812
Smith Abigail Arabelle	Moses Smith & Salla	Aug. 15, 1813.
Studly Warren	Oliver Studly & Elizabeth	Octo 30 1813.
Sargent John	Jno Sargent & Anna	Feb 9 1805.
Sargent Sewall	Same Parents	June 16 1807.
Sargent Zophar	Same Parents	Jany 18 1809.
Sargent Eliza	Same Parents	Mar 24th 1811.
Sargent Nath¹.	Same Parents	July 25 1813.
Sawyer Evelina	Peter & Mary Sawyer	May 16, 1808
Sawyer Peter	Same Parents	Nov. 18, 1811
Sawyer Ezra	Same Parents	July 8, 1814
Smith, Mary Prescott Putnam,	Moses & Sally Smith	Aug. 5, 1816.
Sawyer Charles Ballard	Elias & Nancy Sawyer	Nov. 26 1816.
Sawyer Moses Elias	Peter Sawyer & Mary Sawyer	June 12 1817.

BOOK SECOND.

Name	Parents	Date
Stone Joseph	Jacob Stone & Anna Stone	Feb 19 1797.
Stone James	Same Parents	Aug. 29 1799.
Stone Martha	Same Parents	June 29 1801.
Stone Jacob	Same Parents	Mar. 6 1803.
Anna Stone	Same Parents	Feb 4 [9?], 1805.
Stone Achsah	Same Parents	Apr. 18 1806.
Stone Abel	Same Parents	Apr. 6 1808.
Stone Betsy	Same Parents	Mar. 11 1810
Stone Oliver	Same Parents	Jany. 16 1812.
Stone Betsy	Same Parents	Mar. 3 1814.
Stone Tamar	Same Parents	Dec 30 1815.
Stone Maria	Same Parents	Mar. 23 1818.
114 Sawyer, John Hicks.	Israel Sawyer & Mary his wife	Feby 9, 1797.
Sawyer Henry	Moses Sawyer jun & Betsy his wife	Aug: 31, 1797.
Stearns Hariot	Eli Stearns & Mary his wife	Novr. 21, 1797.
Stedman, William	William Stedman & Almy his wife	July 18, 1799.
Stearns, William	Eli Stearns & Mary his wife	Novr 2^d 1799.
Sawyer, Susan	Israel Sawyer & Mary his wife	Feby 16, 1799.
Sawyer Cynthia	Luther Sawyer & Zilpah his wife	Feby 15, 1800.
Stedman, Francis Dana,	W^m. Stedman & Almy his wife	Feby. 10, 1801.
Sawyer Sally	Oliver Sawyer & Polly his wife	Augt. 9 1801.
Stearns Catharine	Eli Stearns & Mary his wife	Feb. 18 1802
Stevens Charles	Nathan Stevens & Sally Stevens	Aug. 5 1802
Stevens Lucretia	Same Same	Nov 27 1803.
Sargent Susanna	John and Anna Sargent	Apr 24 1803.
Sargent Polly	Stephen and Mary Sargent	Dec 13 1801
Sargent Stephen	Same Same	June 24 1803.
Stearns Sally Whitney	Eli Stearns & Mary his wife	May 13, 1804
Studly Sarah Mann	Consider & Olive Studly	Octo 9th, 1804.
Stedman Charles Harrison	William & Almy Stedman	June 17th 1805.
Sawyer Almy Ellery	Luther and Zilpah Sawyer,	Nov. 12 1805.
Sawyer Eliakim	Same Parents	Jany. 22 1786
Sawyer Zilpah	Same	Jany. 30 1788
Sawyer Luther	Same	Sept. 22 1792
Solindine Adeline	Manasah & Deborah Solindine	March 27 1806.
Smith Sydney	Moses Smith & Sally Smith	Nov. 14 1806.
Sawyer James	Thomas Sawyer & Elizabeth	Feb 14 1797.
Sawyer Elizabeth	Same Parents	Feb 7 1799.
Stearns Nancy	Eli Stearns & Mary his wife	Apr. 15 1806
Stearns Augustus	Same Same	Octo 4 1807
Solindine Susan Wilder	Manasah & Deborah Solindine	Jany. 2 1808
Sawyer Jonas	Paul & Martha Sawyer	Sep 26 1793.
Smith Phillip Augustus	Moses & Sally Smith	Feb 20 1809.
115 Stow Louisa Jane	Aaron & Esther Stow	Jany. 25 1818.
Sawyer Mary Ann	Elias & Nancy Sawyer	Nov. 21, 1820.
Sargent Willard	Stephen & Mary Sargent	Dec 16 1814
Sargent Loisa	Same Parents	Dec 21, 1815
Sargent Curtiss	Same Parents	Octo 12 1815.
1821. Sawyer Fredrick Charles	Peter Sawyer	Dec. 14 1819.
Sawyer Sarah Ann	Eben^r. Sawyer & Sarah	Sep. 3, 1821.
Smith Henry	Moses & Sally Smith	June 15, 1820
1822. Sawyer Emelne	Elias & Nancy Sawyer	Sep. 18 1822.
Sawyer Mary Thurston	Eben Sawyer & Sarah	Nov. 8, 1822
Smith Francis	Moses & Sally Smith	May 20, 1822
Sawyer Sarah Elizabeth	Charles & Eliza Sawyer	September 3, 1823.
Sawyer Henry Hovey	Ezra Sawyer & Eliza	Apr. 18, 1824.
Safford Charles	George & Mary Safford	Sept 14 1817
Safford George Fosdick	Same Parents.	March 19 1819
Safford Roby	Same Parents.	Dec 12 1821
Safford Augustus	Same Parents.	Jany 9 1825.
Sawyer Francis Augustus	Silas & Sarah [Sally] Sawyer,	March 18, 1823.
Sawyer Lucy Ann	Same Parents	August 9, 1825.

LANCASTER RECORDS.

Name	Parents	Date
Solindine Elvira	Manasah & Deborah Solindine	May 10 1820
Solindine Mary	Same Parents.	May 10 1822
Solindine Julia Ann	Same Parents.	Jany — 1824
Sawyer Elmirick	Peter Sawyer	March 31, 1822.
Sawyer Marietta Hayward	Same Parents.	Jany 10 1820.
Sargent Sarah W.	Thomas & Elizabeth,	Octo 19 1826
Sawyer Ezra Thomas	Ezra Sawyer & Eliza	Jan. 4 1827.
Sawyer Abigail Barrett	Elias & Nancy Sawyer	Nov. 26, 1824
Sawyer Louisa Augusta	Same Parents.	Nov. 28 1827.
Sawyer Martha Sophia	Charles & Eliza	April 1, 1825.
Sawyer Charles Francis	Same Parents	Jany. 22, 1827.
Stow Augusta Emily	Levi & Susan Stow	May 7th 1827.
Sargent Lyman	Stephen & Mary Sargent	July 15 1826
116 Sanderson Geo Williams	Sodi & Pamela Sanderson	June 4, 1819.
Sanderson Willm Lowell	Same Parents.	Sept 1. 1822.
Sanderson Nathan Dana	Same Parents	Sept 19 1825.
Sawyer Franklin	Henry & Catharine B.	Feby. 3, 1828.
Sawyer Sarah Elizabeth	Charles & Eliza Sawyer	May 5 1829.
Sawyer Francis Oliver	Ezra Sawyer & Eliza	July 30, 1829.
Stone Christopher Columbus Burditt	James Stone & Eliza.	Nov. 27, 1829.
Seaver Cyrus	Joseph & Persis Seaver	Decr. 15 1828.
Sawyer Catharine Amelia	Henry & Catharine Sawyer	May 11, 1830.
Sargent Emory	Stephen & Mary Sargent	Mar 27, 1821.
Sargent Cordelia	Same Parents	Sept 15 1823.
Stow Edmund	Levi & Susan Stow	Dec 12 1828
Stow Mary Ann	Same Parents	Feb 23, 1831.
Sanderson Edwin Lovejoy	Sodi & Pamela Sanderson	Octo 22 1827.
Sanderson Charles,	Same Parents.	June 29, 1830.
Sanderson Eliza Ann	Same Parents	Augt. 15 1832.
Sawyer Almeida Augusta	Henry & Catharine Sawyer	March 23, 1832
Sawyer George Moses	Charles & Eliza Sawyer	Jany 10 1831.
Sawyer Francina Elsy	Elias & Nancy Sawyer } Twins	Sep 24 1832
Sawyer Frederick Henry	Same Parents	
1833. Sawyer Lucy Caroline	Elijah Sawyer & Martha	Sep 22 1833.
Stow Asa	Luke & Abigail Stow	Sep 16 1829
Stow Abba	Same Parents	May 13, 1832
Stow Andrew	Levi & Susan Stow	May 6, 1833.
1834. Sawyer Francina Eliza Joslyn	Elijah Sawyer	Dec [Oct.] 20. 1834
1835. Stow Luke Stearns	Luke & Abigail Stow	Augt. 9, 1834
Sawyer Emery Thomas	Thomas & Polly Sawyer	March 19, 1835.
Sawyer Mary Katherine	Same Parents	May 13, 1820.
Sargeant Emily,	Merrick & Rebecca Sargeant	Aug. 22, 1835.
Stow Franklin	Moses & Eliza Stow	Octo. — 1831.
Sawyer Nathl. Chandler	Ezra & Eliza Sawyer	August 15, 1831.
Sawyer Sarah Elizabeth	Same Parents.	Augt 7, 1833.
Smith Henry Freeman	Joshua T. Smith & Rebecca	Octo 29 1835.
Sargent Catharine Eliza	Zophar & Catharine Sargent	Jan. 22 1834
117 1836. Sawyer Edmund Houghton	Ezra & Eliza Sawyer	Nov. 16, 1821
Stone Ellen Eliza	James & Elisa Stone	Feb 19, 1836
1837. Stratton Henry Oscar	Geo & Lucinda Stratton	Jan 5th, 1837.
Seargent Henry	Seth & Maria Seargent	Feb 29, 1836
Seargent William Leonard	Merrick & Rebecca Seargent	April 9, 1837
Stone Sarah Louisa	James & Eliza Stone	March 4, 1838
Sawyer Henry Oliver	America & Lucy H. Sawyer	May 4, 1834
Sawyer Lucy Hosley	Same Parents	March 6, 1835
Sawyer Lucinda Matilda	Same Parents	April 27, 1837
Sawyer Eliza Ann	Ezra & Eliza Sawyer	Decr 31, 1838
Sawyer Eliza	Charles & Eliza Sawyer	Nov. 28, 1832
Sawyer John Henry	Same Parents	Jany 16, 1838
Stone Harriet Elizabeth	James & Eliza Stone	Jan 23. 1839
Stone Caroline Louisa	Same Parents	Jany 23, 1839
Stearns Mary Francis	William & Mary Ann Stearns	Oct. 5, 1839

Stearns Martha Ann	Same Parents	Feb 28, 1842
Sargent Laura Ann	Zophar [&] Catharine Sargent	Jany. 26 1836
Sears, Katharine	Edmund H. & Ellen Sears	Feb. 25, 1843
Stratton Geo. Lyman	Geo. & Lucinda Stratton	Nov. 13 1838
Stratton Roselia Jeanette	Same Parents	Jany 4 1841
125 Thompson Abigail	Benj^a. Thompson	May 15, 1796
Thompson Wm Graves	Same.	May 29, 1802
Thompson Caroline	Same.	Dec 24, 1804
Thompson Wm Ramsden	Same.	May 3, 1807.
Thompson Oricy	Same.	Jany. 4, 1810.
Thompson Caroline	Benj^a Thompson & Elizabeth	Jan. 23, 1814.
Tombs Angelina	W^m. & Betsy Tombs	born 20th June 1818.
Tombs Martha Ann	Wm. & Betsy Tombs	born 2^d Feb. 1816.
Tower Mary Eliza	Asahel Tower Jun & Polly his wife.	born 25th Aug. 1818.
Townsend Mary	William Townsend & Martha	Jany. 17, 1816.
Townsend W^m. Prescott	Same Parents	July 25 1818.
Townsend Martha	Same Parents	Jany. 15, 1820.
1821. Tombs William	W^m. & Betsy Tombs	May 20, 1820.
Tower W^m. Henry, altered to Henry Ambrose,	Asahel Tower Jr & Polly	Feb. 5, 1821.
1823. Townshend George	John & Ruth Townshend	Feb. 16, 1807.
Townshend John	Same Parents	Sept. 8, 1808.
Townshend Elvira	Same Parents	Mar 4, 1811.
Townshend Zimri	Same Parents	June 21, 1813.
Townshend William	Same Parents	Nov. 11, 1815.
Thayer Nathaniel	Rev^r Nathl. Thayer & Sarah his wife	Sep. 11, 1808.
Thayer Abigail	Same Parents	Octo 1, 1812.
Thurston an infant	Silas Thurston jun & [Parney]	Mar. 19, 1823.
Tower Julia Ann.	Asahel Tower Jr & Polly	Feb. 21, 1823.
Tilden Henry Partridge,	Josiah & Charlotte Tilden	April 27 1823
Thompson Abigail	Simon Thompson & Lucy	June 13, 1823
126 Thayer. Martha	Revd Nathan^l Thayer & Sarah his Wife	Apr. 25, 1798.
Tower, Lucinda	Asahel & Melicent Tower	Sept. 28, 1798.
Thayer, Mary-Ann	Revd N. Thayer & Sarah his wife	April 13, 1800
Thurston William	Gates Thurston & Betsy his wife	Mar: 6, 1798.
Thurston Thomas Gates	ditto ditto do	Nov. 15 1890.
Tower Daniel Clap	Asahel and Melicent Tower	Nov. 20 1800.
Thurston Abel [Atherton]	Gates & Betsy Thurston	Sep. 15, 1802.
Tower Henry	Asahel & Melicent Tower	Mar 13, 1803.
Townshend Hariot	John & Ruth Townshend	Nov 20 1803.
Townshend Joel Putnam	Same Parents	April 16 1805.
Thayer John	Nathaniel & Sarah Thayer	Aug. 21 1803.
Thayer Christopher Toppan	Same Parents,	June 5 1805.
Thurston Caroline	Peter & Sally Thurston	Sep. 22 1797
Thurston Sally [Sarah Ann]	Same Parents	May 14 1799
Thurston George Peter	Same Parents	March 29 1802.
Tower Christopher	Asahel and Millicent Tower	Sep 10th 1805.
Thurston Sampson Wilder, altered by an act of Court to Wilder [S.] Thurston.	Gates & Betsy Thurston	Octo 8 1806.
Townshend Henry	Robert & Elizabeth Townshend,	Mar. 10th 1793.
Townshend Abigail Holman	Same Parents	April 1st. 1795.
Townshend Nancy Willson	Same Parents	Sep. 25 1797
Townshend Warren	Same Parents	Nov 24th 1800.
Thurston Harriot	Silas & Sarah Thurston	July 24 1797
Thurston David Kendall	Same Parents	July 25 1799
Thurston Mary	Same Parents	June 19 1802
Thurston John	Silas & Mikel Thurston	Mar 20 1808
127 Tower George Franklin	Asahel Tower Jr & Polly	June 3 1825.
Townshend Henry	Warren Townshend & Almira	Octo 4 1824
Townshend Henry	William & Martha	July 4 1823.

Name	Parents	Date
Thnrston Nancy	Gates & Betsy Thurston	Jany 31 1796.
Toombs Elizabeth Cranston	Wm & Betsy Toombs	Feby. 21, 1826
Thurston Martha [H]	Silas Thurston Jr & Parney	Mar. 30, 1824
Thurston Charles Frederic	Same Parents	July 21, 1826.
Thurston Franklin H	David K. Thurston [& Betsy]	Nov 14 1824
Tower Sarah Maria	Asahel & Polly Tower	June 21 1827.
Townshend Abigail Holman	Warren & Almira Townshend	March 13, 1826.
Thurston Caleb	John Thurston Jr & Lucy his Wife	Sept. 14, 1815.
Thurston Mary Ann	Same Parents.	March 27 1817.
Thurston Rebecca	Same Parents.	July 10, 1819.
Toombs Alemeida Cross	Robt C Toombs & Louisa	Dec. 21, 1827.
Thompson Jane	Simon Thompson & Lucy	July 1 1826
Tyler Anthony Hale	Ansel & Mary Tyler	Nov. 12 1823
Tyler Jane Blake	Same Parents	Mar. 27 1826.
Ellen Cross Tombs	daughter of Rob. C and Loisa	Decr 21, 1827
Thurston Harriet Elizabeth	Jno G & Harriet Thurston	March 31, 1829
Tucker Sarah Ann Augusta	Amos & Loisa Tucker	May 30 1829.
Toombs Edward Walker	Wm & Betsy Toombs.	Octo 11, 1828
Thurston Francina Elizabeth	David K. Thurston	Feby 5, 1829.
Tower Rufus Ellis,	Asahel & Polly Tower	Feby 26, 1830.
Thurston Charles	John Thurston Jr & Mehitable	May 12, 1830.
Tower Hannah Sophia	Asahel Tower Jr.	Nov. 3 1831.
1833 Taylor John Franklin	John & Susan Taylor	Jany. 2 1833.
Taylor Susan Jane	Same parents	Jany 24 1834
1834. Townshend Charles	Warren & Almira Townshend	June 23, 1828
Townshend Mary Ann Carter	Same Parents	March 5 1830
Townshend Abigail Holman Sever	Same "	Jany 22 1833.
128 Thurston George Lee,	John G. Thurston & Harriet	Jany. 16, 1831.
Thurston Francis Henry	Same Parents	Dec 21, 1833
Thurston Josephine	Same Parents	Sep. 9, 1832.
Townshend Frederick W.	Willm. Townshend & Martha	March 20 1826
Townshend Francis	Same Parents	Feb. 10, 1830.
Tyler, Eliza Ann	Benjamin & Eliza Tyler New Ipswich	March 10 1820
Tyler Ellen Grace	Same Parents do.	Sept 9, 1827.
1835. Thurston Henry Thomas	John Thurston Jun & Mehitable	Dec 15, 1834
Taylor Henry Thomas	John & Susan Taylor	Jany 19, 1835.
Tower Frances Ellen	Asahel & Polly Tower	May 2, 1835.
Thurston, Russell Gates	Wilder S. & Ann M. Thurston	May 29 1840
Thomson Mary Agnes.	John W. & Ann F. Thomson N.Y.	Aug. 26, 1838
Thurston, Julia Frances	Silas and Parney	January 13, 1834

138

Vose Martha Eliza } twins Peter T. Vose & Ann his Wife August 25, 1816.
Vose Francis Henry }

Virgil Sarah Elizabeth, daughter of Daniel Virgil, and Vashti his wife,
  born May 19th 1831.
Vose Ellen Russell, Samuel J. Sprague Vose & Mary W.Vose January 10, 1841.
139 Winter Lydia daughter of John Winter and Lydia his wife
  born October 22nd, 1809.
White Joseph Carter son of Abel White & Betsy his wife born Dec. 28th 1809.
Wyman Ephraim Son of Benjamin Wyman and Lucretia his second Wife
  born Jany. 26 1809
Willard Isaac son of William & Lucy Willard   born Sept 28th 1809.

Name	Parents	Date
White Mary Chase	Joseph & Rebecca White	May 27 1805.
White James	Same Parents	Octo 12 1806.
Willard Henry	Paul & Martha Willard	Jany. 16 1807.
Wilder Sarah Lee	Abel & Hannah Wilder	June 4 1810
Wilder Anthony	Saml. & Elizabeth Wilder	June 12th 1808
Wilder Malinda	Same Parents.	Mar 8th 1810.
Webb Lucy	Joseph & Lucy Webb	Aug 13 1809
Wilder Abigail Rand	Luke Wilder & Mary	Sep 27 1807
Willard George Anson	Benja. & Sally Willard	June 26 1810.
Willard Salmon	Salmon & Rachel Willard	Octo 11, 1802

BOOK SECOND.

Name	Parents	Date
Willard Rachel	Same Parents	Dec. 7, 1804
Willard Henry	Same Parents	July 5 1810.
Willard Sarah	Same Parents	July 5 1810.
Wilder [Charles] Lewis	Jn° Wilder & Sally Wilder	Feb 20, 1812.
Whittemore Asa Dunbar	Prescott & Lucy Rebecca Whittemore	Aug. 9, 1812.
Willard Horace	Benj^a & Sally Willard	April 19 1812.
140 White Sophia	Jn° White 3^d & Sophia his wife	Septr. 16 1796
Wyman, Benjamin	Benj^a & Martha Wyman	Octr 23^d, 1796
Whiting, Thomas Jefferson	Tim° Whiting jun & Abigail his wife	Decr. 9, 1796.
Wilder, John Warren	John & Sally Wilder	Jany 3^d, 1797
Wheelock, Eli,	Benj^a & Prudence Wheelock.	July 1st, 1797.
Whiting, Solon,	John & Orpah Whiting.	May 13th, 1797.
Whiting, Joseph,	Timothy Whiting jun & Abigail his wife	July 18, 1798.
Wilder Joseph Wales,	John & Sally Wilder	April 16th 1798.
Wilder Samuel	Samuel the 2nd & Elizabeth Wilder	May 16th 1798.
White Patty	Jn° White jun & Sophia his wife	Sept. 19, 1798
Wheelock, Polly	Benj^a & Prudence Wheelock	Jany 4th, 1799.
Woods, Horace	Stephen & Ascenath Woods	Feby 18. 1799.
Whetcomb, Phinehas Willard	Chapman & Rhoda Whetcomb	July 7, 1798.
Willard, Walter.	Paul & Martha Willard	June 7, 1797
Willard, Martha.	Same	May 26, 1799.
Willard, Martha,	Ezra & Susannah Willard	Novr 13, 1799.
Willard, Merrick	William & Sally Willard	Apr: 11, 1797
Whiting, Caroline Lee	John & Orpah Whiting	June 1, 1800.
Wilder, Eliza	Samuel Wilder 2^d & Eliza. his wife	May 3^d, 1800.
Wilder, Sally.	John & Sally Wilder	April 19 1800
Whiting, Hariot,	Timothy & Lydia Whiting.	Decr. 13th 1800
Wheelock, Jonathan	Benj^a. & Prudence Wheelock	July 26, 1800
Willard Eliza.	James & Ame Willard	Aug. 6, 1798
Willard Erastus.	James & Ame Willard	July 4, 1800.
Willard Stedman	William & Sarah Willard	Octo 12 1800
Wilder Henry	Jonathan & Ruth Wilder	Feb 4 1800
Wyman Nathaniel	Benjamin & Martha Wyman	Octo 3, 1801
Wilder Abigail	John & Sally Wilder	March 16th 1802.
Whittemore Benj^a.	Nathl and Polly Whittemore	May 3, 1801
Charles Whiting	Timothy & Lydia Whiting	Novr. 20 1802.
Wilder Daniel Kelsey	Daniel & Lydia Wilder	Jany. 22 1803
Wilder Merrick	Samuel & Elizabeth Wilder	Mar. 13, 1802
Willard Jonas.	Silas & Hannah Willard	May 7, 1795
Willard Silas	Silas & Hannah Willard	Sep. 25 1799.
141 White Luther.	Abijah & Bathsheba White	Nov. 14 1802.
White [Willard?] Peter	Amasa & Fanny Willard	July 6, 1803.
Willard Mary	Paul & Martha Willard	Sep 4 1801.
Willard Lucia	Ditto do.	July 30, 1803.
Wilder John	Jn°. Wilder 3^d.	Aug 6 1795 *obit*
Wilder John	Ditto	June 15 1796.
Wilder Danforth	Ditto.	June 25 1798
Wilder Sally	Ditto.	Jany 12 1801
Willard Sally	William & Sarah Willard	May 25 1803
Washburn Eliphalet	Rufus & Thankful Washburn	June 14 1790
Washburn George	Same	Dec. 5, 1803.
Wilder Benj^a Gowin	John Wilder & Sally his wife	Jany. 3, 1804
Whiting Abigal Kidder	John Whiting 2nd & Nancy his wife	Aug 29 1801
Whiting John	Same Same	July 25 1803.
Willard Stedman	William Willard	April 4th 1804.
Wilder Mary Joslyn	Samuel Wilder 2^d & Elizabeth	April 3 1804
Whittemore Elhanan Winchester	Nathl. Whittemore Jr. & Polly his wife	June 7 1804.
Whetcomb Mary & Maria } twins	Josiah Whetcomb & Dolly his wife	Sep 28 1804
Walker Filenda	Daniel Walker & Sarah	June 11, 1804

LANCASTER RECORDS.

Whiting James	Tim⁰. & Lydia Whiting	Jany. 30 1805
Wilder Alexander	Calvin & Susan Wilder	July 20 1804.
White Lucy Carter	Abel and Betsy White	June 23 1805.
Willard Peter Haskell	William & Lucy Willard	Octo 14 1805
Wilder Holman	Luke Wilder & Mary Wilder	June 8th 1804
Wilder Enos	John Wilder & Sally Wilder	Dec. 24 1805.
Wilder Nancy	Aaron Wilder & Hannah	Sept. 19 1803.
Whitney Mary	Jonas & Mary Whitney	March 7 1804
142 Walker Stephen	Daniel & Sally Walker	May 13th 1806.
White Levi	Abijah & Bathsheba White	Mar 8 1805
Willard Frederic Augustus	Benj. & Sally Willard	March 4th 1807.
Wilder Rebecca Bowers	Abel & Hannah Wilder	June 27 1807
Wilder Josephus	Jn⁰ Wilder & Sally	Sept. 13 1807.
Wyman Charles	Benjª. & Lucretia Wyman	Nov. 26 1807.
Willard Jacob	William & Lucy Willard	Octo. 13 1807
Wilder Hannah Merrit	Abel & Hannah Wilder	Octo 27 1808.
Wilder Filindia	Titus Wilder Jun & Eunice	Nov. 30th 1807.
Wilder Frederick	Jonª. & Ruth Wilder	Jany. 27 1804
Willard Eliza	Amasa & Fanny Willard	Sep 6, 1804
Willard Charles	Benja. & Sally Willard	Octo 18 1808.
Wilder Lucy	John Wilder & Sally	July 21 1809
White Catharine	Abijah & Bathsheba White	Octo 26 1807
White Abijah	Same Parents	Nov 13th 1810.
Wilder William, by act of Court altered to George W. Wilder		
	Elijah & Sophia Wilder	Sep 7, 1810.
Wilder Caroline Amelia	Joel & Lucy Wilder	July 16, 1810.
Wilder Oliver	Titus Wilder jun & Eunice	Nov 15, 1810.
Wyman Martha Thayer	Benjª. & Lucretia Wyman	June 23, 1811.
Willard Henry	Paul & Martha Willard	Jany 16 1807.
Wilder Abel Carter	Elijah & Sophia Wilder	Jany. 17 1812.
Wilder Ebenezer [F.]	Ebenʳ. & Lucena Wilder	Aug. 24 1808.
Wilder Joseph [M.]	Same Parents	Aug. 18, 1811.
Wyman John Richardson	Benjª. & Lucretia Wyman	June 12 1813.
143 Wilder Eliza Ann Wales	John & Sally Wilder	Octo. 26 1813
Whittemore Mary Moore	Nathl Whittemore jun & Polly	Nov. 4 1813.
Whittemore George Prescott	Prescott & Lucy Rebecca Whittemore	Mar. 5, 1814
Whiting Charles Jarvis.	Saml Kidder Whiting & his wife Sarah Russell Whiting	Novr 28 1814.
Wilder Augustus	Saml. 2d & Mary Wilder	Sep 5, 1811.
Wilder Mary Carter	Same Parents	Octo. 31, 1814.
Willard Warren	Darby & Anna Willard	Jany. 17, 1815.
Warner Polly	Nathl. & Polly Warner	June 29 1815.
Wilder Charles Josiah	Joel Wilder & Lucy his wife	Dec 31, 1813.
Wilder Rebecca	Jno Wilder & Sally Wilder	Octo 31, 1815
Willard Fanny	Amasa & Fanny Willard	June 25, 1812
Whittemore Edward Hibbard	Prescott Whittemore and Lucy R. his wife	Feb. 12, 1816.
Wilder Thomas	Thomas & Sarah Wilder	Octo. 7, 1813.
Warner Sally	Nathaniel & Polly Warner	Octo 7 1816
Wilder Mary	Titus Wilder Jun and Eunice Wilder	Dec. 19 1815.
Willard Charles	Darby Willard & Anna	Octo 7 1816
Wheeler Emily	Amos Wheeler & Prudence	May 18, 1819
144		
Weld Margaret Minot.	William G. Weld, and Hannah his wife	Feb. 3, 1817.
Wilder Sidney	Ebenr. & Lucena Wilder	Sep 15 1813
Wilder Charles	Same Parents	Jany 30 1816
Wilder Ephraim Rand	Luke Wilder & Mary Wilder	Jany 14, 1816.

Name	Parents	Date
Whittemore Hariot Augusta	Prescott & Lucy Rebecca Whittemore	Nov. 2, 1817.
Whiting Mary Phelps	Timothy & Lydia Whiting	March 11, 1818.
White Emory Houghton	Abel White & Elizabeth	Octo 30 1813.
Weld, John Gardner Doubleday,	Wᵐ G. Weld & Hannah his wife	Aug. 19, 1818.
Wheeler Mary Parker	Amos & Prudence Wheeler	Nov. 27. 1816.
Wheeler Amos Augustus	Same Parents.	March 29 1818.
Wyman Henry,	Benjᵃ. & Lucretia Wyman	June 23 1818.
Wilder Julia	Abel & Hannah Wilder	Nov. 16, 1816.
Willard Andrew Fuller	Benjᵃ Willard & Sally Willard	Augᵗ. 10 1814
Willard Mary Conant	Same Parents	May 27 1816.
Wilder Ephraim Holman,	Luke Wilder & Mary	Aug. 22, 1818.
Wilder Emily,	Elisha Wilder & Emily	Jany 16 1819.
Willard Mary Ann.	Darby Willard & Anna	May 22 1819
Whittemore Charles Henry	Prescott & Lucy Whittemore	Nov. 17, 1819.
Worster Mary	Samuel & Rebecca Worster	Octo 14, 1815.
Worster Eliza	Same Parents	Nov 20, 1816
Worster Hariot	Same Parents	Sep 3, 1818
Wilder Sewall	Elijah & Sophia Wilder	Jany 17, 1814
Wilder Sophia Ann	Same Parents	Nov 18 1818
145 Wilder Seth	Abel & Hannah Wilder	Sep 25, 1819.
Wilder Almira	Titus Wilder Jr & Eunice	Apr. 19 1820.
Willard Melinda	Derby & Anne Willard	May 9, 1821.
Wilder Edwin Elisha	Elisha & Emily Wilder	Jany. 31, 1821.
Wilder Sarah E.	Jonas Wilder & Sally	Feb. 23, 1821.
Whetcomb Mary Antoinette	Nathˡ. & Abigail B. Whetcomb	Dec 18, 1820.
Whittemore Mary	Prescott Whittemore & Lucy R. his wife	Aug. 3, 1821.
Wilder Rufus [A.]	Ebenʳ Wilder & Lucena	Aug. 26, 1817
Wilder Lucena	Same Parents	May 18, 1819
Wilder Martha Eddy	Joseph Wilder & Eliza	Aug. 25, 1817
Wilder Charles Hanson	Same Parents	July 7, 1819
Wilder Mary Morse Andrews	Same Parents	March 25ᵗʰ, 1821.
Wheeler Roxanna	Amos Wheeler & Prudence	Jany, 21, 1821.
Wilder Annis.	John Wilder	Feb 14, 1804
Wilder Levi.	Same Parents	June 12 1807
Wilder Harriet.	Same Parents	Jany 8, 1812
Wilder Franklin	Same Parents	Sep 11, 1813.
Wilder Warren	Same Parents	Dec 12, 1815
Wilder Lucy Larkin	Same Parents	May 28, 1820.
Weld Hannah Minot	Wm. G. Weld & Hannah	Mar. 19, 1820.
1823. Joseph Wilder	Manassah Wilder	Feb. 8, 1787.
Wilder Sumner	Same Parent	July — 1801
Whetcomb Abigail Baker	Nathˡ & Abigail Whetcomb	Sep. 26, 1822.
Wilder George	Ebenʳ Wilder and Lucena Wilder	Aug. 28, 1822.
Wilder Elizabeth	Same Parents	Mar: 13 1825
146	* * *	
Willard Sarah	Benjᵃ Willard & Sally Willard	April 8 1819
Willard Elizabeth Sophia	Same Parents.	June 2 1820
Willard Sally	Same Parents.	May 20 1822.
Wilder Caroline Matilda	Elisha & Emily Wilder	March 29, 1823.
Wilder Ann Eliza	Joseph & Eliza Wilder	June 7, 1823.
Wetherbee Moses Allen	Salathiel Wetherbee	Jany — 1822
Wetherbee William H.	Same Parents.	Jany 8, 1816
Wetherbee Pamela	Ditto.	Feb 5, 1818
Wetherbee Aurelia	Ditto.	Mar 31, 1806
Wetherbee Electa	Ditto.	Dec. — 1807
Wetherbee Emily	Ditto.	July 12, 1813
Wetherbee Sophronia	Ditto.	June 15, 1811
Wetherbee Hiram Walter	Ditto.	1820
Whitcomb Harriet	Nathˡ & Abigail B. Whitcomb	July 27 1827.
Wilson Emela Augusta	Timothy S & Miranda Wilson	January 9, 1828

Snell Otis Born in Scituate	Snell & Deborah K Wade	Decr 18 1820
Job Paterson in Scituate		Decr 15 1822
Lefy Jacob		Sept 13 1826
Peres Jacob		July 5 1828
Wilder Clarissa	Eben^r. & Clarissa Wilder	Sep 19, 1828
Wilder James	Same Parents	Feby 9, 1830.
White Austin Jonas	Jonas B. White & Nancy	March 21 1830.
Willard Esther Mary	Willm T. Willard & Abigail R	May 8, 1830.
Wilder Emory Pollard	Elisha Wilder & Emily	Nov 4 1827
Wilder Christopher Walker	Same Parents	Jany. 7, 1829.
White Elizabeth Whitcomb	Jonas White & Ann B	Jany 15 1826
White Ann Goodhue	Same Parents	Dec 26, 1827.
White Edwin Clinton	Same Parents	Octo 1, 1829
Wilder Annah	Ebenezer & Clarissa Wilder	April 19, 1832
Whitcomb John Belknap	Capt Nathl. & Abigail Whitcomb	June 8 1832
147 1833. White Laura Sophia	Jonas B. & Nancy White.	January 1, 1833.
Willard William Augustus Putnam,	Putnam & Abigail Willard	Nov: 26 1831.
Wilson Francina Eliza	John & Eliza Ann Wilson	Nov. 10, 1833.
Wilder George Wait	Joel Wilder Jr & Deborah	June 12 1828 [9]
Wilder Francis Whitman	Same Parents.	June 5 1833.
White Jane Gilman	Jonas & Ann B. White	Feb 20, 1832
White Francis Jonas	Same Parents.	Jany 27 1834
White Geo. Washington	Amos & Elizabeth White	March 14, 1830.
White Calvin Dana	Same Parents	March 2, 1833.
1834. Wood Lowell F.	Lowell & Tabitha Wood	May 6, 1826 Acton.
Wood Edwin Hayward	Same Parents	June 5, 1829 Bolton.
Wilder Sarah Harris	Joseph W. Wilder & Ruth	Octo. 21 1832
Wilder George Franklin	Same Parents	Augt. 13, 1834
Wilder John Wm Gamble	Leonard Pollard & Annis	July 16 1833.
Wellington Ann Maria	Thomas H & Lucy Wellington	March 5 1834
Wheelock Albert	Charles & Elizabeth Wheelock	July 15, 1834
Whiting Fabius M.	Solon & Sarah Whiting	May 5. 1831
Whiting Julia E.	Same Parents.	Decr. 6, 1832.
1835. Willard Stedman Alfred	Stedman Willard & Mary his wife	Feby 21, 1834.
Wheeler George Frederick	Jonas & Ruth Wheeler	Octo. 2, 1834.
Worcester Martha	Noah Worcester & Nancy	May 1, 1835.
Wilder Edward Everett	Joel Wilder Jr & Deborah	Augt. 19, 1835.
Wellington Francina	Thomas H & Lucy Wellington,	June 30, 1835
Wheelock Ellen Elizabeth.	Charles & Elizabeth	June 6, 1835
Wade Charlotte O.	Snell Wade & Deborah	Octo. 20, 1834
Wheeler Calvin P.	David & Charlotte Wheeler	Dec. 20, 1831
Wheeler Caroline P.	Same Parents	Octo. 6, 1835.
Willard Sidney	Joseph & Susanna H. Willard	Feby 3, 1831
148 1836. John Wood Wyman	Charles & Nancy Wyman	Sept. 5 1834
Charles Andrew Wyman	Same Parents	July 16 1836.
Mary Worcester	No ah & Nancy Worcester	August 4, 1836
Frederick Irving White	Jonas & Ann B. White	August 18, 1836
Williams Geo. Forrest	G. W. G. Williams & Isabella	April 22^d, 1837
Willard Jerome H.	—	Oct. 26 1818.
Wilder George Lewis	Charles L & Harriet E Wilder	Mar 10th 1837
Wilder Thomas Jefferson	Joseph W. & Ruth Wilder	Oct 3^d 1836
Wetherbee Maria	Alonzo C. & Elizabeth Wetherbee	Aug 5th 1837
Walter Parlin Whittemore	Lorenzo & Loisa Whittemore	Sept — 1838
Whittemore Nathaniel Jun.	Nathl & Nancy Whittemore	March 27, 1839
White Francis Bussey	Jonas & Ann B. White	Oct. 4th 1838
Wyman Mary-ann Lydia	Amos H. & Lucy L. Wyman	Sept. 26th 1838
Washburn Francis	John M. & Harriet W. Washburn	July 6th 1838
Washburn Mary	Same Parents	Decr 10th 1840
Wilder George Endicott	Daniel K & Mary M. Wilder	October 7th 1841
Wilder James Festus	Festus Foster & Eliza Wilder	Novr 30th 1841
Wyman Benj^a. Farnsworth	Charles & Nancy Wyman	May 25, 1839
Washburn Henry Kimball	Jno M & Harriet W. Washburn	Aug 31, 1842.

Wyman Wm. Wilberforce	Charles & Nancy Wyman	Sept 2, 1842
Nancy Francena Whittemore	Nathl & Nancy Whittemore	May 20, 1843
Winchester, Ann Elizabeth	Caleb & Lydia Winchester	Oct. 23, 1843
Winchester Charles	Elhanan and Rhoda Winchr.	April 15 1843
Wilder Ann Eliza Walton	Charles L. & Harriet E. Wilder	Sept. 19, 1839
Wilder Harriet Ellen	Same Parents	June 29, 1841
Wilder Charles Lewis	Same Parents	Decr. 22, 1842
Willard Sarah Jane	Warren & Lucy Willard	March 6, 1840
Willard Samuel		Oct 13 1760
157 Zwier Artemas	Reuben Zwier & Lovisa	April 19, 1799.
Zwier Reuben	Same Parents	May 25, 1801.
Zwier Charles	Same Parents	Aug. 17, 1803.
Zwier Leonard	Same Parents	July 20, 1806.
Zwier Susan	Same Parents	March 17, 1819.

BOOK III.

RECORD OF PUBLISHMENTS AND MARRIAGES.

1815 —

The third volume of records is not paged. Each entry was formally attested by the town clerk, and the certified returns annually received from justices and clergymen were copied in full — commonly following the form of the marriage and publishment certificates first given below. The notices of marriage intentions being usually supplemented within a month by registry of the marriage, those publishments only are here printed which are not followed by a marriage certificate, or which contain information not in the certificate. The following is an accurate transcript of all essential facts in the record, leaving out verbiage. By collation with the original memoranda kept by the Reverends Messrs. Thayer, Sears and Packard, sundry omissions have been made good, and errors noted.

MARRIAGES.

WORCESTER Ss. Mr Samuel Dollison of Lancaster, and Miss Nancy Peirce of West Boylston were married, April 13th, *Anno Domini* 1815.

April 29, 1815. The foregoing is a true return of the persons who have been joined in marriage since the 12th, April, 1814.

By me, TIMOTHY WHITING *Jus. Pacis*

A true Copy, Attest JOSIAH FLAGG *Town Clerk.*

Married before Josiah Flagg, Esq.

1814. Octo. 4. Mr Stephen Wilder to Miss Patience Sargent, both of Lancaster.
1815. Feby. 27. Mr William Larkin of Boylston to Mrs Mehitable Humphrey of Lancaster.

Married before Paul Willard Esq.

1814. May 3. Mr Ephraim Robbins to Miss Polly Gleason, both of Lancaster.

Married before Reverend Nathaniel Thayer.

1814. May 8. Mr Asa Barrett to Miss Sally Bennett, both of Lancaster.
    15. Mr Asa Wood Jun. of Leominster, to Miss Susan Stone of Lancaster.
June 14. Mr Amzi Langdon of Rowe, to Miss Lavina Thayer of Lancaster.
Sept. 13 Mr Samuel Wood Jun. of Keene N. H. to Miss Emily Wyman of Lancaster.
Nov. 15. Revd. Abraham Burnham of Pembroke, N. H. to Miss Martha Barnard of Sterling.

15. Doctor Emory Willard of Marblehead, to Miss Sally Farwell of Lancaster.
24. Mr Jonas Wilder of Sterling, to Miss Sally Fairbank of Lancaster.
1815. April 5. Mr Martin Burpee to Miss Lydia Warner, both of Lancaster.
27. Mr Richard Hildreth of Sterling, to Miss Nancy Osgood of Lancaster.

PUBLISHMENTS.

1815. May 13. Mr Samuel Worster and Miss Rebecca Frothingham both of Lancaster enter their Intentions of Marriage this 13th day of May A. D. 1815. Attest JOSIAH FLAGG, *Town Clerk*.
N. B. No further proceedings in this case, by order of the said Worster, May 15, 1815. Posted again the 10th June, 1815.
May 27. Mr Jesse Ayres and Miss Phebe Franklin, both of Lancaster.
Sep. 30. Mr Joseph Farwell 2d of Lancaster, and Miss Sarah Barnard of Harvard.
Dec. 16. Mr John Burpee of Sterling, and Miss Betsy Stevenson of Lancaster.
18. Mr George Sawyer of Lancaster, and Miss Lucy Hoar of Berlin.
1816 Jany. 19. Mr Willard Barran of Lancaster, and Miss Abigail Hills of Litchfield N. H.
Feb. 19. Mr Joseph Barrett of Lancaster, and Miss Lucy Bartlett of Shirley.
March 6. Mr Isaac Childs of Lancaster, and Miss Polly Kimball of Sterling.

MARRIAGES.

Before Reverend Nathaniel Thayer.

1815. May 3. Deacon Jonathan Cutting of Templeton, to Mrs Mary Prescott of Lancaster.
June 11. Mr John W. Rogers of Boston, to Miss Anstiss D. Pickman of Lancaster.
July 2. Mr Samuel Worcester to Miss Rebecca Franklin, both of Lancaster.
Octo. 19. Mr Elias Sawyer to Miss Nancy Ballard, both of Lancaster
Nov. 28. Mr Amos Adams to Mrs Polly Rugg, both of Lancaster.
1816. Jan. 2 Mr Otis Stearns of Leominster, to Miss Lucy Wilder of Lancaster.
Feb. 7. Mr Samuel Wilder to Mrs Tryphena Corey, both of Lancaster.
23. Mr Jonathan Wood of Westmoreland N. H. to Miss Susan Haskell of Lancaster.
Mar. 13. Mr Hannibal Laughton to Miss Dolly Ballard, both of Lancaster.
Apr. 14. Mr Amasa Willard to Miss Mary Willard, both of Lancaster.

Before Josiah Flagg Esq.

1815. May 16. Mr Moses Chase to Miss Ruth Sargent, both of Lancaster.
Octo 31. Mr Jonathan Kendal of Leominster, to Miss Relief Willard of Lancaster.
Nov. 5. Mr Jesse Cooke to Miss Polly Andrews, both of Lancaster

Before Timothy Whiting Esq.

1816. Jan. 16. Lyman Garfield of Fitchburg, and Nancy Whiting of Lancaster.

Before Paul Willard, Esq.

1815. Nov. 12. Mr Horace Gould and Miss Polly Jones, both of Lancaster.

PUBLISHMENTS.

1816. Nov. 8. Mr Stephen Laughton of Lancaster and Miss Clarissa Cummings of Sutton.
9. Mr Isaac Kilburne of Lancaster and Miss Nancy Edgell of Westminster.

1817. Jany. 11. Mr Amos Butler, and Miss Mary Sargeant, both of Lancaster.
Feb. 20. Mr James Farwell of Lancaster, and Miss Mary Emerson of South Reading.
Sep. 9 Mr Jonathan Barrett Jun. of Lancaster, and Miss Mary Hodgman of Harvard.

MARRIAGES.
Before Paul Willard Esq.

1816. Dec. 29. Mr Leonard Ayres and Miss Lydia Atherton, both of Lancaster.
1817. May 25. Mr Jabez Damon of Reading, and Miss Mary Lewis of Lancaster.

Before Reverend Nathaniel Thayer.

1816. July 8. Mr George Safford to Miss Mary Stevenson, both of Lancaster.
21. Lieutenant Joseph Wilder to Miss Eliza Ann Andrews, both of Lancaster.
25. Mr Caleb Harrington to Miss Martha Gates, both of Lancaster.
Sep. 1. Mr Apollos Osgood of Farmington, Me., to Miss Cynthia Wilder of Lancaster.
10. Mr Elias Gates of Leominster, to Miss Lucy Laughton of Lancaster.
15. Capt. William Cleveland to Mrs Lucy H. Lambert, both of Lancaster.
20. Mr Abel W. Rugg to Miss Hannah Jones, both of Lancaster.
Nov. 24. Mr Abner Pollard of Lancaster, to Mrs Susanna Nurse of Concord.
28. Mr Fisher Ayres to Miss Sally Worcester, both of Lancaster.
1817. Jany. 9. Mr John Carter 2^d. of Lancaster, to Mrs Elizabeth Daby of Harvard.
Feb. 8. Mr Abel Whitney of Boston, to Miss Abigail [H.] Townshend of Lancaster.

PUBLISHMENTS.

1817. Nov. 8. Mr Sodi Sanderson of Lancaster, and Miss Pamela Lovejoy of Milford, N. H.
1818. Feby. 11. Mr Nathan Miller of Lancaster, and Miss Katharine Littaye of Leominster.
March 2. Mr William Nowell of Worcester, and Miss Elizabeth Arnold of Lancaster.
" 7. Mr Asahel Tower Jun. of Lancaster, and Miss Polly Palmer of Sterling.
" " Mr Ephraim Fuller of Lancaster, and Miss Susan Hayward of Acton.
" " Mr Luke Whitcomb of Lancaster, and Miss Nancy Morse of West Boylston.

MARRIAGES.
Before Reverend Nathaniel Thayer.

1817. Sep. 17. Mr Levi Lewis to Miss Abigail Ballard, both of Lancaster.
25. Mr Samuel Merrifield to Miss Hannah Barton both of Lancaster.
Octo. 7. Mr John M. Marston of Boston, to Miss Martha Thayer of Lancaster.
14. Mr John Sweetser of South Reading, to Miss Prudence Hawks of Lancaster.
Nov. 2. Mr John Capen to Miss Anna Edes, both of Lancaster.
Dec. 3. Mr Luke Rugg to Miss Salome Patch, both of Lancaster.
4. Mr Joshua Swan of Waltham to Miss Olive Jones of Lancaster.
1818. March 1. Mr Antipas Bartlett of Northborough, to Miss Abigail Wilder of Lancaster.
April 8. Mr Martin Burpee to Miss Betsy Thompson, both of Lancaster.

BOOK THIRD.   231

Before Timothy Whiting Esq.

1816. June 3. Baxter Wood and Sally Hastings, both of Boylston.

Before Josiah Flagg Esq.

1817. Nov. 27. Mr Thomas Divoll Jun. and Miss Rebecca Kendall, both of Lancaster.
      30. Mr Luke Bennett and Mrs Susanna Divoll, both of Lancaster.
1818. March 30. Mr John Dodd of Princeton, and Miss Rebecca Flagg of Lancaster.

PUBLISHMENTS.

1818. Aug. 8. Mr Harvey Peirce of Lancaster, and Miss Cynthia Allen of Bolton.
  Octo. 23. Mr Elijah Ball of Lancaster, and Miss Olive Plympton of Shrewsbury.
  " 28 Mr William Ballard of Lancaster, and Miss Elsey Holman of Bolton.
1819. Jany. 2. Mr Caleb Houghton of Berlin, and Miss Abigail Meriam of Lancaster.

MARRIAGES.

Before Josiah Flagg Esq.

1818. Sept. 15. Mr Abel M. Godfrey and Miss Sally Corey, both of Harvard.
1819. March 20. Mr Samuel Jones and Mrs Mercy Haskell, both of Lancaster.
" April 14 Mr Jacob Stone and Miss Isabella Bennett, both of Lancaster.

Before Nathaniel Thayer S. T. D.

1818. May 19. Mr Isaac Stearns of Bolton, to Miss Lucy Goss of Lancaster.
  June 3. Mr Ebenezer Pratt to Miss Emily Rice, both of Lancaster.
    10. Mr Francis Faulkner of Keene N. H., to Miss Eliza Stearns of Lancaster.
    14. Mr Jacob Fisher Jun. of Lancaster, to Miss Orricy Hills of Leominster.
  Aug. 11. Mr Elisha Wilder to Miss Emily Pollard, both of Lancaster.
  Octo. 8. Mr Leonard Hartwell to Miss Nabby Peirce, both of Lancaster.
  Nov. 12. Mr Silas Sawyer of Bolton, to Miss Sally Farnsworth of Lancaster.
  Dec. 3. Mr David Smith of Charlestown, to Miss Huldah Kelley of Lancaster.
  " 29. Mr Joseph C. Spear of Concord N. H., to Miss Fanny Sweetser of Lancaster.
1819. March 31. Mr Eliphaz Ballard to Miss Sophronia Willard, both of Lancaster.
  April 11. Mr Joseph Rugg jun. to Miss Olive Studly, both of Lancaster.
  " 25. Mr Nathaniel Wilder of Berlin, to Miss Lucy Osgood of Lancaster.

Before Timothy Whiting Esq.

1818. Aug. 5. Nathan Warner and Mary Phelps both of Bolton.
    16. Danforth Wilder and Dolly Rice, both of Lancaster.
  Sept. 27. Paul Faulkner and Eunice Richardson, both of Lancaster.

PUBLISHMENTS.

1819. Aug. 13. Mr James Carter of Lancaster, and Miss Emma Chase of Leominster.
  Nov. 27. Mr William Willard of Lancaster, and Mrs Patty Harwood of Littleton.
1820. Apr. 8. John Davis Esqr. of Lancaster, and Miss Sylvia Edgarton of Shirley.
  " 8. Mr Ebenezer Haven of Lancaster, and Miss Prissa Draper of Boxboro'.

MARRIAGES.
Before Nathaniel Thayer S. T. D.

1819. June 9. Mr Thomas Safford of Lancaster, to Miss Anna Brigham of Marlboro'.
July 4. Mr Thomas Sawyer Jun. to Miss Polly Wright, both of Lancaster.
8. Mr George Barnard of Worcester, to Miss Silence Moore of Lancaster.
Octo. 8. Mr James Richardson of Poultney Vt., to Miss Mary Fisher of Lancaster.
Dec. 16. Mr Nathaniel Whitcomb to Miss Abigail B. Whiting, both of Lancaster.
1820. Feb. 8. Mr Moses Carlton to Miss Mary Sweetser, both of Lancaster.
Apr. 2. Mr Asahel Harris to Miss Abigail Phelps, both of Lancaster.
18. Mr Abraham C. Willard of Lancaster, to Miss Sarah Follansbee of Leominster.
25. Mr John Goodwin Jr. of Lancaster, to Miss Susannah Smith of Leominster.

PUBLISHMENTS.

1820. May 12. Mr John Ballard of Lancaster, and Mrs Ruth Sawyer of Bolton.
1821. Feb. 9. Mr Jonas White 2^d of Lancaster, and Miss Ann B. Townshend of Bolton.
Apr. 13. Mr Benjamin F. Tidd of Lancaster, and Miss Nancy Keyes of Westford.

MARRIAGES.
Before Josiah Flagg Esq.

1820. June 4. Mr Reuben Zwier Jun. and Miss Nancy Newcomb Phillips, both of Lancaster.
Nov. 20. Mr Alden Spooner of Athol, to Miss Dolly Flagg of Lancaster.

Before Nathaniel Thayer S. T. D.

1820. May 25. Mr Sarsen L. Judd of South Hadley. to Miss Harriet Bennett of Lancaster.
June 15. Mr Isaac E. Hutchins of Leominster, to Miss Lucinda Floyd of Lancaster.
Aug. 13. Mr Coolidge Foster of Leominster, to Miss Dolly Maynard of Lancaster.
Octo. 22. Mr Sewall Tyler to Miss Eunice Houghton, both of Leominster.
Nov. 9. Mr Eben Sawyer to Miss Sarah Ann Thurston, both of Lancaster.
19. Mr Nehemiah Peirce of Hopkinton, to Miss Eliza P. Thomson of Lancaster.
23. Mr Wilkes Geary of Sterling, to Miss Lydia Phelps of Lancaster.
23. Mr Farwell Eager of Westminster, to Miss Althina Bennett of Lancaster.
1821. Jan. 25. Mr Emery Harris to Miss Sally Wilder, both of Lancaster.
Feb. 7. Mr Ezra Sawyer of Sterling, to Miss Eliza Houghton of Lancaster.
" 16. Doctor Theodore Ingalls of Bridgeton Me., to Mrs Sarah Carter of Lancaster.

PUBLISHMENTS.

1821. May 16. Mr Noah Smith of South Reading, to Mrs Mary Willard of Lancaster.
19. Mr Jesse Ayers of Lancaster, and Miss Rebecca Galley of Shirley.
26. Mr Abel Lakin of Lancaster, and Miss Lucy Megett of Pepperell. N. B. This publishment handed into the office in the absence of the Clerk, and disavowed by said Lakin, it being an imposition.

Sep. 14. Mr Samuel W. Burbank of Lancaster, and Miss Hannah Ball of Townshend.
1822. March 2. Mr Josiah Tilden of Lancaster, and Miss Charlotte Bruce of Walpole.
April 1. Mr Charles Chace Jun. of Lancaster, and Miss Mary Tyler of Harvard.

MARRIAGES.

Before Reverend Abisha Samson Pastor of the Baptist Church in Harvard.

1821. Octo. 10. Paul Willard Esq. of Charlestown with Miss Harriet Whiting of Lancaster.
1822. Feb. 28. Mr Nathan Willard of Harvard with Miss Eliza Farwell of Lancaster.

Before Nathaniel Thayer S. T. D.

1821. May 10. Mr Torrey Fitch of Sterling, to Miss Harriet Thurston of Lancaster.
June 7. Mr Ephraim Whitney of Lancaster, to Mrs Mary Nurse of Marlborough.
" 21. Deacon William Burrage of Leominster, to Miss Roxana Sanderson of Lancaster.
July 3. Mr Jonas Haven to Miss Harriet B. Whiting, both of Lancaster.
Dec. 6. Mr Luke Bigelow to Miss Eliza Wilder, both of Lancaster.
1822. Jan. 1. Mr Cephas Carter of Boston, to Miss Abigail Carter of Lancaster.
" 13. Mr John Richards of Boston, to Miss Sally Hawks of Lancaster.
" Mr Phinehas Houghton of Harvard, to Miss Alice Hawks of Lancaster.
Feb. 19. Mr Leonard Pollard to Miss Annis Wilder, both of Lancaster.
Apr. 2. Mr Somes White to Miss Harriet Goodwin, both of Lancaster.

PUBLISHMENTS.

1822. Apr. 23. Mr Oliver Baldwin of Lancaster, and Miss Hannah Patten of Billerica.
" 27. Mr Daniel Burbank of Lancaster, and Miss Elizabeth Hill of Stoneham.
May 2. Mr John Holman of Boston, and Miss Nancy W. Townshend of Lancaster.
10. Mr William Shearer and Miss Rebecca Deputron, both of Lancaster.
Aug. 3. Mr Otis Boynton of Framingham, and Miss Sally Willson of Lancaster.
5. Mr Luther Jones of Lancaster and Miss Charlotte Aldrich of Northbridge.
Sep. 28. Mr Anthony Lane of Lancaster, and Miss Mary Miles White of Westminster.
1823. Jan. 17. [Married Jan. 30, in family records.] Jacob Fisher Esq. of Lancaster, and Miss Betsy Bartlett of Royalston.
March 10. Mr Henry Moore of Lancaster, and Miss Achsah Houghton of Bolton.

MARRIAGES.

Before Nathaniel Thayer S. T. D.

1822. Apr. 23. Mr William H. Lane of Boston, to Miss Harriet Houghton of Sterling.
June 11. Mr Simon Thompson to Miss Lucy Colburn, both of Lancaster.
Aug. 8. Mr William Chadwick to Miss Lucy Thompson, both of Lancaster.
Nov. 28. Mr Charles Sawyer to Miss Eliza Joslyn, both of Lancaster.
Dec. 18. Mr Benjamin B. Otis to Miss Mary Carter, both of Lancaster.
1823. March 31. Mr Nahum Willington of Worcester to Miss Mary N. Ballard of Lancaster.

Apr. 24. Mr Alanson Chace to Miss Maria Harris, both of Lancaster.
  " 27. Mr Jeremiah Barnard of Harvard, to Miss Bilhah Merriam of Lancaster.

Before Josiah Flagg Esq.

1823. Jan. 28. Mr Levi Reed and Miss Sally A. Boynton both of Boston, now residents of Sterling.

PUBLISHMENTS.

1823. Sep. 6. Mr Simeon Bowman Jun. of Lancaster, and Miss Hannah Baily of Berlin.
  " 6. Mr Moses B. Merriam of Lancaster, and Miss Abigail Simonds of Leominster.
  " 20. Mr Elijah Wilder of Lancaster, and Miss Alvina Wilder of Sterling.
Octo. 31. Mr Levi Farwell of Lancaster, and Miss Lucy Bachelder Willard of Harvard.
Dec. 11. Mr Warren Townshend of Lancaster, and Miss Almira Bennett of Sterling.
1824. Apr. 24. Mr Josiah Billings of Lancaster, and Miss Nancy Fife of Bolton.

MARRIAGES.

Before Josiah Flagg Esq.

1824. Apr. 15. Mr Joshua Thomas with the Widow Rebecca Haskell, both of Lancaster.

Before Nathaniel Thayer, S. T. D.

1823. May 14. Mr Reuben Newell Jr. of South Reading, to Miss Emily Rugg of Lancaster.
Octo. 16. Mr Abel Allen of Lancaster, to Miss Harriet L. Larrabee of New Marlboro', N. H.
Dec. 7. Mr Rufus Houghton to Miss Martha Pollard, both of Lancaster.
  " 25. Mr Jonas Colburn of Leominster, to Miss Matilda Parker of Lancaster.
1824. Jan. 21. Mr John McCurdy Jr. of Concord Vt. to Miss Julia Goodwin of Lancaster.
March 4. Mr David K. Thurston to Miss Betsy Howard, both of Lancaster.
Apr. 1. Mr Henry Norcross to Miss Mary Dunn, both of Lancaster.
  " 6. Mr Lucas Dunn to Miss Polly Elliott, both of Lancaster.
  " 6. Mr Timothy W. Draper of Amherst N. H., to Miss Mary Farnsworth of Lancaster.
  " 18. Mr Darius Emery of Lancaster, to Miss Lydia Longley of Shirley.

PUBLISHMENTS.

1824. Apr. 26. Mr William Zwiers of Townshend, and Miss Lovicy Zwiers of Lancaster.
May 14. Mr William Thurston of Lancaster, and Miss Sabra Houghton of Bolton.
Octo. 1. Doctor George Baker of Lancaster, and Miss Elizabeth Dana Hastings of Boston.
1825. March 12. Mr Albert Dyer of Lancaster, and Miss Mary Atherton of Harvard.
April 10. Mr Horace Faulkner of Lancaster, and Miss Emily Holman of Bolton.

MARRIAGES.

Before Reverend Abisha Samson of Harvard.

1824. May 6. Mr Salmon Willard Jr. with Miss Laura Cobb, both of Lancaster.

BOOK THIRD.

Before Nathaniel Thayer, S. T. D.

1824. June 17. Mr Thomas Sargeant to Miss Clarissa Gleason Holbrook, both of Lancaster.
Aug. 3. Mr Frederick A. Lewis of Belfast, Me., to Miss Sally Fisher of Lancaster.
Sep. 30. Mr N. Marcellus Hentz of Northampton, to Miss Caroline Lee Whiting of Lancaster.
Octo. 19. Mr William D. Whitney of Southbridge, to Miss Harriet Hawks of Lancaster.
Nov. 14. Mr Miles Putnam of Bolton, to Miss Rebecca Carter of Lancaster.
1825. Jan. 12. Mr John W. Gamble of West Boylston, to Miss Sally Wilder of Lancaster.
" 18. Mr Gardner Hyde to Miss Almira Jones, both of Lancaster.
March 15. Mr Amos Sawyer to Miss Nancy Fuller, both of Lancaster.
April 7. Mr Henry Phelps to Miss Mary Thurston, both of Lancaster.
" 27. Mr Abel Butler of Lancaster, to Miss Sally Bartlett of Shirley.

Before Josiah Flagg Esq.

1824. Octo. 2. Mr Elisha Copeland and Miss Sophia Willard, both of Sterling.

PUBLISHMENTS.

1825. July 30. Mr Joseph Fletcher of Lancaster, and Miss Eliza Marean of Hubbardston.
Feb. 25. Mr Levi Miles of Lancaster, and Miss Mary Ann Heywood of Concord.

MARRIAGES.

Before Nathaniel Thayer, S. T. D.

1825. May 4. Mr John Henry of Lunenburg to Miss Nancy T. Dollison of Lancaster.
Sep. 28. Mr Thomas Taylor of Hancock N. H., to Miss Elizabeth Daby of Lancaster.
Octo. 27. Mr Peter Osgood to Miss Nancy N. Bridge, both of Lancaster.
Nov 3. Mr Elijah Johnson of Albany Me., to Miss Lucy Goddard of Lancaster.
" 24. Mr Joseph Gerry of Sterling, to Miss Eliza Holmes of Lancaster.
Dec. 1. Mr Edmund Lawrence of Bolton, to Miss Sally Phelps of Lancaster.
" 4. Mr Arad B. Newton to Miss Zilpah Bailey, both of Lancaster.
" " Mr William Divoll to Miss Dolly Houghton, both of Lancaster.
1826. Jany. 12. Mr Edward Wilder Jr. of Leominster to Miss Sarah T. Hunt of Lancaster.
" 17. Mr Charles Bridge to Miss Sophia Whitney, both of Lancaster.
" 24. Mr Jonathan Tarbel Walton of South Reading to Miss Sarah H. Rugg of Lancaster.
March 28. Mr Obadiah Goodale of Sharon N. H., to Miss Martha H. Farwell of Lancaster.

PUBLISHMENTS.

1826. Sep. 2. Mr Henry Sawyer of Lancaster, and Miss Katharine B. Burnett of Warwick.
" 15. Mr Timothy S. Wilson of Lancaster, and Miss Miranda R. Earl of Sudbury.
Octo. 14. Mr Horace Faulkner of Lancaster, and Miss Eliza Holman of Bolton.
Nov. 20. Mr Nathaniel Kingsbury of Lancaster, and Miss Catharine Sawin of Natick.
Dec. 15. Mr George W. Cook of Lancaster, and Miss Charlotte Felton of Marlborough.

1827. March 8. Doctor Right Cummings of Lancaster, and Miss Mary Lawrence of Townshend.
" 9. Mr George Houghton of Lancaster, and Miss Miranda Perry of Worcester.
" 26. Mr John Goodwin Jr. and Miss Catharine L. Willard, both of Lancaster.
April 4. Mr Peter Joslyn and Miss Almira Carter, both of Lancaster. [Married Apr. 21, 1827.]
" 8. Mr Josiah Hayden Vose of Robbinstown Me, and Miss Mary Tucker Vose of Lancaster.
" 27. Mr Horatio Carter of Lancaster, and Miss Emily Norton of Sterling.

MARRIAGES.

Before Joseph Willard Esq.

1826. Nov. 13. Francis Dana Stedman and Harriet Rockwood, both of Lancaster.

Before Reverend Abisha Samson of Harvard.

1827. Jany. 1. Mr Samuel Damon with Miss Rebecca Smith, both of Lancaster.

Before Nathaniel Thayer, S. T. D.

1826. May 10. Mr Arah Ellinwood to Miss Lucretia Tower, both of Lancaster.
" 21. Capt John Thurston to Mrs Lydia Fuller, both of Lancaster.
June 1. Mr Perley Hammond of Lancaster, to Mrs Serephina Bond of Sterling. [colored]
" 1. Mr Murray Waterman to Miss Mary Freeman, both of Lancaster. [colored]
" 4. Mr Stedman Nourse to Miss Patty Howard, both of Lancaster.
July 4. Mr Leonard Bolton to Miss Mary Ann Bennett, both of Lancaster.
13. Mr Henry Low to Miss Mary Gould, both of Lancaster.
Octo. 26. Mr Levi Stow to Miss Susan Harding, both of Lancaster.
Nov. 30. Mr Henry Goss of Lancaster, to Miss Sarah Dexter of Leominster.
Dec. 14. Mr Leander Phelps of Worcester, to Miss Lucy Carroll of Lancaster.
" 24. Mr James G. Barnard to Miss Lavina B. Houghton, both of Lancaster.
1827. Jan. 2. Mr Sewell Carter to Miss Mary T. Locke, both of Lancaster.
Feb. 15. Mr James Stone to Miss Eliza Wilder, both of Lancaster.
April 3. Mr Phinehas Henry of Barre, to Miss Lucy Fairbanks of Lancaster.
" 15. Mr Albert Tufts to Miss Mary L. Newhall, both of Lancaster.
" 17. Capt Cephas Rugg to Miss Lucy K. Allen, both of Lancaster.

Before Reverend George Fisher of Harvard.

1827. March 1. Mr Jeremiah Dyar of Lancaster, and Mrs Lucy Huse of Harvard.

PUBLISHMENTS.

1827. May 9. Mr George Fitch of Lancaster, and Miss Sophronia Willard Houghton of Sterling.
Aug. 17. Mr Ebenezer Wilder of Lancaster, and Miss Clarissa Keyes of Berlin.
Sept. 19. Mr Robert C. Toombs of Lancaster, and Miss Louisa Winn of West Boylston.
1828. March 8. Mr Ward M. Cotton of Lancaster, and Miss Elizabeth M. Lamson of Boylston.
18. Rev. Aaron Burbank of Lancaster, and Miss Chloe Stevens of Townsend.

20. Mr William Larkin of Lancaster, and Miss Mary W. Ball of Northborough.
25. Mr Amos D. Tucker of Lancaster, and Miss Louisa Emerson of Harvard.
29. Mr Luke Stow of Lancaster, and Miss Abigail Houghton of Bolton.
April 21. Doctor George Baker of Lancaster, and Miss Emily Tidd of Medford.
May 13. Mr Isaac Cowdry of Lancaster, and Miss Mary Clisby of Malden.

MARRIAGES.

Before Nathaniel·Thayer, S. T. D.

1827. May 1. Mr James Gordon Carter to Mrs Ann Marsh Packard, both of Lancaster.
31. Mr Daniel Carter of Lowell, to Miss Catharine Phelps of Lancaster.
August 8. Mr Jonas B. White to Miss Nancy Wheelock, both of Lancaster.
Sept. 23. Mr Samuel C. Newhall of Foxcroft Me. to Miss Mary Bennett of Lancaster.
Oct. 7. Mr John A. Haskell of Worcester, to Miss Sarah R. Childs of Lancaster.
" 11. Mr Nathaniel Rand to Miss Nancy E. Thurston, both of Lancaster.
" 22. Mr Varnum Gilson of Cambridge, to Miss Martha Knight of Lancaster.
Dec. 27. Mr Nathaniel Rice to Miss Anna Stone, both of Lancaster.
1828. Jany 17. Mr Benjamin Hawks of Boston, to Miss Eliza Mallard of Lancaster.
" 20. Mr Jeremiah Whittemore of Bolton to Miss Miranda Holmes of Lancaster.
Feby. 27. Mr Ephraim C. Fisher to Miss Sarah Hills, both of Lancaster.
March 5. Jonas Lane Esq. to Miss Lydia Waite, both of Lancaster.
April 9. Mr John Fuller to Miss Sophronia O. W. Adams, both of Lancaster.
" 20. Mr Apollos Houghton of Sterling, to Miss Catharine Rugg of Lancaster.
May 4. Mr Joel Wilder Jr. to Miss Deborah H. Whitman, both of Lancaster.
June 5. Mr John G. Thurston of Lancaster, to Miss Harriet P. Lee of Barre.
Octo. 2. Mr William P. Willard to Miss Abigail R. Wilder, both of Lancaster.
Dec. 25. Mr Horace Maynard of Ashburnham, to Miss Lydia Frothingham of Lancaster.
1829. Jan. 1. Mr Moses Stow to Miss Eliza W. Jones, both of Lancaster.
" " Mr Edmund Parker of Southbridge, to Miss Rebecca Hawks of Lancaster.
Feby. 15. Mr Jonathan H. Park of Stow, to Miss Almira Elliot of Lancaster.
April 26. Mr Benjamin Butler Jr. to Miss Martha Phelps, both of Lancaster.
" 30. Mr Alfred Goodwin of Sterling to Miss Harriet Townshend of Lancaster.

Before Josiah Flagg Esq.

1828. July 2. Mr Edward A. Raymond and Miss Eliza T. Blackman, both of Boston, the said Eliza T. Blackman being resident in Lancaster.
Aug. 10. Mr William Bartlett and Miss Sally Lines, both of Lancaster.

PUBLISHMENTS.

1829. May 23. Mr John Thurston Jun. of Lancaster, and Miss Mehitable C. Alden of Bridgewater.
" 29. Mr Nathaniel Whittemore of Lancaster, and Miss Amelia Stone of Groton.
Octo. 21. Mr Timothy J. Fairbanks of Lancaster, and Miss Lucy A Woods of Boston.
Dec. 21. Joseph Willard Esq. of Lancaster, and Miss Susanna H. Lewis of Boston.
1830. March 24. Mr Thomas Divol of Lancaster, and Miss Mary Whiting of Lunenburg.
" 29. Mr Gilman B. Parker of Lancaster, and Miss Sarah Foster of New Ipswich N. H.
Apr. 20. Mr Joseph Rand of Lancaster, and Miss Meriam Brown of Marlboro', Vt.
" 27. Mr Daniel Virgil of Lancaster, and Miss Vashti Gates of Leominster.

MARRIAGES.

Before Reverend Abisha Samson.

1829. May 10. Mr Charles Goodale of West Boylston, with Miss Sarah Burditt of Lancaster.

Before Nathaniel Thayer, S. T. D.

1829. May 31. Mr David Osgood to Miss Eliza Bridge, both of Lancaster.
Sep. 13. Mr Sidney Harris to Miss Sally Kilburn, both of Lancaster.
Octo. 4. Mr Ira Stearns to Miss Lois Clarke, both of Lancaster.
" 28. Mr Henry Lewis to Miss Sally B. Taylor, both of Lancaster.
Nov. 4. Mr Levi Green to Miss Achsah Stone, both of Lancaster.
" 26. Mr Joel P. Townsend of Lowell, and Miss Sarah Phelps of Lancaster.
1830. Jan. 19. Mr Joseph Rice Jun. to Miss Fanny Adams, both of Lancaster.
Feb. 4. Mr Cyrus Bliss of Granville N. Y. to Miss Susan Fisher of Lancaster.
March 18. Mr Franklin Brigham to Miss Ann W. Taylor, both of Lancaster.
" 25. Mr Alvin Babcock of Berlin, to Miss Hannah A. Wood of Lancaster.
" 31. Capt. Artemas Harrington of Boylston to Miss Martha Stone of Lancaster.
" " Mr Silas Richardson to Miss Annis Smith, both of Lancaster.
April 6. Mr Amory Pollard of Lancaster to Miss Persis Peirce of West Boylston.

PUBLISHMENTS.

1830. Aug. 16. Mr Henry Morse of Leominster, and Miss Miranda Chase of Lancaster.
" 27. Mr Eleazar M. Wilson of Lancaster, and Miss Julia A. Whitney of Petersham.
Octo. 15. Rev[d]. John White Chickering of Lancaster, and Miss Frances Eveline Knowlton of Phillipston.
1831. March 7. Mr Thomas Brown of Lancaster, and Miss Abigail Stone of a place called No Town.
" 11. Mr Jacob Colburn of Lancaster, and Miss Hannah Spaulding of Westminster.
" 26. Mr Joseph Andrews of Lancaster, and Miss Thomazine Phillips Minot of Boston.
April 2. Mr Jotham H. Holt of Lancaster, and Miss Meriam Bartlett of Berlin.

MARRIAGES.

Before Reverend Abisha Samson.

1830. Aug. 15. Mr Vernis Streeter with Miss Eliza H. Burditt, both of Lancaster.

Before Josiah Flagg Esq.

1830. Dec. 26. Henry Barnard with Almira Pratt, both of Sterling.

Before Reverend John W. Chickering.

1831. April 23. Rev^d. George Trask of Framingham, and Miss Ruth Freeman Packard of Lancaster.

Before Nathaniel Thayer S. T. D.

1830. July 26. Solon Whiting Esq. to Miss Sarah S. Savage, both of Lancaster.
Sep. 1. Mr Oren Foster of Newmarket, N. H. to Miss Harriet Mallard of Lancaster.
Octo. 3. Mr Ebenezer Porter of Amesbury, to Miss Caroline C. Plummer of Lancaster.
" " Mr Franklin Woodcock to Miss Hannah C. Plummer, both of Lancaster.
11. Mr America Sawyer to Miss Lucy H. Baldwin, both of Lancaster.
Nov. 4. Mr David Combs Jun. of Dunstable N. H., to Miss Elizabeth Goss of Lancaster.
30. Mr Nathaniel S. Faulkner of Acton, to Miss Sophia Emerson of Lancaster.
Dec. 2. Mr William Cowdrey of Lunenburg, to Miss Lydia Ann W. Phelps of Lancaster.
1831. Feb. 2. Mr Jonathan P. Nurse to Miss Mary Pollard both of Lancaster.
March 31. Capt. Benjamin Houghton to Mrs Sally Keyes, both of Lancaster.
April 12. Mr Marcus Lamb of Worcester, to Miss Nancy Emerson of Lancaster.
28. Mr Levi Harris to Miss Eliza C. Plympton, both of Lancaster.

PUBLISHMENTS.

1831. June 6. Mr Joseph Emerson of Royalston, and Miss Lucy Gould of Lancaster.
Dec. 10. Mr Abel Stone of Lancaster, and Miss Jane Jordan Burrill of Boston.
1832. March 8. Mr Jotham Hastings of Boylston, and Miss Lucy A. Willington of Lancaster.
" 9. Mr Samuel A. Hastings of Lancaster and Miss Olive W. Nurse of Leominster.
" 24. Mr Zophar Sargent of Lancaster & Miss Catharine D. Carter of Westminster.
" 31. Mr Lewis Fletcher and Miss Sally P. Phelps, both of Lancaster.
" " Mr Nathaniel Joslin of Lancaster, and Miss Lovina Farnsworth of Groton.
April 14. Mr Oliver Wilder of Sterling and Miss Mary C. Goddard of Lancaster.

MARRIAGES.

Before Josiah Flagg Esq.

1831. August 15. Mr Abel Richardson Junr. and Miss Elizabeth Osgood, both of Lancaster.

Before Reverend John W. Chickering.

1831. May 31. Moses B Houghton of Cambridge Port, and Almira Pollard of Lancaster.

Before Nathaniel Thayer S. T. D.

1831. May 15. Mr Thomas S. Hildreth to Miss Mary Appleton Verder, both of Lancaster.
Sep. 13. Mr Edward Savage of Waterville Me., to Miss Mary C. Whitman of Lancaster.
" 21. Mr Galen L. Stevenson of Boston, to Miss Sarah Baldwin of Lancaster.
Nov. 2. Mr Jeremiah Foster to Miss Sarah Carpenter, both of Lancaster.
" 6. Mr Edmund Q. Greenleaf to Widow Elizabeth Prouty, both of Lancaster.
" 10. Mr Calvin Phelps to Mrs Prudence Ditson, both of Lancaster.
" 22. Mr Daniel Stowell of Petersham, to Miss Pamela V. Miles of Lancaster.
1832. Jany. 26. Mr Elijah Colburn to Mrs Nancy Taylor both of Lancaster.
March 28. Mr Edmund Jones of Ashburnham, to Miss Betsy Eaton of Lancaster.
April 2. Mr James Wilder Jun. of Sterling, to Miss Martha E. Goss of Lancaster.
" " Mr John Taylor to Miss Susan Newhall, both of Lancaster.
" 3. Mr Parker Longley of Boylston, to Miss Lydia Green of Lancaster.
" 17. Mr Seth French to Miss Fidelia Rugg, both of Lancaster.
" " Mr William Burditt to Miss Sally Tucker, both of Lancaster.

PUBLISHMENTS.

1832. July 28. Mr John Burditt Jun., and Miss Persis Houghton, both of Lancaster.
Aug. 11. Mr Sewall Sergeant of Lancaster, and Miss Cynthia Davis of Ashburnham.
Sep. 22. Mr George Carter of Lancaster, and Miss Nancy Carter of Keene N. H.
Nov. 10. Mr Elijah Sawyer of Lancaster, and Miss Martha A. Joslyn of Leominster.
Dec. 23. Mr John H. Swan and Mary F. Winchester, both of Lancaster.
1833. March 8. Mr Charles A. Lyman of Lancaster, and Miss Sarah Townshend of Bolton.
" 21. Mr George Howard of Lancaster, and Mrs. Elizabeth Buss of Leominster.
April 6. Mr Nathan B. Chamberlain of Lancaster, and Eliza M. Chamberlain of Westboro.

MARRIAGES.

Before Nathaniel Thayer, S. T. D.

1832. May 17. Mr Otis Haskell of Groton to Miss Nancy W. Stearns of Lancaster.
" 31. Mr James Rugg to Miss Nancy Gould, both of Lancaster.
Aug. 23. Mr Jonathan Lovejoy of Lowell, to Miss Louise Atherton of Lancaster.
Sep. 2. Mr Otis Flagg to Miss Althina Hastings, both of Lancaster.
13. Mr Josephus Wilder to Miss Lydia A. Maynard, both of Lancaster.
18. Mr Charles Farwell of Fitchburg, to Miss Ann A. Sanderson of Lancaster.
Octo. 11. Mr Abel Hastings of Boylston, to Miss Emeline Smith of Lancaster.
17. Major John Wilson to Miss Eliza Ann Rugg, both of Lancaster.
Nov. 1. Mr William Daby to Miss Eunice Willard, both of Lancaster.
Dec. 6. Mr Charles Hayes of Cambridge, to Miss Rebecca Goodwin of Lancaster.
25. Mr William Brown Spooner of Boston, to Miss Lucy Huntington of Lancaster.

25. Mr William Davis Ticknor of Boston, to Miss Emeline Staniford Holt of Lancaster.
1833. Jany. 1. Mr William Morse to Miss Mary Ann Goodwin, both of Lancaster.
18. Mr Isaiah Parker to Miss Oraville Atwood, both of Lancaster.
April 4. Mr Caleb Johnson to Miss Mary W. Goss both of Lancaster.
10. Mr Manasseh Putney to Miss Mary E. Parker, both of Lancaster.
21. Mr Williams Greene to Miss Sarah M. Howard, both of Lancaster.
25. Mr Mahlon Snow of Peterborough N. H. to Mrs Martha Gilson of Lancaster.
28. Mr Thomas H. Willington to Miss Lucy Wilder, both of Lancaster.

Before Josiah Flagg, Esq.

1832. Octo. 7. Mr William L. Clark with Miss Charlotte Wetherbee, both of Lancaster.
1833. April 21. Mr Seth Sackett of Southbridge, with Laura P. Burditt of Lancaster.

Before Reverend Hope Brown of Shirley.

1833. April 3. Mr Maynard Loring of Sterling, and Miss Mary Ann Phelps of Lancaster.

PUBLISHMENTS.

1833. May 25. Mr Abraham G. Adams of Lancaster, and Miss Anne Harrington of Weston.
Aug. 2. Mr Merrick Sargeant of Lancaster, and Miss Rebecca Cutting of Templeton.
Aug. 31. Mr Samuel Wright Adams Oliver of Lancaster, and Miss Sarah Ann Welch Hanners of Boston.
Oct. 26. Mr Albert Alden of Lancaster, and Miss Susan Monroe of Barnstable.
Nov. 11. Mr Frederick C. Root of Lancaster, and Miss Rebecca Bridge of Boston.
Nov. 16. Mr William Croome of Lancaster, and Miss Sarah H. Curtis of Roxbury.
1834. March 28. Mr Sumner Wilder of Lancaster, and Miss Susan Maria T. Davis of Holden.
April 5. Mr Abel H. Williams and Miss Rebecca B. Munroe, both of Lancaster.
" 16. Mr John Whipple of Northboro', and Miss Charlotte W. Stone of Lancaster.
" 19. Mr Samuel M. Hinds of Lancaster, and Miss Sarah Cook of Petersham.
' 30. Mr William Davis of Shirley and the Widow Phebe Priest of Lancaster.

MARRIAGES.

Before Reverend Thomas Worcester.

1834. April 8. Mr Noah Worcester and Miss Nancy B. Carter, both of Lancaster.
May 29. Mr Oscar C. B. Carter and Miss Emily Carter, both of Lancaster.

Before Nathaniel Thayer, S. T. D.

1833. Sep. 4. Mr Francis Worcester of Crown Point N. Y., to Miss Martha T. J. Fairbank of Lancaster.
Octo. 29. Mr George Stratton to Miss Lucinda Bailey, both of Lancaster.

	Nov. 28.	Mr Charles H. Grover to Miss Mary Farwell, both of Lancaster.
	Dec. 5.	Mr Charles Wyman to Miss Nancy Farnsworth, both of Lancaster.
	" 31.	Mr Ephraim Fuller to Miss Judith Goss, both of Lancaster.
1834.	Jany. 21.	Mr Thaddeus Balcom to Miss Rebecca Frothingham, both of Lancaster.
	Feb. 25.	Mr Rufus Carter of Berlin, to Miss Sarah E. Goss of Lancaster.
	March 2.	Mr Charles Wheelock of Lancaster, to Miss Elizabeth Hastings of Boylston.
	" 9.	Mr Horatio N. Bridgman to Miss Betsy Pollard, both of Lancaster.
	" 19.	Mr Aaron Collins to Miss Eunice Onthank, both of Lancaster.
	April 6.	Mr Ira G. Childs of Lansingburg N. Y. to Miss Abigail Wilder of Lancaster.
	24.	Mr Joseph F. Smith to Miss Rebecca Arnold, both of Lancaster.
	30.	Mr Oliver Carter 2ᵈ. to Miss Polly Warner, both of Lancaster.

PUBLISHMENTS.

1834.	June 10.	Mr Thomas Jones of Lancaster, and Miss Mary Tweed of Lunenburg.
	Aug. 9.	Mr Hiram Smith of Worcester, and Miss Mary W. Phelps of Lancaster.
	" 30.	Mr David Phelps of Concord, and Miss Laura Meriam of Lancaster.
	Sept. 10.	Mr Abraham Ray of Stow, and Miss Patience Frye of Lancaster.
	Nov. 1.	Mr Haskell McCollum and Miss Silvia Low, both of Lancaster.
	Dec. 3.	Mr Lyman Moore of Lancaster, and Miss Mary Bartlett of Cambridge Port.
1835.	March 14.	Mr George W. Howard of Lancaster, and Miss Elizabeth Houghton of Sterling.
	April 3.	Mr Alfred Knight of Lancaster, and Miss Mary Butterfield of Hollis N. H.
	April 29.	Mr Henry Willard of Lancaster, and Miss Mary Ann Houghton of Sterling.

MARRIAGES.

Before Reverend John W. Chickering of Bolton.

1834 in June. Mr Farnham Plummer and Mrs Abigail Ballard, both of Lancaster.

Before Josiah Flagg Esq.

1834. April 6. Mr Seth Sargent and Miss Maria Temple, both of Shrewsbury.
May 28. Mr Carter Wilder and Miss Susan Fales, both of Lancaster.

Before Reverend Joseph G Binney, West Boylston.

1834. Aug. 3. Mr John Burditt and Widow Sally Carpenter, both of Lancaster.

Before Nathaniel Thayer, S. T. D.

1834.	May 1.	Mr John S. Ward to Miss Olive Phelps, both of Lancaster.
	June 8.	Mr Joseph Wilder 2. to Miss Maria S. Flagg, both of Lancaster.
	Sep. 7.	Mr John Carter to Mrs Mary Gates, both of Lancaster.
	Octo. 1.	Mr Robert Andrews of Boston, to Miss Caroline Amelia Wilder of Lancaster.
	" 16.	Asahel H. Bennett Esq. of Winchester N. H., to Miss Abigail A. G. Smith of Lancaster.
	29.	Mr Joel W. Phelps to Miss Lorinda Davis, both of Lancaster.
	Dec. 10.	Mr George Gray of Boston, to Miss Jane Buttrick of Lancaster.
	" 23.	Mr Nathaniel Whittemore to Miss Nancy Jones, both of Lancaster.

BOOK THIRD. 243

    " 31. Mr Joshua T. Collins of Fitzwilliam N. H., to Miss Elizabeth A. Ballard of Lancaster.
1835. March 2. Mr William Davis to Mrs Nancy Lincoln, both of Lancaster.
    April 7. Mr Charles Wood to Miss Hannah Chapin, both of Lancaster.
    27. Mr Ebenezer Brooks Jr. of Sterling, to Miss Eliza P. Davis of Lancaster.
    29. Mr Wiliam Puffer to Miss Keziah Divoll, both of Lancaster.

PUBLISHMENTS.

1835. May 9. Mr John Townsend of Groton, and Miss Caroline Phelps of Lancaster.
    " June 26. Mr Joseph Morse of Lancaster, and Miss Ann Smith Winchester of Sterling.
    July 31. Mr Watson Wood of Littleton, and Miss Mary Elizabeth Richardson of Lancaster.
    Aug. 5. Mr William Thompson of Lancaster, and Miss Abigail Webb of Sterling.
    " 15. Mr Artemas Barnes of Lancaster, and Miss Alice Stutson of Boston.
    22. Mr Asa D. Farnsworth of Lancaster, and Miss Betsy Sawtell of Groton.
    Sep. 5. Mr Lucien Tiffany of Southbridge, and Miss Julia A. Burditt of Lancaster.
    21. Mr Lowell Hartwell of Groton, and Miss Harriet Worster of Lancaster.
    Nov. 18. Mr George W. Wilder of Lancaster, and Mrs Mercy Stutson of Harwich.
    Dec. 12. Mr Albert G. Thayer of Lancaster, and Miss Sarah Boynton of New Ipswich.
1836. April 18. Mr Edward Warren of Northboro' and Miss Cornelia Stone of Lancaster.
    25. Capt. Salmon Willard and Mrs Mercy Kelly, both of Lancaster.

MARRIAGES.

Before Nathaniel Thayer, S. T. D.

1835. May 6. Mr John W. Barnes to Miss Adeline Mallard, both of Lancaster.
    20. Mr Christopher F. Townsend of Boston to Miss Lucretia Phelps of Lancaster.
    June 14. Mr Jonathan Shattuck of Bolton to Miss Mary W. Knights of Lancaster.
    July 4. Mr George P. Farwell to Miss Ruth Hinkson, both of Lancaster.
    Aug. 4. Mr Joseph Davis to Mrs Mary Warner, both of Lancaster.
    9. Mr Augustus Taylor of Boylston, to Miss Almira Taylor of Lancaster.
    Sep. 8. Mr Charles H. Bridge to Miss Rebecca G. Prouty, both of Lancaster.
    Oct. 8. Mr Charles L. Wilder of Boston, to Miss Harriet E. Harris of Lancaster.
    21. Mr William Joslyn of Holliston, to Miss Elizabeth B. Hunt of Lancaster.
    Nov. 11. Mr Reuben Barrett to Miss Lydia McQuesten, both of Lancaster.
    25. Mr William Fife Jun. of Berlin, to Mrs Sarah Brewer of Lancaster.
1836. Jan. 14. Mr John A. Haskell to Mrs Jane D. Stewart, both of Lancaster.
    April 13. Mr Oliver Greene to Miss Sophia Joslyn, both of Lancaster.

PUBLISHMENTS.

1836. Sep. 10. Mr William Parks of Lancaster, and Miss Dolly S. McIntire of Westminster.
    Oct. 15. Mr Eri B. Bement of Lancaster, and Miss Rosanna Wilder of Fitchburg.

1837. Jan. 3. Mr Charles W. Haskell of Lancaster, and Miss Sarah I. Swain of Ashby.
May 6. Mr Francis Wilcox of Lancaster, & Miss Emily C. Merriam of Fitchburg.

MARRIAGES.

Before Nathaniel Thayer S. T. D.

1836. Aug. 24. Alonzo C. Wetherbee to Miss Elizabeth Fairbank, both of Lancaster.
Sep. 15. Mr Reuben Hastings to Miss Caroline Hall, both of Lancaster.
Oct. 6. Mr Rufus K. Ladd of Boston, to Miss Emily Pollard of Lancaster.
20. Mr James A. Arnold to Miss Angelia Lawrence, both of Lancaster.
Nov. 12. Mr George W. Howe of Detroit Mich. to Miss Sophia Rugg of Lancaster.
Dec. 14. Mr Salmon Houghton to Mrs Frances Jones, both of Lancaster.
1837. April 2. Mr Horace Harrington to Miss Maria Stone, both of Lancaster.

By Joseph W. Huntington Esq.

1836. Sept. 8. Mr Mahlon Snow and Miss Sarah Knights, both of Lancaster.

PUBLISHMENTS.

1838. Jany. 13. Henry Lincoln M. D. of Lancaster and Miss Martha Bond of Sterling. [Married Feb. 14, 1838.]
April 21. Capt. John Whitney of Lancaster, and Miss Rosetta Childs of Henniker N. H.
" 28. Mr Horace Rice and Miss Elcy Morten, both of Lancaster.

MARRIAGES.

Before Reverend John S. Danvenport of Bolton.

1838. March 1. Charles Miller of Springfield, to Matilda Low of Lancaster.

Before Nathaniel Thayer S. T. D.

1837. July 23. Mr Amos H. Wyman to Miss Lucy L. Brimhall, both of Lancaster.
Oct. 12. Mr Francis Piper to Miss Betsy Houghton, both of Lancaster.
25. Capt. Jnoathan B. Webster of Salisbury, to Miss Abigail R. Ballard of Lancaster.
Nov. 1. Capt. Hezekiah M. Grant of Boston, to Miss Martha W. Damon of Lancaster.
22. Mr Thomas Burditt to Miss Sarah E. Woodbury, both of Lancaster.
Dec. 7. Mr Luke W. Carter of Westminster, to Miss Abigail F. Priest of Lancaster.
1838. Jan. 1. Mr Benjamin Tyler to Mrs Mary Phelps, both of Lancaster.
Feb. 7. Mr Edward Hooper of Boston, to Miss Emily W. Rugg of Lancaster.
March 4. Mr John W. Crossman of Boylston, to Miss Evelina Phelps of Lancaster.
April 4. Mr Levi W. Damon of Grafton, to Miss Eliza Ann Chaffin of Lancaster.

PUBLISHMENTS.

1838. May 24. Mr Hollis Davis of Lancaster, and Miss Hannah Hager of Weston.
June 16. Mr William Stearns of Lancaster, and Miss Mary Ann Brown of Sterling.
Aug. 22. Mr Amos Farnum and Miss Mary Harrington, both of Lancaster.
Oct. 20. Mr Erastus B. Bigelow of Lancaster, and Miss Susan W. King of West Boylston.

Nov. 9. Mr Nathan Burditt Jun. of Lancaster, and Miss Mary E. Carter of Lancaster.
1839. March 4. Mr Horace Piper of Lancaster, and Miss Harriet Sargeant of Sterling.
26. Mr John Snow of Leominster, and Miss Emily R. Osgood of Lancaster.

MARRIAGES.

Before Reverend Levi M. Powers of Bolton.

1838. May 8. Joseph Hutchins of Charlestown, and Miss Mary J. Taylor of Lancaster.

Before Reverend Rufus S. Pope of Sterling.

1838. May 29. Mr Benja. Farwell and Miss Grata Johnson, both of Lancaster.
30. Mr Jacob Willard and Miss Eliza Houghton, both of Lancaster.
June 10. Mr William Pitts of Lancaster, and Miss Dolly T. Andrews of Boylston.

Before Reverend Moses Curtis of Harvard.

1838. Sept. 25. Mr Nathaniel Burbank and Miss Eleanor Kelly, both of Lancaster.
Nov. 28. Mr Artemas Hodgman and Miss Sarah P. Townshend, both of Lancaster.
1839. Jany. 2. Mr Warren Willard and Miss Lucy Burbank, both of Lancaster.

Before Nathaniel Thayer, S. T. D.

1838. June 14. Capt. Charles J. Wilder to Miss Eliza Carter, both of Lancaster.
June 21. Mr Thomas Carter of Leominster, to Miss Mary Phelps of Lancaster.
July 4. Mr William Brown to Miss Ann S. Mallard, both of Lancaster.
Aug. 7. Nathaniel Rand Esq. to Miss Ruth Miles, both of Lancaster.
7. Mr Daniel K. Wilder of New Bedford, and Miss Mary M. Andrews of Lancaster.
Sept. 18. Mr Stevens H. Turner and Miss Betsy T. Carter, both of Lancaster.
25. Mr Andrew J. Brown of Bordentown N. J. and Miss Eleanor L Fletcher of Lancaster.
Nov. 29. Mr Jonathan Buttrick to Miss Charlotte Howard, both of Lancaster.
1839. Feby. 18. Mr Henry Knabe of Lancaster, to Mrs Isabella Gilson of Lancaster.

PUBLISHMENTS.

1839. May 9. Mr Fordyce Nourse of Lancaster, and Miss Laura Holman of Bolton.
May 18. Mr Newton Burpee of Sterling, and Miss Rebecca Houghton of Lancaster.
July 21. Mr Samuel J. S. Vose of Lancaster, and Miss Mary W. Richardson of Chester N. H.

MARRIAGES.

Before Reverend John S. Davenport of Bolton.

1838. May 30. Mr Silas S. Greenleaf of Northampton, to Miss Sarah F. Nowell of Lancaster.
1839. May 2. Mr Isaiah Moors to Miss Mary P. Wheeler, both of Lancaster.
July 4. Mr Charles T. Fisher of Templeton, to Miss Martha Ballard of Lancaster.

Before Reverend Isaac Allen of Bolton.

1839. Oct. 15. Nathaniel N. Cowdry of Hinsdale N. H., and Augusta Phelps of Lancaster.

Before Nathaniel Thayer, S. T. D.

1839. June 25. Mr Thomas H. Parker of Shirley, to Miss Nancy P. Crossman of Boylston.
Sept. 12. Mr Calvin Battles of Fitchburg to Miss Sarah Worcester of Lancaster.
25. Mr Moses Gould to Miss Susan W. Boswell, both of Lancaster.
Oct. 6. Mr Mason W. Tisdale to Miss Matilda D. Martin, both of Boston.
Dec. 5. Mr Samuel Jones 2^d to Miss Mary Jane Gooly, both of Lancaster.
1840. Feby. 16. Mr William T. Brabrook of Boston, to Miss Sarah A. Fairbank of Lancaster.

Before Revered David R. Lamson of Berlin.

1839. March 28. Michael Fanning of Lancaster and Harriet Hartwell of Berlin.

PUBLISHMENTS.

1839. Nov. 23. Mr Samuel J. Moors and Miss Elizabeth R. T. Bartlett, both of Lancaster.
1840. Feb. 15. Mr Levi B. Burbank of Lancaster, and Miss Jane Kidder of Townsend.
April 22. Mr Josiah Lawrence of Lancaster, and Miss Relief Annets of Southborough.
25. Mr John B. Parker of Lancaster, and Miss Martha Pollard of Bolton.
26. Mr George C. Robinson of Lancaster, and Abigail L. Atherton of Harvard.
May 26. Mr Warren Nourse of Lancaster, and Miss Nancy Derby of Lunenburg.
June 13. Mr Lucius L Farwell and Miss Mary Barrett, both of Lancaster.
July 16. Mr Curtis Sargent and Miss Huldah Forbes, both of Lancaster.
18. Mr Harrison Johnson and Miss Laura Loisa Cobb, both of Lancaster.
Aug. 5. Mr Silas Coolidge of Marlborough, and Miss Betsy Rugg of Lancaster.
8. Mr Washington Sanderson of Shirley, and Miss Mary Ann Gardner of Lancaster.
Oct. 3. Mr Edmund Fletcher of Andover, and Miss Elizabeth C. Plummer of Lancaster.
1841. Feby. 6. Mr Eber Goddard of Lancaster, and Miss Mary L. Burditt of Leominster.
27. Mr Samuel Adams of Lancaster, and Miss Harriet M. Goddard of Sterling.

MARRIAGES.

Before Esek Whiting Esq. Lunenburg.

1841. Feb. 18. Dexter Bruce Jun. with Louisa Phillips, both of Lancaster.

Before Reverend Lucius R. Paige.

1841. Feb. 22. Mr Benjamin F. Farnsworth and Miss Cynthia Ann Hawks, both of Lancaster.

Before Reverend Charles Packard.

1840. Oct. 7. Joseph M. Wilder of Holliston and Sarah Bruce of Lancaster.
[Oct. 21. William P. Homer of Philadelphia, and Lucy Hastings of Berlin.]
[Revd. Thomas Thomas of Hamilton, Ohio, and Lydia P. Fisher of Northborough.]
Dec. 30. William Phelps and Olive Davis, both of Lancaster.
1841. April 21. Alfred Sawyer of Boylston, and Sarah E. Goss of Lancaster.

BOOK THIRD. 247

Before Reverend Charles Willington of Templeton.

1841. July 1. Mr Emory H. White and Miss Sarah Stone, both of Lancaster.

PUBLISHMENTS.

1841. Oct. 31. Mr Emory Hastings of Lancaster and Miss Maria L. Barton ot Orange.
Nov. 20. Mr Samuel W. Burbank and Miss Mary Ann Rugg, both of Lancaster.
1842. Jany 6. Mr Hiram W. Pitts of Lancaster and Miss Betsy S. Burdit of Leominster.
March 12. Mr Daniel Taylor of Lancaster and Miss Relief S. Taylor of West Boylston.

MARRIAGES.

Before Reverend Edmund H. Sears.

1841. Feb. 2. Mr Phillip Freeman, Jr., of Gardner, to Miss Roxana Bond of Lancaster. (Colored.)
March 4. Mr William C. Carter to Miss Martha Ann R. Bragg, both of Lancaster.
April 28. Mr Thomas Laughton to Miss Nancy P. Dorrison, both of Lancaster.
May 2. Mr Eben Pratt to Miss Betsy Gould, both of Lancaster.
13. Mr Flavel Case of Coventry Conn. to Miss Sally Sawyer of Lancaster.
June 6. Mr Nelson Hutchinson of Norwich Conn., to Miss Hannah Rugg of Lancaster.
Sept. 23. Mr Josiah Wilder of Sterling, and Miss Susan B. Maynard of Lancaster.
30. Dr. William W. Wellington of Cambridge, to Miss Lucy Elizabeth Carter of Lancaster.
Oct. 5. Samuel L. Gardner Esq. of Sag Harbor L. I. to Miss Ann Shaler of Lancaster.
Nov. 25. Mr John Cunningham to Miss Louisa Rice, both of Lancaster.

Before Reverend Charles Packard.

1841. April 21. Mr Alfred Sawyer [of Boylston,] and Miss Sarah A. Goss [of Lancaster.]
28. Sylvanus Reed and Sarah H. Greenleaf, [both of Bolton.]
July 14. Doctor Calvin Carter and Mrs Lucinda W. Cook, [both of Lancaster.]
Sept. 9. Mr Oliver Emerson and Miss Lucy Chapman, [both of Lancaster.]
26. Mr Thomas C. Eustis [of Paxton] and Electa Merrill [of Hudson, N. H.]
Oct. 21. Mr James S. Lawrence [of Seneca Falls N. Y.] and Miss Caroline Lowe [of Lancaster.]

Before Reverend John Harriman.

1841. April 25. In Acton Mr Nathaniel T. Law to Miss Mary Ann Handly, both of Acton.
Oct. 26. In Lancaster Mr Caleb Winchester of Holden, to Miss Mary Ann Greene of Lancaster.
Nov. 25. " Mr Samuel A. Dorrison to Miss Elizabeth F. Green, both of Lancaster.
Dec. 16. " Mr James Pitts to Miss Lucinda Burditt, both of Lancaster.
1842. Jany. 19. Mr Hiram Taylor of Fitchburg to Mrs Martha W. Grant of Lancaster.

Before Reverend Horatio Alger of Chelsea.

1842. May 29. Mr Frederick W. Wilder and Miss Sarah B. Howe, both of Lancaster.

Before Reverend A. Harvey of Westborough.

1841. Sept. 16. Mr Dennis Holt of Lancaster, and Miss Lucy Walker of Westborough.

PUBLISHMENTS.

1842. July 1. Mr Israel Moore of Bolton, and Miss Sarah P. Moore of Lancaster.
    29. Mr John H. Maynard of Lancaster, and Miss Mary Maynard of Concord N. H.
  Aug. 6. Mr William Eaton of Lancaster, and Miss E. J. B. Wetherbee of Boxborough.
    12. Mr Andrew J. Farnsworth of Lancaster, and Miss Catharine M. Phelps of Lunenburg, Vt.
  Oct. 29. Mr Artemas Hodgman and Miss Louisa Hill, both of Lancaster.
1843. Jany. 7. Mr Emory Sargent and Miss Augusta Ann Miller, both of Lancaster.

MARRIAGES.

Before Reverend William Morse of Marlborough.

1843. Jany. 23. Mr Nathaniel Hastings and Miss Ann Elizabeth Packard both of Lancaster.

Before Reverend Edmund H. Sears.

1842. June 23. Mr Jonathan McIntire of Lyndeboro' N. H, to Miss Louisa E. Marshall of Lancaster.
  Dec. 15. Mr Henry Wilder to Miss Anna W. Goodhue, both of Lancaster.
    25. Mr Jonas Goss to Miss Sarah E. Wilder, both of Lancaster.
1843. Jan. 24. Mr Albert S. Carleton to Miss Susannah Damon, both of Lancaster.

Before Reverend John Harriman.

1842. May 27. Mr Silas H. Fairbank of West Boylston, to Miss Mary Ann Woodbury of Lancaster.
  July 24. Mr Francis Noyes of Danvers, to Miss Lucy Rice of Lancaster.
1843. Feb. 16. Mr Elbridge Houghton of Bolton to Miss Emily Richardson of Leominster.
    22. Mr Jonas M. Damon to Miss Hannah H. Carr, both of Lancaster.
  April 3. Mr Alexander Potter to Miss Angelina Chapman, both of Harvard.
  May 30. Mr John Blanchard of Harvard, and Miss Margaret Kennedy of Lancaster.
   "   " Mr Ebenezer W. Howe of Lancaster and Miss Sarah Ann Blanchard of Harvard.

Before Reverend Henry Adams.

1842. October. Mr Loriman Howe of Bolton, and Miss Mary D. Faulkner of Lancaster.

Before Reverend O. G. Hubbard of Leominster.

1842. Jany. 3. Mr George W. Allen of Woburn and Miss Mary L. Tyler of Lancaster.
1843. Nov. 14. Mr David Sawyer of Bolton, and Miss Lorina Kilburne of Lancaster.

Before Reverend Charles Packard.

1842. Feb. 9. Sampson W. Buffum of Winchester N. H. and Miss Mary E. Tower of Lancaster.
  April 5. Jonathan W. Houghton and Abby S. Fay, both of Lancaster.
  Sept. 14. Gilbert Creene and Mary Antoinette Whitcomb, both of Lancaster.

15. Doctor Edwin Adams of Boston, and Anna Gertrude Pollard of Lancaster.
27. John G. Cary and Harriet C. Puffer, both of Boston.

Before Zina Winter Esq. of Stafford, Ct.

1846. April 3. Abel Pollard and Mary Ann Prouty, both of Lancaster.

PUBLISHMENTS.

1843. March 18. Mr Josiah M. Withington of Lancaster and Miss Isabella B. Smith of Boxborough.
Aug. 26. Mr George Brigham 2^d of Marlboro' and Miss Abby Mallard of Lancaster.
Sept. 15. Mr Seth French and Miss Esther Hodgman both of Lancaster.
Sept. 29. Mr Anthony L. Sawyer of Lancaster, and Miss Edith B. Haven of Waltham. [Married October 19, 1843.]
Dec. 13. Mr Warren Ball of Lancaster, and Miss Sophronia Howe of Marlboro'.
23. Mr Joseph Moore of Lancaster, and Miss Adaline Holland of Lowell.
1844. March 4. Mr William B. Rugg of Lancaster, and Miss Mary E. Willis of Littleton.
16. Mr John W. Damon of Lancaster, and Miss Clarazette G. Sanders of Lowell.
May 3. Mr Artemas H Parker of Lancaster, and Miss Susan Elizabeth Peirce of West Boylston.
10. Mr Nathaniel P. Sawtell of Shirley, and Miss Elizabeth Knight of Lancaster.
11. Mr John Townsend of Lancaster, and Miss Elizabeth B. Flagg of Sterling.
June 1. Mr William L. Sanderson and Miss Maria L. Chapin both of Lancaster.
Nov. 1. Mr R. B. Thomas Goodale of Lancaster and Miss Jane R. Chaffin of Holden.
1. Mr David Smith of Lancaster and Miss Mary K. Tozier of Lowell.
1845. Jan. 3. Mr F. Marshall Burdett of Lancaster, and Miss Elizabeth R. Bruce of Southboro'.
March 8. Mr Stilman Houghton of Lancaster and Miss Mercy R. Wetherbee of Boxborough.
April 12. Mr George W. Howe of Lancaster, and Miss Mary Ann Jenness of Lowell.
May 16. Mr Munro Winchester of Lancaster, and Miss Nancy Flagg of Shrewsbury.
19. Mr John T. Dame of Lancaster, and Miss Eliza E. Reeves of Wayland.
22. Mr Samuel W. Burbank of Lancaster, and Miss Olive Ross of Sterling.
July 26. Mr Barney S. Phelps of Lancaster, and Miss Mary A. Taylor of Harvard.
Aug. 2. Mr William Fletcher Jr. of Lancaster, and Miss Drucilla Smith of Henniker, N. H.
9. Mr Jacob C. Bennett and Miss Mary Newton, both of Lancaster.
9. Mr Jonas Goss of Lancaster, and Miss Abbie Fletcher of Acton. [Married Sept. 11.]
Sept. 6. Mr George H. Kendall of Lancaster, and Miss Mary J. Caldwell of Barre.
Dec. 6. Mr James W. Howe of Lancaster, and Miss Harriet Morse of Waterford, Me.
1846. Jan. 7. Mr Elhanan Winchester Whittemore and Miss Margaret Little, both of Lancaster.
Feb. 14. Mr Alvin Sargent and Miss Rebecca Alexander, both of Lancaster.

17

March 7. Mr Matthias F. Chaffin of Lancaster and Miss Amazonia Bolton of W. Boylston.
20. Mr Sewell T. Rugg of Lancaster and Miss Persis Underwood of Templeton.
25. Mr Augustus P. Burdett of Lancaster and Miss Mary E. Stiles of Leominster.
April 23. Mr Thomas E. Lawrence and Miss Adaline E. Howe, both of Lancaster.
May 9. Mr Lucius L. Farwell of Lancaster, and Miss Sarah E. Dickenson of Harvard.
23. Mr John F. Houghton of Lancaster, and Miss Mary C. Hemmenway of Framingham.
Aug. 1. Dr James M. Whittemore of Brighton, and Miss Catharine M. Carter of Lancaster.
Sept. 5. Mr Enos H. Day of Lancaster and Miss Elizabeth Maxwell of Alfred, Me.
17. Mr Sanborn Worthen of Lancaster and Miss Lucinda S. Taylor of Lowell.
Oct. 3. Dr. George W. Burditt of Lancaster, and Miss Elizabeth J. Valentine of Northboro'.
17. Mr Rufus Maynard of Lancaster, and Miss Louisa Jane Houghton of Harvard.
Nov. 6. Mr Reuben Maynard of Lancaster, and Miss Joanna H. Sawyer of Buxton, Me.
Nov. 17. Mr Samuel P. Barrett of Lancaster, and Miss Mary W. Ball of Townsend.
1847. Jan. 30. Mr Alvin Whiting of Lancaster, and Miss Mary Estey of Dedham.
Feb. 11. Mr William T. Merrifield of Lancaster, and Miss Maria C. Brigham of Grafton.
25. Mr Jeremiah Barnard of Lancaster, and Miss Sarah Fletcher of Littleton.
March 6. Mr Otis Houghton of Lancaster, and Miss Susan H. Crouch of Boxborough.
9. Mr Albert Stanwood of Lancaster, and Miss Charlotte M. Morse of Portland, Me.
17. Mr Peter E. Davidson of Lancaster, and Miss Mary Tyler of Leominster.
19. Mr William I. Howe of Lancaster, and Miss Persis Carter of Boylston.
25. Mr Lorey F. Bancroft of Lancaster, and Miss Julia A. Valentine of Northboro'.
26. Mr Charles A. Merriam of Lancaster, and Miss Elima H. Graham of Townsend.
April 14. Mr Daniel Davis of Lancaster, and Cynthia Garfield of Weston.
24. Mr Thomas Hall of Salisbury, and Miss Sarah Townsend of Lancaster.
25. Mr Joseph Green and Miss Cordelia Sargent, both of Lancaster.
May 9. Mr Alfred W. Crossman of Lancaster, and Miss Elizabeth D. Buck of Sterling.
10. Mr George Teasdale of Lancaster, and Miss Mary A. Walcott of Stow.
20. Mr Aratus M. Kelly of Lancaster, and Miss Eliza Robinson of Barre.
20. Mr Andrew Houghton of Lancaster, and Miss Amanda M. Warren of Charlestown.
21. Mr Edwin A. Larkin of Lancaster, and Miss Elizabeth Wright of Mason, N. H.
29. Mr Jonas W. Belcher and Miss Mary E. G. Prouty, both of Lancaster.
June 5. Mr John W. Frost and Miss Finis Barrett, both of Lancaster.

11. Mr Samuel Holland of Leominster, and Miss Eunice Hooper of Lancaster.
19. Mr Ashley H. Wood of Lancaster, and Miss Caroline A. Eager of Webster.
19. Mr Mark Lund of Lancaster and Miss Martha Robbins of Milton.
July 2. Mr Samuel O. McClure and Miss Lucinda G. McKean both of Lancaster.
10. Mr George K. Tuttle of Lancaster, and Miss Martha Ann Hinkley of Bath, Me.
26. Mr William C. Hart of Lancaster, and Miss Elizabeth Fitts of Oxford.
28. Mr John C. Hoadly of Lancaster, and Miss Charlotte S. Kimball of Needham.
Aug. 3. Mr William W. Parker of Lancaster and Miss Emily Walker of Holden.
14. Mr John Commans and Miss Julia Conway both of Lancaster.
Sept. 4. Mr Stillman A. Meeds and Harriet Holman, both of Lunenburg.
20. Mr Calvin R. Wheeler and Miss Lydia D. Norton, both of Lancaster.
Oct. 13. Mr Charles H. Sawyer of Lancaster, and Miss Rosine Sheldon of Holden.
16. Mr Henry A. Howard, and Miss Sally F. Wood, both of Lancaster.
23. Mr Leonard J. Richards and Miss Lydia A. Gordon, both of Lancaster.
23. Mr Newton F. Hayden and Miss Caroline M. Arnold, both of Lancaster.
Dec. 11. Mr Samuel H. Peirce of Lancaster, and Miss Charlotte S. Houghton of Berlin.
25. Mr Samuel H. Gilson of Lancaster, and Miss Caroline Delano of Shirley.
1848. Jan. 3. Mr Calvin Fletcher Jr. of Lancaster and Miss Elizabeth Whitney of Stow.
7. Mr James H. Stone and Miss Betsy Jones both of Lancaster.
18. Mr Andrew J. Farnsworth of Lancaster, and Miss Mary C. Potter of Charlestown.
Feb. 14. Mr Martin Smith and Miss Mary Butler, both of Lancaster.
March 11. Mr Henry F. Haynes of Bolton, and Miss Elizabeth Buss of Lancaster.
24. Mr William McLeran and Miss Cornelia Latham, both of Lancaster.
April 1. Mr George Bowman and Miss Abby M. Hayden, both of Lancaster.
8. Mr George E. Reese and Miss Mary Jane Bailey, both of Lancaster.
15. Mr Elhanan W. Whittemore of Lancaster, and Miss Esther Damon of Lunenburg.
29. Mr Ambrose A. Mason of Lancaster, and Miss Sarah H. Felton of Springfield.
May 6. Mr I. J. Gibson of Lancaster, and Miss Mary A. Gifford of Grafton.
June 7. Mr Nathaniel S. Gilson and Miss Louisa C. Latham, both of Lancaster.
July 6. Mr Silas Peckham and Miss Susan Whitcomb, both of Lancaster.
Aug. 2. Mr Charles Jewett of Lancaster, and Miss Myra Wood of Leominster.
17. Mr Jeremiah Callaghan and Miss Catharine O Roach, both of Lancaster.
19. Mr Elisha B. Frost of Lancaster, and Miss Sarah L. Lawrence of Ashby.
25. Mr Charles L. Swan ot Lancaster, and Miss Lucy W. Haskell of Rochester.

Sept. 6. Mr Patrick F. Moran and Miss Mary Ann Galaher, both of Lancaster.
Oct. 9. Mr Charles S. Patten of Lancaster, and Miss Ellen C. Brown of Milford.
Dec. 9. Mr Martin Shannassy and Mary Fallon, both of Lancaster.
16. Mr Mike Kelly and Miss Mary Bray, both of Lancaster.
18. Mr John Kelly and Miss Eliza Roche, both of Lancaster.
1849. Jan. 6. Mr D. Francis Chaffin and Miss Mary Arvilla Walker, both of Lancaster.
March 10. Mr James Harrington of Lancaster, and Miss Arvilla Augusta Wood of Harvard.
29. Mr Thomas Hastings and Miss Elizabeth T. Houghton, both of Lancaster.
31. Mr Daniel Moran and Miss Mary Lacy, both of Lancaster.
April 15. Mr James Magoun and Miss Margaret Fleming, both of Lancaster.
May 14. Mr Jacob W. Robinson of Lancaster, and Miss Martha Allen of Lowell.
26. Mr Alfred A. Burditt and Miss Matilda A. Boynton, both of Lancaster.
June 9. Mr Joel S. Little of Manchester, N. H., and Miss Lucy Jane Jackman of Lancaster.
13. Mr Amos F. Blood of Lancaster, and Miss Adeline Weston of Acton.
20. Mr Merrick L. Gilson of Lancaster, and Miss Emeline E. Tucker of Boylston.
July 14. Mr George Morrill of Lancaster, and Miss Sarah A. Tolman of Ashby.
16. Mr John Patrick and Miss Dorothy R. Chambers, both of Lancaster.
28. Mr David Dias and Miss Cecilia King, both of Lancaster.
Aug. 25. Mr Frederick E. Lane and Miss Sophia P. Chase, both of Lancaster.
Sept. 1. Mr Joshua C. Jewett and Marion E. Sawyer, both of Lancaster.
Oct. 6. Mr Alexander Grassie of Lancaster, and Miss Sibley Ann Edwards of Boston.
8. Mr Michael Commons and Miss Bridget Kinney, both of Lancaster.
8. Mr John Griffin and Miss Mary Fay, both of Lancaster.
20. Mr Edward B. Rollins of Lancaster, and Asenath D. Joy of Bolton.
23. Mr Joshua Thissell Jr. of Lancaster and Miss M. Sarah Brown of Lowell.
23. Mr Francis Cook and Miss Ednah Buck, both of Lancaster.
29. Mr Stansbury Dunsmoor and Miss Martha S. Evans, both of Lancaster.
Nov. 7. Mr Michael Loughlan and Miss Ann Hobin, both of Lancaster.
10. Mr Edward Agin [Egan?] and Miss Bridget Finnerty, both of Lancaster.
14. Mr Curtis P. Smith and Miss Roena B. Warner, both of Lancaster.
16. Mr John Donelly and Miss Alice Daly, both of Lancaster.

BOOK IV.

MARRIAGES IN LANCASTER. 1843-1849.

The following is an abstract of the register — which is in the regular tabulated form — certain scant details about birth and parentage being here omitted. In many cases corrections have been made, authorized by comparison with publishments and church records.

1843.		*Before Reverend Edmund H. Sears.*
April	9.	Nathaniel L. Howe of Boylston, and Mary A. Howard of Lancaster.
"	12.	James Chandler of Sterling, and Mary Ann Sawyer of Lancaster.
"	16 [17].	Thomas Howe of Boston, and Sarah Fisher of Lancaster.
"	24.	George W. Howard and Martha F. Rugg, both of Lancaster.
May	11.	Lorey F. Bancroft and Ann L. Carter, both of Lancaster.
Oct.	26.	George K. Richards and Nancy Mallard, both of Lancaster.
Dec.	28.	Charles Safford, 26, and Julia A. D. Carter, 24, both of Lancaster.

1843.		*Before Reverend Charles Packard.*
May	16.	Josiah Childs, Jr., and Louisa Toombs, both of Lancaster.
"	23.	James Burpee of Sterling, and Eunice W. Goss of Lancaster.
Sept.	7.	Granville Carter of Boston, and Martha E. Wilder of Lancaster.
[Oct.	3.	Reúben Babcock and Mrs. Priscilla Maynard, both of Berlin.]
[Nov.	7.	Alfred Thomas of Butler Co., Ohio, & Mary Eliza Fisher of Northborough.]
	14.	William H. Young of Leominster, and Sarah Ann Sawyer of Lancaster.

1843.		*Before Reverend John Harriman.*
June	21.	Samuel A. Cutting of Concord, and Harriet S. Rugg of Lancaster.
Dec.	14.	William F. Conant of Berlin, and Mary A. Burditt of Lancaster.

1843.		*Before Reverend Benjamin Whittemore.*
Nov.	30.	Leonard Moseman of Ashburnham, and Clarinda Richardson of Lancaster.

1844.		*Before Reverend Charles Packard.*
Jan.	10.	Nathaniel Rice and Mrs. Rebecca A. A. Crossman, both of Lancaster.
March	20.	Albert S. Carleton and Maria B. Newman, both of Lancaster.
May	14.	Herbert H. Stimson of Boston, 42, and Mary E. Sawyer of Lancaster, 21.
July	4.	Jonathan B. Robinson, 22, and Elizabeth M. Bell, 21, both of Lunenburg.
	25.	Benjamin Daland, 51, and Mary A. Reed, 29, both of Woburn.
Augt.	14.	Charles Emerson, 26, and Mary Townsend, 26, both of Lancaster.
Sept.	19.	Levi Green, 43, and Lucy Harris, 28, both of Lancaster.

1844.   *Before Reverend Edmund H. Sears.*

May   8. Noah Humphrey of Barre, 24, and Lucena Wilder of Holliston, 27.
     13. Silas H. Holland of Cambridge, and Sarah S. Locke of Lancaster, 24.
June 26. Milo Winchester, 22, and [Frances] Malona Phillips, 23, both of Lancaster.
Oct. 10. George F. Safford of Lancaster, 25, and Ardelia A. Graves of Shirley, 20.
     29. Calvin Holman and Elizabeth F. Willard, both of Lancaster.
Dec. 5. George W. Sanderson of Shirley, and Charlotte E. Taylor of Lancaster.
     18. William Moore of Sterling, 26, and Sarah Ann Howard of Lancaster, 20.
     24. John Winditt, Jr., 25, and Mary D. Jones, 30, both of Lancaster.

1844.   *Before Reverend Benjamin Whittemore.*

March 27. John Bennett and Salome Pratt, 26, both of Lancaster.

1845.   *Before Reverend Seth Chandler of Shirley.*

May 31. Doctor James O. Parker of Shirley, 35, and Martha L. Carter of Lancaster, 24.

1845.   *Before Reverend William White of Littleton.*

April 10. Solomon Carter of Boston, 29, and Abby Lewis of Lancaster, 19.

1845.   *Before Reverend John A. Buckingham.*

April 2. Augustine F. Houghton, 23, and Charlotte Barnard, 21, both of Lancaster.

1845.   *Before Reverend Benjamin Whittemore.*

Feby. 4. Jacob R. Bacon, 25, and Sarah M. Farwell, 25, both of Boston.
March 27. Lyman Carr of Harvard, 46, and Fanny Willard of Lancaster, 33.
April 16. Joseph Buckman of Woburn, 20, and Jane B. Tyler of Lancaster, 19.
May 19. Andrew L. Fuller, 21, and Olive Howard, 18, both of Lancaster.
July 1. Samuel Barnes of Sandwich, 41, and Mrs. Mary E. Parker of Boston. 34.
Nov. 20. Seth G. Pitts of Lancaster, 28, and Susan Bennett of Lunenburg, 28.

1845.   *Before Reverend Charles Packard.*

July 31. Albert Whittemore of Nashua, N. H., 28, and Abby Parker of Lancaster, 25.
     "   John P. Hatch, 42, and Sarah Burnham, 29, both of Bolton.
Oct. 21. Hancell C. Hill, 24, of Charlestown, and Mary C. Nowell of Lancaster, 24.

1845.   *Before Reverend J. M. R. Eaton.*

Sept. 14. Horace Loomis 2d, 29, and Susan Eaton, 29, both of Lancaster.

1845.   *Before Reverend Jos. W. Cross of West Boylston.*

Sept. 3. Nathaniel A. Boynton of Lancaster, 22, and Asenath Bliss of Leominster, 23.

1845.   *Before Reverend Henry Adams of Berlin.*

Nov. 19. John Bell, 26, and Elizabeth Tisdale, 22, both of Boston.

1845.   *Before Reverend Edmund H. Sears.*

June 19. Daniel Sawyer of Bolton, 60, and Mrs. Mary Whitney of Lancaster, 60.
Sept. 17. Levi Harris of Lunenburg, 40, and Eliza Ann Wilder of Lancaster, 31.
Oct. 2. John B. Long of Detroit, Mich., 31, and Lucretia Rugg of Lancaster, 19.

	9.	Charles T. Fitch, 22, and Harriet P. Rugg, 21, both of Lancaster.
	19.	[Charles Grove and Nancy W. Whitney, both of Weston.]
	23.	Charles Whitney of Ashburnham, 30, and Susan Davis of Lexington.
Nov.	27.	Eli Sawyer, 23, and Mrs. Sarah E. Carter, 35, both of Lancaster.
Dec.	23.	Elias Danforth, 58, and Mrs. Louisa R. Cary, 39, both of Lancaster.
	31.	Caleb Howard, 27, and Rebecca Thurston, 25, both of Lancaster.

1846.		*Before Reverend Benjamin Whittemore.*
Jan.	8.	James E. Ball of Boylston, 25, and Abigail S. Howe of Lancaster, 26.
	14.	John E. Joslin, 20, and Eliza A. Dorrison, 22, both of Leominster.
Feb.	26.	Samuel Houghton, 2^d, 27, and Lefy Wade, 21, both of Lancaster.
June	17.	Hiram Makepeace, 23, and Sarah Judd, 23, both of Lancaster.
Sept.	3.	John Farr, 25, and Susan C. Royall, 25, both of Lancaster.
Sept.	8.	Rev. Quincy Whitney, 23, of Sterling, and Mandana M. Whittemore, 22, of Lancaster.
Sept.	23.	James C. Parsons, 22, and Jane A. Dorrison, 21, both of Lancaster.
Oct.	17.	Franklin Little, 25, and Mrs. Phebe Ann Rubedeau, 26, both of Lancaster.
	17.	Charles K. Lancey, 23, and Margaret Little, 16, both of Lancaster.
	18.	Joseph Morey, 36, and Sarah H. Chapman, 30, both of Lancaster.
Dec.	1.	Andrew J. Langley of Lancaster, 21, and Maria F. Harwood of Harvard, 18.

1846.		*Before Reverend J. M. R, Eaton.*
May	6.	George W. Hyatt, 22, and Sarah A. Porter, 24, both of Lancaster.
May	14.	Roswell H. Bourne, 21, and Maria N. Houghton, 19, both of Lancaster.
Nov.	17.	Hinckley R. Gray, 28, and Adaline Burditt, 29, both of Lancaster.
	26.	John H. Wood of Northboro', 24, and Mary A. Burditt of Lancaster, 25.

1846.		*Before Reverend Edmund H. Sears.*
April	13.	Josiah Billings, 25, and [Lydia] Ellen Munroe, 22, both of Lancaster.
May	6.	Albert H. Smith, 24, and Susan Fuller, 24, both of Lancaster.
	25.	Caleb W. Bennett, 25, of Scituate, R. I., and Rebecca E. Thompson of Lancaster, 28.
	27.	Ira J. Sawyer of Lancaster, 26, and Abigail M. Houghton of Berlin, 24.
	[27.	George Gleason of Marlboro' and Harriet Burpee of Sterling.]
Oct.	13.	Nathan Burditt of Lancaster, 58, and Deborah H. Ross of Sterling, 37.
[Nov.	12.]	Peder Anderson of Lowell, 36, and Martha Fisher of Lancaster, 27.
Nov.	12.	Abel Sawyer of West Boylston, 33, and Lucy Goss of Lancaster, 30.
	[19.	William S. Locke of Lancaster, and Mary Whitney of Harvard.]

1846.		*Before Reverend Leonard Tracy of West Boylston.*
Feb.	4.	Mansel Haselton, 26, and Lucy Ann Eaton, 21, both of Lancaster.
Dec.	31.	Homer C. Snow, 20, and Lucretia Eddy, 18, both of West Boylston.

1846.		*Before Reverend Joseph W. Cross of West Boylston.*
Aug.	13.	Luke Eddy, 21, and Amanda Holt, 18, both of Lancaster.

1846.		*Before Reverend Clark Sibley of Harvard.*
Oct.	12.	Abram F. Kidder of Lowell, 22, and Sarah M. Burbank of Lancaster, 20.

1846.		*Before Reverend Charles Packard.*
Sept.	22.	Charles Barber, 21, and Elizabeth C. Sartell, 18, both of Lancaster.
Nov.	17.	Nathan Farren, Jr., 35, and Mary Ann Daniels, 27, both of Townsend.
Dec.	2.	Francis P. Pratt of Southbridge, 26, and Maria A. Whitney, 19, of Lancaster.

1846. *Before Reverend Josiah A. Coolidge of Shirley.*
Oct. 8. Calvin Sanderson, 38, and Sarah A. Barnes, 19, both of Lancaster.

1846. *Before Reverend Nathaniel Gage.*
Dec. 10. Washington Sanders[on], 31, of Shirley, and Rhoda Johnson, 35, of Lancaster.

1846. *Before Reverend Samuel Hunt of Concord.*
Dec. 20. Lorenzo F. Wood of Lancaster, 26, and Lucy Ann Brigham of Concord, 22.

1847. *Before Reverend Charles Packard.*
Jan. 5. Horatio B. Howe, 23, and Martha Howe, 23, both of Lancaster.
Feb. 24. Franklin Hayward [of Boxborough,] 27, and Emily A. Wheeler of Lancaster, 29.
Dec. 29. Jerome S. Burditt, 27, and Emily H. Faulkner, 21, both of Lancaster.

1847. *Before Reverend J. M. R. Eaton.*
Jan. 12. Joseph H. Smith, 21, and Janette S. Emery, 21, both of Lancaster.
March 31. Isaac Bell, 40, and Emily Evans, 38, both of Lancaster.

1847. *Before Reverend Benjamin Whittemore.*
Feb. 24. Hiram Ward, 29, and Rebecca P. Rollins, 24, both of Lancaster.
April 13. John Boly [of Worcester,] 20, and Aurelia Little, 19, of Lancaster.
15. Hollis B. Wood, 29, and Sarah G. Richards, 19, both of Lancaster.
May 11. Solomon Jones, 23, of Berlin, and Laura B. Wheeler, 19, of Bolton.
June 16. Mason Wheeler, 30, of Fitchburg, and Sarah Richardson, 31, of Leominster.
July 14. Parsons Cogswell, 24, and Sarah Davis, 22, both of Lancaster.
Aug. 25. Jerome H. Willard, 28, and Mary Ann Blanchard, 24, both of Lancaster.
Oct. 18. Harris Winchester, 23, and Annis K. Lane, 20, both of Lancaster.
Dec. 27. Josiah Moore [of Berlin,] 20, and Ellen L. Keyes, 16, of Lancaster.

1847. *Before Reverend Edmund H. Sears.*
[Jan. 31. Joseph Cushing and Mary A. Arnold, both of Fitchburg.]
March 30. John B. Maynard, 23, and Clara [S.] Flagg, 22, both of Lancaster.

1847. *Before Reverend Nathaniel Gage.*
April 26. Reuben P. Simonds, 27, of Ashburnham, and Rebecca Ballard, 27, of Lancaster.
29. William A. Tower, 23, and Julia Davis, 22, both of Lancaster.

1847. *Before Reverend Clark Sibley of Harvard.*
Jan. 27. Thomas H. Badger, 25, of Boston, and Mary E. Farwell, 21, of Lancaster.

1847. *Before Reverend C. M. Bowers.*
May 30. Avery L. Clapp [of Lowell,] and Ellen E. Houghton of Lancaster.

1847. *Before Elijah Whiton, Esq., of Groton.*
July 14. Samuel Worster, 50, of Lancaster, and Ann Nutting, 31, of Groton.

1847. *Before Reverend George M. Bartol.*
Aug. 5. Charles [Mirick] Carter, 25, and Martha H. Thurston, 22, both of Lancaster.
Sept. 22. George Frederick Chandler, 25, and Susan E. Buss, 24, both of Lancaster.
Oct. 13. Abel W. Longley, 24, and Mary J. Sartell, 25, both of Lancaster.
Nov. 25. Andrew J. Parker, 26, and Abby A. Tapley, 24.

BOOK FOURTH. 257

1847. *Before Reverend Ralph Emerson of Andover.*

Oct. 18. Reverend Alfred Emerson, 35, of South Reading, and M. E. W. Vose, 31, of Lancaster.

1848. *Before Reverend C. M. Bowers.*

Jan. 8. Henry L. Gould, 21, and Priscilla Fiske, 22, both of Lancaster.
Sept. 4. John I. Wilson, 25, and Mary A. Brickett, 18, both of Lancaster.
Oct. 17. John Windle, 40, and Eliza Sargeant, 34, both of Lancaster.

1848. *Before Reverend Charles Packard.*

Feb. 16. Percival W. Bartlett, 26, of Boston, and Margaret E. R. Holt, 25, of Lancaster.
[April 6. Henry F. Haynes of Bolton, and Anne Elizabeth Buss of Lancaster.]
Sept. 11. Edward L. Johnson, 27, and Elizabeth L. James, 27, both of Lancaster.
Oct. 11. Silas Sweatt of Acton, 62, and Mrs. Nancy Heywood, 59, of Lancaster.
Nov. 2. Alfred W. Haynes of Bolton, 25, and Caroline M. Studley, 20, of Lancaster.
Dec. 14. Edward S. Oakes, 27, and Polly D. Newton, 17, both of West Boylston.

1848. *Before Reverend George M. Bartol.*

Feb. 9. Samuel H. Bailey, 22, of Leominster, and Augusta E. Stow, 20, of Lancaster.
    16. Horatio N. Sweet, 24, and Frances McQuestion, 21, both of Lancaster.
March 2. Fred O. Wilder, 21, of Auburn, and Ann James, 21, of Lancaster.
May 4. Daniel Andrew Carter, 23, and Mary A. Davis, 19, both of Lancaster.
June 7. Dane A. Marrett, 26, of Somerville, and Eliza A. Locke, 24, of Lancaster.
    7. Samuel H. Marrett, 26, of Somerville, and Frances A. Locke, 24, of Lancaster.
    11. William Townsend, 61, and Mrs. Rosalinda P. Whitney, 53, both of Lancaster.
Aug. 27. Thomas Dolloff, 26, and Abigail C. Cross, 27, both of Lancaster.
Sept. 28. Wilder S. Thurston, 41, and Caroline M. Laughton, 24, both of Lancaster.
Nov. 28. Edmund Moore, 28, of Sterling, and Susan S. Howard, 19, of Lancaster.

1848. *Before Reverend Benjamin Whittemore.*

March 21. George W. Hackett, 25, and Mrs. Lydia Barrett, 35, both of Lancaster.
April 4. Elijah Bigelow, 25, and Mrs. Sarah Hale, 38, both of Berlin.
    6. Charles H. Arnold, 27, and Sarah Whitney, 21, both of Lancaster.
    27. John Bennett, 37, and Caroline A. Turner, 20, both of Lancaster.
May 7. Joseph R. Bancroft, 23, of Worcester, and Harriet Damon, 24, of Lancaster.
Octo. 19. Jonas H. Brown, 27, and Emeline Holman, 17, both of Lancaster.
Nov. 28. Andrew A. Powers, 19, and Sarah A. Howe, 16, both of Berlin.

1848. *Before Reverend William H. Corning.*

July 3. Angus Walker, 30, and Catharine Orr, 21, both of Lancaster.
Oct. 23. John McNab, 31, and Agnes Walker, 26, both of Lancaster.

1848. *Before Reverend Quincy Whitney.*

Dec. 31. Samuel A. Davis, 38, and Charlotte E. Keyes, 21, both of Sterling.

LANCASTER RECORDS.

1849. *Before Reverend William H. Corning.*

Jan. 1. Levi Houghton, 36, of Berlin, and Lucy A. Conant, 32, of Lowell.
     1. D. L. Willey, 24, of Manchester, N. H., and Helen McAllister, 22, of Lancaster.
Feb. 4. John J. Boynton, 24, and Mary J. Jones, 21, both of Lancaster.
April 21. Samuel Beaver, 24, and Letty J. Eastman, 24, both of Lancaster.
June 1. Niel Carmichael, 27, and Agnes Orr, 21, both of Lancaster.
     1. Jason Gorham, 27, and Eliza Jane Chamberlain, 19, both of Lancaster.
     7. James Wrigley, 34, and Jeanette Sutherland, 26, both of Lancaster.
Dec. 29. Joseph W. Newhall, 24, of Lincoln, and Harriet S. McAllister, 21, of Lancaster.
     29. Henry Moore, 23, and Jane Stewart, 23, both of Holliston.

1849. *Before Reverend Benjamin Whittemore.*

Jan. 7. Stillman A. Sawtell, 25, and Jennett A. Morgan, 23, both of Lancaster.
March 6. James Pitts, 38, and Lucinda Bartlett, 25, both of Lancaster.
     10. Elijah Parmenter, 35, of Westminster, and Abigail Warner, 23, of Lancaster.
June 21. John Clark, 27, of Exeter, Me., and Sarah W. Haven, 28, of Lancaster.
July 3. Charles M. Dorrison, 21, of Lancaster, and Charlotte M. Stoodly, 18, of Londonderry, Vt.
Dec. 30. Nason S. Houghton, 26, of Bolton, and Elizabeth N. Cowdry, 25, of Westford.

1849. *Before Reverend C. M. Bowers.*

Feb. 1. Joshua A. Lane, 27, and Margaret A. Houghton, 23, both of Lancaster.
March 20. Jonathan M. Keyes, 23, of West Boylston, and Esther A. Damon, 20, of Lancaster.
April 11. Alfred D. Kinsman, 26, and Maria C. Houghton, 19, both of Lancaster.
     12. John D. Sawtell, 28, and Angelina Hatch, 25, both of Lancaster.
Nov. 13. Thomas W. Belcher, 22, and Sarah E. Greenleaf, 16, both of Lancaster.

1849. *Before Reverend George M. Bartol.*

March 22. Deacon Peter Osgood, 53, and Mrs. Elizabeth G. White, 50, both of Lancaster.
April 17. Charles Whitcomb, 21, of Bolton, and Rhoena Barnes, 20, of Berlin.
May 2. Charles W. Morse, 25, and Mary A. Warren, both of Lancaster.
June 28. Frederick W. Johnson, 21, and Mary [Eliza] Osgood, 21, both of Lancaster.
July 25. William F. Burrage, 23, of Leominster, and Evelina W. Lawrence, 18, of Lancaster.
Sept. 8. Edward Wright, 26, and Maria Sawin, 23, both of Princeton.
[Sept. 23. Avery D. Sawyer of Lawrence, and Ann G. Wheeler of Bolton.]
Nov. 3. Ferren Martin, 27, and Amanda M. Farr, 21, both of Lancaster.

1849. *Before Reverend Charles Packard.*

April 25. Rufus Arnold, 25, of Sterling, and Caroline A. Johnson, 25, of Lancaster.
May 1. Charles J. Strout, 23, of Lawrence, and Sarah M. Studley, 26, of Lancaster.
Sept. 26. Charles B. Russell, 27, and Mary [Josephine] Brigham, 21, both of Marlboro'.
Nov. 29. William Powers, 23, of Bolton, and Martha Jane Butler, 19, of Lancaster.

BIRTHS. 1843-1849.

A few corrections in dates, and many in names, have been inserted by authority of family records. Numerous duplicate entries have been omitted, and sundry omissions have been discovered and supplied. Doubtless very many other births failed to receive record, for which neglect the heads of families should receive blame, not the town clerks.

1843. July 3. George, son of Reuben Barrett.
" Oct. 9. Caroline B., daughter of Emory Hastings.
1844. Feb. 23. Charles Lewis, son of A. Woodworth.
" Feb. 23. George Thomas, son of Reverend Charles Packard.
" Feb. 12. Louisa Abby, daughter of James Chandler.
1843. Aug. 30 [23?]. Denziel, son of Otis Harrington.
1844. Feb. 14. Samuel Augustus, son of Sam¹. & Sarah [Divoll] Jones.
1843. June 26. Charles William, son of Jesse Gibbs.
1843. July 22. Eudora Savage, daughter of Solon & Sarah Whiting.
1843. Dec. 30. A son of Alfred Knight.
1844. Feb. 14. Oscar Miller, son of James S. & Caroline Lawrence.
" April 26. Joseph Edward, son of Asa D. & Betsy Farnsworth.
1842. Feby. 11. Levi Daniel, son of Levi & Lucy B. Farwell.
1843. Oct. 17. Lovey Melissa, daughter of Levi & Lucy B. Farwell.
1844. July 24. George W., son of Warren & Lucy Willard.
" Jan. 13. Infant son of Lorey F. & Ann M. [Carter] Bancroft.
" Aug. 7. Betsy Louisa, daughter of John & Louisa Cunningham.
" Oct. 6. George William, son of Edmund & Hannah Harris.
1845. Feby. 22. John, son of John & Salome Bennett.
1844. Aug. 18. Elisha Horatio, son of Elisha & Caroline Augusta Turner.
1845. March 6. Walter Henry Knox, son of John & Rosella C. Whitney.
" May 4. Charles Henry, son of Ebenʳ. W. & Sarah Ann Howe.
" Jany. 5. Lewis Franklin, son of George & Lucinda Stratton.
1844. Nov. 11. Emily Louisa, daughter of Horace & Jane Jewett.
1845. July 18. John Murray, son of Nathaniel & Nancy Whittemore.
" March 8. Sarah Lane, daughter of Orion H. & Catharine B. Newton.
1844. Aug. 26. Francis Jerome, son of Henry & Sarah B. Lewis.
" May 2. George Oscar Marcellus, son of Fredᵏ. W. & Sarah B. Wilder.
1843. Sept. 3. Ann Elizabeth, daughter of Jonathan W. & Abby S. Houghton.
1845. Sept. 11. Charles W., son of Jonathan W. & Abby S. Houghton.
" July 11. Samuel Hill, son of Artemas & Louisa Hodgman.
" Oct. 29. Addison Ellis, son of James & Ann M. L. Rugg.
1844. June 17. Franklin Williams, son of Williams & Sarah M. Green.
1845. March 25. Albert, son of James & Lucinda Pitts.
" Nov. 1. Mary Isadore, daughter of Lucius L. & Mary Farwell.
1839. June 6. Edwin Jerome, son of Nathan & Mary Elizabeth Burditt.
1844. March 31. Charles Carter, son of Nathan & Mary Elizabeth Burditt.
1845. Novʳ. 11. Charles Westley, son of Charles & Elizabeth Hapgood.
" June 8. John Edward, son of James S. & Caroline Lawrence.
1846. June 25. Mary E., daughter of Levi B. & Jane Burbank.
1842. April 4. Amanda M., daughter of Levi B. & Jane Burbank.
1846. May 8. Francis Carter, son of Lorey F. & Ann L. Bancroft.
1845. Dec. 1. Emily Jane, daughter of Abel & Lucy B. Rice.
1846. July 29. George Edson Warren, son of William & Drusilla Fletcher.
" May 17. Francis A., son of William B. & Mary E. Rugg.
1845. Nov. 24. Martha Lydia, daughter of Lucius K. & Rebecca Holt.
1846. March 17. John Adams, son of Asa D. & Betsy Farnsworth.
1846. Dec. 2. Erastus Henry, son of John H. & Mary Maynard.
1842. Feb. 20. Charlotte M., daughter of Levi W. Damon.
1844. Sept. 9. Henry W., son of   "   "
1846. Aug. 22. Charles E., son of   "   "
" Oct. 28. George Walter, son of Benja. F. & Cynthia A. Farnsworth.
" March 17. Edwin Augustine, son of Edmund & Harriet P. Harris.

1840.	Oct. 17.	Walter Rice, son of John & Louisa Cunningham.
1847.	June 27.	Edward Godfrey, son of Chas. G. & Laura Stevens.
1847.	Jany. 24.	Mary Rebecca, daughter of Thomas H. & Mary E. Badger.
"	June 20.	Merrill Urwin, son of William B. & Mary E. Rugg.
1845.	Dec. 26.	Angelo Parker, son of [Thos. F. & Caroline Blood.]
1841.	Jan. 10.	Ellen Richardson, daughter of Samuel J. S. & Mary Vose.
1842.	Oct. 7.	Louisa Russell, " " "
1845.	Jan. 25.	John Sprague, son " " "
1847.	Jan. 2.	W^m. Merchant Richardson, son " "
1846.	Nov. 12.	Ellen Martina, daughter of James & Lucinda Pitts.
1847.	Sept. 29.	Emma Adelia, daughter of Joel W. & Lorinda Phelps.
"	Jany. 30.	Clara Augusta, daughter of Henry & Sarah B. Lewis.
1845.	May 26.	Abby Ann, daughter of David & Ann P. Randall.
1847.	Dec. 10.	Mary Elizabeth, " " " "
"	July 21.	Ella Adelia, daughter of Leonard & Jane Newton.
1846.	Nov. 30.	Martha Bond, daughter of Dr. Henry & Martha B. Lincoln.
1847.	Augt. 1.	Alice Marion Leslie, daughter of James & Ann M. L. Rugg.
[1849.	Dec. 6.	Ellen A., daughter of James & Ann M. L. Rugg. *Family records*.]
1847.	Sept. 4.	Walter Lincoln, son of George K. & Nancy Richards.
1848.	July 20.	John Henry, son of John H. & Mary Maynard.
"	Oct. 21.	Caroline Phelps, daughter of John & Elizabeth B. Townsend.
1839.	Sept. 2.	Mary Augusta, daughter of John R. & Harriet A. Wyman.
[1837.	June 13.	John H., son of " " *Wyman genealogy*.]
1842.	Jany. 4.	Ellen Francena, daughter " "
1848.	Feby. 21 [24?].	Albert Carter, son " "
1845.	Jan. 20.	Sarah Wilder, daughter of Jonas & Sarah E. Goss.
1847.	April 27.	Abbie Fletcher, daughter of Jonas & Abbie (Fletcher) Goss.
1848.	Nov. [26].	Harriet [Ella], " " " "
1848.	March 4.	Lydia Ann, daughter of George & Lucinda Stratton.
1846.	March 4.	George Munro, son of Caleb & Lydia Ann Winchester.
1838.	Feb. —.	William W., son of W. W. & Ann H. Bragg.
1839.	Oct. 8.	Henrietta E., daughter of Stephen & Eliza Ann Dana.
1842.	Oct. 14.	Mary Frances, " " " "
1847.	Feb. 16.	Caroline Jane, " " " "
1845.	Feb. 12.	Henry (at Barre), son of Matthew F. & Charlotte A. Woods.
1847.	April 15.	Charlotte Ann, daughter " " "
1849.	April 14.	Mary Spring, daughter " " "
1848.	Jan. 17.	Lauretta J., daughter of William S. & Mary W. Locke.
1843.	Jan. 31.	Frederick F., son of Fordyce & Laura Nourse.
1847.	Oct. 11.	Abby Eliza, daughter of John T. & Eliza E. Dame.
1842.	Sept. 19.	Louisa Millicent, daughter of Wilder S. & Ann M. Thurston.
1845.	March 31.	Ellen Elizabeth, daughter of " " "
1839.	Nov. 20.	Lurenia Jewell, daughter of Stevens H. & Betsy E. Turner.
1841.	Nov. 23.	Charlotte Elizabeth, daughter of " " "
1843.	March 23.	Walter S. Hayward, son of " " "
1845.	October 8.	Emma Julia, daughter of " " "
1848.	Feby. 6.[23].	Sarah Eliza, daughter of " " "
1845.	Sept. 10.	Herbert, son of Albert S. & Maria B. Carleton.
1847.	Aug. 6.	Susan Maria, daughter of " "
1845.	March 13.	George Edwin, son of Edwin A. & Mary Ann Nourse.
1847.	Aug. 24.	Mary Louisa, daughter of " " "
1848.	Nov. 21.	Nathaniel John, son of George F. & Susan E. Chandler.
1844.	Sept. 27.	Enos, son of Charles L. & Harriet E. Wilder.
[1846.	Oct. 15.	Harriet E., daughter of same parents. *Family records*.]
[1849.	January 28.	Frances A., " " " "
1839.	May 8.	Helen, daughter of Hollis & Hannah Davis.
1849.	April 10.	Frank Herbert, son of D. Andrew & Mary A. Carter.
1841.	June 11.	Emma, daughter of Hollis & Hannah Davis.
1847.	July 19.	Emma Frances, daughter of Hollis & Hannah Davis.
1848.	April 25.	Emma Susan, daughter of Andrew L. & Olive H. Fuller.

1839. Nov. 19. Ellen Adelle, ⎫ Children of Elijah & Martha A. [Joslin]
1841. April 9. Clara Elizabeth, ⎬ Sawyer.
1844[3]. Augt. 2. Abby Lizette, ⎪ [Corrected from family records.]
[1849. Nov. 9. Frederick Elijah], ⎭
1844. Sept. 25. Julia Lorinda, daughter of Joel W. & Lorinda Phelps.
1828. Dec. 21. Harriet Sophronia, daughter of Ephraim C. & Sarah Fisher.
1837. Mar. 30. Ellen Sarah,   "   "   "
1841. Feb. 4. Mary Elizabeth,   "   "   "
1844. May 11. William Henry, son   "   "   "
1846. Augt. 27. Louisa, daughter   "   "   "
1829. Octo. 16. Franklin, son of Moses & Eliza W. Stow.
1841. Mar. 29. Henry Harrison, son of   "   "
1845. Aug. 5. Sidney Willard, son of Calvin & Elizabeth F. Holman.
1848. Mar. 14. William Emerson, son of   "   "
1845. Oct. 18. William, son of Jesse & Betsy Gibbs.
1837. Dec. 5. George Robinson, son of Otis R. & Caroline Atherton.
1846. Mar. 26. Keziah Eudora, daughter of Harlow & Catharine C. Lawrence.
1848. Nov. 30. Mary Adelle,   "   "   "
  "   March 2. Herbert Whitney, son of Daniel & Cynthia Davis.
1847. Oct. 25. Caroline Elizabeth, daughter of Thos. F. & Caroline Blood.
  "   Jan. 28. Charles Henry, son of Sewall T. & Persis Rugg.
1842. Oct. 10. Harriet R., daughter of William H. & Lucy Targett.
  "   Jan. 12. Martha, daughter of Galen L. & Sarah Stephenson.
1844. Nov. 16. Sarah Janette, daughter of Alvinzy & Lucy Lane.
——— ——— John Wade, son of Samuel & Lefy Houghton.
1839. Nov. 25. Fabius Harlow, son of James A. & Angelia Arnold.
1843. Sept. 21. Eugenia Kezia, daughter of   "   "
1845. Nov. 25. Florette Sarah,   "   "   "
1847. July 26. Marietta Hastings, daughter of Hastings A. & Rebecca B. Ladd.
1848. Oct. 11. Wilfred Carlton, son of James C. & Almira J. Parsons.
1837. Aug. 29. Mary Elizabeth, daughter of Danforth & Mary G. Lawrence.
1842. July 8. Angelia Josephine,   "   "   "
1847. June 9. John Alvin, son of Alvin & Rebecca A. Sargent.
1844. Sept. 21. William Francis, son of Edward W. & Mary M. Divoll.
1846. Aug. 17. George Dana,   "   "   "
1848. Nov. 7. Mary Louisa, daughter of   "   "   "
1848. April 30. Lizzie and Marietta, twins of Edwin A. & Elizabeth Larkin.
1847. Dec. 19. Malvina Isoria, daughter of George W. & Ann M. Chute.
1835. Oct. 14. Thomas Henry, son of Thomas & Mary Jones.
1837. Aug. 29. Charles Tweed,   "   "   "
1839. Oct. 1. George,   "   "   "
1843. Jan. 23. John Francis,   "   "   "
1844. July 22. Benjamin Walker,   "   "   "
1848. Sept. 9. James, son of Thomas & Bridget Forbes.
1847. Jan. 9. Mary Eliza, daughter of John & Mary E. Windett.
1835. Aug. 22. Mary Jane, daughter of Jonathan & Olive Davis.
1841. Mar. 16. George Henry, son of Jonas M. & Margaret Damon.
1844. Feb. 18. Ann Janette, daughter of   "   "   "
1845. March 29. Charles Hiram, son of   "   "   "
1847. Oct. 2. Margaret, daughter of   "   "   "
1849. Jan. 6. Merrick P., son of Andrew J. & Mary C. Farnsworth.
1845. Oct. 17. Charles Ethan, son of Charles & Julia Ann Safford.
1847. Feb. 16. Sarah Julia, daughter of   "   "   "
1848. June 1. Ellen Frances,   "   "   "
1848. Feb. 13. John, son of Henry & Catharine Hoar.
1838. July 16. Harriet Ann, daughter of Moody B. Haynes & Hannah Carr.
1847. Mar, 30. Charles Calvin, son of Calvin & Sarah Sanderson.
1845. June 1. David Waldo, son of David & Eleanor S. Parker.
1848. June 18. Alfred Hezekiah,   "   "   "
1847. Mar. 23. Sarah Elizabeth, daughter of Asa D. & Betsy Farnsworth.
1849. Dec. 18. Caroline Susan,   "   "   "
1849. Nov. 11. Ellen Frances, daughter of Levi B. & Jane Burbank.

1832. May 28. Harriet E., daughter of Aaron & Chloe S. Burbank.
1837. May 21. Calvin W., son of   "   "   "
1848. Sept. 29. James Otis, son of Otis & Susan H. Houghton.
1842. Apl. 23. Emily Jane, daughter of Thos. B. & Sally Warren.
1847. Feb. 3. Charles Frederick, son   "   "
1839. March 28. Mary Gertrude, daughter of Rufus K. & Emily P. Ladd.
1841. July 23. Lucy Blanche,   "   "   "   "
1844. Feb. 3. George Vivian, son   "   "   "
1846. Oct. 2. Emily Grage, daughter   "   "   "
1849. April 23. Francis Haven, son of Anthony L. & Edith B. Sawyer.
1848. Jan. 14. Harriet, daughter of Rufus W. & Clara Holbrook.
1846. Jan. 15. Ella Gertrude, daughter of Edward E. & Catharine W. Harlow.
1847. Oct. 21. George Edward, son of   "   "   "
1847. Dec. 18. John Henry, son of George W. & Martha T. Howard.
1847. Aug. 10. Lucy Clarissa, daughter of Joseph & Lucy Gleason.
1848. Feb. 18. Persis Lucinda, daughter of Henry A. & Sally F. Howard.
1835. June 11. Edson Dwight, son of Luther & Laura Gaylord.
1837. April 4. Catharine Augusta, daughter of   "   " } Birth place not given.
1848. Mar. 1. Henry Frank, son of   "   "
1841. July 28. Francis Emery, son of James E. & Harriet Gould.
1843. Sept. 6. Harriet Elizabeth, daughter of   "   "
1847. Nov. 18. Lucretia Adelaide,   "   "   "
1849. March 1. George Grandison, son of Henry & Priscilla Gould.
1844. March 28. Almira Peirce, daughter of Nathaniel & Almira Johnson.
1837. Aug. 21. John Edward, son of Henry & Mary Lowe.
1839. June 21. George Washington,   "   "
1841. Nov. 3. Theodore Eliphas,   "   "
1844. Aug. 25. Edgar Augustine,   "   "
——— ——— Edward Francis, son of Milo & Milona Winchester.
1847. March 8. George Thomas, son of Joseph T. & Eliza Sawyer.
1837. Oct. 2. Caroline Louisa, daughter of Haskell & Sylvia McCollum.
1839. June 29. George Haskell, son of   "   "
1841. Oct. 26. Martha Adaline, daughter of   "   "
1842. Dec. 15. Matilda Lowe,   "   "   "
1845. Oct. 31. Harriet Matilda,   "   "   "
1846. May 11. Hanford Laviere, son of Jonas & Eliza Hunt.
1848. Oct. 16. Alice Louisa, daughter of   "   "
1841. July 22. Francis Elizabeth, daughter of Nathan, Jur., & Mary E. Burdett.
1847. Dec. 3. Edward Walter, son of   "   "   "
1849. April 3. George Curtis, son of Austin C. & Mary H. Hill.
1848. Oct. 26. George Augustus, son of Nathaniel A. & Asenath Boynton.
1848. May 24. Eliza Jane, daughter of William & Eliza J. B. Eaton.
1845. July 3. Clara Louisa, daughter of Theodore & Esther L. Jewett.
——— ——— Susan Emily, daughter of Artemas H. & Susan E. Parker.
1847. April 15. Stilman Evander, son of Stilman & Nancy Houghton.
1848. April 20. James Gland, son of John & Janet Wright.
1847. Nov. 23. Jane Eveline, daughter of John W. & Electa Cady.
1844. June 6. Mary Isadore, daughter of Joseph B. & Mary Ann Parker.
1847. July 29. Henrietta Eveline, "   "   "
1848. Nov. 10. Orianna Cornelia, daughter of Robert S. & Zoa Ann Freeman.
1845. March 27. Abby Warren, daughter of Edward W. & Lucy S. Goodale.
1842. Feby. 28. Martha Ann, daughter of William & Mary Ann Stearns.
1843. Aug. 22. Elizabeth Carter,   "   "   "
1846. Mar. 27. Helen Maria,   "   "   "
1847. July 11. Harriet Cutler, daughter of Dr. George M. & Eleanor Morse.
1849. Jan. 15. Francis Edward, son of   "   "   "
1848. Aug. 1. Henry, son of John & Anna Healy.
1844. Jan. 16. Jerome, son of Seth & Maria Sargent.
1844. May 21. Lawson Curtis, son of Merrick & Rebecca Sargent.
1848. July 25. Martha Adaline, daughter   "   "
1847. Dec. 27. Margaret Louisa, daughter of Thomas & Sarah G. Burditt.
1840. Jan. 7. Oscar Marcellus, son of Charles & Matilda Miller.

1845. Nov. 10. Elizabeth Matilda, daughter of Charles & Matilda Miller.
1840. Oct. 21. Sarah Clarissa, daughter of Moses & Susan W. Gould.
1842. Dec. 19. Ellen Augusta, " " "
1847. March 22. Abby Estelle, " " "
1849. Feb. 27. Jane Maria, " " "
1837. May 31. Edwin Algernon, son of Sidney & Sally K. Harris.
1839. Mar. 13. George Sidney. " " "
1847. May 6. Lucinda Adaliza, daughter of Eli & Sarah Sawyer.
1848. June 21. Francis Goss, son of Abel & Lucy G. Sawyer.
1846. Jan. 22. Charles Franklin, son of Benjamin F. & Ann Maria Gould.
1847. Aug. 6. Georgetta Maria, daughter of " " "
1839. Sept. 8. Lovina Ann, daughter of Daniel B. & Miranda Wheeler.
1844. June 29. Sarah Elizabeth, daughter of Nath¹ & Ann Elizabeth Hastings.
1847. Oct. 22. Mary Julia, daughter of " " "
1848. Nov. 20. Angeline Rebecca, daughter of Abel & Mary Ann Pollard.
1846. Nov. 17. Edmund Sears, son of Levi & Eliza Ann Harris.
1848. Apr. 23. Cornelia Vose, daughter of Rev. Chas. M. & Ellen A. Bowers.
1846. May 13. Nathaniel Thayer, son of Augustine F. & Charlotte Houghton.
1848. Jan. 18. Francis Augustine, " " "
1849. May 18. Charlotte Maria, daughter of " " "
1846. Nov. 24. Lizzie Octavia, daughter of Chas. W. & Mary Field.
1834. Nov. 3. Albion Wilder, son of Enoch K. & Martha Gibbs (at Southbridge.)
1836. Oct. 24. Charles Winslow, " " " (at Sturbridge.)
1840. Dec. 7. William Harrison, " " "
1844. June 11. Edward Milton, " " "
1848. Sept. 13. Helen Matilda, daughter " "
1845. June 14. Charlotte Louisa, daughter of Gilbert & Mary A. Greene.
1848. Feb. 27. Edward Gilbert, son of " "
1848. Sept. 16. Anna Martina, daughter of George P. & Susan M. Smith.
1842. April 10. Franklin, son of Mark & Eveline Lund.
1848. May 29. Martha Eveline, daughter of Mark & Martha Lund.
1848. Oct. 8. Enos Abijah, son of Enos H. & Elizabeth M. Day.
1841. Nov. 30. Hiram A., son of George F. & Freelove Chambers.
1847. Nov. 14. Calvin M., " " " "
1848. Mar. 17. Caroline Elmira, daughter of Alvin & Mary Whiting.
1849. Feb. 8. Charles Henry, son of Joseph H. & Jeannette S. Smith.
1848. Dec. 18. Edward Winchester, son of Elhanan W. & Susan Clark.
1848. Apr. 18. George Edward, son of George H. & Mary J. Kendall.
1837. Jan. 15. Franklin C., son of Oliver & Sophia Green.
1839. Aug. 2. Ann Sophia, daughter of " "
1841. Apr. 19. Roscoe F., son of " "
1848. Aug. 29. Willie F., " " "
1847. Jan. 23. Elizabeth Gertrude, daughter of Jacob & Betsy P. Wilson.
1848. March 18. Theodore, son of " " "
1849. Apr. 10. Georgianna, daughter of " " "
1847. Dec. 25. Edward Randall, son of Abel & Lucy Rice.
1848. Nov. 18. Alonzo Peter, son of Peter & Jane Sawyer.
1837. Sept. 23. Eben Ezbon, son of Ebenezer & Betsy Pratt.
1842. March 30. Nelson Lorey Albert, " " "
1843. July 5. Ann Eliza, daughter of " " "
1845. Sept. 27. Oren, son of " " "
1847. Dec. 31. Hiram, son of " " "
1848[9]. Mar. 19. George, son of " " "
1845. Dec. 7. Joseph Allen, son of Camden & Julia A. Maynard.
1845. May 13. Maria, daughter of Elhanan & Rhoda Winchester.
1848. Oct. 30. Sarah, " " "
1836. June 21. Charles, son of Thomas & Lucy Wellington.
1838. Mar. 19. George, " " "
1841. Jan. 10. Enos W., " " "
1846. Apr. 18. Ellen L., daughter of " "
1849. Feb. 24. Ella Maria, daughter of Edward R. & Rebecca Fiske.
1848. Dec. 25. Charles Henry, son of S. H. & Charlotte S. Pierce.

1848.	Jan. 26.	Erastus, son of Horace & Jane Jewett.
1839.	Dec. 25.	William L., son of Abram & Elizabeth Thrower.
1849.	Nov. 21.	Eliza Adaline May, daughter of William & Hannah Matthews.
1849.	Jan. 30.	Frances Ann, daughter of Fred. O. & Ann Wilder.
1849.	Sept. 10.	Edward, son of Calvin Stanley.
1849.	May 19.	Addison Franklin, son of Joseph A. Fletcher.
1849.	Dec. 23.	May Elizabeth, daughter of Samuel A. Dorrison.
1849.	Nov. 20.	Ellen Maria, daughter of Patrick M. Dyer.
1849.	May 19.	Eddy, son of Sawyer A. Fairbanks.
1849.	May 11.	John, son of Peter Freeland.
1848.	June 5.	Jane Eliza, daughter of Josiah Randall.
1849.	June 9.	Elizabeth R., daughter of Caleb W. Bennett (N. Scituate, R. I.)
1849.	July 23.	Edward, son of Patrick Denny.
1849.	June 24.	John, son of John White.
1849.	July 13.	George A., son of Milo Winchester.
1849.	Sept. 24.	Edward F., son of James O. Peirce.
1849.	June 12.	Lucy M., daughter of Seth Sargent.
1849.	Dec. 5.	Elizabeth J., daughter of David Ross.
1849.	Dec. 9.	Emily Ellen, daughter of Rufus K. Ladd.
1849.	Oct. 27.	Angeline Olive, daughter of Addison R. Ball (Bolton).
1849.	Dec. 24.	Eugene, son of Albert S. Carleton.
1849.	Aug. 14.	Austin Elias, son of John E. Joslin (?).
1849.	Nov. 29.	Eunice C., daughter of Edward E. Harlow.
1849.	June 3.	Mary, daughter of John Curran.
1849.	July 23.	Otis Oscar, son of Otis Litchfield.
1849.	May 24.	Mary Ann, daughter of Patrick Carnes (Manchester, N. H.)
1849.	April 23.	George C., son of Camden Maynard.
1849.	Aug. 30.	John Henry, son of Michael Bray (Stow).
1849.	Dec. 16.	Thomas, son of Martin Carey.
1849.	June 3.	Julia, daughter of Dennis O'Brien.
1849.	June 24.	Elizabeth, daughter of William Reed.
1849.	Oct. 24.	Margaret J., daughter of Martin Elbridge.
1849.	July 4.	Agnes Lucretia, daughter of Thomas C. Snow.
1849.	Mar. 1.	Edward, son of Cornelius W. Blanchard.
1849.	Oct. 17.	Julius S., son of Robert S. Freeman.
1849.	March 21.	Francis Hinkley, son of Hinkley R. Gray.
1849.	June 6.	Winslow N., son of Edward W. Goodale.
1849.	Nov. 24.	Jemima Hall, daughter of James Crage.
1849.	Nov. 6.	James, son of Michael Havrety.
1849.	Dec. 3.	Louisa, daughter of Levi Raymond.
1849.	Nov. 13.	Francis L., son of Henry McQuaid.
1849.	Apr. 9.	Margaret D., daughter of Donald Cameron.
1849.	Sept. 30.	Michael, son of John Cummings.
1849.	Dec. 5.	Mary, daughter of Thomas Hinds.
1849.	May 1.	Martin, son of John Ball.
1849.	Dec. 12.	John, son of Michael Dailey.
1849.	Dec. 16.	Thomas, son of Michael Finerty.
1849.	Sept. 18.	Thomas Edward, son of Martin Graham (Roxbury).
1849.	Oct. 2.	Mary E., daughter of George W. Burdett, M. D.
1849.	July 18.	Marion, daughter of Milton Jewett. (Andover.)
1849.	Oct. 25.	Joseph Willard, son of Lucius L. and Sarah E. Farwell.
1849.	May 5.	Charles, son of Horatio N. Bigelow.
1839.	Feby. 8th.	Lyman Augustus, son of Peter & Almira [Carter] Joslyn.
1843.	Nov. 30.	Edward Russell, " " "
1847.	Sept. 13.	Frederick Zaccheus, son of Benj. F. & Cynthia Ann Farnsworth.
1849.	June 14.	Daniel, son of William & Abigail Thompson.
1849.	Aug. 20.	Elmira Mandana, daughter of Rev. Quincy & Mary M. Whitney.
1849.	July 31.	Sylvia Jane Curtis, daughter of Silas L. & Jane Philinda Brown.
1846.	May 3.	Martha, daughter of Samuel, Jr., & Sarah Jones.
1847.	Dec. 18.	Charley, son of " " "
1849.	March 7.	Luther, son of Samuel W. & Olive Burbank.
1847.	Oct. 8.	George A., son of Isaac & Rebecca W. Taylor.

1838. May 14. Henry F., son of Levi M. & Lucinda L. Ball.
1840. June 17. Emily S., daughter of "   "
1849. July 4. Ella Louisa,   "   "   "
1830. Sept. 20. Milton J. ⎫
1833. Feb. 18. Mary H.   ⎬ Children of Joseph M. & Mary Putney
1835. Aug. 2. Lyman K.   ⎪ of Lancaster.
1839. Nov. 30. Warren C.   ⎪ All born in New Hampshire.
1842. Aug. 19. Henry M.   ⎪
1849. Sept. 4. Abby A.   ⎭
1847. Dec. 17. Lucy Ann, daughter of Francis & Mary Ann Shed (in Medford).
1847. Jany. 4. Clara L.   ⎫
1849. Apr. 12. James H.   ⎬ Children of Andrew & Mary W. Bancroft of
1850. July 11. Mary C.   ⎭ Lancaster, born at Madras, East Indies.
1849. Nov. 28. George N., son of Horatio N. & Frances Sweet.
1838. Feb. 5. William.   ⎫
1840. Aug. 1. Francis.   ⎪
1842. Apr. 10. Henrietta. ⎬ Children of William & Lucy Peirce.
1844. Feb. 27. Laura.   ⎪
1847. Apr. 1. Uara.   ⎪
1849. Apr. 1. Mary.   ⎭
1845. July 31. Martha E., daughter of Jeremiah Moore.
1848. Aug. 29. Benjamin, son of Charles & Miranda Cobb.
1839. Dec. 16. Oliver Baldwin.   ⎫
1842. Aug. 10. George Alfred.   ⎬ Children of America & Lucy (Baldwin)
1844. Jany. 23. Alber America.   ⎪ Sawyer.
1846. Dec. 31. Marietta Carter.   ⎪ *Corrected by family records.*
1850. Dec. 27. Elliot Elijah.   ⎭
1849. Jany. 30. Frances Ann, daughter of Frederick & Ann Wilder.
1834. Nov. 9. Emily Elizabeth.   ⎫
1843. Oct. 3. Adrian Trumbull.   ⎬ [Children of Jonathan Puffer and Mary
1846. Aug. 14. Genevieve Amanda.   ⎪ (Pollard) Nourse.
1849. July 4. Eugene Albert.   ⎭ *Corrected by family records.*
1846. June 11. Julia Miller, daughter of Joseph W. and Julia Huntington.
1847. Aug. 28. Joseph Miller, son of   "   "   "
1844. July 16. Frank Wallace.   ⎫
1846. Aug. 24. Harriet Elizabeth.   ⎬ Children of John W. and Adaline (Mal-
1848. Oct. 9. Albert Mallard.   ⎭ lard) Barnes.
[1844. Feb. 15. Sarah Jane, daughter of Jonathan & Charlotte Buttrick.]
[1846. Dec. 8. Ann Elizabeth, "   "   "   "   ]
[1849. Jany. 24. Edward Whitman, son of "   "   "   ]
[1846. Feb. 23. Martha T., daughter of Charles & Nancy Wyman.]
[1849. Oct. 2. Annie C.,   "   "   "   "   ]
[1844. July 30. Jane Maria, daughter of Charles & Jane (Jones) Humphrey.]
[1846. Sept. 24. Clara,   "   "   "   "   ]
[1840. Dec. 19. Joel Thomas, son of Chas. Josiah & Eliza (Carter) Wilder.]
[1842. Dec. 29. George Waite, "   "   "   "   ]
[1846. April 1. Charles Francis, "   "   "   "   ]
[1844. Oct. 3. Sarah M., daughter of Nath. L. & Mary A. Howe.]
[1847. July 20. Mary A., "   "   "   "   ]

DEATHS IN LANCASTER. 1843-1849.

Numerous duplicate records have been omitted, and corrections suggested.

1844. March 15. Walter Austin Davis, son of Austin, 5. Congestion of brain.
  "   April 7. Ann Maria Nourse, daught. of Warren [& Nancy], 3.
  "   "   21. Betty Sawyer, widow of Moses, 94. Old age.
  "   "   24. Davis Whitman, widower, 82.   "
1843. Oct. 12. A child of John Taylor, 3. Typhus fever.
  "   "   21. Achsah Greene, wife of Levi, 37. Consumption.
  "   Nov. 10. Seth Fairbanks, 44. Dropsy.

1844. Jan. 14. Oscar M. Miller, son of Charles, 4. Scarlet fever.
" Feb. 2. Nancy Packard, wife of Rev. Asa, 80. Lung fever.
" April 5. Mrs. Damon, wife of Samuel, 85. Fever.
" May 23. Francis Marion Farwell, son of Levi & Lucy, 9 yrs. 8mo. Inflammation.
" July 30. Abel White, 64 yrs. 8 mo. Dropsy.
1845. April 1. Salome [Pratt] Bennett, wife of John, 26. 5 mo. Consumption.
1844. June 8. Joseph Upton, 70. Infirmity.
" July 12, Miss Hannah Whipple, 70. Dropsy.
" July 28. Martha Ann R. Carter, wife of William, 24.
" [August 24. Martha K. Rugg, daughter of James & Submit. Killed by fall at Niagara Falls.]
" Aug. 25. Joel Thomas Wilder, son of Chasrles J. & Eliza, 3 yrs. 6 mo. Cholera morbus.
" Nov. 4. Emily Davis, daughter of Thomas & Mary, 2 yrs. 6 mo.
" Dec. 13. Lydia Bailey, widow, 77. Typhus fever.
" " 28. Sally Lyon, widow of John, 69.
1845. Jan. 28. Annis Andrews, widow, 81. Dropsy.
" " 28. Sarah E. Goss, wife of Jonas, 24. Disease of heart.
" " 29. Charlotte [E.] Turner, daughter of Stevens H. & Betsy, 4. Scarlet fever.
" Feb. 4. Franklin Warren Fuller, son of Ephraim & Judith, 3. Scarlet fever.
" March 8. Lydia Ann Fuller, daughter of John & Sophronia, 3 mo. Consumption.
" " 14. Mrs. Prudence Phelps, 73. Dropsy.
" Mar. 21. Henry Kimball Washburn, son of John M. & Harriet, 2 yrs. 6 mo. Scarlet fever.
1843. Nov. 7. Mrs. Rebecca [Nichols] Alexander, 61 yrs. 6 mo. Consumption.
1844. Sept. 30. Frances Elizabeth Lewis, daughter of Henry & Sarah B.
" Nov. 9. Ann Elizabeth Houghton, daughter of Jona. W. & Abby S., 18 mo. Scarlet fever.
1845. Dec. 14. Prudence Robbins, widow of John, 90. Old age.
" March —. Miss Caroline M. Newman, d. of Lucy C., 29. Consumption.
1846. May —. Mary Ann King, daughter of Orice. Scarlet fever.
" " 1. Sally Carter, widow of Thomas, 86. Paralysis.
1845. July [7]. Nancy Fay, wife of Josiah. Inflammation.
1846. Sept. 16. Margaret Burditt, wife of Nathan. Typhus fever.
1845. Oct. 25. Thomas Houghton, 69. Dropsy.
" Nov. 15. Jonas Wilder, son of Moses, 58. Dropsy of heart.
" Dec. 17. Lois Bartlett, widow, 74. Old age.
1846. Jan. 9 [8]. Mary Ann (Sawyer) Chandler, wife of James, 25. Consumption.
" Jan. 30. Gardner Phelps, 88. Fever.
" Jan. 14. Capt. Jonas Whitney, son of Jonathan, 74. Dropsy.
1845. Nov. 7. Mary (Barrett) Farwell, wife of Lucius L., 30. Consumption.
1846. March 10. Julia [Lorinda] Phelps, daughter of Joel W. & Lorinda, 1 yr. 7 mo. Lung fever.
" " 18. James Bridge, 53. Lung fever.
" " 28. Lucretia Osgood, widow of Joel, 91. Old age.
" April 6. Hezekiah Davis, 48.
" " 7. A child of Jonathan Bowman, 3 mos. Lung fever.
" " 24. Luther [Tarbell] Bancroft, son of Luther T., 2. Lung fever.
1845. March 18. Henry Oscar Rice, son of Abel & Lucy B., 7 mo. 8 d. Dropsy on brain.
1846. Oct. 9. Mrs. Louisa (Hill) Hodgeman, 40 yrs. 11 mo. Consumption.
" Aug. 4. Moses Barrett, son of Reuben, 62. Consumption.
" May 12. Ann L. [Carter] Bancroft, wife of Lorey F., 24. Child birth.
" June 2. Infant of James Stone.
" June 18 [19]. Francis [Augustus] Sawyer, son of Silas & Sally, 23. Consumption.
" July 9. Williams Green, 38. Consumption.

BOOK FOURTH. 267

1846. Aug. 7. Ellen S. Conant, 7. Typhus fever.
" " 10. Philip Freeman, colored, 33. Broke his neck.
" " 12. Sarah Ann Windett, daughter of John, Jr., 1. Bowel complaint.
" " 19. Luke Stow, 49. Dropsy of the heart.
" Sept. 24. Miss Sarah Windett, daughter of John, 22. Consumption.
" Oct. 12. Elizabeth Derby, 3. Bowel complaint.
" Nov. 22. George L. Gibson, 2. Croup.
" " 28. Betsy Rugg, wife of Ephraim, 65. Consumption.
" Decr. 14. Ann M. Thurston, wife of Wilder S., 28. Consumption.
" Novr. —. —— Barnard, wife of Jeremiah. Typhus fever.
" Dec. 21. John White, 78.
" " 26. Infant child of John Fuller, 1 day.
" " 28. —— Townsend, wife of William, 62. Dropsy.
1847. Jany. 1. Rebecca Rugg, wife of Isaac, 79. General infirmity.
" " 1. Joel J. Rugg, son of Joel & Bathsheba, 28. Typhoid fever.
" " 10. Jonathan Osgood, 71. Lung fever.
" " 19. Elizabeth C. White, daughter of Samuel & Elizabeth, 15. Enlarged kidneys.
" March 18. Miss Parney Howard, daughter of Sidney [& Sally], 27.
" " 25. Rachel G. Wilder, widow, 88. Old age.
" April 9. Calvin Phelps, 76 yrs. 11 mos.
" May 8. Henry B. Barnard, son of Jeremiah, 21. Consumption.
" Feb. 3. Charles Frederick Thurston, son of Silas [& Parney], 20. Fever.
" " 12. [Lucy] Eaton, widow, 96. Old age.
" " 18. Rhoda Bell, wife of William, 46. Disease of liver.
" April 30. Martha Parker, wife of James O. Consumption.
" March 29. Miss Dolly Carr, daughter of John. Consumption.
" " 29. Miss Elizabeth Nowell, 21. Consumption.
" June 23. [Miss] Dickinson, died at alms house. Fever.
" Juiy 5. —— Carter, " " " Consumption.
" " 23. Infant of Jeremiah Moore. Bowel complaint.
" Aug. 19. Infant of Joseph & Sarah Wilder, of Holliston. Bowel complaint.
" " 26. Silas Fairbank, 67.
" " 29. Albert Crane, Esq., of Oswego, N. Y., 49. Bilious fever.
" Sep. 13. Infant of Joseph S. Seaver. Dysentery.
" " 18. Catharine P. Farnsworth, wife of A. J. Typhus fever.
" Oct. 4. Robert C. Houghton, 34. Typhus fever.
" " 13. John W. Dame, son of John T., 1 yr. 6 mos. Bowel complaint.
" " 19. Child of Mr. Van Duser, 4. Croup.
" " 27. Mrs. Eliza Bates, 20. Typhus fever.
" Nov. 6. Lucy Houghton, widow of Robert C., 39.
" " 28. Jonathan F. Houghton, son of R. C. & Lucy, 9. Typhus fever.
" Dec. 13. Patty Maynard, 60. Fever.
" " 18. Infant of Mr. —— Gould, 1. Brain fever.
" Sept. 14. Nancy Dickerson, wife of Moses, 63. Ship fever, at alms house.
" Aug. 19. Zenon Peirce, 42. Consumption.
" Sept. 12. Elias Seaver, son of Joseph S. & Amanda, 4. Cholera morbus.
" " 16. Mary J. Seaver, daughter of " " 2. Cholera morbus.
" " 20. Moses Dickerson, at alms house, 72. Ship fever.
" —— Sarah E. Harris, daughter of Sidney & Sally, 16.
" —— Infant, at alms house, of Patrick & Margaret McLinn.
" Sept. 24. John H. Maynard, son of John H., 3. Scarlet fever.
" " 28. Erastus H. Maynard, son of John H., 9 mo. Scarlet fever.
" Oct. 2. James Stone, 49. Disease of liver.
" " 6. Emma Davis, daughter of Hollis [& Hannah], 6. Killed by fall of cart body.
" " 13. Lucy Allen, wife of Samuel Allen, 80. Consumption.
" " 16. Abby G. Fuller, daughter of John & Sophronia, 7. Fever.
" " 16 [19]. Joel Wilder, son of Samuel, [70]. Consumption.
" " 29. Julia Ann Sargent, d. of Curtis & Huldah. Throat disease.

1847. Nov. 3. Ann Eliza[beth] Buttrick, daughter of Jonathan & Charlotte, 10 mo. 23 days. Teething.
1848. Jany. 1. Mary A. Fairbank, wife of Archibald, 47. Cancer.
[1847. Nov. 23.] Sarah A. Danforth, d. of Elias & Lucy, 26. Consumption.
1848. Feb. 14. A child of William & Hannah Matthews, 8 days.
1847. May 5. Emily Jane Rice, daughter of Abel & Lucy, 1. 5 mo. Lung fever.
1848. Jany. 7. Isaac Miller, 42. Palsy.
" " 27. Mary E. Phelps, daughter of Henry, 22. Consumption.
" Feb. 14. A child of John C. Stiles, 14 mo. Brain fever.
" March 17. Maria Conant, wife of Sherman, 42. Erysipelas.
" April 22. Prudence Haskell, at alms-house, 78. Consumption.
" " 22. Jane Augusta Childs, d. of Isaac & Mary, 20. Consumption.
" May 11. Susan Houghton, wife of Benjamin, 57. Dropsy.
" June 6. Deacon Jonas Lane, 87. Old age.
" " 12. Charlotte K. Hoadley, wife of John C., 24. Consumption.
" July 4. Thomas Watson, 54. Accident.
" Aug. 5. Fordyce Nourse, 39. Typhoid fever.
" " 9. Adelia Freeman, daughter of Philip & Roxy. Dysentery.
" " 15. W[illiam] F. Brabrook, 30. Consumption.
" Sept. 9. Infant of Jeremiah Moore, 1 mo. Bowel complaint.
" " 11. Samuel D. Butler, son of Eldad & Nancy. Dysentery.
" " 14. Elizabeth (Pollard) Thurston, [widow of Gates], 86. Old age.
" Oct. 1. Sylvester Phelps, 79. Consumption.
" " 17. Eunice Bennett, wife of Nathan, 72. Consumption.
" " 27. William A. Ballard, son of William & Elsy, 25. Consumption.
" Nov. —. Seth Larkin, at alms house, 81. Old age.
" " 20. Anna Maria Cummings, d. of Right & Mary, 20. Consumption.
1849. Jan. 10. Winfield Sargent, son of Curtis & Huldah, 3.
" " 16. Elias Sawyer, 47. Consumption.
" " 26. Polly Washburn, widow, 84. Old age.
" Feb. 12. Miss Sally Carter, 68. Influenza.
" " 17. Ann Sargent, widow, 76. Influenza.
" " 19. Rosellina Maria Derby, 7 mo.
1841. Dec. 27. Martha Adaline McCollum, daughter of Haskell & Sylvia.
1845. May 27. Matilda L. McCollum, daughter of Haskell & Sylvia.
1840. Aug. 30. Edwin Jerome Burdett, son of Nathan, Jr.
1844. Jany. 14. Oscar M. Miller, son of Charles & Matilda.
1847. Dec. 25. Ellen A. Gould, daughter of Moses & Susan W.
" " 16. Abby E. Gould, daughter of Moses & Susan W.
1849. March 7. Miss Anna L. Knapp.
" " 11. A child of Horace Whitney.
" April 4. Mrs. Hale.
" " 9. Mr. [Joseph] Davis, [68].
" May 20. Sophronia Ballard, wife of Eliphas.
" " 27. Caroline M. Hayden, wife of Newton F.
" " 28. Martha Laughton, daughter of John, 19. Consumption.
" June 22. Lydia Ann Stratton, daughter of George, 15 mo. 9 d. Croup.
" July 4. Mary Locke, wife of Jonathan, 67. Consumption.
" " 6. —— Lawrence, daughter of Royal.
" " 7. —— Robinson, wife of C. G.
" " 9. Sally Lawrence, wife of Royal, 52. Consumption.
" " 21. David Steuart Robinson, 32. Bilious fever.
" " 23. A child of Luther Gaylord.
" " 31. A child of [John W.?] Cady.
" Aug. 10. Ellen F. Rich, daughter of John, 5 mo.
" " 3. John Henry Howard, son of George W., 2. Dysentery.
" " 12. Elizabeth S. Hastings, daughter of Thomas & Emma, 2. 7 mo.
" " 16. Edgar A. Lowe, son of Henry, 5.
" " 20. Samuel Wilder, 80.
" " 21. Mary Lowe, wife of John, 74. Epilepsy.
" " 25. Georgiana Wilson, daughter of Jacob, 4 mo.
" " 26. Georgianna S. Gibson, daughter of John, 1.

1849.	Aug. 28.	Matilda Worcester, wife of Charles W., 43. Dysentery.
"	Sept. 7.	Ellen Maria Maynard, daughter of Martha, 3.
"	" 7.	Charles H. Lord, son of Absalom, 7 yrs. 2 m.
"	" 11.	Henry Woods, son of Matthew F., 4 yrs. 7 m.
"	" 12.	Mary Frances Phelps, daughter of Mrs. Tabitha, 13.
"	" 13.	William F. Green, son of Oliver.
"	" 17.	A daughter of ——— Townsend, 4.
"	" 19.	Andrew Homer, son of Lawrence, 1 yr. 4 m.
"	" 20.	Ellen A. Bowers, daughter of Rev. Charles M., 4 yrs. 6 m.
"	" "	[Mary A. Howe, daughter of Nathl. L. & Mary A. Howe, 14 mo.]
"	" 24.	Martha Adaline Sargent, daughter of Merrick, 1 yr. 2 m.
1848.	Oct. 23.	Lucinda Pitts, wife of James.
"	" 1.	——— Martin, wife of Deacon Martin.
"	Sept. 8.	A child of S. W. Burbank.
"	Aug. 27.	A child of Daniel Havrety.
1849.	Jan. 10.	——— Farwell, wife of James.
1848.	Sept. 1.	A child of Charles Eddy.
"	" 3.	A child of Anson Lowe.
"	" 17.	A child of Levi Green.
"	Oct. 22.	A child of Calvin Stanley.
"	" 27.	A child of Samuel Osgood.
"	July 24.	A child of Alvinzy Lane.
"	Aug. 28.	A child of Granville [& Martha E.] Carter.
"	Nov. 20.	A daughter of John Carr.
"	" 28.	A child of Jonathan Law.
1849.	Jan. 27.	Mrs. Emily R. Hooper.
"	Feby. 3.	A child of Philip Giles.
"	Sept. 27.	Elijah Colburn, sexton for 40 years, 78 yrs. 9 m. Paralysis.
"	Oct. 26.	Ann E. Pratt, daughter of Ebenezer, 6 yrs. 6 m.
"	Nov. 2.	Caroline M. Thurston, wife of Wilder S., 26. Consumption.
"	" 3.	John Goss, son of Daniel, 64. Consumption.
"	" 18.	William Divoll, 55. Suicide.
"	" 21.	Elizabeth Sawyer, wife of Moses, 84. Old age.
"	" 23.	Amy Fales, wife of Jeremiah, 67.
"	Dec. 1.	William D. Peirce, 37. Liver complaint.
"	" 1.	William Peirce, 36.
"	" 8.	Lucy Fairbanks, wife of Silas, 67.
"	" 17 [16].	Nancy B. Sawyer, wife of Elias, 57. Consumption.
"	May 26.	Luke Wilder. 67. Dropsy on heart.
"	Aug. 14.	Mary E. S. Burditt, wife of A. P., 26. Congestion of brain.
"	Sept. —.	Nancy Newell, widow of David, 80. Old age.
"	Nov. 5.	Joseph Barrett, 94. Old age.
1844.	July 4th.	Joshua Fletcher, son of Timothy & Hannah, 61. Consumption.

RECORDS OF THE FIRST CHURCH.

1708-1847.

Of existing records appertaining to the church in Lancaster, the oldest book opens with a copy of the covenant as renewed at the time of the ordination of Reverend John Prentice, March 29, 1708, and closes with an account of the ordination of Reverend Nathaniel Thayer, October 9, 1793. The second book continues the records to the end of the pastorate of Reverend Edmund Hamilton Sears, April 1, 1847.

Pages of both books devoted to matters of church discipline and polity, and sundry stray items relating to these subjects, are omitted herein as beyond the purpose of this volume, such omissions being noted by asterisks. The marriage lists are the originals of returns made to the town-clerks, and have been given on previous pages.

Reverend John Prentice married Mrs. Mary Gardner, the widow of his predecessor, at Roxbury, December 4, 1705; and second, Mrs. Prudence (Foster) Swan of Charlestown, probably in 1719. Mr. Prentice in 1708 signed the covenant, and added beneath it the names — Thomas Wilder, John Houghton, Joseph Whetcomb, John Wilder, Jeremiah Willson, John Rugg and Jonathan Moor. These eight may have been the only male members of the church at that date. There are also subscribed, not always in their own handwriting, the names of twenty-nine men admitted to membership from time to time — less than one-fourth the number of males accepted as communicants during the pastorate of Mr. Prentice. These were, in order of admission but not of signing: John Priest, Josiah White, Josiah Wheeler, James Wilder, Joseph Wilder, John Warner, Samuel Warner, Jabez Fairbank, Benjamin Wilson, Daniel Rugg, Edward Phelps, John Harris, Jonas Houghton, Jonathan Houghton, Jabez Fairbank [Jr.], Hooker Osgood, Joseph Hutchins, Joshua Osgood, John Bennett, Thomas Houghton, Ephraim Houghton, Joseph Whitcomb, [Jr.], Oliver Moor, Joseph More, David Osgood, Samuel Willard, Joseph Wilder, Jr., Stanton Prentice, Josiah Swan. Then follow the records kept by the pastors.

BOOK I.

¶ Account of those that have been added to the Church of Christ in Lancaster by John Prentice Pastor. viz:

July 25th, 1808. John Keyes & his Wife, James Butler & John Priest & his Wife.
——— 1708. Mary Prentice. 1708–9 March 13, Josiah White Senr.

May 1, 1709. Mary Snow. Nov. 13, Edmund Harris from Sudbury Church.
April 9, 1710. Josiah Wheeler & his Wife from Concord Church.
April 23, Cyprian Stevens & James Wilder. 30, Ruth Stevens.
September 10, Damaris Wilder. Octob. 15, Beatrix Pope Vidua.
January 14th, 1710-11. Sarah Hartwell. 28th. John Glazier & Abigail Wilder.
April 8th. 1711. Mary Glazier & Mercy Wilder. June 3d, Mary Sawyer Wife to Wil—
" 6th. 1712. John Wilder Junr. August, 17. Richard Wiles.
March 22, 1712-13. Elizabeth Rugg Vid. April, 12, 1713. Annah Willard & Elizabeth Rugg. May 30, Hannah Rugg Widdow. July 26. Peter Joslin & Joanna his Wife, also Elizabeth Hutchins. Aug: 30. Mary White wife of Josiah White Senr. Sept. 20th. Joseph Wilder. Novembr. 15, Annah Hynds Wife of John Hynds. Father Snow from Woburn Church the time when forgotten.
1714, April, 11, Samuel Warner. July, 11, Samuel Rugg. Octob, 14, Dorcas Bellows.
1714-15. Feb. 20, Rebekah Whetcomb & Sarah Harris Father Warner from Woburn ye Day forgotten. [John. He was taken into the church at Marlboro', Sept. 20, 1687, as recorded in Rev. William Brinsmead's diary.]
1715, April 17th. Rebekah Beaman. June, 19th. Mary Houghton & Eliz: Harris. July, 31, Lydia Sawtle. Aug: 14th. Hannah Wilson.
1715-16. Jabez Fairbank & Mary his Wife. March, 18th. Samuel Bennet Senr. & Mary his Wife, David Whetcomb, & Ebenezer Warner. 25, Nathl. Sawyer.
1716. April, 1, John Fletcher. May, 6th, Deborah Houghton, Wife of Robert Ho: Junr. 27, John Warner Junr., Benjamin Wilson & Rebekah his Wife. July, 22, Sarah Glazier wife of George Glazier, Elizabeth Rugg, wife of Daniel Rugg, Abigail Houghton Daughter of Robt. Houghton. Nov. 4th. Edward Phelps & his Wife from Andover Church, and Joshua Wheeler. Decemb. 30th. Mary Snow. Father Beaman from Taunton Church the Day & Year forgotten.
1716-17, March, 3d, Daniel Rugg & Hephzibah Brabrook.
1717, May, 26, William Divol & Ruth his Wife. July, 21, Joseph Stone. Sept. 1, John Harris & Ann Willard wife of John Willard.
1718, May, 11, Jonas Houghton Junr. from Marlborough Church, also Joseph Sawyer & Elizabeth Fairbank. 18th, Jacob Houghton, Jonathan Houghton, Hezekiah Townsend & Sarah his Wife, also Dorothy Prescott, wife of John Prescott, & Abigail Wilder, Wife of James Wilder. July, 13, Thomas Sawyer. 17th, Hannah Rugg, wife of Samll. Rugg from Mr Tufts's Church in Newbury. 24th, Isabella Houghton Vidua. Sept. 7th, Mary Kendal & Hannah Priest.
1719, April 19th, Mary Phelps wife of Edward Phelps, Junr. August 9th, Josiah Fairbank & Mary his Wife. Sept. 20th, James Willard & his Wife. Nov. 22, Josiah Sawtle.
1720, May, 22, Jabez Fairbank, Junr. & his Wife. Nov. 6th, Hooker Osgood Senr. & his Wife.
1720-21, January, 1, John Houghton & Mehetabel his Wife.
1721, April, 9th, Jonas Houghton, Senr. June 18th, Josiah Willard. Aug: 13, Eliz: Willard wife of Samuel Willard. Sept. 24, Sarah Houghton wife of Lieut. John Houghton.
1722, March, 25, Edward Broughton. May, 20, Hannah Gooldsberry Vidua.
1723, April 14th. Thomas Tucker & Mary his Wife. Decemb. 1, Joseph Hutchins.
1723-4, March 22, Mary Houghton. April 19th, Eunice Sawyer Wife of Ephraim Sawyer. July, 19th, Elizabeth Priest vidua. Aug. 30. Esther Houghton vidua. Sept. 13, Elizabeth Wilson wife of Jer: Wilson Junr. Sept. 27, Sarah Sawyer Wife of John Sawyer. Nov. 8, Joshua Osgood & Ruth his Wife.
1724-5, January, 3d, Hooker Osgood Junr. & Mary his Wife. 31, Mehetabel Houghton Widow. Feb. 28th, Rebekah Warner Wife of John Warner. April 11, Judith Moor Wife of Fairbank Moor. May 26th, Anna Holman Wife of Jer. Holman.

1726, May, 22, Mary Willard Wife of Abraham Willard. Sept. 25, Joseph Osgood from Mr Barnard's Church in Andover. Octob. 23, Mr Ebenezer Flagg.
1726-7, January 1, Submitt Divoll. 7th, Hannah Osgood.
1727, April 23, Edward Phelps Junr.
1727-8, Feb. 11, Nathaniel Hudson & his Wife, Ebenezer Swan & Mary ye wife of Aaron Willard.

5 1727-8, March, 3d, Lydia Houghton, wife of Daniel Houghton & Mary Bruse.
1728, April 7th, Josiah White & his Wife, & Dorothy Rugg wife of Jonathan Rugg. April, 28, Tabitha Bennett Wife of Samuel Bennet Junr. May, 26, Thomas Prentice, William Pollard & his Wife, the Wife of Edward Broughton & the wife of John Harris. June, 2d, Elizabeth Houghton Wife of Gershom Houghton. 23d, Elizabeth Willard Wife of Joseph Willard. July, 14th, Rachel Prescott Wife of Ebenr: Prescott & Hannah Buss, wife of John Buss. 28, Sarah Kendal Wife of Jonathan Kendal, Eunice Wilder Wife of Jonas Wilder. August, 18th, Eunice White, Vidua. Nov. 17, John Bennett & his Wife. Decemb. 29, Hannah Fletcher Wife of John Fletcher.
1728-9, February 2d. Joseph Wheelock & Elizabeth his Wife.
1729, May 4th; Thomas Houghton of Stilriver & his Wife. June, 29th. Henry Willard Junr. & Abigail his Wife. July, 13, Anna Wheeler Wife of Joshua Wheeler. Octob. 12, James Houghton Senr. & Sarah his Wife. Decemb. 14th. Elizabeth Harris Daughter of ye Wid: Eliz: Harris.
1729-30, Feb. 7, Joshua Houghton & Hasadiah Moor wife of Jo....
1730, April 5, John Beaman. July, 5th. Mehetabel Johnson. July 26th. William Glazier & Martha his Wife. August, 2d, Peter Atherton & Experience his Wife also Rebeckah Sawyer Wife of Ezra Sawyer. 16th. Elizabeth Knight Wife of Amos Knight. Nov. 15, Anes Church the wife of Joshua Church
March 7th, 1730-1, Ephraim Houghton & Sarah his Wife. 14th, Sarah Atherton Daughter of James Atherton.
Octob. 24th, 1731, Hannah Snow, Wife of John Snow. Decemb. 12th, 1731, Elijah Whetney.
Decemb. 13th, Baptized (with the Consent of the Church, several of the Brethren & sev'ral others present,) at the house where William and Elinor White his wife live, their twins (a Son and a Daughter) ye names William and Margaret. This was done at ye Desire of ye Parents, and because the children were both weak and feeble and not able to be brought out and one of them especially under threatening Circumstances by reason of a sore mouth—(This thro' a mistake is noted in a wrong place but being written it must stand.)
February, 6th, 1731-2, Admitted to Church fellowship Joseph Whetcomb & Damaris his Wife. 13, Elizabeth Houghton wife of Joshua Houghton.
July 23d: 1732, Esther White, wife of Jonathan White. August 6th, Mary Ross Wife of Thomas Ross from ye Chh of Christ in Littleton. Also Liberty granted to Elizabeth Patrick a member of the Church in Volenton [Voluntown, Ct.?] to Commune with us whilst Providence casts her lot among us, she promising to attend Duty and walk orderly.
January 14th, 1732-3, Admitted to full Communion Oliver Moor & Abigail his Wife also Thankful Fairbank the wife of Jonas Fairbank. 21st, James Snow & Mary Johnson members of the Chh of Christ in Stow were by a Letter of Recommendation from said Church Admitted members in full Communion with us.

6 May 6th, 1733, Margaret Rugg daughter of Daniel Rugg was admitted to full Communion with the Church, also Betty Sawyer ye wife of Aholiab Sawyer upon a letter of Recommendation from the Revd. Mr Thomas Clap Pastor of the first Church in Windham. July 8th, Joseph Moor & Rebekah his Wife.
August 5th, 1733. Admitted to full Communion David Osgood & Eunice his Wife also Deborah the Wife of Samuel Sawyer.
Sept. 9th, 1733, Anna Ross widdow; at the same time the Brethren present by vote Discovered yr willingness that Joseph Fairbank, Henry Willard, Peter Atherton & Elijah Whitney, all of Harvard should joyn with others in said Town in forming of a Church there, & yt Sarah Smith (heretofore Atherton)

should be Recommended according to her Desire to ye Church of X in Bolton. Nov: 18th. Maj^r. Sam^{ll}. Willard, & Dorothy Richardson Wife of Josiah Richardson. December, 23, 1733, Hannah Powers Wife of Jonathan Powers.

January 6th, 1733-4, The desire of the wife of John Willard, ye Wife of Joseph Willard, the wife of Peter Atherton & ye wife of Joshua Church to have y^r Relations to us transferred to ye Chh of Christ in Harvard, was made known to ye Brethren present and it was Complyed wth by y^m & y^r willingness also signified by ye uplifted hand that they should be Recommended to Communion wth ye Church of X in ye forementioned Place:

January, 27th, 1733-4. Susanna Beaman, Wife of John Beaman Junr. received into full Communion with us upon a Letter of Recommendation from the Chh of Christ in Weston.

April 9, 1734, Dorcas Polley Wife of Eben^r. Polly. 14, Joseph Wilder Junr. & Deborah his Wife, also Lucey Joslin, the wife of John Joslin. 21st, Anna Wilder, the Wife of Ephraim Wilder Junr. May, 19th, Daniel Knight upon a Recommendation from the Chh of Christ in Woburn, ye same Day Samuel Rugg & his Wife upon their desire were Dismissed and by vote of the Brethren were to be Recommended to Communion with the South Church of Christ in Hadley. 26, Mary Houghton, the Wife of Jonas Houghton, & Mary Richardson the Wife of William Richardson. June, 9th. Hannah Woods the wife of Joseph Woods. 23^d, Stanton Prentice.

August 4th, 1734, Joshua Phelps & Rebeccah his Wife. 11th Rebeckah Wilson Wife of Joseph Wilson, and Experience Butler the Wife of Nathan^l Butler. January 5th, 1734-5, Benjamin Harris.

BAPTISMS.

[NOTE. As infants were usually carried to the meeting-house to be baptized at a very tender age, often on the first Sunday after their birth, whatever the weather or the distance, the date of baptism has special value in cases where the birth record cannot be found.]

¶ ENTRED BY ME JOHN PRENTICE THIS SECOND DAY OF DECEMBER, 1730.

THE NAMES OF THOSE THAT HAVE BEEN BAPTIZED BY ME.

It is to be observed that the time of the Baptism of some of them was not noted down, which was an omission in me.

1708. Elizabeth, Jonas, Thomas, Abigail, Children of Jabez Fairbank. Simon, & Amos, Sons of James Atherton, on ye mother's account. Abigail, Daughter of Henry Houghton his Wife having owned the Covenant, at Watertown at Mr Gibbs's Church. Rebeckah Daughter of David Whetcomb. Joseph Jonathan Oliver Mariah Children of Jonathan Moor. May, 30. Simon son of Simon Stevens he having owned the Covenant at Marlborough. Mariah Martha Daughters of George Glazier. Sarah Daugh: of John Keyes. Mary Daughter of John Prescott. Jabez Eunice chil: of John Beaman. Samuel Eunice Nathanael children of Sam^{ll}, Carter. Joanna Sarah Rebekah children of Lieut. Peter Joslin. Joseph Josiah Jonathan Elizabeth children of Samuel Bennett. Sept. 12, Annah Mary Abigail children of John Priest. Octob. 10, James, Mary Eunice Martha Hannah Children of James Butler. 31, Hephzibah Abigail Seth, Children of Caleb Sawyer. John Elizabeth Mary Ruth Submitt, Children of William Divol. Deborah Daughter of Peter Joslin. Nov. 28, Noah Abigail & Sarah Children of John Beaman. William Susannah, Sarah, Children of Joseph Glazier. John, Son of John Bowers. Elizabeth Daughter of Ephr. Wilder. Andrew Son of Joseph Wilder. Abigail Houghton & Mary Houghton upon y^r owning the Covenant. Experience Daughter of Josiah Wheeler. Ephraim Son of Ephraim Wilder. My Daughter Mary.

1709, April 24: William Son of William Divol. Hasadiah Daughter of Henry Houghton. Simon Son of Henry Willard. Octob: 30, Mary Judith Joannah children of Benj[·] Bellows on ye mother's account. Nov. 13, Ruth Daughter of George Glazier. Elizabeth Daughter of John Bowers. Lydia Daughter of John Keyes.

1709-10, Janu: 15, Mary Daughter of James Snow & John Son of James Atherton.   Febr: 5, Thomas Son of Joseph Wilder, & John Son of Joseph Glazier.   12, Beatrix Houghton upon her owning the Covenant.

1710 April, 2, Damaris Daughter of John Priest.   16, Jonathan Son of Simon Stevens.   30, James Son of James Wilder.   May, 21, Hannah Daughter of Jonathan Moor.   June 18, Jonathan Son of Jabez Fairbank.   Sept. 3, Thomas Son of John Prentice & John Son of John Beaman.   24, William Son of Hezekiah Whetcomb.   Nathaniel, Charles chil: of Nath[ll]. Wilder.   Octob. 8th, Tabitha Daughter of John Prescott.   Nov. 19, Hannah Woonsamugg Indian owned the Covenant & was baptized.   26, Benjamin Son of David Whetcomb.   Decemb. 10. John Son of Peter Joslin.   17th, Elizabeth Daughter of Edmund Harris.   21, Nathaniel, Son of James Butler.

1710-11, Feb. 4th, Dorothy Daughter of Samuel Carter.   18, Jonathan Son of Edward Hartwell.   March 25. James Son of Henry Willard

1711, April 8th. Nathanael Son of Jer: Wilson.   22. Benjamin Son of Ebenezer Wilder.   May, 27th, Josiah Son of William Divol.   June 10th Sampson Son of John Bowers.   July, 1, Aholiab, Mary Annah Hephzibah Children of William Sawyer.   Sept. 30, Josiah Wheeler's Twins, Ebenezer & Thankful.   Octob. 21, Abigail Daughter of Samuel Bennet.   28, Martha Daug: of Eph: Wilder.   Nov. 11, Gardner, Son of James Wilder.   18, William Son of William Sawyer & Annah Daughter of Joseph Wilder.   25. Joseph Blood's wive's child Hephzibah.   Decemb. 9. Abigail Daughter of James Snow.

1711-12, Feb. 19. Abigail Daughter of Thomas Carter.   April, 13, Sarah Daughter of Richard Wiles.   27. Grace Daughter of Jabez Fairbank.

1712, May, 25, Josiah White Junr. & his Wife owned the Covenant & had y[r] Children baptized viz: Jonathan Mary Hannah Abigail.   June, 1. Hephzibah Daughter of Ebenezer Wilder.   29th. Nathaniel Son of Simon Stevens.   July 6th, John Bowers's twins John & James.   27. Sarah Daughter of Ed: Hartwell & Abigail Daughter of James Atherton. Mary Wheeler Wife of Jonathan Wheeler owned y[e] Covenant and had her Daughter baptized Mary.   August, 17. Amos Son of Jonathan Moor.   Octob. 19, Amos Son of Edm: Harris.   Octob. 26, Joshua Son of Nathaniel Wilder.   Nov. 23. Benjamin Son of Benj: Bellows.   December, 7, Experience Daughter of Joseph Glazier.

1712-13, Feb. 8th. Thankful Daughter of James Butler.   March, 8th. Esther Daughter of James Wilder.

1713, April, 5. John Son of John Prescott & Jonathan Son of Sam[ll]. Carter May, 3. Thomas Son of Hezekiah Willard & John Son of Thos: Carter.   24. William Son of Henry Willard. Joseph Willard & his Wife owned the Covenant y[e] same time & had y[r]. Son baptized William. Hannah also the Daughter of Jonathan Wheeler.   30. Hannah the Daughter of Hezekiah Whetcomb.   June 21. James Son of Richard Wiles.   August, 2. Abigail Daugh: of Peter Joslin.

8 1713, Octob. 4th. Abigail Laken's Son of Groton Samuel.   Nov. 22. Elizabeth Daughter of John & Mary Prentice & Joseph Son of Joseph & Lucy Wilder.   Decemb. 6th. John & Annah Children of John Hinds,   20th Mary Daughter of John Bowers, & Rachel daugh: of John Priest.   27. Francis Son of John Hinds

1713-14, Janu: 3[d]. Silas Son of Jonas Houghton.   Feb. 28th. Dinah, Daughter of Jonathan Moor.   March 7. Simon, Son of David Whetcomb.   21, Asahel, Son of Ed: Hartwell & Dorothy Daughter of Ephraim Wilder.   28. Joshua, Son of Jabez Fairbank & Ephraim Son of William Divol.

1714, April 11, Josiah Son of Josiah White.   25th. Mary daugh: of George Glazier.   May, 16, Huldah Daughter of John Keyes.   June 6. Ebenezer Prescott & his Wife owned y[e] Covenant and had y[r] Daughter baptized Sarah.   13. Mary Daughter of John Beaman.   27. David Son of Eben[r]. Wilder & Sarah Daughter of James Atherton.   July, 25. Lydia Daughter of Edmund Harris.   Octob. 3, Nathan & Hannah Children of Samuel Warner.   24. Josiah Son of William Sawyer.   Decemb. 12. Phinehas Son of Hezekiah Willard.   26, Dorothy Daugh: of Peter Joslin.

Y⁰ same time John Buss & his Wife owned y⁰ Covenant and had y' Children baptized John & Abigail

1714-15, Janu: 9th. Bezaleel Son of Nathll. Wilder. Feb. 6. Ephraim Son of Samuel Carter. 13. Elizabeth daughter of Simon Stevens. Feb. 20. Thomas Son of Thomas Carter. March, 13, John Whetcomb's Children John & Abigail. 20. Ebenezer Harris's children Sarah Deborah.

1715, May, 15. Hannah Daughter of Eben: Beaman. 22. Thankful daughter of John Wilder & Sarah daughter of Joseph Willard. June, 5. James Butler's Son —— Joseph Glazier's Son Isaiah & Hezekiah Townsend's Son Benjamin. 12. Mary & Abigail Wheelock owned y⁰ covenant & were baptized. 26. Elizabeth Sawyer owned y⁰ Covenant & was baptized. July 3. Margaret Daughter of Richard Wiles, and Jonathan y⁰ Son of Joseph Stone upon his owning y⁰ Covenant. August, 7. Abigail Daughter of Henry Willard. 28. Samuel Son of James Snow. Sept. 25. Abigail Daughter of Samuel Warner. Nov. 6. Lucey daughter of Joseph Wilder.

1715-16, January, 22ᵈ. Manasseh Son of William Divol & Elizabeth Daughter of Ed: Hartwell. March, 4th. Nathanael Son of John Bowers. · 11th, Sarah Daughter of J: & M: Prentice.

1716, April, 1. Thankful daughter of Ebenezer Beaman 8th. Annah daughter of Ebenr. Warner & Hephzibah Daughter of John Priest. 22. Israel Son of Hezekiah Whetcomb. 29. Bette daughter of Jonas Houghton Junr. & Mary Daughter of John Hinds & Ruth Daughter of Josiah White. May 6th. Nathanael Sawyer's children John, Ezra, Nathanael, Thomas, Phinehas, Mary. James Son of James Atherton & Thomas Son of Thomas Carter. 13. Robert Houghton's children Ebenezer & Esther. The same Day John Goss's Wife owned y⁰ Covenant & had her children baptized William & Elizabeth, also Jonathan the Son of Jonathan Sawyer. June, 24. Hannah Daughter of John Whetcomb. July, 1. John Son of John Keyes. 29th. Martha Daughter of Edmund Harris. August 26. Daniel Rugg's Children Reuben, John, Daniel, Elizabeth, Martha, Deborah, Margarett. Sept. 9th. Joseph Stevens's Son Joseph he and his Wife having owned y⁰ Cov. at Sudbury. 23. Hannah Daughter of Ebenezer Harris. 30th the children of John Warner, David John Mary. Octob. 9. Nathanael Son of Simon Stevens, & Hannah y⁰ Daughter of John Buss. Nov. 18th. Annah, Daughter of Jabez Fairbank. Decemb. 3 Samuel Bennet Junr. owned y⁰ Covenant & had his Son baptized Samuel. 9. Elizabeth Daughter of John Beaman Junr. 16. Oliver Son of Sa: Carter.

1716-17. January, 20th. Amos Son of Dan: Rugg, & Mary daughter of John Goss. 27. Lydia, daughter of John Fletcher, & Joseph Son of Mary Snow. Feb. 3ᵈ. Caleb, Son of Joseph Wilder. 10th. Aholiab Son of Nathanael Wilder. March, 24th. Elias Sawyer & his Wife owned y⁰ Covenant and had y' children baptized Elijah & Thankful. 31. Abraham Son of Jonathan Moor.

1717. April, 7th. John & Joseph Sons of Joseph Brabrook, & Thankful Daughter of William Sawyer, & Mary Daughter of Ebenezer Warner.¹ April, 14. Zachariah Son of Joseph Glazier. May, 26. Hezekiah Son of Hezekiah Willard, also Obediah Son of Jonathan Wheeler. June, 16. David Son of Joseph Stone. 30. Dinah daughter of Josiah Wheeler. Septemb. 1. Damaris Daughter of Deacon Joslin, Ebenezer Son of James Snow, Daniel Son of Henry Willard and Jacob Son of Ebenr. Wilder. The same Time John Harris was baptized upon his owning of the Covenant.

9 Sept. 8th John Son of John Willard. 15, John Harris's Daughter Thankful. 29th Edward Son of Edw: Hartwell. Octob. 6. Elizabeth y⁰ Daughter of Jonathan Sawyer. 13. Ruth Daug: of James Wilder. Nov. 3. William Son of John Wilder. Ephraim Son of Samll. Bennett, & Elizabeth Daughter of Joseph Willard. 10th. Simon Son of Samuel Rugg.

1717-18, January 12. Dorothy, Daughter of John Prentice. Feb. 9th. Martha, Daughter of Josiah White.

1718. Apr: 13. Sarah daughter of Hezekiah Townsend. May, 4th. Seth y⁰ Son of John Hinds. 11th. Deborah Daughter of Deborah Houghton vidua. 25. Elkanah Son of John Keyes. June 1st. Bette daughter of

Hezekiah Whetcomb. 22ᵈ, Joseph Sawyer's Children, Joseph Sarah Thomas Abner Asenath Mary. July 6ᵗʰ. Benjamin Wheeler & his Wife owned the Covenant and had their child baptized Hannah. Ebenezer Harris also owned the Covenant & was baptized. 13. Thomas & Joshua Houghton owned yᵉ Covenant and were baptized, also Benj: Houghton & Israel Sons of Jacob Houghton did yᵉ same & were baptized, also on his own account were baptized his Sons Jonathan & John & his Daughters Rebekah & Abigail. Oliver Wilder & his Wife also owned yᵉ Covenant at yᵉ same time and had yʳ children baptized Hannah and Mary. The same time was baptized Mary the Daughter of Hooker Osgood Junr. on her mother's account. at yᵉ same time Rebeckah yᵉ Daughter of Ebenezer Warner was Baptized. 20ᵗʰ. Moses yᵉ Son of James Atherton. Allice Willard & Mary Harris owning yᵉ Covenant were baptized at yᵉ same time. August, 3ᵈ. Gershom Eleazer & Ebenezer Houghton Sons of Robert Houghton owned yᵉ Covenant & were baptized, also of the Sons of Jonas Houghton Benjamin James & Josiah, and on yᵉ mother's account Steven & Jemima. 10ᵗʰ. Ebenezer, Son of Ebenezer Harris, & Lydia Houghton Wife of Daniel Houghton owned yᵉ Covenant & had her children baptized, Simeon & Thaddeus. 17. Elisha Son of Elias Sawyer, yᵉ same time Ruth Wheelock was baptized upon her owning of yᵉ Covenant. 24. Isabella Houghton upon her owning of yᵉ Covenant. 31. John yᵉ Son of yᵉ widow Eliz: Bowers upon her owning of yᵉ Covenant. Sept 7. Joseph Son of Ebenezer Beaman, also John Son of John Goss. Octob. 5. Elizabeth Daughter of John Warner. Nov. 2. Thomas Wilder & his Wife owned yᵉ Covenant and had yʳ children baptized, John Jotham Rachel Prudence Margaret Deliverance Abigail, also Steven Son of John Buss. 9. Jonathan Son of John Priest. Eunice daughter of Hannah Priest and Joseph, Benjamin, Elizabeth, Annah, Sarah, children of yᵉ vid, Isabella Houghton. 23. Annis daughter of Daniel Houghton. 30. Nathan Son of Daniel Rugg, & Ruth Houghton Rachel Houghton & Mary Houghton owning yᵉ Covenant were baptized. Decemb. 14. Isaac Son of Joseph Stevens.

1718–19, Feb. 1. Mary Daughter of Samuel Carter. March, 1. Elizabeth daughter of Thomas Carter. 22. John Bennet & Bathsheba his Wife owned yᵉ Covenant & had yʳ child baptized John.

1719, Apr. 5. Gideon Son of Samuel Rugg. 12. Beulah daugh: of Jo; Wilder, & Dorothy the Daughter of Jethro Eams. 19 Eunice the Daughter of Capt. Ephraim Wilder. 26. Rhoda yᵉ Daugh: of Benj: Wilson. May, 3. Joshua Son of Samˡˡ Warner, & Jonathan Son of Jonathan Houghton. 10ᵗʰ Aaron Willard & his Sister Eunice owned the Covenant & were baptized. 17. Joseph Son of Joseph Glazier. 31. Sarah daughter of Henry Willard. June 14. John the Son of Gabriel Priest, yᵉ mother of yᵉ child having owned yᵉ Covenant at Stow. 28. Annah daughter of Edmund Harris, & Robert yᵉ Son of John Fletcher. July, 5. Martha daughter of William Sawyer. August, 16. Lois daughter of Joseph & Lucey Wilder. Asa Son of John Whetcomb, & Phinehas Son of Joseph Fairbank & Mary daughter of Edward Phelps. Sept. 6. Jonathan Moors twins Isaac & Jacob. 13. Dorothy Daughter of Simon Stevens. 20ᵗʰ John Son of John Kendal. 27. Isaac Son of James Willard. Nov. 1 Tarbel Son of Joseph Willard. 15. Phinehas Son of Samˡˡ. Bennett. 29. Prudence daughter of J. Prentice & Jonathan Son of Edward Hartwell. December 10 6ᵗʰ. Samuel Son of Ebenezer Warner.

1719–20, Feb. 7ᵗʰ. Sarah daughter of James Snow, & Rebeckah daughter of Benj: Corey he owning the Covenant. 14ᵗʰ. Joseph Son of Josiah White & Jerusha daughter of Joshua Houghton. March, 13. Damaris daughter of Nathanael Wilder. 20. Oliver Son of Oliver Wilder & Mary daughter of Hezekiah Townsend.

1720, April, 3ᵈ. Annah daughter of Hezekiah Willard. 24. Allice daugh; of John Harris. May. 29ᵗʰ. Sarah daughter of Jabez Fairbank Junr. June, 5ᵗʰ. Esther Daughter of Amos Sawyer. 19. Caleb Son of Jonathan Sawyer. 26. Jesse Son of Benj: Wheeler, and Sarah daughter of John Goss. July 24ᵗʰ. Gabriel Son of Gabriel Priest, & John yᵉ Son of yᵉ widow Gooldsberry. Aug. 14. Jonathan Son of Ebenezer Harris. 20. Baptized Jonathan Wheeler's child at Shrewsbury where I preacht y* Lecture there. Sept. 25. Nathanael Son of Daniel Houghton. Octob. 9th Lydia daughter of Josiah Sawtle & Robert Son of Eleazer Houghton. 23. Isaac Son of Daniel Rugg. 30. Elizabeth daughter of Sam^ll. Carter. Decemb. 18 Rebeckah daughter of Ebenezer Beaman.

1720–1, Janu: 8th. Azubah daughter of Jonathan Houghton. Mary daughter of John Houghton of Stilriver, & Bathsheba daughter of John Bennett. 30. Joseph Son of Hooker Osgood Junr. Feb. 12. James Son of Thomas Carter. 19. Lieut John Houghton's daughter Elizabeth on her mother's account she having owned the Covenant at Milton. 26. Susannah daughter of Thomas Wilder. March, 19th. Mary daughter of Jonas Houghton Junr. 26. Sarah daug: Hez: Whetcomb.

1721, April 9th. Abigail daughter of James Wilder. 16. Zachariah Son of Samuel Page of Turkey Hill. 30. Benjamin Son of Henry Willard. May 28th Nathan Son of James Butler. June 4th. Ebenezer Son of Ebenezer Warner. 11th. Jerahmeel Son of Nath^ll. Wilder. 25. Asa Son of James Willard. July 2. Abigail daughter of Amos Sawyer, and Anna daug: of Joshua Wheeler. 9. Zerviah Daughter of Benj: Houghton. 30. Mariah dau: of John Priest. August, 6th. Josiah Willard's Children Josiah, Abigail & Susannah, & Sam^ll. Rugg's Son Phinehas. 20. Asahel Son of Edward Phelps. 27th, David Son of William Sawyer. Sept. 10th. Asa Son of Edmund Harris, & Joseph Son of Edward Hartwell. 17th. Jonathan Son of John Buss, & Hannah daughter of John Fletcher. 24th. Mary daughter of John Kendal. Octob. 8th Samuel Willard's Sons Samuel & Abijah. Decemb. 3. Joanna daughter of Josiah White, & Mary daughter of Jab: Fairbank Junr. 31. John Gulliver's Daughter Mille.

1721–2, Janu: 7th. Nathanael Son of John Warner. Feb. 25. Bette daughter of Elias Sawyer.

1722, April, 8th. Moses How of Rutland, a member in full Communion with ye Church of Christ in Brookfield had his Child —— baptized. April 15. Sarah daughter of deacon Joseph Wilder. May, 6th, David Son of James Atherton & Silas Son of Sam^ll. Bennett. 13th. Aaron Son of Samuel Warner. 27. Jethro Eams's children Charles, Prudence. June, 10th. Philip Larkin's Son John on his Wives account. July, 1. Tillee Son of Oliver Wilder, & Saul Son of Joshua Houghton. 8. Ralph Son of John Houghton of Stilriver. 15. Jonathan Son of Ebenezer Prescott, & Jeremiah Son of Gabriel Priest. 22. Nahum Son of Samuel Willard. August, 5th. Prudence daughter of Nath^ll. Wilder, & Ezra Son of Benj Houghton Junr. Sept. 30. Lois daughter of Eleazer Houghton. Decemb. 2. Mary daughter of Hezekiah Willard, & Joseph Son of Jos: Fairbank. 9. Nathan Son of John Bennett. 23. Rufus Son of Jonathan Houghton, & Sarah daugh: of Tho: Carter.

1722–3, January, 13. James Son of James Snow. 27. Jonas Son of Richard Wiles. Feb. 3. Josiah Willard's Daughter Lois. 19. Sarah daughter of Edward Broughton & Sybel daughter of Joseph Willard & Joshua Son of Joshua Wheeler. March, 3^d. David Son of Ebenezer Harris. 10. Lieut. John Houghton's daug: Sarah. 17 Susannah daughter of Daniel Houghton.

1723. April, 7th. Prudence daughter of Samuel Carter. 14. Susannah daughter of Capt. Ephraim Wilder, and Mindwell daughter of Benj. Houghton Senr. 21. Lydia daughter of Sam^ll Rugg & Admonition daughter of Thomas Tucker

11 May, 19, 1723, Jonathan Whetcomb & Rachel his Wife owned the Covenant & had y^r Son baptized Jonas. June, 2. Joseph Son of Daniel Rugg. 9. Jotham Son of Josiah White. Aug. 18, Sam^ll. Son of Seth Walker, he & his Wife having owned the Covenant at Billerica. Sept. 1. David Son of Benjamin Clerk. 8. Cyrus Son of Ebenezer Houghton. Octob 13. Simon Son of Jethro Eams. 20 Aaron Son of Nath^ll. Wilder. Nov. 19. Abijah Son of Benjamin Houghton Junr. 24. Susannah daughter of Jeremiah Bearstow. Decemb. 1. Experience daughter of John Kendall 15. Rebeckah daughter of Jonathan Kendal.

1723-4, January, 12th. Prudence, daughter of Jonas Houghton. Feb. 9th. Sarah daughter of Ebenezer Beaman, & Lois, daughter of Jonathan Sawyer. March 8th. Titus Son of Thomas Wilder. March, 22. John Son of Hooker Osgood Junr.

1724, 29. Asaph Son of James Wilder & John Son of Edward Phelps. April 12, 1724. Ruth & Benjamin children of Joseph Glazier. 1724, April, 19, Ephraim & Eunice Sawyer owned the Covenant & were baptized. Peter the Son of Thomas Houghton. 26. Mary daughter of Ephraim Sawyer. May, 17. Hannah daughter of James Willard. June 17. Nathan Heywood & Esther his Wife owned ye Covenant. 21. Lydia daughter of Henry Willard, & Beulah daughter of Benjamin Wheeler. July 26. Mary daughter of Elizabeth Harris vidua, & Relief daughter of Nathan Heywood. August 23. Abigail daughter of William Sawyer. 30. The antient widow Esther Houghton, Abijah Son of Capt Samll, Willard & Ebenezer Son of John Buss. Sept. 6th. Darius Son of Eleazer Houghton. 27. Widow Eliz: Priest's Children John, Daniel, Eunice, Hasadiah, Bettee, Silence. Octob. 4. Mary daughter of Jonathan Whetcomb. 11. Sarah Daughter of John Sawyer. 18th. Eleazer Son of Hezekiah Whetcomb. Nov: 8. Copia daughter of Edward Broughton. 15. Joshua Son of Joshua Osgood, & John Son of Richard Wiles. Decemb. 20. William Son of William Richardson of Woburn the mother owning the Covenant.

1724-5. Feb. 7th. James Atherton's daughter Submitt, also Amos Son of Amos Sawyer. 14. Mary daughter of Benjamin Coree. 28. Rebekah Warner wife of John Warner owning the Covenant was baptized, also Obadiah Son of Hezekiah Townsend also Eunice daughter of Ephraim Sawyer. March 14, Samuel Son of Nathll. Wilder, Achsah daughter of Jonathan Houghton, & Jerushah daughter of Daniel Houghton. 20. Joshua Son of John Fletcher, & Miriam daughter of James Butler.

1725. April 4th. Josiah Son of Mehetabel Houghton vidua, Orpah daughter of Josh: Houghton. 18th. Keziah daughter of Oliver Wilder. May, 23d. John Son of Samll. Rugg. May, 30th. John Son of Ebenezer Harris. June, 6th. Phinehas Son of John Houghton, & John Son of Hooker Osgood Junr. 20. Matthias Son of Philip Larken. Elizabeth daughter of Joshua Wheeler. 27. Mary daughter of Seth Walker. July 4th. Sarah daughter of Joseph Glazier. 25. Michal daughter of Benj: Houghton Senr. & Silence daughter of Josiah White. August 22. Ebenezer Son of Ebenezer Polley upon his owning the Covenant. Sept. 19th. Lemuel Son of Joseph Willard. Nov. 7th. Sarah daughter of Seth Walker. 14. Aaron Son of Aaron Willard. Decemb. 12. Jonas Son of Fairbank Moor. Decemb. 26. Sarah Daughter of Thomas Carter.

1725-6. March 20. Barnard Son of Richard Wiles, also Eunice daughter of Dav. Osgood he & his Wife owning the Covenant.

1726, April, 3d. Hannah daughter of Jonathan Kendal. 10. Ephraim Son of Josh: Osgood. May 1st, Dorothy daughter of John Sawyer. 29. Olive daughter of Jonath. Sawyer. June, 5th. Ruth daughter of Henry Willard, Abigail daughter of James Willard, & Abraham Son of Abraham Willard. 12. Patience daughter of James Butler. 19th. Jotham Son of John Bennett. 26. Abiathar Son of Gershom Houghton. July, 3d. Josiah Son of Josiah Johnson he having owned the Covenant & his Wife being a member of Mr Barnard's Church in Andover. 10th. Priscilla daughter of Ebenezer Beaman & Joanna daughter of Thomas Houghton. 17. Dorothy daughter of Jonathan Whetcomb. 24. William Son of Thomas Tucker, & Cyrus Son of Joseph Fairbank. Sept. 4. Piercis daughter of Jonas Houghton. Octob. 2d. Zenas Son of Benj: Wheeler. 9th. Moses Son of John Warner. 23. Jacob Houghton & his Wife owned ye Covenant & had yr Son baptized Abraham. Nov. 6th Elizabeth daughter of James Wilder, & Abigail daughter of Jonathan Houghton Junr. Decemb. 11. Martha Houghton wife of Israel Houghton owned ye Covenant & was baptized, & yr children Israel, Benjamin, & Phinehas, also Miriam daughter of Eleazer Houghton. 18. Joseph, Benjamin, John & Peter Atherton owning ye Cov: were baptized, also Ephraim Son of Hez: Willard, Ebenz: Son of Edw: Phelps, & Prudence daughter of Elias Sawyer.

12 1726. Decemb. 25 Relief, daughter of Benjamin Houghton Junr.
1726-7, Janu: 15th. Joseph & John Wheelock owning ye Covenant were baptized.
29, Josiah Son of Sam^ll. Carter, & Patience daughter of Ebenz: Broughton
& Olive daughter of Joseph Wheelock.   Feb. 19th. Molle daughter of
Daniel Houghton.   March, 12, Elias Son of Nathanael Wilder.
1727, April, 16th. Joseph Atherton's children Oliver & Mary.   May, 7th. Lydia
daughter of Edward Phelps.   21. Dinah daughter of Benj: Houghton
Sen.   28th. Levi, Son of Capt. Sam^ll. Willard.   June. 4th. Deborah
daug: of Amos Sawyer.   11. John Son of John Houghton.   18. Ephraim Wheeler & wife owning ye Cov: had &c. Glazier, Ruth, Azubah; also
Elizabeth daug: of Joseph Atherton.   25. Prudence daug: of James Atherton, Hannah daughter of Sam^ll. Rugg, & Vashti dau: of Joshua Houghton.   July, 2. Tamar daughter of Oliver Wilder, & Azubah dau: of Sam^ll.
Bennett Junr.   16. Katharine daughter of Ephraim Sawyer.   30. Sarah
dau: of Jon: Sawyer.   August, 6. Ephah daughter of Jonathan Houghton.
Sept. 3, Elizabeth daugh: of Jabez Fairbanks Junr. Joseph Moor & his
Wife owned ye Covenant and had &c Lucey.   24. Rebekah daugh: of J.
& P. Prentice & Joseph Son of Ephraim Wheeler.   Octob. 1, Peter Son
of Philip Larken, & Timothy Son of Jacob Houghton Junr.   29. Simon
Son of Aaron Willard.   Nov. 5. Thomas Son of Hezekiah Townsend.
12. Phinehas Son of Tho: Carter, & Mary daughter of William Richardson
of Woburn.   Decemb. 10th. Steven Houghton & Henry Houghton Junr.
& yr wives owned the Cov: & had yr children baptized. Abigail daug: of
Steven & Asa Son of Henry Houghton.   24th. Oliver Son of Joseph
Wheelock.
1727-8, January 14.   Ezra Sawyer & his Wife owned ye Covenant and had yr
Daughter Baptized Prudence, also Uriah Holt & his Wife owned ye Covenant at ye same time.   21. Joseph Wilson & his Wife owned ye Covenant
& had yr Son bapt: Joseph.   28. Ruth daughter of Joshua Osgood.   Feb.
4th. Hannah Houghton owning ye Covenant was baptized.   11 David Son
of Abraham Willard.   March, 10. Hannah ye Daughter of John Wright,
father & mother having owned the Covenant at Mr Barnard's in Andover.
17th. Keziah Daughter of Hooker Osgood Junr.   24th. Fairbank Moor
upon his owning of the Covenant, also ye children of Sarah Pratt upon her
doing so also.   Dennis Joseph & Abijah.   Timothy Son of Timothy Knox,
he Submitting to Discipline, also Margarett daught: of William McAllister
upon his owning ye Covenant, also Sarah dau: of Uriah Holt.
1728, April, 1st. Silence daughter of James Houghton Junr. upon his Wives account, she having owned ye Covenant at Concord & submitted to Discipline
with us.   7. John Son of James Butler, & Experience daughter of James
Willard.   21. Silent Son of Richard Wiles. Beckee daug: of Jonathan
Whetcomb.   28. Ruth daughter of John Fletcher.   May, 5. Jonas Son
of Jonas Houghton & Dinah daughter of Hezekiah Whetcomb, & Tamar
daughter of Nath^ll. Hudson.   12. Sarah Sanders owned ye Covenant &
was baptized.   June, 9th. Joseph Son of Henry Houghton Junr.   23. Joseph
Son of Joseph Willard.   July, 7th. Bettee daughter of Seth Walker.

Notandum. August, 4th, 1715. Att a Church meeting att ye house of John
Prentice Captain Peter Joslin & Joseph Wilder were chosen to ye Deacon's office
in the Church of Christ in Lancaster & accepted of said office.

13   July 21, 1728, Baptized Benjamin Houghton Junior's Son Elijah, also David
& Eunice Osgood's Daughter Dorothy.   Aug: 11 Ebenezer Beaman's
twins Ebenezer & Patience, also John Bennett's Son Elisha.   18. Stephen
Houghton's Son Ebenezer.   25. Joshua Wheeler's Daughter Thankful,
& Ezra Sawyer's Daughter Elizabeth.   Also the Widdow Whites children,
Her eldest Daughter Eunice owned ye Covenant, the Rest on her own
Account, viz: John Bette Dorothy Thomas Lois Mary Nathanael.   September, 1, 1728, Fairbank Moor's Son Fairbank, also Jonas Wilder's Children, Joseph & Hannah.   8th. Israel Houghton's Daughter Martha.   15th.
Daniel Rugg's Daughter Sarah, the same time Joshua Wheeler's Wife
owned the Covenant.   22. Thomas Tucker's Daughter, Mary, also Robert
Waite's Son John. Both he and his Wife having in Schadoway in Ireland

made an open profession of Religion and both Submitting to Discipline with us. 29th, Benj: Atherton Junr. owned the Covenant & was Baptized. October, 6th. 1728. Josiah Wilder & Prudence his Wife owned the Covenant. She was Baptized and their two Sons Abner & Rufus. Nov. 10th. Eben: Polley's Son Joseph & John Sawyer's Son John. 17th. Joseph Moor's Son Jacob. 24. Daniel Houghton's Daughter Experience. Decemb. 29th, 1728. Barnard Tewells owned the Covenant and was baptized, also the Son of Joseph Wilson, Solomon.

Febr: 23, 1728-9. The Daughter of Peter Atherton, Experience, he having owned the Covenant, also the Son of Francis Kendal of Woburn, she being with it in Town and Mr Fox being sick, the mother of it a member in full Communion with ye Church in Woburn. March, 9th. Joseph Fairbank's Daughter Mary. 23. Jonathan Houghton's Daughter Zeresh. April, 13. Benj: Osgood's Daughter Hannah. 20th. Ephraim Sawyer's Son Ephraim. May, 11, 1729. Thomas Houghton's Junr. Daughter Hannah. 25th. Deacon White's Son John, Thomas Houghton's Senr. Daughter Esther, Jonas Wilder's Daughter Priscilla. June, 1st. 1729. Jonathan Sawyer's Son Manasseh. 8th. William Pollard's Son John. 15th. Daniel Albert & his Wife owned the Covenant and had yr Daughter Baptized Mary. 29th. Benj: Houghton's Senr. Daughter Keziah. July 20th. Joshua Houghton's Son Solomon; Benj: Atherton's Son, Jonathan, & Henry Willard's Junr. Children, Henry, & Abigail. July 27th, 1729. John Phillip's Son Ethan, he having owned the Covenant at Cambridge and Submitting to Discipline with us. August 3, 1729. Samll. Wright & Ruth his Wife owned the Covenant, & she was Baptized. Aug: 31. Jonathan Kendall's daughter Mary. Henry Houghton's Junr. Son Aretas, Jonathan Houghton's Junr. Ebenezer. Samll. Wright's Daughter, Ruth. Sept. 28th. My Son John Prentice's Son, John. Octob. 26. Joseph Atherton's Son, Joseph, & James Houghton Junr. Son Nathanael. Nov. 2d. Ebenezer Beaman's Son Thomas, Josiah Pratt's Son William. Nov. 9th, 1729. Jonathan Wheelock owned the Covenant & was Baptized. Nov. 23. James Houghton's Children Sarah Bette James, also Joseph Robbins's Daughter Susanna, father & mother members of the Chh at Littleton. Decemb. 7th, 1729. Nathll. Hudson's Son Benaiah, Ephr: Wheeler's Daughter Sarah. 21st. William Glazier owned the Covenant and had his Son baptized William. 28th. Joshua Osgood's Daughter, Sarah.

January, 25th. 1729-30. Capt. Samll. Willard's Son Joshua, the same Day Samll. Carter Junr. owned the Covenant & had his Children baptized viz: Millecent, Lucey, Dorothy. Feb. 15, 1729-30. Uria Holt's Son Uriah. 22. Edward Phelps' Son Edward. March 1st, 1729-30. Aaron Willard's Daughter Mary. 22d. John Houghton's Son David, Seth Walker's Daugh: Lucey, Israel Houghton's Daugh: Mary.

April, 12th, 1730. Joseph Wheelock's Son, Joseph. April, 19. Abraham Willard's Daughter Mary. 26th. James Butler's Son, Asaph, also Jonathan Whetcomb's Son David. May, 10th. Aaron Osgood's Daughter Lois the mother having owned the Covenant. 17th. Benj: Houghton's Junr. Daughter Parnee, also Jonathan Rugg's Son Oliver. May 31, 1730. Samuel the Son of William & Ellinor White who owned the Covenant in Dunbo [Drumbo?] in Ireland, the man Subjected himself to Discipline with us. June 9th, 1730, Phinehas ye Son of Oliver & Mary Wilder. Jacob ye Son of Jacob Houghton Junr. 14th. The Son of William & Mary Richardson, James, the Daughter of Jethro Eams & his Wife Abigail. July 19th. Thomas Fairbank & his Wife owned the Covenant & had yr Son Baptized Samuel. 26. Robert Phelps' Son William & Henry Willard Junr. Daughter, Annis. August, 23, 1730. Shubael Bayley owned the Covenant & had his Son Baptized Joseph. The Son of John Johnson Junr also, Nathanael, on ye mother's account she being a member of the Chh of Christ in Stow. August 30th. 1730. Jabez Fairbank Junr. Daughter Dinah, & Timothy Knox's Son David. Sept. 6th. Amos Knight's Children, viz: Jonathan & Elizabeth, also the same Day Ephraim Houghton & Sarah his Wife owned the Covenant and had yr children Baptized viz. Ephraim & Joseph. Sept. 20th, 1730. James Willard's Daughter Susanna, & Ezra Sawyer's Son Ezra.

Sept. 27th. John Divol & his Wife owned the Covenant & had yr Son Baptized John. Richard Wiles' Daughter Susanna. Octob. 25th. Jonathan Powers owned the Covenant & was Baptized. Nov. 1st: 1730. William Whetcomb & Hephzibah his Wife owned the Covenant & had yt Daughter Baptized, Mary. 8. Joseph Wilson's Son William. 20, Moses the Son of John & Sarah Sawyer, was baptized at ye house of John Sawyer, the child not being capable of being brought out by Reason of a grievous excressence which it was born with upon its belly, and its life being threatened hereby. Several of the members of ye Church were present at ye house at its Baptism. Decemb. 6th. 1730, Baptized Samll. Sawyer & his Daughter Mary, both he & his Wife owning the Covenant. Also, Asa, Son of Josiah Wilder, & Joseph Son of Joshua Church, & John Son of William McAllister, and Elizabeth Daughter of Robert Bratten & Elizabeth his Wife member of a Church of Christ in Fermont in Ireland in ye Countey of Tyrone, the father Submitting to Discipline with us. 20. Nathanael Wilder Junr. & his Wife owned ye Covenant she was baptized, and Nathanael yr Son.
January, 3, 1730-1, Tillee Son of Joseph Moor, the same time Oliver Moor & Abigail his Wife owned the Covenant and had yr Son Baptized Abijah, also Azubah the Daughter of Peter Atherton. 17. Amos Knight's Son Ebenezer, & Jonas Cuttin's Son Absalom he having owned ye Covenant at Mr Warham Williams' Church in Watertown and Submitting to Discipline wth us. 24th. Amee the Daughter of Joseph Willard. Feb. 14. James Houghton's Son Edward, and John Divoll's Phinehas. 28. Fairbank Moor's Son, William, & Robert Whites Daughter Martha. March, 21, 1730-1. Hezekiah Willard's Daughter Elizabeth & John Atherton's Daughter Phebe. 28. Jane Rogers owned the Covenant and was baptized.
April, 11, 1731, Daniel, Son of Daniel Albert. 18. Azubah Daughter of David and Eunice Osgood. 25. Mary the Daughter of Samuel Carter Junr. May 2d. Elisha, Son of Deacon Josiah White. 23. Mercy Daughter of Samuel Wright. June, 6th. 1731, Baptized John ye Son of Thomas Fairbank. 13. Elizabeth Daughter of Henry Houghton Junr. 27th. William Son of William Pollard, & Hannah daughter of Joseph Atherton. July 11th. 1731. Philemon Son of Benj: Houghton Junr. & Annes daughter of Joshua & Annes Church. August 1st. 1731. John Son of Benj: Harris the mother a member of the Chh of Christ in Shrewsbury, also Lydia the Daughter of Matthew Patrick August, 15, 1731, Phillip Larken's Son William, Israel Houghton's Daughter, Lois. Sept. 5th. 1731. Samuel Son of John & Anna Prentice. 12th. Relief Daughter of Nathll. & Mary Wilder. 19. Daniel Son of Daniel Houghton. 26. Ephah Daughter of Jonathan Houghton. Octob. 10th. 1731. Lydia Daughter of Joseph Fairbank, William Son of Nathanael Hudson. Mary Daughter of Jonathan Houghton Junr. & Benjamin Son of Benjamin Osgood. Nov. 7th 1731. Amos, Son of Amos Atherton, the mother a member of the Church. 28 Bette, the Daughter of Benjamin Atherton. Decemb. 12. Joseph & Hannah Woods owned the Covenant & had their Son Baptized. His name, Joseph. Decemb. 19, 1731, Prudence the Daughter of Hooker Osgood Junr. Also Thomas, the Son of Thomas Houghton of Stilriver, and Thomas the Son of Thomas & Abigail Wright, they owning the Covenant at ye same time. 26. Joseph the Son of Ephraim & Sarah Houghton, also, Elias the Son of Elijah Whetney.
January, 2d, 1731-2, Margaret the Daughter of Joseph Robbins. 16th. Abel, Son of Samuel & Elizabeth Willard; also Mary, Daughter of Ebenezer & Dorcas Polley. 23 Abishai, Son of Robert Phelps. February, 13. Amity the Daughter of James Houghton Junr. & his Wife. 20. Phinehas Son of Joseph Wheelock, Abigail daughter of Joseph Whetcomb, and Abigail daughter of Thomas Wright. 27. John Son of Jonas Houghton, & Lydia Daughter of Jonathan Kendal. March 12, 1731-2, Jacob Son of Jonathan & Hannah Powers.
April, 9th. 1732, Nathaniel Son of Aaron Willard, & Aaron Son of Aaron Osgood. 23. Russel Son of Daniel Knight, & Dorothy Daughter of Thomas Houghton yt lives towards Lunenburgh. 30th. Joseph, Son of Joseph Whetcomb. May, 14, 1732. Elisabeth daughter of Joseph Bennett, the mother of the
19

16 child a member of Mr Walter's Chh. in Roxbury. May, 21st, 1732. Tiras, Son of Joshua & Elisabeth Houghton also Hannah, Daughter of Shubael Bayley. 28. Baptized Major Samuel Willard's Negro Caesar, and my own viz, Dorchester, upon their owning to the Covenant. June 25th. 1732. Lydia, Daughter of Seth Phillips, also Levi Son of Oliver Moor. July, 2d. John Moor Junr. & Susannah his Wife owned the Covenant. He was Baptized, and yr children also viz: Samuel Thomas & Abigail also Mr John Martin's Daughter Mary, his Wife being a member in full Communion in the Church of Christ in Cambridge, also Henry Willard Junr's Son Thomas. 30. David Whetcomb & Bette his Wife owned the Covenant & had their Son John Baptized. August, 6th 1732. Jonathan Sawyer's Daughter Lois, & Jabez Fairbank Junr's Daughter Beulah. 13. Mary, Daughter of Ephraim Wheeler, also John Snow's Children viz. Abigail, Mary, Martha. 27th, Joshua Osgood's Son William. Sept. 3d, Baptized with ye Consent of the Brethren taken ye same Day at noon, Jonas the Son of Jonas Wilder, on his Deceased mother's account, who was a member in full Communion. His Grandfather John Wilder who hath ye Care of him promising by divine Help (to ye Church) to give it a Religious Education so long as God in his Providence should give him opportunity herefor. Octob. 1, 1732. Reuben Rugg & his Wife owned the Covenant and had yr Daughter Martha baptized. 22d. Azubah the Daughter of Samuel Sawyer. Nov. 5, 1732. Nahum, Son of Benjamen Houghton Junr. 12th. Hasadiah Moor owned the Covenant and was Baptized, and her child also whose name is Elisabeth. Baptized also at the same time Mary Daughter of Jacob Houghton Junr. Also Abner, Son of Joseph Wilson. 26. Hezekiah Whetcomb & his Wife owned the Covenant and had their Son John baptized, at the same time, Oliver Son of Jonathan Whetcomb. Decemb. 10, 1732. Elisabeth the Daughter of Nathll. Hutson. 31st. Jonathan the Son of Thomas Fairbank. January 14th. 1732-3, Eunice Sawyer Daughter of Bezaleel Sawyer owned the Covenant & was baptized, at ye same time Benjamin the Son of Benj: Houghton Senr. & Martha Daughter of Jonas & Thankful Fairbank. 21st. Phinehas Son of Edward Phelps, & Mary daughter of Amos Knight. February 4th, 1732-3, Ephraim Son of Joseph Moor. March, 11th. Mary Daughter of Timothy Knox, & Katharine Daughter of William White. 18. Margaret, Daughter of Richard Wiles.
April, 1, 1733, David the Son of Amos Atherton. April 8th. 1733. Baptized **17** the following Children viz: Eunice Daughter of Samll. Carter Junr. Rebeckah Daughter of Ezra & Phebe Sawyer. also Isaac the Son of James White upon his owning of the Covenant on sd Day. 15, Martha daughter of Josiah Wilder. Monday April 23, 1733. then Baptized at the house of John Sawyer, Nathll. Son of said Sawyer at the Desire of the Parents, it being under threatening Circumstances by reason of a sore mouth, Deacon Joslin, Nathll. Sawyer and some others present, and they not having opportunity to bring it out to be baptized publickly, by reason of its being taken ill so soon after its birth. It died third Day following. 29. Lois Daughter of Capt. Oliver Wilder. May 6th. 1733. Mary, Daughter of Nathll. Wilder Junr. & Lydia, Daughter of Reuben Rugg. 20th. Joshua, Son of Uriah Holt. June 3d. 1733. Robert, Son of Robert White. 10th. Baptized Jonathan the Son of Jonathan White, Elisabeth Daughter of William Richardson, Henry Son of Daniel Albert, & Abigail Daughter of Henry Houghton Junr. 24th, Jacob Son of Matthew Patrick. July, 15th, 1733. Susannah Daughter of John Moor. 22d. Sarah, Daughter of Ebenr. Dakin a member in full Communion with Mr Loring's Church in Sudbury. August, 5th. Joseph Sawyer Junr. & his Wife owned the Covenant and had their Son Aaron baptized. 19th, Dinah, daughter of Jonas Cuttin, Joseph Son of Israel Houghton & John, Son of John Johnson Junr. 26. Elijah, Son of Joseph & Hannah Wood. Sept. 16. Benjamen, the Son of Fairbank Moor. 23, Levina, Daughter of Jonathan Houghton Junr, & Benjamen Son of Benj. Harris. Octob. 14th. 1733. Keziah, Daughter of John Snow. 21st David, Son of Robert & Elizabeth Bratten. Nov. 11, Susannah Daughter of James Houghton Senr., ye same day ye Brethren manifested their Willingness that Mary Bruce a member in full Communion

with us should, according to her desire be Recommended to Communion with yᵉ Church of Christ in Marlborough. 25. Amos, Son of Amos & Abigail Sawyer. Decemb. 2ᵈ, 1733. Tillee, Son of Josiah & Dorothy Richardson. 16. Tamar, Daughter of Gershom & Elisabeth Houghton. January 20ᵗʰ, 1733-4, Dinah daughter of Hooker Osgood Junr., Jonathan Son of Shubael Bayley, & Eunice Daughter of Benj: Atherton. January, 27,
18 1733-4, Jonas, Son of William Pollard, and Joseph, Son of John Beaman Junr. The father owned yᵉ Covenant, & Susanna the mother was admitted to full Communion by a Letter of Recommendation from Weston church to which she belonged; also, Mary the Daughter of Thomas Wilder Junr, & Mary his Wife, who at the same time owned yᵉ Covenant in order to it. Febr. 3ᵈ. James the Son of James Houghton Junr. Nathˡˡ. Son of Nathaniel Hudson, & Eunice, daughter of David Whetcomb. March 10ᵗʰ, 1733-4, Joel, Son of Robert & Dorothy Phelps. 17ᵗʰ. Moses Son of Joseph Sawyer Junr. 24ᵗʰ. Mary the Daughter of Joseph Bennet, the mother being a member of Mr Walter's Church in Roxbury. 31ˢᵗ. Israel Son of Doctor Daniel Greenleaf, he having owned the Covenant & his Wife a member in full Communion with the Church of Christ at Hingham, also, Sarah, the Daughter of Henry Houghton upon her owning the Covenant.
April, 7ᵗʰ, 1734, Dorcas Polley the Wife of Ebenʳ. Polley upon her owning of the Covenant. Also, Amos, Son of Jonathan Powers, & Isaac, Son of William White. 14. Thomas, yᵉ Son of Aaron Osgood. 21. Ephraim, Son of Ephraim & Anna Wilder, also, Joseph, Son of Joseph & Deborah Wilder. May 5, 1734. Ruth Daughter of Benj: & Ruth Houghton. 19. Israel, Son of Oliver Moor. June 2ᵈ. Oliver, Son of that Thomas Houghton who Lives nigh to Lunenburgh. 9. William, Son of Ephraim Houghton, Elisabeth Daughter of Josiah Richardson & Lucey, Daughter of John Joslin. 16. David, Son of David & Eunice Osgood, & Thankful, Daughter of William Whetcomb. 23. Anna, Daughter of John & Anna Prentice, also, Rebeckah Daughter of Ephraim Wheeler. 30. Josiah, Son of Jonas Fairbank, also Olive, Daughter of Jabez Beaman & his Wife upon their owning the Covenant the same Day. July, 21. John, Son of Joseph Wheelock. 28. Sylvanus, Son of Aholiab Sawyer. August, 4ᵗʰ. Rebeckah, Daughter of Joshua & Rebeckah Phelps. 11ᵗʰ. Elisabeth, the Daughter of Ebenr. Dakin. A member of Mr Loring's Church in Sudbury. 18. Luke, Son of James Richardson, yᵉ mother a member of yᵉ Chh in Woburn. Sept. 8, 1734. Ephraim, Son of Nathˡˡ. & Experience Butler.

19

Att a Chh meeting (duely warned) att the house of Mr John Beaman January, 30ᵗʰ, 1728-9, * * * the following Brethren were chosen Deacons viz: Josiah White & James Wilder, who accepted in the Presence of the Brethren.

20 Aug: 2ᵈ, 1730. Jane Macmullin a member of yᵉ Church of Christ in Dorsenbridge in the County of Londonderry in Ireland, Mr Hugh Wallis Pastor, Desiring Liberty to partake with yᵉ Church in this place whilst her Stay should be in the town in yᵉ ordinance of yᵉ Lord's Supper, she having no Testimonials to shew. It was voted yᵗ in Case she Submitted to Discipline and engaged to attend yᵉ same when it was to be attended & she able to do so, her Desire should be gratified, which she did accordingly before the Church before yᵉ Administration of yᵉ ordinance of yᵉ Lord's Supper.

25 Nov. 14, 1734. Att a Church meeting at the house of John Houghton Esqr. Alexander Scott and his Wife upon the reading of their Testimonial from the Pastor of a Church in Ireland, were allowed by the Brethren present the Priviledge of occasional Communion with us in all ordinances upon their Submitting to Discipline and walking orderly whilst their abode shall be among us.

30 September, 22ᵈ, 1734, David How and Mary his Wife owned the Covenant, upon it she was baptized, also Artemas their Son, at the same time, Jacob, Son of John & Bathsheba Bennett, also John & Sarah Sawyer's twins, Joanna & Damaris. Nov. 3, 1734. Moses Chandler & his Wife owned yᵉ Covenant and had their children baptized, named as followeth : Hannah, Sanborn, Elenor, Eliphalet, Moses, Anna. 24. Sarah, the Daughter of Josiah & Sarah Pratt. Decemb: 8th. Elizabeth, Daughter of Aaron Willard and Mary Daughter of Reuben Rugg. 15th. Oliver, Son of Benj: Osgood. January, 5th, 1734-5, Benj: Harris upon his owning the Covenant. Febr: 9th. Josiah, Son of Thomas Tucker, Dinah daughter of Samll. Carter Junr. & Elizabeth, Daughter of John Beaman Junr. 16. Prudence, the Daughter of Israel & —— Houghton. March, 2d. Elisabeth the Daughter of Joseph Wilson & Rebeckah the Daughter of Joseph Moor. April, 13, 1735. Nathanael, Son of Jonathan Rugg. 20th Ruth, Daughter of Samll. Sawyer, and Keziah Daughter of Ezra Sawyer. May 4th, 1735. Sarah, Daughter of Thomas Wilder Junr. & Mary his Wife. 18th. Levi, Son of Joseph & Hannah Wood. June 8th. William Son of Alexander McBride, a member of a Church in Ireland of which Mr Clark now minister in Nutfield was the Pastor, he hath had by vertue of his Testimonials, the Priviledge of the Special Ordinances of Christ at Concord. The same time baptized Jane, the Daughter of William White. 15. Hiram, Son of Joshua Houghton. 22. Mindwell, the Daughter of Jonathan & Mary Bigelow, the father having owned the Covenant at Weston & the mother a member in full Communion with the Church there.

* * * * *

31 July 6th. 1735, Elisabeth Russel owned the Covenant & was baptized. 13. Margaret Kili owned the Covenant & was baptized, at the same time, Lucey Daughter of Martha Snow. 20. Hephzibah, Daughter of Jabez Fairbank Junr. 27. Hezekiah, Son of Hezekiah Whetcomb. Aug: 17th, 1735. John, Son of John Snow, Deliverance Daughter of Thomas Ross, & Esther, Daughter of Jonathan & Esther White. 24. Magdalen Laggett the Wife of Thomas Laggett owned the Covenant in order to the baptism of her Children. 31. Thomas, & Elisabeth the children of Thomas & Magdalen Laggett, also Abigail the Daughter of Benjamin Houghton. Sept. 14 Piercis the Daughter of Benja. Harris. 21. Caroline the Daughter of Jonathan Houghton Junr., and John the Son of John Joslin.

* * *

Octob. 12. Hannah Daughter of Uriah Holt, & Benjamin, Son of Joseph Whetcomb. 19th. Stephen, Son of Doctor Greenleaf, & Lucey Daughter of Amos & —— Atherton. 26. Lydia Gibbs the wife of Samll. Gibbs upon her owning the Covenant was baptized, and their two Sons also, Elijah & Amasa. The man had before owned the Covenant at Framingham, at the same time baptized also Josiah the Son of James Wilder Junr. Katharine the Daughter of Ephraim Wilder Junr., Sarah the Daughter of William Willard, the mother a member of the Chh in Stow. Nov. 2d. David Son of Richard Wiles, & Lemuel Son of Benj. Houghton Junr. 9th, Capt. William Richardson's Daughter, Lucretia, & Elisabeth the Daughter of John Phillips. 16th. Edmond, Son of Phillip & Mary Larken. 23. Josiah, Son of Josiah Wilder. 30. Hooker, Son of Hooker Osgood Junr. Decemb. 4, 1735. Prudence, the Daughter of David Whetcomb. 1735-6, January, 18th. Kate, the Daughter of James Houghton Junr. Feb. 8 Elijah, Son of Jonas Fairbank, and Bridget Daughter of Jonathan Bayley, the mother a member in full Communion wth a Chh in Rowley.

* * * * *

33 ADMITTED TO FULL COMMUNION.

March 2d. 1734-5, Daniel Power. May 11, 1735, Josiah Swan. Aug: 24th 1735, Elisabeth Prentice. August 31, Abigail Beaman Wife of John Beaman Secundus. Nov. 2, 1735, Ann Barbar wife of Alexander Barbar allowed the Priviledge of Communion in ye ordinance of ye Lord's Supper with us whilst her stay is in Town by vote of the Brethren.

Febr. 15, 1735-6. Benjamin Ballard upon a recommendation from the South Church in Andover, Also Martha Harris, Daughter of ye widow Elisabeth Harris, and Mary Beaman Daughter of John Beaman Junr.

April, 11, 1736. Ruth Ballard the wife of Benj: Ballard. May 9th. Thankful Whetcomb, the wife of Simon Whetcomb. June 6th, 1736. Sarah & Dorothy Prentice. 13. David Nelson upon a Letter of Recommendation from the

Church of Christ in Topsfield, to which he stood related. July 18th. David Whetcomb & Bette his Wife. August, 29th, 1736. Hephzibah Wilson Wife of Jonathan Wilson. Sept. 19th, 1736. Nathaniel Wilson & Eunice his Wife. Octob. 31. Hannah Knight Wife of Amos Knight. Nov. 9th. Mary Houghton Wife of Jacob Houghton Junr. 14. Abigail Wilder Daughter of Deacon James Wilder. Decemb. 19th. Jonathan Osgood and his Wife.

January, 9th, 1736-7. Damaris Carter Wife of Jonathan Carter & Lois White, Wife of John White. 16. Benjn: Houghton Junr. & Ruth Houghton his Wife, and Edward Robbins. March 13th, 1736-7. David Wilder.

June, 19th, 1737. Joshua Fairbank, John Buss, Dinah Beaman wife of Jabez Beaman, Mary Sawyer wife of Abner Sawyer & Prudence Prentice. July, 3d, 1737. Abigail Green, wife of Peter Green. August 14th, 1737. Gardner Wilder and Mary his Wife. Octob. 23d. Thankful Fairbank, Wife of Jonathan Fairbank, Sarah Harris, Daughter of Ebenr. Harris & Anna Harris, Daughter of the Widow Elisabeth Harris. December 25th, 1737, William Goss.

February 5th, Caleb Wilder & Abigail his Wife, also Josiah Sawyer Son of William Sawyer.

34 April 2d. 1738. Admitted to full Communion Daniel Albert, also Bathsheba Robbins wife of Edward Robbins. June 11th, 1738. Annah Knight, Wife of Daniel Knight. July 30th. Nathaniel Butler. Sept. 24th, 1738, John Carter & Abigail his Wife.

March 18th, 1738-9. Robert Phelps.

April 15, 1739. Reuben Rugg & Lydia his Wife. 22d. Thomas Fairbank & Dorothy his Wife. May, 20th, Hephzibah Houghton, Wife of John Houghton Junr., also Samuel & Annah Bayley his Wife upon a Letter of Recommendation from the Church of Christ in Dudley. July 8th. Israel Houghton & Josiah Richardson. 29th. Abigail Ross wife of James Ross. August, 5th, 1739. The Brethren voted yr Consent to ye Desire of Damaris Wilder Wife of Nathaniel Wilder to be Recommended to the Communion of the Chh of Christ in Nichewaug. December 9th. 1739. Mary Sawyer Wife of Phinehas Sawyer. 30. Beulah Carter, Wife of Oliver Carter.

*   *   *   *   *   *

February, 17th, 1739-40, Ebenezer Beaman and vid: Tabitha Sawyer.

April 27th, 1740. Thomas Burpee & Mary his Wife, upon Recommendation from the Second Chh of Christ in Rowley. June 1st, 1740. Jonathan Bayley. 8. Josiah Wilder. August 21, 1740. At a Church meeting at my House: the Brethren present upon hearing the Case of old father Dunsmore a member of ye Church in Ireland of wch Mr Matthew Clark was ye pastor Discovered their Willingness that he should (according to his Desire & upon his Submitting himself to Discipline) have his Priviledge of holding Communion with us in the ordinance of the Lord's Supper.

April, 5th, 1741. Mr Josiah Brown upon a Letter of Recommendation from the Chh of Christ in Lexington. 12. Thomas White and Sarah his Wife. July, 12th, 1741. Mary Houghton Daughter of John Houghton. August, 30th, Mary Moor wife of Isaac Moor of Bolton, and Mary Johnson Sept. 6th, 1741. Hephzibah Kendal widow. 27th. Andrew Wilder. Nov. 1st, 1741. Elizabeth Wilder, Wife of Andrew Wilder.

January 17th, 1741-2. John Herbert & Sarah Wilder Wife of Oliver Wilder Junr. Feby. 28 1741-2. Margaret Bowers, wife of John Bowers.

July 25th, 1742. Rachel Wilder Daughter of Thomas Wilder. Aug: 1st. Ruth Sawyer Wife of Elisha Sawyer. Sept. 12 1742. Thankful Haskal wife of Jer. Haskal.

Octob. 1st, 1742. Att a meeting of the Brethren of ye Chh at the Pastor's House according to his Desire, signified the Sabbath before to Consider Respecting an Addition to ye Number of Deacons &c. 1st Proposed by ye Pastor whether they would now endeavour an Addition to ye Number of Deacons. Voted in the Affirmative. 2ly. Whether they would choose two more. Voted also in the Affirmative. Then by Prayer sought Direction of God in the choice. After this the Brethren brought in yr written votes and upon Counting of them it appeared that Hooker Osgood Junr. and Israel Houghton were the men chosen.   *   *   *   *   *

35 February 29th, 1735-6, John Johnson Junr. owned the Covenant and was baptized. March, 7th, 1735-6, Uriah the Son of Oliver Moor, and Mary ye Daughter of Benjamin Ballard. The same Day the Brethren shewed yr Willingness by ye uplifted hand that our Brother John Warner and his Wife also at yr Desire should be recommended to communion with the Chh of Christ in Harvard. 21. Robert Powers & his Wife owned the Covenant and their Daughter, Named Ruth. was Baptized. 28. Asahel Son of Joshua Osgood, and Abner Son of Joseph Wheelock. April 4th. 1736, Solomon, Son of Nathll. Hudson, and Dorothy Daughter of John Johnson Junr. 11th, Abigail, the Daughter of Daniel Albert. 18. Sarah Daughter of Joseph Sawyer Junr. May, 2d. Josiah Son of Josiah & Sarah Pratt. 9th, Moses, Son of Capt. Oliver Wilder. Relief Daughter of William Whetcomb. Elisabeth, Daughter of Joshua Phelps, & Lydia, Daughter of John Glazier, upon his & his Wives owning of the Covenant. 16. Lois, Daughter of William Pollard, and Mary, Daughter of Simon Whetcomb. 30th, Sarah Daughter of Joseph Bennett & Elisabeth daughter of Jonathan Powers. June 6th. 1736. John, Son of James Richardson & Robert Son of Robert Powers. 13. Eunice, Daughter of Aaron Osgood, July, 4th. Relief Daughter of Benj; Atherton. 11th. Mary, Daughter of David Osgood. August 8th. Thomas, Son of John Bennett. 22d. Susanna, Daughter of Josiah Richardson. 29th. Benjamin, Son of John Sawyer also Jonathan & Lois, Son & Daughter of Jonathan & Hephzibah Wilson. Sept. 5, 1736. The Brethren present manifested their Willingness that Mr Ebenr. Flagg should be Dismist & Recommended to ye Communion of the Chh of Christ in Chester. 19. Eunice Daughter of Hezekiah Snow, and Rhoda, Daughter of Nathaniel & Eunice Wilson, also, Nathaniel & Elizabeth children of Nathll. Carter upon his & his Wife's owning of ye Covenant. Octob. 3d, 1736. Abner, Son of John Moor, Junr. also Prudence, Daughter of Nathaniel Butler. 10. Thomas, Son of Thomas Fairbank. 17. Elijah Son of John Beaman Junr. & Keziah daughter of Simon Whetcomb. 31. Mariah Daughter of Thomas Hough-
36 ton of Harvard. Nov. 7th. 1736. Hannah, ye Daughter of Amos Knight Junr. & Hannah his wife. 14th. Ezra Son of Jabez Beaman. 21. Samuel, Son of Nathll. Hastings and his Wife upon their owning the Covenant the same Day. 28. Deborah, Daughter of Joseph & Deborah Wilder. Decemb. 19th. Jonathan, Son of Jonathan Osgood. 26. Phinehas, Son of Phinehas Willard the mother a member in full Communion. January, 2d. 1736-7. Dorothy, Daughter of Robert Phelps, ye mother in full Communion. 9th. Tillee, Son of John White, ye mother a member in full Communion. 30th. Paul, Son of Fairbank Moor. Feb. 13. Eunice, Daughter of Israel Houghton. 27. Peter Son of Aaron Willard. March 13th. 1736-7. Levi, Son of James Houghton. 20th. Thomas, son of Thomas Ross. 27th. Baptized at the house of Jonathan Osgood the place of meeting, Paul, Son of Samuel Gibbs, also Ame Daughter of Moses Chandler, Elisabeth Daughter of Samuel Burpee, & Sarah Daughter of John Farrar. April 3d, 1737. Thomas, Son of Ephraim Houghton. 10. Samuel, Son of Samuel Carter Junr. & Martha Daughter of James Wilder Junr. 24. Abigail, Daughter of Thomas Munroe, a member of ye Chh of Christ in Charlestown also Samuel Son of John Snow. May, 7th. Baptized by Mr Seccomb of Harvard in my Congregation, Mary, Daughter of Samll Wilson of Nichewaug, the mother a member in full Communion with the Church of Canterbury. Jonathan Son of John Phillips & William Son of John Warner, ye mother a member of ye Chh in Haverhill. June 5th, 1737. Cyrus Son of Jonas Fairbank, and James Son of Benjamin Ballard. 19. Hannah Daughter of Joseph Moor, and Agnus Daughter of Alexander McBride. 26th. Joseph Son of John Joslin & Eunice Daughter of Nathaniel Wilson. July 17, 1737. Mary Resign, Daughter of Benjamin Harris also Damaris, Daughter of Thomas Houghton towards Turkey Hills. 24. David, Son of Doctor Greenleaf. Aug. 7th, 1837. The Brethren manifested (by ye uplifted hand) their willingness that Annah Hinds, wife of John Hinds of Brookfield should according to her desire be dismist and recommended to

37 ye Church of Christ in Brookfield.   August 14th, 1737. Baptized Lucey, Daughter of Saml. Sawyer.   28th. Mary, Daughter of Thomas & Magdalene Laggett.   Sept. 11th, 1737. Oliver Son of Edward Phelps Junr. also, Ruth Daughter of Reuben Rugg.   18th, Elisha, Son of Joseph Wood.   25. Mary, Daughter of Gardner & Mary Wilder   Octob. 2d, 1737. Joshua Son of John & Anna Prentice.   9th, Mary the Daughter of Daniel Howe.   23d. William, Son of Jonathan Fairbank.   Nov. 6th. Benjn: Son of Joseph Whetcomb was baptized by the Revd Mr David Stearns of Lunenburgh in Lancaster.   13. Joel, Son of Benjamin Houghton also Simon Son of Jacob Houghton Junr. & Tamar, Daughter of James Houghton Junr.   27. Jacob, Son of John Glazier.   Decemb. 4th, Jonathan Son of Jonathan Wheelock.   11th Elisabeth Daughter of Aholiab Sawyer.   18th. Jonathan, Son of Jonathan Houghton.
January, 1st. 1737-8, Dinah Daughter of William Goss.   15th. Samuel, Son of Jonathan Osgood, and Elias Son of Nathl. Carter.   29th. Elisabeth, Daughter of David Osgood by me at Jonathan Osgood's house, the same Day Miriam Daughter of Jonathan Bigloe Baptized in Town by Mr Stearns of Lunenburgh.   February, 12th, 1737-8. Tillee Son of David Whetcomb, Annah, Daughter of Jonathan Whetcomb, & Abigail Daughter of Oliver Moors.   26. Baptized at Jonathan Osgoods the place of Publick meeting Sarah Daughter of Josiah Wilder, and by the Revd Mr Seccomb in my pulpit Isaiah Son of Nathl. Butler, Lemuel Son of Uriah Holt and Damaris Daughter of Jonathan Carter.   March 14, 1737-8. Caleb, Son of Caleb Wilder, was baptized privately by reason of some hurt received in ye head at its birth which threatened its Life. Several of the Neighbours were present at its Baptism.   19th, Menasseh Son of Ephraim Wilder Junr.   22d. Abigail, Daughter of Peter Green, the mother in full Communion with us. This child was baptized privately, being under very threatening circumstances by reason of a sore mouth & fitts, at the Desire of the Parents. Several of the neighbours were present.
April, 2d. 1738. Jonathan Son of Jonathan Bayley.   23d Sarah, Daughter of Amos Atherton.   30th, Abel Son of Joshua Osgood.   May, 7th, 1738. Jabez Son of Jonathan Fairbank.   14. Abner Son of Benjamin Osgood.
38 May 21st. 1738. Thomas Sawyer & his Wife owned the Covenant and had their Child Baptized viz yr Son whose Name was Abraham, the same time Nathaniel, Son of Nathl. Hastings.   June 4th, Joseph, Son of Joseph Sawyer.   18th. Levi, Son of Daniel Howe, also Joshua Moor upon his owning of the Covenant.   25th. Nathaniel, Son of Aaron Osgood, and Joshua Son of Joshua Phelps.   July, 2d. 1738, Josiah Son of Josiah Kendall the mother a member of the Church of Christ in Woburn in full Communion.   9. Lois, Daughter of Joshua Moor.   16th. Mary Daughter of Ephraim Carter upon his owning the Cov: 23. Amee, Daughter of Capt. William Richardson.   *   *   *   *   *
August 20th, 1738, Simon Butler & his wife owned the Covenant, also Hannah Daughter of William Whetcomb was baptized.   27th. 1738. William Son of Doctor Daniel Greenleaf.   *   *   *   Sept. 10. Anna, Daughter of Simon Butler.   24th. John, Son of John & Abigail Carter. Octob. 22d. Timothy Ross & Elisabeth his Wife owned the Covenant. The Woman was baptized, also yr Son whose Name is Jesse, at the same time Mary Daughter of Edward & Bathsheba Robbins.   *   *   *
Nov. 5. John Son of John Beaman Junr. Also Lucey Daughter of John Joslin.   Decemb. 10. John Son of John Snow, & Dorothy Daughter of Thomas Fairbank.   17th. Sarah, Daughter of Saml. Bayley & his Wife, members in full Communion with the Chh of Christ in Roxbury.
January, 7th, 1738-9, John, Son of John & Lois White, by Mr Sterns of Lunenburgh in my Pulpit.   21st. Ruth, Daughter of Robert & Dorothy Phelps, also Eunice Daughter of John & Eunice Buss.   28th Esther, Daughter of James & Sarah Richardson.   Febr: 4th. Prudence, Daughter of Joseph Bennet, Mary, Daughter of Josiah Richardson & Darius, Son of Nathaniel Hudson.   11th. Jonathan, Son of Benjamin Townsend, the mother a member in full Communion with the Church of Christ in Byfield, Pastor of which is the Revd. Mr Moses Hale.   18. Cornelius, Son of John

39 & Sarah Sawyer. The Same Day was baptized by y° Rev^d. Mr Cushing of Shrewsbury, who changed with Mr Brown at the meeting of the Neighbourhood at Wonksechaukset, Thomas, Son of Moses Chandler, and Hannah, Daughter of Jonathan & Hannah Powers.   25th. Joshua, Son of Joshua Fairbank, Stanton, Son of Samuel Carter, Thankful, Daughter of Simon Whetcomb, and Lydia, Daughter of Ezekiel Wallingsford.   Feb. 28, 1738-9. James, Son of Richard & Lydia Proutee at the house of Mr House, the child to appearance being not like to live till the Sabbath, both father & mother having owned the Covenant at Hanover & put ymselves under the watch of y° Church y^t of which the Rev^d. Mr Buss is the Pastor. Mach, 18th, 1738-9, Samuel, Son of Thomas Ross.   25th. Gardner, Son of Joseph & Deborah Wilder.
April, 8th. 1739, Frederick, Son of Daniel Albert, & Elisabeth Daughter of Jonathan Wheelock.   15th. Sam^{ll}: Son of Benjamin Ballard, and Abigail Daughter of John Warner.   *   *   *   April 29th. Josiah Son of John Moor, Thomas, Son of Alexander McBride, & Prudence, Daughter of Joshua Church.   May, 13. Samuel, Son of Caleb & Abigail Wilder, & Lucey Daughter of William Goss.   20th. Sarah Prescott owned the Covenant and had her Daughter Susannah baptized.   27th. Susannah, Daughter of Nathaniel Carter.   June, 3^d. Samuel Son of Joseph Wood & Rebeckah Daughter of John Houghton & Hephzibah his wife.   10th. William Pollard's twins, viz, Prudence & Patience, also Katharine, Daughter of Joseph Moor, and Prudence Daughter of Reuben Rugg.   17th. Silas, Son of Jabez Beaman. 24. Jonathan, Son of Jonathan Bigelow and his Wife, also Abigail Daughter of James Wilder.   July 1, 1739. Sylvanus, Son of Benjamin Harris.   July, 8th. Elijah Son of Thomas Houghton of Harvard, & Rhoda Daughter of Jonas Fairbank. The Same Day, the Brethren voted a Dismission & Recommendation for Rebeckah Wilson wife of Joseph Wilson of Nichewaug, to y° Church in sd Place.   29th. James Son of James & Abigail Ross.   *   *   *   *   *   *
Sept. 2^d. 1739. Ezekiel, Son of Hezekiah Snow.   9th. Benjamin, Son of Israel Houghton.   16th. Simon, Son of Timothy Ross.   30. John, Son of Aaron Willard.   Octob. 14, 1739, John Son of John Houghton Junr. Nov. 4th. 1739, Abigail, Daughter of Jonathan Osgood.   11th. Enoch, Son of Amos Jewett. He and his Wife having owned the Covenant at Mr Balch's Church in Bradford.   Decemb. 2^d, 1739. Then baptized Eunice **40** the Daughter of Benjamin Houghton of Woonksechawkset.   9. Levi, Son of David Whetcomb, & Susannah Daughter of Phinehas Sawyer. 16. Levina Daughter of Jonathan Houghton.   30. Tabitha Daughter of John Farrar & Josiah Son of Josiah Sawyer Son of William Sawyer.
January, 6th, 1739-40. Phinehas Beaman owned the Covenant & was baptized, at the same [time] John, the Son of John Buss.   *   *   *   20th. Jabez Fairbank Junr. had his Daughter Eunice baptized, also, Keziah Daughter of Abner Sawyer.   27th. Elisabeth Daughter of Gardner Wilder.   February, 19th. 1739-40. Abigail Daughter of John Carter.   24th. Mary Daughter of Mr Joshua Townsend of Bolton, the mother a member of that Chh. in Boston of which y° Revd. Mr Welsted is y° Pastor.   March, 16th, 1739-40. David Son of David Wilder, & Beulah Daughter of Phinehas Sawyer. 18th. Baptized privately at y° house of John Sawyer his twin Daughters named Mary & Martha, which was done at the Desire of the Parents they being both under threatning Circumstances by reason of the soreness of their mouths.   23^d. Samuel, Son of Samuel Sawyer, Elijah Son of Benj: Osgood, & Oliver Son of William Dunsmore. He and his Wife having owned y° Covenant at Stow.   30th. Levina, Daughter of James Houghton Junr. & Phinehas Son of Amos Atherton.
April, 6th. 1740. Peter, Son of Peter Green, the mother in full Communion. 9th. Ephraim, Son of Ephraim & Abigail Carter, baptized privately, being very ill & like to die.   13. Calvin Son of Doctor Greenleaf, Jonathan Priest Son of Joseph Whetcomb, Mary, Daughter of Uriah Holt, Ruth, Daughter of Richard Wiles, Abigail Daughter of Benjamin Atherton, and Stephen Son of Samuel Burpee, and Jonathan Son of Jonathan Fairbank. 20. Thomas, Son of Thomas Sawyer.   May, 2^d. 1740, Philip, Son of John

Goss at his own house, he being dangerously sick.　11. Mary, Daughter of Samuel Gibbs, and John Son of John Glazier.　June 1, 1740. Benjamin Son of Benjamin Houghton Junr. Tabitha Daughter of ye widow Tabitha Sawyer, also Hephzibah, Daughter of William Whetcomb.　8. Shubael, Son of Jonathan Bayley, & Heman Son of Josiah Kendal.　29. Abigail, Daughter of Ephraim Houghton.　July, 6. Anna, Daughter of Zaccheus Boynton & Lucey, Daughter of Amos Knight Junr.　13. Elizabeth, Daughter of David Jewett who had owned the Covenant in ye first Church in Rowley, and Submitted to Discipline wth us.　27. Matthew Clarke & his wife in Communion with the Irish Church in Worcester upon Submitting to Discipline with us had their Daughter Mary baptized.　August 10th. 1740. Zerviah & Lois Beaman Daughters of Gamaliel Beaman, upon their owning ye Covenant were both of them Baptized.　31. Prudence Daughter of Oliver Moor.　Sept. 14th, 1740.　Abigail Daughter of John Snow, and Lucey Daughter of Ephraim Wilder Junr.　21. Elijah, Son of Joseph Proutee. He and his Wife owned the Covenant at y^t Chh in Hannover of wch Mr Bass is the Pastor　Octob. 12th, 1740. Josiah, Son of David Osgood, Rufus Son of Daniel Powers, and Elijah Son of Phinehas Willard.　26. Rebeckah, Daughter of William Richardson, and Lydia the Daughter of James & Lydia Butler upon y^r owning of ye Covenant.　Nov. 2^d, 1740. Daniel Son of William Goss.　9th. Roger, Son of Thomas Ross.　23^d. Joanna, Daughter of Jonathan & Elisabeth Wheelock.　30th. Thankful, Daughter of Nathaniel Wilson.　December, 14th: 1740. Sarah, Daughter of Joshua Osgood, Silas Son of Aaron Osgood, & Joseph Son of Thomas Fairbank.　21st. Josiah Son of Nehemiah Wood.　This Child was Baptized on its mother Mary Wood's account, she being a member in full Communion, once Mary Johnson & before that Mary Collar.

January, 4th. 1740-1. Abigail Daughter of Lieut. Coll. Oliver Wilder.　25th. Silas, Son of Samuel Carter.　Febr. 22. Ebenezer, Son of Daniel Woodberry, a member in full Communion with the Chh of Christ in Townsend.　March, 2^d. 1740-1. In ye Evening at the house of Joshua Fairbank baptized his Son at his Desire, Named Lemuel, being to appearance nigh unto Death.　22^d. Levina Daughter of Simon Whetcomb.　April, 12. Daniel Son of John Warner, Thomas, Son of Thomas & Sarah White, & Abigail, Daughter of Ephraim and Abigail Carter.　19th. Oliver, Son of Oliver Carter.　April, 26. Att Bolton Experience, Daughter of William Pollard, & Mary Daughter of —— Johnson, ye mother a member of ye Church in Reading.

May, 3^d, 1741. Lucey Daughter of Joseph Moor, & Dorothy Daughter of John Joslin.　10th. Att Woonkseechaukit, Aaron Son of Jonathan Bigelow, Susannah Daughter of Samuel Bayley, Abigail & Prudence Twins & Daughters of Nathaniel Carter, & Bettee Daughter of David Nelson. 24th. Jotham Son of Joseph Woods, Edward Son of Edward Robbins, Rebeckah Daughter of Joseph Wilder Junr. Abijah Son of John White, & Joanna Daughter of Phinehas Beaman.　31st. Robert, Son of Robert Phelps, & Oliver Son of John Beaman.　June, 7th, 1741. Mr Josiah Brown's Son, William, Anna Daughter of John Phillips, Sarah Daughter of Jonathan Ball, Eunice Daughter of Nath^{ll}. Hastings, Lucey Daughter of David Johnson. He and his wife having owned ye Covenant, and Ball having owned the Covenant at Lexington.　14th. Jonathan Priest Son of Hezekiah Whetcomb, & Dinah, Daughter of Moses Osgood & his Wife upon y^r owning of the Covenant.　June, 28th. 1741. Thomas Sawyer and his Wife owned the Covenant and had their Children Baptized, Names, Thomas & Bettee. Also Abigail Carly owned the Covenant & was Baptized.　July 19th, 1741. John Son of James Richardson, George Son of Ephraim Wheeler, and Martha Daughter of Moses Osgood.　26th. Joseph, Son of Benjn: Ballard.　August, 2^d. Caleb, Son of Caleb Wilder, & William Son of Nathan^{ll} Butler.　9th. William, Son of Charles Wilder and his Wife upon y^r owning the Covenant, at ye same time, Hephzibah Daughter of Benjamin Harris.　16th. Hannah, Daughter of Jabez Fairbank of Bolton, and Eunice Daughter of Joseph Bennett.　August, 30th, 1741. Nathan, Son of Timothy Farrar. Both Father & mother having owned the Covenant at Concord, and Caleb, Son of Joshua Church, the mother in Communion with us.

Sept. 13th, 1741. Abigail, Daughter of Mr Caleb Richardson of Bolton, he having owned the Covenant at Roxbury. Peter & Levi, Sons of the Widow Hephzibah Kendal. 27th. Andrew, Son of Andrew & Elisabeth Wilder. Octobr. 4th, 1741. Thomas, Son of Stanton & Mercy Prentice. 25. Oliver Son of Jonathan Powers. The same time Mary & Esther Daughters of Mr Thomas Burpee renewed their Baptismal Covenant. Nov. 1st, 1741. Martha, Daughter of Nathll. Hudson, & Abigail Daughter of Peter Green.

Sundry Brethren manifesting yr Desire of the Consent of ye Church to yr Lying with others in ye foundation of a Chh. at Bolton and being Recommended to yt business viz, Jeremiah Wilson, Jonathan Moor, John Wilder, Jacob Houghton, John Priest, John Fletcher, Jabez Fairbank, David Whetcomb, Nathll. Butler, Nathaniel Wilson, Josiah Sawyer, It was voted by the Brethren present that it should be according to yr Desire.

December, 6th, 1741. Mary Daughter of Ezra and Rebeccah Sawyer. 20th, 1741. Zephaniah Son of John Buss, & Elisabeth Daughter of Reuben Rugg. 27th Mary Daughter of Jonas & —— Fairbank.
January, 10th, 1741-2. Nathanael Sawyer and Mary his Wife owned the Covenant, and had their Children, Oliver & Mary baptized. 17th. Ezra, Son of Oliver Wilder Junr. and Sarah his Wife. 24. Nathan, Son of John Farrar. 31. Peter & Nathaniel, Twins of John & Sarah Sawyer. March, 7th. Baptized at Wooksechauckit meeting at the house of David Osgood, Joshua Son of Samuel Sawyer, and Elijah Son of Samuel Burpee, and Kath-
43 erine Daughter of Thomas Sawyer Junr. March 14th. Israel, Son of Israel Houghton & Timothy Son of Timothy Ross.
April 18th, 1742. Jane, Daughter of Zaccheus Boynton, att Woonksechauksitt. May, 2d. David, Son of James Butler, and Phinehas Son of Phinehas Sawyer. 23d. Richard Son of Richard Proutee. June 6th. Martha, Daughter of John Snow, Sarah, Daughter of Thomas White, & Phinehas Son of Phinehas Beaman. 27th. Peninnah Daughter of Daniel Albert. July 4th. David, Son of David Nelson. 11. Ephraim, Son of Jonathan Nelson, who had owned the Covenant at Rowley & Submitted to Discipline with us. 25th, 1742. Similius, Son of Rachel Wilder Daughter of Thomas Wilder and John Son of John Carter. Aug: 1, 1742. Moses Bayley & his Wife, owned the Covenant, and Sarah yr Daughter was baptized. At ye same time Jonathan Son of Oliver Moor, & Prudence Daughter of Elisha Sawyer. 15. Submit, Daughter of Benj. Osgood. 22. Ephraim, Son of Thomas Fairbank. 29. Baptized at Leominster the first Day of yr meeting in yr new meeting House, David Son of Jonathan White & Elisabeth, Daughter of Matthew Clerk. Sept. 5th. Elisabeth Daughter of Nathanael Sawyer Junr. 12. Thankful, Daughter of Jer: & Thankful Haskall. 26th, 1742. Daniel Priest and his Wife owned the Covenant and had their Son (named Daniel) Baptized, at ye same time the Son of Charles Wilder (named Charles) was baptized. Octob. 10th, 1742. John, Son of John Bowers. His Wife in full Communion. The same time the Brethren by Vote Discovered yr. Willingness that Richard Wilds should be Dismist to Joyn with others in forming a Church in a New Town, known by ye name of ye Road Town. 17. Damaris, Daughter of Jonathan Knight, ye mother of yr Child in full Communion.

The Same Day, (being Sacrament Day) Hooker Osgood Junr. & Israel Houghton who were chosen Deacons on ye 1st of sd month, at a church meeting at ye Pastor's house, and yn desired some time to consider of it, signified that having considered the matter they lookt upon ymselves as called of God to yt service, and Desired prayers that God would Instruct ym. in yr Duty and enable ym. faithfully to attend it, which was made known by ye Pastor to ye Church and accordingly performed, and they took yr Places, or served as Deacons at ye Table of ye Lord.

24. Prudence, Daughter of Josiah & Prudence Brown, also Elisha, Son of Joseph Whetcomb. Novr: 7th, 1742, Abijah, Son of Jonathan Wheelock. 28. Baptized in ye meeting House at Woonksechaukset the first Sabbath of ye meeting in it, as follows: Silas, Son of Benjamin Houghton, & Joseph

Son of Jonathan Osgood.   December 5. Eunice Daughter of Aaron Osgood. 19. Josiah Son of Stanton & Mercy Prentice, also Elisabeth Daughter of Joseph Osgood Junr. & Elisabeth his wife, they both having owned the Covenant in order to it y⁰ Same Day.

44   ADMITTED TO FULL COMMUNION.

December, 12th 1742. In y⁰ forenoon before the Sacrament, Joseph Wood. Feby. 6th 1742-3, Abigail, Wife of Daniel Albert. May, 29, 1743, Daniel Rugg Junr. & Sarah his Wife. August, 21, 1743, The Brethren by vote, signified y^r Willingness that Gardner Wilder & Thomas White should joyn with others in forming a Church in Leominster, & that the wife of Isaac Moor should be Recommended according to her Desire to y⁰ Communion of the Church of X in Bolton, & this Day viz, Aug 28th, the Brethren voted that the wife of Deacon Joseph Fairbank of Harvard should according to her Desire be Recommended to Communion with the Chh of Christ in Harvard.   Decemb. 18, 1743, The Brethren by y^r uplifted hand Signified their Willingness that Martha, the wife of Jonathan Bennett of Shrewsbury North Precinct should according to her Desire be recommended to y⁰ fellowship of the Chh of Christ there, which hath been done.   25. Coll. Oliver Wilder & Mary his Wife were admitted to Communion in all ordinances.
April 29th 1744, Mr Stephen Frost.   May, 13. Zerviah Rugg, wife of Nathan Rugg upon a Letter of Recommendation from y⁰ Chh in Groton.   August 19, 1744. First Baptized & then admitted to Communion Joshua Pierce.
March, 31, 1745, Amos Knight & Benjamin Osgood.   April 21. Asahel Phelps & Elisabeth his Wlfe.   May, 5th 1745, The widow Annah Ross. The wife of Thomas Burpee, the wife of John Snow, the wife of Jonathan Powers, and the wife of James Ross Desired to be Dismist & Recommended to the Communion of the Second Church in Lancaster. It was Consented to by y⁰ vote of y⁰ Brethren on said Day.   June 2^d. Rebeckah Knight wife of Timothy Knight, Relief Prentice & Rebeckah Prentice.   16th.   Jonathan Kendal Junr. & Admonition his Wife.   July 21st, 1745, Mary Sawyer Wife of Nathan^{ll}. Sawyer Junr.   Sept. 22. The Wife of Manasseh Divol.   Octob. 20 Eunice, the wife of Joshua Fairbank.   Nov: 3, 1745. Asaph Wilder & Zipporah his Wife, also the widow Experience Houghton.   December, 8th, 1745, Ruth Wilder Wife of Oliver Wilder Junr. upon a Recommendation from y⁰ Chh of Christ in Lexington.
January 26, 1745-6. Eunice Dunsmore, Wife of John Dunsmore.   March 2, 1745-6. Joshua Fletcher.
April 20, 1746. John Fletcher Junr.   May 4th, The Brethren by uplifted hand Discovered their Willingness y^t Tabitha the wife of Sam^{ll}. Bennett should be Recommended to Communion with y⁰ Church of Christ in Holden.   July 20th. Thomas Kendal & Abigail his wife.   Aug: 24. Rebeckah Phelps Wife of Joshua Phelps.
August 9, 1747 Joanna Fletcher, Wife of John Fletcher Junr. upon a letter of Recommendation from y⁰ Second Chh of Christ in Redding.

45   December 26th, 1742, Baptized, John Son of William Dunsmore.
January 2^d, 1742-3, Then Baptized by Mr Goss of Bolton in my pulpit Oliver, Son of William Goss.   30. Samuel, Son of Samuel Bayley, & Priscilla Daughter of Daniel Jewett in y⁰ meeting House in the New Precinct.   Feb. 6th, Joseph, Son of John Joslin.   13th. Nathan Son of Benjn. Townsend. March, 6th. Dorothy Daughter of Aaron Willard, Elisabeth Daughter of Jonathan Bayley, & Katherine Daughter of Ephraim Wilder Junr.   20th. Jonathan, Son of Jonathan Fairbank & Thomas Son of Amos Rugg.   April 3^d. Joseph Son of Joseph Moor, Lois Daughter of John & Lois White, Elisha Son of Elisha Sawyer, and Susanna Daughter of John Rugg & his Wife who then owned the Covenant in order to y⁰ Baptism of it.   10th. Elisabeth, Daughter of Andrew Wilder.   17th. Susanna, Daughter of Joshua & Eunice Fairbank.   24th. Nathan, Son of Nathan Rugg, the mother of y⁰ Child a member in full Communion with y⁰ Chh of Christ in Groton.

May, 1st, 1743. Oliver Daughter of Moses Osgood & Prudence Daughter of Samuel Carter. 15. Susannah, Daughter of Nehemiah Wood, the mother in full Communion, and John, Son of William & Sarah Whitney at Doctor Dunsmore's house after meeting it being uncapable of being brought out to Baptism in the Congregation. It being dangerously sick and could not bear to be stirred. 29. Susannah Daughter of William Richardson & Mary Daughter of Nath. Hudson & Daniel Son of Daniel Rugg. June 5th. 1743, Lydia Daughter of Gardner Wilder, Esther Daughter of John Glazier, Jacob Son of David Wilder, Ephraim Son of Ephraim Carter, and Thankful Daughter of Zachariah Glazier, upon his wife's owning the Covenant at the same time. 26. Elisabeth, Daughter of Sam^ll Gibbs, & Wife. July 24 Solomon, Son of Benj. Harris. 31. Sarah, Daughter of Ephraim & Sarah Houghton & Josiah Son of Phinehas Beaman. August 14. Baptized in Woonksechauxit meeting house, Tamar Daughter of Thomas Ross, Elisabeth, Daughter of Jonathan Biglow, and James Son of James Ross. 21st. Nahum Son of Caleb Wilder. 28. Grace, Daughter of John Phillips. 28. Elisabeth, Daughter of Ephraim Divol & Wife, they both owning the Covenant on sd Day antecedent to it. Octobr. 9th. Dorothy Daughter of Robert Phelps, & Cornelius Son of Phinehas Willard. 10th Monday Evening, Baptized at the house of Joseph Wilder Junr. his two Sons, Named Peter & John, born on said Day before their time, one of them especially being dangerously ill, and it died quickly after it was baptized, viz, the youngest. 30. Elisabeth, Daughter of Benjamin Houghton Junr. being the first Child that was baptized in the new meeting House. Nov. 6th. Jonas Son of Jonas Fairbank. 13. Eunice Daughter of Peter Green, & Lois, Daughter of Josiah Kendal. 20th Oliver Wilder Junr. His Twins viz. Oliver & Sarah. 27th. Hannah, Daughter of Joseph Abbott & his Wife, **46** both of them having owned the Covenant in Mr Phillips's Church in Andover. December 25, 1743. Then Baptized the Son of Deacon Israel Houghton, named Jonathan.

January 1st, 1743-4. Bathsheba, Daughter of Edward & Bathsheba Robbins. 15. Dorothy, Daughter of Josiah & Dorothy Richardson. February 12th, 1743-4. Ruth, Daughter of Benjamin Ballard. The same time the Brethren manifested their Consent (by vote) to ye Desire of the wife of Gardner Wilder to have her Church Relations removed from us to ye Church of Christ in Leominster. Feb. 26th. The Church manifested the same respecting the Wife of Oliver Carter. March 11th. The Church manifested the same respecting the Wife of Ebenr. Polley, and the wife of Jonathan Carter. The same Day Baptized John, Son of Stanton & Mercy Prentice. 18th. John, Son of Joseph & Hannah Wood. 25. The Church Discovered their willingness that the Wife of Thomas White should be recommended & joyned to ye Church of Christ in Leominster.

April 1, 1744. John Son of John Beaman Junr. 8. Baptized by Mr Gardner of Stow, Nathaniel, Son of Ezra Sawyer, in the meeting house for the Second Precinct in Lancaster. 15. Joseph, Son of Joseph Bennett. 22. Baptized by me in ye Second Precinct, Solomon, Son of David Jewett. 29th. Francis Son of Richard Proutee. May 13th. Paul Son of James Kendall, & Mary Daughter of Thomas Fairbank. 17th. Elisabeth Daughter of Joshua Fairbank at his own House the Child to appearance being nigh to Death. 20th. Mary, Daughter of Nath^ll. Wyman, a member in full Communion with ye Chh of Christ in Woburn. June 3d. 1744. Josiah Son of James Wilder, &c. 10th. Jonathan Son of Zechariah Glazier. 17. Jonathan Son of Jacob Barret, in ye meeting house in the Second Precinct in Lancaster, the man a member of a Chh in Reading, the mother a member of ye Church in Woburn. 24. Baptized by ye Rev^d Mr Loring of Sudbury in ye meeting House in the Second Precinct in Lancaster Anna, the Daughter of Reuben & Lydia Rugg. Sometime in July Baptized by Mr Goss at Chauxit Jonathan, Son of Jonathan Powers. July 1st. Ephraim, Son of Ephraim Divol. 22. Jeremiah, Son of Jeremiah Haskal. the mother in Communion. August, 12th. 1744. Mary Daughter of Capt David Osgood in Chauksit meeting house. 19. Baptized Joshua Pierce and his Son Joshua, upon his father's owning the Covenant at ye same time. 26.

John, Son of Mr Josiah & Prudence Brown. The Same Day Baptized by y⁰ Revd. Mr Barret of Hopkinton at y⁰ meeting house in y⁰ 2ᵈ Precinct Jonathan Son of Jonathan Powers. Sept. 2ᵈ. Mary Daughter of Phinehas
47 Sawyer. Sept. 16, 1744. Rebeckah, Daughter of John Rugg and Mary, Daughter of John Bowers by y⁰ Revd. Mr Loring of Sudbury in my Congregation. 23ᵈ. Mary, Daughter of John & Mary Herbert. 30ᵗʰ. Sarah, Daughter of Daniel & Sarah Rugg. Octob. 11ᵗʰ. Baptized by my hand in the meeting House in y⁰ Second precinct Hannah Daughter of John & Hannah Snow, Bettee, Daughter of Hezekiah Whetcomb, & Joseph Son of Joseph Osgood Junr. Nov. 25ᵗʰ, 1744, Moses, Son of Moses Osgood.

The Day above mentioned, The Desire of David Osgood, Benjⁿ. Houghton Junr. Joseph Moor, Josiah Wilder, Jonathan Osgood, Jonathan Bayley, Thomas Fairbank, Thomas Burpee, Josiah Richardson, Reuben Rugg, Samuel Bayley, David Nelson, William Goss, Oliver Moor, Edward Robbins, Daniel Powers, Brethren of the Church of Christ in Lancaster, was according to yʳ Desire, made Known by y⁰ Pastor to said Church, whose desire was as follows, viz: That they might obtain a dismission from us and a Recommendation to y⁰ Covenanting Brethren in y⁰ West or Second Precinct in Lancaster in order to yʳ Joyning with them in y⁰ founding a Church in sd Precinct, upon which it was voted, that it should be made known by the Pastor in the Name of the Brethren, that they were free that it should be according to yʳ Desire. Upon which, this was (in Proper Time) done by y⁰ Pastor.

January 27ᵗʰ 1744-5. Abijah, Son of John & Lucey Joslin & Jonathan Son of Joshua Pierce. March 3ᵈ, 1744-5. Baptized by Mr Rogers of Leominster in my pulpit, Andrew, Son of Andrew Wilder, Nathaniel, Son of Nathaniel Sawyer, also David Son of Amos Knight Junr. 24. Eunice, Daughter of John White, April, 7ᵗʰ. Keziah, Daughter of Aaron Osgood. 14. Ephraim, Son of Nathaniel Hudson. 21. Mary, Daughter of Jonathan Knight, and Elisabeth, Daughter of Asahel & Elisabeth Phelps.
May, 5ᵗʰ. 1745, Manasseh, Son of Joshua Osgood. 12. Matthew, Son of Matthew Clerk. 26. Att y⁰ 2ᵈ Church, Baptized, Phebe, Daughter of Samˡˡ. Burpee, and a Child of William Goss named ——. June 9ᵗʰ. 1745, Samuel, Son of Timothy Stearns. The father a member of a Church in Reading, the mother a member of a Chh in Wilmington. 16. David & Eunice Wilder's Son Samuel, also Jonathan Kendall Junr. his Daughter, named Sarah. 23. Abijah, Son of Joshua Fairbank, Baptized privately at his house appearing under threatning or Dangerous Circumstances. July 7ᵗʰ, 1745, Jonas, Son of Samuel Carter, the Same Time the Widow Allis Mitchel renewed her Baptismal Covenant. 14. Elisabeth, Daughter of Joshua Phelps. 21. Oliver Son of Ephraim Carter. August, 11ᵗʰ. Abijah, Son of Abijah & Abigail Wyman. Also Zerviah Daughter of Nathan Rugg. 25ᵗʰ. Robert Son of Allis Mitchel. Octob. 6ᵗʰ. Peter Son of Peter Green.
48 20ᵗʰ. John Son of Deacon Israel Houghton. Octob. 27ᵗʰ, 1745. Thomas Son of Stanton & Mercy Prentice. Sarah, Daughter of Jonas Fairbank. The Same Time John Prescott Junr. & his Wife owned the Covenant and had their Daughter Mary baptized. Nov: 3ᵈ, 1745. Hannah Daughter of Nehemiah Wood, on y⁰ mother's account, who is a member in full Communion. 17. Dorothy, Daughter of John Prescott, and Zilpah Daughter of Asaph & Zipporah Wilder. Sept. 8, 1745. Eunice, Daughter of Capt. Ephraim Wilder Junr. by y⁰ hand of y⁰ Revd. Mr John Mellin in my Congregation. Nov. 24ᵗʰ, 1745. Joseph, Son of John Carter.
January 19, 1745 6. Hannah Daughter of Francis Butterick, he having owned the Covenant with us, and his Wife being a member of the Church of Christ in Lunenburgh. This child was Baptized in my Congregation by y⁰ Revd. Mr John Mellin. Feb. 23. Wright, Son of Aaron Willard Baptized by Mr Mellin in my Congregation.
April, 6ᵗʰ, 1746. Martha, Daughter of Charles Wilder. 13. Benjamin, Son of Benjamin Ballard. 27. Abigail, Daughter of Caleb Wilder. May 11, 1746. Joel, Son of Moses Osgood. 18. Joanna, Daughter of John Fletcher, Junr. 25. Damaris, Daughter of Joseph Whetcomb, & Elisabeth Daughter of Ephraim Divol. Baptized in my Congregation by Mr Mellin. June

22ᵈ. Mary, Daughter of Asahel Phelps.   *   *   *   July 6ᵗʰ. Joseph, Son of Mr Josiah & Prudence Brown, Baptized by me, at the Second Precinct in Lancaster. The Same Day Baptized, by Mr Mellin in yᵉ first Precinct, Samuel, Son of Oliver Wilder.   13. Hannah Sawyer Daughter of Bezaleel Sawyer upon her owning the Covenant, & Elisabeth Daughter of Joseph Abbott.   20ᵗʰ. Ephraim Houghton's Son, Elisha, Abigail, Daughter of Amos Atherton, & Rebeckah, Daughter of Thomas & Abigail Kendal.   August, 3ᵈ, 1746. James Son of John Joslin.   17. Abishai, Son of Robert Phelps.   24. Lucey, Daughter of John Rugg.   Sept. 28 Joseph, Son of Joseph Osgood Junr. & Elisabeth his Wife.   30ᵗʰ, Sarah Daughter of John Beaman Junr.   Privately at his house, just before the funeral of one of his children, it being to appearance Dangerously sick.   Octob. 26, 1746. Rebeckah Daughter of Joshua Phelps & Reuben Son of Daniel Rugg Junr.   Nov. 9ᵗʰ. Joshua, Son of Joshua & Eunice Fairbank.   December, 7ᵗʰ. Jonas, Son of Abijah Wyman & Nathaniel Son of Nathaniel Wyman.

49   January 11, 1746-7. Jonathan Son of Jonathan Kendal Junr. & Ruth Daughter of Andrew Wilder.

March, 29ᵗʰ, 1747. Baptized by Mr Mellen in my Congregation John, Son of David & Eunice Wilder, and Stephen, Son of Stanton & Mercy Prentice.   May, 24. Baptized by my hand Timothy Stearns's Son Benjⁿ: Matthew Clerk's Son William, & Zephaniah Williams's Daughter Abigail both father & mother having owned yᵉ Covenant at Marlborough.   June 1ˢᵗ, 1747. Captain William Richardson's Daughter, Eunice, John White's Daughter Lois, and John Gooderidge's Daughter Eunice.   July 26. Baptized by Mr Rogers of Littleton in my pulpit, Luke Son of Aaron Osgood & his Wife, and Eunice Daughter of Phinehas Sawyer & his Wife.   August 9ᵗʰ, 1747. Jonathan, Son of Nathˡˡ. Sawyer Junr.   Sept. 20ᵗʰ, 1747.   Jemima, Daughter of Samuel Carter.   Octob. 25, 1747.   Bulah Daughter of Ephraim Carter, Eunice Daughter of Joshua Fairbank, & Nathaniel Son of John Beaman Junr.   These were baptized by Mr Loring of Sudbury in my pulpit.

[NOTE. This was the last entry made by Reverend John Prentice. He had dropped his pen forever, although he survived until January 6, 1748. For a year his pulpit was supplied by various clergymen, but no memoranda of baptisms or admissions to the church during this period are found until his successor in office, Reverend Timothy Harrington, re-opened the records. Of the thirty-eight said to have been baptized, the names of two only are known.]

BAPTISMS FROM OCTOBR. 25, 1747, TO NOV. 16, 1748.

Augt. 1748.   Ebenezer Son of Benjamin Osgood.
Augt. 1748.   Hannah Daughter of Thomas Kendall per Mr Goss.

[NOTE. Mr. Harrington, in preparing his Century Sermon — preached May 28, 1753 — made a careful enumeration of baptisms and admissions from 1708 to that date, and entered his summaries upon pages 29 and 49 of the Church Book, as given below. In his printed discourse, however, the baptisms by Mr. Prentice are stated to be 1593 instead of 1523.]

By Mr Prentice admitted to full Communion
Males 128   Females 203

From yᵉ Revᵈ. Mr Prentice's Ordination to yᵉ last recorded by him were baptized . . . . 1523 Persons 1523
from October 25ᵗʰ, 1747 to Nov. 16, 1748 . . . 38 without Doubt.

50   REV TIMOTHY HARRINGTON'S RECORDS.
BAPTISMS.

Decem. 4ᵗʰ, 1748.   Joseph Son of John & Mary Herbert.
Decem. 11ᵗʰ, 1748.   David Son of Abraham & Hephzibah Dufore.
Decem. 18ᵗʰ, 1748.   John Son of John & Zipporah Phelps.
Feb. 5, 1748-9.   Abijah Son of Capt. Abijah & Elizabeth Willard ; Abigail Daughter of Andrew & Elizabeth Wilder; Abigail Daughter of Joseph & Patience White.
Feb. 11, 1748.   Mary yᵉ Daughter of Mr Ebenezer Allen.
Feb. 11ᵗʰ, 1748-9.   Kezia Daughter of Sherebiah & Kezia Ballard.
Feb. 19ᵗʰ, 1748-9.   Mary Daughter of John & [Sarah] Osgood.

FIRST CHURCH, BOOK I. 295

Feb. 26th, 1748–9. Eunice Daughter of Josiah & [Deborah] White.
March, 5th, 1748–9. Mary Dr. of Dr Stanton & Mercy Prentice } pr Mr Mellen.
March, 5th, 1748–9. Joshua Son of Joshua & Mary Fletcher.
March, 12th. 1748–9. Mary Dr. of Nehemiah & Mary Wood.
March, 19, 1748–9. { Josiah Son of Joseph & Patience White.
              { Lucy Dr. of Daniel and Sarah Rugg.
March, 26, 1749. Joshua Johnson and Joshua, Abigail, Elizabeth, The Children of sd Joshua Johnson; John Son of ye Widow Kezia Bennet; Mary Dr. of Matthew Clark.
April 9th, 1749. Jonathan Son of Joseph Osgood Junr. per Mr Goss.
April 16th, 1749. John Son of Benja. & Ruth Ballard.
May 21st, 1749. { Hannah Dr. of Joshua Johnson.
              { Dinah my negro maid servant.
June 11th, 1749. Peter Joslyn Junior was baptized.
June 25 1749. Hannah Dr. of Robt. and [Elizabeth] Fletcher.
July 16th 1749. John Son of John & Lydia Rugg.
July 16th. 1749. Mary Dr. of Jacob & Phebe Fowle.
July 18th, 1749. Abel Son of Thomas & Abigail Wright, baptized while sick at Home.
July 9th, 1749. Silence Dr. of Peter & Elisa. Joslyn Junr.
July 23d 1749. Asaph Son of James & [Martha] Wilder.
51 July 30, AD. 1749. Stephen Johnson.
August 20th, 1749. Susanna ye Dr. of John & [Sarah] Osgood.
Sept. 3d. 1749. Abiel Son of Joseph & Hannah Abbot.
Sept. 17th. { Jacob Son of Jacob & Phebe Fowle.
          { William Son of Jonathan Kendall Junior & his wife.
Sept. 24th, 1749. Dorothy Daughter of Aaron & [Eunice] Osgood pr. Mr Seccombe.
October 1st. 1749. Josiah Sawyer and his Daughter Lucy.
Oct. 15th "   Lemuel Son of Josiah Sawyer.
Octob. 22d. 1749. Jane the Wife of Isaac Rugg; Martha, Isaac and Elisabeth, Children of Sd. Isaac & Jane Rugg; Timothy Son of Timothy Harrington.
Novr. 12, 1749. { Stephen Son of Jotham Wilder.
              { Lucy Daughter of Peter Green.
Novr. 19th, 1749. Jacob Son of Isaac & Jane Rugg.
December, 10th, 1749. Titus Son of Jotham & Phoebe Wilder.
December. 17th. 1749, John Son of John & [Mary] Prescott.
December, 24th, 1749. Alice the wife, Abijah the Son of Abijah Houghton.
December, 31st. 1749. Joseph Son of Phinehas & [Mary] Sawyer.   Sum, 53.

1750

Jany. 7th AD. 1749–50. Josiah Son of Josiah & [Sarah] Ballard; Alice Daughter of Abijah & Alice Houghton.
Feb. 11th. AD. 1749–50. Rebecah Dr. of Ephraim Divol.
April 1st. AD. 1750. Dinah Daughter of James Butler; Relief. Daughter of Nathll. Sawyer Junior; Rebecca Daughter of Amasa Turner.
April, 8th. Levi Son of Caleb Wilder.
April 22. Elisabeth Daughter of Jonas Fairbank.
May — William Son of John & [Margaret] Bowers, pr Mr Goss.
May 27. Dorothy Daughter of Ephraim & [Abigail] Carter.
52 June 17th. ADom. 1750. Leafy Dr. of Zephaniah & [Damaris] Williams.
July 1st. William Son of Israel and Desire Nichols.
July 8th. Jonas Son of Amos Knight Junior & [Hannah]
Augt. John Son of Joseph Wilder Junr. Esqr.; Abijah Son of Nathan Rugg.
Septr. 23. Timothy Son of Joshua Fletcher.
Septr. 30. Mary Daughter of Moses & [Martha] Osgood; Molly Daughter of Nathaniel & Lydia White.
Octobr. 14. Frances Daughter of ye Revnd. Josiah & Mrs Jane Swan; Mary ye Daughter of Sherebiah & Kezia Ballard.
October 28th. Abigail, Abijah, Children of John & [Lydia] Phillips.
Novr. 4th. Habijah Son of Capt. Abijah & Elizabeth Willard.
Novr. 11th. Peter Son of Amos Atherton, per Mr Mellen.

Novr. 18th. Stanton Son of Dr Stanton & Mercy Prentice.
Decr. 1750. Nathan Son of Mr Dan¹. Willard.
December. 2d. John Son of Lt. John & [Abigail] Carter. Sum 27
December 9th. Abijah Son of Mr Andrew & [Elizabeth] Wilder. 53
                                                              80

Anno Domini 1751

Feb. 3d. Ephraim Son of Nath¹¹. Wyman.
Feb. 24. Lucy Daughter of Asahel Phelps.
March 3d. { Ephraim Son of Daniel Rugg. } per Mr Mellen.
          { Joseph Son of John Phelps. }
March 24. Annice Dr. of Jonathan Knight.
March 31st. Ruth Dr. of Oliver Wilder Junior, at his own House. In Presence of Some of yᵉ Chh, sd. Child being not likely to live.
April 7. Sarah Dr of John Osgood.
April 14. Samuel Locke; Samuel, Lucretia, Josiah, James, John, William, Children of sᵈ. Samuel Locke.
53 April 14th. Same Day, Thomas, Dorothy, Rebekkah, Sarah, Anna, Children of Hezekiah Gates &c.
Same Day also, Ebenezer Son of Ebenezer Allen Junr.
April 28, Susanna, Dr. of James Wilder, pr. Mr Mellen.
May 3d. John Son of Matthew Clarke, sd child being dangerously Sick was baptised privately.
May 12. Rebekkah Dr. of Matthew Wyman; Elisabeth Dr. of Gershom & Mary Flagg.
May 26th. Lucy Dr. of John & [Lois] White.
June 2d. Eusebia Dr of Timothy & Anna Harrington.
June 16. Pheebe Dr. of Isaac Butler.
June 23. Daniel Son of Peter Joslyn Junior.
June 30. { Ahijah or Abijah Son of Lieut. Joseph Whetcomb } pr. Mr Mellen.
         { Abel Son of John Rugg. }
July 28. David Son of Capt. Jona. Hubbard.
Augt. 11th. { Abel Son of Joshua Phelps } pr. Mr Goss.
           { Abigail Daughter of Thomas Kendall }
Augt. 25. Esther Daught. of Aaron Osgood.
Sept. 1st. John Son of Edwin Robbins; Joseph Son of Joseph White.
October 6. Sarah Daughter of James Carter.
Octob. 13 Timothy Son of Joshua & Hannah Johnson; John Son of Joseph & [Hannah] Abbot.
Novr. 3d. Benjamin Son of Henry and [Rebecca] Haskel.
Decemb. 1. Abigail Daughter of Josiah Sawyer.
December 15. Joseph Son of John & Jane Henderson. 42 yᵉ Sum.

54 Baptisms in 1752.

Jan. 19th Abijah Son of Asa Harris; John Son of Zephaniah Williams.
Feb 23d. Benjamin Son of Benjamin Ballard; Rebekkah Daughter of Robt. Fletcher.
March 15. Daniel Son of Dr. Stanton Prentice; Rebekkah Daughter of Mr John Prescott; Jeremiah Son of Josiah Ballard.
April 5th. Stephen, Abigail, Twins of Abijah & [Abigail] Wyman, per. Mr Mellen.
May 10th. Manasseh Son of Capt. Ephr. Wilder Junr.; Rebekkah Dr. of Abijah Houghton.
May 24th. Amos Sawyer.
May 31. Anna Dr. of Amos Atherton pr. Mr Mellen.
June 7th. Sarah Dr. of Peter Green; Ezra Son of Joseph Osgood Junr.
June 14th. Patience Dr. of Ephraim Divol.
July 26th. Josiah Son of John Bowers. Bapt. pr. Mr Mellen; Lydia Dr. of Israel Nichols. being dangerously sick was baptized in yᵉ Evening pr me.
Augt 9th. { Sarah Dr. of Lt. Caleb Wilder. }
          { Timothy Son of Jonathan Kendall Junr. } pr Mr Marsh.
          { Nathaniel Son of Nath¹¹. White. }

Augt. 16th. Relief Dr. of Ephraim Carter; Martha Dr. of Joseph Wheelock.
Augt. 23. Abijah Son of Jeremiah Haskell; Hephzibah Daughter of James Crosfield.
Octobr. 5th. Daniel ye Son of Matthew Clarke, at ye House of sd Clarke said child being dangerously sick.
Octobr. 15th. Joseph Son of Jacob Fowle; Sarah Daughter of Amasa Turner; Thankful Dr. of Nathanael Sawyer Junr.
55 Octobr. 28th. Joel Son of Isaac Rugg.
Novr. 12th. Ruth Dr. of Daniel Johnson.
December 3d. Abel Son of David & Martha Wilder.
Decem. 10. Samuel Son of James Butler; Levi Son of John Rugg.
Decer. 31. Sherebiah Son of Sherebiah Ballard; Winslow Son of William Phelps; Pheebe Dr. of Jotham Wilder; William Son of Eunice Carter.   38
           122
           ───
           160

1753

Feb. 4th. Lois Daughter of Daniel Rugg.
Feb. 11. Calvin Son of Dean. Joshua Fairbank.
Feb. 25. Nathanael Joslyn, Esther Joslyn.
March 4th. Matthew Wyman; Ruth, Susanna, Children of James & Ruth Richardson.
March 11th. Bezaleel Sawyer Junr.; Eunice his Daughter; Thomas Son of Lt. John Carter; Abner Son of Phinehas Sawyer.
March 18th. Ephraim, Manasseh, Twins of Amos Knight Jur. pr. Mr Mellen.
March 25. Joseph Son of Nathanael Joslyn.
April 1. Lucy Dr. of John White.
April 8. Eunice Goss; Elijah Son of Nathan Rugg.
April 15. { Relief Daughter of John Osgood. } pr. Mr Morse.
         { Elisha Son of Richard Prouty. }
April 22. Mary Dr. of Gershom Flagg.
April 29th. Beulah Daughter of Asahel Phelps.
56 May 7. Joseph Son of Mr Andrew Wilder; Anna Daughter of ye Widow Sarah Hill.
June 3d. Phinehas Son of Joshua Fletcher.
July 1st. John, Dorcas, children of John Solindine he having owned ye Covenant at Groton.
July 8th. Elisabeth Dr. of Peter Joslyn Junr. pr. Mr Mellen.
July 15. James Son of James Richardson; Dorcas Dr. of Moses Osgood; Mary Dr. of Andrew Grymes or Graham.
August 12. Amos Son of Mr Ebenezer Allen.
Augt. 26th. Lydia Daughter of Ensign Joshua Phelps.
Septr. 2d. John Son of John & Prudence Manning.
Septr. 9th. Anna ye Wife of Reuben Lyppenwell.
Septr. 23d. Timothy Son of Timothy & Anna Harrington; Catharine Dr. of Nathl. & [Mary] Wyman; Elisabeth Dr. of Reuben & Anna Lyppenwel; Daniel Son of Russell & Mary Knight; Amos Son of Ebenr. Allen Junr.
Sept. 30th. Patience Dr. of Joseph White.
Octobr. 14th. William Son of Dr Stanton & Mrs Mercy Prentice.
Octobr. 21. Manasseh Son of Jonas & [Thankful] Fairbank; Ebenezer Son of Joseph & [Hannah] Abbot.
Novr. 4th. Eunice Dr. of Asa & [Eunice] Harris.
Novr. 11. Aaron Son of John & Zipporah Phelps.
Novr. 25. James Son of James & [Mary] Carter, pr Mr Seccomb.
Decemb. 9th, 1753. Abigail Nichols.
Decembr. 16. Mary Dr. of Oliver Wilder Junr.; Ruth Dr. of Phineas Houghton.   49
           160
           ───
           209

Anno Donimi 1754.

Jan. 13. Samuel Son of Joshua & [Hannah] Johnson.
Jan. 20th. Elisabeth Dr. of Capt Abijah Willard; Ruth Dr. of Jonathan Knight.
Jan. 27. John Son of Josiah Ballard.
Feb. 10th. Luke Son of Mr David & Mrs Martha Wilder.

Feb. 24th. Relief Dr. of Thomas Kendall.
57 March 25. Israel Son of Daniel Willard at his own House by Reason ——
April 7. Daniel Son of Matthew Wyman. pr. Mr Goss.
April 21. Anna Dr. of Lieut. Joseph Whetcomb; Samuel Son of Jerathmeel Bowers.
April 28th. David Son of Robert Fletcher; Relief Dr. of Abijah Houghton.
May 19th. William Son of Capt. Ephraim Wilder Junr.
Augt. 11th. Jonas Son of Mr John Prescott; Eber Son of Mr Josiah Sawyer.
Augt. 18th. Timothy Adams Son of Mr James Crosfield, pr. Mr Goss.
Septr. 1st. Lydia Daughter of Nathanael & Lydia White.
Septr. 29th. Elisabeth Dr. of Abijah Wyman.
Octobr. 6th. John Son of Joseph Wheelock.
Oct. 28th. Dorothy Dr. of Mr Joseph Osgood Junr. & Elisabeth his wife.
Novr. 3d. John & Seth, Children of John & Hannah Sargeant, and also Elisha Son of Elisha & Lois Bennett.
Novr. 17th. John Johnson, Aetatis 84.
Decembr. 8th. Joseph and Betty Priest ye Parents, and Benjamin, Susanna, Abigail, Joseph, Sarah, Eleazer, John, the Children.   32
                                                                          209
                                                                          ———
                    ANNO DONIMI 1755.   241

January 5th. John ye Son of Lieut. Benjamin Ballard, per Mr Rogers.
January 12th. Lucretia Daughter of Daniel Rugg Junr.; Mary Daughter of Russel Knight.
February 2b. Eunice Daughter of Asa Harris, at Home, being sick.
Feb. 3d. Mary Daughter of Josiah Ballard.
Feb. 16th. John Nichols Junr.; Mercy Nichols; Mary Daughter of John Nichols Junr. and Mercy his Wife; Prudence Daughter of Phinehas Houghton; Sarah Daughter of Reuben Lyppenwell; William Son of William Phelps.
58 Feb. 23d. John Son of William Dunsmoor.
March 9th. Desire Dr. of Israel & Desire Nichols.
April 13. Prudence Dr. of John Osgood, pr. Mr Rogers.
April 27th. Jonathan, Martha, Twins of Mr David & Mrs. Martha Wilder: Mercy Dr. of Dr. Stanton & Mrs Mercy Prentice; Mary Dr. of Mr Zephaniah Williams.
May 4th. Elisha Son of Nathan Rugg; James Son of John Bowers; Subbiear Dr. of Daniel Johnson. * a Hingham Name.
May 11th. William Kendall; Benjamin Son of Benjamin Osgood Junr. and Mary his Wife.
May 18th. Jonathan Son of Mr John White.
May 25th. Oliver Son of Mr Ephraim Carter.
June 15th. Sarah Dr of Matthew Clarke.
June 22. Elisha Son of Joshua Fletcher, pr. Mr Morse.
July 15. Luther Son of Deacon Joshua Fairbank; Abijah Son of Asahel Phelps; Nathanael Son of Nathanael Joslyn; Anna Dr. of Capt. Caleb Wilder.
    One Baptized by Mr Mellen and Amos Atherton forgotten.
July 27. Lois Dr. of Bezaleel Sawyer Junr.
Augt. 3. David Son of Amos Atherton.
Augt. 17th. Peter Son of Ens. Joshua Phelps; Sarah Daughter of Mr Joseph White.
Augt. 20th. Deborah Dr. of Mr Andrew Wilder at his own House by Reason of sickness of which it died.
Sept. 17th. Paul Sawyer on a Lecture Day, because of his going out of [town] in ye Service.
Sept. 28th. Hannah Dr. of Moses Osgood.
Novr. 16th. Thomas Son of Timothy & Anna Harrington; Betty Dr. of Joseph & Betty Priest.   41
December 14th. Luke Son of Phinehas Sawyer.   before. 241
                                                           Sum. 282
                    ANNO DOMINI 1756.

January 11. Rebekah Dr. of James Carter.
January 18. Thomas Son of Thomas Kendall, pr. Mr Rogers.

January 25. Theodora Dr. of Capt. Abijah & Mrs Anna Willard.
59 Feb. 1ʳᵗ. Israel Son of John Manning; Prudence Dr. of Ephraim Divol.
Feb. 15ᵗʰ. Oliver Son of Robert Fletcher.
" 22ᵈ. Ephraim Son of Jonathan Kendall Junr.
" 29ᵗʰ. William Son of George Parkhurst.
March 21ʳᵗ. Josiah Son of John Phelps; Simon Son of James Butler.
April 11. Oliver Son of Benjamin Osgood Jur.; Elisabeth Daughter of Jonathan Knight.
April 25. Jepthah Son of Converse Richardson; Ebenezer Son of Gershom Flagg.
May 2ᵈ. Abel Son of Ebenezer Allen Junr.; Deborah Dr. of Capt. Jno. Carter.
May 9ᵗʰ. pr. Mr Mellen. Francis Son of William Tufts; Samuel Son of John Sarjant; Ephraim Son of Ephraim Wilder Tertius; Ruhamah Dr. of James Richardson.
May 16ᵗʰ. Martha Daughter of Mr Nathanael Wyman.
May 30ᵗʰ. Esther & Relief, Twin Daughters of Daniel Willard; Ruth Kendall.
June 6ᵗʰ. Rebekkah Dr. of William & Mary Tucker.
Augᵗ. 15. John Son of John Nichols Junr.
Augᵗ. 29ᵗʰ. Levi Son of Capt. Levi & Mrs Katharine Willard, per Mr Rogers.
October 17ᵗʰ. Prudence Dr. of Nathˡˡ. & Lydia White; Mary Dr. of James & Mary Ballard.
Octobr. 31. James Son of John Bowers, per Mr Seccomb.
Novr. 21. Lydia Dr. of Sherebiah Ballard.
December 19. Tabitha, Elisabeth, Mary Priest, Daughters of Joseph Priest.
December 26. Susanna Dr. of Peter Green; Sarah Dr. of Abijah Wyman. 282
                                                                       36
60   BAPTISMS ANNO 1757.   318
January 2ᵈ. Anna Dr. of Reuben Lyppenwell.
January 16ᵗʰ. Carter Son of Russel Knight.
January 23ᵈ. Sarah, Deborah, Twins of Timothy Whiting.
Feb. 6ᵗʰ. John Son of Joseph Wheelock.
Feb. 13ᵗʰ. Stephen Son of Daniel Rugg Junr.
Feb. 20ᵗʰ. Joseph Son of Andrew Wilder.
Feb. 27ᵗʰ. Sabre Dr. of Josiah Sawyer. pr. Mr Goss.
March 13. Susanna Dr. of Jotham Wilder.
April 3ᵈ. Richard Baker.
July 3ᵈ. James son of Josiah Ballard; Benjamin, Jacob, Twins of Mrs David Wilder, at Home, one being sick.
July 17. John Son of Zephaniah Williams, per Mr McCarty. Joseph White.
Augt. 21ˢᵗ. { Samuel Son of Benjamin Osgood Junr. } pr. Mr Goss.
           { Ruth Dr. of John Prescott. }
Septr. 4ᵗʰ. Relief Dr. of Daniel Johnson; Lois Dr. of Elisha Bennet.
Septr. 18. Oliver Son of Mr Ephraim Carter.
Sept. 25. Darius Sawyer yᵉ Father; Deborah, Darius, Olive, Jude, Jacob, The Children; Jacob Son of Francis Fullam.
Octobr. 2. Thomas Son of Thomas Kendall; John Son of Joshua Fletcher.
Octobr. 7. Elisabeth Daughter of Deacⁿ. Josh. Fairbank at Home she being Dangerously sick.
Octobr. 16. John Son of Mr John Osgood.
Octobr. 30. Relief Dr. of Mr Joshua Phelps, pr. Mr Morse.
61 Novr. 6. Habijah Son of Capt. Abijah Willard; William Son of William De Putron; Samuel Son, Abiah Dr. of Hannah Churchil.
Novr. 27. Gardner Son of Asahel Phelps.
December 4, per Mr Goss. Mary Dr. of Phinehas Sawyer; Peter Son of John Manning; Rebecca Dr. of Nathanael Joslyn; Timothy Son of Ephraim Wilder yᵉ 3ᵈ.
December 11. Baptized at Leominster a Child of Josiah White & a Child of Oliver Hale.
                                                                       40
Dec. 25. Ephraim Son of Joseph Osgood.   318
                                                                      358

Anno Domini 1758.

1758. January 1. Luke Son of Mr James Carter.
Feb. 26. Jacob Son of Eben^r. Allen Junr.
March 26th. John Son of Capt. Levi Willard.
At Harvard April 9th. Lydia Dr. of Shadrach Hapgood; Jacob Son of John Priest; Zaccheus Son of Silas Farnsworth; Daniel Son of James Burt; Nathan Son of Jonathan Parkhurst; Joel Son of John Sampson; Elisabeth Dr. of Phin^s. Fairbank; Amee Dr. of Benj^a. Bridge; Relief Dr. of Timothy Whitney.
April 16th. Rebecca Dr. of Capt Benjamin Ballard; Bathsheba Dr. of Mr Nathan Bennett; Gershom Son of Mr Gershom Flagg; Kezia Dr. of Mr George Parkhurst; Relief Dr. of Henry Haskell Junior.
May 21st. Relief Dr. of Josiah Whetcomb Junior.
June 13th. Jacob Son of John Phelps, at ye House of sd Phelps, it being feared ye Child would not live to be baptised in public.
June 18th. { Timothy Son of Mr Timothy Whiting. } pr. Mr Mellen.
{ Nathan Son of Nathan Pushee. }
June 25th. Rebekkah Dr. of Jeremiah Haskel.
July 9. Anna Dr. of Timothy and Anna Harrington.
July 30. { Thomas Son of W^m. Tucker. } pr. Mr Goss.
{ Sherebiah Son of Lt. Sherebiah Hunt. }
Septr. 17. Amos Son of Darius Sawyer, pr. Mr Mellen.
Septemb. 24. Samuel Son of Ephraim Divol.
Octobr. 22. Mary Dr. of John Nichols Junior.
Sybil Daughter of Mr Jonathan Knight.
Novr. 12, pr. Mr Mellen. John Son of Zephaniah Williams; James Son of ye Widow Mary Ballard; John Son of Sherebiah Ballard.
62 Nov. 19th. Esther, William, children of William Richardson ye 3^d; John Son of John Warner.
Decembr. 3^d. Benjamin ye Son of Edward Hazzen.
Decembr. 10th. Mary Dr. of Dr. Stanton Prentice.
Decembr. 31. Reuben Son of Reuben Lyppenwell; Abigail Dr. of W^m. Richardson ye 3^d; Phinehas, Luke, Children of Phinehas Houghton by Reason of sickness at his own House.
At Leominster, Decem. 1758. Relief Dr. of W^m. Divol; Abigail Dr. of Abiathar Houghton; Silas Son of Abigail Smith; Elisabeth Dr. of Joseph Wilder.

358
Anno Domini 1759.
31
January 14th. Elisabeth Dr of Isaac Eveleth.   389
February. Eunice Dr. of Nathanael White.
March 4. Sarah Dr. of Russel Knight.
March 11. Anna Dr. of William Phelps.
March 18. Jotham Son of Jotham Wilder; Paul Son of Paul Sawyer.
Joshua, Son of John Rugg; —— of Joseph Wheelock.
April 29. Samuel Son of Joseph Woods; Ruth Dr. of Ensign Joseph White.
May. Martha Dr. of Deacon Joshua Fairbank; Relief Dr. of Mr Joseph Abbot; John Son of Nathan Bennet.
June 3^d. Elisabeth Dr. of Thomas Beaman.
June 17. Catharine Dr. of Capt. Levi Willard.
June 24th. Abijah Son of Lieut. John White; Lois Dr. of Mr. Daniel Willard.
July 8. Elisha Son of Mr Elisha White; Benjamin Son of Mr Abijah Houghton.
Augt. 26. Aaron Son of Mr Daniel Rugg, by Mr Morse.
Sept. 2^d. Elisabeth Dr. of Simon Willard.
Septr. 16th. Relief Dr. of Mr Ephraim Carter; Thomas Son of Mr Thomas Beaman.
Septr. 23. Nathanael Son of Thomas Kendall. Mr Mellen.
Octobr. 14. John Son of Asahel Phelps, pr. Mr Sherman.
63 Octobr. 21. Samuel Son of Coll. Abijah and Mrs Anna Willard.
Novr. 11. Sarah Dr. of William De Putron.
Novr. 18. John Son of Mr Josiah Ballard.
Novr. 25. Mary Dr. of Mr Benjamin Osgood Jur.

Decembr. 2d. Catharine Dr. of Mr Nathan Rugg.
Decembr. 13. Peter Son of Dr. Stanton and Mrs Rebecca Prentice, pr. Mr Wheeler.
Decembr. 30. Otis Son of Mr Mark & Mrs Mary Lincoln; Prudence Dr. of Mr John & Mrs Prudence Warner.

32
389
421

ANNO DOMINI, 1760.

January 6th. Rebecca, Patience, William, Children of Mr Wm. Richardson Junr. and Patience his wife.
January 13. Hannah Dr. of Mr Josiah Sawyer.
Feb. 3. Mary, Dolly, children of Joshua & Dolly Wyman, at Home both being sick.
Feb. 10th. David Son of Nathan & Elisabeth Pushee; Sarah Dr. of Edward & Sarah Hazzen.
March 2d. John son of Mr Timothy Whiting and [Sarah] his wife; Resolved Son of Mr William Richardson Junior and Patience his wife.
April 6. Thankful Dr. of Mr Ebenezer Allen Junr.; Ephraim Son of Mr George Parkhurst.
May 18. Asa Son of Mr James Carter & —— his wife; Anna Daughter of Mr Nathan¹. & Mrs Anna Turner.
June 15. Susanna Dr. of Hooker Osgood Junr. and Mrs Susanna his wife.
June 22. Sarah Dr. of Mr Nathanael Joslyn.
June 29. { Mary Dr. of Mr Joshua Fletcher. } pr. Mr Mellen.
{ Samuel Son of Mr William Richardson. }
July 6th. Tryphena Dr. of Moses and Submit Wilder.
July 13th. Moses Son of Ezekiel and Rebecca Haskel; Lois Dr. of Paul & [Lois] Sawyer.
64 July 20th. Rufus Son of Bezaleel Sawyer Junr. & Wife.
Augt. 10th. Mary ye wife of Richard Baker of Westminster, by Reason of the then unsettled State of that chh.; Thomas Sawyer—both ye children of Bezaleel Sawyer.
August 31st. Margaret Negro maid servant of Ebenezer Allen Junior.
Septr. 28th. Joshua Son of Ensign Joshua Phelps; Catharine Daughter of Mr Thomas Grant; Molly Daughter of Mr Abner Haskel.
October 5th. William Son of Mr John Osgood.
October 12th. James Son of Mr Ephraim Divoll: Prudence Daughter of Mr Ebenezer & Mrs Prudence Knight.
October 26th. Catharine Daughter of Mr Joseph and Mrs Catharine Osgood.
Novr. 2d. Deborah Daughter of Lieut. Sherebiah & Mrs Deborah Hunt.
Novr. 23d. Susanna Dr. of Nathanael & Anna Turner.
December 7. Abel Son of Mr Darius Sawyer.
December 14th. Mary Dr. of Mr Reuben & Mrs Anna Lippenwell, pr. Mr Mellen.
December 28th. John Son of Elijah and Thankful Beeman: Vashti Dr. of Ebenezer and Prudence Knight.

38
421

ANNO DOMINI 1761.

459

January 11th. Martha Dr. of Ensign Joseph & Mrs Patience White.
January 25. John Son of Isaac Evleigh; Jonathan Son of Jonathan Knight.
Feb. 1st. Daniel Son of Daniel Willard.
Feb. 8th. John Son of Peter Larkin.
Feb. 22d. Edward Son of Edward and Sarah Hazzen.
March 1st. Roger Son of Wm. and Mary Phelps, at House he being dangerously wounded in ye Birth.
March 22. Ezra Son of Mr Simon and Mrs Elisabeth Willard.
March 29. Relief Dr. of Joseph and Elisabeth Wilder of Leominster.
April 12th. Peter Son of Mr Andrew and Mrs Elisabeth Wilder; Phinehas Son of Mr Phinehas and Mrs Ruth Houghton.
April 19th. Ephraim Son of Mr Nathanael and Mrs Lydia White; Henry Son of Mr Henry Haskell Junr. and Mrs Rebecca his Wife; Prudence Daughter of Mr John and Mrs Prudence Manning.

April 26th. Sarah Dr. of Mr William & Mrs Mary Tucker.
May 10th. Oliver Son of Mr Joseph & Mrs Olive Wheelock.
May 17th. Elisha Son of Mr Elijah and Mrs Mary Woods.
June 7th. Mary ye Dr. of Mr Elijah & Mrs. Mary Woods.
June 21st. Levi Son of Mr John and Mrs [Hannah] Warner.
June 28th. Lucretia Dr. of Mr Ephraim Wilder 3d, and Mrs Lucretia his Wife.
July 12th, pr. Mr Mellen. Jonathan Son of Mr John & Mrs [Mary] Prescott; Timothy Son of Mr Jonathan and Mrs [Admonition] Kendall.
65 July 19. Samuel Son of Capt. Benja. and Mrs Ruth Ballard; Rachel Dr. of Mr Joseph & Mrs Lucy Woods.
Augt. 9th. Reuben Wheeler, Son of Mr Jotham & [Phebe] Wilder.
Augt. 23d. Jonathan Son of Mr William and Mrs Anna Jewet.
Augt. 30th. John Son of Dr. Stanton & Mrs Rebecca Prentice.
Sept. 13th. Elisabeth Dr. of Col. Abijah & Mrs Anna Willard.
Sept. 20. Abel Son of Deacon Joshua & Mrs Eunice Fairbank; Katharine Dr. of Capt. Levi & Mrs Katharine Willard.
Octob. 11th. Rachel, Sarah, Kezia, Children of ye Widow Rachel Houghton.
Octob. 18th. Allice Daughter of Mr Elisha & Mrs Allice White; Sarah Dr. of Mr Edmond & Mrs Abigail Larkin.
Novr. 15. Anna Dr. of Mr John Nichols Junr. & Mercy his Wife.
Novr. 20th. Christopher [son] of Mr Timothy & Mrs Sarah Whiting; Dolly Dr. of Mr Mark & Mrs Mary Lincoln.
Decembr. 6th. Jude Son of Mr Zephaniah & Mrs —— Williams.
Decemb. 13th. Oliver Son of Mr Francis Fullam & Wife.
Decemb. 20th. Prudence Dr. of Mr Daniel Rugg & Wife.   42
December 27th. Abel Son of Cornet Eph. & Mrs Abigail Carter.   459
                                                                 ―――
                                                                 501

ANNO DOMINI 1762.

January 17. Mary Dr. of Mr Hooker Osgood Junr. & Wife.
January 31. Oliver Son of Mr Benjamin Osgood Junr. & Wife.
Mareh 28. Charlotte Dr. of Mr Paul & Mrs Lois Sawyer.
April 11th. { David Son of Mr Asahel Phelps.
             { Thomas Son of Mr Josiah Ballard. } pr. Mr Mellen.
April 25th. Lemuel Son of Mr Benja. and Mrs Elisabeth Shedd; Mary Daughter of Mr James & Mrs Mary Goss; Mary Dr. of Mr Levi & Mrs Elisabeth Nichols.
May 16th, per Mr Mellen. Ruth Daughter of Mr James & Mrs —— Carter; John Son of Mr Robert & Mrs [Rebecca] Fletcher; Abigail Dr. of Mr James & Mrs Reed; Rebecca Dr. of Mr Henry Haskel Junr. & Wife.
66 May 30. —— of Mr Jonathan Kendall Junr. & wife.
June 27th. Luther Son of Mr Moses & Mrs Submit Wilder.
July 4th. Peter Son ot William Richardson 3d. & wife; Mary Daughter of Josiah and Jane Divol.
July 18th. Bathsheba ye Wife of Thomas Henderson; John, Betty, Thomas, Bathsheba, Children of Bathsheba Henderson.
Augt. 1st. Samuel Son of Mr Ebenezer Allen Junr. & wife; Lois, Lucy Holt.
Augt. 8th. Eunice Dr. of Mr Joseph & Mrs Katharine Osgood.
Septr. 5th. Elisha Son of Mr William & Mrs Mary Phelps.
Septr. 12. Frances Dr. of Capt. Aaron Wiliard on ye mother's acct. who had owned ye Covenant at Sudbury; Hannah Dr. of Mr Reuben & Mrs Anna Lyppenwell.
Septr. 19th. Peter Son of Mr Joshua & Mrs [Mary] Fletcher.
Octobr. 10th. George Son of Mr George & Mrs [Kezia] Parkhurst; Abijah Son of Mr Tilley & Mrs [Keturah] White on her account, a member of a Chh in Haverhill.
Octobr. 17. Peter Son of Lieut. Sherebiah & Mrs Deborah Hunt.
Novr. 14. Phinehas Son of Mr Phinehas & Mrs Sarah Phelps.
Novr. 21st. Luke Son of Mr Phinehas & Mrs [Mary] Sawyer; Daniel Son of Mr Stanton & Mrs Peninnah Carter.
Novr. 28th. Joseph Son of Mr Matthias Larkin & Wife; Benja. Whittemore Son of Wm. Willard Junr. & wife.

Decr. 5th. Mary Dr. of Mr Simon & Mrs Mary Willard; Pheebe Dr. of yᵉ Widow —— Farmer.
Decr. 26th. Dorothy Dr. of Mr Joseph and Mrs Hannah Abbot; Lucretia Dr. of Mr Edward & Mrs Lucretia Houghton; Sarah Dr. of Mr Phinehas & Mrs Sarah Phelps.

501
42
Dorothy Osgood 1754   1
544

ANNO DOMINI 1763.

Jan. 2d. Samuel Joslyn Jan. 2d.
Jan. 16th. Asenath Dr. of Nathanl. Turner & wife; Susanna Dr. of Elijah Beeman & wife; Martha Dr. of Gardner Wilder & wife.
67 March 13th. Sylvester Son of Mr Joel Phelps & wife; Susanna Dr. of Deacon Joseph White & wife; Dorothy Dr. of Lieut. Nathanael Willard & wife.
March 20th. Daniel Son of yᵉ Widow Lydia Johnson.
April 3d. William Son of Mr William & Mrs Anna Jewet.
April 10th. Nathaniel Son of Mr Thomas & Mrs Abigail Kendall; Mary Dr. of Mr Nathaniel & Mrs Martha Joslin.
April 17. Paul Willard Son of Mr Ebenr. and Mrs Sarah Hazzen; Submit Dr. of Mr Elijah & Mrs Mary Osgood.
April 24. Anna Dr. of Mr John & Mrs [Hannah] Warner.
May 1st. { Ephraim Son of Mr Peter & Mrs [Azubah] Larkin. } pr. Mr Mellen.
{ Esther Dr. of Mr Darius & Mrs [Deborah] Sawyer. }
May 8th. Elisabeth Dr. of Mr John Phelps & wife; Ursula Dr. of Mr Joseph Woods & Wife.
May 15th. Ruth and Kezia, Twin children of Mr Phinehas & Mrs Ruth Houghton.
May 29th. Elisabeth Dr. of Mr Levi Nichols and Wife.
June 12th. Mary Dr. of Mrs Wm. Richardson Junr. & Wife.
June 19. Samuel Son of Dr. Stanton & Mrs Rebecca Prentice, pr. Mr Mellen.
July 17th. Elisabeth Dr. of Mr Ephm. Wilder 3d. & Wife.
July 31. Josiah Son of Mr Josiah & Mrs Jane Divol.
Augt. 21. Peter Son of Mr Elisha & Mrs Allice White; Anna Dr. of Col. Abijah & Mrs Anna Willard. Per Mr Wheeler: Joseph Son of Mr John Prescott & Mrs Mary his wife; Jeduthan Son of Mr Josiah and Mrs Abigail Sawyer.
Septr. 4th. Aaron Son of Mr John and Mrs Hannah Sargeant.
Septr. 11th. Martha Dr. of Mr Joseph and Mrs Alice Wheelock.
Sept. 18th. Prudence Dr of Mr John Osgood & Wife.
Octobr. 2d, pr. Mr Morse. Levi Son of Mr Nathaniel & Mrs Lydia White; Zimri Son of Mr Isaac & Mrs Eunice Eveliegh.
Octobr. 23d. John Nichols yᵉ Father and Joseph, Martha, Susanna, Elisabeth, The Children; Unity yᵉ child of John and Prudence Manning.
68 Octobr 3[o]. Calvin Son of Mr Andrew Wilder & Wife; John, Benjamin, Children of Mr Benja. & Mrs Hannah Priest.
Decr. 11th. Nathan Son of Mr Elisha & Mrs Mary Bennet. He was baptised at Home on Lord's Day being at yᵉ Point of Death—and died at night.
Decr. 25. Manasseh Son of Mr Ephr. and Mrs Elisabeth Divol; Lucy Dr. of Mr Cyrus & Mrs Lucy Fairbank.

46
544
590

BAPTISMS 1764.

Jany. 1st. Hannah Dr. of Capt. Levi & Mrs Catharine Willard.
February 12th. Jotham Son of Mr Elijah and Mrs Mary Woods; John Son of Mr Henry Haskel Junr. & wife; Leafy Dr. of Mr John Nichols Junr. & wife.
Feb. 19th. Rebecca Dr. of Mr Thomas & Mrs Abigail Gates.
Feb. 26th. Elijah Son of Mr Ephraim & Mrs Abigail Carter.
March 18th. Burpy Son of Mr Richard & Mrs Prouty.
April 1st, pr. Mr Mellen. William Son of Mr Josiah Ballard & wife; Benjamin Son of Mr Benja. & Mrs Achsah Houghton.
April 15. John Son of Mr Wm. Richardson yᵉ 3d. & wife; Kezia Daughter of Mr Hooker Osgood Junr. & wife: Reuben Son of Mr Nathanael Rugg & wife.
May 13th. Ashbel Son of Mr Robert Fletcher & Wife.

May —. Eben Son of Capt Aaron Willard & wife.
June 3d. Moses Son of Mr Moses Sawyer & wife.
June 10th. James Son of Mr James Goss and wife; Rebekkah Dr. of Mr William De Putron & wife.
July 15. Olive Dr. of Mr Phinehas Phelps & wife; Phebe Dr. of Mr Asa Norcross and wife.
Aug 19th. Dolly, Sophia, Rebecca, children of Mr Philemon & Mrs Rebecca Houghton.
Septr. 2d. Eunice Dr. of Mr Francis Fullam & wife.
69 Septr. 9th. Abel Son of Matthias Larkin & wife; Abigail Dr. of Reuben Lyppenwell & wife.
Sept. 16. Rebecca Dr. of Peter and Dorothy Thirston; Asa Miller Son of Jasher Wyman and wife. On account of sickness baptised in private.
Septr. 30th. Tabitha Gibson Dr. of ye Widow Elisabeth Johnson; Rosanna Dr. of Thomas & Bathsheba Henderson, on ye mother's account.
Octobr. 14th. Aaron Son of Mr John Sargeant & wife; Eunice Dr. of Mr Tilly White and wife.
Octobr. 21st. Rufus Son of Mr Joshua Fletcher & wife, pr. Mr Mellen.
Novr. 4th. Deborah Daughter of Ens. Joshua Phelps and Wife.
Novr. 18. Abigail Dr. of Capt. Benj. Ballard & Wife; Gates Son of Mr Peter Thirston & Wife. 590
Decr. 2d. Molly Dr. of Mr David & Mrs Kezia Baldwin. 36
                                                                                            ———
                                                                                            626

BAPTISMS 1765.

Jany. 13. Cephas Son of Dr. Stanton Prentice & Wife; John Son of Mr Moses Wilder & Wife; Jonathan Son of Mr William Jewet & Wife; Esther Dr. of Mr Asahel Phelps & Wife; Judith Dr. of Mr Paul Sawyer & Wife; Amy Dr. of Mr Levi Houghton & Wife.
Feb. 3d. Prudence Dr. of Mr Joel & Mrs Prudence Phelps.
Feb. 24th. Lucy Daughter of Mr Cyrus & Mrs Lucy Fairbank.
March 10. Peter Son of Mr Elijah Beaman & wife; Betty Dr. of Mr Peter Willard & Wife.
March 31. Mary Dr. of Mr Elisha Bennet & wife; Susanna Dr. of Mr John Warner & wife.
April 14. Lucy Daughter of Mr Thomas Gates & wife.
April 28. Hannah Dr. of Deacn. Joseph White & Wife.
May 5. Peter Son of Mr John Phelps & wife. This child not being like to live was baptised in private.
May 12. Silas Son of Mr Edward Hazzen & wife; Abigail Dr. of Mr Jotham Wilder & wife.
May 26. Lucy Dr. of Mr Peter Larkin and wife; Asa Son of Mr Asa and Mrs Elizabeth Norcross—at Home being sick.
June 30th. Samuel Son of Lieut. Nathanael Willard and Wife.
July 7th. William Son of Lieut. Sherebiah and Mrs Deborah Hunt, per Mr Goss.
70 Sept. 8th. Martha Dr. of Mr Nathanael Joslyn & wife; Rebekkah Dr. of Mr Ephm. Wilder ye 3d. & wife.
Septr. 22. Benjamin Son of Mr Nathanael Wyman & wife.
Septr. 29th, pr. Mr Mellen. Thomas Son of Mr Darius Sawyer & wife; Joshua Son of Mr Elisha White & wife; Elisabeth Daughter of Mr William Phelps & wife.
Octobr. 20. Levi Son of Mr Josiah Divol and Wife.
Novr. 10th. Joseph Son of Mr Abner Haskel & wife.
Novr. 24th. Paul Son of William Willard Junr. and Wife.
Decembr. 1st. Eunice Dr. of Levi Nichols and Wife. 626
Decembr. 29. Rachel Dr. of Mr Robt. Phelps & wife. 32
                                                                                            ———
                                                                                            658

1766

January 19. William Son of Mr Nathaniel White & wife; Huldah Dr. of Mr Henry Haskel Junr. & wife.
26. Molly Dr. of Mr Moses Sawyer & wife.

Feb. 2ᵈ. Archippus Son of Mr Joseph Wheelock & wife.
Feb. 23. Jabez Son of Mr John Prescott and wife.
April 6. Elisabeth Dr. of Mr Asa Norcross & wife.
April 20ᵗʰ. Caesar Negro Servt. to Mr Peter Joslyn.
June 8ᵗʰ. Zilpah Dr. of Mr Abijah Houghton & wife.
June 29ᵗʰ. Isaac Son of Mr John Osgood & wife.
July 27ᵗʰ. Hooker Son of Mr Hooker Osgood and wife.
Augt. 3ᵈ. Catharine Dr. of Mr Thomas Grant and wife.
August 17. Hannah Dr. of Mr Elijah & Mrs Mary Woods.
Augt. 24ᵗʰ. Artemas Son of Mr John Manning & wife; Hannah yᵉ Wife of —
 Lynn Jock Negro.
Augt. 31. Rachel Dr. of Lynn and Hannah Jock, Negroes. —
Septr. 7. Stephen Son of Mr Jacob Eveleigh & wife; Elisabeth Dr. of Mr
 William Richardson 3ᵈ. and wife.
Septr. 14. Susanna Dr. of Mr John Warner and wife.
Sept. 21. Peter Son of Dr. Stanton Prentice & wife; Joseph Son of Lieut. Na-
 thanael Willard & wife.
October 5ᵗʰ. John Son of Mr John Locke and wife.
Novr. 9ᵗʰ. Levi Son of Mr John Nichols and wife; Molly Dr. of Mr Levi Hough-
 ton & wife.
71 Novr. 16. Dolly Dr. of Mr Peter & Mrs Dorothy Thurston. 658
Decembr. 14ᵗʰ, 1766. Hannah Dr. of Mr Christopher Osgood. 25
 ———
 683

1767

January 25. { Lydia Dr. of Mr Reuben Lyppenwel & wife. } by Mr Goss.
 { Bathsheba Dr. of Mr Thomas Bennett & wife. }
Feb. 8ᵗʰ. Susanna Dr. of Mr Danˡ. & Susanna Warner of Swanzy, by Mr
 Adams.
March 15. Cyrus Son of Mr Cyrus Fairbank & wife; William Son of Mr Ed-
 ward Hazzen and wife.
April 5ᵗʰ. Jeduthan Son of Mr Robert Fletcher & wife; Jedidah Dr. of Mr
 Josiah Sawyer & wife; Mehetabel Dr. of Mr James Goss & wife.
April 12ᵗʰ. Rebecca Dr. of Mr. Moses Wilder & wife.
May 3ᵈ. Anne Dr. of Mr Wᵐ. Jewet & wife.
May 10ᵗʰ. Roger Nichols Son of Mr Elijah Beman & wife.
June 14. Betsy Dr. of Mr John White Junr. & Lydia his wife.
June 21ˢᵗ. Wilder yᵉ Son of Mr Thomas Gates & wife: Lucretia Dr. of Mr
 Peter Larkin & wife.
June 28ᵗʰ. James Son of Deacon Joseph White & wife.
July 12ᵗʰ. Joel Son of Mr Ephrm. Wilder yᵉ 3ᵈ. & wife; Mary Daughter of Mr
 William Kendall & wife.
July 26. Levi Son of Mr William Richardson Junr. & wife; Susanna Dr. of Mr
 Ephm. Divol & wife.
Augt. 2ᵈ, Mr Mellen. William Son of Mr William Willard Junr. & wife; Anna
 Dr. of Mr Phinehas Phelps & wife.
Augt. 30. Dolly Dr. of Mr Josiah Ballard & wife.
Septr. 13. Samuel Son of Mr Daniel Rugg Junr. & wife, per Mr Mellen.
Sept. 27. Oliver Son of Mr David Baldwin and wife.
Octo. 4. Anne Dr. of Mr Joshua Fletcher and wife.
Oct. 11. Sarah Dr. of Mr Wyott and Mrs Martha Gunn of Swanzy.
Novr. 1ˢᵗ. Levi Son of Mr Levi Nichols & wife. 683
Dec. 6ᵗʰ. Mercy Dr. of Mr Henry Haskell Junr. and wife. 28
 ———
 711

72 BAPTISMS 1768.

January 17. Stephen Son of Mr Elisha White & wife, pr. Mr Mellen.
 24. Ezekiel Son of Mr Elijah Osgood of Swanzy & wife.
Feb. 28ᵗʰ. Robert Son of Mr Robert Phelps & wife.
March 6ᵗʰ. Betty Dr. of Mr Nathanael White & wife.
March 13ᵗʰ. Molly Dr. of Mr George Parkhurst and wife.
April 3ᵈ. Bezaleel Son of Mr Darius Sawyer & wife, pr. Mr Mellen.

April 10. Sarah Daughter of Mr Jotham Wilder & wife; Asa Son of Mr Josiah Divol & wife.
April 17th. Thomas, David, Mary Holt Children of Thomas Holt and Wife.
April 24. Asa, Lydia, children of Jonas Powers and Wife; Emily Miller Dr. of Arethusa Harrington. [Born Oct. 1, 1766.]
May 8. Sarah Dr. of Mr John Warner & wife, pr. Mr Whitney.
May 15. James Son of Mr James Goodwin and wife; Hannah Dr. of Mr Thomas Grant and wife.
May 22. Robt. Avery Son of Mr Joshua Johnson & wife: Millicent Dr. of ye wife of Mr Joshua Johnson.
May 29th. Rufus Son of Abigail Atherton.
June 5. Dolly Dr. of Mr William Phelps & wife.
June 19th. Christopher Son of Mr Christopher Osgood and wife; Lucretia Dr. of Mr Joel Phelps and wife.
June 26th. Abel Son of Mr Joseph Wheelock and wife.
July 24th. Joseph Son of Mr John and Mrs Prudence Manning; Nabby Smith Dr. of Mr Timothy Goodenough & wife.
July 31. Calvin, Luther, Lydia, Relief, Sarah, Mary, children of ye Widow Mary Sawyer; Elisabeth Dr. of Mr Isaac Eveleth and Wife.
Augt. 14th. James Otis Son of Dr. Stanton Prentice & wife.
Septr. 4th. Amos Son of ye Widow Mary Sawyer.
October 2^d. Hooker Son of Mr Hooker Osgood & wife; Peter Son of Mr Peter Thurston & wife.
9th. Thomas Son of Mr Paul Sawyer & wife.
30. Peter Son of Mr Thomas Page & wife.
Novr. 6. Oliver Son of Lieut. Nathaniel Willard & wife; Nabby Dr. of Mr Thomas Gates & wife. 711
73 Decr. 4. Oliver Johnson Son of Mr Benjamin Priest & wife. 41
752

1769

Jany. 15. John Son of Mr John White Junr. and wife.
Feb. 5th. Thomas Son of Mr Thomas Bennett & wife.
Feb. 19. Elisabeth Dr. of Mr Jonathan Whitney & wife.
March 12. Joshua Son of Mr Elijah Beman & wife.
April 16. Moses Son of Mr William Jewett & wife; Anna Dr of Mr Cyrus Fairbank & wife.
May 7th. Peter Son of Mr Peter Willard and wife, baptised at [home] by Reason of Fits.
May 14th. Achsah Dr. of Mr John Phelps & wife.
May 28th. Samuel Son of Mr Samuel Carter & wife, who owned ye Covenant at White Plains in N. York Government.
June 4th. Ephraim, Lucy, Sally, children of Mr Tilly More & wife; Katy Dr. of Mr Peter Larkin & wife.
June 11th. Eli Son of Mr Jonas Powers and wife, pr. Mr Mellen.
June 25th. Molly Dr. of Mr Phinehas Phelps & wife.
July 2^d. Joseph Son of Mr Daniel Rugg Junr. and wife.
July 16. Jabez, Susanna, children of Thomas Holt; Manasseh Son of John Osgood and wife; Rebecca Dr. of Mr Tilley More and wife.
July 23. Levi Son of Mr Abner Haskel & wife; Martha Dr. of Mr John Phelps & wife.
July 30. Rebekkah Dr. of Mr Reuben Lyppenwell & wife.
Augt. 13. Sarah Dr. of Lynn Jock and wife. Negroes.
Septr. 3^d. Elisabeth Dr. of Dr. William Greenleaf & wife.
Septr. 17. Silence Dr. of Mr Elijah Woods & wife.
Septr. 24. Rebekkah Dr. of ye Widow Esther Locke, Posthumous child of Mr Josiah Locke.
Octobr. 29th. Lydia Dr. of Mr Jonathan Kendall ye 4th. & wife.
Novr. 5th. { Luke Son of Mr Levi Nichols & wife. } pr. Mr Johnson.
{ Abel " of Mr Abel Shead & wife. }
Novr. 19. John Son of Mr Ephraim Carter Junr. & wife.
Novr. 26. Hannah, Sarah, Twins of Mr Benjamin Priest & wife.

Dec. 2ᵈ. Sophia Dr. of Mr Joshua Fletcher and wife.
74 December 10ᵗʰ. Samuel Son of Mr Samuel Ward & wife;   752
     Annice Dr. of Mr William Kendall & wife.   36
                                                          ———
                                                          788

1770

Feb. 11. Dorothy Dr. of Mr Nathaniel Wilder & wife.
Feb. 18. Abigail Dr. of Mr Ephraim Carter Junr. & wife.
March 18. John Son of Mr Moses Sawyer & wife.
April 1ˢᵗ. Ruth Dr. of Mr Ebenezer Knight & wife.
April 15. Sylvester Son of Mr Joel Phelps & wife; Leafy Dr. of Samson and Lucy Ayner, free Negroes.
April 22ᵈ. James Son of Mr Nathaniel Willard & wife.
April 29ᵗʰ. Josiah Son of Mr William Richardson 3ᵈ. and wife.
May 6ᵗʰ. Sarah Dr. of Mr Moses Wilder & wife; Alice Dr. of Mr Joseph Wheelock & wife.
May 13ᵗʰ. Calvin Son of Mr William Phelps & wife; Thurza Dr. of Mary Goodridge.
May 20ᵗʰ. Sarah Dr. of Mr Josiah Divol & wife, pr. Mr Mellen.
June 17. Ephraim Son of Mr Isaac Eveleigh & wife; Annis Dr. of Mr David Greenleafe & wife; Alcy [Elsie?] Dr. of Mr Edward Poor and wife.
June 24. George Son of Mr Thomas Grant and wife.
Jnly 15. Elisabeth Dr. of Mr John Warner and wife; Sarah Dr. of Mr John Hewet and wife.
July 22ᵈ. Josiah Son of Mr Ephraim Wilder & wife.
August 12ᵗʰ. Anna Dr. of Mr Cyrus Fairbank & wife.
Septr. 2ᵈ. John, Phebe, children of Mr Andrew Poor & wife.
Septr. 16. Molly Dr. of Mr Peter Willard and wife.
October 21. Anna Dr. of Mr Thomas Gates & wife.
Octobr. 28. Edward Son of Mr James Goodwin & wife.
Novr. 4ᵗʰ. Anna Dr. of Mr Zephaniah Williams & wife.
Novr. 11ᵗʰ. John Son of Mr Christopher Osgood & wife.
Novr. 25. Sally Dr. of Mr John White Junr. and wife; Luke Son of   30
     Lydia Butler.   788
                                                                    ———
                                                                    818

1771

January 13ᵗʰ. Peter Son of Mr Hooker Osgood and wife.
January 20. Anna Dr. of Mr Elisha White & wife.
January 27. Arethusa Dr. of Mr Joseph Brown & wife.
75 March 17. James Son of Mr James Pratt & wife; Charlotte Dr. of Mr John Prest junior & wife.
March 31. Jonathan Son of Mr Jonathan Whitney & wife; Anna Dr. of Mr Joshua Johnson & wife.
April 14. Abel Son of Mr Timothy Goodenough & wife.
April 21. Fanny Dr. of Mr Tilly Moore & wife.
April 28. John Alldis Son of Mr Asa Haven & wife; Jonathan Son of Jonathan Kendall yᵉ Fourth.
May 12. Israel Son of Mr Paul Sawyer & wife.
May 26. Hannah Dr. of Mr William Jewet & wife.
June 16. Lydia Dr. of Mr Thomas Bennett & wife, pr. Mr Whitney, Northborough.
June 23ᵈ. Joshua yᵉ Son of Mr Joshua Fairbank and wife; Nathaniel Son of Mr Reuben Lyppenwel & wife.
July 14. John Son of Lynn Jock and wife, free Negroes.
July 21. Sarah Dr. of Mr Levi Nichols and wife.
July 28ᵗʰ. Hiram Son of Mr Samuel Carter & wife.
Augt. 4. Sewall Son of Mr Robert Phelps & wife: Sarah Dr. of Mr —— Willson & wife.
Augt. 11. Molly Dr. of Mr John Jones and wife, pr. Mellen.
Sept. 15. John Son of Mr John Hewit & wife.
Sept. 15. John Son of Mr John Hewit & wife.
Sept. 22. Phebe Dr. of Lucy Ayner free Negroe.

Octobr. 6. Jonathan Knight Son of Mr Joseph Blood.
Octobr. 13. Joseph Son of Mr Daniel Rugg junr. and wife; Anna Dr. of ye wife of Mr Simeon Johnson on her Account; Lydia Dr. of Lydia Johnson.
Octobr. 27, 1771. Sarah, Relief, Jabez, Lucy, Hannah, Rhoda, Ephraim, children of Mr Joseph Beeman & wife on her Account; Levi Son of Mr Stephen Wilder and wife; Sophia Dr. of Mr Nathaniel Beeman and wife; Nathaniel Son of Mary Wood.
Nov. 3^d. William Son of Mr George Leason [Gleason] and wife.
Novr. 10th. Thankful Dr. of Widow Thankful Beman.
Novr. 12. Lucy Dr. of Mr John Bennett and wife, at Home sd. child being at ye Point of Death.
Novr. 17. Thankful, Jonathan, Benjamin, Abijah, Peter, Betsy, children of Mr Jonathan Wheelock & wife, on her Account.
76   Decembr. 8. John Son of Mr John Phillips and wife; Anna Dr. of Mr Ephraim Carter junr. and wife.

818
49
867

1772

January 5th. Susanna Dr. of Mr David Greenleaf & wife; Menbah child of Mr Benjamin Priest & wife; Eunice Dr. of Mr Salmon Goodfry and wife.
Feb. 16. Zilpah Dr. of Mr John Phelps and wife.
March 8th. Amasa Son of Mr Simon Willard & wife; Anna Dr. of Mr Phin. Houghton & wife; Isabel Dr. of Mr Joel Phelps & wife; Gardner Son of Mr John Wilder and wife.
April 5. Samuel Son of Mr Jonathan Wheelock & wife.
April 26. Melzar Turner Son of Thomas Grant & wife on ye mother's acct.; Elisabeth Dr. of Mr Nath^{ll}. Joslyn and wife.
May 3^d. Relief, Joel, Children of Mr Russell Knight; Frances Dr. of Mr John Warner & wife.
May 17. Sarah Dr. of Mr Moses Sawyer and wife; Dolly Dr. of Mr Edward Poor and wife.
Lucy Dr. of Mr Joseph Woods and wife. *Day forgotten, to be enquired &c.*
June 28th. Nathan Son of Mr Nathan Newhall and wife.
Augt 2^d. Joel Son of Mr Joshua Fairbank and wife.
Augt. 16th. William Son of Mr Joshua Fletcher and wife.
Augt. 23. Elisabeth Dr. of Lieut. Nathaniel Willard & wife; Molly Dr. of Mr Thomas Holt Junr. and wife.
Augt. 30. Jonas Son of Mr Jonathan Whitney and wife; Luther Son of Mr John Bennet and wife.
Septr. 6. Daniel Son of Mr Daniel Goss and wife.
Septr. 13. Elisabeth Dr. of Mr Andrew Poor and wife, pr. Mr Adams.
Octobr. 4th. Josiah Son of Mr Abishai Phelps and wife.
Octobr 18. Samuel Son of Mr James Pratt & wife.
October 25. Bathsheba Dr. of Mr John Robbins and wife, pr. Mr Whitney Shirley.
Novr. 1. Calvin Son of Mr Sam^{ll}. Wilder and wife.
Novr. 15. Lucy Dr. of Mr Thomas Holt Junr. & wife per Mr Dana.
Novr. 22^d. Rufus Son of Mr William Kendall & wife.   867
Decembr. 29. Damaris Dr. of Mr Joseph Brown and wife.   33
                                                                   900

1773

Jany. 10th. Sarah Dr. of Mr Cyrus Fairbank & wife; Sarah Dr. of Mr John or Joseph Jones & wife.
January 17th. Moses Russell; Moses Phelps Son of sd. Moses Russell.
77 January 31. Molly Dr. of Mr Peter Willard & wife.
Febr. 7th. John Son of Mr Thomas Gates & wife; Jonathan Son of Mr [James] White of Charlemont & wife.
Feb. 14. Levi Son of Mr John Osgood and wife.
Feb. 28. Sally Dr. of Mr William Greenleaf & wife; Sarah Dr. of Mr Salmon Goodfry & wife.
March 14. Deborah Dr. of Nathaniel Beeman & wife.
March 21. Timothy Son of Joshua Johnson & wife.

March 28. James Son of Mr James Wilder Junr. and wife.
April 18th. Charles Son of Capt. Saml Ward and wife.
May 9th. Beulah Dr. of Mr Paul Sawyer & wife.
May 16th. Mary Dr. of Mr William Locke & wife, pr. Mr Mellen.
May 30th. Elijah Son of Mr Joseph Wheelock Junr. and wife, pr. Mr Sparhawk.
June 13. Peter Son of Mr Peter Larkin & wife; Olive Dr. of Mr Reuben Lyppenwell & wife.
June 27. Paul Son of Mr Paul Fitch & wife per Mr Johnson.
July 11. Anna Daughter of Mr Elisha Allen & wife.
July 18. Lucinda Laura Dr. of Mrs Martha Stevens.
July 25th. James Son of Mr Hooker Osgood & wife; John Son of Mr Stephen Wilder & wife.
August 8th. Nathan Son of Mr Thomas Bennet, by Mr Mellen.
Augt. 29. Molly Dr. of Mr John Hewit and wife.
Sept. 5th. Artemas Son of Mr Jonathan Kendall 4th, & wife: Elisabeth Dr. of Mr Daniel Rugg Junr. & wife.
Sept. 19. John Son of Mr James Goodwin & wife; Michael, Elijah, Submit, Daniel, Joel, Children of ye Widow Hannah Ross.
Octobr. 10. Rufus Son of Saml. Carter & wife; Lydia Mansfield Dr. of Patience Wyman.
Octobr. 31, pr. Mr Mellen. Moses Son of Mr Moses Wilder & wife: Ephraim Son of Mr Ephraim Carter Junr. & wife; Polly Dr. of Mr Jonas Wyman & wife.
Novr. 14. David Son of Mr Elisha White & wife.
Novr. 21. Sarah Dr. of Mr John Sprague & wife; Samuel Son of Mr John Phillips & wife; Nathaniel, Jonathan, Eunice, Silas, children of Mr Nathaniel Willard Junr. & wife; Aaron, Jonas, children of Mr Aaron Johnson & wife.
Novr. 28. Hannah Dr. of Mr Daniel Zwier & wife. 900
78 Decembr. 19. Nancy Dr. of Mr Peter Thirston & wife. 51
951

1774.

January 2d. Jotham Son of Mr John Robbins & wife; Charlotte, Arethusa, children of Mr Abijah Houghton Junr. & wife.
January 9th. { John Son of Mr John Kindric and wife. } pr. Mr Mellen.
{ Lucy Dr. of Mr John Bennett & wife. }
January 23d. Ruth Dr. of Mr James & Mrs Ruth White of Charlemont.
January 30. Lucy Dr. of Mr Phinehas Wilder & wife; Jesse Son of Mr Joel Phelps & wife; Samuel Son of Mr Isaac Eveleth & wife.
Febr. 6th. Gershom Son of Mr Gershom Flagg & wife; Susanna Dr. of Mr Mark Heard & wife.
February 20th. Peter Bulkly Son of Mr Moses Russell & wife.
March 13th. Harison Son of Capt. Ephraim Wilder & wife; Zaccheus Son of Mr Jonathan Whitney & wife.
March 26. Jonas Son of Mr Daniel Goss & wife—at Home being dangerously sick.
April 3d. Olive Dr. of Mr John Warner and wife.
April 10th. Jonas Son of Mr Nathaniel Joslyn & wife; Joel Son of Mr Nathaniel Willard Junr. and wife; Alice Dr. of Mr Samuel Wilder and wife; William, Margaret, children of Mr William Shaw & wife.
May 8th. Thomas Son of Mr Titus Wilder, & wife.
May 15. Rebekkah Dr. of Mr Joseph Beeman & wife, pr. Mr Mellen.
May 29th. Joseph Beeman Junr. on his owning ye Covenant; Polly, Lucinda, Sophia, children of Mr Josiah White & wife.
June 5th. Paul, Silas, twin children of Mr Russell Knight & wife.
June 12th. Eleazar Son of Mr Edward Poor and wife. pr. Mr Johnson.
July 17th. David Son of ye Widow Anna Margaret Russell; Eunice Dr. of Mr Samuel Wilder & wife.
July 24th. Peter Son of Mr John Phelps & wife; Luke Son of Mr William Phelps & wife.

310   LANCASTER RECORDS.

July 31. Abigail Dr. of Mr Moses Smith & wife.
Aug⁴. 7. Timothy Son of Mr Timothy Cheney & wife who had owned yᵉ Cov'-
   ant at Stow.
Augt. 14. Lydia Daughter of Mr Timothy Knight junr. & wife.
Augt. 21. Elisha Son of Mr Elisha Allen & wife.
Augt. 28. Ebenezer Son of Mr Ebenezer Allen junr. & wife; Paul Son of Mr
   Moses Dickenson and wife.
Septr. 4ᵗʰ. Nathaniel Son of Mr William Jewet and wife, pr. Mr Morse.
Sept 18. Lois Dr. of Mr Daniel Zwier & wife, pr. Mr Mellen.
Octobr. 2ᵈ. Rebecca Dr. of Mr Joshua Fairbank & wife; Hannah Bachelor Dr.
   of Mr Matthew James and wife.
79 Octobr. 9ᵗʰ. Jonas Son of Mr Cyrus Fairbank & wife.
Novr. 6ᵗʰ. James Son of Mr Abishai Phelps & wife; Phinehas Son of Mr Jos-
   eph Jones & wife.   951
Novr. 27ᵗʰ. Nabby Dr. of Mr Samuel Joslyn & wife.   48
                                                                    ———
                                                                    999

ANNO DOMINI 1775.

January 15. Sarah Dr. of Mr Jotham Woods and wife.
Feb. 19ᵗʰ. Luther Son of Mr William Kendall & wife.
Feb. 26. Submit Dr. of Mr Moses Wilder and wife; Anna Dr. of Mr John Ken-
   drick & wife.
March 5ᵗʰ. Sarah Dr. of Mr Simon Willard and wife.
March 12ᵗʰ. Elisabeth Dr. of Mr Aaron Johnson and wife; Sarah Dr. of Mr
   Benjamin Farmer & wife.
March 19ᵗʰ. Rachel Dr. of Mr Elijah Woods and wife.
April 2ᵈ. Levi Son of Mr Nathaniel Willard and wife.
April 9ᵗʰ. William Son of Mr William Locke & wife.
April 30. John Hancock Son of Mr William Greenleaf & wife; Betsy Dr. of
   Mr Nathaniel Beaman & wife; Anna Dr. of Mr Daniel Goss & wife.
May 7ᵗʰ. Abel Son of Mr John White Junr. & wife; Lucy Dr. of Mr Joseph
   Whitmore & wife.
May 14ᵗʰ. Rebekkah Dr. of Mr Jonathan Wheelock.
May 21ˢᵗ. Mary Dr. of Mr James Wilder junr. and wife.
June 11ᵗʰ. Beulah Dr. of Mr Hooker Osgood and wife.
June 18ᵗʰ. William Pitt Son of Dr. Josiah Wilder and wife; John Son of Mr
   John Robbins & wife.
July 2ᵈ. Olive Wilds Dr. of Mr Elijah Wheelock and wife.
July 16ᵗʰ. Anna Dr. of Mr Daniel Rugg Junr. and wife.
July 30ᵗʰ. Elisabeth Dr. of Mr Jonas Wyman & wife.
Augt. 6ᵗʰ. Polly Dr. of Capt. Thomas Gates & wffe; Rachel Dr. of Mr Joshua
   Johnson & wife: Thankful Dr. of Mr Ebenezer Allen Jnnr. & wife; Stephen
   Haywood Son of Mr Jeremiah Leach & wife.
Augt. 20ᵗʰ. Polly Wilder; Grizzle Apthorpe Flagg.
Augt. 21ˢᵗ. Jeremiah Son of Mr Nehemiah Newton, at his own House in pres-
   ence of divers of yᵉ Chh, being dangerously sick.
Augt. 27. Israel Son of Mr John Hewit and wife.
Septr. 3ᵈ. Sally Sarjeant Dr. of Mr John Newman, at Home dangerously sick.
Septr. 10ᵗʰ. Rebecca Dr. of Mr John Phillips & wife; Salmon or Solomon Son
   of Mr [Salmon] Godfrey and wife; Eliakim Son of Mr Timothy Cheney and
   wife.
Septr. 24ᵗʰ. Peter Son of Mr Samuel Johnson & wife.
Octobr. 8ᵗʰ. Sarah yᵉ wife, Sally and Mary Whitcomb the children of Mr James
   Fuller; Sarah yᵉ Dr. of Mr Mark Heard and wife.
Octobr. 15. Joel Son of Mr Joel Osgood & wife.
Novr. 5. Polly Dr. of Mr John Bennett & wife.   *Turn to page 92*
92 Novr. 12ᵗʰ. Elisabeth Dr. of Mr Joseph Cooledge & wife.
Decembr. 3ᵈ. Eunice Dr. of Mr Jonathan Whitney & wife.   999
December 17. John Son of Mr Nicolas Pierce & wife.   45
                                                                    ———
                                                                    1044

BAPTISMS, ANNO DOMINI 1776.

February 4ᵗʰ. Ruth Dr. of Mr Joel Phelps & wife.

February 18th. Charles Eams Son of Mr Manasseh Knight & wife.
Febry. 25th. Solomon Son of Capt. Ephraim Carter & wife; Joel Son of Mr Benjamin Priest & wife; Polly Dr. of Mr Titus Wilder & wife.
March 3d. Seth Son of Mr Stephen Wilder & wife; Anne Austin Dr. of Mr John Sprague & wife.
March 10th. Sarah Dr. of Capt. Saml. Ward & wife.
March 31st. Peter Son of Mr Nathaniel Joslyn & wife.
April 7th. Ward Son of Mr Elisha White and wife; Joseph Son of Mr Joseph Joslyn and wife.
May 5th. Moses Son of Mr Moses Dickenson & wife; Lucy Dr. of Mr John Warner deceased & wife.
May 12th. Stephen Son of Mr Daniel Goodfry and wife.
July 7th. James Son of Mr Hooker Osgood & wife; Luther Son of Mr Joshua Fairbank & wife; Sarah Dr. of Abner Haskel & wife; Sarah Dr. of Jonathan Kendall 4th. & wife; Sarah Dr. of Mr Joseph Bennett & wife.
July 14th. Peter Son of Mr Ephm. Divol junr. and wife; Abner Son of Mr Abijah Houghton junr. & wife; Nabby Dr. of Mr Samll. Carter & wife.
Sept. 8th. Hannah ye wife of Coll. Joseph North; Sarah Dr. of Mr Thomas Holt Junr.
Septr. 22. Aaron Son of Mr Moses Wilder & wife; Sally ye Dr. of Mr Nathaniel Eaton & wife.
Septr. 29th. Olive Dr. of Mr Nathaniel Willard & wife.
Octobr. 6th. Elisha Son of Mr Elisha Houghton and wife, on her account; Elisha Son of Mr Elisha Bennett & wife, on her account.
Novr. 3d. Mary Dr. of Mr William & Barbara Shaw.
Novr. 10th. Katharine Dr. of Mr Edward Poor & wife.
Decembr. 29. Elisabeth Willard Dr. of Mr Ebenezer Bradish & wife; Sally Dr. of Mr James Pratt and wife.

1044
33
1077

1777.

January 5. Samuel Son of Mr Kendrick & wife; Elisabeth Willard Dr. of Mr Ebenr. Bradish & wife. [Repetition.]
19th. Lemmy Son of Mr Daniel Page & wife.
Feby. 2d. James Son of Mr Gershom Flagg & wife.
Feb. 18th. Joseph Son of Mr Joseph Whitmore and wife, at Home, it being supposed ye child would not live.
March 9th. Anna Dr. of Mr William Locke & wife.
93 March 16. Lydia Dr. of Mr John Phelps and wife.
March 30th. Henry Son of Dr. Josiah Wilder & wife; Joel Son of Mr Samuel Wilder and wife; James Son of Mr Joseph Joslyn and wife.
April 6th. David Son of Mr Samuel Wilder and wife; Peter Son of Mr Danll. Godfry & wife; Anna Dr. of Mr Benja. Farmer & wife.
April 13. Sally, Lucy, children of Mr Manasseh Wilder and wife.
April 20. Joseph Son of Mr Joseph Carter & wife.
April 27. Artemas Son of Mr Timothy Knight Junr. and wife.
May 4th. Luther Son of Mr Jonathan Wheelock & wife.
May 18th. Moses Son of Mr Moses Smith and wife; Daniel Son of Mr Daniel Zwier and wife; Molly Dr. of Mr Ebenr. Allen junr. & wife.
May 25. Jonathan Son of Mr Jonathan Osgood and wife.
June 1st. Joshua Son of Mr Joshua Johnson & wife.
June 8th. Seth Son of Mr Elijah Woods and wife.
June 22d. Sarah Daughter of Mr William Jewet & wife; Lucy Daughter of Mr Daniel Rugg junr. & wife.
June 29th. Maria Dr. of Mrs Maria Houghton & Husband.
July 20th. Patience Dr. of Mr Manasseh Knight & wife.
July 27th. Wiiliam Son of Mr William Kendall and wife; Sally Downe Dr. of Mr Joseph Abbot and wife.
Augt. 17. Moses Son of Cato and Eunice free Negroes, who had owned ye Covenant at Marlborough.
Septr. 7th. Rebekkah Dr. of Mr Salmon Godfry & wife.
Septr. 28. Edward Son of Mr John Robbins and wife.

Octobr. 12. Hephziba Brabrook; Thomas, John Kalsall, children of Mr [John] Baker and wife; Rebecca Dr. of Mr William de Putron & wife; Elisabeth Dr. of Capt. [Daniel] Goss & wife; Bathsheba Dr. of Mr James Goodwin & wife.
Novr. 9th. John Son of Mr Jonas Wyman; Nancy Dr. of Mr James Fuller.
December 21st. Nancy Dr. of Mr Nathaniel Eaton and wife. 1077
December 28. Solomon Son of Mr Benjamin Priest, baptized at Shirley. 43
                                                                    ————
                                                                    1120

1778.

January 4th. Abel Son of Mr Timothy Cheney & wife.
February 1st. William Son of Mr Henry Willard Farmer & wife.
Feb. 22d. Abigail Dr. of Mr Nathaniel Beeman & wife.
March 22d. Samuel Locke Son of Capt. Eph. Wilder & wife; Joseph Nowel Son of Mr Samuel Adams & wife; Mary Daughter of Capt. Ephm. Carter & wife.
94 March 29. Artemas Son of Mr Moses Sawyer & wife; Daniel Son of Mr Daniel Knight & wife; Lucinda Dr. of Mr James Wilder & wife; Betty Dr. [of] Mr Elisha Allen and wife.
April 12th. Thomas, Joseph, twin children of Mr Stephen Wilder & wife; Apphia Dr. of Mr Ephraim Kendall & wife.
April 19th. Joseph Son of Mr Nathaniel Haskell & wife.
May 3. Abigail, Sally, children of Mr Abishai Phelps & wife.
May 10th. Thankful Dr. of Mr Luther Fairbank & wife.
May 17th. James Son of Mr Moses Dickenson & wife.
May 24th. Lucy Dr. of Mr Samuel Joslyn & wife; Nancy Dr. of Mr Joseph Beaman & wife.
June —. John Son of Mr Daniel Godfry &c.
June 28th. George Son of Mr Joel Phelps & wife; Polly Dr. of Mr Jonathan Beaman & wife.
July 12th. John Son of Mr John Carter and wife; Nahum Son of Mr Jonathan Osgood & Wife.
Augt. 29th. Polly Dr. of Dr. Josiah Wilder and wife, at Home for Special Reason, but in Presence of a Number of ye Brethren of ye Chh.
Augt. 30. William Dunsmore Son of Mr Nathaniel Haskell and wife.
Octobr. 4th. Timothy Harrington Son of Mr John Newman & wife.
Octobr. 18. Daniel Son of Wm. Greenleaf Esq.; Billy Son of Mr John More; Kezia Dr. of Mr Abijah Houghton junr.
Novr. 1st. Abel Son of Mr Moses Wilder &c.; Polly Dr. of Mr William Locke &c.; William Son of Mr William Wilder &c.
Novr. 8. Phebe Dr. of Mr John Abbot and wife.
Novr. 22d. { Nancy Dr. of Capt. Joseph Wilder. } pr. Mr Maccarty.
            { Anna Dr. of Mr William Wilder. }
Novr. 29th. John Son of Capt. Thomas Gates &c.
Decr. 20. Luke Son of Mr Joseph Joslyn. 1121
Decr. 31. Solomon Son of Mr Benja. Priest, at Home dangerously sick. 41
                                                                    ————
                                                                    1162

1779.

March 14th. Thomas, Daniel, Ebenezer, Ruthy, Sally Burditt.
March 21st. Jonathan Son of William Henry Farmer & Wife.
April 4. Daniel Son of Lieut. Samuel Wilder &c.; Silas Son of Mr Jonathan Kendall jur. &c.; Martha Dr. of Mr Simon Willard &c.; Emme Dr. of Mr Benja. Haskell &c.
95 April 18. John Son of Mr Joshua Fairbank &c.; Thankful Dr. of ye Widow Mary Allen.
April 25. Polly Dr. of Mr John Kendrick &c.
May 2d. Ephraim Son of Capt. Daniel Rugg &c.
May 9th. Nathan Son of Mr Daniel Page &c.
May 16. Edward Son of Edward Poor &c.; Martha Dr. of Benja. Farmer &c.; Patty Dr. of Manasseh Knight &c.
May 23. William Son of Mr Joseph Carter &c.
August 15. Josiah Son of Mr Jeremiah Ballard and wife.

August 22ᵈ. Rebecca Dr. of Mr Timothy Knight Junr. & wife; Polly Dr. of Mr James Goodwin & wife.
Augt. 29. Sally Dr. of Mr David Hosley & wife.
Septr. 26. Jonas Son of Capt. Daniel Goss and wife.
Octob. 3. Polly Goddard; Sally Nowell Dr. of Mr Samˡˡ. Adams and wife.
Octobr. 10. Louisa Dr. of Dr. R. P. Bridge and wife.
Novr. 14. Augustus Son of Dr. Josiah Wilder & wife.
Novr. 28. Polly Dr. of Mr Samˡ. Wilder and wife.
Decembr. 26. Henry Son of Mr Nathaniel Eaton.   1162
         Daniel Son of Mr Daniel Knight.   31
                                                      1193

BAPTISMS 1780.

March 5. Sewal Son of William Kendall & wife; Betsey Dr. of Mr Samˡˡ. Johnson & wife.
March 19. Samˡ. Son of Mr Jonas Wyman and wife.
April 23ᵈ. Jonas Son of Mr Moses Sawyer & wife; Polly Dr. of Mr Moses Wilder & wife; Nathaniel Son of Mr Nathaniel Beeman and wife; Jonas Son of Mr William Phelps Junr. and wife; Anna Dr. of Mr Thomas Harrington & wife.
April 30. Samuel Son of Capt. Samuel Joslyn & wife.
May 21. Jem Son of Lieut. Salmon Godfrey & wife; Sampson Vryling Stoddard Son of Lieut. Levi Wilder & wife.
May 28. Joseph Son of Mr Caleb Wilder & wife.
June 4ᵗʰ. Abel Son of Capt. John White junr. and wife; Luther Son of Jonathan White & wife.
June 18ᵗʰ. Abner Son of Mr Timothy Cheney & wife, pr. Mr Payson.
July 2ᵈ. Samuel John Son of Mr John Sprague and wife.
July 9ᵗʰ. Bekky Dr. of Mr Moses Dickenson & wife.
July 23ᵈ. Abel Son of Mr Stephen Wilder & wife.
Augt. 20. Katy Dr. of Mr Abishai Phelps & wife.
Augt. 27. Lucy Dr. Mr Abel Phelps and wife.
Septr. 24. James Son of Mr Hooker Osgood & wife, Ashby; Betsey Dr. [of] Manasseh Wilder and wife.
96 Octobr. 1ˢᵗ. Nabby Dr. of Mr Nathˡˡ. Haskel & wife.
Octobr. 8ᵗʰ. Josiah Son of Mr William Locke & wife; Elisabeth Dr. of Mr Joseph Carter & wife.
Octobr. 15. Polly Dr. of Dr. Josiah Wilder & wife.
Octobr. 29. Billy Son of Mr Joseph Joslyn and wife.
Novr. 5. Sally Dr. of Mr Abel Phelps & wife.
Novr. 26. Otis Son of Mr James Wilder & wife.
December 17. James Son of Mr James Carter junr. & wife.
December 24. Lucy Dr. of Mrs Lucy Whitney.
December 31. Nabby Dr. of Deacⁿ. Cyrus Fairbank & wife; Betsy Dr.   1193
of Mr James Pratt & wife.   32
                                                   1225

BAPTISMS 1781.

January 15. Luther Son of Mr Jonathan Wheelock & wife, at Home being dangerously sick.
February 25. Uzziah Son of Mr Benjamin Farmer & wife; Sarah. Dr. of Capt. Ephraim Carter & wife.
March 18ᵗʰ. Ephraim Son of Mr William Wilder & wife.
April 1ˢᵗ. Nahum Son of Mr Abijah Rugg and wife on her Account; Betsy Dr. of Mr Asa Warner and wife on his Account.
April 8ᵗʰ. Moses Son of Mr Joel Osgood and wife.
April 15ᵗʰ. John Son of Mr Thomas and Dolly Cummins.
April 29ᵗʰ. John Son of Mr David and Lucebe Hosley.
May 6ᵗʰ. Caleb Son of Lt. Godfry & wife, pr. Mr Kellogg.
May 20ᵗʰ. Esther Dr. of Mr James Fuller & wife; Polly Dr. of Mr Abijah Houghton junr. & wife.
May 27ᵗʰ. John Son of yᵉ Widow Eunice Poor; Anna Dr. of William Phelps junr. & wife.

21

July 1st, pr. Mr Holcombe. Jonathan Son of Mr Jonathan White; Betsy Dr. of Mr Nathaniel Eaton; Clarissa Dr. of Mr Ed. Johnson, Bolton.
July 22d. Luke Son of Mr Moses Wilder and wife; Samll Son of Mr Samuel Adams & wife.
August 5th. Abel Son of Mr Joshua Fairbank & wife.
Augt. 12. Silence Dr. of Mr Levi Carter and wife.
Augt. 26. John Son of Mr Saml. Wilder & wife; Sally Dr. of Mr Jeremiah Ballard & wife.
Octob. 7. John Son of Mr Ephraim Divol & wife.
Octobr. 28. Polly Dr. of Capt. Daniel Rugg & wife.
Novr. 18. Katy Dr. of Mr William Wyllis and wife.
Dec. 2d. James Son of Mr John Kindrick and wife.
Dec. 9th. Oliver Son of Mr Jacob Phelps & wife.
Betty Dr. of Mr Simon Willard and wife.
Dec. 16. Ebenezer Son of Mr Titus Wilder & wife; Sally Dr. of Mr Levi Wilder and wife.

1225
<u>31</u>
1256

97 BAPTISMS 1782.

Feb. 3d. Patience Dr. of Mr Philip Corey & wife.
Feb. 17. Josiah Son of Mr Jonathan Wheelock & wife.
March 3d. John Son of Deacon Cyrus Fairbank & wife: Emma, Amy Drs. of Timothy Knight Junr. & wife.
March 31. John Son of Capt. Nathaniel Beaman & wife; Deborah Dr. of Mr Samll. Johnson & wife.
April 7. Salley Dr. of Mr Jonathan Whitney & wife; Sarah Dr. of Mr James Goodwin and wife.
April 28. John Son of Capt. Ephraim Carter and wife.
May 5th. Henry Son of Deacn. Josiah Wilder & wife.
May 12th. Amy Dr. of Mr Abijah Rugg & wife, on her Account.
May 26. Sally Phelps on owning ye Covenant.
June 2d. Samuel Son of Putnam Wyman.
June 23d. Sally Dr. of Mr Jonas Wyman & wife.
June 30th. John Son of Capt. Benja. Gould and wife.
July 21st. Salmon Son of Mr Salmon Godfry & wife; Cephas Son of Mr William Kendall & wife; Jacob Son of Mr Jacob Phelps and wife.
Augt. 4. Isaac Son of Mr Samuel Sanderson & wife; Anna Dr. of Mr Joseph Carter & wife.
Augt. 11. Lewis Son of Amos Allen & wife; Samuel Son of Moses Dickenson & wife.
Augt. 25. Katharine Dr. of Mr Thomas Cummins & wife, on her Account.
Septr. 1st. Nathaniel Son of Mr Moses Sawyer & wife; James Son of Mr William Locke & wife.
Sept. 8th. Edward Son of Mr James Wilder & wife.
Sept. 22. John Son of Mr Samuel Adams & wife.
Octobr. 13. John Son of Capt. Timo. Whiting junr. and wife; Nancy Dr. of Mr Aaron Phelps & wife.
Novr. 24. Susanna Dr. of Mr Manasseh Wilder & wife.
Decembr. 8th. Sally Dr. of Mr Gershom Flagg & wife.
Decembr. 22d. Elias Son of Mr Moses Wilder and wife.

1256
<u>32</u>
1288

1783.

Jany. 5th. Joseph, Calvin, Twin Children of Capt. Samll. Joslyn and wife.
January 26th. Amy wife of Mr Elisha Rugg; Luke Son of Levi Carter & wife; Theodora Dr. of Mr Abishai Phelps & wife.
March 2d. Lucy Dr. of Mr Elisha Rugg & wife; Polly Dr. of Mr Asa Carter & wife.
March 9th. Josiah Son of Elisha White Junr.
March 16th. Polly Dr. of Mr Nathaniel Eaton.
March 24. Elisabeth Dr. of Zebulon Butman at Home dangerously sick.
98 April 13. Huldah Dr. of Mr John Robbins &c.; Esther Dr. of Mr Ephraim Divol &c.

April 20th. Sophia Dr. of Mr Joel Osgood, &c.
April 27. Peter Son of Mr Abel Phelps &c.
May 4th. Luther Son of Mr Edward Johnson &c.
May 11th. Lucy Dr. of Mr William Phelps junr. &c.
June 8th. Justin Eliot Son of Dr. Wm. Frink &c.; John Son of Capt. Daniel Goss &c.; Timothy Ballard Son of Mr Thomas Harrington &c.
June 30th. Philip Son of Philip Corey, pr. Mr Adams.
July 27. Henry Son of Mr Winslow Phelps,—on ye mother's Account.
August 24th. Betsy Dr. of Deacon Cyrus Fairbank, pr. Mr Holcomb.
August 31st. Rose Maid Servant to Timothy Harrington on her owning ye Covenant.
Septr. 14. Peggy Dr. of Mr Levi Wilder &c.
Septembr. 28· Mindwell Dr. of Relief Wilder.
October 5. Hannah Dr. of Col. Joseph North & wife on her Account being a member in full Communion.
October 12. Sally, Nancy Clark on their owning ye Covenant.
October 26. Samuel & Sarah, children of Mr Samuel and Mrs Sarah Jones; Josiah Son of Mr Saml. Wilder &c.; Tabby Dr. of Mr Titus Wilder &c.
Novr. 2. Samuel Willard Son of Mr Jonathan Osgood &c.
Novr. 9th. Luther Son of Mr Saml. Jones &c.; Joseph Son of Mr Aaron Phelps &c.
Novr. 16. Stephen Son of Stephen Wilder &c. 1288
December 7. Calvin Son of Dr. James Carter &c. 37
 1325

1784.

Febry. 1st. Betsy Dr. of Mr Samll. Adams &c.
Feb. 8th. Liphas Son of Mr Jeremiah Ballard & wife; Grissel Dr. of Capt. Benjn. Gould & wife.
Feb. 22. Jonas Farnsworth Son of Capt. Nathaniel Beeman &c.; Sally Dr. of Mr Thomas Burditt &c.
March 7. Thomas Son of Lucy Kendall; Salley Dr. of Mr John Kindrick on wife's Account.
March 21st. Jeduthan Son of Mr Nathaniel Haskel &c.; Polly Dr. of Capt. Timothy Whiting junr. &c.
April 4th. Susanna Dr. of Capt. Ephraim Carter &c.
April 11th. Betsy Dr. of Mr Simon Willard &c.
April 18th. John Son of Mr John Ballard his wife a member in full Com.
April 25th. Peter Son of Mr Moses Sawyer & wife.
May 2d. Amos Son of Mr Amos Allen &c.
June 6th. Faithful child of Timothy Knight junr. &c.
June 13th. Elijah Son of Mr William Wilder &c.; Lucy Dr. of Mr Joseph Carter &c.
99 June 20th. Samuel Son of Mr Samuel Johnson &c.
July 11. Samuel Son of Joshua Fairbank &c.
July 18. Ephraim Son of Jacob Phelps &c.
Augt. —. William Son of Thomas Tucker &c.
Augt. 29th. { Nancy Dr. of William Locke &c. } pr. Mr Holcomb.
         { Susanna Dr. of Simon Butler &c. }
Septr. 5th. Nathaniel Son of Asa Warner and Wife.
Septr. 12th. Jonas Son of Jonas Wyman &c.; Lucinda Dr. of Oliver Whcelock &c.
Septr. 26th. Josiah Son of Daniel Rugg Junr. &c.
Octotr. 24th. John Son of Nathll. Eaton &c.; Elisha Son of Elisha Rugg &c.; Anna Dr. of James Goodwin &c.
Nov. 14. Nancy Dr. of Jonathan Whitney &c.
Nov. 28. Susanna Dr. of Abijah Rugg & wife.
Decem. 12. Luke, Lois, Eunice, children of Elisha Bennett & wife on her Account.
Decemr. 19. Benjamin Son of Aaron Rugg &c. 1325
Decemr. 26. Nancy Dr. of Benjamin Wheelock & wife on her Account. 37
 1362

1785.

Jany 2ᵈ. Betsey Dr. of Moses Wilder &c.
Feby. 13. Esther, Sally, children of James White and wife, Charlemont.
March 6ᵗʰ. Samˡˡ. Wright Son of Mr Abishai Phelps & wife; Eusebia Dr. of Mr Wᵐ. Kendall & wife.
May 1ˢᵗ. Oliver Son of Mr Edward Johnson & wife.
May 15. Rebecca Dr. of Mr Jonathan Osgood & wife, pr. Mr Holcomb.
June 19ᵗʰ. Thomas Son of Mr Thomas Harrington & wife.
July 10ᵗʰ. Aaron Son of Mr Joel Osgood & wife, pr. Mr Adams.
July 24. Susanna Dr. of Capt. Ephraim Carter & wife.
Augt. 7. John Son of Mr Aaron Phelps.
Augt. 21. Mary Dr. of Mr Samˡ Jones &c.
Sept. 4. Levi Son of Mr Levi Wilder & wife, at Home &c.; William Son of Mr Samˡ Adams &c.
Septr. 25. Willis, John, Polly, Nancy, children of Mr Willis Wilder &c.
Octo. 2ᵈ. James Son of Col. North & wife — Kenebek; Luke Son of Mr Samuel Wilder & wife; Jacob Son of Mr Thomas Burditt.
Novr. 6ᵗʰ. Esther Dr. of Capt. Benjamin Gould &c.; Alice Dr. of Mr Ephraim Divol Jur. &c.
Novr. 20ᵗʰ. Sophia Dr. of Mr Joseph Carter &c.; Betsy Dr. of Mr Benjamin Wheelock &c.
Decembr. 11. Deborah Dr. of Salmon Godfry &c. 1362
Decemb. 25. Phinehas Son of Mr Jacob Phelps. 27

turn to Page 150 1389

BAPTISMS 1786.

Feb. 12. Joseph Son of Mr Manasseh Wilder & wife.
February 19ᵗʰ. Timothy Danforth Son of Mr John Whiting & wife.
Feb. 26. Sally Upton Dr. of Mr Timothy Whiting junr. & wife.
March 12ᵗʰ. Ezra Son of Mr Moses Sawyer & wife; Charles Son of Mr John Ballard & wife.
April 9ᵗʰ. Asa Son of Mr John Kindrick & wife; Thomas Son of Mr Thomas Tucker & wife; Betsy Dr. of Mr James Fuller & wife.
May 14ᵗʰ. James Son of Thomas Burditt & wife.
May 21ˢᵗ. Patty Dr. of Capt. Thomas Gates & wife.
June 4ᵗʰ. Eunice Dr. of Simon Butler & wife.
June 25. Thomas Son of Titus Wilder & wife.
July 9ᵗʰ. Timothy Wilder Son of Timothy Knight junr. & wife; Jonathan Wright Son of Ezra Willard & wife.
July 16ᵗʰ. Theophilus Son of Nathaniel Eaton and Wife.
Augt. 6ᵗʰ. Abel Son of Elijah Carter & wife; Betsy Dr. of do.
Augt. 13ᵗʰ. James Son of James Divol on his wife's Account.
Septembr 3ᵈ. George Son of Mr Gershom Flagg & wife on her Account.
Octobr. 15ᵗʰ. Anna Dr. of Mr Daniel Goss & wife.
Octobr. 22ᵈ. Sally Dr. of Mr Jonathan Whitney & wife; Sukey Dr. of Mr James Wilder & wife.
Octobr. 29ᵗʰ. { Nathan Son of Mr Elisha Rugg. / Betsey Dr. of Mr Levi Wilder. } pr. Mr Grosvenor.
Novr. 12. { Jonas Son of Mr Moses Wilder / Lydia Dr. of Mr Samuel Johnson. } pr. Mr Bancroft.
Novr. 19. Abel Son of Mr Abel Phelps and wife.
Novr. 26. Lydia Woolcott Dr. of Dr. Wᵐ Frink. 1389
Decembr. 17. Darby Son of Mr Simon Willard Jr. 29

1418

BAPTISMS 1787.

March 14ᵗʰ. Dolly Dr. of Widow Susanna Willson, in private being sick, but in presence of five of yᵉ Brethren.
March 18ᵗʰ. Elisha Dr. [son] of Rufus Fletcher and wife.
March 21. James Son of Mr Jeremiah Ballard and wife at Home dangerously sick.

April 1st. Thomas Son of Mr Thomas Carter, on his wife's Account; David Son of Mr Samuel Jones &c.
May 20th. Julia Dr. of Capt. John Whiting and wife.
June 3d. Betsy Dr. of Mr Jonathan Osgood and wife.
June 10th. Lucretia Dr. of Mr William Locke & wife.
June 17th. Benjamin Son of Capt. Benjamin Gould & wife.
July 1st. Josiah Son of Mr Joseph Carter & wife, pr. Mr Gardner.
Augt. 12. Asahel Son of Mr Asahel Tower and wife.
Sept. 2d. Lydia Dr. of Mr Asa Warner. &c.; Fanny Dr. of Mr Edward Johnson &c.
151 September 9th. Sally Dr. of Mr Aaron Phelps &c.
Novr. 4th. Josiah Son of Mr Nathaniel Haskel &c.
Nov. 11. Abel Son of Mr Jacob Phelps &c.
Decembr. 2d. Samuel Son of Capt. Nathaniel Beeman &c.   20
Deeembr. 23d. Samuel Kidder Son of Capt. Timothy Whiting Junr. &c.   1418
                                                                                  1438
                                      To which add   2
                 1788.   1440

Febr. 10th. James Son of Capt. Daniel Rugg &c.
Feby. 15th. Lucena Dr. of Mr Moses Sawyer & wife, at Home dangerously sick in Presence of three of ye Chh.
March 2d. Esther Dr. of Mr John Locke & wife.
April 6th. James Son of Mr Abishai Phelps &c.
May 11th. Charles Son of Mr Nathaniel Eaton & wife.
May 18th. James Son of Mr John Ballard & wife.
May 25th. Dolly Dr. of Mr Samuel Wilder & wife. By Mr Wright.
June 15. Stephen Son of Mr Jonas Wyman &c.
June 22d. Polly Dr. of Mr Abel Allen & wife; Henry Son of Mr Jacob Sweetser & wife.
July 20th. Timothy Curtiss Son of Mr Nathaniel Haskel &c.; Betsy Dr. of Mr Thomas Tucker &c.
August 24th. Jonas Morse Son of Mr Saml Phelps & wife, pr. Mr Bancroft.
Septr. 28th. Joel Son of Mr Isaac Rugg & wife on her account; Eli, Martha, children of Mr Elisha Bennett & wife on her acct., pr. Mr Nowell.
Novr. 9th. Patty Dr. of Mr William Wilder & wife.
Novr. 16. John Son of Mr Thomas Burditt & Wife, pr. Mr Whitney.
Novr. 23d. Polly Dr. of Mr Samuel Jones & wife.
Novr. 30. Henry Son of Col. John Whiting & wife.   1444
Decembr. 14. James Son of Jeremiah Ballard & wife.   21
                                                                                  1461

                 1789.

January 18. Dolly Dr. of Mr Joel Osgood &c., per Mr Wright.
January 25. Josiah Son of James Wilder &c.
Febry. 1st. Elijah Son of Elijah Rugg &c.
March 1st. Nancy Dr. of Levi Wilder &c.
May 31st. William Son of Asa Warner &c.
June 7th. Betsy Dr. of Titus Wilder &c.; William Son of Samuel Johnson.
June 21st. Alpheus Son of Thomas Carter &c.
June 28th. Daphne Dr. of Capt. Abel Allen &c.
July 26th. Kezia Dr. of Mr Ephraim Divol &c.
Augt. 9. Artemas Son of Mr Elisha Rugg &c.; Sophy Dr. of Mr Rufus Fletcher &c.
Septr. 13. Susanna Dr. of Abijah Rugg.
Sept. 28. Betsy Dr of Jacob Phelps.   1461
152 Decembr. 13th. Cephas Son of Mr Jonathan White &c.   15
                                                                                 1476

                 1790.

January 31. Levi Son of Timothy Whiting Esq. &c.
Feby. 21. Lucy Dr. of Mr John Locke &c., Charlemont.

May 2ᵈ. { Abel Son of Mr Edward Johnson & wife. } pr. Mr Holcomb.
{ Sophia Dr. of Deacon John Whiting and wife. }
May 9ᵗʰ. Joseph Son of Mr Nathaniel Eaton & wife.
June 13ᵗʰ. Edmund Quincy Son of Mr William Greenleaf Junr. & wife; Susa Dr. of Mr Samˡ Allen & wife.
June 20ᵗʰ. Sally Dr. of Deacon Cyrus Fairbank & wife.
July 19ᵗʰ. Polly Dr. of Mr Elijah Rugg, at Home being dangerously sick in Presence of some of yᵉ Chh.
Augt. 15. Katy Dr. of Moses Sawyer and wife, at Home in Danger by Fitts.
August 22ᵈ. Kezia Dr. of Mr Ebenezer Haven & wife; Millicent Dr. of Mr [Asahel] Tower and wife.
Augt. 9ᵗʰ. Cephas Son of Benjamin Wheelock & wife.
Septr. 5ᵗʰ. Patty & Polly, children of Mr Benjamin Wyman & wife.
Septr. 19ᵗʰ. Nabby Dr. of Mr Manasseh Wilder & wife.
Octobr. 10ᵗʰ. Benjamin & Polly, children of Benjamin Houghton junr. & wife.
Octobr. 17ᵗʰ. Artemas Son of Rufus Fletcher and wife; Abigail Dr. of Joseph Carter & wife; Catharine Dr. of Jacob Sweetser & wife.
Octobr. 31ˢᵗ. Daniel Powers Son of Joel Osgood. 1476
Novr. 7ᵗʰ. Cephas Son of Mr Thomas Carter & wife. 23
1499

1791.

March 13. Polly Clarke.
May 1ˢᵗ. John Son of Benjamin Houghton Junr. & wife.
May 29. Betsy Dr. of Benjamin Wyman & wife.
June 26. Harrison Son of Mr Elijah Rugg & wife.
July 10ᵗʰ. William Josephus Son of William Greenleaf & wife.
July 24ᵗʰ. Nabby Dr. of Levi Wilder & wife; Charles & William, children of William Bridge & wife.
Augt. 21ˢᵗ. Elisabeth Dr. of Capt. [Benjamin] Gould & wife. 1499
Novr. 20. Lucinda Dr. of Aaron Phelps & wife. 10
1509

1792.

February. 19ᵗʰ, pr. Mr Bridge of Sudbury East. Josiah Son of Deacon Cyrus Fairbank; John Son of Asa Warner.
April 22ᵈ. Abel Son of Mr Thomas Carter & wife.
April 29ᵗʰ. Cynthia Dr. of Rufus Fletcher & wife.
153 May 13ᵗʰ. Fabius Son of Deacon John Whiting & wife: Louisa, Lavina, Twins of Mr Samuel Jones & wife.
May 10ᵗʰ, 1792. Christopher Ellery Son of William Stedman Esqr. & wife.
July 8ᵗʰ, 1792, pr. Mr Prince, Salem. Phinehas Son of Phinehas Fletcher & wife; Cephas Son of Isaac Rugg & wife; Abiel Son of Samuel Allen & wife; Polly Daughter of Thomas Tucker & wife.
July 13ᵗʰ. Betsy, Joseph, children of Jonathan Osgood and wife, baptised in private yᵉ mother dangerously sick.
July 22ᵈ. Fanny Dr. of Mr [Jacob] Sweetser & wife, pr. Mr Wright.
Septr. 23, 1792. Nancy Dr. of Mr John Ballard & wife.
Octobr. 21. Joel Son of Mr Joseph Carter & wife, per Mr Buckminster of Portsmouth; Jacob Kilburn's child Rebecca.
Novr. 18, 1792. Joel Osgood's Apollos; Timothy Fletcher's Polly; Nathaniel Eaton's Katharine.

BAPTISMS 1793.

March 30ᵗʰ, pr. Mr Wright. Arethusa Dr. of Benjamin Wheelock; Nancy Dr. of Timothy Whiting Esqr. &c.; Charles, Pollard Amos; James Son of William Bridge; Isaac Son of Jacob Kilburn.
Asa Tower.
April 28ᵗʰ, pr. Mr Holcomb. Lucy Dr. of Major Gardner Wilder & wife; Submit Dr. of Mr Benjamin Wyman & wife.
July 14. William, Son of Jacob Phelps.
Suse, Daughter of James Carter Jr.
Baptisms by Mr Harrington 1531 [1549].

80 A Catalogue of the first Chh. in Lancaster on Novr. 16 [1748] with those that have since been added.

Timothy Harrington, Pastor.
Honble. Joseph Wilder Esq. ⎫
Josiah White, ⎪
Hooker Osgood, ⎬ Deacons.
Israel Houghton, ⎪
Sam^ll Willard Esq. Died Novr. 20th, 1752.
Oliver Wilder Esq.
Joseph Wilder, Junior. Esq. Chosen Deacon March 16, 1748-9, and accepted April 2^d, 1749.
Joshua Fairbank. Chosen Deacon and accepted on ye Same Day with Joseph Wilder junior Esq.
Joseph Wheelock,
Jabez Fairbank,
Mrs Prudence Prentice.

John Bennet,
John Beaman,
Eben^r Beaman,
John Prescott,
Robt. Phelps,
Caleb Wilder,
David Wilder,
Thomas Tucker,
Nath^ll. Sawyer,
Stanton Prentice,
Daniel Rugg,
John Carter,
—— Fletcher Senr.
Joshua Fletcher,
Joshua Osgood,

Benjamin Osgood,
Dan^ll. Rugg Junr.
Andrew Wilder,
Aaron Osgood,
Joseph Osgood,
Joseph Whetcomb
Joshua Phelps,
Thomas Kendall,
Daniel Knight,
Amos Knight,
Jonathan Kendall,
Edward Phelps,
Asahel Phelps,
James Houghton,
Amos Knight junr.

81 Those which follow are such as have been received from other churches, or were first received in full communion here.

Males.—Ebenezer Allen, from ye Chh. in Weston; Ebenezer Allen Junior, from ye Chh. in Weston; Nath^ll. Wyman, Abijah Wyman, from ye 1st Chh. in Woburn; Abijah Willard, Jan. 22^d, 1748-9; Joseph White, Feb. 5th, 1748-9; Sherebiah Ballard, Feb. 12th, 1748-9; James Wilder, Nathaniel Sawyer Jun., Ephraim Carter, Robert Fletcher, Joshua Johnson, March 26, 1749; Jonas Fairbanks, John Rugg, July 2^d, 1749; Septr. 7th, 1749. John Prescott was received into full Communion by ye Chh. at his own House, having been confined by sickness and other Infirmities for some years; Amasa Turner, from ye Chh. in Hannover, Sept. 17th, 1749; Isaac Rugg, Octobr. 22^d, 1749; Jotham Wilder, Novr. 12th, 1749; Oliver Wilder Junr., Decr. 31st, 1749; Israel Nichols, May 6th, 1750; Nathanael White, 1750, Sept. 9th; Joshua Houghton, from ye 2^d Chh. in Shrewsbury, Sept. 9th, 1750.

Females.—Sarah ye wife of Eben^r. Allen, received to occas. com. till some just reason appears to ye contrary; Sarah, Mary Allen, from ye Chh. in Weston; Sarah Albert, from ye Chh. in Wilmington; Bethiah Nichols, from ye 2^d Chh. in Hingham; Anna Harrington, Rose Negro Maid Servt. of T. H., from ye Chh. late of ye Lower Ashuelot; Hannah Lyppenwell, from ye first chh. in Woburn; Elizabeth Willard, Jan. 22^d, 1748-9; Patience White, Feb. 5th, 1748-9; Kezia Ballard, Feb. 12th, 1748-9; Silence White, Feb. 12th, 1748-9; Elisabeth Fletcher, Hannah Johnson, Kezia Bennet, Millicent Carter, March 26th, 1749; Widow Lois Pierce, Hannah Fletcher, Ruth Osgood, May 7th, 1749; Lydia Rugg, July 2^d, 1749; Pheebe Fowle, Sarah Beaman, July 16th, 1749; Jane Rugg, Thamar Hudson, Octobr. 22^d, 1749; Pheebe Wilder, Mary Nichols, Novr. 12, 1749; Sarah Rugg, Jan. 7th, 1749-50; Ruth Fletcher, Feb. 25, 1749-50; Mary Harris, April 29th, A. D. 1750. Desire Nichols, May 6th, 1750; Lydia White, Septr. 9th, 1750; Rebekkah Fletcher, Decr. 9, 1750.

82 *Males.*—Samuel Locke, April 14, 1751; Aaron Osgood, Jany. 5th, 1752; Asa Harris, Jan. 19th, 1752; Amos Sawyer, May 24th, 1752; Ephraim Wilder, October 22, 1752; Bezaleel Sawyer, John White, April 8, 1753; Roger Nichols, April 22, 1753; Joseph James, June 17, 1753; Russel Knight, Sept. 23, 1753; Edward Robbins, from ye 2^d Chh., Sept. 23^d, 1753; Moses Osgood, Sept. 30, 1753; Aaron Willard, June 9th, 1754; William Phelps, Septr. 1754; John Sargeant, Elisha Bennett, Novr. 3^d, 1754; John Johnson, Novr. 17, 1754, Ætat: 84; Sam^ll. Willard Esqr., Novr. 24th, 1754, from Petersham alias Nichewaug; Joseph Priest, December 8th, 1754; Josiah Ballard, Jany. 12th, 1755; John Nichols Junr., Feb. 16th, 1755; W^m. Dunsmoor, Feb. 23^d, 1755; Benja. Osgood Junr., May 11, 1755; John Prescott, Joseph Abbot, June 1st, 1755.

Females.—Rebekkah Locke, April 14, 1751; Margaret Stuart, April 22ᵈ, being recommended from yᵉ Presbyter of Bovidy in Ireland; Sarah yᵉ Wife of John Beaman, received May 10, 1752, recommended by yᵉ Chh. in Weston; Sarah Willard, May 23ᵈ, 1752; Elisabeth Wilder, Octobr. 22ᵈ, 1752; Judith Sawyer, April 8ᵗʰ, 1753; Alice Wheelock, from yᵉ Chh. in Lunenburg, May 1753; Mary Knight, Septr. 23ᵈ, 1753; Martha Osgood, Septr. 30, 1753; Wid*, Abigail Woodbury, Novr. 18ᵗʰ, 1753; Mary Bowers, Jan. 13, 1754; Rebecca Phillips, April 14, 1754; Martha Houghton, June 2ᵈ, 1754; Hannah Sargeant, Lois Bennett, Novr. 3ᵈ, 1754; Susanna Willard, Novr. 24, 1754, from Petersham alias Nichewaug; Betty Priest, December 8ᵗʰ, 1754; Margaret Turner, from yᵉ 3ᵈ Chh. in Hingham, Dec. 15, 1754; Sarah Ballard, Jany. 12ᵗʰ, 1755; Mercy Nichols, Feb. 16ᵗʰ, 1755; Hannah Dunsmoor, from yᵉ 1ˢᵗ Chh. in Kellingly, May 11ᵗʰ, 1755; Mary Osgood, May 11ᵗʰ, 1755; Mary Prescott, Hannah Abbot, Mary Flagg, Lucy Butler, June 1ˢᵗ, 1755; Ruth Knight, Augt. 24ᵗʰ, 1755.

83 *Males.*—Reuben Lyppenwel, Decr. 9, 1755; John Bowers, Jan. 11ᵗʰ, 1756; William Richardson Esqr., George Parkhurst, Feb. 29ᵗʰ, 1756; Joseph Wilder 3ᵘˢ, March 7ᵗʰ, 1756; Phinehas Houghton, April 18ᵗʰ, 1756; Converse Richardson, April 25ᵗʰ, 1756; Timothy Whiting, from yᵉ Chh. in Bilerica May 30, 1756; William Tucker, June 6ᵗʰ, 1756; James Ballard, July 4ᵗʰ, 1756; Mr Moses Hemenway, Decembr. 12ᵗʰ, 1756; Henry Haskel Junr., Novr. 13, 1757; Joseph Whitcomb Junr., May 21, 1758; Sherebiah Hunt, Gardner Wilder, June 4ᵗʰ, 1758; Elisha White, May 27, 1759; Jonathan Knight, June 24, 1759; Simon Willard, Sept. 2ᵈ, 1759; Thomas Lyppenwel, Octob. 7, 1759; Edward Phelps Junr., Octobr. 21, 1759; Hooker Osgood Junr., June 15, 1760; Moses Wilder, July 6, 1760; Ezekiel Haskel, July 13ᵗʰ, 1760; Elijah Beeman, July 27ᵗʰ, 1760.

Females.—Anna Lyppenwel, Mary Lyppenwel, Decr. 21ˢᵗ, 1756; Kezia Parkhurst, Abigail Albert, Feb. 29ᵗʰ, 1756; Elisabeth Wilder, March 7ᵗʰ, 1756; Katharine Willard, from yᵉ Chh. in Worcester, April 25ᵗʰ, 1756; Mercy Richardson, April 25ᵗʰ, 1756; Mary Tucker, April 25ᵗʰ, 1756; Mary Tucker, June 6ᵗʰ, 1756; Mary Ballard, July 4ᵗʰ, 1756; Sarah Whiting, October 17ᵗʰ, 1756; Mary & Abigail Carter, Decembr. 12ᵗʰ, 1756; Mary the Wife of James Carter, Augt. 7ᵗʰ, 1757; Dorothy Osgood, Octobr. 23, 1757; Hannah Churchel, Novr. 6, 1757, *Shaker*; Rebecca Haskel, Novr. 13, 1757; Elisabeth Whitcomb, May 21, 1758; Deborah Hunt, June 4ᵗʰ, 1758; Prudence Warner, Novr. 19, 1758, *Shaker*; Anna Willard, Decmbr. 31, 1758; Alice White, May 27, 1759; Elisabeth Willard, Sept. 2ᵈ, 1759; Martha Phelps, Octobr. 21, 1759; Susanna Osgood, June 15, 1760; Submit Wilder, July 6, 1760; Rebecca Haskel, July 13ᵗʰ, 1760; Thankful Beeman, July 27ᵗʰ, 1760.

84 *Males.*—Abner Haskel, Septr. 28ᵗʰ, 1760; Ebenezer Knight, Octobr. 12ᵗʰ, 1760; John Wheelock, Richard Prouty, Novr. 16, 1760; John Manning, May 10ᵗʰ, 1761; Ephraim Divol, May 24ᵗʰ, 1761; William Jewet, July 19, 1761; James Goss, March 28ᵗʰ, 1762; Levi Nichols, Elijah Osgood, April 25ᵗʰ, 1762; Daniel Schwere, a German Protestant after Lecture, June 18ᵗʰ, 1762; Phinehas Phelps, Novr. 14ᵗʰ, 1762; Nathaniel Willard, Jany. 16ᵗʰ, 1763; Mark Lincoln, James Wilder Junr., March 20ᵗʰ, 1763.

Females.—Ruth Ballard, Augt. 17ᵗʰ, 1760; Martha Haskel, Sept. 28ᵗʰ, 1760; Prudence Knight, October 12ᵗʰ, 1760; Hannah Osgood, December 7ᵗʰ, 1760; Martha yᵉ Wife of Gardner Wilder, Abigail the Wife of John Ball, Mary Daughter of Jonas Fairbank, Jany. 25, 1761; Patience Wife of Wᵐ Richardson 3ᵈ, March 29ᵗʰ, 1761; The Widow Lydia House, May 10ᵗʰ, 1761; Prudence Manning, May yᵉ 10ᵗʰ, 1761; Mary yᵉ Wife of Elijah Woods, May 17ᵗʰ, 1761; Elisabeth Divol, Eunice Woods, May 24ᵗʰ, 1761; Anna Jewet, July 19, 1761; Mary Goss, Lucy Knight, March 28ᵗʰ, 1762; Elisabeth Nichols, Mary Osgood, April 25ᵗʰ, 1762; Elisabeth Clarke in Virtue of a Recommendation from Worcester, June 18, 1762, after Lecture; Margaret Schwere a German Protestant, June 18, 1762. after Lecture; Dorothy Richardson, Lucy Wilder, Augt. 15ᵗʰ, 1762; Elisabeth Wilder, Bathsheba Robbins, Octobr. 3ᵈ, 1762; Sarah Phelps, Novr. 14ᵗʰ, 1762; Submit Wyman, Novr. 21ˢᵗ, 1762; Damaris Knight, Novr. 28ᵗʰ, 1762, *Baptist*; Ruth Haskel, Novr. 5ᵗʰ, 1762; Elizabeth Willard, Jany. 16, 1763.

85 *Males.*—John Nichols, Octobr. 23ᵈ, 1763; Cyrus Fairbank, Novr. 6ᵗʰ, 1763; Benjamin Houghton, Feb. 12ᵗʰ, 1764; Thomas Gates, Feb. 12ᵗʰ, 1764; Timo. Knight, from yᵉ Chh. in Worcester, March 10, 1764; Moses Sawyer, April

22, 1764; Joseph Abbot Junr., March 31, 1765; Asa Norcross, May 19, 1765; Caleb Wilder Junr., Feb. 2, 1766; James Goodwin, July 27th, 1766; Jonathan Kendall, Novr. 1st, 1766; John White Junr., June 14, 1767; Daniel Rugg, Junr., June 28th, 1767; William Kendall, July 12th, 1767; Lynn Jock, Negro, from ye Chh. in Concord, Decem. 27, 1767.

Females.—Azubah Wife of Peter Larkin, Katherine Dr. of Capt. Eph. Wilder Jr., May 22d, 1763; Zilpah Wilder, Lucy Holt, July 17th, 1763; Sarah Fairbank, Octobr. 23d, 1763; Lucy Fairbank, Novr. 6th, 1763; Hannah Sawyer, Lois Sawyer, Decr. 18th, 1763; Achsah Houghton, Feb. 12, 1764; Abigail Gates, Feb. 19th, 1764; Mary McClothlin, from the Chh. in Canterbury, Connecticut, April 22, 1764; Mary Sawyer, Eunice Wilder, April 22, 1764; Rebecca Houghton, Augt. 19, 1764; Amy Houghton, Novr. 18, 1764; Elisabeth Norcross, May 19th, 1765; Hannah, Elisabeth Abbot, Septr. 8th, 1765; Rebekkah, Hannah, Drs. of Thomas Kendall, Novr. 10th, 1765; Martha Houghton. Decembr. 1, 1765; Abigail Wilder, Feb. 2d, 1766; Hannah ye Wife of Lynn Jock, Negro, Aug. 24th, 1766; Martha Rugg; Sarah Wilder. Novr. 23, 1766; Mary Bennett, Lydia Bennett, December 7th, 1766; Lydia White, June 14th, 1767; Elisabeth Rugg, June 28th, 1767; Mary Kendall, July 12th, 1767; Henrietta, Arethusa, Eusebia Harrington, April 10th, 1768.

86 *Males.*—Joseph Brown, Septr. 4th, 1767; John Phelps, Thomas Bennett, May 14th, 1769; Tilly More, May 28th, 1769; Josiah Wilder, July 9th, 1769; Jonathan Kendall 4th, Octobr. 29th, 1769; Ephraim Carter Junr., Novr. 19th, 1769; James Pratt, March 17, 1771; Timothy Knight Junr., May 5, 1771; Joshua Fairbank, June 2d, 1771; John Phillips, Augt. 25th, 1771; Joseph Blood, Octobr. 6th, 1771; Asa Haven, from ye 2d Chh. in Mendon, Octo. 20, 1771; Stephen Wilder, October 20th, 1771; Nathaniel Beeman, John Bennett, Octobr. 27, 1771; Salmon Goodfry, Decembr. 22d, 1771; James Carter, from ye Chh. in Bolton, Decemb. 29th; John Wilder, March 1st, 1772.

Females.—Abigail Atherton, May 29th, 1768; Elisabeth, Susanna Phelps, Septr. 11th, 1768; Hannah Johnson, Octobr. 9th, 1768; Mary Whitney, Decembr. 18th, 1768; Achsah Phelps, May 14th, 1769; Zilpah More, May 28th, 1769; Esther Locke, Sept. 24th, 1769; Hannah Kendall, Octobr. 29th, 1769; Abigail Carter, Novr. 19, 1769; Elizabeth Wilder, Decembr. 31st, 1769; Sarah, Lucy Rugg, March 4th, 1770; Esther Poor, September 2d, 1770; Susanna, Eunice Richardson, December 2d, 1770; Mary Priest, January 20th, 1771; Zerviah Pratt, March 17, 1771; Lucy Rugg, April 14, 1771; Sarah Greenleafe, April 28, 1771; Rebekkah Fairbank, May 12, 1771; Anna Phillips, Annis Brown, Augt. 25th, 1771; Betty Blood, Octobr. 6, 1771; Betty Wilder, Octobr. 20th, 1771; Hannah Beeman, Thankful Beeman, Lucy Bennett, Octobr. 27, 1771; Thankful Wheelock, Novr. 17, 1771; Ruth Phelps, Mary Phelps, Novr. 24th, 1771; Rebekkah Goodfry, Decembr. 22d; Abigail Wilder, March 1st, 1772.

87 *Males.*—Abishai Phelps, June 14th, 1772; John Robbins, June 28th, 1772; Samuel Johnson, Novr. 22d, 1772; Nathaniel Joslyn, March 14, 1773; John Wheelock, from Leominster, May 2d; Elisha Allen, July 11th, 1773; Luther Fairbank, Augt. 15, 1773; Jonas Wyman, Octobr. 24th, 1773; Nathaniel Willard Jur., Aaron Joslyn, Novr. 21, 1773; Titus Wilder, April 24, 1774; Josiah White, May 29th, 1774; Joseph Whitmore, Decembr. 4, 1774; Benjamin Farmer, March 5th, 1775; Joel Osgood, Octobr. 8th. 1775; Manasseh Knight, February 11, 1776; Joseph Joslyn, April 7th, 1776.

Females.—Sarah Russell, June 7th, 1772; Katharine Phelps, June 14th, 1772; Lydia Robbins, Mary Ballard, June 28, 1772; Patience Richardson, January 17th, 1773; Martha Stevens, January 31st, 1773; Jemima Wilder, Mary Locke, March 7th, 1773; Alice Joslyn, April 18, 1773; —— Wheelock, May 2d, 1773; Miriam Allen, July 11th. 1773; Katharine Sprague, Elisabeth Wells, Hannah Wyman, Octobr. 24, 1773; Sarah Flagg, Hannah Pitson, Novr. 7th, 1773; Eunice Willard, Elisabeth Johnson, Novr. 21, 1773; Abigail Joslyn, Kezia Kindrick, January 2d, 1774; Rebekkah Fletcher, January 16, 1774; Eunice Wilder, March 27th, 1774; Mary Wilder, April 24th, 1774; Parnee White, May 29th, 1774; Abigail Wife of Mr Moses Smith, July —; Mehetabel ye Wife of Mr Jotham Woods, ——; Ruth Whitmore, Decembr. 4, 1774; Sarah Farmer, March 5, 1775; Mary Ballard, Dr. of Joseph Ballard, Augt. 13, 1775; Polly Wilder, Grizzle Apthorpe Flagg, Thamar, Ruth, Mary Wilder, Augt. 20th, 1775; Lois Osgood, Sally Sargent, Octobr.

8th, 1775; Ruth Goodfry, Decembr. 10th, 1775; Hannah Knight, February 11th, 1776; Dorothy Joslyn, April 7th, 1776.

88 *Males.*—Ephraim Kendall, June 2d. 1776; Manasseh Wilder, March 30th, 1777; William Wilder, April 13th, 1777; Henry Willard Farmer, January 11th, 1778; Jonathan Whitney, April 5th, 1778; Nathaniel Haskell, April 19th, 1778; John Abbott, Novr. 8th, 1778; James Butler, Decembr. 20th, 1778; Benjamin Haskel, Febr. 7th, 1779; Jeremiah Ballard, August 1st, 1779; Levi Wilder, Jonathan White, May 21st, 1780; James Carter Junr.; Novembr. 12th, 1780; Thomas Smith, April 8th, 1781; Aaron Rugg, May 27, 1781; Peter Thurston, Augt. 12, 1781; Jacob Phelps, Decemr. 2d, 1781.

Females.—Relief Divol, May 26, 1776; Elisabeth Kendall, June 2d, 1776; Lydia Knight, Lydia Johnson, July 21st, 1776; Hannah North Wife of Col. Joseph North, Sept. 8th, 1776; Maria Houghton, Octobr. 6th, 1776; Mary Davenport, Novr. 3d, 1776; Anna Wife of Joseph Carter, Martha Wife of John Carter, Decr. 29th, 1776; Anna Gates, Sarah Wilder, March 30, 1777; Rebecca Osgood, May 18th; Mary Baker. Rebecca Ballard, Relief Carter, Octobr. 12, 1777; Sybil Turner, January 11, 1778; Betty Sawyer, April 12th; Abigail Haskell, April 19th, 1778; Thankfull Fairbank, May 3d, 1778; Lois Abbot, Novr. 8, 1778; Mary Allen widow, January 17th, 1779; Susanna Haskell, Feby. 7th, 1779; Mary Knight, May 2d, 1779; Rebecca Ballard, August 1st, 1779; Anna Bridge, Septr. 5th, 1779; Sarah Wilder, July 23d, 1780; Rebecca White, May 21st, 1780; Susy Carter, Novr. 12, 1780; Lucy Whitney, Decembr. 24th, 1780; Mary Fletcher, while sick at Home in Presence of ye Chh. Comtee. March 4, 1781; Susanna Rugg, Wife [of] Abijah Rugg, April 1st, 1781; Lucretia Rugg, May 27th, 1781; Dorothy Thurston, Augt. 12th, 1781; Abigail Flagg, Augt. 19, 1781; Dorothy Phelps, Octobr. 14, 1781; Prudence Phelps. Decembr. 2d, 1781; Abigail Fairbank, Decembr. —

89 Timothy Whiting, from ye Chh. in Bilerica, July 21st, 1782; Amos Allen, Augt. 4th, 1782; Timothy Whiting Junr., Augt. 25th, 1782; Elisha White junr., March 9th, 1783; Samuel Jones, Octobr. 26, 1783; Oliver Wheelock, June 6, 1784; Willis Wilder, July 4th, 1784; Darius Sawyer, Novr. 21st, 1784; Benjamin Gould, John Whiting, February 12th, 1786; Ezra Willard, July 9th, 1786; Elijah Carter, Augt. 6th, 1786; Abel Carter, Augt. 27th, 1786; John Locke, March 2d, 1788; Abel Allen, June 22d, 1788; Elijah Rugg, Feby. 1st, 1789; William Greenleaf Junr., March 21st, 1790; Samuel Allen, June —, 1790; Benjamin Wyman, Augt. 29th, 1790; Benjamin Houghton, Junr., Octob. 3d; Elisha Rugg, Jany. 2d, 1791: William Bridge, July 24th, 1791.

Females.—Patience Wyman, June 2d, 1782; Sarah, Deborah Whiting, from ye Chh. in Bilerica, July 21st, 1782; Rebekkah Allen, Augt. 1782; Abigail Whiting, Augt. 25th; Deborah White, March 9th, 1783; Relief Wilder, September 28, 1783; Sarah Jones, Octobr. 26, 1783; Prudence, Sarah, Ruth, Kezia Houghton, Decembr. 14, 1783; Abigail Baldwin, Lucy Kendall, Feby 1st, 1784; Anna Ballard, Feby. 22d, 1784; Relief Rugg, from ye Chh. in Leominster, March 28, 1784; Lucretia Wheelock, June 6, 1784; Relief Wilder, July 4th, 1784; Charity Carter, August 1st, 1784; Deborah Sawyer, Novr. 21st, 1784; Rebecca Manning, Prudence Wheelock, Decembr. 26, 1784; Dolly Johnson, April 17, 1785; Orpah Whiting, Feby. 12, 1786; Mary Willard, July 9th, 1786; Sarah Carter, Rebecca Wilder, August 6, 1786; Esther Locke, March 2d, 1788; Mary Allen, June 22d, 1788; Hannah Willard, July 27th, 1788, Dr. C. L. W.; Lois Rugg, Feby. 1st, 1789; Maria Greenleaf, March 21st, 1790; Lucy Allen, Junea—, 1790; Martha Wyman, Augt. 29th, 1790; Hannah Houghton, Susanna Osgood, Octobr. 3d, 1790; Elisabeth, Catharine, Anna Willard, Octobr. 17th, 1790; Amy Rugg, Jany. 2d, 1791; Abigail Bridge, July 24th, 1791.

90 *Females.*—Lydia Bennett, Anna Houghton, July 8th, 1792.

Admitted to communion of the Church by Rev. Timothy Harrington, 478.

---

112   DEATHS.

January 20th, 1771. Lucy Wife of John Locke.
                 Child of Mr Thomas Holt.
June 1771. Anna, Wife of Col. Abijah Willard.
July 4th, 1771. Nathaniel, Son of Mr Reuben Lyppenwel & wife.

FIRST CHURCH, BOOK I. 323

July 5, 1771. Molly, Dr. of Mr Peter Willard & wife.
July —, 1771. Eli, Son of Jonas Powers & wife.
Augt. 6, 1771. Ens: Peter Joslin.
Augt. 8, 1771. Still-born Son of Dr. William Greenleaf & wife.
Augt. 12th, 1771. Mr Elijah Beeman.
Augt. 13, 1771. Widow Eunice Fairbank.
Augt. 24th, 1771. Zilpah, Wife of Tilly Moor.
Augt. 27 or 28th. Lucy Davis.
Septr. 1st, 1771. Elisabeth, Dr. of Moses Russell.
Sept. 17 or 18, 1771. Josiah Ballard Junr.
Sept. 24. Abigail White, Wife of Deac. Josiah White.
Octobr. 26th, 1771. Fanny, Dr. of Mr Tilly More.
Novr. 12, 1771. Lucy, Dr. of Mr John Bennett & wife.

COPY OF DEATHS RECORDED BY MR ABIJAH WYMAN FROM DECEMBER 3d 1747 TO NOVR. 1770.

1747.
Mr Edward Phelps, Decembr. 3.
Dr. John Dunsmore, December 7.
The Wife of Jerathmeel Bowers, July 25.
Enoch Hill, December 11.

1748.
The Wife of Mr Ebenr. Harris, June 13.
The Wife of Capt. Oliver Wilder, June 15.
Revd. John Prentice, Jany. 8.
Mr Hooker Osgood, June 30.
Elisabeth Hudson, December 13.
Mr John Bennet Junr., December 30.

1749.
Mr Robert Phelps, March 19.
Mr John Prentice, March —.
Two children of Josiah Sawyer, April.
Abijah, Son of Capt. Abijah Willard, Decemr. 12.

1750.
The Wife of Amasa Turner, Jany. 6th.
The Wife of John Beman, May 9th.
Nathaniel, Son of Thomas Lyppenwell, May 27.
Hannah, Dr. of Nehemiah Woods.
Timothy, Son of Timothy Harrington, June 16.
A child of Matthew Clarke, July 25.

1751.
The Wife of Joseph James, January 4th.
The Wife of Joseph Wheelock, Feby. 9th.
The Wife of David Wilder, Feb. 17.
John, Son of Revd. J. Swan, June 7.
Wife of Aaron Osgood, Augt. 21.
Child of Joshua Fletcher, Augt. 23.
Elisabeth, Wife of Capt. Abijah Willard, Decembr. 6.
The Wife of Asa Harris, December 16.

1752.
Child of William Phelps, Jany. 29.
Abijah, Son of Asa Harris, March 4.
Thomas, Son of Dr. Prentice, May 1.
Joseph Wheelock, July 19.

1753.
Child of John White, killed Feby. 6th.
Benjamin, Son of Benj. Ballard, May 5th.
Dorcas, Wife of John Solandine, May 23.
Abijah, Son of Capt. Abijah Willard, July 25.
Child of John Solandine, Augt. 18.
Ephraim, Son of Amos Knight, Augt. 19.
Similius Wilder, Killed Septr. 26.
Widow R. Divol, Novr. 14.
Wife of Amos Sawyer, Decembr. 1.
Second Wife of Amasa Turner, Decembr. 8.

1754.
Widow Osgood, January 23.
Daughter of Andrew Wilder, Jany. 30.
Wife of Isaac Butler, Feb. 14.
Eunice, Dr. of Asa Harris, March 21.
Child of Daniel Willard, March —.
John, Son of Zeph. Williams, April 22.
Roger, Son of Israel Nichols, Septr. 3d.
Wife of Ebenr. Beeman, Sept. 14.
Wife of Joseph Osgood junr., Oct. 13.
Dr. of Gershom Flagg, October 22.
Wife of Daniel Rugg, December 3.
Sarah Lyppenwell, December 12.

1755.
Nehemiah Woods, January 2.
Widow of Edmund Harris, January 30.
David Atherton, May 2.
Henry Willard, May 16.
Child of ye Wid: Ruth Fletcher, May 16.
Wife of Jabez Fairbank, May 10.
Widow of Neh. Wood, May 31.
Wife of Ebenr. Allen, June 16.
Joseph, Son of Andrew Wilder, Augt. 15.
Elisabeth Joslyn, Septr. 21.
Oliver Osgood, Killed by ye Enemy Sept. 8.

Sam[ll]. Willard Esqr., Octobr. 25.
James Houghton Junr., November.

1756.

Joseph House, July 9th.
Wife of Thomas Wilder, July 21.
Dr. of Nathaniel White, September —.
Wife of Joseph Osgood, October 1.
Child of Ephraim Carter, September—.
Son of Dr. Dunsmore, September —.
Child of Joseph White, Octobr. 12.
Mary, Daughter of Dr. Prentice, October 6.
Elizabeth, Dr. of Capt. Abijah Willard, Octo. 6.
Joseph Osgood, Octobr. 3.
Widow of David Harris, October 7.
Negro Servant of R. Nichols, Octobr. 12.
Daniel Tower, Grandson of R. Nichols, Octob. 10.
Child of Bezal. Sawyer Junr., Octobr. 10.
Theodora, Dr. of Col. Abijah Willard, Octobr. 13.
Thomas, Son of Thomas Kendall, Octobr. 21.
Mercy, Wife of Dr. Prentice, Octobr. 26.
Daughter of Phinehas Sawyer, Octobr. 26.
Child of James Butler, Octobr. 30.
Child of Phinehas Sawyer, Novr. 10.
Nathaniel Sawyer, Novr. 10.
Daniel, Son of Dr. Prentice, Sept. 26.
Wife of John Beeman, December 16.
Amos Sawyer, December 29.

1757.

Wife of Daniel Knight, January 7.
Wife of John Fletcher, March 13.
Hon. Joseph Wilder Esqr., March 29.
Hannah Lyppenwell, April 11.
Child of Joshua Phelps, April 16.
Child of David Wilder, July 11.
Nathaniel, Son of Aaron Osgood, July 23.
John, Son of Henry Haskel, killed Sept. 22.
—— Churchil, September 23.
Hannah Lyppenwell, October 20.
Ruth Kendal, November 10.
Child of Nathaniel Joslyn, Decembr. 26.

1758.

Child of Amos Sawyer, January 12.
Thomas Wilder, February 2.
Jabez Fairbank, March 1.
Dinah, Dr. of Joseph Pierce, April 16.
Joseph James, June 7.
Wife of John Phelps, June 19.
Daniel Rugg, June 23[d].
Wife of Joshua Johnson, August 26.
Amos Knight, September 20.
James Ballard, September —.
Isaac Rugg, October 14.

Gershom Flagg, December 28th.

1759.

Child of Phinehas Houghton, January 6.
Child of Dr. Prentice, January 12.
Wife of Jonathan Harris, April 3.
Samuel Woods, killed by y[e] Enemy.
Tabitha Priest, April 27.
[Mary] Wife of Nathaniel Wyman, May 8.
Child of Benjamin Osgood, May 11.
Wife of Elisha Bennet, May 28.
Dr. of Joseph Priest, Augt. 18.
Wife of Daniel Willard, Sept. 4.
Dr. of William Richardson Junr., Octobr. 15.
Widow Larkin, December 1st.
Child of Levi Willard, December 2[d].

1760.

Child of Simon Willard, Feb. 22.
Widow of James Willard, March 31.
John Fletcher, May 26.
Lydia Phillips, May 31.
John Johnson, July 13.
Wife of Thomas Wright, Augt. 6.
Bezaleel Sawyer, Augt. 25.
Wife of Richard Prouty, Sept. 5.
John, Son of Dr. Prentice, September.
Wife of John Beeman junr., Octobr. 24.
Child of John White, Novembr. 21.
Josiah, Son of Dr. Prentice, ——

1761.

Wife of Ichabod Turner, Feb. 6.
Wife of Nathaniel Wilder.
Child, by y[e] Small-pox, Feb. 1.
Thomas Sawyer, March 2.
Wife of William Phelps, March 22.
Child of Ebenr. Allen, May 9.
Samuel Carter, May 19.
Capt. John Bennett, June 5.
Matthew Clarke, July 9.
Widow of Col. James Wilder, Septembr. 18.
Child of Henry Haskel Junr., Sept. 26.
Negro of Ebenr. Allen, Novr. 28.

1762.

Widow of Capt. Bennet, Feb. 7.
114 Caesar, servant of Col. John Carter, June —.
Child of Elijah Beeman, June 27.
Peter Wilder, July 1st.
Child of Phinehas Houghton, July 4.
Ephraim Reed, killed by a Cart, October 21.
Paul, Son of William Willard, Decemb. 1.
Daniel Johnson, December 14.

1763.

Widow of Matthew Wyman, January 20.

Wife of John Nichols, January 21.
John Phillips, Feb. 1.
Widow of Hon. Jos. Wilder Esq., May 13.
John Beeman, May 3.
Edward Robbins Junr., drowned June 27.
Molly, Negro servt. of Timo. Harrington, Augt. 22.
Hannah Jordan, Octobr. 2.
Third Wife of Amasa Turner, Octobr. 28.
Jotham Robbins, Nov. 24.
Child of Elisha Bennett, Decembr. 11.
Child of John Sargeant, Decembr. 21.

1764.

Child of Cyrus Fairbank, March 1.
Wife of Gardner Wilder, March 7.
Ebenezer Beeman, May 11.
Wife of Capt. Aaron Willard, June 3.
Joshua Johnson, July 1.
Child of William Jewet, Sept. 7.
Andrew Wilder, Decembr. 27.

1765.

Deac. Hooker Osgood, January 5.
Col: Oliver Wilder, March 18.
Child of Phinehas Houghton, March —.
Wife of —— Goodfry, March 30.
Elisabeth Phelps, April 3.
Child of Joel Phelps, April —.
Son of Mr Zweier, killed with a Cart April 30.
Child of Josiah Locke, May 6.
Wife of John Phelps, May 12.
Child of Nathaniel Willard, May 25.
Wife of Benjamin Osgood, May 31.
Roger Nichols, June 3ᵈ.
Child of Philemon Houghton, July 5.
Widow Prudence Prentice, July 10.
Peter, Son of Dr. Prentice, July 9.
Deborah Sawyer, December 16.

1766.

Wife of Philemon Houghton, Feb. 15.
John Solandine, April 17.
Negro Servt. of Mr Divol, April 17..
Col. John Carter, May 8.
Child of Ephraim Wilder, 3ᵈ, May 14.
Elisabeth, Dr. of Abijah Wyman, July 20.
Child of Daniel Rugg Junr., Octob. 14.
Abel, Son of Josiah Locke, Octobr. 15.

1767.

Dinah, Wife of Negro Tim, March 17.
Wife of Aaron Willard, April 27.
Rhoda, Negro Servt. of Dr. Prentice, June 13.
Daniel Knight, October 27.
Child of Elijah Beeman, December —.

1768.

Wife of Deacon Houghton, January 11.
Child of Hooker Osgood, January 7.
Amos, Sawyer, January 25.
Wife of Nathaniel Joslyn, Feb. 13.
Esther, Dr. of Josiah Locke, March 25.
Child of Jonathan Whitney, April 24.
Thomas Tucker, Sept. 19.
Sherebiah Hunt, Novr. 11.
Widow of Joseph House, December —.
Widow of Nathaniel Sawyer, Dec: 28.

1769.

Widow Cory, January 9.
Daniel Albert, January 22.
Elisha Bennet, March 5.
Wife of Thomas Holt, April 12.
Child of Peter Willard, May 19.
Wife of Capt. Ephm. Wilder, May 30.
Wife of Jacob Fowle, June 2.
Josiah Locke, about May 16.
David Atherton, drowned July 3.
Cyrus, Servt. of Levi Willard, July 8.
Wife of Joseph Carter, about Octobr. 23.
Deacⁿ. Joshua Fairbank, Novr. 25.
Dr. Stanton Prentice, December 1.
Capt. Eph. Wilder, Ætas 93, Decemʳ. 14.

1770.

Hannah Sawyer, January 29ᵗʰ.
Ebenezer Harris, January 29.
Capt. Eph: Wilder, March 5.
Juba, Negro Servt. of Mr Ward, February —.
William Richardson Esqr., June 29ᵗʰ.
Oliver Sawyer, July 2.
Ebenezer Allen, July 9ᵗʰ.
Primus Judum, Servt. to yᵉ Widow Willard, July 14.
Susanna Osgood, Augt. 2.
James Houghton, Augt. 9.
Phinehas Phelps, Augt. 12.
Widow of Old Col: Willard, Septr. 28.
Capt. Benjamin Ballard, Octobr. 14.
Asa Rogers, Octobr. 21.
115 Widow of Capt. Benjamin Ballard, Novr. 1.
Widow Green, November —.

The Times when these Persons died are forgotten, but all were between the years 1748 and 1770.

Old Mr Prescott.
Mrs Prescott.
Old Col· Willard.
Mary, Dr. of Dr. Prentice, May, 1750.
Wife of Robt. Fletcher.
Child of Henderson.
Old Mr Larkin.
Matthias Larkin.
Child of Danˡˡ. Albert Junr.
Beulah Wilder.
—— Farmer.

Titus Wilder.
Abigail Woodberry.
Son of Widow Woodberry.
Mr Ebenezer Swan.
Josiah Osgood.
Child of De Putron.
Sarah Wright.
Fleeman's Mother.
John Brazil, drowned.
Hudson, Son to Mrs Eveleigh.
Amos Atherton.
Elijah Atherton.
Anna Jones's Child.
Negro Servt. of Capt. Aaron Willard.
Priscilla Phillips' Child.
Aaron Willard's 2 Children, Shott.
Samson's Child.
Tirus Houghton.
Rachel Houghton.
Sam[ll]. Flood.
Thomas Gates' Child.
Abijah Houghton's Child.
Christopher Osgood's Child.
—— Child.

1772.

January. Jonathan Knight, Son of Joseph Blood & wife.
February 19th, or 20th. Mr Thomas Lyppenwell.
March 8. An Infant of Darius Sawyer's; An Infant of Sam[ll]. Joslin's.
January 19. Submit, ye Wife of Moses Wilder.
January 19. James Locke of ye Second Precinct.
May 5th. Deacon Josiah White, Ætat 90.
The Wife of Mr Moses Russel.
Octobr. 31, 1772. Joseph Fowle.
December 25. Elisha Fletcher.

1773.

Luther, Infant Son of Mr John Bennett, Feb. 15th or 16th.
Wife of William De Putron, March 8, 1773.
March 31. Anna, Dr. of Cyrus Fairbank & wife.
April 21st. Deborah, ye Wife of Col. Joseph Wilder.
Margaret Bowers, June 14th, 1773.
James Goodfry, June 28th, 1773, mortally wounded at a Raising.
—— Ross, August 7, 1773.
David Russell, Augt. 23d, 1773.
December ——. Aaron Johnson's Eldest Child.

1774.

January 5th or 6th. Nathaniel, Son of Mary Wood.

January 19. Hannah Jock, Wife of Lynn Jock.
February 6th, Mr Josiah Brown of Choxet but a member of this Chh.
February 16. Andrew Wilder.
March 6th. Mr Jacob Fowle.
March 19th. The Wife of Major James Wilder.
March 24th, the Widow Judith Sawyer.
Child of Mr Daniel Goss, March 27th.
March 29th, a Child of Peter Willard.
April 4th. Still-born Child of Mr Joel Osgood & wife.
April 12. Mary, y[e] Wife of Mr Moses Sawyer.
April 27, y[e] Wife of Mr Solomon Townsend.
April 30. Mr Joseph Wheelock.
May 8th, the Widow Mary Osgood.
Mr John Goodridge, June 27th, 1774.
Child of Mr Thomas Holt, July 6th, 1774.
Mr Michael Trollett, July 17, 1774.
James, Son of Mr Hooker Osgood, Sept. 13 or 14.
Widow Hannah Lyppenwell, Decembr. 15, 1774.

1775.

Child of Asa Thompson, January, 1775.
The Wife of Mr Jonathan Kendal Sen., Feb. 23d, 1775.
Abigail Cheney, March 27th, 1775.
Mr Solomon Townsend, April 6th, 1775.
James, Son of Frederick Barney, April 12, 1775.
Mr Samuel Locke, April 13, 1775.
Josiah Locke, infant Son of J. & H., April 27, 1775.
Betty Priest and Child, April 30th, 1775.
John, Son of Col. Levi Willard, May 1st, 1775.
May 12th, 1775, the 2d. Wife of Col. J. Wilder.
June 5th. Dr. Fudger's Child, Still-borne.
June 17th. David Robbins, killed in Battle at Charlestown.
June ——. Still-born Child of Mr Gershom Flagg.
July 4th. Rebecca Phelps.
July 11th. Col. Levi Willard.
July 23d, 1775. Elijah Wheelock, mortally wounded by a Fall from a loaded cart.
Augt. 23d, 1775. Jeremiah, Son of Mr Nehemiah Newton.
Augt. 24th, 1775. Susanna, Dr. of Mr John Warner.
Augt. 24th, 1775. Beulah, Dr. of Hooker Osgood.
Robert Phelps, wounded—died at Boston.
September 16th. Rebecca, Dr. of Dr. Atherton.

Stephen Hayward, Son of Jeremiah Leach.
Child of Mark Heald, October 23ᵈ, 1775.
Child of Abijah Hawkes, Novr. 9ᵗʰ or 10ᵗʰ.
Caesar, Negro Servt. of Dr. Dunsmore, Novr. 1775.

DEATHS, 1776.

January 5ᵗʰ. Widow Lydia James.
January 14ᵗʰ. John Phelps junr.
Martha Fairbank, January 17, 1776.
February 23. Thomas Burdit.
Ruth Burditt, March 4ᵗʰ, 1776.
Moses Osgood, March 10ᵗʰ, 1776.
Joel, Son of Mr Joseph Carter & wife.
Joseph Wheelock, March 16, 1776.
John Warner, March 27ᵗʰ, 1776.
Asa Nickson or Nicholson or Nixon, a stranger, May 11, 1776.
John Ballard, in yᵉ Continental service, of yᵉ small-pox.
Nathaniel Wyman, June 5ᵗʰ, 1776. [b. Feb. 26, 1718.]
The Widow Priest, Ætat 80, June —, 1776.
Coll. Caleb Wilder, June 18, 1776.
Abel Wyman, in yᵉ Continental Service, Augt.
Child of Cyrus Fairbank, Sept. —.
Lucy, yᵉ Wife of Cyrus Fairbank, Sept. 16.
Child of Timothy Knight Junr. & wife.
Youngest Child of Mr John Phillips, Octob. 26.
Eldest Child of Mr Phillips, Oct. 29.
Child of Mr Joseph Nichols, Nov. 1.
The other child of Mr John Phillips, Nov. 2ᵈ, 1776.
Deacon David Wilder, Novr. 17ᵗʰ, 1776.
Mr John Phillips, Novr. 24ᵗʰ, 1776.
Mr John Bennett, in yᵉ Service.
James, Son of Mr Hooker Osgood, Decembr. 1ˢᵗ.

1777.

January. Child of Caesar Hammond, free Negro.
January 18ᵗʰ. Still-born Child of James Wilder Junior.
February 23. Joseph, Son of Mr Joseph Whitmore.
Feby. 28ᵗʰ. Deacⁿ. Joseph Wilder.
March 23ᵈ. Andrew Larkin, from Ireland.
April 13 or 14. Elijah Woods' Child, Still-born.
May 15. Mr Ephraim Houghton, Ætatˢ. 75.
June 25ᵗʰ. Mr Stephen Wyman.
June 27. Capt. Hezekiah Gates, Ætatˢ. 77.

June 29ᵗʰ, Deacon Israel Houghton, Ætatˢ. 77.
July or Augt. Lt. Jonathan Sawyer, Killed by Indians.
Augt. 12ᵗʰ or 13ᵗʰ. Ephraim Houghton.
August about 18ᵗʰ. Peter, Infant Son of Mr Danl. Godfry.
Augt. 23ᵈ. Rebekkah, Wife of Timothy Knight.
Augt. 28ᵗʰ. Child of Joseph Nichols & wife.
Augt. 29ᵗʰ. Sylvia, Child of John Willard and wife.
Septr. 9ᵗʰ. Luther, Son of Mr Jonathan Wheelock.
Octobr. 2ᵈ. Elisha, Son of Mr Elisha Allen.
Octobr. 4ᵗʰ. Henrietta, Wife of Mr John Locke & Dr. of T. Harrington; John, Son of Capt. Tho. Gates & wife.
October 20. Jonathan Kendall Junr.
Novr. 1ˢᵗ. Timothy Paine, Son of Mr E. Bradish.
Novr. 2ᵈ. Eunice, Dr. of Mr Jonathan Whitney.
Octob. —. James, Son of Lt. Josiah Ballard.
Mary McClothling or Laughlin, about Octo. 19.
December —. Solomon, Son of Benjamin Priest.
December —. Thomas, Son of Mr — Baker & wife.
December 27. John McGrah, from Ireland.

1778.

Mary, Wife of Jonathan Whitney, Jany. 12ᵗʰ.
John Wheelock, February 7ᵗʰ.
Still-born Child of Prince Davis, February 14.
Sarah, Wife of Gershom Flagg, April 27ᵗʰ.
Eunice White, May 15ᵗʰ, Ætat. 88, 9 or 90.
Anna Harrington, Tuesday, May 19ᵗʰ A. M., 10ʰ. 50ᵐ., Ætat. 60.
The Widow —— Knight, June 9ᵗʰ. 1778, Æ. 92.
Oliver Phelps, June 10ᵗʰ, 1778.
May, 1778, Luke Carter, of yᵉ Small Pox and measles Sebasedegon.
Abel Fairbanks, Joseph Wheelock, in yᵉ army.
Martha, Wife of Nathaniel Eaton, July 5, 1778.
Anna, Dr. of Mr Peter Atherton, August 4ᵗʰ, 1778.
Augt. 23ᵈ, Anna, Augt. 26ᵗʰ, Mary, Children of Mr William Locke & wife.

August 31. Dr. of Capt. Sam¹. Ward & wife.
Septr. 1ˢᵗ. William Pitt, Son of Dr. Josiah Wilder & wife.
117 Septr. 7ᵗʰ. Anna, Dr. of Mr Zeph. Williams &c., and on yᵉ same Day Hannah Ceesar, Maid Servant of Dr. Atherton.
Charles, Son of Capt. S. Ward &c., Septr. 14ᵗʰ.
Polly, Infant Dr. of Dr. J. Wilder, Septr. 17.
Infant of Mr Daniel Godfry, Septr. 18.
Henry, Son of Dr. J. Wilder, Septr. 19.
Thankful Goodridge, Widʷ., Sept. 20ᵗʰ.
Son of Capt. John White junior, Sept. 21.
Thomas, Son of Mr Paul Sawyer, Septr.
Nancy, Dr. of Mr Peter Thirston, Septr. 25.
Peter, Son of Mr Peter Larkin, Sept. 27.
Joseph Wilder Junr., of yᵉ Small Pox, at Sea; Joseph Phelps, died of his wounds in a Sea fight.
Elisabeth, Wife of Dⁿ. Cyrus Fairbank, Octo. 1.
October. Lucy, Cretia, Katy, Children of Mr Peter Larkin; Abigail, Wife of Mr Joshua Smith.
Octobr. 16, the Widow Anna Wilder and the Wife of James Butler.
Novr. 1ˢᵗ. Mary, Wife of Silas Houghton, and a Child of Rebecca Fletcher.
Novr. 27ᵗʰ. Child of Mr Ephraim Cheney.

1779.

Jany. 4ᵗʰ. Solomon, Son of Benjamin Priest.
January 13. Daniel Zweir.
January, 1779. Anna, Dr. of Daniel Goss &c.
Wife of Mr Peter Greene, Feby. 3.
Henry Haskel, April 1ˢᵗ.
Widow Anna Gates, April 23.
Joseph, Son of Caleb Wilder, Augt. 24.
September 13. Widow Jemima Carter.
A Woman at Mrs Phillipses.
Novr. —. Augustus, Son of Dʳ. Jos. Wilder.
Novr. or December. The Wife of Edw. Saunders.
Phinehas Phelps, December 12ᵗʰ.
Stephen Gates.

1780.

January 15 or 16. Majʳ. James Wilder.
February 17ᵗʰ. Ephraim Wyman.
Feb. 29ᵗʰ. Mr Joseph Wheeler.
April 22ᵈ. Youngest Son of Edward Poor.
May 17ᵗʰ. Rebecca Brown from Boston.
July, 1780. Jonathan Phillips.

Sept. or Octobr., a Child of Mr Moses Smith.
Novr. 15ᵗʰ. Deacⁿ. Joseph White.
Josiah Coolledge, December 25ᵗʰ.
Widow Rebecca Phillips, 29 December.

1781.

Elisabeth Jefts, widow, January 21ˢᵗ.
—— Kelly, February —.
Edward Poor, February 14ᵗʰ or 15ᵗʰ.
Asahel Phelps, February 19ᵗʰ.
Child of Sabre Sawyer, abt. Feb. 22ᵈ.
March —. Luther, Son of Jonathan Wheelock.
June 12ᵗʰ. Child of Josiah Coolledge, scalded.
June 13ᵗʰ. Child of Wᵐ. Phelps Junr.
July 16ᵗʰ. Leafy, Dr. of John Nichols junr.
Octobr. 20. Child of Gershom Flagg.
Octobr. 31. The Wife of Amos Knight.
Novr. 2ᵈ. Child of Ephm. Divol Junr.
Decembr. 30. Wife of Capt. Joseph Wilder.

1782.

January 18ᵗʰ. Sarah, Dr. of Daniel Rugg.
March 22ᵈ. John, Inft. Son of Deacon Cyrus Fairbank.
May 6ᵗʰ, yᵉ Wife of Mr Edward Phelps. Ætatis 88.
July 9ᵗʰ, yᵉ Widow Mary Tucker.
July 17ᵗʰ. Anna, Dr. of Mr Joshua Fletcher.
July 19ᵗʰ, an Infant of Stephen Fuller's &c.
July 20. Still-born Infant of Nathˡˡ. Haskell.
Septr. 21ˢᵗ. Edward, Son of James Wilder.
Ruth Wright, Decem. 30.

1783.

January 11ᵗʰ. Patience, Infant Dr. of P. Corey & wife.
April 3ᵈ. Mrs Joanna Alford, Ætatis 83.
Eunice Heard, April 14ᵗʰ, Ætatis 25.
June 7ᵗʰ. John Nichols, Ætatis 85.
Thomas Norton, drowned June 11ᵗʰ, Ætatis 18.
Dinah, Maid-Servant of T. Harrington, June 11ᵗʰ, Ætatis 37.
118 July 2ᵈ. Paul Sawyer, of Fits at Princetown, on a journey Homewards.
July 4ᵗʰ. Infant of Oliver Wheelock.
September, about 25ᵗʰ. Luther, Son of Samuel Jones.
Octor. 28. William, Son of Cyrus Houghton, by yᵉ Bite of a Mad Dog.
Novr. 20ᵗʰ. Jonathan Kendall, Ætatis 93.

1784.

February 7th. —— Stimpson, at Mr G. Flagg's.
March 7th. Mr Edward Phelps, Ætat. 90 or 93.
March 24th. Mr Thomas Cummins, from Ireland.
May 12th. Mr Aaron Willard, Ætats. 84.
May 14th. James Pratt, by Suicide.
May 20th. William Dunsmoor Esq., Ætats. 50.
July 3d. Joshua Phelps, Ætats. 84.
July 7th. Abijah Wyman, Ætats. 69.
July 25. Elisha Marsh Esq., Walpole, Ætatis 71 or 72.
Augt. 21st. James Butler, mortally wounded by a ram.
" " Infant Dr. of Capt. Ephraim Carter.
Septr. 23d. Widow Alice Joslyn, Ætats. 84.
Octobr. 13. Widow Hannah Flagg, Ætats. 73.
Octobr. 27. Anna, infant Dr. of James Goodwin.

1785.

Sarah Wheelock, February 14th.
Oliver Wheelock, April 6th, Ætat. 25.
James, Son of Abishai Phelps, April —— Æt. 10.
Martha, Wife of Levi Page, April 16. Æt. 28.
Son of Nathaniel Beaman, May 4th or 5th.
Election week. Infant Child of Mr Ger. Flagg; Infant Child of Mr Saml. Johnson.
June 10th, Deborah, June 13, Betsy, Children of Mr James Godfry.
July 17th. Sally, Dr. of Jonathan Whitney &c.
Augt. 14. John Phelps, Ætat. 63.
Still born child of John Fletcher.
Child of John Tinny, Septr. 29th.
Octobr. Infant of Capt. S. Joslyn.
Novr. 24th. John, Son of Capt. Thomas Gates.
Novr. 26. Anna, Dr. of Capt. Thomas Gates.
Decembr. 13 or 14. Son of Capt. John Thurston.

1786.

Jany. 25th, John, Jany. 29th, David, children of Mr Jonath. Wilder.
Elisabeth Elithrap, February 14th.
Daniel, Son of Mr Solomon Townsend, February 24.
March 9th. Thomas, Son of Titus Wilder.
March 13th. Widow Elisabeth Clark.
May 19th. Twins of Jonas Wyman & w.

June 20th. Jeremiah Haskel, Ætats. 72, '3 or 4.
June 24th. Widow Hannah Woods, Ætats. 77.
The Widow Rachel Phelps, July 21st, 1786.
Nathan Rugg, Septr. 15th, 1786, Ætats. 68.
Jonathan Rugg, Septr. 17th, 1786, Ætats. 84 or 5.
Infant Child of Eli Stearns, Octobr. 17, 1786.
Child of Saml. Jones, Octobr. 25th.
Infant Child of Deacn C. Fairbank, "
Child of Zebulon Butman, Novr. 23d.

1787.

Widow Dorothy Phelps, Feby. 23, Ætats. 81.
Kezia Houghton, Dr. of Phinias, Ætatis 24, March 26th.
Susanna, Dr. of Hooker Osgood, April 1st, Ætatis 27.
James, Son of Jerh. Ballard, Ætatis 6 months.
Dolly Piper, April 22d, Ætatis 12.
May 5th. Katharine Sprague, Ætatis 4.
Betsy, Dr. of Jonathan Osgood.
Mr Oliver Wilder, Septr. 2d, Ætatis 68.
Infant of Mr Joel Osgood, Septr. 3d.
Widow Zweir, Octobr. 21st, 1787.
Amos Knight, Ætatis 75 or 6, Decemb. 15.
Joseph Taft, Decembr. 25th, Ætatis 66.

1788.

Nathaniel, Son of Mr Moses Sawyer, Feby. 13th, Ætat. 6.
Elisabeth Greenough, Widow, March 13th.
Widow Thankful Haskel, March 30th, Ætatis 73.
Infant Child of Stephen Pratt, April 29th.
John Beaman, June 25th, Ætatis 78.
Sarah, Dr. of Moses Sawyer, September 2, Ætatis 17.
Mary, Wife of John Prescott, Octobr. 19th, Ætatis 65.
Levi, Son of Mr Stephen Wilder, Ætatis 18.
Josiah Wilder Esq., Decembr. 20th, Ætatis 44.

1789.

January 18. Saml. Divoll, Ætatis 31.
Dorothy, wife of Major G. Wilder, Ætatis 46, Feb. 14th, 1789.
March 6th. Eunice Townsend, Ætatis —
March 25th. Mrs Margaret Stoddard, Ætatis 77.
119 Peggy Stone, Negro, found dead in ye Road March 31st.

Widow Sarah Wheeler, April 14, 1789, Ætat. 71.
Widow of Esqr. Richardson, Ætats. 86, at Sterling, March 3ᵈ.
March 3ᵈ. Child of Salmon Godfray, Æ. 8 months.
May 24ᵗʰ. Admonition Kendall, Ætatis 67.
July 18ᵗʰ. Joseph Greenough, Ætatis –
Augᵗ. 14ᵗʰ. Darius Sawyer, Ætatis 69.
Augt. 15. Child of Samˡˡ. Corey, Ætatis 3.
Widow Rebecca Wilder, Ætatis 80.
Wife of Simon Butler, Septr. 25ᵗʰ, Ætatis 30.
Child of Elisha Rugg, Sept. 25ᵗʰ, Infant.
October 18ᵗʰ. Dorothy Widow of Jonathan Rugg, Ætatis 88.
Novr. 7ᵗʰ. Edmund Greenleaf, Ætatˢ. 22.
" John Ballard, junr., Son of John Ballard, drowned in yᵉ well. Ætatis 6.
Novr. 27ᵗʰ. Betsy Dr. of James Fuller, Ætatˢ. 5.
Decembr 18ᵗʰ. Still-born Child of Samˡˡ. Joslyn.

1790.

Sarah, Wife of William Greenleaf Esq. Æ. 53. March 12ᵗʰ, 1790.
Infant of Oliver Tenney, March 22ᵈ, 1790.
May 2ᵈ. Parrot Tenny, Ætatis —.
" Infant child of Abner Pollard & wife.
May 15ᵗʰ. Rachel Wheeler, Ætatis —.
June 9ᵗʰ. Sally, Dr. of Deacon Cyrus Fairbank.
July 16. Jonathan Wheelock, Ætatis –
July 19ᵗʰ. Infant Dr. of Elijah Rugg & wife. Twin.
July 29ᵗʰ, yᵉ other Twin Daughter of Elijah Rugg.

August 16ᵗʰ or 17ᵗʰ. Son of Corbet, free Negro.
Abigail, Wife of Thomas Kendal, Ætatis 66, Novr. 7ᵗʰ.
Novr. 8ᵗʰ. Abel Carter, Ætatis 29.
Decembr. 14. Still-born Child of Samˡ. Jones.
Decembr. 22ᵈ. Lois, Wife of Capt. John White, Æt. 73.

1791.

January 7ᵗʰ. Infant Child of Eli Stearns.
Catharine. Relict of Col. Levi Willard, Jany. 10ᵗʰ, 1791, Ætat. 56.
January 10ᵗʰ. Child of Mr Samˡ. Stevens.
John Prescott, April 1ˢᵗ, Ætatˢ. 79.
Infant Child of Mr — Stone, May 20ᵗʰ.
Thomas Holt, Ætatˢ. 70, July 3ᵈ, 1791.
Mary Phillips, 1791, Shaker.
Edward Clarke, A. B., Ætatis 21, July 5ᵗʰ, 1791.
Edward Robbins, Æ. 79, Octo. 9ᵗʰ, 1791.
Reuben Burnham, Ætatˢ. 18 or 19, November 19, 1791.

1792.

Child of Thomas Ballard, March 3ᵈ, 1792.
Relict of Oliver Wilder, April 6ᵗʰ.
Widow Haven, about April 16, 1792.
Rebecca, Wife of Jonathan Osgood, July 15ᵗʰ.
Mr Jonas Fairbank.
Daniel Rugg, Novr. 1ˢᵗ, 1792, Æt. 78.
Son of Amos Sawyer, " Æt. 4.
Wife of Joel Osgood.
General Greenleafe.

[1793.]

Sarah, Dr. of Moses Wilder, March 17ᵗʰ.
Esq. Ephraim Carter, Octob. 12ᵗʰ, 1793.

---

120   SUCH AS HAVE OWNED Yᴱ COVENANT.

John Osgood and his Wife, Feb. 19ᵗʰ, 1748-9. N.B. he is Son of Deacon Osgood.
Peter Joslyn Junior & his Wife, June 11ᵗʰ, 1749.
Stephen Johnson, July 30ᵗʰ, 1749.
Josiah Sawyer & his Wife, Octr. 1ˢᵗ, 1749.
Abijah & Alice Houghton, Decembr. 24ᵗʰ, 1749.
Hezekiah, Anna Gates, Samuel Locke Junior, Lucretia Locke, April 14ᵗʰ, A. D. 1751.
Gershom, Mary Flagg, May yᵉ 12ᵗʰ, A. Dom. 1751.
John, Jane Henderson, December 15ᵗʰ, 1751.
Eunice Carter, December 31ˢᵗ, 1752.
Nathanael, Martha, Esther Joslyn, Feb. 25ᵗʰ, 1753.
Matthew Wyman, James, Ruth Richardson, March 4ᵗʰ, 1753.
Bezaleel Sawyer Junr., Lois Sawyer his wife, March 11ᵗʰ, 1753.
Eunice Goss, April 8, 1753.
John, Prudence Manning, Sept. 2ᵈ, 1753.
Reuben, Anna Lyppenwell, Sept. 9ᵗʰ, 1753.
Abigail Nichols, December 9ᵗʰ, 1753.

William Kendall, May 11th, 1755.
Paul Sawyer, Sept. 17, 1755. On a Lecture Day being bound into y" Service.
Ruth Kendall, May 30, 1756.
Tabitha, Elisabeth, Mary Priest, December 19th, 1756.
121 Richard Baker, April 3d, A. Dom. 1757.
Darius, Deborah Sawyer, Septr. 25th, 1757.
John Warner and Wife, Novr. 19, 1758.
Thomas, Elisabeth Beaman, June 3d, 1759.
William Richardson Junr., Patience Richardson, January 6th, 1760.
Anna y" Wife of Nathanael Turner, May 18, 1760.
Thomas Sawyer, Mary Baker, y" Children of Bezaleel Sawyer, Augt. 10th, 1760.
Margaret Negro Maid Servant of Ebenr. Allen Junr. Augt. 10th, 1760.
Nathanael Turner, Novr. 23d, A. Dom. 1760.
The Widow Rachel Houghton, Octobr. 11th, 1761.
Mr Edmond Larkin, October 18th, 1761.
Josiah and Jane Divol, July 9th, 1762.
Bathsheba, Wife of Thomas Henderson, July 18th, 1762.
Lois, Lucy Holt, August 1st, 1762.
Stanton, Peninnah Carter, Octobr. 24th, 1762.
William Willard Junr., Mary Willard, Novr. 28th, 1762.
Edward, Lucretia Houghton, Decr. 26th, 1762.
Samuel Joslyn, January 2d, 1763.
Joseph, Martha, Susanna, Elisabeth Nichols, y" Children of John Nichols, Octobr. 23, 1763.
Benjamin, Hannah Priest, Octobr. 30th, 1763.
122 Sept. 16th, 1764. Peter, Dorothy Thirston.
April 20th, 1766. Ceesar, Negro Servant of Mr Peter Joslyn.
Christopher, Hannah Osgood, Octobr 12th, 1766.
Thomas, David, Mary Holt, Children of Thomas Holt and Wife, April 17th, 1768.
Joshua Johnson, May 22d, 1768.
The Widow Mary Sawyer, July 31, 1768.
Thomas Holt. July 16, 1769.
Mr Samuel Ward, December 10th, 1769.
Lucy Ayner, March 11th, 1770.
Mary Goodridge, May 13, 1770.
Eunice Poor, June 17, 1770.
John and Sarah Hewit, July 15, 1770.
Lydia Butler, Novr. 25, 1770.
George, Betty Leason, Octobr. 6, 1771.
Lydia Johnson, October 13, 1771.
Mary Wood, October 27, 1771.
Moses Russell, January 17th, 1773.
Hannah Ross, Widow, Septr. 19, 1773.
Patience Wyman, Octobr. 10th, 1773.
Daniel Zweir, Abigail Zweir, Novr. 28, 1773.
Abijah Houghton Junr., Mary Houghton, January 2, 1774.
William, Barbara Shaw, April 10, 1774.
Joseph Beeman Junr., May 29th, 1774.
Anna Margaret Russell, July 17, 1774.
Ebenezer Allen Junr. & Mary Allen,
Moses Dickenson and Rebekkah Dickenson, } August 28th, 1774.
John Newman, September 3d, 1775.
123 James and Sarah Fuller, October 8th, 1775.
Hephzibah Brabrook, Octobr. 12th, 1777.
Samuel Adams, March 22, 1778.
Thomas, Daniel, Ebenezer, Ruthy, Sally Burditt, March 14th, 1779.
David, Lucebe Hosley, August 22, 1779.
Polly Goddard, Octobr. 3, 1779.
William Phelps Junr., Sarah Phelps, April 23, 1780.
Abel, Lois Phelps, Augt. 6th, 1780.
Dolly Cummins, April 15, 1781.
Sally Phelps, May 26th, 1782.
Amy Rugg, January 26, 1783.

Asa, Mary Carter, Feby. 16th, 1783.
Sally, Nancy Clark, October 12th, 1783.
Thomas, Betty Tucker, July 4th, 1784.
Simon, Elisabeth Butler, Augt. 8, 1784.
Abigail Bennett, Novr. 27, 1785.
Mary Divol, Augt. 6, 1786.
Polly Clarke, March 13, 1791.
William Stedman Esqr., June 18th, 1792.
Phinehas Fletcher & Mary Fletcher.
Jacob Kilburn, November 18, 1792.

165 PERSONS DISMIST TO OTHER CHHS. BY VOTE OF THE CHH.

The Dates Signify ye Times when ye Chh. Voted ye Dismissions. The Persons dismist from Novr: 1748 to ye first Date of this Record, with ye Times of ye Dismission cannot certainly be recollected.

1752. Kezia, ye Wife of David Baldwin, to ye Chh. of Christ in Bilerica.
Joshua Osgood and Wife to ye Chh. in New Rutland.
Israel Nichols and Wife [Desire] to ye Chh. in Leominster. [May 30, 1756.]
Asa Harris to ye Chh. in Leominster. [April 25, 1756.]
John Bowers and Wife to ye Chh. in Stow.
Joseph Wilder 3d & Wife to ye Chh. in Leominster.
Converse Richardson and Wife to ye Chh. in Groton.
Mr Moses Hemenway to ye Chh. in Wells.
Dorothy Osgood to ye Chh. in Bolton.
Mary Houghton to ye Chh. in Bolton.
James Willard to ye Chh. in Harvard.
John Herbert and Wife to ye Chh. in Nicthewogg.
—— Hudson and Wife to ye Chh. in Grafton.
Joseph Whitcomb Junr. & Wife to ye Chh. in Swanzey.
Abigail Ball to ye 2d [church] of Christ in Westborough.
Octob. 11th. Abigail Fairbank to ye Chh. in ye West Precinct.
Mary Kendall to ye Chh. in Lunenburgh.
Edward Phelps Junr. & Wife to ye Chh. in Leominster.
Hannah Willson to ye Chh. in Petersham.
Benja. Osgood Junr. and Wife to ye Chh. of Christ in Keene, Octo. 4, 1767.
Elijah Osgood to ye Chh. of Christ in Swanzey, 1769.
Mrs Susanna Marsh to ye Chh. in Walpole, New Hampshire, March 24, 1771.
Damaris Dickenson to ye Chh. of Christ in Pepperrell.
Lucy Wilder to ye Chh. of Christ in Monadnuck No. 4.
Sarah Eager to ye Chh. of Christ in Paxton, Sept. 8th, 1771.
Benjamin Farmer and Wife to ye Chh. in Alstead, N. H., Jany. 11, 1783.
Deborah Bancroft to ye Chh. in Rindge, N. H., May 29th, 1791.
John Locke and wife to ye Chh. in Charlemont.
1793. Sept. 15. Reuben Leppingwell and Anna his wife to the Chh. in Westminster in Vermont.
171 Septr. 23d, 1750. Experience Sabin to ye first Chh. in Pomfret; Mary Goldsberry to ye Chh. in Grafton.
Thomas Prentice Esq. to ye Chh. in Newton.
Septr. 29th, 1763. Mark & Mary Lincoln to ye first Chh. in Leominster.
Octobr. —, 1767. Bethiah Spooner to ye Chh in Petersham.
May 29th, 1768. { Mary Ball to ye Chh. in Northborough.
Elisabeth Bennett to ye Chh. in Leominster.
June or July, 1773. Lucy Holt to ye Chh. in Westminster.
Ruth White to ye Chh. in Heath, 9th Febry., 1791.

[The following records of marriages solemnized by Mr. Harrington are not included in the town-clerks' lists, the parties not being resident in Lancaster :]

Sept. 1, 1763. The Revd. Mr Ebenezer Sparhawk of Templeton, and Mrs Abigail Stearns of Lunenburgh, and
Mr Noah Dodge and Mrs Sarah Witherby, both of Lunenburgh.
Octobr. 20, 1763. Mr David Stearns and Mrs Mary Low, both of Lunenburgh.
June 6th, 1765. The Revd. Mr Zabdiel Adams, and Mrs Elisabeth Stearns, both of Lunenburgh.

BOOK II.

REVEREND NATHANIEL THAYER'S MINISTRY.

MEMBERS OF THE CHURCH.

1794.

Males.—Jan. 12, John Wilder; Mar. 16, Jonas Fairbank; 23, Nath¹. Sawyer, Thomas Bennett Jr.; April 6, Joseph Wales; July 20, Samuel Wilder, Samuel Rugg; 21, Joseph Osgood, sick, admitted at home; Sep. 28, Samuel Wilder Jr.; Nov. 2, Gates Thurston; Dec. 7, Abner Pollard.

Females.—Mar. 23, Isabel Bennett; May 25, Mercy Manning, Sally White; July 20, Sally Rugg; Aug. 5, Catharine Osgood; Sally Whipple; 31, Eunice Poor, Tabitha Allen, Rebecca Whiting, Zilpah Phelps, Lydia Phelps; Sep. 28, Betsy Wilder, Emma Stevens; Oct. 5, Lucy Wheelock, Sophronia Willard; Nov. 2, Betsy Thurston; Dec. 7, Achsah Pollard, Beulah Phelps, Lucy Fairbank. In 1794. Males 11, Females 20....31.

1795.

Males.—Jan. 18, John Campbell; Feb. 22, Daniel Goss; June 7, John Ballard, Jonas Lane; John Campbell, By certificate from Jaffrey; 21, Reuben Bryant, Certificate from Jaffrey; July 5, Moses Sawyer Jr.; Sep. 13, Joseph Rugg; Nov. 8, Simon Butler; Dec. 27, Oliver Carter.

Females.—Jan. 18, Nancy Campbell; 27, Dolly Lane, sick, admitted at house; June 7, Martha Campbell by Certificate; July 5, Elizabeth Sawyer; Sep. 13, Mary Rugg; Nov. 8, Eunice Butler; Dec. 6, Elisabeth Capen; Dec. 27, Emily Carter.
  In 1795. Males 10, Females 8....18+31=49.

1796.

Males.—Apr. 3, Elijah Houghton, Certificate from Sterling; 17, Gowen B. Newman; May 15, John White 3ᵈ; July 17, Edward Goodwin; Aug. 7, Jacob Fisher; Dec. 4, Samuel Damon, Certificate from Reading.

Females.—Jan. 17, Jemima Stone; Feb. 7, Sarah Thayer; Mar. 20, Bathsheba White; Apr. 17, Lucy Newman; May 15, Sophia White; July 17, Sally Goodwin; Aug. 7, Nancy Fisher; Dec. 4, Abigail Damon, Certificate from Reading.
  Males 6, Females 8....14+49=63.

1797.

Males.—June 4, William Bigelow; Aug. 6, John Phelps; Oct. 1, Daniel Goss Jr.; Dec. 3, Elisha Phelps.

Females.—Oct. 1, Polly Goss; 22, Ruth Carter; Nov. 19, Eunice Lane; Dec. 3, Polly Sargeant, Molly Phelps. Males 4, Females 5....9+63=72.

1798.

Males.—Apr. 1, William Arnold, Certificate from Braintree; July 15, James Goodwin Jr., Ephraim Carter; Aug. 5, William Arnold Jr., Certificate from Braintree.

Females.—Apr. 1, [Mrs.] William Arnold, Certificate from Braintree; July 1, Dolly Flagg, Ruth Phelps; 15, Abigail Goodwin, Mary Carter, Mary Carter; Oct. 14, Alice McLeod; Nov. 4, Eunice Bennett.

Males.—Oct. 14, Thomas McLeod; Nov. 4, Nathan Bennett; 21, Nathaniel Miller, privately, being sick; 25, Joseph Leech.

Females.—Nov. 25, Susanna Leech. Males 8, Females 9....17+72=89.

1799.

Males.—Sept. 29, Timothy Fletcher.
Females.—Mar. 3, Anna Miller; May 26, Elizabeth Rugg, Lucy Rugg; Sep. 1, Diana Eveleth; 29, Hannah Fletcher; Dec. 1, Damaris Johnson: 15, Eunice French. Males 1, Females 7....8+89=97.

1800.

Males.—Jan. 5, Thomas Ballard; Apr. 13, Joseph Rice, Certificate from Boylston; July 6, Amos Sawyer Jr.; Dec. 7, Seth Sargeant.
Females.—Jan. 5, Abigail Ballard; 12, Arethusa Hunt; Mar. 11, Sally Knowlton; Apr. 13, Betsy Rice, Certificate from Boylston; July 6, Polly Sawyer, Esther Phelps, Ruth Phelps; Aug. 3, Martha Wilder; Nov. 16, Triphena Corey, Nancy Corey; Dec. 7, Elizabeth Sargeant; 28, Ann Austin Sprague.
Males 4, Females 12....16+97=113.

1801.

Males.—Aug. 30, George Phelps; Dec. 6, Joseph White.
Females.—Feb. 22, Eleanor Arnold, Deborah Tenney, Sally Phelps; Sept. 27, Elizabeth Fletcher; Oct. 4, Submit Jones; Dec. 6, Rebecca White, privately by reason of sickness.
In 1801. Males, 2. Females, 6....8+113=121.

1802.

Males.—Mar. 14, John Goodwin; July 11, Asa Warner, Certificate from Ipswich; Oct. 24, Oliver Baldwin.
Females.—Mar. 14, Rebecca Goodwin, Lucy Baldwin.
In 1802. Males, 3. Females, 2....5+121=126.

1803.

Males.—Apr. 3, William Stedman; Dec. 4, John Goss.
Females.—Nov. 24, Sophia Sawyer; May 29, Jane Warner; July 3, Rebecca Cowdry; 31, Dolly Divoll; Dec. 4, Mary Goss.
In 1803. Males, 2. Females 5....7+126=133.

1804.

Males.—Mar. 25, Ebenezer Torrey, Certificate from West Church in Boston; June 3, Charles E. Knight; Oct. 7, Luke Wilder; Nov. 11, Edward Fuller, Certificate from Berlin.
Females.—June 3, Sally Knight; Aug. 5, Lucia Selfridge; Oct. 7, Mary Wilder; Nov. 11, Susanna Fuller.
In 1804. Males 4. Females 4....8+133=141.

1805.

Males.—Oct. 27, Calvin Peabody.
Females.—May 12, Elizabeth Joslyn; Oct. 6, Elizabeth Gould; 27, Sarah Farnsworth, Abigail Peabody.
In 1805. Males, 1. Females, 4....5+141=146.

1846.

Males.—March 2, Joel Wilder; May 4, William Fletcher, James Mallard; June 1, John Carter 3d.
Females.—Mar. 2, Lucy Wilder; May 4, Dorcas Fletcher; June 1, Betsy Carter; Oct. 5, Sarah Carter; Nov. 23, Elizabeth Leech, Isabel Englesby, Jemima White. In 1806. Males 4, Females 7....11+146=157.

1807.

Males.—Sep. 6, Israel Haskell.
Females.—Apr. 5, Lucretia Wyman; June 7, Rebecca Leech, Betsy Mallard; July 5, Nancy Bennett, Lucy Arnold; 13, Sarah Whittemore, privately, being sick; Sep. 6, Sally Mallard. In 1807. Males 1, Females 7....8+157=165.

1808.

Males.—Apr. 17, Peter Thurston Jr.
Females.—Apr. 17, Sarah Thurston; June 2, Abigail Whipple, Certificate from Groton; Aug. 7, Sarah Todd; Oct. 2, Anna Maynard.
In 1808. Males 1, Females 4....5+165=170.

1809.

Males.—June 4, Otis Hunt; Aug. 20, Jonas Goss; Sept. 3, John Goss.
Females.—Aug. 20, Judith Goss, Polly Rugg; Sep. 3, Rebecca Goss; Oct. 1, Lucretia McCallum; 3, Ann Rust Parker.
In 1809. Males 3, Females 5....8+170=178.

1810.

Males.—June 3, Eber Goddard; July 1, Josiah Bridge, Certificate from Sudbury; Aug. 5, Jonas Whitney, Horatio G. Buttrick, Eliphaz Ballard, Benja. Hawks; Oct. 7, Solomon Carter.
Females.—Mar. 15, Betsy Allen, privately, by reason of Sickness; June 3, Lucy Goddard, Sophia Allen, Lydia Fales; July 1, Eirene Bridge, Certificate from E. Sudbury; Susanna Hastings; 22, Sophia Durant; Aug. 5, Mary Stearns, Sarah Hildreth, Elizabeth W. Hildreth, Mary Whitney, Nancy Buttrick, Anna Ballard, Polly Hawkes; Sep. 2, Rebecca Kendall, Abigail Kendall; 30, Sally Lane, privately, being very sick; Oct. 7, Lucy Carter, Ann Wilder, Sarah Carter; 28, Betsy Eaton, Catharine Eaton.
In 1810. Males 7, Females 22....29+178=207.

1811.

Males.—June 2, Elijah Wilder; Sept. 1, Robert Phelps.
Females.—Feb. 3, Elizabeth Carter of Fitzwilliam; May 26, Elizabeth Safford, Certificate from Concord. In 1811. Males 2, Females 5....7+207=214.
Females.—June 2, Sophia Wilder; Sep. 1, Polly Phelps, Nancy Todd.

1812.

Males.—Oct. 2, Thomas Carter, At home being sick.
Females.—Aug. 2, Martha Gates; Sep 6, Submit Wilder; Nov. 1, Mary Prescott; Oct. 2, Sally Carter. In 1812. Males 1, Females 4....5+214=219.

1813.

Males.—Oct. 17, Ebenr. Bragg; Dec. 5, Daniel Newhall.
Females.—Apr. 4, Elizabeth White; 25, Catharine Newhall, Certificate from Lincoln; Oct. 17, Susan Howe, Martha Bragg, Lucy Wilder; Dec. 5, Betsy Newhall. In 1813. Males 2, Females 6....8+219=227.

1814.

Males.—May 29, Elisha Sanderson, Certificate from Lunenburg; July 10, Benja. H. Foster.
Females.—Apr. 3, Susanna Spear, Nancy Spear; May 29, Polly Sanderson, Certificate from Lunenburg; July 10, Martha Foster; Aug. 7, Julia Whiting.
In 1814. Males 2, Females 5....7+227=234.

1815.

Males.—Jan. 1, Abijah Rogers; Oct. 1, William Cleveland.
Females.—Jany. 1, Lucy Rogers; Apr. 2, Mary Stearns, Eliza Stearns, Sarah T. Thayer; Sepr. 3, Sally Carter; 17, Elizabeth Chandler.
In 1815. 8....242.

1816.

Females.—Apr. 4, Lucy Manning, Certificate from Billerica; June 2. Prudence Bigelow, Certificate from Westminster; Sep. 26, Susanna Bridge, At home being sick. In 1816. Females 3+242=245.

1817.

Males.—Nov. 2, James Rugg.
Females.—Aug. 3, Rebecca Haskell; Sept. 7, Sophia, Maria and Caroline Whiting, Sophia and Harriet Stearns, Lucy Osgood, Martha and Mary Ann Thayer; Nov. 2, Huldah Homes, Submit Rugg; Dec. 7. Catharine A. Knight, Susanna, Emily and Achsa Pollard.
In 1817. Males 1, Females 15....16+245=261.

1818.

Males.—Nov. 8, Jona. Buttrick.
Females.—Sep. 6, Sally Wilder; Nov. 8, Jane Buttrick, Sally Howe.
In 1818. Male 1, Females 3....4+261=265.

1819.

Males.—Dec. 5, Nath¹. Wilder.
Females.—Aug. 22, Abigail Prescott.

In 1819. Male 1, Female 1....2+265=267.

1820.

Males.—Mar. 19. Tarbel Bancroft, Certificate from West Church in Boston; Apr. 2, Horatio Carter; 23, Asa Packard, Certificate from W. Marlborough; Oct. 21, Ebenezer Wilder.
Females.—Mar. 19, Lucinda Bancroft, Certificate from West Church in Boston; Apr. 17th, Abigail Bridge; 23, Ann M. Packard; Ruthy F. Packard, Certificate from W. Marlboro'; 30, Mary N. Bridge; Aug. 6, Dolly McClallen; Oct. 1, Cynthia Pierce; 21, Lucena Wilder.

In 1820. Males 4, Females 8.... 12+267=279.

1821.

Females.—Aug. 5, Elizabeth P. Peabody; Dec. 2, Ruth Ballard, Certificate from Bolton; Susanna Morse. Female 3+279=282.

1822.

Males.—Apr. 7, James Carter; Oct. 6, Isaac Child.
Females.—June 9, Abigail Wilder; Oct. 6, Polly Child.

In 1822. Males 2, Females 2....4+282=286.

1823.

Females.—July 6, Elizabeth Tidd; Dec. 21, Martha Fletcher.

In 1823. Females 2+286=288.

1824.

Males.—June 6, Silas Thurston, Nath¹. Warner, William Tombs; Aug. 1, Jona. Locke; Sep. 5, Asa Arnold, Oct. 24, Asahel Tower Jr.
Females.—Jan. 5, Almira M. Wilder; June 6, Polly Warner, Betsy Tombs; Aug. 1, Mary Locke, Certificate from Medford; Pamelia Sanderson; Sep. 5, Mary Arnold, Marinda Homes; Oct. 24, Polly Tower; Dec. 5, Sophia White, Martha White, Lucy Carter White.

In 1824. Males 6, Females 11.... 17+288=305.

1825.

Males.—Sep. 4, Christʳ. T. Thayer; Dec. 4, John Fuller.
Females.—— —— Susan Goodwin, At home being sick; Apr. 3, Sarah Baldwin; Sep. 4, Lucy Laughton; Oct. 2, Betsy Townsend; Dec. 4, Sophronia O. W. Adams.

In 1825. Males 2, Females 5....7+305=312.

1826.

Males.—Apr. 2, Richard J. Cleveland.
Females.—Aug. 6, Mary Lane. Male 1, Female 1....2. 314.

1827.

Females.—Sep. 2, Catharine Rugg. In 1827, 1. 315.

1828.

Males.—Apr. 6, Joel Rugg, Peter Osgood, David Osgood.
Females.—Apr. 6, Lydia Lane, Certificate from Roxbury; Sarah Bennett, Bathsheba Rugg: Sep. 7, Catharine Stearns, Sarah W. Stearns; Oct. 6, Lucy Gates, Diana S. Locke. In 1828. Males 3, Females 7.... 10+315=325.

1829.

Males.—June 7, Moses Smith; Dec. 6, Samuel Carter.
Females—June 7, Sarah Smith; Aug. 2, Lucy Thurston, Privately, being sick; Dec. 6, Dilly Carter, Abigail Thayer.

In 1829. Males 2, Females 4....6+325=331.

1830.

Males.—June 6, Samuel F. White; Aug. 1, Ephraim Fuller, Silas Sawyer, Ezra Sawyer.
Females.—Mar. 4, Annis Andrews, Certificate from Boylston; June 6, Elizabeth G. White, Sarah A. White; Aug. 1, Susanna Fuller, Sarah Sawyer, Martha Ballard, Sarah Ann Lane; 15, Eliza Sawyer, Certificate from Sterling.

In 1730. Males 4, Females 8.... 12+331=343.

1831.

Females.—Jan. 23, Prudence Haskell; Nov. 6, Susan Richardson, Privately, being sick. In 1831, 2+343=345.

1832.

Males.—Sep. 2, Sewall Carter.
Females.—Jan. 9, Emily Laughton, Privately, being sick; **108** Apr. 1, Mary T. Carter, Mary Ann Fletcher, Nancy Stearns, Joanna W. Carter, Judith Goss, Martha Ann Hunt; June 3, Elcy Ballard, Almira Townsend, Eleanor L. Fletcher; Oct. 7, Sarah Goodwin; Dec. 2, Betsy Osgood, Mary C. Toppan.
In 1832. Males 1, Females 13....14+345=359.

1833.

Males.—July 7, Artemas Barnes, Certificate from Berlin.
Females.—Oct. 6, Nancy Tidd, Anna W. Goodhue, Irene Lock.
In 1833. Male 1, Females 3....4+359=363.

1834.

Males.—Aug. 3, Elias Sawyer; Sep. 7, Robert Andrews; Dec. 6, William Fletcher Jr.
Females.—June 1, Margaret Sweetzer, Catharine Sweetzer, Nancy E. Rand, Harriet Thurston; 15, Emily Dean; Aug. 3, Nancy Sawyer, Susan Wilder; Sep. 7, Caroline A. Wilder. In 1834. Males 3, Females 8....11+363=374.

1835.

Males.—Aug. 2, Samuel Willard, Certificate from 12th Church in Boston.
Females.—June 7, Lucy C. Newman, Caroline M. Newman; **109** Oct. 4, Betsy Rugg; 18, Alice Barnes.
In 1835. Male 1, Females 4....5+374=379.

1837.

Females.—Apr. 16, Martha B. Carter; June 4, Mary M. Andrews.
In 1837. Females 2+379=381.

1838.

Females.—June 3, Abigail B. Lewis; Harriet W. Washburn, By Certificate from Needham. In 1838. Females 2+381=383.

1839.

Males.—Aug. 4, Luke Bigelow.
Females.—Aug. 4, Eliza Bigelow. In 1839, 2+383=385.

1840.

Males.—June 7, William Stearns.
Females.—June 7, Betsy Rugg, Lucy Wellington.
In 1840. Male 1, Females 2..3
385
388 Whole No. during the ministry of Rev. Dr. Thayer.

* * * * * *

---

119 BAPTISMS.

1793. Oct. 13. Gershom Flagg, Son of Benj^a. Gould.
  Nov. 17. Almira, Daur. of Elijah Rugg.
    24. Elisha, Son of Titus Wilder.
  Dec. 21. Betsy, Daur. of David Pierce. In 1793.—4
1794. Feb. 9. James, Son of Thomas Carter.
    16. Henry, Son of John Ballard.
  Mar. 23. Dorothy, Daur. of Thomas Bennett Jr.
  Apr. 6. Maria, Daur. of John Whiting; Jonathan, Nathaniel, Catharine, Cynthia, Alpheus, John, Children of Nathaniel Sawyer.
    20. Dolly, Daur. of Jeremiah Ballard; Christopher, Son of Rufus Fletcher.

	May	4.	Nabby, Josiah, Children of Daniel Allen; Dolly, Deborah, Eunice, Children of Sam¹. J. Wyman.
	June	15.	Levi, Son of Elizabeth White; Lucy, Daur. of Joel Osgood.
120	July	13.	Olive, Daur. of Samuel Jones.
	Aug.	3.	Cephas, Son of Benja. Houghton, Jr.; David, Son of Jona. White.
		10.	Emily, Daur. of Benja. Wyman.
		17.	Nancy, Daur. of Thomas Tucker.
		24.	Nancy, Daur. of Thomas Burditt.
		31.	Peter, Patty, John, Sally, Susanna, Children of Mercy Manning.
	Sep.	14.	Fidelia, Daur. of Samuel Rugg.
		28.	Nathaniel, Son of Samuel Wilder Jr.
	Oct.	19.	Lucy, Daur. of Jona. Wheelock.
	Nov.	2.	James, Henry, John, Children of Gates Thurston; Mary, William, Children of Samuel Stevens; Mary Ann, Daur. of William Stedman; Cynthia, Daur. of Samuel Allen.
		16.	Eliakim, Zilpah, Luther, Children of Luther Sawyer.
	Dec.	7.	Betsy, Daur. of Phinehas Fletcher; Polly, Emily, Children of Abner Pollard. In 1794—46. In all 50.
121			
1795.	Jan.	11.	David Wilson, Olive, Rufus, Children of Rufus Dresser; Henry, Son of William Bridge.
		27.	Jonas, Anthony, Children of Jonas Lane.
	Feb.	1.	Fanny, Daur. of Widow Mary Willard; Roxana, Daur. of Jacob Phelps.
		8.	Ephraim, Sylvester, Phineas, Children of Mercy Manning.
	Mar.	29.	Achsah, Daur. of Moses Sawyer.
	April	5.	Abel Bartlet, Son of Thomas Chase; John, Son of Thomas Bennett Jr.
	May	15.	Hervey, Son of John Campbell.
	June	23.	Sarah, Rebecca, Mary Hurd, Children of Benja. Gould, born June 21ˢᵗ, baptized privately.
	July	5.	Sally, Daur. of Moses Sawyer Jr.
	Aug.	2.	Augustus, Son of John Ballard.
	Sep.	6.	Thomas, Son of Thomas Safford.
		13.	Dana, Son of David Pierce.
		20.	Nancy, Daur. of John Campbell.
122	Oct.	4.	Mary, Daur. of Ezra Willard.
		18.	Mary, Joseph, Children of Joseph Rugg.
	Nov.	8.	Elizabeth, Daur. of Simon Butler; Charles, Son of Moses Sawyer Jr.
	Dec.	6.	Eli, Son of Thomas Carter; Achsah, Daur. of Abner Pollard.
1796.	Jan.	17.	George, Son of Thomas Burditt. In 1795.30—80.
		24.	Cynthia, Daur. of Samuel Wilder Jr.
	Feb.	7.	Anthony, Son of Elisha Rugg; Samuel, Son of James Divoll; Nancy, Daur. of Gates Thurston.
		21.	Peter, Son of Joel Osgood; Horatio, Son of Oliver Carter.
	Mar.	31.	Lucy, Daur. of Elijah Rugg.
	Apr.	17.	Otis, Son of Benjamin Egerton.
	May	15.	Somes, Son of Abijah White; Jonas Beaman, Son of John White 3ᵈ.
		22.	James, Son of Asahel Tower.
	June	5.	William Stedman, Son of Gowen B. Newman; Sophia, Daur. of James Campbell.
	July	17.	Mary, Phinehas, David, Asa Longley, Lucy, Susanna, Children of Jemima Stone.
123	Aug.	7.	Julia, Daur. of Edwin Goodwin.
		14.	Helena Vander Cruysse, Daur. of Burrill Carnes; Nancy, Jacob, Children of Jacob Fisher.
		21.	Abigail, Daur. of John Carter; Sarah Toppan, Daur. of Nath¹. Thayer.
	Sep.	11.	Sewall, Son of James Carter Jr.
		18.	Sophia, Daur. of John White 3ᵈ.

FIRST CHURCH, BOOK II.

	Sep.	25.	James, Betsy, John, Henry, Sally, Children of James Capen.
	Oct.	2.	Alpheus, Son of Abijah Rugg; Harriet, Daur. of Paul Faulkner.
		9.	Mary, Daur. of Jacob Fisher.
		23.	John Reymore, Son of Samuel Jones; Patty, Daur. of John Campbell; Mary Newell, Daur. of William Bridge.
	Nov.	6.	Benjamin, Son of Benjamin Wyman; Sarah Harriman, Daur. of Joseph Rugg.
		13.	Abel, Son of Samuel Allen.
	Dec.	11.	Thomas Jefferson, Son of Timothy Whiting Jr.; Lucy Channing, Daur. of Gowen B. Newman. In 1796, 44—124
1797.	Jan.	15.	John Warren, Son of John Wilder.
		29.	Dolly Ballard, Daur. of Jonas Lane.
	Apr.	12.	Rufus, Son of Rufus Fletcher.
124		16.	Dolly, Daur. of Thomas Bennett Jr.
		23.	George, Son of Oliver Carter; Catharine, Daur. of Thomas Safford.
	May	21.	Solon, Son of John Whiting.
	June	4.	Abel Warner, Son of Abel Rugg.
		25.	Aaron, Son of Thomas Burbank; James, Son of Thomas Sawyer.
	July	2.	Lydia, Daur. of Jacob Phelps.
		9.	Leonard, Son of Phineas Fletcher.
	Oct.	1.	Elizabeth, Daur. of Rufus Dresser; Amy, Daur. of Samuel Stevens; William, Son of Daniel Goss.
	Dec.	17.	Mary, Daur. of William Arnold. In 1797, 16—140
1798.	Jan	21.	Anna, Daur. of John Campbell.
	Feb.	11.	Charles, Son of Benjamin Houghton Jr.; Parker, Son of Elisha Phelps.
	Mar.	11.	William, Son of Gates Thurston.
	Apr.	1.	David, Son of Joel Osgood.
		8.	Lydia, Daur. of Abner Pollard.
		22.	Lucinda, Daur. of Thomas Carter; Joseph Wales, Son of John Wilder.
		29.	Martha, Daur. of Nath¹. Thayer.
	May	20.	Samuel, Son of Samuel Wilder Jr.
	June	10.	Emily, Daur. of Samuel Rugg; Edward, Son of Joseph Rugg.
		17.	Sally, Daur. of Daniel Allen; Abigail, Daur. of William Bridge.
125	July	1.	Dolly Lovering, Daur. of Ruth Phelps.
		8.	Ephraim Carter, Son of Jacob Fisher.
		15.	William, Sally, Dolly, Rebecca, George Washington, Children of Josiah Flagg.
		22.	Joseph, Son of Timothy Whiting Jr.; Patty Maynard, Daur. of Ephraim Carter; Edmund Minord, Son of James Capen.
	Sep.	2.	Peter Bridge, John Adams, Children of John Prentiss.
		16.	Loring, Son of James Goodwin Jr.
	Oct.	14.	Lucinda, Daur. of Asahel Tower; David, Patty Wilder, Children of Thomas McLeod.
	Nov.	4.	Eunice Bennett, Wife of Nathan Bennett; James Homer, Son of Gowen B. Newman.
		11.	Patty, Daur. of John White Jr.
		18.	Nancy, Daur. of Nathan Bennett.
		25.	Henry, Sarah, Children of Joseph Leech.
	Dec.	2.	Mary Nichols, Daur. of John Ballard.
		16.	Joseph Collis, Son of Thomas Safford.
		30.	Timothy Harrington, Son of Oliver Carter, In 1798, 39—179.
1799.	Jan.	13.	Polly, Daur. of Benjⁿ. Wheelock.
	Feb.	10.	Catharine Whitford, Daur. of Nathl. Arnold.
126		16.	Elizabeth, Daur. of Thomas Sawyer.
	Mar.	3.	Nathan, Anna, Joseph Taylor, Samuel, Children of Widow Anna Miller.
		5.	Thomas, Grandson of Elizabeth Phelps.

	Apr.	14.	Catharine, Daur. of Abel Rugg.
		28.	Mary, Daur. of Elisha Phelps.
	May	19.	Lucy, Daur. of Daniel Goss Jr.
	June	23.	Zophar, Son of Samuel Jones.
	July	28.	Mary, Daur. of Jacob Sweetser; William, Son of William Stedman.
	Aug.	25.	Samuel, Son of Samuel Allen.
	Sep.	1.	Diana Eveleth, Wife of Ephraim Eveleth; Ephraim, Nancy Darling, Children of Ephraim Eveleth.
		22.	Sarah, Daur. of Thomas Bennett Jr.
	Oct.	6.	Joshua, James Fosdick, Thomas, Henry, Charles, George, Mary Ann, Children of Timothy Fletcher.
	Oct.	13.	Mary, Daur. of Joseph Leech.
	Nov.	17.	Martha, Daur. of Ezra Willard.
	Dec.	1.	Damaris Johnson, an adult.
		8.	Horace, Son of Paul Faulkner.
		16.	James, Son of Simon Butler.
127	Dec.	22.	Samuel, Abel, Lucinda, Christopher, Seth, Levi, Children of Widow Eunice French.　　　　　　　In 1799, 37—216.
1800.	Jan.	12.	Mary, Daur. of Rufus Fletcher.
	Feb.	2.	Henry, Son of Jonas Lane.
		16.	Sarah Taft, Daur. of Otis Hunt.
	Mar.	16.	Leonard, Son of Abner Pollard.
		23.	Polly, William, Children of Thomas Ballard: John Adams, Son of Edward Goodwin.
	Apr.	6.	Esther, Daur. of Nathl. Eaton.
		20.	Mary Ann, Daur. of Nath¹. Thayer; Sally, Daur. of John Wilder.
	May	4.	Eliza, Daur. of Samuel Wilder Jr.
		11.	Eli, Son of Thomas Carter.
		18.	Nathaniel, Son of Joseph Rice.
		25.	Cynthia, Daur. of Luther Sawyer.
	June	8.	Caroline, Daur. of John Whiting.
	July	6.	Polly, Dau. of Amos Sawyer; Eliza, Daur. of William Bridge.
		13.	Henry, Hezekiah Patterson, Eliza, Children of Sylvester Phelps.
		20.	Sally, Daur. of Jacob Fisher.
128	July	20.	Otis, Son of Joel Bruce.
		27.	Amos, Son of Amos Sawyer Jr.
	Aug.	3.	Jonathan, Son of Benja. Wheelock; Francis Augustus, Son of Thos. Safford.
		17.	Abigail, Daur. of Thomas Ballard.
		24.	Charles, Son of Oliver Carter.
		31.	Jonas, Tenbrook [Ostenbrook] (a negroe).
	Sep.	7.	Samuel, Son of William Arnold; Lydia, Rhoda, Children of Daniel Johnson; Nancy, Daur. of Joseph Rugg.
	Oct.	5.	Levi, Son of Timothy Fletcher.
	Nov.	9.	Susanna, Daur. of Ephraim Carter.
		16.	Nancy Cory, an adult; Rebecca, Sally, Charles, Children of Triphena Cory; James Baxter, Son of Elisha Phelps; Thomas Gates, Son of Gates Thurston.
	Dec;	7.	Henry, Son of Daniel Johnson.
		14.	Harriet, Daur. of Timothy Whiting.　　　　　In 1800, 42—258.
1801.	Jan.	11.	George Washington, Son of Benja. Houghton Jr.
	Feb.	22.	Francis Dana, Son of William Stedman.
	Mar.	9.	Joseph Arnold, Son of Elisha Rugg.
	Apr.	12.	James Goulding, Son of James Goodwin Jr.
129	May	7.	Catharine, Daur. of Noel Littaye.
		17.	William, Son of John Prentiss; Sarah Wilder, Daur. of Sam. Rugg.
	June	7.	Sally, Deborah, Oliver, Rebecca, Children of Deborah Tenney; Daniel Clap, Son of Asahel Tower.
		21.	Nancy, Oliver, Twins of Elias Emerson.

	Feby. 12.	Delilah, Daughter of Daniel Allen.
	19.	Harriet, Daur. of Paul Faulkner.
	Aug. 2.	Harriet, Daur. of Nathan Bennett.
	23.	Sumner, Son of Manasseh Wilder.
	Sep. 6.	Samuel, Son of Sylvester Phelps; Jesse, Son of George Phelps.
	12.	Elizabeth, Daur. of Benja. Lee.
	27.	Elizabeth Fletcher, an adult.
	Oct. 4.	Polly, Betsy, Charles, Amos Brooks, Cynthia, Children of Moses Jones.
	Oct. 11.	Nathaniel, Son of Benja. Wyman.
	Nov. 1.	James, Son of Daniel Goss Jr.
	15.	Sarah, Daur. of Benja. Whitwell.
130	Dec. 6.	Rebecca, Elizabeth, Joseph, Samuel Farrar, Sally Abbot, William Hunt, Children of Joseph White. In 1801, 36—294.
1802.	Jan. 31.	Mary Ann, Daur. of Nath¹. Williams.
	Mar. 14.	John, Son of John Goodwin.
	21.	Nathaniel, Son of Nathaniel Thayer; Merrick, Son of Samuel Wilder Jr.
	Apr. 4.	Emily, Daur. of Oliver Carter; Sally, Daur. of Abner Pollard.
	25.	Abigail, Daur. of John Wilder.
	May 9.	Oran, Son of Deborah Tenney.
	16.	Abel, Son of Samuel Allen.
	30.	Caroline, Daur. of Thomas Safford.
	June 6.	Grenville, Son of Joseph Rugg.
	13.	Solomon, Son of William Bridge.
	July 11.	John Erwin, Son of Simon Butler.
	Aug. 22.	Mary Ann, Daur. of Jonas Lane.
	Sep. 5.	John, Son of Thomas Bennett Jr.
	12.	Edward Selfridge, Son of Gowen B. Newman.
	19.	Abel, Son of Gates Thurston.
	Oct. 31.	Sarah, Daur. of Oliver Baldwin.
	Nov. 21.	Charles, Son of Timothy Whiting.
131		Otis, Son of Otis Hunt.
	28.	Sally Flagg, Polly Goodwin, Children of Joseph Newman.
		In 1802, 22—316.
1803.	Jan. 9.	Luther, Son of Abigail White.
	Mar. 20.	Joseph, Son of Joseph Rice.
	Apr. 3.	Thomas, Son of Thomas Ballard.
	24.	Sally, Daur. of Daniel Johnson; Sophia Sawyer, an adult.
	May 1.	Samuel Ward, Son of Josiah Flagg.
	22.	Martha, Daur. of Timothy Fletcher.
	29.	Jane Warner, an adult.
	June 5.	Susanna, Daur. of John Sargeant.
	19.	Henry, Son of Asahel Tower.
	July 3.	Rebecca Cowdey, an adult; Eusebius, Son of Amos Sawyer Jr.
	Aug. 7.	Rebecca, Daur. of John Goodwin.
	14.	Sarah Parker, Daur. of Moses Jones.
	Aug. 21.	Leander, Son of James Goodwin Jr.
	31.	John, Son of Nathaniel Thayer.
	Sep. 25.	Henry, Son of Daniel Goss Jr.; Mary Ann, Daur. of Samuel Rugg.
	26.	John, Son of John Goss.
	Oct. 22.	John, Son of Benja. Houghton; Lavina, Daur. of George Phelps.
	[Nov.] 9.	Caroline, Catharine, Twins of Sylvester Phelps.
132	Dec. 4.	Catharine, Daur. of Joseph White. In 1803, 24—340.
1804.	Jan. 1.	Louisa, Daur. of Paul Faulkner.
	8.	Benjamin Gowen, Son of John Wilder.
	Mar. 11.	Nancy Bridge, Daur. of Oliver Carter.
	25.	Emery, Son of Abner Pollard.
	Apr. 29.	Mary Joslyn, Daur. of Sam¹. Wilder.
	May 13.	Edward, Son of Edward Goodwin.

	June	3.	Harriet, Daur. of John Townsend; Merrial, Daur. of Benja. Egerton; Joseph, Son of Joseph Leech; Eliza, Daur. of Joseph Rugg; Charles, Son of Charles E. Knight.
		24.	Charles, Son of Elias Emerson.
	Aug.	5.	Joseph, Son of William Bridge.
		19.	Alexander, Son of Jacob Fisher.
	Oct.	7.	Daniel, Son of Gowen B. Newman; Holman, Son of Luke Wilder.
		21.	John, Son of John Goss.
	Nov.	11.	Caroline, Daur. of Edward Fuller.
		25.	Thomas, Son of Thomas Ballard.
	Dec.	9.	Catherine, Daur. of Thomas Safford.
		16.	Josiah, Son of John Prentiss. In 1804, 21—361.
1805.	Feb.	3.	James, Son of Timothy Whiting.
	Mar.	27.	Susanna, Daur. of James Carter Jr.
	Apr.	28.	Abigail, Daur. of Ephraim Carter.
133			Joel Putnam, Son of John Townsend.
	May	5.	Mary Chase, Daur. of Joseph White; Levi, Son of Abijah White.
		12.	Lucy Kendall, Daur. of Sam¹. Allen.
		19.	Elizabeth, Daur. of Daniel Goss Jr.
	June	16.	Christopher Toppan, Son of Nathaniel Thayer; Eliza, Peter, Children of Jonas Joslyn.
	July	21.	Elizabeth, Daur. of Jonas Lane; Charles Harrison, Son of William Stedman.
		21.	Eliza Ann, Daur. of Amos Sawyer Jr.
	Aug.	4.	Mary Ann, Daur. of Joseph Rice; Lucinda, Daur. of Thomas Bennett Jr.; Sarah, Daur. of George Phelps.
	Sep.	15.	Lydia, Daur. of Benja. Houghton.
	Oct.	6.	John, Son of John Sargeant; Christopher, Son of Asahel Tower.
	Nov.	3.	Joseph Shepard, Son of Edward Fuller.
		10.	James Longley, John Amory, Twins of Calvin Peabody.
		17.	William, Son of Abijah Phelps.
	Dec.	22.	Lewis, Son of Rufus Fletcher. In 1805, 25—386.
1806.	Jan.	5.	Enos, Son of John Wilder.
		12.	Lucretia Murray, Daur. of Joseph Leech.
	Feb.	2.	Joseph, Son of Sylvester Phelps.
		16.	Lucy, Daur. of Joseph Rugg; Palmer, Son of James Goodwin Jr.
134	Feb.	23.	Catharine, Daur. of Oliver Carter.
	Mar.	2.	Lucy Wilder, an adult; Lucy, Joel, Children of Joel & Lucy Wilder.
		9.	Sophia, Daur. of Paul Faulkner; Augustus, Son of Elias Emerson.
	Apr.	20.	Almy Ellery, Daur. of Luther Sawyer; Alfred, Son of John Goodwin.
	May	4.	James Mallard, an adult.
	June	1.	Betsy Carter, an adult; Henry, Rebecca, Children of John & Betsy Carter; Mary Ann, Daur. of Abner Pollard.
		8.	Thomas Curtis, Son of Martin Stevenson.
		22.	John, Son of William Bridge.
	Aug.	17.	James, Son of Jacob Fisher.
	Oct.	12.	Sampson Wilder, Son of Gates Thurston.
		26.	James, Son of Widow Rebecca White.
	Nov.	2.	Maria, Daur. of Otis Hunt.
		23.	Henry, Son of Oiiver Baldwin. In 1806, 25—411.
1807.	Mar.	1.	Rebecca Circum, Daur. of Joseph Leech; George, Son of John Townsend; Mary, Daur. of John Carter.
		8.	Martha, Daur. of Thomas Ballard; Henry, Son of Thomas Safford; Mary, Daur. of Calvin Peabody.
135	Apr.	5.	Sally, Daur. of Charles E. Knight.
		19.	Mary Ann, Daur. of Nathan Bennett; Reuben, Son of Samuel Barrett.

	May 22.	Charles, Son of Benjamin Farnsworth.
	June 7.	Sally, Benjamin, Abijah Haskell, Mary, Children of Benjamin Farnsworth; William, Son of William Fletcher; Eliza Brigham, Daur. of James Mallard; Caleb Strong, Son of Edward Goodwin.
	14.	Martha Bridge, Daur. of John Prentiss.
	21.	Sally, Lucy, Children of Ezekiel Rice; Samuel Chittenden, Son of Gowen B. Newman.
	July 5.	Charles, Son of Widow Nancy Bennett.
	12.	Henry, Son of Thomas Bennett Jr.; Samuel Stillman, Son of Samuel Rugg; Sullivan, Son of Moses Jones.
	19.	Mary Whitcomb, Daur. of John Goss.
	Aug. 30.	Mary Ann, Daur. of Edward Fuller.
	Sep. 20.	Albert, Mary Ann, Children of Abraham Mallard; Josephus, Son of John Wilder.
	Oct. 11.	Abigail Rand, Daur. of Luke Wilder.
	25.	Nancy Jackson, Daur. of Thaddeus Chenery; Louisa, Daur. of George Phelps.
136	Nov. 29.	Charles, Son of Benjamin Wyman. In 1807, 34—445.
1808.	Jan. 24.	Sally Parker, Daur. of Abijah Phelps.
	Feb. 21.	Calvin, Son of Elisha Sanderson; Catharine, Daur. of Abijah White.
	Feb. 28.	Mary Ann Stedman, Daur. of Danl. Goss Jr.
	Apr. 17.	Caroline, Sarah Ann, George Peter, Children of Peter Thurston Jr.
	May 8.	Mary Howe, Daur. of Joseph Leech.
	18.	Mary Pearce, Daur. of Sylvester Phelps.
	June 5.	William, Son of Joseph Rugg.
	19.	Anthony, Son of Saml. Wilder Jr.
	July 3.	Hannah Willard, Daur. of Calvin Peabody.
	24.	Martha Eirene, Daur. of Josiah Bridge.
	31.	Samuel, Son of Samuel Allen.
	Aug. 7.	Clarissa, Daur. of Elias Emerson.
	Sep. 4.	Abel, Son of Joseph Rice; Richard, Son of Oliver Carter.
	11.	David, Son of Jacob Fisher; John, Son of John Townsend; Nathaniel, Son of Nathaniel Thayer.
	Oct. 2.	Charles Angier, Son of Joseph Maynard.
	Nov. 20.	Henry Russell, Son of Richard [J.] Cleveland.
	Dec. 11.	Abel Williams, Son of Abner Pollard; Ephraim, Son of John
137		Carter 3^d. In 1808, 24—469.
1809.	Jan. 22.	James, Son of James Mallard.
	Feb. 19.	Ephraim, Son of Benjamin Wyman; Susan Palmer, Daur. of Thomas Safford.
	Apr. 2.	Abigail Merriam, Daur. of Benjamin Farnsworth.
	23.	Otis, Son of William Fletcher.
	30.	Sarah, Daur. of John Goodwin.
	May 21.	Josiah, Son of Joseph Leech.
	June 4.	Otis Hunt, an adult; George Campbell, Son of Saml. Barrett; John Martin, Son of Martin Stevenson.
	July 9.	Elcy, Daur. of Edward Fuller.
	23.	Lucy, Daur. of John Wilder.
	30.	Olive, Daur. of George Phelps.
	Aug. 20.	Jonas, Son of Jonas Goss; Martha Wyman, Daur. of Josiah Rugg.
	Sep. 3.	Sophia, Daur. of Samuel Rugg; Rebecca White, Daur. of John Goss.
	Oct. 1.	Lucy Ann, Daur. of Thaddeus Chenery; Samuel, Son of Edward Goodwin; Dolly, Eliza Dexter, Charles, Susan Carter, Children of William McClellan.
	22.	Ann Foster, Samuel John Sprague, Edward Henry, Children of Peter T. Vose.
	Nov. 5.	Mary Barron, Daur. of Thomas Bennett Jr.

138
Dec. 19. Josiah Richardson, Son of Thomas Ballard.
Dec. 3. Ann Rust Parker, an adult.
31. Lucy Ann, Daur. of Elias Bennett.   In 1809, 30—499.
1810. Jan. 14. Daniel, Son of Jonas Goss; Elizabeth Beaman, Daur. of Otis Hunt.
28. Harriet, Daur. of Abraham Mallard.
Mar. 11. William Sewall, Son of William Cleveland; Malinda, Daur. of Samuel Wilder Jr.
15. Betsy Allen, an adult. Privately, being sick.
18. Arelah Morse, Son of Josiah Bridge.
19. Nancy Whitney, Daur. of Horatio G. Buttrick.
Apr. 29. Christopher, Augustus, Twins of Joseph Rugg; Joseph, Son of Joseph Maynard.
May 6. Merrial, Daur. of Ephraim Phelps.
20. Betsy, Daur. of Josiah Rugg; Joel Wright, Son of Sylvester Phelps.
June 3. Lucy Rugg, Daur. of Martin Stevenson; Sophia Allen, an adult; Joseph Walker, Sylvia, Asa Johnson, Lucy, Mary Carter, Children of Eber Goddard.
139 June 10. John, Son of John Goss Junr.
17. William Chauncey Wilder, Grandson of Manasseh Knight.
24. Sarah Edwards, Daur. of John Goss.
July 1. Emery, Son of Susanna Hastings; Nathaniel Augustus Kidder, Son of Nathaniel Kidder of Prospect, Maine; William, Daniel Powers, Sons of Sophia Durant; Ann Hague, Daur. of Samuel Plant; Caroline Amelia, Daur. of Joel Wilder.
Aug. 3. Solomon, Son of Sophia Durant.
5. Mary Whitney, Wife of Jonas Whitney; Benjamin Hawks, an adult; Mary, Daur. of Jonas Whitney; Caroline, Daur. of Horatio G. Buttrick; Lewis Ansart, Son of Jonathan Hildreth; Elizabeth Ann, Daur. of Eliphaz Ballard; Thomas Ballard, Son of Benjamin Hawks; Martha Short, Daur. of John Hills.
19. Almy Ellery, Daur. of Gowen B. Newman.
Sep. 2. Rebecca Kendall, an Adult; Abigail Kendall, an Adult.
9. John, Son of Abijah Phelps.
30. Sally Lane, Wife of Jonas Lane, Privately by reason of sickness;
140 Lucy Cotting, Loring, William, [Puffer], Grandchildren of Samuel Joslyn.
Oct. 7. Harriet Carter Puffer, Adopted Child of Solomon Carter; Clifford Callahan, Daur. of Calvin Peabody.
Nov. 11. Mary, Eliza, Sophia, Harriet, William, Catharine, Sally Whitney, Nancy, Augustus, Children of Eli Stearns.
    In 1810, 59—558.
1811. Jan. 6. John, Son of Moses Sawyer.
13. Adeline, Daur. of Thomas Safford.
27. Susanna, Daur. of Jacob Fisher.
Feb. 3. Ebenezer, Joseph, Sons of Elizabeth Carter of Fitzwilliam.
24. James, Son of James Mallard.
Mar. 10. Elvira, Daur. of John Townsend.
24. Judith, Daur. of Jonas Goss.
141 Apr. 21. Nancy, Daur. of John Carter.
June 2. Sophia Wilder, an Adult; William, Son of Elijah Wilder.
9. Joseph White, Son of John Goss.
23. Clarissa, Daur. of Abner Pollard.
30. Martha Thayer, Daur. of Benjamin Wyman.
July 14. Abijah, Son of Abijah White; Mary Ann, Daur. of John Goodwin.
21. Lucy Hosley, Daur. of Oliver Baldwin.
Aug. 4. Sarah Ann, Daur. of Jonas Lane.
25. Nancy, Daur. of Thomas Bennett Jr.

	Sep.	1.	Polly Phelps, an Adult; Nancy Todd, an Adult; Abigail, Daur. of Robert Phelps; Sewall, Son of Robert Phelps.
		8.	Augustus, Son of Samuel Wilder Jr.
	Oct.	6.	Martha, Elmira Ann, Children of Elisha Sanderson.
		13.	Augustus, Son of Benjamin Farnsworth.
	Nov.	10.	Louisa, Daur. of Joseph Rice; James Dexter, Son of Elias Bennett.
		17.	Jeffry, Son of Nathl. Kidder of Prospect, Maine.
	Dec.	22.	James Arthur, Son of William Cleveland; Mary Wilder, Daur.
142			of Charles E. Knight. In 1811, 32—500.
1812.	Jan.	26.	James, Son of Eliphaz Ballard; Abel Carter, Son of Elijah Wilder.
	Feb.	3.	William, Martha, Lincoln, Children of Elizabeth Carter.
	Mar.	15.	Lydia Angier, Daur. of Joseph Maynard; Sally, Daur. of Samuel Allen.
		30.	Rhoda, Betsy, Children of Daniel Johnson.
	Apr.	20.	Sarah, Daur. of Calvin Carter.
	May	10.	Lewis, Son of John Wilder; Evelina Homes, Daur. of Joseph Leech; Louisa Elizabeth, Daur. of Samuel Plant.
		17.	Sewall, Son of Josiah Rugg.
	June	7.	Nancy, Daur. of Josiah Bridge; Martha Ann, Daur. of Otis Hunt.
	Aug.	2.	Nathaniel, William, Sons of Jonas Joslyn.
	Sep.	20.	Edward, Son of Abijah Phelps.
		27.	Warren, Son of Samuel Rugg.
	Nov.	1.	Joseph Cogswell, Son of Samuel Manning; Levi Townsend, Otis Brigham, James Sullivan, Amory, Nancy, Mary Brigham, Hannah Merriam, Children of Levi Prescott.
143	Nov.	15.	Abigail, Daur. of Nathaniel Thayer; Helen Ann Byron, Adopted Child of Rebecca Atherton.
	Dec.	6.	Luther Jones, Son of George Phelps.
		20.	Elizabeth Wimble, Daur. of Jona. Hildreth. In 1812, 31—621.
1813.	Apr.	4.	Mary Hawkes Kendall Ballard, Daur. of Jonas Lane; Mary Ann Peirce, Daur. of Sylvester Phelps.
		20.	Henry Peabody, Son of David Howe.
		25.	Samuel, Son of John Goss 2^4.
	May	16.	Ebenezer, Son of Jonas Goss.
		30.	Nancy Whitney, Daur. of Horatio G. Buttrick.
	June	21.	Pliny Abbot, Son of Pliny Newhall.
		27.	John Richardson, Son of Benjamin Wyman; Julia, Daur. of Joseph Rugg; Zimri, Son of John Townsend.
	Aug.	15.	Alexander, Son of Levi Prescott.
	Sep.	19.	Eber, Son of Eber Goddard.
		26.	Mary, Daur. of Robert Phelps.
	Oct.	17.	William Wilder, Son of Ebenezer Bragg.
		24.	Lydia, Daur. of Thomas Bennett Jr.
		31.	Eliza Ann Wales, Daur. of John Wilder.
	Nov.	21.	Bathsheba, Daur. of John Goodwin.
144	Dec.	19.	Daniel Burt, Son of Daniel Newhall. In 1813, 18—639.
1814.	Jan.	23.	William Stearns, Son of Jonathan Locke Jr.; Sewall, Son of Elijah Wilder.
	Feb.	20.	Levi, Son of John Goss.
		27.	Abigail Ann, Daur. of Joseph Maynard.
	Mar.	6.	Joseph Hiller, Son of William Cleveland.
		20.	Sarah, Daur. of Josiah Bridge; Frederick, Son of David Howe.
		27.	Charles Josiah, Son of Joel Wilder.
	Apr.	3.	Nancy Spear, an Adult; Adeline, Daur. of Abraham Mallard.
		17.	George Poignand, Son of Samuel Plant.
		24.	Elias Dexter, Son of Elias Bennett; Ann Sophia, Daur. of James Mallard.
	May	1.	Elizabeth, Daur. of Joseph Leech.
		29.	Otis Norcross, Son of Morgan Morgan.

	June	5.	Josiah, Son of Eliphaz Ballard.
	July	10.	Caroline, Martha, Children of Benja. H. Foster; Rebecca Pratt, Daur. of Samuel Manning.
		24.	Henry Abbot, Son of Pliny Newhall.
	Aug.	7.	Charles, Son of John Goss, 2^d.
	Oct.	16.	Edward Walker, Son of Abner Pollard.
	Nov.	13.	Mary Carter, Daur. of Samuel Wilder.
	Dec.	4.	George, Son of Jacob Fisher.
145	Dec.	25.	Nancy Darling, Daur. of John Sargeant 2^d. In 1814, 25—664.
1815.	Jan.	1.	Joseph Wilder, Manasseh, Harrison, Moses Chace, Lucy Ann, Emery White, Children of Abijah Rogers.
	Mar.	5.	Lucy Elizabeth, Daur. of Solomon Carter.
	Apr.	9.	Dorcas Warren, Daur. of William Fletcher.
	May	14.	Lucretia, Daur. of George Phelps; Ebenezer Gott, Son of Ebenezer Bragg.
	June	4.	Harriet, Daur. of Joseph Rugg.
	July	19.	Francis, Son of Pliny Newhall.
	Sep.	29.	Charles, Son of Otis Hunt.
	Oct.	1.	James, Son of Benjamin Farnsworth.
		22.	Eliza Ansart, Mary Augusta, Sarah Ann Goodwin, James, Children of Benjamin Chandler.
	Nov.	29.	Rebecca, Daur. of John Wilder.
	Dec.	3.	David, Son of David Howe; Sarah Ann, Daur. of Samuel Plant. In 1815, 21—685.
146			
1816.	Jan.	11.	William, Son of Ruth Townsend.
	Feb.	25.	Solomon, Son of Solomon Carter.
	Mar.	17.	Phebe Rebecca, Daur. of Jonathan Locke.
	Apr.	7.	Haskett Derby Pickman, Son of Charles Bigelow.
		11.	Elizabeth, Dolly, Children of Ephraim Phelps.
	May	10.	Joseph Warren, Son of Joshua Fletcher.
	June	2.	Eliphaz, Son of Eliphaz Ballard; Samuel Andrews, Son of Jonas Goss; Cornelia, Daur. of Robert Phelps; Horace William Shaler, Son of Richard J. Cleveland.
	July	7.	Josiah, Son of Josiah Bridge.
	Aug.	11.	Charles, Son of Elias Bennett; Harriet Maria, Daur. of John Goodwin; Harrison, Son of Levi Prescott.
		18.	Mary, Daur. of —— Wright.
	Sep.	26.	Charles, Henry, Mary Elizabeth, Children of Charles Bridge.
		29.	Abigail, Daur. of James Mallard.
	Oct.	7.	Lucy, Mary, Children of Jonas Joslyn.
		20.	Eliphalet Hill, Son of Calvin Peabody.
	Dec.	1.	Martha, Daur. of Joseph Maynard; Lucy Gates, Daur. of John Goss,
		29.	Benjamin Wyman, Son of Amos Adams. In 1816, 25—710.
1817.	Jan.	5.	Lewis, Son of Benjamin Eager.
	Mar.	23.	Margaret Minot, Daur. of William G. Weld.
	Apr.	13.	Hannah, Daur. of Abraham Mallard.
	May	4.	Eunice Wilder, Daur. of John Goss 2nd.
		25.	Benjamin Hazen, Son of Joseph Rugg; Lydia Whitney, Daur. of Josiah Billings.
	June	1.	Charles Pratt, Son of Samuel Manning.
	July	6.	Charles, Son of Pliny Newhall.
		13.	George, Son of George Phelps; Mary Tucker, Walter Spooner, Catharine Sarah, Martha Eliza, Francis Henry, Children of Peter T. Vose.
	Aug.	3.	Rebecca Haskell, an Adult.
	Sep.	7.	Ephraim Rand, Son of Luke Wilder.
		21.	Susan Augusta, Daur. of Abner Pollard.
	Nov.	9.	Luther Dana, Son of Joseph Leech; Frederick William, Son of Samuel Plant; Emily Wyman, Submit Brooks, Sophia, Children of James Rugg.

FIRST CHURCH, BOOK II. 347

	Nov.	23.	Betsy Thurston, Daur. of John Carter; Susanna Pollard, an Adult; Catharine A. Knight, an Adult.
148	Dec.	7.	Caleb Elijah, Son of Abner Pollard; James Manasseh, Son of Charles E. Knight.
		21.	Edward Warren, Marinda, Children of Huldah Homes.
		28.	Martha, Daur. of Solomon Carter. In 1817, 30—740.
1818.	Jan.	11.	Eliza Ann Sophia, Daur. of Elijah Wilder.
	Feb.	8.	Louisa Jane, Daur. of Abel Stow.
		15.	Charles Carter, Son of Ebenezer Bragg.
	May	24.	Edward Cutter, Son of Jonathan Locke; Mary Ann, Daur. of Ephraim Phelps.
	June	5.	Rebecca, Daur. of Eliphaz Ballard.
	Aug.	2.	Henry, Son of Benjamin Wyman; Sophia, Daur. of Jonas Joslyn.
		23.	Sally Rebecca, Mary White, Charlotte, Children of Nath¹. Kidder.
	Sep.	6.	Sarah, Daur. of Josiah Bridge.
		13.	Francis, Son of John Goss 2ᵈ.
		27.	John Gardner Doubleday, Son of William G. Weld.
	Oct.	4.	Martha Fessenden, Daur. of Josiah Billings; Ephraim Holman, Son of Luke Wilder.
	Nov.	1.	William Augustus, Son of Levi Prescott.
149		8.	Jonathan Buttrick, an Adult.
		15.	Jane, Jonathan, John Whitman, Hannah Elizabeth, Children of Jonathan Buttrick; Thomas Gates, Son of Caleb Harrington; Thomas, William, Francis, Andrew, Children of Thomas Howe. In 1818, 27—767.
1819.	Mar.	21.	Elizabeth, Daur. of James Rugg.
	Apr.	25.	Amos Gilman, Son of Amos Adams.
	June	6.	Lavina, Daur. of Benja. H. Foster.
	Aug.	22.	Barzillai Miles, Son of Thomas Howe.
		29.	Nancy, Daur. of Jonas Goss.
	Sep.	5.	Samuel, Son of Samuel Plant.
	Oct.	17.	William Henry, Son of Solomon Carter.
	Nov.	28.	Ezekiel, Son of Richard Hildreth. In 1819, 8—775.
1820.	Jan.	30.	Clarissa Elizabeth, Daur. of Abner Pollard.
150	Feb.	13.	Aaron Sawyer, Son of Elias Bennett.
	Apr.	30.	Hannah Minot, Daur. of William G. Weld.
	June	4.	Julia Ann Daby, Daur. of John Carter 2ᵈ.
		25.	Sarah, Daur. of John Goss 2ᵈ.
	July	2.	James, Son of James Rugg.
	Aug.	20.	Martha Ann Relief, Daur. of Ebenezer Bragg.
	Sep.	3.	Sarah Shattuck, Daur. of Jonathan Locke.
	Oct.	1.	Samuel Hervey, Son of Hervey Pierce; Rebecca Holmes, Grandchild of Samuel Wilder.
	Dec.	3.	Josiah, Son of Josiah Billings. In 1820, 11—786.
1821.	Apr.	29.	William Frederick, Son of Josiah Bridge; Alfred, Son of Samuel Plant.
	June	17.	William Henry, Son of Solomon Carter.
	July	15.	Levi Whiting, Son of Peter Phelps.
	Aug.	5.	Elizabeth, Daur. of Charles E. Knight.
	Oct.	7.	Ebenezer, Joseph, Sidney, Charles, Rufus, Lucena, Children of Ebenezer Wilder.
	Nov.	11.	Andrew, Son of Tarbell Bancroft.
	Dec.	29.	Christopher Augustine, Son of Abner Pollard.
151			In 1821, 13—799.
1822.	Apr.	7.	Sewall, Zophar, Elizabeth Ann, Nathaniel Miller, Edwin, Children of Anna Sargeant.
		21.	Thomas Porter, Son of Jonathan Butterick.
	May	1.	Joseph Sweetser, Grandson of Jacob Sweetser.
		19.	Nathaniel Lakin, Son of Charles E. Knight.
	June	9.	Josiah Newhall, Son of James Rugg.
	Oct.	6.	Mary Wheeler, Daur. of John Goss 2ᵈ.

	Oct.	27.	Rufus, Sarah Richardson, Mary, Children of Isaac Childs.
	Dec.	8.	Julia Ann, Daur. of Sarah Phelps. In 1822, 14—813.
1823.	Feb.	16.	Benja. Hutchinson, Son of Abijah Rogers.
	Apr.	27.	William Haskell, Son of Samuel Plant.
	July	13.	George Putnam, Son of Solomon Carter.
	Aug.	3.	Samuel Gilman, Son of Amos Adams; Eliza Ann, Frances Augusta, Twins of Jonathan Locke.
		24.	Abigail Allen, Daur. of Josiah Bridge.
152	Sep.	7.	James, Son of Isaac Childs. In 1823, 8—821.
1824.	Jan.	5.	Almira Miranda, Wife of Elijah Wilder.
		11.	Alfred, Son of Daniel Newhall.
	Apr.	4.	Harriet Stearns, Daur. of James Rugg.
	June	6.	William Tombs, an Adult; Polly, Daur. of Nathaniel Warner; Angeline, Martha Ann, William, Children of William Tombs.
	Aug.	1.	Charles Baldwin, Son of Benja. H. Foster.
	Sep.	5.	Mary Arnold, an Adult; Rebecca, James Adams, William, Susan, Charles Henry, Mary Ann, Children of Asa Arnold.
		26.	Nancy, Daur. of Abraham Mallard.
	Oct.	10.	George Williams, William Lowell, Children of Sodi Sanderson.
		24.	Mary Eliza, William Henry, Julia Ann, Children of Asahel Tower Jr.
153	Dec.	5.	Lucy Carter White, an Adult. In 1824, 23—844.
1825.	Feb.	28.	William, Son of John Goodwin Jr.
	Apr.	17.	Abigail Rebecca, Daur. of Solomon Carter.
	May	1.	Levi Edwin, Son of Samuel Brigham.
		22.	John Lucas, Son of Lucas Dunn; Martha, Daur. of James Rugg.
	June	12.	Charles Henry, Son of Hervey Pierce.
	July	3.	Caroline Maria, Daur. of Asa Arnold.
	Sep.	4.	George Franklin, Son of Asa Tower Jr.
		18.	Henry, Son of Samuel Plant.
	Oct.	23.	William Jackson, Son of Charles E. Knight.
		30.	Elizabeth, Daur. of Ebenezer Wilder; Nathaniel, Son of Amos Adams.
	Nov.	20.	Horatio Carter, Son of Ebenezer Bragg. In 1825, 13—857.
1826.	Apr.	23.	Nathan Dana, Son of Sodi Sanderson.
	July	2.	Elizabeth Cranston, Daur. of William Tombs.
		23.	Joseph Fife, Son of Josiah Billings.
	Aug.	28.	Samuel Lane, Son of William Bridge.
	Sep.	3.	George Franklin, Son of Joseph Maynard.
		17.	Marcellus Fabius, Son of N. Marcellus Hentz.
	Oct.	1.	Eleanor Louisa, George Henry, James Fosdick, Julia Abigail, Charles Thornton, Children of Joshua Fletcher; Martha Eddy, Charles Harrison, Mary Morse Andrews, Ann Eliza, Children of Joseph Wilder.
154			
		29.	Lucretia, Daur. of James Rugg; Elizabeth Arnold, Daur. of William Nowell; Sarah Warner, Eliza Ann, Ephraim, Asa Warner, Children of Ephraim Rugg.
	Nov.	5.	Eliza, Daur. of Martha Foster. In 1826, 22—879.
1827.	Mar.	25.	Abigail Carter, Daur. of Peter Osgood.
	June	3.	James, Son of Ephraim Phelps.
		10.	Charles Lowell, Son of Tarbell Bancroft; Ezra Thomas, Son of Ezra Sawyer.
	Aug.	19.	Elizabeth Derby Pickman, Daur. of Samuel Plant.
	Sep.	30.	Jane Augusta, Daur. of Isaac Childs.
	Oct.	7.	Sarah Maria, Daur. of Asahel Tower Jr. In 1827, 7—886.
1828.	Jan.	6.	James Coolidge, Son of Solomon Carter.
	Mar.	11.	Daniel, Son of James Rugg.
155	Apr.	6.	Mary, Elizabeth, Joel Isaac, William Brown, Children of Joel Rugg.
	June	1.	Edwin Lovejoy, Son of Sodi Sanderson.
	Aug.	3.	Mary Eliza, Daur. of Peter Osgood.
	Sep.	7.	Sophia Maynard, Daur. of Charles E. Knight.

	Oct.	5.	Lucy Gates, an Adult.
		12.	Eliza, Daur. of Jacob Fisher.
	Dec.	7.	Lydia Brooks, Adopted Child of John Wilder,

In 1728, 12—898.

1829.	Apr.	5.	Daniel Woodward, Son of Asa Arnold; Edward Walker, Son of William Tombs.
	May	17.	Elizabeth Howland, Daur. of Samuel Jewett.
	June	7.	Sophronia Mehitable, Daur. of John Fuller.
		14.	Charles Robbins, Son of Jeremiah Whittemore.
	July	26.	Abigail Arabella Greene, Mary Prescott Putnam, Henry, Francis, Children of Moses Smith.
	Aug.	2.	Lucy Thurston, an Adult.
	Sep.	6.	Daniel, Son of James Rugg.
156	Dec.	6.	George, Son of Isaac Childs; Francis Oliver, Son of Ezra Sawyer; Oliver, Eliza, Samuel, William, Ann Louisa, Charles Mirick, Andrew, George Augustus, Children of Samuel Carter.
		13.	Levi Lincoln, Son of Abner Pollard. In 1829, 22—920.
1830.	June	6.	Samuel Farrar, Albert Cloyes, Henry Ware, Children of Samuel F. White.
	July	4.	Asa Houghton, Son of Luke Stow.
		18.	Mary Delicia, Daur. of Saml. Plant.
	Aug.	1.	Ephraim Fuller, an Adult; Caroline Maria, Granddaughter of Gowen B. Newman; Anthony Lane, Francis Augustus, Children of Silas Sawyer; Martha Salome, Adopted Child of Silas Sawyer; Susan Hayward, Andrew Lowell, Francis Faulkner, Children of Ephraim Fuller; Sophia Catharine, Daur. of Charles E. Knight; Rufus Ellis, Son of Asahel Tower Jr.
157	Dec.	5.	Adelia Merriam, Daur. of Samuel Carter In 1830, 16—936.
1831.	Jan.	23.	Prudence Haskell, an Adult.
	June	5.	John Thurston, Son of John Fuller.
	Oct.	23.	Nathaniel Chandler, Son of Ezra Sawyer.
	Nov.	6.	Susan Richardson, a Youth. In 1831, 4—940.
1832.	Jan.	9.	Emily Laughton, an Adult.
	June	3.	William Augustus, George Henry, Abigail Sophia, Children of William Ballard; Henry Warren, Charles, Mary Ann, Children of Warren Townsend.
	July	8.	Delicia Amiraux, Daur. of Samuel Plant; Martha Wyman, Daur. of Peter Osgood.
	Aug.	5.	Elizabeth Conant, Daur. of Samuel F. White; Ellen Maria, Mary Susanna, Children of Sewall Carter.
	Sep.	2.	Hannah Sophia, Daur. of Asahel Tower Jr.
158	Oct.	7.	Abigail, Daur. of Luke Stow.
	Nov.	14.	Francis, Son of Joel Rugg. In 1832, 15—955.
1833.	May	3.	Ephraim Hayward, Son of Ephraim Fuller.
	June	2.	Samuel Ebenezer, Son of John Fuller.
	July	7.	Fabius Marcellus, Julia Eliza, Children of Solon Whiting.
	Aug.	4.	Solon Francis, Son of Samuel Carter; Sarah Ellen, Daur. of Artemas Barnes; Abigail Holman, Daur. of Warren Townsend. In 1833, 7—962.
1834.	June	1.	Harriet Thurston, An Adult; Abigail Jane, Daur. of Charles E. Knight; Charles Henry, Ellen Maria, Children of Nathaniel Rand; Harriet Elizabeth, George Lee, Francis Henry, Children of John G. Thurston.
150	June	15.	Samuel Brown, Emily Sarah, Martha Putnam, John Prentiss, Children of John Dean.
	Aug.	10.	Margaret Hanners, Daur. of Samuel W. A. Oliver. In 1834, 12—974.
1835.	Jan.	17.	Mary Ann Augusta, Daur. of Calvin Carter.
		18.	Charles Ballard, Mary Ann, Emeline Amanda, Abigail Barrett, Louisa Augusta, Children of Elias Sawyer.

350   LANCASTER RECORDS.

	June	7.	Mary Elizabeth, Daur. of Tarbell Bancroft; George Walton, Son of Ephraim Fuller.
160	July	5.	Luke Stearns, Son of Luke Stow. In 1835, 9—983.
1836.	July	17.	Sidney Thomas, Son of John Fuller.
	Aug.	7.	Nathaniel Thayer, Son of Samuel White; Sarah Elizabeth, Daur. of Ezra Sawyer. In 1836, 3—983.
1837.	June	3.	Mary Frances, Daur. of George W. Howard.
	July	2.	William Alden, Son of Ephraim Fuller. In 1837, 2—988.
1838.	Sep.	21.	Henrietta Mercy, Daur. of John Fuller.
	Oct.	21.	Francis, Son of John M. Washburn; Martha Sophia, Daur. of Peter Osgood.
161	Nov.	4.	Charles Frederick, Son of Charles Chandler. In 1838, 4—992.
1839.	Feb.	3.	Levi, Abby, Jackson, Crosby, Francis, Martha Jane, Susan Augusta, Lucy Elizabeth and William Augustus (Twins), James Ballard, Children of Levi Lewis.
	Mar.	13.	Mary Elizabeth, Daur. of Mary Tyler.
	Apr.	7.	Eliza Ann, Daur. of Ezra Sawyer.
	Aug.	4.	Lucius Aurelius, Cynthia Wilder Eliza Jane, Theodore Francis, Mary Elizabeth Tyler, Children of Luke Bigelow.
162			In 1839, 17—1009.
1840.	June	7.	William Stearns, an Adult; Adeline Colburn, Daur. of Samuel F. White; Nancy Goss, Daur. of Ephraim Fuller; Emery, Son of Widow Sarah Harris; Francina, Charles, George, Children of Thomas H. Wellington; Mary Frances, Daur. of William Stearns.

In 1840, 8.   Whole number baptized by Doct. Thayer, 1017.

---

178 MEMBERS OF THE CHURCH RECOMMENDED TO OTHER CHURCHES.

1794.	Feb.	9.	Abel and Mary Allen, to the church in Sullivan, N. H.
		23.	Nathaniel and Elizabeth Willard, a general recommendation; Rebecca Harrington, to the church in Heath.
1795.	June	21.	Reuben Bryant, a general recommendation to the churches.
	Oct.	4.	Susanna Osgood, to the church in Sullivan, N. H.
1796.	Feb.	28.	William and Mary Tooker, to the church in Westmoreland, N. H.
1797.	Jan.	29.	Zilpah Kidder, to the church in Winchendon.
	Aug.	27.	Elijah and Lois Rugg, to the church in Sullivan, N. H.
	Sep.	17.	Sarah Adams, to the church in Townsend.
1798.	Aug.	19.	Elisha and Deborah White, to the church in Ashburnham.
179	Sep.	16.	Charity Carter, to the church in Keene, N. H.
1799.	June	9.	William Bigelow, to the first church in Salem.
	Sep.	1.	William Arnold Jr., a Certificate of his regular standing in the church.
1800.	Nov.	2.	Thomas and Alice McLeod, to the church in Sullivan, N. H.; Rebecca Manning, to the church in Pepperell.
	Dec.	7.	Joseph Haynes and Wife, to the church in Rindge, N. H.
1801.	Oct.	18.	Rebecca Fairbank, to the church in Parsonsfield, District of Maine.
1802.	Mar.	7.	Hannah Wyman, to the brethren in Augusta, State of N. York.
1804.	Nov.	25.	Dolly Wyman, to the church in Pittsfield.
1806.	July	6.	Nathaniel and Thankful Beaman, to the brethren in Newport, Canada; Sarah Sawyer, to the church in Wendell.
1807.	Feb.	7.	Mary Carter, to the church in Keene, N. H.
108	1810.	May 25.	Elizabeth Fowle, to the church in Pittsfield.
		July 1.	Rebecca White, to the church in Pittsfield, Ver.
			Mary Phelps, to the church in Sempronius, N. York.
1811.	June	9.	Benjamin and Polly Hawks, to the church in Templeton.
	Sep.	1.	Sarah Carter, to the church in Plymouth, N. H.

1812.	May	3.	Ann Rust Crosby, to the church in Charlestown, N. H.
1813.	Feb.	7.	Lucy Wilder, to the church in Keene, N. H.
1816.	July	21.	Rebecca Thomas, to the church in Sterling.
	Oct.	6.	Amos and Rebecca Allen, to the church in Luzerne, N, York.
1817.	Sep.	14.	Lydia Richardson, to the church in Rutland, Vermont.
1818.	Oct.	11.	Anna and Elizabeth Carter, to the church in Fitzwilliam, N. H. Lucy Shurtleff, to the church in Keene, N. H.; Susanna Barker, to the church in New Marlborough, N. H.
1819.	June	21.	William Greenleaf, to the church in Munson, or elsewhere.
	Aug.	1.	Eliza Faulkner, to the church in Keene, N. H.
1821.	Apr.	5.	Calvin and Abigail Peabody, to the church in Midlesex, N. York.
1822.	May	19.	Benjamin and Grizzle Apthorp Gould, to the first Presbyterian church in Newbury Port.
1827.	June	10.	Achsah Pollard, to the church in Westbrook, Maine.
1828.	Sep.	14.	Sarah Howe, to the Old South Church in Boston.
1831.	July	10.	Lucy Brigham, to the church in Sudbury.
1833.	Sep.	22.	Joseph & Mary Rugg, to the church in Westminster under the pastoral charge of Rev. Mr. Hudson.
	Oct.	3.	Betsy Jones, to the church in Ashburnham.
1839.	Nov.	17.	Artemas & Alice Barnes, to the Unitarian church in Leicester.
1840.	Feb.	23.	Diana S. Locke, to the second church in Lancaster.
	Oct.	4th.	Lucretia Wyman, to the second church in Lancaster.

DEATHS.

1793.	Oct.	12.	Mr Ephraim Carter, 78. Angina Pectoris.
		16.	Mr John Manning, 40. Slow fever.
		18.	Widow Beaman, 84. Angina Pectoris.
		21.	Peggy Davis (a Negroe), 23. Consumption.
		23.	Mrs Prudence Manning, 58. Typhus fever.
		26.	Sally, Daur. of Mercy Manning, 1. Typhus fever.
	Nov.	21.	Mr James Wilder Jr., 20. In a fit.
		23.	Mrs Mary Stratton, 80. Old age. In 1793, 8.
1794.	Jan.	22.	A child of Daniel Keyes, 24 Hours.
	Feb.	27.	Mrs Elizabeth Atherton, 84. Old age.
	Mar.	9.	A Son of Jacob Phelps, 8 mo. Consumption.
	Apr.	10.	Mr James Wilder, 53. Consumption.
		12.	Mrs Sally Phelps, 36. Hemorrhage.
	May	10.	Mrs Martha Sawyer, 30. Consumption.
	July	12.	Mrs Hannah Houghton, 25. Erysipelas.
		14.	Mr Elisha Whitcomb, 80. Dropsy.
		22.	A Daughter of Timothy Fletcher, 2. Worms.
	Aug.	20.	A Son of Thomas Ballard, 1. Dysentery.
		22.	A Child of Jonathan Barrett, 4 days. Fits.
	Oct.	28.	Miss Polly Wheelock, 17. Consumption.
	Nov.	9.	A Daughter of Ignatius Fuller, 2. Dysentery.
			In 1794, 13—21.
1795.	Jan.	20.	Mr David Jones, 78. Mortification.
	Feb.	26.	Mrs Dolly Lane, 27. Consumption.
	Mar.	27.	Miss Abigail Smith, 20. Lung fever.
	Apr.	18.	Mrs Mary Carter, 66. Nervous fever.
	Apr.	29.	A child of Sarah Deputeron, 15 mo.
	May	16.	Mrs Thankful Fairbank, 84. Old age.
		28.	A child of Coffin Chapin, 8 weeks.
	June	9.	An Infant of Rufus Fletcher, a few hours.
		22.	A Son of Asahel Tower, 8 mo. Fits.
	July	4.	Rebecca, 13 days. ⎫
		6.	Mary Hurd, 15 days. ⎬ Children of Benjamin Gould.
		8.	Sarah, 17 days. ⎭

	July	25.	A Daughter of Dr. James Carter, 2. Dysentery.
	Aug.	7.	A Daughter of John Wilder Jr., 4 Hrs. Fits.
		9.	A Son of Ephraim Eveleth, 2. Worms.
		12.	Mr Jonathan Stone, 45. Inflammation of the Brain.
		22.	Mr Peter Green, 81. Apoplexy.
	Oct.	5.	William, Son of Robert Hudson, 15. Bilious cholic.
			A child of Stephen Pratt.
	Dec.	18.	Rev. Timothy Harrington, 79. Old age.
			Mrs Mary Carter, 83. Old age. In 1795, 21—42.
1796.	May	17.	Twins of William Locke, one aged 2 the other 24 Hours.
	June	7.	Mrs Elizabeth Windship, 71. Lung fever.
		9.	A Daughter of Thomas Bennett Jr., 3. Consumption.
		11.	A Son of Thomas Bennett, 14 mo. Lung fever.
			A Son of John Ballard, 10 mos. Fits.
	Aug.	27.	Mrs Elizabeth Temple, 78. Old age.
	Sep.	27.	Mr Eleazer Rider, 82. Mortification.
		29.	A child of Ezekiel Longley, 24 Hours.
	Oct.	5.	Mrs Anna Brewster (of Boston), 29. Putrid fever.
		12.	Mrs Mary Chapin. Nervous fever.
	Nov.	15.	Mrs Mary Locke. By a scald.
188		29.	A Daughter of John Campbell, 10 weeks. Fits.
	Dec.	3.	A Daughter of Paul Faulkner, 13 mo. Influenza.
		25.	A Daughter of Samuel Jones, 4. Worms.
		28.	Miss Polly Gould, 20. Consumption. In 1796, 16—58.
1797.	Feb.	21.	Captain John White, 83. Cancer.
	Mar.	20.	Mrs Anna Rider, 70. In a fit.
	Apr.	1.	Miss Patience Knight, 20. Bilious fever.
		8.	Mr Richard Patten, 65.
		16.	Miss Hannah Fletcher, 76. Cancer.
	June	2.	Mrs Lydia Whittemore, 54. Dropsy.
	July	19.	Miss Lucy Gates, 32. Mortification.
		23.	A child of Daniel Johnson, 9. Dysentery.
		25.	A Daughter of D. Johnson, 3. Dysentery.
		27.	A Daughter of D. Johnson, 1. Dysentery.
		"	Mr Joseph Champney, 22. Ulcerated throat.
	Aug.	8.	A Son of Daniel Johnson, 6. Dysentery.
		28.	Jonas, Son of Jonas Lane, 6. Worms.
	Sep.	9.	Mr John Priest, 88. Mortification.
		11.	Mr Manasseh Divol, 82. Old age.
		24.	Mr Joseph Osgood, 77. Dropsy.
	Oct.	28.	Mrs Britton, 63. Consumption.
	Nov.	6.	A child of Ephraim Eveleth, 6 mo. Worms.
		7.	Mrs Silence Nichols, 72. Very suddenly.
189		10.	Mr Phinehas Houghton, 71. Dropsy. In 1797, 20—78.
1798.	Mar.	1.	Mr John Britton, 80. Mortification.
		8.	A Daughter of Jonas Lane, 14 mo. Worms.
		25.	Mrs Elizabeth Priest, 84. Cramp.
	Apr.	7.	Mr Ephraim Divoll, 84. Old age.
	May	17.	Mr Joseph Priest, 83. Old age.
		19.	Capt. Ephraim Carter, 55. Asthma.
	June	23.	A Daughter of Daneil Allen, 7 weeks. Fits.
	July	4.	A Daughter of Thomas Safford, 15 mo. Bilious fever.
	Aug.	11.	Mr Washington Leech, 22. Drowned.
		24.	A Son of Thomas Carter, 2. Dysentery.
		31.	A Son of Robert Phelps, 3 weeks.
	Sep.	7.	A Son of Calvin Phelps, 1. Scald.
		29.	A Son of Joseph Leech, 19 mo. Dysentery.
	Oct.	1.	Mrs Abigail Whiting, 39. Consumption.
		29.	A Son of Amos Sawyer Jr., 6 weeks. Scrofulous humor.
	Nov.	25.	Mr Nathaniel Miller, 31. Consumption. In 1798, 16—94.
1799.	Jan.	11.	Mr John Rugg, 85. Old age.
	Feb.	12.	A Son of Jonathan Barnard, 3. Quincy.

	Feb.	14.	Mrs Elizabeth Sawyer, 33. Suddenly.
	Mar.	3.	Samuel, Son of Anna Miller, 9 mo. Consumption.
		19.	A Son of Timothy Whiting Jr., 8 mo. Tumor on brain.
		31.	Mrs Sarah Ballard, 73. Old age.
	Apr.	7.	Miss Polly Whiting, 15. Bilious fever.
		19.	Miss Betsy Willard, 15. By discharge of a Gun.
	June	18.	Mrs Nancy Thomas (of Boston), 47. Consumption.
	July	12.	A Son of Isaac Fisher, 2 weeks. Mortification.
			Capt. Timothy Whiting, 68. General Decay.
190	Aug.	6.	Deacon Josiah Ballard, 78. Old age.
		18.	A Daughter of Thomas Ballard, 3. Dysentery.
		26.	A Daughter of Thomas Ballard, 10 mo. Dysentery.
			Mrs Hannah Sargeant, 77. Dysentery.
		31.	A Daughter of Luke Phelps, 1. Dysentery.
	Sep.	1.	A Daughter of Thomas Ballard, 4. Dysentery.
	Dec.	9.	Mr Jotham Woods, 60. By a burn. In 1799, 18—112.
1800.	Apr.	4.	A Son of Samuel Allen, 3. Worms.
	July	18.	Capt. James Carter, 79. Gravel.
		31.	Mrs Eunice Wilder, 54. Consumption.
	Sep.	15.	A Daughter of Jonathan Tenny, 4. From eating cherries.
		28.	Hon. John Sprague, 60. Bilious fever.
	Nov.	29.	Mr Samuel Ward Jr., 31. Dropsy.
	Dec.	30.	James, Son of John Goss, 4. By a Scald.
		31.	Mrs Susanna Leech, 63. Consumption. In 1800, 8—120.
1801.	Feb.	5.	Mr Aaron Sargeant, 36. Killed by a fall.
		28.	Deacon Cyrus Fairbank, 64. Bilious fever.
	Mar.	19.	Mr Josiah Sawyer, 82. Lung fever.
	Apr.	9.	A Daughter of Nathaniel Arnold, 6 Days. Fits.
	May	1.	Miss Nancy Cotting, 22. Consumption.
		9.	Mrs Rebecca Thurston, 39. Consumption.
		11.	A child of Noel Littaye, 6.
	June	18.	A Son of Coffin Chapin, 5.
191		19.	A Son of Coffin Chapin, 8.
	July	1.	A Daughter of Oliver Tenney, 3. Dysentery.
	Aug.	3.	A Son of Thomas Safford, 1. Bilious fever.
		15.	Mr Elisha Bennett, 47. Dropsy.
		16.	A Son of John Dollison, 6. Dysentery.
			A Son of John Goss, 1. Worms.
	Sep.	4.	A Daughter of Simon Keyes, 6 mo.
	Dec.	15.	Mr Nathaniel Wyman, 55. Lung fever.
		27.	A Daughter of Gardner Phelps, 8. Lung fever.
		31.	Mrs Rebecca Allen, 50. Disease of the Liver.
			In 1801, 18—138.
1802.	Jan.	2.	A Daughter of Thomas Durant, 4 Days. Fits.
		10.	A Daughter of Daniel Allen, 8 mo. Consumption.
		21.	A Daughter of Nathan Bennett, 5. Fits.
			Mr Elisha Phelps, 39. Lung fever.
		23.	Mr Abigail Houghton, 79. Bilious fever.
		29.	Miss Patty Knight, 22. Consumption.
	Feb.	2.	Mrs Lydia White, 74. Consumption.
		20.	A Daughter of Joseph Leech, 2. Lung fever.
		22.	Captain Willlam Phelps, 71. Consumption.
	Mar.	2.	Mrs Deborah Sawyer, 74. Old age.
		23.	A Daughter of John Goodwin, 30 Hrs.
	Apr.	27.	A Daughter of Aaron Pollard, 1. Quincy.
		29.	A Son of Nathaniel Thayer, 6 weeks. Fits.
	May	5.	Mrs Martha Wheelock, 94. Old age.
		13.	A Son of Asa Warner, a few months.
	June	20.	Mr Peter Joslyn, 26. Consumption.
	July	5.	Mr John Hosley, 59. Killed by the fall of a Frame.
192	July	27.	Captain Robert Barker, 68. Apoplexy.
		28.	A Son of Sam¹. Dunlap, 6 mo. Mortification.

	July 31.	Deacon Benja. Houghton, 63. Dropsy in the head.
	Aug. 22.	A Son of Jonas Joslyn, 10 mo. Swelling in throat.
	24.	Mrs Rebecca Tenny, 82. Old age.
	Sep. 3.	A Son of Rufus Fletcher, 2 weeks. Fits.
	Oct. 11.	A Son of Benja. Houghton, 11. Measles.
	12.	Mrs Sarah Adams, 80. Measles.
	15.	Mrs Achsah Phelps, 61.
	Nov. 3.	A Daughter of John Dollison, 4. Lung fever.
	4.	Mr Simon Butler, 46. Consumption.
	17.	Mr Thomas Tucker, 77. Old age.
	20.	Mr Jonathan Whitney, 66. Apoplexy.
	23.	Mrs Nabby Puffer, 28. Nervous fever.
	Dec. 12.	Mr Edward Fuller, 86. Old age.
	18.	Mrs Elizabeth Burbank, 83. By a burn.
	21.	Mr John Sargeant, 80. Old age. In 1802, 34—172.
1803.	Feb. 6.	Miss Ruth Phelps, 64. Consumption.
	Apr. 1.	Polly, Daughter of S. Dunlap, 10. Consumption.
	12.	Mrs Sophia White, 32. Consumption.
	17.	A Son of Gates Thurston, 7 mo. Fits.
	May 9.	Mr Joseph Emerson, 81. Numb Palsy.
	June 8.	Mrs Lois Sawyer, 72. Asthma.
	12.	A Son of Elijah Houghton Jr., 8. Scarlet fever.
	24.	Caesar Hammond (a Negroe), 55. Consumption.
193	July 15.	A Daughter of Abner Pollard, 12. Putrid fever.
	24.	Mr Samuel Sanderson, 55. Dropsy.
	Aug. 5.	A Daughter of Abner Pollard, 16 mo. Putrid fever.
	18.	A Daughter of Caleb Russell, 9. Throat distemper.
	20.	A Son of Amasa Willard, 6 weeks. Jaundice.
	31.	A Daughter of Thomas Safford, 1. Dysentery.
	Sep. 22.	Mrs Mary Sprague, 52. Consumption.
	23.	A child of Elisha Sanderson, 2. Dysentery.
	26.	Miss Lucy Carter, 19. Bilious fever.
	28.	A Daughter of Paul Faulkner, 2. Dysentery.
	Oct. 1.	A Son of John Goss, 19 mo. Worms.
	3.	A Son of Timothy Whiting Esq. Canker Rash.
	4.	Mr John Wilder, 56. Apoplexy.
	13.	A Daughter of Gardner Phelps, 14 mo. Dysentery.
	25.	A Son of Philemon Allen, 12. Throat Distemper.
	"	A Son of Gowen B. Newman, 14 mo. Canker Rash.
	Nov. 4.	An Infant of Oliver Balwin, 2 days. Fits.
	8.	Mrs Dinah Holt, 62. Consumption.
	25.	Miss Lydia Thurston. Consumption.
	26.	A Son of Thomas Ballard, 9 mo. Throat Distemper.
		In 1803, 28—200.
1804.	Mar. 26.	A Daughter of Benja. Houghton, 14. Canker Rash.
	May 26.	John Pedro Marshall (a foreigner). Consumption.
	June 3.	A Son of Jonas Joslyn, 6. Dropsy.
	10.	Mr Josiah Ballard, 25. Putrid fever.
	July 3.	A Son of Otis Hunt, 18 mo. Worms.
	25.	A Daughter of Sam¹. Wilder Jr., 4 mo. Consumption.
194	Aug. 6.	A Son of Benja. Lee, 10 Days. Disorder in the head.
	Oct. 2.	Mrs Sally Carter, 22. Consumption.
	9.	An Infant of Josiah Whitcomb, 6 weeks. Tumor in head.
	29.	A child of Stephen Sargeant, 16 mo. Dysentery.
	Nov. 1.	A Son of Ephraim Osgood, 4 weeks. Fits.
	16.	Mrs Abigail Carter, 56. Consumption.
	23.	A Son of John Hunt, 14 mo. Quinsy.
	24 [25].	Mrs Submit Wyman, 74. Consumption.
	Dec. 26.	A Daughter of Oliver Baldwin, A few hours.
	30.	Mrs Patience White. 80. Old age. In 1804, 16—216.
1805.	Jan. 7.	Capt. Elisha Rugg. Injury from a wagon.
	10.	Mrs Ruth Houghton, 78. Dropsy.

	Jan.	12. A Daughter of Joseph Newman, 2. Hooping Cough.
	Mar.	11. Mr Thomas Laughton, 25. Consumption.
		29. A Daughter of James Carter Jr., 3. Dropsy in the head.
	May	18. Mrs Sarah Rugg, 83. Numb Palsy.
		24. Mrs Sarah Whiting, 67. Bilious fever.
	Aug.	10. Miss Lucy Rugg, 22. Consumption.
		20. Mrs Abigail Carter, 84. Old age.
	Sep.	5. A Daughter of Jona. Barnard, 21 mo. Dysentery.
		10, Mr Samuel J. Sprague, 25. Injury by a fall from a carriage.
		11. Mrs Jane Rugg, 92. Old age.
		13. A Daughter of Jonas Lane, 10 weeks. Dysentery.
		15. A Son of Nath'. Low, 19 mo. Worms.
		Mrs Mary Butler, 52. Dysentery.
195	Sep.	23. A Daughter of Jonas Lane, 3. Dysentery.
		26. A Son of Benjamin Thompson, 3. Worms.
		29. Mrs Mary Jones, 85. General Decay.
	Oct.	2. Mr Joseph Sawyer, 25. Dysentery.
		3. Mr Moses Sawyer, 72. Dysentery.
		4. A Son of Jona. Barnard, 7. Dysentery.
		15. A Daughter of John Low, 3. Dysentery.
		22. A Daughter of William Fletcher, 3 weeks.
	Nov.	11. Capt. William Arnold, 61. In 1805, 27—243.
1806.	Jan.	29. A Son of Sir Francis Searle, 6 mo. Fits.
	Feb.	1. A Son of John Wilder Jr., 24 Hrs. Fits.
		7. Mrs Dinah Hudson, 56. Consumption.
		William Flagg, 16. Fever in East Indies.
	Mar.	26. Mr Samuel Thurston, 79. Consumption.
	Apr.	2. Mr Benjamin Egerton, 45. Inflammation on the brain.
		17. Mrs Susanna Divoll, 89. Cancer.
	May	4. Mrs Martha Wyman, 40. Consumption.
		12. An Infant of Aaron Wilder, 12 Days.
		16. A Son of Samuel Barrett, 9 mo. Quincy.
		22. Mrs Zeruiah Pratt, 60. Injury by a fall in a fit of Insanity.
		23. Mr Sparhawk Houghton, 33. Consumption.
		26. Mr Nathaniel Joslyn, 78. Old age.
	June	19. Mrs Sarah Farwell, 86. Old age.
	July	1. Deacon Joseph White, 55. Mortification.
		28. A Son of Jabez Low. 14 Hrs. Fits.
	Sep.	6. A Son of Thomas Ballard, 1. Dysentery.
		16. Mr Isaac Solindine, 75. Consumption.
196	Oct.	28. A Son of Edward Fuller, 1. Consumption.
	Nov.	23. Mr William Deputeron, 83. In a fit. In 1806, 20—263.
1807.	Jan.	20. A Son of Luke Wilder, 2. Worms.
		21. A Son of Samuel Allen, 7. Tumor in bowels.
	Feb.	14. A Daughter of Thomas Safford, 3.
		25. Mr John Solindine, 55. Pleurisy fever.
	Mar.	17. Mr Elisha Bennett, 31. Nervous fever.
	Apr.	1. Mr Charles Ballard, 21. Mortification.
		8. Mrs Zeruiah Rugg, 87. Old age.
		14. Miss Dandridge Hunt, 20. Consumption.
	May	1. A Daughter of Mrs Sarah Egerton, 3. Drowned.
		23. A Son of Benjamin Farnsworth, 7 weeks.
		29. An Infant of William Bridge, a few hours.
	June	10. Col°. Henry Haskell, 73. Gravel.
		23. An Infant of Dr. Calvin Carter, 24 Hours.
	July	17, An Infant of Colo. Jonas Lane, 3 Hours.
	Aug.	1. Miss Mary Ann Stedman, 13. Bilious fever.
		2. Mrs Eunice Lane, 41. Consumption.
		10. Mrs Sarah Cleverly, 61. Cancer.
		21. A Daughter of Jonas Goss, 4 mo.
	Sep.	7. Mr James Ballard, 19. By a fall from a house.
		Mr Samuel Warner, 89. Influenza.

	Sep.	22.	Mrs Mary Phelps, 78. Influenza.
	Oct.	13.	A Daughter of Samuel Cooke, 12. Influenza.
	Nov.	11.	Mrs Lydia Rugg, 91. Old age.
	Dec.	16.	Mrs Mary Willard, 78. Apoplexy.
		20.	A Son of Gowen B. Newman, 3. Bilious fever.

197   In 1807, 25—288.

1808.	Feb.	5.	Mrs Alice Houghton, 82. Pleurisy fever.
		11.	Mrs Mary Taft, 74. Consumption.
		21.	Mr Dunbar Whittemore, 23. Bilious fever.
	Mar.	1.	Mrs Anna Ballard, 50. Consumption.
		4.	Mrs Susanna Solindine, 57. [Suicide.]
		6.	A Son of James Newhall, 9 mo. Dropsy in head.
		14.	A Son of Peter Sawyer, 12 Days. Fits.
	Apr.	7.	A Daughter of John Caldwell, 2. Lung fever.
		17.	A Daughter of Abraham Mallard, 2. Worms.
		24.	Mrs Michal Thurston, 47. Bilious cholic.
	May	24.	A Daughter of Sylvester Phelps, 2 weeks. Fits.
		26.	Mrs Mary Thomas, 68. From the kick of a horse.
	July	14.	Mr Jonathan Osgood, 61. Dropsy.
		28.	An Infant of Oliver Houghton, 2 mo. Consumption.
		30.	Mrs Mary Fletcher, 42. Disease of the Liver.
	Sep.	23.	A Son of Martin Stevenson, 3. Dysentery.
	Oct.	13.	Mrs Sally Emerson, 30. Consumption.
	Nov.	17.	A Son of Jonas Joslyn, 30 Hrs. Fits. In 1808, 18—306.
1809.	Jan.	7.	A Daughter of John Brown, 22 mo. Worms.
	Feb.	27.	A Daughter of Otis Hunt, 2. Lung fever.
	Mar.	5.	An Infant of Samuel Butler, 4 mo. Lung fever.
		7.	A Son of Levi Blood, 16 mo. Lung fever.
		18.	Mrs Sarah Whittemore, 69. Dropsy.
		26.	Louisa, Daughter of George Phelps, 17 mo. Worms.

198

	Apr.	4.	Miss Comfort Low (of Groton, Ver.), 27. Consumption.
		5.	A Infant of John Brown, 12 Hrs. Fits.
	July	23.	A Son of Samuel Allen, 1. Worms.
	Aug.	4.	Christopher E. Stedman, 18. Drowned near Calcutta.
	Oct.	3.	A Son of Oliver Houghton, 3. Dysentery.
	Nov.	26.	Major Gardner Wilder, 70. Old age.
	Dec.	10.	Captain Daniel Goss, 68. Cancer. In 1809, 13—319.
1810.	Jan.	5.	An Infant of Pliny Newhall, 16 Hours.
		13.	A Son of James Mallard, 1. Consumption.
		18.	Mrs Patty Newhall, 22. Puerperal fever.
	Mar.	2.	Mr John Robbins, 72. Consumption.
		18.	Mrs Martha Osgood, 90. Old age.
			Miss Betsy Allen, 24. Consumption.
		19.	A Daughter of Horatio G. Buttrick, 3 weeks. Fits.
	Apr.	16.	Wlliam Stedman, 11. Spotted fever.
		19.	Miss Rebecca Corey, 24. Spotted fever.
		28.	Mrs Rebecca Leech, 39. Spotted fever.
	May	1.	Mr Elijah Rugg, 57. [Suicide.]
		14.	Mrs Eleanor Barrett. Verdict Insanity.
		29.	Mrs Betsy Wilder, 38. Consumption.
	June	2.	Mrs Rebecca Ballard, 52. Consumption.
		22.	Miss Betsy Jones, 16. Consumption.
	July	6.	Mr Aaron Rugg, 51. Consumption.
		7.	Captain Elisha Houghton, 83. Dropsy.
	Aug.	3.	A Son of William Fay, 5 mo. Lung fever.
			Mrs Abigail Bridge, 40. Consumption.
		17.	Mrs Ephraim Divoll. 66. Consumption.

199

		19.	Mrs Betsy Bowman, 20. Consumption.
	Sep.	3.	Colo. John Whiting, 51. Apoplexy. At City of Washington.
		5.	Mrs Abigail Gates, 70. Dysentery.
		23.	Mrs Abigail Faulkner, 23. Consumption.
	Oct.	4.	A Daughter of Samuel Rugg, 15 mo., bilious fever.

	Oct.	5.	A Daughter of G. B. Newman, 3 mo. Consumption.
	Nov.	6.	Miss Charlotte Sawyer, 49. Dropsy.
		20.	A Son of Samuel Wilder 2ᵈ. Disease in head.
	Dec.	18.	Mrs Submit Jones, 39. Consumption.
		22.	Mr Aaron Phelps, 57. Consumption. In 1810, 31—350.
1811.	Jan.	15.	A Daughter of H. G. Buttrick, 12 Hours.
		17.	Mrs Thankful Robbins, 62. Consumption.
		19.	Mrs Phebe Emerson, 81. Apoplexy.
		27.	Mrs Nancy Buttrick, 26. Consumption.
	Mar.	22.	Mr Timothy Stearns, 28. Lung fever.
	May	2.	A Son of Richard Haven, 12. Typhus fever.
		8.	A Son of Paul Nelson, 2. Canker.
		29.	Mrs Nancy Bennett, 32. Consumption.
	Aug.	18.	Capt. John Prescott, 62. Dropsy.
		20.	An Infant of Thomas Phelps, 6 Hours.
			A Daughter of Thomas W. Lyon, 8. Throat Distemper.
		22.	A Daughter of Thomas W. Lyon, 5. Throat Distemper.
	Sep.	8.	A Son of Thomas W. Lyon, 3. Throat Distemper.
		27.	A Son of Eli Stearns. Throat Distemper.
	Nov.	6.	Mrs Martha Wilder, 94. Old age.
		7.	Mrs Priscella Thurston, 83. Old age.
200	Dec.	13.	A Daughter of Benjamin Thompson, 7. Croup.
			In 1811, 17—367.
1812.	Jan.	2.	Mr Peter Divoll, 35. Bilious cholic.
		3.	A Son of Joseph Rugg, 1. Worms.
		26.	Mr Ebenezer Allen, 89. Old age.
			Mrs Abigail Smith, 70. Lung fever.
	Feb.	4.	Mr Moses Smith, 72. Mortification.
		25.	Mrs Polly Allen, 20. Consumption.
	Mar.	5.	Mrs Elizabeth Phelps, 85. Old age.
		15.	A Child of Jeremiah Evans, 2. Lung fever.
		21.	An Infant of Abraham Mallard, 4 Hours.
		28.	A Son of Daniel Johnson, 1. Lung fever.
	Apr.	3.	A Son of Moses Smith, 10 mo. Consumption.
		5.	A Daughter of Abner Pollard, 10 mo. Hooping Cough.
		17.	Mr Samuel Worcester, 69. Lung fever.
		21.	A Son of Abijah Rugg, 15. Lung fever.
		22.	Francis Davis (a Negroe), 86. Lethargy.
	May	2.	Mrs Lydia Knight, 89. Lung fever.
		3.	A Daughter of Vincent, a Mullatto, 9 weeks. Hooping Cough.
	June	8.	Capt. John White, 73. Consumption.
	July	8.	Mrs Fanny Willard, 29. Puerperal fever.
		31.	A Daughter of Thomas Randall, 16 mo. Throat Distemper.
	Aug.	28.	Mr Daniel Laughton, 62. Consumption.
	Sep.	21.	Miss Sally Thurston, —. Consumption.
	Nov.	29.	A Son of Thomas Ballard, 3. Abscess in head.
	Dec.	20.	A Daughter of Joel Pearce, 14 mo.
201		22.	Mr Peter Thurston, 73. Mortification. In 1812, 25—392.
1813.	Jan.	3.	Mr Joshua Fisher, 52. Putrid fever.
		6.	A Son of Elias Bennett, 14 mo. Canker.
		7.	Mrs Eunice Goss, 66. Lung fever.
		13.	Mrs Lydia Emerson, 32. Consumption.
		21.	Mrs Sally Wright, (Insane). In a fit.
	Mar.	12.	Mrs Sally Lane, 34. Puerperal fever.
		17.	A Son of G. B. Newman, 5. Fever.
		23.	John Sullivan Vincent (a Negroe), Lung fever.
	Apr.	1.	Mr Isaac Rugg, 67. Lung fever.
		5.	Mrs Lucy Carter, 35. Consumption.
		17.	Mrs Eunice Butler, 45. Consumption.
		24.	Mr Joseph Beaman, 80. Old age.
	May	7.	Mr David Phelps, 50. Lung fever.
		15.	An Infant of Thomas Burpee, 6 mo. Consumption.

	May	27.	Mr Joel Phelps, 79. Old age.

       May 27. Mr Joel Phelps, 79. Old age.
       June 1. Mrs Sally Knight, 34. Consumption.
             3. Mrs Prudence Phelps, 70. Cancer.
             9. An Infant of Derby Willard, 2 Days. Mortification.
            25. An Infant of Pliny Newhall, 15 Days. Fits.
            28. A Daughter of Gilson Brown, 2. Consumption.
       July 4. Mr Thomas Hastings, 26. } Brothers who were drowned.
                Benjamin Hastings, 16.
            16. Mrs Elizabeth Divoll. 93. Old age.
            25. Mrs Mary Fletcher, 86. Old age.
            31. A Daughter of Jonas Lane, 5 mo. Dysentery.
       Aug. 5. A Daughter of Moses D. Smith, 2. Dysentery.
            10. A Son of James Mallard, 2. Dysentery.
            21. A Daughter of Nahum Rugg, 36 Hours. Fits.
       Sep. 9. Miss Elizabeth Peacock, 56. Consumption.
202   15. A Daughter of John Low, 4. Dysentery.
       Nov. 18. Miss Dolly Phelps, 70. Old age.
            22. Mr Josiah Rugg (In the Army), 29. fever.
       Dec. 9. Mrs Charity Haskell, 68. Consumption.
            12. Miss Jerusha Osgood, 96. Old age.   In 1813, 34—426.
1714. Jan. 7. Mrs Bathsheba Goodwin, 70. Dropsy.
            24. Mr William Larkin, 83. General Decay.
            31. A child of Luke Bennett, 2. Worms.
       Feb. 1. Mr Israel Butler, 68. Consumption.
             2. Mr Lockart Houghton, 43. Consumption.
             9. Major Joseph Hiller, 66. Apoplexy.
       Mar. 30. Mr Moses Wilder, 79. Old age.
       Apr. 11. Mr Aaron Wilder, 37. Mortification.
            15. Mr Samuel Andrews, 64. Consumption.
            22. Mrs Sarah Danforth, 79. Old age.
       May 10. Mr John Pollard, 85. General Decay.
            11. A Daughter of Josiah Bridge, 4 mo. Lung fever.
            22. Mrs Patience Sherin, 62. Croup.
       June 7. A Daughter of Moses Dickinson, 1 week. Fits.
       July 14. Mrs Betty Wilder, 72. Fever.
       Aug. 2. Miss Alice Poor, 44. Dysentery.
             8. Mrs Abigail Joslyn, 65. Consumption.
            12. A Son of Aaron Jones, 2. Scald.
            13. Mr Jonathan Locke, 66. Lung fever.
            18. Miss Polly Wilder, 34. Dropsy.
       Sep. 28. Mr Manasseh Knight, 62. Lung fever.
       Oct. 2. A Child of Farnham Plummer, 4 mo. Abscess in head.
203   22. Mr Josiah Ross, 27. By a fall from a Tree.
       Nov. 3. Mrs Martha Wilder, 70. General Decay.
            14. Mr Joshua Fletcher, 90. Old age.
                Miss Nancy Miller, 20. Consumption.
            20. Mr Richard Townsend, 79. Old age.
       Dec. 21. Mr Nathan Whipple, 82. Old age.
            27. Capt. Thomas Gates, 79. Fever.   In 1814, 29—455.
1815. Jan. 29. An Infant, 4 Hrs. } Twins of Josiah Bridge.
            31. An Infant, 48 Hrs.
       Feb. 2. An Infant of David Richardson, 3 mo. Suffocation.
                An Infant of Abel Wilder, 36 Hrs. Fits.
            18. Mr Nahum Osgood, 36. Asthma.
       Mar. 8. A Daughter of Benjamin Thompson, 13 mo.
             9. An Infant of Asa Barrett, 36 Hrs.
            11. Mrs Abigail Whipple, 75. Consumption.
       Apr. 1. Miss Cynthia Sawyer, 15. Consumption.
            18. Mr Samuel Newton, 27. Drowned.
                Mr Daniel Felton, 23. Drowned.
       May   1. An Infant of Dolly Maynard, 8 Days. Fits.
             8. Mrs Mary Cleveland, 36. Consumption.

	July	2.	Mr John Townsend, 43. [Suicide.]
		5.	Mrs Achsah Houghton, 72. Dropsy.
		17.	An Infant, 8 Hrs. } Twins of Silas Brown.
			An Infant, 20 Hrs. }
		24.	Miss Mary Phelps, 16. Fever.
	Aug.	1.	Mary Ann Jones, 10. Consumption.
	Sep.	29.	An Infant of Otis Hunt, 18 Days.
		30.	Mrs Kezia Baldwin, 91. Old age.
204	Oct.	17.	Mrs Sarah Childs, 34. Consumption.
	Nov.	19.	Mr John Carter, 65. Lung fever.
		28.	Mrs Sally Wilder, 43. Consumption.
	Dec.	7.	A Son of Abner Pollard, 14 mo. Consumption.
		28.	Mrs Betsy Carter, 31. Consumption. In 1815, 26—481.
1816.	Jan.	19.	Parker Phelps, 18. Consumption.
		29.	Mrs Achsah Pollard, 48. Consumption.
	Feb.	2.	Mr Abijah Rugg, 65. Consumption.
		7.	Mrs Mary Carleton, 23. Consumption.
		12.	Mr Gates Thurston, 51. Mortification.
	Mar.	1.	A Son of Hollis Bruce, 2. Measles.
		4.	Mrs Elizabeth Pollard, 78. Old age.
		11.	A Son of Nathaniel Rand, 6. Dropsy in head.
		20.	Mr William Wilder, 62. Typhoid fever.
		24.	Mr Moses Dickinson, 70. General Decay.
	Apr.	2.	Merrick Willard, 19. Lung fever.
	May	1.	A Daughter of David Richardson, 2. Consumption.
		11.	A Son of Joshua Fletcher, 2. Canker.
		27.	Mrs Patty Freeman (a Mulattoe). Consumption.
	July	7.	An Infant of George Safford, 14 Days. Fever.
		9.	Mr Daniel Godfrey, 80. Consumption.
		30.	A Daughter of Samuel Manning, 2. Dysentery.
	Sep.	14.	Mr Isaac Stone, 93. Dysentery.
	Oct.	8.	A Son of Aaron Jones, 2.
	Nov.	18.	A Child of Windsor Barnard, 8 mo.
205	Dec.	30.	Mr Asa Warner, 66. General Decay. In 1816, 22—503.
1817.	Jan.	17.	Doctor James Carter, 63. Organic affection.
		30.	Mr Micah Simmons, 82. Dropsy.
	Feb.	18.	Mrs Alice Allen, 68. Typhus fever.
		19.	Levi Hammond, 39, (a Mulattoe). Consumption.
	Mar.	4.	Mr Philemon Allen, 63. Typhus fever.
		20.	Mr Ephraim Laughton, 27. Consumption.
		23.	Mrs Lydia Burpee, 29. Consumption.
	Apr.	1.	An Infant of John Hawks Jr., 6 mo.
		22.	Loring Goodwin, 19. Ulcers.
		27.	An Infant of David Howe, 3 mo.
	May	22.	Miss Elizabeth Butler, 22. Consumption.
	June	23.	Mrs Nabby Simmons. Typhus fever.
		28.	A Son of William Cleveland, 3. Throat Distemper.
	July	2.	Miss Julia Whiting, 30. Consumption.
	Sep.	12.	A Daughter of Amasa Keyes, 5. Typhus fever.
		24.	A Son of Thomas Thompson, 11 mo. Canker.
		26.	A Daughter of Thomas Thompson, 3. Dysentery.
	Oct.	4.	Mrs Lucy Manning, 37. Consumption.
		11.	Mrs Lucy Whitney, 74. Old age.
		19.	Mr Benjamin Thompson, 51. Consumption.
		24.	Mrs Abigail Rogers, 80. Dysentery.
	Nov.	1.	Mrs Anna Nichols, 77. Consumption.
		2.	A Daughter of Moses Jones, 6. Consumption.
		26.	A Daughter of Moses Emerson, 3. Croup.
	Dec.	13.	An Infant of James Newhall, 24 Hrs. Fits.
206		15.	A Son of Jonas Goss, 4. Croup. In 1817, 26—529.
1818.	Jan.	13.	Mrs Alice Knowlton, 32. Fever.
	Mar.	11.	Mrs Elizabeth Safford, 49. Consumption.

	Mar.	24.	A Daughter of Nathaniel Warner, 1. Worms.
	Apr.	9.	Mrs Elizabeth Fairbank, 70. Lung fever.
		18.	Mrs Elizabeth Leach, 86. Old age.
		30.	Ebenezer Bradish Esq., 73. Suicide. Insane.
	May	16.	A Son of Amos Wheeler, 7 weeks. Lung fever.
		25.	A Son of Farnham Plummer, 5 mo. Hooping Cough.
		31.	A Daughter of Samuel Worcester, 1. Hooping Cough.
	June	22.	Mrs Anna Ballard, 32. Consumption.
		30.	Mr Daniel Stearns, 75. Dropsy.
	July	3.	Mr Prescott Wilder, 23. Hip complaint.
	Aug.	13.	Mr Rufus Geary, 27. Dysentery.
	Sept.	6.	Mrs Sarah Jones, 60. Consumption.
		12.	A Son of Luke Wilder, 2. Dysentery.
	Nov.	10.	Mrs Nancy Jones, 37. Typhus fever.
		11.	An Infant of Moses Osgood, 4 weeks.
		13.	Mr William Blanchard, 56.
	Dec.	31.	Mrs Dolly Ward, 73. General Decay. In 1818, 19—548.
1819.	Feb.	11.	A Son of Titus Wilder Jr. Consumption.
		13.	Mrs Ruth Haven, 55. Dropsy.
		17.	Mrs Catharine Osgood, 91. Old age.
		26.	An Infant of John Capen, 24 Hrs. Fits.
	Mar.	24.	Mr Daniel Johnson, 57. Consumption.
207		29.	A Daughter of Daniel Robbins, 2. Wen on Stomach.
	May	2.	A Daughter of Joshua Fletcher, 2. Worms.
	June	16.	A Daughter of Nathaniel Whittemore Jr., 6. Worms.
		29.	A Son of Jonathan Carleton of Boston, 11. Drowned.
	July	3.	Miss Eloise R. Paine of N. York, 31. Consumption.
		6.	Mr James Clarke. 86. General Decay.
		8.	Mrs Mary Ballard, 53. Consumption.
		21.	Mr Nathaniel Burbank, 73. Numb Palsy.
	Aug.	1.	A Son of John Goss 2^d. Dysentery.
		15.	A Daughter of Ephraim Phelps. Canker.
		31.	Mrs Sarah Wilder, 66. Dropsy.
	Sep.	4.	A Son of Abel W. Rugg, 1. Dysentery.
		16.	A Son of Stephen Laughton, 1. Dysentery.
		24.	Miss Elizabeth Palmer, 59. Dropsy.
	Nov.	20.	Mrs Nancy Hildreth, 32. Consumption. In 1819, 20—568.
1820.	Jan.	7.	Miss Lydia Mansfield, 50. Fits.
		11.	Mrs Essediah Harris, 26. Consumption.
		18.	Mrs Elizabeth Putnam, 50. Consumption.
		23.	Mr Otis Wilder, 41. Sores.
		26.	An Infant of Richard Hildreth, 6 mo. Consumption.
	Feb.	24.	An Infant of Joseph Butler, 7 Weeks. Hooping Cough.
	Mar.	6.	Mrs Rebecca Fletcher, 92. Old age.
		10.	An Infant of Solo. Carter, 7 mo. Consumption.
		30.	A Daughter of Hollis Bruce, 4 Days.
	Apr.	19.	Miss Abigail Thompson, 24. Consumption.
	July	30.	Mrs Lucy Baldwin, 45. Apoplexy.
	Aug.	2.	A Son of John Hyde, 2. Fits.
208	Sep.	6.	Mr James Newhall, 42. Dropsy in chest.
		13.	Mr William Floyd, 52. In a fit.
		20.	Mrs Millicent Tower. 59. Bilious colic.
	Oct.	10.	Mr Stephen Wilder, 72. Gravel.
			Miss Abigail Bridge, 22. Consumption.
	Dec.	3.	Mrs Sarah Deputeron, 93. Old age.
		7.	Mrs Abigail Zweir, 73. Fever.
		17.	Mr John Robbins, 70. Abscess in side.
		29.	A Son of Elias Bennett, 4. Drowned. In 1820, 21—589.
1821.	Jan.	19.	Mrs Rebecca Dickinson, 72. Mortification.
	Mar.	3.	An Infant of Hollis Bruce, 2 Days.
		11.	Mrs Annis Low, 49. Consumption.
		31.	Infant of Leonard Ayres, 2. Fits.

	Apr.	15.	An Infant of Sodi Sanderson, 3 Days.
	May	30.	Miss Catharine Osgood, 61. Consumption.
	June	6.	Infant of Isaac Kilbourn, 24 Hrs.
		13.	Mr Amos Sawyer, 68. Mortification.
		25.	Mr Jeremiah Fales, 76. Disease of the heart.
	July	12.	An Infant of Ephraim Phelps, a few hours.
	Aug.	19.	An Infant of David Howe, 12 Hours.
		22.	Mr George Phelps, 43. Dropsy.
	Sep.	6.	Mrs Polly Thurston, 62. Consumption.
		23.	A Daughter of Stephen Laughton, 13 mo. Dysentery.
	Nov.	7.	Mr Joel Osgood, 75. Disease of the heart.
		13.	A Daughter of John Lyon, 4. Scarlet fever.
		16.	A Son of Nathan Burditt, 4. Croup.
209		17.	Mr John Hyde, 50. General Decay.
	Dec.	23.	Miss Betsy Townsend, 75. Fever. In 1821, 19—608.
1822.	Jan.	5.	Mr Cummings Lincoln, 24. Consumption.
		11.	Mr Rufus Bruce (of Boston), 31. Consumption.
	Feb.	19.	An Infant of Dr. Calvin Carter, 8 Days. Fits.
		22.	A Son of Isaac Childs, 3. Measles.
	Mar.	20.	A Daughter of Dr. Calvin Carter, 2. Canker.
		31.	Mr John Sargeant, 73. General Decay.
	Apr.	15.	Mrs Nancy Fisher, 50. Consumption.
		30.	A Daughter of Amos Wheeler, 15 mo. Measles.
	May	10.	An Infant of Asahel Harris, 3 mo. Fits.
	June	14.	A Child of Benjamin Farnsworth, 9 mo.
		15.	Mrs Sophia Wilder, 30. Consumption.
		29.	An Infant of Hollis Bruce, 2 mo.
		30.	Mr Daniel Knight, 70. Mortification.
	July	20.	Dr. Israel Atherton, 81. Numb Palsy.
		"	Samuel Harris, Indian from Buffalo, 31. Consumption.
	Aug.	6.	Mrs Hannah Billings, 39. Consumption.
		19.	Mrs Elizabeth Wales, 62. Consumption.
	Sep.	17.	An Infant of John Hawks Jr., 2 weeks.
	Oct.	10.	Mrs Prudence Sawyer, 58. Dropsy.
		13.	Mr Edward Rugg, 24. Fever.
		19.	Mr William McClellan, 53. Consumption.
		23.	Capt. Moses Emerson, 48. Dropsy.
210			Major Eben Sawyer, 25. Typhus Fever.
	Nov.	4.	Mr Manasseh Wilder, 70. Fever.
		22.	Mr Henry Townsend, 29. Consumption. In 1822, 25—633.
1823.	Jan.	21.	Capt. John Maynard, 70. General Decay.
		23.	Mr Jacob Sweetser, 76. Consumption.
	Feb.	1.	Mr Thomas Carter, 70. Asthma.
	Mar.	10.	Mrs Roxa Wetherbee, 42. Consumption.
		17.	Major Timothy Fletcher, 72. Numb Palsy.
		21.	An Infant of Silas Thurston Jr., 24 Hours.
	May	15.	Mrs Rebecca Atherton, 86. Lung fever.
		18.	Mrs Moses Peaslee, 36. Lung fever.
	Sep.	24.	Mrs Abigail Whitney of Boston. Consumption.
		25.	Mrs Lydia White, 83. General Decay.
		26.	A Son of Charles E. Knight, 6. Drowned.
	Oct.	5.	A Child of Zaccheus Whitney of Boston, 1. Dysentery.
		24.	A child of Moses Carleton of Groton, 1. Lung fever.
	Nov.	22.	Mrs Mary Thomas, 72. Cancer.
		23.	Mrs Silence Carter, 76. Old age. In 1823, 15—648.
1824.	Feb.	6.	Mrs Almira M. Wilder, 22. Consumption.
		16.	A Daughter of Margaret Atherton, 6. Consumption.
		20.	Mrs Ruth Fletcher, 95. Old age.
			Mrs Catharine Bruce, 56. Consumption.
	May	2.	Mrs Asenath Phelps, 60. Caused by opium.
211	Sep.	2.	Mr Luther Sawyer, 59. Suicide.
		4.	Miss Susan Sargeant, 23. Typhus fever.

24

	Oct.	16.	Mr Newell Whiting, 21. Dropsy.
		20.	A Daughter of John Goodwin Jr., 18 mo. Hooping Cough.
		22.	Mr Samuel Wilder, 79. General Decay.
	Dec.	9.	Mr Peter Thurston, 56. Dropsy in chest. In 1824, 11—659.
1825.	Jan.	9.	Mr Simon Willard, 97. Old age.
		15.	A Daughter of Levi Lewis Esq., 1. Lung fever.
		18.	Capt. Ezra Sawyer, 38. Consumption.
		19.	Mr Aaron Munroe, 69. Lung fever.
		28.	Joseph White, 15. By the fall of a tree.
	Feb.	18.	Mrs Mary Joslyn, 88. General Decay.
		19.	Mrs Susanna Bridge, 35. Typhus fever.
	Mar.	3.	Mrs Eliza D. Baker, 24. Dyspepsy.
		7.	Mr Eli Stearns, 67. Disease of the heart.
		15.	Mr Artemas Laughton, 39. Consumption.
		18.	Mrs Susan Goodwin, 28. Consumption.
		19.	A Child of Nathan Burditt, 1. Lung fever.
		28.	An Infant of Josiah Billings, 36 Hrs.
	Apr.	4.	Mr David Howe, 40. Consumption.
		15.	Mr Jonathan Buttrick, 44. Disease of Liver.
	May	13.	Miss Mary Rice, 19. Typhus fever.
		31.	A Daughter of Elisha Wilder, 6. Disease in head.
	June	5.	A Daughter of Luke Rugg, 4. Poison,
		20.	Mr Thomas Safford. [Suicide.] Insane.
		25.	Mrs Lucena Wilder, 37. Consumption.
	July	18.	Mrs Lydia Wilder, 47. Cancer.
		20.	Mr Joel Tidd, 40. Typhus fever.
	Aug.	8.	Mrs Lydia Houghton, 54. Tumor in bowels.
		24.	Mrs Emily Faulkner, 22. Consumption.
	Sep.	13.	Mr Joseph Damon, 20. Fever.
		14.	Capt. William G. Weld, 50. Diarrhoea.
		29.	Mr Abraham Damon, 22. Bilious fever.
	Oct.	—	A Child of Manasseh Solindine, 17 mo. Dysentery.
		15.	Abel S. Phelps, 14. An ulcerated throat.
		22.	Capt. Caleb Lincoln, 52. Typhus fever.
	Nov.	2.	Mr John Solindine, 51. Consumption.
	Dec.	14.	Mrs Ruth Townsend, 50. Fever. In 1825, 33—692.
1826.	Jan.	4.	A Child of Fisher Ayres, 2. Scald.
		7.	Cuffe Tindy (a negroe), 66. Consumption.
			Elvira Townsend, 14. Typhus fever.
		31.	A Son of Jacob Wilder, 16. Consumption.
	Feb.	2.	Miss Sophia Allen, 43. Consumption.
		5.	Mrs Martha Hammond, 72. Dropsy.
		15.	Capt. Samuel Joslyn, 87. Lung fever.
		24.	Mr Nathaniel Eaton, 81. Consumption.
	Mar.	8.	Mr Joseph Nichols, 82. Lung fever.
		12.	Mr Samuel Whitwell. Abscess in the Hip.
			A Child of Samuel Worcester, 4 mo. Lung fever.
	Apr.	6.	Capt. Jonas Fairbank, 51. Fever.
		8.	A Child of William Nowell, 2. Dropsy in Head.
	May	7.	An Infant of the late Sophia Allen, 5 mo. Consumption.
		10.	Mr Benjamin H. Foster. 42. Cancer.
	June	22.	Mrs Mary Carter, 56. Consumption.
		27.	Miss Sarah Hall, 33. Consumption.
	July	11.	Mr Lemuel Dickenson, 36. Dropsy.
		12.	Mrs Betsy Townsend, 55. Consumption.
	Aug.	8.	Mr Henry Phelps, 30. Inflammation on Brain.
		14.	Samuel Ward Esq., 86. General Decay.
		31.	Mrs Tempe Carter, 42. Mortification.
	Sep.	1.	Mr Robert Townsend, 66. Cancer.
		2.	Mrs Lydia Robbins, 78. Dropsy.
		9.	Mr John Ballard, 68. General Decay.
		13.	Miss Lydia Houghton, 21. Putrid fever.

	Oct.	7.	Mr Amasa Keyes, 53. In a fit.
		14.	Rufus Low, 19. Typhus fever.
	Nov.	3.	Mrs Lucy Rand, 36. Consumption.
		10.	Mr Elijah Wilder, 42. Consumption.
		19.	Mrs Ruth Wilder, 60. Fever.
		21.	A Son of Shadrach Whitney, 10. Fever.
	Dec.	7.	A Son of Ebenezer Bragg, 16 mo. Consumption.
		28.	Perley Hammond (a Negroe). Consumption.
		30.	Deacon Benjamin Wyman, 61. Consumption.

In 1826, 35—727.

1827.	Jan.	8.	Mr James Sawyer, 29. Mortification.
		26.	Mr John Hawkes, 77. Old age.
	Feb.	14.	An Infant of Thomas Sargeant, 4 mo. Fits.
		17.	Mr Joseph Miller, 31. Consumption.
	Mar.	3.	An Infant of Zebediah Tyler, 4 Weeks. Canker.
214	Apr.	4.	Mr Artemas Newhall, 46. Dropsy.
		8.	A Daughter of Henry Moore, 1. Lung fever.
		9.	Mrs Nancy Tyler, 1. Mortification.
		23.	A Daughter of Charles Sawyer, 3.
		29.	Mr Nathaniel Low, 61. Consumption.
	June	19.	Mrs Catharine Kingsbry, 27. Consumption.
		20.	An Infant of Torrey Fitch, 4 Hrs.
	July	2.	Mrs Lucy Thurston, 32. Consumption.
	July	11.	Miss Nancy Butler, 20. Consumption.
		13.	A Son of Hannibal Laughton, 15 mo. Canker.
	Aug.	5.	Miss Lydia Stevenson, 28. Typhus fever.
		31.	Capt. Ephraim Carter, 54. Fever.
	Oct.	3.	Mr Abigail Prescott. Consumption.
	Nov.	7.	Mrs Mercy Manning, 76. Lung fever.
		9.	Mrs Deborah Solindine, 48. Consumption.
		13.	Charlotte Richardson, 16. Apoplexy.
			Mr Samuel Wilder, 81. Old age.
		20.	Peter Davis (a Negroe). Killed by a wagon passing over him.
		26.	A Child of Elisha Wilder, 11 mo. Croup.
	Dec.	1.	Mrs Hannah Chambers, 76. Cancer.
		6.	Mr John Holman, 33. Consumption.
		13.	Mrs Mary Fairbank, 62. Fracture of the Skull by a fall.
215		20.	Clarissa Phelps, 18. Convulsion fits. In 1827, 28—755.
1828.	Jan.	9.	Edward Goodwin Esq., 56. Consumption.
		13.	Mr John Goss 3d, 23. Hip Complaint.
	Mar.	7.	A Child of Charles E. Knight, 6. Consumption.
		16.	A Child of James Rugg, 3 Weeks. Fits.
		19.	An Infant, 48 Hrs. } Twins of James G. Carter. Spasms.
		25.	An Infant, 1 Week.
		27.	Mr Samuel Butler, 44. Consumption.
		28.	Mrs Rebecca White, 66. Lung fever.
	Apr.	21.	Mrs Ann Lawson, 72. Lung fever.
	May	19.	Mr Levi Bennett, 40. Consumption.
		20.	An Infant of Samuel F. White, 3 Days.
		24.	Mrs Mary Stearns, 61. Mortification.
		31.	A Child of Eben. Pratt, 2 mo. Fits.
	July	5.	Mr Holland (of Langdon, N. H.). Mortification.
		13.	Mr Samuel Dickenson, 46. Consumption.
		18.	Mr James Robbins, 79. Lung fever.
	Aug.	11.	Mrs Lydia Thurston, 56. [Wife of Capt. John.]
		26.	A Child of Amos Albee, 2. Worms.
	Sep.	28.	Mrs Patience Wilder, 78. Numb Palsy.
	Oct.	6.	Mr Varnum Gilson, 23. Consumption.
		27.	A Daughter [Elizabeth] of James Rugg, 10. Bilious fever.
	Nov.	22.	An Infant of Martha Gilson, 3 mo. Consumption.
	Dec.	3.	Mr Eli Bruce, 26. Consumption.
		12.	Mrs Mary H. Sawyer, 42. Consumption.

216

Dec.	13.	Mr Ephraim Robbins, 80. Mortification.
	22.	A Child of Charles E. Knight, 6 mo.
	26.	Mr Charles Bigelow, 61. Dropsy in the chest.

In 1828, 27—782.

1829. Feb. 5. Mrs Elizabeth Willard, 89. Old age.
15. An Infant of Ephraim Fuller, 6 Weeks. Fits.
28. A Child of Dalmer Newhall, 5 Days. Fits.
Mar. 1. Miss Martha Sanderson, 20. Consumption.
2. A Child of Phinehas Houghton, 2. Lung fever.
19. Mr Thomas Sawyer, 64. General Decay.
22. A Child of Alvinzy Lane, 3 mo. Spasms.
30. Mrs Ruth Barrett, 72. Pleurisy.
May 29. Miss Martha Fletcher, 26. Consumption.
June 8. Mrs Lucy Gates, 33. Consumption.
10. Miss Lucy C. White, 24. Bilious cholic.
24. Mr Abijah Phelps, 74. Jaundice.
26. Miss Ruth Johnson, 75. Consumption.
27. A Son of Somes White, 15 mo. Disease of bowels.
July 2. A Son of Henry Sawyer, 17 mo. Dysentery.
4. Mrs Sarah Todd, 80. Dropsy.
7. Mr Jonas Fairbank, 86. Old age.
10. Mrs Chloe Lincoln, 63. Ceneral Decay.
20. A Son of Ephraim Fuller, 7. Drowned.
Aug. 4. A Daughter of Ebenezer Haven, 4. Dysentery.
Sep. 8. A Son of Moses Carleton, 4. Dysentery.
10. A Child of Peter Sawyer, 3. Dysentery.
24. Mr Solomon Bridge, 27. Inflammation of the bowels.
Oct. 3. Mrs Anna Clarke, 93. By a burn.
10. Mr Haran Eager, 68. Consumption.
17. Mrs Lucy Pollard, 50. Dyspepsy.

217

28. A Daughter of Silas Sawyer, 4. Fits.
Nov. 8. Major Solomon Carter, 53. Consumption.
21. A Son of Ansel Tyler, 6. Mortification.
Dec. 5. Mr Moses Jones, 60. Consumption.
18. Mrs Rebecca Divoll, 44. Cancer.
19. Mrs Mary Sanderson, 62. Consumption.
28. A Daughter of Joseph Maynard, 16. Brain fever.

In 1829, 33—815.

1830. Mar. 13. Miss Patience Divoll, 77. Numb Palsy.
20. James Carter (Student at Har. College), 17. Typhus fever.
Apr. 11. Capt. Daniel Rugg, 87. Dropsy.
15. Miss Polly Hyde, 32. Decline.
17. Miss Almira Lowe, 24. Consumption.
June 11. Mrs Lucy Severy, 20. At the birth of a child.
14. Mr Edmund Lawrence, 28.
July 3. Mr John Carter 2ᵈ, 48. Consumption.
14. Mrs Sally Butler, 30. Consumption.
Aug. 28. Mr David Poignard, 71. Organic affection of the heart.
Sept. 2. Mrs Submit Rugg, 38. Mortification.
   A Son of Henry Goss, 16 mo. Dysentery.
5. A Child of William Whitney, 11 mo. Dysentery.
8. Mrs Sarah Howard, 39. Dysentery.
22. Mrs Sarah Brown, 76. General Decay.
Oct. 1. Miss Huldah Cleverly, 23. Dropsy.
9. A Son of Joseph Seaver, 2. Consumption.
   Mr Jacob Stone Jr., 27. Consumption.
Nov. 12. Miss Roxana Dexter, 21. Consumption.
28. Mr Seth Sargeant, 78. Bilious cholic.
Dec. 14. Mr Thomas Thurston, 36. Consumption.

218

28. Mrs Elizabeth Goodspeed, 57

In 1830, 22—837.

1831. Jan. 6. Miss Abigail Goddard, 67. Consumption.
17. Miss Lucy Thurston, 31. Consumption.

	Jan.	25.	A Daughter of Jonas Goss, 12. Scarlet fever.
	Feb.	9.	Mrs Sally Colburn, 52. Lung fever.
		15.	A Son of Hervey Pierce, 6. Dropsy in head.
			A Daughter of Nathaniel Rice. Canker.
		16.	Mrs Dorothy Thurston, 92. Numb Palsy.
		19.	Mrs Mary Safford, 36. Puerperal fever.
			Mrs Martha Maynard, 68. Erysipelas.
		20.	A Child of Simeon Bowman, 9 mo. Lung fever.
	Mar.	12.	Mr Moses Sawyer, 66. Lung fever.
		15.	Mr William Whiting, 70. Gradual Decline.
		17.	A Son of Luke Bigelow, 2. Canker Rash.
		26.	Mrs Mary Phelps, 60. Lung fever.
		30.	A Daughter of Joseph Maynard, 11. Canker Rash.
	Apr.	5.	A Daughter of Luke Bigelow, 5. Canker Rash.
		18.	A Daughter of Lucy Carter, 14 mo. Canker Rash.
	May	8.	A Son of Charles Sawyer, 4. Canker Rash.
	June	3.	Mr Peter Sawyer, 47. Consumption.
		"	Miss Hannah Wilson, 24. Disease in the head.
		25.	A Daughter of David K. Thurston, 2. Canker Rash.
	July	22.	Mr James Fuller, 81. Old age.
	Sep.	8.	Mr James Goodwin, 90. General Decay.
		11.	Mrs Lucy Houghton, 46. Tumor in the bowels.
		14.	A Daughter of Joseph Barrett, 14. Canker Rash.
219	Sep.	24.	Mr Zimri Priest, 31. Consumption.
	Oct.	12.	A Child of Peter Joslyn, 21 Hours. Spasms.
	Nov.	19.	Mr Gardner Maynard, 42. Suddenly.
			An Infant of Sally Lawrence, 1. Canker Rash.
		24.	A Son of Levi Lewis Esq., 4. Canker Rash.
		28.	A Daughter of Charles Sawyer, 6. Dropsy.
	Dec.	1.	A Child of Ephraim C. Fisher, 8 mo. Abscess in the head.
		9.	A Daughter of Sam¹. Richardson, 14. Abscess on the Hip.
		16.	Mrs Abby Eliza Barnes, 23. Dropsy.
		20.	Mrs Lucy Brigham, 71. General Decay.
			Miss Sarah T. Thayer, 35. Consumption.
		25.	Miss Sarah Butler, 19. Consumption.
		27.	Mrs Nancy Plummer, 50. Consumption. In 1831, 39—876.
1832.	Jan.	9.	Miss Emily Laughton, 33. Consumption.
		11.	Mrs Susanna Rugg, 77. Influenza.
			Mr David Butler, 95. Old age.
		15.	Mr John Goldthwait, 66. Gradual Decline.
			Almiric, Son of the late Peter Sawyer, 9. Canker Rash.
		21.	Mrs Sarah Thurston, 54. Consumption.
			Mr Jonathan Bruce, 69. General Decay.
		24.	Miss Catharine Miles, 21. Consumption.
	Feb.	11.	Mrs Rebecca Thomas, 73. Lung fever.
		25.	An Infant of Farwell Eager, a few minutes.
	Apr.	16.	Miss Ruth Osgood, 30. Scrofula.
		25.	Miss Rebecca Wilder, 16. Consumption.
			Mr Jacob Zwiers, 93. Influenza.
220	May	1.	A child of Charles Mann, 2. Scarlet fever.
		7.	Mrs Mary Carleton, 32. Consumption.
		24.	A Son of Ephraim Fuller, 2. Mortification.
	June	19.	A Daur. of Samuel Worcester, 3. Canker Rash.
		20.	A Son of Moses Carleton, 4 mo. Consumption.
	July	11.	Mr John Slote, 30. Of N. York. Sudden death.
		16.	Mrs Nancy Barnes, 30. Complicated Disease.
		18.	Mr Sullivan Jones, 24. Brain Fever.
		27.	Mrs Polly Kimball, 64. General Decay.
		28.	A Son of John Rugg, 4. Canker Rash.
	Aug.	14.	Mrs Hannah Fletcher, on a visit at Philadelphia, 75. Cholera.
		16.	Mr Manasseh Solindine, 52. Consumption.
		27.	Mr Abel Willard, 35. Bilious fever.

		Aug.	30.	A Daughter of Peter Osgood, 9 mo. Influenza.

Aug. 30. A Daughter of Peter Osgood, 9 mo. Influenza.
Sep. 2. Mrs Jane Warner, 74. Dropsy in the chest.
    6. An Infant of Galen L. Stevenson (of Boston), 4 mo.
   11. Miss Sally Danforth, 76. Decline.
   17. A Daughter of Charles Sawyer, 3. Influenza.
   18. A Son of John Dean, 3 mo. Influenza.
Oct. 17. An Infant of John G. Thurston, 5 weeks. Influenza.
Nov. 4. Mr Charles Thurston, 35. Consumption.
   13. Mrs Bathsheba Rugg, 42. [Suicide.] Insane.
   23. Miss Nancy Carter, 21. Consumption.
Dec. 28. Mr Oliver Studley, 72. Dropsy.

221
   29. Mr Stephen Cleverly, 72. Consumption.   In 1832. 38—914
1833. Feb. 27. An Infant of Sewell Carter, 4 Days.
Apr. 1. Mr William B. Andrews, 44. Consumption.
May 1. Mrs Susanna Fuller, 35. Fever after birth of a child.
   12. Miss Mary Ann Phelps, 20. Consumption.
      Mr George Grant, 63. Consumption.
July 26. A Infant of Henry Sawyer, 16 mo.
Aug. 3. Capt. Asahel Tower, 72 & 10 mo. Dropsy.
   27. Ezra Sawyer, 19. Scarlet fever.
Sep. 2. A Infant of Elias Sawyer, 1. Dysentery.
   6. Mr Horatio Carter, 37. Consumption.
   11. Mrs Sarah Manly, 84. Dropsy.
   16. An Infant of Ephraim Fuller, 4 mo.
   22. An Infant of Joseph H. Huntington, 4 Wks.
   30. Mrs Delicia Poignand, 68 & 10 mo. Scrofula.
Oct. 11. Mrs Prudence Wheelock, 77. Consumption.
   27. A Child of Jonathan Davis, 4. By a burn.
Nov. 7. Mr Manasseh Divoll, 70. Typhus fever.
   27. Mrs Mercy Adams, 55. Consumption.
Dec. 9. Mr Gowen B. Newman, 65. Inflammation on the Lungs.
   13. Mr Titus Wilder Jr., 55. Sudden death.
   16. Miss Tabitha Allen, 87. Old age.
   23. Mr Hezekiah P. Phelps, 36. Consumption.
   30. An Infant of Abraham Adams, 2 weeks. Canker.
                                                       In 1833, 23—937.

222
1834. Jan. 6. Mr Elijah Whitney, 79. Lung fever.
   25. Miss Betsy Adams, 57. Consumption.
   26. A Daughter of Samuel Plant, 2. Scarlet fever.
Feb. 2. An Infant of John Taylor, 8 days.
   26. A Son of Thomas Shephard, 20 mo. Scarlet fever.
Mar. 15. Mr Ephraim Osgood, 76. Dropsy.
   22. Mr Otis Chamberlain (of Southborough), 28. In a fit.
   24. Mr Nathan Warner, 37. Complaint of bowels.
Apr. 8. Mrs Elizabeth Rugg, 88. Dropsy.
   13. A Daughter of Ephraim C. Fisher, 1. Fits.
      A Son of William Barker, 7 Days.
   16. Mrs Relief Divoll, 86. Old age.
May 9. A Son of Elias Sawyer, 1 & 8 mo. Fits.
June 2. A Daughter of John Dean, 9 mo. Dropsy in the head.
   9. Mr Robert Phelps, 66. Gravel.
      Mr Thomas J. Bethel, 26. Measles.
   11. Mrs Betsy Bridgman of Maine, 21. Mortification.
   22. An Infant of Mrs Mary Warner, 1. Throat Distemper.
   29. Mrs Emily Dean, 35. Consumption.
July 8. Mr George H. Walton, 26. Consumption.
   17. Mr Abel Richardson, 73. Drinking cold water in a time of heat.
Sep. 10. Mrs Anna A. Vose, 58. Consumption.
   13. Miss Martha T. Wyman, 22. Typhus fever.
   17. Mr Joseph Farwell, 75. Dropsy.
   25. A Son of Farwell Eager, 1. Hooping Cough.

	Oct.	10.	Mrs Deborah Stearns, 78. Old age.
223	Nov.	3.	William Barnard, 20. Typhus fever.
		7.	Mr William Gould, 80. General Decay.
		9.	An Infant of Rufus Houghton, 8 mo. Consumption.
	Dec.	4.	An Infant of Charles Sawyer, 1 Day.
		10.	Miss Abigail Thayer, 22. Consumption.
		12.	An Infant of William Larkin, 1. Influenza.
		14.	Mrs Martha Houghton, 31. Consumption.
		22.	Mr James Wilder, 40. Scrofula.
		23.	Mr Stephen Rugg, 78. Influenza. In 1834, 35.—972.
1835.	Jan.	13.	Mr James Pitts, 52.
		14.	Mrs Lucebe Hosley, 75. Cancer.
		16.	Mr Benjamin Houghton, 77. Influenza.
		17.	Miss Mary Ann A. Carter, 17. Lung fever.
		23.	Mrs Lydia A. Wilder, 23. Consumption.
	Feb.	12.	Mrs Almira Townsend, 31. Consumption.
		16.	Mr Stephen Dickenson, 50. Delirium.
		19.	Miss Rebecca Fletcher, 83. Old age.
	Mar.	5.	An Infant of Nathaniel Joslyn, 1 week. Fits.
		17.	Mrs Emily Carter, 68. Lung fever.
			Miss Elizabeth G. Toppan of Hampton, N. H., 32. Hydrocephalus.
		22.	A Son of Abel Butler, 9. Hydrocephalus.
	Apr.	9.	A child of Winsor Barnard, 1. Pleurisy.
		19.	Charles Tucker, 17. In a fit.
	May	1.	Mr Cyrus Fairbank, 68. Consumption.
224		26.	Mr Eber Goddard, 69. Mortification.
		27.	Mrs Hannah Beaman, 99 & 8 mo. By a fall.
	June	1.	Mrs Dolly Flagg, 68. Mortification.
		23.	Miss Evelina Sawyer, 26. Consumption.
		29.	Moses Smith Esq., 58.
	July	15.	Mrs Rachel Fales, 85 & 8 mo. Old age.
		29.	Mrs Jane Gray (of Boston), 24. Typhus fever.
	Oct.	19.	A Child of John Goodwin Jr., 15 mo., bowel complaint.
		24.	An Infant of Lewis Fletcher, 24 Hrs. Fits.
			Mrs Susanna Arnold, 81. Dropsy in the chest.
	Nov.	7.	Ellen Maria, Daughter of Nathaniel Rand, 4. Dropsy.
		27.	Miss Mary Ann Thurston, 18. Consumption.
	Dec.	4.	Mrs Beulah Goodrich, 81. Pleurisy.
		11.	Mr William Carter, 67. Dropsy in the chest.
		22.	Jane Kendall, a Maniac, about 70. Lung fever.
			In 1835, 30—1002.
1836.	Jan.	9.	Capt. John Lyon, 60. Apoplexy.
		13.	Mr Jonathan Wilder, 81. Old age.
	Feb.	3.	A Child of John A. Haskell, 1 & 9 Weeks. Bowel Complaint.
		23.	Mrs Ruth Barnes (of Groton), 58. Disease of the Heart.
		28.	A Infant of George Houghton, 6 mo. Croup.
	Mar.	17.	Sophia, Daughter of Jeremiah Fales, 13. Fever sore.
		19.	An Infant of Charles Wheelock, 9 mo. Influenza.
		21.	A Son of Ephraim Fuller, 1. Ulcerated Throat.
		27.	Mrs Hannah Rugg, 38. Suddenly after the birth of a Child.
225	Apr.	5.	An Infant of Ephraim C. Fisher, 8½ mo. Disorder in the Head.
		16.	An Infant of Rhoda Johnson, 11 Weeks. Dropsy in the Head.
		23.	An Infant of James Gould, 24 Hrs.
	May	20.	Miss Tamar Stone, 20. Consumption.
			Miss Almira Maynard, 28. Consumption.
		25.	Mrs Hannah Whitman, 70 & 7 mo. Suddenly.
	June	13.	Mr Thomas Phelps, 50. Fever.
	July	14.	Mary Childs, 15. Daughter of Isaac Childs. Consumption.
		29.	[Francena E. J.] An Infant of Elijah Sawyer, 1 & 9 mo. Scald.
	Aug.	21.	Capt. Josiah Bowers, 84. [Suicide.]
		31.	Miss Lucretia Murray, 74. Diarrhoea.

	Sep.	17.	A Infant of J. W. Huntington, 11 Weeks.
			Mr Joel Rugg, 48. Consumption.
		19.	Mr Oliver Houghton, 71. Fever.
	Oct.	8.	A Son of John Fuller (of Shirley), 6. Dropsy in the Head.
			A Child of Phinehas B. Howe, 3. Dysentery.
		20.	Mr Ephraim Rugg, 57. Cancer.
	Nov.	4.	Mr Elisha Wilder, —. Consumption.
		13.	An Infant of Farnham Plummer, 7 mo. Decline.
	Dec.	2.	Mrs Rebecca Bowers, 84. Dropsy in the Chest.

226   In 1836, 29—1031.

1837.	Jan.	22.	Miss Mary L. Carleton, 16. Scrofula.
		28.	Miss Sally White, 66. Dropsy.
	Feb.	4.	Mrs Nabby Houghton, 66. Typhus fever.
	Mar.	10.	Mrs Orpah Whiting, 77. Lung fever.
	Apr.	1.	Mrs Mary Fletcher, 75. Influenza.
		10.	Mr Titus Wilder, 87. Gradual Decay.
		17.	An Infant of Alfred Knight, 1 Day.
		30.	Mrs Susanna Carter, 82. General Decay.
	May	2.	Deacon Joel Wilder, 69 & 10 mo. Lung fever.
		4.	Capt. Benjamin Houghton, 73. Dropsy.
		24.	Mrs Elizabeth Sargeant, 74. Spasms.
	June	2.	Mrs Elizabeth Howard, 27. Suddenly.
		10.	Mr Samuel Joslyn, 59. Consumption.
		22.	A child of Aaron Sawin, 8 mo. Lung fever.
	July	1.	A child of Luke Bigelow, 14 mo. Grippe.
		7.	A Daughter of Joshua Fletcher, 6 & 11 mo. Grippe.
			A Daughter of Daniel Virgil, 6. Dropsy in Head.
		23.	Miss Martha Wyman, 81.
	Aug.	11.	A child of Alfred Knight, 19 mo. Wricketts.
	Sep.	26.	Mrs Jemima Whitman, 87. Spasms.
	Oct.	20.	Mrs Lucy Laughton, 81. Old age.
		22.	An Infant of Asa D. Townsend, 10 Weeks. Croup.
	Nov.	5.	Mrs Betsy Fisher, 57.
	Dec.	19.	An Infant of Jonathan Davis, 2 Weeks. Canker.

227   22. An Infant of Ephraim Fuller, 6 Hrs.   In 1837, 25—1056.

1838.	Feb.	17.	A Daughter of Eben. Pratt, 2 & 4 mo. Worms.
		21.	A Daughter of David Wheeler, 4. Canker Rash.
	Mar.	3.	Mrs Tryphena Wilder, 79. Paralysis.
		11.	A Son of Rufus K. Ladd, 7 Weeks. Lung fever.
		16.	Miss Prudence Rugg, 77. Lung fever.
		29.	Mrs Nancy E. Rand, 42. Consumption.
	Apr.	8.	A Daughter of Snell Wade, 3. Consumption.
	May	9.	A Son of Robert M. Bradley, 5. Dropsy on the Brain.
	June	1.	Mr Thomas Ballard, 76. Mortification.
	July	9.	Mrs Margaret Sweetser, 85. General Decay.
		30.	Mrs Martha Carter, 83. General Decay.
	Aug.	2.	Miss Mary Rugg, 24. Consumption.
		5.	Mr Jonas Joslyn, 64. Dropsy.
		9.	A Son of James Arnold, 4 mo. Bowel complaint.
		16.	Mrs Ruth Sawyer, 93. Fever and Age.
	Sep.	7.	Mr Sewall Carter (of Boston), 42. Consumption.
	Oct.	2.	Mr Jeremiah Ballard, 86. Old age.
		12.	Mr George Harris (Died at Wrentham), 23. Typhus fever.
		16.	Nelson Spaulding, 14. Typhus fever.
		22.	Mr Daniel Harris, 80. Cholera Morbus.
	Dec.	7.	Capt. John Thurston, 84. Erysipelas.
		31.	Mr Emory Harris, 50. Premature Decay.

228   In 1838, 22—1078.

1839.	Jan.	20.	Mrs Rebecca Houghton, 70. Numb Palsy.
		26.	Major Jonathan Locke, 60. Numb Palsy.
	Feb.	1.	Mr Farwell Eager, 49. Consumption.
		3.	Miss Louisa Everett, 26. Consumption.

FIRST CHURCH, BOOK II.   369

Feb. 7. Mrs Rebecca Goodwin, 61. Cancer.
8. A child of Felicia Ann Eastman, of Worcester, 15 mo. Lung fever.
9. Mrs Maria S. Wilder, 26. Consumption.
14. William, the Son of Mrs Bray. By the discharge of a Gun.
24. A Son of Phinehas B. Howe, 12. Lung fever.
Mar. 3. Mrs Elizabeth Gould, 84. Old age.
5. Mrs Peggy Davis, supposed 100. Old age.
6. Mrs Laura Phelps, 35. Dropsy.
19. Mrs Mary Tyler, 36. Consumption.
May 8. Mr Joseph Phelps, 33. Consumption.
June 1. A Daughter of Thomas Wellington, 5. Dropsy.
July 2. Levi Lewis Esq., 51. [Suicide.]
10. Mrs Emily Pratt, 42. Consumption.
11. A Daughter of Cyrus Bliss of Granville, N. Y., 9 mo. Bowel complaint.
27. A Daughter of Joseph Maynard Jr., 2. Croup.
Aug. 4. William M. Marston (of Palermo, 16 & 10 mo. Consumption.
14. Mr Amos White, 43. In a Fit.
18. Charles S. Brown, 16 & 10 mo. (of Boston). Consumption.
25. Mr Abel Richardson, 56. Consumption.
26. A Son of Salmon Houghton, 1 & 9 mo. Dysentery.
Sep. 2. A Daughter of Reuben Barrett, 2 & 10 mo. Dysentery.
6. Mrs Prudence Dunsmoor, 87. General Decay.
11. Mrs Frances Houghton, 32. Dysentery.
23. Mr Aaron Jones, 72. Consumption.
25. Mr Jonathan Davis, 36. Typhus fever.
Oct. 1. A Son of Amos H. Wyman, 1. Dysentery.
2. A Son of Levi Pierce, 7. Disorder of the Head.
6. Mr Ebenezer Knowlton, 61. Consumption.
14. Mrs Phebe Atherton, 82. Dysentery.
26. Mrs Betsy Eager, 72. Decline.
Nov. 8. Miss Beulah Phelps, 86 & 9 mo. Old age.
21. A Son of Mrs Alethina Eager, 2. By a burn.
22. Mr John Willard, —. General Decay.
Dec. 25. Mr Baxter Wood, 48 Disease of Kidneys. In 1839, 38—1116.
1840. Jan. 14. Mrs Abigail Fairbank, 88. Old age.
25. Twins (Daughters) of James Stone, 18 Hrs.
Feb. 7. Miss Mary Conquerette, 81. Old age.
11. Josiah Flagg Esq., 79. Influenza.
22. Mr William Gould, 56. Suddenly.
23. Mr Isaac Childs, 65. Lung fever.
29. Mrs Polly Farnsworth, 53. Lung fever.
Mar. 6. Miss Margaret Sweetser, 53. Consumption.
10. A Son of Emeline Sawyer, 7 mo. Lung fever.
23. Mr Silas Thurston, 81. Old age.
May 3. An Infant of Levi Pierce, 1. Scarlet fever.
14. Thomas Davis Esq., 87. Dropsy.
28. Mr Daniel Wilder, 60. Pleurisy.
June 23. Rev. Nathaniel Thayer, D. D., 71. Died at Rochester, N.Y., very suddenly, of spasms on the lungs.
Oct. 18. Mr Jonas Goss, 60. Disease of the liver.
A child of Mr Americus Sawyer.
Nov. 3. Mrs Ann Matthews, 25. Consumption.   In 1840, 18—1134.

337   REV. EDMUND H. SEARS'S RECORD OF DEATHS. 1840-1847.

1840. Dec. 29. Mrs Nancy Sawyer, 63. Cancer.
1841. Feb. 17. An infant child of James Stone.
18. A child of Mrs Williams, 1 year.
20. A daughter of Alfred Knight, 2 years—(throat distemper).
March 24. Miss Sally Ballard, 61—suddenly. Palpitation of the Heart.

	Apl.	16.	A child of Ch⁸. A. Lyman, 18 months. Lung fever.
		17.	A child of Wilder S. Thurston, 1 year. Scrofula.
		17.	Mr Stephen Houghton, 76. Mortification.
	May	11.	Capt. Daniel Goss, 69. Instantly in a fit.
		16.	A child of Oliver Green, 3 yrs. Scarlet fever.
	June	5.	Mr Daniel Lawrence, 52.
	July	2.	Miller, Son of J. W. Huntington, 3 years. Hooping Cough.
		8.	Horatio, son of J. W. Huntington, 1 year. Hooping cough and measles.
		31.	An infant child of Chas. L. Wilder, 1 month. Hooping cough.
338	Aug.	6.	Mr John Carter 63. Consumption.
	Aug.	13.	Samuel B. Wilder, 15. Fits.
		23.	Capt. Joseph Wilder. Dropsy in the chest.
	Sept.	1.	Caroline, dr. of Charles Bridge, of Lowell, 18 months; (died at Lowell of Cholera Infantum, buried here).
		5.	Mr Samuel Adams, 62. Typhus fever.
		18.	Mr John Laughton, 21. Consumption.
	Oct.	11.	Mr Ebenezer W. Fuller, 72. Dysentery.
		19.	Mrs Ruth Miles, 62. Dropsy. In 1840-1, 22.
1842.	Jan.	5.	Mr Jonathan Holman, 78.
	Jan.	25.	Mrs Mary Phelps.
	Feb.	20.	Charles W. Burditt, 6 months. Scarletina. Son of William Burditt.
		27.	Mrs Polly W. Carter, 27. Consumption.
	March	26.	Mrs Abigail Harris, 78. Pleurisy.
339	May	8.	Miss Julia Chandler, 20. Consumption.
		18.	Mr Fabius Whiting, —. Paralysis.
		19.	Mr Oliver Carter, 84. Old age.
	June	2.	Mrs Lucy Newman, 71. Dropsy.
		19.	Laurania S., daughter of Stevens [H.] Turner, 3,—lung fever.
	July	13.	Mr Henry Parker, about 50. Suicide.
		14.	Mrs Eliza Ann Wilson, 30. Consumption.
		30.	Mr Thomas P. Buttrick, 21. Drowned at Lincoln.
	Aug.	9.	Miss Mary Ann Laughton, 21. Consumption.
	Sept.	6.	Mr Ephraim Whitney, 63. Consumption.
		30.	Mr Henry Thurston, 50. Paralysis.
		29.	Mr Cephas Carter, 52. Consumption. (Died at Boston.)
		30.	Mrs Ann Rice, 37. Debility.
	Oct.	3.	Miss Abby Sawyer, 18. Consumption.
		11.	An infant daughter of James Stone.
	Nov.	8.	George W., son of Mr Joel Wilder 2ᵈ, 13. Typhus fever.
		10.	Mr Amasa Willard, 70. Cancer.
		15.	Mr R. M. Bradley, —. Dropsy.
340		24.	Mrs Mary M. Wilder, 39. Consumption.
	Dec.	14.	Miss Martha Townsend, 21. Consumption. In 1842, 24—46.
1843.	Jan.	6.	Mrs Relief Phelps, 83. Consumption.
		28.	Mrs Sarah Wilder, 86. Old age.
		30.	Mrs Hannah W. Upton, 80. Palsy.
		31.	Miss Ann Mitchell, 15. Bowel complaint.
	Feb.	14.	Mr Abel Rugg, 92. Old age.
	March	3.	Miss Cynthia Bigelow, 12. Consumption.
		10.	George W., child of Chs. J. Wilder, 10 weeks. Smothered.
		14.	Mr Elisha Sanderson, 81. Dropsy.
		16.	Dea. Samuel F. White, 50. Consumption.
		24.	Mr John Goss, 73. Dropsy in chest.
		28.	Miss Eliza (Wilder) Harris, 22. Erysipelas.
	May	12.	Mrs Betsy S. Pitts, 29. Consumption.
		23.	Mr Josiah Billings, 58.
	June	2.	Mr Jacob Fisher Senr., 75. Paralysis.
341		5.	Mrs Relief Houghton, 81.
		12.	William Newman, 5. Killed by a limb from a tree.
		26.	Mrs Susannah Carleton, 26. Consumption.

FIRST CHURCH, BOOK II. 371

	July	12.	Mrs Mary Wilder, 95. Old age.
		"	John A., infant son of Luke Bigelow, 4 months. Dysentery.
		26.	Mrs Elizabeth Carter, 54. Consumption.
	Aug.	20.	Mrs Abigail Ballard, 75. Mortification.
		"	Francis, son of Mr Volney Wilder of Boston, 11 months. Dysentery.
		23.	Mr Amos Sawyer, 85. Dysentery.
		25.	Edward, son of Mr Volney Wilder, 11 months. Dysentery.
		31.	George Gerry, a child of Alfred Knight, 1½ years.
	Sept.	4.	Mr Torrey Fitch, 48. Paralysis.
		7.	Lewis Hiram, child of Hiram W. Pitts, 5 months. Dysentery.
		10.	Miss Hannah Larkin, 79. Dysentery.
		18.	Warren, son of Jeremiah Barnard, 1 year 8 mo. Dysentery.
	Oct.	1.	Charles William, son of Mr [Jesse] Gibbs, 3 months. Canker.
		17.	Miss Abigail E. Osgood, 17. Consumption.
		17.	John William, son of George Fitch, 3½ years. Canker.
342	Nov.	2.	Mrs Katharine Rugg, 84. Old Age.
		5.	Mrs Dinah Merriam of Fitchburg, 77.
	Dec.	25.	Mrs Lucy Danforth, 50. Dropsy of the heart.

In 1843, 35—81.

1844.	Jan.	8.	Miss Louisa Sawyer, 16. Consumption.
		14.	Mr Asahel Harris, 50. Consumption.
		14.	Mrs Elizabeth Tidd, 88. Influenza.
	Feb.	1.	Mrs Sarah Farnsworth, 69. Influenza.
		21.	Mrs Sophia Wilder, 64. Influenza.
	March	15.	Walter Austin, son of Austin Davis, 5. Congestion of the brain.
	April	7.	Anna Maria Nourse, 3—suddenly—dr. of Warren Nourse.
		21.	Mrs Betsy Sawyer, 94. Old age.
		24.	Mr Davis Whitman, 82. Old age.
	June	8.	Mr Joseph Upton, 70. General infirmity.
	May	24.	Mrs Dorcas Fletcher, 75. Typhus fever.
	July	12.	Miss Hannah Whipple, 70. Dropsy.
		28.	Mr Abel White, —. Dropsy.
		28.	Mrs Martha Ann R. Carter.
343	Aug.	25.	Joel Thomas, son of Chas. J. Wilder, 3½. Cholera Morbus.
	Oct.	18.	At N. York City, Mr Enos Wilder of Mamaronack, buried in Lancaster—funeral Oct. 23ᵈ, Æ. 39.
	Nov.	4.	Emily, daughter of Thomas Davis, 2½ years.
	Dec.	13.	Mrs Lydia Bailey, 77. Typhus fever.
		28.	Mrs Sally Lyons, 69.
		25.	Drowned at Lowell, George W., son of Chas. Bridge, funeral at Lancaster, Dec. 27ᵗʰ.

In 1844, 18—99.

1845,	Jan.	25.	Mrs Annis Andrews, 81. Dropsy in the chest.
		28.	Mrs Sarah E. Goss, 24. Disease of the heart.
		29.	Charlotte, child of Stevens [H.] Turner, 4. Scarlet fever.
	Feb.	4.	Franklin Warren, child of Ephraim Fuller, 3 yrs. Scarlet fever.
	March	8.	Lydia Ann, child of John Fuller, 3 months. Consumption.
		14.	Mrs Prudence Phelps, 73. Dropsy.
		21.	Henry Kimball, child of John M. Washburn, 2½ yrs. Scarlet fever.
344	March	—.	Miss Caroline M. Newman, 29. Consumption.
	May	—.	Mary Ann, dr. of Orice King, —. Scarlet fever.
		1.	Mrs Sally Carter, 86. Paralysis.
	July	—.	Mrs Nancy Fay, —. Inflammation of the bowels.
	Sept.	16.	Mrs Margaret Burdett, wife of Nathan B., 59. Typhus fever.
	Oct.	25.	Mr Thomas Houghton, 69. Dropsy.
	Nov.	15.	Mr Jonas Wilder, 58. Dropsy of the heart.
	Dec.	14.	Mr Prudence Robbins, 90. Old age.
		17.	Mrs Lois Bartlett, 84. Old age.

In 1845, 16—115.

| 1846. | Jany. | 9. | Mrs Mary Ann Chandler, 25. Consumption. |

	Jany. 14.	Mr Jonas Whitney, 74. Dropsy.
	30.	Mr Gardner Phelps, 88. Fever.
	March 10.	Julia, daughter of Joel [W.] Phelps, 17 months—lung fever.
	18.	Mr James Bridge, 53. Lung fever.
	28.	Mrs Lucretia Osgood. 91. Old age.
345	April 6.	Mr Hezekiah Davis, 48.
	7.	A child of Jonathan Bowman, 3 months. Lung fever.
	24.	Luther Tarbel, grandson of Tarbel Bancroft, 2 years—lung fever.
	May 12.	Mrs Ann L. Bancroft, 24—child birth.
	June —.	An infant child of James Stone.
	" 18.	Mr Francis Sawyer, 23. Consumption.
	July 9.	Mr Williams Greene, 38. Consumption.
	Aug. 7.	Ellen Sophia Conant, 7. Typhus fever.
	10.	Mr Philip Freeman, 33. Neck broken. [Negro.]
	12.	Sarah Ann Windett, 1 year, bowel complaint.
	19.	Mr Luke Stow, 49 years. Dropsy of the heart.
	Sept. 24.	Miss Sarah Windett. 22. Consumption.
	Oct. 12.	Elizabeth Derby, 3—bowel complaint.
	Nov. 22.	George L. Gibson, 2. Croup.
	28.	Mrs Betsy Rugg, 65. Consumption.
	Dec. 14.	Mrs Ann M. Thurston, 28. Consumption.
	Nov. —.	Mrs —— Barnard, —. Typhus fever.
	Dec. 21.	Mr John White, 78.
346	26.	An infant, child of Mr John Fuller, 3 hours.
	28.	Mr William Townsend, 62. Dropsy. In 1846, 26—141.
1847.	Jan. 1·	Mrs Rebecca Rugg, 79. General infirmity.
	"	Mr Joel I. Rugg, 28. Typhoid fever.
	10.	Mr Jonathan Osgood, 71. Lung fever.
	19.	Miss Elizabeth C. White, 15. Enlarged Kidneys.
	Feb. 11.	Mrs Lucy Eaton, 97. Old age.
	15.	Mrs Abigail H. Stow, 51. Inward tumor.
	19.	Addison Ellis Rugg, 15 months. Influenza.
	24.	Mr Benjamin Chandler, 79. Disease of the heart.
	March 7.	Mr Peter Phelps, 72. Paralysis.
	18.	Miss Parney Howard, 27. Fever.

MARRIAGES NOT FOUND RECORDED IN TOWN BOOKS.

Solemnized before Reverend Nathaniel Thayer.

1822.	Aug. 29.	Mr Otis Boynton of Framingham, to Miss Sarah Wilson of Lancaster.
1825.	May 30.	Rev. Ira T. H. Blanchard to Miss Margaret B. Pearson, both of Harvard.
1827.	Apr. 26.	Mr Thomas H. Clark to Miss Eliza Phelps, both of Shirley.
1829.	June 3.	Mr Joseph Hazen to Miss Ann Longley, both of Shirley.
	Nov. 5.	Mr Thomas Lewis 2ᵈ, to Miss Susan Hapgood, both of Sterling.
1831.	Nov. 3.	Lieutenant John Andrews to Miss Mary Elizabeth Dunton, both of Boylston.
1835.	Apr. 21.	Mr Ephraim L. Roper to Miss Caroline Burpee, both of Sterling.
	Aug. 10.	Mr Liberty D. Bigelow to Miss Harriet A. Lawrence, both of Sutton.
1839.	Apr. 23.	Mr Chandler Carter to Miss Nancy Babcock, both of Berlin.

Before Reverend Edmund H. Sears.

1842.	June 1.	Mr Reuben Emery and Miss Mary Joslyn, both of Holliston.
	July 23.	Mr Thomas Hastings of Ashburnham, and Miss Emma S. Chase of Shirley.

1844. May   8. Mr Noah Humphrey of Barre, to Miss Lucena Wilder of Holliston.
1845. Oct. 19. Mr Charles Grove to Miss Nancy W. Whitney, both of Weston.
       23. Mr Charles Whitney of Fitchburg, to Miss Susan Davis of Lexington.
1846. May 27. Mr George Gleason of Marlboro', to Miss Harriet Burpee of Sterling.
1847. Jan. 31. Mr Joseph Cushing to Miss Mary A. Arnold, both of Fitchburg.

DEACONS.

Twenty-three pages of the first Church Book, and one hundred of the second, are devoted to Votes, Regulations, Councils, etc., not hereinbefore copied. The more important portions of them have already been printed by Reverend Abijah P. Marvin in his History of Lancaster. A list of the Deacons of the First Church, compiled from sundry sources, may, however, appropriately be given here.

The first deacon, and probably the only one before the massacre of 1676, was Roger Sumner. Between 1676 and 1715, no deacon is named in existing records:

Capt. Peter Joslyn,	elected	August 4, 1715, died 1759.
Joseph Wilder, Esq.,	"	" " died March 29, 1757.
Josiah White,	"	January 30, 1729, died May 5, 1772.
James Wilder,	"	" " died May 13, 1739.
Hooker Osgood, Jr.	"	Oct. 1, 1742, resigned Sept. 9, 1761, paralytic.
Israel Houghton,	"	" " resigned Sept. 9, 1761.
Joseph Wilder, Jr.,	"	March 16, 1749, died Feb. 28, 1777.
Joshua Fairbank,	"	" " died Nov. 25, 1769.
Joseph White,	"	Sept. 9, 1761, died Nov. 15, 1780.
David Wilder,	"	Sept. 24, 1761, died Nov. 17, 1776.
Josiah Wilder, Esq.,	"	April 2, 1777, died Dec. 20, 1788.
Capt. Benjamin Houghton,	"	" " died July 31, 1802.
Cyrus Fairbank,	"	" " died Feb. 28, 1801.
Josiah Ballard,	"	Sept., 1781, resigned July 31, 1794, infirm.
John Whiting,	"	Sept. 2, 1789, resigned Oct. 23, 1808, removed from town.
Joseph Wales,	"	July 31, 1794, resigned Aug. 24, 1817, do.
Jonas Lane,	"	April 2, 1801, resigned Mar. 25, 1838, infirm.
Joseph White,	"	Dec. 1, 1802, died July 1, 1806.
Joel Wilder,	"	Oct. 3, 1806, died May 2, 1837.
Benjamin Wyman,	"	July 23, 1809, died Dec. 30, 1826.
Josiah Bridge,	"	Sept. 14, 1817, resigned April 1, 1824, removed from town.
Horatio Carter,	"	April 1, 1824, resigned Jan. 12, 1830. (Swedenborgian.)
Tarbell Bancroft,	"	April 5, 1827, died —— 1872.
James G. Carter,	"	April 18, 1830, suspended July 13, 1832.
Peter Osgood,	"	April 19, 1835, resigned —— 1857.
Silas Sawyer,	"	April 5, 1838, declined serving.
Samuel F. White,	"	April 4, 1839, died March 16, 1843.
William Stearns,	"	Dec. 28, 1843, resigned — 1853, removed to Clinton.

BOOK OF RECORDS

FOR

Yᴇ SECOND CHH. IN LANCASTER.

1744 —

The southern part of the Additional Grant to Lancaster was known by its Indian name, Woonksechocksett — usually abbreviated to Chocksett. There a "second church" was gathered, and Reverend John Mellen was ordained pastor over it December 19, 1744. In the political ferment that preceded the rebellion against monarchy, all the pulpits about Lancaster were shaken, and Mr. Mellen's was overturned. A long and bitter wrangle, the details of which occupy about half the pages of the church book, resulted in dismissal of the pastor, November 14, 1774. He served in the relations of minister to the less radical members of the parish, until after its incorporation as a town with the name Sterling, April 25, 1781. Reverend Reuben Holcomb was ordained over the church June 2, 1779. Both Mr. Mellen's and Mr. Holcomb's returns of Lancaster marriages appear on previous pages, as copied into the town's book. If Mr. Mellen kept a record of deaths, it was probably given in to the town-clerks from time to time, but no death list of his appears in the church book.

The records of the Second, or West Precinct Church, open with the usual covenant, the subscribers to which, eighteen in number, were:

John Mellen, Pastor	Jonathan Bayley	Reuben Rugg
David Osgood	Thomas Burpee	Daniel Powers
Joseph Moors	Edward Newton	Edward Robbins
Jonathan Osgood	Josiah Richardson	William Goss
Benjᵃ. Houghton Jun	Thomas Fairbanks	David Nelson
Josiah Wilder	Oliver Moors	Samuel Bayley.

5 Decembr. 31, 1744. The Brethren of yᵉ Chh met att yᵉ house of Capt. David Osgood, & Voted that members should be admitted into the Chh with yᵉ Consent of yᵉ Brethren upon their giving Satisfaction to yᵉ Pastor & publicly consenting to yᵉ Chh Covenant, without offering a written Profession or Relation of their own.

January 13ᵗʰ, 1744-5 Admitted into yᵉ Chh. yᵉ Several persons whose Names are as follows:

Ebenezer Prescott	Jonath. Nelson	Daniel Robbins
Samuel Gibbs	Jonath. Wilder	Hezekiah Whitcomb
Samuel Sawyer	James Kendal	Jonath. Fairbanks
Shubal Bayley	Josiah Kendal	Jonath. Powers

CHOCKSETT CHURCH.

Benja. Houghton
James Houghton
Joseph Bennet

John Wilder
Benja. Wilder

Samuel Burpee
Thomas Burpee Jun.

Feby: 3ᵈ: 1744-5. Admitted into yᵉ Chh yᵉ Several persons whose Names follow:

Jacob Kilburn
Thomas Ross
Ezekiel Kendal
John Glazier

Zacheus Boynton
Anna Boynton his wife
Samuel Kendal
Phebe Kendal his wife

Ezra Houghton
David Jewett
Esther Jewett his wife,

March 3ᵈ. Admitted into yᵉ Chh — John Snow

March 17ᵗʰ. Admitted into yᵉ Chh. yᵉ Several persons whose names are as follows:

Ephraim Sawyer
Amos Rugg
Mary Rugg his wife

Isaac Kilburn
Mary Houghton yᵉ wife of James Houghton
Abigail Wilder yᵉ wife of John Wilder

7 March 18ᵗʰ, 1744-5 Att a Chh Meeting callᵈ. for yᵉ Election of Deacons. Choice was made of our Brother Jonathan Osgood for yᵉ first Deacon & our Brother Oliver Moores for yᵉ Second. And Voted that these were sufficient for yᵉ chhs Service att present.

Likewise voted yᵗ yᵉ Communion Table sh'ld be furnished by a free Contribution, for yᵗ purpose.

April 7ᵗʰ: A Free Collection was made of upwards of five & twenty pounds for yᵉ purpose above sᵈ.

April 21ˢᵗ: Admitted into yᵉ Chh. yᵉ two persons following, namly: James Ross, Esther Glazier yᵉ wife of Jo. Glazier.

May 5ᵗʰ, 1745. The holy ordinance of ye Lord's Supper was Celebrated yᵉ first time in this chh of Christ. Att wch. time was admitted: Mary Bayley yᵉ wife of Moses Bayley. Also received into our Communion from yᵉ 1ˢᵗ. Chh in Rowley: John Crosby, Dorcas Kilburn and Elisabeth Burpee, yᵉ wives of Jacob
8 Kilburn & Samˡˡ. Burpee. Also received into our Communion from yᵉ 2ᵈ Chh. in Rowley: Anna Burpee, yᵉ wife of Thomas Burpee Jun. The Sacrament of yᵉ Lord's Supper is administered every eighth week.

July 7ᵗʰ, 1745. Att wch. time yᵉ Sacrament of yᵉ Lord's Supper was again administered, admitted into yᵉ chh. Gamaliel Beman; also Rec'ved yᵉ relation of yᵉ several persons following from yᵉ first chh of Christ in Lancaster:

The widow Anna Sawyer.
The wife of Thomas Burpee.
The wife of John Snow.

The wife of Jonathan Powers.
The wife of James Ross.

Decembr. yᵉ 15, 1745. Admitted into yᵉ chh. Rachel yᵉ wife of our Brother Hezekiah Whitcomb. Also Recevd into our Communion Jacob Barrett from yᵉ first chh of Christ in Reading.

April yᵉ 6ᵗʰ, 1746. Receivd into our Communion Abigail yᵉ wife of Joseph Wheler, from yᵉ First chh of Christ in Cambridge.

9 June 1ˡ: 1746. Received into our Communion Hannah yᵉ wife of Thomas Dole from yᵉ first Chh of X in Newbury.

July 27. Admitted into this Chh Tilley Wilder & his wife; also Receivd into our Communion Rebeckah yᵉ wife of our Brother Jacob Bennett from yᵉ first chh in Woburn.

Sepʳ 21ˢᵗ. Admitted into this chh Joshua Wilder & his wife.

Novemb. 9. admitted Martha Thompson yᵉ wife of Simon Thompson.

Decemb: 7: admitted Simon Thompson into this chh.

May 3ᵈ, 1747, admitted into this Chh. Aaron Dresser & his wife.

October 18. 1747, admitted Esther the wife of Jacob Smith.

June 19, 1748 admitted Dorothy yᵉ wife of Jonathan Nelson.

July 17. 1748 admitted Ebenezer Prescot Junʳ. & his wife to Communion.

July 24, admitted Jonathan Prescot & his wife.

Octo. 23, 1748, admitted Jeremiah Burpee & his wife.

Decembʳ. 18. Receivd John Brooks into our Communion from yᵉ first Chh. in Wobourn, and Lydia wife of James Kendal.

10 January 22, 1748-9. Admitted yᵉ Wife of Moses Cooper.

Feb: 12 Admitted into our Communion from yᵉ first Chh. in Lancaster yᵉ wife of Capt. David Osgood, Eunice.

Nov*. 19, 1749 Receivd into Communion y* following persons: Ebenezer Burpee & Wife & y* Wife of Jno. Brooks.
May 13, 1750 Admitted Rachel Wheeler to Com*.
July 8, 1750 Admitted to Communion y* following persons. Joseph Palmer, Philip Goss & Wife, Benja Glazier & Wife.
Sep^r: 2 Admitted to Communion. Saul Houghton & Wife, Ezekiel Newton & Wife
Nov^r: 4. Admitted to Communion, the Wife of Jonathan Wilder, Zerviah, the Wife of Ezra Houghton, Dinah, & the Widow Sarah Steward.
Decemb^r. 30, 1750. Admitted Elizabeth Blowers.
April 21, 1751. Admitted Mary y* Wife of Daniel Powers, and Hannah y* Wife of Ezekiel Kendall.
11 Augt. 18, 1751. Admitted Rezina Wilder y* Daughter of Joshua Wilder.
Dec^r: 8th: 1751 Admitted Abner Wilder & Wife.
March 29, 1752 Admitted John Fairbank & Wife.
July 19. Admitted Phinehas Beman.
Sepr. 24. Admitted Joseph Kilbourn & Wife.
Jany. 21, 1753. Admitted Sarah y* wife of Hezekiah Walker.
Decr. 16, 1753. Admitted Abigail wife of Jonathan Bayley.
April 7, 1754. Admitted Nathan Burpee (Son of Thomas Burpee) and his Wife
May 8. Admitted Nathl. Wright & Sam^{ll}. Thurston & Wife.
Augt. 25. Admitted Amity y* Wife of Jonath Gary.
Sepr. 22. Admitted John Whitcomb & Susanna his Wife, also Mary Newton.
Novr. 17. Admitted Stephen Choat & Wife.
May 4, 1755 Nathan Burpee & Wife.
Augt. 31. Admitted Asa Wilder & Wife.
12 Decr. 14, 1755. Admitted Elisha Sawyer, Prudence Rugg & Lydia Glazier.
March 14. 1756. Admitted Nathl Wilder Junr. & Wife.
May 30. Admitted Ruben Wheler.
July 25. Admitted Sarah Bennet.
Augt 8. Admitted Dinah Beman.
Novemb. 14. Admitted Sam^{ll}. Prentice & Wife.
January 9. 1757. Admitted y* following persons, viz: Eph^m. Sawyer Junr. & Wife & Phinehas Wilder & Wife.
March 6, 1757. Admitted Israel Moores & Wife & Prudence Moores.
April 10, 1757. Admitted Jabez Brooks & Wife.
May 1st, 1757. Admitted Sam^{ll}. Snow.
Octob: 15, 1757. Admitted Sam^d. Burpee Junr. & Wife.
13 Augt. 30, 1758. Dismis^d. Deacon Joseph Moores from his office by a vote of y* Chh, after Lecture, agreable to his Desire. At y* same time voted that Elijah Houghton Shold be y* Chorister or Psalm Setter for y* present.
Sept: 3^d. Admitted Mary y* Wife of James Cowey.
Sepr. 24. Admitted Dinah y* Wife of Moses Sawyer.
Octo: 1st Admitted Sibillah y* wife of Amos Powers.
Octo. 29. Admitted y* Widow Mary Wilder, also John Farrar & wife.
Decr. 24. Admitted Jonath: Osgood Junr. & Wife.
June 3, 1759. Admitted Eph^m. Boynton & wife from y* Chh of X in Chester.
June 10. Admitted Elisha Wilder.
Augt. 26, 1759. Admitted y* followin persons. Elijah Houghton, Wid; Priscilla Houghton, Mehitabel Dresser & Eunice Houghton.
14 Octo 21, 1759. Admitted: Moses Burpee & wife; Jabez Fairbanks & wife; Wife of David Nelson, Hannah; Wife of Joseph Bayley, Lydia; Oliver Osgood.
Decr. 16. Admitted David Osgood & wife, & Abigail Conquet.
Feb. 6, 1760 After Lecture made choice of Cap^n: Asa Whitcomb for another Deacon.
Feb. 10. Admitted John Brooks Junr. & wife, also y* wife of Joseph Stewart.
April 13, 1760. Admitted Lemuel Houghton & wife.
July 27. Admitted y* wife of James May.
Novemb^r. 2. Admitted Tilley Littlejohns & Wife.
Decr. 28, 1760, Admitted wife of Jonathan Osgood.

CHOCKSETT CHURCH. 377

March 22, 1761. Admitted y⁰ wife of Thos. Sawyer, the wife of Phinehas Beman & the wife of Jesse Ross.
May 17ᵗʰ, 1761. Admitted William Brown.
Novʳ; 8, 1761. Admitted Abigail y⁰ wife of Josiah Fairbank from y⁰ first Chh in Lancaster.
Decʳ. 20, 1761 Admitted Hezekiah Whitcomb & wife.
March 28, 1762. Admitted Catharine y⁰ wife of Israel Moores.
15 April 18. Admitted Josiah Osgood & Wife.
May 23. Admitted Prudence Brown & Elis: Houghton.
July 18. Admitted Joseph Willoughby & wife and Priscilla Jewet.
Sepʳ. 12 1762 Admitted John Boynton & Thomas Ross Junr. & wife.
Jany. 2, 1763 Admitted Eleanor Ball & Eunice Bennet.
April 17. Admitted Wife of Wᵐ. Judevine.
July 10. Admitted Josiah Houghton, Elizabeth & Anna Rugg.
Octo: 2, 1763 Admitted Joel Houghton & wife
Decr. 25, 1763. Admitted Wife of Ezra Sawyer Junr.
March 11, 1764 Admitted Wife of Fortune Eager, also received Ephraim Boynton from y⁰ Chh in Rowley.
Augᵗ: 12. Admitted Nathˡˡ. Houghton & Wife.
Sepr- 23. Admitted y⁰ Wife of Jonathan Kendal.
Jan: 20, 1765. Admitted Thos. Brooks & Wife
April 21. Admitted Daniel Robbins & Wife.
June 16. Admitted Josiah Winn & Wife, also Joseph Fairbanks & Wife.
Augᵗ. 11. Admitted Tilly Richardson & Wife, Jonathan Whetcomb & Wife and Jonathan Wilder Junr & Wife.
16 Octoʳ. 6, 1765 Admitted John Loring & Wife. also chose y⁰ four Deacons to receive & give a Receipt to y⁰ Executor for y⁰ 200 ₤ old tenor given by Sebastian Smith for purchasing two Silver Tankards for y⁰ Communion Table.
Octʳ. 23. The Chh met according to public appointment and voted that they were not dissatisfied with the Pastor on account of a Complaint exhibited by Josiah Kendal. also voted to dismiss y⁰ Complaint.
17 Feb: 2, 1766 Admitted John Brown & Abijah Worster.
March 30. Admitted Widow Mary Spafford.
Jany. 14, 1767 Chose our Brother Joseph Kilborn, Deacon.
18ᵗʰ Admitted the Wife of Joseph Bennet.
March 15. Admitted Abijah Kendal.
Octobr. 25. Admitted Wife of Samˡˡ. Hancock.
May 22 1768 Admitted Wife of John Boynton.
June 8. Lecture The Chh voted to buy a Clock for y⁰ meeting house, with George Bush's money, ₤6.
Augᵗ. 7 Admitted Bartholomew Peirson & Wife.
Decʳ. 4. Admitted Silas Fairbanks & Wife.
March 26, 1769. Admitted Richard Rand & Wife.
June 4. Admitted Wife of John Glazier, also Samuel Sawyer Junr & wife.
July 30. Admitted Eliphalet Rogers.
May 24. 1770. The Chh. met by appointment, and the Chh. having receiv'd further Intelligence of the Design of George Bush in his Gift of Six pounds to this Chh; they voted to purchas a Silver Vessel for the Comⁿ: Table instead of a Clock, with it, as being more agreable to y⁰ Donor's Intention.
18 Voted that the money sh'd be laid out for the afore mentioned purpose as soon as may be with convenience.
Voted that the Pastor & Deacons be the Committee to procure said Vessel. Josiah Kendal had full Liberty allowed him to offer what he pleased in Reference to a Complaint he formerly Exhibited, & in regard to what the Chh did upon it. The Chh conversed upon the manner of singing the Divine Praises in public, but came to no vote upon it.
July 1, 1770. Admitted Henry Wyman & Wife.
16 Augᵗ: 22, 1770 The Chh met & voted that y⁰ use of y⁰ pitch pipe & taking y⁰ pitches, & keeping time by swinging y⁰ hand in public worship was not acceptable to them. Chose Dea. Moores Chorister in addition to y⁰ former. Voted that they were not willing to sing Dr. Watts' Hymns, together with y⁰ New England Version of y⁰ Psalms, part of y⁰ time.

25

March 14, 1771   The Chh met &c adjourned to Monday next.
March 18.   Chh. met upon adjournment; Voted they were still of yᵉ same mind about yᵉ Pitch pipe & taking yᵉ Pitches, and that they were not willing yᵉ Chorister sh'd beat time according to Discretion.
18   Aug: 26   Admitted Pamela Mellen & Elisabeth Whitney.
Octr 14.   Admitted Joshua Sawyer & Wife, also Silas Wilder & Wife.
Sepr: 15, 1771   Admitted Joseph Mores Junr. & Wife.
March 1, 1772   Ephᵐ. Boynton & Wife from yᵉ Chh in Winchendon.
May 3 1772   Admitted Joseph Wheler from yᵉ Chh in Concord.
19   1772.   July 9.   The Chh met & voted that they were in Charity with yᵉ Chh of Christ in Bolton.
Augᵗ. 22, 1772   Admitted John Mellen Junr. my Son also Mary Hedly.
Nov. 1   Admitted Wife of John Bayly—Oliver Fairbanks & Wife, & Wife of John Moors.

*   *   *   *   *

143   Decʳ: 5, 1773   Admitted Joseph Lewis from yᵉ Chh in Truro.
June 26, 1774   Admitted Wife of Ephm. Willard Junr.
Augᵗ. 14, 1774   Admitted my Daughter Rebecca.
Octr. 6, 1774   Admitted Wife of William Tompson.
Decr. 25, 1774.   Admitted Obediah Groce & wife also yᵉ wife of Joseph House.
Feb. 19, 1775.   Admitted Moses Bayly.
Jany. 14, 1776   Admitted my Daughter Sophia.
Augᵗ 25, 1776   Admitted Moses Gerrish also Prudence Houghton.

*   *   *   *   *   *

139   DISMISSION OF MEMBERS.

Novr. 26, 1752.   Dismisd & recommended Mr Joseph Palmer to yᵉ Second Chh of X in Norton in order to his Ordination to yᵉ pastoral office there.
August 5, 1753.   Dismisd & recommended Edward Robbins to yᵉ Communion of yᵉ first Chh. in Lancaster.
Augᵗ. 8, 1756.   Dismisd & recommended Joshua Wilder to yᵉ Communion of yᵉ Chh. of X in Cold Spring.
Augᵗ. 5, 1759.   Dismisd & recommended Wᵐ. Goss to yᵉ Chh. in Shrewsbury North, and John Fairbank & Wife to yᵉ Chh. in Pequog.
April 27, 1760.   Dismisd. & recomᵈ. Edward Newton to yᵉ 2 Chh. in Shrewsbury.
Sepr. 28, 1760.   Dismisd & recomᵈ. Ebenʳ. Prescot Junʳ & Wife to lie in yᵉ foundation of yᵉ Chh at Roxbury Canada.
Octo: 5 1760.   Dismisd. & recomᵈ. John Farrar & Wife to be admitted into yᵉ Chh. to be gathered in Roxbury Canada.
March 22: 1761   Dismisd & recommended Philip Goss to the Chh of Christ in Roxbury Canada.   Dismisd also soon after yᵉ Wife of sᵈ Philip to sd Chh.
Decr. 9, 1762   Dismisᵈ. & recommended Ephraim Boynton & Wife to Ipswich Canada to lie in yᵉ foundation of yᵉ Chh. there, under Mr Stimson.
140   Decʳ: 9, 1762   Dismisd. also & recommended Joseph Willoughby & Wife to Roxbury Canada.
April 15, 1764.   Dismisd & recommended Stephen Choat & Wife to the Chh in New Ipswich.
August 26, 1764.   Dismisd. & recommended, in order to lie in yᵉ foundation of yᵉ Chh. at Princetown: Tilly Littlejohns & Wife & Elisha Wilder & Wife.
June 8, 1766.   Chh voted to Dismiss & recommend to the Chh of Christ in Westminster: Lemuel Houghton & Wife, & Priscilla Wife of Seth Harrington.
Dec. 4. 1768.   Dismisd John Brown & recommended to the Chh in Charlemont.
March 3, 1771.   Dismisd. Nathˡ Wilder to lie in yᵉ foundation of the Chh at Monadnock No: 4.
March 24, 1771   Dismisd Abijah Kendal to yᵉ Chh. in Templeton, also Wife of Jesse Ross to New Marlboro' so calld.
May 9, 1773.   Dismisd & recommended to yᵉ Chh in Westminster Wife of Joseph Bayly.

141 Octr: 16, 1774 Dismisd James Ross & Wife, Jonathan Osgood & Wife, & John Crosby to lie in y⁰ foundation of a Chh at Irvinshire.

April 27, 1777 Dismisd & recommended Tilly Wilder & Wife to y⁰ Chh of Christ in New Fane, in New York Government.

Octr: 25, 1778 Dismisd & recommended Abigail Hancock to y⁰ Chh in Barre.

Novr. 1, 1778 Dismisd & recommended Sam¹. Prentice to y⁰ Chh in Winchendon.

171   A Record of Baptisms, 1744— J. Mellen.

Decembr: 30ᵗʰ. 1744. Baptis'd y⁰ child of Jonathan Osgood nam'd Asenath.

January 6ᵗʰ: 1745. Baptis'd y⁰ child of William Densmoor named Elisabeth. Jany: 13 Baptisd y⁰ child of Amos Rugg nam'd Amos. Jany; 20ᵗʰ. The Revd Mr Prentice of Lancaster Baptis'd in this chh. y⁰ children of John Wilder nam'd.—Moses, Prudence, Dinah, Sarah, Batrix.

Feb. 17, 1745. Baptis'd y⁰ child of Lieut: Joseph Moores nam'd Rebecca; the Children of Jonathan Wilder nam'd Josiah & Jonathan; the Children of Samuel Kendal nam'd Samuel, Rebecca. Feb: 24. Baptis'd y⁰ child of Aaron Dresser, nam'd Jedediah.

March 3ᵈ: 1745 Baptis'd y⁰ child of Zacheus Boynton nam'd Sarah; also y⁰ child of Thomas Burpee Junr. nam'd Stephen. March 10ᵗʰ. Baptis'd y⁰ child of Ezekiel Kendal nam'd Abijah; also y⁰ child of Isaac Kilburn nam'd Aaron; also y⁰ child of Timothy Ross nam'd Elisabeth.

April 14 Baptis'd y⁰ child of Josiah Wilder, Prudence; also y⁰ child of Thomas Ross nam'd Anna.

May 12ᵗʰ. Baptis'd y⁰ child of Samuel Bayley nam'd Susanna; also y⁰ child of Elisha Sawyer nam'd Jotham. May 26. Baptisd y⁰ child of Samˡˡ. Burpee nam'd Phoebe; also y⁰ child of William Goss nam'd Jonas.

June 16ᵗʰ. Baptis'd y⁰ child of Thomas Dole, Benjamin; also two Adult persons nam'd George, molatto, London negro of Joseph Moores.

July 9ᵗʰ: Baptis'd y⁰ child of David Jewet nam'd Esther. July 21ˢᵗ, 1745 Bap-
173 tiz'd y⁰ child of Amos Rugg namd Elisabeth; July 28. Baptizd y⁰ child of Moses Bayley namd Mary; also y⁰ child of Phinehas Beman namd Elisabeth.

August 18ᵗʰ. Baptizd y⁰ child of Josiah Cook, Israel.

Octoʳ. 6ᵗʰ. Baptizd y⁰ child of Jonath: Bigelow named Sarah. Octʳ. 20ᵗʰ. Baptizd y⁰ child of James Ross, Abigail.

Novembʳ. 23. Baptizd y⁰ child of Jacob Smith, Mary.

Decembʳ. 8ᵗʰ. Baptizd y⁰ child of Jonathan Wilder, Zurvia. Decembr. 15 Baptizd y⁰ child of John Farrar, Elisabeth. Decembʳ. 29ᵗʰ. Baptizd y⁰ child of Jacob Bennett, Joshua.

January the 5, 1746. Baptizd y⁰ children of Benj. Wilder namd as follows: Benjamin, Jane, Mercy, Hepsabeth, Achsah. January 20ᵗʰ. Baptizd y⁰ child of Thomas Sawyer, James.

Feby. y⁰ 2ᵈ: Baptizd y⁰ child of Josiah Richardson, Eunice. Feby y⁰ 16ᵗʰ
174 1745-6. Baptizd y⁰ child of Timothy Ross, named Elisabeth.

March 2ᵈ Baptizd y⁰ child of John Goss, Joseph. March 30ᵗʰ, 1746. Baptiz'd y⁰ child of Jonathan Bayley, namd Hannah.

April 6ᵗʰ. Baptizd y⁰ child of Jonathan Fairbanks, Joshua; also y⁰ child of Edward Robbins, Jotham. April 20ᵗʰ. Baptisd y⁰ child of Deacon Oliver Moores nam'd Hannah; also y⁰ child of John Snow, Hannah; also y⁰ child of Isaac Kilburn namd Jacob. April 27ᵗʰ: Baptizd y⁰ child of Phinehas WIllard namd Elisabeth.

May y⁰ 4ᵗʰ: Baptizd y⁰ child of Deacon Jonathan Osgood namd Asenath.

June y⁰ 8ᵗʰ. Baptizd y⁰ child of Ezekiel Kendal namᵈ Aaron. June 15ᵗʰ: Baptizd y⁰ child of Josiah Wilder, Sarah.

July 20. Baptizd y⁰ child of Samuel Kendal, Abigail. July 27 Baptiz'd y⁰ child of Tilly Wilder, Persis; also Daniel Priests nam'd Elisabeth.

Augᵗ: 17. Baptizd y⁰ child of Ruben Rugg, Sarai.

175 Octr. 12, 1746. Baptizd y⁰ Children of Joshua Wilder nam'd Joshua, Abel, Rezina, Sarai, Phebe, Mary, Damaris.

Novemb. 9ᵗʰ. Baptisd Martha Thompson, yᵉ Wife of Simon Thompson; also yᵉ child of Phinehas Beman nam'd Lemuel.
Decemb: 7. Baptis'd Simon Thompson; also yᵉ child of John Glazier nam'd Ruth. Decemb: 21 Baptisd yᵉ child of David Osgood Capt: named Elisabeth.
January 18. Baptisd yᵉ child of Asa Whitcomb, Eunice.
March 8. Baptisd yᵉ child of John Crosby, namd Jonathan. March 15. Baptisd yᵉ child of Samuel Bayley, Isaac. March 22. Baptisd yᵉ child of Amos Rugg namd Amos.
April 5ᵗʰ, the Child of William Goss, Reuben. April 19, the Child of Jacob Smith, Thomas. April 26, the Child of Jonathan Powers nam'd Lucy.
May 3ᵈ the Child of Moses Bayley nam'd Persis; also yᵉ child of David Nelson, Solomon. May 10ᵗʰ, the Child of Tilly Wilder named Elisabeth. May 24 the Child of Benjamin Wilder namd Rebecca.
176 June 7ᵗʰ, 1747 Baptis'd yᵉ Child of Thomas Fairbanks, Silas; the Child of David Jewet, Hannah; the Child of Jacob Barret, Rebecca. June 21, the Child of Ezra Sawyer nam'd John; of Thomas Ross nam'd Ebenezer; of James Kendall, Peirson.
July 5. Baptis'd yᵉ Child of Jonathan Nelson, Dorothy; the Child of Thomas Dole, Sarai. July 12ᵗʰ. Baptisd yᵉ Children of Simon Thompson named Benjamin, William, Samuel, Isaac, Ebenezer, Elisabeth, Jerusha, Relief; also the Child of Amos Jewet nam'd Ann. July 19, the Child of Isaac Kilburn nam'd Sarai.
August 2ᵈ, the Children of Elisha Sawyer, Elias & Thankful, Twins. August 15, the Child of William Dunsmoor, Joseph. August 23, the Child of Joseph Moores, Relief.
Sepr. 6, the Child of Asa Whitcomb, Ephraim.
Octo: 11, the Child of Ebenezer Bigelow, Ebenezer.
Novʳ. 22, the Child of Aaron Sawyer, Luke.
177 Decemb 13, the Child of Josiah Ballard, Sarai.
April 3ᵈ, 1748, the Child of Samˡˡ Sawyer, Martha; also yᵉ Child of Jonathan Powers, Silas; also of Josiah Houghton, Mehitabil. April 10ᵗʰ, the Child of Jonathan Wilder, Silas. April 17, the Child of John Books, Samuel. April 28, the Child of Nathˡ Wright, Martha.
May 15, the Child of Samˡˡ Kendall, Caleb. May 22 Child of Aaron Dresser, John.
June 19 Child of Jonathan Fairbanks, Jonathan. June 26 Child of Josiah Richardson, Lucy; also of Josiah Wilder, Rufus.
July 17, the Child of Zacheus Boynton, John; also of Ebenezer Prescot Junʳ, Josiah. July 24. Baptis'd yᵉ Child of Jonathan Prescot, Hiram.
Sepr. 25. The Child of Josiah Kendall, Ethan.
Oct. 16 Child of James Ross, John. Octo. 23. The Child of Deacon Jonath: Osgood, Sarah; also yᵉ Child of David Nelson, Mary.
Novʳ 6. The Child of John Bayley, Mary; & Jeremiah Burpee, Molly. Novʳ:
178 6ᵗʰ: 1748 Received into Covenant & Baptis'd Jonathan Goss.
Decembr: 4ᵗʰ. The Child of Thomas Sawyer, Abigail. Decembr: 18. The Child of Timothy Ross, Levi.
Feby: 26, 1748–9 The Child of Abner Sawyer, Relief.
March 5ᵗʰ: The Child of Jacob Barrett, Joshua.
May 7, 1749 Child of Tilly Wilder, Tilly. May 21 The Child of Reuben Rugg, Damaris. May 28. Baptis'd yᵉ Child of Josiah Brown, Elisabeth.
June 11. The Child of Deacon Joseph Moore, Joseph; also of Isaac Kilbourn, Elisabeth. June 18. The Child of Ezekiel Kendal, Joseph. June 25. The Child of Asa Whitcomb, Abigail.
July 9. Child of Ezra Houghton, Dinah. July 16 Child of David Jewet, David. July 23 Children of Ezra Sawyer nam'd Manassah; & Thomas Dole, nam'd John.
Sepʳ. 10 The Children of Moses Cooper, Leonard, Ruth, Phebe. Sepr. 17. Revᵈ Mr Morse Baptisd yᵉ Children of Thomas Ross, William, & of Amos Rugg, Mary.
179 Octo. 15ᵗʰ 1749 Revᵈ: Mr Davis Baptisd yᵉ Child of John Crosby nam'd Hannah.

CHOCKSETT CHURCH.

Nov; 19. Baptisd y⁰ Child of Ebenr: Buss, Hannah.
Jany: 7 1749-50 The Child of John Glazier, Elisabeth.
Feb: 18, 1749-50 The Child of Sam¹¹. Kendall, Bartholomew.
March 11, 1749-50 The Child of David Nelson, Sarah. March 25, 1750 Baptisd y⁰ Children of Elisha Sawyer, Ruth; of Jacob Smith, Asa.
April 1. Baptisd y⁰ Child of Jonathan Powers, Ephraim; y⁰ Child of Jonathan Nelson, Joseph; y⁰ Child of Nath¹ Wright, James. April 8. Baptisd y⁰ Children of Daniel Allen, Henry, Lydia. April 14ᵗʰ. Child of Simon Tompson nam'd Jonathan.
May 20. Child of Jacob Barret, Joseph. May 27. The Child of Josiah Wilder, Josiah.
June 10. Child of Jonath: Prescot, Jonathan. June 17. The Child of Oliver Moores, Thankful.
July 1ˢᵗ The Children of John Steward, John, Jane. July 8, 1750 Baptisd y⁰ Child of Philip Goss, John, and y⁰ Child of Benjamin Glazier, Benjamin, July 15 The Child of Zachariah Harvey, Rachel, and of Sam¹¹ Bayley, Abigail.
Augᵗ: 12 Baptisd y⁰ Child of Jeremiah Burpee, Moses. Augᵗ. 26. The Child of Phinehas Beman, Jonas.
Sepr. 2ᵈ Baptisd Sarah Douglas, Adult, and y⁰ Child of Wᵐ Dunsmoor, Ruth; of Isaac Kilburn, Joanna; of Saul Houghton, Mary; & of Ezekiel Newton, Dorothy. Septemr: 9, 1750 Baptisd my own Child, Pamela; Likewise y⁰ Child of Sam¹¹ Sawyer, Elisabeth. Sepr. 23 The Child of Moses Bayley, Jonas.
Ocfo: 7. Baptisd Elisabeth Blowers, Adult.
Novr: 18 Baptisd y⁰ Children of y⁰ Widow Sarah Steward, Solomon, Sarah.
January 27 1750-1 Child of Aaron Dresser, Elijah; also Child of Asa Whitcomb, Rebecca.
Feb: 17. Child of David Jewet, Phoebe. Feb. 24, 1750-1 Child of John Brooks, Parnee.
March 17. 1750-1 Child of Josiah Brown nam'd Ruhamah; Jonathan Wilder, Martha; Tilly Wilder, Mary; Ephraim Willard, Israel. March 24 Child of Sam¹¹ Kendall, Caleb.
April 28, 1751 The Child of Jonath: Osgood, Mary; also Child of Philip Goss, Nathaniel.
May 5ᵗʰ Baptisd y⁰ Child of Hezekiah Walker, Hezekiah. May 19 Baptisd y⁰ Child of James Ross; Ephraim.
June 16 Child of Jonath: Fairbanks, Lemuel. June 23. Child of Joshua Wilder, Nathanael.
July 7 The Child of John Snow, Elisabeth. July 28. Child of Zacheus Boynton, Ephraim.
Augᵗ: 11 The Child of Thomas Sawyer, Sarah. Augᵗ. 26 Child of Amos Jewet, Samuel.
Sepr. 8. The Child of John Farrar, Daniel. Septembr 22 The Child of Thomas Fairbanks, Oliver. Sepr. 29 Child of Josiah Richardson, Catharine.
Octobr: 6 Child of Ebenezer Bigelow, Hephsebah.
Novm. 3ᵈ The Child of David Nelson, Elisabeth, and Amos Rugg, Stephen.
Novʳ. 1751. Child of Isaac Kilburn, Jacob.
Decr. 8ᵗʰ, 1751 Child of Abner Wilder, Prudence. Decr 29 The Child of Ann Sawyer, Mary.
Feb: 23, 1752 Baptisd y⁰ Child of Jacob Barret, Nathan; also the Child of Jacob Smith, Mary.
March 8, 1752 Child of Josiah Houghton, Hephzibah. March 22 Child of Joseph Moores, Elisabeth. March 29 the Child of Ruben Rugg, Asa; also y⁰ Child of John Fairbanks, Relief.
April 5. Child of Benja: Wilder, Bulah; also Child of Thomas Ross, Hannah; also Child of John Crosby, Levi.
May 10ᵗʰ. Child of Nathanael Wright, Thomas. May 24. Child of Thomas Dole, Jeremiah.
June 28. Baptisd my own Son nam'd John; also y⁰ Child of Josiah Kendall, Esther.

August 16. The Child of Simon Tompson, Asa.
Octobr 15. The Child of Zachariah Harvey, Daniel; also of Jeremiah Burpee, Ebenezer.
183 Nov: 5, 1752. Baptised ye Children of John Hedly namd John, Josiah, Mary; also ye Child of Joseph Kilbourn nam'd Ruth. Novr. 19. The Child of Phinehas Beman, Josiah. Novr. 26. Child of Ezekiel Newton, Ephraim.
Decr. 10 Child of Elisha Sawyer, Martha. Dec. 24. Children of Tilly Wilder, Lydia & Rebecca, Twins.
Jany: 21, 1753. Child of Ebenezer Buss, Eunice.
Feb: 11. The Child of Sam^{ll} Bayley, Isaac. Feb: 18 Child of Jonathan Osgood, Dorothy.
March 18th. Child of Jonathan Nelson, Jonathan. March 4th. Child of Saul Houghton, Joshua.
April 29 Child of Jonath: Wilder, Hannah.
May 6. Child of Ezekiel Kendall, Noah; also of Daniel Allen, Daniel. May 13th. Child of Abijah Moores, Barshebah. May 20 Child of Abner Wilder, Levi. May 27 Child of Josiah Brown, Timothy.
June — Child of Jonath: Prescot, Vashti. June 17, 1753. Baptisd ye Child of **184** Josiah Wilder, Isaac; also of Isaac Kilborn, John.
July 1. Child of Asa Whitcomb, Catharine. July 15. The Child of Stephen Stearns, Mary. July 22 Child of John Glazier, Jonas.
Aug^t: 26 Child of Jonath: Fairbanks, Thankful, & Child of Philip Goss, Sarah.
Sepr. 9. Child of Joshua Wilder, Solomon. Sepr 30 Child of Ephraim Willard, Asubah; also of John Fairbanks, Nahum.
Octo. 7 Child of John Hedly, Elisabeth.
Decr. 9. Baptisd Child of John Farrar, Hannah; also ye Child of John Peirson, Sarah.
Jan; 6, 1754 Child of David Jewet, Stephen.
March 3, 1754 Child of Sam^{ll} Sawyer, Ruth. March 24 Child of Amos Rugg, Solomon. March 31 Child of Jonath: Powers, Manassah; also of David Nelson, David.
April 14 Child of Jacob Smith, Benjamin; also of Nathan Burpee, Asubah.
185 April 21, 1754. Baptisd my own Child, Rebecca.
May 29, 1754. Child of Phinehas Beman, Benjamin; also Hezekiah Walker, Sarah. May 26 Child of James Ross, Prudence.
June 2 Child of Benjamin Wilder, Jacob. June 16 Children of Sam^{ll} Thurston, Priscilla; of David Willard, Martha.
July 6 Children of Aaron Gary, Moses, and Benja: Glazier, Susanna. July 21 Child of Joseph Gary, Lois.
Augt. 4 Child of Thomas Ross, Jonathan; also of John Crosby, Sarah.
Sepr. 1. The Children of Jonath: Gary, Jonathan & Mary. Sepr. 29 The Children of John Whitcomb, Anna & Susanna; also Child of Mary Newton, Submit.
Octo 13. Baptisd ye Child of Nath^{ll} Kendal, William; also Child of Ezra Houghton, Lucy.
Nov^r: 10. Child of Thomas Sawyer, Cornelius; also Child of Jonath: Gary, Phebe.
186 Novr. 24, 1754 Child of Sam^{ll} Thurston, John.
Jan: 5 1755 Baptis'd Child of Tim^y: Ross, Olive. Jan: 19 Child of Stephen Choat, Patience.
March 16, 1755 Child of Josiah Brown, Stanton. March 30 Child of Lieut Asa Whitcomb, Hannah.
April 6. Child of Ezekiel Kendall, Elisabeth; also Child of Josiah Houghton, Bethesda. April 13 Baptis'd ye Children of Joseph Motes, Calvin; Abner Sawyer, Olive; Eben^r: Buss, Abigail. April 20. Child of John Whitcomb, Anna.
May 4 Child of Zachariah Harvey, Darius, & Child of Thomas Dole, Elijah. May 18 Child of Dorchester Negro nam'd Margaret. May 29 Child of John Fairbanks, John.
June 1. Child of Tilly Wilder, Lucy; also Child Isaac Kilborn, Isaac. June 22 Child of Abijah Moor, Tamar.
July 13 Child of Jonath Wilder, Calvin.

187 Augt: 10: 1755 Baptis'd Child of Daniel Allen, Obadiah.
Octo: 12. Child of Eben^r: Prescot, Benjamin. Octo 19 Child of Jeremiah Burpee, Jeremiah.
Novr 9 Child of Joseph Kilbourn, Joseph.
Decr 7. Child of Jonath: Gary, Nathan. Decr. 28 Child of Jonath: Fairbanks, Seth; Child of Phinehas Beman, Mary; Child of Nathan Burpee, Martha; & Child of Asa Wilder, Reuben.
January 25, 1756. Baptisd my own Child, Sophia; also Child of David Jewet, Hannah.
Feb: 29. Child of David Willard, David.
March 20. Child of John Brooks, Elisabeth; Child of Ephraim Willard, Lois; Child of John Bayley, Ephraim.
188 April 25, 1756 Twins of Nathl: Wright, Thomas & Ephraim; Child of Isaac Kilborn, Elisabeth; Child of Jonathan Prescot, Joanna; Child of Nath^ll Wilder Jr., Timothy.
May 23 Child of Josiah Wilder, Martha.
June 6 Child of Amos Rugg, Phoebe. June 13 Child of Nathan Burpee Junr., Elijah. June 27 Child of John Pearson, Josiah.
July 11 Child of John Headly, Charles; Child of Dorchester Negro, Ishmael.
Augt: 8 Baptisd Dinah Beman, Adult. Augt: 29 Child of Joseph Gary, Joseph; also of Daniel Robbins, Hannah.
Octo: 3 Child of Benja Wilder, Anna. Octo: 17 Child of Widow Lydia Glazier, Ebenezer.
Novemb. 14 Child of Sam^ll Prentice, Prudence.
189 Decr. 5 Child of Abner Wilder, David. Decr. 19 Child of Josiah Brown, Rebecca.
Jany: 16, 1757 Children of Ephraim Sawyer Junr., Ephraim, Dorothy. Jany: 30 Child of Ephraim Sawyer Junr., Josiah.
Feb: 20 Child of Sam^ll Thurston, Judith, and Child of Stephen Choat, William. Feb: 27 Child of Ezekiel Kendall, David.
March 20 Child of John Fairbanks, Samuel.
April 10 Child of Ezra Houghton, Prudence, & Child of Saul Houghton, David.
May 1: Child of Asa Wilder, Elijah. May 22 Child of Abner Sawyer, Prudence. May 29 Child of Joseph Kilborn, Timothy; also Child of Jabez Brooks, Lucy Cutter.
June 12 Child of Daniel Allen, Salmon. June 19 Child of Jacob Smith, Esther; also of Thomas May, Benjamin.
190 July 3, 1757 Child of Phinehas Beman, Elisha, & of Sam^ll Kendall, Phoebe. July 10 Children of John McBride, John & Mary; also ye Child of Isaac Eveleth, William. July 17 Child of Israel Moores, Oliver. July 31. Child of Josiah Houghton, Bethesda; also of Thomas May, Thomas.
Sepr: 18 Child of Elisha Sawyer, Thomas; also of Joseph Gary, Ruth.
Octo: 30 Baptisd my own Son, Henry.
Nov^r: 6 Child of Philip Goss, Philip.
Decr: 4 Child of Asa Hill, Betty, & of John Crosby, Levi. Decr: 25. Child of Nath^ll. Wilder Junr., Lydia.
Jan: 15 1758 Child of Uriah Holt, Annis; also of Ezekiel Newton, Asubah. Jan: 29 Child of Jeremiah Burpee, Ebenezer.
Feb: 5 Child of Sam^ll Burpee Junr., Hannah. Feb: 12 Child of Daniel Robbins, Mary.
191 Ap^l. 2^d 1758. Twins of David Willard, Jonathan & Rebecca. April 9 Child of John McBride, Anna; also Child of Jonathan Prescot, Peter. April 16. Child of Asa Whitcomb, Mary. April 23 Child of Dorchester Negro, David.
June 25 Child of Eben^r Prescot, Ebenezer. June 28. Wednesday, preached a Lecture at Rutland East Wing & Baptisd the Child of Zachariah Harvey, Isaiah; the Child of Peter Goodens, Hopestill; the Child of Abijah Moores, Abijah.
July 2^d Child of Sam^ll. Prentice, Anna. July 16. Child of Nath^ll Wright, Joseph.
Aug^t: 13. Child of Abner Wilder, Levi.
Sepr. 3 Child of Amos Rugg, Stephen; of James Richardson, Relief; of James

Cowey, John. Sepr: 24 Baptisd ye Children of Moses Sawyer, Paul, Judith, Ruth.
192 Octo. 1st: Baptisd ye child of John May Junr., John. Octo: 29, the Child of John Farrar, John.
Nov^r: 12. Child of Elisha Sawyer, Beatrix. Nov^r: 26 Child of David Nelson, Nathan; Child of Nathan Burpee, Mary; Child of Israel Moores, Betty.
Dec^r: 3. Child of Amos Powers, Thankful. Dec^r: 10 Child of Phinehas Beman, David. Decr. 24. Child of Sam^{ll}. Burpee Junr., Nathan. Dec^r: 31. Child of Sam^{ll}. Thurston, Silas.
Feb: 5, 1759 Child of Phin^s: Wilder, Adam.
March 26. Child of Benj: Wilder, at his house, Submit.
April 22. Child of Aaron Geary, Oliver, & Child of Eph^m. Willard, Joshua.
Apr: 29 Child of Jabez Brooks, Eunice.
May 6 Child of Jona: Fairbanks, William. May 20. Child of Nathan Eager, Zerobabel.
June 3. Child of Eben^r Buss, Lucy. June 10 Baptisd Elisha Wilder, Adult; also Child of John Crosby, Zervia; also Child of John Peirson, Joseph.
193 June 17, 1759. Child of Jona. Osgood, Jonathan. June 24. Child of Ezekiel Kendall, Sarah.
July 27. Child of Thos. May, Levi.
Augt. 12 Child of Ephraim Boynton, Sarah. Augt. 26 Child of Joseph Kilbourn, Ruth; Child of Asa Wilder, Prudence; & Child of Widow Priscilla Houghton, Priscilla.
Sepr. 2 Child of Tilly Wilder (pr Mr Woodard), Hannah. Sepr. 16. Child of Ephraim Sawyer, John; and Child of Jane Houghton, Persis.
Octo: 21 Child of Moses Burpee, Hittie, & Children of Joseph Bayley, Joseph & Stephen.
Jan: 6, 1760 Baptisd Elisabeth Wittemore, adult; also ye child of Josiah Brown, Samuel, & child of Jabez Fairbank, Abigail.
Feb: 10. Child of Sam^{ll} Kendall, Lucy; also of John Brook Junr., John. Feb. 24 Child of John Headly, Abram; also child of Nathan Eager, Zilpah.
March 16, 1760. Child of Jona: Wilder, Elihu. March 23 Child of Ezra Houghton, Dinah. March 30 Child of David Willard, Jonathan; also of Ephm. Goss, Elihu.
194 April 13, 1760 Child of Amos Rugg, Olive; Child of Abner Wilder, Nathan; Child of David Osgood Junr., Asubah; Child of Lemuel Houghton, Olive; & Child of Lewis Conqeret, Mary. April 27 Child of Daniel Robbins, Susanna.
June 1st: Child of Nath^{ll} Wright, Joseph. June 8 Child of Lemuel Houghton, Elijah. June 22. Child of Elisha Sawyer, Susanna.
July 27 Children of Joseph Stewart, Benjamin & Joseph; also Child of Phinehas Beman, Abigail; also Child of Joseph Gary, Joseph; also Child of John May Junr., Kezia.
Augt: 3 Baptisd Moses Sawyer, adult; also his Child nam'd Dinah. Augt: 17. Child of Jona. Prescot, Joanna. Augt: 29 Children of James May, James & David.
Octo: 5 Child of Henry Prentice, William; Child of Josiah Houghton, Jonas; Child of James May, Aaron; & Child of Nath^{ll}: Wilder, Sarah. Octo: 26. Baptisd my own Child nam'd Mary.
195 Nov. 2^d: 1760 Child of Tilly Littlejohns, Hannah. Novr. 16 Child of Jeremiah Burpee, Jeremiah.
Decr. 14 Child of Sam^{ll} Prentice, John. Decr. 28 Child of Widow Stewart, [Joseph] Mary; also of David Nelson, Anna.
Jan: 25, 1761 Child of Elisha Wilder, Hannah; also of Jonathan Bayley Junr., Eunice.
Feb: 1. Child of Ezekiel Newton, Elisabeth.
March 8 Child of Phinehas Wilder, Phinehas; also child of Sam^{ll} Burpee Junr., Elijah. March 15 Child of Moses Burpee, Ebenezer. March 22. Child of Joseph Bayley, Shubael.
April 12. Child of John Brooks Junr., William; Child of Jesse Ross, Lemuel; Child of Jabez Fairbanks, Hannah. April 19. Child of James Richardson, Abel; Child of Daniel Bixbee, Levinah.

CHOCKSETT CHURCH.

May 3. Child of Sam[ll]. Snow, John. 17. Child of Jona: Osgood, Abigail. 31 Child of Stephen Choat, Bathsheba.
July 5 Child of Nathan Agur, Nathan. July 19 Child of David Osgood Junr., Nathan.
Augt. 2[d] Child of Jona: Fairbanks, Rebecca. Augt. 9 Child of John Glazier, Jacob. Augt. 30 Child of Thos. Willard, John.
Octo: 11 Child of Israel Moores, Thomas.
Novr. 2 Child of Benjamin Shed at his house, Eleazer. Novr. 15 Child of Sam[ll] Thurston, Mary, & Child of Josiah Fairbank, Josiah; also Child of Ephraim Willard, Experience. Nov[r]. 15 Child of David Willard, Artemas.
Dec[r]: 13th Child of Eph[m]. Sawyer, James. Dec[r]. 27 Child of Hezekiah Whitcomb, David Ross.
Jan. 3, 1762 Child of Jesse Ross, Reuben.
Feb: 7. Child of Josiah Brown, Rebecca. Feb: 14. Child of Eben[r]. Buss, Benjamin; also Child of Eph[m]. Boynton Jun[r]., Irena; also Child of Jabez Brooks, Deborah.
March 28 Child of Asa Wilder, Reuben; also Child of Hezekiah Whitcomb, Mary.
April 11 Child of John Crosby, Joel. April 18 Child of Amos Rugg, Pamela. 25. Child of Josiah Osgood, Eunice.
May 23 Child of John Headly, Sarah. May 30 Child of Joseph Kilborn, Samuel; also of Josiah Osgood, Mary.
June 6 Child of John Brooks, Benjamin.
July 4, 1762 Child of John Peirson, Hannah; & of Warren Snow, Pliny. July 11 Child of Elijah Houghton, Katharine. July 18. Child of Joseph Willoughby, Joseph, & Child of Daniel Robbins, Jemima.
Sep[r]: 5 Child of Abner Wilder, Samuel; Child of Moses Sawyer, Thomas; also Child of Jona: Bayly Junr., Zurvia. Sep[r]: 12 Child of Widow Dinah Goodell, Nathan; also of Thomas Ross Junr., Betty. Sep[r]: 19 Baptisd my own Child, Thomas, & Child of John May Junr:, Phoebe. 26 the Child of Jonathan Osgood, Elihu.
Octobr: 3 Child of Ezra Houghton, Salmon; of Nath: Wright, Lucy; of Jabez Fairbanks, Meriam. 31. Child of Jane Houghton, Tyrus.
Novr: 14 Child of Sam[ll]. Kendall, Lucretia. 21 Child of Jona: Prescot, Elisabeth.
[1763] March 13 Twins of Ezekiel Kendal, Ezekiel & Elisabeth.
March 20 Child of Jonas Maison, Ruhamah; also child of Job Spafford, Samuel; also child of Israel Moores, Abigail; also child of Sam[ll]. Burpee Junr:, Mary.
April 3[d]: Child of James Mirick, Dolly. 10 Child of Thos: May, Prudee.
May 1st: Child of James May, Sarah.
June 12 Children of William Judevine, Calven, Luther. June 19 Child of Henry Prentice, Sam[ll]. June 22 Child of Thos: Willard at his house, Mary.
July 3[d]: 1763 Child of John Glazier, Oliver; also Child of Nathan Eager, Haran; also Child of Joseph Tower, Lorana. July 10 Child of Nath[ll]. Wilder, Peter. 24 Child of Nathan Burpee, Thomas; also child of Sam[ll]. Prentice, Samuel.
Augt. 21. Child of Eph[m]. Sawyer, Peter; Child of Phinehas Beman, Gedion; also Child of Oliver Dresser, Oliver. 28th: Child of Josiah Fairbank, Abigail; also Child of James Richardson, Lucy.
Sepr. 4 Child of John Brooks Junr., Hannah. 11th Child of John Boynton, Jewet. 18 Child of Samuel Snow, Samuel.
Octo. 2 Child of Jesse Ross, Jesse. Octo. 16 Child of Jeremiah Burpee, Elisabeth.
Novr. 13. Child of John Bayly, William; Child of Moses Burpee, Hepsebah; also Child of Roger Ross, Jonathan.
Dec[r]: 4 Baptisd wife of John Gibbs, adult, Elisabeth; also child of Stephen Choat, Rebecca; also child of David Willard, Lucy. 18. Child of D[r] Enoch Dole, Dolly Richardson. 25 Child of James Houghton Junr., Abel.

Feb: 5, 1764 Child of Roger Ross, Abigail. 12th: Child of Ezra Sawyer Junr,, Abner. 26: Child of Deacon Asa Whitcomb, Asa.
March 4 Child of Ephraim Willard, Nancy. 11 Child of Jabez Brooks, Mary. 18 Child of Jonathan Osgood Junr., Silence. 25 Child of Ezra Sawyer Junr., Ezra.
April 15. Child of Fortune Eager, Ephraim; also Child of Daniel Robbins, Elisabeth; also Child of Hezekiah Whitcomb, Hezekiah.
May 6 Child of David Osgood, Anna; also Child of Josiah Osgood, Samuel. 20 Child of Jonathan Bayly, Benjamin.
200 June 24, 1764. Child of Amos Rugg, Hannah; also Child of John Gibbs, Naomi, and his Wive's Children by her former husband, Isaac & Prudence; also at ye same time, Child of Nathll. Jones, Phoebe Payson.
Augt: 26, 1764 Children of Nathl: Houghton, Nathaniel & Ephraim; also Child of Fortunatus Eager, Mehitabel.
Octor: 7 Child of Ebenr. Buss, Silas. Octobr: 14 my own Son named Prentice; also children of Jona: Kendall, Ebenezer & Jonathan, 28. the Child of Jonas Mason, Ebenezer.
Novr: 18 Child of John May, Kezia.
Decr. 9 Child of John Boynton, Ephraim.
Jan: 20: 1765 Child of Wm. Judevine, William. 27. Child of Elijah Houghton, Oliver.
Feb: 24. Child of Nath: Wilder, Lucy.
March 10 Child of Moses Sawyer, Louisa. 17 Child of Israel Moores, Catharine. 31 Children of John Peirson, Twins, Lucinda & Dorinda; also Child of Thomas Brooks, Thomas; also Child of Stephen Keys, Calvin.
April 7 Child of Thomas Ross Junr., Moses.
201 April 21, 1765. Child of Josiah Houghton, James. 28 Child of Jesse Ross, Martha.
May 5th Child of Ephraim Sawyer, Susanna. May 12 Child of Nathl. Houghton, Stephen. 19 Child of James Houghton Junr., Mary; also Child of Thomas Cleland, Pamela. May 26. Child of John Hedly, John; also Child of Asa Wilder, Isaac.
June 16. Child of Capn. Elisha Sawyer, Hannah; also Child of Ezra Houghton, Ruth.
July 7 Child of Thomas Willard, Joseph. 21 Child of Joseph Fairbanks, Joseph.
Augt: 11. Child of John Crosby, John; also Child of Joseph Kilborn, Joshua. Augt. 18 All the Children of Tilly Richardson, Josiah, Tilly, John, Elisabeth, Kezia, Lucy, Dorothy; Also Children of Jonathan Whitcomb, Jonathan & Thomas. Augt: 25 Child of Josiah Fairbank, Manassah.
Sepr. 8 Child of John Palmer, Hitte. 15 Child of Tilly Richardson, Ezra.
202 Sepr. 22, 1765 Child of Jona. Whitcomb, John. Sepr. 29 Child of John Brooks Junr., Ammi.
Octobr 20 Child of Joseph Tower, Justus. 27 Child of Roger Ross, Willis. Octobr 10 Child of Samuel Snow, Joseph. 17 Child of Jonathan Wilder, Junr., Deborah.
Decr. 28 Child of Widow Spafford at her house sick, Mary. 29 Child of John Loring, Lucy.
Jan: 19, 1766 Child of David Osgood, Susee; also Child of Moses Burpee, Nathaniel.
Feb: 9 Child of David Willard, Elisabeth. 16 Child of Josiah Osgood, Josiah.
March 2 Child of Dea: Asa Whitcomb, Cate; also Child of David Nelson, Mary; also Child of John Glazier, Jonas; also Child of Samll. Prentice, Thomas. March 16 Child of Jabez Brooks, Hannah. 23 Child of Jonathan Osgood, Samuel. 30 Child of Saul Houghton, Eunice.
April 6 Child of Ebenr. Knight, Salmon; also Child of Timothy Goodens, Asa. 20 Child of Ezra Sawyer, Thomas.
May 1 Child of Nathan Burpee, Nathan.
203 May 18, 1766 Child of Ezekiel Kendal, Hannah. 25 Child of Jonathan Kendal, Lucina.
June 1. Child of Enoch Dole, Dunsmore. 8th. Child of Ephraim Willard, Anna. 22d. Child of Hezekiah Whitcomb, Samuel.

CHOCKSETT CHURCH.

Augt. 3ᵈ Child of Jabez Fairbanks, Alpheus.
Sepr: 21 Child of John Brooks, Sylvia; also Child of Thomas Brooks, Helon.
Oct. 5. Child of Joel Houghton, Sarah. 19. Child of Samˡˡ. Burpee Junr., Stephen.
Novr. 2 Child of John May, Molly. 16 Child of Thomas May, Daniel; also Child of Thos. Ross Junr., Phoebe. 23 Child of James Richardson, Manassah. 30 Child of Roger Ross, Mary.
Decr: 14. Child of Nathˡˡ. Wright, Aaron.
Jany: 4, 1767 Child of James Kendal Junr., Peirson. 11 Child of Nathˡˡ. Wilder, Sarah. 18 Child of Elijah Houghton, Elijah; also Child of Joseph
204 Bennet, Prudence. Jan: 25. Child of Ephm. Sawyer, Daniel Greenleaf; also Child of William Judevine, Luther; also Child of Joseph Fairbank, Molly.
Feb: 8 Child of James May, Moses. 15 Child of Jonas Maison, Rebecca. 22 Child of Fortunatus Eager, Winslow; also Child of Jotham Sawyer, John; also Child of Edward Newton, Edward.
March 26 Child of Israel Moore at his house, James.
April 26 Child of Nathˡˡ. Jones, Phoebe.
May 3. Child of Daniel Perry, Joseph. 10. Child of Tho. Geary, Thomas; also Child of Jonath. Whitcomb, Betty. 20 Child of James Houghton, Silas; also Children of Jonathan Bayly, Twins, Molly, Prudence.
June 8. Child of Thomas Willard, Dolly. 28 Child of Mathias Larkin, Seth.
July 5 Child of Phinehas Wilder, Lois; also Child of Stephen Keyes, Gerrish. 19 Child of Samˡˡ. Thurston, Sally.
Augt 2 Child of John Peirson, Frances. 9ᵗʰ: Child of John Glazier, Jason. 30 Child of Tilly Richardson, Rebecca.
205 Sepr: 6, 1767 Child of Jona: Osgood, Phinehas; also Child of John Boynton, Beman. 13 Child of Ebenʳ. Buss, John.
Novʳ: 1. Child of Ezra Houghton, Nahum. 29. Child of Cap. Elisha Sawyer, Elisabeth; also Child of Nathaniel Houghton, Josiah Richardson; also Child of Jonathan Kendal, Patience.
Decr: 6ᵗʰ. Child of Jabez Fairbank, Sally. 13. Children of Samˡˡ. Handcock, Thomas, William. 20ᵗʰ: Child of Shubael Bayly, Dolly
Jan: 3, 1768. Child of Asa Wilder, Asa.
Feb: 14 Child of John Brooks Junr., Eunice. 28 my own Child named Charlotte; also Child of James Kendal Junr., Augustus.
March 6. Child of Joseph Wesson, Hannah; also Child of Ebenr. Knight, Phoebe; also Child of Jabez Brooks, Rhoda; also Child of Josiah Fairbanks, Martha. 27. Child of Samuel Snow, Sarah; also Child of Joseph Tower, Jonas.
April 17 Child of Josiah Osgood, Joseph.
May 8. Child of Samˡˡ. Prentice, Levi.
206 May 22. Child of Dea: Asa Whitcomb, Betty; also Child of Dea: Joseph Kilborn, Dorcas.
June 5. Child of Tho: Geary Junr., Phoebe. 12 Child of Thomas Brooks, Alpheus.
July 3 Child of David Osgood, Rebecca; also Child of Hezekiah Whitcomb, Submit. 10. Baptised Francis Prouty's wife, Mary; also their Child named Abel. 17 Child of Moses Burpee, Phoebe; also Child of Jotham Sawyer, Dinah. 24 Child of John Loring, Joseph.
Augt. 7 Child of Bartholomew Peirson, Enos. 21 Child of Ephm. Willard, Lucy.
Sepr. 11 Child of Dr Enoch Dole, Illsly. 25 Child of Capⁿ: Elijah Houghton, Maverick; also Child of Edward Newton, Ephraim.
Octobr: 16. Child of Thomas Willard, Molly. 23 Child of Samˡˡ. Rice, Polly.
Novr. 27 Child of George Hybrus, Jabez.
Dec. 4. Child of John Brooks, tertius, Daniel Brown. 18 Child of Tho: Cleland, Lydia.
207 1768 Decr: 25 Child of Ezekiel Kendal, Ephraim.
Jany: 1, 1769. Child of Jonath: Wilder Junr., Dolly; also Children of Benjamin Dole, Relief, Dolly. 22 Child of Joseph Fairbank, Thomas; also Child of Samˡˡ. Burpee Junr., Azubah.

Feb: 5. Child of Daniel Robbins, Daniel. 12. Child of David Nelson, Solomon; also Child of Nath[ll]. Jones, Sally; also Child of Silas Fairbanks, Dolly.
March 12 Child of Tho. Ross Junr., Ruth.
April 16. Child of Ephm. Sawyer, Eunice; also Child of William Judevine, Jane Rogers; also Child of Nath[ll]. Wilder, Zebina; also Child of Francis Prouty, Tirza. 30. Child of Jona[n]: Whetcomb, Annis; also Children of Thomas Rugg, Thomas & Eunice.
May 7th Child of James Houghton, Eli. 21 Child of Phinehas Wilder, Jonaathan. 28 Child of Sam[ll]. Thurston, Susanna; also Child of David Willard, Zilpah.
June 11. Child of Fortunatus Eager, Fortunatus; also Child of Thomas Rugg, Willm: Stickney. June 18 Child of Sam[ll]. Sawyer Junr., Cooper. 25 Child of Richard Rand, Luke Sawyer.
July 16 Baptis'd Elisabeth Kendal, adult; also Child of Sam[ll]: Rice, Samuel. 30 Child of Roger Ross, Dolly.
August, 6 Child of Jonas Mason, Lydia; also Child of James May, Jacob. 20th Child of Josiah Houghton, Abigail.
Sepr. 17 Child of Cap[n]: Ezra Sawyer, Nathaniel.
Octr. 15. Child of John May Junr:, Betty. 22. Child of Ebenr: Buss, Rebecca. 29. Child of Jona: Bayly Junr:, Michal.
Nov[r]: 5 Child of James Kendal Junr., James.
Decr. 17 Child of Shubal Bayly, Paul.
1770 Feb: 11th. Child of John Peirson, Charlotte.
March 11th. Child of Tho. Brooks, Phoebe. 18th: Child of Josiah Fairbanks, Ephraim.
April 8. Child of Edward Newton, Annis. 15 Child of Silas Fairbanks, Lydia. April 22, 1770 Child of Asa Wilder, Mary; also Child of Tho. Willard, Annis.
May 6. Child of John Brooks Junr., Almeria. 27. Child of Dea: Asa Whitcomb, John; also Child of Tho: Geary, David.
June 24 Child of Dea: Joseph Kilborn, Levi.
July 1. Children of Henry Wyman, Sarah & Mary. 8 Child of Amos Boynton, Edna. 15 Child of Sam[ll]. Prentice, Luke.
Augt: 5 Child of Moses Burpee, Sarah; also Child of Bart[w]: Peirson, Hovey. 19th. Child of Tho. Cleland, Elisabeth.
Sepr. 9. Child of John Loring, John; also Child of Benjamin Dole, Benjamin. 23 Child of Aaron Sawyer, Submit; also Child of Hezakiah Whitcomb, Lois; also Child of Joseph Wesson, Stephen. 30th: Child of David Osgood Junr., Eunice.
Octr. 14 Child of Sam[ll]. Sawyer Junr., Samuel; also Child of Joshua Sawyer, Solomon; also Child of John Brooks tertius, John. Octr: 28. Child of Sam[ll]. Snow, Moses.
Novr. 11 Child of Jonathan Osgood, Betty. 17 Child of Silas Wilder, Silas; also Child of Sam[ll]. Herring, Solomon. 24 Child of Caleb Whitney, Lucy; also Child of Joseph Sawyer, Jabez; also Child of Nath[l]. Jones, Eunice.
Decr. 30 Child of Jona: Whitcomb, Nathan.
Jany. 6, 1771 Child of Caleb Church, Silas. 27 Child of Jabez Fairbank, Elisabeth.
Feb: 3 Child of Capt. Elijah Houghton, Lockheart.
March 17. Child of Roger Ross, Jonathan.
April 14 Child of Ephraim Willard, Cate; also Child of Joseph Fairbanks, Ephraim. 21. Child of Sam[ll]. Burpee Junr., Elisabeth; also Child of Nath[ll]. Houghton, Menassah; also Child of Israel Moores, Eunice.
July 14. Child of Joseph Tower, John; also Child of Francis Prouty, Isaac. 21 Child of Thomas May, Hannah.
Augt. 11 Child of W[m]. Judevine, Patience. 18 Child of Enoch Dole, Polly. 25 Child of Ezra Houghton, Benjamin; also Child of Ephraim Sawyer, Artemas.
Sepr. 8 Child of Sam[ll]. Thurston, Hepzibeth. 15 Child of Phins: Wilder, Hannah; Child of Jonas Mason, Sarah; Child of Silas Fairbanks, Silas; also

Child of Thomas Brooks, Hannah Cutter. 22 Child of Joseph Moores Junr., Abel.
Octr: 6 Child of Zechariah Eager, Elisabeth. 20 Child of Tho: Ross Junr:' Leonard.
Nov:r 10. Child of Joseph Moores Junr., Jonathan Bush. 17 Child of James Houghton, James.
Decr: 15 Child of James Kendal Junr., Mary; also Child of Thomas Rugg, Mary.
212 1772. Jany. 5 Child of Shubael Bayly, Enos.
Feb: 2 Baptisd Joshua Kendall, adult. 16 Child of James Richardson, Elisabeth; also of Child Jona^n: Wilder Junr., Mary.
March 1. Child of Henry Wyman, Rebecca.
April 8 Benja. Roper, at Joel Hotons, Adult. 26 Child of Josiah Fairbanks, James.
May 17 Child of John May, Ezra. 31 Baptisd James Taylor, adult; also Child of Eben^r: Knight, Betty; also Child of Nath^{ll}. Jones, Samuel.
June 7. Child of William Eaton, Rebecca. 14. Child of Dea: Asa Whetcomb, Sarah. 21. Child of Benja Dole, Betty Plumber. 28. Child of Robert Fletcher, Peirsis; also Child of Jabez Fairbanks, Jabez.
July 12 Child of Joshua Kendal, Dolly. 19 Child of Caleb Whitney, Oliver.
Aug^t: 9 Child of Thos: Geary, John. 30 Child of James Curtis, Sophia.
Sepr: 6 Child of Jona^n: Whetcomb, Ebenezer. 13 Child of John Brooks Junr., **213** Jonathan. Sepr: 20 Child of Joshua Sawyer, Elisabeth. 27. Child of Israel Cook, Ruth.
Novr. 1 Baptisd Children of Benjamin Tompson, Benjamin, Susanna, Lucy.
Nov:r 8 Children of John Moores, John, Samuel, James; also Child of Oliver Fairbanks, Oliver. Nov:r 29 Child of Jonathan Osgood, Sophia.
Decr: 20. Child of Sam^{ll}. Sawyer Junr., Martha.
1773. Jany 3 Child of David Osgood, Sarah. 10 Child of David Nelson, Dolly; also Child of John Brooks, William. 17 Baptisd Negro Woman of David Osgood, Phillis; also her Child named Peter.
March 14 Child of John Loring, Jonathan.
April 4 Child of Moses Burpee, Elisabeth. 15 Baptisd in private, Ebenezer Taylor Junr., adult. 18 Child of Israel Moores, Cornelius; also Child of Silas Fairbanks, Cate.
214 May 30 Child of Cap^n: Elijah Houghton, Sparhawk; also Child of Jedediah Boynton, Lucy; also Child of Benja: Tompson, Thomas.
June 6. Child of Tho: Brooks, Jabez. 20 Child of Ephm: Sawyer, Abraham.
July 18. Child of Fortunatus Eager, Tamar.
Octr. 4 Baptisd Jonathan Taylor in private, adult. Octr: 10. Child of Joseph Moores Junr., Jotham. 31 Child of Joseph Fairbanks, Anna; also Child of Bartholomew Peirson, ——.
Novr. 7. Child of Jonas Mason, Elisabeth.
Decr. 5. Child of Nath^{ll}. Houghton, Mary.
1774. Feb. 20 Child of Sam^{ll}. Burpee Junr., Martha.
March 27 Child of Sam^{ll}. Thurston, Lydia; also Child of Ephraim Willard, Peter.
April 10 Child of Jona^n: Whitcomb, Lucy: also Child of Richard Rand, Mary.
April 24 Child of Shubael Bayly, Sampson; also Child of Hezekiah Whitcomb, Relief.
215 May 8. Child of Sam^{ll}. Rice, Pamela; also Child of Sam^{ll}. Snow, Jotham; also Child of Daniel Allen, Daniel. 15. Child of Eph^m: Sawyer, Timothy. 22 Child of Joseph Bennet. Enoch.
July 3: Children of Ephm Willard Junr., Dolly & Abel; also Child of Daniel Allen, Molly. July 24. Child of Josiah Fairbank, Beaulah.
Augt. 7 Child of Israel Cook, Charity. 14 Child of Ebenr. Knight, Annis: also Child of Joshua Kendal, Ephraim. 21. Child of Dr Enoch Dole, Barnet Wate. 28 Child of John Moore, Thomas.
Sepr. 18 Child of Jona^n: Bayly, at ye House, Sarah; also Child of Daniel Robbins, Sarah; also Child of James Houghton, ——; also Child of Joshua Sawyer, ——.

Octr. 9. Child of Jabez Fairbanks, Thankful; Child of Thomas Geary, Joseph; Child of Thomas Ross Junr., Thomas; Child of Heman Kendal, Eunice; Child of Sam¹¹. Sawyer Junr., Phoebe; of Oliver Fairbanks, Susee. Oct.
216 23 Child of Thomas Willard, Silas; also Child of Capⁿ: Joseph Lewis, Hannah.
Novr: 13. Children of Willm: Tompson, Anna Jewet, Mary.
Decr. 25 Child of Obediah Groce, Daniel Whiting.
April 30, 1775. Children of Joseph House, Joseph, John, Allice.
June 18 Child of Capn. Elijah Houghton, Sophia.
July 23 Child of John Brooks, Enos.
April 21, 1776 Baptisd yᵉ Negro Girl of Edmund Quincy Esq., Eunice; also her little Boy, named James. N B the Negro Girl confest Fornication & made Profession.
June 23. Baptisd Child of Obediah Groce, Lucy.
Augt. 4 Child of Daniel Allen, Allice.
Octr: 27 Child of Sam¹¹: Prentice, Prudence.
Jany: 12 1777 Child of Capn: Peter Bubier, John.
Feb: 16 Child of Josiah Fairbanks, Levi.
217 June 14 1778 Child of Joseph Woodbury, Joseph.
August 23 Child of Daniel Allen, Joseph House.
1779 Jany: 31 Child of Sam¹¹: Clark, Hovey.
Decr: 5 1779 Child of John Brooks, James; Child of Obediah Groce, Nahum Houghton; also Child of Joseph Moores, William.
1780 April 2 Child of Capn: Peter Bubier namd Sophia Mellen.
1780 July 6ᵗʰ Child of Sam¹¹. Clark, Hubberd; also Child of Daniel Allen, Rebecca.
Octr: 22 Child of Joseph Woodbury, John.
Novʳ: 18, 1781 Child of John Brooks, Catharine; also Child of Obediah Groce, Sophia; also Child of Daniel Allen, Cynthia.
Octr: 6 1782 Child of Joseph Woodbury, Relief.
July 27 1783 Child of Daniel Allen, Elijah.
Augt. 1 Child of Sam¹¹. Clark, Rebecca.
Octr: 12, 1773 Baptis'd Child of Peter Green Esqʳ., Thomas Mellen.
967 since 1744.

BAPTISMS BY REVEREND REUBEN HOLCOMB, IN 1779.

Child presented by Eph. Willard junr., Joseph; Benjn. Thompson, Joseph; Jonath: Whitcomb, Sally; Edward Newton, David; Benja. Roper, Cata; Tho. Blotchet, Lydda; Cpt. Richardson's Wife, Serena; Jabez Fairbanks, Patience; Benj. Thompson, Ebenezer; Lemuel Fairbank, Thankfull, Barak-Beckwith; Joseph Lowes, Martha; Samˡ. Bayley, Dolly; Joseph Bayley, Joshua Houghton; do., Sally; Samˡ. Thompson's Wife, Josiah; Timothy Brown, Josiah Prentice; Widdow Betty Dresser, David Nelson, Mehitable, Betty; Wid. Betty Jewet, Betty, Samuel; Jonas Mason, Azubah; Heman Kendal, Nathan; Mrs Wright, Pamela, Abel; Jonathⁿ. Wilder Junr:, Eunice; Phineas Wilder, Edward; Reuben Gary, Benjamin, Ruth, Polly; Eunice Brooks, Mary; Jonth. Prescot, Levi, Jonathan; Judith Mears was Baptised on her own account; The Wife of Tho. Mears, Polly, John, Richard, Hannah, Dolly, Thomas, Nabby; David Osgood, Josiah.

IN 1780.

Samuel Snow, Anna; Moses Burpee, Moses; Sam¹¹. Bayley Junr., James; Thomas Sawyer Junr., Elias; Joshua Kendall, Joanna; Benjⁿ. Richardson, Eunice; Jonas Brooks, Susy; John Loring, Betsey; Wife of John Wheler, Sarah, Ruth, John; Reuben Geary, Joseph; Shubael Bayley, Betty; Edward Waldron, Hannah; Thos. Brooks, Amos; Thos. Sawyer Junr., Thomas; Moses Burpee, Thomas; Ethan Kendall, Ethan, Wyman, Oliver, Prudence; Seth Fairbanks, Amos; Elijah Wilder, Lucrecia; Joseph Bayley, Polly; Jonth. Moore, Prudence, Dolly, Nabby; Edward Newton, Ezekiel; Mary Eaton, Collins; Ethan Kendall, Joel.

* * * * * *

CHOCKSETT CHURCH.

The following marriages, solemnized before Reverend John Mellen, are not to be found, or are differently recorded, in the town books:

June 23, 1748. Married Ezra Houghton & Dinah Houghton.
1751. July 10. John Fairbank & Relief Houghton.
1774. April 24. Abel Wright & Lydia Richardson.
Tilley Richardson & Elizabeth Sawyer, January 31, 1750-1. [July 10 in town book.]
Samuel Newton & Sarah Douglas, December 18, 1751. [Dec. 19 in town book.]

MISCELLANEOUS RECORDS.

THE HILLSIDE CHURCH.

June 9, 1828, the corner stone of a house for religious worship was laid at a commanding site upon Wataquodock Hill, in Bolton. Here the "Evangelical Congregational Church of Bolton, Lancaster, Sterling and Stow," was organized March 17, 1830, the first pastor, Rev. J. W. Chickering, being ordained over it on April 14 of that year. Of the thirty-six original members of the society, those resident in Lancaster were :

Reverend Asa Packard.
Mrs. Nancy Packard.
Ruth F. Packard.
Widow Abigail Ballard.
William Stedman.
Sophia Stearns.

Widow Naomi Pollard.
Mrs. Elizabeth Nowell.
Almira Pollard.
Anson Lowe.
Elizabeth B. Hunt.

Walter S. Vose.
Ann F. Vose.
Paul Faulkner.
Mrs. Eunice Faulkner.
Levi Wilder.

ADMISSIONS FROM LANCASTER.

1831. Jan. 2. Mrs. Hannah Hastings, Mrs. Frances E. Chickering, Charles Priest, and Mrs. Nancy Priest.   Mar. 6. Charles Wyman.   July 3. Horace Faulkner and Mrs. Eliza Faulkner, Sylvia Lowe, Francis M. Moore. Sept. 4. Thomas Sawyer and Mrs. Polly Sawyer, Mrs. Phebe Emerson, Caroline Farnsworth, Hollis Hastings.   Nov. 2. Rufus Fletcher, Samuel Jewett and Mrs. Betsey Jewett, Mrs. Lucy Ann Fairbank, Louisa Faulkner.
1832. Jan. 1. Asa Dunn and Mrs. Luzima Dunn, Mary Faulkner, Harriet Priest, Eliza Dudley, Isaiah Moore, Ephraim Smith, Martha Lowe, Caroline Lowe, Haskell McCollom, Hiram Smith, Frederick Barnett.   March 4. Amos Wheeler and Mrs. Prudence Wheeler, Gilman B. Parker and Mrs. Sarah Parker, David Osgood and Mrs. Eliza Osgood.   May 6. Mrs. Lydia Stephenson, Esther Eaton.   Sept. 2. Mrs. Mary Lowe, John Lowe.
1833. Jan. 6. John D. Fisk, Laura Matilda Wheeler.   March 10. Mrs. Esther Eliza Dudley, Sarah Stearns Priest, Helen Amanda Jewett.   April 28. Joseph Breck and Mrs. Sarah Breck, Mrs. Eliza Shattuck.   Nov. 3. Stewart Hastings, Mary Maynard, Rhoda Francina Priest.
1834. May 4. Martha Ballard.   Sept. 7. Lorinda Lowe, Ira G. Childs and Mrs. Abigail W. Childs, William Nowell and Mrs. Sarah Nowell.
1836. Nov. 6. Sarah Bruce.
1837. March 5. Mrs. Nancy Wyman.   July 2. Catharine Sarah Vose.   October 22. Martha Eliza Vose.
1838. January 7. Mrs. Mary Tower.   September 2. Mrs. Rosella C. Whitney.   Nov. 4. Nathan M. Goodale and Mrs. Lucy Goodale.
1839. May 5. Sarah Goss.
1840. May 3. Nancy Elizabeth Priest.

CONGREGATIONAL CHURCH. 393

BAPTISMS OF LANCASTER CHILDREN.

1830. May 23. Mary Daniells, child of Paul & Eunice Faulkner; John William, child of W^m. & Elizabeth Nowell. Oct. 10. Louisa Christmas, child of W^{dw}. Abigail Ballard.
1831. Jan: 2. Stewart, child of S. & H. Hastings. Mar: 20. Silvanus Chickering, child of Charles and Nancy Priest. Oct. 2. John White, child of John W. and Frances E. K. Chickering. Nov. 6. Frances Evelina Chickering, child of Saml. & Betsey Jewett.
1832. Aug. 5. Ann Hubbard, child of S. & B. Jewett. Sept. 2. Lucy, child of W. & E. Nowell. Nov. 25. Mary Parker, Emily and Ellen, children of A. & P. Wheeler; Gilman Cornelius, child of G. B. & S. Parker.
1833. Mar. 10. Martha Ann, child of T. & L. Fairbank. Mar. 31. Sarah Lewis, Martha Ann, Nathan Augustus Munroe, Caroline Moore and Charles Henry, children of E. S. Dudley. Nov. 24. Electa Maria, child of C. & N. Priest.
1834. Aug. 17. Frances Electa, child of J. W. & F. E. Chickering. Oct. 12. Samuel Abbot, Child of G. B. & S. Parker. Nov. 9. John Wood, child of Charles Wyman.
1835. Nov. 1. Emery Thomas, child of Thos. & Polly Sawyer.
1836. April 24. Josiah Goodell, child of Ira G. & Abigail W. Childs. July 17. Catharine Ann, child of W^m. & Elizabeth Nowell. Aug. 21. Mary Frances, child of H. & S. McCollum. Oct. 16. Charles Andrew, child of Charles Wyman.
1837. May 28. Mary Jane, child of G. B. & S. Parker. April 23. John Edwin, child of Esther Dudley.
1838. June 3. Caroline Louisa, child of H. & S. McCollum. Aug. 26. Josiah, child of Ira G. & A. W. Childs. Oct. 21. Sarah Isabella, child of G. P. & S. Parker; Frances Ellen, child of Mrs. Mary Tower.

NOTE. Rev. Henry Adams, the last pastor over the church, preached his farewell sermon May 7, 1843. No register of births, marriages or deaths is found in the church books.

THE EVANGELICAL CONGREGATIONAL CHURCH.

April 24, 1839, the Lancaster members of the Evangelical Congregational Church of Bolton, Lancaster, Sterling and Stow, in a letter asking consent to their separation for the founding of a new church, stated that they had "become members of a religious society legally organized in Lancaster," had "a convenient and comfortable house for their solemnities," and that their pulpit was "regularly supplied." The petitioners were thirty-one in number:

Rev^d. Asa Packard.
Mrs. Nancy Packard.
Amos Wheeler.
Mrs. Prudence Wheeler.
Charles Wyman.
Mrs. Nancy Wyman.
William Nowell.
Mrs. Elizabeth Nowell.
Anson Lowe.
Mrs. Phebe Emerson.

Caroline Farnsworth.
Rufus Fletcher.
Mrs. Lucy Ann Fairbanks.
Emma W. Goss.
Isaiah Moore.
Mrs. Martha [Lowe] Gibbs.
Caroline Lowe.
Haskell McCollum.
Mrs. Sylvia [Lowe] McCollum
Mrs. Lydia Stevenson.
Esther Eaton.

John Lowe.
Mrs. Mary Lowe.
Charles Miller.
Martha Ballard.
Lorinda Lowe.
Ira G. Childs.
Mrs. Abigail W. Childs.
Sarah Bruce.
Mrs. Mary Tower.
Mrs. Rosella C. Whitney.

These, with eight others — Erastus B. Bigelow, Mrs. Susan W. Bigelow, Mrs. Polly [Brigham] Bigelow, Horatio N. Bigelow, Mrs. Emily W. Bigelow, Charles Humphrey, Mrs. Jane Humphrey and Sarah Goss — were the original members, organized May 22, 1839, as the Evangelical Congregational Church of Lancaster.

Admissions to Membership.

1839. Joseph Wilder, Jr.
1840. Mrs. Ruth Wilder, Mary C. Nowell, Mrs. Sarah Carter, Joseph Marshall, Mrs. Caroline V. Marshall, Diana S. Locke, Elthina Eager, James S. Lawrence, Mrs. Susan Davis, Sarah Stone, Joseph D. Huntington, Mrs. Rebecca P. Packard, Mrs. Lucretia Wyman, Mary Anne Osgood, Marietta Mills, Nancy Hayward, Lucy S. Stevenson.
1841. Mrs. Mary P. Bradley, Mary E. Tower, Mary Townsend, Mrs. Lucinda W. Cook, Mrs. Ann M. Carter, Dorcas Fletcher, John Carr, Mrs. Mary Carr, Martha White, Daniel Haverty, Josiah Childs, Jr., Harriet Olds.
1842. Mary Fletcher, Julia A. Tower, Rachel Damon, Martha A. Maynard, Oliver Studley, Mrs. Elizabeth Studley, Joseph B. Parker, Mrs. Mary Newman, Catharine P. Farnsworth.
1843. Martha E. Wilder, Lydia Warner, Mrs. Jonas White, Maria Newman, Louisa Toombs, Polly Sawyer, Mary C. Sawyer, Charles Packard, Sewall P. Talman, Abigail Wilder, Levi Greene, Mrs. Achsah Greene, Nathaniel Rice, Eliza H. Sawyer, Lucy Harris, Jonathan Holt, Jr., Eunice Wellington, Levi Houghton, Eliza Houghton, Eliza Ellen Houghton, James T. Sawyer, Sophia Greene, Mary C. Packard.
1844. Isaac F. Woods, William Grassie, Caleb T. Symmes, Mrs. Nancy R. Symmes, Horace Faulkner, Mrs. Eliza Faulkner, Emily H. Faulkner, Loramon D. Howe, Mrs. Mary D. Howe.
1845. Anna P. Lee, Nathan S. Robinson, Mrs. Lucy T. Robinson, Mrs. Harriet Whitney, Thomas H. Whitney, Mrs. Salome Whitney, Elizabeth Grassie, Alexander Grassie, George Grassie, Mrs. Elizabeth Grassie, Mrs. Charlotte A. Woods, Gilbert Greene, Mrs. M. Antoinette Greene, Eliza Ann Tyler, Timothy J. Fairbanks.
1846. Robert C. Houghton, Mrs. Lucy Houghton.
1847. Mrs. Elizabeth Buss, Edward L. Johnson, Mrs. Sibyl Miller, Mrs. J. C. Stiles, R. Francina Priest, Nancy Elizabeth Priest, Thomas B. Nichols, Martha B. Wilder, Mary Ann Townsend, Norton E. Pratt, Clarissa M. Pratt, Lydia Pratt.
1848. Elizabeth D. Clark.
1849. Thomas G. Grassie.

Death Register.

Kept by Reverend Charles Packard, 1840-1849.

Reverend Charles Packard, first pastor of the First Evangelical Congregational Church in Lancaster, was ordained January 1, 1840. His memoranda of marriages, in the first record book of the church, have been used to correct his returns as copied into the town books, and need not be repeated here. His list of deaths was irregularly kept, and is as follows:

1843. Feb. 1. Mrs. Warren Damon, 30.
" Feb. 24. Infant child of Henry Low, 3 days.
" Mar. 20. Rev. Asa Packard, 84.
" May 14. Mrs. Rufus Fletcher, 74; Fever.
" May 14. Mrs. Fidelia French, 47; consumption.
" Oct. 12. Infant child of John Taylor, 3; typhus.
" Oct. 21. Mrs. Levi Green; consumption.
" Nov. 10. Seth Fairbanks, 44; dropsy of heart.
1844. Jan. 14. Oscar Marcellus Wilder, 4; scarlet fever.
" Jan. 27. Mrs. Lorenzo Woodbury of Bolton, 42; lung fever.
" Feb. 2. Mrs. Nancy Packard, 80; lung fever.
" Feb. 14. Mrs. Anne Woodbury of Bolton, 81; lung fever.
" Apr. 5. Mrs. Samuel Damon, 85; fever.
" May 4. Infant child of Woodworth, 3 mos.
" July 31. Infant child of Caleb & Nancy Sawyer, 8 mos.; humour.
" Dec. 4. Child of Silas & Sarah Greenleaf, 6 years; typhus fever.
1847. Feb. 12. Mrs. Eaton, 96.
" " 18. Rhoda Bell, 46; Liver.

UNIVERSALIST CHURCH.

	Mar. —.	Dolly Carr, —; consumption.
	Apr. 30.	Mrs. Martha Parker, —; consumption.
	May 29.	Elizabeth Nowell, 21; consumption.
	June 23.	Miss Dickenson at Alms House; fever.
		Carter at Alms House; consumption.
	July 23.	Infant child of Jeremiah Moore; bowel complaint.
	Aug. 19.	Infant child of Joseph & Sarah Wilder; bowel complaint.
	Aug. 22.	Woodbury, 91. Farmer.
	Aug. 26.	[Silas] Fairbanks. Farmer.
	Aug. 29.	Albert Crane, Esq., of Oswego, 49; bilious fever.
	Sept. 15.	Infant child of Mr. Seaver, 1; Dysentery.
	Sept. 18.	Mrs. C. P. Farnsworth; Typhus fever.
	Oct. 4.	Robert C. Houghton, 34; Typhoid.
	Oct. 13.	John W. Dame, 1½; Bowel complaint.
	Oct. 19.	Child of Vanduser, 4; Croup.
	Oct. 27.	Mrs. Eliza A. Bates, 20; Typhus.
	Nov. 6.	Mrs. Lucy Houghton, 30; Typhoid.
	Nov. 28.	Jona. F. Houghton, 9; Typhoid.
	Dec. 4.	Jonas Houghton, 87.
	Dec. 13.	Patty Maynard, 60; Fever.
	Dec. 18.	Infant child of Mr. Gould, Clintonville, 1 year.
1848.	Jan. 7.	Isaac Miller, 42; Palsy and Insane.
	Jan. 27.	Mary E. Phelps, 22; Consumption.
	Feb. 14.	Infant child of John C. Stiles, 14 mo.; Brain.
	Aug. 15.	Brabrook, 30; Consumption.
	Sep. 9.	Child of Jer. Moors, 4 wks.
1849.	April 9.	Joseph Davis, 68; Bowels.
	Aug. 22.	Mary Low, Clintonv*, 74; Epilepsy.
	Aug. 28.	Mrs. Matilda Worcester, Clintonv*, 43; Dysentery.
	Sep. 9.	Mary E. Maynard, 2; Dysentery.
	Sep. 12.	Henry Woods, 4; Dysentery.
	Oct. 14.	Olive Haynes (Bolton), 82; Old age.
	Dec. 1.	Henry D. Pierce, 37; Intemperance.

FIRST UNIVERSALIST CHURCH.

In the books of the First Universalist Society of Lancaster no register of baptisms, marriages or deaths is found. A list of those who signed their names to the constitution as adopted April 30, 1838, follows:

Josiah Fay.
John Hawks.
Jonas Wheeler.
John Bennett.
John Richards.
Suell Wade.
J. P. Nurse.
Joseph Whitney.
William W. Bragg.
William Pitts.
Joshua Fletcher.
James Pitts.
Benjamin Wilder.
J. M. Damon.
Nathan Whitney.
Aaron Sawin.
Charles Wood.
Henry Norcross.
Christopher Jones.

Alice Hawks.
Cynthia K. Hawks.
Bela Marsh.
John Swan. *Voted out.*
James S. Lawrence.
Sally H. Hawks.
Samuel Damon.
Harriet B. Fay.
Julia A. Fletcher.
George Sawyer.
Sampson W. Evans.
John W. Damon.
Henry Sawyer.
Moses Stow.
John Lawton.
Joseph Farwell.
John R. Wyman.
Lucinda Pitts.
Almira Johnson.
Harriet Damon.

Assenath Barbour.
Mary P. Nourse.
Elizabeth A. Ross.
Nancy Dorrison.
Eliza A. Dorrison.
Eliza W. Osgood.
Nabby W. Fletcher.
Eliza W. Stow.
Almira J. Hide.
Sarah W. Haven.
Sarah Richards.
Salome Pratt.
Luther Gaylord.
Miles Gaylord.
Garry Sanford.
David Randall.
Elisha Turner.
E. W. Richards.
John M. Whitney.

The members of the church in 1850 were:

Benjamin Whittemore.	Eliza Stow.	Sarah Ann Howe.
Mandana M. Whittemore.	William Pitts.	Elmira Hyde.
John Bennett.	Seth G. Pitts.	Andrew J. Brown.
Orion Newton.	Susan B. Pitts.	Sarah A. Willard.
Catharine B. Newton.	Susan Bennett.	Louisa Fleming.
Samuel Chickering.	Stilman A. Sawtell.	Luther Grover.
Susan Chickering.	Benj. B. Whittemore.	Edward J. Crossman.
Luther Gaylord.	Billings H. Ridley.	Susan Crossman.
Laura Gaylord.	Henry F. Newton.	Harriet B. Fay.
Moses Stow.	Elisha Turner.	Rosella C. Whitney.
	Caroline A. Turner.	

DEATH REGISTER.

Kept by Reverend George M. Bartol, First Church, 1847-1849.

1847. Aug. [19.] Zenon Pierce, 42. Consumption.
Sept. 12. Silas, son of Joseph S. & Amanda Seaver, 4. Chol. Morb.
Sept. 14. Nancy, wife of Moses Dickinson, at Alms House, 63. Ship Fever.
Sept. 16. Mary Janette, dr. of Joseph S. & Amanda Seaver, 2. Chol. Morb.
Sept. 21. Moses Dickinson, at Alms House, 72. Ship Fever.
Sept. 23. Sarah E., dr. of Sidney & Sally Harris, 16 yrs. Typhus Fever.
Sept. 24. Patrick, son of Patrick & Margaret McLinn, 6 mos., at Alms House.
Sept. 24. John Harrison, son of John H. & Mary Maynard, 3 yrs. 10 mos. Scarlet Fever.
Sept. 26. Erastus Henry, " " " " 9 months. Scarlet Fever.
Oct. 2. James Stone, 48. Disease of Liver.
Oct. 6. Emma, dr. of Hollis & [Hannah] Davis, 6 yrs. 4 mos. Accident, Falling Cart Body.
Oct. 13. Lucy, wife of Samuel Allen, 84 yrs. 9 mos. Consumption.
Oct. 16. Abby Goddard, dr. of John & Sophronia Fuller.
Oct. 16. Joel Wilder.
Oct. 29. Julia Ann, dr. of Curtis & Huldah Sargent. Throat Distemper.
Nov. 3. Ann Elizabeth, dr. of Jonathan & Charlotte Buttrick, 11 mo. 23 days.
Nov. 23. Sarah Ann, dr. Elias & Lucy Danforth, 26. Consumption.
1848. Jan. 1. Mary A., wife of Archibald Fairbanks, 47. Internal Cancer.
Feby. 14. Eliza Adeline, child of W^m. & Hannah Matthews, 8½ days.
Mar. 17. Maria, wife of Sherman Conant, 42. Erysipelas.
April 5. Prudence Haskell, at Alms House, 78. Consumption.
April 22. Jane Augusta, dr. of Widow Mary Childs, 20. Consumption.
May 11. Susan, wife of Benjamin Houghton, 57. Cancer.
June 6. Deacon Jonas Lane, 87. Old age.
June 12. Charlotte Kimball, wife of John C. Hoadley, 24. Consumption.
July 4. Thomas Watson. Accident. Fell & run over by his Cart & Oxen.
Aug. 5. Fordyce Nourse, 39. Typhoid Fever.
Aug. 9. Adelina, dr. of Widow Roxy Freeman (col^d.). Dysentery.
Sept. 11. Samuel Davis, son of Eldad & Nancy Butler, 5 mos. Dysentery.
Sept. 14. Elizabeth, widow of Gates Thurston, 86. Old age.
Oct. 1. Sylvester Phelps, 79.
Oct. 17. Eunice, wife of Nathan Bennett, at Alms House, 72. Consumption.
Oct. 27. William A., son of W^m. & Elsey Ballard, 25. Consumption.
Nov. 20. Anna Maria, dr. of Dr. Right & Mary Z. Cummings, 20. Consumption.

1849. Jany. 10. Winfield, son of Curtis & Huldah Sargent, 3 months.
" 16. Elias Sawyer, 47. Consumption.
Jan. 26. Polly Washburn, 84. Old age.
Feby. 12. Miss Sally Carter, 68. Influenza.
Feby. 17. Ann, widow of John Sargent, 76. Lung Fever.
Feby. 19. Rosellina Maria, child of Wᵐ. & Eunice Derby, 7 m. Influenza.
May 18. Sophronia W., wife of Eliphaz Ballard, Sr., 75.
May 26. At Sterling in Rev. Mr. Mellen's absence, Luke Wilder, 67. Dropsy of the Heart.
May 28. Martha Butler, dr. of John & Nancy Laughton, 19. Consumption.
June 23. Lydia Ann, dr. George & Lucinda B. Stratton, 15 m. 19 d. Croup.
July 4. Mrs. Mary Locke, 67. Consumption.
July 10. Mrs. Sarah Lawrence, 52. Consumption.
July 21. David Steuart Robertson, formerly of Foveran, Aberdeenshire, Scotland, 32. Bilious Fever.
Aug. 5. John Henry, son of Geo. W. & Martha R. Howard, 19 m. Dysentery.
Aug. 14. Mary E. S., wife of Augustus P. Burditt, 26 yrs. Congestion of the Brain. Burial in Leominster.
Aug. 20. Samuel Wilder.
Aug. ? Nancy, widow of David Newell, 80. Old Age.
Sept. 27. Elijah Colburn, 78. Paralysis.
Oct. 20. Mrs. Sally Smith, died at Boston. Dysentery.
Nov. 2. Caroline M., wife of Wilder S. Thurston. Consumption.
Nov. 3. John Goss, at Alms House, 66. Consumption.
Nov. 5. At Northborough, —— Barrett. Old Age.
Nov. 20. Elizabeth, widow of Moses Sawyer, 84. Old Age.
Dec. 16. (At Sterling) Nancy, widow of Elias Sawyer, 57. Consumption.

JUDGE JOSEPH WILDER'S MEMORANDA.

In the Lancaster Library is a memorandum book used by Judge Joseph Wilder chiefly for record of public business transacted by him. Scattered through the volume are the following entries not found in the town-clerks' books:

Joseph Wilder, the Son of Joseph and Lucy Wilder, was born yᵉ 17 of November, 1173.
Lucy Wilder, Otober yᵉ 31ˢᵗ, 1715.

MARRIAGES CONSUMMATED.

Thomas Styles with Sarah Hartwill, May yᵉ 14, 1728.
—— Holland with —— Temple, ——
—— Homes with Ruth Farnsworth, ——
Jonathan Beman and Martha Smith of Lancaster about yᵉ 16ᵗʰ or 23ᵈ of March, 1732.
Samuel Gibs and Lediah Moor of Lancaster, April yᵉ 12ᵗʰ, 1732.
Ebenezer Dakin and Abigail Beman Jr., ——
William Sawyer and Hannah Whetcomb of Lan., August yᵉ 25, 1732.
Jonathan Bellows and Judith Tezer of Southborough, —— 27, 1732.
James Smith of Coventry and Sarah Atherton of Harvard, May yᵉ 29ᵗʰ, 1733, pr Joseph Wilder, Justice of peace.
Obadiah Cooley of Brookfield and Martha Wilder of Lancaster, April yᵉ 24ᵗʰ, 1734, pr Joseph Wilder, J. P.
Samuel Johnson & Mary Snow, July yᵉ 25ᵗʰ, 1734, pr J. Wilder.
Benjamin Wilder and Jane Robins, January yᵉ 9, 1734-5.
Jonathan Fairbank and Thankful Sawyer, April yᵉ 8ᵗʰ, 1735.
John Chenery and Keziah Kendal was married Sept. yᵉ 11ᵗʰ, 1745, pr J. Wilder.
July yᵉ 3, 1746. Jonathan Prescott married to Vashti Houghton.
July yᵉ forth, 1746. John Bennet Jr. and Keziah Wilder was married.

EPITAPHS IN LANCASTER BURIAL GROUNDS OF DATE PRIOR TO 1850.

THE OLD BURIAL FIELD.

The founders of the town, and their descendants during the 17th century at least, buried their dead without formal services—following the custom of the Puritans in England—and perhaps a plot of ground for the family graves was sometimes selected within the home lot or orchard. Early in the present century ancient graves were visible near the sites of both the Roper and the Prescott garrisons. But in the infancy of the Nashaway Plantation, land adjoining the meeting-house site was set apart for common use as a "burying place." The practice of marking graves by incribed headstones probably did not begin until after the resettlement, one apparent exception being that of Mrs. Dorothy Prescott, who died in 1674. The oldest date now to be found is that over the grave of the first John Houghton—1684. For half a century all memorial stones were but fragments of slate riven from some ledge, or rough granite slabs, upon which unskilled hands rudely incised name and date,—the latter being often upon a foot-stone or on the back of the head-stone. Many of the older inscriptions are illegible to most eyes. In his History of Lancaster, Reverend A. P. Marvin has given a plan of this ancient burial place, upon which the marked graves are located and numbered, and has added literal copies of the epitaphs. In the following carefully revised list of inscriptions the same numbering is adopted. Their arrangement is indicated by division lines. Numbers omitted are of stones not lettered, or of misplaced foot-stones found to belong with other numbers.

1. In Memory of A | Father, & 4 Children. | Mr Andrew Wilder died Dec: | ye 28th. AD, 1764, in ye 56th. | year of his Age.
    Death is a Debt, to Nature due, | Whic I have paid: & so must You.
Andrew, Son of Mr. An | drew & Mrs. Elizabeth | Wilder, was Still Born | Sept: ye 4th. 1741. Ruth, Dau^t. of Mr. A. & | Mrs. E. Wilder, died Jan: | ye 19th. 1753, in ye 8th. | Year of her Age. | Joseph, Son of Mr. A. & | Mrs. E. Wilder, died | Aug: ye 15th, 1775,[55] in ye 3 | Year of his Age. | Deborah, Dau^t. of Mr A. & | Mrs. E. Wilder, died Aug: | ye 22^d, 1755, Aged | 11 Days.

2. In Memory of Mr. | JOHN PHILLIPS, | Who died Nov. y^e | 23^d, Anno-Dom. 1776: | Aged 56 Years. | And also two of his Sons; | John, died Oct. ye 29th, | 1776: Aged 5 years. | Samuel, died Nov. ye 2^d, | 1776: Aged 3 years. | Likewise, of his Daughter, | Rebecca, died Oct. ye 26th, | 1776: Aged 22 Months.

3. In Memory of | BATHSHEBA ROBBINS | widow of | Mr EDWARD ROBBINS, | who died | Oct. 16, 1805, | in the 86 year of | her age.

4. In Memory of | Mr EDWARD ROBBINS, | who depated this life | Octr. 9th, 1791, in y^e | 78th. Year of his age

5. Here lies interred | ye Body of Mr. | JOHN PHILLIPS | Who departed | this Life January | ye 31st, Anno-Dom. | 1763, Aged 70 Years.

6. In Memory of Mrs | LYDIA PHILLIPS, | who departed this | Life May y° 31ʳᵗ. | Anno-Dom. 1760: | Aged 29 Years.

7. In Memory of | REBECCA PHILLIPS | who died July y° | 4ᵗʰ. Anno-Domini, 1775 | Aged 53 Years.

8. In Memory of Mʳ. | JONATHAN PHILLIPS, | who departed this | Life July y° 20ᵗʰ. | Anno-Domini 1780: | Aged 44 years.

9. In Memory of | Jotham Robbins, Son | of Mr Edward & | Mrs. Bathsheba | Robbins, who died | November y° 24ᵗʰ. | 1763, Aged 17 years, | 7 Months and 24 Days.

10. Mr. Edward | Robbins, Junʳ. | 1763. [On a foot-stone.]

11. Here Lyes the | Body of Jacob | Waters of | Charls Town | Aged 65 Years & | 7 Mo Who Died | at Lankester | Decembʳ y° 15ᵗʰ 1714

12. Here lies interred | y° Body of |Mr. | EPHRAIM WYMAN, | who deceased on y° | 17ᵗʰ, of Febʸ. Ano-Do. | 1780: in y° 30ᵗʰ | Year of his Age.

> Death levels All, both the wicked | and the just: Man's but a flower, and his | end is dust.

13. ERECTED | in Memory of | Mʳ. NATHANIEL WYMAN, | who died | Dec 15, 1801, | Aged 55. | A Pattern of Honesty & Industry.

14. Here lies interred | Y° Body of Mrs. | MARY WHITNEY | (y° Wife of Mr. JONATHAN WHIT | NEY) who deceas'd | Jan. y° 12ᵗʰ, AD. 1778: | in y° 34ᵗʰ. Year | of her Age.

15. Sacred | To the Memory of Mr. | NATHANIEL WYMAN, | who died June y° 5ᵗʰ, AD. | 1776, in y° 58ᵗʰ Year | of his Age.

> The stroke of Death hath laid my Head, | Down in this dark and silent Bed; The Trump shall sound, I hope to rise, | And meet my SAVIOUR in the Skies.

16. Here lies Buried | y° Body of Mrs. MARY | WYMAN y° Wife of | Mr. Nathaniel Wyman | who died on May y° | 8ᵗʰ. 1759, in y° 37ᵗʰ. | Year of her Age. | Her Father deceased | the same Day.

17. ERECTED | In Memory of | Mrs. SUBMIT WYMAN, | (Relict of Mr. Nathanˡ. Wyman) | who died | Novʳ, 25, 1804, in the | 74ᵗʰ year of her | age.

18. In Memory of | Elizabeth Daughᵗ. | of Mr Abijah & | Mrs. Abigail | Wyman who | died July y° 20 | 1766, Aged 11 | Years, & 10 Month.

19. HERE LIES BURIED | YE BODY OF MR | JOHN BENNIT WHO DEPARTED | THIS LIFE | DECEMᵇʳ YE 30ᵗʰ | A. D. 1748. | AGE 29 YEAR | 11 M & 10 DS.

20. In Memory of Mrs. | Bathsheba Bennitt, y° | Wife of Capt. John | Bennitt, who died | Febʳʸ. y° 7ᵗʰ. 1762, | Aged 67 years. | Remember Death.

21. In Memory of Capt. | John Bennitt, who | died June y° 5ᵗʰ. 1761. | Aged 68 years.

> O Death Thou'st Conquer'd me, | I by thy Dart am Slain; But CHRIST has conquer'd thee, | And I shall Rise again.

22. HERE LIES BURIED | Y° BODY OF MR | SAMUEL BENNIT | WHO DEPARTED | THIS LIFE JULY 6ᵗʰ. | A.D. 1742. | AGE | IN Y° 77ᵗʰ. YEAR OF HIS AGE.

23. MARY MOORE | DECEASED | SEPTEMBER 26 | 1705

24. ANNA SERS

26. HERE LYES THE BODY | OF LEVI THE SON OF SALM | ON & REBECAH GODFREY | WHO DEPARTED THIS | LIFE MAY 3 1789 | AE 7 M & 8 DAYS.

27. In Memory of A | Father, & 4 Children. | Mr Mathew Clark, died | July y° 9ᵗʰ, ADom: 1760. | in the 56ᵗʰ. Year of his | Age. | Mary, died Janʳʸ. | y° 27ᵗʰ, 1749, in y° | 9ᵗʰ year of | her Age. | John, died | May y° 15ᵗʰ, | 1751, Age | 3 Weeks. | Mathew, died | July y° 24ᵗʰ, 1750, | in y° 9ᵗʰ. Year | of his Age. | Sarah, died | October y° 6ᵗʰ, | 1758, in y° 3ᵈ | Year of her Age.

28. In Memory of Mrs. | Martha Wilder, Wife of | Mr Gardner Wilder, who, | died March y° 7ᵗʰ, ADomi. | 1764, Aged 27 years.

> My Loveing friends, as you pass by, | On my cold Grave but cast your Eye; Your Sun like mine may set at Noon, | Your Soul be call'd for Very soon; In this dark Place you'll quickly be; | Prepare for death & Follow me.

29. In Memory of | Gardner, Son of | Mr. Gardner & | Mrs. Martha | Wilder, who | was Stillborn | Sept. ye 17th, | 1761.

30. Here lies Buried | The Body of M^rs. Hannah Buss | Y^e Wife of | Mr John Buss, | Who Died | March ye 14 A D | 1738 | in ye 56 | Year of Her Age.

31. Here lies Buried | The Body of Mr | John Buss Who | Died April | The 30 A D | 1734 Aged | About 55 | Years.

32. ERECTED | in memory of | Mrs. MARY LOCKE, | Wife of Mr. Wm Locke, | who died Nov 17th | 1796: in the 50th. | Year of her Age.
    The sweet remembrance of the just | Shall flourish when they sleep in dust.

33. ERECTED | in Memory of Mrs. | REBECCA WILDER, | Wife of Joseph Wilder, Esq. | who died Sepr. 10th. | 1789: in the 80th. Year | of her Age.
    Here sleeps the flesh, unconscious, close confin'd,
    But far, far distant, dwells th' immortal Mind.

34. Here lies interred y^e | Body of Mr. | JAMES LOCKE, | who deceased on | ye 19th of March AD. | 1772, in ye 33^d. Year | of his Age.
    Behold the numerous Croud | That's Mouldering in the Ground
    Ready to Start when CHRIST commands ; The awful Trump to Sound.

35. Here lies interred y^e | Body of Mr. | SAMUEL LOCKE, | who died April ye 13th, | A D. 1775, in ye 73^d. | Year of his Age.
    The stroke of death hath laid my Head, | Down in this dark and silent bed;
    The Trump shall sound, I hope to rise, | And meet my SAVIOUR in the Skies.

36. Here lies interred y^e | Body of Mr. | JOSIAH LOCKE | who died May ye 16 | A D. 1769, Ætat^s. 33.
    Every Man at his best | State; is altogether Vanity | Cease ye from Man, whose Breath is in his Nostrils; and | trust in ye EVER LIVING GOD.

37. Esther, Dau^t. of | Mr. Joseph & Mrs. | Esther Locke, | died March ye 25th, | 1768. Aged | 6 Months & 1 | Day.

38. Abel, second Son | of Mr Josiah and | Mrs. Esther Locke, | died Oct: ye 13th. | 1766. Aged 2 | Months & 1 Day.

39. In Memory of | Rebecah Dau^t. of Mr. | Ephraim Wilder ye 3^d. | & Mrs Lucretia | his Wife, who died | May ye 14th. 1766. | Aged 8 Months & | 7 Days.

40. Abel, first Son | of Mr. Josiah and | Mrs. Esther Locke, | died May ye 6th. | 1765, Aged 3 | Months, & 20 Days.

42. In Memory of, | Mr JOHN WARNAR, | Who Departed this | Life March the 27th. AD | 1776, in the 41st Year | of his age:
    To the, O Stone, We Recommend this Dust,
    Commanding the in Faith to Keep Your trust.
    Take this Body and secure in entomb
    Until the Day of Resurrection comes.

43. Here lies interred ye Body | of Col. OLIVER WILDER. | who died March y^e | 16 ADomini 1765, | in the 71 Year of | his Age.
    The stroke of Death hath laid my Head, | Down in this Dark & Silent Bed;
    The Trump shall sound, I hope to rise | And meet my SAVIOUR in the Skies.

44. HERE LIES BURIED | Y^e BODY OF MRS | MARY WILDER | WIFE OF CO^ll | OLIVER WILDER | ESQ^r WHO DEPARTED | THIS LIFE JUNE Y^e | 15th A-D 1748 | IN Y^e 53^d YEAR | OF HER AGE.

45. In Memory of | Timothy son of | ye Rev^d. Timothy | and Mrs. Anna | Harrington, who | Dec^d. June ye 16th. | 1749. Ætat^s 7, | Months & 25, Days.

46. Sacred | to the Memory of Mrs. | ANNA HARRINGTON, | Ye amiable consort of ye Rev^d. TIMOTHY HARRINGTON, | who, resigned to the Will of | GOD, & depending entirely | on the LORD JESUS for | Salvation, deceased on | May ye 19th AD. 1778. | Ætat^s. 62

47. The Reverend | TIMOTHY HARRINGTON | Etatis 80, | Fourth Pastor of the Church in Lancaster, | Died December 18, 1795. | Endued with superior abilities, he happily | united the manners of the Gentleman, with | the unaffected gravity of the Divine, and was | especially distinguished for | benevolence of heart. | The sacred doctrines he taught, were enforced | by an uniform example in the practice of the | domestic, social, and moral | virtues. | A con-

sistent and rational view of the Gospel; | a faith in the Saviour of the world; | and a reliance on the mercy of GOD, | inspired him with y⁰ joyful hope | of a resurrection to | eternal life.

" Be thou faithful unto death, and | I will give thee a crown of life."

48. HEAR LY | ETH THE BODY | OF ABIGAIL | THE WIFE OF | HENRY HO | UGHTON. | AGE 31 | 1711

49. HASADIAH | THE DAUGHTER | OF HENRY AND | ABIGAIL HO | UGHTON: | AGE 2 · Y | 2 · M · D | 1711

51. In Memory of Mr. | HENRY HASKELL | who died April | yᵉ 1ˢᵗ. A Dom, 1779. | in yᵉ 73ᵈ Year | of his Age.

The sweet Remembrance | of the Just, | Shall Flourish when they | sleep in Dust.

52. John | Swan | ÆT 3½ Y.

54. HERE LIES | BURIED yᵉ BODY | OF MRS MARY CARTER, | yᵉ WIFE OF | MR. EPHRAIM CARTER | WHO DECᵈ MAY | yᵉ 30ᵗʰ, 1738, & IN yᵉ | 21ˢᵗ YEAR OF HIR AGE.

55. Here lies Buried the | Body of Mrs. Eliza | beth, yᵉ Wife of Mr. | Joseph Osgood who | Died October yᵉ 9ᵗʰ | 1755, in the | 34ᵗʰ Year of her | Age.

57. In Memory of | The Reverend John Whiting, | second minister of Lancaster, | Killed by the Indians | September 11, A. D. 1697. | This Stone in place | Of one broken and decayed | is set by the Town, A. D. 1878. [See 66.]

58. HENRY | HOUGHT | ON THE | SON OF | HENRY & | ABIGAIL | HOUGHTON | AGE 1 · Y | 6 M · D | 1702

59. A SON OF | HENRY & | ABIGAIL HO | UGHTON. | A. 6 w | 1708

60. JOHN | HOUGHTON | DECEASED | APRIL | 29. Day | 1684.

61. ABIGA | IL D OF | J. M. H.

63. In | MEMORY | of | Dr: Stanton Prentice, who | deceased on yᵉ first of Deceʳ. | Anno Domini 1769. Æts: | 58.

"This Life's a Dream, an empty show; | But yᵉ bright World to which I go, Hath Joys substantial & sincere: | When shall I wake & find me there?"

64. HERE LIES INTERRD | THE BODY | OF | Mʳ EBENEZER SWAN | WHO DECEASED | AUGUST Yᵉ 22ᵈ | A DOM. 1750 | AET 42.

65. Here lyes Buried | yᵉ Body of yᵉ Revⁿᵈ. Mr. | ANDREW GARDNER, | Who Decᵈ. Octoʳ. 26ᵗʰ | Anno Domi 1704, in yᵉ | 30ᵗʰ Year of His Age.

66. MR | JOHN....ITING | PAST....OF THE | CHURCH....LANʳ | DECEASED | SEPTEMBER | 11 DAY | 1697. [See 57.]

67. Yᵉ REVᵈ. Mʳ JOHN PRENTICE | PASTOR OF Yᵉ FIRST CHURCH | IN LANCASTER | DIED JAN. 6ᵗʰ A. D. 1747-8. | ÆTAT. 66. IN HIS DOCTRINE | HE WAS LEARNED, JUDICIOUS, | PLAIN, SEASONABLE, & UNREPROUEABLE. | IN HIS CONUERSATION, STEADY, | SOBER, TEMPERATE, PEACEABLE, | WATCHFUL, INSTRUCTIUE, | PRUDENT AND BLAMELESS | IN HIS HOUSE RULING WITH ALL | GRAUITY A TENDER HNSBAND, | A GOOD FATHER, A KIND MASTR, | & GIUEN TO HOSPITALITY. | IN HIS PUBLIC CHARECTER, A TRUE GOSPEL BISHOP, | IN HIS PRIUATE CAPACITY—A GENTⁿ. & AN EXEMPLARY | CHRISTIAN: HIS MEMORY IS PRECIOUS, | & HIS PRAISE IN Yᵉ CHURCHES.

68. Here Lyes the | Body of Mrs. Mary | Prentice, Wife to | yᵉ Revᵈ. Mr. John | Prentice, Who | Decᵉᵈ March yᵉ | 9ᵗʰ. 1717-8, in yᵉ 37ᵗʰ | Year of Her Age.

69. In | Memory of | Mrs Mercy, yᵉ wife of Dʳ Stanton Prentice | who Deceased on yᵉ 26 of Octobʳ. AD. | 1756, in the 40ᵗʰ Year of her Age. | In the Character | of a wife, she was kind and faithful. | of a Parent tender, Provident, & conssientious: | Of a Christian, chearful, charitable, & generous, | humble, & self-denying. | In Her | The poor have lost a Benefactress: | The Sick a skillful Assistant: | and her acquaintance a much regretted Friend. | Her husband, he praiseth her: | and her Children | Rise up. and call her Blessed.

70. Here lies Buried | yᵉ Body of | Thomas prentice | Son of Doctʳ. | Stanton & Mʳˢ. | Marcy prentice, | Who Decᵈ. May 2ᵈ | A D. 1752, Age | 6 years 7 Mo.

71. HERE LIES BURIED | Yᵉ BODY OF | THOMAS PRENTIES | SON OF DOCᵗʳ | STANTON & MRS. | MERCY PRENTICE | WHO DECᵈ. AUGUST | Yᵉ 17ᵗʰ 1745 | AGE 3 YEARS | 10 M AND 19 D.

72. HERE LIES BURIED | YE BODY OF MARY | PRENTICE. DAFTʳ | OF DOCᵗʳ. STANTON | & MRS MERCY | PRENTICE WHO | DECᵈ. MAY 23ᵈ | A D 1749 | AGE 1 YEAR & 3 Mᵒ.

73. Here lies the | Body of Daniel | Prentice, son of | Dr: Stanton Pren | tice and Mrs; Mercy, | his wife, who | died Sepᵗ. 21ˢᵗ, 1756. | Aged 5 years.

74. Here Lies the | Body of Mercy | Prentice, Daughter | of Dr: Stanton | Prentice and Mrs. Mercy his wife, | who died Octʳ. | 6ᵗʰ, 1756, aged 2 Y.

75. Here lies the | Body of Mercy | Prentice, Daugh | ter of Dr. Stanton | Prentice, and Mrs. | Rebecca his wife, | who died January | 12ᵗʰ: 1759, aged 3 M.

76. Here Lies the Body | of Peter Prentice, | son of Dr Stanton | Prentice and Mrs. | Rebecca his wife | who died July, | 1766, Aged 5 years | and 6 months.

77. In Memory of | Susannah Carter, | daugʳ. of Docʳ. James | & Mrs. Susannah Carter, | Who died July 28ᵗʰ. | 1795, Aged 2 years | & 17 days.

78. In Memory of Mr. | Thomas Sawyer, | who died March | yᵉ 1ˢᵗ. AD: 1760. Aged 22 Years, | 9 Months, and 27 | Days.

79. HERE LIETH THE BODY OF | EUNICE SAWYER, THE WIFE | OF BEZALEEL SAWYER, | WHO DECEASED THE 4; DAY OF | MARCH 1712: 13. AGED ABO | UT 26 YEARS: ALSO THE BO | DY OF HER DEAD BORN | INFANT.

80. In Memory of Mr | Bezaleel Sawyer, | who died August | yᵉ 25ᵗʰ. AD. 1760, | Aged 75 Years, | 3 Months, and | 12 Days.

82. T W.

83. HERE LIES | BURIED Yᵉ BODY | OF JOHN CARTᴿ. | Yᵉ SON OF MR | JOHN & MRS | ABIGAIL CARTER, | WHO DECᵈ. OCTOBʳ | Yᵉ 18ᵗʰ 1739 AGE | 1 YEAR 9 M & 9 D.

84. In Memory | of Elisha | Son of Capt. | John & Mrs Abi | gail Carter | who was | still born.

85. HERE LIES BURIED | Yᵉ BODY OF | JOHN CARTER | SON OF LIEUᵗ | JOHN & MRS | ABIGAIL CARTER | WHO DECᵈ DECEMᵇʳ. | Yᵉ 21ˢᵗ A' D 1746 | IN Yᵉ 5ᵗʰ YEAR | OF HIS AGE.

86. HERE LIES BURIED | Yᵉ BODY OF | ABIGAIL CARTER | DAUGHᵗʳ OF LIEUT. | JOHN & MRS | ABIGAIL CARTER | WHO DECᵈ. DECEMᵇʳ | Yᵉ 25ᵗʰ, A. D. 1746 | IN Yᵉ 7ᵗʰ YEAR | OF HER AGE.

87. Here lies interred the | Body of Col: JOHN | CARTER, who deceased | May yᵉ 8ᵗʰ, ADom: 1766, | Ætatˢ. 53.

> Every Man at his best | State; is altogether Vanity. | Cease yᵉ | from Man whose Breath | is in his Nostrils; and | trust | in yᵉ EVER LIVING GOD.

88. L——— | Bod—— | Abo—— [A broken stone.]

89. Caleb Townsend

90. HERE LIES BURIED | Yᵉ BODY OF Yᵉ | WIDOW RUTH | CARTER, RELIKS | OF CAPᵗ. THOMAS | CARTER, WHO DECᵈ | DECEMBʳ Yᵉ 25ᵗʰ, | ANNO DO 1739 | AGE 55 YEARS, | 7 M. & 16 D

91. HERE LIES BURIED | THE BODY OF | CAPTAIN THOMAS | CARTER. | AS YOU ARE | SO WERE WE | AS WE ARE | SO YOU WILL BE. | WHO DIED | MARCH THE | 31 1737 | & WAS 55 | YEARS OLD

93. HERE LIES BURIED | Yᵉ BODY OF | MR SAMUEL CARTER | WHO DECSED | AUGUST Yᵉ 22ᵈ, | ANNO DOM. 1738 | & IN Yᵉ 61ˢᵗ YEAR | OF HIS AGE.

94. Erected | In Memory of | Mrs. Elizabeth Temple, | Relict of Mr. Isaac Temple, | Who died Aug. 27ᵗʰ | 1796, in the 78ᵗʰ | Year of her Age.

95. Here lies interred the | Body of Mr. | Josiah Ballard Junr | who died Sepᵗ. yᵉ 17ᵗʰ, | A. D. 1771, in the 22ᵈ. | year of his Age.

> No Age exempted from the Grave; | No Sex in Nature freed; Her mouth wide open gaping Stands | For to Receive the Dead.

96. Here: Lies | THE BODY | OF JOHN | BOWARS | D : 1718

OLD BURIAL FIELD.

97. Here lies interred y* | Body of Mr. | ROGER NICHOLS | who died June | y* 3ᵈ. A D. 1765. | in the — Year of | his Age.

98. In Memory of | John, Son of Mr. | John & Mrs Anna | Ballard who died | Novʳ. 7ᵗʰ, 1789: in | the 6ᵗʰ. Year of | his age.

99. In | memory of two | Sons of Mr. Thomas | and Mrs. Abigail Ballard | John died | March 3ᵈ | 1792, aged | 4 months | & 10 days. | John died | August 20ᵗʰ. | 1794, aged | 19 months | & 20 days.

100. IN MEMORY OF | THOMAS SON OF MR. | THOMAS KENDALL | & ABIGAIL HIS WIFE | DIED OCTʳ, 25ᵗʰ, | 1756 | IN Yᵉ 1ˢᵗ YEAR | OF HIS AGE.

102. In Memory of two Children | of Capt. Daniel and Mrs. Eunice Goss. | Jonas Goss | died May y* | 27ᵗʰ, Anno Do. | 1774: Aged | 3 Days. | Anna Goss | died January | y* 17ᵗʰ A D. 1779: | Aged 3 Years, | 8 Months & | 19 Days.

103. In Memory of Capt. | EPHRAIM WILDER, | who died December y* | 13ᵗʰ, A D: 1769, in y* 94ᵗʰ, | Year of his Age.

    O Death, Thou'st conquer'd me, | I by thy Dart am Slain;
    But CHRIST has conquer'd thee, | And I shall rise again.

104. In Memory of Mrs. | Elizabeth, y* Wife of | Capt. Ephraim Wilder, | who died May y* 28 | 1769, in y* 89ᵗʰ. year | of her Age.

    The Stroke of Death hath laid my Head, | Down in this dark and Silent Bed.
    The Trump shall Sound I hope to rise, | And meet my SAVIOUR in the Skies.

105. In Memory of Capt. | EPHRAIM WILDER, Junʳ. | who died March y* 7ᵗʰ | A D. 1770, in the 63ᵈ. | Year of his Age.

    Every Man at his best state, is altogether Vanity. | Cease y* from Man whose Breath is in his Nostrils: and trust | in the Ever living GOD.

106. Here lies interred | y* Body of Mrs. | ANNA WILDER, | Consort of Capt. | Ephraim Wilder, | who died Oct y* 16ᵗʰ. | A D: 1778, in the 67ᵗʰ. | Year of her Age.

    The Sweet remembrance of the Just, | Shall flourish when they Sleep in Dust.

107. Here lies interred | y* Body of Mrs. | Anna Gates, | (Wife of Capt. Hezekiah | Gates) who died April | y* 23ᵈ, Anno-Do. 1779: | Aged 70 years.

    Ye Aged, awake, improve your short Liv'd day,
    Improve your Time and Talents whilst you may.

108. In Memory of Mr. | Joseph House, who | Died July y* 9ᵗʰ. | 1756, in y* 61ˢᵗ. Year of his Age— | Elizabeth Daughter | of Mr Joseph House, | & Lydia his wife | who Died in | October 1739, in | y* 14ᵗʰ year of | her Age.

109. In Memory of | Nancy (Dauᵗ. | of Mr. Peter | & Mrs. Dorothy | Thurston) who | died Sept. y* 25ᵗʰ, | 1778: in the | 5ᵗʰ Year of | her Age.

110. Here lies interred | Yᵉ Body of Capᵗ. | HEZEKIAH GATES, | Who departed this Life | June y* 27ᵗʰ. Anno-Dom. | 1777, in y* 73ᵈ | Year of his Age.

    My Flesh shall slumber in y* Ground | Till y* last Trumpets joyful Sound:
    Then shall awake with sweet surprise | And in my SAVIOURS Image rise.

111. In Memory of Mrs. | Rebekah y* Wife of Mr. | Philimon Houghton, | Who died Febʳʸ. y* 15ᵗʰ, | A D: 1766, Ætatis 26.

    Now sleeps, God rest her Soul; | A vertuous wife Her hapless Husband's | only Pride in Life. | Triumphant mount where | Happy Plannets role, And open Paradise to her | Immortal Soul.

112. Rebekah Dauᵗ | of Mr. Philimon | & Mrs. Rebekah | Houghton, died | July y* 5 1765 | Aged 1 Year, 5 | Months and 5 Days.

113. Memento Mori. In Memory of | Mʳˢ. Martha Page | wife of | Mr. Levi Page | who departed this Life, | April y* 16ᵗʰ 1785. | In the 28 year of | her Age.

114. In Memory of | David Atherton, | Son of Mr. Amos | & Mrs. Elizabeth | Atherton, who | died July y* 4ᵗʰ. | 1769, in y* 14ᵗʰ. Year | of his Age.

    When this you Se, | Remember me.

115. In Memory of Mr Edmond | Harriss, who Died Decᵇᵉʳ | Y* 10ᵗʰ, 1726, in y* 53 year | of his Age. | Mrs Elizabeth his wife | Died Janʳʸ y* 31, 1755 | & in y* 73 year | of her Age.

116. Amos Harris | April 4 Day | 1713.

117. Here lies interred y^e | Body of ye Honble | ELISHA MARSH Esqr. | (of Walpole in the | State of New Hampshire,) who | died July ye 25th. | Anno Domini, 1784. | Ætatis 71.

118. Here Lies Buried | The Body of the | Honourable Co^{ll}. | SAMUEL WILLARD, | Esq. Who Departed | This Life Novem^{br}. 20th | Anno Domini 1752 | In the 63^d year | of His Age.

119. Wilder, Son of | Mr Thomas & | Mrs Abigail | Gaits, died July | ye 20th 1766. | Aged 1 Month & | 2 Days.

121. John, Son of Capt. | Thomas Gates & | Abigail his wife | Died Novr 24th | 1785: In his 7th Year | So fades the flower, | Their 3^d onely son.

122. Anna Daugh^r. of | Capt. Thomas Gates | & Abigail his wife: | Died Novr 27th 1785: In her 16th year.

> Death with his warrant in his hand, | Comes rushing on amain;
> We must obey ye Summons yn | & so return to dust again.

123. Thomas, Son of | Capt. John Thurston, | & Beca his wife, | Died Decr 14th 1785: | Aged 2 Years 5 | Months & 8 Days.

124. In memory of | Miss Lucy Gates. | Dau^t of Capt Thomas, | & Mrs Abigail Gates, | who died July 19th, | 1797, in the 33^d. | Year of her age.

125. In Memory of | Mr. ELIJAH WHEELOCK. | Who Died July the 27th. | A D. 1775; | in the 35th. Year | of his age.

> For Though his Soul Know Soars With Wings on high,
> Yet here his Body Must Forgotten lie;
> And youer Commanded, While he here Dose Sleep,
> The Silent Watches of Each Hour to Keep.

126. Here lies interred | ye Body of Mrs. | ELISABETH FAIRBANK, | ye Wife of Deaⁿ. CYRUS FAIRBANK, | who departed this | Life, Oct. ye 1st, Anno. | 1778. in ye 39th. | Year of her Age.

> Death is a debt to Nature due, | Which I have paid & so must you.

127. Here lies interred | the Body of M^{rs} | LUCY FAIRBANK, | ye wife of Deacⁿ. | CYRUS FAIRBANK, | who died Sept. ye 16th. | 1776, Aged 36 | Years & 8 Days. | Likewise Ephraim, Son of the | Deceas'd, still born, Sep^t. ye 1st, 1776.

> The Small and Great are here.

128. ERECTED | in memory of Deaⁿ. | CYRUS FAIRBANK, | who departed this life | Feby. 28th, 1801. | Aged 63 years.

> The sweet remembrance of the just, | Shall flourish when they sleep in dust.

130. Mr Jonas Fairbank | Died Novr the 4th, | 1792: | In his 89th. Year.

> The Memory of the Just | is blessed.

131. In Memory of Mr. | Isaac Rugg, who | Died October ye 14th, | ADom: 1758, in ye 38th | Year of his Age.

> Thou hast by Death cut short his days,—But him, Immortal, Thou shalt raise.

132. In Memory of | THANKFUL FAIRBANK, | Wife of | Jonas Fairbank, | who died | May 13, 1795, | aged 81 years.

> "She looked well to the ways of her household, | and eateth not the bread of idleness."

133. In Memory of | Lucy, Dau^t. of Mr. | Cyrus, & Mrs Lucy | Fairbank, who died | March, ye 1st, 1764, | in ye 3^d. Month of | her Age.

134. Anna, Daught of | Mr. Cyrus & Mrs. | Lucy Fairbank, | died July ye 17th, | 1769, Aged 3 Mon | & 8 Days.

135½. Sally Daugh^r of Deac. | Cyrus and Lucy Fair | bank, died June 9th 1790: | in her 18th. year. | When this you see, remember me

136. In Memory of | Anna (Dau^t. of | Mr. Cyrus & | Mrs Lucy | Fairbank) died | March ye 31st, | 1773, Aged 2 | Years, 7 Months, | & 20 Days.

137. In Memory of Lieu^t. | JABAZ FAIRBANK, who | died in March 1758. | Aged about 84 Years. | Mrs MARY, his first Wife died | in March 1718 Aged 42 years | Mrs ELIZABETH his Second Wife, died May ye 11th, 1755. | Aged 80 Years 7 Months.

138. HERE LIES THE BODY | OF | MARY FAIRBANK | THE WIFE OF | JABEZ FAIRBANK | DESSCED FEBRUARY | 21: DAY IN | YEAR 1718. | DIED IN | THE 43 YEAR OF | HIR AGE.

139. HERE LIES | THE BODY | OF | GRASE FAIRBANK.

140. HERE LIES | THE BODY | OF THE DAF | TER OF JOSEPH FAIRBANK.

145. ERECTED | to the Memory of | WILLIAM DUNSMOOR Esqr. | who departed this Life | May ye 20th, 1784: | in the 51st year | of his age.

Life how short, Eternity how long.

How lov'd, how valu'd, once avales thee not, | To whom related or by whom begot;
A heap of dust alone remains of thee, | Tis all thou art, & all that die shall be.

146. John Dunsmoor, Son of | William Dunsmoor Esqr. | & Mrs. Hannah his wife; who died Oct. 29th, | 1756: Aged 1 Year | & 8 Months.

Happy the babe, who preveleg'd by fate, | To shorter labour, and a lighter weight,
Receiv'd but yesterday the Gift of breath, | Order'd to-morrow to return to death.

147. In Memory of | Mr. Darius Sawyer, | who died Augt. 13th, | 1789: in the 69th | Year of his | Age

148. In Memory of | Mrs. Deborah, Daught. | of Mr. Darius, and Mrs. | Deborah Sawyer, | Who died Dec^{ber}. y^e | 16th. A D: 1765. Aged | 21 Years, 9 Months | & 26 Days. | Remember Death.

149. In Memory of a Father & 3 Children. | Doc^t. JOHN | DUNSMOOR | Departed this | Life, Dec^{br}. ye 7th, | 1747, in y^e. 45th. | Year of his | Age. | Eunice Died | Sep. y^e. 9th, 1745. | in y^e. 3^d. Year | of her | Age. | Olive Died | Sep. y^e. 19th. 1745, | in y^e. 8th. Year | of her | Age. | John Died | Sep. y^e. 26th. 1745, | in y^e. 5th. Year | of his | Age.

150. In Memory of | Sylvester, Son | of Mr. Joel, & | Mrs. Prudence | Phelps who | died April, ye 7th. | 1765, Aged | 2 Years and 1 Mon.

151. In memory of | EBENEZER ALLEN, | who died July 9th, | 1770. Æ. 94 | Years.

152. HERE LIES BURIED | THE BODY OF M^{rs}. | SARAH ALLEN | WIFE OF M^r. | EBENEZER ALLEN, | DIED JUNE 15th. 1755, | IN Y^e 71st YEAR | OF HER AGE.

153. In Memory of | Mr Phinehas Phelps | the Son of Dr. | Phinehas & | Mrs. Sarah Phelps | who Departed this | Life Decr. ye 12, 1784: | in the 19th Year of | his age.

154. In Memory of | D^r. Phinehas Phelps | who Departed this | Life Augt. ye 12th, | 1770; | in the 37th, Year | of his age.

156. PHILIP | GOSS | DECÆSED | MAY 1698

157. JONATHAN FAIR | BANKS AND HIS | DAUGHTER GRACE | FAIRBANKS | WHO DECEA | SED SEPTEM | BER THE 11 | 1697.

158. JONAS | FAIRBANKS | WHO DECEA | SED SEPTEM | BER THE 13th | 1697.

159. HANNAH | FAIRBANKS DESAS | ED DEC | EMBER 11, | 1704.

160. In Memory— | Amos Sawyer— | died [1768]—Remember Death. [A broken stone.]

162. In Memory of M^{rs}. | ABIGAIL SAWYER, | ye wife of M^r. | AMOS SAWYER | who Died Nov^{br}. | ye 20th. 1753, Aged | 65 Years 7 Months | & 13 Days.

163. In Memory of | Thomas Allen, Son of | Mr. Amos & Mrs. Rebecca | Allen, who died Jan^y. | the 23rd. 1793: aged 5 | Years, 7 months, & 16 | days.

Who was his Father's Son, tender | and well-beloved in the eyes | of his Mother.

164. Here Lies Buried | the Body of Mr. | John Prescott, | who Died | Oct. ye 11th, 1749, | in ye 77th. Year | of his | Age.

165. Here Lies Buried | ye Body of Mrs. | Dorothy Prescott | ye wife of Mr. | John Prescott, | who Died Sep. | ye 28th, 1749, in | ye 73^d. Year of | her Age.

166. ERECTED | In Memory of | Mr John Prescott, | who departed this life, | April 1st: 1791: | In the 79th: year | of his age.

Death like an overflowing flood, | Doth sweep us all away: ·
The young, the old, the middle aged | To death becomes a prey

167. ERECTED | In Memory of | Mrs. Mary Prescott, | Consort of | Mr. John Prescott, | who departed this life | Oct\[r\]. y\[e\] 20\[th\]. 1788, | In the 66\[th\], year | of her age.

    Forbear my friends to weep | Since death to me is gain;
    Those Christians who in Jesus sleep | Shall with the Lord remain.

168. EXPERIE | NCE | PRESCO | TT | DASES | ED | THIS LIFE—

170. Abijah Willard Junr. | Son of Capt. Abijah, | & Mrs Elisabeth | Willard, died | December y\[e\] 12\[th\], | 1749, Aged 10 | Months.

171. Here lies interred y\[e\] Body | of Mrs. ELISABETH | y\[e\] Wife of Capt. | ABIJAH WILLARD, | who died December | y\[e\] 6\[th\], ADom. 1751. | in y\[e\] 29\[th\], Year of | her Age.

172. In Memory of Mrs. | CATHERINE WILLARD | Relict of | Levi Willard, Esq\[r\]. | who died Jan\[ry\]. 10\[th\]. 1791. | Aged 56.

    Illum'd by piety and grace divine, | Through various woes we saw her sweetly shine;
    In every scene Omnipotence she view'd, | And calm, and steady, virtuous ways pursu'd.
    For thee bless'd shade, thy Children oft shall weep, | Till life is hush'd in death's eternal sleep.

173. In Memory of | LEVI WILLARD, Esq\[r\]. | Who died July y\[e\] 11\[th\], | AD. 1775. | Aged 48.

    Virtue and worth, with humane feelings join'd | Enlarg'd, improv'd, and dignify'd his mind.

174. In Memory of Mr. | JOHN WILLARD, | who died May y\[e\] | 1\[st\]. AD. 1775. | Aged 17.

    Early this Youth the path of Virtue trod, | And left with joy, this world to join his God.

175. In Memory of | KATHARINE, Dau\[t\]. | of Capt. Levi, & | Mrs. Katharine | Willard, who | died Dec\[r\]. y\[e\] 3\[d\]. | ADom. 1759, Aged | 5 Months & 14 Days.

176. Theodorah Daugh\[t\]. | of Capt. Abijah & | Mrs Anna Willard, | died Oct: y\[e\] 14\[th\]. | 1756, Aged 9 | Months.

177. Elisabeth, Daugh\[t\]. | of Capt. Abijah & | Mrs Anna Willard, | died Oct: y\[e\] 6\[th\]. | 1756, in y\[e\] 3\[d\] | Year of her | Age.

179. THOMAS | SAWYER | DIED SEP | TEMBER 12 | 1706 | ABOUT | THE 90 | YEAR OF | HIS AGE.

180. In Memory of Mrs. | MARY SAWYER, | Wife of Lieut. | Moses Sawyer, who | died April y\[e\] 12\[th\] AD. | 1774, in y\[e\] 33\[d\]. Year | of her Age

181. Here lyes Buried | y\[e\] Body of Mr. | THOMAS SAWYER, | Who Died Septemb\[r\]: | 5\[th\]; 1736, in y\[e\] 89\[th\] | Year of His Age.

182. HERE LIES BURIED | Y\[e\] BODY OF | MR JOSEPH SAWYER | WHO DEC\[d\]. | JULY Y\[e\] 10\[th\], 1737 | & IN Y\[e\] 55\[th\] YEAR | OF HIS AGE.

183. Here Lyes y\[e\] | Body of | Sarah Sawyer, | Wife to Joseph | Sawyer, Aged | 37 Years. Died | March y\[e\] 7\[th\], 1717-18.

184. Here Lyes the | Body of Mrs Priscilla | Beman, Wife to | Mr. John Beman, | Who Dec\[d\]. Aug\[st\] | 6\[th\], 1729, in y\[e\] 73\[d\]. | Year of Her Age.

185. HERE LIES BURIED | Y\[e\] BODY OF M\[r\]. | JOHN BEAMAN, | WHO DEPARTED | THIS LIFE JANUARY | Y\[e\] 15\[th\], A: D. 1739-40. | IN Y\[e\] 90\[th\]. YEAR | OF HIS AGE.

186. July | 17 Day | 1700   [A foot-stone.]

187. SARAH | PRESCOT | HVR BLAS | ED SOUL | ASANDED | UP TO HEA | VEN JULY 14 | 1709 | AGED | ABOUT | 63 | YEARS.

188. MARY PRE | SCOT DAP | ARTED THIS | LIFE | FEB 23 1718.

*IOHN PRESCOTT | DESASED.—[The foot-stone broken.]

  ☛ [This marks the grave of the Founder of Lancaster, who died in 1681.]

189. HERE LIETH THE | BODY OF DOROTHY | THE DAUGHTER OF | JOHN PRESCOT & | DOROTHY HIS WI | FE WHO | DESEASED T | HE 27 DAY OF | MARCH 1713 | AGED – 7 – YEARS.

189. *bis.* HERE LIES | DOROTHY THE | WIFE OF JONATH | AN PRESCOTT | WHO DECEASED......

    [Mrs. Prescott died in 1674. Foot-stone missing.]

OLD BURIAL FIELD. 407

190. Here lies interred the | Body of Mrs. | DEBORAH WILDER, | (Consort of the Honble. | JOSEPH WILDER, Esq;) | who departed this Life, | on ye 20th. of April AD: 1773, | in ye 65th. Year of her Age.
> The Stroke of Death hath laid my Head | Down in this Dark & Silent Bed:
> The Trump shall Sound; I hope to rise, | And meet my SAVIOUR in the Skies.

191. HERE LIES | BURIED THE BODY | OF MRS. HANNAH | FLETCHER, THE | WIFE OF MR JOHN | FLETCHER, WHO | DIED APRIL | THE 10th, 1737. | IN THE 52 YEAR | OF HER AGE.

192. Here lies interred y^e | Body of Mrs Rebecca | ye Wife of M^r. | James Locke who | died March ye 9th AD. | 1769, in ye 28 Year of | her Age.
> My flesh shall slumber in the Ground, | Till ye last Trumpets joyful Sound;
> Then shall awake in sweet surprize, | And in my SAVIOUR Image rise.

193. In Memory of | Peter and John, Twin | Children of Col. Joseph | & Mrs. Deborah Wilder. | Peter died July ye 1st, | 1762 Ætatis. 19. | & John died on ye Day | of his Birth.
> Death levels all, ye Wicked and ye Just. | Man's but a Flower, and his End is Dust.

194. In Memory of Mrs. | Martha Sawyer, | (Wife of Mr Paul Sawyer,) | who died May 10th. | 1794: Aged 31 years.
> Behold and see as you pass by, | As you are now so once was I;
> As I am now so you must be; | Prepare for death, and follow me.

195. In Memory of Mrs. | Martha Joslin, Wife | of Mr Nathaniel Joslin, | who died February | ye 13th, AD: 1768, in y^e | 37th. Year of her Age.
> The stroke of Death hath laid my Head, | Down in this dark and silent Bead;
> The Trump shall Sound, I hop to rise, | And meat my SAVIOUR in the Skyes.

197. In Memory of Mrs. | Joanna Joslin y^e | wife of Capt. | Peter Joslin | who Died Sep. | ye 24th. 1717 | in ye 44th year | of her Age.

198. In Memory of | Dorothy Joslin, | Daughter of Capt. | Peter Joslin & | Joanna his wife | who Died April | 20th, 1732, in y^e | 18th year of | her Age

199. In Memory of Mrs. | Hannah Joslin ye wife | of Capt. Peter Joslin | who died Augt. y^e. | 14th, 1739, in y^e | 71st Year of | Her Age.

201. HERE LIES BURIED | Y^e BODY OF | REBEKAH RUGG, | DAUGHTR OF | MR JOHN & MRS | LYDIA RUGG | WHO DEC^d. JULY | Y^e 6th, 1747, | AGED 2 YEARS | 9 M & 27 D.

202 a. To the Memory of | ANN AUSTIN | wife of | Peter Thacher Vose, | and daughter of | Hon. John Sprague, | Born | Feb. 26, 1776. | Died | Sept. 10, 1834

202 b. PETER THACHER VOSE | Born in | Milton, | Sept. 4, 1769, | Died | March 4, 1851.

202 c. FRANCIS HENRY VOSE. | Born | August 25, 1816 | Died | July 22, 1841.

202 d. SAMUEL SPRAGUE VOSE | Born in | Augusta, Maine, | Died in Lancaster, | March 1826, | Aged 27.

202 e. EDWARD HENRY | Son of | Peter Thacher & | Ann Austin Vose, | Died | June 23, 1810, | Aged 3 yrs.

204. MRS KATHARINE SPRAGUE, | the amiable Consort of y^e | Honble JOHN SPRAGUE, Esqr. | And a daughter of the late | RICHARD FOSTER, Esqr, | Died May 5th AD. 1787. | in the 49th. year of her age, | And is here interred.
> Blessed are the pure in Heart, | for they shall see God.

205. The Remains | of the | Hon'ble John Sprague, Esqr. | Chief Justice of the Court | of Common Pleas for the | County of Worcester, | who deceased Sept. 28, AD. 1800, | Ætatis 61, | are here deposited.
> Blessed are the peace-makers, for they | shall be called the children of God.

206. In Memory of | SAMUEL JOHN SPRAGUE, A. M. | attorney at law, only son of the | late honourable JOHN SPRAGUE, and | KATHERINE his wife | who died Sept. 10, | A D. 1805, in the | 26 year of his | Age.
> "A safe companion & an easy friend, | Unblam'd through life, lamented in thy end."

207. In Memory of | Amos, Son of Mr. | Amos and Mrs. Prud | ence Sawyer, | Who died Nov. | 1st. 1792, Aged | 3 Years 2 Mon & 5 Days.

THE OLD-COMMON BURIAL GROUND.

When in 1706, after long debate, the third meeting-house was built, far from the old site, upon the east side of the river, a suitable lot of land across the highway near it was given to the town for burials by Captain Thomas Wilder, second of the name. The donor's grave is the oldest in the enclosure, the date of which is known. Inscriptions prior to 1850, beginning with those of the Wilder family, are as follows — the first given being upon a cenotaph of modern erection:

SACRED | to the Memory of | THOMAS WILDER, | from Lancaster in England, | who first settled at Hingham | in 1641, and came to this Town | July 1, 1659, and died Oct. 23, | 1667, leaving three sons — viz | THOMAS, JOHN and NATHANIEL, | from whom are derived all | of the name of Wilder in | this Town and vicinity.

Here Lyes Buried | ye Body of Capt. | THOMAS WILDER | who dec^d August. 7th. | 1716, about ye 70th | Year of His Age.

In Memory of the | Honble. JOSEPH WILDER ESQ^r, | who died MARCH 29th. A Domi 1757. | Ætatis 74.

 He was enrich'd with strong Powers, and good Accomplishments, which were | exerted in his numerous public, | & private Connections. He was | pleasant in Conversation; in Life exemplary: & a steady Friend | to his Country, to ye Good, to | the Poor, to Virtue, and to GOD.

In Memory of M^{rs}. | LUCY WILDER, Relict of y^e. | Honble: JOSEPH WILDER Esqr, | who died May ye 13th, AD: | 1763, Ætatis 84.

 HARK | from the Tombs a doleful Sound; | My Ears attend the Cry,
 Ye living Men, come view the Ground, | Where you must shortly lie.

ERECTED | In Memory of | Col CALEB WILDER, | who died | June 19, 1776, | Æt. 59. | Also of his wife, Mrs. ABIGAIL WILDER. | who died | Oct 1, 1804, | Æt. 92 | And of their daughter, | ABIGAIL SMITH.

ERECTED | to the memory of | MRS. ABIGAIL WILDER, | wife of Caleb Wilder, | who died | Oct. 1, 1804, | Aged 92.

ERECTED | to the memory of | MRS. | ABIGAIL SMITH | daughter of | Caleb Wilder, | who died Sept. 8, | 1778, Aged 32.

SACRED | to the memory of | MRS. SARAH WILDER, | who was transfer'd | from time to eternity, | on the 31 day of Augt. | 1819, | Aged 66 years.

 Hope wipes the tear from sorrow's eye, | While faith points upward to the Sky.

ERECTED | In Memory of | Mr LEVI WILDER, | who departed this life | January 5th: 1793, | aged 42 years.

 How lov'd, how valu'd, once avail'd thee not, | To whom related or by whom begot:
 A heap of dust alone remains with thee, | 'Tis all thou art and all we soon shall be.

HERE LIES Y^e BODY | OF MRS. PRUDANCE | WILDER Y^e WIFE OF | MR. JOSIAH WILDER, AGED | 33 YEARS, 1 M, WITH 4 | OF THEIR CHILDREN, | ALL BETWEEN 12 & 2 | YEARS OF AGE VIZ. | RUFUS MARTHA | JOSIAH & SARAH | ALL DIED BY FIRE | JANUARY Y^e 23^d 1739.

HERE LIES BURIED Y^e BODY OF | CO^{ll} JAMES WILDER, | ESQ^r, WHO DEPARTED | THIS LIFE MAY | Y^e 13th A D 1739 | & IN Y^e | 59th YEAR | OF HIS AGE.

In Memory of Mrs. | ABIGAIL WILDER Relict of | Col: James Wilder Esqr, | Who deceas'd on ye 18th. | Day of Sep^t. A Dom: 1761, | Ætatis. 80.

 O Death, thou'st conquer'd me, | I by thy Dart am Slain.
 But CHRIST has conquer'd thee, | And I shall Rise again.

Sacred | To the Memory of | JOSIAH WILDER Esqr. | who deceased on y^e | 20th. of December, AD. | 1788 in ye 45th. Year | of his Age.

 Every Man at best state | is altogether Vanity: | Cease ye from Man, whose breath | is in his Nostrils: | And trust in | the ever living GOD.

Here lies Buried y^e | Body of Mr | Titus Wilder Son | of Mr Thomas and M^{rs}. Susanna Wilder | Who Dec^d May ye 1st, | A. D. 1749 | Age 25 Years | & 4 M^o.

OLD COMMON BURIAL GROUND.

JONATHAN | WILDER, | DIED | Jan. 13, 1836, | Æt 80. | RUTH | PRESCOTT, | his wife, | DIED | Nov. 19, 1826. | Æt 69.

IN Memory | of | David Wilder, | (Son of Lieu^t, | Jonathan Wilder | & M^{rs}. Ruth | Wilder who died | Jan^r: 29th: 1786; | Aged 4 years & | 4 months. | IN Memory | of | John Wilder, | Son of Lieu^t, | Jonathan Wilder | & M^{rs}. Ruth | Wilder who died | Jan^r: 25th: 1786; | Aged 3 years & | 3 months.

> Death like an overflowing stream, | Sweeps us away, our life's a dream,
> An empty tale, a morning flower, | Cut down and wither'd in an hour.

Here Lies Buried | ye Body of M^r | ASAPH WILDER | Who Departed | This Life July ye 8th | Anno Domini 1747 | Age 23 years | 7 M & 12 D^s.

In Memory of M^{rs}. Zipporah, ye Wife of | M^r. John Phelps, and | formerly ye Wife of | M^r. Asaph Wilder, who | died June ye 20th, ADomi | 1758, Ætatis, 34.

> Thou hast by Death, cut short my Days, | But I Immortal, Thou shalt rais.

Here Lyes ye Body | of Hannah Willder, | Daugh^{tr}, of M^r. John | & M^{rs}. Sarah Willder; | Who Dec^d. Sept^r. | 30th, 1723, in ye 16 | Year of her Age.

HERE LIES BURIED | Y^e BODY OF MR | EBENEZ^R WILDER | WHO DEPARTED | THIS LIFE | DECEM^{br} Y. 25th | A-D 1745 | IN Y^e 65th YEAR | OF HIS AGE | HERE LIES BURIED | Y^e BODY OF MR^s | MARY WILDER | Y^e WIFE OF MR | EBEN^{zr} WILDER | WHO DEC^d | JANUARY Y^e 6th | A-D 1733-4 | AGE 54 YEARS | 9 M & 22 D^s.

HERE LIES BURIED | Y^e BODY OF MRS | ANNA WILDER | Y^e WIFE OF MR | DAUID WILDER | WHO DEC^d | SEPTEM^{br} Y^e 20th | A-D 1744 | IN Y^e 35 YEAR OF HER AGE

HERE LIES BURIED | Y^e BODY OF MR^s | EUNICE WILDER | Y^e WIFE OF MR | DAUID WILDER | WHO DEC^d FEBR^y Y^e 17th | A-D 1750-1 | IN Y^e 30th YEAR | OF HER AGE

In Memory of | Josiah Son of | Capt. James, & | M^{rs}. Martha | Wilder, who | died April, y^e | 4th. 1736, Aged | 5 Mon^s & 16 D^s.

In Memory of | Manasseh, Son of | Capt, Ephraim & M^{rs}. | Anna Wilder, who died December, ye 17, | 1741, in ye 4th. Year | of his Age.

Ephraim, Son of | Capt. Ephraim & | M^{rs}. Anna Wilder, | was Born June y^e | 17th. 1732, and | Died on the Day | of his Birth;

In Memory of | Katharine Daugh^t. of | Capt. Ephraim & M^{rs}. | Anna Wilder, who died | December ye 21st. 1741, | in ye 7th. Year of her Age.

> The small and Great are there. Job.

ANNA MARIA, | daughter of S. V. S. & | Electa Wilder, | died June 20, 1834, | Aged 18 months.

> The blood of Christ, a ransom paid, | Ere death with friendly care;
> The opening bud to heaven conveyed, | And bade it blossom there.

SAMPSON VRYLING | STODDARD, | only son of S. V. S. & | Electa Wilder, | died Feb. 20, 1832, | Aged 3 years 8 months.

> The LORD gave, and the | LORD hath taken away; | blessed be the name of | the LORD.

SARAH VRYLING | STODDARD, | daughter of S. V. S. & | Electa Wilder, | died July 23, 1823, | Aged 23 months.

> Jesus said, Suffer little | children to come unto me, | and forbid them not; | for of such is the kingdom | of God.

SACRED | to the memory of | FRANCINA MELANIE, | daughter of S. V. S. & | Electa Wilder, died in Paris, March 20, 1818, | Aged 8 months.

> Except ye be converted, and | become as little children ye | shall not enter into the | kingdom of heaven. Matt. XVIII, 3.

Here Lyes ye Body | of Rhoda Willson, | Daug^{tr} of Mr Benja^n | & Mrs Rebeckah | Willson; Died Augt 1st, 1732, | in ye 15th | Year of her Age.

MORS vincit omnes | Here lies interred y^e | Body of Capt. | NATHANIEL WILSON, | who departed this Life | August ye 19th, AD. 1778. | in ye 67th, Year of | his Age.

> Death with his warrant in his hand, | Came rushing on amain;
> And I was forced to obey, | But shall arise again.

HERE LIES BURIED | Yᵉ BODY OF MR | JEREMIAH WILSON | WHO DEPARTED | THIS LIFE | MARCH Yᵉ 22ᵈ | A D 1743 | IN Yᵉ 77ᵗʰ YEAR | OF HIS AGE

HERE LIES | THE BODY OF | JOSIAH WHE | TCOMB SEN. D | ECEASED IN H | IS 80 YEAR | JW DYED | MARCH THE | 21 1718

Here Lyes Buried | yᵉ Body of Mʳ | DAVID WHETCOMB | Who Died April | 11ᵗʰ 1730 in yᵉ 62ᵈ | Year of His Age

Here lies Buried | yᵉ Body of Mʳˢ. Mary | Whetcomb Wife to | Mʳ. David Whetcomb, | Who Died Januʳʸ | 5ᵗʰ, 1733-4 in yᵉ 67ᵗʰ | Year of Her Age.

Here Lyes Buried | yᵉ Body of Mʳ. | HEZEKIAH WHETCOMB | Who Died May 6ᵗʰ. | 1732 in yᵉ 31ˢᵗ Year | of His Age

HERE LIES | THE BODY OF RE | BEKAH WARNER | THE DAUGHTER OF | JOHN WARNER AND | SARAH HIS WIFE | R W | WHO DECE | ASED MARCH | THE 30 DAY 1718 | AGED 20 YEARS.

In Memory of | Dorothy W. Daughᵗ. | of Lieut Nathˡ. & | Mʳˢ Elizabeth Willard | She died May yᵉ | 25ᵗʰ, 1765, Aged 2 Yr, 2 M, & 17 D.

Here lies yᵉ | Bodys of Wright & | Dorothy children of | Mr Aaron & Mrs Mary | Willard Died March | 28 1754 yᵉ Son | Age 8 y & 24 | Dˢ. The Girl | 11 y & 18 Dˢ.

HERE LIES BURIED | Yᵉ BODY OF | ELIZABETH | WILLARD DAUGH | OF ENSⁿ AARON | & MRˢ MARY | WILLARD WHO | DECᵈ SEPTMᵇʳ 25 | A D 1746 | AGE 11 YEARS | 10 M & 25 Dˢ.

Here lyes Buried | yᵉ Body of | Mʳˢ. Mary Wiilard: | Wife to Mr Aaron | Willard she died | April yᵉ 27ᵗʰ, AD 1767, | Aged 63 Years, 2 months, & 8 days.

Here Lies Buried yᵉ. | Body of Mʳˢ, MARTHA | JOSLYN yᵉ. wife of | Capᵗ. PETER JOSLYN | & Formerly yᵉ. wife of | Mʳ. JOSIAH WHEELER | she Died May yᵉ. 21ˢᵗ. | 1748. in yᵉ. 69ᵗʰ. | Year of her Age.

HERE LIES BURIED | Yᵉ BODY OF | Mʳ. JOSIAH WHEELER | WHO DIED | DECEMBER Yᵉ 8ᵗʰ | 1738 & IN | Yᵉ 64ᵗʰ YEAR | OF HIS AGE

Miss. | REBECAH | Daughter of | Mr. Samuel and | Mrs. Rebecah Woodberry | died | Febr. 25, 1815, | Æt. 24.

TIMOTHY WHITING, | Obt, | Jan. 12, 1826. | Æ. 67. | ABIGAIL, | Wife of | Timo Whiting, | Obt. Oct. 1, 1798, | Æ. 39, | Resurgamus. | Lydia, | Wife of | Timo. Whiting, | Obt Jan. 15, 1851, | Æ 75. | In Memoriam.

ERECTED | In Memory of | Miss OLIVE BUTLAR, | who died | Feb. 24, 1822, | aged 59.

<blockquote>
Come my Friends, behold, | This bed of clay how cold:
But let us look above | And see our Saviour drest in love.
Oh! happy it would be to meet a smileing God.
</blockquote>

WILLIAM J. | died May 23, 1806; | Æt. 9 months, | Son of | Mr. Charles & | Mrs. Ruth Chase.

ALBERT R. | died April 4, 1825; | Æ. 8 months, | son of | Mr: Alanson & Mrs. | Maria Chase.

<blockquote>O envy not his blest estate, He's happiness complete.</blockquote>

In memory of | AMIA ANN CHACE, | who died | Feb. 4, 1831: | Æt. 21.

IN Memory of | Mrs. Mary Carter, | wife of | Capᵗ. James Carter, | who died April 18ᵗʰ. 1795. Aged 66 years | and 15 days.

Capt. | JAMES CARTER, | who died | July 15, 1800 | Æ. 79.

In Memory of Mʳˢ. | PRUDENCE CARTER, | Wife of Capᵗ, James | Carter, who died | Janʳʸ. yᵉ 10ᵗʰ, AD. 1747 | Aged 19 Years 3 Monᵗʰˢ. | and 16 Days.

<blockquote>My Youthful Days cut short by Thee | are lengthen'd to Eternity.</blockquote>

IN | Memory | of | MARY LOUISA CARLETON, | died Jan. 22, 1837, | aged 16 years.

<blockquote>"Oh blest! thus pure to pass away."</blockquote>

SACRED | To the memory of | MRS. MARY CARLETON, | wife of Mr. Moses Carleton, | who died May 7, 1832. | Æt. 32.

<blockquote>In the death of Mrs. Carleton, | her Husband is bereft of an | affectionate and amiable | Companion, and her Children | of a kind and tender Mother.</blockquote>

OLD COMMOM BURIAL GROUND. 411

GEORGE HENRY, | son of | Mr. Moses and | Mrs. Mary Carleton, | died | Sept. 8, 1829, | Æt. 4 years.
> No taint of earth, no thought of sin, | Ere dwelt thy stainless breast within,
> And God hath laid thee down to sleep | Like a pure pearl below the deep.

THEODORE, | Son of Mr. Moses & | Mrs. Mary Carleton | died | Oct. 23, 1823, | Æt. 1 year.
> Unclose thy narrow portals silent tomb! | Take this fair flower blighted in earliest bloom,
> Pure, as when first its infant charms had birth | It faded, ere it caught one stain from earth.
> The cherub came to show what angels are, | Then fled to heaven to ope a pathway there.

SACRED | To the Memory of | Mrs. MARY CARLETON, | Wife of Mr. Moses Carleton; | who died Feb. 7, 1816: | Æt. 23
> In deaths calm shade beneath this sculptur'd stone—Sleeps lovely Mary, silent and alone,
> But wasted in the grave, her precious dust, | Shall live again when God revives the just,
> Then dry your tears, her upward flight pursue, | She waits in heaven, ere long to welcome you.

JAMES, | Son of Jonathan | Carleton of Boston, | he was a pupil at the | Academy in this | Town, and was drowned while bath | ing near the centre | Bridge June 29, | 1819, in his 12 year.

MARY CLEVELAND, | wife of | William Cleveland, | died May 7, 1815, | aged 36.

JOSEPH HILLER, ESQ. | Died Feb. 9, 1814: | Aged 66.

JOSEPH HILLER, | Son of | W^m. & Mary Cleveland, | Died June 28, 1817, | Aged 3 years.

MOSES EMERSON | died Oct. 22, 1822, aged 48. | Judith Kelly died Dec. 5, 1798, aged 23. | Sally Carleton died Oct. 16, 1808, aged 29. | Lydia Carleton died Jan. 13, 1813, aged 32. | Eunice Wright died Sept. 27, 1844, aged 58. | Hazen died April 4, 1807 aged 3 years. | Sally C. died Nov. 26, 1817, aged 3 years. Moses K. died Oct. 27, 1825, aged 27 years. | Francis P. died Aug. 24, 1835, aged 25 yrs. | Children of | Moses Emerson.

Here Lies Buried | ye Body of M^{rs} | Deliverance Fife | Wife of Mr Willm. | Fife who Dec^d. | November ye 4th. | A.D. 1750 | Age 37 years, | 10 M & 4 D^s.

Memento Mori. | ERECTED | In Memory of M^r. WILLIAM FIFE, | Who departed this life, May y^e | 5th. 1790, in ye 74th. | Year of his Age.
> Friends and physicians could not save, | My mortal body from the Grave;
> Nor can the Grave confine me here, | When Christ shall call me to appear.

Memento Mori. | ERECTED | In Memory of M^{rs}. | ABIGAIL FIFE, | Wife of William Fife | who departed this life, | April ye 30th, 1790, | in ye 69th. Year of | her age.
> Retire, my friends dry up your tears, | Here I must lie till Christ appears.

IN Memory of | Mr. Joseph Fife, | who died Nov^r. | 3. 1810, | Aged 22 years.
> Friends and physicians could not save, | My mortal body from the grave.
> Nor shall the grave confine me here, | When Christ shall call me to appear.

Here lies interred | ye Body of M^{rs}. CHARITY FALLAS, | ye Wife of M^r. | WILLIAM FALLAS, | who departed this | life Oct: ye 29th. A D. | 1786, in the 65th. | Year of her Age.
> "Blessed are the dead | which die in the Lord."

HERE LIES THE | BODY OF M^r | EPHRAIM FARNWORTH | WHO DIED FEBRUARY | THE 18th 1737 | IN THE 35 | YEAR OF HIS | AGE.

In Memory | of Jonathan | son of Mr Jona | than and | Thankfull | Fairbank | who Died Septr 14 1741 | in ye 2 | year of | his Age.

MARTHA, | wife of | Silas Fairbanks, | died Dec. 8, 1849, | Æt. 68.

SILAS FAIRBANKS | died Aug. 26, 1847. | Æt. 67.

IN Memory of | M^{rs}. HANNAH FLAGG, | Relict of M^r. | Gershom Flagg, | who died Oct. | ye 13th. 1784, | Aged 73.

In memory of | MR. | PAUL FAULKNER, | died Feb. 9. 1841, | aged 75 yrs. | Also of his wives | MRS ABIGAIL F. | died Sept. 23, 1811, | aged 42 yrs. | MRS. HANNAH F. | died Oct. 4. 1817, | aged 46 yrs. | MRS EUNICE F. | died Oct. 5, 1846, | aged 62 yrs.

Mrs. | Emily Faulkner | wife of | Mr. Horace Faulkner, | died Aug. 24, 1825, | Æt 22.

Here lies Buried | ye Body of | Mr JOHN GOOS | who Dec^d. | October ye 5th | A. D. 1747 | In ye 30 year of His Age.

MR | JOHN GOSS, | died March 24, 1843, | Æt. 73.

> Farewell, fond wife, and children too | For Christ hath called me home;
> In a short time he'll call you, | Prepare yourselves to come.

In Memory of | MR. JOHN GOSS JR. | Son of Mr. John and | Mrs. Mary W. Goss, | who died | Jan. 13, 1828, | Æt. 23.

> And is he gone? 'tis true he is, | His glass bow soon 'tis run,
> How pleasant were his youthful ways, | But now his work is done.

In Memory of | John Goss, Son of | Mr John & Mrs | Mary W. Goss | who died Octr. 1, | 1803, aged 1 year 7 | Mo. & 22 days.

> Sleep on my babe & take thy rest, | God call'd the hom, he thought it best.

In memory of | Joseph Goss, Son of | Mr. John & Mrs. Mary | W. Goss, who died | Aug. 16th, 1801, Aged | 1 Year, 10 months & 2 days.

> So fades the lovely blooming flower, | Frail smiling solace of an hour.

In memory of | James Goss, Son of | Mr. John & Mrs. Mary | W. Goss, who died | Dec. 30th, 1800, Aged 3 | Years, 18 months & 2 days.

> So soon our transient comforts fly, | An pleasures only bloom to die.

Here lyes ye Body of | Dinah Houghton Daug^{tr} | of Mr Jonas & Mrs Mary | Houghton Who Died | Sep^t 23^d 1723 Aged | 12 Years & 5 M^o.

Here lyes ye Body | of Mr JONAS | HOUGHTON; Who | Died Sep^t. 20th, 1723 | Aged 60 Years & 5 M^o.

Here Lyes the | Body of M^s. Mary | Houghton, Wife to | M^r. Jonas Houghton | Senr. Dec^d. Dece^{mbr} | 31st 1720 in ye 60th | Year of har Age.

HERE LIES | BURIED Y^e BODY | OF CAP^t JONAS | HOUGHTON WHO | DEPATED THIS | LIFE AUGUST | Y^e 15th A. D 1739 | JN Y^e 57th YEAR | OF HIS AGE

HERE LIES | BURIED Y^e BODY | OF Mr JOSIAH | HOUGHTON WHO | DEC^d SEPTEMBER Y^e | 29th 1723 | AGED 24 YEARS | & 11 M

Ephah Houghton, | Daug^{tr}. of Lieu^t. | Jonathan & M^{rs}. | Thankful Houghton | Died Sep^{tr}. 27th, 1729 | Aged 2 Years & 3 M^o.

HERE LIES BURIED | Y^e BODY OF | MARY HOUGHTON | DAUGHT'R OF ENSIGN | JACOB & MRS | MARY HOUGHTON | WHO DIED | AUGUST Y^e 30th | 1736 AGE | 3 YEARS 10 M | & 29 D

Here Lyes Buried | ye Body of Lieu^t. | JOHN HOUGHTON; | Who Dec^d April | ye 5th, 1724. | Aged 51 Years.

Here Lyes y^e | Body of M^s. | Mary Albert | Wife to Mr. | Daniel Albert | Who Dec^d. Octo^r | 23^d. 1726: in y^e 25 | Year of Her Age

HERE LIES Y^e | BODY OF | LEVINAH HOUGHTON | Y^e DAUGHTER OF | MR JONATHAN & | MR^s MARY HOUGHTON | WHO DIED | JULY Y^e 5th | 1738 & JN | Y$_e$ 5th YEAR OF HER AGE

HERE LIES Y^e | BODY OF SILANCE | HOUGHTON Y^e | DAUGHTER OF MR | JONATHAN & MRS | MARY HOUGHTON | WHO DIED | SEPTEMBER | Y^e 4 | 1728

Here Lies Buried | The Body of | Mrs Rebekah | Houghton Wife of | Mr Jacob Houghton | Died October y^e | 22 A-D 1752 | Age 80 yers 10. M | & 29 D^s

HERE LIES BURIED | Y^e BODY OF | JOHN HOUGHTON | ESQUIR, AS YOU | ARE SO WARE WE | AS WE ARE SO | YOU WILL BE | WHO DIED FEBRUARY | YE 3^d ANNO DOMINY | 1736-7 AND | IN Y^e 87th YEAR | OF HIS AGE

HERE LIES | BURIED Y^e BODY | OF MRS MARY | HOUGHTON Y^e | WIFE OF JOHN | HOUGHTON ESQ^r | WHO DIED APRIL | Y^e 7th ANO DM 1724 | & JN Y^e 76 YEAR | OF HER AGE

HERE LIES BURIED | Y^e BODY OF | MR WILL^m HOUGHTON | AS . YOU . ARE . SO . WERE . WE . | AS . WE: ARE: SO; YOU: WILL: BE | WHO DEPARTED | THIS LIFE | JULY Y^e 15th | ANNO DM 1743 | AGE 48 YEARS | 2 M & 20 D

OLD COMMON BURIAL GROUND. 413

HERE LIES BURIED | Y^e BODY OF MR | ROBART HOUGHTON | WHO DEC^d | NOVEMB^r Y^e 7th | A-D 1723 | JN Y^e 65 YEAR | OF HIS AGE:

Here Lyes ye Body | of Mr. EBENEZER | HOUGHTON; | Who | Dec^d. Octo^{br}. ye 13th | 1723, in the 24th | Year of His Age.

HERE LIES BURIED | Y^e BODY OF MRS | ESTHER HOUGHTON | RELICT WIDOW | OF MR ROBART HOUGHTON WHO | DEC^d JANUARY | 13th A-D 1740-41 | JN Y^e 82th YEAR | OF HER AGE

RUFUS HOUGHTON | Born Nov. 28, 1796: | Died May 31, 1846. | Solon | Georgiana

MARTHA P. | Wife of | Rufus Houghton, | Born June 12, 1803: | Died Dec. 17, 1835.

SACRED | to the memory of | Mr. SIMON HOUGHTON, | of Weare, N. H. | & a native of Bolton, Mass. | who died | July 7, 1814 Æt. 41.

> In peace here rests a traveler's dust, | His journey's at an end:
> He prais'd esteem among the just | A censure from a friend,
> Broke loose from time's tenacious chains, | And Earth's revolving gloom,
> To range, at large, in vast domains | Of radient worlds to come:

SACRED | to the memory of | MRS. MARTHA HOUGHTON, | wife of | Mr. Simon Houghton, of Bolton | who died April 3, 1823. | in the 73 Year | of her age.

> No pain, no grief, no anxious fear, | Invade thy bounds; no mortal woes
> Can reach the peaceful sleeper here, | Whilst angels watch her soft repose.
> So Jesus slept; God's dying son | Pass'd through the grave and blest the bed;
> Then rest, dear saint, till from his throne, | The morning break & peirce the shade.

SACRED | to the memory of | Mr. SIMON HOUGHTON | of Bolton, | who departed this life | March 25, A D: 1814, in | 77th. year of | his age.

> The dust and ruins, that remain, | Are precious in our eyes:
> These ruins shall be built again, | And all this dust shall rise.

IN Memory of Lieu^t. | THOMAS HOOKER, | Who died September | ye 18th 1768, in y^e | 79th. year of his age.

> when Death unto you calls, | your Soul Rejoined must,
> To God that judgeth all, | Both Wicked and the just.

HERE LIES BURIED | Y^e BODY OF | MR URIAH HOLT | WHO DEPARTED | THIS LIFE AUGUST | Y^e 24th A D 1741 | AGE 40 YEARS | 2 M & 10 D.

IN | Memory of | MRS. PHEBE JENKS, | Relict of | Mr. William Jenks, | of Wrentham | who died | Oct. 11, 1822, | Aged 88.

IN | Memory of | Miss. Mary Jenks, | who died | May 17, 1817, | Aged 44.

Her Lies THE BODY OF Mrs | SARAH KNIGHT THE WIF OF Mr | DANIEL KNIGHT died APRIL The | 30 1722 DIED In The 38 | YEAR OF HER AGE

GEORGE. | son of George & | Eunice Marshall | formerly of England. | Died | May 17, 1847. | Aged 18 months.

> Suffer little children to come unto | me; and forbid them not, for of such is | the kingdom of God.

HERE LIES BURIED | Y^e BODY OF | JOSEPH MOORS | SON OF DEAC^n JOSEPH & MR^s | REBEKAH MOORS | WHO DEC^d | OCTOB^r Y^e 25th | A-D 1746 | AGE 3 YEARS | 6 M & 28 D^s

HERE LIES Y^e | BODY OF REBEKAH | MOORS DAUGHTER | OF DEAC^n JOSEPH | & MR^s REBEKAH MOORS WHO DEC^d | SEPTEMB^r Y^e 22^d | A D 1746 | AGE 1 YEAR | 7 M & 10 D^s

HERE LIES | Y^e BODY OF | REBEKAH MORES | Y^e DAUGHT^r OF | MR JOSEPH & MR^s | REBEKAH MORES | WHO DEC^d | JUNE Y^e 26th | 1740 IN Y^e | 6th YEAR OF | HER AGE

HERE LIES | Y^e BODY OF | CATHORIGN MORES | DAUGHT^r OF MR | JOSEPH & MR^s | REBEKAH MORES | WHO DIED | JUNE Y^e 23^d | 1740 IN Y^e | 2^d YEAR OF | HER AGE

HERE LIES BURIED Y^e | BODIES OF EPHRAIM & | HANNAH & JACOB MORES | Y^e CHILDREN OF | MR JOSEPH MORES & | MR^s REBEKAH HIS WIFE | WHO DEC^d JUNE Y^e 15th & | Y^e 17th & 18th 1740 AGE OF | E 7 YEARS 6 M & 22 D | & H M 3 YEARS 1 M & 7 D | & J M 11 YEARS 8 M & 6 D

HERE LIES BURIED | Yᵉ BODY OF | LUCY MOORS | DAUGHTʳ OF DEAᶜᵒⁿ | JOSEPH & MRˢ | REBEKAH MOORS | WHO DECᵈ | OCTOBʳ Yᵉ 7ᵗʰ | A-D 1744 | AGE 3 YEARS | 6 M & 15 Dˢ

HERE LIES BURIEᵈ | Yᵉ BODY OF | LUCY MORES | Yᵉ DAUGHTʳ OF | MR JOSEPH & MRˢ | REBEKAH MORES | WHO DECᵈ | AUGUST Yᵉ 22ᵈ | A-D 1740 | IN Yᵉ 14ᵗʰ YEAR | OF HER AGE

HARRIET, | Daughter of | Mr. Henry and | Mrs. Achsah Moore | died | April 8, 1826, | Æt. 14 mo. & 14 da.

In Memory of | DAVID STEUART ROBERTSON, | Second son of the late John Robertson, Esqʳ. | of Foveran House, Aberdeenshire. | Born in Scotland, | Educated at Rugby in England, | And at Giessen, in Germany, | In which country, as well as in Sicily, | He had spent several years, | At the age of twenty-three, | He came to America. | Having, after various experience of the Old World, | Acquired an ardent love for the New, | He settled in this town of Lancaster, | And became a citizen of the United States. | Deceased on the twenty first of July, | A. D. MDCCCXLIX. | In the thirtieth year of his age.

  Here Steuart sleeps—and should some brother Scot
  Wander this way, and pause upon the spot,
  He need not ask, now life's poor show is o'er,
  What arms he carried, or what plaid he wore;
  So small the value of illustrious birth,
  Brought to this solemn, last assay of earth:
  Yet, unreproved, his epitaph may say,
  A royal soul was wrapt in Steuart's clay,
  And generous actions consecrate his mound
  More than all titles, though of kingly sound.

Mrs. Ann Quincy, | Relict of | Josiah Quincy | Esq. | Late of | Braintree. | Died Feb. 17, | 1805. | Æ. 80.

A chearful heart was hers, and free from guile; | She showed that piety and age could smile; Religion had her heart, her cares, her voice, | Twas her last refuge as her earliest choice Like a tir'd traveler, with sleep oppress'd | Within her children's arms she sank to rest. Heaven did her life prolong to spread its praise, | And bless'd her with a patriarch's length of days.

Here lie the remains of | ELOISE RICHARDS PAYNE, | Who departed this life | July 3 1819, | Æt. 31. | She will be talked of | but a little while, | and | forgotten by society, | will survive only in a few hearts, | where the memory of such a Being | is immortal.

  Sink into dust, | frail covering of a purified spirit! | Parent earth receive thine own!
  God in Heaven, | Take her soul to thee!

Here sleeps | what was mortal | of | ELIZA | QUINCY | PACKARD, | dauᵗ. of Rev. Asa Packard. | She died suddenly | Novʳ. 18ᵗʰ. A. D. 1816 | Ætat. 24.

An | improved mind, | a heart and Life | enriched with early | Piety, endeared her | where she was known, | and rendered her death | deeply lamentable. | Thy will Father, be done! | I am the resurrection | and the life! | Listening for the triumph of the Arch Angel. | In CHRIST they sleep | who bore on earth his cross. | Till from the tomb their dust shall rise | In his own image to the skies.

ANN GUILD. | Daughter of | Rev. Charles & | Rebecca P. Packard, | died Apr. 28, 1846; | aged 10 weeks.

  Transplanted.

Anna Marsh Packard, | Eldest child of | Revᵈ. Asa Packard, | sleeps here, | she died June 6ᵗʰ. 1796 | Aged 5 years.

  Of such is the kingdom of God.

Memento mori. | Here lies | Buried the Body | of Mʳ. John Phelps | who departed | this Life | January, 14ᵗʰ: 1776. In the 28 year of his age.

ERECTED | in memory of | Mrs. SALLY PHELPS | Wife of Mr. Aaron Phelps, | who died April 12ᵗʰ. | 1794: Aged 36 | Years.

  Behold and see, as you pass by, | As you are now, so once was I;
  As I am now, so you must be; | Prepare for death & follow me.

MR. PETER PHELPS | DIED | MARCH 7. 1847 | AGED 72 YRS. | ABIEL S. PHELPS, | DIED | OCT. 15, 1825, | AGED 14 yrs. * * * *

OLD COMMON BURIAL GROUND.   415

CHARLES, Son of | Farnham & Nancy | Plummer died | May 25, 1818 | Æt. 9 mo.

Thomas 2ᵈ. Son | of Farnham & Nancy | Plummer died Oct. | 2, 1814, Æt 5 mo. | Also Thomas 1ˢᵗ. Son | died at Beverly June | 12, 1808, Æt. 9 mo.

Here Lies Buried | The Body of Mʳ | JOHN PREIST, | who Departed this | Life, Sepᵇʳ. 29, A. D. | 1756, in yᵉ 75ᵗʰ | Year of his Age.

Here Lies Buried | The Body of Mʳˢ. | ANNA PRIEST, | Wife of Mʳ John | Priest Who Departed | This Life April 3 | Anno Domini 1751, | In yᵉ 67 year | of Her Age.

HERE LIES BURIED | Yᵉ BODY OF | JONATHAN PRIEST | Yᵉ ONLY SON OF | MR JOHN & MRˢ ANNA | PRIEST WHO DECᵈ | APRIL Yᵉ 23ᵈ 1738 | AGED 12 YEARS | & 7 M

Here Lyes yᵉ Body | of Abigail Priest, | Daughᵗʳ. of Mr John | & Mʳˢ. Anna Priest; | Who Decᵈ. Septʳ. | 25ᵗʰ. 1723, in yᵉ 17ᵗʰ. | Year of her Age.

In memory of | CHARLOTTE RICHARDSON | daughʳ. of Mr. Ephraim & | Mrs. Eunice Richardson | who died | Nov. 13, 1827, | aged 15 years.
    Like roses crop'd before their bloom | She's carried to the silent tomb.

ABIGAIL H. | wife of | Luke Stowe, | died Feb. 15, 1847, | aged 54 years.
    Farewell dear friends, and children too, | For Christ has called me home,
    In a short time he'll call for you, | Prepare yourselves to come.

LUKE STOWE | died Aug. 19, 1846. | aged 49 years.
    Friends and physicians could not save, | My mortal body from the grave;
    Nor can the grave confine me here, | When Christ shall call me to appear.

HERE LIES | THE BODY OF | MR JOHN | SAWYER WHO | DIED OCTOBER | THE 2ᵈ 1731 | IN THE | 43 YEAR | OF HIS | AGE

HEAR . LYES | THE . BODY . OF | SARAH . THE | DAUGHTER | OF . JOHN . & | RUTH | SAWYER | DECEASED | DESEMBER | THE 21 - D | 1717

Here lyes yᵉ Body | of Mʳˢ Dinah Sawyer | Wife of Mr Seth | Sawyer; Who Decᵈ. | Octoᵇʳ. 25ᵗʰ 1727 | in yᵉ 23ᵈ Year | of her Age

Here Lies Buried | The Body of | Mʳ Elias Sawyer | Who Died Novembʳ | yᵉ 20, A D 1752, | In yᵉ 63 | Year of His Age.

HERE LIE˙ BURIED | Yᵉ BODY OF | MR MOSES SAWYER | WHO DEPARTED | THIS LIFE | NOVEMBʳ Yᵉ 24ᵗʰ | A-D 1739 AGE | 27 YEARS | 2 M & 29 D.

Here Lies Buried | The Body of | Mʳ Thos Sawyer. | Who Died Novembʳ | yᵉ 29 A˙ D 1752 | In yᵉ 63 | year of His Age

ERECTED in memory | of | Mrs. Lydia Sawyer, | Relict of Mr Elijah Sawyer, | of Bolton, | who died May 5ᵗʰ, | A. D. 1799, aged 72 years | 6 months & 1 day.

ERECTED | in memory of Mrs. | Elizabeth Sawyer, | Wife of Mr. Thomas | Sawyer, who died | Feb. 14, 1799, in | the 34ᵗʰ. year | of her age.

AMOS SAWYER, | a native of Danvers Ms. | died June 13, 1821: | Æt. 68.

In memory of | MRS. | ELIZABETH SAFFORD, | wife of Thomas Safford, | who died | March 11, 1818, | Æt. 49.

In memory of | MR. THOMAS SAFFORD | who died | June 20, 1825, | Æt. 59.

IN Memory of | Catharine Safford, | daughʳ. of Mr. Thomas | & Mrs. Elizabeth Safford, | who died July 4ᵗʰ: 1798, | Aged 15 months.
    Now she is numbered among the | children of God and her lot is among | the Saints.

IN Memory | of | Mr. JOSHUA TOWNSEND | (a native of Boston,) | who departed this life | Janʸ. 20ᵗʰ. 1790, In | the 90ᵗʰ year | of his age.

Here lies interred | yᵉ Body of Mʳˢ. | ELIZABETH TOWNSEND | (yᵉ Wife of Mʳ. | JOSHUA TOWNSEND) | who departed this | Life Feb. yᵉ 8ᵗʰ. Anno. | Dom. 1779: in yᵉ | 76ᵗʰ. Year of her | Age.

THE CHOCKSETT PRECINCT BURIAL GROUND. 1736–1781.

The first meeting-house in the Second Parish of Lancaster was opened for public use November 28, 1742; but during five or more years previous to this date, the families in that quarter of the town had grown sufficiently numerous to organize neighborhood meetings under the leadership of Josiah Brown, a young clergyman there resident. From this fact, and from the evidence of the memorial to the Dresser children, it may be inferred that the third place of burial in Lancaster was public ground as early as 1736. Throwing doubt upon such inference, however, is the statement of a historian in the Worcester Magazine of 1826, that Gamaliel Beaman's burial in 1745 was the first within the parish.

In Memory of 3 Children of M^r: | Samuel & M^{rs}: Anna Bayley, | Anna Died | Feb^{ry}, ye 25th; | 1756, in y^e, | 19th; Year | of her | Age. | Susannah Died | Oct^{ber}; y^e, 5th; | 1750 in y^e, | 6th; Year | of her | Age. | Isaac Died | Nov^{ber}; ye 2nd; | 1750, in y^e. | 4th; Year | of his | Age.

Here Lies Buried | the Body of M^r; | Gamaliel Beaman | who Died October | 26th: 1745. in y^e | 61st; Year of | his Age.

HERE LIES BURIED | Y^e BODY OF MR^s | ANNAH BOYNTON | Y^e WIFE OF MR | ZACCHEUS BOYNTON | WHO DEC^d | MAY Y^e 5th | A. D 1746 | IN Y^e 30th YEAR | OF HER AGE.

In Memory of | M^r; SETH BROOKS, | who Died January | ye 16th, AD. 1776, | Aged 23 Years, 5 | Months, & 6 Days.

> Behold & see as you pass by, | As you are now so once was J,
> As I am now so you must be, | Prepare for Death & follow me.

ERECTED | in memory of | Josiah Brown A. M. | Preacher of the Gospel, | who departed this life | Feb. 6th. 1773, in the | 57th. Year of his age.

> Kind as a parent, and a friend sincere; | A generous heart disposed to feed the poor; | But cruel death has shorten'd his career, | His chearing converse we shall hear no more. | No more his tongue shall sacred truths impart, | Each virtue's fled which glow'd within his breast; | The graves great herald wing'd its cruel dart, | And now he sleeps within his bed of rest.

In Memory of | Rebekah, Dau. | of Mr. Josiah | & Mr^s. Prudence Brown, who | died August, y^e | 11th, 1761, in y^e | 5th. Year of her | Age.

In Memory of | John Brown, | Son of M^r. John & M^{rs} | Gen. Brown, who died | February ye 24th 1781 | in ye 6th year of his | Age.

IN MEMORY OF | ELIZABETH BURPE | DAU^r OF Mr SAMUEL | & M^{rs}: ELIZth: BURPE | DIED OCT^r: 1749, | IN Y^e 13th: YEAR | OF HER AGE.

IN MEMORY OF | ELIJAH BURPE, | SON OF M^r. | SAMUEL & M^{rs}: | ELIZth: BURPE | DIED NOV^r. 17th. 1750. | IN YE 9 YEAR | OF HIS AGE.

IN MEMORY OF | HANNAH BURPE | DAU^r. OF M^r. SAMUEL | & M^{rs}. ELIZth. BURPE | DIED OCT^r. 13th. 1756. | IN Y^e 24th. YEAR | OF HER AGE.

Ebenezer died | Augst, 31st, | 1756, in ye 4th | Year of his | Age. | Jeremiah died | Sep 2nd, 1756, | in ye 11th month | of his | Age. | Molly died | Sep 6th, 1756, | in ye 8th, Year | of her | Age. In Memory of 3 Children of Mr. | Jeremiah Burpe & Elizabeth his wife.

IN MEMORY OF M^r; | NATHAN BURPE | DIED SEP^t 30th, 1756 | IN Y^e 25th. | YEAR | OF HIS AGE. | This man wife & child | in 14 days did die | his house left Disolate | Being ye whole Family.

IN MEMORY OF | ELIJAH BURPE | SON OF M^r. | NATHAN BURPE | & M^{rs}. AZUBAH HIS | WIFE, DIED SEP^t. 20th. | 1756. AGED 3 | MONTHS & 10 D^s.

IN MEMORY OF | AZUBAH BURPE | WIFE OF M^r. | NATHAN BURPE | DIED SEP^t. 16th. 1756, | IN Y^e 26th. YEAR | OF HER AGE.

[NOTE. In 1756 Chocksett was ravaged by an endemic dysentery, singularly fatal in its attacks. Within two months more than one-twentieth of the population died.]

CHOCKSETT BURIAL GROUND.

Here Lies y* | Body of Ruth | Cooper, Dafter | of Mr Moses & Mrs Ruth | Cooper Who | Died Sep^t. y* | 27, 1750, Age 6 | Years 7 M^s & | 14 D^s.

Here Lies y* | Body of Lenard | Cooper y* Son of | M^r. Moses & M^{rs} | Ruth Cooper | Who Died Sep^t. | y* 1 1750 Aged | 4 Years 9 Months.

John Son of M^r. Aaron & M^{rs}. | Mehetabal Dresser, who | died Feb^r. 25th. 1737, in y* 4th | Year of his Age. | And Jedediah There Son | who died Sep^t. y* 30th. 1736, in | y* 2nd. Year of his Age. & Aaron There Son who | was Born Sep^t. y* 29th, 1753, | & died in 1 Hour.

Hannah Daugh^t. of | M^r. Aaron and M^{rs}. | Mehetabal Dresser, | who died Jan. y* | 18th. 1749, in y* 12th. | Year of her Age.

In Memory of M^{rs}. | Mehetabeel Wife | of M^r. Fortunatus | Eager, who Died | March y* 29th. 1759, | in the 26th. Year | of her Age.

Jonathan died | Oct^{br}. y*. 19th: | 1747, in y* | 5th: year of | his Age. | Joshua died | Oct^{br}. y*. 21st: | 1747, in y* | 2nd: year of | his Age. | Jonathan died | Dec^{br}. y* 14th. | 1750, in | y* 2nd: year | of his Age. | In Memory of 3 Children of | M^r. Jonathan & M^{rs}. Thankfull Fairbanks.

In Memory | of M^{rs}: Mercy | Gates who | Died Feb^{ry}: | y* 4th: 1756, | In y*. 44th: | Year of her | Age.

IN MEMORY OF M^{rs}. | ESTHER GLAZIER | WIFE OF M^r. | JOHN GLAZIER | DIED JULY 9th: 1753. | IN Y* 38th: YEAR | OF HER AGE.

In Memory of M^r: | Nathan Goodell, | who died Sep^t. y* 10th: | 1762, in y*. 26th. Year | of his Age.

Thou Shortned hast, | His youthful days ; | But him Immortal, | Thou shalt raise.

DEO PATRIÆ AMICIS. | In Memory of M^r. | WILLIAM HARRIS, | who fled from y* destruction | of Charlestown, A·D·1775, | where he was Public School | Master 11 Years; and came | to this town, where he died, | Octr. 30th, 1778, aged 34 | Years & 3 months; he left | behind a Wife & 4 children, | who raised this stone to perpe | tuate y* memory of a man | justly beloved.

O ye whose cheek y* tear of pity stains | Draw near with pious reverence & attend ;
Here lie y* loving Husband's dear remains, | The tender Father, & the generous Friend ;
The pitying heart that felt for human woe ; | The dauntless heart oppos'd to human pride ;
The friend of man to vice alone a foe, | "For e'en his failings lean'd to virtue's side."

Here is deposited what was | mortal of ANN (who died Feb^r. | 8th, 1778, aged 3 years 3 m'ths & | 11 days,) & of WILLIAM (who died | on the 16th. of the same month, aged | 5 months & 21 days,) the children of M^r. WILLIAM | & M^{rs}. REBECCAH HARRIS.

"Beneath this stone two infants lie, | To mingle with the dust ;
Yet they shall mount above the sky ;—And dwell among the just.
When flames of wrath shall burn y* seas, | And nature groan its last,
Millions on earth will wish their days | As swiftly too had past."

Here lies y* Body of M^{rs}: | BETHESDA HOUGHTON | wife of M^r: | JOSIAH HOUGHTON | died APRIL 20th: 1755. | In y* 37th: year | of her Age. | Also BETHESDA DAU^r: | to y* above nam'd | died APRIL 10, 1756, | Aged 1 Year & 21 D^s:

Dinah Dau^r. of | M^r. Ezra & | M^{rs}. Dinah | Houghton | who Died | October y* 17th, | 1756. Aged | 7 Years 3 Mon | ths & 4 Days. | Mary Dau^r. | of M^r. Ezra & | M^{rs}. Dinah | Houghton | who was | Still Born | November | y* 12th, 1753.

In Memory of | M^r. Benjamin | Houghton who | Died April y* 25th. | 1759, | in the 27th | Year of his | Age.

HEAR LIES BURIED THE | BODY OF MR BENIAMIN | HOUGHTON WHO | DEPARTED THIS | LIFE FEBRUARY Y* 28. | 1764, IN Y* 74 | YEAR OF HIS AGE.

When death unto you calls | Your soul Resine you must
to God that judgeth all | Both Wicked and the just
Death is a Debt to Nature Due | Which I have paid & so must you.

Joshua House | died Aug. 8th. 1786, | in his 62^d. Year. | Joshua House Jun. | died Aug. 4th. 1778. | Aged 20 Years.

ESTHER KENDAL | DAU^r: OF M^r: | JOSIAH & M^{rs}. | TABITHA KENDALL | DIED MARCH 10th. 1756. | IN Y* 4th YEAR | OF HER AGE.

In Memory of | Peirson, Son of M^r. | James Kendal, & | Lydia his Wife, | Who Died Sepr. ye 22 | 1756, Aged, 9 years | & 3 Months.

Here lies inter'd | ye Body of M^{rs}. | MARY LEAVITT, | Wife of Doct. | Josiah Leavitt, | who died May y^e | 20th. 1778. in ye 34th. | Year of her Age.

The sweet Remembrance of the Just, | Shall florish when they Sleep in Dust.

In Memory of | Marah Littlejohn, | Dau. of M^r. Tilley & | M^{rs}. Hannah Littlejohn, | who died March 23^d | 1776: Aged 11 | years & 6 weeks.

Youth forward slips, | Death soonest nips:

Deposited | In this grave | Are the Remains | of MISS SOPHIA MELLEN, | 3^d. dau^{tr}. of the Rev. John | and M^{rs}. Rebecca Mellen. | She died Dec 17th. 1778 | in the 23^d Year | of her age.

Wisdom is the gray hair,—and | an unspotted life is old age.

Here lies interred y^e | body of Thomas, | third Son of ye Rev'd: | JOHN & M^{rs}. REBECCA | MELLEN of Lancaster, | who deceased August | ye 11th. 1766, Aged 3 | Years & 11 Months.

The small & great are there.

HERE LIES BURIED | Y^e BODY OF | HANNAH MOOR | DAUGHT^r OF DEAC | OLIVER & MR^s | ABIGAIL MOOR | WHO DEC^d SEPT'M | Y^e 1st A D 1749. | AGE 3 YEARS | & 5 M.

IN MEMORY OF Mrs ABIGAIL MOORE | WIFE OF M^r | ISRAEL MOORE | DIED DEC^r. 20th. 1759, | IN Y^e 21st: YEAR | OF HER AGE.

Here lies interred y^e | Body of Deacon | OLIVER MOOR, | who deceased Dec^m. | ye 23^d, AD. 1774, in | ye 67th. Year of | his Age.

Death is a Debt to Nature due, | Which I have paid & so must you.

In Memory of | M^{rs}. Asenath Osgood | ye wife of Dea. | Jonathan Osgood | who Died feb y^e | 25th; 1753, in y^e | 39th: Year of her | Age.

Here lies interred | the Body of Deac^n. | JONATHAN OSGOOD | who deceased Feb^{ry}. y^e | 10th. AD 1766, in ye 70th. | Year of his Age.

Ye Aged awake improve ye short liv'd Day:
Improve your time and Talents whilst you may.

In Memory of M^{rs}. | Abigail Wife of | M^r. Jonathan Os | good who Died | June ye 12th. 1759, in | ye 27th. year of her Age.

Here lies interred | the Body of | DAVID OSGOOD ESQ. | who deceased Feb^{ry}. y^e | 20th. AD. 1771. in ye 73^d. | Year of his Age.

Down to the impartial Grave's | devouring shade;
Sinks human Honours and the hoary head.

Here Lies Buried | Y^e Body Of | Rufus Powers | Son Of M^r. Daniel & M^{rs}. | Mary Powers | Who Dec^d Aug 27 | 1750 Age | 10 Years 18 D^s.

IN MEMORY OF M^r, | JOSIAH RICHARDSON | WHO DIED SEP^{br}. | Y^e 1st 1752 IN | THE 47th: YEAR | OF HIS | AGE.

When Sovereign Power Ascends ye throne | Then Feeble Mortals Tumble Down.

In Memory of M^r. | DANIEL ROBBINS | who Died March | ye 31st. 1755 | in ye 47 year | of his Age

Here Lies Buried | The Body of M^{rs} | Mary Ross Wife of | Mr Thomas Ross | Who Died November | ye 29 1765 | Aged 54 Years 6 | Months & 16 Days.

In Memory of | Priscilla Graves | (Dau^r. of M^r. | Ebenezer & M^{rs}. | Achsah Ross) | who died | April ye 20th, | 1776. Aged | 7 Months & | 11 Days. | In Memory of Ebenezer (Son | of M^r. Ebenezer | & M^{rs}. Achsah | Ross) who | died April ye 20th. 1776. | Aged 2 Years | 9 Months | 21 Days.

In Memory | of two Children | of M^r. Thos & Mrs Priscilla Ross. | Betty died | Sep. 20^{tb}. | 1769: in | the 9th. year | of her age. | The 2^d. Betty | died Sep. | 4th. 1782: in | the 5th year | of her age.

AMOS RUGG DIED SEPT. 15 | 1746 IN Y^e 2^d YEAR | OF HIS AGE. | STEPHEN RUGG DIED OCT^r. 19 | 1756 IN Y^e 5 YEAR | OF HIS AGE. | SOLOMON RUGG DIED NOV^r. 5 | 1756 IN Y^e 3^d YEAR | OF HIS AGE. | the Children of M^r. AMOS | and M^{rs}. MARY RUGG.

CHOCKSETT BURIAL GROUND.

HERE LIES INTER'D | THE BODY OF | PRUDENCE RUGG | DAU^r. OF ENSIGN REUBEN & M^{rs}. | LYDIA RUGG | DIED MAY 20th. 1758. | Ætat 19,

HERE LIES INTER'D | THE BODY OF | MARTHA RUGG | DAU^r. OF ENSIGN | REUBEN & M^{rs}. | LYDIA RUGG | DIED APRIL 1st 1758 | ÆTAT 26.

HERE LIES BURIED | Y^e BODY OF M^{rs} | EUNICE SAWYER | Y^e WIFE OF | LIEUT. EPHRAIM SAWYER | WHO DEC^d | JUNE 24th | A-D 1748 | AGE 52 YEARS | 3 M & 24 D^s.

Here Lies Buried | the Body of | Ruth Sawyer the | Daught^r. of ^{mr} Sam^{ll} | & Mrs Debora Sawyer | Who Dec^d Augst 9th | A. D. 1751. In y^e | 17 Year of Her Age.

Here Lies Buried | The Body of M^{rs}. | Anna Sawyer Wife | of Mr Thomas Sawyer | Who Died Nouember | ye 5: 1753. In y^e | 17 Year of her Age.

SARAH | SAWYER | DIED SEP^t. 26 | 1756. | IN Y^e 6 YEAR | OF HER AGE. | THOMAS | SAWYER | DIED SEP^t. 28 | 1756. | IN Y^e 17 YEAR | OF HIS AGE. | JAMES | SAWYER | DIED OCT^r. 3^d. | 1756] IN Y^e 11 YEAR | OF HIS AGE | THE CHILDREN OF M^r. THOMAS | & M^{rs}. ABIGAIL SAWYER.

In Memory of Olive | Dau: of M^r. Abner | Sawyer & Mary his | wife, Died Octr. 6 | 1756, in ye 2nd. | Year of her | Age.

HERE LIES BURIED | THE BODY OF M^r. | ABNER SAWYER | DIED DEC^r: 6th: | 1758. | IN Y^e 47th: YEAR | OF HIS AGE.

ERECTED | in memory of M^r; EZRA SAWYER, | who deceas'd Octr. 23^d, 1765: in the 63^d. | Year of his Age.

Calm sleeps ye flesh, far distant unconfin'd,
In worlds unbounded dwells the immortal mind.

ERECTED | in memory of Cpt. | EZRA SAWYER, | who departed this life | March 4th. 1776: | in the 47th. Year of | his Age.

"GOD's word commands our flesh to dust, | Return ye sons of men;
All nations rose from earth at first | And turn to earth again."

In memory of | Mr AARON SAWYER | who died Decemb^{er}. | ye 15th. AD: 1744. | Aged 42 Years, 6 | Months & 22 Days.

In Memory of | DOLLEE, Daugh^t. of | M^r. Aaron & M^{rs}. | Abigail Sawyer, who | died May ye 21st. | 1782, Aged 14 Years, | 5 Months, & 9 Days.

The Days of my Youth | hast Thou Shortened.

Here lies Buried, the Body | of M^r. John SCOOT, who | died on Novr. ye 16th. 1760, & | in ye 80th. Year of his Age.

O Death Thous't Conquer'd me, | I by thy Dart am Slain.
But CHRIST has Conquer'd thee, | And I shall Rise again.

IN MEM⊕RY OF | M^r.. SEBASTIAN | SMITH WHO DIED | MARCH 24. 1765 | ABOUT 73 YEAR | OF HIS AGE.

IN MEMORY OF M^r: CHARLES STEWART | DIED JULY 31st. 1750. | IN Y^e 32^d. YEAR OF HIS AGE. | ALSO 3 CHILDREN OF M^r. CHARLES | AND M^{rs}. SARAH STEWART. | SAMUEL DIED | AUGst. 9th. | 1750, | IN Y^e 9th YEAR | OF HIS AGE. | PHEBE DIED | AUGst. 9th. | 1750, | IN Y^e 7th. YEAR | OF HER AGE. | HULDA DIED | AUGst. 10th. | 1750, | IN Y^e 5th. YEAR OF HER AGE.

In Memory of | Jndith Dau^r. of | M^r. Samuel & M^{rs}. | Priscilla Thurston | who died June | ye 20th, AD. 1774, in y^e | 18th. Year of her Age.

In Memory of M^{rs}. | Eunice Whetcomb. | Wife of Dea^c. Asa | Whetcomb, who died | on Sept. ye 7th. 1760, in ye 37th. | Year of her Age.

HERE LIES BURIED | Y^e BODY OF | MARTHA WILDER | DAUGHTER OF MR JOHN & MR^s PRUDANCE WILDER | OF NECHOWOG | WHO DEC^d SEPT^m | 28th. 1747 | AGE 5 YEARS | 3 M & 2 D^s.

IN MEMORY | OF | TIMOTHY | WILDER | SON OF M^r | NATHANAEL AND | M^{rs}. LYDIA WILDER | WHO DIED OCTOBER | THE 7. 1756 AGED 5 | MONTHS AND 28 | DAYS.

THE MIDDLE CEMETERY.

In May, 1798, a committee, elected to procure and lay out new burial grounds, bought of Reverend Nathaniel Thayer and Honorable John Sprague one acre and twenty-four rods of land lying in rectangular form, sixteen rods in length on the highway, and eleven and one-half rods in width. According to their report, they "agreed to pay Mr Thayer fifty dollars on his executing a deed to Mr Sprague of the Gore of Land between the old and new burying fields, which he agrees to receive in exchange for what the Town will have of him, and each of them giving a deed to the Town, agreeably to the plan." In 1842, this field being crowded with graves, about one-half acre was added to it, on the west end, by purchase of the widow of Nathaniel Thayer, D. D.; and space for two tiers of lots along the whole front was gained by enclosing common land on the highway, removing therefrom the hearse-house and town pound which had for many years been obtrusive features of this locality. The following is a carefully revised transcript of all inscriptions in this populous field bearing date earlier than 1850:

In memory of | MRS. LUCY ALLEN, | wife of | Mr. Samuel Allen; | Died | Oct. 13, 1847, | aged 80 yrs. & | 9 mo.

MRS. ANNIS, | wife of | Samuel Andrews, | DIED | Jan. 25, 1845, | Æt. 81.

WILLIAM B. ANDREWS.| died | April 1, 1833, | aged 44 years.

In memory of | Abel Allen, | Son of Mr. Samuel | and Mrs. Lucy Allen, | who died | April 4th. 1800: aged 3 Years | & 5 months.

In memory of | SAMUEL ALLEN, | Son of Mr. Samuel & | Mrs Lucy Allen, | who died | Jan. 21st. 1807, Æ. 8 Years.

ELIZABETH, | Daughter of | Ferdinand and | Elizabeth Andrews; died | Jan. 13, 1831, | Æt. 6 mos.

In memory of | MRS. SARAH B. | wife of Mr John Burditt, | who died | March 17, 1832, | Æt 47.

FRANKLIN C. | Son of | Mr. John & Mrs. | Sally Burditt, | died Nov. 24, 1837; | Æt 2 yrs.

F. WENTWORTH, | son of | John & Sarah | BURDITT, | DIED | June 18, 1849, | Æt. 21.

In memory of | CHARLES A. | Son of Thomas & | Sarah E. Burditt, | who died | Feb. 21, 1842, | aged 6 mo.

JOSEPH BEAMAN | died Apr'l 7, 1813, | Æt 72. | HANNAH BEAMAN | died May 29, 1835, Æt. 99.

NATHAN BURDITT * * * * * MARGARET, | His wife | Died Sept. 16, 1845, | Æt. 59 yrs. 6 mos. | & 19 dys.

RHODA P. | wife of | William Bell, | died | Feb. 18, 1847, | Æt. 48.

    Her happy spirit took its flight, | From this vain world of sorrow;
    But oft she wished she might depart, | Before the coming morrow.

SAMUEL W. | Son of | Jona. and | Sarah Bowman, | who died | April 7, 1846, | aged 4 mo. & | 5 days.

    Thy spirit in glory, now | Shines with the blest.

WILLIAM A. | eldest son of | William & Elsey | BALLARD, | DIED | Oct. 27, 1848, | Æt. 25.

ANN ELIZABETH, | dau't of | Jonathan & | Charlotte | BUTTRICK, | DIED | Nov. 3, 1847, | Æ. 11 mo's.

LUTHER T. | only son of | L. T. & S. J. | BANCROFT, | died | Apr. 24, 1846, Æt. 22 ms.

    Go with thy Savior, my child; Thy Father in heaven hath sent for thee.

LUTHER T. BANCROFT | DIED | in Boston, | June 29, 1844, | Æt. 26.

MIDDLE CEMETERY. 421

SALOME PRATT, | Wife of | John Bennett, | Died Apr. 1, 1845, | Æ. 26 ys. | JOHN, | Their only Child, | Died Mar. 16, 1846, | Æ 1 yr. 22 ds.

ANN L. | wife of, | LOREY F. BANCROFT, | died May 12, 1846, | aged 27 years.

IN MEMORY OF | LYDIA B. | daur. of | Joseph & Lucy | BARRETT, | who died Sept. 14, 1831, | Æ 4 yrs. 2 mo. | & 28 ds.

IN | memory of | MR. JONATHAN BRUCE, | who died | Jan. 20, 1832, | aged 69.

MRS. CATHARINE | wife of | Mr. Jonathan Bruce; | who died | Feb. 20th: 1824, | aged 56.
She was an affectionate wife, | a kind mother, and a faithful friend.

HORATIO C. | son of | Capt. Ebenezer & | Mrs. Martha Bragg, | died Dec. 7, 1826, | Æt. 16 months.

ALONZO. | Son of Mr. Josiah & | Nancy Billings, | who died | March 28, 1825, | Æt. 36 hours.

IN | memory of | Mrs. HANNAH, | wife of | Mr Josiah Billings | who died | Augt. 6, 1822, | Æt. 39.
Hope looks beyond the bounds of time | When what we now deplore
Shall rise in full immortal prime | And bloom to fade no more.

IN | Memory of | MR. JOSIAH BILLINGS, | who died | May 23, 1843, | aged 60.
Farewell dear wife and children too, | For Christ has called me home;
In a short time he'll call for you | Prepare yourselves to come.

Erected by Mr. | Martin Burpee Jr. | in memory of | his mother | MRS. LYDIA, | wife of | Mr. Martin Burpee, | who died | March 23, 1817, | aged 29.

SARAH, | Daughter of Josiah | & Eirene Bridge, | Died May 11, 1814: | Æ. 3 months.

IN | Memory of | MRS. LUCY BRIGHAM, | wife of | Mr Jotham Brigham; | who died Dec. 20, 1830, | aged 71.
There is a calm for those who weep.

FRANKLIN | son of | R. M. & M. P. | Bradley, | Died May 9, 1838, | Æ. 5 ys.

ROBERT M. BRADLEY | DIED | Nov. 15, 1842, | Æ. 48.

In Memory of | MRS. | REBECKAH BOWERS, | wife of | Capt. Josiah Bowers | who died | Nov. 30, 1836, | aged 85.

In Memory of | CAPT. | JOSIAH BOWERS, | who died | Aug. 22, 1836, aged 84.

SACRED | to the memory of | MRS. LUCY BALDWIN, | wife of | Mr. Oliver Baldwin. | She died July 30, 1720, Æt. 45.
There is a calm for those who weep, | A rest for weary pilgrims found;
They softly lie and sweetly sleep, | —— low in the ground.

MARTHA JANE, | daugh. of Cyrus, & | Susan Bliss; | who died | July 11, 1839, | aged 9 months.

WINSOR | Son of | Winsor & Phebe | BARNARD, | died | Apr. 9, 1835, | Æ. 2 yrs.

IN | Memory of | MR. | WILLIAM BARNARD, | who died | Nov. 4, 1834, | aged 20 years, & 7 mo.

CALEB S. | Son of | Winsor & Phebe | BARNARD, | died Nov. 4, 1816, | Æ. 3 ms.

In memory of | MR. | JONATHAN BARNARD, | who died | March 5, 1824, | aged 60.

In memory of | BENIJAH BARNARD, | Son of Mr. Jonathan, & | Mrs. Annas Barnard, | who died Octr: 4th: | 1805, Æ. 7 Years & | 21 days.

In memory of | Julia Barnard, | Daut. of Mr. Jonathan | & Mrs. Annas | Barnard who died | Sept. 5th. 1805, Æ. 1 | Year & 9 months, | & 8 days.

In memory of | Jonathn. Barnard, | Son of Mr. Jonathan & | Mrs. Annas Barnard, | who died Feb. 12th. | 1799; Aged 3 Years, | 2 months & 20 days.

MRS. | SOPHRONIA W. | wife of | Eliphas Ballard, | died | May 18, 1849, | Æt. 75.

MRS. | ANNA G. | wife of | Eliphas Ballard, | died | June 22, 1818, | Æt. 32.

ERECTED | in memory of | Miss | SALLY BALLARD, | who died March 25, 1841, | aged 60 years.
"Blessed are the pure in heart, | for they shall see God."

ERECTED | in memory of Mr. | JOSIAH BALLARD, | Son of Mr Jeremiah, & | Mrs. Rebeckah Ballard, | who died June 10th, 1804. | Æt. 25 Years.

SACRED | to the memory of | MRS. REBECCA BALLARD | wife of | Mr. Jeremiah Ballard, | who died June 2, 1810, | Æt. 52.

In memory of | JEREMIAH BALLARD, | died | Oct. 2, 1838, | aged 86.
Blessed are the dead who die in the Lord, | from henceforth and forever.

ERECTED | in memory of | Dea^n. Josiah Ballard, | who died Aug. 6th. | 1799, in the 78th. | Year of his age.
Let worms devour my wasting flesh, | And crumble all my bones to dust.
My God shall raise my frame anew, | At the revival of the just.

ERECTED | in memory of Mrs. | Sarah Ballard, | Wife of Dea^n. Josiah Ballard, | who died March 31st. | 1799, in the 74th. | Year of her age.
Death's the last point of many lingering years, | We live in sadness, and we part in tears.

THOS BALLARD | died Jan. 1, 1838, | aged 76 years.
Prepare to meet thy God.

MRS. ABIGAIL, | wife of the late | MR. | Thomas Ballard, | who died | Aug. 20, 1843, | aged 75 yrs. & | 4 mo.

In memory of | Sophia Ballard, | Dau^{tr}. of Mr. Thomas | and Mrs. Abigail Bal | lard, who died Sept. | 1799, aged 4 Years, | 8 months, & 4 days.

In memory of | Lucy Ballard, | Dau^{tr}. of Mr. Thos. & Mrs. | Abigail Ballard, | who died | Aug. 19th, 1799, aged | 2 Years, 9 mo^s. 9 days.

In memory of | Abigail Ballard, | Dau. of Mr. Thomas & | Mrs. Abigail Ballard, | who died Aug. 25th. 1799, | aged 9 months and 13 days.

ERECTED | in memory of | MRS. NANCY BATES, | wife of | Stephen Bates Esq. | She died | at Dunstable N. H. | Oct. 1, 1821, | Æt. 33.
Though natural ties of love are strong, | Yet sure they must be broke;
We can't expect to tarry long, | Before death's fatal stroke.

IN | Memory of | MR. JOHN BALLARD, | who died | Sept. 9, 1826, | Æt. 66.

ERECTED | In Memory of | MRS. ANNA BALLARD, | wife of | Mr John Ballard, | who died March 1, 1808, | Æt. 49.
A feeble but an agreeable companion, | A fond mother & a sincear Christian.

In memory of | MR. CHARLES BALLARD, | who died | April 1, 1807, | Æt. 21.
Virtues like thine when lost to earth, | Found memory's tear will ever gain,
The tender tribute due to worth; | But they shall give to others birth,
Nor their example be in vain.

IN | memory of | Mrs Molly, | wife of | Mr. John Ballard. | She died | July 8, 1819, | Æt. 53.
A humble and sincere Christian.

In Memory of | MR. | HENRY BALLARD, | who was killed instantly | in felling a tree | Jan. 12, 1830, Æt 36.
"There was but a step between me & death."
"Watch therefore, for ye know neither the day, nor the hour, when the son of man cometh."

JOHN AUGUSTUS | Son of Mr. Henry & | Mrs. Abigail Ballard, | died May 31, 1830: Æ. 6 yrs.
So fades the early blooming flower.

SARAH ELIZABETH, | daugh. of Henry & | Abigail Ballard, | Died | Feb. 19, 1841, | aged 14 years.
Leaves have their time to fall, | And flowers to wither at the north wind's breath,
And stars to set—but all, | Thou hast, all seasons for thine own Oh! Death.

H. G. BUTTRICK. | NANCY WHITNEY, | March 19, 1810; Æt. 3 wks. | SARAH AUGUSTA, | Jan. 15, 1811; Æt. 14 hours; | NANCY, | Jan. 27, 1811: Æt. 26 yrs.
A household's tomb; | To faith how dear; | A part have gone; | Part linger here;
United all | In love and hope, | One household still.

MR. | HENRY BRIDGE, | who died at Woburn | Oct. 31, 1824, | aged 30.

MIDDLE CEMETERY.

Miss. | ABIGAIL BRIDGE | died Oct. 10, 1820, | aged 22.

ERECTED | in memory of | Mrs ABIGAIL BRIDGE, | wife of Mr. | WILLIAM BRIDGE, | who died Aug | ust 13, 1810; in the 41st. year | of her age.
> After a long and distressing illness which she bore with unexampled patience, and Christian fortitude and cheerfully resigned her spirit into the hands of God who gave it, She was a pattern of patience, industry, frugality, and economy, an amiable partner, an affectionate parent, a kind neighbor, and a sincere Christian. May her memory be ever blessed.
> Friend nor physicians could not save | My mortal body from the grave,
> Nor can the grave confine me here, | When Christ shall call me to appear.

In Memory of | Mrs. CATHERINE BENNETT, | wife of | Mr. Luke Bennett | who died | Oct. 4, 1814, | Æt. 24.
> When Christ communicates his word | And bids the world apppear,
> Thrones are prepared for all his friends, | That humbly lov'd him here.

In Memory of | MR. ELISHAH BENNETT, | who died | Augt. 14, 1801, | Aged 46 years.

GEORGE W. BRIDGE, | Son of | Charles & Sophia | BRIDGE, | Drowned Dec. 25, 1844, | Æt. 10 yrs. 10 mos | & 22 days.

FRANKLIN T. | Son of | Charles & Sophia | BRIDGE, | died May 6, 1844, | Æt. 17 mos. & 24 ds.

CAROLINE T. | dau of | Charles & Sophia | BRIDGE, | died Aug. 31, 1841, | Æt. 1 yr. 6 mos. & 5 ds.

MRS. SUSAN, | wife of | Mr Charles Bridge, | who died | Feb. 19th. 1825, | aged 35.
> A virtuous woman is a crown to her husband.

MR. | SOLOMON BRIDGE | died | Sept. 24, 1829, | aged 27.
> Death with his dart has pierc'd my heart, | When I was in my prime;
> When this, you see grieve not for me, | 'Twas God's appointed time.

MR. | JAMES BRIDGE | Died | March 18, 1846, | aged 53 yrs.
> Sweet is the memory of the just, | When they are slumbering in the dust.

Emily S. Ball, | daugh. of | Levi M. & | Lucindia L Ball, | Born June 17, 1840 | Died June 17, | 1845, | aged 5 yrs.

In Memory of | Nancy Bennett | Dau of Mr. Nathan | & Mrs Eunice Bennett | who died Jan 21st. | 1802, Aged 5 years, | 1 month & 12 days.
> Her life was like a morning flower, | Cut down and wither'd in an hour.

In memory of MARY, | 3^d Daughter of Capt. | John, & Mrs. Polly Brown, | who died Jan. 7, 1809, | Æ. 22 months. | Also her Infant Sister, | who died April 5, 1809, | Æ. 12 hours.
> When on our Graves you cast you Eye, | Remember like us you are born to die.

H. EMMA, | A dearly beloved child | of Granville and | Martha E. Carter, | who died in Boston | Aug. 29, 1848; | Æt. 13 months.

In memory of | BENJAMIN CHANDLER | who died | Feb. 24, 1847, Æ. 79.

Miss. JULIA LOUISA, | daughter of | Mr. Benjamin & | Elizabeth Chandler; | Died | May 8, 1842, | aged 19 yrs.

DOLLY H. | dau. of | John & Mary | CARR, | Died | March 1, 1847, | Æ. 23.
> She's gone but we would not recall her again, | So sweet are her slumberings now;
> No sorrow, nor sickness can enter the tomb, | To injure her beautiful brow.

ATTOSA CARR, | DIED | Nov. 20, 1848, | Æt. 27.

ANNA MARIA, | only child of | Dr. Wright & Mary L. | Cummings; | born March 6, 1828; | died Nov. 20 1848. |
> "Multis lachrymis composita es."

M. A. R. BRAGG | wife of W. C. CARTER | Died | July 28, 1844, | Æ. 24 yrs. 18 ds.

In memory of | MRS. | POLLY W. CARTER | wife of Mr. | Oliver Carter 2^d. | who died | Feb. 28, 1842, | aged 27.

To the | memory of | JANE AUGUSTA | daugh. of | Mr. Isaac and | Mrs. Polly Childs, | Died | April 22, 1848, | aged 20 years.

In memory of | MARY, | daugh. of | Mr. Isaac & | Mrs. Polly Childs. | who died July 14, 1836, | aged 15 yrs.

JAMES | Son of Mr. Isaac & | Mrs. Polly Childs; | he died | Feb. 22. 1822, | Æ. 3 yrs. & 2 mo.

To the | Memory of | Mr. ISAAC CHILDS, | who died | Feb. 23, 1840, aged 65.

SACRED | to the memory of | MRS. SARAH CHILDS, | who died | Octr. 17, 1815, | Æt. 34.

> Behold and see as you pass by, | As you are now so once was I.
> As I am now so you must be. | Prepare for death and follow me.

ELIJAH COLBURN | DIED | Oct. 17, 1849, | Æt. 78.

MRS. SALLY COLBURN, | wife of | Elijah Colburn; Died | Feb. 9, 1831 | aged 53.

REBECCA W. CARTER | daugh. of George, & | Nancy Carter, | died | Sept. 18, 1842, | aged 7 months.

ERECTED | in memory of | MR. HORATIO CARTER | who died | Sept. 6, 1833, | aged 37.

ERECTED | in memory of | MRS. EMILY CARTER, | wife of | Mr. Oliver Carter, | who died | March 17, 1835, | aged 68.

ERECTED | in memory of | MR. OLIVER CARTER | who died | May 18, 1842, | aged 84.

MISS. | MARY CONQUERETTE, | died | Feb. 7. 1840, | aged 81.

In Memory of | Mr JOHN CARTER, | who died | Nov. 19, 1815, | Æt. 65.

> This spot contains the ashes of the just, | Who sought not honours and betray'd not trust;
> This truth he prov'd in every path he trod, | An honest man's the noblest work of God.

ERECTED | in memory of | MRS. MARTHA CARTER | wife of | Mr. John Carter, | who died | July 30, 1838, | aged 83.

In memory of | MR. JOHN CARTER, | who died | Augt. 6, 1841, | aged 63.

MRS. | TEMPE CARTER; | wife of Mr John Carter; | who died | August 31st. 1826, | aged 43.

MARIETTA C. | only child of | Cephas & | Abigail Carter | died June 17, 1847, | aged 13 yrs.

IN | Memory of | MR. | CEPHAS CARTER | who died | Sept. 29, 1842, | aged 52 years.

ERS. | SALLY CARTER, | wife of Thomas Carter; | died May 1, 1845, | aged 86.

MR. | THOMAS CARTER | died | Feb. 1, 1823, | aged 70.

In memory of | Eli Carter, | Son of Mr. Thomas | and Mrs. Sally Carter, | who died Aug. 24, | 1798, in the 3^d | Year of his age.

NANCY, | Dau^r. of John 3^d & | Betsy Carter, | died | Nov. 22, 1832, | Æt. 21 yrs. 7 mos.

> Not lost, but gone home.

In memory of | MR. JOHN CARTER 2, | who died | July 3, 1830: | Æt. 48.

> Around this monumental stone, | Let friendship drop a sacred tear;
> The husband kind, the parent fond, | The upright man lies buried here.

ERECTED | In Memory of | Mrs BETSY CARTER, | Wife of Mr John Carter 2^d. | who died Dec. 28, 1815; | Æt. 31.

> She was a pattern of the Christian virtues; died in the Christian faith and hope; and her memory is blessed.

CAPTAIN EPHRAIM CARTER | died May 19, 1798 aged 55.

> He was a comfort & staff to aged | Parents, a guide to Children, | a faithful & affectionate Consort, | a Patron & Lover of Free Masonry, | & a constant Benefactor to the Poor. | Animated with public Spirit, | he promoted the good of Society; | and in his numerous private and | public employments, acted with | strict integrity. | He was a sincere Christian & his | memory shall long be cherished.

IN | memory of | MRS. ABIGAIL CARTER | widow of | Cap. Ephraim Carter, | who died | Nov. 16, 1804, | Æt. 56.
> She was sincere & faithful in performing the relative & christian duties, & "fell on sleep, believing as Jesus died & rose again, even so them also, who sleep in Jesus will God bring with him."

MRS. MARY CARTER | wife of Capt. Ephraim Carter, | who died June 22 1826, | Æt. 55.

CAPT. | EPHRAIM CARTER | died August 31, 1827 | Æ 54.

In memory of | ELIZABETH, | wife of Solomon Carter, | who died | July 26, 1843, Æt. 56.

In memory of | SOLOMON CARTER, | who died Nov. 8, 1829, Æt. 56.

MRS. LUCY CARTER, | Wife of Solomon Carter, | Died | April 5th. 1813, | Æt. 35.
> She was amiable in her temper; circumspect in her conversation; faithful in domestic life, a pattern of well regulated affection in the conjugal state; given to cheerfulness and hospitality as a neighbour; humble and sincere in her christian profession; patient in sickness; serene in death, believing that her Redeemer liveth. "Be ye followers of them, who thro' faith and patience inherit the promises."

CALVIN CARTER, M. D. * * * * SALLY PERRY, | his wife | died Apr. 30, 1840, | aged 56 yrs. 4 ms. | JAMES, | died at Cambridge | Mar. 20, 1830, | aged 17 yrs. | MARIANNE AUGUSTA, | died Jan. 17, 1835, | aged 17 yrs. 4 ms. | children of | Calvin & Sally P. Carter. | MARTHA LINCOLN, | died Mar. 20, 1822, | aged 2 yrs. | TWO INFANTS, | died 1807–1822. | children of | Calvin & Sally P. Carter. MARTHA LINCOLN, | died Apr. 30, 1847, | aged 23 yrs. 8 ms.

In Memory of | Susanna Carter, | daug^r. of James Carter | & Sarah his wife who | died March 29, 1805, | aged 8 months & 6 ds.
> Fairwell sweet child a long adue. | No more with pleasure shall we look on you.

Ens^n. | James Carter | died March 12, 1814, | aged 33 years.
> Blessed are the merciful for they shall obtain mercy. Blessed are the peacemakers for they shall be called the children of God.

DR JAMES CARTER | born Nov. 9 1753 | died Jan. 17 1817

SUSANNA KENDALL | wife of | James Carter | born Nov. 9 1755 | died Apr. 30 1837

SEWALL CRRTER, | Son of Dr. James Carter, | Sept. 9, 1796–Sept. 7, 1838.
> "I know that my Redeemer liveth."

IN | Memory of | REBECCA COREY, | Daughter of | Stephen & Triphena Corey | who died April 19, 1810, | Aged 24 years.
> "Her neighbours & friends stood weeping | and showing the coats & garments | which she made while she | was with them."

WILLIAM DIVOLL | DIED | Nov. 18, 1849, | in his 50 yr.
> Thou art gone from us, dear Father, | And thy voice no more we hear. Thou hast left our kindred circle, | A brighter home to cheer.

MRS LUCY, | wife of | Elias Danforth, | DIED | Dec. 25, 1843, | Æt. 50.

MISS SARAH ANN, | Daughter of Elias & | Lucy Danforth, | DIED | Nov. 23, 1847, | Æt. 26.

MR. | LEMUEL DICKENSON | died July 10, 1826: | Æt. 36.

MRS. | EMILY DEAN, | wife of Mr. John Dean; | who departed this life | June 29, 1834, | aged 35.

CHARLES, | Son of John & | Emily Dean; | who died | Sept. 18, 1832, | aged 3 months.

SARAH B. | daught. of John & | Emily Dean; | who died | June 2, 1834, | aged 9 months.

In memory of | Mrs. REBECAH DAMON, | wife of Mr Samuel Damon, | who died | April 4, 1844, | aged 86.

In memory of | MRS. ABIGAIL, wife of | Mr Samuel Damon, | who died | Oct. 8, 1826, | Æt. 74.

In memory of | Mr. SAMUEL DAMON, | who died | June 1, 1845, | aged 89.

ABRAHAM P. | son of Mr. William and | Mrs Abigail Damon; | who died | Sept. 29, 1825, | aged 21 years and | 8 months.

    Friends nor physicians, could not save, | My mortal body from the grave.
    Nor can the grave confine me here, | When Christ shall call me to appear.

MARGARET ANN, | daugh. of Jonas M. & | Margaret Damon, | who died Sept. 18, 1840. | Æt. 1 year 3 mo. & | 23 days.

MRS. MARGARET, | wife of | Mr. Jonas M. Damon, | died Sept. 22, 1842, | aged 33 yrs. 6 mo. & | 4 days.

    We shall all meet again.

To | The memory of | MRS. SARAH, | Relict of | Doctor F. Danforth, | who died | April 19, 1814; | Æt. 79.

To | The memory of | MISS | SARAH DANFORTH, | who died | Sept. 4, 1832; | Æt. 76.

WALTER AUSTIN, | son of Austin & | Sally Davis, | died March 15, 1844; | aged 5½ years.

    The bloom of life doth soon decay, | The brightest flowers the soonest fades.

EMMA, | Daughter of | Hollis & Hannah | DAVIS, | Was killed by the falling | of a Cart Body, | Oct. 6, 1847, | Æt. 6 yrs. & 4 ms.

    "One Sparrow Shall not fall on | the ground without your Father."
    "Tis but the Casket that lies here, | The Gem that filled it sparkles yet."

ERS. PHEBE | wife of | Elias Emerson, | died | Dec. 16, 1840, | Æt. 72.

    Cease ye mourners, case to languish | Oer the grave of those you love;—
    Pain, and death, and night, and anguish, | Enter not the world of love.

In memory of | MR. | ELIAS EMERSON, | who died | June 16, 1835; | Æt. 76.

    Cease, weeping friends your tears refrain, | He sweetly sleeps, to rise again;
    Sleep on dear husband take thy rest, | Let thy example make us bless'd.

In memory of | MR JOSEPH EMERSON, | who died May 9, 1803; | Æt. 81: | Also MRS PHEBE, | his wife, died Jan. 19, | 1811; Æt. 81.

In memory of | Mr. BENJAMIN EDGERTON, | who died April 1st, | 1806, in the 45 year | of his age.

Maryann dau. of Mr. | Benjamin & Mrs. Sarah | Edgerton, died May 1, | 1807; aged 2 yrs. 11 Mo. | & 14 days.

MISS. | SARAH A. EAGER | died Nov. 27, | 1840, aged 18 years, | daugh. of Mr. Farwell, | & Mrs. Althina Eager.

    Dearest sister, thou hast left us, | Here thy loss we deeply feel,
    But 'tis God that hath bereft us, | He can all our sorrows heal
    Yet again we hope to meet thee, | When the day ot life is fled.
    Then in Heaven with joy to greet thee, | Where no farewell tear is shed.

Miss | CAROLINE EAGER | died Dec. 2, | 1842, | aged 21 yrs. | Daugh. of Mr. Farwell & | Mrs. Althina Eager.

    Sister thou was't mild and lovely | Gentle as the summer's breeze,
    Pleasant as the air of evening, | When it floats among the trees.
    Peaceful be thy silent slumber, | Peaceful in thy grave so low;
    Thou no more wilt join our number | Thou no more our songs shall know.

NATHANIEL EATON | died | Feb. 24, 1826, | Æ. 82.

    "I know that my Redeemer liveth." | Hail, glorious Gospel! Heavenly light!
    Whereby we live with Comfort, | and with hope we die."

LUCY, | wife of NATHANIEL EATON | died Feb. 11, 1847, | Æ. 96.

    Descended from the Pilgrims, she lov'd their doctrines, and practic'd their virtues.
    Jesus my God, I know his name. | His name is all my trust!

CATHARINE M. | wife of | Andrew J. Farnsworth | DIED | Sept. 19, 1847, | Æt. 30 yrs. 4 ms. & 19 ds.

    Weep not for the youthful, the pious, the just;
      Though the heart of the mourner with sorrow is riven.
    The lov'd one's frail body low slumbers in dust,
      But her spirit released now triumphs in heaven.

MARY | wife of | James Farwell, | daughter of | Elias & Phoebe Emerson, | died Jan. 9th. 1849, | aged 55 years.

MR. | BENJAMIN H. FOSTER | died May 10, 1826, | aged 42.

SACRED | To the Memory of | MRS. MARY FLETCHER | Wife of Mr Rufus Fletcher | who died | Aug. 30, 1808, | Æt. 42.
> Habitual resignation to the severe | trials of Providence and a christian | faith gave her peace in death, and a hope of seeing the glory of God.

SACRED | to the memory of | MR. | THOMAS FLETCHER, | who died at Boston | June 23, 1832, | aged 22 years.
> His mind was tranquil and serene, | No terrors in his looks were seen;
> His Saviour's smiles dispell'd the gloom, | And smoothed his passage to the tomb.

IN | Memory of | MRS. | MARY FLETCHER, | wife of the late | Deac. Joel Fletcher | of Templeton, | who died | April 1, 1837, | aged 74.
> Farewell dear friends and children too, | For Christ hath call'd me home.

SACRED | to the memory of | MARTHA FLETCHER, | who died | May 29, 1829, | aged 26 years & 29 days.
> Peace, peace, no murmur, 'tis the will of God,
> That God who orders all things for the best;
> 'Tis ours to bow and kiss th' aflicting rod,
> 'Twas hers to seek the mansions of the blest.

HANNAH | FOSDICK, | Relict of | Timothy Fletcher, | died Aug. 14, 1832, | Æ. 75.

TIMOTHY FLETCHER ESQ. | Died March 17, 1823: | Aged 72.
> Thou shalt come to thy grave | in a full age, like as a shock | of corn cometh in in his season.

ERECTED | In Memory of | Mr. JOSHUA FLETCHER, | Who died Nov. 14, 1814, | Æt. 90.
> When I am buried in the dust, | My flesh shall be thy care;
> These with'ring limbs with thee I trust, | To raise them strong and fair.

ERECTED | In Memory of | Mrs. MARY FLETCHER, | wife of | Mr Joshua Fletcher, | who died | July 25, 1813, | Æt. 86.
> "Remembering her Creator, and confessing her Saviour in the days of her youth, her whole life was sanctified by piety. She was patient and resigned in sickness and death, and had a humble hope of entering on the joy of her LORD."

DORCAS | Wife of | W^m. Fletcher, | died May 21, 1844, | aged 75.
> Could prayers or tears or public offerings save | A wife, a mother from the mouldering grave?
> Ah no! her form in dust uncouscious lies; | Within our hearts her name immortalized.

ROXANA, | daugh^r. of Mr. W^m: & | Mrs. Dorcas Fletcher, | who died | Oct. 22, 1805 | aged 21 days.
> We had a daughter darling of our love, | She is an angel in the realms above.

In memory of | MR. | JOSHUA FLETCHER, | who died | July 4, 1844, | aged 61.
> He left the world, his toils were oer, | Free from all sorrow, care, or pain;
> To us he will return no more, | But we shall meet with him again.

JOSEPH WARREN, | son of Joshua & | Nabby Fletcher, | died May 11, 1816, | Æt. 2 yrs. & 6 mos.

JULIA MARIA, | dau. of Joshua & | Nabby W. Fletcher, | died May 2, 1819, | Æt. 2 yrs. 1 mo. & 11 d's.

MARTHA CELESTINE, | dau. of Joshua & | Nabby W. Fletcher, | died July 7, 1837, | Æt. 6 yrs. & 11 mos.
> Little children come to me, | That is what the Savior said.

JEREMIAH FALES | DIED | April 22, 1848, | Æt. 69.

AMY, | widow of | JEREMIAH FALES, | DIED | Nov, 23, 1849, | Æt. 67.

SOPHIA, | Dau. of | Jeremiah & Amy | FALES, | died | Mar. 17, 1836, | Æt. 12 yrs.

WARREN FALES | DIED IN BOSTON, | April 4, 1848, | Æt. 34.

JOHNNIE | Son of George | & Sophronia W. | FITCH, | died Oct. 17, 1843, | Æt. 4 yrs. 7 ms.

Mr. | TORREY FITCH | DIED | Sept. 4, 1843, | Æt. 48.

In memory of two | Infant children of | Torrey & Harriet | Fitch, | died June 16, 1828, | and June 20, 1829.

E. FULLER.——FRANKLIN W. 1842-1845..GEORGE W. 1835-1836..FRANCIS F. 1830-1832..EPHRAIM H. 1833-1833..ABIGAIL L. 1829-1829..FRANCIS F. 1822-1829..SUSAN | wife of Ephraim. | 1798-1829..EBENEZER W. 1769-1841.

IN | Memory of | MR JONAS FAIRBANK, | who died July 7, 1829, | Æt. 86.

In memory of | ELISABETH FAIRBANK, | wife of | Jonas Fairbank, | who died | April 9, 1818, | aged 70 years.

"She openeth her mouth with wisdom; | and in her tongue was the law of kindness,"

Capt. | JONAS FAIRBANKS | died April 6, | 1826, | aged 51.

MRS. | MARY FAIRBANK | wife of Mr. Cyrus Fairbank, who died | Dec. 13, 1827, | aged 63 years.

An affectionate wife, and | a tender friend.

Mr. | CYRUS FAIRBANK, | died | April 30, 1835; | Æt. 68.

To the memory of | MRS. | NANCY F. FAY, | wife of Josiah Fay; | who died | July 7, 1845, | Æt. 52 yrs.

She hath gone home.

SACRED | to the memory of | JACOB FISHER ESQ. | who died | June 2, 1843, | aged 75.

SACRED | to the memory of | MRS. NANCY FISHER, | wife of Jacob Fisher Esq. | She died April 15, 1822, | Æt. 50.

She opened her mouth with wisdom; | and in her tongue was the law of kindness. The heart of her husband did safely trust in her. | She hath done him good & not evil all the days | of her life. Her children shall rise up and bless her memory.

ERECTED | in memory of | MRS. BETSY FISHER, | second wife of | Jacob Fisher Esq. | who died | Nov. 6, 1837, | aged 57.

ELIZABETH, | died Dec. 1, 1831, | aged 11 mo's. | SOPHRONIA, | died Apr. 13, 1834, | aged 11 mo's. | CHARLES, | died Apr. 4, 1836, | aged 8 mo's. | Children of | Ephr. C. & Sarah H. | Fisher.

EDWARD E. | son of Mr. Asa D. & | Mrs. Betsy Farnsworth, | who died | Oct. 22, 1837, | aged 10 weeks.

JAMES, | son of Mr. Benj. 2ᵈ. | and Mrs. | Dorcas Farnsworth. | he died June 11, 1822, | Æ. 9 ms. & 25 d.

JOSIAH FLAGG ESQ. | Born in Boston, Nov. 12, 1760; | Died in Lancaster, Feb. 11, 1840. | DOLLY FLAGG, | his wife | Born in Lancaster, Nov. 6, 1766; | Died June 1, 1835. * * * *

In memory of | MRS. FIDELIA, | wife of | Mr. Seth French | who died | May 14, 1843, | aged 49.

In memory of | MRS. | SALLY FARNSWORTH | who died | Feb. 1, 1844, | aged 68, | wife of Mr. Benj. | Farnsworth who died | in Francistown N. H, | Aug. 1830.

In memory of | LYDIA B. GOULD, | daughter of | Benjamin and Sarah Gould, | who died | August 17, 1841; | aged 5 years.

"Suffer little children to come unto me and forbid them not, for of such is the kingdom of heaven."

ERECTED | in memory of | MRS. | ELIZABETH GOODSPEED, | daughʳ. of Capt. Daniel, | and Mrs. Elizabeth Rugg, | who died | Dec. 28, 1830, | aged 57.

MR. | JONAS GOSS, | died | Oct. 18, 1840, | In his 61, year.

"An honest man is the noblest work of God."

JUDITH GOSS | died | Augᵗ. 21, 1807, | Æt. 4 months. | EBENEZER GOSS | died | Dec. 15, 1817, | Æ. 4 years and | 6 months. | Children of Mr. Jonas | & Mrs. Judith Goss.

IN | Memory of | NANCY GOSS, | daughter of Mr. Jonas, | and Mrs. Judith Goss, | who died Jan. 25, 1831, | aged 12 years & | 2 months.

The blooming youth departs in peace; | She leaves her friends and is at rest.

MIDDLE CEMETERY.

SACRED | To the memory of | CAPT. DANIEL GOSS | who died | Dec. 10, 1809, Æt. 69.
    He was a just man, and perfect in | his generation & he walked with God.

SACRED | To the Memory of | MRS. EUNICE GOSS, | Relict of Capt. Daniel Goss; | who died | Jan. 7, 1813; | Æt. 66.
    "A virtuous woman is a crown | to her husband." "A woman that feareth the Lord she shall be praised."

CAPT. | DANIEL GOSS JR. | died June 11, 1841, | Æt. 81 yrs. & 11 ms.

In Memory of | HENRY LAWTON, | Son of Mr Henry, and | Mrs Sarah D. Goss, | who died Sept. 2, 1830, | aged 16 months.
    Sleep on sweet babe and be at rest, | To call the hom, God saw it best.

In memory of | MR. WILLIAM GOULD JR. | who died | Feb. 21, 1840, | aged 56 yrs.

ERECTED | in memory of | Mrs. ELIZABETH | wife of | Mr W^m. Gould | who died | March 3, 1839, | aged 84.
    Death gives more than was in Eden lost.

ERECTED | in memory of | MrW^m GOULD, | who died | Nov. 7, 1834. | aged 80.
    The thought of death, sole victor of its dread.

SACRED | To the memory of | MR. EBER GODDARD, | A Revolutionary Soldier; [?] | Died May 26, 1835. | Æt. 67.
    "I am the resurrection and the life, he that believeth in me, though he were dead yet shall he live."

MARTHA ANN | daugh^r. of Mr Varnum, & | Mrs. Martha Gilson | who died | Nov. 23, 1828. | Æt. 3 months.
    Like roses crop'd before they bloom | She's carried to the silent tomb.
    Lie here sweet child and take thy rest, | To call thee home, God saw it best.

MR. | VARNUM GILSON | died Oct. 6, 1828, | Æt. 23 years.
    My tender wife don't mourn for me, | 'Tis here my earthly sorrows end ;
    Prepare thyself in youthful days, | In silence here to meet your friend.

MRS. | REBECCA GOSS; | wife of Capt. John Goss; | who died | Jan. 27, 1827, | aged 43 years.
    She was an exemplary, and humble christian.

IN | Memory of | MRS. ABIGAIL GATES, | wife of Capt. Thomas Gates, | who died Sept. 5th; 1810, | Æt. 70.
    "The days of our years are three-score years and ten."
    Jesus said: I am the resurrection and the iife, he that believeth in me though he were dead, yet shall he live ; and whosoever liveth and believeth in me, shall never die."

SACRED | to the Memory of | Capt. THOMAS GATES, | who died | Dec. 27, 1814, | Æt. 79.
    "Blessed are they that do his commandments, that they may have right to the tree of life, and may enter in through the Gates into the city."

IN | Memory of | MR. | JAMES GOODWIN | who died Sept. 8, 1831, | aged 90.
    His mind was tranquil and serene, | No terrors in his looks were seen :
    His Saviour's smile dispell'd the gloom, | And smoothed his passage to the tomb.

IN | memory of | MRS. BATHSHEBA GOODWIN | wife of | Mr. James Goodwin, | who died | Jan. 7, 1814, | Æt. 70.
    Fare well vain world I am gone home, | My Saviour smil'd & call'd me come ;
    Bright Angels carried me away | To sing God's praise in endless day.

JOHN | GOODWIN | Died | SEPT. 1, 1812 | Æ. 69. | REBECAH | GOODWIN, | Died | FEB. 7, 1839. | Æ. 62. | BATHSHEBA | GOODWIN, | Died | JUNE 11, 1833 | Æ. 22. | HARRIET | M. GOODWIN, | Died | FEB. 6, 1836. | Æ. 20.

MARSHALL F. | died Aug. 24, 1845, | Æt. 5 yrs. & 10 mo. | EDWARD E. | died Feb. 5, 1839, | Æt. 1 year, | An Infant Son | died Apr: 21, 1836, | Æt. 2 days. | Children of James F. & Harriet | GOULD.

Otis Hunt Junr. | died July 3, 1804. | Aged 1 year, 8 months, | & 13 days. | Maria Hunt | died Feb. 27, 1809. | Aged 2 years, 4 months, | 2 days. | Son and Daughter of Mr. Otis | & Mrs. Arrethuse Hunt.

In memory of | MRS. ELIZABETH, | wife of Mr. | George W. Howard, | who died | June 2, 1837, | Æt. 27.

In memory of | MRS. SARAH M. | wife of | Mr. George Howard, | who died | Sep. 7, 1830, | Æt. 39.

In Memory of | ASA W. HOWARD, | son of George & | Sarah M. Howard; | who died in Boston | July 27, A. D. 1843, | Aged 28.

IN | Memory of | MRS. HEZEDIAH L. | wife of | Mr Emory Harris, | who died | 11th: Jan. 1820, | aged 26 yrs.

 And they rest not day & night, saying | Holy, Holy, Holy is the Lord God, Almighty, which was & is, & is to come. Rev. 4th. 8th.

IN | Memory of | Mr EMORY HARRIS | who died | 31st: Dec. 1838, | aged 50 yrs.

 In him the poor & fatherless | ever found a friend.

IN HEAVEN THERES REST. | IN | Memory of | GEORGE, | Son of Emory & | Hezediah L. Harris: | who graduated at | B. U. P. Sept. 1837, & died at Wrentham | 12th: Oct. 1838, | aged 23 yrs.

 Such the mysterious calls of Providence.

ELIZA H. HARRIS, | died | Mar. 28, 1843, | Æt. 22.

CAPT. | ASAHEL HARRIS, | died | Jan. 14, 1844, | Æt. 50.

In memory of | MR. JOHN HOLMAN, | who died | Dec. 6, 1827, | Æt. 33.

In Memory of | MRS. NANCY W. | wife of Mr John Holman, | and daughter of | Mr. Robert and | Mrs. Betsey Townsend, | who died | Jan. 25, 1827, | Æt. 29.

JOHN EDWARD | Son of Mr. John A. & | Mrs. Sarah R. Haskell, | who died | Feb. 3, 1836, | aged 21 months & | 3 days.

in memory of Mr. | DAVID HOSLEY, | who was killed by | the fall of a Frame; | July 5th, 1802, | Aged 59 Years.

Luceba, | wife of | DAVID HOSLEY, | DIED | Jan. 14, 1834, | Æt. 72.

ELIZABETH HOLLAND | Died Oct. 18, 1847, | Æ. 22 ys.

ERECTED | In Memory of | Capt. ELIJAH HOUGHTON, | who died | July 7, 1810; | Æt. 82.

 Around this monumental stone, | Let friendship drop a sacred tear;
 The husband kind, the parent fond, | The upright man lies buried here.

In Memory of | MRS. MARY HOUGHTON, | wife of | Capt Elijah Houghton, | who died | May 21, 1818, | Æt. 82.

OLIVER HOUGHTON | died | Sept. 20, 1836, | aged 70 years.

ABIGAIL | HOUGHTON | wife of Oliver Houghton, | departed this life | Feb. 4, 1837, | aged 66 years.

In memory of | MR. SALMON HOUGHTON | who died | May 28, 1844, | aged 63.

In memory of | MRS. LUCY, | wife of Mr. Salmon Houghton, | who died | Sept. 12. 1831; | Æt. 46.

In memory of | MRS. FRANCES, | second wife of | Mr Salmon Houghton; | who died Sept. 11, 1839, | aged 32 years.

SALMON J. | son of Mr. Salmon & | Frances Houghton, | who died Aug. 26, 1839, | aged 1 year & | 10 months.

In Memory of | SARAH ABBY, | daugh. of Mr. Samuel A. & | Mrs. Olive W. Hastings | who died | March 13, 1841, | aged 7 years & | 10 mo.

 Sweet Innocent, | Welcom'd to the regions of Bliss.

ERECTED—in memory of | CAPT. | BENJAMIN HOUGHTON, | who died | May 4, 1837, | aged 73.

Mrs. LYDIA HOUGHTON, | wife of Capt Benjm. Houghton; | who died | August 8th: 1825, | aged 54.

 "Her children rise up and call her blessed. | Her husband also and he praiseth her."

MISS. | LYDIA HOUGHTON | daughr. of Capt. Benjn. | and Mrs. | Lydia Houghton, | who died | Sept. 13, 1826, | aged 21.

 She openeth her mouth with wisdom, | and in her tongue is the law of kindness.

MIDDLE CEMERERY. 431

JOHN HAWKES | died | Oct. 8, 1847, | Æt. 74.

REBECCA | Wife of C. B. Hale | Died | Feb. 20, 1849; | Æ. 29 yrs.

MRS. | NANCY, | Wife of | Richard Hildreth, | died, | Nov. 20, 1819, | Æ. 32 yrs. & | 6 mo. | Also, EZEKIEL, their son, | died JAN. 26, 1820, | Æ. 6 mo.

ERECTED | In Memory of | Mr. THOMAS HASTINGS, | Æt. 28. | Also | BENJAMIN HASTINGS, JR. | Æt. 16, | who were drowned | July 4, 1813, | Sons of Mr. Benjamin & Mrs. Experience Hastings, | of Sulivan N. H.

" Time like an everrunning stream, | Bears all its sons away;
" They fly forgotten, as a dream | Dies at the opening day.
" Then cease, fond nature, dry thy tears, | Religion points on high;
" There everlasting spring appears, | And joys that never die.

EMILY W. | Wife of | Edward Hooper | Died | Jan. 26, 1849, | Æ. 35.

O, gently rest, sweet spirit, rest, | Thy worldly toil is o'er:
God called thee home, he thought it best, | To dwell on Earth no more.
Thy lovely voice no more we hear, | Thy form no more we see;
Till we in Heaven, at last, appear, | Clothed in immortality.

PARNEY, | daughter of | Sidney & Sally | Howard, | died March 18, | 1847, | aged 27 years.

MARY M. | died | March 2, 1829, | Æt. 2 yrs. * * * Daughters of Phineas | & Allice Houghton.

SOLON, Æt. 2 yrs. | MARY ANN, Æt. 11 yrs. | EDWIN, Æt. 2 yrs. | BENJ. F. Æt. 20 yrs. | children of | Aaron & Sally Jones.

AARON JONES | died | Sept. 23, 1839, | Æt. 72.

MR. SULLIVAN JONES, | son of Mr. Moses, & | Mrs. Submit Jones, | who died | July 18, 1832, | aged 25.

IN | Memory of | MR. | MOSES JONES, | who died | Dec. 5th, 1829, | aged 60 years.

In memory of | SUBMITTEE JONES, | wife of Moses Jones, | who died | Decr. 19, 1810, aged 36 years.

" Them that sleep in Jesus will God bring with him."

IN | Memory of | Mrs. Abigail Joslyn, | wife of | Capt. Samuel Joslyn, | who died | Aug. 8, 1814; | Æt. 65.

CAPT. SAMUEL JOSLYN | died 15th. Feb. 1826, | aged 88.

ERECTED | in memory of | Mrs. MARY JOSLYN, | wife of Mr. Nathaniel Joslyn, | who died | Feb. 18th, 1825, | aged 88.

ERECTED | In memory of | MR. NATHANIEL JOSLYN, | who died | May 28, 1806, | Æt. 78.

In memory of | MR. PETER JOSLYN, | who died | June 20, 1802, | Æt. 26.

Ye weeping mourning friends retire, | No more indulge your greef,
Releas'd from earthly pains & cares. | Thy friend has found relief.

MR. JONAS JOSLYN | Died | Aug. 5, 1838, | aged 64 yrs.

Luther Jones * * * Charlotte * * * Their children. | MARCUS L. | DIED | Oct. 11, 1842, | Æ. 14 yrs. | SARAH J. | DIED | Oct. 23, 1826, | Æ. 1 yr. 1 mo.

SARAH L. Daughter of | Amasa & | Sally B. Keyes, | died Sept. 12, 1817, | Æt. 5 yrs. 2 mos.

ERECTED | In memory of | Mr. AMASA KEYES | who died Oct. 7, 1826, | aged 53 years.

SOPHIA M. | daughr. of Mr. Charles E. | & Mrs. Catherine A. Knight | who died | Dec. 26, 1828, | Æt. 6 mo. & 10 days.

Happy infant early blest | Sleep on now, and take thy rest
Early freed from worldly cares | Which increase in growing years.

NATHANIEL L. | son of Mr. Charles E. & | Mrs. Catherine A. Knight, | who died | March 7, 1828, | Æt. 6 yrs & 2 mo.

'Tis fruitless now for me to weep | He can't come back to me,
My lot is now to go to him, | He shall not come to me.

JAMES M. | son of Mr Charles E. & | Mrs Catherine Knights, | who was drowned | Sept. 26, 1823, | Æt. 6 years.
When this you see remember me.

In | Memory of | Mrs. Sally Knight, | wife of | MR. CHARLES E. KNIGHT | who died | 1 June 1813; | Æt. 34.

In memory of | MISS PATTY KNIGHT, | 2 Daughter of | Mr. Manasseh and | Mrs. Hannah Knight, | who died Jan^r. 29, 1802, | Æt. 22.

And is the lovely shadow fled, | The blooming wonder of her years;
So soon inthronge among the dead, | She justly claims our pious tears,
Farewell bright soul a short farewell, | Till we shall meet again above,
In the sweet groves where pleasures dwell | And trees of life bare fruits of love.

In memory of | MR. MANASSEH KNIGHT | who died Sep. 28, 1814, | Æt. 63.

Possessing the integrity and goodness of the honest & upright man, his memory will be embalmed in the affections of all who knew his worth; and while virtue itself shall be revered, his virtues shall be held in remembrance by the righteous and the good.

EVELINE B. | wife of | MARK LUND, died | May 16, 1846, | Æt. 29.

CHARLES B. | Son of | Mark & Eveline B. | LUND | died Apr. 7, 1846. | Æt. 4 mos.

EDGAR A. Son of | Henry & Mary | LOWE. | Died | Aug. 17, 1849. | Æt. 5 yrs.

In memory of | MR. | NATHANIEL LOW, | who died | April 29, 1827, | aged 63.

In memory of | MRS. ANNES LOW, | wife of Mr. Nathaniel Low | who died. | March 11, 1821, | aged 49. | POLLY LOW died Sept. | 15, 1805, aged 6 years. | SAXON LOW died Sept. | 16, 1805, aged 10 mons. | Children of | Nathaniel & Annes Low.

In memory of | RUFUS LOW, | son of Nathaniel | and Annes Low, | who died | Oct. 14, 1824, | aged 19 years.

Alas! not youth, with all its rose and bloom | Can save from death, or rescue from the tomb,
But this fair flower, untimely snatched away, | We trust will rise in an immortal day.

SACRED | to the memory of | MISS ALMIRA LOW | who died | April 17th, 1830, | Æt. 24.

In the midst of life we are in death.
Each lone scene shall thee restore; | For thee, the tear be duly shed;
Belov'd till life could charm no more, | And mourn'd till pity's self be dead.

MARY E. | Dau. of | Anson & Emeline | LOWE, | died | Aug. 31, 1848, | Æt. 8 mos.

ERECTED | To the Memory of | MR. JONATHAN LOCKE, | who died | Aug. 13, 1814; | Æt. 66.

Though length of age has laid me low, | In youth how many thousands go;
Then stop young friend Ah! giddy youth, | This place breaths forth a solemn truth.

ERECTED | in memory of | Maj. | JONATHAN LOCKE, | Died | Jan. 26, 1839, | aged 61 y'rs.

Hope wipes the tears from sorrows eye.

ERECTED | in memory of | MRS. MARY LOCKE, | wife of Maj. Jon^a. Locke; | Died | July 4, 1849, | aged 67 yrs.

While faith points upward to the sky.

In memory of | MRS. CHLOE LINCOLN, | wife of Mr. Jacob Lincoln | who died | July 10, 1829, | Æ. 63.

In memory of | MR. | CUMMINS LINCOLN, | who died | Jan. 5, 1822, | Æt. 24.

In memory of | Mr. Washington Litch, | Son of | Mr. John Litch, and | Mrs Lydia his wife; | who died | Aug. 11th. 1798; Æ. 22.

Friends, do not tremble to convey | My Body to the tomb,
There the dear flesh of Jesus lay, | And left a long perfume.

MRS. SALLY, | wife of | Edmund Lawrence, | Died | July 6, 1849, | aged 52 years.

To | the memory | of | MR JOHN LYON, | who died | Jan. 3, 1836; | aged 61.

To | the memory | of | MRS. SALLY LYON, | wife of | Mr. John Lyon, | who died | Dec. 28, 1844, | aged 69.

MIDDLE CEMETERY.

MARTHA ANN, | daur. of Capt. John, & | Mrs Sally Lyon; | She died Nov. 13, 1821 | Æ 4 years & 7 mo.
> Lie here sweet child, and take thy rest. | To call thee home, God thought it best.

SACRED | to the memory of | MRS. ABIGAIL M. | wife of | Mr Eliab Leach, of Boston; | who died Dec. 4, 1835, | aged 27.
> The rose beside thy bed shall bloom, | And sweetly twine around thy tomb.
> Fit emblem, dearest, of thy worth, | Of faithful love and early death.

B. LEE | son of B. & L. Lee | Aged 1 month.

Capt. | CALEB LINCOLN | died Oct. 21, 1825, | Æt. 52.
> "An honest man's the | noblest work of God."

To the | memory of | MRS. REBECCA LEA | CH, the wife of Mr. | Joseph Leach, who | departed this life | April 28th, 1810, | Æ. 39.
> If christian piety and Conjugal affection, | Could have averted thy stroke O death!
> She would have still lived on Earth, But | Alas! No warning given! unceremonious Fate!
> A sudden Rush from life's meridian Joys!
> Unveil thy bosom faithful Tomb, | Take this new treasure to thy trust;
> And give these sacred relicks room, | To slumber in the silent dust.
> In thy fair Book of life divine, | My God! inscribe her name,
> There let it fill some humble place, | Beneath the slaughtered lamb.

In Memory of | MRS. SUSANNAH LEACH, wife | of Mr. JOSEPH LEACH, | who departed this life Decr. | 31st, 1800, in the 34th. year of | her age. Also Collins Leach | their son, who died Septr. 28th: | 1789, aged 18 months.
> How lov'd, how valu'd once avails thee not, | To whom related or by whom begot.
> A heap of dust alone remains of thee. | Tis all thou art & all that we shall be.
> Make the extended skies your tomb, | Let stars record your worth:
> Yet know vain mortals all must die | As natures sickliest birth.
> Thy saints while ages roll away, | In endless fame survive,
> Their glories o'er the wings of time, | Greatly triumphant live.

In memory of | MARTHA B. LAUGHTON | daugh. of Mr. John, & | Mrs. Nancy Laughton; | who died | May 28, 1849, | aged 19 yrs.
> Weep not for me my parents dear, | I am not dead but sleeping here;
> My glass is run, my grave you see, | And oh! prepare to follow me.

In memory of | MISS. | MARY ANN LAUGHTON | eldest daughter of Mr. John | & Mrs. Nancy Laughton, | who died | Aug. 9, 1842, | aged 21 yrs.
> Precious in the sight of the Lord, | is the death of his saints.
> Her mind was tranquil and serene, | No terrors in her looks were seen;
> Her Saviour's smiles dispell'd the gloom, | And smoothed her passage to the tomb.

In memory of | MR. JOHN LAUGHTON JR. | Only son of Mr. John & | Mrs. Nancy Laughton | who died | Sept. 18, 1841, | aged 21 yrs.
> Blessed are the dead, | who die in the Lord.
> The blooming youth, the man of life | Was called by God to stop—to die;
> Away from scenes of earth-born strife, | He's gone to dwell with God on high.

IN | Memory of | MR. WILLIAM LEWIS, | who died | Oct. 9, 1836, | Aged 24.

MR. | ARTEMAS LAUGHTON | died | March 15, 1825, | aged 39.
> An honest man's the noblest work of God.

Here are buryed the children of | Mr Stephen & Clarissa Laughton. | LUCY ANN | died | Sept. 22, 1822 | Æt. 13 months. | EPHRAIM | died | Sept. 14, 1820, | Æt. 22 months.
> Like roses crop'd before their bloom | They are carried to the silent tomb.

ABIGAIL A. | Died Dec. 28, 1829, | Æt. 15 yrs. | CAROLINE E. | Died Mar. 30, 1831, | Æt. 11 yrs. | Children of | Joseph & Anna | MAYNARD.

EDWARD A. | only son of | Jeremiah & Mary | H. MOORS, | died | July 24, 1847, | Æt. 15 ms. 16 ds.
> So this dear bud was early torn, | And left its Parents here to mourn,
> An object of their love; | But Parents, let your tears be dry,
> This tender plant now lives on high, | And blooms with Christ above.

MARGARET ANN | Dau. of | Jerh: & Mary H. | Moors, died | Sept. 9, 1848, | Æt. 26 ds.
> Lay here sweet babe | And take thy rest, | For God who gave thee | Thought it best.

JOHN HARRISON, | died Sept. 25, 1847, | Æt. 3 yrs. & 10 ms. | ERASTUS HENRY, | died Sept. 26, 1847, | Æt. 9 ms. & 24 ds, | only Children of John H. & Mary | MAYNARD.

 Parents dear, weep not for us, | We are with Jesus, free from care,
 Make God your friend, & heaven your aim, | And soon you'll meet your children there.

OSCAR M. | Son of Charles & | Matilda Miller, | died | Jan. 14, 1844, | Æt. 4 yrs.

 Sleep on, sleep on, my only son, | Thy life is gone, thy course is run,
 Thine eyes are clos'd to open no more, | And we thy loss must now deplore.

Mrs. ANN MATTHEWS | wife of | David Matthews, and daugh. of | John and Phebe | Winditt, | Died Nov. 3, 1840, | aged 25 years.

 Blessed are they who die in the Lord.

SACRED | to the memory of | MRS LUCY MANNING, | wife of | Doct. Samuel Manning, | who died | Oct. 4, 1817. | Æt. 38.

REBECCA PRATT, | daughter of | Samuel & Lucy Manning. | Obt. July 30, 1816; | Æt. 2 yrs. & 3 mo.

In memory of | MR. AARON MUNROE, | who died | Jan. 17, 1825, | Æt. 69.

In memory of | Maryann Mallard, | Daughter of | Mr. Abraham & | Mrs. Sally Mallard, | who died April 17, 1808, | Aged 2 years, 6 months.

ERECTED | In Memory of | JAMES MALLARD, | Son of Mr. James & Mrs. Betsy Mallard; | who died Jan. 11, 1810, | Æt. 11 mo. & 21 da. | Also | JAMES MALLARD, | who died Au. 10, 1813: | Æt. 2 yrs. 5 mo. & 26 da.

 Happy infants early blest, | Rest in peaceful slumber, rest.
 Early rescued from the cares, | Whitch increase with growing years.

SACRED | To the memory of | MISS. CATHERINE MILES, | daughter of Mr. Thomas & | Mrs. Ruth Miles; | who died Jan. 24, 1832, | aged 21.

 Prepare to meet thy God.

RUTH | wife of | Thomas Miles, | died | (in the blessed hope of a | happy immortality,) | Oct. 19, 1841, | Æt. 67.

MISS. | MARY E. MAYNARD, | daugh. of Mr. Joseph & | Mrs. Betsy Maynard, | who died Jan. 27, 1841, | aged 23 years.

 Peaceful be thy silent slumber, | Peaceful in the grave so low;
 Thou no more will join our number, | Thou no more our songs shall know,
 Yet again we hope to meet thee, | When the day of life is fled;
 Then in Heaven with joy to greet thee | Where no farewell tear is shead.

MISS ALVIRA MAYNARD | daugh^r. of Mr. Joseph, and | Mrs. Betsy Maynard: | who died May 19, 1836, | aged 28 years.

 I would not live always; no; welcome the tomb;
 Since Jesus hath lain there, I dread not its gloom;
 There sweet be my rest, till he bid me arise,
 To hail him in triumph descending the skies.

ERECTED | in memory of | JOHN MAYNARD ESQ. | who died | Jan. 21, 1823, | Æt. 70.

 He was a true friend to his country; | and as a revolutionary officer, he did much | towards gaining her Independence, and liv'd | many years to enjoy the fruits of his labour.

SACRED | to the memory of | MRS. MARTHA MAYNARD, | consort of John Maynard Esq. | and daugh^r. of Maj. Gardner | Wilder, | who died Feb. 19, 1836, | in the 69th; year of | her age.

What though affliction here would heave a sigh, | That one so lov'd and so revered should die—
Calm resignation clasps a saviour's cross, | And mourns, but does not murmur at the loss,
This mouldering dust shall here repose in peace, | Till that great day, when time itself shall cease.
Her spirit is with God; and this its plea— | "My Saviour liv'd, my Saviour died for me!"

 Not unto us, O Lord, not unto us, but unto thy name | give glory, for thy mercy and for thy truth's sake.

MR. | JOSEPH T. MILLER | died Feb. 17, 1827, | aged 31.

 Blessed are the dead | Who die in the Lord.

MIDDLE CEMETERY.   435

IN | memory of | Mr. | WILLIAM MCLALLEN | who died | Oct. 19, 1822, | Æt. 55.

IN | Memory of | widow | SARAH MANLEY, | who died | Sept. 11, 1833, | aged 84.

FORDYCE NOURSE | died Aug 6, 1848, | aged 39 years.

In memory of | MISS. ELIZABETH A. | daugh^r. of | William and | Elizabeth Nowell, | who died | May 28, 1847, | aged 21 years.

JOHN W^M. | Son of | Mr. William & Mrs. | Elizabeth Nowell, | died | March 9, 1832, | Æt. 3 ys. & 15 d.

ELIZABETH A. | daughter of | Mr. William & Mrs. | Elizabeth Nowell, | died | April 8, 1826, | Æt. 2 yrs. & 3 ms.

WILLIAM NICHOLS, | Son of | William H. & | Mary Newman; | who died | June 12, 1843, | aged 5 years.
No prayers no tears its flight could stay, | 'Twas Jesus called the soul away.

MR. GOWEN B. NEWMAN | died | the 9th. of Dec. 1833, | aged 64.
"The memory of the just is blessed."

MRS. | LUCY NEWMAN, | relict of | Gowen B. Newman, | died | June 2, 1842, | aged 71.
"Death cannot the soul imprison."

Erected in memory of | JAMES HOMER NEWMAN, | who died | in Savannah Georgia, | June 24, 1822, | aged 24. | And of | CAROLINE M. NEWMAN | died March 29, 1845, | aged 29.
"'Tis in heaven that spirits dwell, | Glorious though invisible."

IN | Memory of | MRS. PATTY, | wife of | Mr. Pliny Newhall, | who died | Jan. 18, 1810; | In the 23, year | of her age. | An infant died Jan. 1810, | aged 15 days.

In memory of | MR. | JONATHAN OSGOOD, | Died Jan. 10, 1847, | aged 71.

MISS ALMIRA, | daugh. of | Mr. Jonathan & Mrs. Anna Osgood: | died July 15. 1845, | aged 39 yrs. & | 8 mo.
Lift thy hopes to Heaven above thee, | Think that there in bliss I roam;
I would live and live to love thee, | But my Father calls me home.

MRS. MARY N. | wife of Dea. | Peter Osgood; | who died | June 11, 1847, | aged 50 years.
A partner tender, and a parent dear' | To none an enemy, to all sincere,
Cheerful she liv'd, and on the bed of death | Kiss'd submissively the rod, and yielded up her breath.

ERECTED | In memory of | ABIGAIL C. OSGOOD, | daugh. of Dea. Peter | & Mrs. Mary N. Osgood, | who died | Oct. 17, 1843, | aged 17 years.
Dust to its narrow house beneath, | Soul to its rest on high.
Those that have seen thy smiles in death, | No more may fear to die.

MARTHA W. | daughter of | Deac. Peter, and | Mrs. Mary N. Osgood, | died Aug. 29, 1832, | Aged 9 months.
Ere sin could blight or sorrow fade | The opening bud to Heaven's conveyed.

IN | memory of | MR. JOEL OSGOOD | who died | Nov. 7, 1821, | Æt. 75.

IN | memory of | Mrs. | LUCRETIA OSGOOD, | wife of | Joel Osgood, | who died | March 28, 1846, | aged 91 yrs.

IN | Memory of | MR. JONATHAN OSGOOD, | who died | July 14, 1808, | Aged 59.

MR. NAHUM OSGOOD | Died | Feb. 18, 1815, | Aged 36.

In memory of | MR. | EPHRAIM OSGOOD, | who died | March 16, 1834, | aged 76.

LUCINDA, | wife of | JAMES PITTS, | & daughter of Hervey Burditt. | DIED | Oct. 23, 1848, | Æt. 30 yrs. & 3 ms.
"Then shall the dust return to the earth as it was, | and the spirit shall return unto God who gave it." | For the Lord will not cast off forever.

SACRED | to the memory of | DAVID POIGNAND, | Born in the Island | of Jersey, | Jan. 12, 1759; | Died in Lancaster, | Aug. 28, 1830.

"Is death uncertain? therefore thou be fix'd. | Fix'd as a centinel, all eye, all ear, | All expectation of the coming foe."

SACRED | to the memory of | DELICIA AMIRAUX | POIGNAND, | Born in the Island | of Jersey, | Dec. 17, 1764; | Died in Lancaster, | Sept. 30, 1833.

She stretcheth out her hand to the poor, yea, she reacheth forth her hands to the needy; She openeth her mouth with wisdom; and in her tongue is the law of kindness.

DELICIA AMIRAUX, | daughter of Samuel and | Delicia M. Plant, | died Jan. 26, 1834; | Æt. 2 yrs. & 20 days.

Thy thread of life, has soon been spun, | Thy little race has soon been run; Thou darling of thy father's eye. | Thy sister's pet and mother's joy, Thy brother's plaything; thou are gone, | And left a painful void at home. We weep—but thou O God art just, | May we in thee put all our trust.

JULIA L. | Dau^r. of | Joel W. & Lorinda | PHELPS, | DIED | Mar. 10, 1846, | Æt. 17 months.

MERIEL PHELPS, | daut. of Mr. Eph^m. Phelps; | & Mrs. Dolly Phelps, | who died | Aug. 15, 1819, | Æ. 12 years & | 7 months.

Surviving friends weep not for me, | Weep for yourselves you soon must be. Where time itself will die; | Prepare for death, watch ye and pray, Was Christ's command; his voice obey, | And you shall reign on high.

MR. | MOSES PEASLEE | died May 8, 1823. | Æt. 36.

Death but entombs the body; | life the soul.

MRS. EMELY PRATT, | wife of | Mr. Eben Pratt, | and daugh. of | Mr. Joseph and Betsy Rice: | who died July 10, 1839, | aged 42. | Also their daugh. | EMELY F. PRATT, | aged 2 yrs.

But her soul in beauty of holiness pass'd, | Displaying its banner of hope to the last; No shadow of darkness of doubt or of fear, | E'er shaded her brow or extracted a tear.

ROBERT PHELPS | died | June 9, 1834, | Æt. 66.

In memory of | MISS ELIZABETH PEACOCK | who died | Se^r. 9, 1813. | Æt. 56.

She was for many years an assistant in the | family of Mr. Manasseh Knight by whome | She was beloved and respected.
She was a friend who gave relief | To him whose heart was fill'd with grief; Although her hand no wedlock ever bound, | Yet true to God and man was found. Ye weeping, mourning friends retire, | No more indulg your grief, Releas'd from earthly care and pain, | Thy friend has found sweet relief.

BETSY S. | wife of Hiram W. Pitts, | and dau. of James Burditt, | DIED | May 12, 1843, | Aged 29. | LEWIS HIRAM, | Their son | died Sept. 7, 1843, | Aged 4 ms. & 15 ds.

JAMES PITTS, | DIED | Jan. 13, 1835. | Aged 52.

In memory of | MRS. ABIGAIL, | wife of Mr Jabez Prescott & | daugh. of Mr. Thomas Gates, | who died | Oct. 4, 1827, Æt. 59.

In Memory of | MRS. ABIGAIL, | wife of | Farnham Plummer, | formerly wife of Henry Ballard, | Died Feb. 5, 1842, | aged 42 years.

I am the resurrection and the life; he that believeth in me, though he were dead, yet shall he live.

ABIGAIL, Wife of Nathan Puffer | and dau. of Samuel & Abigail Wilder Joslyn. | Born in Lancaster Nov. 24, 1774, | Died Nov. 23, 1802.

"Knowest thou the ordinances of heaven? Canst thou | set the dominion thereof in the earth?"

MARY E. PHELPS, | DIED | Jan. 26, 1848, | Æt. 22 yrs.

MR. | HENRY PHELPS | died | Aug. 18, 1826, | aged 30 years.

ERECTED | in memory of | MR. | JOSEPH PHELPS, | who died | May 8, 1839, | aged 33.

ERECTED | in memory of | Miss. | MARY ANN P. PHELPS, | who died | May 11, 1833, | aged 20.

ERECTED | in memory of | MR. HEZEKIAH P. PHELPS, | who died | Dec. 25, 1833, | aged 36.

MIDDLE CEMETERY.

MARY P. | daugh'. of Mr. Sylvester | and Mrs. Esther Phelps, | who died | May 22, 1814; | Æt. 20 days.

FATHER & MOTHER | Died Oct. 1848, | Æt. 80 | And | Died June 1857 | Æt 83½.

MRS. | MARY PHELPS, | wife of | Mr Abijah Phelps; | who died | March 26, 1831. | aged 59.
> The humble christian's rest is here, | The tender parent fond & dear.
> A faithful wife was summoned home, | Prepare thyself to follow soon.

MR. | ABIJAH PHELPS | died June 23, 1829, | aged 74.
> Farewell dear friends and children too, | For Christ has call'd me home,
> In a short time he'll call for you, | Prepare yourselves to come.

REED * * * MARY ELIZABETH | Born April 19, 1839, | Died Oct. 20, 1840. | GEO. FRANCIS | Born Feb. 12, 1841, | Died Feb. 6, 1846.

MISS. | SARAH WILDER | daugh. of | Samuel and | Sally Rugg: | died Feb. 23, 1846,—aged 45 yrs.
> Pleasant, cheerful, kind at heart, | On her brow a smile was laid,
> Lov'd by all 'twas hard to part, | Lo not a murmur she betray'd.

MR. DAVID RICHARSON, | who died | April 5, 1818, | Æt. 30.

ERECTED | in memory of | MRS. PRUDENCE ROBBINS, | who died | Dec. 14, 1845, | aged 90 yrs.

LUCY | wife of | Nathaniel Rand | Died Nov. 3, 1826, | Æ. 37. | HARRY | their son | Died Mar. 10, 1816; | Æ. 6 yrs. 6 ms. | NANCY ELIZABETH | wife of | Nathaniel Rand | Died Mar. 29, 1838, | Æ. 42. | ELLEN MARIA | their daughter | Died Nov. 7, 1835, | Æ. 4 ms.

In memory of | MISS. | MARY ANN RICE, | daughter of Mr Joseph & | Mrs. Betsy Rice. | who died | May 13, 1825: | aged 20 years.

MRS. BETSEY, | wife of | Ephraim Rugg, | died | Nov. 28, 1846, | Æt. 66.

EPHRAIM RUGG | died Oct. 20, 1836, Æt. 57.

MRS. | ELIZABETH RUGG | wife of | Capt. Daniel Rugg | who died | April 8, 1834, | aged 88.

IN | memory of | Capt. | DANIEL RUGG, | who died | April 11, 1830, | aged 87.

To the memory of | MISS. | PRUDENCE RUGG, | who died | March 16, 1838, | aged 77 yrs.

ERECTED | in memory of | MR. | STEPHEN RUGG, | who died | Dec. 23, 1834. Aged 78.

MR. JOEL I. RUGG | son of Joel & | Bathsheba Rugg, | Died | Jan. 1, 1847, aged 28.

MRS. REBEKAH, | wife of | Mr Isaac Rugg, | Died | Jan. 1, 1847, | aged 79.

IN | memory of | Mr ABIJAH RUGG, | who died | Feb. 12, 1816, | Æt. 65

In memory of | MRS. | SUSANNA RUGG, | wife of | Mr. Abijah Rugg; | who died | Jan. 11, 1832, aged 77.

MR. | ISAAC RUGG | Died April 1, 1813, | aged 67.

MR. AARON RUGG, | who died | July 6, 1810, | aged 50 years & | 11 months.
> Sweet is the memory of the just, | While they lie buried in the dust.

MRS. BATHSHEBA RUGG, | wife of Mr. Joel Rugg; | who died | Nov. 13, 1832, | aged 42.

MR. JOEL RUGG, | died | Sept. 17, 1836, | Æt. 48.

MISS. MARY | Daughter of Joel & | Bathsheba Rugg, | died | Aug. 2, 1838; | Æt. 24.

FRANCIS, | Son of Joel & | Bathsheba Rugg | Died | Nov. 21, 1839, | aged 7 yrs.

ERECTED | in memory of | MISS LUCY RUGG, | who died Aug. 10 | th, 1805, Æ. 22 | Years.
> She is not dead but sleepeth.

ERECTED | in memor of Capt. | ELISHA RUGG, | who died Jan. 7th: | 1805 | Æ. 49 Years.
> Faithful to himself, affectionate to | his family; just to his neighbour, | and sincere to his God, he was | fortified against the agonies of | long sickness, and triumphed in | hope of sharing the Redeemer's love

Mr. ABEL, & | Mrs. KATHARINE RUGG, | died Feb. 14, & | Nov 2, 1843, | aged 91 & | 84 years.

HANNAH JONES | wife of | Abel W. Rugg | DIED | Mar. 27, 1836, | Æ. 38 yrs. 4 ds. * * *

MARTIN RUGG | Died Sept. 4, 1819, | Æ. 15 mos. 15 ds.

ERECTED | In Memory of | MR JOSIAH ROSS, | Son of Mr. Seth & | Mrs. Abigail Ross | of Petersham; | who died Oct. 22, 1814; Æt. 27.

ADDISON E. | only son of | James & | A. M. L. Rugg, | died | Feb. 20, 1847, | Æt. 15 months.

MRS. SUBMIT, | wife of | Mr. James Rugg, | DIED | Sept. 1, 1830, | Æt. 38.
> Weep not for me, but for yourselves.
> The body returns to dust as it was, | and the spirit to God who gave it.

In memory of | MRS. MARY SAWYER, | wife of | Daniel Sawyer, | who | died Dec. 31, 1848, | aged 64 years.
> Peaceful be thy silent slumber, | Peaceful in the grave so low;
> Thou no more will join our number, | Thou no more our songs shall know.

SARAH JULIA, | Daur. of | Charles & Julia | SAFFORD | DIED | June 22, 1847, | Æt. 4 months.

THOMAS SAWYER | DIED | June 10, 1846, | Æ 49.
> "Blessed are the dead, which die in the Lord."

MARTHA A. | dau. of | Merrick & Rebecca | SARGENT, | DIED | Sept. 26, 1849, | Æ. 1 yr. 2 ms.

JULIA ANN, | Daur. of Curtis & | Huldah Sargent, | died Oct. 30, 1847, | Æt. 1 yr. 8 ms. 22 ds.

WINFIELD P. | Son of Curtis & | Huldah Sargent, | died Jan. 10, 1849, | Æt. 3 mos.

LYDIA ANN, | Daur. of George & | Lucinda Stratton, | Died June 23, 1849, | Æ. 1 yr. 3 mos. | & 19 dys.

HENRY H. SAWYER | SON OF EZRA & ELIZA | DIED JAN. 30, 1842, AGED 18.

FRANCENA E. | died | Sept. 2, 1833, | Æt. 11 mo. & 19 days. | FREDERICK H. | died | May 9, 1834. | Æt. 20 mo. & | 21 days. | Children of Mr. Elias & | Mrs. Nancy Sawyer.
> Happy infants early bless'd | And in peaceful slumbers rest.

MISS ABBY B. | daughter of | Mr. Elias & | Nancy B. Sawyer, | died | Oct. 3, 1842, | Æt. 18 yrs.
> Dust to its narrow house beneath, | Soul to its place on high.
> They that have seen thy look in death, | No more may fear to die.

MISS LOUISA A. | daughter of | Mr. Elias & | Nancy B. Sawyer, | died | Jan. 8, 1844, | Æt. 16 yrs.
> Calm on the bosom of thy God, | Dear spirit rest thee now;
> Een while with us thy footsteps trod, | His seal was on thy brow.

MARY ANN, | wife of | James Chandler, | & daughter of Elias & | Nancy B. Sawyer, | died January 8, 1846, | aged 25 years.
> ✝ Weep not.
> Lord she was thine, & not my own. | Thou hast not done me wrong.
> I thank thee for the precious loan, | Afforded me so long.

ELIAS SAWYER | DIED | Jan 16, 1849, | Æt. 57.
> "To die is to go home."

NANCY B. | WIFE OF | ELIAS SAWYER | DIED | DEC. 16, 1849, | Æt. 57.
> "We shall meet again."

MIDDLE CEMETERY. 439

SALLY | widow of | Howell Smith, | died in Boston, | Oct. 20, 1849, | aged 59 yrs.
    Yet, dear mother, not forever, | Are our words of parting given,
    Time nor death itself can sever | Hearts that strive to meet in heaven.

EBEN SAWYER | DIED | Oct. 23, 1822, | aged 25 years.

JACOB SWEETSER, | Died | Jan. 23, 1823, | Æt. 76 yrs. | MARGARET, | his wife | Died July 9, 1838, | Æt. 85 yrs. | MARGARET, | Died | March 6, 1840 | Æt. 53 yrs. * * *

MRS. | DEBORAH SOLLENDINE | wife of Mr. Manasseh Sollendine | who died | Oct. 9, 1827, | aged 46.
    Blessed are the dead | who die in the Lord.

ELI STEARNS | BORN | NOV. 12, 1757, | DIED MAR. 7, 1825. | MARY WHITNEY | HIS WIFE | BORN | JAN. 14, 1767, | DIED | MAY 24, 1828. | AUGUSTUS, | DIED | SEPT. 27, 1811, | Æ. 4 YRS.

MR. | GARRY C. SANFORD | died | Oct. 23, 1847, | Æt. 32.

SARAH E. | daughter of | Charles & Eliza Sawyer, | died Apr. 23, 1827, | Aged 3 yrs. & 8 ms.

CHARLES F. | son of Charles & | Eliza Sawyer, | died May 8, 1831. | Aged 4 yrs. & 3 ms.

MARTHA S. | daughter of | Charles & | Eliza Sawyer, | died Nov. 28, 1831, | Aged 6 yrs. & 8 ms.

SARAH E. | daughter of | Charles & | Eliza Sawyer, | died Sept. 17, 1832, | Aged 3 yrs. & 4 ms. | Also their infant, | died Dec. 4, 1834, | Aged 4 days.

SYMMES, | June 21, 1844. Oct. 10, 1842.

MARY, | wife of | GEORGE SAFFORD, | DIED | Feb. 19, 1831, Æ. 36.

In memory of | MRS. | LYDIA STEVENSON, | wife of | Mr. Martin Stevenson; | who died | June 5, 1840, | aged 72.

In memory of | MR. | MARTIN STEVENSON, | who died | March 20, 1839, | aged 73.

LUCY ANN, | only daughter of | Silas & | Sally Sawyer, | died | Oct. 28, 1829, | Æt. 4 yrs. 3 ms.

FRANCIS A. youngest son of | Silas and Sally Sawyer | died June 19, 1846, | aged 23. years.
    Virtue never dies.
    All peaceful was his bed of death. | To heaven he raised a smiling eye,
    Calm and composed resigned his breath | For him we trust 'twas gain to die.

In memory of | MR. MOSES SAWYER, | who died | Mar. 12, 1831, | in his 67 year.
    The memory of the just is blessed.

ELISABETH, | Wife of | MOSES SAWYER, | Died | Nov. 20, 1849, Æ. 84 yrs. 8 ms.
    She had hope in death.

ERECTED | In memory of | MR. MOSES SMITH, | who died | Feb. 4, A. D. 1812, | Æt. 72.

ERECTED | In Memory of | MRS. ABIGAIL SMITH, | wife of Mr. Moses Smith; | who died Jan. 26, A. D. 1812, | Æt. 70.

To | the Memory | of the | HON. MOSES SMITH, | who died June 27, | 1835, | aged 58.

In Memory of | CHARLES HENRY SMITH, | Son of Moses Smith Esq. | & Mrs Sarah his wife | who died April 3, 1812. | Æt. 10 mos & 8 days

MRS. ELIZA H. | wife of | Vernis Streeter, | died Oct. 15, 1845, | aged 36 years.
    Jesus said unto her: I am the resurrection, and the life; he that believeth in me, though he were dead, yet shall live.

MR. DANIEL STEARNS | died June 30, 1818, | Æ. 74. | MRS. DEBORAH, | his wife, died Oct. 10, 1834 | Æ. 78.

ELLEN C. | daugh. of Mr. Aron & | Mrs. Phebe Sawin, | who died | Nov. 23, 1840, | aged 2 yrs. & 4 mo.
> By angels borne she flyes to rest, | We know 'tis well nay more 'tis best.
> When we our pilgrim's path have trod | O may we find her with our God.

ERECTED | In memory of | MR. JOHN SARGEANT, | who died | Dec. 21, 1802; | Æt. 80.
> 'Tis but a few whose days amount | To three-score years and ten;
> And all beyond that short account, | Is sorrow, toil and pain.

ERECTED | In Memory of | MRS HANNAH SARGEANT, | Wife of | Mr John Sargeant; | who died | Aug. 26, 1799: | Æt. 77.
> Forbare my friends thy tears to shed, | Rejoice to think my troubles cease;
> Lo! since this vale of death I tread, | I traverse in eternal peace.

ERECTED | In Memory of | MR AARON SARGEANT, | who died | Feb. 5, 1801: | Æt. 36.
> So Jesus slept; Gods dying son | Past through the grave and blest the bed;
> Then rest dear saint till from his throne, | The morning breaks, and pierces the shade.

In memory of | MISS. | LYDIA STEPHENSON, | who died | Aug. 5, 1827, | Æt. 28.

MOSES SAWYER | DIED | Oct. 5, 1805, Æ. —
> Our Grandfather.

ELIZABETH | wife of MOSES SAWYER | Died | Apr. 21, 1844, | Æ. 94.
> Our Grand mother.

JOHN SARGEANT | DIED | Apr. 1, 1822, | Æt. 73. | ANN, | his wife | DIED | Feb. 17, 1849, | Æt. 76.

In memory of | MRS. | ELIZABETH, | wife of | Seth Sargent, | Died | May 24, 1837, | aged 74.

IN | Memory of | MR. SETH SARGENT, | who died | Nov. 28, 1830, | aged 77.

In memory of | CHRISTOPHER ELLERY | STEDMAN, | son of William & Almy, Stedman, | who was drowned at sea, | on a voyage from Boston | to Calcutta, Aug. 9, 1809, | Aged 17 years.
> This tie was sacred when the | Promise of fidelity & usefulness | was accomplishing.
> "Gods way is in the sea & his path in the great waters & his footsteps are not known."

In Memory | of | Mary Ann Stedman, | only daughter | of | William and Almy Stedman; | who died August 1, A. D. 1807, | in the 13 year of her age.
> Early, bright, transient, chaste as morning dew, | She sparkled, was exhal'd, and went to Heaven.

IN | Memory of | WILLIAM STEDMAN Jun. | Son of William & Almy | Stedman, | who died April 16, 1810, | Aged 11 years.
> He was intelligent, affectionate, and dutiful. "He remembered his creator in the days of his youth."

N. THAYER [A tomb.]

LURENIA J. | died | June 19, 1842, | Æ. 3 yrs. 7 mos. | CHARLOTTE E. | died | Jan. 29, 1845, | Æ. 4 yrs. 2 mos. | * * * | children of S. H. & B. T. Turner.

CHARLES F. | son of Silas & Parney H. Thurston, | DIED | Feb. 3, 1847, | Æt. 20 yrs. 6 mo's. | & 10 d's.

JOSEPHINE | Infant Dau^r. of | J. G. & H. L. Thurston | Died Oct. 15, 1832.

MRS. ELIZABETH TIDD, | DIED | JAN. 14, 1844, | AGED 88 YRS. | JOEL TIDD, | A SOLDIER IN | THE WAR OF 1812, | DIED JULY 20, 1825, | AGED 40 YRS. | GEORGE C. TIDD, | DIED NOV. 8, 1834, | AGED 41 YRS. * * *

MRS. MARTHA TOWNSEND, | wife of | William Townsend, | Died | Dec. 29, 1846, | aged 62 yrs.

MISS. | MARTHA TOWNSEND, | daugh. of William & | Martha Townsend, | Died | Dec. 14, 1842, | aged 23 yrs.

CAPTAIN | GEORGE K. TUTTLE * * * * EUNICE EMILY, | his wife | Died Feb. 5, 1847, | Æ. 38. | Children of | Geo. K. & EUNICE E. Tuttle: | LYDIA B. | Died Mar. 30, 1834, | Æ. 13 mos. 22 ds. * * *

MIDDLE CEMETERY. 441

PETER THURSTON, | DIED | Dec. 9, 1824, | aged 56 years. | SALLIE, HIS WIFE, | DIED | Jan. 21, 1832, | aged 54 years.

ERECTED | In Memory of | MR. PETER THURSTON, | Who died | Dec. 22, 1812: | Æt. 73.

MRS. DOROTHY, | Relict of | Mr. Peter Thurston, Senr. | Died | Dec. 20, 1831, | Æt. 92 years.

ERECTED | In Memory of | Mr GATES THURSTON, | who died | Feb. 12, 1816; Æt. 51.

How lov'd, how valu'd once, avails thee not; | To whom related, or by whom begot;
A heap of dust alone remains of thee; | 'Tis all thou art! and all we soon shall be.

MRS. ELIZABETH, | Relict of the late | Mr. Gates Thurston, | DIED | Sept. 14, 1848, | Æt. 86.

CAPT. | HENRY THURSTON, | DIED | Sept. 30, 1842, | Æt. 50.

MR. | ROBERT TOWNSEND, | died | Sept 1st. 1826, | aged 66.

MRS. | BETSY TOWNSEND, | wife of Mr. Robert Townsend; | who died | July 12th, 1826, | aged 55.

MR. | HENRY TOWNSEND, | who died | Nov. 22, 1822, | aged 29.

MRS | ALMIRA TOWNSEND, | wife of | Capt. Warren Townsend, | who died Feb. 12, 1835, | aged 31.

Awhile here pensive let me bend, | And mourn my fair departed friend.
When passing where thy ashes sleep, | Whose heart so hard that will not weep.

ABIGAIL H. | daugh^r. of Capt. Warren | and | Mrs. Almira Townsend: | who died Sept. 11, 1831, | aged 5 years & 6 m.

I know my babe is blest, | Her bliss by Jesus given;
She's early gone to rest, | She's found an early Heaven.

JAMES NEWHALL TAYLOR | Died | Oct. 14, 1843. | Age, 4 yrs. 8 mo. | SUSAN | Died Feb. 1, 1834, | Age 8 days.

In memory of | CAROLINE M. | second wife of | Wilder S. Thurston, | who died | Nov. 2, 1849, | aged 25 years.

In memory of | MRS. | ANN M. THURSTON, | wife of | Wilder S. Thurston, | who died | Dec. 14, 1846, | aged 29 years.

"Blessed are the meek."

Those who knew her need no | sounding phrase to tell her virtues. | To those who knew her not, | No sounding phrase can tell them

In Memory of | RUSSELL GATES | Son of | Wilder S & | Ann M. Thurston, | who died | April 17, 1841, | aged 10½ mos.

SACRED | To the Memory of | Mrs. REBECKAH THURSTON, | Wife of Capt. John Thurston; | who died | May 9, 1801; | Æt. 39.

Thou dear departed soul adieu, | Thy lifeless clay must here remain;
Till Christ thy body shall renew, | Then both with joy shall meet again.'

Sacred to the memory of | CAPT. JOHN THURSTON, | who died Dec. 7, 1838, | Æt. 84 yrs.

MARY ANN, | dau't of | John & Lucy | THURSTON, | DIED | Nov. 27, 1835, | Æ. 19 yrs.

MRS. LUCY, | wife of John | THURSTON JR. | DIED | July 2, 1827, | Æ. 32 ys.

ERECTED | in memory of | MRS. | MARY TYLER, | second wife of | Mr. Benjamin Tyler; | who died | March 19, 1839, | aged 36 yrs. & 10 mo.

ERECTED | in memory of | MRS. ELIZA H. TYLER, | Consort of | Mr. Benjamin Tyler, | and daughter of | Roswell Hubbard Esq. | of Sullivan N. H. | who died | May 15, 1835, aged 40.

Blessed are the dead, | Who die in the Lord.

In memory of | MRS. CAROLINE P. | wife of Mr. | John Townsend Jr. | who died | March 5, 1840, Æt. 36.

Jesus saith I am the resurrection | and the life; he that believeth on me, though he were dead, yet shall he live.
Therefore stay your tears dear friends, | Weep not for me, but for your sins,
Die to the world, and live to God, | And heaven will soon be your abode.

Mr. John Townsend | died | July 2, 1815, | aged 42.

Mrs. Ruth Townsend, | consort of | Mr. John Townsend | who died | Dec. 14, 1825 | aged 50.

Elvira | daughter of John & | Ruth Townsend, | who died | Jan. 7. 1826, | aged 14 years.

In | Memory of | Capt. Asahel Tower | Died Aug. 3, 1833, | Æ. 73.

In Memory of | Mrs. Meliscent Tower, | Wife of | Capt. Asahel Tower, | who died | Sept. 20, 1820, | aged 59.

> Come hither mortals, cast an eye, | Then go thy way, prepare to die;
> Think on thy doom, for die thou must, | One day like me, be turn'd to dust.

In | memory of | Mrs. Phebe Upton, | wife of | Mr Joseph Upton, | who died | June 11, 1812, | Æt. 33.

> Friend nor physician could not save | My mortal body from the grave.
> Nor can the grave sonfine me here | When Christ doth call me to appear.

Mrs. Mary M. | wife of | Daniel K. Wilder, | died Nov. 24, 1842, | Æt. 39.

> Calm on the bosom of thy God, | Fair Spirit rest the now!
> E'en while with ours thy footsteps trod, | His seal was on thy brow.
> Dust to its narrow house beneath, | Soul to its place on high!
> They that have seen thy look in death, | No more may fear to die.

Sarah, | Daur. of | Samuel & Sarah Winchester, | died Oct. 23, 1846, | Æt. 18.

Cleora Ann, | Dau. of | David & Sarah A. | Wallace, | died | April 1, 1848, | Æt. 9 yrs.

Henry | Son of | Matthew F. | & Charlotte A. | Woods | Died | Sept. 12, 1849, | Æ. 4 yrs. 7 mos.

Sarah,—daugh. of | John and Phebe | Winditt, | Died Sept. 24; 1846, | aged 22 years.

O Lord remember me.

Mary E. | died | Nov. 23, 1858, | Aged 12 yrs. | Sarah A. | died Aug. 11, 1846, | Aged 1 yr. | Children of | J. W. Jr. & M. E. Winditt.

> O cease dear parents, | Cease your weeping | Above the spot, | Where we are sleeping.

Samuel Ward, | Born Sept. 25, 1739, | Died Aug 14, 1826. | Dolly Ward, | Born Sept. 16, 1745, | Died Dec. 31, 1818. | Samuel Ward Jr. | Born 1769, | Died Nov. 29, 1800. | Sarah C. Hall, | Born 1793. | Died June 27, 1826. | Lucretia Murray, | Born June 1762, | Died Aug. 30, 1836.

George Waite, | Son of | Joel & Deborah H. | Wilder, | died Nov. 8, 1842, | Æt. 13 yrs.

Erected | In memory of | Mr Jonas Wilder | Died | Nov. 15, 1845, | Aged 58.

Mrs. Sarah E. Goss, | wife of | Mr. Jonas Goss. | Died | Jan. 28, 1845, aged 24.

Hannah Whipple | Died | July 12, 1844, | aged 70.

Erected | In Memory of | Mr William Wilder, | who died | March 20, 1816: | Æt. 61.

> Look, down upon this sacred spot and see | What death can do to you as well as me;
> Sweet bosom Friend, your falling sand is nigh; | Children, prepare, 'tis God that calls on high.

In | memory of | Mrs. | Sophia Wilder, | wife of | Mr Elijah Wilder, | who died | June 1822; Æt. 30

Joseph Wilder | died | Aug. 23, 1841, | aged 55 yrs.

Sally | died March, | 24, 1818, | Æt 18 months daughter of Capt. | Nathaniel & | Mrs. Polly Warner.

> This lovely child begining to expand | Was soon transplanted to a happy land.
> She has gone & left her parents here to mourn | Gone, gone forever never to return.

Erected | In Memory of | Mr. Asa Warner, | who died | Decr. 31, 1816, | Æt. 67.

> The dust & ruins that remain | Are precious in our eyes;
> These ruins shall be built again, | And all this dust shall rise.

MIDDLE CEMETERY. 443

Mrs. | Abigail H. Whitney | daug^r. of Mr. Robert & | Mrs. Betsy Townsend; | who died | Sept. 24, 1823, | aged 27.

In memory of | Amos Augustus, | son of Amos & Prudence | Wheeler, who died | May 16th. 1818; | aged 7 weeks.

> So fades the lovely blooming flower, | Fond smiling solace of an hour,
> So soon our transient comforts fly, | And pleasures only bloom to die.

Roxanna | daur. of Mr. Amos | & Mrs Prudence Wheeler. | She died | April 30, 1822, | Æ. 15 mo. & 8 days.

> This lovely bud so young so fair, | Call'd hence by early doom,
> Just came to show how sweet a flower | In Paradise may bloom.

Mrs. Lusena, | wife of | Mr. Ebenezer Wilder, | who died | June 25, 1825, | aged 37, | daughter of Moses and Betsy Sawyer.

In memory of | Mr. | Joel Wilder | died | Oct. 19, 1847. | aged 70.

In memory of | Mrs. Sophia Wilder | wife of | Mr. Joel Wilder | who died | Feb. 21, 1844, | aged 64.

Mrs. Susanna | wife of | Mr Calvin Wilder, | died | March 24, 1847, | Æt. 73.

In memory of | Mr. | Calvin Wilder, | who died | April 5, 1832, | Æt. 59.

In memory of | Mrs. Martha, | wife of | Mr. Samuel Wilder, | who died | Nov. 13, 1814, | Æt. 72.

In memory of | Mr. Samuel Wilder, | who died | Nov. 3, 1827, | Æt. 81.

In memory of | Mrs. Eliza Ann, | wife of Col. John Wilson, | who died | July 14, 1842, | aged 30 years.

> The humble christian's rest is here, | The tender parent fond and dear,
> A faithful wife was summon'd home. | Prepare thyself to follow soon.

Frances, | died Aug. 20, and | Edward, | Aug. 25, 1843, | Aged 11 months. | Twin sons of | Volney & Charlotte | Wilder.

"Suffer little children, and forbid them not, to come unto me; for of such is the kingdom of Heaven."

Erected | In memory of | Mrs. Mary Willard, | Widow of the | Hon. Abijah Willard Esq. | who died Dec. 16, 1807; | Æt. 77.

Mrs. Elizabeth, | Wife of | Joseph Wales Esq. | died Aug. 19, 1822, | Æ. 61.

An example of Piety, | Benevolence, Usefulness, Rectitude.

Erected | In memory of Mrs. | Lydia Wilder, | wife of | Mr Daniel Wilder, | who died | July 18, 1825, | aged 47.

Mr. James Wilder | died, | Dec. 22, 1834, | Æt. 40.

Ann Maria | daughter of | Capt. Thomas H. & | Mrs. Lucy Wellington | who died June 1, 1839, | aged 5 years & | 3 mo.

Charlotte O. | daughter of | Mr Snell, and Mrs. Deborah R. Wade, | who died | April 8, 1838, aged 3 years & | 6 months.

To | the memory of | Mr. Davis Whitman | who died April 24, 1844 | aged 81 yrs. & 11 mo.

Mrs. Hannah Whitman, | wife of Mr. Davis Whitman, | and grandmother | to George Walton; | who died May 25, 1836, | aged 70 years, & | 7 months.

George Henry, | son of Jotham & | Eliza C. Walton, | Died July 9, 1834, | Aged 26 years.

Ephraim R. | son of Mr. Luke & | Mrs. Mary Wilder, | who died | Sept. 12, 1818, | Æt. 2 years & 8 mo.

> Sleep on sweet Child take thy rest | To call thee home, God saw it best.

Holman Wilder, | son of Luke & Mary | Wilder; | died Jany. 20, 1807, Aged 2 years | & 8 months.

> He cometh forth like a | flower and is cut down.

Jerome Willard | died Sept. 30, 1846, | Æt. 12.

Amasa Willard | died Nov. 10, 1842, | Æt. 71 * * *

Mrs. | Fanny Willard, | wife of Mr Amasa Willard; | who died | July 8 1812, | aged 29.

In memory of | Betsy Willard, | Daut. of Mr. Simon and | Mrs. Elizabeth Willard, | who died April 19th. | 1799, Aged 15 Years | and 22 days.

MR. SIMON WILLARD | died Jan. 9, 1825, | aged 97.

ERECTED | In Memory of | MRS. SALLY WILDER, | Wife of Mr John Wilder; | who died Nov. 28, 1815; | in the 46, year of | her age.

> Lo! where this silent Tomb-stone weeps, | A Friend a Wife a Mother sleeps;
> A heart within whose sacred cell. | The peaceful virtues lov'd to dwell;
> Affection warm and faith sincere, | And soft humanity was there;
> Sudden her death with many a groan, | In giving life she lost her own.

EEBEKAH | Daughter of Mr. | John & Mrs Sally Wilder; | died April 25, | 1832, Æt. 16 | years and 6 months.

> Like brilliant stars her virtues glowed, | While from her lips wise counsel flowed
> But when the close of life she knew | Smiling she bade the world adieu.

In memory of MR. ENOS WILDER, | who died in N. Y. | Oct. 19, 1844, | aged 39 yrs.

MRS. LYDIA A. | wife of | Mr Josephus Wilder, | who died | Jan. 23, 1835, | aged 23 years. | Also FRANCENA O. | their only Child, | died Feb. 6, 1834. | aged 3 months & 7 d.

> In the midst of life we are in death.
> Each lonely scene shall thee restore, | For thee the tear be duly shed.

To | the memory of | MRS. ORPAH, | Relict of | Col. John Whiting, | U. S. Army, | who died | March 10, 1837; | Æt. 78.

To | the memory of | COL. | JOHN WHITING, | U. S. Army, | who died | and was buried | at Washington D. C. | Sept. 3, 1810; | Æt. 50.

To | the memory of | MAJOR | FABIUS WHITING, | U S Army, | who died | May 16, 1842, | Æt. 50.

To | The memory of | MISS. JULIA, | Daughter of John | and Orpah Whiting, | who died | July 2, 1817; | Æt. 30.

ERECTED | In memory of | DEACON | JOEL WILDER, | who died | May 2, 1837; | Æt. 70.

> The righteous shall be in | everlasting remembrance.

GEORGE W. WILDER | son of | Charles J. and | Eliza C. Wilder; | who died | March 10, 1843, | aged 10 wks.

JOEL THOMAS, | son of | Charles J. and | Eliza C. Wilder, | Died | Aug. 24, 1844, | aged 3 years & | 8 mo.

SACRED | To the Memory of | DEA. JOSEPH WHITE | who died July 1, 1806, | Æt. 55.

> He was a man of honest report, | ruled his children and his own | house well; and in the use of the | office of Deacon was found blameless.
> "Blessed are the dead who die in the Lord."

Deac. | SAMUEL F. WHITE, | Died | March 15, 1843, | Aged 50.

ELIZABETH C. WHITE | daugh. of | Dea. S. F. & | E. G. White, | Died Jan. 19, 1847, | aged 14 yrs. & | 9 mo.

> Strew with bright flowers this early grave | The bright and innocent lies here;
> Our Father's hand the blossom gave, | And early took it to his care.

In Memory of | Mr. Asa Dunbar Whittemore, | Son of Mr. Nathaniel | & Mrs. Lydia Whittemore, | who died | Feby. 21, 1808, | Æt 23 years & 6 months.

> Sure never till my latest breath | Shall I forget your looks my tender friends
> I must leve thee | And go to Christ that died for me.

In memory of | MR. | NATHANIEL WHITTEMORE, | who died | Jan. 3, 1822; | Æt. 80 ys. & | 6 ms.

In memory of | MRS. AMELIA, | wife of Mr. | Nathaniel Whittemore, | who died | April 18, 1834, | Æt. 45.

IN | Memory of | MRS. MARY, | wife of | Mr. Nathaniel Whittemore, | who died | Aug. 15, 1828; | Æt. 49. | Also MARY M. | her Daughter died June 16, | 1819: | Aged 5 ys & 6 ms.

In memory of | MARY M. | daughter of Mr. | Nathaniel & Mrs. | Mary Whittemore, | who died | June 16, 1819, | Æt. 5 ys. & 7 ms

In memory of | NATHANIEL WHITTEMORE | Junr. | Son of Mr. Nathaniel, & | Mrs. Mary Whittemore | who died | Dec 14, 1831, | aged 15 years.

<small>Adieu dear Youth, God calls thee home, | From this dark vale of sin and wo;
No adverse cloud, can shade thy joys— | Or sorrow cause thy tears to flow.
The christian faith presents a balm, | To heal the parents wounded heart.
A hope that they shall live again | And meet their child, no more to part.</small>

SARAH EMORY, | only Daughter of | E. H. & S. S. White, | died Nov. 15, 1842, | Æt. 3 days.

In memory of | Miss. | LUCY C. WHITE, | who died | June 10, 1829, | Æt. 24.

JOSEPH C. WHITE | killed by a Tree, | Jan. 28, 1825, | Æt. 16 ys..1 mo.

ABEL WHITE | died | July 30, 1844. | Æt. 64 ys. 8 ms.

GARDNER WILDER Esq. | died on the | 26th. of Nov. 1809, | aged 70 years. | And his wife, | MRS. CATHERINE WILDER, | died on the | 23d: of Sept. 1845, | aged 93 years.

SACRED | to the memory of | Mr. Jonathan Whitney, | who departed this life | November 20th: 1802, | Aged 66 years.

<small>Possessing the integrity and goodness of the upright man; his memory will be embalmed in the affections of all who knew his worth; and while virtue itself shall be revered, his virtues shall be had in remembrance of the virtuous and the good.</small>

In memory of | MRS LUCY WHITNEY, | widow of Mr. Jon*. Whitney, | who died | Oct. 11, 1817: | Æt. 74.

"Blessed are the dead | Who die in the Lord."

EPHRAIM WHITNEY, | died | Sept. 6, 1842, | Æt. 62.

JONAS WHITNEY, | DIED | Jan. 14, 1846, | Æt. 74.

"I am the resurrection and the life."

Erected | in memory of | William S. | son of Zaccheus & | Fanny Whitney, | who died | Oct. 4, 1823; | aged 15 mo.

DEA. BENJAMIN WYMAN | died Dec. 30, 1826, | Æt. 61. | MARTHA JOSLYN | died May 4, 1806, | Æt. 40. * * * Wives of Dea. Benj. Wyman.

MISS. | MARTHA T. WYMAN | died Sept. 13, 1834, | aged 23 years.

CAPT. SAMUEL WILDER, | Died Aug. 20, 1849, | AGED 80 YEARS.

He rests from his labours.

In memory of | MRS. ELIZABETH WILDER, | wife of Capt. Samuel Wilder, | who died | May 22, 1810, | Æt. 38.

<small>"She was an affectionate wife, a faithful parent, an honest friend, and a humble christian. She had hope in death and her memory is blessed."</small>

THE BURIAL PLACE OF THE SHAKER COMMUNITY.

In 1781 Mother Ann Lee and the Shaker elders came from Watervliet to eastern Massachusetts upon a proselyting tour. During the two years of her sojourn here, she won, in Lancaster, Harvard and Shirley, numerous converts to her peculiar doctrines, who soon organized a community, choosing for their place of residence a fertile valley near the junction of the three towns. A field for their dead was selected within the bounds of Lancaster, a few rods from the Shirley line. In it, running north and south, are long rows of graves, each with its little head and foot-stone about eighteen inches in height. These memorials are all of rough slate from a quarry near by, save the few erected since 1860, which are of white marble. A large majority of the inscriptions, especially of the older ones, consist of two letters only. The following list includes all of dates before 1850, and begins with the western-most row.

M. BROCKLEBANK. | DIED July 30th, 1838, Æ. 85.
L. KILBURN. | Died March 24th. | 1835, Æt. 88.

| H.W. | L.W. | A.A. | G.P. | A.L. | S.W. | L.T. | E.W. | S.C. | S.L. | E.W. |

O. Burt, | Died Nov. 24th. 1834. | Æt. 19.
D. M.
R. Barrett, | Died Dec. 5th. 1833, | Æt. 82.
H. Grover, | Died Oct. 12th. 1832, | Æt. 22.
Æ. 80. | N Willard, | Died July 12th. 1832.
E. Osgood, | died 1831, Æt. 82.
ASA | Brocklebank, | 1831, Æt. 59.
M. Hayward.
E. Wild.
P. Pratt.

| P.M. | J.K. | S.K. | E.P. | M.B. | P.P. | M.M. | H.A. |
| B.B. | L.C. | L.P. | M.P. | H.K. | | | |

P. Warner.
S. Kinney.
M. Osgood, | Died Dec. 3d. 1834, | Æt. 87.
Sarah Safford, | Died Jan. 24th. 1838, | Æt. 75.
Percis Warner, | Died Dec. 28th. 1836, Æt. 72.
J. Temple, | Died July 30th. 1834, Æt. 80.
E. Priest.
E. Pierce.
D. M.
R. Robbins, | dec'd March 1822, | Æt. 65.

| R.M. | S.L. | W.W. | D.C. | J.C. | E.P. | J.M. |
| W.P. | S.B. | H.W. | L.P. | M.B. | R.K. | D.L. |

L. Hayward, | dec'd. March 1822. | Æt. 75.
L.K.   A.P.
B. Burt | Æt. 81, 1820.
R.H.   M.M.
S. Edmands.
M. Lyon, | died Jan. 9th. 1834, | Æt. 73.

| S.W. | S.B. | S.F. | W.T. | H.W. | B.D. | J.P. |

A. Beckwith, | died 1812.
I. Wilds, | died Sept. 13th. 1817, | Æt. 65.
M.W.   N.T.
Geo. Persons, | Died Sept. 11, 1841, | Æt. 17.
G. Hammond, | Died Nov. 29th. | 1835 Æt. 76.
S. Barrett, | Died Sept. 1, 1835, Æt. 83.
A. Worster, | Died May 5th 1835, Æt. 88.
Ellin G. Prevot | died | Feb. 17, 1848, | Æt. 26.
B. Abbott, | 1840, Æt. 38.
S. Clark. | 1840, Æt 21.
A. Wheelock, | Died Sept. 28th. 1838, | Æt. 89.
M. Prouty, | died March 16th. 1833, | Æt. 31.
R. Williams, | Died Nov. 8th. 1829, Æt. 56.

THE NORTH BURIAL GROUND.

At a town-meeting in April, 1800, the fourth article of the warrant was: "To consider the expediency of appropriating a certain piece of land at the north part of the town, where a number of persons are buried, for the purpose of a burying field." A committee, to whom the matter was intrusted with full powers to act, reported, in the following May, that they had "Received a quitclaim Deed of Mr Elijah Wiles of 112 Rods of Ground, being 16 Rods in length bounding on the Road leading by Col. Henry Haskell to Harvard, and 7 Rods deep." The deed found in the town's archives, however, is dated February 20, 1805, whereby Elijah Wilds conveys to the town 144 rods of land, measuring 8 rods along the highway, and 18 rods in depth. In the public burial place thus established are numerous graves mostly undistinguished by monuments. The epitaphs dating prior to 1850 are:

In memory of Mrs | REBECCA ALEXANDER, | wife of Mr. Nathaniel Alexander, | who died | Nov. 7, 1843, | aged 61 years & | 6 mo.
 Farewell dear friends and children too, | For Christ has call'd me home :
 In a short time he'll call for you. | Prepare yourself to come.

ELIZABETH, | died | Dec. 19, 1807, | Æt. 10 months. | Daughter of Mr. W^m. | & Mrs. Eliz^b: Blanchard.
 Farewell sweet child we part in pain, | We only part to meet again.

In memory of MR. | WILLIAM BLANCHARD | who died | Nov. 13, 1818, Æt. 56.
 Dangers stand thick thro' all the ground | To push us to the tomb:
 And diseases wait around | To hurry mortals home.

JACOB R. BACON | Died | Nov. 3^d. 1845 | Aged 25 years.
 Hope points to Heaven.

ERECTED | In memory of | MR. REUBEN BARRETT JR | who died | July 26, 1816. | Æt. 34.
 Peaceable, patient, honest & upright | He trusted God, & upward took his flight.

In memory of | MOSES BARRETT | who died | Aug. 4, 1846, Aged 62 yrs.

MRS | REBECCA BARRETT | Died | Sept. 27, 1847, | Aged 85 years & 4 months.

In memory of | SAMUEL P. BARRETT, | who died | Sept. 23, 1847, | Aged 29½ yrs. | Also an Infant Child.
 Tis thus our earthly comforts fly, | And prospects brighten but to die.

MISS NANCY, | daughter of | Mr Samuel & | Mrs Nancy Butler, | died July 11, 1827, | Æt. 20 yrs. 4 ms.
 All thy toils and cares are over. | Weary Sister take thy rest;
 God in mercy hath recalled thee; | To thy place among the blest.

MR. SAMUEL BUTLER, | DIED | March 27, 1828 Æt. 44.
 Here shall I rest in sweet repose, | Till through the midst of heaven,
 The Angel's trump shall sound aloud | And life to all be given.

MRS. NANCY, | wife of Mr. | Samuel Butler, | DIED | Aug. 11, 1849, | Æt. 64.
 Dear as thou wert and justly dear, | We will not weep for thee ;
 One thought shall check the starting tear, | It is that thou art free.

MISS SALLY, | daughter of | Mr. Samuel & | Mrs. Nancy Buttler, | died | Dec. 25, 1831, | Æt. 20.
 Sister sleep on, thou art at rest. | At rest with Jesus and the blest;
 Although from us you have been riven, | We soon shall meet again in heaven.

In memory of | SARAH | wife of Mr. Abel Butler, | who was born | March 16, 1800, | and died | July 14, 1830. | Erected by her mother Lois Bartlet.

JEREMIAH | BARNES | Died July 27, 1845, | Æt. 34.
 May thy flesh rest in hope.

To | the memory of | MRS. RUTHY, | wife of | Mr. Isaac Cowdry; | who died | Jan. 19, 1828, | Aged 50.
 Lo beneath this sacred mound, | A friend, a wife, a mother's found;
 A heart's within this silent cell, | Where perfect virtue loved to dwell.
 Affection warm and faith sincere, | And soft humanity were there.

In memory of | Aaron Cook Jr. | son of Mr. Aaron & | Mrs. Betsy Cook, | who died | July 3, 1803, | Aged 2 years & | 4 months.

IN | Memory of Miss Harriot Cook, | Daur. of | Mr. Aaron & | Mrs Betsy Cook | who died Octr. 12, 1807. | Aged 12 years.

In memory of | BETSY | daughter of | Mr. Aaron & | Mrs Elizabeth Cook; | who died Feb. 20, 1830; | Æt. 33.

AARON COOK | died | Oct. 20, 1845, | Æt. 74.

MRS. | ELIZABETH, | wife of | Mr Aaron Cook, | died | Jan. 17, 1842, | Æt. 67.

SUSAN, | Dau. of Aaron & | Elizabeth Cook, | Died | Feb. 17, 1844, | Aged 26.
She was a dear and beloved child, | A sister kind, affectionate and mild.

MRS. REBECKAH P. | Relict of | Mr. James Cutler, | died, | July 9, 1840, in her 69th, | year.

Beneath this stone | rest the loved remains of | MRS SUSAN DYAR, | wife of | MR JEREMIAH DYAR, | who died | Feb. 16, 1824, Aged 47.
The storms of life are o'er, thy night of rest is come. | Sleep sweetly sainted mother! in thy lonely tomb. | "Blessed are the dead who die in the Lord." | Here friends have we on earth, and when they part; | The nerve unwinds whos tension tears the heart. | A little while and we shall meet no more to part.

ANN ELIZABETH, | Daughter of Capt. Joseph | and Mrs Sarah Farwell, | died Aug. 31, 1842, | Æt. 17 yrs. & 2 ms.
When the bonds of earth are riven, | And the reign of death is o'er,
In the light and joy of Heaven, | We shall meet to part no more.

In | memory of | MRS SARAH FARWELL, | wife of Mr Leonard Farwell, | who died June 1, 1809, | in the 51 year of her | age.
She was a tender mother, friend & wife, | She practis'd virtue all her life
And she is gone to realms above, | Where all is harmony and love.
HARK FROM THE TOMB.
Beneath this stone I rest my head, in slumber sweet Christ blest the bed,
Weep not for me my pains are o'er, we soon shall meet to part no more.
Friends quit this stone and look above the skys. | The dust lies here, but virtue never dies.

In memory of | MR LEONARD FARWELL | died in Milton N. Y. | Born Oct. 2, 1760, | Died Oct. — 1822, | Aged 62.

MARY | wife of | Lucius L. Farwell, | Died Nov. 7, 1845, | Aged 30 years. | Also Mary I. Farwell | their Daugh. | Died Aug. 5, 1846 | Aged 9 mo. & 4 days.

ERECTED | In Memory of | Mr ELIAS HASKELL, | who died | July 2, 1811, | Æt. 76.
Although my body sleeps awhile | Beneath this barren clod;
Yet I hope to awake and smile | To see my Saviour God.

MR | LUTHER JOHNSON | died | April 22, 1822, | Aged 33.
MR | AARON JOHNSON | died | Feb. 6, 1820, | aged 79.
SEWELL | son of Calvin and | Abigail Johnson | died | Nov. 22, 1845, | Æt. 28.
MRS. ABIGAIL, | wife of | Mr Calvin Johnson, | died | Feb. 13, 1845, Æt. 54.
HARRISON | JOHNSON | died Oct. 13, 1842, | Æt. 28.
WM. GIBBS | son of Mr Joseph, | and | Mrs. Lucy Morse; | who died | March 6, 1832. | Aged 7 years.

IN | Memory of | Mr Abijah Nichols, | son of | Mr. Joseph & Mrs. | Anna Nichols, | died Augt. 19. 1801, | Æ. 23.

ELISHA | SANDERSON, | DIED | March 14 1843, | Æt. 81.

In memory of | MRS. MARY, | wife of Mr. Elisha Sanderson, | who died | Dec. 18, 1829; | Æt. 63.

In memory of | MARTHA. | Daughter of Mr. Elisha | & Mrs. Mary Sanderson, | who died | March 1, 1829, | Æt. 20.
Youth's emblem is a fleeting flower, | Which called to life by some soft shower,
Doth raise its tender head;
Scarce had its leaves begun to bloom, | Scarce shed around its sweet perfume,
When life and beauty fled.

In memory of | MRS. ANNA THOMAS | wife of | DOCT. JOSHUA THOMAS | of Boston | Who died June 18, 1799, | Æt. 47.
Blessed are the merciful; | For they shall obtain mercy.

ERECTED | in memory of | MR. | JOSHUA THOMAS, | who was born | March 14, 1745, | and died | Feb. 4, 1831.

IN | Memory of | Mrs. | MARY THOMAS, | wife of | Mr. Joshua Thomas, | who died May 25, 1808, | aged 67.
The sweet remembrance of the just, | Shall flourish while they sleep in dust.

NORTH VILLAGE CEMETERY.

In memory of | Mary, daughter of Samuel | & Rebecca Worster, who died | Octr. 10, 1815; | Also Elizabeth, | who died May 31, 1818; | aged 1 year & eight months.
> The little strangers soon did go, | Fled from the scene of care and wo,
> Early did take their speedy flight, | To reach the mansions of delight.

In Memory of | Mrs. Sarah Willard, | wife of | Mr. William Willard, | who died June 2d. | 1803 in the 36 year | of her age
> Beneath these clods my body lies, | And mouldering back to dust,
> My soul has gone beyond the skys, | And hear'd its sentence just.

ERECTED | In memory of | PAUL WILLARD ESQ. | who died | Aug. 2, 1817, | Æt. 52.
> An honest man's the noblest work of God. | In God is my Salvation and my glory.

ERECTED | In Memory of | Mrs. MARTHA WILLARD | wife of | Mr. PAUL WILLARD. | who died | May 22, 1808, | in the 34 year | of her age.
> Farewell vain world, I am gone home. | My Saviour smil'd & call'd me, come,
> Bright angels carried me away | To sing God's praise in endless day.

In Memory of | Mary Willard | Daur. of | Mr. Paul & | Mrs. Martha Willard, | Who died | Octr. 4, 1803. | Aged 2 years & | 1 month.

SACRED | to the memory of | MISS LUCIA WILLARD, | Daug. of Paul Willard Esq. | who died | Nov. 14, 1818. | Æt. 15.
> Clasp'd in my Heavenly Father's arms, | I would forget my breath;
> And lose my life among the charms | of so divine a death.

SACRED | to the memory of | MR. DEXTER WILLARD | son of Paul Willard Esq. | who died | July 6, 1810, Æt. 17.
> Death like an overflowing stream, | Sweeps us away; our life's a dream,
> An empty tale, a morning flower, | Cut down and wither'd in an hour.

SARAH F. | wife of Dr. Amory | WILLARD | born Feb. 6, 1787, | died July 9, 1834. | S. JOSEPHINE, | dau of Dr. A. & S. F. | WILLARD | born Jan. 24, 1825, | died Apr. 24, 1830.
> Is it well with thee and thy child? It is well.

In | memory of | MR. LUKE WILLARD | who died | Sept. 17, 1813, | Æt. 20.
> This flesh and blood I want no more, | I land upon a blissful shore;
> Its work is done, and I resign | That dust which is no longer mine.

WILLIAM | WILLARD | died May 18, 1837, | Æt. 70.

In memory of | MRS LUCY WILLARD, | wife of | Mr. William Willard | who died | June 27, 1819, | Æt. 41.
> Friends & Physicians could not save | My mortal body from the grave.
> Nor can the grave confine me here, | When Christ shall call me to appear.

HENRY WILLARD | DIED | June 11, 1847, Aged 37. | MARY ANN | his wife, died | Feb. 20, 1847, Aged 41.

ABIGAIL | wife of | BENJA. WILLARD, | DIED | Oct. 12, 1848, Æt. 74.

THE NORTH VILLAGE CEMETERY.

This burial ground contains about four acres, and was not opened for public use until 1855 — the first interment being made in September of that year. The following memorial inscriptions are, however, found therein, being mostly upon cenotaphs, though several families removed their dead from other cemeteries to this:

SOLON FRANCIS | Died Mar. 17, 1831, | Æ. 2 yrs. 7 ms. | JANE ELIZA | Died Apr. 5, 1831, | Æ. 6 yrs. 8 ms. | CORNELIA ASENATH | Died July 1, 1837, | Æ. 1 yr. 1 mo. | CYNTHIA WILDER | Died Feb. 24, 1843, | Æ. 12 yrs. 6 ms. | JOHN ALANSON | Died July 9, 1843. | Æ. 5 ms. | Children of Luke & Eliza | BIGELOW. *

MR. | NATHANIEL BURBANK | died July 22, 1818, | aged 73.

MRS. | RUTH BURBANK, | wife of | Mr. Nathaniel Burbank | who died June 5, 1835, | aged 82.

SAML. W. BURBANK, | * * * HANNAH, | His wife died Feb. 17, 1840, | Æt. 39 yrs. | MARY A. | His wife died July 29, 1844, | Æt. 41 yrs. | SUSAN E. | Died July 20, 1825, | Æt. 2 yrs. 10 mos. | H. ELIZABETH, | Died Mar. 23, 1843, | Æt. 15

yrs. | LUCIANNE, | Died May 23, 1848, | Æt. 17 yrs. 1 mo. | Children of Sam¹ W. & | Hannah Burbank. | HARVEY, | Died Dec. 26, 1842, | Æt. 4 mos. | ELLEN, | Died Apr. 26, 1844, | Æt. 3 mos. | Children of Sam¹. W. & | Mary A. Burbank. | HENRY L. | Son of Sam¹. W. & | Olive R. Burbank, | Died Sept. 9, 1848, | Æt. 10 mo.

FRANCES ANNIE, | Died March 24, Aged 2 yr's & | 5 Mo's and 17 days. And | JAMES HARVEY, | Died March 28, 1849, Aged 4 yrs | 10 Mo's and 3 days. | Children of ANSON & | ELIZABETH C. BURTON.

Ee'r sin could taint the infant mind, | Hath Death life's tendrils riven, These two sweet buds together twin'd, | And planted them in Heaven.

SALLY WILSON, | wife of George Dodge, | died Mar. 26, 1847, | aged 38 yrs.

H. HARRISON | Son of | J. W. & J. M. | HUNTINGTON | born July 24, 1840 | died July 8, 1841.

JOSEPH M. Son of | J. W. & J. M. | HUNTINGTON | born June 20, 1838 | died July 2, 1841.

HORATIO M. Son of | J. W. & J. M. | HUNTINGTON | born June 26, 1836 | died Sept. 17, 1836.

JULIA MARIE | Dau. of | J. W. & J. M. | HUNTINGTON | born Aug. 25, 1823 | died Sept. 23, 1833.

DEA. JONAS LANE | died Jan. 6, 1848, | Æ. 87. | Rest weary Pilgrim. | DOLLY BALLARD, | wife of | DEA. JONAS LANE, | died Feb. 26, 1795, | Æ. 27. | Early called but sadly mourned, | Their children, | JONAS | died Sept. 5, 1791, Æ. 1 yr. 8 ms. | JONAS | Aug. 29, 1797, Æ.. 5 yrs. 10 ms.

EUNICE KENDALL, | wife of | DEA. JONAS LANE, | died Aug. 12, 1807, | Æ. 41. | Husband and children, Farewell. | Their children, | DOLLY BALLARD | died Mar. 10, 1798, Æ. 1 yr. 1 mo. | ELIZABETH | Sept. 13, 1805, Æ. 2 ms. | MARY ANN | Sept. 23, 1805, Æ. 3 yrs. 1 mo. | An Infant Son | born & died July 17, 1807.

SALLY HAWKES, | wife of | DEA. JONAS LANE, | died Mar. 12, 1813, | Æ. 34. | She is not here, but above. | MARY H. K. B | Their Dau. died July 30, 1814, | Æ. 1 yr. 5 ms.

FATHER & MOTHER | JOSIAH LAWRENCE | DIED | May 19, 1848, | Æt. 71 yrs. | TABITHA, | His wife | Died Jan. 7, 1835, | Æt. 57 yrs.

WILLIE J. | Son of | Harlow & Catherine C. | LAWRENCE, | BORN | Mar. 20 1843, | DIED | Mar. 8, 1845.

EUGENIA C. | Dau. of | Harlow & Catherine C. | LAWRENCE, | BORN | Mar. 26, 1846, | DIED | July 9, 1846.

LEVI LEWIS | DIED | June 28, 1839, | Æ. 51. | Children of Levi & Abigail Lewis. | MARTHA | Died Jan. 15, 1825, | Æ. 11 ms. | AUGUSTUS | Nov. 24, 1831, | Æ. 4 yrs. 8 ms. * * *

BENJAMIN B OTIS | * * * | MARY C. his wife | Died Nov. 15, 1849, | Æ. 42. | Children of | Benj. B. & Mary C. Otis. | MARY ELIZABETH, | died June 26, 1824, | Æ. 14 ms. | NANCY CARTER, | died Oct. 10, 1832, | Æ. 15 ms. * * *

CHARLES A. | Son of Alexander & | Angelina Potter, | died | Aug. 29, 1848, | Æt. 1 Yr. 1 Mo.

"Lo, Children are a heritage of the Lord,,

FRANKLIN | Son of Moses & | Eliza W. Stowe | DIED | Sept. 23, 1847 | Æ. 18.

IN | Memory of | MISS MARY WARES, | who died | Nov. 28, 1820, | Aged 21 yr. & 5 mo.

The human heart repines and grieves | To part with kindred dear; But faith in God the mind relieves, | And wipes away the tear.

HENRY K. WASHBURN | died March 21, 1845, | aged 2 years & 6 months.

Ere sin could blight, or sorrow fade, | Death timely came with friendly care; The opening bud to Heaven conveyed, | And bade it bloom forever there.

NEHEMIAH B. WILLARD | died in Harvard, Oct. 1, 1838, | Æt. 42 yrs. * *

ANDREW J. WILLARD | died in Harvard, Jan. 25, 1831, | Æt. 13 mos. | SIDNEY G. WILLARD | died in Harvard, July 22, 1834, | Æt. 1 mo. | Children of Nehemiah B & | Hannah E. Willard. * * *

APPENDIX.

The following lists of Marriages and Births in Lancaster families, not found in preceding pages, being mostly of dates when town, county and church registers fail us, are supplementary to those of Deaths and Marriages on pages 19 and 20. They have been made up from sundry sources supposed reliable.

MARRIAGES.

Daniel Hudson, Jr., and Mary Maynard of Sudbury, —— 1674.
Jonathan Prescott and Elizabeth Hoar of Concord, December 23, 1675.
Henry Kerley and Elizabeth How, at Charlestown, 2^m. 18^d., 1677.
Ephraim Roper and Widow Hannah Goble of Concord, November 20, 1677.
Joseph Rice of Marlboro' and Widow Sarah (Prescott) Wheeler, at Dedham, 12^m. 22^d., 1677.
James Sawyer and Mary Marble, February 4, 1678.
Joshua Sawyer and Sarah Potter, at Woburn, —— 1678.
Josiah White and Mary Rice of Marlborough, 9^m. 28^d., 1678.
George Hewes and Widow Lydia Bennett, at Concord, 5^m. 3^d., 1679.
John Hinds and Widow Mary Butler, February 9, 1681–2.
Nathaniel Wilson and Thankful Beaman, —— 1683.
Caleb Sawyer and Sarah Houghton, December 28, 1687.
Thomas Wilder and Mary Houghton, June 25, 1688.
Jonathan Fairbank and Mary Hayward, —— 1688.
Henry Willard and Dorcas Cutler, —— 1689.
John Ball and Hannah Rugg, at Concord, —— 1690.
Philip Goss and Mary Prescott, at Concord, March 29, 1690.
Joseph Houghton and Jane Vose, at Milton, October 31, 1693.
Nathaniel Hudson and Rebecca Rugg, —— 1693.
William Divoll and Ruth Whitcomb, —— 1695.
John Moore and Hazadiah Fairbank, at Concord, January 1, 1698.
Samuel Prescott and Esther Wheeler, May 5, 1698.
Ephraim Wilder and Elizabeth Stevens, —— 1698.
Henry Willard and Abigail Temple, at Concord, July 21, 1698.
John Willard and Mary Hayward, at Concord, October 31, 1698.
John Houghton, Jr., and Widow Mary Goss, at Concord, November 20, 1698.
John Wilder and Sarah Sawyer, —— 1699.
Philip Goss and Judith Hayward, August 30, 1699.
David Whitcomb and Widow Mary Fairbank, May 31, 1700.
Simon Willard and Mary Whitcomb, —— 1700.
George Glazier and Sarah Barrett, at Chelmsford, December 17, 1700.
Samuel Carter and Dorothy Wilder, March, 1701.
Rev. Timothy Stevens and Widow Alice Whiting, —— 1701.
Simon Stevens and Mary Wilder —— 1701.
Joseph Wilder and Lucy Gardner, —— 1702.
Ebenezer Wilder and Mary ——, —— 1702.
Benjamin Bellows and Widow Dorcas Willard, —— 1703.
Thomas Wilder and Susanna Hunt, —— 1704.
Daniel Rugg and Elizabeth Priest, —— 1704.
Rev. John Prentice and Widow Mary Gardner, December 4, 1705.
Samuel Farnsworth and Widow Mary (Whitcomb) Willard, December 12, 1706.

Jonathan Wilder and Mary ——, —— 1706.
Nathaniel Wilder and Damaris Whitcomb, —— 1707.?
John Bowers and Elizabeth Stevens, —— 1707.
Thomas Carter and Ruth Phelps, —— 1707.
Jabez Fairbank and Mary Wilder dau. of Thomas,
Edward Hartwell and Sarah Wilder, " "
Hezekiah Willard and Anna Wilder, " " } between 1707 & 1712.
Joseph Hutchins and Elizabeth Wilder, "
James Wilder and Abigail Gardner, October 20, 1709.
Henry Willard and Sarah Nutting of Groton, —— 1710. ?
John Fletcher and Hannah Phelps, —— 1712. ?
Oliver Wilder and Mary Fairbank, —— 1713.
Samuel Bennett and Tabitha Wheeler, at Concord, April 5, 1715.
Josiah Willard and Hannah Wilder, —— 1715.

BIRTHS.

Adam, son of Lawrence and Ann (Linton) Waters, —— 1645.?
Jonathan, son of John and Mary (Platts) Prescott, —— 1646.?
Jonas, son of " " " " —— 1648.
Amos, son of John and Alice Tinker, October 28, 1657.
Samuel, son of " " " April 1, 1659.
Joseph, son of Jacob and Ann Farrar, August 6, 1660.
Benjamin, son of Simon and Mary Willard, —— 1665.
Samuel, son of Jonathan and Dorothy Prescott, —— 1674.
Mary, daughter of Jonas and Mary (Loker) Prescott, February 3, 1674.
Elizabeth, daughter of " " " " January 23, 1676.
Jonas, son of " " " " at Sudbury, Oct. 25, 1678.
Joanna, daughter of John and Sarah Prescott, January 6, 1676.
Elizabeth, daughter of " " " at Concord, 9^m. 27^d., 1678.
Sarah, daughter of John and Mary Whitcomb, —— 1674.
Elizabeth, Mary, Katharine, Ruth, daughters of Jonathan and Hannah Whitcomb, born between 1675 and 1692.
Mary and Damaris, daughters of Josiah and Rebecca Whitcomb, born between 1675 and 1682.
Israel, son of John and Mary (Farrar) Houghton, —— 1676.
Benjamin, son of " " " " —— 1678.
Daniel, son of John and Hannah Rugg, at Concord, 9^m. 15^d., 1678.
Jonathan, son of " " " " 10^m. 12^d., 1680.
Nathaniel, son of Nathaniel and Mary (Sawyer) Wilder, —— 1675.
Ephraim, son of " " " " at Sudbury, Apr. 16, 1677.
Mary, daughter of " " " " " May 12, 1679.
Elizabeth, " " " " " " Feb. 14, 1680-1.
Dorothy, " " " " " " —— 1686.
Nathaniel, son of " " " " " —— 1688. ?
Eunice, daughter of " " " " " —— 1690. ?
Oliver, son of " " " " " —— 1694. ?
Thomas, son of John and Hannah Wilder, at Charlestown, 1^m. 2^d., 1676.
Hannah, daughter of " " " " " October 31, 1679.
James, son of " " " " " —— 1681.
Anna, or Hannah, " " " " " —— 1690.
Simon, son of Cyprian and Mary (Willard) Stevens, at Boston, August 13, 1677.
Dorothy, daughter of " " " died in infancy. ?
Elizabeth, " " " " —— 1681.
Joseph, son of " " " " —— 1683.
Priscilla, daughter of Ephraim and Hannah (Goble) Roper, at Concord,
2^m. 5^d., 1679.
Ruth, " " " " " " 1^m. 7^d., 1681.
Elizabeth, " " " " " " 1^m. 17^d., 1683.
Bathsheba, " " " " " " ——
Ephraim, son of " " " " " ——
James, son of Thomas and Mary Wilder, at Marlboro', 4^m. 28^d., 1680.

Elizabeth, daughter of Thomas and Mary Wilder, ——— ——— 1687.
Anna,   "   "   "   "   ——— ——— 1689.
Mary,   "   "   "   "   ——— ——— 1691. ?
Isabel, daughter of Robert and Esther Houghton, June 6, 1687.
Abigail,   "   "   "   "   April 18, 1689.
Eleazar, son of   "   "   "   ——— 1691.
Joshua,   "   "   "   "   ——— 1695.
John, son of Henry and Mary Willard, September 3, 1682.
Sarah, daughter of   "   "   "   ———
Hezekiah and Joseph, sons of do.,   ———
James, Josiah and Jonathan, Abigail, Susanna and Tabitha, children of Henry and Dorcas Willard, born between 1690 and 1703.
Mary, daughter of Philip and Mary Goss, ——— 1691.
John, son of   "   "   "   ——— 1693.
Gershom, son of Joseph and Jane Houghton, ——— 1691.
Ebenezer, son of   "   "   "   August 25, 1693.
Nathaniel, son of   "   "   "   ——— 1696.
Esther, daughter of Samuel and Esther Prescott, ——— 1699.
Dorothy,   "   "   "   "   ——— 1702.
Amos, son of   "   "   "   May 20, 1705.
Mary, daughter of   "   "   "   January 5, 1708.
Jonathan, son of Josiah and Mary White, ——— 1692.
Benjamin, son of Jacob and ——— Houghton, ——— 1700.
Aaron, son of Simon and Mary (Whitcomb) Willard, ——— 1701.
Moses, son of   "   "   "   ——— 1702.
Alice, Eunice and Miriam, daughters of do., between 1703 and 1708.
Abraham, Henry, Mary, children of Henry and Abigail (Temple) Willard, born about 1707.
Cyprian and Mary, children of Simon and Mary (Wilder) Stevens, born about 1707.
Benjamin, David, Hephzibah, children of Ebenezer and Mary Wilder, born between 1702 and 1708.
Ephraim, 1707; Asaph, 1714; Elizabeth, Martha, Dorothy, Eunice, Susanna, children of Ephraim and Elizabeth (Stevens) Wilder, 1699-1718.
John Francis Thurston, son of John and Mehitabel C. (Alden) Thurston, born May 16, 1832.

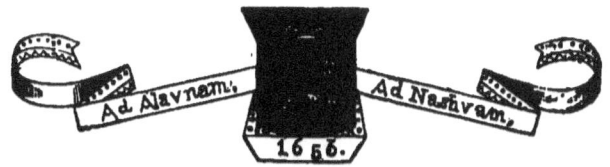

INDEX.

PLACES.

Aberdeenshire, Scot., 414.
Acton, 230, 239, 247, 249, 252, 257.
Albany, Me., 235.
Alfred, Me., 250.
Alstead, N. H., 128, 144, 332.
Amesbury, 339.
Amherst, N. H., 154, 166, 234.
Andover, 33, 44, 246, 257, 264, 271, 272, 278, 279, 284, 292.
Ashby, 127, 136, 139, 143, 147, 244, 251, 252, 313.
Ashburnham, 40, 100, 117, 127, 128, 130, 140, 141, 145, 237, 240, 253, 255, 256, 350, 351, 372.
Ashuelot, 319.
Athol, 232.
Augusta, Me., 106, 152, 165, 407.
Augusta, N.Y., 350.
Avon, N.Y., 183.
Barnstaple, 241.
Barre, 150, 236, 237, 249, 250, 254, 373, 379.
Batavia, E. I., 121, 180.
Bath, Me., 251.
Belfast, Me., 154, 235.
Berlin, 130, 143, 151, 153, 155, 162, 164, 170, 229, 231, 234, 236, 238, 242, 243, 246, 251, 253, 255, 256, 257, 258, 334, 337, 372.
Bernardston, 124.
Beverly, 415.
Billerica, 20, 36, 38, 39, 85, 100, 104, 141, 143, 151, 172, 179, 233, 277, 320, 322, 332, 335.
Bolton, 23, 27, 28, 29, 30, 31, 32, 34, 35, 37, 38, 41, 43, 45, 87, 93, 99, 102, 103, 104, 105, 126, 127, 128, 129, 130, 131, 133, 134, 135, 138, 141, 143, 145, 148, 149, 150, 151, 152, 153, 154, 155, 161, 162, 163, 164, 165, 166, 168, 169, 170, 171, 231, 232, 233, 234, 235, 237, 240, 242, 243, 244, 245, 246, 247, 248, 251, 252, 254, 256, 257, 258, 264, 285, 288, 290, 291, 314, 321, 334, 336, 378, 392, 394, 395, 413, 415.
Boston, 19, 40, 46, 124, 128, 131, 145, 146, 147, 149, 150, 152, 155, 161, 162, 166, 167, 168, 169, 171, 173, 175, 178, 192, 196, 229, 230, 233, 234, 237, 238, 239, 240, 241, 242, 243, 244, 246, 249, 252, 253, 254, 256, 257, 273, 288, 328, 332, 334, 336, 351, 352, 361, 366, 369, 370, 371, 397, 411, 415, 420, 422, 427, 428, 433, 452.
Boxborough, 145, 149, 150, 163, 231, 248, 249, 250, 250.
Bordentown, N. J., 245.
Boxford, 33.
Boylston, 130, 132, 145, 146, 148, 149, 151, 152, 154, 155, 162, 164,

165, 166, 167, 169, 170, 228, 231, 236, 238, 240, 242, 243, 244, 245, 246, 247, 250, 252, 253, 255, 334, 335, 336, 372.
Bradford, 288.
Braintree, 333, 414.
Brattleboro', Vt., 167, 173.
Brighton, 250.
Bridgeton, Me., 232.
Bridgewater, 238.
Brimfield, 126, 138.
Brookfield, 18, 30, 32, 43, 87, 88, 277, 286, 287, 397.
Brookline, 167, 173.
Brownstown, 124.
Buffalo, N.Y., 361.
Burlington, 167, 173.
Butler Co., Ohio, 253.
Buxton, Me., 250.
Byfield, 287.
Calcutta, E. I., 120, 190, 356, 440.
Canterbury, Ct., 286, 381.
Cambridge, 19, 20, 35, 40, 151, 154, 178, 237, 240, 247, 254, 280, 282, 375, 425.
Cambridgeport, 239, 242.
Carlisle, 155.
Castine, Me., 152.
Charlemont, 44, 104, 127, 142, 308, 309, 317, 332, 378.
Charlestown, N. H., 351.
Charlestown, 19, 20, 37, 46, 141, 152, 155, 165, 197, 231, 233, 245, 250, 251, 254, 270, 399, 417, 451, 452.
Chelmsford, 18, 33, 88, 134, 139, 451.
Chelsea, 247.
Chester, N. H., 245, 286, 376.
Chesterfield, N. H., 151.
Chittenden, Vt., 131, 147.
Chocksett, 292, 326, 374, 416.
Clinton, 373, 395.
Cold Spring, N.Y., 378.
Coleraine, 104.
Concord, 19, 20, 23, 28, 35, 41, 87, 93, 131, 133, 146, 148, 155, 166, 168, 171, 230, 235, 242, 253, 256, 271, 289, 321, 335, 378, 451, 452.
Concord, N. H., 136, 231, 248.
Concord, Vt., 234.
Coventry, Ct., 247, 397.
Crown Point, N.Y., 241.
Danvers, 129, 138, 248, 415.
Dedham, 113, 250, 451.
Detroit, Mich., 246, 254.
Dorchester, 19, 20.
Dorsenbridge, Ireland, 283.
Dracut, 138, 153, 154.
Drumbo, Ireland, 280.
Dublin, N. H., 145, 155.
Dudley, 285.

Dunstable, 46, 239, 422.
East Sudbury, 144.
Ervingshire, 136, 379.
Exeter, N. H., 258.
Farmington, Me., 230.
Fermont, Ireland, 281.
Fitchburg, 104, 128, 129, 130, 134, 141, 143, 145, 149, 154, 162, 168, 172, 180, 229, 240, 243, 244, 246, 247, 256, 371, 373.
Fitzwilliam, N. H., 127, 141, 143, 152, 171, 243, 335, 344, 351.
Fort Ann, N.Y., 133, 148.
Foxcroft, Me., 237.
Framingham, 23, 31, 40, 44, 127, 140, 144, 147, 233, 239, 250, 372.
Francistown, N. H., 428.
Gardner, 152, 347.
Grafton, 33, 83, 244, 250, 251, 332.
Granville, N.Y., 238, 369.
Groton, 19, 20, 21, 29, 32, 33, 34, 35, 36, 38, 39, 84, 86, 88, 98, 100, 103, 132, 137, 147, 150, 151, 153, 154, 168, 171, 172, 200, 238, 239, 240, 243, 256, 274, 291, 297, 332, 334, 361, 366.
Guadeloupe, W. I., 160.
Guilford, Vt., 128, 144.
Hadley, 273.
Hamilton, Ohio, 246.
Hampton, N. H., 148, 366.
Hancock, N. H., 235.
Hanover, 288, 289, 319.
Harvard, 25, 28, 30, 31, 33, 34, 35, 36, 37, 39, 40, 43, 44, 45, 46, 84, 85, 87, 93, 99, 100, 102, 106, 127, 128, 129, 130, 136, 140, 142, 143, 144, 145, 146, 149, 150, 152, 155, 161, 163, 164, 168, 172, 173, 229, 230, 231, 233, 234, 236, 237, 245, 246, 248, 249, 250, 252, 254, 255, 273, 286, 288, 332, 372, 397, 445, 450.
Hardwick, 150, 163.
Harwich, 243.
Haverhill, 286, 302.
Heath, 131, 146, 147, 167, 173, 332, 350.
Henniker, N. H., 130, 150, 162, 244, 249.
Hingham, 23, 30, 283, 298, 319, 408.
Hinsdale, N. H., 245.
Holden, 33, 86, 104, 141, 144, 179, 241, 247, 249, 251, 291.
Hollis, N. H., 36, 105, 152, 164, 242.
Holliston, 243, 246, 254, 258, 267, 372, 373.
Hopkinton, 39, 139, 232, 293.
Hubbardston, 235.
Hudson, N. H., 247.

INDEX.

Ipswich, Canada, 334, 378.
Ireland, 320, 327, 329.
Jaffry, 137, 138, 333.
Jersey, 436.
Keene, N. H., 40, 100, 105, 130, 135, 137, 143, 145, 169, 228, 231, 240, 332, 350, 351.
Kennebec, 316.
Killingly, Ct., 23, 87, 320.
Kingsbury, N.Y., 147.
Lancaster, N. H., 141.
Langdon, N. H., 363.
Lansingburgh, N.Y., 242.
Lawrence, 258.
Leicester, 151, 351.
Leominster, 21, 23, 27, 30, 31, 32, 33, 34, 35, 38, 39, 40, 42, 43, 44, 45, 46, 83, 84, 86, 87, 88, 98, 99, 102, 103, 104, 124, 130, 132, 134, 135, 136, 139, 142, 145, 146, 147, 148, 150, 151, 152, 153, 154, 155, 161, 162, 166, 168, 170, 171, 175, 178, 189, 228, 229, 230, 231, 232, 233, 234, 235, 236, 238, 239, 240, 245, 246, 247, 248, 250, 251, 253, 254, 255, 256, 257, 258, 290, 291, 292, 293, 299, 300, 301, 321, 322, 332, 397.
Lexington, 19, 22, 31, 40, 83, 93, 137, 255, 285, 289, 291, 373.
Lincoln, 143, 171, 174, 177, 258, 335, 370.
Litchfield, N. H., 229.
Littleton, 25, 38, 39, 40, 43, 45, 102, 134, 145, 231, 243, 249, 250, 272, 280, 294.
Londonderry, Vt., 258.
Londonderry, N. H., 29, 31, 172.
Lowell, 175, 198, 238, 240, 249, 250, 252, 255, 256, 258, 370, 371.
Lunenburg, 21, 23, 26, 27, 28, 30, 31, 32, 33, 34, 35, 38, 40, 42, 45, 44, 46, 83, 84, 86, 87, 98, 102, 104, 128, 130, 132, 134, 135, 143, 145, 147, 151, 152, 154, 164, 172, 173, 235, 238, 239, 242, 246, 251, 253, 254, 281, 283, 287, 293, 320, 332, 335.
Lunenburg, Vt., 248.
Luzerne, N.Y., 351.
Lyme, Ct., 22, 28, 31.
Lyndeboro', N. H., 248.
Madras, E. I., 265.
Malden, 126, 140, 237.
Mamaroneck, N.Y., 371.
Manchester, N. H., 252, 258, 264.
Marblehead, 149, 162, 167, 169, 173, 229.
Marlboro', 17, 19, 20, 23, 34, 35, 38, 40, 41, 42, 45, 99, 126, 131, 134, 137, 139, 146, 154, 168, 170, 172, 180, 232, 233, 235, 246, 248, 249, 255, 258, 271, 273, 283, 294, 311, 373, 451, 452.
Marlboro', Vt., 167, 172, 238.
Mason, N. H., 169, 250.
Medford, 237, 265, 336.
Medway, 45.
Mendon, 29, 135, 321.
Methuen, 172.
Middlesex, N.Y., 351.
Milford, 252.
Milford, N. H., 230.
Milton, 29, 106, 251, 277, 407, 451.
Milton, N.Y., 280, 448.
Monadnock, No. 4, 103, 332, 378.
Munson, 351.
Narraganset, No. 2, 23, 30, 31, 34, 35, 83, 84, 86, 87, 88, 99.
Narraganset, No. 6, 87, 99.
Nashua, N. H., 254.
Natick, 137, 172, 235.

Needham, 251, 337.
New Bedford, 245.
New Braintree, 44, 140, 152, 165.
Newbury, 30, 127, 142, 271, 375.
Newburyport, 351.
Newfane, N.Y., 379.
New Ipswich, N. H., 43, 104, 130, 222, 238, 243, 378.
New Market, N. H., 239.
New Marlboro', N. H., 41, 44, 129, 139, 145, 234, 351, 378.
New Milford, Ct., 139.
Newport, Canada, 350.
Newton, 148, 168, 171, 332.
Niagara Falls, 266.
Nichewaug, 285, 286, 288, 319, 320, 332.
Northampton, 235.
Northboro', 43, 44, 104, 130, 230, 237, 241, 243, 246, 250, 253, 255, 307, 332, 397.
Northbridge, 233.
North Scituate, R. I., 264.
Norton, 378.
Norwich, Ct., 247.
Notown, 238.
Nottingham, 135.
Nutfield, 284.
Orange, 244.
Orrington, Me., 167.
Oswego, N.Y., 267, 395.
Oxford, 251.
Palermo, 369.
Paris, France, 409.
Parsonsfield, Me., 350.
Paxton, 44, 103, 247, 332.
Peckerfield, N. H., 147.
Pelham, 87.
Pembroke, N. H., 127, 140, 228.
Pepperell, 232, 332, 350.
Pequog, 378.
Peterboro', N. H., 104, 241.
Petersham, 35, 36, 37, 39, 40, 99, 102, 141, 147, 152, 165, 169, 238, 241, 319, 320, 332, 438.
Philadelphia, Pa., 180, 246, 365.
Phillipston, 238.
Pittsfield, Vt., 350.
Plymouth, N. H., 350.
Pomfret, Ct., 31, 139, 332.
Portland, Me., 152, 250.
Portsmouth, N. H., 318.
Poultney, Vt., 232.
Princeton, 45, 98, 99, 102, 103, 104, 132, 139, 146, 149, 155, 168, 171, 231, 258, 328, 378.
Prospect, Me., 155, 167.
Reading, 40, 170, 230, 289, 291, 292, 293, 333, 375.
Rhode Island, 146.
Rindge, N. H., 126, 127, 129, 138, 140, 142, 145, 332, 350.
Roadtown, 290.
Robinston, Me., 236.
Rochester, N.Y., 193, 251, 369.
Rowe, 170, 228.
Rowley, 30, 33, 284, 285, 289, 290, 375, 377.
Royalston, 142, 154, 166, 233, 239.
Roxbury, 154, 161, 166, 241, 264, 270, 283, 287, 290, 336.
Roxbury, Canada, 378.
Rutland, 19, 40, 85, 99, 133, 148, 185, 277, 332, 351, 383.
Sag Harbor, L. I., 247.
St. Armand, Canada, 151, 163.
Salem, 153, 165, 350.
Salisbury, 244, 250.
Sandwich, 254.
Savannah, Ga., 435.
Schadoway, Ireland, 279.
Scituate, R. I., 136, 182, 285.

Sempronius, N.Y., 350.
Seneca Falls, N.Y., 247.
Sharon, N. H., 235.
Sherborn, 20, 36.
Shirley, 34, 36, 37, 40, 83, 84, 87, 98, 102, 135, 137, 139, 141, 145, 146, 147, 148, 149, 152, 162, 169, 170, 171, 229, 231, 232, 234, 235, 241, 246, 249, 251, 254, 256, 312, 372, 445.
Shrewsbury, 21, 31, 32, 33, 34, 35, 36, 37, 38, 39, 42, 45, 83, 84, 85, 98, 99, 102, 127, 129, 131, 134, 135, 136, 137, 138, 139, 140, 141, 143, 146, 147, 163, 168, 172, 231, 242, 249, 281, 288, 291, 319, 378.
Simsbury, Ct., 140.
Somerville, 257.
Sodus, N.Y., 169, 170.
Southboro', 31, 38, 104, 131, 134, 146, 246, 249, 305, 397.
South Brimfield, 138.
Southbridge, 235, 237, 241, 243, 255, 263.
South Hadley, 232.
South Reading, 230, 232, 234, 235, 257.
Springfield, 146, 179, 251.
Sterling, 124, 127, 129, 130, 131, 133, 142, 144, 145, 150, 154, 155, 161, 162, 163, 165, 166, 168, 169, 171, 175, 184, 196, 228, 229, 230, 232, 233, 234, 235, 236, 237, 239, 240, 241, 242, 243, 244, 245, 246, 247, 249, 250, 253, 254, 255, 257, 258, 330, 335, 336, 351, 372, 373, 392, 397.
Still River, 277, 281.
Stillwater, N.Y., 152.
Stoneham, 233.
Stow, 18, 19, 23, 31, 35, 38, 40, 44, 85, 102, 129, 137, 153, 237, 242, 250, 251, 264, 272, 284, 288, 310, 332, 392, 393.
Sturbridge, 263.
Sudbury, 20, 23, 31, 35, 38, 40, 44, 85, 99, 124, 125, 126, 135, 136, 140, 141, 144, 146, 167, 172, 173, 235, 271, 282, 283, 292, 294, 302, 318, 335, 351, 451, 452.
Sullivan, N. H., 133, 148, 152, 182, 350, 431, 441.
Surry, N. H., 170.
Sutton, 139, 146, 229, 372.
Swanzey, N. H', 37, 39, 43, 99, 102, 104, 125, 134, 241, 305, 332.
Taunton, 271.
Templeton, 40, 41, 42, 44, 45, 46, 99, 102, 104, 135, 150, 154, 163, 229, 245, 247, 250, 332, 350, 378, 427.
Tewksbury, 38, 99.
Thompson, Ct., 148, 161.
Topsfield, 127, 141, 285.
Townsend, 38, 128, 143, 144, 145, 169, 171, 233, 234, 236, 246, 250, 255, 289, 350.
Truro, 378.
Turkey Hill, 277, 286.
Upton, 172.
Uxbridge, 136.
Voluntown, Ct., 272.
Walpole, N. H., 233, 329, 332, 404.
Waltham, 139, 188, 230, 249.
Warren, Me., 167, 173.
Warwick, 99, 115, 235.
Washington, D. C., 194, 356, 444.
Waterford, Me., 249.
Watertown, 19, 20, 273, 281.
Watertown, N.Y., 168, 171.
Waterville, Me., 240.

INDEX. 457

Watervliet, 445.
Wayland, 249.
Weare, N. H., 413.
Webster, 251.
Wells, 332.
Wendell, 128, 144, 350.
Westboro', 31, 35, 38, 83, 87, 99, 100, 132, 134, 149, 240, 248, 332.
West Boylston, 169, 228, 230, 235, 236, 238, 242, 244, 247, 248, 249, 250, 255, 257, 258, 332.
Westbrook, Me., 351.
West Cambridge, 155, 166.
Westford, 232, 258.
West Marlboro', 336.

Westminster, 35, 38, 39, 44, 45, 46, 87, 98, 99, 102, 125, 134, 136, 150, 162, 172, 229, 232, 233, 238, 239, 243, 244, 258, 301, 335, 351, 378.
Westminster, Vt., 332.
Westmoreland, N. H., 229, 350.
Weston, 46, 78, 135, 179, 241, 244, 250, 255, 273, 284, 319, 320, 373.
Wethersfield, Ct., 20, 127.
White Plains, N.Y., 306.
Wilmington, 30, 293, 319.
Winchendon, 39, 46, 105, 129, 135, 137, 139, 149, 350, 378, 379.
Winchester, N. H., 41, 103, 242,

248.
Windham, 138, 272.
Woburn, 15, 18, 19, 28, 29, 33, 36, 43, 83, 89, 128, 137, 248, 253, 254, 271, 273, 280, 283, 287, 292, 319, 375, 422, 451.
Woonksechocksett, 288, 289, 290, 374.
Woonsocket Falls, R. I., 191.
Worcester, 15, 30, 41, 43, 44, 45, 99, 102, 104, 124, 125, 127, 130, 132, 136, 139, 140, 141, 147, 150, 151, 163, 171, 230, 232, 233, 236, 237, 239, 242, 256, 289, 320, 369.
Wrentham, 183, 368, 430.

NAMES.

ABBOT, Abiel, 74, 295.
B——, 446.
Dorothy, 92, 303.
Ebenezer, 78, 297.
Elizabeth, 23, 126, 138, 294, 321.
Hannah, 23, 34, 69, 74, 76, 78, 89, 92, 105, 113, 135, 292, 295, 296, 297, 303, 320, 321.
John, 34, 76, 125, 135, 296, 312, 322.
Joseph, 23, 34, 69, 74, 76, 78, 89, 92, 113, 135, 149, 162, 292, 294, 295, 296, 297, 300, 303, 311, 319, 321.
Lois, 322.
Mary, 138.
Phebe, 312.
Priscilla, 44.
Relief, 89, 300.
Sally Down, 113, 311.
William, 152, 165.
ADAMS, Abraham G., 241, 366.
Amos, 174, 197, 229, 346, 347, 348.
Amos G., 174, 197, 347.
Benjamin, 14.
Benj. Wyman, 197, 346.
Betsey, 315, 366.
Daniel, 143.
Edwin, 249.
Elizabeth, 123, 174.
Fanny, 153, 238.
George, 14, 20.
Hannah, 172.
Rev. Henry, 248, 254, 393.
John, 154, 314.
Joseph N., 312.
Mercy, 366.
Nathaniel, 197, 348.
Polly, 197.
Sally N., 313.
Samuel, 123, 125, 137, 174, 246, 312, 313, 314, 315, 316, 331, 370.
Saml. Gilman, 197, 348.
Sarah, 174, 350, 354.
Sophronia O. W., 237, 336.
William, 316.
Zabdiel, 332.
AKELEY, Almus, 197.
Harriet, 197.
Lucinda Elizabeth, 197.
ALBEE, Amos, 363.
ALBERT, Abigail, 57, 59, 60, 63, 66, 67, 74, 99, 115, 118, 160, 286, 291, 320.
Daniel, 19, 24, 31, 57, 59, 60, 63, 66, 67, 74, 84, 115, 156, 160, 280, 281, 282, 285, 286, 288, 290, 291, 325, 412.
Frederick, 43, 66, 108, 115, 116,

118, 130, 146, 160, 288.
Henry, 60, 108, 282.
Joseph, 115, 116.
Mary, 57, 108, 115, 116, 156, 160, 280, 412.
Molly, 115, 116.
Penninah, 36, 67, 74, 99, 290.
Peter, 118.
Sarah, 319.
ALDEN, Albert, 241.
Mehetabel C., 238, 453.
ALDIS, Mehetabel, 104, 134.
ALDRICH, Charlotte, 233.
Faithful, 172.
ALEXANDER, Jonas, 197.
Joseph N., 197.
Nathaniel, 167, 173, 178, 197, 447.
Rebecca, 197, 249, 266, 447.
William, 102.
ALFORD, Joanna, 328.
ALLARD, Lois, 88.
ALLEN, Abel, 80, 127, 143, 174, 197, 234, 299, 317, 322, 339, 341, 350, 420.
Abiel, 318.
Abigail, 14.
Abraham, 121.
Alice, 133, 148, 174, 359, 390.
Amos, 78, 127, 141, 297, 314, 315, 322, 351, 405.
Anna, 110, 149, 309.
Benjamin, 13, 14, 20.
Betsey, 110, 123, 174, 312, 335, 344, 356.
Cheney, 197.
Cynthia, 121, 231, 338, 390.
Daniel, 10, 11, 13, 20, 46, 74, 197, 338, 339, 341, 352, 353, 381, 382, 383, 389, 390.
Daphne, 317.
Delilah, 174, 197, 341.
Ebenezer, 46, 78, 80, 82, 89, 91, 110, 112, 156, 159, 174, 294, 296, 297, 299, 300, 301, 302, 310, 311, 319, 323, 324, 325, 331, 357, 405.
Elijah, 390.
Elisha, 45, 78, 110, 309, 310, 312, 321, 327.
Elnathan, 11.
George W., 248.
Hannah, 13.
Henry, 381.
Jacob, 82, 300.
James, 197.
John, 123, 167, 173, 174, 197.
Joseph H., 390.
Josiah, 338.
Lewis, 314.
Lois, 197.
Lucy, 121, 174, 197, 267, 322, 396,

420.
Lucy Kendall, 197, 236, 342.
Lydia, 381.
Martha, 252.
Mary, 10, 11, 13, 14, 21, 32, 38, 78, 98, 104, 105, 110, 112, 133, 135, 197, 294, 312, 319, 322, 331, 350.
Miriam, 110, 321.
Molly, 112, 311, 389.
Nabby, 338.
Obadiah, 383.
Philemon, 123, 129, 141, 174, 354, 359.
Polly, 133, 148, 174, 197, 317, 357.
Rebecca, 152, 164, 174, 197, 322, 351, 353, 390, 405.
Sally, 174, 197, 339, 345.
Salmon, 383.
Samuel, 10, 91, 121, 128, 145, 174, 197, 267, 302, 318, 322, 338, 340, 341, 342, 343, 345, 353, 355, 356, 396, 420.
Sarah, 39, 82, 100, 159, 319, 405.
Silas, 146.
Sophia, 123, 174, 335, 344, 362.
Sparhawk, 123, 174.
Susay, 121, 318.
Susanna, 167, 173.
Tabitha, 78, 80, 82, 89, 91, 156, 174, 333, 366.
Thankful, 89, 112, 156, 301, 310, 312.
Thomas, 13, 405.
AMES, Abigail, 30.
Hannah, 135.
Prudence, 32.
AMORY, John, 131, 146.
ANDERSEN, Peder, 255.
ANDERSON, Margaret, 29.
ANDREWS, Anes, 266, 336, 371, 420.
Dolly T., 245.
Eliza Ann, 230.
Elizabeth, 420.
Ferdinand, 420.
John, 372.
Joseph, 238.
Judith, 154.
Mary M., 245, 337.
Polly, 229.
Robert, 242, 337.
Samuel, 174, 358, 420.
William B., 174, 366, 420.
ANGEL, Augustus, 95.
Christian, 84, 85, 95.
Diadem, 95.
Hannah, 95.
Henry, 95.
Patience, 95.
Stephen, 95.

INDEX.

ANNETS, Relief, 246.
ANSART, Eliza. Wimble, 153.
ARMOND, Jenny, 150.
ARMSTRONG, Mary, 173.
ARNOLD, Angelia, 261.
  Asa, 173, 197, 336, 348, 349.
  Caroline M., 197, 251, 348.
  Catherine W., 339.
  Charles, 197.
  Charles H., 257, 348.
  Daniel W., 197, 349.
  Eleanor, 153, 165, 334.
  Elizabeth, 230.
  Eugenia K., 261.
  Fabius H., 261.
  Florette S., 261.
  James, 174, 368.
  James A., 197, 244, 261, 348.
  Lucy, 167, 173, 334.
  Mary, 197, 336, 339, 348.
  Mary Ann, 197, 348, 373.
  Mary A., 256.
  Nathaniel, 339, 353.
  Rebecca, 197, 242, 348.
  Rufus, 258.
  Samuel, 340.
  Sophia, 197.
  Susan, 197, 348.
  Susanna, 367.
  William, 174, 197, 333, 339, 340, 348, 350, 355.
ASPINWALL, Louisa E., 197.
  Thomas, 169, 171, 197.
ATHERTON, Abel, 174,
  Abigail, 15, 42, 47, 72, 104, 129, 274, 288, 294, 306, 321.
  Abigail L., 246.
  Amos, 25, 47, 61, 72, 77, 84, 91, 273, 281, 282, 284, 287, 288, 294, 295, 296, 298, 325, 403.
  Amy, 149.
  Anes, 197.
  Anna, 37, 77, 296, 327.
  Azubah, 59, 281.
  Benjamin, 24, 49, 66, 278, 280, 281, 283, 286, 288.
  Betty, 49, 281.
  Caroline, 261.
  Caroline W., 174.
  Charles, 197.
  David, 47, 62, 91, 277, 282, 298, 323, 325, 403.
  Deborah, 13,
  Elijah, 326.
  Elizabeth, 11, 12, 47, 55, 57, 62, 72, 77, 91, 279, 351, 403.
  Eunice, 49, 66, 283.
  Experience, 57, 59, 272, 280.
  George R., 261.
  Hannah, 9, 11, 12, 13, 14, 53, 55, 57, 59, 281.
  Israel, 46, 104, 124, 174, 187, 326, 328, 361.
  James, 9, 11, 12, 13, 14, 15, 20, 272, 273, 274, 275, 276, 277, 278, 279.
  John, 25, 59, 274, 278, 281.
  Jonathan, 49, 280.
  Joseph, 14, 18, 53, 55, 57, 59, 278, 279, 280, 281,
  Joshua, 9,
  Louisa, 240.
  Lucy, 47, 284,
  Lydia, 230.
  Margaret, 174, 361.
  Mary, 11, 14, 17, 53, 126, 234, 279.
  Mary D., 197.
  Moses, 276.
  Oliver, 53, 279.
  Otis R., 261.
  Peter, 24, 47, 57, 59, 140, 174, 272, 273, 278, 280, 281, 295, 327.

  Phebe, 59, 153, 165, 174, 281, 369.
  Phineas, 47, 288.
  Prudence, 279.
  Rebecca, 152, 165, 174, 326, 345, 361.
  Relief, 66, 286.
  Rufus, 306.
  Sally, 155, 167.
  Samuel, 151.
  Sarah, 25, 47, 272, 274, 287, 397.
  Simon, 273.
  Submit, 278.
ATWOOD, Oraville, 241.
AVERY, Hannah, 35, 98.
  Luceby, 124.
  Millicent, 306.
AYNER, Leafy, 307.
  Lucy, 307, 331.
  Phebe, 307.
  Sampson, 43, 104, 307.
AYRES, Fisher, 230, 362.
  Jesse, 229, 232.
  Leonard, 230, 360.
  Maria, 145.
  Peter, 174.
BABBITT, Sally, 143.
BABCOCK, Alvin, 238.
  Nancy, 372.
  Reuben, 253.
BACHELOR, Lucy, 145, 234.
BACON, Jacob R., 254, 447.
BADGER, Mary E., 260.
  Mary R., 260.
  Thomas H., 256, 260.
BAGNALL, Nancy, 133, 148.
BAILEY & BAYLEY.
  Abigail, 45, 104, 112, 160, 376, 381.
  Anna, 48, 70, 71, 112, 285, 416.
  Benjamin, 28, 93, 386.
  Betty, 390.
  Bridget, 38, 66, 69, 72, 159, 160, 284.
  Dinah, 112.
  Dolly, 116, 387, 390.
  Dudley, 46, 73.
  Elijah, 81, 105, 136.
  Elizabeth, 24, 69, 291.
  Enos, 110, 389.
  Ephraim, 80, 383,
  Eunice, 90, 91, 93, 95, 100, 112, 114, 142, 384,
  Hannah, 48, 68, 72, 84, 86, 110, 114, 234, 282, 379,
  Isaac, 112, 380, 382, 416,
  James, 116, 390.
  John, 73, 80, 81, 97, 378, 380, 383, 385.
  Jonas, 75, 381.
  Jonathan, 21, 32, 48, 66, 69, 72, 88, 90, 91, 93, 95, 100, 112, 114, 159, 160, 283, 284, 285, 287, 289, 291, 293, 374, 376, 379, 384, 385, 386, 387, 388, 389.
  Joseph, 34, 48, 80, 85, 114, 136, 280, 376, 378, 384, 390.
  Joshua H., 114, 390.
  Lucinda, 241.
  Lydia, 266, 371, 376.
  Mary, 30, 69, 73, 74, 75, 80, 81, 97, 101, 138, 375, 379, 380.
  Mary Jane, 251.
  Michal, 100, 388.
  Molly, 95, 387.
  Moses, 29, 69, 74, 75, 290, 375, 378, 379, 380, 381.
  Paul, 388.
  Persis, 44, 74, 103, 380.
  Phineas, 112.
  Polly, 114, 390.
  Prudence, 95, 387.
  Rachel, 114.

  Ruth, 73.
  Sally, 114, 390.
  Sampson, 389.
  Samuel, 68, 70, 71, 112, 116, 137, 285, 287, 289, 291, 293, 374, 379, 380, 381, 382, 390, 416.
  Samuel H., 257.
  Sarah, 68, 69, 88, 287, 290, 389.
  Shubael, 24, 28, 40, 48, 69, 101, 110, 280, 282, 283, 289, 374, 384, 387, 388, 389, 390.
  Stephen, 384.
  Susanna, 68, 71, 289, 379, 416.
  Thankful, 116.
  William, 97, 385.
  Zerviah, 91, 141, 385.
  Zilpah, 235.
BAKER, Dinah, 143.
  Elizabeth D., 176, 362.
  George, 176, 234, 237.
  John, 135, 312.
  John K., 312.
  Mary, 301, 322.
  Richard, 99, 299, 301, 327, 331.
  Sally, 130.
  Stephen, 131, 146.
  Thomas, 312, 327.
BALCOM, Rebecca, 198.
  Rebecca J., 198.
  Thaddeus, 198, 242.
BALDWIN, Abigail, 322.
  David, 86, 93, 129, 142, 167, 173, 304, 305, 332.
  Henry, 199, 342.
  Kezia, 45, 93, 304, 332, 359.
  Lucy, 129, 142, 176, 198, 199, 265, 334, 336, 421.
  Lucy H., 198, 239, 344.
  Molly, 93, 127, 143, 304.
  Oliver, 151, 176, 198, 199, 233, 305, 334, 341, 342, 344, 354, 421.
  Polly, 139.
  Sarah, 199, 240, 336, 341.
BALL, Abigail, 30, 200, 320, 332.
  Addison R., 264.
  Angeline O., 264.
  Betty, 141.
  Deborah, 41, 103.
  Eleanor, 377.
  Eleazar, 24.
  Elijah, 44, 103, 109, 231.
  Elizabeth, 16.
  Ella Louisa, 265.
  Emily S., 265, 423.
  Ephraim E., 200.
  Experience, 129.
  Hannah, 32, 233.
  Henry F., 265.
  James E., 255.
  John, 16, 35, 99, 264, 320, 451.
  Jonathan, 77, 134, 289.
  Levi, 169, 171.
  Levi M., 265, 423.
  Lucinda I., 265, 423.
  Margaret, 44.
  Martha, 77.
  Martin, 264.
  Mary, 150, 163, 332.
  Mary Thomas, 169.
  Mary W., 237, 250.
  Nahum, 149, 161.
  Nathan, 141, 200.
  Patience, 31.
  Phineas, 29.
  Rebecca, 44, 104, 109.
  Sarah, 284.
  Stephen, 38, 100.
  Thankful, 141.
  Warren, 249,
  William, 141, 169, 170.
BALLARD, Abigail, 119, 161, 175, 177, 199, 200, 201, 230, 242, 304.

INDEX. 459

334, 340, 371, 392, 393, 403, 422.
Abigail R., 244.
Abigail S., 349.
Anna, 117, 175, 322, 356, 403, 422.
Anna G., 198, 199, 335, 360, 421.
Asa W., 200.
Augustus, 117, 338.
Benjamin, 26, 62, 64, 66, 67, 75, 76, 78, 81, 158, 159, 284, 286, 288, 289, 292, 293, 295, 296, 298, 300, 302, 304, 323, 325.
Charles, 117, 175, 316, 355, 422.
Dolly, 96, 117, 130, 145, 229, 305, 337.
Eliphas, 117, 167, 173, 175, 198, 199, 231, 268, 315, 335, 344, 345, 346, 347, 397, 421.
Elizabeth A., 198, 243, 344.
Elsy, 268, 337, 396, 420.
George H., 349.
Henry, 117, 176, 179, 200, 201, 337, 422, 436.
James, 64, 83, 87, 91, 96, 117, 175, 198, 286, 299, 300, 316, 317, 320, 324, 327, 329, 345, 355.
Jeremiah, 76, 96, 117, 126, 138, 172, 175, 176, 177, 192, 296, 312, 314, 315, 316, 317, 322, 329, 337, 368, 422.
John, 75, 78, 96, 117, 119, 127, 141, 155, 161, 167, 175, 176, 232, 295, 297, 298, 300, 315, 316, 317, 318, 322, 327, 330, 333, 337, 338, 339, 352, 362, 403, 422.
John A., 176, 422.
Joseph, 67, 289, 321.
Josiah, 30, 74, 75, 76, 96, 117, 175, 199, 295, 296, 297, 298, 299, 300, 302, 303, 305, 312, 319, 323, 327, 346, 353, 354, 373, 380, 402, 422.
Josiah R., 175, 199, 344.
Kezia, 75, 77, 79, 294, 295, 319.
Louisa C., 200, 393.
Lucy, 175, 199, 422.
Luther, 200.
Lydia, 76, 299.
Martha, 199, 245, 336, 342, 392, 393.
Mary, 45, 62, 75, 91, 96, 104, 125, 127, 130, 140, 158, 286, 295, 298, 299, 300, 320, 321, 360.
Mary N., 117, 233, 339.
Molly, 175, 422.
Nancy, 117, 175, 198, 199, 229, 318.
Polly, 119, 167, 172, 340.
Rebecca, 81, 117, 127, 140, 175, 199, 200, 256, 300, 322, 347, 356, 422.
Ruth, 44, 62, 64, 66, 67, 75, 76, 78, 81, 158, 159, 284, 292, 295, 302, 320, 336.
Sally, 117, 177, 314, 369, 422.
Samuel, 66, 288, 302.
Sarah, 41, 74, 75, 76, 96, 103, 175, 295, 320, 353, 380, 422.
Sarah Elizabeth, 201, 422.
Sherebiah, 21, 32, 75, 77, 79, 294, 295, 297, 299, 300, 319.
Sophia, 119, 175, 422.
Sophronia W., 268, 397, 421.
Thirza, 31.
Thomas, 96, 119, 145, 161, 175, 176, 177, 189, 199, 302, 330, 334, 340, 341, 342, 344, 351, 353, 354, 355, 357, 368, 403, 422.
William, 96, 119, 128, 144, 231, 268, 303, 340, 349, 396, 420.
William A., 268, 349, 369, 422.
BANCROFT, Andrew, 200, 265, 347.
Ann L., 259, 266, 372, 421.

Benjamin, 127, 142.
Chas. Lowell, 198, 348.
Clara L., 265.
Deborah, 332.
Francis C., 259.
James H., 265.
Joseph R., 257.
Lorey F., 250, 253, 259, 266, 420.
Lucinda, 198, 336.
Luther T., 266, 372, 421.
Mary C., 265.
Mary E., 198, 350.
Mary W., 265.
Sarah J., 420.
Tarbell, 198, 200, 336, 347, 348, 350, 372, 373.
BARBER, Alexander, 284.
Ann, 284.
Asenath, 395.
Charles, 255.
BARKER, Charles, 154, 165.
Robert, 175, 353.
Susanna, 351.
William, 366.
BARNARD, Anes, 175, 421.
Benijah, 175, 200, 421.
Bilhah, 198.
Caleb S., 176, 200, 421.
Charlotte, 254.
Elizabeth, 172.
George, 232.
Henry, 239.
Henry B., 267.
James G., 236.
Jeremiah, 177, 198, 234, 250, 267, 371.
John, 41, 103.
Jonathan, 175, 352, 355, 421.
Josiah, 151, 164.
Julia, 175, 421.
Lucy, 198.
Lydia, 152.
Martha, 228.
Mary, 168, 171.
Mrs. ——, 267, 372.
Phebe, 176, 200, 198, 421.
Polly, 143.
Robert, 24.
Sarah, 229.
Warren, 177, 198, 371.
William, 151, 164, 176, 200, 367, 421.
Winsor, 169, 170, 176, 191, 198, 200, 359, 367, 421.
BARNES, Abby E., 176, 200, 365.
Adeline, 197, 265.
Albert M., 265.
Alice, 337, 351.
Anna, 162.
Artemas, 176, 200, 201, 243, 337, 349, 351.
Betsey M., 200.
Frank W., 265.
George Abram, 197.
Harriet E., 265.
Ira, 176, 200.
Jeremiah, 197.
John W., 197, 243, 265.
Levina, 137.
Nancy, 176, 200, 201, 365.
Nancy J., 200.
Rebecca, 33.
Rhoena, 258.
Ruth, 367.
Sabra, 200.
Samuel, 254.
Sarah A., 197, 255.
Sarah E., 200, 349.
Wm. Merriam, 201.
BARNEY and BARNETT.
Frederick, 326, 392.
James, 326.

BARRETT, Asa, 170, 199, 228, 358.
Daniel B., 198.
Eleanor, 175, 198, 356.
Elias, 198.
Elisha, 198.
Finis, 250.
George, 259.
George C., 198, 343.
Jacob, 47, 71, 73, 75, 76, 292, 375, 380, 381.
John, 47.
Jonathan, 47, 122, 147, 230, 292, 351.
Joseph, 75, 122, 176, 200, 229, 269, 365, 381, 421.
Joshua, 71, 73, 380.
Lemuel, 127, 143.
Lucy, 176, 200, 421.
Lydia, 257.
Lydia B., 176, 421.
Mary, 199, 246.
Mehetabel B., 198.
Moses, 169, 199, 201, 266, 447.
Nathan, 76, 381.
Nathan E., 198.
Polly, 122.
Rebecca, 47, 71, 73, 75, 76, 155, 380, 447.
Reuben, 153, 175, 177, 198, 243, 259, 266, 342, 369, 447.
Ruth, 122, 176, 364.
R——, 446.
Sally, 199.
Samuel, 136, 153, 165, 168, 172, 175, 198, 342, 343, 355.
Samuel A., 175, 198.
Samuel Prescott, 201, 250, 447.
Sarah, 198, 199, 201, 451.
S——, 446.
——, 397.
Timothy, 145.
BARRON, Willard, 229.
BARSTOW, Jeremiah, 277.
Susanna, 277.
BARTLET, Antipas, 44, 104, 230.
Betsy, 233.
Elizabeth R. T., 246.
Emory A., 200.
Ezekiel, 110, 160.
Hannah, 106.
John, 106, 166, 200.
Lois, 266, 371, 447.
Lucinda, 258.
Lucy, 229.
Mary, 200, 242.
Miriam, 238.
Moses, 106, 160.
Percival W., 257.
Roger, 106, 110, 112, 116, 160.
Sally, 235.
Tamazin, 106, 110, 112, 116, 160.
William, 257.
BARTOL, George M., 256, 257, 258.
BARTON, Hannah, 230.
Maria L., 247.
BATES, Eliza A., 267, 395.
Nancy, 422.
Stephen, 155, 166, 422.
BATTLES, Calvin, 246.
BEAMAN, Abigail, 100, 113, 156, 273, 284, 312, 384, 397.
Abraham, 23.
Benjamin, 100, 382.
Betsy, 113, 148, 161, 210.
David, 84.
Deborah, 113, 308.
Dinah, 56, 61, 64, 84, 86, 285, 376, 383.
Ebenezer, 50, 83, 157, 275, 276, 277, 278, 279, 280, 285, 319, 323,

325.
Elemuel, 72.
Elijah, 69, 90, 99, 160, 286, 301, 303, 304, 305, 306, 320, 323, 324, 325.
Elisha, 100, 383.
Elizabeth, 27, 28, 34, 37, 69, 72, 82, 86, 98, 275, 284, 300, 331, 379.
Ephraim, 38, 113, 308.
Eunice, 19, 373.
Ezra, 64, 286.
Gamaliel, 10, 12, 15, 20, 56, 74, 136, 271, 289, 375, 416.
Gideon, 100, 385.
Hannah, 26, 50, 92, 95, 113, 275, 308, 321, 367, 420.
Jabez, 25, 61, 64, 92, 144, 273, 283, 285, 286, 288, 308.
Joanna, 68, 72, 74, 88, 100, 289.
John, 15, 21, 33, 36, 69, 70, 73, 86, 90, 117, 156, 157, 159, 272, 273, 274, 275, 283, 284, 286, 287, 289, 292, 294, 301, 314, 319, 320, 323, 324, 325, 329, 400.
Jonas, 100, 381.
Jonas F., 117, 315.
Jonathan, 312, 397.
Joseph, 50, 69, 83, 92, 95, 113, 175, 276, 283, 308, 309, 312, 331, 357, 420.
Joshua, 306.
Josiah, 100, 292, 382.
Judith, 26.
Lemuel, 72, 103, 133, 380.
Lois, 21, 31, 289.
Lucy, 92, 127, 142, 308, 321.
Mary, 25, 29, 56, 58, 274, 284, 383.
Mary M., 166.
Mehetabel, 12.
Nancy, 113, 152, 164, 312.
Nathaniel, 6, 43, 73, 113, 117, 294, 308, 310, 312, 313, 314, 315, 317, 321, 329, 350.
Noah, 10, 273.
Olive, 61, 283.
Oliver, 69, 156, 298.
Patience, 50, 157, 279.
Peter, 304.
Phineas, 27, 29, 68, 72, 74, 100, 133, 288, 289, 290, 292, 376, 377, 379, 380, 381, 382, 383, 384, 385.
Polly, 312.
Priscilla, 15, 31, 50, 157, 278, 406.
Rebecca, 30, 50, 113, 149, 157, 162, 271, 277, 309.
Relief, 128, 144, 308.
Rhoda, 113, 308.
Roger N., 305.
Samuel, 317.
Sarah, 10, 12, 15, 50, 99, 126, 134, 139, 156, 159, 273, 278, 294, 308, 319, 320.
Silas, 288.
Silence, 72, 103, 134.
Sophia, 113, 132, 147, 308.
Susanna, 69, 70, 73, 156, 273, 283, 303.
Thankful, 12, 27, 29, 50, 90, 113, 117, 275, 301, 308, 320, 321, 350, 451.
Thomas, 34, 50, 82, 280, 300, 331.
Widow ——, 351.
Zerviah, 289.
BEARD, Lucy, 46.
BEAVER, Samuel, 258.
BECKWITH, A——, 446.
Lucy, 196.
BELCHER, Jonas W., 250.
Thomas W., 258.
BELKNAP, Deborah, 150.
Jeremiah, 24.

Joseph, 136.
Mary, 43.
Mittie, 130.
BELL, Elizabeth M., 253.
Isaac, 256.
John, 254.
Rhoda P., 267, 394, 420.
William, 267, 420.
BELLOWS, Benjamin, 51, 273, 274, 451.
Dorcas, 51, 271.
Joanna, 273.
Jonathan, 397.
Judith, 18, 273.
Mary, 273.
Ruth, 134.
BEMENT, Eri B., 243.
BEMIS, Hannah, 153, 165.
Sally, 147.
Zaccheus, 98.
BENNETT, Aaron S., 200, 347.
Abigail, 34, 86, 274, 332.
Abner, 96.
Amira, 234.
Althina, 232.
Asa, 93.
Asahel H., 242.
Azubah, 54, 279.
Bathsheba, 27, 53, 94, 130, 145, 159, 276, 277, 283, 300, 305, 399.
Benjamin, 127, 141.
Caleb W., 255, 264.
Caroline, 175.
Catherine, 423.
Charles, 176, 199, 343, 346.
Clorinda, 200.
David, 46, 127, 142.
Dolly, 175, 198, 339.
Dorathy, 122, 337.
Eli, 317.
Elias, 108, 175, 198, 199, 200, 344, 345, 346, 347, 357, 360.
Elias D., 199, 345.
Elisha, 33, 36, 53, 82, 94, 112, 135, 150, 159, 163, 175, 176, 199, 279, 298, 299, 303, 304, 311, 315, 317, 319, 324, 325, 353, 355, 423.
Elizabeth, 17, 22, 33, 61, 63, 68, 76, 141, 156, 198, 273, 281, 332.
Elizabeth R., 264.
Enoch, 389.
Ephraim, 54, 93, 275.
Eunice, 45, 68, 76, 103, 199, 268, 289, 315, 333, 339, 377, 396, 423.
George, 10, 11, 12, 14, 16.
Hannah, 84, 85.
Harriet, 199, 232, 341.
Henry, 198, 343.
Isabella, 122, 175, 198, 231, 333.
Jacob, 37, 41, 53, 99, 103, 283, 375, 379.
Jacob C., 249.
James D., 175, 198, 345.
John, 11, 17, 23, 44, 53, 82, 104, 111, 122, 127, 142, 159, 175, 198, 254, 257, 259, 266, 270, 272, 276, 277, 278, 279, 283, 286, 295, 300, 308, 309, 310, 319, 321, 323, 324, 326, 327, 338, 341, 395, 396, 397, 399, 421.
Jonathan, 273, 291.
Joseph, 39, 61, 63, 68, 76, 156, 273, 281, 283, 286, 287, 289, 292, 311, 375, 377, 387, 389.
Joshua, 379.
Josiah, 24, 84, 85, 93, 96, 108, 273.
Jotham, 53, 278.
Kezia, 86, 295, 319.
Laban, 198.
Levi, 176, 363.
Lois, 82, 125, 135, 153, 159, 165, 298, 299, 315, 320.

Lucinda, 198, 342.
Lucy, 111, 126, 132, 138, 147, 308, 309, 321, 323.
Lucy Ann, 198, 344.
Luke, 166, 175, 231, 315, 358, 423.
Lutner, 308, 326.
Lydia, 10, 11, 12, 14, 42, 94, 97, 101, 102, 149, 162, 198, 307, 321, 322, 345, 451.
Martha, 291, 317.
Mary, 11, 17, 35, 61, 76, 85, 93, 94, 96, 104, 108, 112, 131, 140, 237, 271, 283, 303, 304, 321.
Mary Ann, 236, 342.
Mary B., 198, 343.
Mary M., 166.
Molly, 93.
Nancy, 175, 198, 199, 334, 339, 343, 344, 357, 425.
Nathan, 53, 149, 162, 175, 199, 268, 277, 300, 303, 309, 333, 339, 341, 342, 353, 390, 423.
Otis, 200.
Patience, 39, 101, 108.
Phineas, 54, 276.
Polly, 310.
Prudence, 68, 76, 156, 287, 387.
Rebecca, 375.
Roxa, 198.
Sally, 170, 199, 200, 228.
Solomon P., 259, 266, 421.
Samuel, 10, 54, 139, 271, 272, 273, 274, 275, 276, 277, 279, 291, 399, 452.
Sarah, 44, 63, 68, 76, 88, 198, 286, 311, 336, 340, 360.
Silas, 54, 277.
Susan, 254, 396.
Tabitha, 54, 272, 291.
Thomas, 39, 53, 94, 96, 97, 101, 102, 122, 132, 146, 175, 180, 198, 286, 305, 306, 307, 309, 321, 333, 337, 338, 339, 340, 341, 342, 343, 344, 345, 352.
Walter F., 198.
William, 14.
BERBEAN, Mary, 15.
BERNARD, se Barnard.
BETHEL, Thomas J., 176, 366.
BEWNEY, John, 84, 86.
BIGELOW, Aaron, 67, 289.
Abel, 81, 137.
Abigail, 139.
Ann, 87.
Anna, 74.
Charles, 199, 264, 346, 364.
Cornelia A., 177, 197, 449.
Cynthia, 174, 370.
Cynthia W., 177, 197, 350, 449.
Daniel, 45, 104.
Ebenezer, 21, 31, 32, 74, 75, 81, 380, 381.
Elijah, 257.
Eliza, 176, 177, 197, 200, 337, 449.
Eliza Jane, 197, 350.
Elizabeth, 292, 298.
Emily W., 393.
Erastus B., 244, 393.
Hasket, D. P., 199, 346.
Hepzibah, 75, 81, 381.
Horatio N., 264, 393.
Jacob, 125, 136.
Jane Eliza, 176, 200, 449.
John A., 177, 198, 371, 449.
Jonathan, 33, 59, 62, 64, 66, 67, 69, 72, 86, 284, 287, 288, 289, 292, 379.
Jotham, 86.
Liberty D., 372.
Lucius A., 200, 350.
Lucy, 75.
Luke, 174, 176, 177, 197, 200, 233,

337, 350, 365, 368, 371, 449.
Mary, 59, 62, 64, 66, 67, 69, 72, 98, 284.
Mary E. T., 197, 350.
Mindwell, 62, 284.
Miriam, 64, 69, 287.
Polly B., 393.
Prudence, 335.
Richardson, 167, 173.
Sarah, 35, 72, 199, 379.
Solon F., 176, 197, 449.
Susan W., 393.
Theodore F., 197, 350.
William, 333, 350.
BILLINGS, Alonzo, 421.
Hannah, 176, 200, 361, 421.
Horace, 200.
Joseph F., 198, 348.
Josiah, 176, 177, 198, 200, 234, 255, 346, 347, 348, 362, 370, 421.
Luther, 200.
Lydia W., 200, 346.
Martha F., 200, 347.
Nancy, 421.
BINNEY, Joseph G., 242.
BIXBX, Daniel, 384.
Elizabeth, 94.
Ephraim, 94.
John, 106.
Joseph, 42, 94, 97, 108.
Levina, 384.
Manasseh, 39, 94, 99.
Martha, 29, 43, 94.
Mary, 38, 94, 99, 106.
Miriam, 97, 108.
Nathaniel, 29.
Priscilla, 108.
Rachel, 97.
Samuel, 36, 94, 98, 134.
William, 106.
BLACKENDON, Jenny, 128, 143.
BLACKMAN, Eliza T., 237.
BLAKE, Francis, 133, 148.
BLANCHARD, Cornelius W., 264.
Edward, 264.
Eliza, 175.
Elizabeth, 175, 199, 447.
Ira T. H., 372.
John, 248.
Mary Ann, 256.
Sarah Ann, 248.
William, 175, 199, 360, 447.
BLISS, Asenath, 254.
Cyrus, 176, 238, 369, 421.
Martha J., 421.
Susan, 421.
BLODGET, Lydia, 390.
Samuel, 42, 102.
Sarah, 44.
Thomas, 45, 390.
Timothy, 103.
BLOOD, Amos F., 252.
Angelo P., 260.
Betty, 321.
Caroline, 260, 261.
Caroline E., 261.
Hepzibah, 274.
Jonathan K., 308, 326.
Joseph, 274, 308, 321, 326.
Levi, 155, 166, 356.
Lucy, 151, 163.
Mary, 43.
Thomas, 175.
Thomas F., 260, 261.
BLOWERS, Elizabeth, 83, 87, 376, 381.
BODGE, Rebecca, 142.
BOLEY, John, 256.
BOLTON, Amazonia, 250.
Leonard, 236.
BOND, Lucy, 46.
Martha, 244.

Roxana, 247.
Seraphina, 236.
BOOKS, see Brooks.
BOSWELL, Susan W., 246.
BOSWORTH, Beatrix, 14.
Benjamin, 14.
Jonathan, 46, 104.
BOURNE, Henry W., 198.
Mary Ann, 198.
Mary S., 198.
Roswell, 198.
Roswell H., 255.
William R., 198.
BOUTELL, Kendall, 98, 130.
BOWERS, Charles M., 256, 257, 258, 263, 269.
Cornelia V., 263.
Elizabeth, 273, 276.
Ellen A., 263, 269.
Hannah, 98.
James, 274, 298, 299.
Jerahmeel, 31, 34, 78, 298, 323.
John, 68, 114, 273, 274, 275, 276, 285, 290, 293, 295, 296, 298, 299, 320, 332, 402, 452.
Josiah, 114, 130, 145, 176, 296, 367, 421.
Margaret, 68, 114, 285, 295, 326.
Mary, 78, 274, 293, 320.
Nathaniel, 275.
Rebecca, 176, 368, 421.
Sampson, 274.
Samuel, 78, 298.
William, 295.
BOWKER, Oliver, 126, 139.
Phebe, 44.
BOWMAN, Betsy, 356.
Charles, 201.
George, 201, 251.
Hannah, 176, 198, 200, 201.
Henry, 176, 198, 200.
Jonathan, 266, 372, 420.
Samuel Mirick, 198.
Samuel W., 420.
Sarah, 420.
Simeon, 176, 198, 200, 201, 234, 365.
BOYNTON, Anna, 37, 68, 99, 289, 375, 416.
Amos, 388.
Asenath, 262.
Beaman, 387.
Edna, 388.
Elizabeth, 98.
Ephraim, 76, 137, 166, 376, 377, 378, 381, 384, 385, 386.
George A., 262.
Hannah, 71, 74, 76.
Irena, 385.
Jane, 35, 68, 87, 290.
Jedediah, 45, 103, 389.
Jewett, 387.
John, 36, 37, 74, 98, 377, 380, 385, 386, 387.
John J., 258.
Joseph, 39, 101.
Lucy, 389.
Matilda A., 252.
Nathaniel A., 254, 262.
Otis, 233, 372.
Paul, 136, 137.
Sally A., 234.
Sarah, 71, 243, 379, 384.
Zaccheus, 21, 27, 28, 31, 68, 71, 74, 76, 289, 290, 375, 379, 380, 381, 416.
BRABROOK, Bethesda, 32.
Hepzibah, 271, 312, 331.
John, 20, 275.
Joseph, 275.
Thankful, 46, 103.
William, 84.

William F., 246, 268, 395.
BRACKET, Mary, 40.
BRADISH, Ebenezer, 175, 311, 327, 360.
Elizabeth W., 311.
Timothy P., 327.
BRADLEY, Franklin, 421.
Mary P., 394, 421.
Robert F., 176.
Robert M., 176, 177, 368, 370, 421.
Sarah, 154.
BRADSTREET, Relief, 135.
BRAGG, Abigail A., 260.
Ann H., 260.
Charles Carter, 199, 347.
Ebenezer, 168, 172, 176, 199, 200, 201, 335, 345, 346, 347, 348, 363, 421.
Ebenezer Gott, 199, 346.
George F., 201.
Horatio C., 176, 201, 348, 421.
Joseph M., 201.
Martha, 199, 200, 201, 335, 421.
Martha A. R., 200, 247, 347.
William W., 260, 345, 395.
BRATTEN, David, 282.
Elizabeth, 281, 282.
Robert, 281, 282.
BRAY, John H., 264.
Mary, 252.
Mrs. ———, 369.
Michael, 264.
William, 176, 369.
BRAZIL, John, 326.
BRECK, Joseph, 392.
Sarah, 392.
BREWER, Elizabeth, 36.
Sarah, 150, 243.
BREWSTER, Anna, 175, 352.
Oliver, 128, 175.
BRICKETT, Mary A., 257.
BRIDE, Betsy, 198.
James Henry, 198.
Wilson, 198.
BRIDGE, Abigail, 175, 176, 199, 322, 336, 339, 356, 360, 423.
Abigail A., 200, 348.
Amy, 300.
Anna, 140, 322.
Asarelah M., 199, 344.
Benjamin, 300.
Catharine M., 198.
Caroline T., 177, 198, 370, 423.
Charles, 167, 173, 175, 176, 177, 198, 199, 200, 235, 318, 346, 370, 371, 423.
Charles Henry, 198, 243.
Eirene, 175, 198, 199, 200, 335, 421.
Eliza, 199, 238, 340.
Ellen A., 198.
Franklin T., 175, 198, 423.
George W., 175, 198, 371, 423.
Henry, 338, 346, 422.
James, 266, 318, 372, 423.
James W., 200.
John, 198, 199, 341.
John H., 198.
Joseph, 199, 342.
Josiah, 175, 198, 199, 200, 335, 343, 344, 345, 346, 347, 348, 358, 373, 421.
Louisa, 313.
Martha Eirene, 199, 343.
Mary Elizabeth, 199, 346.
Mary Jane, 198.
Mary N., 199, 336, 339.
Nancy, 198, 345.
Nancy N., 235.
Rebecca, 241.
R. Perkins, 126, 138, 313.

INDEX.

Samuel L., 348.
Sarah, 128, 144, 198, 199, 345, 347, 421.
Solomon, 176, 199, 341, 364, 423.
Sophia, 175, 177, 198, 200, 423.
Susan, 176, 364, 423.
Susanna, 198, 335, 362.
William, 128, 145, 170, 175, 176, 199, 318, 322, 338, 339, 340, 341, 342, 348, 355, 423.
William A., 198.
William F., 200, 347.
BRIDGMAN, Betsy, 176, 366.
Horatio N., 176, 242.
BRIGGS, Calvin, 167, 173.
BRIGHAM, Almira L., 200.
Ann, 198, 200.
Anna, 232.
Artemas, 155, 166.
Betsy, 154.
Dandridge H., 200,
David, 71.
Eber, 167, 173.
Francis, 199.
Francis L., 200.
Franklin, 198, 200, 238.
George, 249.
Hannah, 134.
Harriet A., 198.
Jabez, 151, 163, 199, 200.
Jotham, 421.
Levi E., 348.
Lucy, 351, 365, 421.
Lucy A., 255.
Maria C., 250
Mary, 75, 136.
Mary Ann, 199.
Mary J., 258.
Mindwell, 72.
Samuel, 348.
Sarah Ann, 200.
Silas, 30, 71, 72, 75.
Sophia, 199.
Tabitha, 71, 72, 75.
Widow ——, 176.
BRIMHALL, Lucy L., 244.
BRINSMEAD, William, 15, 271.
BRITTAIN and BRITTON.
John, 147, 175, 352.
Polly, 47, 175, 352.
BROCKLEBANK, Asa, 446.
Eunice, 45.
Martha, 83, 85, 445.
Mr ——, 196.
BROCKWAY, Gideon, 21, 31.
BROOKINS, Philip, 24.
BROOKS, Almeria, 388.
Alpheus, 97, 387.
Ammi, 386.
Amos, 390.
Benjamin, 91, 385.
Betsy W., 101.
Beulah, 111.
Catharine, 82, 90, 390.
David, 105, 135.
David C., 112.
Daniel B., 97, 387.
Deborah, 98, 101, 126, 128, 138, 385.
Ebenezer, 42, 102, 111, 243.
Elizabeth, 79, 383.
Enos, 390.
Esther, 101, 112.
Eunice, 98, 384, 387, 390.
Hannah, 84, 85, 97, 101, 112, 385, 386.
Hannah C., 112, 389.
Helon, 97, 387.
Isaac, 93.
Jabez, 81, 84, 85, 98, 101, 112, 376, 383, 384, 385, 386, 387, 389.
Jacob, 93.

James, 390.
Joanna, 112.
Jonas, 83, 112, 390.
John, 22, 32, 40, 75, 79, 82, 84, 87, 90, 91, 96, 97, 106, 375, 376, 380, 381, 383, 384, 385, 386, 387, 388, 389, 390.
Jonathan, 93, 389.
Joshua, 128, 138.
Lucy, 81, 98, 101, 112.
Lucy C., 81, 104, 134, 383.
Lydia, 349.
Mary, 35, 93, 97, 101, 106, 137, 386, 390.
Mittie, 131, 146.
Parney, 43, 75, 79, 91, 96, 381.
Phebe, 112, 388.
Polly, 112.
Rhoda, 101, 387.
Samuel, 43, 380.
Sarah, 93, 138.
Seth, 93, 416.
Submit, 36, 89.
Susy, 390.
Sylvia, 96, 387.
Thankful, 108.
Thomas, 37, 97, 112, 150, 163, 377, 386, 387, 388, 389, 390.
William, 43, 90, 104, 108, 111, 134, 384, 389.
BROUGHTON, Copia, 31, 54, 278.
Ebenezer, 279.
Edward, 54, 271, 272, 277, 278, 279.
Martha, 26, 54, 77.
Patience, 32, 54, 279.
Sarah, 27, 28, 54, 277.
BROWN, Andrew J., 245, 396.
Anes, 101, 110, 121.
Ann S., 197.
Arethusa, 101, 307.
Asaph, 199.
Bathsheba, 168, 171.
Betty, 200.
Charles S., 177, 369.
Damaris, 110, 308.
Deliverance, 17.
Eleazer, 125.
Elizabeth, 47, 105, 380.
Ellen C., 252.
Ellen S., 197.
Elmer, 135.
Ephraim, 17.
Eunice, 116.
Mrs. Gen——, 416.
Gilson, 358.
Hope, 241.
Jane P., 264.
John, 44, 47, 104, 105, 175, 198, 293, 356, 377, 378, 416, 423.
Jonas H., 257.
Joseph, 25, 43, 47, 101, 104, 105, 110, 294, 307, 308, 321.
Josiah, 27, 29, 47, 105, 285, 288, 289, 290, 293, 294, 326, 380, 381, 382, 383, 384, 385, 416.
Josiah P., 116, 390.
Julia, 199.
Kezia, 199.
Lois, 83, 85.
Lydia, 28.
Mary, 17, 40, 175, 423.
Mary Ann, 244.
Mary B., 199.
Miriam, 238.
Moses, 200.
M. Sarah, 252.
Nathaniel, 103, 134.
Oliver, 155, 167, 199.
Polly, 175, 198, 423.
Prudence, 37, 47, 99, 105, 290, 293, 294, 377, 416.

Rachel, 145.
Rebecca, 105, 150, 163, 328, 383, 385, 416.
Ruhamah, 104, 381.
Ruth, 198.
Samuel, 105, 384.
Sarah, 137, 176, 364.
Silas, 359.
Silas L., 199, 264.
Stanton, 105, 382.
Susan, 199.
Sylvia J. C., 264.
Thomas, 197, 238.
Timothy, 105, 116, 135, 382, 390.
William, 37, 47, 98, 105, 245, 289, 377.
BRUCE, Abigail, 200.
Catharine, 176, 361, 421.
Charlotte, 233.
Christopher, 200.
Dexter, 246.
Eli, 363.
Elizabeth R., 249.
Hollis, 200, 359, 360, 361.
Jerusha, 200.
Joel, 340.
Jonathan, 176, 365, 421.
Lydia, 40.
Mary, 34, 272, 282.
Otis, 340.
Rufus, 176, 361.
Sarah, 200, 246, 392, 393.
BRUNSON, Lydia, 45.
BRYANT, Anna, 45.
Grace, 130.
Micah, 44, 104.
Miriam, 42.
Reuben, 333, 350.
BUBIER, John, 390.
Capt. Peter, 390.
Sophia M., 390.
BUCK, Edna, 252.
Elizabeth D., 250.
Isaac, 126, 140.
BUCKINGHAM, John A., 254.
BUCKMAN, Joseph, 254.
BUFFUM, Jedediah, 155, 166, 199.
Nancy, 199.
Sampson W., 199, 248.
BULL, Mary, 15.
BULLARD, Prudence, 36.
BULLEN, Lois, 42, 102.
BUNSON, Rhoda, 137.
BURBANK, Aaron, 236, 262, 339.
Amanda M., 259.
Calvin W., 262.
Chloe S., 262.
Daniel, 233.
Eliza J., 198.
Elizabeth, 354.
Ellen, 450.
Ellen F., 261.
George W., 200.
Hannah, 176, 177, 198, 200, 449, 450.
Hannah E., 200.
Harvey, 450.
Harriet E., 262, 449.
Henry L., 450.
Hosea H., 198.
Jane, 259, 261.
Levi B., 246, 259, 261.
Lucy, 169, 171, 245.
Lucy Ann, 200, 450.
Luther, 264.
Mary A., 449, 450.
Mary E., 259.
Mehetabel, 168, 172, 198.
Nathaniel, 175, 176, 245, 360, 449.
Olive R., 264, 450.
Ruth, 449.
Samuel W., 176, 177, 198, 200.

INDEX. 463

233, 247, 249, 264, 269, 449, 450.
Sarah M., 200, 255.
Susan E., 176, 200, 449.
Thomas, 339.
Widow and Mrs., 175, 176.
BURDITT, Abel, 111.
Adeline, 200, 255.
Alfred A., 201, 252.
Augustus P., 250, 269, 397.
Betsy S., 247.
Charles A., 177, 198, 420.
Charles Carter, 259.
Charles W., 370.
Christopher C., 176, 200.
Daniel, 312, 331.
Ebenezer, 312, 331.
Edward W., 262.
Edwin J., 259, 268.
Eliza, 199.
Eliza H., 239.
Frances E., 262.
Francis W., 201, 420.
Franklin C., 198, 420.
Frederick W., 200.
F. Marshall, 249.
George, 338.
George W., 200, 250, 264.
Hervey, 435.
Henry H., 198.
Jacob, 316.
James, 200, 316, 436.
Jerome S., 256.
Jerome W., 198.
John, 176, 200, 198, 201, 240, 242, 317, 420.
John M., 198.
Joshua, 111, 133, 147.
Julia A., 200, 243.
Laura P., 241.
Louisa J., 200.
Lucinda, 247.
Margaret, 176, 198, 199, 200, 201, 266, 371, 420.
Margaret L., 262.
Martha A., 200.
Mary Ann, 200, 253, 255.
Mary E., 259, 262, 264.
Mary E. S., 269, 397.
Mary L., 246.
Nancy, 338.
Nathan, 167, 172, 176, 198, 199, 200, 201, 245, 255, 259, 262, 266, 268, 361, 362, 371, 420.
Persis, 198, 200.
Polly, 111.
Ruth, 111, 312, 327, 331.
Sally, 143, 198, 200, 312, 315, 331, 420.
Sarah, 238.
Sarah A., 200.
Sarah B., 176, 200, 201, 420.
Sarah E., 117, 198, 420.
Sarah E. W., 198.
Sarah G., 262.
Sarah M., 176.
S. W., 269.
Thomas, 111, 129, 140, 177, 198, 199, 244, 262, 312, 315, 316, 317, 327, 331, 338, 420.
Thomas E., 198.
Thomas M., 200.
William, 198, 200, 240, 370.
William D., 198.
BURNETT, Catharine B., 235.
BURNHAM, Abraham, 228.
Reuben, 330.
Ruth, 128.
Sarah, 254.
BURPEE, Anna, 375.
Azubah, 80, 82, 90, 92, 94, 109, 382, 387, 416.
Betsy, 200.

Caroline, 372.
Ebenezer, 77, 90, 91, 159, 376, 382, 383, 384, 416.
Elijah, 69, 80, 109, 290, 383, 384, 416.
Elizabeth, 67, 69, 74, 75, 77, 79, 90, 92, 107, 109, 159, 286, 375, 385, 388, 389, 416.
Esther, 21, 290.
Hannah, 109, 129, 138, 383, 416.
Harriet, 255, 373.
Hephzibah, 92, 97, 385.
Hester, 30.
Hitty, 91, 384.
James, 253.
Jeremiah, 75, 77, 79, 90, 92, 159, 375, 380, 381, 382, 383, 384, 385, 416.
John, 200, 229.
Lydia, 175, 199, 359, 421.
Marah, 109.
Margaret, 91, 92, 95, 109.
Martha, 82, 109, 110, 126, 140, 383, 389.
Martin, 175, 199, 200, 229, 230, 421.
Mary, 26, 29, 82, 137, 285, 290, 384, 385.
Molly, 159, 380, 416.
Moses, 75, 91, 92, 95, 97, 109, 135, 376, 381, 384, 385, 386, 387, 388, 389, 390.
Nathan, 34, 80, 82, 85, 90, 92, 94, 109, 376, 382, 383, 384, 385, 386.
Nathaniel, 95, 386.
Newton, 245.
Phebe, 37, 74, 98, 107, 293, 379, 387.
Polly, 175.
Priscilla, 33.
Samuel, 67, 69, 74, 83, 85, 107, 109, 110, 286, 288, 290, 293, 375, 376, 379, 383, 384, 385, 387, 388, 389, 416.
Sarah, 109, 388.
Stephen, 67, 71, 109, 288, 379, 387.
Thomas, 29, 71, 92, 154, 175, 285, 290, 291, 293, 357, 374, 375, 376, 379, 385, 390.
BURRAGE, William, 233.
William F., 258.
BURRILL, Jane J., 239.
BURT, Daniel, 300.
B——, 446.
James, 300.
O——, 446.
Polly, 149.
BURTON, Anson, 450.
Elizabeth C., 450.
Frances A., 450.
James H., 450.
BUSH, George, 377.
Hephzibah, 42, 102.
John, 20.
Lucy, 129.
Persis, 129, 140.
BUSS, Abigail, 27, 28, 48, 80, 275, 382.
Anne E., 257.
Benjamin, 91, 385.
Ebenezer, 22, 32, 48, 74, 77, 79, 80, 82, 91, 93, 96, 106, 278, 381, 382, 384, 385, 386, 387, 388.
Elizabeth, 240, 251, 394.
Eunice, 66, 68, 77, 136, 158, 287, 382.
Hannah, 29, 48, 74, 133, 272, 275, 381, 400.
John, 28, 48, 66, 68, 96, 157, 158, 272, 275, 276, 277, 278, 285, 287, 288, 290, 387, 400.

Jonathan, 45, 48, 103, 277.
Kezia, 74, 77, 79, 80, 82, 91, 93, 96, 106.
Lucy, 82, 384.
Rebecca, 106, 388.
Stephen, 30, 48, 276.
Silas, 93, 386.
Susan E., 256.
Zephaniah, 68, 290.
BUTLER, Abel, 123, 198, 201, 235, 367, 447.
Abijah, 123.
Achsa, 894.
Albert, 201.
Almira, 200.
Amos, 81, 200, 230.
Amos J., 200.
Anes, 81.
Anne, 199.
Anna, 65, 123, 287.
Asaph, 58, 81, 89, 280.
Benjamin, 123, 176, 198, 109, 237.
Charles, 201.
David, 68, 176, 199, 290, 365.
Deborah, 66, 68, 80.
Dinah, 129, 140, 175, 295.
Ebenezer, 143, 175.
Eldad, 268, 396.
Elizabeth, 127, 142, 332, 338, 359.
Ephraim, 61, 283.
Eunice, 131, 146, 155, 166, 175, 273, 316, 333, 357.
Experience, 61, 63, 65, 273, 283.
Frederick A., 198.
George W., 201.
Granville, 200.
Hamilton E., 200.
Hannah, 52, 55, 58, 273.
Harriet, 201.
Isaac, 27, 29, 296, 323.
Isaiah, 65, 287.
Israel, 123, 126, 137, 175, 358.
James, 18, 20, 27, 52, 55, 58, 66, 68, 80, 156, 270, 273, 274, 275, 277, 278, 279, 280, 289, 290, 295, 297, 299, 322, 324, 328, 329, 340.
Jane, 81.
Janette, 89.
John, 55, 123, 144, 279.
John E., 341.
Joseph, 176, 200, 360.
Josiah, 287.
Lucy, 31, 84, 87, 320, 384.
Luke, 307.
Lydia, 66, 156, 176, 289, 307, 331.
Margaret, 200.
Martha, 18, 200, 273.
Martha J., 258.
Martha P., 198.
Mary, 24, 175, 176, 199, 200, 251, 273, 355, 451.
Mary J., 258.
May, 200.
Merrick, 201.
Miranda, 201.
Miriam, 278.
Nancy, 176, 201, 258, 363, 396, 447.
Nathan, 277.
Nathaniel, 26, 61, 63, 65, 150, 273, 274, 283, 285, 286, 287, 289, 290.
Olive, 410.
Patience, 52, 278.
Phebe, 129, 296.
Polly, 199.
Prudence, 63, 286.
Rachel, 199.
Rufus, 201.
Sally, 198, 201, 364, 447.
Samuel, 123, 176, 201, 297, 356, 363, 447.
Samuel D., 268, 396.

464 INDEX.

Sarah, 364, 447.
Sherman, 201.
Sidney S., 198.
Simon, 27, 28, 65, 80, 127, 136, 142, 146, 175, 287, 299, 315, 316, 330, 332, 333, 338, 340, 341, 354.
Stephen, 176, 200.
Susanna, 315.
Thankful, 27, 274.
William, 289.
William B., 201.
Widow, 176.
BUTMAN, Elizabeth, 314.
Zebulon, 314, 329.
BUTTERFIELD, Elijah, 147.
Mary, 151, 242.
BUTTRICK, Ann E., 265, 268, 396, 420.
Asa, 198, 199.
Caroline, 199, 344.
Charles, 198.
Charlotte, 197, 265, 268, 396, 420.
Cornelius W.,
Edward W., 265.
Francis, 30, 71, 293.
George Thomas, 197.
Hannah, 71, 198, 199, 293.
Hannah E., 199, 347.
Harriet P., 199.
Horatio G., 153, 165, 168, 171, 175, 199, 335, 344, 345, 356, 357, 422.
Jane, 198, 199, 242, 335, 347.
John W., 199, 347.
Jonathan, 46, 103, 176, 191, 197, 198, 199, 245, 265, 268, 335, 347, 362, 396, 420.
Nancy, 175, 199, 335, 357, 422.
Nancy W., 175, 199, 344, 345, 422.
Sarah A., 422.
Sarah J., 265.
Susan, 168, 171.
Thomas P., 174, 177, 199, 347, 370.
William, 25.
BYAM, Jesse, 42.
BYRON, Helen A., 124, 345.
CÆSAR, 282, 305, 324, 327, 331.
Hannah, 328.
CADY, Electa, 262.
Jane E., 362.
John W., 262, 268.
CALAHAN, Jeremiah, 251.
Rebecca, 147.
CALDWELL, John, 177, 202, 356.
Mary J., 249.
Lydia, 177, 202.
CAMERON, Donald, 264.
Margaret D., 264.
CAMPBELL, Alice, 42.
Anna, 339.
Hannah, 147.
Hervey, 338.
James, 120, 132, 147.
John, 132, 147, 177, 333, 338, 339, 352.
Martha, 333.
Nancy, 333, 338.
Patty, 339.
Polly, 146.
Sophia, 120, 338.
CANOUSE, John, 129.
CANTERBURY, Rose, 34, 86.
CAPEN, Betsy, 121, 339.
Dolly,
Edmund M., 339.
Elizabeth, 121, 333.
Henry, 121, 339.
James, 121, 339.
John, 121, 230, 339, 360.
Sally, 121, 129, 141, 339.

CAREY, John G., 249.
Louisa R., 255.
Martin, 264.
Thomas, 264.
CARLETON, Albert S., 178, 248, 253, 260, 264.
Eugene, 264.
Eunice, 140.
Frances S.,
George Henry, 178, 411.
Herbert, 260.
James, 177, 411.
Jonathan, 177, 360, 411.
Lydia, 172.
Maria B., 260.
Mary, 177, 178, 359, 365, 410, 411.
Mary L., 368, 410.
Moses, 177, 178, 232, 361, 364, 365, 410, 411.
Susan M., 260.
Susanna, 178, 370.
Theodore, 178, 411.
William, 148, 161.
CARLEY, also see Kerley.
Abigail, 289.
Elizabeth, 26.
Martha, 26.
William, 29.
CARMICHAEL, Niel, 258.
CARNES, Burrill, 338.
Mary Ann, 264.
Helena V. C., 338.
Patrick, 264.
CARPENTER, Sally, 242.
Sarah, 240.
CARR, Attosa, 423.
Dolly H., 267, 395, 423.
Hannah, 261.
Hannah H., 248.
Harriet A., 261.
John, 267, 269, 394, 423.
Lyman, 254.
Mary, 394, 423.
CARROLL, Lucy, 236.
CARRUTH, James, 42.
CARTER, Abel, 91, 121, 302, 316, 318, 322, 330.
Abigail, 27, 35, 40, 55, 65, 66, 67, 68, 71, 73, 76, 77, 80, 82, 90, 93, 98, 99, 100, 108, 114, 121, 128, 158, 159, 177, 202, 233, 274, 285, 287, 288, 289, 295, 296, 302, 303, 307, 318, 320, 321, 338, 342, 354, 355, 402, 424, 425.
Abigail A., 202, 348.
Adelia M., 202, 349.
Almira, 210, 236.
Alpheus, 121, 178, 317.
Ann M., 202, 394.
Anna, 26, 108, 115, 308, 314, 322, 351.
Anne L., 253, 266, 349.
Asa, 89, 127, 142, 301, 314, 332, 347.
Betsy, 153, 165, 177, 178, 202, 316, 334, 342, 359, 424.
Betsy T., 201, 245, 347.
Beulah, 42, 66, 73, 103, 285, 294.
Calvin, 123, 154, 178, 201, 202, 247, 315, 345, 349, 355, 361, 425.
Caroline, 201.
Catharine, 342.
Catharine D., 239.
Catharine M., 250.
Catharine P., 202.
Cephas, 121, 178, 233, 318, 370, 424.
Chandler, 372.
Charity, 322, 350.
Charles, 201, 202, 340.
Charles M., 202, 256, 349.
Damaris, 65, 87, 285, 287.
Daniel, 237, 302.

Daniel Andrew, 202, 257, 260, 349.
Deborah, 80, 130, 145, 299.
Delia, 202, 336.
Dinah, 36, 62, 88, 284.
Dorothy, 24, 32, 40, 54, 57, 77, 100, 274, 280, 295.
Ebenezer, 344.
Eli, 121, 177, 201, 338, 340, 424.
Elias, 64, 287.
Elijah, 93, 128, 144, 303, 316, 322.
Elisha, 402.
Eliza, 245, 349.
Elizabeth, 27, 28, 29, 55, 63, 70, 115, 177, 178, 201, 202, 276, 277, 280, 313, 335, 344, 345, 351, 371, 425.
Ellen M., 349.
Emily, 178, 201, 202, 241, 333, 341, 367, 424.
Emily B., 202.
Ephraim, 27, 28, 40, 65, 67, 68, 73, 76, 77, 82, 90, 93, 98, 100, 108, 114, 115, 149, 158, 159, 162, 177, 178, 180, 186, 201, 202, 275, 287, 288, 289, 292, 293, 294, 295, 297, 298, 299, 300, 302, 303, 306, 307, 308, 309, 311, 312, 313, 314, 315, 316, 319, 321, 324, 329, 330, 333, 339, 340, 342, 343, 351, 352, 363, 401, 424, 425.
Eunice, 19, 60, 77, 273, 282, 297, 330.
Frank H., 260.
George, 201, 202, 240, 339, 424.
George A., 202, 349.
George P., 202, 348.
Granville, 253, 269, 423.
Henry, 114, 202, 342.
H. Emma, 423.
Hiram, 307.
Horatio, 178, 202, 236, 336, 338, 366, 373, 423.
James, 55, 76, 78, 79, 83, 89, 96, 121, 123, 139, 152, 160, 161, 165, 177, 178, 179, 181, 182, 185, 190, 194, 201, 231, 277, 296, 297, 298, 300, 301, 302, 313, 315, 318, 320, 321, 322, 336, 337, 338, 342, 352, 353, 355, 359, 364, 402, 410, 425.
James Coolidge, 202, 348.
Jas. Gordon, 202, 237, 263, 373.
Jemima, 40, 44, 55, 57, 59, 60, 62, 64, 67, 69, 71, 72, 100, 294, 328.
Joanna W., 337.
Joel, 115, 318, 327.
John, 20, 27, 55, 66, 68, 71, 73, 77, 80, 98, 105, 114, 115, 121, 135, 153, 154, 158, 165, 166, 177, 178, 201, 202, 230, 242, 274, 285, 287, 288, 290, 293, 296, 297, 299, 306, 312, 314, 319, 322, 324, 325, 334, 338, 342, 343, 344, 347, 359, 364, 370, 402, 424.
Jonas, 71, 293.
Jonathan, 39, 44, 65, 102, 274, 285, 287, 292.
Joseph, 42, 71, 103, 115, 135, 153, 165, 293, 311, 312, 313, 314, 315, 316, 317, 318, 322, 325, 327, 344.
Josiah, 31, 54, 279, 317.
Julia Ann, 202.
Julia A. D., 253, 347.
Levi, 103, 134, 178, 314.
Lincoln, 345.
Lucinda, 201, 339.
Lucy, 32, 55, 115, 177, 202, 280, 315, 333, 334, 335, 354, 357, 365, 425.
Lucy E., 202, 247, 346.
Luke, 83, 160, 300, 314, 327.
Luke W., 244.

INDEX. 465

Marietta C., 424.
Martha, 121, 178, 201, 322, 345, 347, 368, 424.
Martha A. R., 266, 371, 423.
Martha B., 337.
Martha E., 209, 423.
Martha L., 178, 201, 202, 254, 425.
Mary, 26, 34, 59, 65, 76, 78, 79, 83, 84, 86, 87, 89, 96, 132, 147, 158, 160, 161, 168, 172, 202, 233, 276, 281, 287, 297, 312, 320, 332, 333, 342, 350, 351, 352, 362, 401, 410, 425.
Mary A., 260.
Mary Ann A., 178, 201, 349, 367, 425.
Mary E., 245.
Mary S., 349.
Mary T., 337.
Milicent, 21, 27, 33, 54, 280, 319.
Nabby, 145, 311.
Nancy, 132, 146, 151, 163, 164, 178, 202, 240, 344, 424.
Nancy B., 202, 241, 341, 366.
Nathaniel, 35, 63, 64, 66, 273, 286, 287, 288, 289.
Oliver, 28, 66, 82, 133, 148, 159, 178, 201, 202, 242, 275, 285, 289, 292, 293, 298, 299, 333, 338, 339, 340, 341, 342, 343, 349, 370, 423, 424.
Oliver W., 202.
Oscar C. B., 241.
Patty, 150, 163.
Patty M., 201, 339.
Peninnah, 302, 331.
Persis, 250.
Phinehas, 55, 84, 87, 279.
Polly, 115, 178, 201, 202, 314.
Polly W., 370, 423.
Prudence, 30, 69, 277, 289, 292, 410.
Rebecca, 79, 83, 127, 143, 202, 235, 298, 342.
Relief, 76, 82, 114, 126, 137, 297, 300, 322.
Richard B., 202, 343.
Rufus, 242, 309.
Ruth, 24, 55, 96, 156, 302, 333, 402.
Sally, 121, 177, 178, 201, 202, 266, 268, 335, 354, 371, 397, 424.
Sally P., 425.
Samuel, 19, 20, 54, 55, 57, 59, 60, 62, 64, 67, 69, 71, 72, 158, 202, 273, 274, 275, 276, 277, 279, 280, 281, 282, 284, 286, 288, 289, 292, 293, 294, 306, 307, 309, 311, 324, 336, 349, 402, 451.
Sarah, 30, 55, 76, 114, 156, 201, 232, 277, 278, 296, 313, 322, 334, 335, 345, 350, 394, 425.
Sarah C., 202.
Sarah E., 255.
Sarah F., 202.
Sewall, 123, 178, 201, 236, 337, 338, 349, 366, 368, 425.
Silas, 41, 67, 100, 289.
Silence, 178, 314, 361.
Solomon, 115, 153, 165, 169, 170, 177, 178, 188, 201, 202, 254, 311, 335, 344, 346, 347, 348, 360, 364, 425.
Solon F., 202, 349.
Sophia, 115, 316.
Stanton, 36, 67, 99, 288, 302, 331.
Susan, 168, 172, 318, 322.
Susanna, 66, 115, 123, 167, 173, 177, 201, 287, 315, 316, 340, 342, 402, 425.
Susanna K., 201, 368, 402, 425.

Tempe, 178, 202, 362, 424.
Thankful, 63, 64, 66.
Thomas, 28, 55, 77, 121, 128, 144, 156, 158, 177, 201, 245, 266, 274, 275, 276, 277, 278, 279, 297, 317, 318, 335, 337, 338, 339, 340, 352, 361, 402, 424, 452.
Timothy H., 201, 339.
William, 77, 115, 152, 164, 177, 178, 297, 312, 345, 349, 367.
William C., 247, 266, 423.
Wm. Henry, 177, 201, 202, 347.
———, 267, 395.
CASE, Flavel, 247.
CATO, 311.
CHADWICK, William, 233.
CHAFFIN, D. Francis, 252.
Eliza A., 244.
Jane R., 249.
Matthias F., 250.
CHAMBERLAIN, Eliza J., 258.
Eliza M., 240.
John, 26.
Nathan B., 240.
Otis, 178, 366.
Samuel, 18.
CHAMBERS, Aaron, 202.
Calvin M., 263.
Catharine, 202.
David, 178.
Dorothy R., 252.
Freelove, 263.
George F., 263.
Hannah, 178, 363.
Hiram, 202.
Hiram A., 263.
CHAMPNEY, Joseph, 177, 352.
CHANDLER, Amy, 286.
Anna, 84, 87, 284.
Benjamin, 153, 165, 201, 346, 372, 423.
Charles, 350.
Charles F., 350.
Dolly, 41.
Eleanor, 284.
Eliphalet, 284.
Eliza A., 133, 148, 201, 346.
Elizabeth, 201, 335, 423.
Elizabeth F., 202.
Geo. Frederick, 256, 260.
Hannah, 283.
Henry D., 201.
James, 201, 253, 259, 266, 346, 438.
John, 125, 136.
Julia L., 178, 370, 423.
Louisa A., 259.
Mary A., 201, 266, 346, 371, 438.
Mary E., 202.
Moses, 283, 284, 286, 287.
Nathaniel, 152, 165.
Nathaniel J., 260.
Samuel W., 202.
Sanborn, 283.
Sarah A. G., 201, 346.
Seth, 254.
Susan E., 260.
Thomas, 287.
William D., 201.
CHANNING, Widow, 177.
CHAPIN, Coffin, 132, 177, 351, 353.
Hannah, 243.
Leonard, 177.
Maria L., 249.
Mary, 177, 352.
Orcily, 177.
CHAPLIN, Ann, 29.
CHAPMAN, Angelina, 248.
Lucy, 247.
Sarah H., 255.

CHASE, Abby, 148.
Abel B., 338.
Abigail, 127, 133, 142.
Alanson, 178, 202, 234.
Albert R., 178, 202, 410.
Amy A., 178, 410.
Charles, 178, 183, 233, 410.
Charles H., 202.
Dolly, 126, 138.
Emery, 202.
Emma, 231.
Emma S., 372.
George, 178.
Maria, 178, 202, 410.
Maria A., 202.
Mary, 202.
Miranda, 238.
Moses, 130, 143, 201, 202, 229.
Mrs., 178.
Oliver, 128, 144.
Relief, 150, 163.
Ruth, 201, 202, 410.
Sophia P., 252.
Thomas, 146, 338.
William J., 410.
CHENERY, John, 397.
Lucy A., 202, 343.
Nancy J., 202, 343.
Polly, 202.
Thaddeus, 202, 343.
CHENEY, Abel, 312.
Abigail, 326.
Abner, 313.
Eliakim, 310.
Ephraim, 328.
John, 31.
Timothy, 310, 312, 313.
CHICKERING, John W., 238, 244, 392, 393.
Frances E. K., 392, 393.
Frances E., 393.
Samuel, 396.
Susan, 396.
CHILDS, Abigail W., 392, 393.
George, 349.
Ira G., 242, 392, 393.
Isaac, 177, 178, 201, 229, 268, 336, 348, 349, 361, 367, 369, 424.
James, 177, 201, 348, 424.
Jane A., 268, 348, 396, 424.
Josiah, 253, 393, 394.
Josiah G., 393.
Mary, 201, 268, 348, 367, 396, 424.
Polly, 201, 336, 424.
Rosetta, 244.
Rufus, 348.
Sarah, 177, 359, 424.
Sarah R., 237, 348.
CHOATE, Bathsheba, 385.
Patience, 382.
Rebecca, 385.
Stephen, 376, 378, 382, 383, 385.
William, 383.
CHURCH, Alice, 31.
Anes, 57, 59, 64, 272, 281.
Caleb, 31, 289, 388.
Joseph, 31, 57, 281.
Joshua, 24, 31, 38, 57, 59, 64, 99, 272, 273, 281, 288, 289.
Mary, 31.
Prudence, 31, 85, 288.
Silas, 31, 102, 288.
Vashti, 31, 64.
CHURCHILL, Abiah, 115, 299.
Hannah, 23, 88, 99, 115, 299, 320, 324.
Samuel, 23, 115, 299.
———, 324.
CHUTE, Anna M., 261.
George W., 261.
Malvina I., 261.

32

CLAPP, Avery L., 256.
  Thomas, 272.
CLARK, Anna, 142, 178, 364.
  Anne, 129.
  Benjamin, 277.
  Betsy, 145.
  Catharine, 149, 162.
  Daniel, 126, 128, 297.
  David, 277.
  Edward, 330.
  Edward W., 263.
  Elhanan W., 263.
  Elizabeth, 67, 128, 144, 290, 320, 329.
  Elizabeth D., 394.
  Eunice, 149, 162.
  Hovey, 390.
  Hubbard, 390.
  Isaac, 135.
  James, 84, 177, 178, 360.
  Joanna, 30.
  John, 258, 296, 399.
  Lois, 238.
  Lucy, 153, 165.
  Mary, 67, 289, 295, 399.
  Matthew, 67, 285, 289, 290, 293, 294, 295, 296, 297, 298, 323, 324, 399.
  Nancy, 315, 332.
  Polly, 131, 146, 318, 332.
  Rebecca, 390.
  S——, 446.
  Sally, 128, 144, 315, 332.
  Samuel, 390.
  Sarah, 298, 399.
  Susan, 263.
  Sybil, 145.
  Thomas H., 372.
  William, 294.
  William L., 241.
CLELAND, Elizabeth, 388.
  Hannah, 22.
  Helen, 68.
  James, 22, 27, 28, 68, 80, 82.
  John, 22, 82.
  Jonas, 22.
  Lydia, 387.
  Mary, 22.
  Pamela, 386.
  Samuel, 22.
  Thankful, 22, 68, 80, 82.
  Thomas, 68, 101, 386, 387, 388.
CLEVELAND, Henry R., 343.
  Hiller, 177.
  Horace W. S., 346.
  James A., 345.
  Joseph H., 345, 411.
  Mary, 177, 358, 411.
  Richard J., 181, 336, 343, 346.
  Thomas, 38.
  William, 177, 230, 335, 344, 345, 359, 411.
  William S., 344.
CLEVERLY, Huldah, 364.
  Sarah, 177, 355.
  Stephen, 155, 178, 366.
CLISBY, Mary, 237.
COBB, Benjamin, 265.
  Charles, 265.
  Laura, 234.
  Laura L., 246.
  Miranda, 265.
COBLEIGH, John, 99.
  Joseph, 88.
COBURN and COLBURN.
  Charles, 202.
  David H., 202.
  Elijah, 149, 162, 178, 202, 240, 269, 397, 424.
  Jacob, 238.

Jonas, 202, 234.
Jonathan, 86.
Lucy, 233.
Lucy H., 202.
Nancy W., 202.
Sally, 178, 202, 365, 424.
Sarah, 83.
COFFIN, Ralph, 133, 148.
COGSWELL, Charles, 170.
  Parsons, 256.
COLLAR, Mary, 289.
COLLINS, Aaron, 242.
  Joshua T., 243.
CONANT, Ellen S., 267, 372.
  Lucy A., 258.
  Maria, 268, 396.
  Sally, 154.
  Sherman, 268, 396.
  Sophia, 372.
  Thomas, 34.
  William F., 253.
COMMONS, John, 251.
  Michael, 252.
CONQUERETTE, Abigail, 139, 140, 376.
  Louis, 82, 85, 88, 384.
  Mary, 82, 178, 369, 384, 424.
CONSTANTINE, Jesse, 172.
CONVERSE, Josiah, 21, 27, 32.
CONWAY, Julia, 251.
COOK, Aaron, 148, 177, 201, 447, 448.
  Betsy, 447.
  Caroline, 201.
  Charity, 389.
  Daniel, 38.
  Elizabeth, 201, 417.
  Francis, 252.
  George W., 201, 235.
  Harriet, 177, 447.
  Horatio N., 201.
  Israel, 379, 389.
  Jas. Madison, 201.
  Jesse, 229.
  Jonathan, 197.
  Josiah, 379.
  Lucia, 201.
  Lucinda W., 247, 394.
  Ruth, 389.
  Samuel, 356.
  Sarah, 46, 104, 231.
  Susan, 448.
COOLEY, Aaron, 155, 166.
  Obadiah, 397.
COOLEDGE, Elizabeth, 310.
  Esther, 129.
  Flavel, 154.
  John, 126, 139.
  Jonas, 162.
  Joseph, 310.
  Josiah, 328.
  Josiah A., 256.
  Margaret, 125.
  Silas, 246.
COOMBS, David, 239.
COOPER, Leonard, 380, 417.
  Moses, 80, 375, 380, 417.
  Phebe, 41, 80, 380.
  Priscilla, 85, 88.
  Ruth, 80, 380, 417.
COPELAND, Almira, 202.
  Charles, 202.
  Charles Henry, 202.
  Delia, 202.
  Elisha, 235.
  Mary, 202.
CORBET, Cæsar, 130, 330.
COREY, Benjamin, 26, 276, 278.
  Charles, 340.
  Dinah, 43.

Frances, 46.
Mary, 278.
Molly, 44.
Nancy, 334, 340.
Patience, 314, 328.
Philip, 129, 141, 314, 315, 328.
Rebecca, 177, 276, 340, 356, 425.
Sally, 231, 340.
Samuel, 142, 330.
Stephen, 129, 141, 177, 425.
Triphena, 229, 334, 340, 425.
Widow, 325.
CORNING, William H., 257, 258.
CORTHALL, Lettice, 136.
COTTING, Katy, 146, 150, 163.
  Nancy, 177, 353.
  Thankful, 150, 163.
COTTON, Ward M., 236.
COURSER, Archelaus, 11, 12, 13, 20.
  Mary, 13.
  Rachel, 11, 12, 13.
  Simon, 12, 13.
COY, Abigail, 24.
COWEY, James, 83, 85, 376, 384.
  John, 384.
  Mary, 376.
COWDRY, Elizabeth N., 258.
  Isaac, 237, 447.
  Nathaniel N., 245.
  Rebecca, 155, 334, 341.
  Ruth, 447.
  William, 239.
CRAIG, James, 264.
  Jemima H., 264.
  William, 148, 162.
CRANE, Albert, 267, 395.
CRAWFORD, Robert, 102.
  William, 84.
CREFORD, John, 29.
CROOKER, Sally, 154, 165.
CROOME, William, 241.
CROSBY, Ann R., 351.
  Hannah, 380.
  Joel, 385.
  John, 31, 76, 375, 379, 380, 381, 382, 383, 384, 385, 386.
  Jonathan, 73, 380.
  Levi, 76, 381, 383.
  Mindwell, 73, 76.
  Samuel, 45, 104.
  Sarah, 382.
  Zervia, 384.
CROSFIELD, Adam, 79.
  Elizabeth, 79.
  Hephzibah, 79, 297.
  James, 79, 297, 298.
  Timothy A., 298.
CROSMAN, Alfred W., 250.
  Edward J., 396.
  Elijah, 96.
  James, 41, 96, 97, 103.
  John W., 244.
  Jonathan, 98.
  Mary, 96, 97.
  Nancy P., 246.
  Rebecca A. A., 253.
  Susan, 396.
CROSS, Abigail C., 257.
  Joseph W., 254, 255.
CROUCH, David, 64.
  John, 64.
  Jonathan, 60.
  Mary, 64.
  Susan H., 250.
CUMMINGS, Anna M., 202, 268, 396, 423.
  Catharine, 314.
  Clarissa, 229.
  Dolly, 313, 331.

John, 264, 313.
Mary L., 202, 248, 268, 396, 423.
Michael, 264.
Right, 202, 236, 268, 396, 423.
Susanna, 128.
Thomas, 126, 138, 313, 314, 329.
CUNNINGHAM, Betsy L., 259.
Christiana, 202.
John, 202, 247, 259, 260.
Louisa, 202, 259, 260.
Walter R., 260.
CURRAN, John, 264.
Mary, 264.
CURTIS, James, 109, 389.
John, 35, 85.
Moses, 245.
Sarah H., 109, 241.
Sophia, 109, 389.
Timothy H., 151, 163.
CUSHING, Job, 24, 288.
Joseph, 256, 373.
CUTLER, Dorcas, 451.
James, 448.
Rebecca P., 448.
CUTTER, Hannah, 37.
CUTTING, Absalom, 59, 281.
Dinah, 59, 61, 282.
Jonas, 59, 61, 130, 281, 282.
Jonathan, 229.
Joseph, 129, 139.
Josiah, 21, 34, 83, 86, 131, 146.
Orpha, 136.
Persis, 46.
Rebecca, 241.
Samuel A., 253.
Stephen, 178, 202.
CYRUS, ——, 325.
DABY, Elizabeth, 230, 235.
John, 39.
Phebe, 140.
William, 240.
DAILY, Alice, 252.
John, 264.
Michael, 264.
DAKIN, Abigail, 61, 62, 64, 67.
Ebenezer, 61, 62, 64, 67, 282, 283, 397.
Elizabeth, 62, 283.
Jesse, 67.
John, 28.
Lydia, 27, 32.
Sarah, 61, 282.
DALAND, Benjamin, 253.
DALTON, John P., 173.
DAME, Abby E., 260.
Eliza E., 260.
John T., 249, 260, 267.
John W., 267, 395.
DAMON, Aaron A., 179, 203.
Abigail, 203, 333, 425, 426.
Abraham, 362.
Abraham P., 179, 203, 426.
Ann J., 261.
Betsy, 168, 172.
Caroline L., 203.
Charlotte M., 259.
Charles E., 259.
Charles H., 261.
Darius, 20.
Edwin H., 203.
Esther, 251.
Esther A., 258.
George H., 261.
Hannah, 149.
Harriet, 257, 395.
Harriet H., 179, 203.
Henry W., 259.
Jabez, 230.
Jerophas E., 203.

John Warren, 179, 202, 203, 249, 394, 395.
Jonas M., 202, 248, 261, 395, 426.
Joseph, 362.
Joseph W., 179, 203.
Levi W., 203, 244, 259.
Margaret, 261, 426.
Margaret Ann, 426.
Martha W., 203, 244.
Mary L., 203.
Michael S., 203.
Nancy M., 179, 203, 394.
Polly, 173, 179, 202, 203.
Rachel, 394.
Rachel R., 203.
Rebecca, 266, 425.
Samuel, 154, 166, 172, 179, 202, 203, 236, 266, 333, 394, 395, 425, 426.
Susanna, 248.
William, 153, 165, 179, 203, 426.
DANA, Caroline J., 260.
Eliza A., 260.
Henrietta E. 260.
Mary F., 260.
Stephen, 260.
Tabitha, 172.
DANFORTH, Doctor F., 179, 426.
Elias, 179, 203, 255, 268, 396, 425.
Eliza L., 203.
Lucy, 179, 203, 268, 371, 396, 425.
Nancy, 203.
Octa, 203.
Orphan, 143.
Roxana, 203.
Sarah, 179, 358, 366, 426.
Sarah A., 203, 268, 396, 425.
DANIELS, Mary A., 255.
DARBY and DERBY.
Elizabeth, 267, 372.
Eunice, 307.
Mary, 86, 88.
Nancy, 246.
Oliver, 168, 171, 172.
Rosellina M., 268, 397.
Simon, 155, 166.
Thomas, 154, 166.
William, 397.
DARLING, Margaret, 167, 172.
Mary, 127, 140.
DAVENPORT, Elizabeth, 85.
Eunice, 25.
John, 166.
John S., 244, 245.
Mary, 322.
Sarah, 27.
Submit, 34.
DAVIDSON, Peter E., 250.
DAVIS and DAVIES.
Austin, 255, 371, 426.
Betsy, 203.
Catharine. 203.
Cynthia, 240, 261.
Daniel, 250, 261.
Elisha, 203.
Eliza P., 243.
Emily, 266, 371.
Emma, 260, 267, 396, 426.
Emma F., 260.
Francis, 41. 103, 179, 357.
Franklin, 203.
Hannah. 260, 267, 396, 426.
Harriet A., 203.
Helen, 260.
Herbert W., 261.
Hezekiah, 266, 372.
Hollis, 244, 260, 267, 396, 426.
John, 203, 231.
John Buxton, 203.

Jonathan, 179, 261, 366, 368, 369.
Joseph, 243, 268, 395.
Julia, 256.
Levi, 148.
Lois, 103, 134.
Lorinda, 241.
Lucy, 323.
Mary, 10, 266.
Mary A., 257.
Mary J., 261.
Miriam, 85.
Olive, 246, 261.
Peggy, 179, 351, 369.
Peter, 363.
Prince, 327.
Ruth, 129.
Sally, 426.
Samuel, 10, 20.
Samuel A., 257.
Sarah, 256.
Sumner, 203.
Susan, 203, 255, 373, 394.
Susan M. T., 241.
Sylvia, 203.
Thomas, 179, 266, 369, 371.
Tryphosa, 203.
Walter A., 265, 371, 426.
William, 241, 243.
DAY, Elizabeth M., 263.
Enos A., 263.
Enos H., 263, 263.
Stephen, 19.
DEACONS, list of, 373.
DEAN, Charles, 179, 203, 425.
Dolly, 203.
Emily, 179, 203, 337, 366, 425.
Emily S., 349.
Francis P., 203.
George B., 203.
George C., 203.
John, 179, 203, 349, 366, 425.
John P., 203, 349.
Martha P., 349.
Samuel B., 349.
Sarah B., 179, 203, 425.
DELANO, Caroline, 251.
DEMERRY, Clarissa, 155.
DENNY, Edward, 251.
Patrick, 264.
DEPUTRON, Becky, 116.
Polly, 209.
Rebecca, 233, 304, 312.
Sarah, 110, 126. 179, 300, 351, 360.
William, 83, 87, 110, 116, 127, 135, 142, 178, 299, 300, 304, 312, 320, 355.
DEXTER, Roxana, 179, 364.
Sarah, 236.
DIAS, David, 252.
DICKERSON and DICKENSON.
Alfred, 203.
Damaris, 332.
Eliza, 203.
James, 119, 312.
Lemuel. 119, 312.
Lois, 203.
Lucy, 119, 153.
Miss, 267, 395.
Moses, 119, 168, 171, 179, 203, 267, 310, 311, 312, 313, 314, 331. 358, 359, 396.
Nancy, 203, 267, 396.
Paul, 39, 100. 119, 310.
Rebecca, 119, 179, 313, 331, 360.
Samuel, 119, 126, 137, 314, 363.
Sarah, 40, 88.
Sarah E., 250.
Stephen, 119, 179, 367.
DIGGINS, James, 42, 102.
DINAH, 21, 295, 325, 328.

INDEX.

DITSÓN, Prudence, 240.
DIVOLL, Abigail, 74, 133, 148.
 Alice, 114, 154, 165, 316.
 Arethusa, 150, 163.
 Asa, 306.
 Caroline C., 203.
 Dolly, 154, 165, 203, 334.
 Edward, 203.
 Edward W., 261.
 Elizabeth, 17, 39, 70, 74, 76, 77, 79, 89, 92, 96, 100, 132, 146, 161, 179, 273, 292, 293, 303, 320, 358.
 Ellen M., 203.
 Emily O., 203.
 Ephraim, 39, 70, 74, 76, 77, 79, 89, 92, 96, 112, 114, 134, 161, 178, 179, 274, 292, 293, 295, 296, 299, 300, 301, 303, 305, 311, 314, 316, 317, 320, 328, 352, 356.
 Esther, 114, 154, 165, 179, 314.
 Frances A., 203.
 George, 203.
 George D., 261.
 Hannah, 12, 14, 16.
 James, 89, 128, 144, 301, 316, 338.
 Jane, 93, 302, 303, 331.
 John, 11, 12, 14, 16, 24, 34, 56, 59, 63, 86, 273, 281, 314.
 Josiah, 12, 16, 32, 93, 274, 302, 303, 304, 306, 307, 331.
 Julia A., 203.
 Kezia, 114, 243, 317.
 Levi, 93, 304.
 Luke, 147.
 Manasseh, 27, 28, 92, 178, 179, 275, 291, 303, 352, 366.
 Mary, 18, 93, 273, 302, 332.
 Mary L., 361.
 Mary M., 261.
 Mr. ——, 325.
 Patience, 77, 179, 296, 364.
 Peter, 112, 154, 166, 179, 202, 311, 357.
 Phineas, 59, 281.
 Prudence, 79, 142, 299.
 Rebecca, 76, 77, 125, 136, 179, 203, 295, 364.
 Relief, 112, 114, 142, 300, 322, 366.
 Ruth, 18, 271, 273, 323.
 Samuel, 79, 161, 300, 329, 338.
 Sarah, 56, 59, 63, 125, 203, 259, 307.
 Submit, 272, 273.
 Susan, 179.
 Susanna, 96, 139, 152, 163, 178, 202, 231, 305, 355.
 Thomas, 129, 142, 179, 203, 231, 238.
 William, 14, 27, 203, 235, 269, 271, 273, 274, 275, 300, 425, 451.
 William C., 203.
 William F., 251.
DIXON, Sarah, 155.
DODD, John, 231.
DODGE, George, 450.
 Noah, 332.
 Sally W., 450.
 Sarah, 196.
DOLE, Anna, 38.
 Barnet W., 389.
 Benjamin, 40, 71, 379, 387, 388, 389.
 Betty P., 389.
 Dolly, 127, 387.
 Dolly R., 100, 143, 385.
 Dunsmoor, 100, 386.
 Elijah, 81, 386.
 Enoch, 37, 98, 100, 385, 386, 387, 388, 389.
 Eunice, 100, 126, 138.
 Hannah, 71, 73, 81, 375.
 Illsley, 100, 387.
 Jeremiah, 381.
 John, 380.
 Polly, 100, 131, 146, 388.
 Relief, 387.
 Sarah, 39, 73, 380.
 Thomas, 39, 71, 73, 81, 375, 379, 380, 381, 382.
DOLLISON and DORRISON.
 Almira J., 203.
 Barzillai, 203.
 Charles M., 203, 258.
 Daniel, 179, 203.
 Eliza Ann, 203, 355, 395.
 Eliza W., 169, 171.
 Elizabeth F., 203.
 Elizabeth W., 203.
 Ellen E., 203.
 Esther, 179, 203.
 George A., 203.
 Jane A., 255.
 John, 128, 144, 178, 179, 203, 353, 354.
 Levi P., 203.
 Lucy, 178, 179, 203.
 Margaret B., 203.
 Mary Ann, 203.
 Mary E., 264.
 Nancy, 203, 395.
 Nancy P., 203, 247.
 Nancy T., 203, 235.
 Oscar A., 203.
 Samuel, 169, 174, 203, 228.
 Samuel A., 203, 247, 264.
DOLLOFF, Thomas, 257.
DONELLY, John, 252.
DORCHESTER, Daniel, 91, 282, 382, 383.
 David, 85, 383.
 Ishmael, 91, 383.
 Margaret, 36, 85, 91, 98, 382.
DORRITY, Elizabeth, 88.
DOUGLAS, Sarah, 22, 34, 381, 391.
DRAPER, Prissa, 231.
 Timothy, 234.
DRESSER, Aaron, 41, 73, 375, 379, 380, 381, 417.
 Betty, 116, 390.
 David N., 111, 390.
 David W., 338.
 Elijah, 129, 128, 381.
 Elizabeth, 111, 116, 339.
 Hannah, 417.
 Hitty, 111.
 Jedediah, 379, 417.
 John, 46, 73, 111, 116, 380, 417.
 Mehetabel, 73, 88, 376, 390, 417.
 Olive, 338.
 Oliver, 37, 98, 385.
 Rufus, 338, 339.
DRUSE, Betty, 197.
DUDLEY, Andrew J., 179, 203.
 Caroline M., 393.
 Charles Henry, 203, 393.
 Eliza, 392.
 Esther E., 179, 203, 392, 393.
 E. S., 393.
 James, 87.
 John, 179, 203.
 John E., 205, 393.
 Martha A., 393.
 Nathan A. M., 393.
 Sarah L., 393.
DUFORE, Abraham, 294.
 David, 41, 42, 294.
 Hephzibah, 21, 32, 294.
DUNLAP, Betsy, 149, 262.
 Elizabeth, 202.
 Paulina, 178.
 Polly, 354.
 Samuel, 162, 178, 202, 353, 354.
 Tyler, 178, 202.
DUNN, Asa, 392.
 John L., 348.
 Lucas, 234, 348.
 Luzima, 392.
 Mary, 234.
DUNSMOOR, Agnus, 36, 98.
 Anes, 106.
 Betty, 30, 112.
 Catharine, 84, 87.
 Father, 285.
 Elizabeth, 73, 99, 379.
 Eunice, 62, 84, 87, 291, 405.
 Hannah, 130, 145, 320, 405.
 Jane, 73, 81.
 John, 40, 62, 73, 96, 101, 106, 112, 130, 145, 291, 298, 323, 405.
 Joseph, 42, 73, 102, 106, 380.
 Martha, 33, 34, 86.
 Mary, 84.
 Olive, 81, 405.
 Oliver, 73, 288.
 Phebe, 106.
 Prudence, 179, 369.
 Reuben, 101.
 Ruth, 44, 97, 103, 106, 381.
 Sarah, 96, 101, 106, 112.
 Silvanus, 106.
 Stansbury, 252.
 William, 33, 40, 62, 73, 81, 87, 97, 160, 288, 291, 292, 298, 319, 324, 327, 329, 379, 380, 381, 405.
DUNTON, Mary E., 372.
DUPEE, Naomi, 37, 87.
DURANT, Daniel P., 344.
 Solomon, 344.
 Sophia, 168, 171, 335, 344.
 Thomas, 152, 164, 353.
 William, 344.
DURSTER, Ruhamah, 46.
DUTTON, Thankful, 84.
DYER, Albert, 234.
 Ellen M., 264.
 Jedediah, 179.
 Jeremiah, 236, 448.
 Patrick M., 264.
 Susan, 179, 448.
EAMS, Abigail, 280.
 Charles, 277.
 Dorothy, 276.
 Jethro, 17, 276, 277, 280.
 Prudence, 277.
 Simon, 277.
EAGAN, Edward, 252.
EAGER, Abigail, 108.
 Althina, 204, 369, 394, 426.
 Benjamin, 204, 346.
 Betsy, 179, 204, 369.
 Caroline, 426.
 Caroline A., 251.
 Dinah, 111.
 Eliza, 204.
 Elizabeth, 108, 389.
 Ephraim, 91, 386.
 Ephron, 111.
 Farwell, 179, 204, 232, 365, 366, 368, 426.
 Fortunatus, 89, 91, 92, 95, 99, 100, 110, 111, 112, 114, 377, 386, 387, 388, 389, 417.
 Francis, 41, 103.
 Hannah, 112.
 Haran, 111, 149, 162, 179, 187, 204, 364, 385.
 John B., 204.
 Lewis, 204, 346.
 Mehetabel, 89, 92, 386, 417.
 Mercy, 204.
 Molly, 114.

Nathan, 46, 89, 90, 111, 384, 385.
Sally, 204.
Samuel, 204.
Sarah, 89, 90, 111, 332.
Sarah A., 426.
Tamar, 91, 92, 95, 100, 110, 112, 114, 389.
Winslow, 95, 387.
Zachariah, 108, 389.
Zerababel, 89, 384.
Zilpah, 89, 384.
EARL, Miranda R., 235.
EASTMAN, Felicia A., 179, 369.
Letty J., 258.
EATON, Betsy, 204, 240, 314, 335.
Catharine, 318, 335.
Catharine M., 204.
Charles, 204, 317.
Collins, 390.
Eliza J., 262.
Eliza J. B., 262.
Esther, 204, 340, 492, 393.
Henry, 124, 204, 313.
Rev. J. M. R., 254, 255, 256.
John, 129, 139, 204, 315.
Joseph, 204, 318.
Lucy, 124, 204, 267, 372, 394, 426.
Lucy Ann, 255.
Martha, 327.
Mary, 204, 390.
Nancy, 162, 204, 312.
Nathaniel, 124, 126, 132, 138, 146, 179, 204, 311, 312, 313, 314, 315, 316, 317, 318, 327, 340, 362, 426.
Polly, 314.
Rebecca, 389.
Sally, 149, 162, 204, 311.
Susan, 254.
Theophilus, 204, 316.
William, 248, 262, 389.
EDDY, Charles, 269.
Lucretia, 255.
Luke, 255.
EDES, Anna, 230.
EDGELL, Nancy, 229.
EDGERTON, Benjamin, 179, 338, 342, 355, 426.
Maryann, 426.
Merrial, 179, 342.
Otis, 338.
Sarah, 171, 179, 355, 426.
Sylvia, 231.
EDMUNDS, Rebecca, 33.
EDWARDS, S——, 446.
Sibley Ann, 252.
ELBRIDGE, Margaret J., 264.
Martin, 264.
ELDER, James, 43, 104.
Nancy, 151, 164.
Rebecca, 152, 164.
Sally, 148, 161.
ELITHRAP, Elizabeth, 329.
ELLENWOOD, Arah, 204, 236.
Eliza A., 204.
Elizabeth, 204.
ELLERY, Almy, 146.
ELLIOTT, Almira, 237.
Polly, 234.
ELLIS, Catharine, 45.
Joseph, 133, 148.
EMERY, Darius, 234.
Janette S., 256.
Reuben, 372.
EMERSON, Alfred, 257.
Augustus, 342.
Charles, 204, 253, 342.
Clarissa, 204, 342.
Daniel, 105.
Elias, 179, 203, 204, 340, 342, 343, 426, 427.

Eunice, 179, 204.
Eunice W., 411.
Francis B., 204.
Francis P., 411.
Hazen, 411.
Hiram, 204.
Jacob, 39.
Joseph, 154, 166, 239, 354, 426.
Judith K., 411.
Louisa, 237.
Lydia, 179, 204, 357.
Lydia C., 411.
Mary, 230.
Moses, 171, 172, 179, 204, 359, 361, 411.
Moses K., 411.
Nancy, 203, 239, 340.
Oliver, 204, 247, 340.
Phebe, 203, 204, 357, 392, 393, 426, 427.
Ralph, 257.
Sally, 179, 356.
Sally C., 179, 204, 411.
Sophia, 204, 239.
ENGLESBY, see Ingoldsby.
ESTERBROOKS, Hannah, 137.
ESTY, Mary, 250.
EUERS, Samuel, 154, 166.
EUNICE, 311, 390.
EUSTIS, Thomas C., 247.
EVANS, Emily, 256.
George W., 204.
Jeremiah, 204, 357.
Martha S., 252.
Sampson W., 395.
Sarah, 204.
Sarah O., 204.
EVELETH, Anna, 37, 98.
Diana, 334, 340.
Elizabeth, 97, 300, 306.
Ephraim, 109, 179, 307, 340, 352.
Eunice, 89, 92, 95, 97, 109, 110, 129, 141, 150, 163, 303, 326.
Hudson, 326.
Isaac, 83, 87, 89, 92, 95, 97, 109, 110, 300, 301, 303, 306, 307, 309, 383.
Jacob, 305.
John, 89, 301.
Nancy D., 340.
Samuel, 110, 309.
Stephen, 95, 305.
William, 89, 383.
Zimri, 92, 143, 303.
EVERETT, Louisa, 179, 368.
FAIRBANK, Abel, 302, 314, 327.
Abigail, 24, 83, 101, 107, 137, 181, 273, 332, 369, 377, 384, 385.
Abijah, 22, 293.
Alpheus, 107, 387.
Amos, 390.
Ann, 101.
Anna, 27, 28, 113, 275, 306, 307, 326, 389, 404.
Archibald, 268, 396.
Augustus A., 117.
Barakbakworth, 114, 390.
Betsey, 168, 171, 315.
Beulah, 60, 101, 282, 389.
Calvin, 297.
Charles T., 206.
Cyrus, 6, 22, 37, 54, 99, 113, 114, 126, 127, 131, 137, 140, 146, 180, 181, 184, 278, 286, 303, 304, 305, 306, 307, 308, 310, 313, 314, 315, 318, 320, 325, 326, 327, 328, 329, 330, 353, 367, 373, 404, 428.
Deborah, 83, 165.
Dinah, 58, 280.
Dolly, 111, 130, 388.
Dorothy, 51, 66, 67, 72, 74, 285, 287.
Eddy, 264.
Elijah, 22, 284.
Eliza, 107.
Elizabeth, 17, 22, 41, 58, 103, 114, 180, 206, 244, 271, 273, 279, 292, 295, 299, 300, 328, 360, 388, 404, 428.
Elisha, 111.
Ephraim, 72, 101, 114, 290, 388, 411.
Eunice, 43, 74, 104, 288, 291, 294, 302, 323.
Francis L., 206.
Grace, 10, 17, 25, 274, 405.
Hannah, 89, 107, 289, 384, 405.
Hasadiah, 12, 451.
Hepzibah, 58, 60, 62, 284.
Jabez, 13, 17, 35, 58, 60, 62, 65, 83, 85, 87, 89, 106, 107, 112, 270, 271, 273, 274, 275, 276, 277, 279, 280, 282, 284, 287, 288, 289, 290, 319, 323, 324, 376, 384, 385, 387, 388, 389, 390, 404, 405, 452.
James, 101, 389.
Joel, 308.
John, 33, 51, 117, 281, 312, 314, 328, 376, 378, 381, 382, 383, 391.
Jonas, 10, 11, 12, 13, 14, 16, 17, 22, 25, 44, 62, 104, 113, 180, 189, 272, 273, 282, 283, 284, 286, 288, 290, 292, 293, 295, 297, 310, 319, 320, 330, 333, 362, 364, 404, 405, 428.
Jonathan, 11, 17, 23, 51, 57, 63, 65, 71, 85, 106, 107, 158, 160, 274, 282, 285, 287, 288, 291, 292, 374, 379, 380, 381, 382, 383, 384, 385, 397, 405, 411, 417, 451.
Joseph, 17, 38, 53, 54, 57, 59, 67, 101, 151, 156, 272, 276, 277, 278, 280, 281, 289, 291, 377, 386, 387, 388, 389, 405.
Joshua, 10, 16, 27, 43, 71, 74, 101, 106, 117, 160, 274, 285, 288, 289, 290, 291, 293, 294, 297, 298, 299, 300, 302, 307, 308, 310, 311, 314, 315, 319, 321, 325, 373, 379, 417.
Josiah, 22, 35, 62, 99, 101, 271, 283, 318, 377, 385, 386, 387, 388, 389, 390.
Katie, 111, 389.
Laura P., 206.
Lemuel, 104, 106, 114, 289, 381, 390.
Levi, 101, 390.
Lucy, 113, 114, 155, 167, 236, 269, 303, 304, 321, 327, 333, 404.
Lucy A., 206, 392, 393.
Luther, 125, 137, 298, 311, 312, 321.
Lydia, 10, 11, 12, 14, 59, 111, 281, 388.
Manasseh, 101, 297, 386.
Martha, 22, 34, 62, 86, 101, 206, 282, 300, 327, 387, 411.
Martha A., 206, 393.
Martha T., 206, 241.
Mary, 10, 17, 22, 38, 53, 54, 57, 59, 72, 100, 101, 156, 180, 271, 277, 280, 290, 292, 320, 363, 404, 405, 428, 451, 452.
Mary A., 268, 396.
Mercy, 54, 156.
Miriam, 83, 89, 107, 112, 385.
Molly, 101, 387.
Nabby, 153, 165, 313.
Nahum, 382.
Olive, 112.
Oliver, 45, 378, 381, 389, 390.
Patience, 390.

INDEX.

Phebe, 114.
Phineas, 53, 276, 300.
Rebecca, 101, 106, 117, 310, 321, 350, 385.
Relief, 381.
Rhoda, 288.
Sally, 107, 169, 229, 318, 330, 387, 404.
Samuel, 51, 111, 280, 315, 383.
Sarah, 22, 28, 41, 103, 113, 205, 206, 276, 293, 308, 321.
Sarah A., 246.
Sawyer A., 264.
Seth, 106, 128, 265, 383, 390, 394.
Silas, 40, 74, 103, 111, 205, 206, 267, 269, 377, 380, 388, 389, 395, 411.
Silas H., 248.
Susan, 390.
Susanna, 291.
Thankful, 22, 43, 62, 63, 65, 71, 106, 114, 158, 160, 272, 282, 285, 297, 312, 322, 351, 382, 390, 404, 411, 417.
Thomas, 24, 51, 66, 67, 72, 74, 101, 273, 280, 281, 282, 285, 286, 287, 289, 290, 292, 293, 374, 380, 331, 387.
Timothy J., 206, 238, 293, 394.
William, 63, 106, 126, 139, 160, 287, 384.
FALES, Amy, 153, 165, 204, 205, 206, 269, 427.
Anna,
Daniel, 205.
Ephraim, 205.
Jeremiah, 168, 171, 180, 187, 204, 205, 206, 269, 361, 367, 427.
Loisa, 205.
Lydia, 335.
Martha, 205, 206.
Mary Ann, 205.
Nancy, 155, 167.
Olive, 205.
Rachel, 367.
Sophia, 206, 367, 427.
Susan, 242.
Susanna, 204.
Tempe, 154, 166.
Warren, 205, 427.
FALLASS, Charity, 411.
William, 411.
FALLON, Mary, 252.
FANNING, Michael, 246.
FARMER, Anna, 311.
Benjamin, 104, 134, 310, 311, 312, 313, 321, 332.
Hannah, 137.
Henry W., 125, 136, 312, 322.
Jonathan, 312.
Martha, 312.
Phebe, 303.
Sally, 180.
Sarah, 310, 321.
Uzziah, 313.
Widow, 303.
William, 312.
William H., 312.
——, 325.
FARNSWORTH, Abigail, 150, 181.
Abigail M., 204, 343.
Abijah H., 205, 343.
Andrew J., 204, 206, 248, 251, 261, 267, 426.
Angelina, 205.
Asa, 117.
Asa D., 180, 206, 243, 259, 261, 428.
Augustus, 204, 345.
Benjamin, 148, 154, 161, 165, 180, 181, 204, 205, 343, 345, 346, 355, 361, 428.

Benjamin F., 205, 206, 247, 259, 264.
Benjamin S., 206.
Betsy, 180, 206, 259, 261, 428.
Caroline, 392, 393.
Caroline S., 261.
Catharine M., 206, 426.
Catharine P., 267, 394, 395.
Charles, 180, 205, 343.
Cynthia A., 206, 259, 264.
Dorcas, 204, 205, 428.
Edward E., 180, 206, 428.
Elias, 103, 117, 134.
Ephraim, 117.
Frederick Z., 264.
George W., 259.
Hannah, 152, 164.
James, 180, 204, 205, 346, 428.
James D., 206.
John A., 259.
John E., 206.
Jonas, 205.
Joseph, 126.
Joseph E., 259.
Lois, 117.
Lovina, 239.
Lydia, 205.
Mark A., 206.
Mary, 205, 234, 343.
Mary C., 261.
Merrick P., 261.
Nancy, 204, 242.
Nathaniel F., 149, 162.
Polly, 181, 369.
Ruth, 397.
Sally, 180, 204, 205, 231, 343, 428.
Samuel, 451.
Sarah, 181, 334, 371,
Sarah E., 261.
Silas, 300.
Thankful, 43.
William H., 206.
Zaccheus, 300.
FARNUM, Amos, 244.
FARR, Amanda M., 258.
John, 255.
FARRAR, Adam H., 70.
Ann, 13, 452.
Daniel, 381.
David, 28, 66.
Derias, 77.
Dinah, 24.
Elizabeth, 66, 72, 379.
George, 13.
Hannah, 13, 17, 78, 80, 134, 382.
Henry, 16.
Jacob, 13, 16, 17, 19, 452.
Joanna, 39.
John, 12, 13, 14, 17, 64, 66, 68, 70, 72, 74, 77, 78, 80, 84, 87, 286, 288, 290, 376, 378, 379, 381, 382, 384.
Joseph, 13, 341, 452.
Mary, 22, 13, 64, 66, 68, 70, 72, 74, 77, 78, 80, 452.
Nathan, 68, 116, 138, 289, 290.
Nathaniel, 74, 134.
Salme, 116.
Sarah, 64, 116, 286.
Tabitha, 66, 288.
Timothy, 289.
FARREN, Nathan, 255.
FARRINGTON, Abner, 103, 134.
FARWELL, Abel, 205.
Abigail, J., 206.
Ann E., 181, 205, 448.
Augusta M., 206.
Benjamin, 120, 245.
Betsy, 120.
Charles, 240.
Daniel W., 181, 206.

Elbridge, 205.
Eliza, 233.
Eliza W., 206.
Eunice, 37, 102.
Frances M., 180, 206.
Francis M., 206, 266.
Frederick H., 205.
George P., 206, 243.
Henry, 149, 162.
James, 205, 230, 269, 427.
Jonathan, 154, 166, 205.
Joseph, 120, 126, 139, 180, 181, 205, 229, 366, 395, 448.
Joseph W., 264.
Leonard, 120, 141, 180, 448.
Levi, 120, 180, 181, 206, 234, 259, 266.
Levi D., 259.
Lorey M., 259.
Lucius A., 206.
Lucius L., 205, 206, 246, 250, 259, 264, 266, 448.
Lucy B., 180, 181, 205, 206, 259, 266.
Martha H., 205, 235.
Mary, 205, 206, 242, 246, 259, 266, 427, 448.
Mary A. R., 206.
Mary E., 205, 256.
Mary I., 259, 448.
Molly, 205.
Ruth, 206.
Sally, 120, 169, 229.
Sarah, 120, 135, 168, 172, 180, 205, 355, 448.
Sarah E., 204.
Sarah M., 205, 254.
Susanna, 133.
FASSETT, Rebecca, 164.
FAULKNER, Abigail, 180, 204, 205, 356, 411.
Amory, 206.
Augustus, 205.
Bathsheba, 206.
Eliza, 205, 351, 392, 394.
Emily, 362, 412.
Emily H., 205, 256, 394.
Eunice, 205, 392, 393, 411.
Francis, 231.
George A., 206.
Hannah, 180, 411.
Harriet, 180, 205, 339, 341.
Horace, 204, 205, 234, 235, 340, 392, 394, 412.
Louisa, 205, 341, 392.
Mary, 392.
Mary D., 205, 248, 393.
Nathaniel S., 239.
Paul, 133, 148, 162, 168, 171, 180, 181, 189, 204, 205, 231, 239, 340, 341, 342, 352, 354, 392, 393, 411.
Sophia, 342, 354.
FAY, Abbie S., 248.
Harriet B., 395, 396.
Josiah, 168, 172, 206, 395, 428.
Mary, 43, 252.
Nancy F., 266, 371, 428.
William B., 56.
FELTON, Charlotte, 235.
Daniel, 358.
Mathias, 127, 143.
Mr. ——, 186.
Sarah H., 251.
FIELD, Charles W., 263.
Lizzie O., 263.
Mary, 263.
FIFE, Abigail, 411.
Deliverance, 411.
Joseph, 211.
Nancy, 234.
Polly, 155.

INDEX. 471

William, 31, 34, 243, 411.
FINNERTY, Bridget, 252.
Michael, 264.
Thomas, 264.
FISHER, Alexander, 205, 342.
Andrew, 205.
Betsy, 205, 368, 428.
Caroline, 205.
Charles, 428.
Charles T., 245.
Charlotte, 205.
David, 204, 343.
Eliza, 205, 349.
Elizabeth, 428.
Elizabeth H., 206.
Ellen S., 261.
Emily, 206.
Ephraim C., 180, 204, 237, 261, 339, 365, 366, 367, 428.
George, 204, 236, 346.
Harriet S., 261.
Isaac, 144, 180, 353.
Jacob, 6, 122, 132, 146, 180, 181, 204, 205, 206, 231, 233, 333, 338, 339, 340, 342, 343, 344, 346, 349, 370, 428.
James, 205, 342.
Joshua, 180, 357.
Louisa, 261.
Lydia P., 246.
Martha, 205, 255.
Mary, 204, 232, 339.
Mary E., 253, 261.
Nancy, 122, 168, 172, 180, 204, 205, 333, 338, 361, 428.
Orricy, 205, 206.
Sally, 120, 235, 340.
Sarah, 205, 253.
Sarah H., 261, 428.
Sophronia, 428.
Susan, 238.
Susanna, 204, 344.
William H., 261.
FISKE, Edward R., 263.
Ella M., 263.
John D., 392.
Jonathan, 151, 164.
Moses, 129.
Priscilla, 257.
Rachel, 38.
Rebecca, 263.
FITCH, Andrew L. H., 206.
Charles T., 205, 255.
Ebenezer, 129, 140.
Edwin Raymond, 206.
Francis G., 205.
George, 181, 205, 206, 236, 371, 427.
Harriet, 205, 206, 428.
Harriet L., 206.
Helen S., 206.
John W. H., 181, 206, 371, 427.
Louisa M. T., 206.
Paul, 309.
Sophronia W., 205, 206, 427.
Torrey, 181, 205, 206, 233, 363, 371, 428.
FITTS, Elizabeth, 251.
FLAGG, Abigail, 322.
Clara S., 256.
Dolly, 121, 180, 204, 205, 232, 333, 339, 367, 428.
Ebenezer, 81, 272, 286, 299.
Elizabeth, 296.
George, 316.
George W., 121, 204, 339.
Gershom, 21, 33, 81, 133, 139, 296, 297, 299, 300, 309, 311, 314, 316, 323, 324, 326, 327, 328, 329, 330, 411.
Grizzle A., 127, 141, 310, 321.

Hannah, 329, 411.
James, 311.
Josiah, 6, 9, 121, 130, 145, 151, 180, 181, 204, 205, 339, 341, 369, 428.
Jotham, 94.
Marian S., 242.
Mary, 36, 81, 88, 296, 297, 320, 330.
Nancy, 249.
Otis, 206, 240.
Polly, 105, 135.
Rebecca, 94, 121, 152, 231, 339.
Sally, 121, 150, 162, 314, 339.
Samuel W., 121. 192, 205, 341.
Sarah, 321, 327.
Sarah E., 206.
Theresa, 206.
William, 16, 121, 180, 339, 355.
Zenobia, 64.
FLEEMAN and FLEMING.
Adam, 79, 89, 91, 92, 107.
Daniel, 89, 91.
David, 79.
Elizabeth, 92.
Eunice, 113.
Louisa, 396.
Margaret, 79, 89, 91, 92, 107, 113, 252.
Mary M., 113.
Solomon, 91.
———, 326.
FLETCHER, Abbie, 249.
Addison F., 264.
Anna, 96, 124, 305, 328.
Artemas, 118, 318.
Ashbel, 303.
Betsy, 120, 338.
Calvin, 251.
Charles, 122, 340.
Charles Thornton, 205, 348.
Christopher, 337.
Cynthia, 118, 318.
David, 79, 298.
David B., 206.
Dorcas, 180, 181, 204, 205, 334, 371, 394, 427.
Dorcas W., 204, 346.
Drusilla, 259.
Edmund, 246.
Edward I... 206.
Eleanor L., 204, 245, 337, 348.
Elijah, 180, 204.
Elisha, 118, 124. 156, 298, 316, 326.
Elizabeth, 74, 159, 295, 319, 334, 341.
Faithful, 181.
George, 122, 340.
George E. W., 259.
George H., 205, 348.
George W., 180, 206.
Hannah, 51, 74, 122, 158, 180, 204, 269, 272, 277, 295, 319, 334, 352, 365, 407.
Hannah F., 427.
Henry, 206.
James F., 205, 340, 348.
Jane A., 206.
Jeduthan, 305.
Joanna, 72, 291, 292.
Joanna B., 206.
Joel, 427.
John, 30, 51, 72, 81, 91, 106, 124, 130, 143, 158, 271, 272, 275, 276, 277, 278, 279, 290, 291, 293, 299, 302, 324, 329, 407, 452.
Jonas, 21, 33, 86.
Joseph, 154, 166, 235.
Joseph A., 264.
Joseph W., 179, 204, 346, 427.

Joshua, 21, 32, 51, 74, 75, 78, 81, 89, 91, 93, 96, 100, 110, 124, 156, 179. 180, 204, 205, 206, 269, 278, 291, 295, 297, 298, 299, 301, 302, 304, 305, 307, 308, 319, 323, 328, 340, 346, 348, 358, 359, 360, 368, 395, 427.
Julia A., 205, 348, 395.
Julia M., 180, 204, 427.
Leonard, 204, 339.
Levi, 204, 340.
Lewis, 180, 205, 206, 239, 342, 367.
Lucy, 106.
Luke, 90.
Lydia, 29, 51, 275.
Martha, 122, 180, 204, 336, 341, 364, 427.
Martha C., 206, 427.
Mary, 74, 75, 78, 81, 89, 91, 93, 96, 100, 110, 120, 124, 147, 156, 179, 180, 204, 205, 295, 301, 302, 322, 332, 340, 356, 358, 368, 394, 427.
Mary Ann, 204, 337, 340.
Nabby W., 179, 180, 204, 205, 206, 395, 427.
Oliver, 79, 299.
Otis, 204, 206, 243.
Persis, 389.
Peter, 91, 124, 128, 144, 302.
Phineas, 78, 120, 124, 146, 204, 297, 318, 332, 338, 339.
Polly, 118, 120, 132, 180, 204, 318.
Rachel, 106, 134.
Rebecca, 79, 90, 91, 180, 296, 302, 319, 321, 328, 360, 367.
Robert, 21, 32, 33, 51, 74, 79, 90, 91, 159, 276, 295, 296, 298, 299, 302, 303, 305, 319, 325, 369.
Roxana, 180, 205, 427.
Rufus, 93, 118, 124, 130, 144, 172, 180, 181, 204, 205, 304, 316, 317, 318, 337, 339, 340, 342, 351, 354, 392, 393, 394, 427.
Ruth, 21, 33, 51, 86, 180, 279, 319, 323, 361.
Sally P., 180, 206.
Sarah, 250.
Sarah A., 206.
Sophia, 100, 118, 124, 132, 147, 307, 317.
Thomas, 340, 427.
Timothy, 51, 75, 122, 124, 180, 204, 269, 295, 318, 334, 340, 341, 351, 361, 427.
William, 110, 124, 153, 165, 180, 181, 204, 205, 249, 259, 308, 334, 337, 343, 346, 355, 427.
FLOOD, Samuel, 326.
William, 139, 145, 180.
FLOYD, Lucinda, 232.
William, 360.
FOLLANSBEE, Sarah, 232.
FORBES, Bridget, 261.
Huldah, 246.
James, 261.
Thomas, 261.
FOSKETT, Abigail, 25.
FOSTER, Alvan C., 206.
Benjamin H., 172, 180, 205, 335, 346, 347, 348, 362, 427.
Calvin, 153.
Caroline, 205, 346.
Catharine, 46.
Charles B., 205, 348.
Coolidge, 232.
Eliza, 205, 348.
Ephraim, 43.
James, 104.
Jeremiah, 206, 240.
Lavina, 205, 347.

INDEX.

Martha, 205, 335, 346, 348.
Nabby, 150, 163.
Oren, 239.
Prudence, 270.
Richard, 407.
Sarah, 206, 238.
FOWLE, Elizabeth, 350.
Jacob, 27, 28, 44, 73, 75, 126, 138, 295, 297, 325, 326.
Joseph, 297, 326.
Mary, 45, 73, 104, 295.
Phebe, 73, 75, 295, 319.
Ruth, 38, 102.
FRANKLIN, Phebe, 229.
Rebecca, 229.
FREELAND, John, 264.
Peter, 264.
FREEMAN, Adelina, 268, 396.
Amos, 167, 173, 180.
Ann, 84.
Julius S., 264.
Mary, 236.
Mercy, 180.
Orianna C., 262.
Patty, 359.
Philip, 151, 164, 247, 267, 268, 372.
Robert S., 262, 264.
Roxana, 268, 396.
Zoa A., 262.
FRENCH, Abel, 340.
Abigail, 126, 128, 137.
Christopher 340.
Desire, 42.
Eunice, 334, 340.
Fidelia, 181, 394, 428.
Levi, 340.
Lucinda, 340.
Samuel, 130, 143, 340.
Seth, 240, 249, 340, 428.
FRINK, Justin E., 117, 315.
Lydia W., 316.
Sarah, 117.
William, 117, 315, 316.
FROST, Elisha B., 251.
John W., 250.
Patience, 36.
Submit, 84, 86, 95, 105.
Stephen, 291.
Zervia, 29.
FROTHINGHAM, Daniel, 155.
Lydia, 237.
Rebecca, 229, 242.
FRYE, Patience, 242.
FUDGER, Doctor, 326.
FULLAM, Eunice, 94, 304.
Francis, 79, 91, 94, 299, 302, 304.
Jacob, 79, 299.
Oliver, 91, 302.
Susanna, 79, 91, 94.
Timothy, 39, 101.
FULLER, Abby G., 267, 396.
Abigail L., 428.
Abner, 204.
Alcy, 204.
Andrew L., 205, 254, 260, 349.
Betsy, 316, 330.
Caroline, 205, 342.
Ebenezer W., 181, 370, 428.
Edward, 153, 180, 204, 205, 334, 342, 343, 354, 355.
Elsie, 126, 128, 343.
Emma S., 260.
Ephraim, 180, 205, 206, 230, 242, 266, 336, 349, 350, 364, 365, 366, 367, 368, 371, 428.
Ephraim H., 180, 206, 349, 428.
Esther, 313.
Francis F., 180, 205, 206, 349, 428.
Franklin W., 266, 371, 428.
George W., 206, 350, 428.

Henrietta M., 330.
Ignatius, 145, 351.
James, 180, 204, 310, 312, 313, 316, 330, 331, 365.
John, 206, 237, 266, 267, 336, 349, 350, 368, 371, 372, 396.
John T., 206, 349.
Joseph, 204.
Joseph S., 205, 342.
Judith, 206, 266.
Lydia, 236.
Lydia A., 266, 371.
Mary Ann, 205, 343.
Mary W., 310.
Mrs., 180.
Nancy, 235, 312.
Nancy G., 350.
Olive H., 260.
Polly, 151, 164.
Sally, 204, 310.
Samuel Ebenezer, 206, 349.
Sarah, 127, 140, 310, 331.
Sidney T., 350.
Sophronia O., 206, 266, 267, 396.
Sophronia M., 206, 349.
Stephen, 129, 141, 328.
Susan, 180, 205, 206, 255, 428.
Susan H., 205, 349.
Susanna, 204, 205, 334, 336, 366.
William A., 350.
FURBUSH, Eunice, 46, 104.
GAFFEL, Elizabeth, 31.
GAGE, Nathaniel, 256.
GANIES, Daniel, 16.
GALLAGHER, Mary Ann, 252.
GALLEY, Rebecca, 232.
GAMBLE, John W., 235.
GARDNER, Abigail, 54, 452.
Andrew, 20, 401.
Lucy, 451.
Mary, 270, 451.
Mary Ann, 246.
Samuel L., 247.
GARFIELD, Cynthia, 250.
Lyman, 229.
GATES, Abigail, 92, 95, 101, 109, 117, 181, 303, 321, 356, 404, 429.
Anna, 64, 66, 68, 70, 75, 101, 109, 124, 296, 307, 322, 328, 329, 330, 403, 404.
Dorothy, 36, 66, 99, 296.
Elias, 230.
Elizabeth, 60, 144.
Hezekiah, 9, 25, 59, 60, 64, 66, 68, 70, 75, 157, 185, 296, 327, 330, 403.
John, 109, 117, 308, 312, 327, 329, 404.
Lucy, 95, 181, 304, 336, 349, 352, 364, 404.
Martha, 230, 335.
Mary, 20, 59, 60, 157, 242.
Mercy, 417.
Miriam, 30.
Nabby, 97, 130, 145, 306.
Patty, 316.
Polly, 148, 161, 310.
Rebecca, 26, 68, 84, 87, 92, 122, 127, 142, 296, 303.
Sarah, 11, 26, 43, 70, 104, 296.
Stephen, 11, 19, 328.
Susanna, 45.
Thomas, 36, 64, 88, 89, 92, 95, 97, 101, 109, 117, 181, 296, 303, 304, 305, 306, 307, 308, 310, 312, 316, 320, 326, 327, 329, 358, 404, 429, 436.
Vashti, 238.
Wilder, 95, 305, 404.
GAYLORD, Catharine A., 262.
Edson D., 262.

Henry F., 262.
Laura, 262, 396.
Luther, 262, 268, 395, 356.
Miles, 395.
GEARY and GARY.
Aaron, 46, 110, 382, 384.
Amity, 376.
Benjamin, 112, 150, 390.
Catharine, 35, 88.
David, 388.
Ephraim, 151.
Hannah, 39.
Hepsy, 148, 161.
Ichabod, 40, 101.
John, 389.
Jonathan, 376, 382, 383.
Joseph, 79, 80, 89, 382, 383, 384, 390.
Kezia, 23.
Lois, 44, 79, 103, 382.
Lucy, 42, 110.
Lucy C., 112.
Mary, 382.
Moses, 382.
Nathan, 38, 98, 383.
Oliver, 384.
Phebe, 39, 101, 382, 387.
Polly, 390.
Prudence, 127, 142.
Reuben, 104, 112, 134, 390.
Rufus, 181, 360.
Ruth, 79, 80, 89, 383, 390.
Sarah, 44.
Susanna, 22, 33.
Thomas, 39, 44, 83, 85, 101, 387, 388, 389, 390.
Wilkes, 232.
GEER, Lucy R., 171.
GEMWELL, Samuel, 84, 87.
GEORGE, ——, 376.
GERRISH, Abigail, 110, 111.
Betty, 111.
Molly, 110.
Moses, 378.
Samuel, 45, 103, 110, 111.
GERRY, Joseph, 235.
GIBBS, Albion W., 263.
Amasa, 62, 284.
Betsy, 261.
Charles W., 182, 259, 263, 371.
Edward M., 263.
Elijah, 60, 284.
Elizabeth, 91, 292, 385.
Enoch K., 263.
H——, 182.
Helen M., 263.
Jesse, 259, 261, 371.
John, 35, 87, 91, 385, 386.
Joseph, 31.
Lydia, 60, 62, 64, 66, 284.
Martha, 263, 393.
Mary, 66, 289.
Naomi, 91, 138, 386.
Paul, 45, 64, 286.
Samuel, 60, 62, 64, 66, 284, 286, 289, 292, 374, 397.
Sibyl, 35.
William, 98, 261.
William H., 263.
GIBSON, George L., 267, 372.
Georgiana S., 268.
I. J., 251.
John, 268.
GIFFORD, Mary A., 251.
GILES, Philip, 269.
GILLET, Azubah, 150, 162.
GILSON, Hannah, 30.
Isabella, 245.
Martha, 241, 363, 429.
Martha Ann, 429.
Merrick L., 252.

INDEX. 473

Nathaniel S., 251.
Samuel H., 251.
Varnum, 237, 363, 429.
GLAZIER, Aaron, 136.
Benjamin, 27, 32, 75, 77, 78, 79, 159, 278, 376, 381, 382.
Ebenezer, 79, 383.
Elizabeth, 75, 381.
Esther, 53, 64, 66, 68, 75, 78, 99, 292, 375, 417.
Experience, 26, 274.
George, 271, 273, 274, 451.
Isaiah, 275.
Jacob, 64, 90, 287, 385.
Jason, 96, 387.
John, 20, 35, 63, 64, 66, 68, 75, 78, 90, 91, 94, 96, 271, 274, 286, 287, 289, 292, 375, 377, 380, 381, 382, 385, 386, 387, 417.
Jonas, 78, 94, 382, 386.
Jonathan, 70, 77, 292.
Joseph, 159, 273, 274, 275, 276, 278.
Lydia, 63, 77, 78, 79, 84, 137, 159, 286, 376, 383.
Maria, 18, 273.
Martha, 57, 67, 272, 273.
Mary, 26, 90, 91, 94, 96, 271, 274.
Olive, 136.
Oliver, 91, 385.
Ruth, 27, 28, 273, 278, 380.
Sarah, 159, 271, 273, 278.
Susanna, 78, 159, 273, 382.
Thankful, 70, 292.
William, 57, 272, 273, 280.
Zachariah, 27, 67, 70, 275, 292.
GLEASON, George, 255, 308, 373.
Joanna, 98.
Joseph, 262.
Lucy, 262.
Lucy C., 262.
Polly, 170, 228.
William, 308.
GLOVER, Betsy, 144.
GOBLE, Hannah, 16, 451.
GODDARD, Abigail, 364.
Artemas W., 207.
Asa J., 344.
Eber, 131, 146, 181, 206, 207, 246, 335, 344, 345, 367, 429.
Harriet M., 246.
Joseph W., 344.
Lucy, 206, 207, 335, 344.
Lucy M., 207.
Mary C., 207, 239, 344.
Mary L., 207.
Nabby, 181.
Polly, 133, 148, 313, 331.
Sylvia, 344.
GODFREY, Abel M., 231.
Abigail, 37.
Betsy, 329.
Caleb, 313.
Daniel, 41, 134, 181, 311, 312, 327, 328, 359.
Debenjah, 119.
Deborah, 316, 329.
Eunice, 86, 119, 147, 308.
Hannah, 31.
James, 40, 100, 119, 132, 147, 152, 165, 313, 326, 329.
John, 312.
Levi, 399.
Mary, 87, 138.
Mrs. ——, 325.
Peter, 311, 327.
Rebecca, 119, 150, 162, 311, 321, 399.
Ruth, 322.
Salmon, 43, 104, 119, 153, 165, 308, 310, 311, 313, 314, 316, 321,

325, 330, 399.
Sarah, 119, 149, 162, 308.
Solomon, 119, 310.
Stephen, 311.
GOLDEN and GOULDING.
James B., 207.
Mary, 207.
Patrick, 207.
Patty, 163.
GOLDSBURY, Hannah, 271, 279.
John, 276.
Mary, 332.
GOLDTHWAIT, Eunice, 206.
Hannah, 206.
John, 181, 206, 365.
Mehetabel, 206.
GOODALE and GOODELL.
Abby W., 262.
Charles, 238.
David, 45, 103, 112.
Dinah, 39, 101, 107, 385.
Dorothy, 112.
Edward W., 262, 264.
Eunice, 112.
Lucy, 392.
Lucy S., 262.
Martha F., 207.
Miriam, 45.
Nathan, 107, 385, 417.
Nathan M., 392.
Obadiah, 207, 235.
R. B. Thomas, 249.
Solomon, 44, 103.
Winslow N., 264.
GOODENS, Asa, 386.
Hopestill, 383.
Peter, 383.
Timothy, 386.
GOODHUE, Anna W., 248, 337.
Benjamin, 153, 165.
GOODMAN, John, 17.
GOODNOW and GOODENOUGH.
Abel, 307.
Abigail S., 97, 306.
Anna, 129, 139.
Asa, 94.
Elizabeth, 37, 98.
Jonas, 36.
Peter, 98.
Sarah, 94, 97, 307.
Timothy, 94, 97, 306, 307.
GOODRICH and GOODRIDGE.
Benjamin, 25.
Beulah, 182, 367.
Doctor, 182, 195.
Eunice, 42, 104, 294.
John, 294, 326.
Joshua, 42, 104.
Mary, 135, 307, 331.
Thankful, 328.
Thirza, 307.
GOODSPEED, Elizabeth, 181, 364, 428.
GOODWIN, Abigail, 207, 333.
Alfred, 207, 237, 342.
Anna, 315, 329.
Bathsheba, 97, 109, 111, 113, 118, 151, 164, 181, 182, 312, 345, 358, 429.
Caleb S., 207, 343.
Catharine, 207.
Cynthia J., 182, 207.
Edward, 109, 118, 122, 133, 148, 181, 187, 207, 307, 333, 338, 340, 341, 343, 363.
George T., 207.
Harriet, 233.
Harriet M., 206, 346, 429.
James, 38, 97, 100, 109, 111, 113, 118, 181, 207, 306, 307, 309, 312, 313, 314, 315, 321, 329, 333, 339,

340, 341, 342, 365, 429.
James G., 207, 340.
James S., 207.
John, 111, 118, 150, 162, 181, 182, 194, 206, 207, 232, 236, 309, 334, 341, 342, 343, 344, 345, 346, 348, 353, 362, 367, 429.
John A., 207, 340.
Julia, 122, 234, 338.
Leander, 207, 341.
Loring, 181, 207, 339, 359.
Mary Ann, 206, 241, 344.
Palmer, 207, 342.
Polly, 118, 152, 165, 313.
Rebecca, 182, 206, 207, 240, 334, 341, 369, 429.
Sally, 122, 207, 333.
Samuel, 207, 343.
Sarah, 118, 152, 164, 206, 314, 337, 343.
Susan, 181, 206, 336, 362.
Susan E., 181, 206, 207.
William, 348.
William S., 206.
GOOLEY, Mary J., 246.
GOOS, John, 412.
GORDON, Lydia A., 251.
GORHAM, Jason, 258.
Goss, Abbie F., 260.
Abigail, 34, 207.
Anna, 167, 173, 310, 316, 328, 403.
Asa, 116.
Charles, 206, 346.
Daniel, 30, 45, 69, 104, 148, 161, 181, 182, 188, 207, 269, 289, 308, 309, 310, 312, 313, 315, 316, 326, 328, 333, 339, 340, 341, 342, 343, 344, 356, 370, 403, 429.
Dinah, 30, 69, 257.
Dorothy, 30.
Ebenezer, 181, 206, 345, 428.
Elihu, 384.
Elizabeth, 27, 28, 153, 165, 207, 239, 275, 312, 342.
Elizabeth A., 207.
Emma W., 393.
Ephraim, 23, 34, 384.
Eunice, 181, 297, 330, 357, 403, 428.
Eunice W., 207, 253, 346.
Francis, 347.
Hannah, 77, 81.
Harriet E., 260.
Henry, 179, 181, 207, 236, 341, 364, 429.
Henry L., 181, 207, 429.
James, 36, 181, 207, 302, 304, 305, 320, 341, 353, 412.
John, 30, 70, 77, 106, 167, 173, 181, 182, 206, 207, 269, 275, 276, 288, 315, 334, 335, 341, 342, 343, 344, 345, 346, 347, 353, 354, 360, 363, 370, 379, 381, 397, 412, 429, 453.
Jonas, 154, 181, 182, 206, 207, 248, 249, 260, 266, 330, 313, 335, 343, 344, 345, 346, 347, 355, 359, 305, 300, 379, 403, 428, 442.
Jonathan, 70, 380.
Joseph, 41, 106, 109, 116, 181, 207, 379, 412.
Joseph W., 206, 344.
Judith, 181, 206, 207, 242, 335, 337, 344, 429.
Kezia, 38, 99.
Levi, 206, 345.
Lucy, 30, 69, 109, 231, 255, 288, 340.
Lucy G., 206, 346.
Martha E., 207, 240.
Mary, 70, 181, 206, 207, 275, 302,

33

INDEX.

320, 334, 451, 453.
Mary A. S., 207, 343.
Mary W., 207, 241, 343, 347, 412.
Mehetabel, 305.
Nancy, 181, 347, 428.
Nathaniel, 181.
Oliver, 30, 69, 291.
Philip, 20, 30, 32, 77, 81, 288, 376, 378, 381, 382, 383, 405, 451, 453.
Polly, 207, 333.
Rebecca, 206, 207, 335, 429.
Rebecca W., 207, 343.
Reuben, 380.
Samuel, 206, 345.
Samuel A., 346.
Sarah, 106, 109, 116, 276, 347, 382, 392, 393.
Sarah A., 247.
Sarah D., 181, 207, 429.
Sarah E., 207, 242, 246, 260, 266, 344, 371, 442.
Sarah W., 207, 260.
Stephen, 129, 138.
Susan P., 207.
William, 26, 30, 69, 126, 139, 207, 275, 285, 287, 288, 289, 291, 293, 339, 374, 378, 379, 380.
William D., 207.
GOULD, Abby E., 263, 268.
Anna M., 263.
Benjamin, 117, 127, 141, 314, 315, 316, 317, 318, 322, 337, 338, 351, 428.
Benjamin F., 263.
Betsy, 247.
Charles F., 263.
Edward E., 182, 429.
Elizabeth, 168, 172, 182, 318, 334, 369, 429.
Ellen A., 263, 268.
Esther, 117, 316.
Frances E., 262.
George G., 262.
Georgetta M., 263.
Gershom F., 337.
Grizzel, 117, 315.
Grizzel A., 117, 321.
Harriet, 262, 429.
Harriet E., 262.
Henry, 262.
Henry L., 257.
Horace, 229.
James, 307.
James E., 182, 262, 429.
Jane M., 263.
John, 117, 314.
Lucretia A., 262.
Lucy, 239.
Lydia, 84, 132, 147.
Lydia B., 428.
Marshall E., 429.
Mary, 236.
Mary H., 338, 351.
Moses, 246, 263, 268.
Miss, 182.
Mr., 267, 395.
Nancy, 240.
Nathaniel, 182.
Polly, 181, 352.
Priscilla, 262.
Rebecca, 338, 351.
Sarah, 338, 351, 428.
Sarah C., 263.
Susan W., 263, 268.
William, 181, 182, 267, 369, 429.
GRAGE, James, 264.
Jemima H., 264.
GRAHAM, Arthur, 31.
Elima H., 250.
Martin, 264.

Thomas E., 264.
GRANT, Catharine, 115, 301, 305.
Hannah, 115, 306.
George, 115, 307, 366.
Hezekiah M., 244.
Martha W., 247.
Melzar T., 115, 308.
Thomas, 88, 99, 115, 301, 305, 306, 307, 308.
William, 115.
GRASSIE, Alexander, 252, 394.
Elizabeth, 394.
George, 394.
Thomas G., 394.
William, 394.
GRAVES, Ardelia A., 254.
Luther, 46, 103.
GRAY, Francis H., 264.
George, 242.
Hinkly R., 255, 264.
Jane, 367.
GREGG, Margaret, 29.
GREGORY, Ruth, 42.
GREEN, Abigail, 44, 73, 103, 159, 285, 287, 290.
Achsa, 207, 265, 394.
Ann S., 263.
Asa W., 207.
Charles F., 207.
Charlotte L., 263.
Daniel W., 207.
Dolly, 152, 165.
Edward G., 263.
Eliza A. H., 207.
Elizabeth F., 247.
Ellen M., 207.
Elsy Ann, 207.
Esther, 95.
Eunice, 39, 73, 102, 292.
Franklin C., 263.
Franklin W., 259.
Gilbert, 248, 263, 394.
George M., 207.
Israel, 95.
John D., 207.
Joseph, 250.
Joshua, 95.
Levi, 207, 238, 253, 265, 269, 394.
Lucy, 45, 104, 295.
Lydia, 240.
M. Antoinette, 394.
Margaret, 135.
Mary Ann, 247, 263.
Michael B., 168, 171.
Oliver, 243, 263, 269, 370.
Oliver E., 182.
Peter, 73, 105, 136, 159, 285, 287, 288, 290, 292, 293, 295, 296, 299, 328, 352, 390.
Roscoe F., 263.
Sarah, 104, 134, 207, 296.
Sarah M., 207, 259.
Sophia, 263, 394.
Susanna, 125, 137, 299.
Thomas M., 390.
Widow ——, 325.
William F., 263, 269.
Williams, 207, 241, 259, 266, 372.
GREENLEAF, Anes, 307.
Calvin, 288.
Daniel, 37, 61, 62, 64, 98, 283, 284, 286, 287, 288, 312.
David, 64, 286, 307, 308.
Edmund, 330.
Edmund Q., 124, 207, 240, 318.
Elizabeth, 32, 64, 306.
Elizabeth W., 207.
George R., 207.
Israel, 61, 283.
John Hancock, 310.
Levi, 128, 145.

Maria, 124, 322.
Sally, 146, 308.
Sarah, 321, 330, 394.
Sarah E., 207, 258.
Sarah H., 247.
Silas, 394.
Silas S., 245.
Silence, 61, 62.
Stephen, 62, 284.
Susanna, 308.
William, 6, 124, 145, 287, 306, 308, 310, 312, 318, 322, 323, 330, 351.
Wm. Josephus, 124, 318.
GREENOUGH, Elizabeth, 160, 329.
Joseph, 330.
GRIFFIN, John, 252.
GRIMES, Andrew, 34, 78, 136, 297.
Mary, 78, 297.
Submit, 78.
William, 43, 104.
GROSS and GROCE, Anna, 99.
Daniel W., 111, 390.
Lucy, 111, 390.
Margaret, 23.
Nahum H., 390.
Obadiah, 46, 103, 111, 378, 390.
Sophia, 390.
GROUT, Phebe, 42, 102.
GROVE, Charles, 255, 373.
GROVER, Charles H., 242.
H——, 446.
Luther, 396.
GUILD, Mrs., 181.
GULLIVER, John, 277.
Milke, 277.
Sarah, 18.
GUNN, Martha, 305.
Sarah, 305.
Wyatt, 39, 102, 305.
HACKETT, George W., 257.
HADLEY and HEADLEY.
Abraham, 90, 129, 141, 384.
Catharine, 166.
Charles, 90, 383.
Deborah, 90, 92, 93.
Elizabeth, 90, 168, 171, 172, 382.
John, 38, 90, 92, 93, 382, 383, 384, 385, 386.
Josiah, 43, 90, 382.
Mary, 90, 378, 382.
Sarah, 92, 385.
HAGER, Elizabeth, 136.
Hannah, 244.
HALE, C. B., 431.
Ephraim, 41.
Ezra, 103.
Lydia, 42, 102.
Moses, 287.
Mrs., 268.
Oliver, 299.
Rebecca, 431.
Sarah, 257.
HALL, Caroline, 244.
Ezra, 46.
George, 40.
Nancy, 161.
Sally, 152, 165.
Sarah, 167, 173.
Sarah G., 362, 442.
Thomas, 250.
HAMMOND, Cæsar, 182, 327, 354.
G——, 446.
John, 41, 102.
Levi, 182, 359.
Martha, 362.
Mercy, 167, 173, 180, 183.
Patty, 151, 164.

INDEX.

Perley, 183, 236, 363.
HANCOCK, Abigail, 379.
  Samuel, 37, 99, 377, 387.
  Thomas, 387.
  William, 387.
HANDLEY, Mary Ann, 247.
HANNAHS or HANNERS.
  Sarah A. W., 241.
  Sally, 131.
HAPGOOD, Charles, 259.
  Charles W., 259.
  Elizabeth, 259.
  Lydia, 300.
  Mercy, 56.
  Nathaniel, 56.
  Sarah, 56.
  Shadrack, 300.
  Susan, 372.
HARDING, Susan, 236.
HARLOW, Catharine W., 262.
  Edward E., 262, 264.
  Ella G., 262.
  Eunice C., 264.
  George E., 262.
HARPARD, John, 74.
  Joseph, 74.
  Mary, 74.
HARPER, Elizabeth, 87.
HARRIMAN, Edwin, 209.
  John, 183, 247, 248, 253.
  John A., 183, 209.
  Julia A., 183, 209.
HARRINGTON, Anna, 22, 126, 138, 296, 297, 298, 300, 313, 319, 327, 400.
  Anne, 241.
  Arethusa, 22, 306, 321.
  Artemas, 238.
  Caleb, 230, 347.
  Denziel, 259.
  Emily, 113, 148.
  Emily M., 306.
  Eusebia, 41, 103, 296, 321.
  George, 16.
  Henrietta, 22, 46, 104, 321, 327.
  Horace, 244.
  James, 252.
  Mary, 244.
  Otis, 259.
  Priscilla, 378.
  Rebecca, 350.
  Seth, 35, 87, 378.
  Thomas, 127, 140, 298, 313, 315, 316.
  Thomas G., 347.
  Timothy, 21, 22, 127, 140, 161, 295, 296, 297, 298, 300, 315, 319, 323, 325, 327, 328, 352, 400.
  Timothy B., 315.
HARRIS, Abigail, 78, 183, 209, 370.
  Abijah, 76, 159, 296, 323.
  Alfred P., 209.
  Alice, 30, 276.
  Amos, 274, 403.
  Ann, 417.
  Anna, 31, 276, 285.
  Asa, 30, 34, 76, 78, 86, 159, 277, 296, 297, 298, 319, 323, 332.
  Asahel, 183, 191, 209, 232, 361, 371, 430.
  Benjamin, 24, 59, 61, 62, 66, 273, 281, 282, 284, 286, 288, 289, 292.
  Bradford, 209.
  Charles B., 210.
  Christopher C., 209.
  Daniel, 151, 164, 183, 368.
  David, 277, 324.
  Deborah, 27, 59, 61, 62, 66, 275.
  Ebenezer, 32, 275, 276, 277, 278, 285, 323, 325.

Edmund, 156, 210, 259, 271, 274, 275, 276, 277, 323, 403.
Edmund S., 263.
Edwin A., 259, 263.
Eliza, 209, 271.
Eliza A., 263.
Eliza H., 183, 430.
Eliza W., 370.
Elizabeth, 25, 272, 274, 278, 284, 285, 403.
Emory, 170, 176, 182, 183, 208, 210, 232, 350, 368, 430.
Eunice, 76, 78, 159, 297, 298, 323.
Essediah, 360.
Francis A., 209.
Frederick, 210.
Frederick A., 209.
George, 183, 208, 368, 430.
George S., 263.
George W., 259.
Hannah, 269, 275.
Hannah P., 210, 259.
Harriet, 208.
Harriet E., 243.
Hepzibah, 289.
Hasadiah L., 182, 208, 430.
Jane A., 209.
John, 59, 158, 270, 271, 272, 275, 278, 281.
Jonathan, 21, 32, 276, 324.
Julia M., 209.
Levi, 239, 254, 263.
Lucy, 253, 394.
Luther, 130.
Lydia, 126, 128, 274.
Maria, 234.
Martha, 275, 284.
Mary, 276, 278, 319.
Mary R., 286.
Persis, 62, 284.
Rebecca, 126, 140, 417.
Sally, 209, 210, 267, 396.
Sally K., 263.
Samuel, 183, 361.
Sarah, 27, 29, 271, 275, 285, 350.
Sarah E., 267, 396.
Sidney, 209, 238, 263, 267, 396.
Sidney A., 209.
Solomon, 292.
Sylvanus, 66, 288.
Thankful, 31, 275.
William, 417.
HART, Polly, 154, 166.
  William C., 251.
HARTHAN, David, 97.
  Eunice, 97.
  Lois, 97.
  Lucy, 97.
  Lydia, 97.
  Micah, 97.
  Olive, 97.
  Samuel, 97.
  Sarah, 97.
HARTWELL, Abigail L., 209.
  Asahel, 274.
  Edward, 274, 275, 276, 277, 452.
  Elizabeth, 275.
  Emily P., 209.
  Harriet, 246.
  Jonathan, 274, 276.
  Joseph, 277.
  Leonard, 209, 231.
  Lowell, 243.
  Sarah, 271, 274, 397.
HARVEY, Anna, 88.
  Rev. A., 248.
  Daniel, 382.
  Darius, 382.
  Isaiah, 383.
  Mary, 172.
  Rachel, 102, 381.

Sarah, 86.
Zachariah, 98, 381, 382, 383.
HARWOOD, Ebenezer, 129, 139.
  Maria F., 255.
  Patty, 231.
HASELTON, Mansell, 255.
HASKELL, Abigail, 322.
  Abijah, 77, 297.
  Abner, 89, 94, 100, 301, 304, 306, 311, 320.
  Abraham, 71, 104, 134.
  Andrew, 42, 73, 102, 113.
  Benjamin, 137, 296, 312, 322.
  Charity, 182, 358.
  Charles W., 244.
  Dorinda, 168, 171.
  Elias, 182, 448.
  Elizabeth, 36.
  Emma, 312.
  Ezekiel, 88, 90, 301, 320.
  Henry, 68, 71, 83, 86, 141, 182, 192, 296, 300, 301, 302, 303, 304, 305, 320, 324, 328, 355, 401, 440.
  Huldah, 68, 71, 304.
  Israel, 334.
  Jeduthun, 315.
  Jeremiah, 27, 29, 68, 70, 73, 77, 136, 285, 290, 292, 297, 300, 329.
  John, 68, 113, 154, 165, 303, 324.
  John A., 183, 209, 237, 243, 367, 430.
  Jno. Edward, 183, 209, 430.
  Joseph, 94, 304, 312.
  Josiah, 317.
  Lemuel, 45, 104.
  Levi, 100, 306.
  Lois, 113.
  Lucy, 153, 165, 169, 170.
  Lucy W., 251.
  Lydia, 45, 104.
  Martha, 89, 94, 100, 147, 320.
  Mary, 31, 126, 207.
  Mercy, 207, 231, 305.
  Molly, 89, 139, 301.
  Moses, 90, 301.
  Nabby, 313.
  Nathaniel, 125, 136, 312, 313, 315, 317, 322, 328.
  Otis, 240.
  Polly, 154.
  Prudence, 113, 144, 145, 268, 337, 349, 396.
  Rebecca, 90, 126, 138, 149, 153, 234, 296, 300, 301, 302, 320, 335, 346.
  Relief, 300.
  Ruth, 68, 103, 320.
  Sarah, 113, 145, 148, 161, 183, 209, 311.
  Sarah R., 430.
  Susan, 229.
  Susanna, 322.
  Thankful, 68, 70, 73, 77, 84, 87, 285, 290, 329.
  Timothy C., 317.
  William, 207.
  William D., 312.
HASTINGS, Abel, 240.
  Abigail, 125, 136.
  Althina, 240.
  Amory, 208.
  Ann E., 263.
  Benjamin, 129, 182, 358, 431.
  Caroline B., 259.
  David, 102.
  Elizabeth, 242.
  Elizabeth D., 234.
  Elizabeth S., 268.
  Emma, 268.
  Emory, 247, 259, 344.
  Ephraim, 169, 170.

INDEX.

Eunice, 36, 289.
Experience, 431.
Hannah, 392, 393.
Hollis, 392.
John, 37.
Jonathan, 43.
Jotham, 239.
Katy, 130.
Laura L., 209.
Lucy, 246.
Mary J., 263.
Nathaniel, 37, 98, 248, 263, 286, 287, 289.
Olive W., 209, 430.
Parney, 130, 143.
Reuben, 244.
Ruth, 129.
Sally, 231.
Samuel, 286.
Samuel A., 183, 209, 239, 430.
Sarah, 83.
Sarah A., 183, 209, 430.
Sarah E., 263.
Stewart, 392, 393.
Susanna, 208, 335, 344.
Thomas, 167, 173, 182, 208, 252, 268, 358, 372, 431.
Timothy F., 132.
HATCH, Angelina, 258.
John P., 254.
Turner, 182.
HAVEN, Asa, 110, 307, 321.
Caroline, 208.
Ebenezer, 119, 128, 144, 182, 208, 209, 231, 318, 364.
Edith B., 249.
Eunice, 110.
Harriet, 208, 209.
John, 208.
John A., 110, 307.
Jonas, 208, 233.
Jubal H., 208.
Kezia, 119, 155, 167, 318.
Nancy, 209.
Prissa, 209.
Richard, 147, 182, 208, 357.
Ruth, 119, 182, 208, 360.
Sally, 182, 208.
Sarah W., 209, 258, 395.
Waldo, 209.
Widow ——, 330.
William, 209.
William I., 208.
HAVERTY, Daniel, 210, 269, 394.
Emma I., 210.
James, 264.
Michael, 264.
Robert E., 210.
HAWKES, Abijah, 327.
Alice, 182, 208, 209, 233, 395.
Anstiss, 182,
Benjamin, 167, 172, 208, 237, 335, 344, 350.
Catharine, 168, 172.
Cynthia, 182, 208.
Cynthia A., 209, 246, 395.
Daniel, 208.
Hannah, 147.
Harriet, 208, 235.
James, 208.
John, 133, 148, 182, 183, 208, 209, 359, 361, 363, 395, 431.
Mary, 153, 165.
Mary P., 208.
Polly, 208, 335, 350.
Prudence, 230.
Rebecca, 208, 237.
Sally, 167, 172, 208, 233.
Sally H., 395.
Sewall, 182, 208.
Thomas B., 208, 344.

HAYDEN, Abby M., 251.
Caroline M., 268.
Newton F., 251, 268.
Tamazin, 154, 165.
HAYES, Charles, 240.
HAYNES, Alfred W., 257.
Eleanor, 148, 161.
Eli, 120.
Harriet A., 261,
Harriet M., 210.
Henry F., 251, 257.
John A., 210.
Joseph, 350.
Mary, 210.
Moody B., 261.
Moses, 168, 171.
Olive, 395.
Sarah, 120,
HAYWARD and HEYWOOD.
Anna, 107.
Benjamin, 107,
Eleazer, 24.
Elizabeth, 23, 38, 98.
Esther, 278.
Franklin, 256.
Hannah, 13.
James, 108.
John, 24, 35, 98.
Judith, 451.
Lois, 183, 446.
Louis, 197.
Lucy, 152.
Martha, 107.
Mary, 107, 451.
Mary Ann, 235.
Moses, 183, 197, 446.
Nancy, 257, 394.
Nathan, 278.
Patience, 108, 110.
Phineas, 108.
Relief, 278.
Reuben, 110.
Sarah, 13, 107.
Seth, 107.
Stephen, 44, 103.
Susan, 230.
Thomas, 86.
Timothy, 42, 108, 110.
William, 42, 104.
HAZEN, Benjamin, 300.
Ebenezer, 303.
Edward, 84, 300, 301, 304, 305.
Joseph, 372.
Mary, 132, 147.
Nathaniel, 147.
Paul W., 303.
Sarah, 301, 303.
Silas, 304.
William, 305.
HEALD, Abigail, 63.
Elizabeth, 27.
Ezra, 65.
Israel, 63, 65.
Lucy, 26.
Mark, 327.
Mary, 63.
Mercy, 25.
HEALY, Anna, 262.
Henry, 262.
John, 262.
HEARD and HURD.
Edmund, 6, 132, 147.
Eunice, 328.
Isaac, 131, 146, 160.
Mark, 309, 310.
Sarah, 146, 310.
Susanna, 309.
HEMMENWAY, Mary C., 250.
Moses, 320, 332.
Vashni, 146.
HENDERSON, Bathsheba, 93,

302, 304, 331.
Betty, 302.
Jane, 76, 296, 330.
John, 32, 76, 296, 302, 330.
Joseph, 76, 296.
Rosanna, 93, 304.
Thomas, 93, 302, 304, 331.
——, 325,
HENRY, Betsy, 151.
Charles, 140.
George, 135.
John, 235.
Mary, 46, 151, 163,
Phineas, 236.
HENTZ, Caroline L., 235.
Marcellus F., 348.
N. Marcellus, 235, 348.
HERBERT, John, 29, 285, 293, 294, 332.
Joseph, 294.
Mary, 293, 294.
HERRING, Lucy, 107.
Samuel, 107, 388.
Solomon, 107, 388.
HERSEY, Mary, 126.
HEWES, George, 451.
Lucy, 236.
HEWITT, Israel, 310,
John, 42, 100, 307, 309, 310. 331.
Molly, 309.
Sarah, 307, 331.
HIBRESS, Dury, 97.
George, 97, 387.
Jabez, 97, 387.
HICKS, Mary, 148.
HIGGINS, Mathias, 141.
HIGLEY, Pliny, 167, 172.
HILDREEH, Ann V., 209.
David, 154.
Elizabeth W., 335, 345.
Ezekiel, 182, 209, 347, 431.
Jonathan, 153, 344, 345.
Lewis A., 344.
Martha, 209.
Mary, 209.
Nancy, 182, 209, 360, 431.
Richard, 182, 209, 229, 347, 360, 431.
Sarah, 335.
Thomas, 209.
Thomas S., 240.
HILL and HILLS, Abigail, 229.
Anna, 78, 297.
Asa, 383.
Austin C., 262.
Betty, 383.
Ebenezer, 37, 99.
Eliphalet, 127, 142.
Elizabeth, 233.
Enoch, 78, 86, 323.
George C., 262.
Hancell C., 254.
John, 344.
Louisa, 248, 266.
Martha S., 344.
Mary H., 262.
Orricy, 231.
Sarah, 35, 78, 169, 237, 297.
Willard, 151, 163.
HILLER, Joseph, 182, 358.
Lucy, 154, 166.
HILT, Peter, 37, 99.
HINDS, Anna, 271, 274, 286.
Francis, 274.
John, 15, 20, 27, 28, 271, 274, 275, 286, 451.
Mary, 15, 264, 275.
Samuel M., 241.
Seth, 275.
Thomas, 264.

HINKLEY, Martha Ann, 251.
HINKSON, Ruth, 243.
HOADLEY, Charlotte K., 268, 396.
 John C., 251, 268, 396.
HOAR, Catharine, 261.
 Elizabeth, 451.
 Henry, 261.
 John, 125, 136, 261.
 Lucy, 229.
 Oliver, 85.
 Rebecca, 143.
HOBART, William, 128, 145.
HOBIN, Ann, 252.
HODGMAN, Artemas H., 183, 210, 245, 248, 259.
 Esther, 249.
 Louisa, 210, 259, 266.
 Mary, 230.
 Oren, 210.
 Samuel H., 259.
 Sarah P., 183.
HOLBROOK, Clara, 262.
 Clarissa G., 235.
 Harriet, 262.
 Rufus W., 262.
HOLCOMB, Reuben, 126, 140, 374, 390.
HOLDEN, Joanna, 102.
HOLLAND, Adaline, 249.
 Elizabeth, 430.
 Mr. ——, 363, 397.
 Samuel, 251.
 Sarah, 135.
 Silas H., 254.
HOLMAN, Amanda M., 209.
 Anna, 271.
 Calvin, 254, 261.
 Charles A., 209.
 David, 111.
 Eliza, 235.
 Elizabeth F., 261.
 Elizabeth J., 209.
 Elsey, 231.
 Emeline, 257.
 Emily, 234.
 Harriet, 251.
 Helen M., 209.
 James H., 209.
 Jeremiah, 18, 271.
 John, 111, 183, 233, 363, 430.
 Jonathan, 183, 370.
 Katy, 125, 136.
 Laura, 245.
 Martha, 110, 112.
 Mary, 17.
 Nancy W., 430.
 Orion, 209.
 Reuben, 110.
 Rufus, 112.
 Ruth, 140.
 Samuel, 45.
 Sarah, 43, 111.
 Sidney W., 261.
 Solomon, 111.
 Stephen, 110, 112.
 William E., 261.
HOLMES, Barzillai, 150, 162.
 Edward, 152, 164, 207, 208.
 Edward W., 207, 347.
 Eliza, 235.
 Huldah, 207, 208, 335, 347.
 Miranda, 208, 237, 336, 347.
 Rebecca, 347.
 William, 133.
 ——, 397.
HOLT, Abiel, 72, 92, 130.
 Amanda, 255.
 Anes, 383.
 Barzillai, 27, 28, 72, 88, 91, 92, 94.

 David, 44, 47, 103, 120, 306, 331.
 Dennis, 248.
 Dinah, 120, 182, 354.
 Elizabeth, 45, 72.
 Emeline S., 241.
 Hannah, 62, 284.
 Jabez, 47, 306.
 James, 72.
 Jonathan, 394.
 Joshua, 61, 282.
 Jotham, 94.
 Jotham H., 238.
 Lemuel, 66, 287.
 Levi, 91.
 Lois, 71, 91, 92, 94, 138, 302, 331.
 Lucius K., 259.
 Lucy, 72, 302, 308, 321, 331, 332.
 Margaret E. R., 257.
 Martha L., 259.
 Mary, 46, 47, 67, 104, 288, 306, 331.
 Molly, 308.
 Rebecca, 259.
 Samuel, 138.
 Sarah, 33, 57, 58, 61, 62, 66, 67, 157, 279, 311.
 Susanna, 47, 71, 72, 306.
 Thomas, 30, 43, 44, 47, 71, 72, 120, 182, 306, 308, 311, 322, 325, 326, 330, 331.
 Uriah, 53, 57, 58, 61, 62, 66, 67, 157, 279, 280, 282, 284, 287, 288, 383, 413.
HOMER, Andrew, 269.
 Lawrence, 269.
 William P., 246.
HOOKER, Thomas, 413.
HOOLEY, John, 130.
HOOPER, Edward, 244, 431.
 Emily W., 269, 431.
 Eunice, 251.
HOSLEY, David, 114, 123, 137, 182, 313, 331, 430.
 John, 123, 313, 353.
 Joseph, 39.
 Luceby, 114, 123, 183, 313, 331, 367, 430.
 Lucy, 151.
 Sally, 114, 123, 149, 162, 313.
HOSMER, Josiah, 39, 101.
 Mary, 23.
HOUGHTON, Abby S., 259, 266.
 Abel, 92, 138, 168, 171, 385.
 Abia, 53.
 Abiathar, 21, 27, 33, 52, 278, 300.
 Abigail, 10, 17, 23, 24, 25, 54, 55, 57, 63, 85, 97, 108, 136, 268, 271, 273, 276, 278, 279, 282, 284, 289, 300, 353, 388, 401, 430, 453.
 Abigail M., 255.
 Abijah, 32, 42, 47, 102, 182, 183, 277, 295, 296, 298, 300, 305, 309, 311, 312, 313, 326, 330, 331.
 Abner, 311.
 Abraham, 55, 125, 278.
 Achsa, 52, 92, 182, 233, 278, 303, 321, 359.
 Alice, 41, 103, 182, 295, 330, 356, 431.
 Amity, 60, 281.
 Avery, 94, 304, 321.
 Andrew, 250.
 Andrew R., 209.
 Anes, 21, 32, 276.
 Anna, 15, 24, 53, 92, 94, 95, 98, 108, 125, 276, 308, 322.
 Ann E., 259, 266.
 Apollos, 237.
 Aretas, 58, 280.
 Arethusa, 309.
 Asa, 54, 279.

 Augustine F., 254, 263.
 Azubah, 27, 52, 277.
 Beatrix, 11, 12, 14, 15, 274.
 Benjamin, 12, 18, 29, 37, 45, 47, 53, 54, 56, 58, 59, 60, 63, 64, 66, 69, 80, 84, 85, 92, 97, 99, 101, 118, 126, 128, 138, 145, 149, 158, 160, 161, 162, 168, 171, 182, 183, 207, 208, 239, 268, 276, 277, 278, 279, 280, 281, 282, 283, 284, 285, 287, 288, 289, 290, 292, 293, 300, 303, 318, 320, 322, 338, 339, 340, 341, 342, 354, 367, 368, 373, 374, 375, 388, 396, 417, 430, 452, 453.
 Bethesda, 73, 76, 80, 82, 382, 383, 417.
 Betsy, 118, 244.
 Betty, 33, 50, 51, 86, 143, 108, 275, 280.
 Caleb, 231.
 Caroline, 284.
 Catharine, 63, 91, 159, 385.
 Cephas, 118, 338.
 Charles, 208, 339.
 Charles W., 259.
 Charlotte, 133, 147, 263, 309.
 Charlotte M., 263.
 Charlotte S., 251.
 Cyrus, 183, 209, 277, 328.
 Damaris, 64, 286.
 Daniel, 272, 276, 277, 278, 279, 280, 281.
 Darius, 53, 278.
 David, 58, 79, 280, 383.
 Deborah, 18, 271, 275.
 Deliverance, 80, 82, 90, 92, 95, 97.
 Dinah, 32, 58, 74, 76, 79, 89, 91, 93, 96, 101, 156, 279, 376, 380, 384, 391, 412, 417.
 Dolly, 95, 235, 304.
 Dorcas, 19,
 Dorothy, 60, 281.
 Ebenezer, 18, 57, 275, 276, 277, 279, 280, 413, 453.
 Edward, 24, 35, 50, 88, 209, 281, 303, 331.
 Edmund W., 208.
 Elbridge, 248.
 Eleazer, 17, 53, 276, 277, 278, 453.
 Eli, 388.
 Elijah, 35, 38, 47, 56, 91, 98, 106, 107, 110, 123, 159, 182, 183, 208, 279, 288, 333, 354, 376, 384, 385, 386, 387, 388, 389, 390, 430.
 Elisha, 294, 311, 356.
 Eliza, 208, 209, 232, 245, 394.
 Eliza E., 394.
 Elizabeth, 21, 32, 37, 52, 53, 54, 56, 57, 58, 59, 60, 61, 62, 69, 87, 98, 127, 143, 242, 272, 276, 277, 281, 282, 283, 292, 377.
 Elizabeth T., 252.
 Ellen E., 256.
 Emeline, 182, 208.
 Ephah, 52, 157, 279, 281, 412.
 Ephraim, 24, 56, 60, 93, 105, 270, 272, 280, 281, 283, 286, 289, 292, 294, 327, 386.
 Esther, 15, 29, 55, 58, 271, 275, 278, 280, 413, 453.
 Eunice, 64, 66, 88, 126, 139, 232, 286, 288, 376, 386.
 Experience, 9, 19, 31, 280, 291.
 Ezra, 32, 47, 74, 76, 79, 89, 91, 93, 96, 101, 105, 277, 375, 379, 380, 382, 383, 384, 385, 386, 387, 388, 391, 417.
 Frances, 183, 369, 430.
 Francis A., 263.
 Frederick, 183, 209.
 Gardner P., 209.

INDEX.

George, 236, 367.
George W., 208, 209, 340.
Georgiana, 413.
Gershom, 19, 52, 61, 272, 276, 278, 283, 453.
Grace, 82, 90, 159.
Hannah, 12, 15, 20, 57, 118, 158, 161, 279, 280, 322, 351.
Harriet, 123, 233.
Harriet W., 209.
Hasadiah, 273, 401.
Henry, 19, 53, 54, 56, 58, 59, 125, 273, 279, 280, 281, 282, 283, 401.
Hephzibah, 64, 76, 285, 288, 381.
Hiram, 62, 92, 284.
Isabella, 24, 271, 276, 453.
Israel, 18, 42, 53, 57, 61, 62, 64, 66, 68, 70, 71, 104, 157, 158, 159, 276, 278, 279, 280, 281, 282, 284, 285, 286, 288, 290, 292, 293, 319, 327, 373, 453.
Jacob, 14, 19, 55, 125, 271, 276, 278, 279, 280, 182, 285, 287, 290, 412, 453.
James, 37, 44, 50, 53, 55, 57, 60, 61, 63, 64, 70, 75, 92, 94, 95, 97, 98, 272, 276, 279, 280, 281, 282, 284, 286, 287, 288, 319, 324, 325, 375, 385, 386, 387, 388, 389.
James O., 262.
Jane, 9, 10, 11, 12, 384, 385, 453.
Jeffery A., 208.
Jemima, 19, 276.
Jerusha, 29, 54, 276, 278.
Joanna, 53, 56, 58, 60, 61, 64, 67, 157, 278.
Joel, 36, 64, 98, 99, 287, 377, 387, 389.
John, 6, 9, 11, 12, 14, 15, 17, 18, 19, 20, 26, 29, 52, 53, 56, 58, 60, 64, 71, 118, 125, 156, 182, 270, 271, 276, 277, 278, 279, 280, 281, 283, 285, 288, 293, 318, 341, 398, 401, 412, 451, 452.
John F., 250,
John W., 261,
Jonas, 15, 51, 52, 60, 90, 105, 156, 159, 270, 271, 273, 274, 275, 276, 277, 278, 279, 281, 384, 395, 412.
Jonathan, 6, 15, 19, 23, 31, 52, 54, 56, 57, 59, 61, 65, 70, 97, 157, 158, 270, 271, 276, 277, 278, 279, 280, 281, 282, 284, 287, 288, 292, 412.
Jonathan F., 267, 395.
Jonathan W., 248, 259, 266.
Joseph, 9, 36, 53, 56, 60, 61, 98, 102, 135, 157, 276, 279, 280, 281, 282, 451, 453.
Joshua, 17, 31, 54, 57, 60, 62, 77, 126, 128, 272, 276, 277, 278, 279, 280, 282, 284, 319, 325, 382, 453.
Josiah, 15, 32, 35, 37, 73, 76, 80, 82, 85, 90, 97, 105, 108, 128, 144, 156, 159, 209, 276, 278, 377, 380, 381, 382, 383, 384, 386, 388, 412, 417.
Josiah R., 387.
Judah, 129.
Kate, 63, 284.
Kezia, 22, 32, 52, 58, 91, 126, 139, 161, 280, 302, 303, 312, 322, 329.
Lavina B., 236.
Leafy, 261.
Lemuel, 47, 85, 88, 284, 376, 378, 384.
Levi, 37, 50, 70, 75, 94, 99, 258, 286, 304, 305, 394.
Levina, 43, 61, 67, 102, 282, 288, 412.

Lockheart, 107, 182, 358, 388.
Lois, 53, 82, 84, 87, 136, 277, 281.
Louisa J., 250.
Lucretia, 303, 331.
Lucy, 46, 79, 103, 267, 365, 382, 394, 395, 430.
Lucy H., 209.
Lucy J., 209.
Luke, 82, 300.
Lydia, 183, 207, 208, 272, 276, 342, 362, 430.
Manasseh, 105, 388,
Margaret, 45.
Margaret A., 258.
Maria, 123, 208, 286, 311, 322.
Maria C., 258.
Maria N., 255.
Martha, 39, 53, 57, 61, 62, 64, 66, 68, 70, 71, 102, 157, 158, 159, 183, 209, 278, 279, 320, 321, 307.
Martha P., 413.
Martha E., 209.
Mary, 9, 13, 14, 15, 19, 21, 26, 29, 32, 34, 51, 52, 53, 55, 56, 57, 59, 60, 61, 63, 64, 65, 67, 77, 79, 82, 86, 90, 93, 94, 105, 106, 107, 110, 125, 156, 157, 158, 182, 183, 208, 271, 273, 276, 277, 280, 281, 282, 285, 328, 331, 332, 375, 381, 386, 389, 412, 417, 430, 451, 452.
Mary Ann, 242.
Mary N., 431.
Maverick, 107, 146, 387.
Mehetabel, 43, 53, 56, 58, 73, 103, 271, 278, 380.
Meriel, 208.
Merviah, 131.
Michal, 22, 32, 58, 278.
Mindwell, 31, 58, 277.
Miranda, 209.
Miriam, 31, 53, 278.
Molly, 44, 80, 279, 305.
Moriah, 57, 63.
Moses B., 239.
Nabby, 183, 208, 368.
Nahum, 47, 95, 96, 282, 387.
Nancy, 122, 151, 163, 168, 171, 208, 262.
Nason S., 258.
Nathaniel, 57, 82, 88, 93, 105, 277, 280, 377, 386, 387, 388, 389, 458.
Nathaniel T., 263.
Olive, 384.
Oliver, 61, 107, 182, 183, 208, 283, 356, 368, 386, 430.
Orpah, 21, 34, 54, 86, 278.
Otis, 250, 262.
Parmer, 32.
Parney, 22, 47, 59, 280.
Persis, 52, 90, 240, 278, 384.
Peter, 53, 278.
Philemon, 47, 84, 87, 90, 95, 281, 304, 325, 403.
Phineas, 53, 78, 80, 82, 86, 89, 91, 108, 159, 161, 182, 233, 278, 297, 298, 300, 301, 303, 308, 320, 324, 325, 329, 352, 364, 431.
Polly, 118, 313, 318.
Priscilla, 35, 80, 87, 376, 384.
Prudence,, 22, 34, 52, 62, 78, 151, 164, 278, 284, 298, 322, 378, 383.
Rachel, 136, 276, 302, 326, 331.
Ralph, 3, 4, 6, 9, 10, 11, 12, 20, 53, 277.
Rebecca, 24, 46, 64, 67, 95, 125, 183, 245, 276, 288, 296, 304, 321, 368, 403, 412.
Relief, 33, 47, 54, 129, 147, 183, 279, 298, 370, 391.
Robert, 15, 53, 55, 271, 275, 276, 277, 413, 453.

Robert C., 267, 394. 395.
Rufus, 52, 183, 209, 234, 277, 367, 413.
Ruth, 18, 23, 47, 54, 56, 59, 69, 78, 80, 82, 85, 89, 91, 93, 108, 125, 128, 144, 147, 159, 160, 182, 208, 276, 283, 285, 297, 301, 303, 322, 354, 386.
Sabra, 234.
Salmon, 91, 166, 244, 369, 385, 430.
Salmon J., 430.
Samuel, 255, 261.
Samuel F., 123.
Sarah, 11, 14, 19, 31, 50, 56, 60, 70, 75, 80, 99, 125, 129, 138, 150, 163, 271, 272, 276, 277, 280, 281, 283, 292, 302, 322, 387, 451.
Saul, 31, 54, 77, 79, 90, 277, 376, 381, 382, 383, 386.
Silas, 29, 41, 51, 95, 101, 128, 129, 274, 290, 328, 387.
Silence, 34, 55, 56, 85, 157, 279, 412.
Simon, 287, 413.
Simeon, 28, 276.
Solomon, 22, 33, 57, 80, 82, 90, 92, 95, 97, 139, 183, 280.
Solon B., 209, 413.
Sophia, 95, 106, 122, 138, 304, 390.
Sophronia W., 208, 236.
Sparhawk, 106, 110, 122, 133, 148, 182, 208, 355, 389.
Stilman, 249, 262.
Stilman E., 262.
Stephen, 54, 57, 93, 105, 183, 276, 279, 370, 386.
Susan, 268, 396.
Susan H., 262.
Susanna, 34, 50, 86, 277, 282.
Tabitha, 56, 157.
Tamar, 46, 61, 64, 80, 99, 102, 283, 287.
Thaddeus, 276.
Thankful, 26, 52, 157, 412.
Thomas, 19, 53, 56, 57, 58, 60, 61, 63, 64, 67, 128, 144, 157, 178, 266, 270, 272, 276, 278, 280, 281, 283, 286, 288, 371.
Tilly, 105.
Timothy, 55, 279.
Tiras, 23, 60, 87, 282, 326, 385.
Vashti, 31, 57, 279, 397.
William, 19, 283, 328, 412.
Zerish, 52, 286.
Zerviah, 27, 28, 29, 58, 60, 63, 64, 66, 73, 277, 376.
Zilpah, 130, 143, 305.
HOUSE, Alice, 129, 141, 350.
Deborah, 27, 28.
Elizabeth, 403.
Hannah, 34, 86.
John, 390.
Joseph, 41, 103, 288, 324, 325, 378, 390, 403.
Joshua, 21, 31, 417.
Lydia, 320, 403.
Persis, 30.
Rachel, 23, 87.
Sarah, 32.
HOWARD, Amasa, 183, 209.
Asa W., 430.
Betsy, 234.
Caleb A., 209, 255.
Charlotte, 245.
Daniel M., 209.
Elizabeth, 183, 209, 368, 430.
Francina, 210.
George, 183, 186, 209, 240, 430.
George F., 209.
George W., 183, 209, 242, 253.

INDEX.

262, 268, 350, 397, 430.
Henry A., 251, 262.
John H., 262, 268, 397.
Levi, 183, 209.
Louisa M., 209.
Martha F., 262, 397.
Mary, 183, 209.
Mary A., 253.
Mary F., 209, 350.
Moses, 197.
Olive, 254.
Parney, 209, 267, 372, 431.
Patty, 236.
Persis L., 262.
Rebecca, 88.
Sally, 209, 267, 431.
Sally F., 262.
Sarah, 364.
Sarah A., 209, 254.
Sarah E., 209.
Sarah M., 183, 209, 241, 430.
Sidney, 209, 210, 267, 431.
Sidney T., 209.
Susan S., 209, 257.
HOWE, Abigail, 35, 61, 63, 64, 67, 85, 92, 95, 96, 106, 109, 116.
Abigail S., 255.
Abraham, 17, 129, 139.
Adaline E., 250.
Andrew, 209, 347.
Artemas, 61, 283.
Barzillai M., 209, 347.
Betty, 37, 67.
Bezaleel, 35, 63, 97.
Charles H., 258.
Daniel, 287.
David, 61, 168, 172, 183, 208, 209, 283, 345, 346, 359, 361, 362.
Dolly S., 209.
Ebenezer W., 248, 259.
Elizabeth, 103, 451.
Ephraim, 98.
Francis, 208, 347.
Frederick, 208, 345.
George W., 244, 249.
Hannah, 209.
Henry P., 209, 345.
Horatio B., 256.
James W., 249.
Levi, 92, 209, 287.
Loriman D., 248, 394.
Martha, 256.
Mary, 61, 283, 287.
Mary A., 265, 269.
Mary D., 394.
Mehetabel, 28.
Moses, 277.
Nancy, 209.
Nathaniel L., 253, 265, 269.
Oliver, 34.
Persis, 132.
Phineas, 61, 63, 64, 67, 97.
Phineas B., 183, 209, 368, 369.
Rebecca, 44.
Sally, 208, 209, 335.
Sarah, 16, 97, 351.
Sarah A., 257, 259, 396.
Sarah B., 247.
Sarah M., 265.
Sibilla, 28.
Silas, 37, 64, 92, 95, 96, 106, 109, 116.
Sophronia, 249.
Susan, 183, 208, 209, 335.
Tabitha, 31.
Tamer, 38, 109, 116.
Thomas, 97, 155, 208, 209, 253, 347.
William, 183, 208, 209, 347.
William J., 250.
HOWLAND, Ellen M., 209.
Harriet L., 209.

Henry J., 209.
HUBBARD, David, 296.
Jonathan, 296.
Rev. O. G., 248.
Roswell, 441.
Ruth, 26.
Thomas, 137.
HUCK, Susanna, 35, 85.
HUDSON, Abigail, 12, 15.
Ann, 12.
Benaiah, 280.
Beriah, 47.
Daniel, 12, 14, 16, 19, 451.
Darius, 47, 287.
Dinah, 182, 355.
Elizabeth, 12, 16, 47, 282, 323.
Ephraim, 293.
Eunice, 83, 87.
Ezekiel, 47.
Fanny, 168, 171.
Jane, 47.
Joanna, 12, 14, 16.
John, 12.
Lucy, 119.
Martha, 47, 290.
Mary, 12, 19, 47, 292.
Nathaniel, 14, 16, 47, 158, 272, 279, 280, 283, 282, 283, 286, 287, 290, 292, 293, 451.
Rebecca, 16.
Robert, 129, 140, 155, 170, 181, 209, 352.
Sarah, 12, 209.
Solomon, 47, 286.
Tamar, 47, 279, 319.
William, 12, 47, 119, 281, 352.
———, 332.
HUMPHREY, Charles, 265, 393.
Clara, 265.
Jane, 265, 393.
Jane M., 265.
Mehetabel, 238.
Noah, 254, 373.
HUNT, Alice Z., 262.
Arethusa, 208, 334, 429.
Charles, 346.
Daudridge, 182, 200, 355.
Deborah, 44, 102, 127, 141, 301, 302, 304, 320.
Eliza, 262.
Elizabeth B., 208, 243, 344, 392.
Emeline, 210.
Hanford L., 262.
Jeremiah, 208.
John, 152, 164, 208, 354.
Jonas, 262.
Maria, 182, 342, 429.
Martha Ann, 208, 337, 345.
Nancy, 210.
Otis, 150, 163, 182, 208, 335, 340, 341, 342, 343, 344, 345, 346, 354, 356, 359, 429.
Peter, 132, 147, 302.
Polly, 208.
Samuel, 256.
Sarah T., 208, 235, 340.
Sherebiah, 85, 87, 129, 140, 300, 301, 302, 304, 320, 325.
Sophia, 151, 163, 169.
Susanna, 57, 64, 451.
Thomas T., 210.
Titus, 208.
William, 131, 146, 304.
HUNTINGTON, George M., 209.
Horatio H., 183, 370, 450.
Horatio M., 183, 209, 450.
Joseph D., 394.
Joseph M., 183, 265, 370, 450.
Joseph W., 6, 183, 209, 265, 366, 368, 370, 450.
Julia, 265.

Julia M., 183, 209, 265, 450.
Lucy, 240.
HURD, see HEARD.
HUSE, see HEWES.
HUSTON, Caleb, 145.
Jane, 56.
Nathaniel, 56.
Tamar, 56.
HUTCHINS, Benjamin, 17.
Elizabeth, 271.
Isaac E., 232.
Joseph, 245, 270, 271, 452.
HUTCHINSON, Nelson, 247.
HYATT, George W., 255.
HYDE, Almira J., 395, 396.
Cardner, 235.
John, 182, 183, 360, 361.
Julia, 181.
Polly, 364.
Solon W., 182.
INDIANS, 15, 17, 19, 274, 361.
INGALLS, Theodore, 232.
INGOLDSBY, Isabel, 334.
IVERS, Anne, 128.
Mary, 145.
IVORY, John, 152.
JACKSON, Josiah, 86, 88.
JACKMAN, Lucy J., 252.
JACOBS, Emeline, 110.
Gardner, 210.
George S., 210.
Ira G., 210.
Sullivan, 210.
JAMES, Ann, 257.
Elizabeth L., 257.
Hannah B., 310.
Joseph, 33, 319, 323, 324.
Lydia, 327.
Mathew, 310.
Thomas, 12.
———, 390.
JEFTS, Elizabeth, 328.
Lydia, 39.
JENKS, Mary, 183, 413.
Phebe, 413.
William, 413.
JENNESS, Mary Ann, 249.
JENNISON, Eunice, 30.
Israel, 125.
JEWELL, Sarah, 19.
JEWETT, Amos, 41, 74, 76, 109, 288, 289, 380, 381.
Anna, 90, 92, 93, 96, 100, 108, 111, 302, 303, 320.
Anne, 74, 305, 380.
Ann H., 393.
Betsy, 116, 392, 393.
Betty, 390.
Charles, 251.
Clara L., 262.
Daniel, 291.
David, 27, 28, 29, 30, 46, 73, 74, 76, 111, 113, 116, 289, 292, 375, 379, 380, 381, 382, 383.
Ebenezer, 109.
Elizabeth, 30, 43, 74, 98, 103, 116, 289.
Elizabeth H., 349.
Emily L., 259.
Enoch, 74, 99, 288.
Erastus, 264.
Esther, 30, 41, 73, 74, 76, 101, 375, 379.
Esther I., 262.
Frances E. C., 393.
Hannah, 74, 108, 126, 128, 307, 380, 383.
Helen A., 392.
Horace, 210, 259, 264, 309.
Jane, 210, 259, 264.
John S., 210.

480 INDEX.

Jonathan, 90. 93. 302, 304.
Joshua C., 252,
Marion, 264.
Mary, 40, 74, 76, 101.
Milton, 264.
Moses, 100. 306.
Nathaniel, 111, 310.
Phebe, 46, 76, 103. 381.
Priscilla, 30, 39, 101, 109, 291, 377.
Ruth, 111, 113, 116.
Samuel, 76, 90, 109, 116, 135. 184, 191, 349, 381, 390, 392, 393.
Sarah, 311.
Sarah C., 210.
Solomon, 40. 126, 140, 292.
Stephen, 352.
Theodore, 262.
William, 40, 92. 93, 96, 100, 108, 111, 302, 303, 304, 306, 307, 310, 311, 320, 325.
William H. S., 184.
JIPE, Esther, 23.
JOCK, Hannah, 22, 97, 108, 305, 231, 326.
John, 108. 307.
Lynn, 22, 97, 108, 305, 306, 307, 321, 326.
Rachel, 12, 305.
Sarah, 97. 305.
JOHNSON, Aaron, 121, 184, 186, 187, 309, 310, 326, 448.
Abel, 117. 318.
Abigail, 47, 295, 448.
Almira, 262, 395.
Almira P., 210, 262.
Anes, 24, 52.
Anna, 121, 168, 172, 307, 308.
Betsy, 117, 313, 345.
Caleb, 241.
Caroline A., 258.
Calvin, 121, 168, 171, 210, 448.
Charles F., 210.
Clarissa, 314.
Damaris, 116. 334. 340.
Daniel, 21. 33. 75. 79. 92, 96. 184, 297, 298, 299, 303, 324, 340, 341, 345, 352, 357, 366.
David, 27, 289.
Deborah, 117, 121, 314.
Dorothy, 51, 64, 286, 322.
Ebenezer, 136.
Edward, 314, 315, 316, 317, 318.
Edward L., 257, 394.
Elijah, 235.
Elizabeth, 47, 121, 148, 295, 304, 310, 321.
Elizabeth R., 210.
Fanny, 317.
Francis, 210.
Frederick W., 258.
Grata, 245.
Hannah, 35, 41, 47, 98, 100, 295, 296, 297, 319, 321.
Harrison, 210, 246, 448.
Henry, 340.
Jemima, 45.
John, 51, 64, 158, 280, 286, 298, 319, 324.
Jonathan, 131, 146.
Jonas, 45, 103, 116, 121, 152, 210, 309.
Joseph, 42.
Joshua, 35, 47, 98, 147, 295, 296, 297, 306, 307, 308, 310, 311, 319, 324, 325, 331.
Josiah, 52, 157, 278,
Julia Ann, 210.
Lucy, 116, 131, 146, 289.
Luther, 121, 170, 184, 210, 315, 448.

Luther S., 210.
Lydia, 75, 79, 92, 96, 112, 117, 127, 142, 155, 166, 303, 308, 316, 322, 331, 340.
Mary, 26, 29, 51, 64, 210, 272, 285, 289.
Mary S., 210.
Mehetabel, 272.
Millicent, 306,
Nabby, 210.
Nathaniel, 51, 64, 210, 262, 280.
Oliver, 316.
Orson, 210.
Peter, 112, 310.
Prudence, 153, 165.
Rachel, 310.
Relief, 96, 146, 299.
Rhoda, 216, 256, 340, 345, 367.
Robert A., 306.
Rollin, 210.
Ruth, 297, 364.
Sally, 168, 172, 341.
Samuel, 47, 92, 105, 112, 117, 127, 135, 143, 297, 310, 313, 314, 315, 316, 317, 321, 329, 397.
Sarah, 121, 210.
Sewell, 210, 448.
Simeon, 308.
Sophia, 210.
Stephen, 295, 330.
Subbiear, 79, 151, 163, 298.
Tabitha G., 304.
Tamar, 134.
Timothy, 296, 308.
William, 19, 317.
JONES, Aaron, 149, 162, 181, 183, 184, 210, 358, 359, 369, 431.
Almira, 210, 235.
Amos Brooks, 210, 341.
Anna, 326.
Benjamin F., 210.
Benjamin W., 261.
Betsy, 184, 210, 251, 341, 351, 356.
Betty, 107.
Charlotte, 184, 210, 431.
Charlotte A., 210.
Charles, 183, 210, 264, 341.
Charles T., 261.
Christopher, 210, 395.
Cynthia, 210. 341.
David, 138, 184, 317, 351.
David W., 210.
Edmund, 240.
Edward, 210.
Edwin, 183, 210, 431.
Eliza, 210.
Eliza W., 237.
Eunice, 107, 388.
Frances, 244.
George, 261.
Hannah, 111, 230.
Jane, 205.
John, 42, 104, 307, 308.
John F., 261.
John R., 339.
Joseph, 308, 310.
Lavina, 318.
Lavina J., 210.
Louisa, 318.
Luther, 184, 210, 233, 315, 328, 431.
Marcus L., 184, 210, 431.
Martha, 264.
Mary, 184, 261, 316, 335.
Mary Ann, 183, 359, 431.
Mary D., 254.
Mary J., 258.
Mehetabel, 103.
Molly, 307.
Moses, 131, 146, 171, 174, 183,
184, 210, 341, 343, 359, 364, 431.
Nancy, 184, 210, 242, 360.
Nathaniel, 37, 98, 107, 111, 153, 356, 387, 388, 389.
Olive, 230, 338.
Phebe, 107, 111, 387.
Phebe P., 386.
Phineas, 310.
Polly, 167, 173, 184, 210, 229, 317, 341.
Priscilla, 41.
Sally, 107, 151, 164, 183, 388, 431.
Samuel, 107, 155, 167, 183, 184, 210, 231, 246, 259, 264, 315, 316, 317, 318, 322, 328, 329, 330, 355, 359, 340, 352, 389.
Samuel A., 259.
Sarah, 183, 259, 264, 315, 322, 360.
Sarah J., 184, 210, 431.
Sarah P., 210, 341.
Solomon, 256.
Solon, 184, 210, 431.
Submit, 184, 210, 334, 357, 431.
Sullivan, 184, 210, 343, 365, 431.
Thomas, 242, 261.
Thomas H., 261.
Zophar, 340.
JORDAN, Hannah, 325.
JOSLIN, Aaron, 321.
Abigail, 27, 110, 184, 274, 321, 358, 431, 436.
Abijah, 293.
Abraham, 10, 14, 16, 19.
Alice, 32, 46, 158, 321, 329.
Almira, 210, 264.
Ann, 14, 16.
Austin E., 264.
Beatrix, 10, 14, 16.
Betsy, 132, 147, 184, 210.
Billy, 313.
Calvin, 168, 171, 314.
Catharine E., 210.
Damaris, 275.
Daniel, 296.
Deborah, 25, 72, 273.
Dorothy, 11, 156, 274, 289, 322, 407.
Edward R., 264.
Eliza, 210, 233, 342.
Elizabeth, 12, 122, 295, 297, 308, 323, 334.
Esther, 297, 330.
Hannah, 407.
Hester, 46.
James, 184, 210, 294, 311.
Joanna, 271, 273, 407.
John, 25, 61, 63, 156, 255, 264, 273, 274, 283, 284, 286, 287, 289, 291, 293, 294.
John E., 255, 264.
Jonas, 148, 161, 184, 210, 309, 342, 345, 346, 347, 354, 356, 368, 431.
Joseph, 10, 19, 46, 125, 136, 158, 286, 291, 297, 311, 312, 313, 314, 321.
Lucy, 61, 63, 153, 156, 165, 273, 283, 287, 293, 312, 346.
Luke, 312.
Lyman A., 264.
Martha, 128, 303, 304, 330, 407, 410.
Martha A., 240.
Mary, 10, 11, 20, 127, 176, 184, 303, 346, 362, 372, 431.
Mary Ann, 210.
Mary D., 254.
Nabby, 110, 148, 161, 310.
Nathaniel, 10, 11, 12, 13, 14, 20, 34, 44, 46, 86, 104, 176, 184, 210,

INDEX. 481

239, 297, 298, 299, 301, 303, 304, 308, 309, 311, 321, 324, 325, 330, 345, 355, 367, 407, 431.
Patty, 144, 170.
Peter, 11, 15, 16, 18, 32, 46, 156, 158, 184, 210, 236, 264, 271, 273, 274, 275, 279, 295, 296, 297, 305, 311, 323, 330, 331, 342, 353, 365, 373, 407, 410, 431.
Polly, 142.
Rebecca, 11, 14, 126, 138, 273, 299.
Samuel, 46, 102, 110, 184, 303, 310, 312, 313, 314, 326, 329, 330, 331, 344, 362, 368, 431, 436.
Sarah, 10, 12, 14, 15, 16, 127, 142, 273, 301.
Silence, 295.
Sophia, 243, 347.
Thomas, 14.
William, 210, 243, 345.
William C., 210.
JOY, Asenath D., 252.
David, 147.
JOYNER, Anna, 38.
Anne, 40.
JUBA, 325.
JUDEVINE, Calvin, 106, 385.
Cornelius, 112.
Jane R., 388.
Luther, 385, 387.
Patience, 106, 108, 112, 388.
William, 106, 108, 112, 377, 385, 386, 387, 388.
JUDD, Sarah, 255.
Sarsen L., 232.
JUDUM, Primus, 325.
KEECH, Benjamin, 39.
Mehetabel, 39.
Zerviah, 39.
KELLY, Aratus M., 250.
Eleanor, 245.
Huldah, 231.
John, 252.
Maurice, 173.
Mercy, 243.
Mike, 252.
——, 328.
KELSEY, Lydia, 152, 164.
KENDALL, Aaron, 45, 78, 104, 379.
Abiathar, 48.
Abigail, 39, 45, 48, 71, 74, 78, 79, 91, 102, 291, 294, 296, 303, 330, 335, 344, 379, 403.
Abijah, 78, 377, 378, 379.
Admonition, 70, 73, 75, 77, 79, 90, 291, 302, 330.
Anes, 101, 307.
Apphia, 312.
Artemas, 110, 309.
Augustus, 96, 114, 387.
Bartholomew, 381.
Benjamin, 48.
Caleb, 130, 145, 380, 381.
Cephas, 314.
David, 93, 383.
Dolly, 110, 389.
Dorothy, 110, 116.
Ebenezer, 72, 75, 159, 386.
Elizabeth, 35, 46, 87, 94, 96, 97, 109, 112, 114, 135, 322, 382, 385, 388.
Ephraim, 65, 79, 106, 112, 116, 125, 135, 299, 312, 322, 387, 389.
Esther, 77, 381, 417.
Ethan, 45, 77, 102, 109, 110, 112, 380, 390.
Eunice, 48, 148, 390.
Eusebia, 316.
Experience, 277.

Ezekiel, 26, 29, 34, 78, 85, 93, 94, 106, 375, 376, 379, 380, 382, 383, 384, 385, 386, 387.
Frances, 280.
George E., 263.
George H., 249, 263.
Hannah, 44, 72, 74, 75, 78, 97, 101, 103, 104, 110, 112, 121, 129, 134, 278, 294, 321, 376, 386.
Heman, 38, 67, 101, 289, 390.
Henry, 121.
Hephzibah, 65, 285, 290.
Hester, 46.
Isaac, 386.
James, 39, 64, 70, 96, 97, 109, 114, 157, 292, 374, 375, 380, 387, 388, 389, 418.
Jane, 184, 367.
Joanna, 116, 390.
Joel, 390.
John, 121, 276, 277.
Jonas, 22, 33.
Jonathan, 30, 36, 41, 70, 73, 75, 77, 79, 90, 97, 100, 101, 110, 112, 131, 146, 229, 272, 277, 278, 280, 281, 291, 293, 294, 295, 296, 299, 302, 306, 307, 309, 311, 312, 319, 321, 326, 327, 328, 377, 386, 387.
Joseph, 46, 78, 136, 380.
Joshua, 44, 110, 116, 389, 390.
Josiah, 65, 67, 71, 77, 88, 287, 289, 292, 374, 377, 380, 381, 417.
Kezia, 31, 397.
Levi, 65, 88, 290.
Lois, 71, 292.
Lucretia, 385.
Lucina, 386.
Lucy, 37, 77, 98, 130, 140, 145, 315, 322, 384.
Luke, 112.
Luther, 111, 310.
Lydia, 23, 70, 82, 87, 97, 114, 281, 306, 375, 418.
Mary, 30, 40, 78, 87, 93, 94, 95, 101, 106, 109, 111, 114, 127, 143, 271, 277, 280, 305, 321, 332, 389.
Mary J., 263.
Nabby, 121.
Nathan, 390.
Nathaniel, 48, 91, 121, 142, 300, 303, 382.
Noah, 78, 382.
Oliver, 112, 390.
Patience, 387.
Paul, 40, 70, 101, 292.
Peter, 26, 65, 290.
Phebe, 126, 139, 375, 383.
Pierson, 96, 114, 380, 387, 418.
Prudence, 136, 386, 390.
Ralph, 48.
Rebecca, 30, 42, 71, 104, 121, 231, 277, 294, 321, 335, 344, 379.
Relief, 78, 121, 127, 143, 298.
Rufus, 111, 308.
Ruth, 48, 299, 324, 331.
Samuel, 121, 375, 379, 380, 381, 383, 384, 385.
Sarah, 29, 64, 70, 94, 112, 122, 144, 157, 272, 293, 311, 384.
Sewall, 313.
Silas, 72, 312.
Stephen, 116.
Susanna, 139.
Tabitha, 65, 67, 71, 77, 417.
Thankful, 109, 110, 112.
Timothy, 77, 90, 98, 126, 139, 296, 302.
Thomas, 30, 48, 71, 74, 78, 79, 91, 121, 129, 142, 291, 294, 296, 298, 299, 300, 303, 315, 319, 321, 324, 330, 403.

Uzziah, 48.
William, 40, 75, 84, 87, 95, 100, 101, 111, 137, 295' 298, 305, 307, 308, 310, 311, 313, 314, 316, 321, 331, 382.
Wyman, 110, 390.
KENDRICK, Anna, 310.
Asa, 316.
James, 314.
John, 45, 110, 112, 309, 310, 311, 312, 314, 315, 316.
Kezia, 110, 112, 321.
Polly, 312.
Sally, 315.
Samuel, 112, 311.
KENNEDY, Margaret, 248.
KENNEY, Bridget, 252.
Joshua, 155, 167.
Lydia, 106.
S——, 446.
Sarah, 135.
KENT, Eunice, 30.
KERLEY, Ann, 12.
Bridget, 12.
Elizabeth, 9, 10, 11, 13, 14, 16.
Hannah, 11.
Henry, 9, 10, 11, 13, 14, 16, 20, 451.
Joseph, 13, 16.
Martha, 14.
Mary, 11.
William, 10, 11, 12, 13, 16, 20.
KETTLE, Elizabeth, 13.
John, 13, 16.
Jonathan, 13.
Joseph, 16.
KEYES, Amasa, 184, 359, 363, 431.
Calvin, 93, 386.
Clarissa, 236.
Charlotte E., 257.
Daniel, 121, 132, 210, 351.
Dorcas, 184.
Elizabeth, 93.
Elkanan, 275.
Ellen I., 256.
Gerrish, 387.
Huldah, 274.
Jedidah, 121, 210.
John, 210, 270, 273, 274, 275.
Jonathan M., 258.
Lucinda, 210.
Lydia, 273.
Martha, 210.
Mary, 210.
Nancy, 232.
Prudence, 19.
Sally B., 184, 239, 431.
Sarah, 24, 61, 64, 121, 273.
Sarah I., 184, 431.
Simon, 184, 353.
Stephen, 93, 386, 387.
Thomas, 129.
KIBBY, Lydia, 11.
KID, Alexander, 33.
KIDDER, Abigail, 141.
Abraham F., 255.
Charlotte, 347.
Heywood, 149, 161.
Jane, 246.
Jeffrey, 345.
Mary W., 347.
Nathaniel, 155, 167, 344, 345, 347.
Nathaniel A., 344.
Rebecca, 141.
Sally R., 347.
Zilpah, 350.
KILBURN, Aaron, 71, 379.
Calvin, 91, 211.
Dorcas, 96, 101, 375, 387.

34

482 INDEX.

Elizabeth, 27, 29, 91, 380, 383.
Hannah, 91.
Isaac, 30, 71, 91, 211, 229, 318, 361, 375, 379, 380, 381, 382, 383.
Jacob, 132, 137, 147, 318, 332, 375, 379, 381.
Joanna, 71, 103, 134, 381.
John, 91, 382.
Joseph, 21, 34, 79, 86, 93, 96, 101, 376, 377, 382, 383, 384, 385, 386, 387, 388.
Joshua, 386.
Levi, 101, 388.
Lorena, 248.
Lydia, 184, 445.
Mary, 79, 91, 93, 96, 101.
Mary Jane, 211.
Nancy, 211.
Rebecca, 318.
Ruth, 93, 126, 128, 382, 384.
Sally, 238.
Samuel, 46, 93, 104, 385.
Sarah, 91, 150, 380.
Timothy, 79, 129, 138, 383.
William, 91.
KILI, Margaret, 284.
KIMBALL, Aaron, 184.
Benjamin, 127, 140.
Charlotte S., 251.
Polly, 184, 229, 365.
KING, Cecilia, 252.
Charles E., 211.
Mary Ann, 211, 266, 371.
Orice, 181, 211, 266, 371.
Sarah, 20.
Susan W., 244.
Thomas, 19.
KINGSBURY, Catharine, 184, 363.
Nathaniel, 184, 235.
KINNEY, see KENNEY.
KINSMAN, Alfred D., 258.
KITTRIDGE, Esther, 38, 99.
KNABE, Henry, 245.
KNAPP, Anna L., 268.
Charles M., 211.
Horace, 211.
Martha T., 211.
KNIGHT, Abel B., 107.
Abidan, 168, 172.
Abigail, 161.
Abigail J., 211, 349.
Alfred, 184, 242, 259, 368, 369, 371.
Amos, 26, 44, 56, 59, 60, 63, 67, 68, 71, 73, 75, 77, 127, 142, 184, 272, 280, 281, 282, 285, 286, 289, 291, 293, 295, 297, 319, 323, 324, 328, 329.
Amy, 314.
Anes, 43, 76, 104, 111, 296, 389.
Anna, 285.
Artemas, 311.
Betsy, 161.
Betty, 108, 389.
Carter, 112, 299.
Catharine A., 184, 211, 335, 347, 431, 432.
Charles, 112, 210, 342.
Charles E., 152, 169, 170, 184, 210, 211, 311, 334, 342, 345, 347, 348, 349, 361, 363, 364, 431, 432.
Damaris, 39, 56, 70, 100, 290, 320.
Daniel, 26, 29, 60, 87, 112, 125, 137, 157, 273, 281, 285, 297, 312, 313, 319, 324, 325, 361, 413.
David, 71, 293.
Ebenezer, 59, 82, 85, 90, 107, 108, 111, 281, 301, 307, 320, 386, 387, 389.

Elizabeth, 32, 56, 59, 60, 79, 125, 127, 135, 141, 211, 249, 272, 280, 299, 347.
Eunice, 314.
Ephraim, 77, 297, 323.
Faithful, 315.
George G., 184, 371.
Hannah, 63, 67, 68, 71, 73, 75, 77, 83, 112, 119, 285, 286, 295, 322, 432.
James, 184.
James M., 211, 347, 432.
Joel, 308.
Jonas, 75, 295.
Jonathan, 26, 29, 70, 71, 74, 76, 79, 82, 91, 159, 280, 289, 293, 296, 297, 299, 300, 301, 320.
Joseph, 68, 75, 295.
Joseph, 68, 75, 295.
Lucy, 36, 67, 92, 99, 289, 320.
Lydia, 111, 184, 310, 322, 357.
Manasseh, 77, 112, 119, 135, 184, 297, 311, 312, 321, 344, 358, 432.
Mary, 40, 60, 70, 71, 74, 76, 79, 82, 88, 91, 99, 100, 112, 119, 128, 153, 159, 165, 282, 293, 297, 298, 320, 322.
Mary W., 211, 243, 345.
Martha, 237.
Matthew, 36, 99.
Nancy, 171.
Nathaniel L., 184, 211, 347, 431.
Patience, 119, 184, 311, 352.
Patty, 119, 184, 210, 312, 353, 432.
Paul, 309.
Phebe, 107, 387.
Prudence, 82, 90, 107, 108, 111, 301, 320.
Rebecca, 170, 291, 313, 317.
Relief, 308.
Russell, 34, 60, 112, 281, 297, 298, 299, 300, 308, 309, 319.
Ruth, 79, 104, 107, 134, 297, 307, 320.
Sally, 152, 184, 210, 211, 334, 342, 358, 432.
Salmon, 107, 386.
Sarah, 25, 60, 83, 87, 112, 157, 244, 300, 413.
Silas, 301.
Sophia C., 211, 349.
Sophia M., 184, 348, 431.
Sybil, 82, 125, 136, 300.
Timothy, 30, 104, 111, 134, 291, 310, 311, 313, 314, 315, 316, 320, 321, 327.
Timothy W., 316.
Vashti, 90, 301.
William J., 211, 348.
Widow ——, 327.
KNOWLTON, Alice, 359.
Asa, 154, 165.
Charles, 210.
Deborah, 155, 167.
Ebenezer, 184, 369.
Frances E., 238.
Rebecca, 127, 143.
Relief, 210.
Sally, 334.
Sarah, 83, 131.
Seth, 210.
KNOX, David, 280.
Jane, 57.
Mary, 282.
Timothy, 57, 279, 280, 282.
LACY, Mary, 252.
LADD, Emily E., 264.
Emily G., 262.
Emily P., 185, 212, 261.
George V., 185, 212, 262.

Hastings A., 261.
Lucy B., 262.
Marietta H., 261.
Mary G., 262.
Rebecca B., 261.
Rufus K., 185, 212, 244, 262, 264, 368.
LAHEY, Peggy, 41, 103.
LAKIN, Abel, 232.
Abigail, 274.
Catharine A., 169, 170.
Samuel, 274.
LAMB, Marcus, 239.
LAMBERT, Lucy H., 230.
William, 154, 166.
LAMSON, David R., 246.
Elizabeth M., 236.
LANCEY, Charles K., 255.
LANE, Alfred L., 212.
Alvinzy, 185, 212, 261, 269, 364.
Alvinzy W., 212.
Annis K., 212, 256.
Anthony, 233, 338.
Clarissa, 185.
Diancy T., 212.
Dolly, 119, 185, 333, 351.
Dolly B., 185, 339, 450.
Elizabeth, 185, 342, 450.
Eunice K., 185, 333, 355, 450.
Frederick E., 252.
George Hy, 212.
Helen M., 212.
Henry, 340.
Jonas, 119, 130, 145, 148, 167, 172, 177, 185, 237, 268, 333, 338, 339, 340, 341, 342, 344, 345, 352, 355, 358, 373, 396, 450.
Joshua A., 258.
Lucy, 185, 212, 261.
Lydia, 336.
Mary, 336.
Mary Ann, 185, 341, 450.
Mary H. K. B., 345, 450.
Sally H., 185, 335, 344, 357, 450.
Sarah Ann, 336, 344.
Sarah J., 261.
William H., 233.
LANGDON, Amzi, 170, 228.
LANCLEY, Andrew J., 255.
LARKIN, Abel, 304.
Abigail, 302.
Andrew, 327.
Azubah, 80, 81, 82, 89, 91, 93, 95, 128, 303, 321.
Benjamin, 151, 164, 184.
Betty, 125, 137.
Edwin A., 250, 261.
Edmund, 52, 99, 284, 302, 331.
Elizabeth, 261.
Ephraim, 91, 143, 303.
Hannah, 186, 371.
Hasadiah, 80, 136, 170.
John, 52, 89, 144, 277, 301.
Joseph, 302.
Katy, 306, 328.
Lizzie, 261.
Lucretia, 95, 305, 328.
Lucy, 93, 304, 328.
Marietta, 261.
Mary, 36, 52, 284.
Matthias, 21, 33, 52, 278, 302, 304, 325, 387.
Mehetabel, 185.
Molly, 81, 129, 139.
Mr. ——, 325.
Persis, 80.
Peter, 33, 52, 80, 81, 82, 89, 91, 93, 95, 279, 301, 303, 304, 305, 306, 309, 321, 328.
Philip, 52, 277, 278, 279, 281, 284.
Polly, 184.
Sarah, 302.

INDEX.

Seth, 268, 387.
Widow, 324.
William, 52, 185, 228, 237, 281, 358, 367.
LARRABEE, Harriet L., 234.
Sarah, 197.
LATHAM, Louisa C., 251.
Cornelia, 251.
LAUGHTON, Andrew, 212.
Artemas, 362, 433.
Austin A., 212.
Caroline, 212.
Caroline M., 212, 257.
Clarissa, 212, 433.
Daniel, 184, 185, 212, 357.
Dolly, 185, 212.
Emily, 185, 212, 337, 349, 365.
Ephraim, 185, 359, 433.
Hannibal, 185, 212, 229, 363.
Hannibal D., 212.
James, 212.
John, 186, 268, 370, 395, 397, 433.
Lucy, 212, 230, 336, 368,.
Lucy A., 433.
Martha B., 268, 397, 433.
Marshall, 185, 212.
Mary Ann, 186, 370, 433.
Mary W., 212.
Nancy, 397, 433.
Nancy P., 212.
Olive, 155, 166.
Rebecca, 212.
Stephen, 212, 229, 360, 361, 433.
Thomas, 185, 212, 247, 355.
LAW, Jonathan, 269.
Nathaniel T., 247.
LAWRENCE, Angelia, 244.
Angelia J., 261.
Caroline, 259.
Catharine C., 261, 450.
Danforth, 261.
Daniel, 186, 370.
Edmund, 185, 212, 235, 364, 432.
Eugenia C., 450.
Evelina W., 258.
George, 212.
Harlow, 261, 450.
Harriet A., 372.
James S., 247, 259, 394, 395.
John E., 259.
Josiah, 246, 450.
Kezia E., 261.
Mary, 236.
Mary A., 261.
Mary E., 261.
Mary G., 261.
Oscar M., 259.
Royal, 268.
Sally, 212, 268, 365, 397, 432.
Sarah L., 251.
Tabitha, 450.
Thomas E., 250.
Willie J., 450.
LAWSON, Ann, 363.
Mary, 172.
Nancy, 172.
LEACH and LEITCH.
Abigail M., 433.
Collins, 185, 211, 433.
Eliab, 433.
Elizabeth, 102, 185, 334, 345, 360.
Evelina H., 345.
Henry, 122, 339.
Jeremiah, 310, 327.
John, 40, 432.
Joseph, 122, 146, 152, 172, 184, 185, 211, 333, 339, 340, 342, 343, 345, 346, 355, 433.
Josiah, 211, 343.
Lucretia M., 211, 342.
Luther D., 211, 346.

Lydia, 432.
Mary, 185, 211, 340.
Mary H., 211, 343.
Rebecca, 184, 211, 334, 356, 433.
Rebecca Luscomb, 211, 342.
Sally, 122.
Sarah, 339.
Stephen H., 310, 327.
Susanna, 122, 185, 211, 333, 353, 433.
Tabitha, 211.
Washington, 185, 352, 432.
LEASON, Betty, 331.
George, 308, 331.
William, 308.
LEAVITT, Josiah, 6, 105, 128, 138, 418.
Mary, 418.
LEE, Ann, 185, 445.
Anna P., 394.
Benjamin, 193, 211, 341, 354, 433.
Elizabeth, 211, 341.
George W., 212.
Harriet P., 237.
Harriet T., 212.
Laura S., 212.
LEESE, Patience, 129, 141.
Richard, 129, 139.
LEGATE, Elizabeth, 23, 83, 85, 284.
Magdalen, 22, 23, 284, 287.
Mary, 22, 287.
Robert, 22.
Thomas, 22, 23, 284, 287.
LEWIS, Abby, 254, 350.
Abigail, 185, 211, 212, 450.
Abigail B., 337.
Augustus, 185, 212, 450.
Barrachia, 13.
Bethia, 11.
Charles, 149.
Charles A., 212.
Clara A., 260.
Crosby, 212, 350.
Delia Ann, 212.
Frances E., 212, 266.
Francis, 212, 350.
Francis J., 259.
Frederick A., 235.
George H., 212.
Hannah, 11, 12, 13, 14, 390.
Henry, 212, 238, 259, 260, 266.
Jackson, 211, 350.
James B., 212, 350.
John, 11, 12, 13, 14.
Joseph, 103, 134, 378, 390.
Levi, 185, 211, 212, 230, 350, 362, 365, 369, 450.
Lucy E., 212, 350.
Lydia, 15.
Martha, 185, 212, 450.
Martha J., 212, 350.
Mary, 230.
Patience, 13.
Rebecca, 11, 12.
Sarah B., 212, 259, 260, 266.
Sarah J., 212.
Susan A., 212, 350.
Susannah H., 238.
Thomas, 150, 372.
Timothy, 150, 163, 185.
William, 14, 433.
William A., 212, 350.
LILLY, Sarah, 83.
LINCOLN, Betsy, 211.
Caleb, 150, 163, 185, 362, 433.
Chloe, 185, 211, 364, 432.
Cummings, 185, 361, 432.
Dolly, 302.
Ellen S., 212.
Elizabeth, 13, 14.
Henry, 212, 244, 260.

Jacob, 185, 211, 432.
Levi, 127, 141.
Maria, 211.
Mark, 83, 84, 87, 301, 302, 320, 332.
Martha B., 212, 260.
Mary, 83, 301, 302, 332.
Mary C., 212.
Nancy, 243.
Otis, 83, 301.
William, 13, 14.
William H., 212.
LINES, Sally, 237.
LINTON, Ann, 452.
Richard, 12.
LIPPENWELL, Abigail, 92, 127, 143, 304.
Anna, 82, 91, 92, 96, 97, 101, 129, 141, 297, 299, 301, 302, 320, 330, 332.
Elizabeth, 82, 129, 139, 297.
Hannah, 91, 302, 319, 324, 326.
Lydia, 90, 128, 145, 305.
Mary, 84, 87, 301, 320.
Nathaniel, 101, 307, 322, 323.
Olive, 309.
Rebecca, 97, 306.
Reuben, 34, 82, 86, 91, 92, 96, 97, 101, 128, 144, 297, 298, 299, 300, 301, 302, 304, 305, 306, 307, 309, 320, 322, 330, 332.
Sarah, 82, 104, 134, 298, 323.
Thomas, 320, 323, 326.
LITCHFIELD, Otis, 264.
Otis O., 264.
LITTAYE, Catharine, 185, 211, 230, 340.
Dolly, 211.
Katy, 211.
Noel, 131, 185, 211, 340, 353.
Sally, 185, 211.
LITTLE, Aurelia, 256.
Fortune, 143.
Franklin, 255.
Joel S., 252.
Margaret, 249, 255.
LITTLEJOHN, Hannah, 384, 418.
Mary, 56, 58, 60, 62.
Marah, 418.
Sarah, 60.
Simeon, 60.
Thomas, 24, 56, 58, 60, 62.
Tilley, 62, 84, 85, 376, 378, 384, 418.
LOCKE, Abel, 93, 94, 325, 400.
Anna, 118, 161, 311, 327.
Diana S., 336, 351, 394.
Edward C., 211, 347.
Eliza Ann, 211, 257, 348.
Esther, 93, 94, 125, 136, 306, 317, 321, 322, 325, 400.
Frances A., 211, 257, 348.
Henrietta, 326, 327.
Irene, 337.
James, 36, 43, 98, 118, 296, 314, 326, 400, 407.
John, 38, 46, 79, 94, 99, 104, 128, 144, 296, 305, 317, 322, 326, 327, 332.
Jonathan, 185, 195, 211, 212, 268, 336, 345, 346, 347, 348, 358, 368, 432.
Josiah, 38, 93, 94, 99, 118, 296, 306, 313, 325, 326, 400.
Lauretta J., 260.
Lucretia, 83, 87, 91, 118, 296, 317, 330.
Lucy, 94, 317, 322.
Martha, 103, 134.
Mary, 111, 118, 161, 185, 211, 212, 268, 309, 321, 327, 336, 352, 397, 400, 432.

INDEX.

Mary T., 236.
Mary W., 260.
Nancy, 118, 315.
Phebe R., 212, 346.
Polly, 118, 312.
Rebecca, 74, 79, 81, 125, 136, 306, 320, 407.
Samuel, 74, 79, 81, 296, 319, 326, 330, 400.
Sarah S., 211, 254, 347.
William, 45, 74, 81, 104, 111, 118, 148, 161, 185, 296, 309, 310, 311, 312, 313, 314, 315, 317, 327, 352, 400.
William S., 212, 255, 260, 345.
LOKER, Mary, 452.
LONDON, ——, 379.
LONG, John B., 254.
LONGLEY, Abel W., 256.
Ann, 372.
Ezekiel, 185, 352.
John, 18.
Lydia, 39, 102, 234.
Mary, 43, 104.
Parker, 240.
Sarah, 36, 86.
Susanna, 139.
William, 37, 102.
LOOMIS, Horace, 254.
LORD, Absalom, 269.
Charles H., 269.
LORING, Betsy, 116, 390.
Daniel, 116.
Elizabeth, 97, 110, 111, 116.
John, 97, 110, 111, 116, 377, 386, 387, 388, 389, 390.
Jonas, 111.
Jonathan, 110, 389.
Joseph, 97, 387.
Lucy, 97, 386.
Maynard, 241.
LOTHROP, Deborah, 30.
LOUGHLAN, Michael. 252.
LOVEJOY, Jonathan, 240.
Pamela, 230.
LOWE, Abigail, 185, 211.
Albert W., 212.
Alfred, 212.
Almira, 185, 211, 364, 432.
Anes, 185, 211, 212, 360, 432.
Anson, 211, 269, 392, 393, 432.
Caroline, 212, 247, 392, 393.
Charles F., 212.
Comfort, 185, 356.
David, 168, 172.
Edgar A., 262, 268, 432.
Eliphas, 211.
Emeline, 432.
Francis, 212.
George W., 262.
Henry, 212, 236, 262, 268, 394, 432.
Jabez, 355.
John, 185, 211, 212, 268, 355, 358, 392, 393.
John E., 262.
John W., 212.
Jonathan, 211.
Joseph, 390.
Lorinda, 392, 393.
Martha, 211, 390, 392, 393.
Mary, 185, 211, 262, 268, 332, 392, 393, 395, 432.
Mary E., 432.
Matilda, 211, 244.
Nathaniel, 185, 211, 212, 355, 363, 432.
Polly, 185, 211, 212, 432.
Rufus, 185, 211, 363, 432.
Sally, 147.
Saxton, 185, 211, 432.

Susan, 211.
Sylvia, 211, 242, 392, 393.
Theodore E., 262.
Thomas, 211.
William, 211.
LUE and LEW, Lucy, 43, 104.
Primus, 34, 86.
LUND, Charles B., 432.
Eveline B., 263, 432.
Franklin, 263.
Mark, 251, 263, 432.
Martha, 263.
Martha E., 263.
LUXFORD, Margaret, 13.
Reuben, 13.
LYMAN, Alfred A., 212.
Charles A., 185, 212, 240, 370.
Maria L., 212.
LYON, Aaron, 185.
Amory W., 211.
Augustus, 211.
Charles, 211.
Deborah, 196.
Elizabeth, 98.
Jonn, 154, 165, 185, 211, 266, 361, 367, 432, 433.
Lawson, 211.
Luther, 211.
Maria, 185, 211.
Martha A., 211, 433.
Mary, 152, 211.
Mary A., 211.
Matilda, 185, 446.
Nancy, 185, 211.
Sally, 211, 266, 371, 432, 433.
Sophia, 211.
Thomas, 211.
Thomas W., 180, 185, 211, 357.
Willard, 185, 211.
William, 211.
MCALLISTER, Harriet S., 258.
Helen, 258.
John, 281.
Margaret, 279.
William, 279, 281.
MCBRIDE, Agnes, 64, 286.
Alexander, 62, 64, 284, 286, 288.
Anna, 383.
John, 383.
Mary, 62, 64, 383.
Thomas, 288.
William, 62, 284.
MCCALLUM, Lucretia, 335.
MCCARTY, John, 36, 99.
MCCLELLAN and MCLELLAN.
Charles, 212, 343.
David, 141.
Dolly, 336, 343.
Eliza D., 343.
Lucretia, 212.
Susan, 6, 212, 343.
William, 132, 147, 186, 212, 343, 361, 435.
MCCLURE, Samuel O., 251.
MCCOLLISTER, Margaret, 25.
MCCOLLUM, Caroline L., 262, 393.
George H., 262.
Harriet M., 262.
Haskell, 213, 242, 262, 268, 392, 393.
Matilda L., 262, 268.
Martha A., 262, 268.
Mary F., 213, 393.
Sylvia, 213, 262, 268, 393.
MCCURDY, John. 234.
MCELWAIN, Andrew, 38.
Jenny, 35.
MCFADDEN, Francis, 62.
Margaret, 62.
Sarah, 62.
MCFARLAND, George, 21, 34,

Margaret, 36, 99.
MCGAW, Arabella, 212,
John, 172, 212.
Hannah, 212.
MCGRAH, John, 327.
MCGREGOR, David, 151.
MCINTIRE, Dolly S., 243.
Jonathan, 248.
Levi, 170.
Peletiah, 197.
MCKEAN, Lucinda G., 251.
MCKOWN, Mary, 46.
MCLAUGHLIN, Mary, 321, 327.
MCLEOD, Alice, 212, 333, 350.
David, 212, 339.
Hannah, 13, 15.
John, 16.
Lydia, 13, 14, 15, 16.
Mordecai, 13, 14, 15, 16.
Patty W., 339.
Thomas, 149, 162, 212, 333, 339, 350.
MCLERAN, William, 251.
MCLINN, Margaret, 267, 396.
Patrick, 267, 396.
MCMULLIN, Jane, 283.
MCNABB, John, 257.
MCQUAID, Francis L., 264.
Henry, 264.
MCQUESTION. Frances, 257.
Lydia, 243.
MAGOUN, James, 252.
MAKEPEACE, Hiram, 255.
MALLARD, Abby, 249.
Abigail, 346.
Abraham, 186, 212, 213, 343, 344, 345, 346, 348, 356, 357, 434.
Adaline, 213, 243, 265, 345.
Albert, 212, 343.
Ann S., 245, 345.
Betsy, 186, 212, 334, 434.
Eliza B., 212, 237, 343,
Hannah D., 213, 346.
Harriet, 213, 239, 344.
James, 154, 170, 186, 212, 334, 342, 343, 344, 345, 346, 356, 358, 434.
Mary Ann, 186, 212, 343, 434.
Nancy, 253, 348.
Sally, 186, 212, 213, 334, 434.
MANLEY, Sarah, 186, 366, 435.
MANN, Anna, 136.
Charles, 365.
MANNING, Artemas, 109, 305.
Charles F., 213, 346.
Ephraim, 119, 338.
Eunice, 142.
Israel, 109, 119, 126, 141, 299, 119, 186, 297, 299, 301, 303, 305, 360, 329, 330, 338, 351.
Joseph, 109, 300.
Joseph C., 213, 345.
Lucy, 213, 335, 359, 434.
Mercy, 108, 110, 119, 186, 333, 338, 351, 363.
Patty, 119, 338.
Peter, 109, 119, 127, 138, 143, 299, 338.
Phineas, 119, 338.
Polly, 110.
Prudence, 81, 109, 297, 301, 303, 306, 320, 330, 351.
Rebecca, 322, 350.
Rebecca P., 186, 213, 346, 434.
Sally, 119, 338, 351.
Samuel, 186, 213, 345, 346, 359, 434.
Susanna, 119, 338.
Sylvester, 119, 338.
Unity, 109, 303.
MANSFIELD, Lydia, 186, 360.

INDEX. 485

MAABLE, Joseph, 196.
Mary, 451.
MARGARET, ——, 301, 331.
MAREAN, Eliza, 235.
MARRETT, Dane A., 257.
  Samuel H., 257.
MARSH, Bela, 395.
  Elisha, 30, 84, 87, 329.
  Susanna, 332.
MARSHALL, Caroline V., 394.
  Eunice, 413.
  George, 413.
  Louisa E., 248.
  John Pedro, 354.
  Joseph, 394.
  Pierre, 186.
MARSTON, John M., 230.
  William M., 186, 369.
MARTIN, Deacon, 269.
  Ferren, 258.
  John, 152, 282.
  Matilda D., 246.
  Mary, 282.
MARVIN, Abijah P., 373.
MASON, Ambrose A., 251.
  Azubah, 390.
  Ebenezer, 386.
  Elizabeth, 39, 389.
  Jonas, 385, 386, 387, 388, 389, 390.
  Lydia, 150, 388.
  Rebecca, 387.
  Ruhamah, 385.
  Samuel, 40, 103.
  Sarah, 40, 388.
MATTHEWS, Ann, 186, 369, 434.
  David, 434.
  Eliza A. M., 264, 396.
  Hannah, 264, 268, 396.
  Jerusha, 31.
  Mary, 31.
  Thankful, 87, 88.
  William, 264, 268, 396.
MAY, Aaron, 384.
  Benjamin, 93, 129, 383.
  Betty, 97, 388.
  Daniel, 108, 387.
  David, 80, 384.
  Ephraim, 116.
  Esther, 111.
  Ezra, 109, 389.
  Hannah, 40, 116, 388.
  Jacob, 388.
  James, 80, 83, 376, 384, 385, 387, 388.
  John, 48, 81, 84, 85, 91, 93, 94, 97, 109, 111, 384, 385, 386, 387, 388, 389.
  Joseph, 170.
  Kezia, 48, 81, 91, 93, 94, 97, 109, 111, 384, 386.
  Levi, 93, 384.
  Lucy, 166.
  Mary, 34, 85.
  Molly, 94, 387.
  Moses, 387.
  Noah, 112.
  Phebe, 91, 385.
  Prude, 93, 385.
  Sarah, 22, 32, 80, 385.
  Thankful, 93, 108, 112.
  Thomas, 23, 93, 108, 112, 383, 384, 385, 387, 388.
MAYNARD, Abigail, 213.
  Abigail A., 345, 433.
  Alvira, 213, 367, 434.
  Ann, 186.
  Anna, 95, 121, 186, 212, 334, 433.
  Betsy, 186, 213, 434.
  Camden, 213, 263, 264.
  Caroline, 186.
  Caroline E., 433.

Catharine E., 213.
Charles A., 212, 343.
David H., 213.
Dolly, 121, 232, 358.
Ebenezer, 83, 87.
Elisha, 95.
Elizabeth, 212, 213.
Ellen M., 269.
Elvira, 213.
Erastus H., 259, 267, 396, 434.
Esther, 186.
Eunice, 38.
Gardner, 40, 95, 101, 121, 365.
George C., 264.
George F., 348.
Horace, 237.
Jacob, 40.
John, 20, 121, 127, 144, 185, 186, 212, 261, 434.
John B., 256.
John H., 213, 248, 259, 260, 267, 396, 434.
Joseph, 137, 170, 186, 195, 212, 213, 343, 344, 345, 346, 348, 364, 365, 369, 433, 434.
Joseph A., 263.
Joseph W., 212.
Julia A., 213, 263.
Lydia A., 240, 345.
Martha, 121, 186, 212, 213, 269, 346, 434, 365.
Martha A., 394.
Mary, 149, 162, 213, 248, 259, 260, 392, 396, 434.
Mary E., 213, 395, 434, 451.
Nabby, 212.
Oliver, 149.
Patty, 121, 267, 395.
Polly, 121.
Priscilla, 253.
Reuben, 250.
Rufus, 213, 250.
Sally F., 212.
Sophia, 212.
Susan B., 247.
Susanna, 44, 153.
MAXWELL, Elizabeth, 250.
MAZE, Alice, 13.
  Henry, 13.
MEAD and MEED, Lydia, 130.
  Sarah, 213.
  Stillman A., 231.
MEARS, Dolly, 100, 390.
  Hannah, 100, 390.
  John, 100, 390.
  Judith, 100, 390.
  Mary, 100.
  Molly, 100.
  Nabby, 100, 390.
  Polly, 100.
  Richard, 100, 390.
  Thomas, 38, 100, 390.
MEGETT, Lucy, 212.
MELLEN, Charlotte, 93, 387.
  Henry, 81, 93, 383.
  John, 21, 22, 33, 81, 86, 93, 140, 374, 378, 381, 418.
  Mary, 93, 384.
  Pamela, 22, 44, 81, 93, 103, 378, 381.
  Prentice, 93, 386.
  Rebecca, 22, 81, 93, 105, 136, 378, 382, 418.
  Sarah, 39.
  Sophia, 81, 93, 378, 383, 418.
  Thomas, 93, 385, 418.
MERRIAM, Abigail, 231.
  Bilhah, 234.
  Charles A., 250.
  Dinah, 186, 371.
  Emily C., 244.

Laura, 242.
Lydia, 83.
Moses B., 234.
Nathan, 23.
Sarah, 141.
Susnna, 153.
Thomas, 102.
MERRICK, Tilley, 18.
MERRIFIELD, Samuel, 230.
  William T., 250.
MERRILL, Electa, 247.
MERRITT, Hannah, 154.
MILES, Catharine, 186, 365, 434.
  Levi, 235.
  Pamela V., 240.
  Reuben, 35.
  Ruth, 186, 245, 370, 434.
  Sally, 155.
  Thomas, 186, 434.
MILLER, Anna, 152, 164, 186, 334, 339, 353.
  Augusta A., 248.
  Charles, 244, 262, 263, 266, 268, 393, 434.
  Elizabeth M., 263.
  Isaac, 268, 395.
  Joseph, 186, 363.
  Matilda, 262, 263, 268, 434.
  Nancy, 119, 186, 358.
  Nathan, 119, 230, 339.
  Nathaniel, 119, 146, 186, 333, 352.
  Oscar M., 262, 266, 268, 434.
  Samuel, 186, 339, 353.
  Sibyl, 394.
MILLS, Marietta, 394.
MINOT, Thomasine P., 238.
MIRICK, Dolly, 385.
  James, 385.
MITCHELL, Abner, 128, 143.
  Alice, 293.
  Ann, 186, 370.
  Esther, 98.
  Robert, 30, 293.
MOFFAT, Dolly, 85.
MOLLY, ——, 325.
MONOCO, alias One-eyed John, 15, 19.
MORE, MOORE and MOORS.
  Aaron, 111.
  Abel, 389.
  Abigail, 22, 23, 37, 45, 58, 60, 61, 63, 65, 75, 79, 82, 85, 91, 103, 159, 272, 281, 282, 287, 385, 418.
  Abijah, 22, 58, 101, 130, 145, 281, 382, 383.
  Abraham, 275.
  Abner, 64, 75, 286.
  Achsah, 186, 213, 414.
  Achsah A., 213.
  Amos, 274.
  Anna, 109, 274.
  Anne, 9, 11, 12, 13, 14.
  Archibald, 124.
  Artemas, 124.
  Barsheba, 382.
  Benjamin, 61, 282.
  Betty, 384.
  Billy, 312.
  Calvin, 80, 128, 382.
  Catharine, 66, 90, 91, 93, 97, 108, 110, 111, 113, 158, 288, 377, 386, 413.
  Charlotte, 116.
  Cornelius, 110, 389.
  David, 37, 98.
  Dinah, 25, 274.
  Dolly, 151, 390.
  Ebenezer B., 382.
  Edmund, 257.
  Edward A., 433.
  Elizabeth, 9, 42, 77, 102, 112,

486 INDEX.

282, 381.
Ephraim, 60, 93, 158, 282, 306, 413.
Eunice, 108, 109, 388.
Ezra, 94.
Fairbank, 18, 49, 61, 64, 271, 278, 279, 281, 282, 286.
Fanny, 101, 307, 323.
Francis, 41.
Francis M., 392.
Hannah, 22, 23, 64, 90, 105, 135, 158, 274, 286, 379, 413, 418.
Harriet, 186.
Hasadiah, 272, 282.
Henry, 124, 186, 213, 233, 258, 363, 414.
Hugh, 135.
Isaac, 276, 285, 291.
Isaiah, 244, 392, 393.
Israel, 22, 35, 61, 79, 82, 85, 88, 90, 91, 93, 97, 108, 110, 111, 113, 159, 248, 283, 376, 377, 383, 384, 385, 386, 387, 388, 389, 418.
Jacob, 56, 158, 276, 280, 413.
James, 109, 124, 168, 171, 387, 389.
Jeremiah, 265, 267, 268, 395, 433.
John, 9, 11, 12, 13, 14, 15, 18, 20, 61, 64, 109, 124, 282, 286, 288, 312, 378, 389, 451.
Jonadab, 151, 164.
Jonas, 49, 278.
Jonathan, 12, 22, 24, 45, 103, 112, 270, 273, 274, 275, 276, 290, 390.
Jonathan B., 289.
Joseph, 11, 24, 42, 56, 59, 60, 62, 64, 66, 67, 69, 71, 72, 74, 77, 80, 102, 158, 159, 249, 270, 272, 273, 279, 280, 281, 282, 284, 286, 288, 289, 291, 293, 374, 376, 378, 379, 380, 389, 390, 413.
Joshua, 287.
Josiah, 256, 288.
Jonathan, 389.
Judith, 49, 61, 64, 271.
Levi, 22, 34, 60, 85, 90, 94, 101, 109, 111, 117, 140, 282.
Lois, 287.
Lucy, 56, 67, 92, 140, 158, 159, 169, 170, 279, 289, 306, 414.
Lydia, 11, 397.
Lyman, 243.
Margaret A., 433.
Maria, 13, 19, 273.
Martha E., 265.
Mary, 9, 99, 126, 139, 173, 285, 399.
Mary H., 433.
Molly, 90, 140, 155, 167.
Nabby, 390.
Nancy, 124.
Oliver, 22, 25, 58, 60, 61, 63, 65, 75, 79, 160, 270, 272, 273, 281, 282, 283, 286, 287, 289, 290, 293, 374, 375, 379, 381, 383, 418.
Patience, 64.
Paul, 64, 286.
Prudence, 22, 90, 112, 117, 289, 376, 390.
Rachel, 130.
Rebecca, 44, 56, 59, 60, 62, 64, 66, 67, 69, 71, 72, 74, 77, 80, 82, 90, 94, 97, 101, 103, 109, 111, 117, 158, 159, 272, 284, 306, 379, 413.
Relief, 42, 72, 102, 380.
Reuben, 129.
Rufus, 130.
Ruth, 40.
Sally, 96, 132, 146, 306.

Samuel, 61, 75, 109, 116, 124, 125, 136, 282, 389.
Samuel J., 246.
Sarah, 111, 117, 148, 167.
Sarah P., 248.
Silas, 97.
Silence, 232.
Susanna, 61, 64, 282.
Tamar, 382.
Thankful, 45, 75, 102, 381.
Thomas, 90, 109, 124, 282, 385, 389.
Tilley, 37, 59, 92, 93, 96, 97, 99, 101, 281, 306, 307, 321, 323.
Uriah, 22, 63, 101, 286.
William, 49, 124, 254, 281, 390.
Zerish, 75.
Zerviah, 18.
Zilpah, 92, 93, 96, 97, 101, 321, 323.
MORAN, Daniel, 252.
Patrick F., 252.
MOREY, Joseph, 255.
MORGAN, Caroline, 213.
Janette A., 258.
Louis, 213.
Morgan, 213, 345.
Otis N., 213, 345.
MORRILL, George, 252.
MORRIS, Charles, 83, 85.
Lincoln, 169, 171.
MORRISON, Lucy, 147.
MORSE and MOSS.
Charles W., 258.
Charlotte M., 250.
Curtis G., 213.
Eleanor, 262.
Francis E., 262.
George M., 262.
Harriet, 249.
Harriet C., 262.
Henry, 238.
Joseph, 186, 243, 448.
Lucy, 448.
Mary Ann, 213.
Nancy, 230.
Paltiel, 139.
Samuel L., 169, 170.
Sarah, 38.
Susan, 186.
Susan M., 213.
Susanna, 336.
William, 213, 241, 248.
William G., 448.
MORTON, Elsie, 244.
MOSES, ——, 311.
MOSMAN, Ann, 98.
Joshua, 40.
Leonard, 253.
Moses, 125, 135.
Timothy, 46.
MOTT, Eliza, 169.
MOWER, Samuel, 125, 136.
MUNROE, Aaron, 186, 362, 434.
Abigail, 64, 286.
Elizabeth, 64.
Ephraim, 64.
John, 127, 142.
Lucy, 132.
Lydia, 144.
Lydia E., 255.
Mary, 197.
Rebecca, 167, 173.
Rebecca B., 241.
Susan, 241.
Thomas, 64, 286.
MURRAY, Lucretia, 186, 367, 442.
NEGROES and MULATTOES, see AYNER, Leafy, Lucy, Phebe, and Sampson.
AYRES, Peter.
BLACKENDON, Jenny.

BOND, Roxana and Seraphina.
CÆSAR, ——, Hannah.
CANTERBURY, Rose.
CATO, ——.
CORBET, Cæsar.
CYRUS.
DAVIES, Francis, Peggy, Peter.
DINAH, ——.
DORCHESTER, Daniel, David, Ishmael, Margaret.
EUNICE, ——.
FREEMAN, Adelia, Amos, Mary, Mercy, Patty, Philip, Roxy.
GEORGE.
HALL, Nancy.
HAMMOND, Cæsar, Levi, Mercy, Patty, Perley.
HENRY, Charles.
JAMES, ——.
JOCK, Hannah, John, Lynn, Rachel, Sarah.
JUBA, ——.
JUDUM, Primus.
LAHEY, Peggy.
LONDON.
LEW, Lucy, Primus.
MARGARET.
MITCHELL, Abner.
MOLLY.
MOSES.
OSTENBROOKS, Jonas.
PETER.
PETERSON, George.
PHILLIS.
RHODA.
ROSE.
SMITH, Happy.
STONE, Peggy.
TIM.
TINDY, Cuffee.
VINCENT, Apica, John, Levi N., Lovina, Sylvia.
WATERMAN, Murray.
WOODS, Phebe.
——, 324, 325, 326.
NELSON, Anna, 91, 384.
Betty, 67, 156, 289.
David, 29, 67, 68, 70, 72, 74, 75, 82, 84, 86, 91, 94, 97, 109, 156, 284, 289, 290, 293, 374, 376, 380, 381, 382, 384, 386, 388, 389.
Dolly, 109, 389.
Dorothy, 75, 78, 375, 380.
Elizabeth, 46, 381.
Ephraim, 68, 290.
George, 186, 213.
Hannah, 68, 70, 82, 91, 94, 97, 109, 376.
Horatio, 213.
Jonathan, 29, 68, 75, 78, 290, 374, 375, 380, 381, 382.
Joseph, 75, 381.
Louisa, 213.
Margaret, 67, 72, 74, 75, 156.
Mary, 74, 94, 156, 380, 386.
Mary Ann, 213.
Mercy, 72, 91, 156.
Michal, 154, 166.
Nathan, 70, 72, 82, 156, 384.
Paul, 186, 213, 357.
Polly, 130.
Rachel, 68.
Rhoda, 186, 213.
Sarah, 75, 381.
Solomon, 72, 97, 131, 147, 380, 388.
Thankful, 78, 137.
NEWHALL and NEWELL.
Albert, 124.
Alfred, 348.
Artemas, 363.

INDEX.   487

Betsy, 213, 335.
Catharine, 213, 335.
Charles, 346.
Dalmer, 124, 213, 364.
Daniel, 171, 213, 335, 345, 348.
Daniel B., 213, 345.
Daniel R., 168.
David, 269, 397.
Frances, 346.
Hannah, 112, 128, 145.
Henry A., 213, 346,
James, 124, 186, 213, 356, 359, 360.
Jerome, 124, 213.
Joseph W., 258.
Martha A., 124, 213.
Mary, 124, 213.
Mary L., 124, 236.
Moreton, 124.
Moses, 103, 112, 134.
Nancy, 269, 397.
Nathan, 308.
Onesimus, 130.
Patty, 356, 435.
Pliny, 154, 165, 171, 213, 345, 346, 356, 358, 435.
Pliny A., 345.
Reuben, 234.
Samuel C., 237.
Susan, 124, 213, 240.
Susanna, 146.
NEWMAN, Almy E., 344.
Betsy, 213.
Betsy S., 213.
Caroline M., 266, 337, 349, 371, 435.
Daniel, 186, 342.
Edward S., 186, 213, 341.
Gowen B., 132, 147, 186, 213, 333, 338, 339, 341, 342, 343, 344, 349, 354, 356, 357, 366, 435.
James Homer, 213, 339, 435.
John, 310, 312, 331.
Joseph, 149, 162, 213, 341, 355.
Lucy, 186, 213, 333, 370, 435.
Lucy A., 213.
Lucy C., 213, 266, 337, 339.
Maria, 213.
Maria B., 213, 253, 394.
Mary, 213, 394, 435.
Mary Ann, 213.
Polly G., 213, 341.
Sally F., 213, 341.
Sally S., 310.
Samuel C., 186, 213, 343.
Timothy H., 312.
William H., 186, 213, 370, 435.
William N., 186, 213, 370, 435.
William S., 338.
NEWTON, Anes, 106, 388.
Arad B., 235.
Azubah, 383.
Catharine B., 259, 396.
David, 117, 390.
Dorothy, 45, 103, 381.
Edward, 106, 109, 112, 117, 374, 378, 387, 388, 390.
Elizabeth, 384.
Ellen A., 260.
Ephraim, 106, 382, 387.
Ezekiel, 22, 32, 117, 376, 381, 382, 383, 384, 390.
Hannah, 128, 144.
Henry F., 396.
Huldah, 99.
James, 112.
Jane, 260.
Jeremiah, 310, 326.
Leonard, 260.
Mary, 38, 101, 249, 376, 382.
Naomi, 141.

Nathaniel, 25,
Nehemiah, 310, 326.
Orion H., 259, 396.
Patience, 38.
Polly D., 257.
Ruth, 42, 102,
Samuel, 22, 34, 109, 186, 358, 391.
Sarah, 106, 109, 112, 117.
Sarah L., 259.
Submit, 382.
NICHOLS, Abigail, 37, 99, 297, 330.
Abijah, 448.
Anna, 302, 359, 448.
Bethia, 40, 102, 319.
Daniel, 40, 101.
David, 141.
Desire, 80, 295, 298, 319, 332.
Elizabeth, 109, 302, 303, 320, 331.
Eunice, 109, 304.
Israel, 80, 295, 296, 298, 319, 323, 332.
Jane, 80.
John, 18, 33, 38, 77, 79, 83, 298, 299, 300, 302, 303, 305, 319, 320, 325, 328, 331.
Joseph, 105, 186, 303, 327, 331, 362, 448.
Leafy, 303, 328.
Levi, 87, 88, 109, 302, 303, 304, 305, 306, 307, 320.
Lucy, 80.
Luke, 109, 306.
Lydia, 80, 296.
Martha, 303, 331.
Mary, 21, 77, 86, 109, 128, 144, 298, 300, 302, 319.
Mercy, 77, 79, 83, 87, 298, 302, 320.
Rebecca, 167, 173, 266.
Roger, 80, 319, 323, 324, 325, 403.
Sarah, 109, 307.
Silence, 186, 352.
Susanna, 39, 102, 303, 331.
Thankful, 99.
Thomas B., 394.
William, 80, 295.
NICKERSON, Asa, 327.
NIMS, David, 40, 100.
NORCROSS, Asa, 304, 305, 321.
Betsy, 155.
Daniel, 43, 103.
Elizabeth, 304, 305, 321.
George H., 213.
Henry, 213, 234, 395.
Lucy Maria, 213.
Mary, 83, 98.
Nathaniel F., 213.
Phebe, 304.
Polly, 213.
Samuel, 102.
Sarah A., 213.
NORTH, Hannah, 211, 315, 322.
James, 316.
Joseph, 311, 315, 316, 322.
NORTON, Emily, 236.
Hephzibeth, 142.
Lydia D. 251.
Thomas, 328.
NOURSE, Adrian T., 265.
Anne Elizabeth, 214.
Ann M., 265, 371.
Byron H., 213.
Edwin A., 260.
Emily E., 265.
Eugene A., 265.
Fordyce, 214, 245, 260, 268, 396, 435.
Francis E., 214.
Frederick F., 260.
Genevieve A., 265.
George E., 260.

Henry S., 1, 3, 213.
Jonathan P., 213, 214, 239, 265, 395.
Laura, 214, 260.
Mary, 149, 233.
Mary Ann, 260.
Mary L., 260.
Mary P., 213, 214, 265, 395.
Nancy, 265.
Olive W., 239.
Patty H., 213, 214.
Roscoe H., 214.
Stedman, 176, 213, 214. 236.
Susanna, 169, 230.
Warren, 246, 265, 371.
NOWELL, Catharine A., 213, 393.
Elizabeth, 125, 137, 186, 213, 267, 392, 393, 395, 435.
Elizabeth A., 186, 213, 348, 435.
John W., 186, 213, 393, 435.
Lucy B., 213, 393.
Mary C., 254, 394.
Sarah, 392.
Sarah F., 245.
William, 186, 213, 230, 348, 362, 392, 393, 435.
NOYES, Francis, 248.
NUTTING, Ann, 256.
Phineas, 168, 171.
Sarah, 452.
OAKES, Edward S., 257.
O'BRIEN, Dennis, 264.
Julia, 264.
OLDS, Harriet, 394.
OLIVER, Abigail, 214.
Esther, 214.
Joel, 154, 165, 214.
Margaret H., 349.
Samuel W. A., 241, 349.
ONTHANK, Eunice, 242.
ORR, Agnes, 258.
Catharine, 257.
OSBORN, Betsy, 165.
James, 129.
OSGOOD, Aaron, 25, 35, 62, 64, 65, 67, 68, 73, 74, 76, 86, 123, 156, 158, 280, 281, 283, 286, 287, 289, 291, 293, 294, 295, 296, 316, 319, 323, 324.
Abel, 65, 287.
Abigail, 37, 66, 82, 98, 156, 160, 288, 385, 418, 435.
Abigail C., 214, 348.
Abigail E., 187, 371.
Abner, 287.
Almira, 214, 435.
Amy, 214.
Anna, 92, 386, 435.
Apollos, 123, 230, 318.
Asahel, 63, 286.
Asenath, 63, 65, 66, 70, 71, 73, 76, 379, 418.
Azuoah, 34, 58, 85, 89, 128, 138, 281, 384.
Benjamin, 34, 79, 82, 86, 280, 281, 284, 287, 288, 290, 291, 294, 298, 299, 300, 319, 324, 325, 332.
Betsy, 214, 317, 318, 329, 337.
Betty, 106, 388.
Beulah, 310, 326.
Catharine, 79, 89, 91, 187, 301, 302, 333, 360, 361.
Christopher, 95, 97, 108, 305, 306, 307, 326, 331.
Daniel P., 123, 187, 214, 318.
David, 19, 56, 58, 61, 63, 65, 70, 72, 88, 89, 90, 92, 94, 97, 112, 123, 158, 238, 270, 272, 278, 279, 281, 283, 286, 287, 289, 290, 292, 293, 336, 339, 374, 375, 376, 380, 384, 385, 386, 387, 388, 389, 390, 392, 418.

INDEX.

Dinah, 71, 85, 88, 283, 289.
Dolly, 123, 167, 173, 214, 317.
Dorcas, 44, 297.
Dorothy, 22, 32, 51, 56, 74, 80, 84, 87, 125, 136, 279, 295, 298, 320, 332, 382.
Ebenezer, 197, 294, 446.
Elihu, 91, 385.
Elijah, 35, 91, 99, 288, 303, 305, 320, 332.
Eliza W., 392, 395.
Elizabeth, 26, 40, 65, 69, 71, 72, 75, 80, 126, 138, 158, 239, 287, 291, 294, 298, 380, 401.
Emily, 214.
Emily R., 245.
Ephraim, 58, 79, 85, 144, 187, 214, 278, 299, 354, 366, 435.
Esther, 76, 296.
Eunice, 22, 33, 56, 58, 61, 62, 63, 64, 65, 67, 68, 70, 72, 73, 74, 76, 90, 91, 127, 142, 156, 158, 159, 272, 278, 279, 281, 283, 286, 291, 295, 302, 375, 385, 388.
Ezekiel, 305.
Ezra, 80, 127, 143, 214, 296.
Gilson, 214.
Hannah, 35, 95, 97, 99, 108, 187, 214, 272, 280, 298, 305, 320, 331.
Hooker, 23, 51, 88, 99, 149, 157, 159, 162, 270, 271, 276, 277, 278, 279, 281, 283, 284, 285, 290, 301, 302, 303, 305, 306, 307, 309, 310, 311, 313, 319, 320, 323, 325, 326, 327, 329, 330, 373.
Isaac, 305.
James, 214, 309, 311, 313, 326, 327.
Jane, 91, 93, 96, 159.
Jerusha, 187, 358.
Joanna, 91, 92, 95, 100, 106, 109.
Joel, 72, 104, 113, 123, 132, 134, 147, 149, 162, 187, 293, 310, 313, 315, 316, 317, 318, 321, 326, 329, 330, 338, 339, 361, 435.
John, 51, 75, 76, 78, 80, 82, 108, 157, 278, 294, 295, 296, 297, 298, 299, 301, 303, 305, 306, 307, 308, 330.
Jonathan, 26, 63, 65, 66, 70, 71, 73, 75, 76, 82, 85, 86, 88, 91, 92, 95, 100, 106, 109, 112, 118, 123, 125, 136, 153, 156, 159, 160, 165, 187, 214, 267, 285, 286, 287, 288, 291, 292, 295, 311, 312, 315, 316, 317, 318, 329, 330, 356, 372, 374, 375, 376, 379, 380, 381, 382, 384, 385, 386, 387, 388, 418, 435.
Joseph, 6, 23, 29, 35, 51, 69, 71, 72, 75, 79, 80, 85, 89, 91, 96, 123, 158, 187, 214, 272, 277, 290, 291, 293, 294, 295, 296, 298, 299, 301, 302, 318, 319, 323, 324, 333, 352, 387, 401.
Josiah, 35, 87, 91, 93, 96, 159, 289, 326, 377, 385, 386, 387, 390.
Joshua, 18, 32, 58, 61, 63, 65, 67, 71, 73, 270, 271, 278, 279, 280, 282, 286, 287, 289, 293, 319, 332.
Kezia, 21, 32, 51, 132, 147, 279, 293, 303.
Lemuel, 73.
Levi, 308.
Lois, 62, 113, 126, 150, 280, 321.
Lucretia, 123, 266, 372, 435.
Lucy, 123, 167, 173, 187, 214, 231, 335, 338.
Luke, 73, 294.
Manasseh, 71, 293, 306.
Martha, 38, 71, 72, 76, 99, 187, 289, 295, 320, 356.
Martha S., 350.

Martha W., 187, 214, 349, 435.
Mary, 27, 45, 51, 63, 70, 75, 76, 79, 82, 91, 102, 128, 157, 158, 187, 271, 276, 286, 292, 294, 295, 298, 300, 302, 303, 320, 326, 381, 385, 446.
Mary Ann, 214, 394.
Mary E., 214, 258, 348.
Mary N., 214, 435.
Moses, 27, 28, 71, 72, 76, 123, 141, 152, 164, 187, 214, 289, 292, 293, 295, 297, 298, 313, 319, 327, 360.
Nahum, 118, 187, 312, 358, 435.
Nancy, 214, 229.
Nathan, 90, 385.
Nathaniel, 65, 287, 324.
Olive, 37, 71, 98.
Oliver, 79, 284, 292, 299, 302, 323, 376.
Peter, 123, 187, 189, 214, 235, 258, 307, 336, 338, 348, 349, 350, 366, 373, 435.
Phebe, 27, 28.
Phineas, 100, 387.
Polly, 145.
Prudence, 23, 80, 87, 140, 281, 298, 303.
Rebecca, 97, 112, 118, 123, 316, 322, 330, 387.
Relief, 78, 137, 297.
Roland, 214.
Ruth, 58, 61, 63, 65, 67, 71, 73, 86, 214, 271, 279, 319, 365.
Samuel, 65, 82, 87, 88, 93, 95, 96, 269, 287, 299, 386.
Samuel W., 118, 214, 315.
Sarah, 24, 58, 67, 73, 75, 76, 78, 80, 82, 89, 90, 92, 94, 97, 105, 112, 135, 280, 289, 294, 295, 296, 380, 389.
Silas, 67, 289.
Silence, 92, 386.
Sophia, 109, 123, 152, 164, 315, 389.
Submit, 91, 290, 303.
Susey, 94, 386.
Susanna, 75, 295, 301, 320, 322, 325, 329, 350.
Thomas, 62, 214, 283.
Vryling, 214.
Widow ——, 323.
William, 61, 214, 282, 301.
OSTENBROOKS, Jonas, 152, 164, 340.
OTIS, Benjamin B., 214, 233, 450.
Mary C., 213, 450.
Mary E., 214, 450.
Nancy C., 450.
PACKARD, Ann E., 248.
Anna M., 237, 336, 414.
Anna G., 414.
Asa, 266, 336, 392, 393, 394, 414.
Charles, 259, 394, 414.
Eliza Q., 414.
George T., 259.
Mary C., 394.
Nancy, 266, 392, 393, 394.
Rebecca P., 394, 414.
Ruth F., 239, 336, 392.
PAGE, Alice, 33.
Betsy, 152.
Daniel, 311, 312.
Joseph, 41, 103.
Lemuel, 311.
Levi, 117, 127, 143, 329, 403.
Martha, 117, 329, 403.
Nathan, 312.
Peter, 306.
Samuel P., 129, 138, 277.
Sarah, 21, 33, 86.
Thomas, 88, 99, 306.
Zachariah, 277.

PAIGE, Lucius R., 246.
PALMER, Elizabeth, 360.
Hitty, 386.
John, 386.
Joseph, 376, 378.
Mr. ——, 188.
Polly, 230.
PANSEY, Julia Ann, 141.
PARKEE, Abby, 254.
Abigail, 64.
Alfred F., 261.
Andrew J., 256.
Ann R., 335, 344.
Anna, 44, 214.
Artemas H., 249, 262.
Czarina, 188.
David, 261.
David W., 261.
Deborah, 9.
Edmund, 9, 12, 215, 237.
Edward S., 188.
Eleanor S., 261.
Elizabeth, 9, 12.
Esther, 9.
Francis, 64.
Gilman B., 216, 217, 238, 392, 393.
Gilman C., 216, 393.
Hannah, 129, 140, 214.
Henrietta E., 262.
Henry, 188, 370.
Isaiah, 241.
James, 40.
James O., 254, 267.
Joel, 188, 214.
John, 152, 215.
John B., 246.
Joseph B., 262, 394.
Lewis, 155.
Lydia, 33, 34, 85, 215.
Martha, 267, 395.
Mary Ann, 262.
Mary E., 241, 254.
Mary I., 262.
Mary J., 217, 393.
Matilda, 214.
Mercy, 9.
Otis, 149.
Parney, 140.
Phillis, 127, 140.
Polly, 149, 162.
Samuel, 19.
Samuel A., 217, 393.
Samuel S., 150.
Sarah F., 216, 217, 392, 393.
Sarah I., 217, 393.
Susan E., 262.
Susanna, 30.
Thomas H., 246.
William W., 251.
PARK and PARKS, George, 35.
Jonathan H., 237.
William, 243.
PARKHURST, Ephraim, 90, 301.
George, 79, 81, 87, 90, 299, 300, 301, 302, 305, 320.
Jonathan, 300.
Kezia, 79, 81, 90, 300, 302, 320.
Molly, 305.
Nathan, 300.
William, 79, 299.
PARMENTER, Edmund, 99.
Elijah, 258.
John N., 105, 135.
Molly, 99.
PARSONS, Almira J., 261.
James C., 255, 261.
Wilfred C., 261.
PATCH, Salome, 230.
PATRICK, Elizabeth, 272.

INDEX. 489

Jacob, 282.
John, 252.
Lydia, 281.
Matthew, 281, 282.
PATTEN, Charles S., 252.
Hannah, 233.
Richard, 187, 352.
PATTERSON, Alexander, 130.
Esther, 148.
PAYNE, Eloise R., 177, 360, 414.
PEABODY, Abigail, 334, 351.
Calvin, 153, 165, 187, 214, 215, 334, 342, 343, 344, 346, 351.
Clifford C., 215, 344.
Elizabeth H., 214, 346.
Elizabeth P., 336.
Hannah, 21, 31.
Hannah W., 215, 343.
James A., 215.
James L., 215, 342.
John A., 342.
Mary, 215, 342.
Nabby, 214, 215.
PEACOCK, Elizabeth, 358, 436.
Jane, 151.
PEARSON and PERSON.
Anna, 100, 126, 139.
Bartholomew, 39, 97, 101, 106, 110, 377, 387, 388, 389.
Charlotte, 100, 388.
Dolly, 188.
Dorinda, 386.
Elizabeth, 97, 106, 110.
Enos, 97, 387.
Frances, 387.
George J., 188, 446.
Hannah, 385.
Hovey, 106, 388.
John, 100, 110, 382, 383, 384, 385, 386, 387, 388.
Joseph, 384.
Josiah, 383.
Love, 40.
Lucinda, 386.
Margaret B., 372.
Mary, 83, 85.
Sarah, 36, 98, 382.
PEASE, Abby E., 217.
Catharine W., 217.
Lorey, 217.
PEASLEE, Martha A., 216.
Moses, 188, 216, 361, 436.
Sarah, 216.
PECKHAM, Silas, 251.
PEGGY, 85, 315.
PEIRCE, Betsy, 120, 337.
Charles, 216.
Charles H., 188, 216, 263, 348.
Charlotte S., 263.
Clarissa, 187.
Cynthia, 188, 216, 336.
Dana, 120, 338.
David, 120, 337, 338.
Dinah, 324.
Edward F., 264.
Eleanor, 197, 446.
Frances M., 217.
Francis, 265.
Gilbert, 217.
Harvey, 188, 216, 231, 347, 348, 365.
Henrietta, 265.
Henry, 216.
Henry D., 395.
James O., 264.
Joel, 187, 357.
John, 310.
Jonathan, 70, 293.
Joseph, 324.
Joshua, 69, 70, 291, 292, 295.

Laura, 265.
Levi, 188, 369.
Lois, 69, 70, 319.
Lucy, 173, 265.
Mary, 129, 265.
Nabby, 231.
Nancy, 169, 228.
Nathan, 169.
Nehemiah, 232.
Nicholas, 310.
Persis, 238.
Rhoda, 216.
Sally, 216.
Sally A., 216.
Samuel, 38, 138.
Samuel H., 216, 251, 263, 347.
Sarah, 31, 120.
Susan E., 249.
Susanna, 154, 166.
Uara, 265.
William, 265, 269.
William D., 269.
Zenon, 267, 396.
PERRY, Daniel, 38, 101, 387.
Joseph, 165, 387.
Miranda, 236.
Rachel, 163.
Sally, 154.
Simeon, 128, 144.
PETER ——, 389.
PETERSON, George, 36, 98.
PHELPS, Aaron, 78, 81, 115, 129, 141, 150, 163, 187, 215, 297, 314, 315, 316, 317, 318, 357, 414.
Abel, 94, 115, 126, 138, 296, 313, 315, 316, 317, 331.
Abiel S., 188, 362.
Abigail, 215, 216, 232, 312, 345.
Abijah, 153, 165, 187, 188, 214, 298, 342, 343, 344, 345, 304, 437.
Abishai, 43, 60, 72, 102, 159, 281, 294, 308, 310, 312, 313, 314, 316, 317, 321, 329.
Achsa, 97, 145, 187, 306, 321, 354.
Anna, 82, 117, 127, 141, 187, 215, 300, 305, 313.
Ann P., 345.
Anthony, 168, 172.
Asa, 30.
Asahel, 50, 72, 187, 188, 215, 277, 291, 293, 294, 296, 297, 298, 299, 300, 302, 304, 319, 328.
Asenath, 187, 188, 215, 361.
Augusta, 245.
Barney S., 249.
Bathsheba, 17, 23.
Betsy, 119, 143, 214, 215, 216, 217, 317.
Beulah, 188, 297, 333, 369.
Calvin, 108, 187, 188, 215, 240, 267, 307, 352.
Caroline, 215, 243, 341.
Catharine, 215, 237, 321, 341.
Catharine M., 248.
Charles, 214.
Clarissa, 188, 215, 363.
Cornelia, 216, 346.
Darwin, 215.
David, 187, 215, 242, 302, 357.
Deborah, 94, 127, 143, 304.
Dolly, 108, 131, 147, 187, 188, 215, 216, 306, 346, 358, 436.
Dolly I., 187, 339.
Dorothy, 59, 60, 63, 66, 68, 69, 72, 159, 283, 286, 287, 292, 322, 329.
Ebenezer, 278.
Edward, 17, 49, 50, 64, 120, 156, 159, 214, 270, 271, 272, 276, 277, 278, 279, 280, 282, 287, 319, 320, 323, 328, 329, 332, 345.
Elisha, 108, 143, 149, 162, 187,

214, 215, 302, 333, 339, 340, 353.
Eliza, 215, 340, 372.
Elizabeth, 42, 49, 64, 71, 72, 92, 94, 104, 108, 127, 132, 147, 187, 216, 217, 286, 291, 293, 303, 304, 321, 325, 339, 346, 357.
Elizabeth W., 214.
Emma A., 260.
Ephraim, 119, 154, 165, 188, 215, 216, 315, 344, 346, 347, 348, 360, 361, 436.
Esther, 128, 144, 187, 215, 216, 304, 334, 437.
Evelina, 215, 244.
Gardner, 124, 127, 143, 187, 188, 215, 266, 299, 353, 354, 372.
George, 124, 151, 164, 187, 188, 195, 214, 215, 216, 312, 334, 341, 342, 343, 345, 346, 356, 361.
Hannah, 452.
Henrietta E., 217.
Henry, 117, 188, 215, 216, 235, 268, 315, 340, 362, 436.
Hezekiah P., 215, 340, 366, 436.
Isabel, 113, 132, 146, 308.
Jacob, 81, 119, 127, 140, 187, 188, 215, 300, 314, 315, 316, 317, 318, 322, 338, 339, 351.
James, 216, 310, 317, 329, 348.
James B., 215, 340.
Jesse, 113, 215, 309, 341.
Joel, 37, 63, 99, 113, 124, 160, 187, 283, 303, 304, 306, 307, 308, 309, 310, 312, 325, 358, 405.
Joel W., 215, 217, 242, 260, 261, 266, 344, 372, 436.
John, 21, 32, 37, 39, 50, 75, 78, 81, 92, 97, 99, 103, 115, 154, 187, 214, 215, 278, 294, 296, 297, 299, 300, 303, 304, 306, 308, 309, 311, 316, 321, 324, 325, 327, 329, 333, 344, 409, 414.
Jonas, 115, 154, 166, 313.
Jonas M., 115, 317.
Joseph, 75, 81, 115, 188, 215, 296, 315, 328, 342, 369, 436.
Joshua, 30, 62, 64, 65, 71, 73, 94, 144, 157, 158, 273, 283, 286, 287, 291, 293, 294, 296, 297, 298, 299, 301, 304, 319, 322, 324.
Josiah, 81, 149, 162, 299, 308.
Julia A., 216, 348.
Julia L., 261, 266, 372, 436.
Katy, 313.
Laura, 188, 369.
Lavina, 115, 188, 215, 341.
Leander, 236.
Levi W., 216, 347.
Lois, 115, 127, 140, 331.
Lorinda, 217, 260, 261, 266, 436.
Louisa, 187, 215, 343, 356.
Lucinda, 115, 215, 318.
Lucretia, 113, 119, 132, 144, 147, 168, 171, 214, 243, 363, 346.
Lucy, 44, 104, 115, 187, 215, 296, 313, 315.
Luke, 187, 309, 353.
Luther J., 216, 345.
Lydia, 21, 29, 33, 50, 86, 94, 105, 120, 135, 151, 163, 215, 232, 279, 297, 311, 333, 339.
Lydia A. W., 239.
Maria, 216.
Martha, 97, 130, 146, 215, 237, 306, 320.
Martha S., 217.
Mary, 26, 50, 64, 72, 77, 80, 82, 90, 108, 121, 124, 153, 159, 165, 187, 188, 214, 215, 216, 231, 244, 245, 271, 276, 294, 301, 302, 321, 344, 345, 350, 356, 359, 365, 370,

35

490 INDEX.

Mary A., 188, 216, 217, 241, 347.[437.]
Mary A. P., 216, 345, 366, 436.
Mary B., 216.
Mary E., 216, 268, 395, 436.
Mary F., 269.
Mary P., 187, 215, 343, 437.
Mary W., 242.
Meriel, 188, 218, 344, 436.
Molly, 306, 333.
Nabby, 121.
Nancy, 115, 154, 166, 215, 314.
Olive, 93, 129, 142, 215, 217, 242, 304, 343.
Oliver, 64, 119, 187, 287, 314, 327.
Parker, 214, 139, 359.
Patterson H., 188.
Peter, 94, 115, 188, 216, 298, 304, 309, 315, 347, 372, 414.
Phineas, 50, 93, 120, 282, 302, 303, 304, 305, 306, 316, 320, 325, 328, 405.
Polly, 215, 335, 345.
Prudence, 113, 119, 124, 131, 146, 160, 187, 215, 266, 304, 322, 358, 371, 405.
Rachel, 94, 96, 101, 130, 304, 329.
Rebecca, 24, 43, 62, 64, 65, 71, 73, 94, 104, 115, 117, 157, 158, 215, 273, 283, 291, 294, 326.
Relief, 94, 129, 143, 188, 299, 370.
Robert, 38, 59, 60, 63, 66, 68, 69, 72, 94, 96, 100, 101, 121, 133, 148, 159, 174, 187, 188, 192, 216, 280, 281, 285, 286, 287, 289, 292, 294, 304, 305, 307, 319, 323, 326, 333, 345, 346, 352, 366, 436.
Roger, 90, 301.
Roxana, 120, 168, 171, 338.
Ruth, 49, 66, 113, 152, 159, 164, 187, 287, 310, 321, 333, 334, 339, 354, 452.
Sally, 115, 187, 214, 215, 216, 235, 312, 213, 314, 317, 331, 334, 351, 414.
Sally P., 214, 239, 343.
Samuel, 80, 115, 188, 215, 216, 317, 341.
Samuel W., 316.
Sarah, 25, 40, 73, 94, 102, 115, 143, 188, 215, 238, 302, 303, 320, 331, 342, 348, 405.
Sewall, 101, 188, 216, 307, 345.
Susanna, 104, 134, 321.
Sylvester, 113, 148, 160, 187, 188, 215, 216, 268, 303, 307, 340, 341, 342, 343, 344, 345, 356, 396, 405, 437.
Tabitha, 269.
Theodora, 314.
Thomas, 155, 188, 214, 215, 216, 217, 339, 357, 367.
William, 21, 36, 59, 77, 80, 82, 86, 88, 90, 108, 115, 119, 120, 126, 139, 159, 187, 214, 217, 246, 280, 297, 298, 300, 301, 302, 304, 306, 307, 309, 313, 315, 318, 319, 323, 324, 328, 331, 342, 353.
Winslow, 77, 117, 141, 297, 315.
Zilpah, 149, 161, 308, 333.
Zipporah, 75, 78, 81, 294, 297, 409.
PHILLIPS, Abigail, 40, 295.
Abijah, 295.
Anna, 101, 105, 110, 126, 137, 160, 289, 321.
Damson, 149, 162.
Elizabeth, 284.
Ethan, 196, 280.
Frances Malona, 254.
Grace, 292.
John, 44, 101, 110, 134, 160, 280, 284, 286, 289, 292, 295, 308, 309, 310, 321, 325, 327, 398.
Jonathan, 150, 163, 286, 328, 399.
Levina, 159, 162.
Louisa, 246.
Lydia, 282, 295, 324, 399.
Mary, 330.
Mrs. ——, 328.
Mulford, 151.
Nancy, N., 232.
Patty, 126, 140.
Polly, 151.
Priscilla, 326.
Prudence, 149, 162.
Rebecca, 160, 310, 320, 328, 398, 399.
Samuel, 110, 160, 309, 398.
Seth, 282.
PHILLIS ——, 389.
PICKMAN, Anstiss D., 229.
PIERPONT, Hannah, 26, 29.
PIKE, Anes, 109.
David, 90.
Ebenezer, 84, 90, 109.
Elijah, 109.
Ephraim, 90.
Lydia, 90, 109.
Susanna, 109.
William, 109.
PIPER, Betty, 46.
Dolly, 329.
Francis, 244.
Horace, 217.
Joshua, 43, 103.
Jude, 126, 128, 138.
Sally, 128, 144.
PITSON, Hannah, 135, 321.
PITTS, Albert, 259.
Anna L., 216.
Betty S., 188, 370, 436.
Dolly T., 217.
Ellen E., 217.
Ellen M., 260.
Hiram W., 188, 247, 371, 436.
James, 188, 216, 247, 258, 259, 260, 269, 367, 395, 435, 436.
Lewis H., 188, 371, 436.
Lucinda, 259, 260, 269, 395, 438.
Prudence, 216.
Seth G., 216, 254, 396.
Susan B., 396.
William, 217, 245, 395, 396.
PLANT, Alfred, 216, 347.
Ann H., 216, 344.
Delicia A., 188, 216, 349, 436.
Delicia M., 188, 214, 216, 436.
Elizabeth D. P., 216, 348.
Frederick W., 214, 346.
George P., 214, 345.
Henry, 216, 348.
Louisa E., 216, 345.
Mary D., 216, 349.
Samuel, 188, 214, 216, 344, 345, 346, 347, 348, 349, 366, 436.
Sarah A., 214, 346.
William M., 216, 348.
PLATTS, Mary, 452.
PLUMMER, Abigail, 188, 217, 436.
Caroline C., 239.
Charles, 188, 216, 415.
Elizabeth C., 214, 246.
Farnham, 187, 188, 214, 216, 217, 242, 358, 360, 368, 415, 436.
Francis J., 217.
Hannah, 30.
Hannah C., 239.
John C., 188, 217.
Mary M., 217.
Nancy, 187, 188, 214, 216, 365, 415.
Thomas, 187, 216, 415.
PLYMPTON, Eliza C., 239.
Olive, 231.
POIGNAND, David, 188, 192, 364, 436.
Delicia A., 188, 366, 436.
Louisa E., 169, 171.
POLLARD, Aaron, 150, 353.
Abel, 249, 263.
Abner, 120, 130, 145, 187, 214, 215, 216, 230, 330, 333, 338, 339, 340, 341, 342, 343, 344, 346, 347, 349, 354, 357, 359.
Abner W., 215, 343.
Achsa, 120, 187, 214, 215, 216, 333, 335, 338, 351, 359.
Adelaide E., 216.
Almira, 215, 239, 392.
Alvah H., 216.
Amory, 215, 216, 238, 341.
Amos, 130, 146, 318.
Anes, 188, 216.
Angeline R., 263.
Anna G., 249.
Betsy, 130, 145, 216, 242.
Caleb E., 347.
Charles, 318.
Charles F., 216.
Christopher A., 216, 347.
Clarissa, 187, 216, 344.
Clarissa E., 216, 347.
Edward W., 187, 214, 216, 346.
Elizabeth, 188, 268, 359.
Ellen A., 216.
Emily, 120, 214, 231, 244, 335, 338.
Experience, 54, 57, 59, 61, 63, 289.
Gardner, 152, 188, 214, 215, 216.
George Amory, 216.
Henry L., 216.
John, 57, 187, 188, 280, 358.
John W. G., 188.
John G., 217.
Jonas, 61, 283.
Leonard, 188, 215, 216, 233, 340.
Leonard L., 216.
Levi, 215, 216, 217.
Levi L., 340.
Lois, 63, 286.
Lucy, 188, 214, 215, 216, 364.
Lydia, 131, 214, 216, 217, 339.
Martha, 234, 246.
Mary, 215, 239.
Mary Ann, 215, 263, 342.
Nancy, 216.
Nancy W., 216.
Naomi, 392.
Oliver, 54.
Patty, 215.
Patience, 288.
Persis, 216.
Peter, 188.
Polly, 120, 187, 338.
Prudence, 288.
Sally, 187, 215, 341.
Seth H., 216.
Susan A., 214, 346.
Susanna, 152, 165, 214, 216, 335, 347.
Sylvia A., 216.
William, 24, 54, 57, 58, 61, 63, 188, 272, 280, 281, 283, 286, 288, 289.
POLLEY, Dorcas, 54, 58, 60, 273, 281, 283.
Ebenezer, 19, 54, 58, 60, 273, 278, 280, 281, 283, 292.
Joseph, 58, 280.
Mary, 60, 281.
POND, Lois, 154, 166.
Prentiss, 169, 170.
Sally, 133.

INDEX. 491

POOR, Alice, 187, 358.
Andrew, 40, 102, 307, 308.
Catharine, 112, 311.
Dolly, 110, 308.
Edward, 42, 104, 108, 110, 112, 117, 307, 308, 309, 311, 212, 328.
Eleazer, 110, 309.
Elizabeth, 308.
Elsie, 108, 307.
Esther, 321.
Eunice, 108, 110, 112, 117, 313, 331, 333.
John, 117, 307, 313.
Phebe, 307.
POPE, Beatrix, 15, 271.
Ebenezer, 126, 141.
John, 15.
Rufus S., 245.
Susanna, 15.
PORTER, Ebenezer, 239.
Sarah A., 255.
POTTER, Alexander, 248, 450.
Angelina, 450.
Charles A., 450.
Harvey, 215.
Jacob, 215.
Lucy, 215.
Mary C., 251.
Sarah, 451.
POWERS, Amos, 35, 61, 83, 99, 283, 376, 384.
Andrew A., 257.
Anna, 116.
Asa, 306.
Daniel, 26, 67, 284, 289, 293, 374, 376, 418.
Eli, 306, 323.
Elizabeth, 39, 63, 101, 286.
Ephraim, 129, 139, 381.
Hannah, 36, 60, 61, 63, 70, 71, 73, 273, 281, 288.
Henry, 105, 135.
Jacob, 60, 97, 281.
Jesse, 113.
John, 135.
Jonas, 113, 306, 323.
Jonathan, 25, 40, 60, 61, 63, 70, 71, 73, 273, 281, 283, 286, 288, 290, 291, 292, 293, 374, 375, 380, 381, 382.
Levi M., 245.
Lucy, 41, 73, 102, 380.
Lydia, 97, 112, 113, 306.
Manasseh, 382.
Martha, 27, 28.
Mary, 67, 376, 418.
Molly, 144.
Oliver, 41, 70, 97, 101, 112, 290.
Peter, 113.
Rhoda, 116.
Robert, 26, 286.
Rufus, 67, 289, 418.
Ruth, 286.
Sarah, 128.
Silas, 380.
Sybil, 83, 376.
Thankful, 83, 384.
Tryphena, 113.
William, 258.
POWNAL, Harriet, 155, 166.
PRATT, Abel S., 216.
Abijah, 57, 279.
Almira, 239.
Anna, 125, 136.
Ann E., 263, 209.
Betsy, 117, 216, 263, 313.
Charity, 141.
Clarissa M., 394.
Curtis, 216.
Dennis, 279.
Ebenezer, 188, 197, 216, 217, 231, 247, 263, 269, 363, 368, 436.
Ebenezer E., 263.
Elizabeth, 153, 165.
Elsy F., 217.
Emily, 188, 216, 217, 369, 436.
Emily F., 436.
Francis P., 255.
George, 263.
Harriet, 122.
Hiram, 263.
James, 42, 104, 106, 109, 117, 122, 132, 147, 181, 214, 307, 308, 311, 313, 321, 329.
Jesse, 216.
Joseph, 279.
Joseph W., 216.
Josiah, 57, 64, 280, 284, 286.
Lydia, 122, 214, 394.
Mary, 40, 100, 134.
Mary L., 217.
Nabby, 214.
Nelson L. A., 263.
Norton E., 394.
Oren, 263.
Phineas, 24, 197, 446.
Polly, 216.
Sally, 122, 133, 142, 148, 311.
Salome, 216, 254, 266, 395.
Samuel, 109, 151, 163, 308.
Sarah, 57, 64, 279, 284, 286.
Solomon, 130.
Stephen, 329, 352.
William, 57, 280.
Zerviah, 106, 109, 117, 187, 321, 355.
PREBLE, Ebenezer, 151, 164.
PRENTICE and PRENTISS.
Anna, 27, 28, 34, 57, 62, 86, 90, 214, 281, 283, 287, 383.
Anna R., 214.
Caleb, 44, 103.
Cephas, 95, 304.
Daniel, 296, 324, 402.
Dorothy, 275, 284.
Elizabeth, 27, 29, 274, 284.
Henry, 44, 384, 385.
James Otis, 95, 214, 306.
Jeffrey Otis, 168, 172.
John, 56, 57, 62, 90, 95, 158, 214, 215, 216, 270, 274, 275, 276, 279, 280, 281, 283, 287, 292, 294, 302, 323, 324, 339, 340, 342, 343, 384, 401, 451.
John A., 214, 339.
Joshua, 287.
Josiah, 215, 291, 324, 342.
Levi, 16, 387.
Luke, 109, 388.
Martha, 214, 215.
Martha B., 214, 343.
Mary, 24, 270, 273, 274, 275, 295, 300, 324, 325, 401, 402.
Mary A. W., 215.
Mercy, 68, 95, 290, 291, 292, 293, 294, 295, 296, 297, 298, 324, 401, 402.
Peter, 95, 301, 305, 325, 402.
Peter B., 339.
Prudence, 27, 29, 56, 90, 93, 94, 96, 109, 276, 279, 285, 319, 325, 383, 390.
Rebecca, 21, 33, 46, 56, 86, 95, 104, 279, 291, 301, 302, 303, 402.
Relief, 21, 33, 86, 291.
Samuel, 23, 87, 90, 93, 94, 96, 109, 281, 303, 370, 379, 383, 384, 385, 386, 387, 388, 390.
Sarah, 29, 275, 284.
Stanton, 68, 84, 95, 174, 270, 273, 290, 291, 292, 293, 294, 295, 296, 297, 298, 300, 301, 302, 303, 304, 305, 306, 319, 323, 324, 325, 401, 402.
Stephen, 95, 294.
Thomas, 27, 68, 94, 272, 274, 290, 293, 323, 332, 386, 401, 402.
William, 95, 215, 297, 340, 384.
PRESCOTT, Abigail, 188, 336, 363, 436.
Alexander, 214, 345.
Amory, 215, 345.
Amos, 453.
Azubah, 114.
Benjamin, 81, 383.
David, 117.
Dorothy, 13, 14, 19, 72, 159, 271, 293, 405, 406, 452, 453.
Ebenezer, 15, 31, 73, 81, 272, 274, 277, 374, 375, 378, 380, 383.
Elizabeth, 32, 92, 385, 452.
Esther, 453.
Eunice, 45, 73, 104.
Experience, 406.
Hannah, 13, 16.
Hannah M., 214, 345.
Harrison, 214, 346.
Hiram, 44, 73, 380.
Jabez, 130, 145, 305, 436.
James S., 215, 345.
Jerusha, 73, 81.
Joanna, 81, 90, 383, 384, 452.
John, 13, 14, 15, 20, 70, 72, 73, 75, 77, 89, 92, 104, 125, 136, 159, 187, 271, 273, 274, 293, 295, 296, 298, 299, 302, 303, 305, 319, 325, 329, 330, 357, 405, 406, 452.
Jonas, 4, 14, 89, 92, 126, 138, 298, 452.
Jonathan, 4, 13, 14, 19, 31, 73, 76, 81, 90, 92, 94, 114, 116, 117, 136, 277, 302, 375, 380, 381, 382, 383, 384, 385, 390, 397, 406, 451, 452.
Joseph, 92, 303.
Josiah, 380.
Jotham, 94.
Levi, 114, 214, 215, 216, 345, 346, 347, 390.
Levi T., 214, 345.
Lois, 94.
Lydia, 4, 11.
Martha, 20.
Mary, 13, 14, 20, 70, 72, 73, 75, 77, 89, 92, 104, 116, 117, 134, 159, 214, 215, 216, 229, 273, 293, 295, 302, 303, 320, 329, 335, 406, 451, 452, 453.
Mary B., 214, 345.
Mrs. ——, 325.
Nancy, 214, 345.
Otis B., 214, 345.
Peter, 81, 383.
Rachel, 272.
Rebecca, 77, 130, 145, 296.
Ruth, 89, 92, 115, 127, 140, 299.
Samuel, 451, 452, 453.
Sarah, 11, 13, 14, 15, 32, 274, 288, 406, 451, 452.
Sophia, 152, 165.
Susanna, 288.
Tabitha, 25, 274.
Vashti, 73, 76, 81, 90, 92, 136, 382.
William A., 216, 347.
PREVOT, Ellen G., 446.
PRIEST, Abigail, 44, 50, 104, 273, 298, 415.
Abigail F., 244.
Adolphus M., 217.
Anna, 18, 273, 415.
Bathsheba, 60.
Benjamin, 35, 53, 98, 298, 303, 306, 308, 311, 312, 327, 328, 331,

INDEX.

Betty, 197, 278, 298, 320, 326.
Charles, 216, 217, 392, 393.
Charlotte, 307.
Damaris, 19, 67, 274.
Daniel, 27, 29, 156, 278, 290, 379.
Eleazer, 53, 298.
Electa M., 217, 393.
Elizabeth, 135, 187, 271, 278, 299, 331, 352, 379, 446, 451.
Eunice, 24, 135, 276, 278.
Gabriel, 50, 276, 277.
Hannah, 43, 104, 126, 139, 271, 276, 303, 306, 331.
Harriet, 392.
Hasadiah, 278.
Hephzibah, 26, 275.
Jacob, 300.
Jeremiah, 50, 277.
Joel, 311.
John, 20, 43, 50, 104, 187, 270, 273, 274, 275, 276, 277, 278, 290, 298, 300, 303, 307, 352, 415.
Jonathan, 67, 158, 276, 415.
Joseph, 52, 53, 56, 60, 67, 187, 298, 299, 319, 324, 352.
Maria, 27, 277.
Mary, 18, 41, 52, 53, 56, 60, 103, 273, 299, 321, 331.
Meribah, 308.
Nancy, 216, 217, 392, 393.
Nancy E., 392, 394.
Oliver J., 306.
Phebe, 241.
Rachel, 241, 274.
Rhoda F., 392, 394.
Sarah, 42, 100, 144, 298, 306.
Sarah S., 392.
Silence, 278.
Solomon, 312, 327, 328.
Susanna, 38, 53, 99, 298.
Sylvanus C., 216, 393.
Tabitha, 56, 299, 324, 331.
Widow ——, 327.
Zimri, 365.
PROCTER, Anna, 197.
Betty, 43, 103.
Robert, 38, 102.
Sarah, 29.
PROUTEE, Abel, 108, 387.
Burpee, 97, 303.
Elijah, 289.
Elisha, 137, 297.
Elizabeth, 216, 240.
Esther, 97.
Francis, 40, 108, 292, 387, 388.
Isaac, 108, 388.
James, 288.
Jason, 216.
Joseph, 289.
Lydia, 40, 103, 288.
Martha, 188, 446.
Mary, 108, 387.
Mary A., 249.
Mary E. G., 216, 250.
Rebecca G., 243.
Richard, 36, 97, 98, 288, 290, 292, 297, 303, 320, 324.
Thirza, 108, 388.
PUFFER, Abigail, 187, 436.
Harriet, 123.
Harriet C., 249, 344.
Loring, 123, 344.
Lucy Cutting, 123, 344.
Martha, 24.
Nabby, 123, 354.
Nathan, 123, 148, 161, 187, 436.
William, 123, 243, 344.
PUSHEE, David, 301.
Elizabeth, 300.
Nathan, 301.
PUTNAM, Ebenezer, 188.

Elizabeth, 188, 360.
Miles, 235.
Rebecca, 129, 138.
Ruth, 102.
PUTNEY, Abby A., 265.
Henry M., 265.
Joseph M., 265.
Lyman K., 265.
Manasseh, 216. 241.
Marietta, 216.
Mary, 216, 265.
Mary H., 265.
Milton J., 265.
Warren C., 265.
QUARLS, Joanna, 20.
QUINCY, Ann, 414.
Edmund, 390.
Josiah, 414.
RAMER, Polly, 132.
RAND, Charles H., 218, 349.
Elizabeth, 19.
Ellen M., 349, 367, 437.
Hananiah, 38, 99.
Harry, 189, 437.
Jonathan, 18.
Joseph, 238.
Josephine A., 218.
Luke S., 100, 388.
Lucy, 155, 166, 189, 363, 437.
Mary, 153, 389.
Nancy E., 189, 218, 337, 368, 437.
Nathaniel, 189, 218, 237, 245, 349, 359, 367, 437.
Relief, 100.
Richard, 41, 100, 101, 377, 388, 389.
Ruth, 28.
William D., 218.
RANDALL, Abby A., 260.
Ann P., 260.
David, 260, 395.
Jane E., 264.
Josiah, 129, 264.
Mary E., 260.
Thomas, 357.
RAY, Abraham, 242.
RAYMOND, Edward A., 237.
Levi, 264.
Louisa, 264.
Nathan, 37, 98.
REED, Abigail, 93, 302.
Anna, 145.
Catharine, 19.
Elizabeth, 93, 264.
Ephraim, 93, 324.
George F., 437.
Hannah, 129, 139.
James, 302.
Joshua, 34, 86.
Levi, 234.
Mary A., 253.
Mary E., 437.
Sylvanus, 247.
William, 264.
William C., 152, 165.
REESE, George E., 251.
REEVES, Eliza E., 249.
RENIE, Henry, 12.
REVOLUTION, Soldiers of, 179, 180, 181, 182, 183, 187, 189, 191, 192, 193, 195, 196.
REYNOLDS, Sarah H., 168, 172, 194, 195.
RHODA ——, 325.
RICE, Abel, 218, 259, 263, 266, 268, 343.
Abraham, 114.
Ann, 35, 370.
Anna, 189, 218.
Anna M., 218.
Benjamin, 107.

Benj. Franklin, 218.
Betsy, 217, 218, 334, 436, 437.
Daniel, 85, 88.
David, 107.
Dolly, 107, 231.
Edward R., 263.
Eliakim, 107, 129.
Elijah, 104.
Elisha, 107.
Eliza, 217.
Elizabeth, 107, 169, 170.
Emily, 231.
Emily J., 259, 268.
Ezekiel, 217, 343.
Harriet A., 218.
Harriet M., 189, 218.
Henry, 138.
Henry O., 266.
Horace, 244.
Jacob E., 218.
John, 107.
Jonas, 107.
Joseph, 107, 149, 162, 217, 218, 238, 334, 340, 341, 342, 343, 345, 436, 437, 451.
Josiah, 107, 156, 189, 218.
Jotham, 40, 99.
Lois, 33.
Louisa, 218, 247, 345.
Louisa E., 218.
Lucy, 248, 263, 268, 343.
Lucy B., 259, 266.
Luke, 107.
Luther, 141.
Mary, 23, 100, 114, 218, 362, 451.
Mary Ann, 189, 217, 218, 342, 437.
Mary E., 218.
Merrick, 152.
Molly, 107.
Nathaniel, 189, 217, 218, 237, 253, 340, 365, 394.
Pamela, 389.
Polly, 387.
Reuben, 107.
Sally, 217, 343.
Samuel, 35, 85, 100, 114, 387, 388, 389.
Sarah, 83, 87.
Sarah J., 218.
Silas, 31, 136.
Simeon, 107.
Stephen, 107.
Susanna, 107, 156.
William, 163.
Zebulon, 107, 156.
RICH, Ellen F., 268.
John, 268.
RICHARDS, E. W., 395.
George K., 253, 260.
Jane, 144.
John, 233, 395.
Leonard J., 251.
Mary, 134.
Mitchell, 98.
Nancy, 260.
Sarah, 395.
Sarah G., 256.
Walter L., 260.
William, 27.
RICHARDSON, Abel, 107, 189, 218, 239, 366, 369, 384.
Abigail, 83, 145, 290, 300.
Amy, 66, 99, 287.
Anna, 37.
Benjamin, 126, 128, 137, 390.
Betsy, 218.
Caleb, 390.
Catharine, 43, 102, 381.
Charlotte, 189, 363, 415.
Clorinda, 218, 253.

Converse, 80, 83, 87, 299, 320, 332.
David, 170, 358, 359, 437.
Dorothy, 37, 38, 60, 62, 71, 98, 99, 129, 273, 283, 292, 320, 386.
Elizabeth, 40, 45, 60, 62, 86, 95, 103, 218, 282, 283, 305, 386, 389.
Emily, 248.
Ephraim, 39, 96, 107, 108, 415.
Esther, 65, 79, 83, 90, 92, 95, 108, 287, 300.
Eunice, 37, 71, 78, 98, 231, 294, 321, 379, 390, 415.
Gardner, 108.
Harriet M., 218.
James, 34, 43, 58, 61, 63, 65, 68, 80, 86, 107, 153, 158, 165, 232, 280, 283, 286, 287, 289, 297, 299, 330, 383, 384, 385, 387, 389, 390.
Jepthah, 80, 299.
John, 39, 63, 68, 92, 102, 158, 286, 289, 303, 386.
Joseph O., 218.
Josiah, 25, 60, 62, 71, 108, 273, 283, 285, 286, 287, 292, 293, 307, 374, 379.
Kezia, 138, 386.
Levi, 305.
Lucretia, 35, 63, 88, 284.
Lucy, 41, 101, 107, 129, 144, 380, 385, 386.
Luke, 61, 87, 283.
Lydia, 134, 351, 391.
Manasseh, 109, 387.
Martha W., 218.
Mary, 33, 58, 60, 63, 66, 67, 69, 78, 81, 86, 88, 273, 279, 280, 287, 303.
Mary E., 243.
Mary W., 245.
Mercy, 80, 320.
Patience, 81, 129, 139, 301, 320, 321, 331.
Paul, 41, 103.
Person, 126, 128.
Peter, 92, 302.
Polly, 107.
Rachel, 38, 100.
Rebecca, 37, 43, 67, 81, 98, 130, 280, 301, 387.
Relief, 107, 129, 138, 383.
Resolved, 301.
Ruhamah, 299.
Ruth, 43, 80, 103, 107, 297, 330.
Samuel, 90, 169, 189, 218, 301, 365.
Sarah, 33, 61, 63, 65, 68, 96, 107, 108, 158, 256, 287.
Serena, 390.
Silas, 238.
Susan N., 189, 337, 349.
Susanna, 34, 41, 69, 80, 85, 286, 292, 297, 321.
Thomas, 96.
Tilley, 12, 33, 60, 129, 142, 283, 377, 386, 387, 391.
Widow ——, 189.
William, 6, 18, 23, 32, 58, 60, 63, 66, 67, 69, 78, 79, 81, 83, 90, 92, 95, 98, 108, 273, 278, 279, 280, 282, 284, 287, 289, 292, 294, 300, 301, 302, 303, 305, 307, 320, 324, 325, 330, 331.
RIDER, Anna, 189, 352.
Eleazar, 189, 352.
RIDLEY, Billings H., 396.
RIGBY, Elizabeth, 12, 13.
John, 12, 13.
ROACH, Catharine O., 251.
Eliza, 252.
ROBB, Margaret, 28.
ROBBINS, Bathsheba, 38, 69, 77, 109, 132, 147, 189, 285, 287, 292, 308, 320, 398, 399.
Daniel, 6, 27, 29, 83, 94, 97, 111, 160, 360, 374, 377, 383, 384, 385, 386, 388, 389, 418.
David, 31, 33, 127, 140, 326.
Edward, 27, 69, 77, 113, 189, 285, 287, 289, 292, 293, 296, 311, 319, 325, 330, 374, 378, 379, 398, 399.
Eleazer, 149, 217.
Elizabeth, 35, 85, 94, 386.
Ephraim, 102, 170, 228, 364.
Hannah, 94, 103, 134, 168, 171, 217, 383.
Huldah, 152, 164, 314.
Jacob, 23, 108, 138.
James, 151, 163, 363.
Jane, 70, 397.
Jemima, 94, 385.
John, 45, 77, 104, 108, 113, 153, 165, 189, 266, 296, 308, 309, 310, 311, 314, 321, 356, 360.
Joseph, 280, 281.
Jotham, 77, 149, 162, 309, 325, 379, 399.
Jude, 108.
Kezia, 25.
Levi, 108.
Lucy, 23, 108, 129, 139.
Luke, 23, 108.
Lydia, 113, 189, 321, 362.
Margaret, 281.
Martha, 251.
Mary, 68, 83, 87, 94, 97, 111, 217, 287, 383.
Prudence, 266, 371, 437.
R——, 446.
Robba, 217.
Roger, 23, 30, 108.
Sarah, 111, 389.
Sarah M., 217.
Silas, 23, 108.
Susanna, 94, 280, 384.
Thankful, 357.
ROBERTSON, David S., 268, 397, 414.
Sarah, 144.
ROBINSON, C. G., 268.
Eliza, 250.
George, 153.
George C., 246.
Jacob W., 252.
Jonathan B., 253.
Lucy T., 394.
Nathan S., 394.
ROBY, Reuel, 168, 171.
ROCKWOOD, Harriet, 236.
ROGERS, Abiah, 10, 12, 14, 20.
Abigail, 13, 20, 24, 189, 359.
Abijah, 150, 163, 335, 346, 348.
Amos, 151.
Asa, 325.
Bathsheba, 12, 20.
Benjamin, 9.
Benjamin H., 348.
Dorcas, 14.
Eliphalet, 45, 103, 377.
Elizabeth, 39.
Emery W., 346.
Hannah, 18.
Harrison, 346.
Ichabod, 10.
Israel, 13.
Jane, 281.
Jeremiah, 10, 12, 13, 14, 19, 20.
Jehosaphat, 12.
John, 21, 33, 86.
John W., 229.
Joseph, 140, 189.
Joseph W., 346.
Lucy, 335.
Lucy Ann, 346.
Manasseh, 346.
Mehetabel, 12, 13.
Moses C., 346.
Samuel, 24.
Susannah, 14.
ROLLINS, Edward B., 252.
Rebecca P., 256.
ROLPH, Hannah, 34.
ROOT, Frederick C., 241.
ROPER, Asa, 79.
Bathsheba, 452.
Benjamin, 77, 78, 105, 135, 389, 390.
Cata, 390.
Elizabeth, 16, 452.
Enoch, 89.
Ephraim, 14, 16, 22, 32, 77, 78, 79, 89, 95, 117, 451, 452.
Ephraim L., 372.
Hannah, 16, 452.
John, 16.
Joseph, 95.
Lucy, 95.
Manasseh, 77, 78.
Michal, 77, 78, 79, 89, 95, 117.
Naomi, 117.
Nathaniel, 89, 117, 138.
Priscilla, 14, 16, 452.
Rachel, 20.
Ruth, 452.
Silas, 78.
Sylvester, 95.
ROSE, ——, 315, 319.
Ross, Abigail, 42, 66, 70, 73, 74, 77, 81, 92, 111, 285, 288, 379, 386, 438.
Achsa, 111, 116, 160, 418.
Anna, 26, 27, 28, 40, 101, 272, 291, 379.
Benjamin W., 116, 160.
Betty, 91, 385, 418.
Daniel, 309.
David, 264.
Deborah H., 255.
Deliverance, 22, 33, 63, 88, 284.
Dolly, 106, 388.
Ebenezer, 41, 73, 74, 89, 102, 111, 116, 160, 380, 418.
Elijah, 309.
Elizabeth, 66, 69, 71, 76, 287, 379.
Elizabeth A., 395.
Elizabeth J., 264.
Ephraim, 77, 111, 381.
Hannah, 24, 77, 89, 104, 135, 309, 331, 381.
James, 27, 28, 39, 66, 70, 73, 74, 77, 81, 101, 285, 288, 291, 292, 375, 379, 380, 381, 382.
Jesse, 22, 88, 90, 92, 287, 377, 378, 384, 385, 386.
Joanna, 134.
Joel, 309.
John, 218, 380.
Jonathan, 76, 89, 91, 108, 382, 385, 388.
Josiah, 189, 358, 438.
Lemuel, 90, 384.
Leonard, 108, 389.
Levi, 380.
Lois, 102.
Luther, 117.
Lydia, 25.
Margaret, 74.
Martha, 386.
Mary, 61, 63, 64, 66, 67, 69, 73, 76, 77, 84, 85, 88, 89, 91, 92, 95, 106, 108, 272, 387, 418.
Micah, 117, 140.

INDEX.

Michael, 309.
Molly, 117.
Moses, 95, 386.
Olive, 249, 382.
Phebe, 95, 387.
Polly, 218.
Priscilla, 91, 95, 108, 112, 418.
Priscilla G., 111, 418.
Prudence, 81, 382.
Reuben, 90, 385.
Roger, 36, 67, 89, 91, 92, 95, 98, 106, 108, 289, 385, 386, 387, 388.
Ruth, 90, 92, 108, 388.
Samuel, 35, 66, 88, 89, 288.
Seth, 111, 438.
Silas, 111.
Simeon, 111, 218.
Simon, 42, 66, 111, 288.
Submit, 23, 85, 309.
Tamar, 36, 69, 89, 98, 111, 292.
Thomas, 20, 61, 63, 64, 66, 67, 69, 73, 74, 75, 77, 85, 88, 89, 91, 95, 108, 112, 272, 284, 286, 288, 289, 292, 375, 377, 379, 380, 381, 382, 385, 386, 387, 388, 389, 390, 418.
Timothy, 66, 69, 71, 76, 287, 288, 290, 379, 380, 382.
William, 76, 89, 111, 134, 380.
Willis, 386.
———, 320.
Rowe, Prudence, 103, 133.
ROWLANDSON, Bridget, 11.
Joseph, 9, 11, 12, 16, 20.
Mary, 9, 11, 12.
Sarah, 12, 16.
Thomas, 12, 16.
ROYALL, Susan C., 255.
RUBEDEAU, Phebe A., 255.
RUCK, Hephzibah, 26.
RUGG, Aaron, 82, 142, 189, 300, 315, 322, 356, 437.
Abel, 76, 147, 161, 180, 189, 217, 296, 339, 340, 370, 438.
Abel W., 189, 217, 218, 230, 339, 360, 438.
Abijah, 75, 117, 122, 139, 189, 217, 295, 313, 314, 315, 317, 322, 339, 357, 359, 437.
Addison E., 259, 372, 438.
Alice M. L., 260.
Almira, 337.
Alpheus, 189, 217, 339.
Amos, 26, 29, 42, 56, 70, 73, 75, 76, 79, 80, 89, 91, 95, 159, 275, 291, 375, 379, 380, 381, 382, 383, 384, 385, 386, 418.
Amy, 117, 167, 168, 171, 173, 217, 314, 322, 331.
Ann M. L., 259, 260, 438.
Anna, 69, 74, 101, 120, 292, 310, 377.
Anthony, 120, 338.
Artemas, 120, 317.
Asa, 46, 76, 381.
Asa W., 217, 348.
Augustus, 189, 218, 344.
Bathsheba, 189, 217, 218, 267, 336, 366, 437.
Benjamin H., 217, 315, 346.
Betsy, 122, 217, 218, 246, 267, 337, 344, 372, 437.
Catharine, 89, 147, 161, 189, 217, 237, 301, 336, 340, 371, 438.
Cephas, 236, 318.
Charles F., 218.
Charles H., 261.
Christopher, 218, 344.
Damaris, 45, 74, 103, 380.
Daniel, 26, 29, 39, 56, 71, 72, 74, 76, 77, 78, 80, 82, 83, 90, 94, 96, 97, 100, 101, 124, 156, 189, 218,
270, 271, 272, 275, 276, 277, 279, 291, 292, 293, 294, 295, 296, 297, 298, 299, 300, 302, 305, 306, 308, 309, 310, 311, 312, 314, 315, 317, 319, 321, 323, 324, 325, 328, 330, 348, 349, 364, 437, 451, 452.
Daniel W., 218.
Deborah, 24, 275.
Dorothy, 62, 272, 330.
Edward, 189, 217, 339, 361.
Elijah, 77, 142, 145, 155, 167, 189, 217, 297, 317, 318, 322, 330, 337, 338, 350, 356.
Elisha, 79, 120, 129, 142, 189, 217, 298, 314, 315, 316, 317, 322, 330, 338, 340, 354, 438.
Eliza, 189, 218, 342.
Eliza A., 217, 240, 348.
Elizabeth, 19, 56, 68, 73, 94, 96, 97, 101, 105, 124, 134, 156, 189, 217, 271, 275, 290, 295, 309, 321, 334, 347, 363, 366, 377, 379, 437.
Ellen A., 260, 348.
Emeline E., 218.
Emily, 217, 234, 339.
Emily W., 217, 244, 346.
Ephraim, 76, 153, 165, 217, 218, 267, 296, 312, 348, 368, 437.
Eunice, 100, 388.
Fidelia, 122, 240, 338.
Francis, 218, 349.
Francis A., 259.
George H., 217.
Gideon, 276.
Granville, 217, 341.
Hannah, 12, 13, 14, 17, 20, 38, 95, 189, 217, 218, 247, 271, 279, 367, 386, 438, 451, 452.
Hannah M., 217.
Harriet, 217, 346.
Harriet P., 218, 255.
Harriet S., 217, 253, 348.
Harrison, 318.
Henry H., 218.
Isaac, 29, 70, 73, 75, 77, 128, 144, 188, 267, 277, 295, 297, 317, 318, 319, 324, 357, 403, 437.
Jacob, 75, 132, 295.
James, 124, 169, 170, 189, 217, 218, 240, 259, 260, 266, 317, 335, 346, 347, 348, 349, 363, 438.
Jane, 70, 73, 75, 77, 189, 295, 319, 355.
Joel, 77, 168, 171, 189, 217, 218, 267, 297, 317, 336, 348, 349, 368, 437.
Joel I., 217, 267, 348, 372, 437.
John, 9, 11, 12, 13, 14, 17, 20, 29, 32, 68, 70, 72, 74, 76, 77, 82, 156, 189, 218, 270, 275, 278, 291, 293, 294, 295, 296, 297, 300, 319, 352, 365, 407, 452.
Jonathan, 62, 272, 280, 284, 329, 330, 452.
Joseph, 12, 17, 27, 28, 97, 101, 122, 132, 147, 189, 217, 218, 231, 277, 306, 308, 333, 338, 339, 340, 341, 342, 343, 344, 345, 346, 351, 357.
Joseph A., 217, 340.
Joshua, 82, 300.
Josiah, 155, 166, 218, 315, 343, 344, 345, 358.
Josiah N., 217, 347.
Julia, 217, 345.
Kezia, 81.
Lewis, P., 217.
Levi, 77, 297.
Lois, 77, 104, 134, 297, 322, 350.
Lucinda M., 218.
Lucretia, 78, 127, 142, 218, 254,
298, 322, 348.
Lucy, 32, 44, 72, 74, 104, 120, 135, 151, 163, 189, 217, 294, 295, 311, 314, 321, 334, 338, 342, 355, 437.
Lucy H., 218.
Luke, 122, 189, 217, 218, 239, 362.
Lydia, 23, 32, 60, 62, 64, 66, 68, 69, 70, 72, 74, 76, 77, 79, 82, 85, 156, 189, 277, 282, 285, 292, 295, 319, 356, 407, 419.
Margaret, 29, 272, 275.
Marah, 12.
Martha, 9, 11, 24, 45, 60, 70, 104, 189, 275, 282, 295, 321, 348, 419.
Martha F., 217, 253.
Martha K., 218, 266.
Martha W., 218, 343.
Martin, 189, 438.
Mary, 23, 62, 70, 73, 75, 79, 80, 87, 89, 91, 95, 122, 159, 189, 217, 218, 284, 333, 338, 351, 368, 375, 380, 389, 418, 437.
Mary Ann, 217, 247, 341.
Mary E., 218, 259, 260, 348.
Mary T., 218.
Merrill U., 260.
Molly, 36, 98.
Nahum, 117, 168, 171, 218, 313, 358.
Nancy, 132, 147, 340.
Nathan, 29, 69, 72, 73, 75, 77, 79, 81, 89, 120, 189, 276, 291, 293, 295, 297, 298, 301, 316, 329.
Nathaniel, 62, 284, 303.
Olive, 89, 384.
Oliver, 280.
Pamela, 91, 385.
Persis, 261.
Phebe, 79, 383.
Phineas, 277.
Polly, 167, 172, 218, 229, 314, 318, 335.
Prudence, 66, 90, 189, 196, 288, 302, 368, 376, 419, 437.
Rebecca, 14, 70, 72, 156, 267, 293, 372, 437, 437, 451.
Relief, 73, 134, 322.
Reuben, 25, 60, 62, 64, 66, 68, 69, 72, 74, 76, 275, 282, 284, 285, 287, 288, 290, 292, 293, 294, 303, 374, 379, 380, 381, 419.
Ruth, 19, 22, 64, 88, 287.
Sally, 333, 437.
Salome, 189, 217, 218.
Samuel, 20, 96, 122, 131, 146, 188, 217, 218, 271, 273, 275, 276, 277, 278, 279, 305, 333, 338, 339, 340, 341, 343, 345, 356, 437.
Samuel S., 218, 343.
Sarah, 49, 56, 71, 72, 74, 76, 77, 78, 80, 82, 86, 90, 101, 122, 128, 217, 279, 291, 293, 295, 319, 321, 328, 355, 379.
Sarah H., 217, 235, 339.
Sarah W., 217, 218, 340, 348, 437.
Sewall, 218, 345.
Sewell T., 218, 250, 261.
Simon, 275.
Solomon, 80, 95, 159, 382, 418.
Sophia, 188, 217, 244, 343, 346.
Stephen, 76, 80, 89, 159, 189, 299, 367, 381, 383, 418, 437.
Submit, 189, 217, 218, 266, 335, 364, 438.
Submit B., 217, 346.
Susan W., 189, 217, 218.
Susanna, 38, 68, 72, 100, 117, 122, 125, 167, 173, 189, 217, 291, 315, 317, 322, 365, 437.
Thomas, 12, 39, 43, 70, 100, 103, 291, 388, 389.

INDEX. 495

Warren, 217, 345.
William, 218, 343.
William B., 217, 249, 259, 260, 348.
William S., 100, 388.
Zerviah, 42, 69, 72, 73, 75, 77, 79, 81, 89, 104, 189, 291, 293, 355.
Russ, Joseph, 38, 99.
Russell, Anna M., 110, 114, 309, 331.
Caleb, 189, 354.
Charles B., 258.
David, 110, 309, 326.
Elizabeth, 26, 284, 323.
Esther, 129.
Ezekiel, 129.
John, 31.
Katy M., 114.
Lucretia, 189.
Moses, 40, 102, 104, 134, 308, 309, 323, 326, 331.
Moses P., 308.
Peter B., 309.
Ruth, 30.
Sarah, 321.
Sabin, Experience, 332.
Timothy, 31.
Sachwell, Jeremiah, 104, 134.
Sackett, Seth, 241.
Safford, Adeline, 344.
Augustus, 219.
Caroline, 341.
Catharine, 190, 339, 342, 415.
Charles, 219, 253, 261, 438.
Charles E., 261.
Eliza, 168, 171.
Elizabeth, 190, 335, 359, 415.
Ellen F., 261.
Francis A., 340.
George, 191, 219, 230, 359, 439.
George F., 219, 254.
Henry, 342.
Joseph C., 339.
Julia A., 261, 438.
Mary, 219, 365, 439.
Polly, 191.
Roby, 219.
Sarah, 446.
Sarah J., 261, 438.
Susan P., 343.
Thomas, 190, 191, 232, 338, 339, 340, 341, 342, 343, 344, 352, 353, 354, 355, 362, 415.
Sampson, Abisha, 234, 236, 238, 239.
Catharine, 89.
Elijah, 81.
Joel, 300.
John, 32, 77, 79, 81, 89, 300.
Levi, 79.
Mindwell, 116.
Mr. ——, 191.
Nathaniel, 116.
Prudence, 77, 79, 81, 89.
Silas, 116.
Thomas, 78.
William, 79.
——, 326.
Sanborn, Sarah, 60.
Tristam, 161.
Zadock, 25, 60.
Sanders, Clariette G., 249.
Edward, 328.
Sarah, 279.
Sanderson, Ann A., 240.
Calvin, 256, 261, 343.
Charles, 220.
Charles C., 261.
Edwin I., 220, 348.
Elisha, 190, 335, 343, 345, 354, 370, 448.

Eliza Ann, 220.
Elmira A., 345.
Eunice, 33.
George W., 220, 254, 348.
Isaac, 314.
Martha, 345, 364, 448.
Mary, 364, 448.
Nathan D., 220, 348.
Pamela, 220, 336.
Polly, 335.
Roxana, 233.
Samuel, 190, 314, 354.
Sarah, 261.
Sodi, 220, 230, 348, 361.
Washington, 246, 256.
William L., 220, 249, 348.
Sanford, Garry C., 395, 439.
Sargent, Aaron, 93, 133, 148, 190, 303, 304, 353, 440.
Alvin, 249, 261.
Ann, 268, 397, 440.
Anna, 218, 219, 347.
Catharine, 220, 221.
Catharine E., 220.
Cordelia, 220, 250.
Curtiss, 219, 246, 267, 268, 396, 397, 438.
Ebenezer, 150, 163.
Edwin, 347.
Eliza, 218, 257.
Elizabeth, 220, 334, 368, 440.
Elizabeth A., 347.
Emily, 220.
Emory, 220, 248.
Hannah, 76, 79, 93, 122, 152, 164, 190, 298, 303, 320, 353, 440.
Harriet, 245.
Henry, 220.
Huldah, 267, 268, 396, 397.
Jerome, 262.
John, 76, 79, 93, 122, 152, 164, 171, 190, 218, 219, 298, 299, 303, 304, 319, 325, 341, 342, 346, 354, 361, 397, 440.
John A., 261.
Julia Ann, 267, 396, 438.
Laura A., 221.
Lawson C., 262.
Louisa, 219.
Lucy M., 264.
Lyman, 220.
Maria, 220, 262.
Martha A., 262, 269, 438.
Mary, 122, 219, 220, 230.
Merrick, 220, 241, 262, 269, 338.
Nancy D., 346.
Nathaniel M., 218, 347.
Patience, 170, 228.
Polly, 152, 165, 219, 333.
Rebecca, 220, 262, 438.
Rebecca A., 261.
Richard, 190.
Ruth, 229.
Sally, 321.
Samuel, 79, 122, 127, 140, 299.
Sarah W., 220.
Sewall, 218, 240, 347.
Seth, 76, 122, 132, 147, 191, 220, 242, 262, 264, 298, 334, 364, 440.
Stephen, 152, 190, 219, 220, 354.
Susan, 191, 361.
Susanna, 219, 341.
Thankful, 151, 164.
Thomas, 220, 235, 363.
Willard, 219.
William, 122.
William L., 220.
Winfield P., 268, 297, 438.
Zophar, 218, 220, 221, 239, 347.
Savage, Edward, 240.
Sarah S., 239.
Sawin, Aaron, 368, 395, 440.

Catharine, 235.
Ellen C., 440.
Maria, 258.
Phebe, 440.
Sawtell, Betsy, 243.
Elizabeth C., 255.
John D., 258.
Josiah, 271, 277.
Lydia, 271, 277.
Mary J., 256.
Nathaniel P., 249.
Richard, 132, 147.
Stillman A., 258, 396.
Susan, 172.
Sawyer, Aaron, 23, 50, 63, 81, 85, 90, 93, 96, 105, 109, 111, 129, 138, 157, 160, 282, 380, 388, 419.
Abby L., 261.
Abel, 90, 255, 263, 301.
Abigail, 24, 27, 29, 46, 55, 70, 74, 76, 81, 90, 93, 96, 103, 109, 111, 125, 139, 157, 190, 273, 277, 278, 283, 296, 303, 380, 405, 419.
Abigail B., 190, 220, 349, 370, 438.
Abner, 26, 67, 82, 92, 97, 112, 276, 285, 288, 297, 380, 382, 383, 386, 419.
Abraham, 287, 389.
Achsa, 114, 169, 170, 338.
Agnes, 91, 94, 96, 105, 109, 116.
Aholiab, 60, 61, 272, 274, 283, 287.
Abner A., 265.
Alfred, 246, 247.
Almiric, 365.
Almeida A., 220.
Alonzo P., 263.
Almy E., 219, 342.
Alpheus, 337.
Amariah, 94.
America, 190, 191, 220, 239, 265, 369.
Amos, 17, 23, 55, 82, 87, 92, 94, 111, 127, 133, 142, 148, 157, 159, 160, 190, 191, 235, 276, 277, 278, 279, 283, 296, 300, 306, 319, 323, 324, 325, 330, 334, 340, 341, 342, 352, 361, 371, 405, 407, 415.
Anna, 274, 375, 381, 419.
Anthony L., 249, 262, 349.
Artemas, 114, 312, 388.
Asenath, 26, 276.
Avery D., 258.
Azubah, 60, 85, 282.
Beatrix, 54, 110, 384.
Benjamin, 63, 286.
Betsy, 149, 162, 219, 371, 443.
Betty, 28, 36, 43, 60, 61, 70, 98, 109, 114, 161, 162, 191, 265, 272, 277, 289, 322.
Beulah, 288, 309.
Bezaleel, 48, 96, 282, 294, 297, 298, 301, 305, 319, 324, 330, 331, 402.
Caleb, 10, 273, 276, 394, 451.
Calvin, 92, 129, 142, 147, 306.
Catharine, 35, 41, 70, 85, 88, 104, 220, 279, 290, 337.
Catharine A., 220.
Catharine B., 220.
Charles, 131, 191, 219, 220, 233, 338, 363, 365, 366, 367, 439.
Charles B., 218, 349.
Charles F., 191, 220, 439.
Charles H., 251.
Charlotte, 190, 302, 357.
Clara E., 261.
Cooper, 97, 388.
Cornelius, 67, 71, 136, 287, 382.
Cynthia, 190, 219, 337, 340, 358.
Damaris, 21, 33, 55, 61, 283.

INDEX.

Daniel, 254, 438.
Daniel G., 387.
Darius, 30, 44, 48, 81, 82, 90, 91, 94, 96, 299, 300, 301, 303, 304, 305, 322, 326, 330, 331, 405.
David, 55, 114, 157, 248, 277, 383.
Deborah, 12, 30, 38, 55, 58, 60, 62, 64, 66, 70, 76, 81, 82, 90, 91, 94, 96, 99, 101, 159, 190, 272, 279, 299, 303, 322, 325, 331, 353, 405, 419.
Deliverance, 50, 72.
Dinah, 46, 55, 107, 376, 384, 387, 415.
Dolly, 96, 111, 319.
Dorothy, 50, 94, 278, 383.
Eber, 298.
Eben, 190, 219, 232, 361, 439.
Edith B., 262.
Edmund H., 220.
Edward, 15.
Eli, 255, 263.
Eliakim, 124, 218, 219, 338.
Elias, 54, 72, 134, 190, 218, 219, 220, 229, 268, 269, 275, 276, 277, 278, 337, 349, 366, 380, 390, 397, 415, 438.
Elijah, 29, 220, 240, 261, 275, 367, 415.
Elisha, 27, 35, 39, 43, 70, 72, 76, 77, 85, 101, 110, 113, 276, 285, 290, 291, 376, 379, 380, 381, 382, 383, 384, 386, 387.
Eliza, 191, 219, 220, 262, 336, 438, 439.
Eliza Ann, 220, 342, 350.
Eliza H., 394.
Elizabeth, 10, 22, 33, 42, 59, 69, 71, 76, 87, 88, 102, 106, 110, 121, 158, 190, 218, 219, 269, 275, 279, 287, 290, 333, 339, 353, 381, 387, 389, 391, 397, 415, 439, 440.
Ellen A., 201.
Elliot E., 265.
Elmirick, 191, 220, 365.
Emeline A., 191, 219, 349, 369.
Emery T., 220, 393.
Ephraim, 10, 16, 33, 34, 85, 94, 105, 135, 150, 163, 271, 278, 279, 280, 375, 376, 383, 384, 385, 386, 387, 388, 389, 419.
Esther, 55, 71, 88, 91, 106, 109, 111, 114, 128, 144, 157, 276, 303.
Eunice, 21, 30, 41, 48, 70, 101, 271, 278, 282, 294, 297, 388, 402, 419.
Eusebius, 341.
Evelina, 124, 218, 367.
Ezra, 19, 35, 59, 71, 88, 92, 97, 112, 114, 191, 218, 219, 220, 232, 272, 275, 279, 280, 282, 284, 290, 292, 316, 336, 348, 349, 350, 362, 366, 377, 380, 386, 388, 419, 438.
Ezra Thomas, 220, 348.
Fairbank, 113.
Francina E., 220, 367, 438.
Francina E. J., 220.
Francis A., 219, 266, 349, 372, 439.
Francis G., 263.
Francis H., 262.
Francis O., 220, 349.
Franklin, 191, 220.
Frederick C., 219.
Frederick E., 261.
Frederick H., 220, 438.
George, 229, 395.
George A., 265.
George M., 220.
George T., 262.
Hannah, 14, 24, 48, 82, 110, 124, 141, 218, 294, 301, 321, 325, 386.

Hannah W., 46, 103.
Henry, 191, 219, 220, 235, 364, 369, 395.
Henry H., 219, 438.
Henry O., 191, 220.
Hephzibah, 17, 25, 273, 274.
Ira J., 255.
Israel, 146, 219, 307.
Jabez, 109, 388.
Jacob, 81, 129, 299.
James, 10, 74, 94, 191, 219, 339, 363, 379, 385, 419, 451.
James T., 394.
Jane, 263.
Jedidah, 132, 305.
Jeduthan, 303.
Joanna, 61, 157, 283.
Joanna H., 250.
John, 11, 15, 50, 55, 61, 63, 67, 71, 72, 94, 107, 113, 114, 116, 156, 157, 158, 159, 218, 271, 275, 278, 280, 281, 282, 283, 286, 287, 288, 290, 307, 337, 344, 380, 384, 387, 415.
John H., 219, 220,
Jonathan, 67, 275, 276, 278, 279, 280, 282, 294, 327, 337.
Jonas, 219, 313.
Joseph, 17, 25, 36, 63, 65, 91, 94, 96, 98, 105, 109, 114, 116, 158, 190, 271, 276, 282, 283, 286, 287, 295, 355, 388, 406.
Joseph T., 262.
Josiah, 27, 28, 29, 37, 46, 48, 74, 94, 99, 125, 137, 190, 274, 285, 288, 290, 295, 296, 298, 299, 301, 303, 305, 323, 330, 353, 383.
Joshua, 10, 41, 60, 101, 106, 109, 111, 114, 190, 378, 388, 389, 451.
Jotham, 39, 72, 101, 107, 379, 387.
Jude, 81, 299.
Judith, 48, 304, 320, 326, 384.
Katy, 114, 155, 166, 318.
Kezia, 35, 67, 71, 82, 84, 85, 88, 92, 97, 112, 129, 150, 284, 288.
Lemuel, 125, 136, 295.
Lois, 129, 140, 190, 278, 282, 298, 301, 302, 321, 330, 354.
Louisa, 380.
Louisa A., 190, 220, 349, 371, 438.
Lucena, 114, 155, 166, 317.
Lucinda A., 263.
Lucinda M., 220.
Lucy, 41, 64, 83, 84, 85, 100, 265, 287, 295.
Lucy A., 124, 191, 219, 439.
Lucy C., 220.
Lucy G., 263.
Lucy H., 191, 220.
Luke, 298, 302, 380.
Luther, 92, 130, 143, 190, 191, 219, 336, 338, 340, 342, 361.
Lydia, 92, 126, 128, 137, 306, 415.
Manasseh, 41, 100, 101, 280, 380.
Marietta C., 260.
Marietta H., 220.
Marion E., 252.
Martha, 14, 27, 43, 67, 68, 77, 109, 158, 191, 219, 276, 288, 351, 380, 382, 389, 407.
Martha A., 220, 261.
Martha S., 220, 349, 439.
Mary, 10, 11, 12, 13, 14, 15, 18, 21, 25, 27, 29, 34, 37, 42, 46, 55, 58, 63, 65, 67, 69, 70, 77, 79, 82, 84, 86, 87, 92, 93, 94, 98, 99, 102, 110, 111, 113, 114, 130, 139, 156, 158, 159, 161, 218, 219, 271, 274, 275, 276, 278, 281, 285, 288, 290, 291, 293, 295, 299, 302, 306, 321,

326, 331, 381, 406, 438, 452.
Mary A., 219, 253, 266, 349, 438.
Mary B., 331.
Mary C., 394.
Mary H., 155, 166, 363.
Mary K., 220.
Mary T., 219, 353.
Miriam, 50, 157.
Molly, 114, 145, 304.
Moses, 37, 48, 50, 63, 93, 98, 114, 121, 125, 132, 137, 146, 157, 161, 190, 191, 218, 219, 268, 269, 281, 283, 304, 307, 308, 312, 313, 314, 315, 316, 317, 318, 320, 326, 329, 333, 338, 344, 355, 365, 376, 384, 385, 386, 397, 406, 415, 439, 440, 443.
Moses E., 218.
Nancy, 190, 369, 394.
Nancy B., 218, 219, 220, 269, 337, 397, 438.
Nathaniel, 13, 26, 45, 55, 63, 65, 69, 70, 71, 77, 97, 114, 149, 158, 161, 271, 275, 282, 290, 291, 292, 293, 294, 295, 297, 314, 319, 324, 325, 329, 333, 337, 388.
Nathaniel C., 220, 349.
Olive, 81, 128, 138, 278, 299, 382, 419.
Oliver, 63, 90, 149, 151, 164, 219, 290, 325.
Oliver B., 265.
Parney, 90, 129, 139.
Patience, 110.
Paul, 48, 84, 87, 110, 129, 142, 190, 219, 298, 300, 301, 302, 304, 306, 307, 309, 328, 331, 384, 407.
Persis, 105.
Peter, 94, 114, 155, 166, 191, 218, 219, 220, 263, 290, 315, 356, 364, 365, 385.
Phebe, 97, 106, 109, 112, 113, 117, 282, 390.
Phineas, 21, 27, 79, 104, 134, 275, 285, 288, 290, 293, 294, 295, 297, 298, 299, 302, 324.
Polly, 130, 144, 219, 220, 334, 340, 392, 393, 394.
Prudence, 21, 31, 54, 59, 70, 71, 82, 129, 190, 278, 279, 290, 301, 383, 407.
Putnam, 113.
Rebecca, 26, 59, 71, 85, 159, 272, 282, 290.
Relief, 41, 82, 92, 101, 138, 159, 295, 306, 380.
Rufus, 301.
Ruth, 43, 46, 55, 62, 70, 72, 76, 77, 117, 159, 191, 232, 284, 285, 368, 381, 382, 384, 415, 419.
Sabra, 142, 299, 328.
Sally, 121, 154, 165, 219, 247, 266, 338, 439.
Samuel, 24, 41, 58, 60, 62, 64, 66, 70, 76, 97, 106, 109, 112, 113, 117, 154, 159, 272, 281, 282, 284, 287, 288, 290, 374, 377, 380, 381, 382, 388, 389, 390.
Samuel F., 110.
Sarah, 13, 14, 24, 48, 50, 61, 63, 67, 71, 73, 76, 92, 114, 156, 157, 158, 159, 161, 191, 219, 263, 271, 276, 278, 279, 281, 283, 286, 288, 290, 306, 308, 329, 336, 350, 381, 406, 415, 451.
Sarah A., 219, 253.
Sarah E., 191, 219, 220, 350, 439.
Seth, 24, 25, 273, 415.
Silas, 191, 219, 231, 266, 336, 349, 364, 373, 439.
Silence, 111.
Silvanus, 61, 84, 283.

INDEX. 497

Solomon, 106, 388.
Sophia, 334, 341.
Submit, 109, 388.
Susan, 219.
Susanna, 88, 94, 99, 110, 141, 288, 384, 386.
Tabitha, 30, 63, 65, 285, 289.
Thankful, 25, 43, 67, 72, 77, 103, 135, 275, 297, 380, 397.
Thomas, 10, 11, 12, 13, 14, 16, 17, 20, 26, 27, 70, 74, 76, 94, 97, 110, 126, 138, 149, 156, 162, 190, 191, 219, 220, 232, 271, 275, 276, 287, 288, 289, 290, 301, 304, 306, 324, 328, 331, 339, 364, 377, 379, 380, 381, 382, 383, 385, 386, 390, 392, 393, 402, 406, 415, 419, 438.
Timothy, 389.
Uri, 131.
William, 46, 96, 110, 163, 271, 274, 275, 276, 277, 278, 285, 288, 397.
Zilpah, 190, 219, 338.
SCARLET, John, 147.
SCATE, John, 16.
SCOOT, John, 119.
SCOTT, Alexander, 28, 283.
 Eleanor, 31.
 William, 29.
SEARLE, Sir Francis, 355.
SEARS, Anna, 399.
 Edmund H., 221, 270, 369.
 Ellen, 221.
 Katherine, 221.
SEAVER, Amanda, 267, 396.
 Cyrus, 191, 220.
 Elias, 267.
 Elizabeth, 155.
 Joseph, 46, 103, 191, 220, 364.
 Joseph S., 267, 395, 396.
 Mary J., 267, 396.
 Nathaniel, 23.
 Persis, 220.
 Rebecca, 38.
 Silas, 396.
SECCOMBE, John, 286, 287.
SELFRIDGE, Lucia, 334.
 Lucy, 364.
SEVERY, John, 126, 139, 191.
 Lydia, 115.
 Phebe, 169, 170.
SHAKERS, 185, 187, 188, 196, 197, 320, 329, 445, 446.
SHATTUCK, Eliza, 392.
 Jonathan, 243.
 William, 36.
SHALER, Ann, 247.
SHAUGHNESSY, Martin. 252.
SHAW, Barbara, 311, 331.
 Margaret, 309.
 Mary, 130, 146, 311.
 William, 42, 104, 309, 311, 331.
SHEARER and SHERIN.
 Patience, 190, 358.
 William, 148, 161, 233.
SHED, Abel, 103, 306.
 Benjamin, 83, 87, 302, 385.
 Eleazer, 302.
 Elizabeth, 302.
 Francis, 265.
 Lemuel, 302.
 Lucy A., 265.
 Martha, 172.
 Mary Ann, 265.
 Solomon, 98.
SHELDON, Rosine, 251.
SHEPHERD, Thomas, 366.
 Thomas W., 191.
SHERMAN, Samuel, 153, 165.
SHOLAN, alias Showanon, 19.
SHOSHANIM, alias Sagamore

Sam, 19.
SHURTLEFF, Lucy, 351.
SIBLEY, Clark, 255, 256.
SIMMONS and SYMONDS.
 Abigail, 234.
 Henry, 19.
 Mary, 127, 143.
 Micah, 190, 359.
 Nabby, 190, 359.
 Reuben P., 256.
SINGLETARY, Richard, 17.
SLOTE, John, 365.
SMITH, Abigail, 39, 110, 190, 300, 310, 321, 328, 351, 357, 439.
 Abigail A. G., 218, 242, 349.
 Albert H., 255.
 Alice, 27, 28.
 Anes, 238.
 Ann, 20.
 Anna, 135.
 Anna M., 263.
 Asa, 45, 103, 380.
 Benjamin, 89, 116, 382.
 Betsy, 166.
 Charles Hy., 190, 218, 263, 439.
 Curtis P., 252.
 David, 231, 249.
 Dolly, 128, 145.
 Drusilla, 249.
 Ebenezer, 139.
 Effie, 98.
 Emeline, 240.
 Ephraim, 392.
 Esther, 36, 89, 103, 116, 134, 375, 383.
 Ezekiel, 150, 162.
 Francis, 10, 219, 349.
 George P., 263.
 Gideon, 98.
 Hannah, 45.
 Hannah S., 116.
 Happy, 140.
 Henry, 219, 349.
 Henry F., 220.
 Hiram, 242, 392.
 Howell, 439.
 Isabella B., 249.
 Jacob, 21, 30, 89, 375, 379, 380, 381, 382, 383.
 James, 20, 25, 397.
 Jeannette S., 263.
 Jesse, 152, 164.
 Joanna, 10.
 John, 10, 12, 13, 18.
 Jonathan, 19.
 Joseph F., 242.
 Joseph H., 256, 263.
 Joshua, 29, 44, 104, 328.
 Joshua T., 220.
 Lucretia, 127, 142.
 Lucy, 30, 128, 129, 132, 137, 139, 145, 147.
 Martha, 397.
 Martin, 251.
 Mary, 10, 12, 89, 379, 381.
 Mary P. P., 218, 349.
 Moses, 44, 103, 110, 154, 190, 191, 218, 219, 310, 311, 321, 328, 336, 349, 357, 367, 439.
 Moses D., 358.
 Noah, 232.
 Peter, 126, 141.
 Philip A., 219.
 Polly, 129, 142.
 Rebecca, 220, 236.
 Richard, 10, 12, 20.
 Sally, 190, 218, 219, 397, 439.
 Samuel, 142.
 Sarah, 116, 162, 272, 336, 439.
 Sebastian, 377, 419.

Silas, 43, 102, 300.
Stephen, 37, 98.
Susan M., 263.
Susanna, 143, 232.
Sydney, 219.
Thomas, 322, 380.
 Widow ——, 191.
 William, 34, 86.
SNOW, Abigail, 37, 39, 68, 99, 158, 274, 282, 289.
 Agnes I., 264.
 Anna, 390.
 Ebenezer. 26, 275.
 Elizabeth, 77, 381.
 Esther, 40, 102.
 Eunice, 64, 286.
 Ezekiel, 288.
 Hannah, 31, 40, 59, 63, 64, 68, 72, 77, 99, 157, 158, 272, 293, 379.
 Hannah B., 72.
 Hezekiah, 26, 64, 286, 288.
 Home C., 255.
 James, 272, 274, 275, 276, 277.
 John, 24, 31, 59, 63, 64, 68, 72, 77, 129, 140, 157, 158, 245, 271, 272, 282, 284, 286, 287, 289, 290, 291, 293, 375, 379, 381, 385.
 Joseph, 275, 386.
 Jotham, 149, 162, 389.
 Kezia, 63, 85, 88, 282.
 Lucy, 133, 284.
 Mahlon, 241, 244.
 Martha, 36, 63, 64, 98, 158, 282, 284, 290.
 Mary, 59, 83, 85, 271, 274, 275, 282, 397.
 Moses, 59, 157, 388.
 Peter, 86.
 Pliny, 385.
 Samuel, 64, 88, 129, 275, 286, 376, 385, 386, 387, 388, 389, 390.
 Sarah, 26, 276, 387.
 Thomas C., 264.
 Warren, 88, 385.
SOAMES, Keturah, 36.
SOLLENDINE, Adaline, 219.
 Deborah, 191, 219, 220, 363, 439.
 Dorcas, 297, 323.
 Elvira, 220.
 Isaac, 190, 355.
 John, 133, 190, 191, 297, 323, 325, 355, 361.
 Julia Ann, 191, 220.
 Manasseh, 153, 165, 191, 219, 220, 361, 365, 439.
 Mary, 220.
 Susan, 148, 161.
 Susan W., 219.
 Susanna, 27, 28, 29, 190, 356.
SOUTHWICK, Mrs. ——, 185.
SPAFFORD, Hannah, 41.
 Job, 96, 385.
 John, 129, 139.
 Mary, 43, 96, 377, 386.
 Samuel, 96, 385.
 Widow ——, 386.
SPARHAWK, Catharine, 35.
 Ebenezer, 332.
SPAULDING, Hannah, 238.
 John, 17.
 Nelson, 191, 368.
SPEAR, Joseph C., 231.
 Nancy, 335, 345.
 Susanna, 335.
SPOONER, Alden, 232.
 Bethia, 332.
 Daniel, 40, 102.
 William B., 240.
SPRAGUE, Ann A., 106, 116, 152, 165, 311, 334.

INDEX.

Catharine, 110, 116, 321, 329, 407.
John, 46, 110, 116, 145, 175, 190, 193, 309, 311, 313, 353, 407.
Mary, 190, 354.
Samuel J., 116, 190, 313, 355, 407.
Sarah, 110, 133, 148, 309.
STACY, Anna, 135, 237.
STANLEY, Calvin, 264, 269.
Edward, 264.
STANWOOD, Albert, 250.
STEARNS, Aaron, 99.
Abigail, 332.
Alice, 85.
Augustus, 190, 219, 344, 439.
Benjamin, 27, 28, 294.
Catharine, 219, 336, 344.
Charles, 121.
Daniel, 123, 130, 145, 190, 191, 360, 439.
David, 26, 287, 332.
Deborah, 123, 191, 363, 367, 439.
Dinah, 71, 74, 76.
Eli, 121, 128, 144, 190, 191, 219, 329, 330, 344, 357, 362, 439.
Eliza, 231, 335, 344.
Elizabeth, 76, 121, 332.
Elizabeth C., 262.
Freeborn, 155.
Hannah, 155, 167.
Harriet, 219, 335, 344.
Helen M., 262.
Henry, 121.
Ira, 238.
Isaac, 74, 231.
John, 38.
Martha, 123.
Martha A., 221, 262.
Mary, 121, 190, 191, 219, 335, 344, 363, 382, 439.
Mary A., 220, 262.
Mary F., 243, 350.
Nancy, 219, 337, 344.
Nancy W., 240.
Otis, 229.
Sally W., 219, 336, 344.
Samuel, 25, 71, 293.
Sophia, 121, 335, 344, 392.
Stephen, 382.
Thomas, 44, 104.
Timothy, 71, 74, 76, 190, 293, 294, 357.
Widow ——, 195.
William, 219, 220, 244, 262, 337, 344, 350.
STEBBINS, Patience, 42.
STEDMAN, Almy, 120, 190, 219, 440.
Charles H., 219, 342.
Christopher E., 120, 190, 318, 356, 440.
Francis D., 219, 236, 340.
Mary Ann, 120, 190, 338, 355, 440.
William, 6, 120, 130, 146, 148, 190, 219, 318, 332, 334, 338, 340, 342, 356, 373, 392, 440.
STEVENS, Amy, 339.
Azubah, 24.
Charles, 219.
Charles G., 260.
Chloe, 236.
Cyprian, 3, 6, 14, 271, 452, 453.
Dorothy, 276, 452.
Edward G., 260.
Elizabeth, 275, 451, 452, 453.
Emma, 333.
Isaac, 276.
John V., 161.
Jonathan, 274.
Joseph, 275, 276, 452.

Laura, 260.
Lucinda L., 309.
Lucretia, 219.
Martha, 127, 143, 309, 321.
Mary, 14, 338, 452, 453.
Nathan, 219.
Nathaniel, 274, 275.
Pardon, 190.
Rebecca, 84.
Ruth, 271.
Sally, 219.
Samuel, 130, 144, 146, 330, 338, 339.
Simon, 273, 274, 275, 276, 451, 452, 453.
Timothy, 451.
William, 338.
STEVENSON, Betsy, 229.
Galin L., 240, 261, 366.
John M., 343.
Lucy R., 344.
Lucy S., 394.
Lydia, 191, 363, 392, 393, 439, 440.
Martha, 261.
Martin, 190, 191, 342, 343, 344, 356, 439.
Mary, 230.
Sarah, 261.
Thomas C., 190, 342.
STEWART and STUART.
Anna, 81.
Benjamin, 384.
Catharine, 112.
Charles, 78, 419.
Dinah, 376.
Dolly, 154.
Elizabeth, 112.
Hannah, 36, 98.
Huldah, 419.
Jane, 81, 258, 381.
Jeremiah, 36, 98.
John, 81, 381.
Joseph, 83, 85, 376, 384.
Margaret, 320.
Mary, 38, 45, 103, 384.
Nathan, 168, 171.
Phebe, 419.
Polly, 112.
Samuel, 212, 419.
Sarah, 45, 78, 103, 112, 376, 381, 419.
Solomon, 42, 78, 102, 112, 381.
Widow ——, 384.
STICKNEY, Eunice, 39.
Mary, 36.
Peter, 141.
STILES, Hannah, 132.
John C., 268, 394, 395.
Mary E., 250.
Thomas, 397.
STIMPSON, Herbert H., 253.
——, 329.
STODDARD, Margaret, 329.
Sally, 139.
STONE, Abel, 191, 219, 239.
Abiel, 97.
Abigail, 238.
Abraham, 45.
Achsah, 219, 238.
Amelia, 238.
Anna, 190, 191, 219, 237.
Asa L., 338.
Betsy, 162, 190, 219.
Caroline I., 220.
Charlotte W., 241.
Christopher C. B., 220.
Cornelia, 243.
Daniel, 97.
David, 275, 338.

Deborah, 148.
Eliza, 191, 220, 261.
Elizabeth, 149.
Ellen E., 220.
Harriet E., 220.
Isaac, 38, 167, 359.
Jacob, 162, 190, 191, 219, 231, 364.
James, 190, 191, 219, 220, 236, 266, 267, 369, 370, 372, 396.
James H., 251.
Jemima, 149, 162, 333, 338.
Jonathan, 275, 352.
Joseph, 28, 219, 271, 275.
Lucy, 338.
Mr. ——, 330.
Maria, 219, 244.
Martha, 219, 338.
Mary, 154, 166, 338.
Mercy, 97.
Oliver, 27, 219.
Peggy, 7, 329.
Phineas, 338.
Polly, 151.
Samuel, 137.
Sarah, 150, 247, 394.
Sarah L., 191, 220.
Susan, 170, 228.
Susanna, 137, 338.
Tamar, 191, 219, 367.
STOWE, Aaron, 219.
Abel, 347.
Abigail, 220, 349.
Abigail H., 220, 372, 415.
Andrew, 220.
Asa H., 220, 349.
Augusta E., 220, 257.
Benjamin, 129.
Edmund, 220.
Eliza W., 220, 261, 395, 396, 450.
Esther, 219.
Franklin, 220, 261, 450.
Henry H., 261.
Levi, 220, 236.
Louisa J., 219, 347.
Luke, 220, 237, 267, 349, 350, 372, 415.
Luke S., 220, 350.
Mary Ann, 220.
Moses, 220, 237, 261, 395, 396, 450.
Silence, 38.
Susan, 220.
STOWELL, Daniel, 240.
STRATTON, George, 220, 221, 241, 259, 260, 268, 397, 438.
George Lyman, 221.
Hannah, 168, 171.
Henry O., 220.
Lewis F., 259.
Lucinda B., 220, 221, 259, 260, 397, 438.
Lydia Ann, 260, 268, 397, 438.
Margaret, 41.
Mary, 351.
Nabby, 133, 148.
Rosella Jeanette, 221.
STREETER, Eliza H., 439.
Vernis, 239, 439.
STRONG, Jane, 140.
STROUT, Charles J., 258.
STUDLEY, Caroline M., 257.
Charlotte M., 258.
Consider, 191, 219.
Elizabeth, 218, 394.
Frederick G., 218.
Nabby, 168, 171.
Olive, 219, 231.
Oliver, 168, 172, 218, 366, 394.
Sarah M., 219, 258.
Warren, 218.
William, 174.

INDEX.   499

STUTSON, Alice, 243.
  Mercy, 243.
SUMNER, Esther, 139.
  Hannah, 23, 87.
  Jaazoniah, 12.
  Mary, 11, 12, 13, 14.
  Rebecca, 13.
  Roger, 11, 12, 13, 14, 20, 373.
  Waitstill, 11.
  William, 14.
SUTHERLAND, Janette, 258.
SWAIN, Sarah I., 244.
SWAN, Charles L., 251.
  Ebenezer, 272, 326, 401.
  Francis, 295.
  Jane, 295.
  John, 323, 395, 401.
  John H., 240.
  Josiah, 270, 284, 295, 323.
  Joshua, 230.
  Prudence, 270.
SWEET, Frances, 265.
  George N., 265.
  Horatio N., 257, 265.
  Silas, 257.
SWEETSER, Catharine, 318, 337.
  Elizabeth D., 151, 163.
  Fanny, 231, 318.
  Henry, 317.
  Jacob, 191, 317, 318, 340, 347, 361, 439.
  John, 230.
  Joseph, 347.
  Margaret, 191, 337, 368, 369, 439.
  Mary, 232, 340.
  Sally, 149, 162.
  William, 190.
SYMMES, Caleb T., 349, 439.
  Nancy R., 394, 439.
TAFT, Elizabeth, 136.
  Joseph, 139, 329.
  Mary, 192, 356.
TALMAN, Sewall P., 394.
TANNER, Lorana, 143.
TAPLEY, Abby A., 256.
TARGET, Harriet R., 261.
  Lucy, 261.
  William H., 261.
TAYLOR, Almira, 243.
  Anna, 150.
  Ann W., 238.
  Augustus, 243.
  Charlotte E., 254.
  Daniel, 247.
  David, 33, 86.
  Ebenezer, 21, 32, 76, 86, 90, 106, 154, 165, 389.
  Elizabeth, 28.
  Elnathan, 106.
  George A., 264.
  Henry T., 232.
  Hiram, 247.
  Isaac, 264.
  James, 76, 389.
  James N., 441.
  Jerusha, 28.
  John, 169, 170, 222, 240, 265, 366, 394.
  John F., 222.
  Jonathan, 76, 389.
  Lucinda S., 250.
  Mary, 76, 90, 106.
  Mary A., 249.
  Mary J., 245.
  Nancy, 146, 240.
  Nathaniel, 90, 127, 140.
  Rebecca W., 264.
  Relief S., 247.
  Sally B., 238.
  Submit, 116.

Susan, 222, 441.
Susan J., 222.
Thomas, 235.
TEMPLE, Abigail, 451, 453.
  Deborah, 24.
  Elizabeth, 162, 352, 402.
  Isaac, 127, 143, 402.
  J——, 446.
  Joseph, 83.
  Lucy, 162.
  Maria, 246.
  Mary, 25, 152.
  Timothy, 41, 103.
  ——, 397.
TENNEY, Betsy, 119.
  Deborah, 334, 340, 341.
  John, 166, 329.
  Jonathan, 119, 130, 143, 192, 353.
  Oliver, 127, 143, 330, 340, 353.
  Oren, 341.
  Parrot, 330.
  Rebecca, 192, 340, 354.
  Sally, 340.
  Susanna, 150, 163.
  William, 103.
TEWELLS, Barnard, 280.
TEZER, Judith, 397.
THAYER, Abigail, 192, 221, 336, 345, 367.
  Albert G., 243.
  Christopher T., 221, 336, 342.
  Jacob, 155, 167.
  John, 221, 341.
  Jonathan, 127, 142.
  Levina, 170, 228.
  Lucretia, 132, 147, 155, 166.
  Martha, 221, 230, 335, 339.
  Mary Ann, 221, 335, 340.
  Nathaniel, 121, 148, 186, 192, 193, 221, 270, 338, 339, 340, 341, 342, 343, 345, 353, 369, 440.
  Sarah, 121, 221, 333.
  Sarah T., 121, 192, 335, 338, 365.
THISSELL, Joshua, 252.
THOMAS, Anna, 448.
  Alfred, 253.
  David, 87.
  Joshua, 117, 173, 192, 234, 448.
  Mary, 117, 149, 161, 192, 356, 361, 448.
  Moses, 150, 162.
  Nancy, 192.
  Rebecca, 150, 192, 351, 365.
  Thomas, 246.
THOMPSON, Abigail, 192, 221, 264, 360.
  Ann F., 222.
  Anna Jewett, 110, 390.
  Asa, 96, 105, 135, 326, 382.
  Benjamin, 39, 42, 101, 191, 192, 221, 355, 357, 358, 359, 380, 389, 390.
  Betsy, 230.
  Caroline, 191, 221.
  Cynthia, 170.
  Daniel, 264.
  Ebenezer, 69, 380, 390.
  Eliza P., 232.
  Elizabeth, 39, 101, 110, 112, 191, 192, 221, 380.
  Eunice, 116.
  Isaac, 137, 380.
  Jane, 222.
  Jerusha, 67, 380.
  John W., 222.
  Jonathan, 96, 140, 381.
  Joseph, 390.
  Josiah, 116. 390.
  Lucy, 221, 222, 233, 389.
  Martha, 67, 69, 71, 96, 375, 380.

Mary, 105, 112, 136, 390.
Mary A., 222.
Nancy, 166, 353.
Oricy, 221.
Rebecca E., 255, 351.
Relief, 40, 71, 380.
Samuel, 96, 116, 126, 138, 380, 390.
Sarah, 96, 105, 134.
Simon, 67, 69, 71, 96, 221, 222, 233, 375, 380, 381, 382.
Susanna, 42, 389.
Thomas, 359, 389.
William, 43, 103, 110, 112, 243, 264, 378, 380, 390.
William G., 191, 192, 221.
William R., 221.
THROWER, Abraham, 264.
  Elizabeth, 264.
  William L., 264.
THURSTON, Abel A., 192, 221, 341.
  Anna M., 193, 222, 260, 267, 372, 441.
  Anna, 122.
  Betsy, 122, 123, 153, 165, 192, 221, 222, 333.
  Caleb, 222.
  Caroline, 221, 343.
  Caroline M., 269, 397, 441.
  Charles, 122, 192, 222, 366.
  Charles F., 222, 267, 440.
  Cynthia, 122, 168, 171.
  David K., 122, 221, 222, 234, 365.
  Dolly, 130, 145, 305.
  Dorothy, 94, 108, 192, 304, 305, 322, 331, 365, 403, 441.
  Elizabeth P., 268, 396, 441.
  Ellen E., 260.
  Francina E., 222.
  Francis H., 222, 349.
  Franklin H., 222.
  Gates, 94, 123, 130, 145, 192, 221, 222, 268, 304, 333, 338, 339, 340, 341, 342, 354, 359, 396, 441.
  George L., 222, 349.
  George P., 221, 343.
  Gilman, 150, 162.
  Hannah, 162.
  Harriet, 122, 221, 233.
  Harriet E., 222, 349.
  Harriet L., 192, 222, 337, 349, 440.
  Henry, 123, 193, 338, 370, 441.
  Henry T., 222.
  Hephzibah, 113, 154, 388.
  James, 123, 338.
  John, 92, 122, 123, 127, 142, 152, 165, 169, 170, 181, 192, 193, 221, 222, 236, 238, 329, 338, 368, 382, 404, 441, 453.
  John G., 6, 192, 221, 222, 237, 349, 366, 440.
  Josephine, 192, 222, 440.
  Judith, 92, 383, 419.
  Julia F., 222.
  Louisa M., 260.
  Lucy, 122, 192, 222, 336, 349, 363, 364, 441.
  Lydia, 113, 354, 363, 389.
  Martha H., 222, 256.
  Mary, 92, 122, 129, 221, 235, 385.
  Mary Ann, 193, 222, 367, 441.
  Mehetabel C., 222, 453.
  Michal, 192, 221, 356.
  Nancy, 155, 166, 222, 237, 309, 328, 338, 403.
  Parney, 221, 222, 267, 440.
  Pearson, 92.
  Peter, 36, 94, 99, 108, 149, 162, 192, 221, 304, 305, 306, 309, 322,

328, 331, 334, 343, 357, 362, 403, 441.
Polly, 142, 192, 361.
Priscilla, 92, 112, 136, 192, 357, 382, 419.
Rebecca, 94, 122, 127, 141, 192, 222, 255, 304, 353, 404, 441.
Russell G., 192, 222, 441.
Sally, 112, 122, 191, 221, 357, 387, 441.
Sampson W., 221, 342.
Samuel, 33, 92, 112, 122, 192, 355, 376, 382, 383, 384, 385, 387, 388, 389, 419.
Sarah, 122, 192, 221, 334, 365.
Sarah Ann, 221, 232, 343.
Silas, 92, 122, 144, 154, 166, 167, 173, 191, 192, 193, 221, 222, 267, 336, 361, 369, 384, 440.
Sophia, 122, 168, 173.
Stephen, 128, 145.
Susanna, 112, 146, 388.
Thomas, 122, 192, 364, 404.
Thomas G., 221, 340.
Wilder S., 193, 221, 222, 257, 260, 267, 269, 370, 397, 441.
William, 221, 234, 339.
TICKNOR, William D., 241.
TIDD, Benjamin F., 232.
Elizabeth, 193, 336, 371, 440.
Emily, 237.
George C., 440.
Joel, 192, 362, 440.
Nancy, 337.
TIFFANY, Lucien, 243.
TILDEN, Charlotte, 221.
Henry P., 221.
Josiah, 221, 233.
TILLEY, Susanna, 39, 101.
TIM ——, 325.
TINDY, Cuffee, 192, 362.
TINKER, Alice, 452.
Amos, 452.
John, 4, 6, 19, 452.
Samuel, 452.
TISDALE, Elizabeth, 254.
George, 250.
Mason W., 246.
TITUS, Samuel, 87.
TODD, John, 135, 192.
Nancy, 335, 345.
Polly, 133, 148.
Sarah, 192, 334, 364.
TOLMAN, Sarah A., 252.
TOOMBS, Almeida C., 222.
Angelina, 221, 348.
Betsy, 221, 222, 336.
Edward W., 222, 349.
Elizabeth C., 222, 348.
Ellen C., 222.
Louisa, 222, 253, 394.
Martha A., 221, 348.
Robert C., 222, 236.
William, 221, 222, 336, 348, 349.
TOPPAN, Elizabeth G., 192, 367.
Mary C., 337.
Sarah, 148.
TORRANCE, Margaret, 21, 34.
TORREY, Abigail, 151, 164.
Ebenezer, 334.
TOWER, Asa, 318, 348.
Asahel, 118, 192, 221, 222, 230, 317, 318, 336, 338, 339, 340, 341, 342, 348, 349, 351, 366, 442.
Christopher, 221, 342.
Daniel, 324.
Daniel C., 221, 340.
Frances F., 222, 393.
George F., 221, 348.
Hannah S., 222, 349.
Henry, 221, 341.
Henry A., 221.

Hepzibeth, 96, 109.
James, 118, 338.
John, 109, 388.
Jonas, 96, 387.
Joseph, 96, 109, 385, 386, 387, 388.
Julia A., 221, 348, 394.
Justus, 386.
Lorana, 385.
Lucinda, 221, 339.
Lucretia, 236.
Mary, 392, 393.
Mary E., 221, 248, 348, 394.
Millicent, 118, 192, 221, 318, 360, 442.
Polly, 221, 222, 336.
Rufus E., 222, 349.
Sarah M., 222, 348.
William, 118.
William A., 256.
William H., 221, 348.
TOWNSEND, Abigail H. S., 222.
Abigail H., 221, 222, 230, 349, 441.
Almira, 192, 221, 222, 337, 367, 441.
Ann B., 232.
Asa D., 368.
Benjamin, 27, 52, 69, 275, 287, 291.
Betsy, 192, 336, 361, 362, 430, 441, 443.
Caleb, 157, 402.
Caroline P., 260, 441.
Charles, 222, 349.
Christopher F., 243.
Daniel, 329.
Elisha, 155, 166.
Elizabeth, 192, 221, 415.
Elizabeth, B., 260.
Elvira, 192, 221, 344, 362, 442.
Eunice, 329.
Francis, 222.
Frederick W., 222.
George, 221, 342.
Harriet, 221, 237, 342.
Henry, 183, 192, 221, 361, 441.
Henry W., 349.
Hezekiah, 52, 55, 157, 271, 275, 276, 278, 279.
James, 128, 138.
Joel P., 221, 238, 342.
John, 43, 104, 152, 164, 192, 221, 243, 249, 260, 342, 343, 344, 345, 359, 441, 442.
Jonathan, 69, 99, 287.
Joshua, 288, 415.
Luther, 167, 173.
Martha, 193, 221, 222, 370, 440.
Mary, 52, 221, 253, 276, 288, 394.
Mary Ann, 349, 394.
Mary A. C., 222.
Mr. ——, 269.
Nancy W., 221, 233.
Nathan, 69, 291.
Obadiah, 32, 52, 278.
Richard, 192, 358.
Robert, 192, 195, 221, 362, 430, 441, 443.
Ruth, 192, 221, 346, 362, 442.
Sarah, 27, 28, 52, 55, 69, 240, 250, 271, 275.
Sarah F., 245.
Solomon, 326, 329.
Thomas, 55, 192, 221, 222, 279.
Warren, 192, 221, 222, 234, 349, 441.
William, 169, 170, 193, 221, 222, 257, 267, 346, 372, 440.
William P., 221.
Zimri, 221, 345.

TOZIER, Mary K., 249.
TRACY, Leonard, 255.
TRASK, George, 239.
Hannah, 32.
TREADWAY, Judith, 23.
TROLLET, Michael, 160, 326.
TUCKER, Admonition, 30, 51, 277.
Amos D., 222, 217.
Betsy, 120, 317, 332.
Charles, 367.
Daniel, 131.
Emeline E., 252.
Josiah, 62, 284.
Loisa, 222.
Mary, 37, 51, 52, 58, 62, 79, 81, 89, 99, 271, 279, 299, 302, 320, 328, 350.
Nancy, 120, 338.
Polly, 120, 318.
Rebecca, 79, 126, 138, 299.
Sally, 151, 240.
Sarah, 89, 127, 141, 302.
Sarah A. A., 222.
Thomas, 18, 51, 52, 58, 62, 81, 120, 143, 271, 277, 278, 279, 284, 300, 315, 316, 317, 318, 319, 325, 332, 338, 354.
William, 52, 79, 81, 87, 89, 120, 192, 278, 299, 300, 302, 315, 320, 350.
TUFTS, Albert, 236.
Francis, 299.
William, 299.
TURNER, Amasa, 23, 33, 137, 295, 297, 319, 323, 325.
Anna, 197, 301, 331.
Asenath, 303.
Betsy T., 260, 266, 440.
Caroline A., 257, 259, 396.
Charlotte E., 260, 266, 371, 440.
Elisha, 259, 395, 396.
Elisha H., 259.
Emma J., 260.
Ichabod, 324.
Jane, 32.
Joshua, 151, 163.
Lauriana S., 193, 370.
Lurena J., 260, 440.
Margaret, 320.
Nathaniel, 99, 301, 303, 331.
Rebecca, 295.
Sarah, 297.
Sarah, E., 266.
Stevens H., 193, 245, 260, 266, 370, 371, 440.
Susanna, 301.
Sybil, 322.
Walter S. H., 260.
Zilpha, 34, 36.
TUTTLE, Eunice E., 400.
George K., 251, 440.
Lydia B., 440.
TWEED, Mary, 242.
TYLER, Ansel, 172, 222, 364.
Anthony H., 222.
Benjamin, 193, 222, 244, 441.
Eliza A., 222, 394.
Eliza H., 193, 222, 441.
Ellen G., 222.
Graty, 170.
Jane B., 222, 254.
Mary, 193, 222, 233, 250, 350, 369, 441.
Mary E., 350.
Mary L., 248.
Nancy, 363.
Rachel, 133.
Sewell, 232.
William, 192.
Zebediah, 172, 363.

INDEX. 501

UNDERWOOD, Persis, 250.
UPTON, Hannah W., 193, 370.
  Joseph, 169, 170, 193, 266, 371, 442.
  Phebe, 193, 442.
VALENTINE, Elizabeth J., 250.
  Julia A., 250.
VANDUSER, Mr., 267, 395.
VENHAM, Abigail, 29.
VERDER, Mary A., 240.
VINCENT, Apica, 115.
  John, 115, 357.
  John S., 115, 193, 357.
  Levi N., 115.
  Lovina, 115.
  Lydia S., 115.
  Sylvia, 115.
VIRGIL, Daniel, 222, 238, 368.
  Sarah E., 222.
  Vashti, 222.
VOSE, Ann A., 106, 193, 222, 366, 407.
  Ann F., 106, 343, 392.
  Catharine S., 106, 346, 392.
  Edward H., 106, 343, 407.
  Ellen R., 222, 260.
  Francis H., 106, 193, 222, 346, 407.
  Jane, 451.
  John S., 260.
  Josiah H., 236.
  Louisa R., 260.
  Martha E., 106, 222, 257, 346, 392.
  Mary T., 106, 236, 346.
  Mary W., 222, 260.
  Peter T., 106, 152, 165, 193, 222, 343, 346, 406.
  Samuel J. S., 106, 222, 245, 260, 343.
  Walter S., 106, 346, 392, 407.
  William M. R., 260.
WADE, Charlotte O., 196, 226, 443.
  Deborah R., 196, 226, 443.
  Job P., 226.
  Lefy J., 226, 255.
  Perez J., 226.
  Snell, 196, 226, 368, 395, 443.
  Snell O., 226.
WAITE, John, 279.
  Lucretia, 128.
  Lydia, 237.
  Nathaniel, 43.
  Robert, 279.
  Samuel, 126, 140.
WALCOT, Mary A., 250.
WALDO, Martha, 127, 141.
WALES, Elizabeth, 195, 361, 443.
  Joseph, 6, 132, 147, 195, 333, 373, 443.
WALDRON, Edward, 116, 390.
  Hannah, 116, 390.
WALKER, Agnes, 257.
  Angus, 257.
  Betty, 279.
  Daniel, 223, 224.
  Eleanor, 59.
  Elizabeth, 37, 99.
  Emily, 251.
  Filenda, 223.
  Hezekiah, 32, 75, 376, 381, 382.
  Isabel, 13.
  Lucy, 59, 248, 280.
  Lydia, 42, 45, 103.
  Mary, 278.
  Mary A., 252.
  Rachel, 75.
  Samuel, 277.
  Sarah, 75, 223, 224, 278, 376, 382.
  Seth, 59, 277, 278, 279, 280.
  Stephen, 224.
  Vashti, 41.
WALLACE and WALLIS.
  Cleora A., 442.
  David, 442.
  Hugh, 283.
  Jonathan, 126, 138.
  Mary, 144.
  Sarah A., 442.
WALLINGFORD, Ezekiel, 23, 28, 65, 75, 288.
  Lucy, 23, 38, 75.
  Lydia, 23, 32, 37, 65, 75, 102, 288.
  Mary, 23, 35, 75, 99.
WALTON, Eliza C., 443.
  George H., 195, 366, 443.
  Jonathan T., 235.
  Jotham, 443.
WARD, Charles, 109, 309, 328.
  Dolly, 97, 109, 194, 360, 442.
  Hiram, 256.
  John S., 242.
  Samuel, 6, 41, 97, 109, 194, 195, 307, 309, 311, 325, 328, 331, 353, 362, 442.
  Sarah, 311.
WARES, Mary, 450.
  Moses, 152, 164.
  Polly, 195.
WARNER, Aaron, 277.
  Abigail, 113, 258, 275, 288.
  Abijah, 126, 128.
  Anna, 92, 113, 275, 303.
  Asa, 151, 194, 195, 313, 315, 317, 318, 334, 353, 359, 442.
  Betsy, 153, 165, 313.
  Daniel, 38, 68, 100, 289, 305.
  David, 275.
  Dorothy, 44.
  Ebenezer, 156, 193, 271, 275, 276, 277.
  Elizabeth, 113, 276, 307.
  Frances, 113, 308.
  Hannah, 35, 68, 86, 274, 302, 303.
  Izze, 152, 164.
  Jane, 195, 334, 341, 366.
  John, 48, 53, 68, 84, 92, 93, 94, 113, 157, 159, 270, 271, 275, 276, 277, 278, 286, 288, 289, 300, 301, 302, 303, 304, 305, 306, 307, 308, 309, 311, 318, 326, 327, 331, 400, 410.
  Joshua, 276.
  Levi, 48, 113, 302.
  Lucy, 113, 311.
  Lydia, 229, 317, 394.
  Mary, 27, 157, 166, 243, 275, 366.
  Mercy, 33, 154.
  Moses, 53, 278.
  Nathan, 195, 231, 274, 366.
  Nathaniel, 167, 172, 194, 224, 277, 315, 336, 348, 360, 442.
  Olive, 113, 309.
  Persis, 446.
  Polly, 194, 224, 242, 336, 348, 442.
  Prudence, 48, 92, 93, 94, 113, 159, 196, 301, 320, 446.
  Rachel, 84.
  Rebecca, 53, 157, 271, 276, 278, 410.
  Rowena B., 252.
  Sally, 194, 224, 442.
  Samuel, 193, 270, 211, 274, 275, 276, 277, 355.
  Sarah, 306, 410.
  Susanna, 93, 94, 159, 304, 305, 326.
  William, 286, 317.
WARREN, Amanda M., 250.
  Benjamin, 38, 98.
  Charles F., 262.
  Edward, 243.
  Emily J., 262.
  Mary A., 258.
  Polly, 149.
  Sally, 262.
  Thomas B., 262.
WASHBURN, Eliphalet, 223.
  Francis, 226, 350.
  George, 223.
  Harriet W., 226, 266, 337.
  Henry K., 226, 266, 371, 450.
  John M., 226, 266, 350, 371.
  Luther, 150, 163.
  Mary, 226.
  Polly, 268, 397.
  Rufus, 150, 163, 223.
  Thankful, 223.
WATERMAN, Murray, 236.
WATERS, Adam, 4, 452.
  Ann, 10, 12, 20, 452.
  Elizabeth, 15.
  Ephraim, 10, 12.
  Jacob, 10, 399.
  Joanna, 10, 12.
  Joseph, 4, 10, 15.
  Laurence, 4, 10, 12, 20, 452.
  Martha, 15.
  Mary, 14, 20.
  Rachel, 4, 10, 12.
  Rebecca, 11.
  Samuel, 10, 14.
WATKINS, John, 150.
WATSON, Thomas, 268, 396.
WEBB, Abigail, 154, 165, 243.
  Joseph, 167, 173, 222.
  Lucy, 222.
WEBSTER, Jonathan B., 244.
WEDGE, Deborah, 12, 13.
  John, 12.
  Joshua, 13.
  Mary, 12.
  Thomas, 12, 13.
WELD, Hannah, 224, 225.
  Hannah M., 225, 347.
  John G. D., 225, 347.
  Margaret M., 224, 346.
  William G, 195, 224, 225, 346, 347, 362.
WELLINGTON, Ann M., 226, 443.
  Charles, 247, 263, 350.
  Ellen L., 263.
  Enos W., 263.
  Eunice, 394.
  Francina, 226, 350.
  George, 263, 350.
  Lucy, 226, 263, 337, 443.
  Lucy A., 239.
  Nahum, 263.
  Thomas H., 196, 226, 241, 263, 350, 390, 443.
  William W., 247.
WELLS, Elizabeth, 125, 136, 321.
WESSON, Eunice, 107.
  Hannah, 107, 387.
  Joseph, 107, 387, 388.
  Stephen, 107, 388.
WESTON, Adaline, 252.
WETHERBEE, Aaron, 56, 157.
  Alice, 157.
  Alonzo C., 226, 244.
  Aurelia, 225.
  Catharine, 23, 28, 58.
  Charlotte, 241.
  Electa, 225.
  Elizabeth, 52, 56, 58, 157, 226.
  E. J. B., 248.
  Emily, 225.
  Hannah, 169, 170.
  Hiram W., 225.
  John, 52, 56, 58, 157.

INDEX.

Jonathan, 52, 157.
Maria, 226.
Mercy R., 249.
Moses A., 225.
Oliver, 157.
Pamela, 225.
Reuben, 150, 163.
Roxana, 195, 361.
Salathiel, 195, 225.
Sarah, 332.
Sophronia, 225.
Thomas, 27.
William H., 225.
WHEELER, Abigail, 15, 85, 88, 375.
Abraham, 15, 16, 152, 164.
Amos, 188, 194, 195, 224, 225, 360, 361, 392, 393, 443.
Amos A., 194, 225, 443.
Anna, 65, 272, 277.
Anne G., 258.
Azubah, 33, 279.
Benjamin, 57, 58, 276, 278.
Beulah, 57, 278.
Calvin P., 226.
Calvin R., 251.
Caroline P. 226.
Charlotte, 226.
Daniel B., 263.
Daniel G., 151, 163.
David, 226, 368.
Dinah, 27, 28, 275.
Ebenezer, 274.
Elizabeth, 13, 65, 278.
Ellen, 393.
Emily A., 224, 256, 383.
Ephraim, 18, 279, 280, 282, 283, 289.
Esther, 451.
Experience, 15, 23, 273.
George, 289.
George F., 226.
Glazier, 279.
Hannah, 57, 58, 274, 276.
Isaac, 15.
Jacob, 11, 12.
Jesse, 57, 276.
John, 15, 116, 390.
Jonas, 226, 395.
Jonathan, 274, 275, 277.
Joseph, 16, 39, 100, 126, 279, 328, 375, 378.
Joshua, 65, 271, 272, 277, 278, 279.
Josiah, 270, 271, 273, 274, 275, 410.
Laura B., 256.
Laura M., 392.
Lovina A., 263.
Martha, 410.
Mary, 24, 64, 274, 282.
Mary P., 225, 245, 393.
Mason, 256.
Miranda, 263.
Obadiah, 275.
Phebe, 31, 73.
Prudence, 194, 195, 224, 225, 392, 393, 443.
Rachel, 330, 376.
Rebecca, 283.
Reuben, 155, 166, 376.
Richard, 11, 12, 13, 16, 20.
Roxana 195, 225, 443.
Ruth, 116, 226, 279, 390.
Samuel, 13, 20.
Sarah, 11, 12, 13, 27, 116, 280, 330, 390, 451.
Tabitha, 15, 452.
Thankful, 25, 65, 274, 279.
Zebediah, 11.
Zenas, 58, 278.

Zipporah, 31, 71.
WHEELOCK, Abel, 96, 108, 306, 445.
Abigail, 17, 49, 53, 275.
Abijah, 130, 145, 290, 308.
Abner, 280.
Albert, 226.
Alice, 77, 78, 80, 82, 90, 92, 94, 96, 108, 140, 303, 307, 320.
Archenus, 108.
Archippus, 94, 305.
Brethusa, 122, 318.
A——, 446.
Benjamin, 122, 142, 223, 308, 315, 316, 318, 339, 340.
Betsy, 122, 308, 316.
Cephas, 122, 318.
Charles, 276, 242, 367.
Eli, 223.
Elijah, 108, 135, 309, 310, 326, 404.
Elizabeth, 23, 51, 226, 272, 288, 289.
Ellen E., 226.
Joanna, 289.
John, 49, 78, 80, 108, 126, 139, 279, 283, 298, 299, 320, 321, 327.
Jonathan, 26, 84, 87, 137, 142, 223, 280, 287, 288, 289, 290, 308, 310, 311, 313, 314, 327, 328, 330, 338, 340.
Joseph, 33, 49, 51, 53, 77, 78, 80, 82, 90, 92, 94, 96, 108, 272, 279, 280, 281, 283, 286, 297, 298, 299, 300, 302, 303, 305, 306, 307, 309, 319, 323, 326, 327.
Joseph C., 445.
Josiah, 314.
Lucinda, 315.
Lucretia, 322.
Lucy, 333, 338.
Luther, 311, 313, 327, 328.
Martha, 18, 77, 92, 108, 129, 142, 194, 297, 303, 353.
Mary, 23, 51, 275.
Nancy, 122, 237, 315.
Olive, 49, 53, 279, 302.
Olive W., 310.
Oliver, 49, 80, 108, 127, 142, 279, 302, 315, 322, 328, 329.
Peter, 308.
Phineas, 49, 281.
Polly, 223, 339, 351.
Prudence, 84, 122, 223, 322, 366.
Rebecca, 310.
Relief, 129, 138.
Ruth, 18, 276.
Samuel, 308.
Sarah, 329.
Thankful, 125, 137, 308, 321.
——, 321.
WHIPPLE, Abigail, 194, 334, 358.
Dorcas, 153, 165.
Hannah, 266, 371, 442.
John, 241.
Nabby, 150, 162.
Nathan, 194, 358.
Sally, 148, 161, 333.
WHITAKER, David, 137.
Joseph, 44, 103.
WHITBORN, William, 20.
WHITCOMB, Abigail, 14, 42, 49, 56, 60, 65, 75, 85, 86, 225, 226, 275, 281, 380.
Abigail B., 225.
Abijah, 76, 296.
Achsa, 37, 99.
Anes, 107, 388.
Anna, 65, 287, 298, 382.
Asa, 21, 30, 36, 75, 78, 98, 276, 376, 380, 381, 382, 383, 386, 387, 388, 389, 419.
Becky, 56, 279.
Benjamin, 62, 63, 65, 66, 274, 284, 287.
Betty, 37, 59, 61, 63, 65, 70, 107, 275, 282, 285, 293, 387.
Catharine, 78, 382, 386, 452.
Chapman, 223.
Charles, 258.
Cyrus, 57.
Damaris, 39, 56, 61, 62, 66, 68, 73, 74, 76, 102, 272, 293, 452.
Daniel, 55, 157.
David, 12, 25, 58, 59, 61, 63, 65, 157, 271, 273, 274, 280, 282, 283, 284, 285, 287, 288, 290, 410, 451.
David R., 385.
Deborah, 15.
Dinah, 55, 279.
Dolly, 139, 193, 223.
Dorothy, 53, 63, 65, 66, 129, 278.
Ebenezer, 389.
Eleazer, 278.
Elijah, 68.
Elisha, 290, 351.
Elizabeth, 17, 25, 49, 56, 57, 79, 98, 320, 452.
Enoch, 127, 141.
Ephraim, 380.
Eunice, 39, 61, 75, 78, 101, 283, 380, 419.
Frances, 14.
Hannah, 12, 13, 14, 15, 16, 49, 55, 57, 59, 65, 274, 275, 287, 382, 397, 452.
Harriet, 225.
Hephzibah, 58, 60, 61, 63, 65, 67, 281, 289.
Hezekiah, 15, 24, 55, 60, 64, 67, 70, 85, 274, 275, 276, 277, 278, 279, 282, 284, 289, 293, 374, 375, 377, 385, 386, 387, 388, 389, 410.
Israel, 27, 275.
James, 49, 57, 59.
Joanna, 14.
Job, 13.
John, 12, 13, 14, 15, 20, 22, 26, 33, 59, 60, 65, 107, 275, 276, 282, 376, 382, 386, 388, 452.
John B., 226.
Jonas, 277.
Jonathan, 12, 13, 14, 15, 16, 18, 20, 36, 53, 56, 58, 60, 65, 98, 107, 277, 278, 279, 280, 282, 287, 377, 386, 387, 388, 389, 390, 452.
Jonathan P., 67, 288, 289.
Joseph, 15, 19, 23, 56, 57, 61, 62, 66, 68, 73, 74, 76, 79, 104, 270, 272, 281, 284, 287, 288, 290, 293, 296, 298, 319, 320, 332.
Josiah, 11, 12, 13, 14, 15, 49, 55, 56, 59, 60, 62, 84, 87, 156, 157, 193, 223, 300, 354, 410, 452.
Joshua, 45, 104.
Kezia, 35, 64, 87, 286.
Levi, 288.
Levina, 289.
Lois, 59, 388.
Lucy, 149, 389.
Luke, 230.
Maria, 193, 223.
Mary, 13, 14, 15, 49, 57, 58, 62, 65, 157, 223, 278, 281, 286, 383, 385, 410, 451, 455.
Mary A., 225, 248.
Nancy, 149, 162.
Nathan, 107, 388.
Nathaniel, 225, 226, 232.
Oliver, 60, 282.
Paul, 60.
Philemon, 43, 74.

INDEX. 503

Phineas W., 223.
Prudence, 63, 284.
Rachel, 53, 56, 58, 60, 64, 65, 67, 79, 277, 375.
Rebecca, 11, 12, 13, 14, 15, 18, 19, 49, 56, 75, 125, 271, 273, 279, 381, 452.
Relief, 63, 79, 286, 300, 389.
Rhoda, 223.
Ruhamah, 55, 56, 59, 60, 62, 157.
Ruth, 14, 451, 452.
Sally, 390.
Samuel, 386.
Sarah, 57, 59, 277, 389, 452.
Silas, 60.
Simon, 26, 62, 64, 274, 284, 286, 288, 289.
Submit, 387.
Susan, 251.
Susanna, 84, 376, 382.
Tamar, 63, 107.
Thankful, 23, 61, 62, 64, 283, 284, 288.
Thomas, 107, 386.
Tilley, 65, 287.
Timothy, 57.
William, 25, 58, 60, 61, 63, 65, 67, 274, 281, 283, 286, 287, 289.
WHITE, Abel, 113, 114, 153, 165, 195, 222, 224, 225, 266, 310, 313, 371.
Abigail, 27, 49, 50, 78, 125, 136, 157, 160, 274, 294, 323, 341.
Abijah, 68, 72, 82, 92, 122, 132, 147, 223, 224, 289, 300, 302, 338, 342, 343, 344.
Adaline C., 350.
Albert C., 349.
Alice, 302, 303, 320.
Amos, 106, 226, 369.
Ann B., 226.
Ann G., 226.
Anna, 307.
Austin J., 226.
Bathsheba, 122, 223, 224, 333.
Betsy, 95, 128, 130, 144, 193, 222, 224, 305.
Betty, 25, 279, 305.
Calvin D., 226.
Catharine, 171, 224, 282, 341, 343.
Cephas, 317.
David, 120, 290, 309, 338.
Deborah, 295, 322, 350.
Dorothy, 279.
Edwin C., 226.
Eleanor, 272, 280.
Elisha, 50, 85, 127, 141, 281, 300, 302, 303, 304, 305, 307, 309, 311, 314, 320, 322, 350.
Elizabeth, 16, 20, 34, 123, 149, 162, 169, 176, 225, 226, 267, 335, 338, 341.
Elizabeth C., 267, 349, 372, 444.
Elizabeth G., 258, 338, 330, 444.
Elizabeth W., 226.
Emory H., 225, 247, 445.
Ephraim, 127, 143, 193, 301.
Esther, 66, 67, 158, 272, 284, 316.
Eunice, 25, 41, 71, 72, 75, 92, 103, 130, 143, 272, 279, 293, 295, 300, 304, 327.
Francis B., 226.
Francis J., 196, 226.
Frederick I., 226.
George W., 226.
Hannah, 11, 25, 49, 131, 146, 274, 304.
Henry W., 349.
Isaac, 282, 283.
Jacob, 120.
James, 25, 44, 50, 123, 157, 222,

282, 305, 308, 309, 316, 342.
Jane, 284.
Jane G., 226.
Jemima, 334.
Joanna, 12, 27, 29, 50, 277.
John, 12, 15, 19, 26, 39, 50, 64, 65, 68, 69, 71, 72, 73, 75, 76, 78, 79, 80, 82, 95, 97, 108, 113, 114, 120, 132, 147, 156, 157, 159, 193, 194, 195, 223, 264, 267, 279, 280, 285, 286, 287, 289, 291, 293, 294, 296, 297, 298, 300, 305, 306, 307, 310, 313, 319, 321, 323, 324, 328, 330, 333, 338, 339, 352, 357, 372.
Jonas, 226, 232, 394.
Jonas B., 120, 226, 237, 338.
Jonathan, 17, 26, 49, 66, 67, 80, 117, 120, 126, 138, 156, 158, 272, 274, 282, 284, 290, 298, 308, 313, 314, 317, 322, 338, 453.
Joseph, 15, 31, 50, 78, 80, 90, 123, 143, 193, 222, 276, 294, 295, 296, 297, 298, 299, 300, 301, 303, 304, 305, 319, 324, 328, 334, 341, 342, 355, 362, 373, 444.
Joseph C., 195, 222.
Joshua, 304.
Josiah, 15, 17, 27, 28, 43, 49, 50, 52, 78, 150, 156, 157, 160, 270, 271, 272, 274, 275, 276, 277, 278, 280, 281, 283, 295, 299, 309, 314, 319, 321, 323, 326, 373, 451, 453.
Jotham, 32, 50, 277.
Keturah, 92, 302.
Kezia, 18.
Laura S., 226.
Levi, 131, 146, 193, 224, 303, 338, 342.
Lois, 44, 64, 65, 68, 69, 71, 72, 73, 75, 76, 78, 79, 80, 82, 104, 137, 159, 279, 285, 287, 291, 294, 296, 330.
Lucinda, 309.
Lucretia, 138.
Lucy, 76, 78, 127, 142, 159, 296, 297.
Lucy C., 195, 224, 336, 348, 364, 445.
Luther, 223, 313, 341.
Lydia, 95, 97, 108, 113, 195, 295, 298, 299, 301, 303, 305, 319, 321, 353, 361.
Margaret, 272.
Martha, 21, 33, 50, 79, 86, 90, 127, 128, 139, 143, 275, 281, 301, 336, 394.
Mary, 15, 17, 20, 29, 49, 52, 156, 271, 274, 279, 453.
Mary C., 123, 222, 342.
Mary M., 233.
Molly, 44, 104, 295.
Nancy, 226.
Nathaniel, 21, 33, 86, 194, 279, 295, 296, 298, 299, 300, 301, 303, 304, 305, 319, 324.
Nathaniel T., 350.
Parney, 321.
Patience, 78, 80, 90, 105, 135, 193, 294, 295, 297, 301, 319, 354.
Patty, 145, 223, 339.
Peter, 12, 146, 303.
Polly, 309.
Prudence, 127, 140, 194, 299.
Rebecca, 117, 120, 123, 167, 173, 222, 322, 334, 341, 342, 350, 363.
Robert, 281, 282.
Ruth, 27, 29, 50, 90, 129, 140, 275, 300, 309, 333.
Sally, 108, 196, 307, 316, 333, 368.
Sally A., 123, 341.

Samuel F., 123, 196, 267, 280, 336, 341, 349, 350, 363, 370, 373, 444.
Sarah, 15, 67, 68, 80, 90, 105, 135, 285, 289, 290, 298.
Sarah A., 336.
Sarah E., 445.
Sarah S., 445.
Silence, 35, 50, 98, 278, 319.
Somes, 122, 233, 338, 364.
Sophia, 120, 194, 223, 309, 333, 336, 338, 354.
Stephen, 305.
Susanna, 127, 143, 303.
Thankful, 23, 52.
Tilley, 36, 64, 92, 286, 302, 304.
Thomas, 27, 28, 67, 38, 279, 285, 289, 290, 291, 292.
Ward, 311.
William, 272, 280, 282, 283, 284, 304.
William H., 123, 254, 341.
WHITING, Abigail, 117, 119, 193, 223, 322, 352, 410.
Abigail B., 232.
Abigail K., 223.
Achsa, 39.
Alice, 20, 451.
Alvin, 250, 263.
Caroline E., 263.
Caroline Lee, 223, 235, 335, 340.
Charles, 223, 341.
Charles J., 224.
Christopher, 91, 302.
Deborah, 79, 127, 142, 299, 322.
Esek, 246.
Eudora S., 259.
Eunice, 20.
Fabius, 118, 196, 318, 370, 444.
Fabius M., 226, 349.
Fanny, 20, 169, 170.
Harriet, 223, 233, 340.
Harriet B., 233.
Henry, 118, 319.
James, 224, 342.
John, 16, 20, 91, 117, 118, 143, 151, 194, 223, 300, 314, 316, 317, 318, 322, 337, 339, 340, 356, 373, 401, 444.
Joseph, 193, 223, 339.
Julia, 118, 194, 317, 335, 359, 444.
Julia E., 226, 349.
Levi, 119, 317.
Lucy, 168, 171.
Lydia, 194, 223, 224, 225, 410.
Maria, 118, 335, 337.
Mary, 238, 263.
Mary P., 194, 225.
Nancy, 119, 223, 229, 318.
Newell, 195, 362.
Orpah, 118, 179, 223, 322, 368, 444.
Paul, 195.
Polly, 117, 193, 315, 353.
Rebecca, 150, 162, 333.
Sally U., 117, 316.
Samuel K., 117, 224, 317.
Sarah, 79, 91, 193, 226, 259, 299, 301, 320, 322, 355.
Sarah R., 224.
Solon, 223, 226, 239, 259, 339, 349.
Sophia, 118, 318, 335.
Thomas J., 223, 339.
Timothy, 79, 91, 117, 119, 141, 151, 163, 193, 194, 195, 223, 224, 225, 229, 300, 301, 302, 314, 315, 316, 317, 318, 320, 322, 339, 340, 341, 342, 353, 354, 410.
Timothy D., 116, 316.
William, 365.
Zilpha, 37, 99.

INDEX.

WHITMAN, Davis, 195, 265, 371, 443.
  Deborah H., 237.
  Hannah, 367, 443.
  Jemima, 368.
  Mary C., 240.
WHITNEY, Abel, 195, 230.
  Abigail, 18, 21, 32, 361.
  Abigail H., 195, 443.
  Abraham, 28.
  Alice, 34, 58, 61.
  Anes, 109.
  Betsy, 144, 170.
  Caleb, 58, 109, 388, 389.
  Charles, 255, 373.
  Daniel, 30.
  David, 35.
  Elias, 281.
  Elijah, 25, 195, 272, 281, 366.
  Elizabeth, 25, 108, 128, 138, 251, 306, 378.
  Elmira M., 264.
  Eliphalet, 136.
  Ephraim, 108, 128, 144, 196, 233, 370, 445.
  Eunice, 310, 327.
  Fanny, 445.
  Grace, 35, 85.
  Harriet, 394.
  Hephzibah, 25.
  Horace, 268.
  John, 18, 56, 244, 259, 292.
  John M., 395.
  Jonas, 46, 108, 153, 165, 224, 266, 308, 335, 344, 372, 445.
  Jonathan, 17, 39, 58, 61, 100, 108, 129, 139, 194, 266, 306, 307, 308, 309, 310, 314, 315, 316, 322, 325, 327, 329, 354, 399, 445.
  Joseph, 395.
  Josiah, 25.
  Julia A., 238.
  Levi, 164.
  Lucy, 108, 109, 194, 313, 322, 359, 388, 445.
  Maria A., 255.
  Mary, 44, 103, 108, 128, 224, 254, 255, 321, 327, 335, 344, 399, 439.
  Mary M., 264.
  Nancy, 108, 153, 165, 315.
  Nancy W., 255, 373.
  Nathan, 395.
  Nathaniel, 17, 44.
  Oliver, 61, 389.
  Phineas, 58.
  Polly, 144, 353.
  Quincy, 255, 257, 264.
  Rachel, 147.
  Rebecca, 18, 56, 129.
  Relief, 300.
  Reuben, 195.
  Rosalinda P., 257.
  Rosella C., 259, 392, 393, 396.
  Sally, 108, 155, 160, 314, 316, 329.
  Salome, 394.
  Samuel, 168, 171, 196.
  Sarah, 28, 46, 56, 103, 257, 292.
  Shadrach, 195, 363.
  Sophia, 235.
  Thomas H., 394.
  Timothy, 34, 300.
  Walter A. K., 259.
  William, 292, 364.
  William D., 235.
  William S., 445.
  Zaccheus, 108, 309, 361, 445.
WHITON, Elijah, 256.
WHITTEMORE & WHITMORE.
  Albert, 254.
  Amelia, 195, 444.
  Asa D., 193, 223, 444.

Benjamin, 105, 111, 134, 223, 396.
Benjamin B., 396.
Charles H., 225.
Charles R., 349.
Dorcas, 154, 165.
Dunbar, 356.
Edward H., 224.
Elhanan W., 223, 249, 251.
Elizabeth, 144, 384.
George P., 224.
Hannah, 40, 101.
Harriet A., 225.
James M., 250.
Jeremiah, 237, 349.
John M., 259.
Joseph, 134, 310, 311, 321, 327.
Josiah, 133.
Lorenzo, 226.
Louisa, 226.
Lucy, 310.
Lucy R., 223, 224, 225.
Lydia, 154, 166, 193, 352, 444.
Mandana M., 255, 396.
Mary, 83, 225, 444, 445.
Mary M., 194, 224, 444.
Nancy, 226, 227, 259.
Nancy F., 227.
Nathaniel, 150, 151, 193, 194, 195, 223, 224, 226, 227, 238, 242, 259, 300, 444, 445.
Perley, 148, 161.
Polly, 194, 223, 224.
Prescott, 171, 223, 224, 225.
Ruth, 321.
Sarah, 111, 193, 334, 356.
Walter P., 226.
WHITWELL, Benjamin, 133, 148, 341.
Samuel, 193, 362.
Sarah, 341.
WILCOX, Francis, 244.
WILDER, Aaron, 48, 105, 113, 153, 165, 193, 194, 224, 277, 311, 355, 358.
  Abel, 64, 78, 105, 110, 124, 154, 222, 224, 225, 297, 312, 313, 358, 379.
  Abel Carter, 224, 345.
  Abigail, 17, 28, 35, 36, 44, 51, 54, 60, 61, 64, 65, 66, 68, 69, 70, 72, 75, 77, 80, 88, 89, 99, 102, 104, 158, 223, 230, 242, 271, 276, 277, 285, 288, 289, 293, 294, 304, 321, 336, 341, 375, 394, 408.
  Abigail Rand, 222, 237, 343.
  Abijah, 76, 130, 145, 290.
  Abner, 22, 33, 52, 76, 90, 91, 280, 376, 381, 382, 383, 384, 385.
  Abraham, 113.
  Achsa, 41, 70, 102, 379.
  Adam, 79, 384.
  Aholiab, 28, 48, 275.
  Alexander, 224.
  Alice, 110, 149, 162, 309.
  Almira, 195, 225.
  Almira M., 336, 348, 361.
  Alvina, 234.
  Andrew, 27, 28, 68, 70, 73, 76, 78, 81, 89, 93, 273, 285, 290, 291, 293, 294, 296, 297, 298, 299, 301, 303, 319, 323, 325, 326, 398.
  Anes, 225, 226, 233.
  Ann Eliza, 225, 348.
  Ann E. W., 227.
  Anna, 22, 25, 61, 63, 65, 66, 67, 68, 71, 74, 76, 80, 114, 127, 140, 226, 273, 274, 283, 298, 312, 328, 383, 403, 409, 452, 453.
  Anne, 129, 264, 265, 335.
  Anna M., 409.

Anthony, 194, 222, 343.
Asa, 39, 59, 79, 82, 85, 90, 96, 113, 281, 376, 383, 384, 385, 386, 387, 388.
Asaph, 23, 31, 71, 77, 278, 291, 293, 295, 409, 453.
Augustus, 118, 160, 224, 313, 328, 345.
Beatrix, 30, 379.
Benjamin, 38, 70, 73, 74, 76, 78, 159, 274, 299, 375, 379, 380, 381, 382, 383, 384, 395, 397, 453.
Benjamin G., 223, 341.
Betsy, 106, 118, 166, 194, 313, 316, 317, 333, 356.
Betty, 112, 124, 194, 321, 358.
Beulah, 28, 76, 104, 134, 276, 325, 381.
Bezaleel, 48, 275.
Bridget, 96, 97, 101, 110, 112.
Caleb, 27, 65, 66, 68, 69, 72, 75, 80, 158, 275, 285, 287, 288, 289, 292, 293, 295, 296, 298, 313, 319, 321, 327, 328, 408.
Calvin, 78, 93, 110, 114, 148, 161, 190, 195, 224, 303, 308, 382, 443.
Caroline A., 224, 242, 337, 344.
Caroline M., 225.
Carter [Abel C.], 242.
Catharine, 37, 63, 68, 99, 120, 151, 164, 284, 291, 321, 409, 445.
Cephas, 115.
Charles, 27, 48, 68, 69, 224, 274, 289, 290, 293, 347.
Charles Francis, 265.
Charles Hanson, 225, 348.
Charles Josiah, 196, 224, 245, 265, 266, 345, 370, 371, 444.
Charles Lewis, 196, 223, 226, 227, 243, 260, 370.
Charlotte, 443.
Christopher W., 216.
Clarissa, 226.
Cynthia, 122, 230, 338.
Damaris, 48, 157, 271, 276, 285, 379.
Danforth, 223, 231.
Daniel, 116, 152, 163, 164, 195, 196, 223, 312, 309, 443.
Daniel K., 196, 223, 226, 245, 442.
David, 21, 27, 28, 30, 33, 67, 71, 73, 78, 79, 86, 90, 96, 115, 151, 194, 274, 285, 288, 292, 293, 294, 297, 298, 299, 311, 319, 323, 324, 327, 329, 373, 383, 409, 453.
Deborah, 65, 72, 81, 85, 87, 94, 97, 108, 111, 114, 116, 273, 283, 286, 288, 298, 326, 386, 398, 407.
Deborah H., 226, 442.
Deliverance, 31, 276.
Dinah, 64, 379.
Dolly, 97, 120, 139, 154, 317, 387.
Doris, 166.
Dorothy, 25, 274, 307, 329, 451, 452, 453.
Ebenezer, 15, 74, 136, 155, 157, 166, 195, 224, 225, 226, 236, 274, 275, 314, 336, 347, 348, 409, 443, 453, 451.
Ebenezer F., 224, 347.
Edward, 196, 235, 314, 328, 371, 390, 443.
Edw. Everett, 226.
Edwin Elisha, 225.
Electa, 409.
Elias, 48, 106, 155, 279, 314.
Elihu, 83, 384.
Elijah, 79, 128, 168, 173, 195, 224, 225, 234, 315, 335, 344, 345, 347, 348, 363, 383, 390, 442.
Elisha, 88, 195, 225, 226, 231, 337,

INDEX. 505

362, 363, 368, 376, 378, 384.
Eliza, 155, 223, 225, 226, 233, 236, 340, 370.
Eliza Ann, 254.
Eliza Ann S., 347.
Eliza A. W., 224, 345.
Eliza C., 265, 266, 444.
Elizabeth, 18, 22, 30, 41, 42, 44, 54, 66, 68, 70, 73, 74, 76, 78, 81, 89, 93, 103, 104, 106, 109, 122, 222, 223, 225, 273, 278, 285, 288, 290, 291, 294, 296, 300, 301, 303, 320, 321, 348, 380, 398, 403, 445, 452, 453.
Emily, 195, 225, 226.
Emory Pollard, 226.
Enos, 224, 260, 342, 371, 444.
Ephraim, 22, 25, 61, 63, 65, 68, 71, 74, 76, 83, 87, 91, 109, 129, 139, 156, 273, 274, 276, 277, 283, 284, 287, 289, 291, 293, 296, 298, 299, 302, 303, 304, 305, 307, 309, 312, 313, 319, 321, 325, 400, 403, 409, 443, 451, 452, 453.
Ephr. Holman, 225, 347.
Ephr. Rand, 194, 224, 346.
Esther, 26, 274.
Eunice, 27, 45, 54, 57, 59, 71, 73, 90, 91, 104, 110, 111, 113, 116, 132, 146, 157, 193, 194, 224, 225, 272, 276, 293, 294, 309, 321, 353, 390, 409, 452, 453.
Ezra, 67, 290.
Festus F., 226.
Filindia, 224.
Frances A., 260, 264, 265.
Francina M., 409.
Francina O., 444.
Francis, 196, 371, 443.
Francis W., 226.
Franklin, 215.
Frederick, 115, 193, 195, 224.
Frederick O., 257, 264, 265.
Frederick W., 247, 259.
Gardner, 26, 35, 38, 64, 66, 72, 91, 98, 99, 120, 146, 193, 274, 285, 287, 288, 291, 292, 303, 308, 318, 320, 325, 329, 356, 399, 434, 445.
George, 225.
Geo. Endicott, 226.
Geo. Franklin, 226.
George Lewis, 226.
George O. M., 259.
George W., 196, 224, 226, 243, 265, 370, 442.
Hannah, 14, 15, 19, 42, 49, 51, 54, 78, 101, 156, 193, 222, 224, 225, 276, 279, 382, 384, 388, 409, 452.
Hannah M., 224.
Harriet, 225.
Harriet E., 196, 226, 227, 260.
Harrison, 109, 309.
Henry, 113, 115, 118, 160, 223, 248, 311, 314, 328.
Hephzibah, 26, 38, 70, 98, 274, 379, 453.
Holman, 194, 224, 342, 443.
Horace, 195.
Isaac, 39, 382, 386.
Jacob, 78, 126, 128, 137, 195, 275, 292, 299, 362, 382.
James, 26, 45, 54, 63, 77, 106, 111, 113, 158, 159, 160, 195, 226, 240, 270, 271, 274, 275, 277, 278, 283, 284, 285, 286, 288, 292, 295, 296, 309, 310, 312, 313, 314, 316, 317, 319, 320, 324, 326, 327, 328, 351, 367, 373, 408, 409, 443, 452.
James Festus, 226.
Jane, 70, 73, 74, 76, 78, 159, 379.
Jemima, 111, 321.
Jerahmeel, 48, 277.

Joel, 109, 116, 152, 165, 174, 196, 224, 226, 237, 267, 305, 311, 334, 342, 344, 345, 368, 370, 373, 396, 443, 443, 444.
Joel Thos., 265, 266, 371, 444.
John, 14, 15, 30, 41, 45, 48, 49, 60, 61, 64, 65, 67, 68, 70, 71, 72, 73, 95, 102, 104, 105, 115, 148, 153, 156, 158, 161, 165, 194, 195, 223, 224, 225, 270, 271, 275, 276, 282, 290, 292, 294, 295, 304, 306, 309, 314, 316, 321, 329, 333, 339, 340, 341, 342, 343, 345, 346, 349, 352, 354, 355, 375, 379, 407, 408, 409, 419, 444, 451, 452.
John Warren, 223, 339.
John W. G., 226.
Jonas, 19, 49, 54, 57, 59, 106, 157, 169, 225, 229, 266, 272, 279, 280, 282, 316, 371, 442.
Jonathan, 15, 17, 27, 28, 38, 48, 49, 73, 74, 75, 78, 79, 83, 90, 94, 97, 101, 108, 111, 114, 115, 116, 127, 140, 194, 195, 196, 223, 224, 298, 329, 307, 374, 376, 377, 379, 380, 381, 382, 384, 386, 387, 388, 389, 390, 409, 452.
Joseph, 6, 15, 23, 25, 54, 65, 72, 78, 81, 104, 125, 134, 136, 142, 151, 183, 196, 225, 230, 242, 267, 270, 271, 273, 274, 275, 276, 277, 279, 283, 286, 288, 289, 292, 295, 296, 299, 300, 301, 312, 313, 316, 319, 320, 323, 324, 325, 326, 327, 328, 332, 347, 348, 370, 373, 394, 395, 397, 398, 407, 408, 442, 451.
Joseph M., 224, 246.
Joseph W., 176, 223, 226, 339.
Josephus, 195, 224, 240, 343, 444.
Joshua, 48, 61, 64, 274, 375, 376, 378, 379, 381, 382.
Josiah, 30, 37, 48, 52, 56, 59, 60, 63, 65, 71, 73, 77, 80, 98, 105, 109, 113, 114, 118, 135, 136, 159, 160, 224, 280, 281, 282, 284, 285, 287, 292, 293, 307, 310, 311, 312, 313, 314, 315, 317, 321, 328, 329, 373, 374, 379, 380, 381, 382, 383, 408, 409.
Jotham, 31, 73, 74, 79, 80, 90, 140, 276, 295, 297, 299, 300, 302, 306, 319.
Julia, 225.
Kate, 120, 164.
Kezia, 51, 96, 278, 397.
Leonard P., 226.
Levi, 75, 80, 90, 118, 139, 194, 225, 295, 308, 313, 314, 315, 316, 317, 318, 322, 329, 382, 383, 392, 408.
Lewis, 115, 345.
Lois, 26, 33, 62, 79, 92, 96, 145, 276, 282, 387.
Lucina, 195, 224, 225, 254, 336, 347, 362, 373, 443.
Lucinda, 312.
Lucretia, 91, 109, 126, 141, 302, 390, 400.
Lucy, 25, 37, 38, 72, 92, 93, 96, 97, 99, 110, 114, 120, 150, 163, 170, 224, 229, 241, 274, 275, 276, 289, 309, 311, 318, 320, 332, 334, 335, 342, 343, 350, 382, 386, 397, 408.
Lucy Larkin, 225.
Luke, 78, 106, 115, 129, 153, 172, 194, 222, 224, 225, 269, 297, 314, 316, 324, 342, 343, 346, 347, 355, 360, 397, 443.
Luther, 95, 105, 302.
Lydia, 39, 79, 82, 90, 96, 104, 113, 134, 195, 223, 292, 362, 382, 383,

Lydia A., 195, 367, 444.
Lydia B., 349.
Malinda, 194, 222, 344.
Manasseh, 65, 76, 105, 114, 135, 195, 225, 287, 296, 311, 313, 314, 316, 318, 322, 341, 361, 409.
Margaret, 276.
Maria S., 196, 369.
Martha, 35, 60, 63, 68, 69, 75, 77, 78, 79, 80, 90, 91, 98, 105, 110, 116, 127, 135, 137, 159, 160, 168, 169, 170, 172, 194, 274, 282, 286, 293, 295, 297, 298, 303, 320, 334, 357, 358, 381, 383, 397, 399, 400, 408, 409, 419, 443, 453.
Martha B., 394.
Martha E., 225, 253, 348, 394.
Mary, 14, 15, 17, 18, 20, 26, 49, 51, 58, 62, 63, 64, 65, 66, 76, 82, 88, 98, 99, 108, 110, 111, 141, 156, 172, 194, 196, 222, 224, 225, 276, 280, 281, 282, 283, 284, 285, 287, 291, 297, 310, 321, 334, 371, 376, 379, 381, 388, 389, 400, 409, 443, 451, 452, 453.
Mary Carter, 224, 346.
Mary Joslin, 193, 223, 341.
Mary M. A., 196, 225, 226, 348, 370, 442.
Mercy, 70, 106, 113, 157, 271, 379.
Merrick, 223, 341.
Mindwell, 315.
Miriam, 71, 73, 80.
Moses, 23, 46, 60, 63, 84, 86, 95, 104, 105, 106, 110, 113, 193, 194, 266, 286, 301, 302, 304, 305, 307, 309, 310, 311, 312, 313, 314, 316, 320, 326, 330, 358, 379.
Nabby, 118, 318.
Nahum, 69, 80, 292.
Nancy, 115, 118, 150, 155, 163, 166, 169, 170, 224, 312, 316, 317.
Nathan, 90, 141, 384.
Nathaniel, 14, 15, 17, 20, 23, 25, 36, 48, 58, 82, 87, 92, 93, 96, 97, 99, 122, 157, 231, 274, 275, 276, 277, 278, 279, 281, 282, 285, 307, 324, 336, 338, 376, 378, 381, 383, 384, 385, 386, 387, 388, 408, 419.
Oliver, 27, 28, 30, 33, 51, 62, 63, 67, 69, 72, 73, 76, 82, 96, 150, 158, 194, 224, 274, 276, 277, 278, 279, 280, 282, 285, 286, 289, 290, 291, 292, 294, 296, 297, 319, 323, 325, 329, 330, 400, 452.
Oscar Marcellus, 394.
Otis, 195, 313, 360.
Patience, 363.
Patty, 114, 115, 144, 317.
Peggy, 118, 315.
Persis, 79.
Peter, 72, 89, 92, 292, 301, 324, 385, 407.
Peter Haskell, 224.
Phebe, 73, 74, 79, 80, 90, 161, 295, 297, 302, 319, 379.
Phineas, 38, 51, 79, 83, 85, 92, 96, 97, 101, 110, 112, 280, 309, 376, 384, 387, 388, 390.
Polly, 113, 114, 118, 131, 146, 151, 152, 160, 164, 194, 310, 311, 312, 313, 316, 321, 328, 358.
Prescott, 115, 194, 360.
Priscilla, 57, 84, 85, 280.
Prudence, 42, 56, 57, 59, 60, 61, 63, 65, 67, 68, 71, 76, 82, 136, 137, 138, 276, 277, 289, 379, 381, 384, 419.
Rachel, 276, 285, 290.
Rachel G., 267.
Rebecca, 36, 72, 73, 74, 95, 98,

37

INDEX.

106, 109, 128, 144, 195, 224, 289, 304, 305, 322, 330, 340, 365, 380, 382, 400, 444.
Rebecca B., 224.
Rebecca H., 347.
Relief, 46, 103, 114, 281, 301, 315, 322.
Reuben, 79, 90, 129, 383, 385.
Reuben W., 90, 142, 302.
Rezina, 70, 158, 376, 379.
Rosanna, 243.
Rufus, 56, 73, 136, 280, 347, 380, 408.
Rufus A., 225.
Ruth, 26, 72, 73, 74, 76, 82, 226, 275, 291, 294, 296, 321, 363, 394, 398.
Ruth Prescott, 115, 195, 223, 224, 409.
Sally, 114, 118, 131, 146, 147, 149, 162, 194, 223, 224, 225, 232, 235, 314, 335, 340, 359, 444.
Sampson V. S., 118, 313, 409.
Samuel, 40, 41, 45, 48, 66, 67, 71, 72, 80, 91, 100, 103, 104, 110, 116, 122, 132, 147, 157, 158, 168, 172, 193, 194, 195, 196, 222, 223, 224, 229, 267, 268, 278, 288, 293, 304, 308, 309, 311, 312, 313, 314, 315, 316, 317, 333, 338, 339, 340, 341, 343, 344, 345, 346, 347, 354, 357, 362, 363, 385, 397, 445.
Samuel B., 196, 370.
Samuel Lock, 109, 312.
Sarah, 15, 26, 29, 30, 41, 48, 49, 61, 64, 65, 67, 69, 72, 80, 96, 102, 106, 110, 114, 126, 127, 137, 140, 156, 158, 194, 196, 224, 267, 277, 284, 285, 287, 290, 292, 296, 306, 307, 321, 322, 330, 336, 370, 379, 384, 387, 395, 408, 409.
Sarah B., 259.
Sarah E., 215, 248.
Sarah H., 226.
Sarah Lee, 222.
Sarah V. S., 409.
Seth, 225, 311.
Sewall, 225, 345.
Sidney, 224, 347.
Silas, 42, 73, 74, 102, 106, 378, 380, 388.
Similius, 290, 323.
Solomon, 382.
Sophia, 195, 224, 225, 335, 344, 361, 371, 442.
Sophia Ann, 225.
Sophia P., 196.
Stephen, 43, 73, 124, 155, 166, 170, 194, 195, 228, 295, 308, 309, 311, 312, 313, 315, 321, 329, 360.
Submit, 95, 105, 106, 110, 113, 301, 302, 310, 320, 326, 335, 384.
Sumner, 225, 241, 341.
Susan, 224, 316, 337.
Susanna, 29, 57, 64, 77, 80, 126, 138, 277, 296, 299, 314, 408, 443, 453.
Tabitha, 168, 172, 315.
Tamar, 51, 74, 130, 145, 279, 321.
Thankful, 22, 27, 28, 49, 275.
Thomas, 13, 15, 57, 64, 65, 66, 70, 110, 224, 270, 274, 276, 277, 278, 283, 284, 285, 290, 304, 309, 312, 316, 324, 329, 408, 451, 452, 453.
Thomas J., 226.
Tilley, 30, 51, 76, 277, 375, 379, 380, 381, 382, 384.
Timothy, 91, 299, 383, 419.
Titus, 74, 104, 110, 133, 155, 166, 194, 195, 196, 224, 225, 278, 295, 309, 311, 314, 315, 316, 317, 321,

326, 329, 337, 360, 366, 368, 408.
Triphena, 105, 129, 141, 196, 301, 368.
Volney, 196, 371, 443.
Warren, 225.
William, 49, 68, 114, 126, 137, 152, 164, 194, 224, 275, 289, 298, 312, 313, 315, 317, 322, 344, 359, 442.
William C., 344.
William Pitt, 114, 118, 160, 310, 328.
Willis, 129, 138, 316, 322.
Zebina, 97, 388.
Zerviah, 39, 73, 74, 75, 78, 83, 90, 101, 379.
Zilpah, 40, 71, 99, 293, 321.
Zipporah, 21, 32, 71, 291, 293, 409.
WILDS and WILES, Anna, 135.
Barnard, 278.
David, 284.
Elijah, 446.
Ivory, 137, 446.
James, 274.
John, 158, 278.
Jonas, 277.
Margaret, 275, 282.
Nancy, 154.
Richard, 18, 58, 158, 271, 274, 275, 277, 278, 279, 281, 282, 284, 288, 290.
Ruth, 58, 158, 288.
Sarah, 274.
Silent, 279.
Susanna, 58, 281.
WILKER, George, 128, 145.
WILLARD, Aaron, 19, 36, 40, 54, 57, 60, 66, 68, 71, 92, 124, 159, 272, 276, 278, 279, 280, 281, 284, 286, 288, 291, 293, 302, 304, 319, 325, 326, 329, 410, 453.
Abel, 6, 39, 49, 124, 152, 164, 281, 365, 389.
Abigail, 27, 28, 43, 52, 55, 58, 89, 124, 153, 165, 220, 272, 275, 277, 278, 280, 449, 453.
Abigail R., 220.
Abijah, 32, 34, 46, 49, 76, 78, 81, 86, 157, 193, 277, 278, 294, 297, 299, 300, 302, 303, 319, 322, 323, 324, 406, 443.
Abraham, 18, 31, 57, 272, 278, 279, 280, 294, 295, 453.
Abraham C., 123, 232.
Adonijah, 56, 157.
Alice, 17, 276, 453.
Amasa, 111, 115, 153, 165, 194, 196, 223, 224, 229, 308, 354, 370, 443.
Amory, 169, 229, 449.
Amy, 59, 111, 130, 146, 223, 281.
Andrew, 96.
Andrew J., 450.
Andrew Fuller, 225.
Anes, 118, 142, 155, 280, 388.
Anna, 27, 52, 54, 59, 78, 81, 153, 165, 224, 225, 271, 276, 299, 300, 302, 303, 320, 322, 386, 406.
Anne, 271.
Artemas, 385.
Asa, 168, 171, 277.
Azubah, 75, 78, 89, 105, 135, 382.
Barzillai, 56.
Benjamin, 31, 89, 96, 118, 123, 154, 194, 195, 222, 223, 224, 225, 277, 449, 452.
Benj. Whittemore, 92, 118, 142, 302.
Betsy, 114, 199, 315, 353, 444.
Betty, 90, 130, 143, 304, 314.
Caleb, 59, 163.
Calvin, 169.

Catharine, 79, 81, 82, 95, 131, 146, 161, 290, 300, 302, 303, 320, 322, 330, 388, 406.
Catharine L., 236, 322.
Charles, 194, 224.
Cornelius, 69, 292.
Cyrus, 116, 124.
Daniel, 31, 73, 75, 78, 88, 89, 120, 129, 143, 145, 275, 296, 298, 299, 300, 301, 323, 324.
Darby, 114, 168, 172, 224, 225, 316, 358.
David, 22, 32, 57, 137, 279, 382, 383, 384, 385, 386, 388.
Dexter, 121, 194, 449.
Dolly, 100, 387, 389.
Dorcas, 49, 451, 453.
Dorothy, 68, 92, 100, 110, 291, 303, 410.
Dorothy W., 410.
Eben, 92, 304.
Elijah, 68, 289.
Eliza, 132, 147, 223, 224, 271, 281.
Elizabeth, 49, 56, 59, 76, 78, 90, 92, 94, 97, 99, 100, 110, 111, 114, 116, 157, 159, 272, 275, 281, 284, 294, 295, 297, 300, 301, 302, 308, 309, 320, 322, 323, 324, 350, 364, 379, 386, 406, 410, 444.
Elizabeth F., 254.
Elizabeth Sophia, 225.
Emily, 213.
Ephraim, 44, 54, 75, 78, 89, 103, 278, 378, 381, 382, 383, 384, 385, 386, 387, 388, 389, 390.
Erastus, 223.
Esther, 299.
Esther Mary, 226.
Eunice, 105, 131, 146, 240, 276, 309, 321, 453.
Experience, 55, 279, 385.
Ezra, 111, 115, 127, 143, 150, 163, 223, 301, 316, 322, 338, 340.
Fanny, 153, 165, 194, 223, 224, 254, 338, 357, 443.
Frances, 92, 302.
Fredk. Augustus, 224.
George A., 222.
George W., 259.
Habijah, 81, 295, 299.
Hannah, 11, 52, 55, 58, 95, 96, 223, 278, 303, 322, 388.
Hannah E., 450.
Henry, 24, 29, 49, 53, 55, 58, 96, 222, 223, 224, 242, 272, 273, 274, 275, 276, 277, 278, 280, 282, 323, 449, 451, 452, 453.
Hezekiah, 52, 54, 59, 274, 275, 276, 277, 278, 281, 452, 453.
Hope, 13.
Horace, 223.
Isaac, 222, 276.
Israel, 139, 298, 381.
Jacob, 114, 118, 224, 245.
James, 26, 36, 52, 55, 58, 67, 86, 92, 94, 101, 149, 225, 271, 274, 276, 277, 278, 279, 280, 307, 324, 332, 453.
Jerome H., 226, 256, 443.
Jesse, 124, 150.
Joel, 105, 309.
John, 66, 81, 90, 95, 97, 116, 124, 195, 196, 271, 273, 275, 288, 300, 326, 327, 369, 385, 406, 451, 453.
Jonas, 223.
Jonathan, 13, 18, 56, 59, 105, 129, 139, 144, 157, 309, 383, 384, 453.
Jona. Wright, 115, 316.
Joseph, 10, 56, 59, 94, 100, 226, 236, 238, 272, 273, 274, 275, 276,

INDEX. 507

277, 278, 279, 281, 305, 326, 386, 390, 453.
Joshua, 49, 39, 141, 280, 384.
Josiah, 19, 124, 271, 277, 452, 453.
Judah, 89.
Kezia, 56, 59, 157.
Lemuel, 56, 278.
Levi, 6, 49, 79, 81, 82, 95, 124, 161, 279, 299, 300, 302, 303, 310, 324, 325, 329, 330, 406.
Lois, 89, 103, 126, 134, 137, 138, 277, 300, 383.
Longley, 94.
Lovey, 120.
Luceby, 124, 168, 171.
Lucia, 194, 223, 449.
Lucy, 73, 75, 78, 97, 116, 120, 124, 126, 141, 154, 165, 194, 222, 224, 227, 259, 385, 387, 449.
Lucy B., 234.
Luke, 119, 449.
Lydia, 21, 33, 278.
Martha, 116, 121, 193, 194, 222, 223, 224, 312, 340, 382, 449.
Mary, 10, 11, 13, 14, 19, 21, 33, 43, 54, 57, 60, 66, 68, 69, 71, 73, 77, 92, 99, 100, 101, 104, 111, 114, 115, 116, 124, 125, 128, 135, 151, 167, 173, 193, 194, 223, 226, 229, 232, 272, 277, 280, 303, 322, 331, 338, 356, 385, 410, 443, 449, 451, 452, 453.
Mary Ann, 225, 449.
Mary C., 194, 225.
Melinda, 225.
Merrick, 194, 223, 359.
Miriam, 453.
Molly, 100, 145, 307, 308, 323, 387.
Moses, 453.
N——, 446.
Nahum, 49, 277.
Nancy, 386.
Nathan, 78, 233, 296.
Nathaniel, 36, 37, 60, 73, 92, 94, 97, 100, 102, 105, 110, 281, 303, 304, 305, 306, 307, 308, 309, 310, 311, 320, 321, 325, 350, 410.
Nehemiah B., 450.
Olive, 311.
Oliver, 97, 110, 306.
Paul, 73, 99, 121, 147, 173, 193, 194, 222, 223, 224, 233, 304, 324, 449.
Peter, 66, 194, 223, 286, 304, 306, 307, 308, 323, 325, 326, 389.
Peter II., 224.
Pethula, 56, 157.
Phineas, 52, 68, 69, 87, 274, 286, 289, 292, 379.
Polly, 119.
Putnam, 226.
Rachel, 123, 124, 194, 222, 223.
Rebecca, 67, 83, 86, 87, 138, 383.
Relief, 229, 299.
Ruth, 53, 278.
Sally, 119, 120, 132, 194, 195, 222, 223, 224, 225.
Salmon, 123, 147, 194, 196, 222, 234, 243.
Samuel, 6, 29, 49, 94, 157, 159, 227, 270, 271, 273, 277, 278, 279, 280, 281, 282, 300, 304, 319, 324, 325, 337, 357, 404.
Sarah, 42, 53, 73, 77, 84, 92, 94, 111, 147, 194, 195, 223, 225, 275, 276, 284, 310, 320, 449, 453.
Sarah A., 396.
Sarah F., 449.
Sarah J., 227, 449.
Sibyl, 277.
Sidney, 226.

Sidney G., 450.
Silas, 77, 105, 147, 223, 309, 390.
Simon, 10, 11, 13, 19, 64, 99, 111, 114, 116, 193, 195, 273, 279, 300, 301, 303, 308, 310, 312, 314, 315, 316, 320, 324, 302, 444, 451, 452, 453.
Sophia, 235.
Sophronia, 231, 236, 333.
Stedman, 193, 223, 226.
Stedman A., 226.
Susanna, 18, 58, 84, 87, 223, 277, 280, 320, 453.
Susanna H., 226.
Sylvia, 124, 327.
Tabitha, 453.
Tarbel, 276.
Theodora, 299, 324, 406.
Thomas, 85, 99, 100, 274, 282, 385, 386, 387, 388, 390.
Walter, 223.
Warren, 224, 227, 245, 259.
William, 26, 37, 73, 77, 92, 99, 101, 114, 119, 145, 153, 165, 193, 194, 222, 223, 224, 231, 274, 284, 302, 304, 305, 324, 331, 449.
William A. P., 226.
William P., 237.
William T., 226.
Wright, 71, 293, 410.
Widow ——, 325.
Zilpah, 388.
WILLEY, D. L., 258.
WILLIAMS, Abel H., 241.
Abigail, 294.
Anna, 106, 307, 328.
Damaris, 80, 81, 106, 295.
David, 81.
Dinah, 102.
George Forrest, 226.
G. W. G., 226.
Isabella, 226.
Jacob, 86, 88.
John, 81, 296, 299, 300, 323.
Jude, 302.
Leafy, 104, 295.
Mary, 80, 298.
Mary Ann, 341.
Mrs. ——, 196, 369.
Nathaniel, 341.
R——, 446.
Warham, 281.
William, 40, 99.
Zephaniah, 80, 81, 106, 294, 295, 296, 298, 299, 300, 302, 307, 323, 328.
WILLIS, Jesse, 140.
Katy, 314.
Mary E., 249.
Sally, 139.
William, 314.
WILLOUGHBY, Joseph, 377, 378, 385.
WILLS, Jiles, 46, 103.
WILSON, Abner, 282.
Benjamin, 157, 270, 271, 276, 409.
Betsey P., 263.
David, 44.
Dolly, 13, 16.
Eleazer M., 238.
Eliza Ann, 196, 226, 370, 443.
Elizabeth, 136, 271, 284.
Elizabeth G., 263.
Emily Augusta, 225.
Eunice, 64, 285, 286.
Francina E., 226.
Georgiana, 263, 268.
Hannah, 18, 195, 271, 332, 365.
Hepzibah, 285, 286.
Jacob, 263, 268.
Jeremiah, 270, 271, 274, 290, 410.

John, 196, 226, 240, 443.
John I., 257.
Jonathan. 26, 285, 286.
Joseph, 24, 35, 57, 59, 99, 126, 137, 273, 279, 280, 281, 282, 284, 288.
Lois, 286.
Mary, 65, 286.
Mehetabel, 17.
Miranda, 235.
Nathaniel, 26, 64, 274, 285, 286, 289, 290, 409, 451.
Paul, 128.
Rebecca, 57, 59, 157, 271, 273, 288, 409.
Rhoda, 64, 157, 276, 286, 409.
Roxa, 193.
Samuel, 65, 286.
Sarah, 233, 307, 372.
Solomon, 57, 280.
Susanna, 316.
Thankful, 289.
Theodore, 263.
Timothy S., 225, 235.
William, 59, 281.
WINCH, Jonathan, 150.
WINCHESTER, Ann E., 227.
Ann S., 243.
Caleb, 227, 247, 260.
Charles, 227.
Edw. Francis, 262.
Elhanan, 227, 263.
George A., 264.
George M., 260.
Harris, 256.
Henry, 127, 140.
Lydia A., 227, 260.
Maria, 263.
Mary F., 240.
Milo, 254, 262, 264.
Milona, 262.
Munroe, 227.
Rhoda, 227, 263.
Sally, 170.
Samuel, 168, 172, 442.
Sarah, 263, 442.
WINDITT, John, 254, 261, 267, 434, 442.
Mary E., 261, 442.
Phebe, 434, 442.
Sarah, 267, 372, 442.
Sarah Ann, 267, 372, 442.
WINDLE, John, 257.
WINN and WING.
Elizabeth, 126, 137.
Jacob, 42, 89, 92, 102.
John, 89.
Josiah, 377.
Louisa, 236.
Lydia, 41, 101.
Prudence, 92.
Sarah, 40, 89, 92.
William, 45.
WINSHIP, Elizabeth, 352.
WINSLOW, Worcester, 127, 140.
WINTER, John, 127, 141, 222.
Lydia, 222.
Zina, 249.
WITHINGTON, Josiah M., 249.
WOOD and WOODS, Aaron, 144.
Alice, 18.
Arvilla A., 252.
Asa, 170, 228.
Asenath, 223.
Ashley H., 251.
Baxter, 196, 231, 369.
Betty, 130.
Charles, 243, 395.
Charlotte A., 260, 394, 442.
David, 140, 162.
Edwin H., 226.

INDEX.

Elijah, 60, 82, 87, 90, 92, 95. 116, 282, 302, 303, 305, 306, 310, 311, 320, 327.
Elisha, 64, 82, 287, 302.
Elizabeth, 29.
Eunice, 320.
Hannah, 51, 60, 62, 64, 66, 68. 69, 95, 160, 273, 281, 282, 284, 292, 293, 305, 323, 329.
Hannah A., 238.
Henry, 260, 269, 395, 442.
Hollis B., 256.
Horace, 223.
Isaac F., 394.
Jedediah, 38, 99.
John, 69, 292.
John H., 255.
Jonathan, 229.
Joseph, 25, 60, 62, 64, 66, 68, 69, 84, 87, 96, 273, 281, 282, 284, 287, 288, 289, 291, 292, 300, 302, 303, 308.
Josiah, 74, 145, 289.
Jotham, 68, 92, 104, 117, 134, 193, 289, 303, 310, 321, 353.
Levi, 62, 102, 284.
Lorenzo F., 256.
Lowell, 226.
Lowell F., 226.
Lucy, 96, 302, 308.
Lucy A., 238.
Mary, 28, 51, 74, 82, 90, 92, 95, 116, 125, 137, 289, 295, 302, 303, 305, 308, 320, 326, 331.
Mary S., 260.
Matthew F., 260, 269, 442.
Mehetabel, 117, 321.
Myra, 251.
Nathaniel, 308, 326.
Nehemiah, 51, 74, 289, 292, 293, 295, 323.
Phebe, 152, 164.
Rachel, 18, 96, 130, 143, 302, 310.
Sally F., 251.
Samuel, 66, 96, 130, 169, 228, 288, 300, 324.
Sarah, 117, 197, 310.
Seth, 116, 311.
Silence, 306.
Stephen, 223.
Susanna, 51, 292.
Tabitha, 226.
Ursula, 96, 303.
Watson, 243.
WOODBURY, Abigail, 31, 67, 320, 326.
Anne, 394.
Daniel, 67, 289.
Ebenezer, 67, 289.
Israel, 168, 172.
John, 390.
Joseph, 390.
Lorenzo, 394.
Mary Ann, 248.
Mr. ——, 395.
Mehetabel, 87.
Rebecca, 410.
Relief, 390.
Samuel, 410.
Sarah E., 244.
Widow ——. 326.
WOODCOCK, Elkanah, 39, 102.
Franklin, 239.
WOODWARD, Hannah, 197.
WOODWORTH, A., 259, 394.
Chas. Lewis, 259.
WOONSAMUG, Hannah, 274.
WORCESTER, Abijah, 377.
A ——, 446.
Charles W., 269.

Eliza, 195, 225.
Elizabeth, 449.
Francis, 241.
Harriet, 225, 243.
Martha, 226.
Mary, 195, 225, 226, 449.
Matilda, 269, 395.
Molly, 196, 269.
Nancy, 226.
Noah, 226, 241.
Rebecca, 225, 449.
Sally, 230.
Sampson, 161.
Samuel, 146, 194, 195, 225, 229, 256, 357, 360, 362, 365, 449.
Sarah, 246.
Thomas, 241.
WORTHEN, Sanborn, 250.
WRIGLEY, James, 258.
WRIGHT, Aaron, 95, 387.
Abel, 134, 295, 390, 391.
Abigail, 58, 281, 295, 390.
Edward, 258.
Elizabeth, 250.
Ephraim, 83, 383.
Eunice, 171.
Experience, 24.
Hannah, 55, 279.
Isaac, 14.
James, 75, 105, 134, 381.
James G., 262.
Jane, 29.
Janette, 262.
John, 55, 262, 279.
Joseph, 89, 383, 384.
Lucy, 91, 385.
Lydia, 120, 141.
Martha, 43, 75, 83, 89, 91, 95, 380.
Mary, 19, 346.
Mercy, 59, 281.
Nathaniel, 43, 75, 83, 89, 91, 95, 103, 376, 380, 381, 383, 384, 385, 387.
Pamela, 390.
Phebe, 25, 127, 141.
Polly, 232, 310.
Ruth, 57, 59, 280, 328.
Sally, 357.
Samuel, 57, 59, 280, 281.
Sarah, 194, 326.
Thomas, 24, 58, 83, 127, 142, 281, 295, 324, 381, 383.
William, 132, 147.
WYMAN, Abel, 79, 327.
Abigail, 71, 72, 73, 75, 77, 78, 79, 86, 88, 119, 127, 140, 293, 296, 309.
Abijah, 30, 71, 73, 78, 79, 127, 143, 293, 294, 296, 298, 299, 319, 325, 329, 399.
Albert C., 269.
Amos H., 196, 226, 244, 369.
Anna, 34, 86.
Annie C., 265.
Asa Miller, 144, 304.
Benjamin, 94, 115, 120, 128, 144, 155, 166, 193, 195, 222, 223, 224, 225, 304, 318, 322, 338, 339, 341, 343, 344, 345, 347, 363, 373, 445.
Benj. Farnsworth, 226.
Betsy, 118, 120, 168, 171, 318.
Catharine, 45, 94, 104, 297.
Charles, 224, 226, 227, 242, 265, 343, 392, 393.
Charles A., 226, 393.
Daniel, 75, 298.
Deborah, 338.
Dolly, 83, 119, 128, 144, 301, 338, 350.
Elizabeth, 78, 79, 298, 310, 325,

399.
Ellen F., 260.
Emily, 120, 169, 228, 338.
Ephraim, 77, 222, 296, 328, 343, 399.
Eunice, 73, 126, 137, 338.
Hannah, 118, 321, 350.
Harriet A., 260.
Henry, 40, 71, 110, 225, 307, 377, 388, 389.
Jasher, 83, 85, 304.
John, 118, 127, 143, 165, 312.
John H., 260.
John R., 224, 260, 345, 395.
John Wood, 226, 393.
Jonas, 45, 73, 79, 118, 294, 309, 310, 312, 313, 314, 315, 317, 321, 329.
Joseph, 128, 134, 145.
Joshua, 301.
Lucretia, 222, 224, 225, 334, 351, 394.
Lucy L., 226.
Lydia M., 309.
Martha, 94, 115, 120, 193, 223, 299, 322, 355, 368, 445.
Martha Thayer, 195, 224, 265, 344, 366, 445.
Mary, 39, 70, 73, 77, 83, 94, 100, 110, 127, 139, 142, 292, 297, 301, 324, 388, 399.
Mary Ann L., 226.
Mary Augusta, 260.
Matthew, 27, 28, 71, 72, 75, 77, 119, 296, 297, 298, 324, 330.
Nancy, 226, 227, 265, 392, 393.
Nathaniel, 29, 36, 70, 73, 77, 89, 94, 223, 292, 294, 296, 297, 299, 304, 319, 324, 327, 341, 353, 399.
Patience, 75, 107, 116, 148, 161, 309, 322, 324, 331.
Patty, 115, 120, 154, 165, 193, 318.
Phebe, 104.
Polly, 118. 120, 155, 166, 309, 318.
Putnam, 314.
Rachel, 18.
Rebecca, 71, 77, 110, 296, 389.
Sally, 118, 314.
Samuel, 107, 118, 119, 313, 314.
Samuel D. [H?], 40, 107, 116.
Samuel Johnson, 119, 338.
Sarah, 41, 72, 79, 110, 127, 142, 299.
Stephen, 78, 79, 118, 135, 296, 317, 327.
Submit, 94, 120, 169, 170, 193, 318, 320, 354, 399.
William W., 227.
Zebadiah, 126, 127.
YOUNG, William H., 253.
ZWIER and SCHWERE.
Abigail, 149, 162, 196, 331, 360.
Artemas, 227.
Barbara, 42, 104.
Betsy, 151.
Charles, 227.
Daniel, 43, 309, 310, 311, 320, 328, 331.
Hannah, 309.
Jacob, 44, 104, 153, 196, 365.
Leonard, 227.
Lois, 310.
Lovicy, 227, 234.
Margaret, 37, 99, 320.
Mr. ——, 325.
Peter, 143.
Reuben, 150, 162, 196, 227, 232.
Susan, 150, 163, 227.
William, 234.
Widow ——, 329.

www.ingramcontent.com/pod-product-compliance
Lightning Source LLC
Chambersburg PA
CBHW030103010526
44116CB00005B/71